THE INTERNATIONAL ENCYCLOPEDIA OF EDUCATION

SECOND EDITION

THE INTERNATIONAL ENCYCLOPEDIA OF EDUCATION

SECOND EDITION

Volume 12

Editors-in-Chief

TORSTEN HUSÉN
University of Stockholm, Sweden

T. NEVILLE POSTLETHWAITE
University of Hamburg, Germany

PERGAMON

UK	Elsevier Science Ltd, The Boulevard, Langford Lane, Kidlington, Oxford OX5 1GB, England
USA	Elsevier Science Inc, 660 White Plains Road, Tarrytown, New York 10591-5153,USA
JAPAN	Elsevier Science Japan, Tsunashima Building Annex, 3-20-12 Yushima, Bunkyoku, Tokyo 113, Japan

Second edition 1994

Library of Congress Cataloging in Publication Data
International encyclopedia of education (2nd ed.)
The international encyclopedia of education / editors-in-chief Torsten Husén, T. Neville Postlethwaite. — 2nd ed.
p. cm.
1. Education—Dictionaries. 2. Education—Research—Dictionaries. I. Husén, Torsten, 1916– II. Postlethwaite, T. Neville.
LB15.I569 1994
370'.3—dc20 94–3059

British Library Cataloguing in Publication Data
A catalogue record for this book is available from the British Library.

ISBN 0–08–041046–4 (cloth : set : alk. paper)

∞™ The paper used in this publication meets the minimum requirements of the American National Standard for Information Sciences—Permanence of Paper for Printed Library Materials, ANSI Z39.48–1984.

Printed in Great Britain by BPC Wheatons Ltd, Exeter

CONTENTS

Honorary Editorial Advisory Board	vii
Editorial Board	ix
Classified List of Entries	1
List of Contributors	23
Name Index	69
Subject Index	205
List of Major Education Journals	479

HONORARY EDITORIAL ADVISORY BOARD

EDITORIAL BOARD

CLASSIFIED LIST OF ENTRIES

The Classified List of Entries, which is supplementary to the Subject Index, groups the contents of the *Encyclopedia* by article title into a number of broad fields, alphabetically organized, from **Administration of Education** to **Technical and Vocational Education and Training.** Within these broad groups entries are further subdivided into appropriate subheadings. The reader is thus presented with a general overview of the contents of the *Encyclopedia*.

Inevitably some articles can be categorized equally well under more than one heading. Rather than make an arbitrary decision as to which section they belong, each article has been listed wherever appropriate. For example; "Prior Knowledge and Learning" is listed both under *Processes and Outcomes of Learning* under the main heading INSTRUCTIONAL PSYCHOLOGY, and under *Learning Processes: Students* under the heading of TEACHING.

Articles are grouped under the following general headings: Administration of Education; Adult Education; Anthropology of Education; Children with Special Needs; Comparative and International Education; Curriculum; Economics of Education; Educational Evaluation; Educational Research, Methodology, and Measurement; Educational Technology; Girls and Women in Education; History and Historiography of Education; Human Development; Instructional Psychology; National Systems of Education; Philosophy of Education; Preschool Education; Sociology of Education; Teacher Education; Teaching; and Technical and Vocational Education and Training. These headings provided the basis for the organizing scheme which was used in commissioning articles for the *Encyclopedia*.

ADMINISTRATION OF EDUCATION

Accountability and Inspection

Education Indicators: Use in Policy and Management
School Inspectors and Supervision
See also ECONOMICS OF EDUCATION *(Production of Education)*

Administration at School Level

Organization of Schools
School Administration, History of
School Principals: Role in Restructured Schools
School-based Management

Administrative Recruitment, Training, Selection, and Careers

Administrative Preparation: Inservice
Administrative Preparation: Preservice
Administrator Recruitment, Selection, and Careers

Finance and Resource Allocation

Resource Allocation in Schools and School Systems
School Business Management and Budgeting
School Finance

Governance and Politics of Schools

Decentralization in Educational Government and Management
Governance and Management of Schools: International Developments
Governance: Relations among Level of Government
Labor Relations in Education
Local Education Authorities, School Boards, and School Councils
Micropolitics of Schools
Ministries and State Departments of Education
Politics and Governance of Education
School–Community Relations
School Reform and Restructuring

Issues in Educational Administration

Ability Grouping and Tracking in Schools
Alternative Schools and Programs
Authority and Power in Educational Organizations
Desegregation in Schools
Discipline in Schools
Dropouts, School Leavers, and Truancy
Law and Administration in Education
Public versus Private Schools: Research Controversies
Religious Issues in Education
School Choice and Privatization
School Size and Small Schools
Urban Education: Changing Ecology, Politics, and Reform
Urban Schools

School Effectiveness and Improvement

Bureaucracy and School Effectiveness

Educational Reforms, Implementation of
Effective Schools, Management of
Effective Schools Research: Methodological Issues
Institutional Self-evaluation and Renewal
Organizational Development and Consultancy in Education
School as a Workplace: Implications for Reform
School Climate and Culture
School District or Regional Management and School Improvement
School Improvement
School Organizational Effects on Student Outcomes
Secondary Schools: Effective

Services and Tasks of Administration

Community Education and Community Schools
Distance Education at the School Level
Facilities and Physical Plant
Information Technology Use in Educational Management Systems
Personnel Administration in Education
School–Business Partnerships

Teachers and Educational Administration

Teacher Unions
Teachers and Policy: Implications for Management

Theory of Educational Administration

Administration of Education as a Field of Study
Administration of Education: Critical Approaches
Conflict and its Management in Educational Organizations
Decision-making Theory
Employee Motivation and Incentives in Schools
Evolution and Contemporary Developments of Organization Theory
Globalization of Educational Policy and Reform
International Associations: Role in Educational Administration
Leadership in Educational Administration
Management Information Systems
Management of Change and Innovation
Management of Contraction in Public Education
Organizational Theory in Education: Comparative Management Perspectives
School Administration, History of
Schools as Sociocultural Systems

ADULT EDUCATION

Adult and Continuing Education, The Field of

Adult Education: Concepts, Purposes, and Principles
Adult Education: Disciplinary Orientations
Adult Education, History of
Adult Education: Overview
Adult Literacy Programs in Developing Nations
Andragogy
Community Education and Community Development
Conscientization Mobilization
Critical Approaches to Adult Education
Education for Peace
Formal, Nonformal, and Informal Education
Human Resource Development
Ideologies in Adult Education
Lifelong and Continuing Education
Literacy and Numeracy: Concepts and Definitions
Nonformal Education, Economics of
Occupational Training, Economics of
On-the-Job Training
Population Education
Psychology of Adult Education
Recurrent and Alternation Education
Sociology of Adult Education
Technical and Vocational Education and Training

Adult Education Programs

Adult Education: Information Sources
Adult, Recurrent and Lifelong Education: Comparative and International Studies
Africa, Anglophone: Adult Education
Africa, Francophone: Adult Education
Arab Countries: Adult Education
Asia, East and Southeast: Adult Education
Australia and New Zealand: Adult Education
Caribbean and Central America: Adult Education
Central and Eastern Europe: Adult Education
China, People's Republic of: Adult Education
European Community Programs in Continuing Vocational Education
Indian Subcontinent: Adult Education
Interchange in Adult Education: North–South Dialogue
International Adult Education
Japan: Adult Education and Training
Japan: Vocational Education and Training
Latin America: Adult Education
Latin America: Articulation of Education, Training, and Work

Nongovernmental Organizations: Adult Education
Nordic Countries: Adult Education
North America: Adult Education
Professional Associations for Adult Education
Russia (Soviet Union): Adult Education
Southern and Western Europe: Adult Education
Technical–Vocational Education: Comparative and International Studies
UNESCO and Adult Education
United Nations Organizations: Research and Service in Comparative and International Education

Costs and Financing

Costs of Continuing Education: Industrialized Countries
Lifelong Education: Financing Mechanisms
Paid Educational Leave and Collective Bargaining
Partnerships: Initial and Adult Education
Payroll Levies for Training
Private Sector Training, Education and Performance Contracting in
Training with Production
See also ECONOMICS OF EDUCATION

Curriculum and Teaching

Curriculum and Materials in Adult Literacy
Curriculum in Adult Education
Design of Training Programs: Effectiveness
Distance Education, Educational Technology in
Individual Techniques for Teaching and Learning
Teacher Education and Adult Development
Teacher Roles and Teaching Styles: Adult Education
Teaching Methods for Adults
Training of Adult Educators

Demand and Supply of Learning Opportunities

Adult and Continuing Higher Education
Adult Basic Education
Adult Secondary Education
Broadcast Education in Adult Education
Community Colleges
Counseling Adult Students
Distance Education
Dropout in Adult Education
Female Access to Vocational Education and Training
Folk High Schools
Language and Communication Education for Adults
Libraries as Learning Resources
Nontraditional Students: Third-age and Part-time
Open University
Outreach in Adult Education
Participation in Adult Education: Antecedent Factors
Participation Motivation in Adult Education
Polytechnical Education
Populations and Special Clienteles: Adult Education
Proprietary Further Education
Providers of Adult Education
Student Support Systems: Adult Education
Study Circles
University Adult Education
Women and Adult Education
Worker Education and Labor Education

Human Development and Adult Learning

Adult Learning: Overview
Aging and Adult Development
Experiential and Open Learning for Adults
Group Learning
Human Development: Research and Educational Practice
Human Development: Research and Social Policy
Human Development: Research Methodology
Intellectual Development across the Lifespan
Learning across the Lifespan, Development of
Learning Environments
Learning in Industrial Settings
Learning to Learn: Adult Education
Lifespan Development
Lifespan Learning: Implications for Educators
Memory Development
Problems and Crises in Human Development
Self-directed Adult Learning
Study Habits and Strategies
Taxonomies of Skill Development
Transfer of Learning

Measurement and Evaluation

Adult and Nonformal Education: Statistics
Certification of Adult Education
Continuing Education: Effects of
Cost-effectiveness of Training Courses
Distance Education: Economic Evaluation
Evaluation of Adult Education
Evaluation of Public Training: Industrial Countries
Job Analysis in Corporate Education
Literacy: Research and Measurement
Measurement of Adult Education
Measurement of Industry Training
Participatory Research
Selection Bias in Educational Research

Task Analysis
Training Concepts and Statistics
Training Costs: Measurement

Policies for Adult and Continuing Education

Adult Education and Training Markets
Adult Education for Development
Adult Education, Reform Strategies in
Education and Labor Markets in Developing Nations
Employment Policy: Adult Education and Training
Further Education and Training: Demand, Supply, and Finance
Legislation in Adult Education
Leisure: Adult Education
Market Failure in Firm-based Education and Training
Nonformal Education Policy in Developing Nations
Overeducation
Postliteracy: Concepts and Policies
Time Policies and Lifelong Education
Training, Government Role in

See also HUMAN DEVELOPMENT; TECHNICAL AND VOCATIONAL EDUCATION AND TRAINING

ANTHROPOLOGY OF EDUCATION

Applied Anthropology in Education

Anthropological Programs in Education
Anthropology Teaching at the Precollege Level
Bilingual Education: Anthropological Perspectives
Community–School Relations, Anthropological Study of
Cultural Transformation: Ethnological Information to Education Programs
Education of Indigenous Peoples, Anthropological Study of
Multicultural Education: Anthropological Perspectives

Selected Areas of Anthropology Inquiry in Education

Anthropology of Education: History and Overview
Classroom Culture and Social Organization, Anthropological Study of
Cross-cultural Study of Education
Culture and Achievement Motivation in Education
Culture, Cognition, and Education, Perspectives on
Ethnographic Evaluation in Education
Literacy and Numeracy, Anthropological Study of
School Culture and Peer Groups
Social Change and Education: Anthropological Perspectives
Social Stratification and Education: Anthropological Perspectives

Theoretical Perspectives

Cultural Continuities and Discontinuities in Education
Education as Culture Transmission and Acquisition
Ethnography of Education: Anthropological Approach
Human Learning, Evolution of: Anthropological Perspectives
Language in Education, Changing Views of: Anthropological Perspectives

CHILDREN WITH SPECIAL NEEDS

Alternative Approaches to Service Delivery

Deinstitutionalization
Health Needs and Adaptations in Education Services Delivery

Children and Youth at Risk

Abused and Neglected Children and Youth
Children and Youth at Risk
Delinquent and Adjudicated Youth
Education for Street Children

Children and Youth with Mild and Moderate Handicapping Conditions

Behavioral Disorders: Emotional
Behavioral Disorders: Social
Deaf and Hearing Impaired Youth, Education of
Deaf–Blind Children and Youth, Education of
Learning Characteristics of Students with Special Needs
Mild Mental Retardation
Specific Learning Disability
Visually Handicapped Children and Youth, Education of

Curricular Considerations of Children with Special Needs

Cognitive Strategy Instruction: Special Education
Literacy Development in Children with Special Needs: Role of Parents

Microcomputer Technology for Students with Special Needs
Peer Tutoring
Reading and the Mildly Handicapped
Social Skills

See also CURRICULUM *(Curriculum Development and Implementation)*

Diagnosis and Classification of Children with Special Needs

Children and Youth with Special Needs, Diagnosis and Classification of
Developmental Disabilities: Severe
Early Childhood Developmental Screening
Neurological Bases of Learning Problems

Education of Children with Special Needs

Children and Youth with Special Needs, Education of
Cognitive Modifiability
Disability Statistics
Infants, Toddlers, and Preschoolers, Programs for
Integrated Services for Children and Youth with Special Needs
Integration of Students with Special Educational Needs in Regular School Environments
International Cooperation in Special Education
Mainstreaming
Mildly Handicapped Students: Noncategorical Approach
Pharmacotherapy in Schoolchildren
Prereferral Intervention for Students with Special Needs
Resource Room Programs as a Special Education Model
Teaming Arrangements in Special Education

Families and Children with Special Needs

Children Caring for Children
Empowering of Families of Children and Youth with Special Needs

Gifted and Talented

Gifted and Talented Learners in Special Populations
Gifted Children, Development of
Identification and Programming of the Gifted and Talented
Social–Emotional Development and Adjustment in Gifted Students

Special Education and Personnel Training

School "Related Services" Personnel
Teacher Education and Special Education Needs

Speech Disorder and Language Development

Augmentative and Alternative Communication
Language Differences versus Language Disorders
Language Disorders among Bilingual Students
Language Disorders and Autism
Programs that Foster Resilience among Children at Risk
Specific Language Disorders of Childhood
Speech and Language Disorders and the Hard of Hearing
Speech and Language Handicapped: Overview
Speech–Sound Disorders: Articulation and Phonology
Voice Disorders in Schoolchildren

Vocational Education

Career Education for Special Needs Students
Transition to Adult and Working Life for Persons with Handicaps

See also INSTRUCTIONAL PSYCHOLOGY

COMPARATIVE AND INTERNATIONAL EDUCATION

Activities of Professional Government and International Organizations

Comparative Education and International Education: Organizations and Institutions
Comparative Education Societies
European Community: Educational Goals and Plans
International Conferences, Commissions, and Reforms in Education
Organisation for Economic Co-operation and Development (OECD): Educational Activities
United Nations Organizations: Research and Service in Comparative and International Education

Comparative and International Education as a Field of Study

Area Studies: Comparative and International Education

Comparative and International Education: Overview and Historical Development
Comparative and International Education: Paradigms and Theories
International Education
Population Education

Comparative Studies in Education

Adult, Recurrent, and Lifelong Education: Comparative Studies
Attitudes toward Schooling: Comparative Studies in
Basic Education: Comparative and International Studies
Education and Development
Education for Peace
Educational Achievement: Comparative Studies
International Adult Education
Nonformal and Alternative Approaches to Basic Education: Comparative Studies
Political Work of Teachers
Teaching and Teacher Education: Comparative and International Studies
Technical–Vocational Education: Comparative and International Studies

Concepts, Methods, and Data Resources in Comparative and International Educational Research

Comparative Methodology in Education
Comparative Statistics in Education
Development Education
Documentation and Information in Comparative and International Education
Educational Policy and Decision-making: Comparative Data
International Baccalaureate

CURRICULUM

Curriculum Components

Syllabus
Teachers' Guide
Textbooks

Curriculum Development and Implementation

Community and Parents' Participation in Curriculum Decisions
Computer and Information Sciences: Educational Programs
Core Curriculum
Curriculum Adaptation
Curriculum Development at School Level
Curriculum Development Centers
Curriculum Management
Curriculum Planning Models
Curriculum Politics and Policies
Curriculum Renewal
Educational Objectives: Use in Curriculum Development
Educational Psychology: Impact on Curriculum
Forecasting, Education, and Its Impact on Curriculum
Hidden Curriculum
Knowledge: Conceptions of and Impact on the Curriculum
Legal Factors Affecting Curriculum
Minorities and Immigrant Children, Curriculum for
Nongraded Curriculum
Social, Cultural, and Economic Factors Affecting Curriculum
Teachers as Curriculum-makers
See also CHILDREN WITH SPECIAL NEEDS *(Curricular Considerations of Children with Special Needs)*

Curriculum as a Field of Study: Concepts and Principles

Curriculum as a Field of Study
Curriculum Inquiry, Forms of
Curriculum: Sociological Perspectives
Curriculum Theory

Curriculum Evaluation

Courseware Evaluation
Curriculum Evaluation Models
Curriculum Evaluation: Qualitative
Curriculum-based Assessment
Curriculum-specific Evaluation Criteria
Measurement-driven Curriculum
See also EDUCATIONAL EVALUATION

Curriculum History

Curriculum History: National Profiles
Curriculum, History of

Curriculum Processes

School Subjects: Studying
Students' Curriculum Experiences

Foreign Languages

Foreign Language Acquisition, Process of
Foreign Language Education
Foreign Language Education: Primary School Programs
Foreign Language Education: Secondary School Programs
Learning Strategies in Second Language Learning
Reading Comprehension in Second and Foreign Language

Humanities and Arts

Aesthetic Education
Art Education Programs
Children's Literature
Geography: Educational Programs
History: Educational Programs
Humanities: Educational Programs
Literature: Educational Programs
Mass Media Literacy: Educational Programs
Music Education: Programs and Mehods
Performing Arts: Education Programs
Religious Education

Language Arts

Language across the Curriculum
Linguistics and Language Learning
Listening and Speaking Instruction
Spelling and Grammar Instruction
Writing and Composition Instruction

Mathematics Education

Mathematical Applications in School Curriculum
Mathematics and Language
Mathematics Education, Affective Issues in
Mathematics Education, History of
Mathematics Instruction: Contemporary Research
Mathematics: Primary School Programs
Mathematics: Secondary School Programs
Mathematics: Topics of Instruction

Physical Education

Sport Pedagogy, Research in

Reading

Beginning Reading: Grapheme Systems and Orthography
Reading Comprehension in Second and Foreign Language
Reading Comprehension, Learning of
Reading, Learning and Instruction of
Reading Teacher Education

Science Education

Agricultural and Rural Education
Environmental and Ecological Education
Integrated and General Science
Language and the Science Curriculum
Life Sciences: Secondary School Programs
Physical Sciences: Secondary School Programs
Science: Attitudes toward
Science Education, History of
Science Education: Primary School Programs
Scientific Literacy
Technology: Educational Programs

Social Studies

Civic Education
Drug Prevention Education
Drugs and Education
Education for the Life of Work
Family Life Education
Health and Education
Health Education
Political Education
Social Studies in Primary School
Social Studies: Secondary School Programs

ECONOMICS OF EDUCATION

Benefits of Education

Agricultural Productivity and Education
Benefits of Education
Consumption Benefits of Education
Education and Economic Growth
Education and Fertility
Education and Productivity
External Benefits of Education
Vocational Education and Productivity

Costs of Education

Cost Analysis in Education
Private and Public Costs of Schooling in Developing Nations
Student Fees

Education and Discrimination

Education and Female Labor Force Participation in Industrializing Countries
Gender and Education Choices, Economics of
Gender and Occupational Segregation
Gender Differences in Earnings
Immigrants' Education and Economic Performance
Race Earnings Differentials

Education and Income Distribution

Education and Earnings
Education, Occupation, and Earnings
Family Status and Economic Status
Income Distribution and Education
Kinship Studies

Education and Labor Markets

Brain Drain, Economics of
Demand and Supply Elasticities for Educated Labor
Education and Informal Labor Markets
Education and Labor Markets in Developing Nations
Education and the Employment Contract
Education and the Labor Market
Human Capital Concepts
Internal Labor Markets and Education
Internal Migration and Education
Job Information and Education
Labor Market and Educational Expansion
Labor Market Segmentation and Education
Public Sector Employment and Education
Screening Models and Education
Vintage Effects and Education

Education and Technological Change

Education and the New International Division of Labor
Technical Change and the Demand for Educated Labor
Technological Change and Deskilling
Technological Change and Education

Evaluating Educational and Training Investment

Apprenticeship, Economics of
Cost–Benefit Analysis
Cost-effectiveness Analysis
Manpower Forecasting and Educational Planning
Market Failure in Firm-based Education and Training
Occupational Training, Economics of
On-the-job Training
Overeducation
Rates of Return to Education
Returns to Vocational Education in Developing Nations

Financing of Education

Community Financing of Education
Educational Finance and Economic Adjustment in Developing Nations
Educational Financing
International Educational Expenditures
International Educational Indicators
International Financing of Education
Public–Private Division of Responsibility for Education
School Finance
Student Loans

Production of Education

Childcare, Economics of
Education Production Functions
Educational Technology, Economics of
Industrial Restructuring and Educational Reforms
Joint Production of Education
Macroeconomics of Educational Time and Learning
Microeconomics of School Production
Political Economy of Educational Production
Preschool Education, Economics of
School Choice: Market Mechanisms
School Dropouts
School Enterprise, Economics of
Supply of Teachers
Teacher Education, Economics of
Teacher Unionization, Economics of

See also ADULT EDUCATION *(Market Policies and Finance)*; EDUCATIONAL POLICY AND PLANNING; TECHNICAL AND VOCATIONAL EDUCATION AND TRAINING *(Provision, Location, and Financing)*

EDUCATIONAL EVALUATION

Curriculum Evaluation

Curriculum-based Assessment

Evaluation Models and Approaches

Data Envelopment Analysis
Delphi Technique
Ethics of Evaluation Studies

Evaluation: A Tylerian Perspective
Evaluation Design, Evolution of
Evaluation, Empirical Framework for
Evaluation: Formative, Summative, and Goal-free
Evaluation Models and Approaches
Evaluation, Nature of
Fourth Generation: Evaluation
Needs Assessment
Program Evaluation
Theory-based Evaluation

National Standard Setting and Assessment

Evaluation of National Comparisons
Monitoring National Standards: United Kingdom
National Assessment of Educational Programs
National Standard Setting and Reporting
Professional Standards for Educational Evaluation: United States

Purposes and Goals of Evaluation Studies

Decision-oriented Evaluation and Beyond
Evaluation of Adult Education
Evaluation of Educational Personnel
Evaluation of Preschool Programs
Evaluation of Public Training: Industrial Countries
Informing Evaluation for Local School Improvement
International Educational Indicators

See also ADULT EDUCATION *(Measurement and Evaluation)*; CURRICULUM *(Curriculum Evaluation)*; ECONOMICS OF EDUCATION *(Evaluating Educational and Training Investment)*; EDUCATIONAL RESEARCH, METHODOLOGY, AND MEASUREMENT; EDUCATIONAL TECHNOLOGY *(Evaluation, Diffusion, and Implementation)*; TEACHING *(Teacher Effectiveness)*

EDUCATIONAL POLICY AND PLANNING

Development and Implementation of Educational Policy

Adult Education, Planning Public Policy for
Decentralization of Schooling in Developing Nations
Demography in Educational Planning
Dissemination of Educational Research
Documentation Systems: Regional Education
Educational Planning: Differing Models
Educational Planning: Implementation Problems
Educational Planning: Models and Methods
Educational Policy Studies: Overview
Facilities Planning and Policy: Macro Level
Planning Education: History
Planning Education: Overview
School Mapping
Textbook Development in Developing Nations, Planning for

Economic Aspects of Educational Planning

Educational Efficiency and Effectiveness, Concepts of
Educational Planning, Economics of

See also ECONOMICS OF EDUCATION

Educational Reform

Adult Education, Reform Strategies in
Educational Reform: Impact of Indigenous Forms of Knowledge
Planning Educational Reforms: Use of Contingency Approach
Quality of Education in Developing Nations: Policies for Improving
Social Equality and Educational Expansion in Developing Nations

Planning Education Worldwide

Planning Education: Arab World
Planning Education: Asia
Planning Education: Latin America
Planning Education: North America and Europe
Planning Education: Sub-Saharan Africa

Politics and Policy Development

International Cooperation and Assistance in Education
International Knowledge Networks
Legitimacy in Educational Policy
Meritocracy
Nonformal Education Policy in Developing Nations
Politics of Educational Planning
School Law and Educational Planning

Teacher Supply and Demand

Planning for Effective Teaching in Developing Nations
Teacher Preparation, Conceptions of Teaching, and Evaluation: Alternative Policies

See also EDUCATIONAL RESEARCH, METHODOLOGY, AND MEASUREMENT *(Information and Policy in Educational Research)*

EDUCATIONAL RESEARCH, METHODOLOGY, AND MEASUREMENT

Aptitude Tests

Vocational Interests and Aptitudes, Measures of

Attitude and Environmental Measurement

Attitudes, Measurement of
Descriptive Scales for Measuring Educational Climate
Family and School Environmental Measures
Judgments, Measurement of
Thurstone Scales

Information and Policy in Educational Research

Census and National Survey Data
Data Banks and Data Archives
Dissemination of Educational Research
Educational History in Biographies and Autobiographies
Educational Research and Policy-making
Educational Research, History of
Policy Analysis
Policy-oriented Research
Politics of Educational Research
Research in Education: Nature, Needs, and Priorities

Measurement Models and Methods

Adaptive Testing
Approaches to Learning, Nature and Measurement of
Assessment in Schools, Methods of
Criterion-referenced Measurement
Developmental Levels, Measurement of
Item Sampling in Testing
Item Writing Techniques
Latent Trait Measurement Models
Measurement in Educational Research
Measurement of Social Background
Models of Intelligence
Partial Credit Model
Partial Order Scalogram Analyses of Nonmetric Data
Portfolios, Profiles, Records, Reports, and Certification
Q-Methodology
Questionnaires
Scaling Methods
Selection Mechanisms in Secondary Education

Measurement Theory

Classical Test Theory
Criterion-referenced Measurement
Generalizability Theory
Item Response Theory
Measurement in Educational Research
Rasch Measurement, Theory of
Reliability in Educational and Psychological Measurement
Repertory Grid Technique
Validity

Research Methodology

Action Research
Biographical Research Methods
Case Study Methods
Change, Measurement of
Cross-sectional Research Methods
Event History Analyses
Experimental Studies
Facet Theory
Feminist Research Methodology
Hermeneutics
Historical Methods in Educational Research
Human Development: Research Methodology
Interviewing for Selection and Clinical Research
Legitimatory Research
Longitudinal Research Methods
Microcomputers in Educational Research
Missing Data and Nonresponse in Survey Research
Mobility Tables
Models and Model Building
Narrative Inquiry
Oral History in Educational Research
Participant Observation and Verification
Participatory Research
Phenomenography
Quasi-experimentation
Research in Education: Epistemological Issues
Research Methodology: Scientific Methods
Research Paradigms in Education
Sampling in Survey Research
Selection Bias in Educational Research
Self-report in Educational Research
Semiotics in Educational Research
Simulation as a Research Technique
Single Case Research: Measuring Change
Sociometric Methods
Survey Research Methods
Training of Research Workers in Education
Triangulation in Educational Research
Twin Studies
Unintended Effects in Educational Research
Videotape and Audiotape Recording in Educational Research

Statistical Analysis and Data Management

Bayesian Statistics in the Analysis of Data
Canonical Analysis
Cluster Analysis
Concept Mapping
Configural Frequency Analyses of Categorized Data
Content and Text Analysis
Contingency Tables
Correlational Procedures in Data Analysis
Correspondence Analysis of Qualitative Data
Data Envelopment Analysis
Database Management Systems in Education
Decision Theory in Educational Testing
Descriptive Data, Analysis of
Discriminant Analysis
Educational Research, Moderating and Mediating Effects in
Expectancy Tables in Educational Prediction
Exploratory Data Analysis
Factor Analysis
Factorial Modeling
Galois Lattices
Hierarchical Linear Models
Hypothesis Testing
Interaction and Detection of its Effects in Educational Research
Log–Linear Models
Measures of Variation
Meta-analysis
Missing Scores in Survey Research
Multilevel Analysis
Multitrait–Multimethod Analysis
Multivariate Analysis
Nonparametric and Distribution-free Statistics
Partial Order Scalogram Analyses of Nonmetric Data
Path Analysis and Linear Structural Relations Analysis
Path Analysis with Latent Variables
Prediction in Educational Research
Profile Analysis
Projections of Educational Statistics
Rating Scale Analysis
Regression Analyses of Quantified Data
Robust Statistical Procedures
Sampling Errors in Survey Research
Secondary Data Analysis
Significance Testing
Smallest Space Analysis
Social Network Analysis
Variance and Covariance, Analysis of

Testing and Tests

Achievement Test Scales
Adaptive Testing
Computerized Educational Testing
Criterion-referenced Measurement
Educational Achievement: Comparative Studies
Essays: Equating of Marks
Essays, Scoring of
Examinations: Public
Foreign Language Testing
Individualized Testing in the Classroom
Item Banking in Testing and Assessment
Item Bias
Item Sampling in Testing
Learning Potential and Learning Potential Tests
Literacy, Numeracy, and Oracy Testing
Measures of Variation
Missing Scores in Survey Research
Mother Tongue Language Tests
Multiple Choice Tests, Guessing in
Objective Tests in Measurement
Personality Inventories
Practical Mathematics and Science Testing
Projective Testing Techniques
Rating Scales
Student Progress, Charting of
Test Administration
Test Bias
Testing and the Curriculum
Tests and Attitude Scales, Translation of
Tests and Examinations, Coaching for
Tests: Different Types
Tests, Equating of
Test-taking Anxiety and Expectancy of Performance

See also COMPARATIVE AND INTERNATIONAL EDUCATION *(Concepts, Methods, and Data Resources in Comparative and International Educational Research)*; EDUCATIONAL EVALUATION

EDUCATIONAL TECHNOLOGY

Applications and Institutional Settings

Computerized Educational Testing
Distance Education, Educational Technology in
Educational Technology in Elementary and Secondary Education
Educational Technology in Technical Training for Youth and Adults
Gender and New Technology
Media and Learning

Media in Education: Role of Still, Audio, and Audiovisual
Media Program Administration
Microcomputer Technology for Students with Special Needs
New Information Technology and the Curriculum
New Information Technology in Language Education
New Information Technology in Mathematics Education
New Information Technology in Science Education
Preschool Educational Television Programs
Technology in Educational Planning
Videotape and Audiotape Recording in Educational Research

Delivery Options

Computer Simulations and Modeling
Computer-assisted Learning
Computer-managed Learning
Computers in Education
Databases, Instructional Uses of
Hypertext, Educational Applications of
Individual Techniques for Teaching and Learning
Logo, Educational Applications of
Modular Curricula
Programmed Learning

Delivery Systems

CD Technology
Computer Networking for Education
Information Storage and Retrieval
Instructional Radio
Instructional TV and Video
Language Laboratories
Telecommunication in Education
Videodisk Technology: Interactive

Design Functions, Tools, and Resources

Courseware Design
Idea Generation and Decision-making Techniques
Information Systems for Education
Instructional Design Theories
Job Analysis in Corporate Education
Libraries as Learning Resources
Media Selection
Message Design in Learning
Motivation in Instructional Design
Prototyping as a Design Activity
Software Tools in Courseware Design

Educational Technology as a Concept and as a Field of Study

Artificial Intelligence as a Contributing Field to Instructional Design
Communication, Media, and Instrumentation
Educational Technology: Conceptual Frameworks and Historical Development
Educational Technology: Scope of the Field
Ergonomics
Instructional Psychology (as a Contributing Field to Instructional Design)
Systems Approach to Design and Development

Evaluation, Diffusion, and Implementation

Cost-effectiveness of Training Courses
Designing Innovations from an Implementation Perspective
Dissemination and Diffusion of Knowledge and Innovation
Evaluating Implementation of Educational Programs and Innovations
Innovations, Implementation of
Program and Project Management
Project Evaluation and Monitoring

Impact of Educational Technology

Broadcasting and Technology: Effects on Children and Youth
Computer Literacy
Computer Networking for Education
Copyright
Educational Technology Activities of International Organizations
Educational Technology: Developing Nations
Publishing: Transnational Influences
Social Implications of Educational Technology
Visual Literacy

Media Production

Audio Media, Production of
Audiovisual Programs, Production of
Educational Computer Software, Production of
Electronic Publishing
Multimedia Packages, Production of
Print Media, Production of
Software Publishing
Still Media, Production of

Media Specific Organizations and Journals

Computers in Education, Organizations and Journals on
Distance Education, International Organizations and Journals on
Educational Media, Organizations and Journals on
Libraries, Organizations and Journals on

Methodology

Laboratory Packages for Science Learning
Media in Education: Role of Still, Audio, and Audiovisual
Microcomputer-based Laboratories and Science Education
Multimedia Systems in Education
Printed Materials in Education

See also INSTRUCTIONAL PSYCHOLOGY *(Computers, Media, and Learning)*

GIRLS AND WOMEN IN EDUCATION

History of Women's Education

Women's Education, History of: Australia
Women's Education, History of: Francophone Countries
Women's Education, History of: German-speaking Europe
Women's Education, History of: India
Women's Education, History of: Islamic Countries
Women's Education, History of: North America

Sex Roles and Gender in Education

Coeducation versus Single-sex Schooling
Female Access to Vocational Education and Training
Gender and Education
Gender and Educational Management in Developing Nations
Gender and New Technology
Gender and School Learning: Mathematics
Gender and School Learning: Science
Minority Women and Education
School Texts and Gender, Analysis of
Women and Academic Careers
Women and Adult Education
Women and the Professionalization of Teaching
Women in Educational Administration: United States
Women's Studies Programs

Theoretical Perspectives on Women's Education

Feminist Approaches and the Curriculum
Feminist Ethics and Moral Education
Feminist Research Methodology
Gender Theories in Education
Sex Education, Conceptions of
Sex Equity: Assumptions and Strategies
Women in Education: New Scholarship

HISTORY AND HISTORIOGRAPHY OF EDUCATION

History of Education

Adult Education, History of
Anthropology of Education: History and Overview
Contemporary History of Education
Curriculum, History of
Education as a Field of Study, Origins of
Educational History in Biographies and Autobiographies
Educational Research, History of
Historiography of Education
Instructional Psychology, History of
Mathematics Education, History of
Philosophy of Education: Historical Overview
Preschool Education, History of
Science Education, History of
Special Education, History of
Vocational Training, History of

Thinkers and Practitioners in Educational History

Comenius and Education
Descartes and Education
Erasmus and Education
Froebel and Education
Herbart and Education
Kerschensteiner and Education
Locke and Education
Luther and Education
Montessori and Education
Pestalozzi and Education
Plato and Education
Quintilian and Education
Rousseau and Education
Saint Augustine and Education
Saint Ignatius Loyola and Education
Saint Thomas Aquinas and Education

Spencer and Education
See also GIRLS AND WOMEN IN EDUCATION *(History of Women's Education)*

HUMAN DEVELOPMENT

Biological Approaches to Human Development

Abnormal Prenatal Development
Brain Development and Human Behavior
Genetics and Human Development
Physical Growth and Development: Universal Changes and Individual Differences
Sex Differences in Behavior and Behavioral Development

Cognitive Development

Cognitive Development and the Acquisition of Expertise
Cognitive Development: Individual Differences
Cognitive Development: Overview
Gifted Children, Development of
Intellectual Development across the Lifespan
Language Development
Learning across the Lifespan, Development of
Motor Development and Skill Acquisition
Perceptual Development
Play: Developmental Stages, Functions, and Educational Support
Reasoning in Childhood, Development of
Social Cognition, Development of

General Issues in Human Development

Developmental Psychopathology
Human Development: Cross-cultural Approaches
Human Development: Overview
Human Development: Research and Educational Practice
Human Development: Research and Social Policy
Human Development: Research Methodology

Personality Development

Achievement Motivation, Development of
Aggression, Development and Socialization of
Early Experience and Human Development
Emotional Development
Family Influence on Human Development
Gender Roles
Moral Development
Peer Relations and Development
Personality Development
Problems and Crises in Human Development
Prosocial Behavior, Development of
Self-concept, Development of
Self-related Cognition, Learned Helplessness, Learned Optimism, and Human Development
Social Development
Temperament Development

Theories and (Prescientific) Concepts of Human Development

Behaviorist Approaches to Human Development
Cognitive Development: Information-processing Approach
Ecological Models of Human Development
Evolutionary Theory: Ethological and Sociobiological Aspects
Human Development: Cultural and Religious Concepts
Humanistic Models of Human Development
Piaget's Theory of Human Development
Psychodynamic Theories of Human Development
Social Cognitive Theory of Human Development

Stages of Human Development in the Lifespan

Adolescence
Aging and Adult Development
Childhood
Human Development, Stages in
Infancy
Lifespan Development
See also ADULT EDUCATION *(Human Development and Adult Learning)*; INSTRUCTIONAL PSYCHOLOGY *(Processes and Outcomes of Learning)*; TEACHING *(Learning Processes, Students)*

INSTRUCTIONAL PSYCHOLOGY

Assessment and Learning

Assessment in the Service of Learning
Learning Potential and Learning Potential Tests

Computers, Media, and Learning

Computer Programming, Learning and Instruction of
Computers and Learning

Media and Learning
Problem-solving and Learning: Computer Modeling
See also EDUCATIONAL TECHNOLOGY

Curriculum and the Psychology of Learning and Instruction

Attitudes and Values, Acquiring
Mathematics, Learning and Instruction of
Motor Skills, Learning and Instruction of
Problem-solving and Thinking, Development of Learning Skills in
Reading Comprehension, Learning of
Reading, Learning and Instruction of
Science, Learning and Instruction of
Social Sciences, Learning and Instruction of
Visual and Performing Arts, Learning and Instruction of
Writing, Learning and Instruction of

History of Instructional Psychology

Instructional Psychology, History of

Individual Differences and Learning and Instruction

Abilities and Aptitudes
Cognitive Styles and Learning
Individual Differences and Instruction
Intelligence, Learning, and Instruction

Knowledge and Skill Acquisition in Different Domains

Expert Level of Understanding

Learning Environments

Group Processes in the Classroom
Home Environment and School Learning
Learning Environments
Learning in Industrial Settings

Processes and Outcomes of Learning

Adult Learning: Overview
Architecture of Cognition
Attention in Learning
Bilingualism
Cognition and Learning
Concept Learning
Constructivism and Learning
Creativity
Declarative and Procedural Knowledge
Development, Learning, and Instruction
Feedback in Learning
Knowledge Representation and Organization
Language and Learning in Education
Learning Processes and Learning Outcomes
Learning Strategies and Learning to Learn
Literacy
Metacognition
Motivation and Learning
Perception and Learning
Preconceptions and Misconceptions
Prior Knowledge and Learning
Reasoning
Self-regulation in Learning
Task Analysis
Transfer of Learning

Social, Cultural, and Affective Aspects of Learning

Affect, Emotions, and Learning
Culture and Learning
Peer Relations and Learning
Personality, School, and Social Environment as Learning Determinants
Social and Communication Skills
Social Interaction and Learning
Stress, Coping, and Learning

Theories and Models of Learning in Educational Settings

Instructional Psychology, Paradigms in
Learning Activity
Learning Theories: Historical Overview and Trends
Models of Learning
See also ADULT EDUCATION *(Human Development and Adult Learning)*; HUMAN DEVELOPMENT; TEACHING; TEACHER EDUCATION

NATIONAL SYSTEMS OF EDUCATION

Africa

Benin
Botswana
Burkina Faso
Burundi
Cameroon
Central African Republic

Chad
Côte d'Ivoire
Egypt
Ethiopia
Gambia
Ghana
Guinea, Republic of
Guinea-Bissau
Kenya
Lesotho
Liberia
Libya
Madagascar
Malawi
Mali
Mauritania
Mauritius
Morocco
Mozambique
Namibia
Niger
Nigeria
Rwanda
Seychelles
Sierra Leone
South Africa
Sudan
Swaziland
Tanzania
Togo
Tunisia
Uganda
Zaire
Zimbabwe

Americas Including Caribbean

Antigua and Barbuda
Argentina
Bahamas
Barbados
Belize
Canada
Chile
Colombia
Costa Rica
Cuba
Dominica
El Salvador
Guadaloupe and Martinique
Guatemala
Honduras
Jamaica
Mexico
Nicaragua
Panama
Paraguay
Peru
Senegal
Suriname
United States
Uruguay
Venezuela

Asia

Afghanistan
Bangladesh
Bhutan
China, People's Republic of
Hong Kong
India
Japan
Korea, Democratic People's Republic of
Korea, Republic of
Laos
Macau
Malaysia
Maldives
Mongolia
Myanmar
Nepal
Pakistan
Singapore
Sri Lanka
Thailand
Vietnam

Australasia and Pacific

American Samoa
Australia
Brunei
Fiji
Indonesia
Kiribati
New Zealand
Papua New Guniea
Philippines
Tonga
Tuvalu
Vanuatu

Europe

Albania
Austria

Belgium
Bulgaria
Cyprus
Denmark
Estonia
Finland
France
Germany
Greece
Hungary
Iceland
Ireland, Republic of
Italy
Latvia
Lithuania
Luxembourg
Malta
Netherlands, The
Norway
Poland
Portugal
Romania
Russia
Slovenia
Spain
Sweden
Switzerland
Turkey
United Kingdom

Middle East

Bahrain
Iran
Israel
Jordan
Kuwait
Lebanon
Oman
Saudi Arabia
Syria
United Arab Emirates
Yemen

PHILOSOPHY OF EDUCATION

Analytical Traditions in the Philosophy of Education

Critical Theory and Education
Critical Thinking: Philosophical Issues
Curriculum: Philosophical Perspectives
Dewey, Pragmatism, and Education
Educational Administration: Ethical and Philosophical Issues
Philosophy of Education: Analytic Tradition
Philosophy of Education: Historical Overview
Philosophy of Education: Western European Perspectives

Epistemological Issues in Education and Philosophy of Science

Epistemology and Education
Hermeneutics
Philosophy of Science and Science Education
Positivism, Anti-Positivism, and Empiricism
Postmodernism and Education
Relativism and Realism
Research in Education: Epistemological Issues
Teacher Education: Philosophical Issues
Values in Educational Inquiry: Philosophical Issues

Political, Social, and Moral Philosophy

Equality of Educational Opportunity: Philosophical Issues
Ethics, Moral Philosophy, and Education
Marxism and Educational Thought
Moral Education: Philosophical Issues
Phenomenology and Existentialism
Political Philosophy and Education

Theories of Human Nature of Major Religious Traditions

Buddhist Theory of Human Nature and Development
Christian Theory of Human Nature and Development
Confucian Theory of Human Nature and Development
Hindu Theory of Human Nature and Development
Islamic Theory of Human Nature and Development
Judaic Theory of Human Nature and Development
Shinto Theory of Human Nature and Development

PRESCHOOL EDUCATION

Early Childhood Education

Childcare and Preschool Effects
Early Childhood Interventions
Early Childhood Personnel, Preparation of
Emergent Literacy
Gender Roles and Preschool Education

Infant Programs
Preschool Educational Television Programs
Toddler Programs

Evaluation of Preschool Education

Assessment in Early Childhood
Evaluation of Preschool Programs
School Readiness

Parents and Preschool Education

Parent Education for Early Childhood Education
Parent Involvement in Preschool Programs

Policy Issues in Early Childhood Education

Childcare Policies and Programs: International Overview
Preschool Education: Worldwide Trends

See also HUMAN DEVELOPMENT; TEACHER EDUCATION; TEACHING

SOCIOLOGY OF EDUCATION

Family and Schooling

Family and School Environmental Measures
Family and Schooling
Family, School, and Cultural Capital
Family, School, and Social Capital
Family Status and Economic Status
Measurement of Social Background

School Processes

Aspirations and Expectations of Students
Dropouts, School Leavers, and Truancy
Empowerment Skills, Acquisition of
Political Socialization and Education
Race and Ethnicity in Education
School and Classroom Dynamics
School Dropouts
Sex Differences and Educational Outcomes
Social Mobility, School Stratification, and Education
Socialization

Social Theories in the Study of Education

Classical Sociological Theories of Education
Contemporary Sociological Theories of Education
Critical Theory and Education
Reproduction Theory
Resistance Theory
Sociology of Education: Overview

Sociological Fields in the Study of Education

Curriculum: Sociological Perspectives
Learning in School, Sociology of
Sociology of Adult Education
Sociology of Teaching
Special Education, Sociology of

Structure of Educational Systems

Ability Grouping and Tracking in Schools
Coeducation versus Single-sex Schooling
Discipline in Schools
Loose Coupling and Educational Systems
Public and Private Schools: Sociological Perspectives
Second Chance Education and Alternative Routes

Teachers and Society

Teacher Burnout
Teachers' Expectations
Teachers' Roles
Teachers' Work and Political Action

The School as a Social System

Education and the State
Multicultural Education
School Choice, Foundations of
Schools as Sociocultural Systems
Stratification in Educational Systems

Youth in Schools

Student Friendships and Conflict in School
Student Political Activism and Student Movements
Youth and Leisure
Youth Cultures and Subcultures
Youth Unemployment

TEACHER EDUCATION

Accreditation, Certification, and Evaluation

Accreditation and Standards: Teacher Education
Teacher Certification and Standards

Teacher Education, Evaluation in
Teacher Preparation, Conceptions of Teaching, and Evaluation: Alternative Policies

Concepts and Topics in Teacher Education

Teacher Education and Adult Development
Teacher Education, Case Methods in
Teacher Education, Economics of
Teacher Education, Governance of
Teacher Education: Philosophical Issues
Teacher Education: Professional Ethics
Teacher Education, Technology in
Teaching and Teacher Education: Comparative and International Studies

Educating Special Categories of Teachers

Early Childhood Personnel, Preparation of
Mathematics Teacher Education
Music Teacher Education
Physical Education Teacher Education
Reading Teacher Education
Science Teacher Education
Social Studies Teacher Education
Teacher Education and Special Education Needs
Teacher Education for Language Arts and Literature
Teacher Training for Vocational Technical Subjects
Visual Arts Teacher Education

Inservice and Onservice Teacher Education

Teacher Education: Inservice
Teacher Education: Onservice
Teacher Recruitment and Induction
Teachers, Professional Socialization of

Preservice Teacher Education

Laboratory Experiences in Teacher Education
Schools for Laboratory and Professional Development
Student Teaching and Field Experiences
Teacher Education, Microteaching in
Teacher Education Programs: Curriculum
Teacher Education Programs: Structure
Teacher Education, Supervision in
Teacher Educators, Characteristics of

Teacher Characteristics

Teachers, Characteristics of Prospective

TEACHING

Classroom Contexts and Constraints

Age Grouping of Students
Class Size
Classroom Environments
Classrooms: Grouping of Students
Frame Factors
Goal Structures
Grade Repeating
Learning Environments
Lesson Structure
Paraprofessionals, Availability and Use of
Seating Arrangements in Classrooms
School Culture and Peer Groups
Student Diversity and Classroom Teaching
Student Roles in Classrooms
Students in Classrooms, Gender and Racial Differences among
Teaching, Realities of
Time: Allocated and Instructional

Classroom Management and Control

Behavior, Analysis and Modification of
Classroom Rules and Routines
Group Dynamics
Reinforcement
Teacher Managerial Behaviors

Concepts and Theories of Teaching and Teachers

Research into Practice: Translating
Sociology of Teaching
Teachers as Artists
Teachers as Clinicians
Teachers as Professionals
Teachers as Researchers
Teaching: Aptitude–Treatment Interaction Model
Teaching: Behavioral Theories
Teaching, Cognitive Developmental Theories of
Teaching: Heuristic Models
Teaching: Implicit Theories
Teaching: Informational Processing Theories
Teaching: Linguistic and Sociolinguistic Theories
Teaching, Paradigms for Research on
Teaching: Social Psychological Theories
Teaching, Synthesizing Research on
Women and the Professionalization of Teaching

Evaluation and Assessment

Assessment in the Service of Learning

Classroom Assessment
Individualized Testing in the Classroom
Questioning Strategies
Students, Grading and Evaluation of
Teacher Certification and Standards
Teacher Evaluating Behavior

Learning Processes: Students

Academic Learning Time
Affect, Emotions, and Learning
Aspirations and Expectations of Students
Attention in Learning
Cognitive Styles and Learning
Comprehension, Teaching and Testing for
Concept Learning, Teaching and Testing for
Creativity, Teaching and Testing for
Critical Reading: Teaching and Assessing
Learning Strategies, Teaching and Testing for
Memory, Teaching and Testing for
Metacognitive Strategies, Teaching and Testing for
Motor Skills, Learning and Instruction of
Prior Knowledge and Learning
Problem-solving, Teaching and Testing for
Student Cognitive Processing and Learning
Student Perceptions of Classrooms
Study Habits and Strategies
Written Composition, Teaching and Testing for

Teacher Characteristics

Teacher Development
Teacher Expertise
Teachers' Beliefs and Belief Systems
Teachers' Knowledge
Teaching: Social Status

Teacher Effectiveness

Classroom Observation
Substitute Teachers
Teacher Evaluation
Teaching, Student Evaluation of

Teacher Planning and Decision Making

Homework
Instructional Alignment
Instructional Pacing
Student Needs: Diagnosing
Teacher Planning, Approaches to
Teachers and Policy: Implications for Management

Teaching as an Occupation

School–Parent Relationships
Teacher Burnout
Teacher Responsibility
Teacher Roles and Teaching Styles: Adult Education
Teacher Stress and Burnout
Teacher Unionization, Economics of
Teacher Unions
Teachers' Expectations
Teachers, Professional Socialization of
Teachers' Work and Political Action

Teaching Methods and Instructional Strategies

Assessment in the Service of Learning
Classroom Discussion
Cooperative Learning
Direct Instruction
Discovery Learning and Teaching
Feedback in Learning
Individualized Instruction
Individualized Testing in the Classroom
Mastery Learning
Nonverbal Classroom Behavior
Open Education
Questioning Strategies
Science Laboratory Instruction
Seatwork, Assignment and Supervision of
Simulations and Games
Student Influences on Teaching
Teacher Evaluating Behavior
Teaching and Learning, Demonstration Methods of
Teaching and Learning, Explanation in
Teaching: Diagnostic–Prescriptive
Teaching in Small Groups
Teaching Methods for Adults
Teaching: Reflective
Technology and the Classroom Teacher
Tutoring

Theories and Models of Teaching

Teaching: Aptitude–Treatment Interaction Model
Teaching: Behavioral Theories
Teaching, Cognitive Developmental Theories of
Teaching: Heuristic Models
Teaching: Implicit Theories
Teaching: Informational Processing Theories
Teaching: Linguistic and Sociolinguistic Theories
Teaching, Paradigms for Research on
Teaching: Social Psychological Theories

See also INSTRUCTIONAL PSYCHOLOGY

TECHNICAL AND VOCATIONAL EDUCATION AND TRAINING

Industrialized and Developing Country Perspectives

Africa: Traditional Apprenticeship
China, People's Republic of: Vocationalizing Education
Japan: Vocational Education and Training
Latin America: Articulation of Education, Training, and Work
Latin America: National Training Agencies
Soviet Union: Vocational Education and Training
Technical and Vocational Education and Training: Eastern and Southern Africa
United States: Federal Vocational Education Policy
Vocational Education and Training: Eastern and Central Europe
Vocational Education and Training in Germany: National and International Dimensions
Vocational Education and Training: Western Europe
Vocational Training Initiatives: United Kingdom

Provision, Organization, and Financing

European Community: Vocational Training Qualifications
International Labour Organisation (ILO): Vocational Training
Payroll Levies for Training
Planning for Vocational Education and Training
Quality Assurance in Vocational Education and Training
Teacher Training for Vocational Technical Subjects
Training, Government Role in
Training with Production
Vocational Education and Training and the Macroeconomic Environment
Vocational Education and Training: Improving Cost-effectiveness in Developing Nations
Vocational Education and Training, International Assistance for

School-based, Institution-based, and Industry-based Technical and Vocational Education and Training

Education and Productive Work
Enterprise Education: Small Business Training
Informal Sector: Vocational Education and Training
Modularization in Vocational Education and Training
Nongovernmental Organizations (Latin America): Training for Disadvantaged Groups
Primary School Agriculture in Sub-Saharan Africa
Private Sector Training, Education and Performance Contracting in

Theoretical and Conceptual Issues

Taxonomies of Skill Development
Technical and Vocational Education and Training
Training and Education, Convergence between
Vocationalism: Theoretical Assumptions

Traditions of Training

Apprenticeship, History and Development of
Technician Training
Vocational Education and Training: Anglo-German Comparisons
Vocational Training Modes: Sweden, Germany, and Japan
See also ADULT EDUCATION

LIST OF CONTRIBUTORS

Contributors are listed in alphabetical order together with their affiliations. Titles of articles which they have authored follow in alphabetical order, along with the respective volume and page numbers. Where articles are co-authored, this has been indicated by an asterisk preceding the article title.

ABDULLAH, D. H. A. (Ministry of Education, Bandar Seri Begawan, Brunei Darussalam)
Brunei Darussalam: System of Education **1**: 570–77

ABE, Y. (Kokuga Kuin University, Tokyo, Japan)
Broadcast Education in Adult Education **1**: 561–64

ABRAHAMSSON, K. (University of Stockholm, Stockholm, Sweden)
Time Policies and Lifelong Education **11**: 6390–95

ADAMS, A. V. (World Bank, Washington, DC, USA)
Vocational Education and Training and the Macroeconomic Environment **11**: 6633–38

ADAMS, D. (University of Pittsburgh, Pittsburgh, Pennsylvania, USA)
Comparative Methodology in Education* **2: 948–58; *Educational Planning: Differing Models* **3**: 1804–10

ADAMS, R. J. (Australian Council for Educational Research, Hawthorn, Victoria, Australia)
Student Progress, Charting of* **10: 5783–91

ADDOU, H. (Teachers College, Columbia University, New York, USA)
Agricultural Productivity and Education* **1: 244–54

ADLER, S. A. (University of Missouri, Kansas City, Missouri, USA)
Social Studies Teacher Education **10**: 5583–85

AHMED, M. (UNICEF, New York, USA)
Nonformal Education, Economics of **7**: 4136–41

AINSCROW, M. (University of Minnesota, Minneapolis, Minnesota, USA)
Children and Youth with Special Needs, Education of* **2: 719–30

AIRASIAN, P. W. (Boston College, Chestnut Hill, Massachusetts, USA)
Classroom Assessment **2**: 792–96; **Test Administration* **11**: 6311–15

AL-BAADI, H. M. (Ministry of Education, Riyadh, Saudi Arabia)
Planning Education: Arab World **8**: 4483–85; *Saudi Arabia: System of Education* **9**: 5142–51

AL-NAYADI, M. A. (United Arab Emirates University, Abu Dhabi, United Arab Emirates)
United Arab Emirates: System of Education **11**: 6511–15

AL-SHANFARI, A. M. (Ministry of Education, Muscat, Oman)
Oman: System of Education **7**: 4201–06

AL-SUBAIE, A. A. T. (Ministry of Education, Doha, Qatar)
Qatar: System of Education **8**: 4849–55

ALBAN-METCALF, R. J. (Trinity and All Saints College, Leeds, UK)
Repertory Grid Technique **9**: 5013–16

ALEXANDER, T. J. (Organisation for Economic Co-operation and Development, Paris, France)
Organisation for Economic Co-operation and Development (OECD): Educational Activities **7**: 4225–27

ALGOZZINE, B. (University of North Carolina, Charlotte, North Carolina, USA)
Children and Youth With Special Needs, Diagnosis and Classification of* **2: 711–19

ALI, M. M. (Ministry of Education, Dhaka, Bangladesh)
Bangladesh: System of Education **1**: 450–57

ALKIN, M. C. (University of California, Los Angeles, California, USA)
Curriculum Evaluation Models **3**: 1279–83

ALLAL, L. (University of Geneva, Geneva, Switzerland)
Generalizability Theory* **5: 2458–62

ALLERUP, P. (Danish Institute for Educational Research, Copenhagen, Denmark)
Rasch Measurement, Theory of **8**: 4902–13

ALLINGTON, R. L. (State University of New York, Albany, New York, USA)
Reading and the Mildly Handicapped* **8: 4930–36

ALMANNAI, L. (Ministry of Education, Manama, Bahrain)
Bahrain: System of Education* **1: 444–50

ALMEIDA, C. (Department of Education, Macau)
Macau: System of Education* **6: 3539–45

ALMOTAWA, A. (Ministry of Education, Manama, Bahrain)
Bahrain: System of Education* **1: 444–50

ALTBACH, P. G. (State University of New York, Buffalo, New York, USA)
International Knowledge Networks **5**: 2993–98; *Student Political Activism and Student Movements* **10**: 5775–83

ALTEN, S. R. (Syracuse University, Syracuse, New York, USA)
Audio Media, Production of **1**: 396–400

ALTRICHTER, H. (University of Innsbruck, Innsbruck, Austria)
Austria: System of Education* **1: 423–32

ALVERMANN, D. E. (University of Georgia, Athens, Georgia, USA)
Reading Teacher Education **8**: 4945–48

AMMERMAN, R. T. (Western Pennsylvania School for Blind Children, Pittsburgh, Pennsylvania, USA)
Abused and Neglected Children and Youth **1**: 15–20

ANDER, C. (National Institute for Education, Budapest, Hungary)
Galois Lattices* **4: 2395–400

ANDERSON, D. S. (Australian National University, Canberra, ACT, Australia)
Public and Private Schools: Sociological Perspectives **8**: 4824–31

ANDERSON, J. (The Flinders University of South Australia, Bedford Park, South Australia, Australia)
Content and Text Analysis **2**: 1074–79; **Data Banks and Data Archives* **3**: 1377–81

ANDERSON, L. (University of Illinois at Chicago, Chicago, Illinois, USA)
Data Envelopment Analysis* **3: 1381–87

ANDERSON, L. M. (Michigan State University, East Lansing, Michigan, USA)
Seatwork, Assignment and Supervision of **9**: 5359–63

ANDERSON, L. W. (University of South Carolina, Columbia, South Carolina, USA)
Attitudes, Measurement of **1**: 380–90; *Individualized Instruction* **5**: 2773–79; **Instructional Pacing* **5**: 2867–70; **Substitute Teachers* **10**: 5832–34; *Time, Allocated and Instructional* **11**: 6388–90

ANDERSON, R. H. (University of South Florida, Tampa, Florida, USA)
Nongraded Curriculum* **7: 4155–57

ANDRICH, D. (Murdoch University, Murdoch, Western Australia, Australia)
Essays: Equating of Marks **4**: 2012–17; *Rating Scale Analysis* **8**: 4918–23; *Thurstone Scales* **11**: 6385–88

ANT, M. (National Institute for the Development of Professional Training, Luxembourg)
Luxembourg: System of Education **6**: 3531–38

ANWARD, J. (Stockholm University, Stockholm, Sweden)
Semiotics in Educational Research **9**: 5411–17

ARRIAGADA, A-M (World Bank, Washington, DC, USA)
Occupational Training, Economics of* **7: 4197–201

ARTERO-BONAME, M. T. (University of Guam, Mangilao, Guam, USA)
Questioning Strategies* **8: 4875–82

ARVIDSON, L (University of Linköping, Linköping, Sweden)
Folk High Schools* **4: 2324–27

ASENDORPF, J. B. (Max Planck Institute, Munich, Germany)
Social Development **9**: 5523–28

ASSIÉ-LUMUMBA, N. T. (Cornell University, Ithaca, New York, USA)
Women's Education, History of: Francophone Countries **11**: 6735–41

ASTON, M. H. (The Advisory Unit, Computers in Education, Hatfield, UK)
Software Publishing **10**: 5618–22

ATHERLEY, L. (UNESCO, Paris, France)
Barbados: System of Education* **1: 458–65

AZIZ, A. A. (Ministry of Education, Kuala Lumpur, Malaysia)
Malaysia: System of Education* **6: 3564–72

AZIZ-ZADEH, H. (Tehran, Iran)
Iran: System of Education **5**: 3007–11

BAILIN, S. (University of Manitoba, Winnipeg, Manitoba, Canada)
Critical Thinking: Philosophical Issues **2**: 1204–08

BAKER, C. D. (University of Queensland, St Lucia, Queensland, Australia)
School Texts and Gender, Analysis of **9**: 5299–302

BAKER, D. (University of Brighton, Brighton, UK)
Literacy and Numeracy: Concepts and Definitions **6**: 3453–59

BAKER, E. L. (University of California, Los Angeles, California, USA)
Measurement-driven Curriculum **7**: 3722–26

BALL, S. (University of Sydney, Sydney, New South Wales, Australia)
Unintended Effects in Educational Research **11**: 6507–11

BALL, S. J. (University of London, London, UK)
Micropolitics of Schools **7**: 3821–26; *Participant Observation and Verification* **7**: 4316–19

BALLSTAEDT, S-P. (University of Tübingen, Tübingen, Germany)
Comprehension, Teaching and Testing for* **2: 964–69

BANDURA, A. (Stanford University, Stanford, California, USA)
Social Cognitive Theory of Human Development **9**: 5513–18

BANK, B. J. (University of Missouri, Columbia, Missouri, USA)
Student Friendships and Conflict in School **10**: 5754–59

BARNETT, W. S. (Rutgers State University, New Brunswick, New Jersey, USA)
Evaluation Of Preschool Programs **4**: 2141–45; *Preschool Education, Economics of* **8**: 4662–66

BARR, R. (National College of Education, Evanston, Illinois, USA)
Classrooms: Grouping of Students **2**: 821–25

BARRINGTON, J. M. (Victoria University of Wellington, Wellington, New Zealand)
New Zealand: System of Education **7**: 4104–11

BARROW, R. (Simon Fraser University, Burnaby, British Columbia, Canada)
Philosophy of Education: Analytic Tradition **8**: 4442–47

BATES, A. W. (Open Learning Agency, Burnaby, British Columbia, Canada)
Distance Education, Educational Technology in **3**: 1573–80

BÁTHORY, Z. (National Institute of Public Education, Budapest, Hungary)
Hungary: System of Education **5**: 2697–706

BEARE, H. (University of Melbourne, Melbourne, Victoria, Australia)
School Reform and Restructuring* **9: 5275–81

BEATON, A. E. (Boston College, Chestnut Hill, Massachusetts, USA)
Item Sampling in Testing **5**: 3055–61; *Missing Scores in Survey Research* **7**: 3858–62

BEEN, V. R. (Ministry of Education, Kingston, Jamaica)
Jamaica: System of Education* **6: 3067–74

BEHRMAN, J. R. (University of Pennsylvania, Philadelphia, Pennsylvania, USA)
Kinship Studies* **6: 3138–44

BÉLANGER, P. (UNESCO Institute for Education, Hamburg, Germany)
UNESCO and Adult Education* **11: 6501–07

BELLER, E. K. (Freie Universität Berlin, Berlin, Germany)
Infant Programs **5**: 2803–06

BELLI, H. (Ministry of Education, Managua, Nicaragua)
Nicaragua: System of Education **7**: 4111–17

BEN JABALLAH, H. (Ministry of Education, Tunis, Tunisia)
Tunisia: System of Education* **11: 6466–76

BENGTSSON, J. (Organisation for Economic Co-operation and Development, Paris, France)
Recurrent and Alternation Education* **8: 4957–64

BENNETT, J. (UNESCO, Paris, France)
Preschool Education: Worldwide Trends **8**: 4670–77

BENNETT, J. A. (Ministry of Education, Belize City, Belize)
Belize: System of Education **1**: 504–10

BENNETT, N. (University of Exeter, Exeter, UK)
Group Processes in the Classroom **5**: 2532–36

BEN-PERETZ, M. (University of Haifa, Haifa, Israel)
Curriculum-specific Evaluation Criteria* **3: 1359–67; *Teacher Education Programs: Curriculum* **10**: 5991–95; *Teachers as Curriculum-makers* **10**: 6089–92

BENSON, C. S. (University of California, Berkeley, California, USA)
Educational Financing **3**: 1789–93; *Taxonomies of Skill Development* **10**: 5914–19

BENSON, J. (University of Georgia, Athens, Georgia, USA)
Evaluation Design, Evolution of* **4: 2079–89

BENTON, L. (New Jersey Institute of Technology, Newark, New Jersey, USA)
Postliteracy: Concepts and Policies **8**: 4634–39

BERG, D. L. (Council of Ministers of Education, Toronto, Ontario, Canada)
Canada: System of Education **2**: 618–26

BERGMANN, H. (German Institute for International Educational Research, Frankfurt, Germany)
Niger: System of Education **7**: 4117–24

BERKHOUT, S. J. (University of Pretoria, Pretoria, South Africa)
South Africa: System of Education* **10: 5625–35

BERLINER, D. C. (Arizona State University, Tempe, Arizona, USA)
Teacher Expertise **10**: 6020–26

BERMAMET, T. (Ministry of Education, Amman, Jordan)
Jordan: System of Education* **6: 3106–13

BERNARD, D. C. (UNESCO, Bangkok, Thailand)
Vietnam: System of Education* **11: 6608–14

BEYNON, J. (UNESCO, Paris, France)
Facilities and Physical Plant **4**: 2219–25

BIALYSTOK, E. (York University, North York, Ontario, Canada)
Reading Comprehension in Second and Foreign Language **8**: 4936–40

BIDDLE, B. J. (University of Missouri, Columbia, Missouri, USA)
Teachers' Roles **10**: 6127–32; *Youth and Leisure* **11**: 6794–98

BIERVLIET, W. E. (CESO, The Hague, The Netherlands)
Training with Production **11**: 6445–52

BIGGS, J. B. (University of Hong Kong, Hong Kong)
Approaches to Learning: Nature and Measurement of **1**: 318–22

BIJOU, S. W. (University of Nevada–Reno, Reno, Nevada, USA)
Behaviorist Approaches to Human Development **1**: 495–97

BIKLEN, D. (Syracuse University, Syracuse, New York, USA)
Language Disorders and Autism **6**: 3232–35

BIKLEN, S. K. (Syracuse University, Syracuse, New York, USA)
Women in Education: New Scholarship **11**: 6723–27

BILLARD, L. (University of Georgia, Athens, Georgia, USA)
Women and Academic Careers **11**: 6709–12

BIRCH, I. K. F. (University of Western Australia, Perth, Western Australia, Australia)
Legal Factors Affecting Curriculum **6**: 3356–60; *School Law and Educational Planning* **9**: 5252–55

BISHOP, J. (University of Warwick, Coventry, UK)
Overeducation **7**: 4249–55

BJORKLUND, D. F. (Florida Atlantic University, Boca Raton, Florida, USA)
Childhood* **2: 701–06

BJØRNDAL, I. R. (Ostfold Board of Higher Education, Halden, Norway)
Norway: System of Education **7**: 4185–92

BLAUG, M. (University of Exeter, Exeter, UK)
Education and the Employment Contract **3**: 1695–703

BLEISTEIN, C. A. (Educational Testing Service, Princeton, New Jersey, USA)
Item Bias* **5: 3043–51

BLOCK, J. H. (University of California, Santa Barbara, California, USA)
Teachers' Beliefs and Belief Systems* **10: 6099–103

BLUM, A. (Hebrew University, Rehovot, Israel)
Integrated and General Science **5**: 2897–903

BOEHM, U. (University of Bremen, Bremen, Germany)
Vocational Education and Training in Germany: National and International Dimensions **11**: 6653–60

BOEKAERTS, M. (University of Leiden, Leiden, The Netherlands)
Affect, Emotions, and Learning **1**: 199–204; *Stress, Coping, and Learning* **10**: 5735–38

BOGIN, B. (University of Michigan-Dearborn, Dearborn, Michigan, USA)
Human Learning, Evolution of Anthropological Perspectives **5**: 2681–85

BOLAM, R. (University College, Swansea, UK)
Administrative Preparation: Inservice **1**: 67–73; *Teacher Recruitment and Induction* **10**: 6044–48

BONDESIO, M. J. (University of Pretoria, Pretoria, South Africa)
South Africa: System of Education* **10: 5625–35

BOONCHUAY, T. (Office of the National Education Commission, Bangkok, Thailand)
Thailand: System of Education* **11: 6371–78

BOOT, P. A. (Ministry of Labor, The Hague, The Netherlands)
Evaluation of Public Training: Industrial Countries* **4: 2145–50

BORDIA, A. (Lok Jumbish Parishad, Jaipur, India)
India: System of Education **5**: 2744–53

BORICH, G. (University of Texas, Austin, Texas, USA)
Students, Grading and Evaluation of* **10: 5818–22

BORKENAU, P. (University of Bielefeld, Bielefeld, Germany)
Genetics and Human Development **5**: 2462–65

BOTTANI, N. (Organisation for Economic Co-operation and Development, Paris, France)
International Educational Indicators* **5: 2984–89

BOURKE, S. F. (University of Newcastle, Newcastle, New South Wales, Australia)
Literacy, Numeracy, and Oracy Testing **6**: 3468–74

BOURQUE, M. L. (National Assessment Governing Board, Washington, DC, USA)
National Standard Setting and Reporting **7**: 4054–56

BOWERS, N. (Joint Economic Committee of the United States Congress, Washington, DC, USA)
Training Concepts and Statistics **11**: 6416–20

BOWLAND, D. (International Labour Organisation, Geneva, Switzerland)
International Labour Organisation (ILO): Vocational Training* **5: 2998–3003

BOWMAN, M. J. (University of Chicago, Chicago, Illinois, USA)
On-the-job Training **7**: 4206–11

BOYD, W. L. (Pennsylvania State University, University Park, Pennsylvania, USA)
Educational Policy Studies: Overview* **4: 1835–41; **Local Education Authorities, School Boards, and School Councils* **6**: 3491–96; **Management of Contraction in Public Education* **6**: 3603–08; **Politics and Governance of Education* **8**: 4587–95

BOYDEN, J. (Children in Development, Oxford, UK)
Education for Street Children* **3: 1733–36

BRAAKSMA, J. (University of Twente, Enschede, The Netherlands)
Libraries, Organizations and Journals on **6**: 3399–401

BRANDHORST, T. (ERIC Processing and Reference Facility, Rockville, Maryland, USA)
Information Systems for Education **5**: 2823–27

BRANSON, R. K. (Florida State University, Tallahassee, Florida, USA)
Program and Project Management **8**: 4754–58

BRAUNGART, M. M. (State University of New York, Syracuse, New York, USA)
Political Socialization and Education* **8: 4575–81

BRAUNGART, R. G. (Syracuse University, Syracuse, New York, USA)
Political Socialization and Education* **8: 4575–81

BRAY, M. (University of Hong Kong, Hong Kong)
Community Financing of Education **2**: 910–14; *Hong Kong: System of Education* **5**: 2636–43; **Macau: System of Education* **6**: 3539–45; *School Size and Small Schools* **9**: 5291–94

BREDESON, P. V. (University of Wisconsin–Madison, Madison, Wisconsin, USA)
Organizational Theory in Education: Comparative Management Perspectives **7**: 4240–46

BREHMER, I. (Universitat Bielefeld, Bielefeld, Germany)
Women's Education, History of: German-speaking Europe **11**: 6741–48

BRENNER, M. E. (University of California, Santa Barbara, California, USA)
Cultural Transformation: Ethnological Information to Educational Programs **3**: 1233–36

BROADFOOT, P. (University of Bristol, Bristol, UK)
Learning in School, Sociology of **6**: 3306–12

BROLIN, D. E. (University of Missouri, Columbia, Missouri, USA)
Career Education for Special Needs Students **2**: 631–35

BRONFENBRENNER, U. (Cornell University, Ithaca, New York, USA)
Ecological Models of Human Development **3**: 1643–47

BROOKFIELD, S. D. (University of St Thomas, St Paul, Minnesota, USA)
Adult Learning: Overview **1**: 163–68; *Teacher Roles and Teaching Styles: Adult Ed* **10**: 6054–58

BROOKS-GUNN, J. (Columbia University, New York, USA)
Early Experience and Human Development* **3: 1636–43

BROWN, C. (University of California, Berkeley, California, USA)
Industrial Restructuring and Educational Reforms **5**: 2792–99

BROWN, D. J. (University of British Columbia, Vancouver, British Columbia, Canada)

Decentralization in Educational Government and Management **3**: 1407–12

BRYK, A. S. (University of Chicago, Chicago, Illinois, USA)
Hierarchical Linear Models* **5: 2590–96

BUCKBY, M. (University of York, York, UK)
Foreign Language Education: Secondary School Programs* **4: 2351–57

BULLOCK, M. (Max Planck Institute for Psychological Research, Munich, Germany)
Reasoning in Childhood, Development of **8**: 4951–57

BURBULES, N. C. (University of Illinois at Urbana-Champaign, Champaign, Illinois, USA)
Marxism and Educational Thought **6**: 3617–22

BURETTA, B. N. V. (Ministry of Education, Dar es Salaam, Tanzania)
Tanzania: System of Education **10**: 5903–10

BURKE, G. (Monash University, Clayton, Victoria, Australia)
Census and National Survey Data **2**: 649–53

BURKHARDT, H. (University of Nottingham, Nottingham, UK)
Mathematical Applications in School Curriculum **6**: 3631–34

BURNS, R. B. (University of California, Riverside, California, USA)
Models of Learning **7**: 3880–86; *Teaching, Paradigms for Research on* **10**: 6202–08

BURSTYN, J. N. (Syracuse University, Syracuse, New York, USA)
Electronic Publishing **4**: 1954–58; **Women's Education, History of: North America* **11**: 6761–65

BUTLER, D. L. (University of British Columbia, Vancouver, British Columbia, Canada)
Student Cognitive Processing and Learning* **10: 5738–45

BUTLER, K. G. (Syracuse University, Syracuse, New York, USA)
Speech and Language Handicapped: Overview **10**: 5691–94

BYSTRÖM, J. (SISU, Stockholm, Sweden)
Study Circles **10**: 5827–29

CAILLODS, F. (IIEP, Paris, France)
School Mapping **9**: 5255–59; *Technician Training* **11**: 6266–72

CAIRNS, L. (Monash University, Gippsland, Victoria, Australia)
Behavior, Analysis and Modification of **1**: 483–86

CALDERHEAD, J. (University of Bath, Bath, UK)
Teachers as Clinicians **10**: 6086–88

CALDWELL, B. J. (University of Melbourne, Melbourne, Victoria, Australia)
School-based Management **9**: 5302–08

CALDWELL, G. (Australian National University, Canberra, ACT, Australia)
Australia and New Zealand: Adult Education **1**: 409–15

CALERO-BRECKHEIMER, A. (University of Hamburg, Hamburg, Germany)
Specific Learning Disability* **10: 5681–86

CAMPBELL, P. H. (Temple University, Philadelphia, Pennsylvania, USA)
Infants, Toddlers, and Preschoolers, Programs for **5**: 2806–14

CAPKOVÀ, D. (Academy of Education, Prague, Czech Republic)
Comenius and Education **2**: 880–84

CARDINET, J. (Institut Romand de Recherches et de Documentation Pédagogiques, Neuchâtel, Switzerland)
Generalizability Theory* **5: 2458–62

CARNOY, M. (Stanford University, Stanford, California, USA)
Education and Productivity **3**: 1690–95; *Education and the New International Division of Labor* **3**: 1707–13; *Joint Production of Education* **6**: 3101–06; *Political Economy of Educational Production* **8**: 4562–68; *Race Earnings Differentials* **8**: 4896–902; *Rates of Return to Education* **8**: 4913–18; *Technological Change and Education* **11**: 6277–83

CARR-HILL, R. (University of York, York, UK)
Basic Education: Comparative and International Studies **1**: 465–75

CASSEL, W. S. (Florida Atlantic University, Boca Raton, Florida, USA)
Childhood* **2: 701–06

CEESAY, M. (Ministry of Education, Youth Sports, and Culture, Banjul, The Gambia)
Gambia: System of Education **4**: 2401–07

CHADWICK, A. (University of Surrey, Guildford, UK)
Training of Adult Educators* **11: 6431–38

CHAMOT, A. U. (Georgetown University, Washington, DC, USA)
Learning Strategies in Second Language Learning* **6: 3329–35

CHAPMAN, J. D. (University of Western Australia, Perth, Western Australia, Australia)
Governance and Management of Schools: International Developments **5**: 2504–09

CHARLESWORTH, W. (University of Minnesota, Minneapolis, Minnesota, USA)
Evolutionary Theory: Ethological and Sociobiological Aspects **4**: 2167–72

CHENG, KAI-MING (University of Hong Kong, Hong Kong)
Asia, East and Southeast: Adult Education* **1: 348–53

CHEUNG, K. C. (University of Macau, Macau)
Practical Mathematics and Science Testing **8**: 4643–48

CHIPMAN, S. F. (US Office of Naval Research, Arlington, Virginia, USA)
Gender and School Learning: Mathematics **4**: 2432–36

CHISWICK, B. R. (University of Illinois at Chicago, Chicago, Ilinois, USA)
Immigrants' Education and Economic Performance **5**: 2737–40

†CHOPPIN, B. H. (University of California, Los Angeles, California, USA)
Objective Tests in Measurement **7**: 4193–97

CHU, S. K. (UNESCO, Paris, France)
Adult and Nonformal Education: Statistics **1**: 94–100

CIBULKA, J. G. (University of Wisconsin, Milwaukee, Wisconsin, USA)
Urban Education: Changing Ecology, Politics, and Reform **11**: 6551–58

CIPOLLONE, P. (Stanford University, Stanford, California, USA)
Education and Earnings **3**: 1655–60

CLANDININ, D. J. (University of Alberta, Edmonton, Alberta, Canada)
Curriculum Inquiry, Forms of* **3: 1316–20; **Narrative Inquiry* **7**: 4046–51; **Teacher Preparation, Conceptions of Teaching, and Evaluation: Alternative Policies* **10**: 6035–44

CLARK, R. E. (University of Southern California, Los Angeles, California, USA)
Instructional Psychology, History of **5**: 2874–80; *Media and Learning* **7**: 3739–44

CLAYCOMB, C. L. (Pennsylvania State University, University Park, Pennsylvania, USA)
Local Education Authorities, School Boards, and School Councils* **6: 3491–96

CLIFTON, R. A. (University of Manitoba, Winnipeg, Manitoba, Canada)
Race and Ethnicity in Education **8**: 4891–96

† deceased.

COBB, P. (Vanderbilt University, Nashville, Tennessee, USA)
Constructivism and Learning **2**: 1049–52

COHEN, A. M. (University of California, Los Angeles, California, USA)
Community Colleges **2**: 893–900

COHEN, S. A. (University of San Francisco, San Francisco, California, USA)
Instructional Alignment **5**: 2852–56

COLARDYN, D. (OECD, Paris, France)
Certification of Adult Education **2**: 662–65

COLEMAN, J. S. (University of Chicago, Chicago, Illinois, USA)
Family, School, and Social Capital **4**: 2272–74

COLEMAN, P. (Simon Fraser University, Burnaby, British Columbia, Canada)
School District or Regional Management and School Improvement **9**: 5221–24

COLES, G. S. (Robert Wood Johnson Medical School, Piscataway, New Jersey, USA)
Neurological Bases of Learning Problems **7**: 4077–81

COLLETTA, N. J. (World Bank, Washington, DC, USA)
Formal, Nonformal, and Informal Education **4**: 2364–69; **Technology in Educational Planning* **11**: 6292–98

COLLINS, A. (Bolt Beranek and Newman, Inc., Cambridge, Massachusetts, USA)
Cognition and Learning* **2: 835–38

COLLINS, A. (Northwestern University, Evanston, Illinois, USA)
Learning Environments* **6: 3297–302

COLLINS, J. (State University of New York, Albany, New York, USA)
Family, School, and Cultural Capital* **4: 2267–72

COLLINS, M. T. (Perkins School for the Blind, Watertown, Massachusetts, USA)
Deaf-Blind Children and Youth, Education of* **3: 1402–07

COLLIS, B. A. (University of Twente, Enschede, The Netherlands)
Computers in Education **2**: 1007–12; *Teacher Education, Technology in* **10**: 6005–09

COLLOPY, R. M. B. (University of Michigan, Ann Arbor, Michigan, USA)
Student Influences on Teaching* **10: 5759–62

COMBER, L. C. (Kenilworth, Warwickshire, UK)
Teaching and Learning, Demonstration Methods of* **10: 6140–43

COMINGS, J. P. (World Education, Boston, Massachusetts, USA)
Nongovernmental Organizations: Adult Education **7**: 4146–48

COMSTOCK, G. (Syracuse University, Syracuse, New York, USA)
Broadcasting and Technology: Effects on Children and Youth **1**: 564–70

CONBOY, I. (Victoria Ministry of Education, Melbourne, Victoria, Australia)
Social Implications of Educational Technology* **9: 5539–45

CONLEY, S. (University of Maryland, College Park, Maryland, USA)
School as a Workplace: Implications for Reform **9**: 5176–81

CONNELLY, F. M. (Ontario Institute for Studies in Education, Toronto, Ontario, Canada)
Curriculum Inquiry, Forms of* **3: 1316–20; **Narrative Inquiry* **7**: 4046–51; **Teacher Preparation, Conceptions of Teaching, and Evaluation: Alternative Policies* **10**: 6035–44

COOK-GUMPERZ, J. (University of California, Santa Barbara, California, USA)
Language in Education, Changing Views of: Anthropological Perspectives* **6: 3235–38

COOLAHAN, J. (Maynooth University College, Maynooth, Republic of Ireland)
Ireland, Republic of: System of Education **5**: 3011–20

COOPER, B. S. (Fordham University, New York, USA)
Alternative Schools and Programs **1**: 260–66; **Labor Relations in Education* **6**: 3189–97

COOPER, J. M. (University of Virginia, Charlottesville, Virginia, USA)
Teacher Education, Supervision in **10**: 6000–04

COOPER, M. (University of New South Wales, Kensington, New South Wales, Australia)
Nonparametric and Distribution-free Statistics **7**: 4157–63

COPLAN, R. J. (University of Waterloo, Waterloo, Quebec, Canada)
Play: Developmental Stages, Functions, and Educational Support* **8: 4536–42

CORBETT, H. D. (Research for Better Schools, Philadelphia, Pennsylvania, USA)
School Climate and Culture* **9: 5206–11

CORTENBACH, K. E. T. (Monroe School, Santa Barbara, California, USA)
Drugs and Education* **3: 1611–19

CORVALÁN-VÁSQUEZ, O. (CIDE, Santiago, Chile)
Nongovernmental Organizations (Latin America): Training for Disadvantaged Groups **7**: 4148–55

COSGROVE, M. (University of Technology, Sydney, New South Wales, Australia)
Laboratory Packages for Science Learning* **6: 3202–05

COURTENAY, B. C. (University of Georgia, Athens, Georgia, USA)
Evaluation of Adult Education **4**: 2119–23

COX, J. (Furman University, Greenville, South Carolina, USA)
Foreign Language Education: Primary School Programs* **4: 2346–51

COX, M. J. (King's College, London, UK)
Computer Simulations and Modeling **2**: 985–88

CRAELIUS, M. H. (Forsbacka, Sweden)
Namibia: System of Education **7**: 4039–46

CRAHAY, M. (University of Liège, Liège, Belgium)
Childcare and Preschool Effects **2**: 678–88

CRANSTON, M. (University of London, London, UK)
Locke and Education **6**: 3496–99

CREEMERS, B. P. M. (University of Groningen, Groningen, The Netherlands)
Effective Schools, Management of* **4: 1929–34

CREER, B. (University of Quebec, Montreal, Quebec, Canada)
Mathematics: Topics of Instruction* **6: 3671–86

CRELLIN, C. T. (Oxford, UK)
Bhutan: System of Education **1**: 525–31; *Myanmar: System of Education* **7**: 4030–38

CRITICOS, C. (University of Natal, Durban, South Africa)
Media Selection **7**: 3756–60

CROW, G. M. (Louisiana State University, Baton Rouge, Louisiana, USA)
School Principals: Role in Restructured Schools* **9: 5268–73

CROWSON, R. L. (Vanderbilt University, Nashville, Tennessee, USA)
School–Community Relations **9**: 5211–17

CRUICKSHANK, D. R. (Ohio State University, Columbus, Ohio, USA)
Teaching and Learning, Explanation in* **10: 6143–49

CRUZ CÁRDENAS, R. E. (Ministry of Education and Culture, Montevideo, Uruguay)
Uruguay: System of Education* **11: 6563–67

CUDWORTH, A. L. (Nottingham Trent University, Nottingham, UK)
Simulations and Games **9**: 5472–76

CUI, J. P. (University of California, Los Angeles, California, USA)
Proprietary Further Education* **8: 4792–96

CUNNINGHAM, P. M. (Northern Illinois University, DeKalb, Illinois, USA)
Community Education and Community Development **2**: 900–07

DAMON, W. (Brown University, Providence, Rhode Island, USA)
Peer Relations and Learning **8**: 4368–72

DARKENWALD, G. G. (Rutgers State University, New Brunswick, New Jersey, USA)
Group Learning **5**: 2529–32

DAVID, Y. M. (University of Michigan, Ann Arbor, Michigan, USA)
Cognitive Strategy Instruction: Special Education* **2: 861–68

DAVIES, B. (University of New England, Armidale, New South Wales, Australia)
Gender Theories in Education **5**: 2453–58

DAVIES, C. T. (University of Manchester, Manchester, UK)
Population Education **8**: 4608–10

DAVIES, L. (University of Birmingham, Birmingham, UK)
Gender and Education Management in Developing Nations **4**: 2419–23

DAVIS, D. J. (University of North Texas, Denton, Texas, USA)
Visual Arts Teacher Education **11**: 6618–21

DAVIS, R. B. (Rutgers State University, New Brunswick, New Jersey, USA)
Mathematics Teacher Education* **6: 3668–71

DAVIS, R. G. (Harvard University, Cambridge, Massachussetts, USA)
Educational Planning: Models and Methods **3**: 1825–30

DAVIS, W. E. (University of Maine, Orono, Maine, USA)
Children and Youth At Risk* **2: 706–11

DE CORTE, E. (University of Leuven, Leuven, Belgium)
Computers and Learning* **2: 1002–07; **Mathematics, Learning and Instruction of* **6**: 3652–55

DE KEYSER, R. (Catholic University of Leuven, Leuven, Belgium)
History: Educational Programs **5**: 2618–23

DE LANDSHEERE, G. (Université de Liège, Liège, Belgium)
Educational Research, History of **4**: 1864–73; *European Community: Educational Goals and Plans* **4**: 2053–59

DE MOURA CASTRO, C. (World Bank, Washington, DC, USA)
Training and Education, Convergence between* **11: 6412–16

DE OLIVEIRA, J. B. (World Bank, Washington, DC, USA)
Training and Education, Convergence between* **11: 6412–16

DE RIBAUPIERRE, A. (University of Geneva, Geneva, Switzerland)
Piaget's Theory of Human Development* **8: 4479–83

DE VALLE, A. L. (Contiguo ESNACIFOR, Comayagua, Honduras)
Honduras: System of Education **5**: 2631–36

DE VOS, G. A. (University of California, Berkeley, California, USA)
Culture and Achievement Motivation in Education* **3: 1236–41

DE WOLF, H. C. (Open University, Heerlen, The Netherlands)
Distance Education **3**: 1557–63; *Distance Education, International Organizations and Journals on* **3**: 1580–84

DEFREITAS, G. (Hofstra University, Hempstead, New York, USA)
Labor Market Segmentation and Education **6**: 3184–89

DELAMONT, S. (University of Wales, Cardiff, UK)
Teachers as Artists **10**: 6083–86

DELQUADRI, J. (University of Kansas, Lawrence, Kansas, USA)
Peer Tutoring* **8: 4372–76

DEMETRIOU, A. (Aristotelian University of Thessaloniki, Thessaloniki, Greece)
Human Development: Research and Educational Practice **5**: 2666–70

DENNING, C. (International Book Development Ltd., London, UK)
Printed Materials in Education* **8: 4694–98

DENO, S. L. (University of Minnesota, Minneapolis, Minnesota, USA)
Curriculum-based Assessment* **3: 1355–59

DENZIN, N. K. (University of Illinois at Urbana-Champaign, Urbana, Illinois, USA)

Biographical Research Methods **1**: 537–43; *Triangulation in Educational Research* **11**: 6461–66

DESHLER, D. (Cornell University, Ithaca, New York, USA)
Participation Motivation in Adult Education **7**: 4325–30

DESSEY, J. A. (Tel Aviv University, Tel Aviv, Israel)
Mathematics: Topics of Instruction* **6: 3671–86

DIALLO, A. O. (Nouakchott, Mauritania)
Mauritania: System of Education **6**: 3686–90

DIALLO, H. A. B. (Ministry of Education, Conakry, Republic of Guinea)
Guinea, Republic of: System of Education **5**: 2552–56

DÍAZ DÍAZ, V. H. (Lima, Peru)
Peru: System of Education **8**: 4409–15

DILLON, J. T. (University of California, Riverside, California, USA)
Classroom Discussion **2**: 803–07

DIORIO, J. A. (University of Otago, Otago, New Zealand)
Sex Education, Conceptions of **9**: 5435–41

DISINGER, J. F. (Ohio State University, Columbus, Ohio, USA)
Environmental and Ecological Education **4**: 1991–96

DLAMINI, E. (Ministry of Education, Mbabane, Swaziland)
Swaziland: System of Education **10**: 5862–66

DOCHY, F. J. R. C. (University of Heerlen, Heerlen, The Netherlands)
Prior Knowledge and Learning **8**: 4698–702

DOERINGER, P. B. (Boston University, Boston, Massachusetts, USA)
Internal Labor Markets and Education **5**: 2937–42

DONG, MING CHUAN (China State Education Commission, Beijing, People's Republic of China)
China, People's Republic of: Adult Education **2**: 746–49

DONN, G. (University of Edinburgh, Edinburgh, UK)
Feminist Approaches and the Curriculum **4**: 2287–92

DREWES, M. G. (Ministry of Labor, The Hague, The Netherlands)
Evaluation of Public Training: Industrial Countries* **4: 2145–50

DREYFUS, A. (Hebrew University of Jerusalem, Rehovot, Israel)
Agricultural and Rural Education **1**: 240–44

DRONKERS, J (University of Amsterdam, Amsterdam, The Netherlands)
Social Mobility, Social Stratification, and Education **9**: 5548–54

DUBERG, R. (Research Development International, Stockholm, Sweden)
Laos: System of Education **6**: 3241–47; *Liberia: System of Education* **6**: 3389–94

DUCCI, M. A. (CINTERFOR, Montevideo, Uruguay)
Latin America: National Training Agencies **6**: 3262–67

DUCHARME, E. R. (Drake University, Des Moines, Iowa, USA)
Teacher Educators, Characteristics of **10**: 6009–12

DUIT, R. (University of Kiel, Kiel, Germany)
Preconceptions and Misconceptions **8**: 4648–52

DUKE, C. (University of Warwick, Coventry, UK)
Adult and Continuing Higher Education **1**: 89–94; *International Adult Education* **5**: 2945–51

DULBERG, L. (State University of New York, Buffalo, New York, USA)
Hypothesis Testing* **5: 2709–14

DUNKIN, M. J. (University of New South Wales, Oatley, New South Wales, Australia)
Teaching and Teacher Education: Comparative and International Studies **10**: 6149–55; *Teaching, Synthesizing Research on* **10**: 6235–40

DUNN-RANKIN, P. (University of Hawaii, Honolulu, Hawaii, USA)
Scaling Methods **9**: 5151–59

DWARKASING, W. W. (Training Department Suralco, Paramaribo, Suriname)
Suriname: System of Education **10**: 5846–54

DWECK, C. S. (Columbia University, New York, USA)
Achievement Motivation, Development of* **1: 28–32

DWOMOH, Y. (Ministry of Education, Accra, Ghana)
Ghana: System of Education **5**: 2480–86

DWORKIN, A. G. (University of Houston, Houston, Texas, USA)
Teacher Burnout **10**: 5919–25

EASH, M. J. (University of Massachusetts, Boston, Massachusetts, USA)
Syllabus **10**: 5883–87; *Teachers' Guide* **10**: 6113–17

EBBESEN, S. (University of Copenhagen, Copenhagen, Denmark)
Saint Thomas Aquinas and Education **9**: 5121–24

EBERTS, R. W. (University of Oregon, Eugene, Oregon, USA)
Teacher Unionization, Economics of* **10: 6068–73

EDGERTON, S. H. (University of Illinois at Urbana-Champaign, Urbana, Illinois, USA)
Curriculum Politics and Policies **3**: 1334–38

EFLAND, A. (Ohio State University, Columbus, Ohio, USA)
Art Education Programs **1**: 338–43

EICHER, J-C. (University of Burgundy, Dijon, France)
International Educational Expenditures **5**: 2978–84

EIGER, N. (Rutgers University, New Brunswick, New Jersey, USA)
Worker Education and Labor Education **11**: 6769–75

EISENBERG, N. (Arizona State University, Tempe, Arizona, USA)
Prosocial Behavior, Development of **8**: 4796–99

EISNER, J. P. (University of Pennsylvania, Philadelphia, Pennsylvania, USA)
Self-related Cognition, Learned Helplessness, Learned Optimism, and Human Development* **9: 5403–07

EKSTRAND, H. (School of Education, Malmö, Sweden)
Multicultural Education **7**: 3960–70

ELEN, J. (University of Leuven, Leuven, Belgium)
Instructional Psychology (as a Contributing Field to Instructional Design)* **5: 2870–74

ELLIOTT, M. (University of Kansas, Lawrence, Kansas, USA)
Peer Tutoring* **8: 4372–76

EL-SANABARY, N. (Kensington, California, USA)
Women's Education, History of: Islamic Countries **11**: 6753–61

ELSHOUT, J. (University of Amsterdam, Amsterdam, The Netherlands)
Architecture of Cognition **1**: 328–31; *Creativity* **2**: 1175–78

ELSOM-COOK, M. T. (Electric Brain Company, Leeds, UK)
Artificial Intelligence as a Contributing Field to Instructional Design **1**: 343–48

ELY, D. P. (Syracuse University, Syracuse, New York, USA)
Educational Technology: Scope of the Field **4**: 1924–29

EMANUELSSON, I. (University of Gothenburg, Mölndal, Sweden)
Integrated Services for Children and Youth with Special Needs **5**: 2903–07; *Mainstreaming* **6**: 3556–60; *Special Education, History of* **10**: 5658–63

EMIHOVICH, C. (Florida State University, Tallahassee, Florida, USA)
Cultural Continuities and Discontinuities in Education **3**: 1227–33

EMMER, E. T. (University of Texas, Austin, Texas, USA)
Teacher Managerial Behaviors **10**: 6026–31

ENTWISTLE, H. (Concordia University, Montreal, Quebec, Canada)
Ideologies in Adult Education **5**: 2732–37

ENTWISTLE, N. (University of Edinburgh, Edinburgh, UK)
Adult Study Strategies **1**: 184–94

EPSTEIN, E. H. (Ohio State University, Columbus, Ohio, USA)
Comparative and International Education: Overview and Historical Development **2**: 918–23

ERAUT, M. (University of Sussex, Brighton, UK)
Educational Technology: Conceptual Frameworks and Historical Development **4**: 1882–99; *Programmed Learning* **8**: 4766–75; *Teacher Education: Inservice* **10**: 5966–73

ERICKSON, F. (University of Pennsylvania, Philadelphia, Pennsylvania, USA)
Schools as Sociocultural Systems **9**: 5308–13

ERICKSON, P. A. (Saint Mary's University, Halifax, Nova Scotia, Canada)
Anthropology Teaching at the Precollege Level **1**: 297–300

ERIKSON, R. (University of Stockholm, Stockholm, Sweden)
Mobility Tables **7**: 3862–64

ESPIN, C. A. (University of Minnesota, Minneapolis, Minnesota, USA)
Curriculum-based Assessment* **3: 1355–59

EVANS, D. R. (University of Massachusetts, Amherst, Massachusetts, USA)
Conscientization and Mobilization **2**: 1045–49

EVANS, J. L. (Aga Khan Foundation, Geneva, Switzerland)
Early Childhood Interventions **3**: 1624–29

EVANS, P. L. C. (Organisation for Economic Co-operation and Development, Paris, France)
Integration of Students with Special Educational Needs in Regular School Environments **5**: 2907–10

EVERITT, B. S. (University of London, London, UK)
Cluster Analysis **2**: 825–31; *Contingency Tables* **2**: 1079–84

EVERS, C. W. (Monash University, Melbourne, Victoria, Australia)
Educational Administration: Ethical and Philosophical Issues* **3: 1769–75; **Research in Education: Epistemological Issues* **9**: 5021–31

EVERTSON, C. M. (Vanderbilt University, Nashville, Tennessee, USA)
Classroom Rules and Routines **2**: 816–20

EYLON, B-S. (Weizmann Institute of Science, Rehovot, Israel)
Physical Sciences: Secondary School Programs **8**: 4474–79; **Science, Learning and Instruction of* **9**: 5338–42

FÄGERLIND, I. (University of Stockholm, Stockholm, Sweden)
Education and Development* **3: 1648–55

FAGNANO, C. L. (Milken Institute for Job and Capital Formation, Santa Monica, California, USA)
Benefits of Education* **1: 510–21

FAGOT, B. I. (University of Oregon, Eugene, Oregon, USA)
Gender Roles and Preschool Education **4**: 2449–52

FAIRLEY, J. (Scottish Local Authorities Management Centre, University of Strathclyde, Glasgow, UK)
Vocational Training Initiatives: United Kingdom **11**: 6685–90

FAROOQ, R. A. (Ministry of Education, Islamabad, Pakistan)
Pakistan: System of Education* **7: 4263–70

FARRELL, J. P. (Ontario Institute for Studies in Education, Toronto, Ontario, Canada)
Demography in Educational Planning* **3: 1449–53; *Planning Education: Overview* **8**: 4499–510; *Planning for Effective Teaching in Developing Nations* **8**: 4519–26; *Social Equality and Educational Expansion in Developing Nations* **9**: 5532–39; **Textbook Development in Developing Nations, Planning for* **11**: 6360–66

FARRUGIA, C. J. (University of Malta, Msida, Malta)
Malta: System of Education **6**: 3586–93

FAXAS, Y. F. (University of Havana, Havana, Cuba)
Cuba: System of Education* **3: 1221–27

FELDHUSEN, J. F. (Purdue University, West Lafayette, Indiana, USA)
Creativity, Teaching and Testing for **2**: 1178–83

FERBER, M. A. (University of Illinois, Urbana, Illinois, USA)
Gender Differences in Earnings **4**: 2440–46

FERGUSON, D. L. (University of Oregon, Eugene, Oregon, USA)
Developmental Disabilities: Severe **3**: 1504–08

FETTERMAN, D. (Stanford University, Stanford, California, USA)
Ethnographic Evaluation in Education **4**: 2043–46

FIELDS, G. S. (Cornell University, Ithaca, New York, USA)
Labor Market and Educational Expansion **6**: 3179–84

FINK, A. H. (Indiana University, Bloomington, Indiana, USA)
Behavioral Disorders: Social* **1: 490–95

FINN, J. D. (State University of New York, Buffalo, New York, USA)
Class Size* **2: 770–75; **Hypothesis Testing* **5**: 2709–14; *Variance and Covariance, Analysis of* **11**: 6586–91

FISCHBEIN, E. (Tel Aviv University, Tel Aviv, Israel)
Mathematics: Topics of Instruction* **6: 3671–86

FISCHBEIN, S. (Department of Special Education, Stockholm Institute of Education, Stockholm, Sweden)
Twin Studies **11**: 6488–92

FISCHER, K. W. (Harvard University, Cambridge, Massachusetts, USA)
Human Development, Stages in* **5: 2677–81

FISCHGRUND, J. E. (The Pennsylvania School for the Deaf, Philadelphia, Pennsylvania, USA)
Deaf and Hearing Impaired Youth, Education of **3**: 1398–402

FISHER, C. W. (University of Northern Colorado, Greeley, Colorado, USA)
Academic Learning Time **1**: 20–23

FLORIO-RUANE, S. (Michigan State University, East Lansing, Michigan, USA)
Classroom Culture and Social Organization: Anthropological Study of **2**: 796–803

FLUITMAN, F. (International Labour Organisation, Geneva, Switzerland)
Africa: Traditional Apprenticeship **1**: 221–27

FORDHAM, P. (University of Warwick, Coventry, UK)
International Conferences, Commissions, and Reforms In Education **5**: 2957–61

FOSTER, P. (State University of New York, Albany, New York, USA)
Area Studies: Comparative and International Education **1**: 331–32

FOSTER, W. (Indiana University, Indiana, USA)
Administration of Education: Critical Approaches **1**: 60–67

FRASER, B. J. (Curtin University of Technology, Perth, Western Australia, Australia)
Classroom Environments **2**: 807–11; *Student Perceptions of Classrooms* **10**: 5772–75

FREEDMAN, K. (University of Minnesota, Minneapolis, Minnesota, USA)
Visual And Performing Arts, Learning And Instruction of **11**: 6616–18

FREEDMAN, S. W. (University of California, Berkeley, California, USA)
Written Composition, Teaching and Testing For **11**: 6781–85

FREEMAN, D. (Advisory Unit: Computers in Education, Hatfield, UK)
Databases, Instructional Uses of **3**: 1394–98

FREEMAN, R. B. (Harvard University, Cambridge, Massachusetts, USA)
Demand and Supply Elasticities for Educated Labor **3**: 1443–49

FROESE, V. (University of British Columbia, Vancouver, British Columbia, Canada)
Language across the Curriculum **6**: 3205–09

FULIGNI, A. J. (University of Michigan, Ann Arbor, Michigan, USA)
Home Environment and School Learning* **5: 2624–28

FULLAN, M. G. (University of Toronto, Toronto, Ontario, Canada)
Innovations, Implementation of **5**: 2839–47

FULLER, B. (Harvard University, Cambridge, Massachusetts, USA)
Quality of Education in Developing Nations: Policies for Improving **8**: 4865–73

GALL, J. P. (University of Oregon, Eugene, Oregon, USA)
Group Dynamics* **5: 2523–29

GALL, M. D. (University of Oregon, Eugene, Oregon, USA)
Group Dynamics* **5: 2523–29; **Questioning Strategies* **8**: 4875–82

GALLART, M. A. (CENEP, Buenos Aires, Argentina)
Latin America: Articulation of Education, Training, and Work **6**: 3256–62

GALLUZZO, G. R. (University of Northern Colorado, Greeley, Colorado, USA)
Teacher Education, Evaluation in **10**: 5954–58

GALTON, M. (University of Leicester, Leicester, UK)
Classroom Observation **2**: 811–16

GALVIN, P. (University of Utah, Salt Lake City, Utah, USA)
Employee Motivation and Incentives in Schools* **4: 1967–72

GANDÁSEGUI, M. A. (CELA, Panama City, Panama)
Panama: System of Education **7**: 4270–75

GARDNER, C. (University of South Carolina, Columbia, South Carolina, USA)
Substitute Teachers* **10: 5832–34

GARDNER, R. (University of London, London, UK)
Teacher Education: Onservice **10**: 5977–82

GARRISON, D. R. (University of Calgary, Calgary, Alberta, Canada)
Dropout in Adult Education **3**: 1599–602

GATAWA, B. S. M. (Harare, Zimbabwe)
Zimbabwe: System of Education **11**: 6814–21

GAYESKI, D. (Ithaca, New York, USA)
Multimedia Systems in Education **7**: 3991–96

GENNAOUI, A. (National Planning Office, Port Vila, Vanuatu)
Syria: System of Education **10**: 5887–95

GERALD, D. E. (National Center for Education Statistics, United States Department of Education, Washington, DC, USA)
Projections of Educational Statistics* **8: 4783–88

GEZI, K. (California State University, Sacramento, California, USA)
Libya: System of Education **6**: 3402–07

GHAFOOR, A. (Ministry of Education, Islamabad, Pakistan)
Pakistan: System of Education **7**: 4263–70

GHISLANDI, P. (University of Milan, Milan, Italy)
CD Technology **2**: 646–49; *Multimedia Packages, Production of* **7**: 3987–91

GIBNEY, L. (Stanford University, Stanford, California, USA)
Education and Fertility **3**: 1672–76

GIDEONSE, H. D. (University of Cincinnati, Cincinnati, Ohio, USA)
Teacher Education, Governance of **10**: 5961–65

GIERE, U. (UNESCO Institute of Education, Hamburg, Germany)
Caribbean and Central America: Adult Education* **2: 635–40

GIL, G. A. (Center for Educational Research, Documentation and Evaluation (CIDE), Ministry of Education and Science, Madrid, Spain)
Spain: System of Education **10**: 5650–58

GILBERT, R. (James Cook University, Townsville, Queensland, Australia)
Empowerment Skills, Acquisition of* **4: 1980–85

GILTROW, D. (Santa Fe, New Mexico, USA)
Educational Media, Organizations and Journals on **3**: 1797–800

GIMMESTAD, M. J. (University of Northern Colorado, Greeley, Colorado, USA)
Teacher Education Programs: Structure* **10: 5995–6000

GINSBURG, M. B. (University of Pittsburgh, Pittsburgh, Pennsylvania, USA)
Political Work of Teachers* **8: 4581–87

GLASER, R. (University of Pittsburgh, Pittsburgh, Pennsylvania, USA)
Assessment in the Service of Learning* **1: 370–74; **Expert Level of Understanding* **4**: 2194–99

GLATTHORN, A. (East Carolina University, Greenville, North Carolina, USA)
Teacher Development **10**: 5930–35

GLENN, C. L. (Boston University, Boston, Massachusetts, USA)
School Choice and Privatization **9**: 5192–97

GLOVER, R. (University of Texas, Austin, Texas, USA)
Apprenticeship, Economics of* **1: 306–10

GLUCK, P. G. (Brooklyn College, CUNY, New York, USA)
Aesthetic Education **1**: 194–99

GODFREY, M. (University of Sussex, Brighton, UK)
Planning for Vocational Education and Training **8**: 4526–32

GOLDRING, E. B. (Vanderbilt University, Nashville, Tennessee, USA)
Community and Parents' Participation in Curriculum Decisions **2**: 888–93

GOLDSTEIN, B. (Temple University, Philadelphia, Pennsylvania, USA)
Language Differences versus Language Disorders* **6: 3225–28; **Speech and Language Disorders and the Hard of Hearing* **10**: 5686–91

GONON, P. (University of Bern, Bern, Switzerland)
Kerschensteiner and Education **6**: 3133–38

GONZÁLEZ II, H. V. (Stanford University, Stanford, California, USA)
Legitimacy in Educational Policy* **6: 3367–68

GOOD, T. L. (University of Arizona, Tucson, Arizona, USA)
Teachers' Expectations **10**: 6106–12

GOODALE, G. (International Labour Organisation, Geneva, Switzerland)
Female Access to Vocational Education and Training **4**: 2281–87

GOODLAD, J. I. (University of Washington, Seattle, Washington, USA)
Curriculum as a Field of Study **3**: 1262–67

GOODSON, I. (University of Western Ontario, London, Ontario, Canada)
School Subjects: Studying **9**: 5294–99

GOPINATHAN, S. (Institute of Education, Singapore, Republic of Singapore)
Publishing: Transnational Influences **8**: 4845–48

GORDON, D. (Ben-Gurion University, Beersheba, Israel)
Hidden Curriculum **5**: 2586–89

GÖTTELMANN-DURET, G. (IIEP, Paris, France)
United Nations Organizations: Research and Service in Comparative and International Education* **11: 6523–30

GOTTLIEB, G. (University of North Carolina, Greensboro, North Carolina, USA)
Abnormal Prenatal Development* **1: 12–15

GRABOWSKI, B. L. (Pennsylvania State University, University Park, Pennsylvania, USA)
Videodisk Technology: Interactive **11**: 6600–04

GRAEBER, A. (University of Quebec, Montreal, Quebec, Canada)
Mathematics: Topics of Instruction* **6: 3671–86

GRAF, W. D. (University of Washington, Seattle, Washington, USA)
Pharmacotherapy in Schoolchildren* **8: 4419–24

GRAYDON, S. (Simon Fraser University, Burnaby, British Columbia, Canada)
Preschool Educational Television Programs* **8: 4677–80

GRAYSON, D. (University of Sydney, Sydney, New South Wales, Australia)
Multitrait–Multimethod Analysis* **7: 4000–07

GREEN, B. (Queens University, Belfast, UK)
Mathematics, Learning and Instruction of* **6: 3652–55

GREEN, L. W. (University of British Columbia, Vancouver, British Columbia, Canada)
Health Education* **5: 2567–72

GREEN, P. S. (University of York, York, UK)
Foreign Language Education: Secondary School Programs* **4: 2351–57

GREENO, J. G. (Stanford University, Stanford, California, USA)
Learning Environments* **6: 3297–302

GREENWOOD, C. R. (University of Kansas, Lawrence, Kansas, USA)
Peer Tutoring* **8: 4372–76

GRETLER, A. (Swiss Coordination Center for Research in Education, Aarau, Switzerland)
Switzerland: System of Education **10**: 5873–83

GRIFFITH, W. S. (University of British Columbia, Vancouver, British Columbia, Canada)
North America: Adult Education **7**: 4180–85

GRIMM, H. (University of Bielefeld, Bielefeld, Germany)
Language Development **6**: 3219–24

GROEBEN, N. (Heidelberg University, Heidelberg, Germany)
Humanistic Models of Human Development **5**: 2689–92

GROOT, W. (Leiden University, Leiden, The Netherlands)
Screening Models and Education* **9: 5350–55

GROOTINGS, P. (European Centre for the Development of Vocational Training (CEDEFOP), Berlin, Germany)
Vocational Education and Training: Eastern and Central Europe **11**: 6641–48

GROSS, M. U. M. (University of New South Wales, Sydney, New South Wales, Australia)
Social–Emotional Development and Adjustment in Gifted Students **9**: 5528–32

GROSSMAN, P. L. (University of Washington, Seattle, Washington, USA)
Teachers' Knowledge **10**: 6117–22

GRUBEL, H. G. (Simon Fraser University, Burnaby, British Columbia, Canada)
Brain Drain, Economics of **1**: 554–61

GRUMET, M. (Brooklyn College, Brooklyn, New York, USA)
Humanities: Educational Programs **5**: 2692–97

GUBA, E. G. (Indiana University, Bloomington, Indiana, USA)
Fourth Generation: Evaluation* **4: 2369–75

GUMPERZ, J. J. (University of California, Berkeley, California, USA)
Language in Education, Changing Views of: Anthropological Perspectives* **6: 3235–38

GUNDEM, B. B. (University of Oslo, Oslo, Norway)
Curriculum, History of **3**: 1301–08

GUSKEY, T. R. (University of Kentucky, Lexington, Kentucky, USA)
Mastery Learning **6**: 3625–31

GUSTAFSON, K. L. (University of Georgia, Athens, Georgia, USA)
Instructional Design Models **5**: 2856–62

GUSTAFSSON, C. (Uppsala University, Uppsala, Sweden)
Montessori and Education **7**: 3912–14

GUSTAFSSON, J-E. (University of Gothenberg, Mölndal, Sweden)
Models of Intelligence **7**: 3873–80

GUSTAVSSON, B. (University of Linköping, Linköping, Sweden)
Folk High Schools* **4: 2324–27

GUTHRIE, J. W. (University of California, Berkeley, California, USA)
Globalization of Educational Policy and Reform **5**: 2495–500

GWANG-CHOL CHANG (International Institute for Educational Planning, Paris, France)
Korea, Democratic People's Republic of: System of Education **6**: 3155–60

HABELOW, E. (Temple University, Philadelphia, Pennsylvania, USA)
Learning Characteristics of Students with Special Needs* **6: 3292–97

HAERTEL, G. D. (Temple University, Philadelphia, Pennsylvania, USA)
Educational Psychology: Impact on Curriculum **4**: 1841–48

HAIG, B. D. (University of Canterbury, Christchurch, Canterbury, New Zealand*)
Feminist Research Methodology **4**: 2297–302

HAILEY, J. (Cranfield School of Management, Bedford, UK)
Enterprise Education: Small Business Training **4**: 1985–91

HAKEEM, A. H. A. (Ministry of Education, Male, Republic of Maldives)
Maldives: System of Education **6**: 3572–78

HAKUTA, K. (Stanford University, Stanford, California, USA)
Bilingualism **1**: 535–37

HALL, B. L. (Ontario Institute for Studies in Education, Toronto, Ontario, Canada)
Participatory Research **7**: 4330–36

HALL, G. E. (University of Northern Colorado, Greeley, Colorado, USA)
Teacher Education Programs: Structure* **10: 5995–6000

HALLAK, J. (International Institute for Educational Planning, Paris, France)
United Nations Organizations: Research and Service in Comparative and International Education* **11: 6523–30

HALLINAN, M. T. (University of Notre Dame, Notre Dame, Indiana, USA)
School and Classroom Dynamics **9**: 5169–76; *School Choice, Foundations of* **9**: 5197–201

HALLS, W. D. (University of Oxford, Oxford, UK)
Contemporary History of Education **2**: 1056–64; *International Baccalaureate* **5**: 2955–57; *United Kingdom: System of Education* **11**: 6515–23

HALT, D. (University of Southampton, Southampton, UK)
Missing Data and Nonresponse in Survey Research **7**: 3853–58

HAMADACHE, A. (Lavardin, France)
Nonformal and Alternative Approaches to Basic Education: Comparative Studies **7**: 4132–36

HAMBLETON, R. K. (University of Massachusetts, Amherst, Massachusetts, USA)
Criterion-referenced Measurement **2**: 1183–89; *Standard Setting in Criterion-referenced Testing* **10**: 5721–26; **Tests and Attitude Scales, Translation of* **11**: 6328–34

HAMERS, J. H. M. (University of Utrecht, Utrecht, The Netherlands)
Learning Potential and Learning Potential Tests* **6: 3312–15

HAMEYER, U. (University of Kiel, Kiel, Germany)
Curriculum Theory **3**: 1348–55

HAMILTON, S. F. (Cornell University, Ithaca, New York, USA)
Apprenticeship, Economics of* **1: 306–10

HANNA, J. H. (University of Maryland, College Park, Maryland, USA)
Social Change and Education: Anthropological Perspectives **9**: 5508–10

HANSEN, D. T. (University of Illinois at Chicago, Chicago, Illinois, USA)
Curriculum History: National Profiles* **3: 1288–301

HANSON, D. J. (State University of New York, Potsdam, New York, USA)
Drug Prevention Education **3**: 1607–10

HANSON, E. M. (University of California, Riverside, California, USA)
Governance: Relations among Levels of Government **5**: 2509–12

HANUSHEK, E. A. (University of Rochester, Rochester, New York, USA)
Education Production Functions **3**: 1756–62; **Educational Efficiency and Effectiveness, Concepts of* **3**: 1779–84

HAQ, F. (Ministry of Education, Kabul, Afghanistan)
Afghanistan: System of Education **1**: 204–10

HARASIM, L. M. (Simon Fraser University, Burnaby, British Columbia, Canada)
Computer Networking for Education **2**: 977–82

HARDCASTLE, A. J. (University of California, Los Angeles, California, USA)
Private Sector Training, Education and Performance Contracting in* **8: 4708–15

HARDMAN, M. L. (University of Utah, Salt Lake City, Utah, USA)
Transition to Adult and Working Life for Persons with Handicaps* **11: 6457–61

HARGREAVES, A. (Ontario Institute for Studies in Education, Toronto, Ontario, Canada)
Teaching, Realities of **10**: 6208–15

HARLEN, W. (Scottish Council for Research in Education, Edinburgh, UK)
Science Education: Primary School Programs **9**: 5328–35

HARMAN, G. (University of New England, Armidale, New South Wales, Australia)
Ministries and State Departments of Education **7**: 3833–40

HARNISCHFEGER, A. (Northwestern University, Evanston, Illinois, USA)
Attention in Learning **1**: 374–77

HÄRNQVIST, K. (University of Gothenburg, Mölndal, Sweden)
Training of Research Workers in Education **11**: 6438–45

HAROUTUNIAN-GORDON, S. (Northwestern University, Evanston, Illinois, USA)
Plato and Education **8**: 4532–36

HART, K. (University of Quebec, Montreal, Quebec, Canada)
Mathematics: Topics of Instruction* **6: 3671–86

HARTMAN, D. (The Shalom Hartman Institute, Jerusalem, Israel)
Judaic Theory of Human Nature and Development **6**: 3113–20

HARTMAN, W. T. (Pennsylvania State University, University Park, Pennsylvania, USA)
School Business Management and Budgeting **9**: 5181–86

HARTOG, J. (University of Amsterdam, Amsterdam, The Netherlands)
Screening Models and Education* **9: 5350–55

HATANO, G. (Dokkyo University, Saitama, Japan)
Cognitive Development and the Acquisition of Expertise **2**: 838–42

HATIVA, N. (Tel Aviv University, Tel Aviv, Israel)
Technology and the Classroom Teacher **11**: 6283–87

HAWKRIDGE, D. G. (Open University, Milton Keynes, UK)
Educational Technology: Developing Nations **4**: 1899–903

HAYWOOD, H. C. (Vanderbilt University, Nashville, Tennessee, USA)
Cognitive Modifiability* **2: 857–61

HAZEL, E. (University of Technology, Sydney, New South Wales, Australia)
Laboratory Packages for Science Learning* **6: 3202–05; *Science Laboratory Instruction* **9**: 5335–38

HAZELIP, K. (University of California, Santa Barbara, California, USA)
Teachers' Beliefs and Belief Systems* **10: 6099–103

HEALY, C. (University of California, Los Angeles, California, USA)
Student Support Systems: Adult Education* **10: 5805–08

HECKHAUSEN, J. (Max Planck Institute for Human Development and Education, Berlin, Germany)
Lifespan Development **6**: 3425–28

HECKMAN, P. E. (University of Arizona, Tucson, Arizona, USA)
Age Grouping of Students* **1: 227–30

HELLER, K. A. (University of Munich, Munich, Germany)
Identification and Programming of the Gifted and Talented* **5: 2725–32

HELMKE, A. (University of Landau, Landau, Germany)
Self-concept, Development of **9**: 5390–94; *Student Needs: Diagnosing* **10**: 5768–72; **Teaching: Diagnostic–Prescriptive* **10**: 6169–73

HENCKE, R. (Harvard University, Cambridge, Massachusetts, USA)
Human Development, Stages in* **5: 2677–81

HENDRICKS-LEE, M. S. (University of Cincinnati, Cincinnati, Ohio, USA)
Teacher Planning, Approaches to* **10: 6031–35

HENRIOT-VAN ZANTEN, A. (Université René Descartes, Paris, France)
Community–School Relations, Anthropological Study of **2**: 914–18

HENRY, G. (University of Liège, Liège, Belgium)
Correspondence Analysis of Qualitative Data **2**: 1117–21

HERMAN, J. L. (University of California, Los Angeles, California, USA)
Item Writing Techniques **5**: 3061–66

HERRANEN, M. (Ministry of Education, Helsinki, Finland)
Finland: System of Education **4**: 2316–24

HERSCHBACH, D. R. (University of Maryland, College Park, Maryland, USA)
Quality Assurance in Vocational Education and Training **8**: 4858–65

HERSHKOWITZ, R. (Tel Aviv University, Tel Aviv, Israel)
Mathematics: Topics of Instruction* **6: 3671–86

HEYMAN, G. D. (University of Illinois at Urbana-Champaign, Champaign, Illinois, USA)
Achievement Motivation, Development of* **1: 28–32

HEYNEMAN, S. P. (World Bank, Washington, DC, USA)
Textbook Development in Developing Nations, Planning for* **11: 6360–66

HICKS, N. L. (World Bank, Washington, DC, USA)
Education and Economic Growth **3**: 1660–66

HIELSCHER, S. (UNESCO Institute of Education, Hamburg, Germany)
Caribbean and Central America: Adult Education* **2: 635–40

HIEMSTRA, R. (Syracuse University, Syracuse, New York, USA)
Self-directed Adult Learning **9**: 5394–99

HIGGINS, P. J. (State University of New York, Plattsburgh, New York, USA)
Anthropological Programs in Education **1**: 277–80

HILDYARD, A. (Ontario Institute for Studies in Education, Toronto, Ontario, Canada)
Writing, Learning and Instruction of **11**: 6778–81

HILL, J. (University of Illinois at Urbana-Champaign, Champaign, Illinois, USA)
School Culture and Peer Groups **9**: 5217–20

HINCHLIFFE, K. (University of East Anglia, Norwich, UK)
Education and the Labor Market **3**: 1703–07; *Manpower Forecasting and Educational Planning* **6**: 3608–13; *Public Sector Employment and Education* **8**: 4836–39

HIRSCH, D. (OECD/CERI, Paris, France)
Partnerships: Initial and Adult Education **8**: 4337–39

HODSON, B. W. (Wichita State University, Wichita, Kansas, USA)
Speech–Sound Disorders: Articulation and Phonology **10**: 5694–97

HOI, N. (Department of Education, Port Moresby, Papua New Guinea)
Papua New Guinea: System of Education* **7: 4275–82

HOLLINGSWORTH, S. (Michigan State University, East Lansing, Michigan, USA)
Teachers as Researchers **10**: 6096–99

HOLMBERG, B. (Fern Universität, Hagen, Germany)
Open University **7**: 4215–20

HOLTE, R. (University of Uppsala, Uppsala, Sweden)
Saint Augustine and Education **9**: 5115–17

HOPES, C. (German Institute for International Educational Research, Frankfurt, Germany)
Administrator Recruitment, Selection, and Careers* **1: 78–83

HOPKINS, D. (University of Cambridge, Cambridge, UK)
Institutional Self-evaluation and Renewal **5**: 2847–52

HOPPERS, W. (CESO, The Hague, The Netherlands)
Education and Productive Work **3**: 1685–90

HORE, T. (Monash University, Clayton, Victoria, Australia)
Nontraditional Students: Third-age and Part-time **7**: 4163–71

HOUSE, E. R. (University of Colorado, Boulder, Colorado, USA)
Ethics of Evaluation Studies **4**: 2033–37

HOUTKOOP, W. (Dutch Advisory Council for Adult Education, Bunnik, The Netherlands)
Southern and Western Europe: Adult Education **10**: 5635–44

HOWE, K. R. (University of Colorado, Boulder, Colorado, USA)
Equality of Educational Opportunity: Philosophical Issues **4**: 2001–04

HOWE, M. J. A. (University of Exeter, Exeter, UK)
Learning across the Lifespan, Development of **6**: 3285–88

HOWE, W. (University of Richmond, Richmond, Virginia, USA)
Leadership **6**: 3276–84

HOWIESON, C. (University of Edinburgh, Edinburgh, UK)
Modularization in Vocational Education and Training **7**: 3890–95

HOYLE, E. (University of Bristol, Bristol, UK)
Evolution and Contemporary Developments **4**: 2156–67; *Teachers as Professionals* **10**: 6092–96; *Teaching: Social Status* **10**: 6224–27

HÜFNER, K. (Free University of Berlin, Berlin, Germany)
Planning Education: North America and Europe **8**: 4495–99

HUGHES, M. G. (University of Birmingham, Birmingham, UK)
International Associations: Role in Educational Administration **5**: 2951–55

HURSH, D. (University of Rochester, Rochester, New York, USA)
Civic Education **2**: 767–70

HUSEIN, M. G. (Ministry of Education, Kuwait, State of Kuwait)
Kuwait: System of Education **6**: 3170–77

HUSÉN, T. (University of Stockholm, Stockholm, Sweden)
Educational History in Biographies and Autobiographies **3**: 1793–97; *Educational Research and Policy-making* **4**: 1857–64; *International Education* **5**: 2972–78; *Meritocracy* **7**: 3769–71; *Research Paradigms in Education* **9**: 5051–56

HUSSAR, W. J. (National Center for Education Statistics, United States Department of Education, Washington, DC, USA)
Projections of Educational Statistics* **8: 4783–88

HUTCHINGS, D. E. (New York State Psychiatric Institute, New York, USA)
Abnormal Prenatal Development* **1: 12–15

HUTTUNEN, I. (University of Oulu, Oulu, Finland)
Language and Communication Education for Adults **6**: 3209–13

HUYNH HUYNH (University of South Carolina, Columbia, South Carolina, USA)
Robust Statistical Procedures **9**: 5077–82

HYAMS, B. K. (Flinders University of South Australia, Bedford Park, South Australia, Australia)
Oral History in Educational Research **7**: 4220–25

HYNDS, S. (Syracuse University, Syracuse, New York, USA)
Teacher Education for Language Arts and Literature **10**: 5958–61

ICHILOV, O. (Tel Aviv University, Tel Aviv, Israel)
Political Education **8**: 4568–71

IDOL, L. (Institute for Learning and Development, Austin, Texas, USA)
Teaming Arrangements in Special Education **10**: 6240–44

IGLESIAS, A. (Temple University, Philadelphia, Pennsylvania, USA)
Language Differences versus Language Disorders* **6: 3225–28; **Speech and Language Disorders and the Hard of Hearing* **10**: 5686–91

IMEL, S. (ERIC Clearinghouse on Adult, Career, and Vocational Education, Ohio State University, Columbus, Ohio, USA)
Adult Education: Information Sources **1**: 139–42

JACKSON, G. A. (Massachusetts Institute of Technology, Cambridge, Massachusetts, USA)
Decision-making Theory **3**: 1421–25

JACKŪNAS, Ž. (Vilnius, Lithuania)
Lithuania: System of Education* **6: 3484–91

JACOB, E. J. (George Mason University, Fairfax, Virginia, USA)
Culture, Cognition, and Education, Perspectives on **3**: 1246–53

JAEGGI, E. (Technische Universität Berlin, Berlin, Germany)
Psychodynamic Theories of Human Development **8**: 4812–16

JALLADE, J.-P. (European Institute of Education and Social Policy, Paris, France)
Vocational Education and Training: Western Europe **11**: 6664–69

JAMES, E. (World Bank, Washington, DC, USA)
Public–Private Division of Responsibility for Education **8**: 4831–36

JAMIESON, I. (University of Bath, Bath, UK)
Education for the Life of Work **3**: 1736–40

JANOWSKI, A. (Institute for Educational Research, Warsaw, Poland)
Poland: System of Education* **8: 4542–49

JANSEN, M. (Danish National Institute for Educational Research, Copenhagen, Denmark)
Denmark: System of Education* **3: 1453–61

JANSSEN, K. N. (Eastern Kentucky University, Richmond, Kentucky, USA)
Behavioral Disorders: Social* **1: 490–95

JANSSEN REINEN, I. (University of Twente, Enschede, The Netherlands)
Computer Literacy* **2: 973–77; **Gender and New Technology* **4**: 2423–27

JANTZI, D. (Ontario Institute for Studies in Education, Toronto, Ontario, Canada)
School Organizational Effects on Student Outcomes* **9: 5259–64

JARVIS, P. (University of Surrey, Guildford, UK)
Sociology of Adult Education **10**: 5591–96; **Training of Adult Educators* **11**: 6431–38

JAWORSKI, J. (BBC Open University Production Centre, Milton Keynes, UK)
Audiovisual Programs, Production of **1**: 400–04

JENKINS, E. W. (University of Leeds, Leeds, UK)
Science Education, History of **9**: 5324–28; *Scientific Literacy* **9**: 5345–50

JIMENEZ, E. (World Bank, Washington, DC, USA)
Financing Public Education: Practices and Trends **4**: 2310–16

JIYONO (Office of Education and Cultural Research and Development, Jakarta, Indonesia)
Indonesia: System of Education* **5: 2784–92

JOHANNESSON, K. (University of Uppsala, Uppsala, Sweden)
Quintilian and Education **8**: 4887–90

JOHANSSON, E. (University of Umeå, Umeå, Sweden)
Luther and Education **6**: 3528–31

JOHANSSON, J-E. (University of Gothenburg, Mölndal, Sweden)
Froebel and Education **4**: 2385–88

JOHNSON, D. W. (University of Minnesota, Minneapolis, Minnesota, USA)
Goal Structures* **5: 2500–04; **Teaching: Social Psychological Theories* **10**: 6219–24

JOHNSON, L. J. (University of Cincinnati, Cincinnati, Ohio, USA)
Prereferral Intervention for Students with Special Needs* **8: 4657–62

JOHNSON, R. T. (University of Minnesota, Minneapolis, Minnesota, USA)
Goal Structures* **5: 2500–04; **Teaching: Social Psychological Theories* **10**: 6219–24

JOHNSON, S. M. (Harvard University, Cambridge, Massachusetts, USA)
Teachers and Policy: Implications for Management **10**: 6079–83

JOHNSON, T. G. (The Flinders University of South Australia, Bedford Park, South Australia, Australia)
Science: Attitudes Toward* **9: 5318–24

JOHNSTON, A. (SIDA, Stockholm, Sweden)
Adult Literacy Programs in Developing Nations* **1: 169–76

JOHNSTONE, J. N. (Australian Planning and Training Associates Pty Ltd, Sydney, New South Wales, Australia)
Kiribati: System of Education **6**: 3144–48; *Tuvalu: System of Education* **11**: 6484–88; *Vanuatu: System of Education* **11**: 6580–86

JONATHAN, R. (University of Edinburgh, Edinburgh, UK)
Vocationalism: Theoretical Assumptions **11**: 6699–704

JOÓ, A. (National Institute for Education, Budapest, Hungary)
Galois Lattices* **4: 2395–400

JUAN, S. (University of Sydney, Sydney, New South Wales, Australia)
Education of Indigenous Peoples, Anthropological Study of **3**: 1750–56

KAESTLE, C. F. (University of Wisconsin–Madison, Madison, Wisconsin, USA)
Historical Methods in Educational Research **5**: 2601–07

KAGAN, S. L. (Yale University, New Haven, Connecticut, USA)
Human Development: Research and Social Policy **5**: 2670–73; *School Readiness* **9**: 5273–75

KAHN, L. (Canisius College, Buffalo, New York, USA)
Cross-cultural Study of Education **2**: 1208–13

KAIL, R. (Purdue University, West Lafayette, Indiana, USA)
Cognitive Development: Information-processing Approach **2**: 847–52

KAISER, H. J. (University of Hamburg, Hamburg, Germany)
Music Education: Programs and Methods **7**: 4016–27; *Music Teacher Education* **7**: 4027–30

KALA, U. (Tallinn Pedagogical University, Tallinn, Estonia)
Estonia: System of Education* **4: 2025–29

KALVERBOER, A. F. (State University, Groningen, The Netherlands)
Developmental Psychopathology **3**: 1514–20

KAMAT, S. G. (University of Pittsburgh, Pittsburgh, Pennsylvania, USA)
Political Work of Teachers* **8: 4581–87

KAMERMAN, S. B. (Columbia University, New York, USA)
Childcare Policies and Programs: International Overview **2**: 693–701

KAMPER, G. (Berlin, Germany)
Curriculum and Materials in Adult Literacy **3**: 1257–62

KANAYA, T. (Sonoda Women's College, Amagasaki, Japan)
Japan: System of Education **6**: 3078–86

KANJEE, A. (University of Massachusetts, Amherst, Massachusetts, USA)
Tests and Attitude Scales, Translation of* **11: 6328–34

KAPLAN, A. (University of Haifa, Haifa, Israel)
Research Methodology: Scientific Methods **9**: 5043–50

KASWORM, C. E. (University of Tennessee, Knoxville, Tennessee, USA)
University Adult Education **11**: 6547–51

KEATS, D. M. (University of Newcastle, Newcastle, New South Wales, Australia)
Interviewing for Selection and Clinical Research **5**: 3003–07

KEATS, J. A. (University of Newcastle, Newcastle, New South Wales, Australia)
Classical Test Theory **2**: 785–92; *Measurement in Educational Research* **7**: 3698–707

KEEVES, J. P. (The Flinders University of South Australia, Bedford Park, South Australia, Australia)
Achievement Test Scales **1**: 32–42; *Assessment in Schools, Methods of* **1**: 362–70; **Attitudes toward Schooling, Comparative Studies in* **1**: 390–96; **Canonical Analysis* **2**: 626–31; **Comparative Methodology in Education* **2**: 948–58; **Cross-sectional Research Methods* **2**: 1213–20; **Descriptive Data, Analysis of* **3**: 1464–75; **Descriptive Scales for Measuring Educational Climate* **3**: 1475–83; *Examinations: Public* **4**: 2172–80; *Legitimatory Research* **6**: 3368–73; *Longitudinal Research Methods* **6**: 3512–24; **Measurement of Social Background* **7**: 3715–22; *Measures of Variation* **7**: 3726–39; *Models and Model Building* **7**: 3865–73; **Multilevel Analysis* **7**: 3978–87; *Multivariate Analysis* **7**: 4007–16; **Path Analysis and Linear Structural Relations Analysis* **8**: 4339–52; **Path Analysis with Latent Variables* **8**: 4352–59; *Profile Analysis* **8**: 4752–54; **Research in Education: Nature, Needs, and Priorities* **9**: 5031–38; **Science: Attitudes Toward* **9**: 5318–24; **Sex Differences and Educational Outcomes* **9**: 5423–33; **Teaching and Learning, Demonstration Methods of* **10**: 6140–43; *Testing and the Curriculum* **11**: 6321–28; *Tests: Different Types* **11**: 6340–49

KELLAGHAN, T. (St Patrick's College, Dublin, Republic of Ireland)
Family and Schooling **4**: 2250–58

KELLER, J. M. (Florida State University, Tallahassee, Florida, USA)
Motivation in Instructional Design **7**: 3943–47

KELLER, M. (Max Planck Institute, Berlin, Germany)
Social Cognition, Development of* **9: 5510–12

KELLY, D. M. (University of British Columbia, Vancouver, British Columbia, Canada)
School Dropouts **9**: 5224–28

KELLY, R. (Singapore Polytechnic, Singapore)
Foreign Language Testing **4**: 2357–64

KELLY, T. F. (National Planning Department, Colombo, Sri Lanka)
Vocational Education and Training: Improving Cost-effectiveness in Developing Nations **11**: 6648–53

KEMMERER, F. (State University of New York, Albany, New York, USA)
Decentralization of Schooling in Developing Nations **3**: 1412–16

KEMMIS, S. (Deakin University, Geelong, Victoria, Australia)
Action Research **1**: 42–48

KENNEDY, J. J. (Ohio State University, Columbus, Ohio, USA)
Log-Linear Models* **6: 3499–508

KENNEDY, M. (University of London, London, UK)
Women's Studies Programs **11**: 6765–69

KERCHNER, C. T. (Claremont Graduate School, Claremont, California, USA)
Labor Relations in Education* **6: 3189–97

KERDEMAN, D. (University of Washington, Seattle, Washington, USA)
Hermeneutics* **5: 2579–86

KESSELS, J. W. M. (Foundation for Corporate in Education, Terschuur, The Netherlands)
Job Analysis in Corporate Education* **6: 3092–96

KGOMANYANE, G. (Ministry of Education, Gaborone, Botswana)
Botswana: System of Education **1**: 543–52

KHANIYA, T. R. (Ministry of Education and Culture, Kathmandu, Nepal)
Nepal: System of Education* **7: 4060–67

KIBBY, M. R. (University of Strathclyde, Glasgow, UK)
Hypertext, Educational Applications of **5**: 2706–09

KIERAN, C. (University of Quebec, Montreal, Quebec, Canada)
Mathematics: Topics of Instruction* **6: 3671–86

KIERNAN, M. A. (Ministry of Education and Culture, Kathmandu, Nepal)
Nepal: System of Education* **7: 4060–67

KILLEN, M. (Wesleyan University, Middleton, Connecticut, USA)
Social Cognition, Development of* **9: 5510–12

KILPATRICK, J. (University of Georgia, Athens, Georgia, USA)
Mathematics Education, History of **6**: 3643–47; *Mathematics Instruction: Contemporary Research* **6**: 3647–52

KIM, E-Y. (University of California, Berkeley, California, USA)
Ethnography of Education: Anthropological Approach* **4: 2046–53

KING, E. M. (World Bank, Washington, DC, USA)
Gender and Education Choices, Economics of **4**: 2412–19

KING, K. (University of Edinburgh, Edinburgh, UK)
Dissemination of Educational Research **3**: 1553–57; *Technical and Vocational Education and Training* **11**: 6245–51

KINUNDA, M. (UNICEF, Nairobi, Kenya)
Kenya: System of Education **6**: 3125–33

KLEES, S. J. (Florida State University, Tallahassee, Florida, USA)
Educational Planning, Economics of **3**: 1810–21; *Educational Technology, Economics of* **4**: 1903–11

KLEIN, P. (Bar Ilan University, Ramat Gan, Israel)
Cognitive Modifiability* **2: 857–61

KLOOSTERMAN, P. (Indiana University, Bloomington, Indiana, USA)
Mathematics Education, Affective Issues in **6**: 3639–43

KLOVDAHL, A. S. (The Australian National University, Canberra, ACT, Australia)
Social Network Analysis **9**: 5554–60

KNIGHT, S. L. (University of Houston, Houston, Texas, USA)
Schools for Laboratory and Professional Development* **9: 5313–18

KNOERS, A. (Catholic University of Nijmegen, Nijmegen, The Netherlands)
Instructional Psychology, Paradigms in **5**: 2880–84

KNOWLES, J. (Ministry of Education, Culture and Youth Affairs, St John's, Antigua and Barbuda)
Antigua and Barbuda: System of Education **1**: 300–06

KNOWLTON, M. (University of Minnesota, Minneapolis, Minnesota, USA)
Visually Handicapped Children and Youth, Education of **11**: 6625–28

KOHNSTAMM, G. A. (University of Leiden, Leiden, The Netherlands)
Temperament Development* **11: 6307–11

KOKORA, P. (Georgetown University, Washington, DC, USA)
Côte d'Ivoire: System of Education **2**: 1152–61

KOLEN, M. J. (American College Testing, Iowa City, Iowa, USA)
Tests, Equating of **11**: 6349–55

KOMOROWSKA, H. (University of Warsaw, Warsaw, Poland)
Poland: System of Education* **8: 4542–49

KOMOSKI, P. K. (EPIE Institute, Hampton Bays, New York, USA)
Computer-managed Learning **2**: 998–1002

KONTOGIANNOPOULOU–POLYDORIDES, G. (University of Patras, Patras, Greece)
Greece: System of Education* **5: 2515–23

KÕRGESAAR, J. (Tartu University, Tartu, Estonia)
Estonia: System of Education* **4: 2025–29

KORNADT, H. J. (University of the Saarland, Saarbrücken, Germany)
Human Development: Cross-cultural Approaches* **5: 2647–51

KOTTE, D. (University of Hamburg, Hamburg, Germany)
Sex Differences and Educational Outcomes* **9: 5423–33

KOZMA, R. B. (University of Michigan, Ann Arbor, Michigan, USA)
Computer and Information Sciences: Educational Programs **2**: 969–73; *Mass Media Literacy: Educational Programs* **6**: 3622–25

KRASKA, K. (University of Osnabrück, Osnabrück, Germany)
Self-regulation in Learning* **9: 5400–03

KRATOCHWILL, T. R. (University of Wisconsin-Madison, Madison, Wisconsin, USA)
Reinforcement* **9: 4974–77

KRAUSE EHEART, B. (University of Illinois at Urbana–Champaign, Champaign, Illinois, USA)
Toddler Programs **11**: 6395–98

KREINER, S. (Danish National Institute for Educational Research, Copenhagen, Denmark)
Denmark: System of Education* **3: 1453–61

KRISTOFF, W. (University of Hamburg, Hamburg, Germany)

Configural Frequency Analyses of Categorized Data **2**: 1031–37

KUBISZYN, T. (University of Texas, Austin, Texas, USA)
Students, Grading and Evaluation of* **10: 5818–22

KUH, G. D. (Indiana University, Bloomington, Indiana, USA)
Student Support Systems: Administration **10**: 5796–805

KUHL, J. (University of Osnabrück, Osnabrück, Germany)
Self-regulation in Learning* **9: 5400–03

KUTNER, M. A. (Pelavin Associates Inc., Washington, DC, USA)
Adult Basic Education **1**: 100–03

KWONG, Y. H. (World Bank, Washington, DC, USA)
Technology in Educational Planning* **11: 6292–98

LA BELLE, T. J. (West Virginia University, Morgantown, West Virginia, USA)
Nonformal Education Policy in Developing Nations* **7: 4141–45

LACEY, C. (University of Sussex, Brighton, UK)
Teachers, Professional Socialization of **10**: 6122–27

LAGERWEIJ, N. (University of Utrecht, Utrecht, The Netherlands)
School Improvement* **9: 5241–47

LAKIN, K. C. (University of Minnesota, Minneapolis, Minnesota, USA)
Deinstitutionalization* **3: 1434–38

LAKOMSKI, G. (University of Melbourne, Melbourne, Victoria, Australia)
Critical Theory and Education **2**: 1199–204; **Educational Administration: Ethical and Philosophical Issues* **3**: 1769–75

LAKSHMI, T. K. S. (M. S. University of Baroda, Baroda, India)
Women's Education, History Of: India* **11: 6748–53

LAMBERT, N. M. (University of California, Berkeley, California, USA)
Seating Arrangements in Classrooms **9**: 5355–59

LAMINE, B. (Ministry of Education, Tunis, Tunisia)
Tunisia: System of Education* **11: 6466–76

LAMM, Z. (Hebrew University of Jerusalem, Jerusalem, Israel)
Knowledge: Conceptions of and Impact on the Curriculum **6**: 3148–51

LAMOURE, J. (Ecole Normal Supérieure, Cachan, France)
Youth Unemployment **11**: 6803–08

LANCASTER, F. W. (University of Illinois at Urbana–Champaign, Urbana, Illinois, USA)
Information Storage and Retrieval **5**: 2819–23

LANCY, D. F. (Utah State University, Logan, Utah, USA)
Literacy and Numeracy, Anthropological Study of **6**: 3446–53

LAND, R. (Education Department of Queensland, Brisbane, Queensland, Australia)
Empowerment Skills, Acquisition of* **4: 1980–85

LANDER, R. (Gothenburg University, Mölndal, Sweden)
Management of Change and Innovation **6**: 3597–603

LANE, S. (University of Pittsburgh, Pittsburgh, Pennsylvania, USA)
Assessment in the Service of Learning* **1: 370–74

LANGEWAND, A. (Free University of Berlin, Berlin, Germany)
Herbart and Education **5**: 2575–79

LARSON, K. A. (University of California, Santa Barbara, California, USA)
Delinquent and Adjudicated Youth **3**: 1438–41

LÁRUSSON, H. (Ministry of Culture and Education, Reykjavik, Iceland)
Iceland: System of Education **5**: 2715–21

LAUGLO, J. (The Research Council of Norway, Oslo, Norway)
Vocational Training Modes: Sweden, Germany, and Japan **11**: 6690–99

LAUTERBACH, U. (German Institute of International Educational Research, Frankfurt, Germany)
Apprenticeship, History and Development of **1**: 310–18

LAWSON, M. J. (The Flinders University of South Australia, Bedford Park, South Australia, Australia)
Concept Mapping **2**: 1026–31; *Experimental Studies* **4**: 2186–94

LAYNE, A. (University of the West Indies, Cave Hill, Barbados)
Barbados: System of Education* **1: 458–65

LAYTON, D (University of Leeds, Leeds, UK)
Technology: Educational Programs **11**: 6287–92

LE THAC CAN (Hanoi, Vietnam)
Vietnam: System of Education* **11: 6608–14

LEACH, F. (University of London, London, UK)
Sudan: System of Education **10**: 5834–43

LEAL FILHO, W. D. S. (University of Bradford, Bradford, UK)
Guinea-Bissau: System of Education **5**: 2556–62

LEE, V. E. (University of Michigan, Ann Arbor, Michigan, USA)
Coeducation versus Single-sex Schooling* **2: 831–34; **Public versus Private Schools: Research Controversies* **8**: 4839–45; *Secondary Schools: Effective* **9**: 5373–79

LEEPER, H. A. (University of Western Ontario, London, Ontario, Canada)
Voice Disorders in Schoolchildren **11**: 6704–07

LEHMANN, R. H. (University of Hamburg, Hamburg, Germany)
Essays, Scoring of **4**: 2018–25; *Germany: System of Education* **5**: 2470–80

LEIGHFIELD, K. (University of Virginia, Charlottesville, Virginia, USA)
Student Teaching and Field Experiences* **10: 5808–12

LEINHARDT, G. (University of Pittsburgh, Pittsburgh, Pennsylvania, USA)
Exploratory Data Analysis* **4: 2199–208; **Videotape and Audiotape Recording in Educational Research* **11**: 6604–08

LEINHARDT, S. (University of Pittsburgh, Pittsburgh, Pennsylvania, USA)
Exploratory Data Analysis* **4: 2199–208

LEITHWOOD, K. A. (Ontario Institute for Studies in Education, Toronto, Ontario, Canada)
Evaluating Implementation of Educational Programs and Innovations **4**: 2070–74; **School Organizational Effects on Student Outcomes* **9**: 5259–64

LENS, W. (University of Leuven, Leuven, Belgium)
Motivation and Learning **7**: 3936–42

LERNER, R. M. (Michigan State University, East Lansing, Michigan, USA)
Adolescence* **1: 83–89

LÊ THÀNH KHÔI (Université René Descartes, Paris, France)
Planning Education: History **8**: 4489–91

LEVIN, H. M. (Stanford University, Stanford, California, USA)
Cost–Benefit Analysis **2**: 1127–31; *Cost-effectiveness Analysis* **2**: 1131–36; *School Choice: Market Mechanisms* **9**: 5201–06; *School Finance* **9**: 5233–41

LEVIN, T. (Tel Aviv University, Tel Aviv, Israel)
Courseware Evaluation **2**: 1170–75

LEVINE, D. U. (University of Nebraska, Omaha, Nebraska, USA)
Desegregation in Schools **3**: 1483–86

LEVY, G. (University of Wyoming, Laramie, Wyoming, USA)
Gender Roles* **4: 2446–49

LEWY, A. (Tel Aviv University, Tel Aviv, Israel)
Curriculum-specific Evaluation Criteria* **3: 1359–67

LEYTON SOTO, M. (SIMAC, Guatemala City, Guatemala)
Guatemala: System of Education **5**: 2544–51

LIAW, F. (Columbia University, New York, USA)
Early Experience and Human Development* **3: 1636–43

LIETZ, P. (The Flinders University of South Australia, Bedford Park, South Australia, Australia)
Cross-sectional Research Methods* **2: 1213–20

LIMBASSA, D. (University of Bangui, Bangui, Central African Republic)
Central African Republic: System of Education **2**: 653–56

LIN HUEY-YA (Fu-Jen Catholic University, Taipei, Taiwan, Republic of China)
Confucian Theory of Human Nature and Development **2**: 1042–45

LINACRE, J. M. (University of Chicago, Chicago, Illinois, USA)
Individualized Testing in the Classroom **5**: 2779–84; *Judgments, Measurement of* **6**: 3120–24

LINCOLN, Y. S. (Texas A&M University, College Station, Texas, USA)
Fourth Generation: Evaluation* **4: 2369–75

LIND, A. (SIDA, Stockholm, Sweden)
Adult Literacy Programs in Developing Nations* **1: 169–76

LINDBORG, R. (University of Lund, Lund, Sweden)
Descartes and Education **3**: 1461–64

LINDMAN, H. R. (Indiana University, Bloomington, Indiana, USA)
Bayesian Statistics in the Analysis of Data **1**: 475–80

LINDSEY, J. K. (Limburg University, Diepenbeck, Belgium)
Significance Testing **9**: 5460–67

LINN, M. C. (University of California, Berkeley, California, USA)
Gender and School Learning: Science **4**: 2436–40; **Science, Learning and Instruction of* **9**: 5338–42

LIPSITT, L. P. (Brown University, Providence, Rhode Island, USA)
Infancy **5**: 2799–802

LIPSMEIER, A. (University of Karlsruhe, Karlsruhe, Germany)
Vocational Training, History of* **11: 6678–84

LLAMAS, I. (Universidad Autónoma Metropolitana, Mexico City, Mexico)
Education and Labor Markets in Developing Nations **3**: 1681–85

LLOYD, L. L. (Purdue University, West Lafayette, Indiana, USA)
Augmentative and Alternative Communication* **1: 404–09

LOCKHEED, M. E. (World Bank, Washington, DC, USA)
Coeducation versus Single-sex Schooling* **2: 831–34; **Educational Efficiency and Effectiveness, Concepts of* **3**: 1779–84

LOHMAN, D. F. (University of Iowa, Iowa City, Iowa, USA)
Intelligence, Learning, and Instruction **5**: 2916–22

LOHNES, P. R. (State University of New York, Buffalo, New York, USA)
Discriminant Analysis **3**: 1544–49; *Factorial Modeling* **4**: 2241–45

LOKAN, J. J. (Australian Council for Educational Research, Hawthorn, Victoria, Australia)
Vocational Interests and Aptitudes, Measures of **11**: 6669–78

LOMPSCHER, J. (Academy of Educational Sciences, Berlin, Germany)
Learning Activity **6**: 3289–92

LONG, H. B. (University of Oklahoma, Norman, Oklahoma, USA)
Professional Associations for Adult Education **8**: 4731–36

LONG, M. H. (University of Hawaii at Manoa, Honolulu, Hawaii, USA)
Foreign Language Acquisition, Process of **4**: 2331–39

LOPEZ, A. L. (University of Illinois at Chicago, Chicago, Illinois, USA)
Students' Curriculum Experiences* **10: 5813–18

LOUIS, K. S. (University of Minnesota, Minneapolis, Minnesota, USA)
School Improvement* **9: 5241–47

LOWE, J. (University of Warwick, Coventry, UK)
Legislation in Adult Education **6**: 3360–67; *Leisure: Adult Education* **6**: 3373–78

LOWYCK, J. (University of Leuven, Leuven, Belgium)
Computers and Learning* **2: 1002–07; **Instructional Psychology (as a Contributing Field to Instructional Design)* **5**: 2870–74; *Learning in Industrial Settings* **6**: 3302–06

LOXLEY, W. (International Association for the Evaluation of Educational Achievement, The Hague, The Netherlands))
Comparative Education and International Education: Organizations and Institutions **2**: 933–42

LUGG, C. A. (Pennsylvania State University, University Park, Pennsylvania, USA)
Management of Contraction in Public Education* **6: 3603–08

LUKE, A. (James Cook University of North Queensland, Townsville, Queensland, Australia)
Critical Reading: Teaching and Assessing* **2: 1194–98

LUKŠIENÉ, M. (Vilnius, Lithuania)
Lithuania: System of Education* **6: 3484–91

MACDONALD, M. (University of British Columbia, Vancouver, British Columbia, Canada)
Health Education* **5: 2567–72

MACDONALD-ROSS, M. (Open University, Milton Keynes, UK)
Print Media, Production of **8**: 4688–94

MACKERACHER, D. (Ontario Institute for Studies in Education, Toronto, Ontario, Canada)
Lifespan Learning: Implications for Educators* **6: 3428–35

MACLEOD, G. (University of New England, Lismore, New South Wales, Australia)
Teacher Education, Microteaching in **10**: 5973–77

MAGABE M. (Catholic University of Bukavu, Bukavu, Rwanda)
Zaire: System of Education **11**: 6809–14

MAGNUSSON, D. (Stockholm University, Stockholm, Sweden)
Personality Development* **8: 4388–95

MAHER, C. A. (Rutgers State University, New Brunswick, New Jersey, USA)
Mathematics Teacher Education* **6: 3668–71

MAHROUSE, M. E. (Assiut University, Sohag City, Egypt)
Egypt: System of Education **4**: 1939–47

MAIMUNAH, S. (Ministry of Education, Kuala Lumpur, Malaysia)
Malaysia: System of Education* **6: 3564–72

MANGUBHAI, F. (University of Southern Queensland, Toowoomba, Queensland, Australia)
Fiji: System of Education **4**: 2302–10

MANLEY-CASIMIR, M. (Simon Fraser University, Burnaby, British Columbia, Canada)
Preschool Educational Television Programs* **8: 4677–80

MAREK, J. C. (University of California, Santa Barbara, California, USA)
Buddhist Theory of Human Nature and Development **1**: 577–81

MARENTIČ POŽARNIK, B. (University of Ljubljana, Ljubljana, Slovenia)
Slovenia: System of Education **9**: 5490–97

MARGALIT, M. (Tel Aviv University, Tel Aviv, Israel)
Empowering Families of Children and Youth with Special Needs **4**: 1976–80

MARJORIBANKS, K. (University of Adelaide, Adelaide, South Australia, Australia)
Family and School Environmental Measures **4**: 2245–50; *Interaction and Detection of its Effects in Educational Research* **5**: 2922–31

MARKLUND, S. (University of Stockholm, Stockholm, Sweden)
Sweden: System of Education **10**: 5866–73

MARKOWITSCH, H. J. (University of Bielefeld, Bielefeld, Germany)
Brain Development and Human Behavior **1**: 552–54

MARKS, H. M. (University of Wisconsin, Madison, Wisconsin, USA)
Public versus Private Schools: Research Controversies* **8: 4839–45

MARLAND, P. W. (University of Southern Queensland, Toowamba, Queensland, Australia)
Teaching: Implicit Theories **10**: 6178–83

MARSDEN, W. E. (University of Liverpool, Liverpool, UK)
Geography: Educational Programs **5**: 2465–70

MARSH, H. W. (University of Western Sydney, Macarthur, New South Wales, Australia)
Multitrait–Multimethod Analysis* **7: 4000–07; *Teaching, Student Evaluation of* **10**: 6227–35

MARSHALL, J. (University of Auckland, Auckland, New Zealand)
Postmodernism and Education* **8: 4639–42

MARTIN, C. L. (Arizona State University, Tempe, Arizona, USA)
Gender Roles* **4: 2446–49

MARTIN, E. (University of Havana, Havana, Cuba)
Cuba: System of Education* **3: 1221–27

MARTIN, H. (California State University, Los Angeles, California, USA)
Student Support Systems: Adult Education* **10: 5805–08

MARTIN, L. G. (University of Wisconsin, Milwaukee, Wisconsin, USA)
Adult Secondary Education **1**: 181–84

MARTIN, R. P. (University of Georgia, Athens, Georgia, USA)
Temperament Development* **11: 6307–11

MARTON, F. (University of Gothenburg, Mölndal, Sweden)
Phenomenography **8**: 4424–29

MARX, R. W. (University of Michigan, Ann Arbor, Michigan, USA)
Student Influences on Teaching* **10: 5759–62

MASEMANN, V. L. (University of Toronto, Toronto, Ontario, Canada)
Comparative Education Societies **2**: 942–48; *Educational Reform: Impact of Indigenous Forms of Knowledge* **4**: 1848–52

MASON, E. J. (University of Kentucky, Lexington, Kentucky, USA)
Gifted Children, Development of* **5: 2492–95

MASON, G. (National Institute of Economic and Social Research, London, UK)
Vocational Education and Training: Anglo–German Comparisons **11**: 6638–40

MASRI, M. (Ministry of Education, Amman, Jordan)
Jordan: System of Education* **6: 3106–13

MASSIALAS, B. G. (Florida State University, Tallahassee, Florida, USA)
Arab Countries: Adult Education **1**: 322–28; *Social Studies: Secondary School Programs* **9**: 5578–82

MASTERS, G. N. (Australian Council for Educational Research, Hawthorn, Victoria, Australia)

Partial Credit Model **7**: 4302–07; **Student Progress, Charting of* **10**: 5783–91

MATEEV, M. D. (University of Sofia, Sofia, Bulgaria)
Bulgaria: System of Education **1**: 581–88

MATTHEWS, M. R. (University of New South Wales, Sydney, New South Wales, Australia)
Philosophy of Science and Science Education **8**: 4461–64

MAYER, R. E. (University of California, Santa Barbara, California, USA)
Computer Programming, Learning and Instruction of **2**: 982–85; *Feedback in Learning* **4**: 2279–81; *Problem-solving and Thinking, Development of Learning Skills in* **8**: 4722–28; *Problem-solving, Teaching and Testing for* **8**: 4728–31; *Study Habits and Strategies* **10**: 5829–31

MCANINCH, A. R. (Knox College, Galesburg, Illinois, USA)
Teacher Education, Case Methods in **10**: 5943–48

MCCARTHEY, S. J. (University of Texas, Austin, Texas, USA)
Student Roles in Classrooms* **10: 5791–96

MCCAUL, E. J. (University of Maine, Orono, Maine, USA)
Children and Youth At Risk* **2: 706–11

MCCOMBE, R. J. (Australian Bureau of Statistics, Canberra, ACT, Australia)
Measurement of Industry Training **7**: 3711–15

MCCONNELL, S. R. (University of Minnesota, Minneapolis, Minnesota, USA)
Social Skills* **9: 5563–67

MCCORMICK, A. (Stanford University, Stanford, California, USA)
Videotape and Audiotape Recording in Educational Research* **11: 6604–08

MCDONNELL, J. (University of Utah, Salt Lake City, Utah, USA)
Transition to Adult and Working Life for Persons with Handicaps* **11: 6457–61

MCDOUGALL, A. (Monash University, Clayton, Victoria, Australia)
Software Tools in Courseware Design **10**: 5622–25

MCFADDEN, M. G. (Charles Sturt University, Mitchell, Queensland, Australia)
Resistance Theory* **9: 5056–61

MCGAW, B. (Australian Council for Educational Research, Hawthorn, Victoria, Australia)
Meta-analysis **7**: 3775–84

MCGILL-FRANZEN, A. (State University of New York, Albany, New York, USA)
Reading and the Mildly Handicapped* **8: 4930–36

MCGINN, N. F. (Harvard University, Cambridge, Massachusetts, USA)
Politics of Educational Planning **8**: 4595–602

MCGRANE, P. A. (Yale University, New Haven, Connecticut, USA)
Intellectual Development across the Lifespan* **5: 2910–16

MCKENZIE, P. A. (Australian Council for Educational Research, Hawthorn, Victoria, Australia)
Australia: System of Education **1**: 415–23; **Research in Education: Nature, Needs, and Priorities* **9**: 5031–38

MCLEAN, M. (University of London, London, UK)
Bahamas: System of Education **1**: 439–44

MCMAHON, W. W. (University of Illinois at Urbana-Champaign, Urbana, Illinois, USA)
Consumption Benefits of Education **2**: 1052–56

MEBRAHTU, T. (University of Bristol, Bristol, UK)
Development Education **3**: 1494–501

MEDLEY, D. M. (University of Virginia, Charlottesville, Virginia, USA)
Teacher Evaluation* **10: 6015–20

MEDWAY, F. J. (University of South Carolina, Columbia, South Carolina, USA)
Tutoring **11**: 6481–84

MEEK, V. L. (University of New England, Armidale, New South Wales, Australia)
Education and the State **3**: 1713–20

MEHAUT, P. (CNRS University of Nancy II, Nancy, France)
Employment Policy: Adult Education and Training **4**: 1972–76

MEISELS, S. J. (University of Michigan, Ann Arbor, Michigan, USA)
Assessment in Early Childhood **1**: 358–62; *Early Childhood Developmental Screening* **3**: 1621–24

MEISTER, C. (University of Illinois at Urbana–Champaign, Champaign, Illinois, USA)
Direct Instruction* **3: 1524–30

MEKETE, B. (Addis Ababa University, Addis Ababa, Ethiopia)
Ethiopia: System of Education **4**: 2037–43

MÉRÖ, L. (National Institute for Education, Budapest, Hungary)
Galois Lattices* **4: 2395–400

MESSICK, S. (Educational Testing Service, Princeton, New Jersey, USA)
Cognitive Styles and Learning **2**: 868–72

METCALF, K. K. (Indiana University, Bloomington, Indiana, USA)
Laboratory Experiences in Teacher Education **6**: 3197–202; **Teaching and Learning, Explanation in* **10**: 6143–49

MEYER, D. K. (University of Texas, Austin, Texas, USA)
Learning Strategies, Teaching and Testing for* **6: 3335–40

MICHAEL, W. B. (University of Southern California, Los Angeles, California, USA)
Evaluation Design, Evolution of* **4: 2079–89; **Prediction in Educational Research* **8**: 4652–57

MICHEL, C. (University of California, Santa Barbara, California, USA)
Guadeloupe and Martinique: System of Education* **5: 2536–44

MIDDLETON, J. (World Bank, Washington, DC, USA)
Vocational Education and Training, International Assistance for **11**: 6660–64

MIKLOS, E. (University of Alberta, Edmonton, Alberta, Canada)
Administrator Recruitment, Selection, and Careers* **1: 78–83

MILLER, K. M. (Miller and Tyler Ltd., London, UK)
Personality Inventories* **8: 4395–99

MILLOT, B. (World Bank, Washington, DC, USA)
Macroeconomics of Educational Time and Learning **6**: 3545–50

MILLSAP, M. A. (Abt Associates, Cambridge, Massachusetts, USA)
United States: Federal Vocational Education Policy* **11: 6530–38

MILOFSKY, C. (Bucknell University, Lewisburg, Pennsylvania, USA)
Special Education, Sociology of **10**: 5663–68

MINGAT, A. (Institut de Recherche sur l'Economie de l'Education, Dijon, France)
Togo: System of Education **11**: 6398–403

MIRANDA, G. V. DE (Federal University of Minas Gerais, Belo Horizonte, Brazil)
Education and Female Labor Force Participation in Industrializing Countries **3**: 1666–72

MITCHELL, D. E. (University of California, Riverside, California, USA)
Authority and Power in Educational Organizations* **1: 432–37; **Contemporary Sociological Theories of Education* **2**: 1064–74

MIURA, S. (Fukuhara Gakuen University Consortium, Kita-Kyushu City, Fukuoka, Japan)
Japan: Adult Education and Training **6**: 3074–78

MOADJIDIBAYE, T. D. (University of Chad, N'Djamena, Chad)
Chad: System of Education **2**: 665–70

MOBARAK, H. (UNESCO, Paris, France)
UNESCO and Adult Education* **11: 6501–07

MOEGIADI (Office of Education and Cultural Research and Development, Jakarta, Indonesia)
Indonesia: System of Education* **5: 2784–92

MOLENDA, M. (Indiana University, Bloomington, Indiana, USA)
Educational Technology in Elementary and Secondary Education **4**: 1911–18; **Media in Education: Role of Still, Audio, and Audiovisual* **7**: 3744–53

MONCHABLON, A. (Paris, France)
France: System of Education **4**: 2377–85

MONK, D. H. (Cornell University, Ithaca, New York, USA)
Microeconomics of School Production **7**: 3816–21; *Resource Allocation in Schools and School Systems* **9**: 5061–66

MÖNKS, F. J. (University of Nijmegen, Nijmegen, The Netherlands)
Gifted Children, Development of* **5: 2492–95; **Identification and Programming of the Gifted and Talented* **5**: 2725–32

MONSON, D. L. (University of Minnesota, Minneapolis, Minnesota, USA)
Children's Literature **2**: 733–38

MONTADA, L. (University of Trier, Trier, Germany)
Problems and Crises in Human Development **8**: 4715–19

MOOCK, P. R. (World Bank, Washington, DC, USA)
Agricultural Productivity and Education* **1: 244–54

MOONEN, J. (University of Twente, Enschede, The Netherlands)
Prototyping as a Design Activity **8**: 4799–803

MOORE, G. A. B. (University of Guelph, Guelph, Ontario, Canada)
Telecommunication in Education **11**: 6298–307

MOORE, M. G. (Pennsylvania State University, University Park, Pennsylvania, USA)
Distance Education at the School Level **3**: 1563–67

MORA, J. (Del Valle University, Cali, Colombia)
Colombia: System of Education **2**: 872–80

MORALES-GÓMEZ, D. A. (International Development Research Center, Ottawa, Ontario, Canada)
International Cooperation and Assistance in Education **5**: 2961–65

MORAN, K. A. (State University of New York, Buffalo, New York, USA)
Learning Theories: Historical Overview and Trends* **6: 3340–45

MORGAN, G. (Australian Council for Educational Research, Hawthorn, Victoria, Australia)
Expectancy Tables in Educational Prediction **4**: 2180–83; *Portfolios, Profiles, Records, Reports, and Certification* **8**: 4617–23

MORGENSTERN, C. (University of Hamburg, Hamburg, Germany)
Attitudes toward Schooling, Comparative Studies in* **1: 390–96; **Descriptive Scales for Measuring Educational Climate* **3**: 1475–83

MORINE-DERSHIMER, G. (University of Virginia, Charlottesville, Virginia, USA)
Student Teaching and Field Experiences* **10: 5808–12

MORRIS, R. R. (Ministry of Education, Kingston, Jamaica)
Jamaica: System of Education* **6: 3067–74

MOSES, Y. T. (California State University, Dominguez Hills, California, USA)
Multicultural Education: Anthropological Perspectives* **7: 3971–74

MOTTAHAR, M. M. (University of Sana'a, Sana'a, Yemen)
Yemen: System of Education **11**: 6787–94

MUKHOPADHYAY, C. C. (San Jose State University, San Jose, California, USA)
Multicultural Education: Anthropological Perspectives* **7: 3971–74

MULDER, M. (University of Twente, Enschede, The Netherlands)
Cost-effectiveness of Training Courses **2**: 1136–39; *Design of Training Programs: Effectiveness* **3**: 1486–91

MULVIHILL, T. M. (Syracuse University, Syracuse, New York, USA)
Women's Education, History of: North America* **11: 6761–65

MUNBODH, S. (Industrial and Vocational Training Board, Rose Hill, Mauritius)
Mauritius: System of Education **7**: 3691–98

MURASKIN, L. D. (SMB Economic Research, Washington, DC, USA)
United States: Federal Vocational Education Policy* **11: 6530–38

MURNANE, R. J. (Harvard University, Cambridge, Massachusetts, USA)
Supply of Teachers **10**: 5843–46

MURPHY, J. (Vanderbilt University, Nashville, Tennessee, USA)
Administrative Preparation: Preservice **1**: 73–77

MUSGRAVE, P. W. (Monash University, Clayton, Victoria, Australia)
Curriculum: Sociological Perspectives **3**: 1343–48

MUST, O. (Tartu University, Tartu, Estonia)
Estonia: System of Education* **4: 2025–29

MYLONAS, T. (University of Patras, Patras, Greece)
Greece: System of Education* **5: 2515–23

NAMUDDU, K. (Kampala, Uganda)
Children Caring for Children **2**: 730–33

NAPITUPULU, W. P. (UNESCO Ministry of Education and Culture, Jakarta, Indonesia)
Literacy Education: Southeast Asia **6**: 3463–67

NÄRMAN, A. (Gothenburg University, Mölndal, Sweden)
Technical and Vocational Education and Training: Eastern and Southern Africa **11**: 6251–56

NATRIELLO, G. (Columbia University, New York, USA)
Dropouts, School Leavers, and Truancy **3**: 1602–07

NAYLOR, F. D. (University of Melbourne, Parkville, Victoria, Australia)
Test-taking Anxiety and Expectancy of Performance **11**: 6355–60

NDENGEJEHO, P. B. (National University of Rwanda, Ruhengeri, Rwanda)
Rwanda: System of Education **9**: 5107–14

NELSON, R. P. (University of Iowa, Iowa City, Iowa, USA)
Health Needs and Adaptations in Education Services Delivery **5**: 2572–75

NEURURER, J. (University of South Carolina, Columbia, South Carolina, USA)
Teachers, Characteristics of Prospective **10**: 6103–06

NEVO, D. (Tel Aviv University, Tel Aviv, Israel)
Evaluation of Educational Personnel* **4: 2123–32

NG, E. K. L. (Ontario Institute for Studies in Education, Toronto, Ontario, Canada)
New Information Technology in Language Education **7**: 4088–95

NHAVOTTO, A. (Ministry of Education, Maputo, Mozambique)
Mozambique: System of Education **7**: 3953–60

NIEMI, J. A. (Northern Illinois University, Dekalb, Illinois, USA)
Human Resource Development **5**: 2685–89

NIITURA, R. (University of California, Santa Barbara, California, USA)
Shinto Theory of Human Nature and Development* **9: 5449–53

NIKANDROV, N. D. (Russian Academy of Education, Moscow, Russia)
Russia: System of Education **9**: 5098–107

NISBET, J. (University of Aberdeen, Aberdeen, UK)
Policy-oriented Research **8**: 4556–62

NODDINGS, N. (Stanford University, Stanford, California, USA)
Ethics, Moral Philosophy, and Education **4**: 2029–33

NOFFKE, S. E. (University of Illinois at Urbana–Champaign, Champaign, Illinois, USA)
Multicultural Education, Curriculum for **7**: 3974–78

NOMBRE, J. D. (Ouagadougou, Burkina Faso)
Burkina Faso: System of Education* **1: 594–98

NUNNER-WINKLER, G. (Max Plank Institute, Munich, Germany)
Moral Development **7**: 3914–20

NUTHALL, G. (University of Canterbury, Christchurch, New Zealand)
Teaching: Heuristic Models **10**: 6173–78

NUTTALL, D. L. (University of London, London, UK)
Monitoring National Standards: United Kingdom **7**: 3906–12

NYIRENDA, S. (Ministry of Education and Culture, Lilongwe, Malawi)
Malawi: System of Education **6**: 3560–64

OAKES, J. (University of California, Los Angeles, California, USA)
Ability Grouping and Tracking in Schools **1**: 6–12; **Age Grouping of Students* **1**: 227–30

OBEID, R. A. (Ahfad University College for Women, Omdurman, Sudan)
Islamic Theory of Human Nature and Development **5**: 3020–23

OBIAKOR, F. E. (Emporia State University, Emporia, Kansas, USA)
Children and Youth With Special Needs, Diagnosis and Classification of* **2: 711–19

OBORNE, D. J. (University College of Swansea, Swansea, UK)
Ergonomics **4**: 2007–12

ODAET, C. F. (Makerere University, Kampala, Uganda)
Uganda: System of Education **11**: 6493–501

ODMAN, P-J. (University of Stockholm, Stockholm, Sweden)
Hermeneutics* **5: 2579–86

OELKERS, J. (Institute of Education, Bern, Switzerland)
Rousseau and Education **9**: 5087–91

OGAWA, R. (University of California, Riverside, California, USA)
Employee Motivation and Incentives in Schools* **4: 1967–72

OGBU, J. U. (University of California, Berkeley, California, USA)
Anthropology of Education: History and Overview **1**: 280–97; **Ethnography of Education: Anthropological Approach* **4**: 2046–53; *Language and Learning in Education* **6**: 3213–16; *Social Stratification and Education: Anthropological Perspectives* **9**: 5567–72

OGLESBY, K. L. (Lancaster University, Lancaster, UK)
Women and Adult Education **11**: 6712–19

OHLSSON, S. (University of Pittsburgh, Pittsburgh, Pennsylvania, USA)
Declarative and Procedural Knowledge **3**: 1432–34

OJA, S. N. (University of New Hampshire, Durham, New Hampshire, USA)
Teacher Education and Adult Development **10**: 5935–39

OKEDARA, J. T. (University of Ibadan, Ibadan, Nigeria)
Africa, Anglophone: Adult Education **1**: 210–15

OLIVE, J. (University of Georgia, Athens, Georgia, USA)

New Information Technology in Mathematics Education **7**: 4095–100

OLSON, D. R. (Ontario Institute for Studies in Education, Toronto, Ontario, Canada)
Literacy **6**: 3443–46

O'MALLEY, J. M. (Prince William County Schools, Manassas, Virginia, USA)
Learning Strategies in Second Language Learning* **6: 3329–35

ÖNEY, B. A. (Boğaziçi University, Istanbul, Turkey)
Turkey: System of Education **11**: 6476–81

ONUSHKIN, V. G. (Russian Academy of Pedagogical Sciences, St Petersburg, Russia)
Russia (Soviet Union): Adult Education **9**: 5091–98

OPWIS, K. (University of Freiburg, Freiburg, Germany)
Problem-solving and Learning: Computer Modeling* **8: 4719–22

ORIVEL, F. (University of Burgundy, Dijon, France)
Distance Education: Economic Evaluation **3**: 1567–73

ORTIZ, A. (University of Texas, Austin, Texas, USA)
Language Disorders among Bilingual Students **6**: 3228–32

OSBORN, M. (University of Bristol, Bristol, UK)
Outreach in Adult Education **7**: 4246–49

OSBORNE, C. (Middlesex University, London, UK)
Educational Technology Activities of International Organizations **4**: 1878–82

OSER, F. K. (University of Fribourg, Fribourg, Switzerland)
Attitudes and Values, Acquiring **1**: 377–80; **Moral Education: Philosophical Issues* **7**: 3920–25; **Teacher Responsibility* **10**: 6048–53

OSTERWALDER, F. (University of Bern, Bern, Switzerland)
Pestalozzi and Education **8**: 4415–19

OUANE, A. (UNESCO Institute for Education, Hamburg, Germany)
Africa, Francophone: Adult Education **1**: 215–21; *Mali: System of Education* **6**: 3578–86

OUEDRAOGO, N. M. (Ouagadougou, Burkina Faso)
Burkina Faso: System of Education* **1: 594–98

PACHOCIŃSKI, R. (Institute for Educational Research, Warsaw, Poland)
Central and Eastern Europe: Adult Education **2**: 656–62

PALINCSAR, A. S. (University of Michigan, Ann Arbor, Michigan, USA)
Cognitive Strategy Instruction: Special Education* **2: 861–68

PALMA, D. (CEAAL, Santiago, Chile)
Latin America: Adult Education* **6: 3253–56

PALMER, D. J. (Texas A&M University, College Station, Texas, USA)
Specific Learning Disability* **10: 5681–86

PAPANASTASIOU, C. (University of Cyprus, Nicosia, Cyprus)
Cyprus: System of Education **3**: 1367–75

PASHCAL, R. A. (Northern Illinois University, De Kalb, Illinois, USA)
Homework* **5: 2628–31

PATRY, J-L. (University of Fribourg, Fribourg, Switzerland)
Teacher Responsibility* **10: 6048–53

PAUL, R. H. (Laurentian University, Sulbury, Ontario, Canada)
Experiential and Open Learning for Adults **4**: 2183–86

PAULSTON, R. G. (University of Pittsburgh, Pittsburgh, Pennsylvania, USA)
Comparative and International Education: Paradigms and Theories **2**: 923–33

PAYNE, M. A. (University of Waikato, Hamilton, New Zealand)
School–Parent Relationships **9**: 5264–68

PEASE-ALVAREZ, L. (University of California, Santa Cruz, California, USA)
Bilingual Education: Anthropological Perspectives **1**: 531–35

PEKRUN, R. (University of Regensburg, Regensburg, Germany)
Emotional Development **4**: 1963–67

PELLEGRINO, J. W. (Vanderbilt University, Nashville, Tennessee, USA)
Abilities and Aptitudes **1**: 1–6

PENDLEBURY, S. (University of the Witwatersrand, Johannesburg, South Africa)
Minority Women and Education **7**: 3848–53

PENG, S. S. (Temple University, Philadelphia, Pennsylviania, USA)
Disability Statistics **3**: 1530–34

PENNA FIRME, T. (Federal University of Rio de Janeiro, Rio de Janeiro, Brazil)
Education for Street Children* **3: 1733–36

PEREIRA, P. (De Paul University, Chicago, Illinois, USA)
Logo, Educational Applications of **6**: 3508–12

PERFETTI, C. A. (University of Pittsburgh, Pittsburgh, Pennsylvania, USA)
Reading, Learning and Instruction of **8**: 4942–45

PERKINS, D. N. (Harvard Graduate School of Education, Cambridge, Massachusetts, USA)
Transfer of Learning* **11: 6452–57

PERNER, J. (University of Sussex, Brighton, UK)
Cognitive Development: Overview **2**: 852–57

PERRY, D. G. (Florida Atlantic University, Boca Raton, Florida, USA)
Aggression, Development and Socialization of **1**: 230–34

PERRY, E. (University of Oregon, Eugene, Oregon, USA)
Organizational Development and Consultancy in Education* **7: 4236–40

PESCHAR, J. L. (Groningen University, Groningen, The Netherlands)
Stratification in Educational Systems **10**: 5730–35

PETERS, M. (University of Auckland, Auckland, New Zealand)
Postmodernism and Education* **8: 4639–42

PETERS, M. E. (Dominica Teachers' Training College, Roseau, Dominica)
Dominica: System of Education **3**: 1593–99

PETERSEN, A. C. (University of Minnesota, Minneapolis-St Paul, Minnesota, USA)
Sex Differences in Behavior and Behavioral Development* **9: 5433–35

PETERSON, K. D. (University of Wisconsin, Madison, Wisconsin, USA)
School Principals: Role in Restructured Schools* **9: 5268–73

PETERSON, P. L. (Michigan State University, East Lansing, Michigan, USA)
Student Roles in Classrooms* **10: 5791–96

PETTERSSON, R. (Tullinge, Sweden)
Message Design in Learning **7**: 3771–75; *Visual Literacy* **11**: 6622–25

PETTY, M. A. (Universidad Católica de Córdoba, Córdoba, Argentina)
Argentina: System of Education **1**: 332–38

PHILIPPART, A. (Ministry of Education, Research, and Training, Brussels, Belgium)
Belgium: System of Education **1**: 497–504

PHILLIPS, D. C. (Stanford University, Stanford, California, USA)
Philosophy of Education: Historical Overview **8**: 4447–56; *Positivism, Antipositivism, and Empiricism* **8**: 4630–34; **Relativism and Realism* **9**: 4977–81; *Spencer and Education* **10**: 5705–08

PHILLIPS, G. W. (National Center for Education Statistics, Washington, DC)
National Assessment of Educational Programs* **7: 4051–54

PIEBALGS, A. (Ministry of Education, Riga, Latvia)
Latvia: System of Education **6**: 3267–72

PIÉRON, M. (University of Liège, Liège, Belgium)
Sport Pedagogy, Research in **10**: 5708–13

PIETERS, J. M. (University of Twente, Enschede, The Netherlands)
Psychology of Adult Education **8**: 4816–24

PIGEON, G. (University of California, Santa Barbara, California, USA)
Guadeloupe and Martinique: System of Education* **5: 2536–44

PIMM, D. (Open University, Milton Keynes, UK)
Mathematics and Language **6**: 3634–39

PINNELL, G. S. (Ohio State University, Columbus, Ohio, USA)
Discipline in Schools* **3: 1534–38

PLANK, D. N. (Michigan State University, East Lansing, Michigan, USA)
Educational Policy Studies: Overview* **4: 1835–41; **Politics and Governance of Education* **8**: 4587–95

PLOMP, T. (University of Twente, Enschede, The Netherlands)
Computer Literacy* **2: 973–77; **Gender and New Technology* **4**: 2423–27

PÖGGELER, F. (Technical University of Aachen, Aachen, Germany)
Adult Education, History of **1**: 135–39

PONTECORVO, C. (University of Rome (La Sapienza), Rome, Italy)
Social and Communication Skills **9**: 5504–08

PORRAS-ZÚÑIGA, J. (UNESCO, Paris, France)
Comparative Statistics in Education **2**: 958–64

POSCH, P. (University of Klagenfurt, Klagenfurt, Austria)
Austria: System of Education **1**: 423–32

POSNER, G. (Cornell University, Ithaca, New York, USA)
Curriculum Planning Models **3**: 1328–34

POST, D. (Pennsylvania State University, University Park, Pennsylvania, USA)
Conflict and its Management in Educational Organizations **2**: 1037–42

POSTER, C. D. (Consultancy in Education Management, Bristol, UK)
Community Education and Community Schools **2**: 907–10

POSTLETHWAITE, T. N. (University of Hamburg, Hamburg, Germany)
Educational Achievement: Comparative Studies **3**: 1762–69

POTTER, J. (University of New Brunswick, Fredericton, New Brunswick, Canada)
Counseling Adult Students **2**: 1161–65

POUNDER, D. (University of Utah, Salt Lake City, Utah, USA)
Personnel Administration in Education **8**: 4404–08

POWELL, D. R. (Purdue University, West Lafayette, Indiana, USA)
Parent Involvement in Preschool Programs **7**: 4296–302

POWERS, D. E. (Educational Testing Service, Princeton, New Jersey, USA)
Tests and Examinations, Coaching for **11**: 6334–40

PRAKASH, B. (Asian Development Bank, Manila, The Philippines)
Planning Education: Asia **8**: 4485–89

PRATT, D. (Queen's University, Kingston, Ontario, Canada)
Curriculum Management* **3: 1320–25

PRESSLEY, M. (University of Maryland, College Park, Maryland, USA)
Memory, Teaching and Testing for* **7: 3763–69

PRINCE, B. (Furman University, Greenville, South Carolina, USA)
Foreign Language Education: Primary School Programs* **4: 2346–51

PRYZWANSKY, W. B. (University of North Carolina, Chapel Hill, North Carolina, USA)
School "Related Services" Personnel **9**: 5281–91

PUGACH, M. C. (University of Wisconsin, Milwaukee, Wisconsin, USA)
Resource Room Programs as a Special Education Model* **9: 5066–71

PURDOM, D. M. (University of South Florida, Tampa, Florida, USA)
Nongraded Curriculum* **7: 4155–57

PURVES, A. C. (State University of New York, Albany, New York, USA)
Literature: Educational Programs **1**: 3–3; *Beginning Reading: Grapheme Systems and Orthography* **1**: 480–83; *Writing and Composition Instruction* **11**: 6775–78

QUAZI, S. (Ontario Institute for Studies in Education, Toronto, Ontario, Canada)
Facilities Planning and Policy: Macro Level* **4: 2225–30

RADI, M. (Ministry of Education, Rabat, Morocco)
Morocco: System of Education **7**: 3925–30

RAKOTONDRAZAKA, R. (Ministry of Universities, Antananarivo, Madagascar)
Madagascar: System of Education **6**: 3550–56

RAMPAUL, W. E. (University of Manitoba, Winnipeg, Manitoba, Canada)
International Cooperation in Special Education **5**: 2965–72

RANAWEERA, A. M. (UNESCO, Hamburg, Germany)
Sri Lanka: System of Education **10**: 5713–21

RATHS, J. (University of Delaware, Newark, Delaware, USA)
Accreditation and Standards: Teacher Education **1**: 24–28

RAU, J. M. (Ministry of Education, Lisbon, Portugal)
Portugal: System of Education **8**: 4623–30

RAUDENBUSH, S. W. (Michigan State University, East Lansing, Michigan, USA)
Effective Schools Research: Methodological Issues* **4: 1934–39; **Hierarchical Linear Models* **5**: 2590–96

READ, A. (International Book Development Ltd., London, UK)
Printed Materials in Education* **8: 4694–98

REED, R. J. (Pennsylvania State University, University Park, Pennsylvania, USA)
Urban Schools **11**: 6558–63

REEVE, R. A. (University of Illinois at Chicago, Chicago, Illinois, USA)
Secondary Data Analysis* **9: 5367–73

REICHENBACH, R. (University of Fribourg, Fribourg, Switzerland)
Moral Education: Philosophical Issues* **7: 3920–25

REIGELUTH, C. M. (Indiana University, Bloomington, Indiana, USA)
Instructional Design Theories **5**: 2862–67; **Task Analysis* **10**: 5910–14

REIMERS, F. (Harvard University, Cambridge, Massachusetts, USA)
Costa Rica: System of Education **2**: 1139–46; *Educational Finance and Economic Adjustment in Developing Nations* **3**: 1784–89; *Venezuela: System of Education* **11**: 6591–600

RESCHLY, D. J. (Iowa State University, Ames, Iowa, USA)
Mild Mental Retardation **7**: 3826–30

RESNICK, L. B. (University of Pittsburgh, Pittsburgh, Pennsylvania, USA)
Cognition and Learning* **2: 835–38; **Learning Environments* **6**: 3297–302

REYES, M. E. (International Institute for Educational Planning, Paris, France)
Mexico: System of Education **7**: 3792–802

REYNOLDS, A. J. (Pennsylvania State University, University Park, Pennsylvania, USA)
Theory-based Evaluation* **11: 6378–85

REYNOLDS, B. P. (University of South Carolina, Columbia, South Carolina, USA)
Paraprofessionals, Availability and Use of **7**: 4290–93

REYNOLDS, D. (University of Wales, Cardiff, UK)
Effective Schools, Management of* **4: 1929–34

REYNOLDS, M. C. (University of Minnesota, Minneapolis, Minnesota, USA)
Children and Youth with Special Needs, Education of* **2: 719–30; *Delphi Technique* **3**: 1441–43; *Mildly Handicapped Students: Noncategorical Approach* **7**: 3830–33

RICHARDSON, W. (University of Warwick, Coventry, UK)
School–Business Partnerships **9**: 5186–92

RICHTER, I. (University of Hamburg, Hamburg, Germany)
Law and Administration in Education **6**: 3272–76

RIEBEN, L. (University of Geneva, Geneva, Switzerland)
Piaget's Theory of Human Development* **8: 4479–83

RIEDMILLER, S. (GTZ Project, Tanga, Tanzania)
Primary School Agriculture in Sub-Saharan Africa **8**: 4680–88

RINK, J. E. (University of South Carolina, Columbia, South Carolina, USA)
Physical Education Teacher Education **8**: 4464–68

RIVAROLA, D. M. (Centro Paraguayo de Estudios Sociológicos, Asunción, Paraguay)
Paraguay: System of Education **7**: 4282–90

ROCHE, A. F. (Wright State University, Yellow Springs, Ohio, USA)
Physical Growth and Development: Universal Changes and Individual Differences **8**: 4468–74

RODRÍGUEZ, C. (Santiago College, Santiago, Chile)
Chile: System of Education **2**: 738–46

ROGERS, A. (Education for Development, Reading, UK)
Interchange in Adult Education: North–South Dialogue **5**: 2931–37

ROGERS, H. J. (Columbia University, New York, USA)
Multiple Choice Tests, Guessing in **7**: 3996–4000

ROMBERG, T. A. (University of Wisconsin–Madison, Madison, Wisconsin, USA)
Mathematics: Primary School Programs **6**: 3655–61

ROMISZOWSKI, A. J. (Syracuse University, Syracuse, New York, USA)
Individual Techniques for Teaching and Learning **5**: 2770–73; *Systems Approach to Design and Development* **10**: 5895–901

ROSEN, S. (University of Chicago, Chicago, Illinois, USA)
Job Information and Education **6**: 3096–101; *Vintage Effects and Education* **11**: 6614–15

ROSENSHINE, B. (University of Illinois at Urbana–Champaign, Champaign, Illinois, USA)
Direct Instruction* **3: 1524–30

ROSIER, M. J. (University of Melbourne, Melbourne, Victoria, Australia)
Data Banks and Data Archives* **3: 1377–81; *Survey Research Methods* **10**: 5854–62

ROSS, K. N. (Deakin University, Geelong, Victoria, Australia)
Sampling Errors in Survey Research* **9: 5124–31; **Sampling in Survey Research* **9**: 5131–42

ROTH, G. L. (Northern Illinois University, Dekalb, Illinois, USA)
Educational Technology in Technical Training for Youth and Adults **4**: 1918–24

ROUSE, M. (Cambridge Institute of Education, Cambridge, UK)
Transition to Adult and Working Life for Persons with Handicaps* **11: 6457–61

ROWLAND, G. (Ithaca College, Ithaca, New York, USA)
Task Analysis* **10: 5910–14

RUBENSON, K. (University of British Columbia, Vancouver, British Columbia, Canada)
Adult Education: Disciplinary Orientations **1**: 120–27

RUBIN, K. H. (University of Waterloo, Waterloo, Quebec, Canada)
Play: Developmental Stages, Functions, and Educational Support* **8: 4536–42

RUBTSOV, V. V. (Russian Academy of Education, Moscow, Russia)
Social Interaction and Learning **9**: 5545–48

RUIJSSENAARS, A. J. J. M. (University of Leuven, Leuven, Belgium)
Learning Potential and Learning Potential Tests* **6: 3312–15

RUIZ-ESPARZA, R. (Albuquerque, New Mexico, USA)
El Salvador: System of Education **4**: 1947–54

RUMBERGER, R. W. (University of California, Santa Barbara, California, USA)
Technical Change and the Demand for Educated Labor **11**: 6256–61

RUSSELL, A. (The Flinders University of South Australia, Bedford Park, South Australia, Australia)
Educational Research, Moderating and Mediating Effects in **4**: 1873–77

RUSSELL, J. D. (Purdue University, West Lafayette, Indiana, USA)
Media in Education: Role of Still, Audio, and Audiovisual* **7: 3744–53

RUST, K. (Westat Corporation, Rockville, Maryland, USA)
Sampling in Survey Research* **9: 5131–42

RWEHERA, M. (Paris, France)
Burundi: System of Education **1**: 598–607

SABAR, N. (Tel Aviv University, Tel Aviv, Israel)
Curriculum Development at School Level **3**: 1267–72

SABOT, R. H. (Williams College, Williamstown, Massachusetts, USA)
Internal Migration and Education* **5: 2942–45

SACK, R. (Paris, France)
Benin: System of Education **1**: 521–25

SADKER, D. (The American University, Washington, DC, USA)
Sex Equity: Assumptions and Strategies* **9: 5441–45

SADKER, M. (The American University, Washington, DC, USA)
Sex Equity: Assumptions and Strategies* **9: 5441–45

SAHA, L. J. (Australian National University, Canberra, ACT, Australia)
Aspirations and Expectations of Students **1**: 354–58; **Classical Sociological Theories of Education* **2**: 775–85; **Education and Development* **3**: 1648–55; **Measurement of Social Background* **7**: 3715–22; *Sociology of Education: Overview* **10**: 5596–607; *Sociometric Methods* **10**: 5614–18

SAKO, M. (London School of Economics and Political Science, London, UK)
Japan: Vocational Education and Training **6**: 3086–92

SÄLJÖ, R. (University of Linköping, Linköping, Sweden)
Culture and Learning **3**: 1241–46; *Self-report in Educational Research* **9**: 5407–11

SALOMÉ, B. (World Bank, Washington, DC, USA)
Informal Sector: Vocational Education and Training* **5: 2814–19

SALOMON, G. (University of Haifa, Haifa, Israel)
Transfer of Learning* **11: 6452–57

SALT, A. (International Labour Organisation, Geneva, Switzerland)
International Labour Organisation (ILO): Vocational Training* **5: 2998 3003

SALVO PAYSSÉ, M. T. (Ministry of Education and Culture, Montevideo, Uruguay)
Uruguay: System of Education* **11: 6563–67

SAMS, J. (Jordanhill College of Education, Glasgow, UK)
Soviet Union: Vocational Education and Training **10**: 5644–50

SAMUELS, M. (The Learning Center, Calgary, Alberta, Canada)
Cognitive Modifiability* **2: 857–61

SARACHO, O. N. (University of Maryland, College Park, Maryland, USA)
Early Childhood Personnel, Preparation of* **3: 1629–36

SATO, N. E. (University of California, Berkeley, California, USA)

Ethnography of Education: Anthropological Approach **4**: 2046–53

SAUVÉ, J. W. (Association of Jesuit Colleges and Universities, Washington, DC, USA)
Saint Ignatius Loyola and Education **9**: 5118–21

SCANNELL, D. P. (University of South Carolina, Columbia, South Carolina, USA)
Teacher Certification and Standards* **10: 5925–30

SCANNELL, M. M. (South Carolina Commission on Higher Education, Columbia, South Carolina, USA)
Teacher Certification and Standards* **10: 5925–30

SCHAIE, K. W. (Pennsylvania State University, University Park, Pennsylvania, USA)
Aging and Adult Development **1**: 234–39

SCHEERENS, J. (University of Twente, Enschede, The Netherlands)
Decision-oriented Evaluation and Beyond **3**: 1425–31; *Education Indicators: Use in Policy and Management* **3**: 1740–46

SCHEUNEMAN, J. D. (Educational Testing Service, Princeton, New Jersey, USA)
Item Bias* **5: 3043–51

SCHICKEDANZ, J. A. (Boston University, Boston, Massachusetts, USA)
Emergent Literacy **4**: 1958–63

SCHIEFELBEIN, E. (UNESCO–OREALC, Santiago, Chile)
Documentation Systems: Regional Education **3**: 1589–93; *Educational Planning: Implementation Problems* **3**: 1821–25; *Educational Policy and Decision-making: Comparative Data* **3**: 1830–34; *Planning Education: Latin America* **8**: 4491–95

SCHLEICHER, A. (University of Hamburg, Hamburg, Germany)
Database Management Systems in Education **3**: 1387–94; *Microcomputers in Educational Research* **7**: 3810–16

SCHLEISMAN, J. L. (University of Minnesota, Minneapolis, Minnesota, USA)
Adaptive Testing* **1: 48–53

SCHMUCK, R. (University of Oregon, Eugene, Oregon, USA)
Organizational Development and Consultancy in Education* **7: 4236–40

SCHNEEWIND, K. A. (University of Munich, Munich, Germany)
Family Influence on Human Development **4**: 2258–61

SCHNEIDER, W. (University of Würzburg, Würzburg, Germany)
Memory Development **7**: 3760–63

SCHNOTZ, W. (University of Jena, Jena, Germany)
Comprehension, Teaching and Testing for* **2: 964–69; *Reading Comprehension, Learning of* **8**: 4940–42

SCHRADER, F-W. (University of Landau, Landau, Germany)
Teaching: Diagnostic–Prescriptive* **10: 6169–73

SCHROEDER, H. (University of Karlsruhe, Karlsruhe, Germany)
Vocational Training, History of* **11: 6678–84

SCHUBERT, W. H. (University of Illinois at Chicago, Chicago, Illinois, USA)
Curriculum History: National Profiles* **3: 1288–301; **Students' Curriculum Experiences* **10**: 5813–18

SCHÜTZE, H. G. (University of British Columbia, Vancouver, British Columbia, Canada)
Paid Educational Leave and Collective Bargaining **7**: 4257–63

SCHWAB, R. L. (Drake University, Des Moines, Iowa, USA)
Teacher Stress and Burnout **10**: 6058–62

SCIARONE, A. G. (Delft University of Technology, Delft, The Netherlands)
Language Laboratories **6**: 3238–41

SCOTT MURRAY, T. (Statistics Canada, Ottawa, Ontario, Canada)
Measurement of Adult Education **7**: 3707–11

SCRIVEN, M. (Western Michigan University, Kalamazoo, Michigan, USA)
Evaluation: Formative, Summative, and Goal-free **4**: 2097–101

SEDDON, T. (Monash University, Clayton, Victoria, Australia)
Teachers' Work and Political Action **10**: 6132–39

SEIDL, B. L. (University of Wisconsin, Milwaukee, Wisconsin, USA)
Resource Room Programs as a Special Education Model* **9: 5066–71

SEITLHEKO, A. N. (Ministry of Education, Maseru, Lesotho)
Lesotho: System of Education **6**: 3378–85

SELIGMAN, M. E. P. (University of Pennsylvania, Philadelphia, Pennsylvania, USA)
Self-related Cognition, Learned Helplessness, Learned Optimism, and Human Development* **9: 5403–07

SELLIN, B. (CEDEFOP, Berlin, Germany)
European Community: Vocational Training Qualifications **4**: 2063–70

SELLIN, N. (University of Hamburg, Hamburg, Germany)
Multilevel Analysis* **7: 3978–87; **Path Analysis with Latent Variables* **8**: 4352–59

SESAY, A. B. (Ministry of Education, Youth, and Sport, Freetown, Sierra Leone)
Sierra Leone: System of Education* **9: 5453–60

SHAKESHAFT, C. (Hofstra University, Hempstead, New York, USA)
Women in Educational Administration: United States **11**: 6727–31

SHAMLAYE, B. (Ministry of Education, Mont Fleuri, The Seychelles)
Seychelles: System of Education **9**: 5445–49

SHANE, H. G. (Indiana University, Bloomington, Indiana, USA)
Forecasting, Education, and Its Impact on Curriculum **4**: 2327–31

SHANNON, D. M. (Auburn University, Auburn, Alabama, USA)
Teacher Evaluation* **10: 6015–20

SHARAN, S. (Tel Aviv University, Tel Aviv, Israel)
Teaching in Small Groups **10**: 6183–87

SHARPLEY, C. F. (Monash University, Clayton, Victoria, Australia)
Single Case Research: Measuring Change **9**: 5486–90

SHEPARD, L. A. (University of Colorado, Boulder, Colorado, USA)
Grade Repeating **5**: 2512–15

SHIMONI, R. (Hebrew University, Jerusalem, Israel)
Parent Education for Early Childhood Education **7**: 4294–96

SHIN, SE-HO (Korean Educational Development Institute, Seoul, Republic of Korea)
Korea, Republic of: System of Education **6**: 3161–70

SHMUELI, E. (Jerusalem, Israel)
Israel: System of Education **5**: 3023–28

SHORT, E. C. (Pennsylvania State University, University Park, Pennsylvania, USA)
Curriculum Management* **3: 1320–25

SHUELL, T. J. (State University of New York, Buffalo, New York, USA)
Learning Theories: Historical Overview and Trends* **6: 3340–45

SHUTE, V. J. (Brooks Air Force Base, Texas, USA)
Learning Processes and Learning Outcomes **6**: 3315–25

SHYE, S. (Israel Institute of Applied Social Research, Jerusalem, Israel)
Facet Theory **4**: 2213–19; *Partial Order Scalogram Analyses of Nonmetric Data* **7**: 4308–16; *Smallest Space Analysis* **9**: 5497–504

SIAROON, M. (Office of the National Education Commission, Bangkok, Thailand)
Thailand: System of Education* **11: 6371–78

SICHEL, B. A. (Long Island University, Brookville, New York, USA)
Feminist Ethics and Moral Education **4**: 2292–97

SIEGEL, H. (University of Miami, Coral Gables, Florida, USA)
Relativism and Realism* **9: 4977–81

SILVER, H. (University of Plymouth, Plymouth, UK)
Historiography of Education **5**: 2607–18

SIMONS, P. R-J. (University of Nijmegen, Nijmegen, The Netherlands)
Metacognition **7**: 3784–88; *Metacognitive Strategies, Teaching and Testing for* **7**: 3788–92

SINGER, J. D. (Harvard University, Cambridge, Massachusetts, USA)
Event History Analyses* **4: 2150–56

SINOFSKY, E. R. (Los Angeles Unified School District, Los Angeles, California, USA)
Copyright **2**: 1099–102

SIROTNIK, K. (University of Washington, Seattle, Washington, USA)
Informing Evaluation for Local School Improvement **4**: 2381–89

SITKO, C. J. (University of Western Ontario, London, Ontario, Canada)
Microcomputer Technology for Students with Special Needs* **7: 3802–08

SITKO, M. C. (University of Western Ontario, London, Ontario, Canada)
Microcomputer Technology for Students with Special Needs* **7: 3802–08

SKEEL, D. J. (Peabody Center of Education, Vanderbilt University, Nashville, Tennessee, USA)
Social Studies in Primary School **9**: 5572–78

SKILBECK, M. (Organisation for Economic Co-operation and Development, Paris, France)
Curriculum Renewal **3**: 1338–43; *Social, Cultural, and Economic Factors Affecting Curriculum* **9**: 5518–23

SLADECZEK, I. E. (University of Wisconsin–Madison, Madison, Wisconsin, USA)
Reinforcement* **9: 4974–77

SLAVIN, R. E. (Johns Hopkins University, Baltimore, Maryland, USA)
Cooperative Learning **2**: 1094–99

SMALL, R. (Monash University, Clayton, Victoria, Australia)
Phenomenology and Existentialism **8**: 4429–33

SMEYERS, P. (University of Leuven, Leuven, Belgium)
Philosophy of Education: Western European Perspectives **8**: 4456–61

SMIT, C. A. (Foundation for Corporate Education, Terschuur, The Netherlands)
Job Analysis in Corporate Education* **6: 3092–96

SMITH, H. A. (Queen's University, Kingston, Ontario, Canada)
Nonverbal Classroom Behavior **7**: 4171–75

SMITH, N. L. (Syracuse University, Syracuse, New York, USA)
Evaluation Models and Approaches **4**: 2101–09; *Project Evaluation and Monitoring* **8**: 4780–83

SMITH, R. M. (Northern Illinois University, De Kalb, Illinois, USA)
Learning to Learn: Adult Education **6**: 3345–49

SMITH, T. H. (Hofstra University, Hempstead, New York, USA)
Teacher Education: Professional Ethics **10**: 5985–91

SMYLIE, M. A. (University of Illinois at Chicago, Chicago, Illinois, USA)
Curriculum Adaptation **3**: 1253–57

SNOW, R. E. (Stanford University, Stanford, California, USA)
Individual Differences and Instruction **5**: 2759–69; *Teaching: Aptitude–Treatment Interaction Model* **10**: 6155–59

SOLMON, L. C. (Milken Institute for Job and Capital Formation, Santa Monica, California, USA)
Benefits of Education* **1: 510–21

SOLOMAN, J. (University of Patras, Patras, Greece)
Greece: System of Education* **5: 2515–23

SOLTIS, J. F. (Teachers College, Columbia University, New York, USA)
Dewey, Pragmatism, and Education **3**: 1520–24

SOREN, B. J. (Ontario Institute for Studies in Education, Toronto, Ontario, Canada)
Performing Arts: Education Programs **8**: 4384–88

SOSNIAK, L. A. (Washington University, St Louis, Missouri, USA)
Educational Objectives: Use in Curriculum Development **3**: 1800–04

SOTO, G. (Purdue University, West Lafayette, Indiana, USA)
Augmentative and Alternative Communication* **1: 404–09

SOW, M. (Ministry of National Education, Dakar, Senegal)
Senegal: System of Education **9**: 5417–23

SOWDEN, S. (The Flinders University of South Australia, Bedford Park, South Australia, Australia)
Descriptive Data, Analysis of* **3: 1464–75

SPADA, H. (University of Freiburg, Freiburg, Germany)
Problem-solving and Learning: Computer Modeling* **8: 4719–22

SPAULDING, S. (University of Pittsburgh, Pittsburgh, Pennsylvania, USA)
Mongolia: System of Education **7**: 3895–906

SPAULL, A. D. (Monash University, Clayton, Victoria, Australia)
Teacher Unions **10**: 6073–79

SPEARRITT, D. (University of Sydney, Sydney, New South Wales, Australia)
Evaluation of National Comparisons **4**: 2132–40; *Factor Analysis* **4**: 2230–41; *Mother Tongue Language Tests* **7**: 3930–36

SPENCE, L. E. (Tel Aviv University, Tel Aviv, Israel)
Mathematics: Topics of Instruction* **6: 3671–86

SPENCER, D. A. (Arizona State University, Tempe, Arizona, USA)
Sociology of Teaching **10**: 5607–14

SPENNER, K. I. (Duke University, Durham, North Carolina, USA)
Technological Change and Deskilling **11**: 6272–77

SPERNA-WEILAND, J. (Erasmus University, Rotterdam, The Netherlands)
Erasmus and Education **4**: 2004–07

SPICUZZA, R. J. (University of Minnesota, Minneapolis, Minnesota, USA)
Social Skills **9**: 5563–67

SPIEL, C. (University of Vienna, Vienna, Austria)
Human Development: Research Methodology* **5: 2673–77

SPODEK, B. (University of Illinois at Urbana–Champaign, Urbana, Illinois, USA)
Early Childhood Personnel, Preparation of* **3: 1629–36

SPOLSKY, B. (Bar Ilan University, Ramat Gan, Israel)
Foreign Language Education **4**: 2339–46; *Linguistics and Language Learning* **6**: 3435–39

SPRINTHALL, N. A. (North Carolina State University, Raleigh, North Carolina, USA)
Teaching, Cognitive Developmental Theories of **10**: 6164–69

SQUIRES, D. (King's College, London, UK)
Educational Computer Software, Production of **3**: 1775–79

STAAB, C. (University of British Columbia, Vancouver, British Columbia, Canada)
Listening and Speaking Instruction **6**: 3439–43

STACEY, N. (US Department of Education, Washington, DC, USA)
Adult Education and Training Markets* **1: 103–11

STALLINGS, J. A. (Texas A&M University, College Station, Texas, USA)
Schools for Laboratory and Professional Development* **9: 5313–18

STANCHEV, I. (University of Twente, Enschede, The Netherlands)
Computers in Education, Organizations and Journals on **2**: 1012–16

STEFFE, L. P. (University of Quebec, Montreal, Quebec, Canada)
Mathematics: Topics of Instruction* **6: 3671–86

STEMMLER, M. (Pennsylvania State University, University Park, Pennsylvania, USA)
Sex Differences in Behavior and Behavioral Development* **9: 5433–35

STEPHENS, M. D. (University of Nottingham, Nottingham, UK)
Teaching Methods for Adults **10**: 6198–202

STERN, D. (University of California, Berkeley, California, USA)
Market Failure in Firm-based Education and Training **6**: 3614–17; *School Enterprise, Economics of* **9**: 5228–33

STERNBERG, R. J. (Yale University, New Haven, Connecticut, USA)
Intellectual Development across the Lifespan* **5: 2910–16

STEVENSON, H. W. (University of Michigan, Ann Arbor, Michigan, USA)
Home Environment and School Learning* **5: 2624–28

STOCKING, M. L. (Educational Testing Service, Princeton, New Jersey, USA)
Item Response Theory **5**: 3051–55

STOKKING, K. M. (University of Utrecht, Utrecht, The Netherlands)
Dissemination and Diffusion of Knowledge and Innovation **3**: 1549–53

STONE, J. A. (University of Oregon, Eugene, Oregon, USA)
Teacher Unionization, Economics of* **10: 6068–73

STONE, V. I. (Federal University of Maranhão, Maranhão, Brazil)
Education for Street Children* **3: 1733–36

STRAW, S. B. (University of Manitoba, Winnipeg, Manitoba, Canada)
Spelling and Grammar Instruction **10**: 5697–705

STREUNER, J. N. (University of Twente, Enschede, The Netherlands)
Curriculum in Adult Education* **3: 1308–15

STRIKE, K. A. (Cornell University, Ithaca, New York, USA)
Epistemology and Education **4**: 1996–2001

STROBER, M. H. (Stanford University, Stanford, California, USA)
Childcare, Economics of **2**: 688–93; *Gender and Occupational Segregation* **4**: 2427–32

STROMQUIST, N. P. (University of Southern California, Los Angeles, California, USA)
Gender and Education **4**: 2407–12

STUFFLEBEAM, D. L. (Western Michigan University, Kalamazoo, Michigan, USA)
Evaluation of Educational Personnel* **4: 2123–32; *Professional Standards for Educational Evaluation: United States* **8**: 4736–51

STUKÁT, K-G. (University of Gothenburg, Mölndal, Sweden)
Preschool Education, History of **8**: 4666–70

STURMAN, A. (University of Southern Queensland, Toowoomba, Queensland, Australia)
Case Study Methods **2**: 640–46; *Loose Coupling and Educational Systems* **6**: 3524–28; *Socialization* **10**: 5586–91

SUAREZ, T. M. (University of North Carolina, Chapel Hill, North Carolina, USA)
Needs Assessment **7**: 4056–60

SUÁREZ-OROZCO, M. M. (University of California, San Diego, California, USA)
Culture and Achievement Motivation in Education* **3: 1236–41

SULZBACHER, S. (University of Washington, Seattle, Washington, USA)
Pharmacotherapy in Schoolchildren* **8: 4419–24

SULZER-AZAROFF, B. (University of Massachusetts, Amherst, Massachusetts, USA)
Teaching: Behavioral Theories **10**: 6159–64

SUPPLE, M. (Trinity College, Dublin, Republic of Ireland)
Specific Language Disorders of Childhood* **10: 5674–81

SUTARIA, M. C. (INNOTECH, Quezon City, The Philippines)
Philippines: System of Education **8**: 4433–42

SUTTON, C. (Leicester University, Leicester, UK)
Language and the Science Curriculum **6**: 3216–19

SUTTON, P. J. (UNESCO Institute for Education, Hamburg, Germany)
Lifelong and Continuing Education **6**: 3416–22

SWAMINATHAN, H. (University of Massachusetts, Amherst, Massachusetts, USA)
Latent Trait Measurement Models **6**: 3247–53

TACHIBANAKI, T. (Kyoto University, Kyoto, Japan)
Education, Occupation, and Earnings **3**: 1746–50

TALL, D. (Tel Aviv University, Tel Aviv, Israel)
Mathematics: Topics of Instruction* **6: 3671–86

TAM, HAK PING (Ohio State University, Columbus, Ohio, USA)
Log-Linear Models* **6: 3499–508

TAMIR, P. (Hebrew University, Jerusalem, Israel)
Discovery Learning and Teaching **3**: 1538–44; *Life Sciences: Secondary School Programs* **6**: 3407–16

TAPSOBA, S. (International Development Research Center, Ottawa, Ontario, Canada)
Planning Education: Sub-Saharan Africa **8**: 4510–14

TATSUOKA, M. M. (Educational Testing Service, Princeton, New Jersey, USA)
Regression Analyses of Quantified Data **9**: 4965–74

TAUBMAN, P. (University of Pennsylvania, Philadelphia, Pennsylvania, USA)
Family Status and Economic Status **4**: 2274–79; **Kinship Studies* **6**: 3138–44

TAUFE'ULUNGAKI, A. M. (Ministry of Education, Nuku'alofa, Tonga)
Tonga: System of Education **11**: 6403–12

TAYLOR, W. A. (Ministry of Education, Youth, and Sport, Freetown, Sierra Leone)
Sierra Leone: System of Education* **9: 5453–60

TEESE, R. (University of Melbourne, Parkville, Victoria, Australia)
Reproduction Theory **9**: 5016–21

TELEM, M. (Tel Aviv University, Tel Aviv, Israel)
Information Technology Use in Educational Management Systems **5**: 2828–31

TELFORD, H. (Carey Baptist Grammar School, Kew, Victoria, Australia)
School Reform and Restructuring* **9: 5275–81

TEMO, S. (Tirana, Albania)
Albania: System of Education **1**: 254–60

TENG TENG (Chinese Academy of Social Sciences, Beijing, People's Republic of China)
China, People's Republic of: System of Education **2**: 750–55

TENNYSON, R. D. (University of Minnesota, Minneapolis, Minnesota, USA)
Concept Learning **2**: 1016–20; *Concept Learning, Teaching and Testing for* **2**: 1020–26

TERRASI, S. (Boston College, Chestnut Hill, Massachusetts, USA)
Test Administration* **11: 6311–15

THEOBALD, M. R. (University of Melbourne, Melbourne, Victoria, Australia)
Women's Education, History of: Australia **11**: 6731–35

THIBADEAU, G. (Indiana University of Pennsylvania, Indiana, Pennsylvania, USA)
Open Education **7**: 4211–15

THOMAS, A. M. (Ontario Institute for Studies in Education, Toronto, Ontario, Canada)
Adult Education, Planning Public Policy for **1**: 152–58; *Adult Education, Reform Strategies in* **1**: 158–63

THOMAS, R. M. (University of California, Santa Barbara, California, USA)
American Samoa: System of Education **1**: 266–74; *Christian*

Theory of Human Nature and Development **2**: 760–67; **Drugs and Education* **3**: 1611–19; *Educational Reforms, Implementation of* **4**: 1852–57; *Health and Education* **5**: 2563–67; *Hindu Theory of Human Nature and Development* **5**: 2597–601; *Human Development: Cultural and Religious Concepts* **5**: 2651–56; *Organization of Schools* **7**: 4227–36; *Religious Education* **9**: 4995–5008; **Shinto Theory of Human Nature and Development* **9**: 5449–53

THOMPSON, A. R. (Bristol University, Bristol, UK)
Teacher Training For Vocational Technical Subjects **10**: 6063–68

THOMPSON, F. (Temple University, Philadelphia, Pennsylvania, USA)
Family, School, and Cultural Capital* **4: 2267–72

THOMSON, J. D. (Australian Council for Educational Research, Hawthorn, Victoria, Australia)
Canonical Analysis* **2: 626–31

THORKILDSEN, R. J. (Utah State University, Logan, Utah, USA)
Special Education, Use of Technology in **10**: 5668–74

†THORNDIKE, R. L. (Columbia University, New York, USA)
Reliability in Educational and Psychological Measurement* **9: 4981–95

THORNDIKE, R. M. (Western Washington University, Bellingham, Washington, USA)
Correlational Procedures in Data Analysis **2**: 1107–17; **Reliability in Educational and Psychological Measurement* **9**: 4981–95

TIENE, D. (Kent State University, Kent, Ohio, USA)
Instructional TV and Video **5**: 2891–97

TILAK, J. B. G. (National Institute of Educational Planning and Administration, New Delhi, India)
Indian Subcontinent: Adult Education **5**: 2753–59; *Training Costs: Measurement* **11**: 6420–25

TILSON, T. D. (Academy for Educational Development, Washington, DC, USA)
Instructional Radio **5**: 2884–91

TIMMERMANN, D. (University of Bielefeld, Bielefeld, Germany)
Lifelong Education: Financing Mechanisms **6**: 3422–25

TIMPANE, P. M. (Columbia University, New York, USA)
Politics of Educational Research **8**: 4602–04

† deceased.

TIROSH, D. (Tel Aviv University, Tel Aviv, Israel)
Mathematics: Topics of Instruction* **6: 3671–86

TITMUS, C. J. (University of Leeds, Leeds, UK)
Adult Education: Concepts, Purposes, and Principles **1**: 111–20; *Adult, Recurrent, and Lifelong Education: Comparative Studies* **1**: 176–80

TITTLE, C. K. (City University of New York, New York, USA)
Test Bias **11**: 6315–21

TO, D–L. (US Department of Education, Washington, DC, USA)
Adult Education and Training Markets* **1: 103–11

TO NGOC CHAU (International Institute for Educational Planning, Paris, France)
Demography in Educational Planning* **3: 1449–53

TOMIYASU, Y. E. (Keio University, Tokyo, Japan)
Deinstitutionalization* **3: 1434–38

TOOMEY, D. (La Trobe University, Bundoora, Victoria, Australia)
Literacy Development in Children with Special Needs: Role of Parents **6**: 3459–63

TÖRESTAD, B. (Stockholm University, Stockholm, Sweden)
Personality Development* **8: 4388–95

TORPER, U. (University of Lund, Lund, Sweden)
Frame Factors **4**: 2375–77

TORRES, C. A. (University of California, Los Angeles, California, USA)
Adult Education for Development **1**: 127–35

TORREY, P. (University of South Carolina, Columbia, South Carolina, USA)
Instructional Pacing* **5: 2867–70

TRAVERS, K. (National Science Foundation, Washington, DC, USA)
Mathematics: Secondary School Programs **6**: 3661–68

TREIMAN, J. E. (University of California, Riverside, California, USA)
Authority and Power in Educational Organizations* **1: 432–37

TROLLIP, S. R. (S. R. Trollip and Associates Inc., Minneapolis, Minnesota, USA)
Courseware Design **2**: 1165–70

TROMMSDORFF, G. (University of Konstanz, Konstanz, Germany)

Human Development: Cross-cultural Approaches* **5: 2647–51

TROW, M. (University of California, Berkeley, California, USA)
Policy Analysis **8**: 4550–56

TSANG, M. C. (Michigan State University, East Lansing, Michigan, USA)
China, People's Republic of: Vocationalizing Education **2**: 755–60; *Cost Analysis in Education* **2**: 1121–27; *Costs of Continuing Education: Industrialized Countries* **2**: 1146–52; *Private and Public Costs of Schooling in Developing Nations* **8**: 4702–08

TUEROS, M. (International Labour Organisation, Dar Es Salaam, Tanzania)
Education and Informal Labor Markets **3**: 1676–81

TUIJNMAN, A. C. (University of Twente, Enschede, The Netherlands)
Adult Education: Overview **1**: 143–52; *Continuing Education, Effects of* **2**: 1084–94; **Curriculum in Adult Education* **3**: 1308–15; **Lifespan Learning: Implications for Educators* **6**: 3428–35; **Path Analysis and Linear Structural Relations Analysis* **8**: 4339–52; *Populations and Special Clienteles: Adult Education* **8**: 4610–16; *Providers of Adult Education* **8**: 4803–12; **Recurrent and Alternation Education* **8**: 4957–64; *Selection Bias in Educational Research* **9**: 5379–85

TURNER, J. H. (University of California, Riverside, California, USA)
Contemporary Sociological Theories of Education* **2: 1064–74

TYLER, B. (Miller and Tyler Ltd, London, UK)
Personality Inventories* **8: 4395–99

TYLER, R. W. (Stanford University, Stanford, California, USA)
Core Curriculum* **2: 1102–07; *Evaluation: A Tylerian Perspective* **4**: 2074–79

UMAR, J. (Ministry of Education and Culture, Jakarta, Indonesia)
Item Banking in Testing and Assessment **5**: 3036–43

UPTON, G. (University of Birmingham, Birmingham, UK)
Teacher Education and Special Education Needs **10**: 5939–43

UTRIA, B. (World Bank, Washington, DC, USA)
Informal Sector: Vocational Education and Training* **5: 2814–19

VAIDEANU, G. (Bucharest, Romania)
Romania: System of Education **9**: 5082–87

VALVERDE, G. A. (Michigan State University, East Lansing, Michigan, USA)
United States: System of Education **11**: 6538–47

VAN BRUGGEN, J. C. (National Institute for Curriculum Development, Enschede, The Netherlands)
Core Curriculum* **2: 1102–07; *Curriculum Development Centers* **3**: 1272–78

VAN CROMBRUGGE, H. (Catholic University of Leuven, Leuven, Belgium)
Family Life Education* **4: 2262–67

VAN DEN AKKER, J. (University of Twente, Enschede, The Netherlands)
Designing Innovations from an Implementation Perspective **3**: 1491–94

VAN DER KAMP, M. (University of Groningen, Groningen, The Netherlands)
Participation in Adult Education: Antecedent Factors **7**: 4319–25

VAN DER LINDEN, W. J. (University of Twente, Enschede, The Netherlands)
Computerized Educational Testing **2**: 992–98; *Decision Theory in Educational Testing* **3**: 1416–21

VAN DER SANDEN, J. M. M. (Tilburg University, Tilburg, The Netherlands)
Motor Skills, Learning and Instruction of **7**: 3950–53

VAN DUSEN, L. M. (Utah State University, Logan, Utah, USA)
Evaluation, Nature of* **4: 2109–19

VAN GEEL, T. (University of Rochester, Rochester, New York, USA)
Religious Issues in Education **9**: 5008–13

VAN GENT, B. (University of Leiden, Leiden, The Netherlands)
Andragogy **1**: 274–77

VAN LIESHOUT, C. F. M. (University of Nijmegen, Nijmegen, The Netherlands)
Peer Relations and Development **8**: 4364–68

VAN MASTER STONE, G. (University of Texas, Austin, Texas, USA)
Learning Strategies and Learning to Learn* **6: 3325–29

VAN METER, P. (University of Maryland, College Park, Maryland, USA)
Memory, Teaching and Testing for* **7: 3763–69

VANDEMEULEBROECKE, L. (Catholic University of Leuven, Leuven, Belgium)
Family Life Education* **4: 2262–67

VANGUNDY, A. B. (University of Oklahoma, Norman, Oklahoma, USA)
Idea Generation and Decision-making Techniques **5**: 2721–25

VANTASSEL-BASKA, J. (College of William and Mary, Williamsburg, Virginia, USA)
Gifted and Talented Learners in Special Populations **5**: 2486–91

VELLOSO, J. (University of Brasília, Brasília, Brazil)
Income Distribution and Education **5**: 2740–44

VERGIDIS, D. (University of Patras, Patras, Greece)
Greece: System of Education* **5: 2515–23

VERMA, A. (M. S. University of Baroda, Baroda, India)
Women's Education, History Of: India* **11: 6748–53

VERSCHAFFEL, L. (University of Leuven, Leuven, Belgium)
Computers and Learning* **2: 1002–07; **Mathematics, Learning and Instruction of* **6**: 3652–55

VERSPOOR, A. M. (World Bank, Washington, DC, USA)
Planning Educational Reforms: Use of Contingency Approach **8**: 4514–19

VILLAR, L. M. (University of Seville, Seville, Spain)
Teaching: Reflective **10**: 6215–19

VILLARREUL, F. A. (Michigan State University, East Lansing, Michigan, USA)
Adolescence* **1: 83–89

VIO GROSSI, F. (CEAAL, Santiago, Chile)
Latin America: Adult Education* **6: 3253–56

VISALBERGHI, A. (University "La Sapienza," Rome, Italy)
Italy: System of Education **5**: 3028–36

VLCEK, C. (Central Washington University, Ellensburg, Washington, USA)
Media Program Administration **7**: 3753–56

VOELKL, K. E. (State University of New York, Buffalo, New York, USA)
Class Size* **2: 770–75

VON EYE, A. (Michigan State University, East Lansing, Michigan, USA)
Human Development: Research Methodology* **5: 2673–77

VON HOFSTEN, C. (Umeå University, Umeå, Sweden)
Motor Development and Skill Acquisition **7**: 3947–50

VOOGT, J. C. (University of Utrecht, Utrecht, The Netherlands)
School Improvement* **9: 5241–47

VOOGT, J. M. (University of Twente, Enschede, The Netherlands)
Microcomputer-based Laboratories and Science Education **7**: 3808–10; *New Information Technology in Science Education* **7**: 4100–04

VOSNIADOU, S. (University of Athens, Athens, Greece)
Knowledge Representation and Organization **6**: 3151–55

VOSS, J. F. (University of Pittsburgh, Pittsburgh, Pennsylvania, USA)
Reasoning **8**: 4948–51; *Social Sciences, Learning and Instruction of* **9**: 5560–63

VUYK, E. J. (Ministry of Education and Science, Zoetermeer, The Netherlands)
Netherlands, The: System of Education **7**: 4067–77

WAGEMANS, J. (University of Leuven, Leuven, Belgium)
Perception and Learning **8**: 4376–79

WAGNER, A. (Organisation for Economic Co-operation and Development, Paris, France)
Teacher Education, Economics of **10**: 5948–54

WAGNER, D. A. (University of Pennsylvania, Philadelphia, Pennsylvania, USA)
Literacy: Research and Measurement **6**: 3474–80

WAHBE, N. (Ministry of Education, Manama, Bahrain)
Bahrain: System of Education* **1: 444–50

WAHLGREN, B. (The Royal Danish School of Educational Studies, Copenhagen, Denmark)
Nordic Countries: Adult Education **7**: 4175–80

WALBERG, H. J. (University of Illinois at Chicago, Chicago, Illinois, USA)
Data Envelopment Analysis* **3: 1381–87; **Homework* **5**: 2628–31; **International Educational Indicators* **5**: 2984–89; **National Assessment of Educational Programs* **7**: 4051–54; *Personality, School, and Social Environment as Learning Determinants* **8**: 4400–04; **Secondary Data Analysis* **9**: 5367–73; **Theory-based Evaluation* **11**: 6378–85

WALKER, D. F. (Stanford University, Stanford, California, USA)
New Information Technology and the Curriculum **7**: 4081–88

WALKER, J. C. (University of Canberra, Canberra, ACT, Australia)

Research in Education: Epistemological Issues **9**: 5021–31; **Resistance Theory* **9**: 5056–61

WALLINGTON, C. J. (Rochester Institute of Technology, Rochester, New York, USA)
Still Media, Production of **10**: 5726–30

WALSH, J. J. (Boston College, Chestnut Hill, Massachusetts, USA)
Projective Testing Techniques **8**: 4788–91

WALTHER, R. (FORCE, Brussels, Belgium)
European Community Programs in Continuing Vocational Education **4**: 2059–63

WALTON, C. (Northern Territory University, Darwin, Northern Territory, Australia)
Critical Reading: Teaching and Assessing* **2: 1194–98

WANG, M. C. (Temple University, Philadelphia, Pennsylvania, USA)
Learning Characteristics of Students with Special Needs* **6: 3292–97; *Student Diversity and Classroom Teaching* **10**: 5745–50

WARD, C. R. (University of Pittsburgh, Pittsburgh, Pennsylvania, USA)
Nonformal Education Policy in Developing Nations* **7: 4141–45

WARI, P. (Department of Education, Port Moresby, Papua New Guinea)
Papua New Guinea: System of Education* **7: 4275–82

WARWICK, D. (Education for Enterprise, Farnham, UK)
Modular Curricula **7**: 3886–89

WATKINS, W. H. (University of Utah, Salt Lake City, Utah, USA)
Minorities and Immigrant Children, Curriculum for **7**: 3840–48

WATSON, D. M. (King's College, London, UK)
Computer Assisted Learning **2**: 988–92

WATSON, J. K. P. (University of Reading, Reading, UK)
School Administration, History of **9**: 5159–69; *School Inspectors and Supervision* **9**: 5247–52

WATSON, L. (University of Northumbria, Newcastle, UK)
Polytechnical Education **8**: 4604–08

WATT, J. (Murdoch University, Murdoch, Western Australia, Australia)
Political Philosophy and Education **8**: 4571–75

WAYSON, W. W. (Ohio State University, Columbus, Ohio, USA)
Discipline in Schools* **3: 1534–38

WEBB, J. (Research for Better Schools, Philadelphia, Pennsylvania, USA)
School Climate and Culture* **9: 5206–11

WEIFANG MIN (Beijing University, Beijing, People's Republic of China)
Vocational Education and Productivity **11**: 6628–33

WEILER, H. N. (Stanford University, Stanford, California, USA)
Legitimacy in Educational Policy* **6: 3367–68

WEILER, K. A. (Tufts University, Medford, Massachusetts, USA)
Women and the Professionalization of Teaching **11**: 6719–23

WEINER, G. (South Bank University, London, UK)
Students in Classrooms, Gender and Racial Differences Among **10**: 5822–27

WEINERT, F. E. (Max Planck Institute for Psychological Research, Munich, Germany)
Cognitive Development: Individual Differences **2**: 842–47; *Development, Learning, and Instruction* **3**: 1501–04; *Human Development: Overview* **5**: 2656–65; *Research into Practice: Translating* **9**: 5038–43

WEINSTEIN, C. E. (University of Texas, Austin, Texas, USA)
Learning Strategies and Learning to Learn* **6: 3325–29; **Learning Strategies, Teaching and Testing for* **6**: 3335–40

WEISS, D. J. (University of Minnesota, Minneapolis, Minnesota, USA)
Adaptive Testing* **1: 48–53

WERNER, E. E. (University of California, Davis, California, USA)
Programs that Foster Resilience among Children at Risk **8**: 4775–80

WESTWOOD, S. (University of Leicester, Leicester, UK)
Critical Approaches to Adult Education **2**: 1189–94

WHITE, J. (University of London, London, UK)
Curriculum: Philosophical Perspectives **3**: 1325–28

WHITE, P. (University of London, London, UK)
Teacher Education: Philosophical Issues **10**: 5982–85

WHITE, P. B. (La Trobe University, Bundoora, Victoria, Australia)
Social Implications of Educational Technology* **9: 5539–45

WHYTE, J. (Trinity College, Dublin, Republic of Ireland)
Specific Language Disorders of Childhood* **10: 5674–81

WILCOX, R. R. (University of Southern California, Los Angeles, California, USA)
Simulation as a Research Technique **9**: 5467–71

WILKENING, F. (University of Tübingen, Tübingen, Germany)
Perceptual Development **8**: 4379–84

WILLETT, J. B. (Harvard University, Cambridge, Massachusetts, USA)
Change, Measurement of **2**: 671–78; **Event History Analyses* **4**: 2150–56

WILLIAMS, J. H. (Harvard University, Cambridge, Massachusetts, USA)
Documentation and Information in Comparative and International Education **3**: 1584–89

WILLIS, G. (University of Rhode Island, Kingston, Rhode Island, USA)
Curriculum Evaluation: Qualitative **3**: 1284–88

WILLKE, I. (University of Bochum, Bochum, Germany)
Education as a Field of Study, Origins of **3**: 1720–24

WILLMS, J. D. (University of British Columbia, Vancouver, British Columbia, Canada)
Effective Schools Research: Methodological Issues* **4: 1934–39

WILLOWER, D. J. (Pennsylvania State University, University Park, Pennsylvania, USA)
Administration of Education as a Field of Study **1**: 53–60

WILMS, W. W. (University of California, Los Angeles, California, USA)
Private Sector Training, Education and Performance Contracting in* **8: 4708–15; **Proprietary Further Education* **8**: 4792–96

WILSON, B. (University of Melbourne, Melbourne, Victoria, Australia)
Youth Cultures and Subcultures **11**: 6798–803

WILSON, B. L. (Research for Better Schools, Philadelphia, Pennsylvania, USA)
School Climate and Culture* **9: 5206–11

WILSON, D. N. (Ontario Institute for Studies in Education, Toronto, Ontario, Canada)
Facilities Planning and Policy: Macro Level* **4: 2225–30; *Technical-Vocational Education: Comparative and International Studies* **11**: 6261–66

WILSON, M. (University of California, Berkeley, California, USA)
Developmental Levels, Measurement of **3**: 1508–14; **Sampling Errors in Survey Research* **9**: 5124–31; **Student Progress, Charting of* **10**: 5783–91

WINDHAM, D. M. (State University of New York, Albany, New York, USA)
International Financing of Education **5**: 2989–93; *Management Information Systems* **6**: 3593–97

WINN, W. D. (University of Washington, Seattle, Washington, USA)
Communication, Media, and Instrumentation **2**: 884–88

WINNE, P. H. (Simon Fraser University, Burnaby, British Columbia, Canada)
Student Cognitive Processing and Learning* **10: 5738–45; *Teaching: Informational Processing Theories* **10**: 6187–93

WISEMAN, D. L. (Texas A&M University, College Station, Texas, USA)
Schools for Laboratory and Professional Development* **9: 5313–18

WOLCOTT, H. F. (University of Oregon, Eugene, Oregon, USA)
Education as Culture Transmission and Acquisition **3**: 1724–29

WOLF, R. M. (Columbia University, New York, USA)
Evaluation, Empirical Framework for **4**: 2089–97; **Prediction in Educational Research* **8**: 4652–57; *Program Evaluation* **8**: 4758–66; *Q-Methodology* **8**: 4855–57; *Quasi-experimentation* **8**: 4873–75; *Questionnaires* **8**: 4882–87; *Rating Scales* **8**: 4923–30

WOLFE, B. L. (University of Wisconsin–Madison, Madison, Wisconsin, USA)
External Benefits of Education **4**: 2208–12

WONG, B. (Simon Fraser University, Burnaby, British Columbia, Canada)
Children and Youth With Special Needs, Diagnosis and Classification of* **2: 711–19

WONG, K. K. (University of Chicago, Chicago, Illinois, USA)
Bureaucracy and School Effectiveness **1**: 589–94

WONG, P. L. (Stanford University, Stanford, California, USA)
Internal Migration and Education* **5: 2942–45; **Occupational Training, Economics of* **7**: 4197–201

WONG, SUK-YING (International Christian University, Tokyo, Japan)
Asia, East and Southeast: Adult Education* **1: 348–53

WOOD, F. H. (University of Minnesota, Minneapolis, Minnesota, USA)
Behavioral Disorders: Emotional **1**: 486–90

WOODHALL, M. (University of London, London, UK)
Human Capital Concepts **5**: 2643–47; *Student Fees* **10**: 5750–54; *Student Loans* **10**: 5762–68

WOODWARD, A. (The Norman Howard School, Rochester, New York, USA)
Textbooks **11**: 6366–71

WOOLLS, B. (University of Pittsburgh, Pittsburgh, Pennsylvania, USA)
Libraries as Learning Resources **6**: 3394–99

WORTHEN, B. R. (Utah State University, Logan, Utah, USA)
Evaluation, Nature of* **4: 2109–19

WRAGG, E. C. (Exeter University, Exeter, UK)
Lesson Structure **6**: 3385–89

WULF, C. (Free University of Berlin, Berlin, Germany)
Education For Peace **3**: 1729–33

WURZBURG, G. K. (Organisation for Economic Co-operation and Development, Paris, France)
Further Education and Training: Demand, Supply, and Finance **4**: 2388–95

YAGER, R. E. (University of Iowa, Iowa City, Iowa, USA)
Science Teacher Education **9**: 5342–45

YEMBE, O. W. (University of Yaounde, Yaounde, Cameroon)
Cameroon: System of Education **2**: 609–18

YEOH, O. C. (National Institute of Nanyang Technological University, Singapore, Republic of Singapore)
Singapore: System of Education **9**: 5476–85

YINGER, R. J. (University of Cincinnati, Cincinnati, Ohio, USA)
Teacher Planning, Approaches to* **10: 6031–35

YOGEV, A. (Tel Aviv University, Tel Aviv, Israel)
Second Chance Education and Alternative Routes **9**: 5363–67

YOLOYE, E. A. (Amoye Institute for Educational Research and Development, Ibadan, Nigeria)
Nigeria: System of Education **7**: 4124–32; *Selection Mechanisms in Secondary Education* **9**: 5385–89

YOUNG, R. (University of Sydney, Sydney, New South Wales, Australia)
Teaching: Linguistic and Sociolinguistic Theories **10**: 6193–97

YUE-PING CHUNG (Chinese University of Hong Kong, Hong Kong)
Returns to Vocational Education in Developing Nations **9**: 5071–76

ZAHORIK, J. A. (University of Wisconsin, Milwaukee, Wisconsin, USA)
Teacher Evaluating Behavior **10**: 6012–15

ZAMBONE, A. M. (Perkins School for the Blind, Watertown, Massachusetts, USA)
Deaf-Blind Children and Youth, Education of* **3: 1402–07

ZECHA, G. (University of Salzburg, Salzburg, Austria)
Values in Educational Inquiry: Philosophical Issues **11**: 6576–80

ZEITZ, C. M. (University of Pittsburgh, Pittsburgh, Pennsylvania, USA)
Expert Level of Understanding* **4: 2194–99

ZELLER, R. A. (Bowling Green State University, Bowling Green, Ohio, USA)
Validity **11**: 6569–76

ZHOU, NAN-ZHAO (National Institute for Educational Research, Beijing, People's Republic of China)
Asia, East and Southeast: Adult Education* **1: 348–53

ZIDERMAN, A. (Bar Ilan University, Ramat Gan, Israel)
Payroll Levies for Training **8**: 4359–64; *Training, Government Role in* **11**: 6425–31

ZINS, J. E. (University of Cincinnati, Cincinnati, Ohio, USA)
Prereferral Intervention for Students with Special Needs* **8: 4657–62

ZOUAIN, G. (UNESCO, Paris, France)
Lebanon: System of Education **6**: 3349–56

ZUBRZYCKI, J. (Australian National University, Canberra, ACT, Australia)
Classical Sociological Theories of Education* **2: 775–85

NAME INDEX

The Name Index has been compiled so that the reader can proceed either directly to the page where the named person is cited, or to a reference in the bibliography. For each name, the volume and page numbers for the bibliographic citation are given first, followed by the page number(s) in parentheses where that reference is cited in text. Where a name is referred to only in text, and not in the bibliography, the page number appears only in parentheses.

The accuracy of the spelling of authors' names has been affected by the use of different initials by some authors, or a different spelling of their name in different papers or review articles (sometimes this may arise from a transliteration process), and by those journals which give only one initial to each author.

Aamodt P O, **2:** 665; **11:** 6551 (6550)
Aarkrog V, **7:** 4179 (4179)
Aaro L E, **5:** 2572 (2568)
Aaron H J, **3:** 1761; **9:** 5240 (5238)
Aaron I E, **4:** 1962 (1962)
Aaron J, **11:** 6768
Aaron J H, **4:** 1863 (1860)
Aaron P G, **5:** 2767; **8:** 4935 (4934)
Aarons A, **2:** 892 (891)
Aaronson D, **9:** 5416
Abadan-Unat N, **11:** 6760 (6754)
Abagi J O, **10:** 5762 (5761)
Abbey D, **1:** 158 (154, 156)
Abbott R, **5:** 2851 (2849)
Abbott R D, **10:** 5795 (5793)
Abbs P, **8:** 4388 (4384)
Abderhalden E, **1:** 15
Abdessalem A, **11:** 6476
Abdul-Dayem A, **8:** 4485 (4485)
Abdul-Ghani N, **8:** 4485
Abe Y, **2:** 899 (898)
Abel E L, **5:** 2567
Abelard P, **2:** (804)
Abeles R P, **8:** 4824
Abelson R P, **6:** 3155
Abel-Struth S, **7:** 4026, 4030
Abernethy D B, **1:** 332 (332)
Aboitiz F, **7:** 4081 (4078)
Abou-Rejeily K, **6:** 3356
Abou-Zeid A W, **8:** 4473 (4471)
Abraham B, **8:** 4788
Abraham H, **3:** 1544 (1540, 1541)
Abraham J, **3:** 1501
Abraham K G, **6:** 3616 (3614)
Abraham M R, **6:** 3416; **8:** 4479 (4476), 4652 (4649, 4652)
Abraham R, **4:** 2363 (2362)
Abraham R G, **6:** 3335 (3330)
Abrahamsen A A, **1:** 408 (407)
Abrahamson R F, **2:** 737 (734)
Abrahamson S, **8:** 4751
Abrahamsson K, **1:** 93 (90, 93), 103, 157 (154, 155), 162 (161); **5:** 2951 (2949); **6:** 3366 (3363); **7:** 4180; **8:** 4638 (4638); **11:** 6394, 6395, 6551 (6548, 6549)
Abrami P C, **10:** 6234 (6230)
Abrams P, **5:** 2831 (2831)
Abramson L Y, **7:** 3942 (3940); **9:** 5406 (5404, 5405)
Abramson T Y, **9:** 5240
Abreu de Armengol M, **7:** 4136 (4133)
Absy C A, **6:** 3334 (3330)
Abt C C, **9:** 5475 (5473, 5474)
Abu Nasr J, **1:** 328; **11:** 6760 (6759)
Abu-Rabi I M, **9:** 5008 (5005)
Ach N, **2:** 856 (852); **5:** (2875, 2881); **9:** 5403 (5400)
Achenbach T M, **9:** 5528 (5527)
Achilles C M, **2:** 775 (773, 774); **4:** 1938 (1936)
Achinstein P, **8:** 4634
Achio F, **2:** 1160 (1159)
Achtenhagen F, **3:** 1354 (1354); **9:** 5562 (5562)
Acioly N M, **8:** 4951 (4949)
Acker S, **4:** 2286 (2284), 2291 (2289, 2290); **7:** 3826 (3825); **9:** 5432; **10:** 5613 (5609, 5612), 5826, 6042 (6040), 6214 (6210, 6212); **11:** 6726 (6724), 6727
Ackerman B P, **8:** 4956 (4952)
Ackerman P L, **1:** 5 (2), 377 (375); **2:** 847; **5:** 2767 (2762), 2768 (2763), 2769, 2884, 2921 (2920); **6:** 3325; **7:** 3942; **9:** 5043, 5403, 5563; **10:** 5762, 6159
Ackerman W B, **4:** 2245
Ackoff R L, **3:** 1745 (1741); **10:** 5900 (5895)
Ackum S, **4:** 2150 (2148)
Acland H, **10:** 5607 (5601)
Acosta J M, **10:** 6034 (6033)
Adair J G, **11:** 6511 (6509)
Adam C, **3:** 1464 (1462, 1463)
Adam R, **10:** 6078 (6077)
Adam-Moodley K, **7:** 3970 (3969)
Adams A, **2:** 866 (862); **10:** 5934 (5933), 6042 (6037), 6043
Adams A V, **8:** 4519 (4515); **10:** 5919; **11:** 6431 (6430), 6638 (6633), 6663 (6660, 6661, 6662, 6663)
Adams C, **5:** 2457 (2454)
Adams C T, **5:** 2512 (2509)
Adams D, **2:** 932 (925, 929, 932); **3:** 1501 (1495), 1819 (1810), 1829 (1826); **5:** 2792; **6:** 3463, 3467, 3608; **8:** 4509 (4500), 4601 (4595, 4600); **9:** 5055 (5054), 5191 (5189)
Adams D K, **3:** 1809 (1804); **8:** 4595 (4588)
Adams D M, **9:** 5475 (5472, 5473)
Adams F, **2:** 729 (721)
Adams G R, **1:** 88 (86)
Adams G S, **1:** 389 (387)
Adams J, **3:** (1723)
Adams J A, **4:** 2281 (2280); **7:** 3953 (3952)
Adams M A, **4:** 2286 (2285)
Adams M J, **4:** 1962 (1960, 1962); **8:** 4936, 4944 (4944)
Adams R, **1:** 158 (155, 156); **3:** 1513 (1511), 1514 (1511); **10:** 5957 (5954, 5955)
Adams R E, **10:** 5900 (5900)
Adams R J, **4:** 2180 (2174, 2177); **5:** 2783 (2782); **7:** 4307 (4305, 4306); **9:** 5432 (5428, 5430); **10:** 5790 (5789); **11:** 6320 (6319)
Adams R S, **10:** 6132 (6131)
Adams R W, **9:** 5358 (5357)
Adams V M, **1:** 204; **6:** 3642, 3643, 3655 (3653)
Adams W, **1:** 560 (554)
Adamski W W, **1:** 310 (306); **4:** 2257 (2252); **11:** 6647 (6641, 6643, 6647)
Adamson J W, **8:** 4715 (4708)
Adamson R, **3:** (1723)
Adamson-Macedo C, **11:** 6415 (6412)
Adamu H A, **9:** 5008 (4999)
Addams J, **5:** (2614); **7:** (3843)
Addinall E, **5:** 2773 (2771)
Addou H, **3:** 1695 (1693)
Adelman C, **1:** 47 (45); **2:** 645, 816 (812, 813)
Adelman I, **7:** 4200 (4199)
Adelman N E, **10:** 5953 (5950)

Adelson J, **1:** 88 (87); **8:** 4581 (4576, 4579)
Adelstein D, **8:** 4446 (4445)
Adema J J, **1:** 52 (49); **2:** 998 (996); **5:** 3061 (3058)
Ader H J, **5:** 3051 (3046)
Adey P, **5:** 2669 (2667); **6:** 3416; **8:** 4478 (4476), 4652; **9:** 5327 (5325)
Adger C R, **9:** 5358 (5356)
Adioetomo S M, **4:** 2418 (2415)
Adkison J, **4:** 2423 (2423)
Adler A, **3:** (1261); **8:** 4816 (4815, 4816)
Adler B, **1:** 553 (553)
Adler I, **7:** 4315 (4313)
Adler M, **1:** 594 (591); **5:** 2697 (2693); **9:** 5196 (5194); **11:** 6557 (6556)
Adler M J, **2:** 784 (776)
Adler P, **9:** 5232 (5230); **11:** 6276 (6272)
Adler S A, **3:** 1636 (1633); **6:** 3227 (3225); **10:** 5585 (5584)
Adoni H, **9:** 5518 (5514)
Adorno T W, **7:** (4331); **8:** (4419), (4454); **9:** (5052); **10:** (5600); **11:** 6579
Adsett M, **8:** 4638 (4635)
Aebli H, **2:** 846 (844); **3:** 1434 (1432, 1433)
Afer D, **8:** (4887)
Agar J, **4:** 2423 (2421)
Agar M, **3:** 1729 (1728)
Agarwal S M, **11:** 6282 (6278)
Agbenyega C O, **9:** 5389 (5388)
Agee J L, **9:** 5275 (5274)
Ager C L, **1:** 494 (491)
Aggarwal Y P, **9:** 5358 (5357)
Agne R, **10:** 6012 (6009, 6010, 6011)
Agresti A, **6:** 3507 (3500, 3507)
Aguiar N, **3:** 1671 (1667)
Agyekum S, **1:** 127 (124, 125)
Ahamad B, **3:** 1824 (1822); **6:** 3613 (3610, 3611, 3612); **8:** 4531 (4527)
Ahern N F, **11:** 6712 (6709, 6710, 6711)
Ahier J, **3:** 1347 (1345)
Ahlbrand W, **10:** 6197 (6195)
Ahlgreen M, **4:** 2286 (2285)
Ahlgren A, **9:** 5323 (5318)
Ahlstrom A, **5:** 2851 (2848)
Ahluwalia N T, **10:** 5726 (5725)
Ahmed M, **1:** 152 (144); **4:** 2369 (2365); **5:** 2960 (2959), 2961 (2959); **6:** 3261 (3257); **7:** 4136, 4140 (4137, 4139, 4140), 4145 (4141, 4142), 4200 (4197, 4199); **10:** 5596 (5592)
Ahuja Y L, **7:** 4205
Ahwesh E, **9:** 5563 (5562)
Aigner D J, **4:** 2445 (2444)
Aiken D R, **9:** 5323 (5320)
Aiken L, **4:** 2088 (2086); **6:** 3638 (3635)
Aiken L R, **6:** 3642 (3639); **9:** 5323 (5320), 5432 (5430)
Aiken L S, **5:** 2931 (2927)
Aiken W M, **10:** 6168 (6168)
Aikenhead G S, **9:** 5338 (5336); **11:** 6292 (6291)
Aikin W M, **3:** 1482 (1475); **10:** (5814)
Ainley J, **6:** 3527 (3525)
Ainley J A, **11:** 6677 (6676)
Ainley J G, **6:** 3373 (3372)
Ainley P, **11:** 6690 (6686)
Ainscow M, **2:** 729 (723, 724, 728, 729), 730; **5:** 2971 (2966, 2967, 2968); **6:** 3297 (3292); **10:** 5942 (5940)
Ainslie R C, **2:** 687
Ainsworth L K, **6:** 3096
Ainsworth M D S, **1:** 234 (232); **5:** 2806
Ainsworth R G, **1:** 157 (156)
Airasian P W, **2:** 796 (793, 794, 795)
Aitken L S, **9:** 4974
Aitken M, **4:** 1933 (1929, 1932); **7:** 4015 (4012)
Aitkin M A, **1:** 520 (516); **2:** 831 (830); **4:** 1938 (1937); **5:** 2595 (2590, 2593, 2595); **6:** 3389 (3387); **7:** 3986 (3979, 3982, 3983)
Ajayi-Dopemu Y, **11:** 6608 (6605)
Ajchariyakul N, **5:** 2890 (2886)
Ajello A M, **9:** 5562 (5561)
Ajeyalemi D, **11:** 6292 (6291)
Ajzen I, **1:** 358 (354, 356), 389 (380, 381, 382, 386); **7:** (4322); **10:** 6103 (6100)
Akahori K, **7:** 3946 (3945)
Akaike H, **6:** 3508 (3504)
Akenson D H, **5:** 3020
Akenson J E, **9:** 5577 (5573)
Aker G F, **7:** 4185; **8:** 4616 (4610), 4736, 4812
Akerlof G A, **3:** 1703, 1750 (1750); **9:** 5354 (5351)
Akhalkin S, **10:** 5649 (5645)
Akhtar R, **7:** 4270
Akin J S, **7:** 3820 (3816)
Akiner S, **7:** 3906
Akinnaso F N, **1:** 482 (482)
Akinsanya S K, **1:** 295, 296, 297 (288); **2:** 1212, 1213
Akiyama T, **5:** 2897 (2895)
Akker J J H van den, **3:** 1278 (1274), 1354 (1351), 1355 (1350)
Akpati E T I, **6:** 3227 (3226)
Akrawi M, **10:** 5895
Al Jarrash A, **2:** 733 (731)
Al Khabori B K, **7:** 4205
Al Ougaly A, **7:** 4205
Al Raesi I, **7:** 4205
Al Shanfari S M, **7:** 4205
Al-Abidi S H, **1:** 328
al-Baadi H, **9:** 5151 (5150)
Al-Barwani T, **1:** 327 (326)
Al-Bassam A-A, **8:** 4485 (4483)
Al-Baṭrīq M K, **11:** 6627 (6626)
Al-Chehoumi A M, **6:** 3356
Al-Ghanim A M, **11:** 6628 (6626)
al-Hammad M A, **9:** 5151
Al-Hariri R, **11:** 6760 (6753)
Al-Jabr S M, **10:** 5585 (5583)
Al-Jeraisi A, **9:** 5151 (5146)
Al-Khalifa E, **11:** 6730 (6729)
al-Minawi N, **8:** 4485
Al-Nayadi M, **11:** 6515
al-Rasheed M, **9:** 5151 (5150)
Al-Uqaili R, **9:** 5151 (5146)
Alaluf M, **1:** 503
Alatis J E, **4:** 2345
Alatis J L, **4:** 2351 (2348)
al-Zaid A M, **9:** 5151
Alavosius M P, **9:** 5489 (5488)
Alba R D, **6:** 3507 (3502)
Albach H, **8:** 4359
Albelda R P, **4:** 2431 (2429)
Albert M, **3:** 1819 (1818)
Albert R S, **2:** 1182
Alberto P A, **10:** 6164
Alberts J R, **1:** 15 (12); **8:** 4383
Alberty H, **10:** 5817 (5814)
Albisetti J C, **11:** 6747 (6746)
Albrecht D, **10:** 5767 (5766, 5767)
Albrecht J W, **9:** 5354 (5354)
Alchian A A, **3:** 1702 (1697); **4:** 1972 (1970, 1971, 1972)
Alcock P, **11:** 6557 (6553)
Alcorn S, **3:** (1404)
Aldenderfer M S, **9:** 5158 (5158)
Alder T F, **9:** 5432 (5429)
Alderman D L, **5:** 3050 (3046); **11:** 6339 (6337, 6338)
Alderman H, **5:** 2945 (2943)
Alderson G, **3:** 1778 (1778)
Alderson J C, **4:** 2363 (2361, 2362, 2363), 2364; **5:** 2784; **8:** 4939 (4937)
Aldrich J L, **4:** 1995
Alesandrini K, **2:** 1170 (1168)
Alessi S M, **2:** 1011 (1008), 1170 (1166, 1168, 1169); **7:** 4094 (4093), 4100
Alexander C, **1:** 157 (155); **8:** 4824
Alexander D J, **4:** 2123 (2121, 2122)
Alexander G, **2:** 1012 (1009)
Alexander the Great, **8:** (4888)
Alexander H A, **3:** 1271 (1270)
Alexander J, **1:** 28; **2:** 933
Alexander J C, **1:** 59 (54, 58)
Alexander K, **3:** 1606 (1606), 1778 (1776); **10:** 5613
Alexander K L, **1:** 11 (10), 358 (357); **2:** 824 (822, 824); **4:** 2249; **5:** 2627 (2624); **8:** 4830 (4827), 4844 (4840, 4841)
Alexander L, **3:** 1829 (1826); **4:** 2330 (2329)
Alexander P, **10:** 5795 (5794)
Alexander P A, **1:** 193, 194 (186, 187); **2:** 1026; **6:** 3329 (3327), 3339; **8:** 4823 (4821); **10:** 5745 (5740, 5741), 6192 (6188)
Alexander of Villedieu, **9:** (5123)
Alexander W, **8:** 4509 (4503)
Alexander W M, **3:** 1315 (1312); **7:** 4249
Alexandersson C, **7:** 4179 (4179)
Alexson J, **1:** 490 (487)
Alford R, **8:** 4568
Alfthan T, **11:** 6430 (6425)
Alger C, **3:** 1501 (1497)
Algina J, **2:** 1189 (1188); **7:** 4056 (4055)
Algozzine B, **2:** 719 (712, 714, 715, 716); **6:** 3297 (3294); **7:** 3833 (3831), 4081; **9:** 5071 (5069)
Ali A Y, **5:** 3023
Ali H A, **7:** 4205
Alibali M W, **2:** 856 (855)
Alie J A D, **9:** 5460
Alikperov V G, **9:** 5532 (5528)

Alin Åkerman B, **11:** 6492 (6489)
Alinsky S, **2:** 1194
Alkin M C, **1:** 60, 152; **2:** 933; **3:** 1283 (1279, 1280, 1283), 1431 (1425, 1426, 1428); **4:** 2108 (2101, 2102, 2105, 2108); **5:** 2779; **6:** 3496; **9:** 5210; **10:** 5613
Allaart P, **4:** 2150
Allal L, **5:** 2462 (2460, 2461)
Allan R, **4:** 2131
Alleman J, **2:** 796 (794); **3:** 1283 (1279); **9:** 5363 (5359, 5361)
Alleman-Brooks J, **9:** 5362 (5359, 5361)
Allen D A, **10:** 5680 (5675, 5676, 5677)
Allen D W, **10:** 5977 (5973, 5974, 5975)
Allen E L, **6:** 3096
Allen G, **2:** 906; **11:** 6360 (6356)
Allen G E, **2:** 718 (717)
Allen I M, **10:** 5681 (5676)
Allen J, **9:** 5441
Allen J D, **10:** 6031 (6030)
Allen J P B, **6:** 3439 (3438)
Allen K R, **4:** 2266 (2265)
Allen L, **4:** 2445 (2444, 2445)
Allen M, **5:** 2692
Allen P B, **4:** 2346 (2344)
Allen R P, **3:** 1394 (1388)
Allen V, **8:** 4395
Allen V L, **10:** 6159 (6155); **11:** 6484 (6482, 6484)
Allen-Meares P, **9:** 5290 (5288, 5289)
Allensworth D D, **5:** 2571 (2569, 2570)
Allerup P, **8:** 4912 (4903, 4908, 4911)
Allexsaht-Snider M, **6:** 3452 (3448)
Alley R, **10:** 6132 (6130)
Allinder R M, **3:** 1359 (1358)
Allington R L, **2:** 824 (823), 868 (865); **6:** 3484 (3481); **8:** 4935 (4932, 4933); **9:** 5070 (5069), 5071 (5069); **11:** 6777 (6776)
Allinson C, **1:** 321 (319)
Allison B, **1:** 343 (341)
Allison C, **7:** 4282; **10:** 6012 (6011)
Allison G T, **3:** 1431 (1427)
Allison P D, **4:** 2156 (2154, 2155, 2156)
Allman J, **1:** 194 (192)
Allman P, **1:** 277 (276); **2:** 1165
Allmendinger D F, **10:** 5782 (5777)
Allmendinger J, **10:** 5735 (5732, 5734)
Alloy L B, **9:** 5406 (5404, 5405)
Allport G, **2:** 1098 (1097)
Allport G W, **1:** 379 (378), 389 (381); **3:** 1485 (1484), 1797; **5:** 2692 (2690); **7:** 3706 (3704); **8:** 4394 (4392); **9:** 5175 (5171)
Allred J, **6:** 3398 (3395)
Allsop T, **8:** 4648 (4645)
Allwright R L, **4:** 2357 (2353, 2356); **6:** 3213 (3211)
Almeida R, **4:** 2225 (2219)
Almond B, **11:** 6580
Almond G A, **3:** 1654 (1650)
Almond L, **10:** 5713 (5708)
Almy M, **3:** 1635 (1631); **7:** 4300 (4298)
Alonsoconchiero, **4:** 2331
Alpert B, **8:** 4881 (4877); **9:** 5060 (5058, 5059)
Alpert P, **3:** 1820 (1810)
Alpert R, **11:** 6360 (6356)
Alrabaa S, **10:** 5895
Alschuler A S, **7:** 3946 (3943)
Alston A, **6:** 3671 (3668, 3669, 3670)
Altbach P G, **2:** 932 (927, 929); **3:** 1300 (1289), 1589 (1586), 1655 (1653), 1712 (1707); **4:** 1851 (1849, 1850); **5:** 2753, 2998 (2995, 2997); **8:** 4509, 4586, 4698, 4848 (4846); **9:** 5060, 5539; **10:** 5782 (5776, 5778, 5779, 5780), 5783, 5929 (5925, 5926); **11:** 6366, 6371
Alten S R, **1:** 400
Altenbaugh R J, **9:** 5180 (5179, 5180); **10:** 5613 (5609); **11:** 6775
Althof W, **1:** 380; **7:** 3920 (3919), 3925 (3923); **10:** 6053 (6051, 6052)
Althusser L, **2:** 784 (780), 932 (925), 1072 (1067), 1193 (1191); **3:** (1346), 1720 (1715); **6:** 3621 (3618, 3619); **9:** 5060 (5056); **10:** 5596 (5592), 5606 (5597)
Altmaier E, **10:** 5925 (5921, 5922, 5923)
Altman I, **10:** 6207
Altmann J, **5:** 2685 (2682)
Altonji J G, **6:** 3143 (3139), 3616 (3614)
Alton-Lee A, **6:** 3345 (3344)
Altrichter H, **1:** 47 (45), 431 (430, 431), 432 (431)
Altwerger B, **6:** 3452 (3448)
Alutto J A, **9:** 5180 (5179)
Alvarez B, **4:** 2250, 2257 (2250, 2253, 2255, 2256); **9:** 5268
Alvarez-Buylla A, **1:** 554
Alvermann D E, **2:** 806 (804), 866 (863, 865); **8:** 4947 (4946, 4947)
Alves A J, **3:** 1735 (1734)
Alves Pinto M C, **6:** 3544 (3540)
Alvey W, **3:** 1425
Alwin D F, **7:** 4007
Alwitt L, **6:** 3625 (3623)
Amabile T M, **2:** 1182 (1178, 1180)
Amadeo J, **1:** 338
Amader J V, **11:** 6437 (6436)
Amado A N, **3:** 1438 (1436)
Amaj A M, **1:** 210
Amar R, **7:** 4316 (4310); **9:** 5504 (5501)
Amato J, **8:** 4694
Amatruda C S, **5:** 2680 (2677)
Amaya-Williams M, **9:** 5403 (5400)
Ambroise J, **1:** 139 (137)
Ambron S R, **2:** 687 (687), 1012
Ambrosoli L, **5:** 3036
Ames C, **1:** 31 (28, 31); **2:** 866 (866), 867; **7:** 3942; **10:** 5745, 6103 (6100)
Ames G, **8:** 4372 (4371)
Ames L, **9:** 5275 (5274)
Ames R, **2:** 867; **10:** 5745, 6103 (6100)
Ames R E, **7:** 3942
Amidon E J, **2:** 816
Aminah S, **10:** 5943 (5940)
Amir R, **6:** 3415 (3410)
Amir Y, **3:** 1486; **7:** 3970 (3967)
Amirs, **8:** 4901 (4901)
Amjad R, **6:** 3613; **8:** 4531 (4527, 4528)
Ammar H, **3:** 1755 (1753)
Ammerman R T, **1:** 19 (17, 18)
Ammon P, **8:** 4482 (4482)
Ammon U, **2:** 968
Amonoo R F, **5:** 2486
Amon-Tanoh Y, **1:** 221 (218); **6:** 3586
Amos V, **7:** 3852 (3849)
Amsden A, **3:** 1712 (1707); **11:** 6282 (6278)
Amsel E, **8:** 4957 (4953)
Amudson K J, **9:** 5008
Amyot M, **11:** 6814 (6812)
An C B, **4:** 2212 (2210)
an-Noori A-G, **8:** 4485 (4483)
Anagnos M, **3:** (1402)
Anandalingam G, **5:** 2798 (2793)
Anastasi A, **4:** 2257 (2253); **7:** 3970 (3967); **8:** 4399, 4657 (4654); **9:** 4995 (4991), 5432 (5424, 5427); **11:** 6315 (6313, 6315), 6339 (6335, 6337), 6677 (6670), 6678
Anastasi P, **5:** 2767 (2760, 2761)
Anastasiow N J, **3:** 1623 (1621), 1624
Anchor K N, **7:** 4296 (4295)
Andel J J, **6:** 3377 (3375)
Anders P, **3:** 1257 (1256); **8:** 4948 (4946)
Andersen D G, **10:** 5929 (5928)
Andersen E, **6:** 3213
Andersen E B, **4:** 2017 (2012); **6:** 3507 (3501); **8:** 4912 (4902, 4908), 4923 (4920)
Andersen H B, **10:** 5913 (5913)
Andersen V, **1:** 408 (405)
Anderson A, **3:** 1820 (1811), 1824; **6:** 3209 (3208); **11:** 6684
Anderson A A, **5:** 2819
Anderson A B, **7:** 3861 (3858); **10:** 5862 (5860)
Anderson B, **3:** 1641 (1640), 1643 (1639); **7:** 3861
Anderson B D, **10:** 5924 (5923)
Anderson C, **1:** 193 (192); **2:** 760, 824 (824); **3:** 1820 (1812)
Anderson C A, **1:** 474 (467, 468); **2:** 932 (923, 927, 932); **3:** 1655 (1653), 1695 (1692), 1768 (1762); **4:** 2257, 2278 (2276), 2369; **5:** 2647; **6:** 3312, 3458 (3454); **7:** 4211; **8:** 4509 (4504), 4688; **9:** 5076; **10:** 6227; **11:** 6251, 6265, 6425
Anderson C S, **4:** 1938 (1936); **9:** 5210 (5207)
Anderson C W, **6:** 3416 (3410, 3413, 3414); **9:** 5363 (5360)
Anderson D, **5:** 2572, 2595 (2590, 2593), 2897 (2895); **6:** 3625 (3623); **7:** 3986 (3983)
Anderson D A, **5:** 2595 (2595)
Anderson D R, **1:** 570; **6:** 3625; **8:** 4680 (4677, 4678)
Anderson D S, **4:** 1840 (1836, 1837); **7:** 4170 (4168); **8:** 4830 (4828); **9:** 5201 (5197); **10:** 6239 (6236, 6237); **11:** 6797 (6796, 6797)
Anderson D W, **3:** 1266 (1264)
Anderson E, **2:** 700
Anderson G, **1:** 474 (471); **2:** 802 (799)

Anderson G J, **2:** 811 (808, 809); **3:** 1482 (1478); **9:** 4973 (4972)
Anderson G L, **9:** 5272 (5269); **10:** 5745 (5738)
Anderson H, **9:** 5246 (5242)
Anderson J, **1:** 103 (101); **2:** 913 (911), 973 (972), 1079 (1075, 1076, 1077, 1078); **3:** 1628 (1627); **9:** 5302 (5300)
Anderson J C, **11:** 6384 (6381, 6382)
Anderson J E, **6:** 3284; **7:** 3706 (3705)
Anderson J F, **8:** 4887
Anderson J G, **4:** 2165 (2157)
Anderson J H, **10:** 5790 (5785)
Anderson J R, **1:** 330 (328, 329), 347 (343); **2:** 851 (849), 1006 (1003), 1031 (1029); **3:** 1434 (1432, 1433); **4:** 2199 (2198); **5:** 2921 (2919, 2920); **6:** 3301 (3300), 3324 (3317, 3318, 3320), 3329 (3328), 3334 (3332), 3335; **7:** 3768 (3766, 3767), 3953 (3953); **8:** 4722 (4720, 4721), 4731 (4729), 4823 (4821)
Anderson K, **7:** 3991, 4336 (4332); **11:** 6603 (6601)
Anderson L, **2:** 816 (812, 813, 814, 815); **3:** 1820; **7:** 3886 (3881); **8:** 4509, 4873 (4869, 4871); **9:** 5308; **10:** 6015 (6014); **11:** 6298
Anderson L M, **2:** 820 (816, 817, 818), 867 (861); **9:** 5362 (5359, 5361)
Anderson L W, **1:** 23, 389 (381, 383, 389); **2:** 775 (772), 796 (792); **3:** 1482 (1475), 1768 (1764); **4:** 2140 (2135), 2165 (2163); **5:** 2778 (2774, 2777), 2869 (2868, 2869); **6:** 3631 (3627); **7:** 3872 (3867), 4030, 4236; **9:** 5043 (5038, 5041); **10:** 5861 (5856), 6095 (6095), 6155 (6150, 6151, 6152, 6153, 6154), 6173 (6172), 6239 (6238, 6239); **11:** 6390 (6388, 6389)
Anderson M, **4:** 2411 (2407); **11:** 6690 (6686)
Anderson M B, **9:** 5228 (5225, 5227); **10:** 5924 (5922), 6062 (6061)
Anderson M L, **1:** 277 (275)
Anderson O R, **6:** 3416 (3409, 3410)
Anderson P P, **5:** 2812 (2807)
Anderson R, **2:** 973, 1084 (1079), 1152 (1147, 1150); **3:** 1355 (1350), 1602 (1600); **7:** 4329 (4326)
Anderson R C, **2:** 968 (967); **5:** 3066; **7:** 3768 (3765, 3766); **9:** 5363; **10:** 5795 (5791)
Anderson R E, **2:** 977 (974), 1011; **11:** 6390 (6389), 6424
Anderson R H, **1:** 230 (227, 228); **7:** 4157
Anderson R O, **8:** 4783 (4780)
Anderson S, **3:** 1784 (1782)
Anderson S A, **2:** 1011 (1009, 1010)
Anderson S B, **11:** 6511 (6508)
Anderson S C, **11:** 6798 (6795, 6796)
Anderson S E, **6:** 3602 (3600)
Anderson T, **7:** 3970 (3969); **11:** 6306 (6305)
Anderson T H, **1:** 193 (185); **2:** 968 (966); **10:** 6149 (6145); **11:** 6370 (6369)
Anderson T W, **3:** 1548 (1545, 1546); **4:** (2233); **7:** 3858 (3854, 3857); **9:** 5559 (5558)
Anderson V, **10:** 6192 (6191)
Anderson-Levitt K M, **1:** 294 (283); **2:** 918, 1212 (1210); **4:** 2272 (2268); **5:** 2514 (2514); **9:** 5312 (5311)
Anderssen N, **5:** 2571 (2571)
Anderssen O, **3:** (1724)
Andersson B, **8:** 4429 (4425, 4429)
Andersson T, **4:** 2351 (2347)
Andrae J, **7:** 4214 (4211, 4212)
Andre K, **1:** 554
Andre P, **8:** 4835 (4834)
Andre T, **7:** 3809 (3809)
Andreotti E, **3:** 1619
Andrew I, **10:** 5973
Andrews D, **5:** 2861 (2860)
Andrews D F, **9:** 5081 (5078, 5079, 5080, 5081)
Andrews D H, **3:** 1315 (1313), 1490 (1487); **4:** 1898 (1888), 1924; **5:** 2874 (2873)
Andrews F M, **2:** 1094
Andrews G, **7:** 3783 (3778); **10:** 5693 (5692)
Andrews G J, **4:** 2123 (2120)
Andrews G R, **1:** 31 (31)
Andrews H A, **4:** 2131 (2127)
Andrews I, **10:** 5973
Andrich D, **1:** 389 (385, 387); **4:** 2017 (2012); **6:** 3124 (3123), 3252 (3251), 3253 (3251); **7:** 3706 (3704), 4307 (4304, 4305); **8:** 4912 (4902), 4923 (4920, 4921, 4922); **9:** 5323 (5320); **11:** 6387 (6386, 6387)
Andrioli G C, **1:** 554
Ang W H, **9:** 5485
Angleitner A, **11:** 6310 (6310)
Anglin G J, **2:** 888; **5:** 2773, 2874; **7:** 3756 (3755)
Angoff W H, **1:** 41 (41); **2:** 792 (787); **5:** 3050 (3044), 3061 (3058); **7:** 4000 (3997), 4056 (4054, 4056); **8:** 4394 (4390); **10:** 5725 (5723); **11:** 6355 (6350, 6352)
Angula N, **7:** 4046
Angus L, **6:** 3474
Anjali M, **3:** 1266 (1265)
Ankenmann R, **1:** 374 (373)
Anker R, **3:** 1671 (1666), 1672, 1676; **4:** 2431 (2430), 2432
Ankerhus J, **6:** 3224 (3219)
Ankhara-Dove L, **10:** 5846 (5843, 5845)
Ankonina D B, **4:** 1980 (1978, 1979)
Ankrah-Dove L, **8:** 4526
Annesley F R, **9:** 5070 (5068), 5071 (5068)
Annett J, **6:** 3096 (3093)
Ansen A R, **11:** 6563 (6562)
Ant M, **6:** 3538
Antaki C, **8:** 4951
Antel J, **4:** 2212
Anthias F, **7:** 3852 (3849)
Anthony E J, **8:** 4779 (4776, 4777)
Anthony H, **10:** 6015 (6014)
Anthony H M, **2:** 867 (861)
Anthony P, **10:** 5613 (5611); **11:** 6558
Anthony R N, **5:** 2831 (2828)
Antler J, **11:** 6722
Antonovsky A, **4:** 1979 (1976, 1977)
Antrobus J, **10:** 5759
Anward J, **9:** 5416 (5414, 5416)
Anweiler O, **5:** 2479 (2472); **11:** 6647 (6641)
Anyon J, **2:** 1072 (1067); **3:** 1347 (1346); **6:** 3621 (3618); **10:** 5613 (5608), 5817 (5816), 6103 (6101)
Anzai Y, **2:** 842 (839)
Anzalone S, **4:** 1910 (1904, 1905, 1906, 1907, 1908, 1909)
Aoki M, **5:** 2942 (2939, 2940)
Apel K-O, **5:** 2585 (2585); **7:** 3924 (3921, 3922, 3923)
Apfel N, **7:** 4301 (4299)
Aphek E, **6:** 3334 (3330)
Appel M H, **8:** 4957
Appelbaum M I, **1:** 362 (361); **7:** 3706 (3702)
Appelhans P, **5:** 2910 (2908)
Appell L S, **7:** 3807 (3806)
Apple M, **2:** 933; **4:** 1910 (1909, 1910), 2292; **7:** 4088 (4082); **8:** 4574 (4573); **9:** 5543 (5540); **10:** 6214 (6209); **11:** 6722 (6720)
Apple M W, **2:** 1072 (1067, 1068), 1074, 1203 (1199); **3:** 1300 (1288), 1315, 1337 (1334, 1335), 1347 (1346, 1347); **4:** 1852; **5:** 2589 (2587); **6:** 3621 (3618); **7:** 4246 (4242); **8:** 4586 (4582, 4583), 4848 (4846); **9:** 5180 (5180), 5298 (5295), 5327 (5326), 5523; **10:** 5606 (5600), 5613 (5608), 6096 (6094), 6139 (6133, 6136)
Applebee A N, **6:** 3208 (3208), 3209 (3208), 3483 (3481); **7:** 3725 (3724), 4050 (4047); **10:** 5961 (5959); **11:** 6777 (6776), 6780 (6779, 6780), 6784 (6784), 6785 (6783)
Applebee R, **6:** 3484 (3481)
Applegate J H, **3:** 1635 (1631, 1632)
Appleton I, **6:** 3377 (3374), 3378
Appleton S, **2:** 1160; **11:** 6740 (6739)
Apps J W, **1:** 127 (121), 151 (149); **5:** 2937 (2935); **7:** 4170 (4163, 4166); **8:** 4811 (4804, 4806), 4812; **11:** 6551
Apter S J, **1:** 490 (489)
Aquinas T St, **9:** 5124 (5121)
Arabie P, **9:** 5158 (5158), 5503 (5500)
Arabsheibani G, **9:** 5354 (5352)
Arai I, **3:** 1553 (1550)
Aramburo D, **2:** 718 (717)
Aranya N, **4:** 2218 (2216)
Arasteh J, **5:** 2571
Arboleda J, **3:** 1824 (1823); **8:** 4509 (4508)
Arbuthnott J, **7:** 4162 (4158)
Arcavi A, **11:** 6608 (6604)
Archambault R D, **8:** 4455 (4455)
Archbald D A, **7:** 3725 (3724)
Archer D, **2:** 640 (638), 906 (903)
Archer J, **2:** 866 (866); **4:** 2423 (2420)
Archer M, **1:** 332 (332); **2:** 932 (929), 957 (951), 1072 (1071); **6:** 3550; **11:** 6647 (6641)

Archer M S, **2:** 784 (782); **4:** 2257; **8:** 4601 (4596), 4602; **9:** 5168 (5160); **10:** 5606 (5599, 5602)
Archer P, **3:** 1624 (1622)
Arcus M, **4:** 2266 (2262), 2267 (2262)
Aregger K, **3:** 1355 (1349)
Arends R, **6:** 3202 (3198)
Arendt H, **1:** 437 (432)
Arensberg C M, **2:** 918
Arey W, **7:** (3843)
Arfwedson G, **4:** 2376 (2376)
Argles M, **9:** 5327 (5324)
Argumedo M, **3:** 1821 (1818)
Argyle M, **10:** 5977 (5975)
Argyris C, **4:** 2165 (2158); **6:** (3280), 3349 (3348)
Arias A Jr, **2:** 982 (978, 981)
Arias-Godinez B, **4:** 1910 (1906, 1910)
Aries P, **1:** 230 (227)
Ariès P, **5:** 2617 (2613)
Aries P, **8:** 4677
Ariotti P, **6:** 3219
Aristotle, **1:** (195); **2:** (776), (825); **3:** (1432); **4:** (2031); **6:** (3499); **7:** (3920), (3924); **8:** (4535), (4575), (4671), (4888), (4889), (4948), (4950); **9:** (5051), (5122), (5339), (5395); **11:** (6622)
Arivaratne A T, **8:** 4811 (4809)
Arlin M, **5:** 2664 (2662), 2869 (2868); **10:** 6031 (6029)
Armbruster B B, **1:** 193 (185); **2:** 969 (966); **8:** 4942 (4941); **10:** 6149 (6145); **11:** 6370 (6369)
Armenian H, **6:** 3356
Armento B J, **9:** 5563, 5577 (5577)
Armer M, **3:** 1655 (1650)
Armitage J, **8:** 4844 (4843)
Armitage S, **7:** 4336 (4332)
Armon C A, **6:** 3434 (3432), 3435; **8:** 4824
Armon-Thomas E, **11:** 6608
Armor D J, **3:** 1761 (1759); **9:** 5201 (5198)
Armstrong H E, **9:** (5325)
Armstrong N, **10:** 5713 (5710)
Armstrong P F, **4:** 2123 (2120, 2121); **10:** 6058 (6055)
Armstrong R, **7:** (3841)
Armstrong S C, **7:** (3841)
Armytage W H G, **8:** 4715 (4708)
Arneaud P, **4:** 2339
Arnheim R, **1:** (340)
Arnkoff D B, **11:** 6360 (6358, 6359)
Arnold A, **2:** 1048
Arnold C, **4:** 2432 (2428, 2431)
Arnold M, **2:** (776); **3:** (1294)
Arnold R, **5:** 2732 (2726); **11:** 6659 (6659)
Arnold V, **6:** 3334 (3330)
Arnot M, **4:** 2291, 2292 (2287); **7:** 3852 (3849, 3850); **10:** 5826 (5823), 5827; **11:** 6723
Arnott M, **9:** 5307 (5307)
Arnott R, **7:** 3820 (3816, 3818)
Arnove R, **2:** 932 (929); **4:** 1910 (1904, 1905); **8:** 4586, 4602, 4639; **9:** 5539
Arnove R F, **1:** 135 (131, 132), 175 (169); **2:** 640 (639); **4:** 1910; **5:** 2759; **8:** 4509; **9:** 5060, 5367 (5366)
Arnove R J, **6:** 3531
Arnove R S, **10:** 6139 (6139)
Arns F, **3:** 1253 (1249)
Aronoff S, **3:** 1829 (1829)
Aronowitz S, **3:** 1315; **4:** 2249 (2249); **6:** 3621 (3619); **10:** 6197 (6194)
Arons S, **9:** 5196 (5195)
Aronson E, **1:** 358; **2:** 1079, 1098 (1096), 1099 (1098); **5:** 2665, 3061; **8:** (4369); **9:** 5130; **10:** 5617, 5925 (5920), 6062 (6060); **11:** 6575 (6574)
Aronson L R, **1:** 15
Arosemena D, **7:** 4275
Arredondo D E, **6:** 3631 (3629, 3630)
Arriagada A M, **1:** 423; **3:** 1680 (1677); **4:** 2419; **6:** 3074; **7:** 4200 (4198), 4201 (4200); **9:** 5076; **11:** 6260 (6260)
Arriagazzi L, **9:** 5076 (5072, 5074)
Arrien J B, **2:** 640
Arrieta Gallastegui J, **1:** 48 (45)
Arrow K J, **3:** 1694 (1691), 1750 (1748); **4:** 2445 (2442, 2444); **5:** 2798 (2793); **6:** 3616 (3614); **9:** 5354 (5350, 5352); **11:** 6424 (6420)
Arruda N F C, **8:** 4751 (4745)
Arsenio W F, **7:** 4300 (4300)
Arter J A, **10:** 6173 (6169, 6170)
Arthur C J, **2:** 1073 (1067)
Arthur J, **1:** 88 (85)
Arthur J A, **5:** 2945 (2943, 2945)
Arthur W B, **11:** 6615
Artzt A F, **11:** 6608
Aruri F, **6:** 3113
Arvey R D, **8:** 4408 (4405)
Arvidson L, **7:** 4179 (4179); **10:** 5829
Arvizu S F, **1:** 535; **7:** 3973 (3972)
Arwady J, **5:** 2897 (2896)
Ary D, **9:** 5490 (5488)
Aryal C N, **7:** 4067
Asante M K, **7:** 3977 (3976)
Ascham R, **5:** (2608)
Ascher W, **8:** 4787 (4787)
Asendorpf J B, **7:** 3919 (3919); **9:** 5528 (5525, 5526)
Asensio M, **9:** 5562 (5560, 5561)
Ashby E, **10:** 6164 (6162)
Ashcraft M H, **2:** 851 (849)
Ashcroft B, **2:** 1193 (1192)
Ashcroft L, **4:** 1984 (1980); **5:** 2856 (2854); **6:** 3434 (3430)
Ashdown R, **11:** 6461
Ashe J, **4:** 1990 (1989)
Ashe K, **9:** 5008 (5006)
Asheim I, **6:** 3531
Ashenden D, **3:** 1739 (1738)
Ashenden D J, **3:** 1347 (1346); **4:** 2249 (2248), 2272 (2269, 2270, 2271); **9:** 5060 (5057, 5058), 5312 (5311); **10:** 5606 (5603), 5613 (5608), 5758 (5758)
Ashenfelter O A, **3:** 1750; **4:** 2445; **5:** 2942; **6:** 3106; **7:** 4200 (4199); **9:** 5355, 5385
Asher J W, **5:** 2732 (2730)
Asher S J, **9:** 5528 (5527)
Asher S R, **8:** 4368 (4365); **9:** 5567 (5566); **10:** 5758
Asher W, **8:** 4787 (4783)
Asher W J, **5:** 2495 (2493)
Ashfar H, **4:** 2432
Ashford M, **8:** 4736 (4734)
Ashizawa K, **8:** 4473 (4470)
Ashley J, **1:** 494 (491)
Ashman A F, **8:** 4376
Ashraf S A, **9:** 5008 (4998, 5001)
Ashton D, **10:** 6099 (6098)
Ashton D N, **3:** 1739 (1737)
Ashton P, **8:** 4873 (4872); **9:** 5056; **10:** 6012 (6011), 6214 (6208, 6211, 6214)
Ashton P T, **10:** 5965, 6047
Ashworth J, **9:** 5196 (5194)
Ashworth R, **2:** 982 (981)
Asiamah F, **5:** 2486
Askew J, **9:** 5334 (5333)
Askew J M, **3:** 1768 (1765); **9:** 5497 (5496); **11:** 6334 (6332)
Aslanian C B, **7:** 4329 (4326)
Aslin R N, **5:** 2802 (2801); **8:** 4383 (4381)
Asmus W, **3:** 1300 (1290)
Asok C, **9:** 5142
Asoko H M, **8:** 4479 (4477), 4652
Aspinwall L C, **5:** 2768 (2763)
Asplund R, **7:** 4255
Asplund-Carlsson M, **8:** 4429 (4426)
Asquith P D, **8:** 4464
Assefa A M, **2:** 900
Assié N T, **11:** 6740 (6737, 6739), 6741
Assié-Lumumba N T, **11:** 6740 (6736, 6738), 6741
Assor A, **5:** 2589 (2588)
Assouan U, **2:** (1159)
Astin A W, **2:** 834 (832); **10:** 5782
Astin H S, **10:** 5782; **11:** 6712 (6711)
Astington J W, **8:** 4956 (4952); **9:** 5512
Astleitner H, **9:** 5216 (5213, 5215)
Aston M H, **10:** 5621
Astuto T A, **4:** 2165 (2165); **5:** 2847 (2840); **6:** 3284 (3277); **8:** 4594 (4587); **9:** 5281 (5276)
Athanassopulous M, **4:** 1980 (1978)
Atistole, **11:** (6742)
Atkin J, **9:** 5215 (5214)
Atkin R, **2:** 991 (990)
Atkins E, **3:** 1354 (1352)
Atkinson A B, **9:** 5355
Atkinson C, **1:** 296 (292)
Atkinson E P, **9:** 5338 (5336)
Atkinson J, **10:** 6223 (6222)
Atkinson J W, **3:** 1240 (1236, 1237, 1238); **7:** 3942 (3937, 3939, 3940)
Atkinson N, **11:** 6821
Atkinson P, **1:** 295 (283); **4:** 2052 (2047, 2048); **7:** 4319 (4316); **9:** 5312 (5310, 5311); **10:** 6085 (6085), 6197; **11:** 6465 (6463)
Atkinson P A, **10:** 6085 (6085)
Atkinson R, **9:** 5544
Atkinson R C, **1:** 52; **2:** 1011 (1008); **5:** 2714 (2709); **7:** 4006; **8:** 4727
Attard P, **4:** 1898 (1896); **6:** 3593
Atterbury B W, **7:** 4025 (4022, 4023)

Attermeir S M, **5:** 2813 (2810)
Attwood L, **4:** 2412 (2410)
Atutov P R, **3:** 1690 (1686, 1687, 1689)
Atwood V A, **9:** 5577
Au K H, **1:** 294 (293); **2:** 802 (800), 866 (865); **4:** 2052 (2049, 2050); **6:** (3451); **8:** 4881 (4878); **9:** 5313, 5363 (5362); **10:** 5795 (5792)
Au W K, **6:** 3512 (3511)
Aubert V, **6:** 3196 (3192)
Aubrecht J D, **10:** 6234 (6233)
Aubrey C, **10:** 5972
Aubrey R F, **9:** 5290 (5283)
Audet L, **8:** 4509
Auraham R, **3:** 1610
Aussiker A, **2:** 820 (817); **10:** 6031 (6030)
Auster L, **10:** 5886 (5884)
Auster R, **4:** 2212 (2209)
Austin A G, **11:** 6735 (6733)
Austin B, **6:** 3096 (3094)
Austin G A, **4:** 2281 (2280); **10:** 6202 (6199)
Austin G R, **4:** 2452 (2450)
Austin J L, **8:** 4446 (4442, 4444)
Ausubel D P, **1:** (3); **2:** 968 (965), 1031 (1027); **3:** 1544; **6:** 3416 (3409, 3415); **8:** 4652 (4648), 4702 (4698); **9:** (5326); **10:** 6015 (6014)
Avakov R, **8:** 4491
Avalos B, **2:** 933 (930); **8:** 4526 (4525)
Averch H S, **8:** 4568 (4563); **10:** 5590 (5590)
Averill M, **5:** 3050 (3045, 3049)
Averitt R, **6:** 3189 (3187)
Avi-Itzhak T E, **6:** 3283 (3283)
Avinashillingham T S C, **5:** 2971 (2967)
Avis G, **4:** 2412; **10:** 5650
Avis J, **9:** 5512 (5512)
Avoseh O, **10:** 6106 (6104)
Avraham Y, **4:** 1980 (1978, 1979)
Awuwoloye E O, **9:** 5389 (5388)
Axtell R E, **7:** 4175
Ayala F J, **4:** 2172 (2168)
Ayalon H, **7:** 3852 (3849); **9:** 5367 (5365); **11:** 6265 (6262)
Ayer A J, **3:** 1464; **8:** 4446 (4442), (4450), 4634 (4633)
Ayers D, **7:** 3935 (3931)
Ayers T, **8:** 4779 (4776, 4778)
Ayers W C, **3:** 1325 (1325), 1337 (1336); **10:** 5818 (5816)
Ayles R, **5:** 2491 (2489), 2495 (2493)
Ayoub M A, **4:** 2011 (2011)
Ayres I, **4:** 2445 (2444)
Ayres L, **9:** 5175 (5170)
Ayres L P, **4:** 1871 (1868)
Ayres R, **2:** 942
Ayres R L, **8:** 4601 (4599)
Azariadis C, **3:** 1703 (1697)
Azhar R A, **1:** 254 (246)
Aziz-zadeh H, **5:** 3011
Azuma H, **2:** 842; **4:** 1898 (1896), 2140 (2138), 2199, 2412 (2411); **5:** 2627 (2625), 2656; **6:** 3312 (3310); **9:** 5216 (5213); **10:** 5591 (5590)
Azzam M, **10:** 5895
Azzaretto J F, **2:** 665 (662)

Baas S M, **5:** 2462 (2460)
Bååth J A, **7:** 4220 (4218)
Babad E Y, **10:** 5762 (5761); **11:** 6511 (6509)
Baca L M, **6:** 3232
Bacchus K, **1:** 244; **3:** 1343, 1739 (1737)
Bach R, **6:** 3189 (3188)
Bacharach S B, **1:** 437 (435); **4:** 2165 (2163); **7:** 3826 (3823); **8:** 4408; **9:** 5180 (5176), 5210 (5207), 5308; **10:** 6062
Bachelard G, **9:** (5056)
Bachelor P, **2:** 1182 (1179, 1180)
Bachman J G, **11:** 6797 (6795)
Bachman L, **4:** 2363 (2361, 2362)
Bachtiar H, **10:** 5782 (5779)
Backus J M, **10:** 6004
Bacon F, **2:** (804), (883); **3:** (1540); **8:** (4535)
Baczewski P, **4:** 1957 (1955)
Badawood A S, **9:** 5151 (5146)
Baddeley A D, **1:** 330 (329), 376 (375); **6:** 3324 (3317); **8:** 4951
Badgio P, **8:** 4956 (4956)
Badiane F, **1:** 221 (218)
Badinter, **8:** 4676 (4675)
Badri B, **3:** 1623 (1622)
Badri G, **7:** 4296 (4294)
Baduel P R, **7:** 3691
Baecher R, **6:** 3232
Baeck L, **8:** 4676 (4672)
Baer D M, **1:** 497 (495)
Baer K E von, **10:** (5706)
Baethge M, **1:** 317 (311); **11:** 6647 (6647)
Baghurst P A, **5:** 2571 (2569)
Baglivo J, **2:** 1084 (1081)
Bagozzi R P, **1:** 389 (381); **7:** 4006 (4005, 4006)
Bagunywa A, **8:** 4586 (4583)
Bahr K, **7:** 4282
Baier A, **4:** 2296 (2296)
Baier H, **10:** 5686 (5684)
Bailar B A, **9:** 5372 (5370)
Bailey A J, **1:** 72 (70)
Bailey C, **11:** 6704
Bailey D B, **1:** 362 (360, 361)
Bailey D B Jr, **5:** 2814 (2808)
Bailey F G, **7:** 3826 (3822)
Bailey G D, **4:** 1924
Bailey K, **5:** 2813 (2808)
Bailey K D, **9:** 5050
Bailey M, **7:** 4007 (4003), 4255; **10:** 6234 (6230)
Bailey M N, **3:** 1703 (1697)
Bailey P, **6:** 3459 (3457, 3458)
Bailey S, **5:** 2732
Bailey T, **8:** 4638 (4636); **11:** 6415
Bailin S, **2:** 1207 (1206), 1208; **8:** 4447
Baillaud J, **10:** (5681)
Bailyn B, **5:** (2603), 2607, 2617 (2609, 2611, 2613, 2616)
Bain A, **4:** 1871 (1865)
Bain B, **4:** 1851 (1850, 1851)
Bainbridge L, **6:** 3434 (3433)
Bainton R H, **6:** 3531
Baird B F, **3:** 1425
Baird J R, **6:** 3205; **8:** 4652 (4652); **9:** 5327 (5326), 5338 (5337, 5338)
Bajbi A S, **1:** 244 (241)
Bakeman R, **4:** 2452 (2451)
Baker A C, **4:** 1848; **7:** 3726
Baker C, **5:** 2457 (2454)
Baker C D, **2:** 1198 (1196); **9:** 5302 (5300, 5301); **10:** 6117 (6113)
Baker D, **5:** 2628 (2626)
Baker D A, **6:** 3458 (3458)
Baker D N, **5:** 2607
Baker D P, **4:** 2249 (2248)
Baker E, **3:** 1283 (1280); **6:** 3204 (3202, 3203)
Baker E L, **1:** 370 (370), 374 (371, 372, 373); **3:** 1266 (1264); **4:** 1848 (1847); **6:** 3416 (3411); **7:** 3725 (3724), 3726 (3724, 3725), 4016 (4011); **8:** 4623 (4619, 4622); **10:** 5887, 6035 (6032); **11:** 6320 (6315), 6349 (6343)
Baker E T, **2:** 1139; **5:** 2910 (2908); **9:** 5071 (5068)
Baker F B, **2:** 998 (992); **5:** 2784, 3043 (3038); **6:** 3507 (3507)
Baker I, **5:** (2888)
Baker J, **4:** 2351 (2349)
Baker L, **2:** 969 (966), 1198 (1195); **8:** 4408 (4404), 4942 (4941); **10:** 5795 (5792)
Baker L A, **5:** 2465 (2464)
Baker R, **3:** 1635 (1632)
Baker R J, **7:** 4015 (4015)
Baker V J, **1:** 244
Baker-Ward L, **7:** 3768 (3764)
Bakhtin M M, **3:** (1250)
Bakke E W, **8:** 4839
Bakker B F M, **8:** 4830 (4827); **9:** 5553; **10:** 5606 (5600)
Bakvis H, **5:** 2512
Balacheff N, **1:** 347 (346)
Balassa B, **3:** 1789; **11:** 6638 (6634, 6637)
Balay E E, **3:** 1567 (1565)
Baldé M, **1:** 157 (156)
Balderston J, **3:** 1793
Balding J, **10:** 5713 (5710)
Baldwin A L, **3:** 1240 (1236)
Baldwin A Y, **5:** 2491 (2486)
Baldwin E E, **2:** 1203 (1199)
Baldwin J M, **1:** (377)
Baldwin R S, **2:** 803; **6:** 3209 (3207)
Baldwin S, **2:** 1094; **3:** 1610 (1610)
Baldwin T T, **3:** 1490 (1490)
Bale J, **3:** 1501; **5:** 2470
Bales R, **5:** 2529 (2524)
Bales R F, **2:** 1074 (1065)
Bales S, **1:** 199 (198)
Balestri D, **2:** 973
Balibar R, **3:** 1347 (1345)
Balicki C, **11:** 6265 (6263)
Balke G, **6:** 3602 (3598)
Balke-Aurell G, **5:** 2767 (2761, 2762), 2768 (2761)
Ball C J, **9:** 5180 (5178)
Ball D L, **3:** 1257 (1256); **9:** 5363 (5360); **10:** 6121 (6118), 6239 (6238)
Ball R J, **8:** 4359 (4357)

Ball S, **3:** 1784 (1782); **4:** 2165 (2160), 2423 (2422); **6:** 3496 (3494, 3495); **8:** 4642 (4642); **9:** 5312 (5311); **10:** 5829, 6139 (6132); **11:** 6511 (6508), 6563 (6559, 6560, 6561, 6562)
Ball S E, **5:** 2903 (2898)
Ball S J, **1:** 11 (8, 9), 594 (592); **3:** 1307 (1307); **4:** 2165 (2159); **5:** 2509; **6:** 3496; **7:** 3826 (3822, 3823, 3825), 4180, 4246 (4244), 4319 (4317, 4318, 4319); **8:** 4616; **9:** 5065 (5061), 5180 (5179); **10:** 6139 (6137, 6138); **11:** 6557 (6556)
Balla J R, **4:** 2241 (2238); **7:** 4006 (4002); **8:** 4359 (4357)
Ballard C L, **4:** 2315 (2311, 2312)
Ballard K D, **2:** 729 (728); **6:** 3559 (3558)
Ballard M, **9:** 5577
Ballarin A A, **1:** 82 (79, 80)
Ballauf T, **8:** 4419 (4419)
Ballentine J H, **10:** 5606 (5601)
Baller W, **7:** 3830 (3829)
Ballion R, **9:** 5196 (5194)
Ballou G M, **1:** 400
Ball-Rokeach S, **9:** 5518 (5514)
Ballstaedt S-P, **2:** 968 (967)
Balogh T, **8:** 4839 (4838)
Baloğlu Z, **11:** 6481 (6476)
Balota D A, **8:** 4939
Baltes M M, **6:** 3427 (3427); **8:** 4824
Baltes P B, **1:** 239, 362; **2:** 846; **3:** 1513 (1512), 1647 (1646); **4:** 1877, 2261; **5:** 2664 (2660), 2665, 2676 (2673, 2674, 2675, 2676), 2677 (2675), 2768, 2916 (2915); **6:** 3288, 3427 (3426, 3427), 3428 (3427), 3435 (3432), 3523 (3513, 3514, 3519, 3522); **7:** 3763 (3762, 3763); **8:** 4719 (4716), 4823 (4817, 4819), 4824; **9:** 5518 (5517), 5528; **11:** 6394 (6391)
Baltzell D, **1:** 82 (80)
Bamberger P, **4:** 2165 (2163)
Banathy B H, **4:** 1917 (1914); **5:** 2861 (2858), 2867 (2862, 2863, 2866); **8:** 4758 (4754, 4755); **10:** 5900 (5900)
Bandura A, **1:** 88 (85, 86), 203 (200), 234 (231, 233), 376 (376), 497 (495), 570; **4:** 1847 (1842, 1846), 1980 (1979), 2449 (2446); **6:** 3345; **7:** 3942 (3939, 3942), 3946 (3943); **8:** 4394 (4390, 4393); **9:** 5518 (5513, 5514, 5515, 5516, 5517), 5528 (5524); **10:** 5977 (5974), 6223 (6222); **11:** 6360 (6358)
Banerjee S, **5:** 2758 (2757)
Banfield J, **7:** 3889 (3888)
Bangert W V, **9:** 5121
Bangert-Drowns R L, **1:** 230 (228); **5:** 2779 (2777); **6:** 3631 (3625, 3630); **7:** 4104 (4101); **9:** 5043 (5042); **10:** 5673 (5671); **11:** 6339 (6336)
Bank A, **4:** 2388 (2382), 2389; **6:** 3597
Bank B J, **10:** 5758 (5756), 6132 (6130); **11:** 6797 (6796, 6797)
Bank L, **1:** 234 (233)
Banker R D, **3:** 1386 (1384)
Bank-Mikkelsen N E, **3:** 1507 (1435, 1505); **10:** (5662)
Banks D, **9:** 5350 (5348)
Banks D K, **10:** 5862 (5855)
Banks J, **1:** 294 (294)
Banks J A, **7:** 3970 (3960, 3961), 3977 (3974, 3975); **10:** 5585
Banks O, **3:** 1347 (1344); **10:** 5606 (5598, 5599)
Banks P D, **11:** 6461 (6459)
Bannister D, **9:** 5016 (5016)
Bantock G H, **3:** 1328 (1326); **6:** 3389 (3387)
Bany M A, **1:** 486 (483)
Baptiste H P, **6:** 3284
Baptiste H P Jr, **5:** 2509
Barakett J M, **10:** 5762 (5761)
Baranes R, **6:** 3453 (3450)
Barash D P, **3:** 1733
Baratz J, **6:** 3215 (3214)
Barba R, **8:** 4881 (4878)
Barbalet M, **11:** 6735 (6734)
Barber L, **10:** 6086
Barber M, **10:** 6079
Barber N S J, **5:** 3020
Barber P J, **1:** 376 (375)
Barbera-Stein L, **9:** 5441 (5436, 5437)
Barbre J W, **5:** 2457 (2456)
Barbuto D M, **6:** 3401 (3401)
Bardon J I, **9:** 5290 (5286)
Bareet A, **2:** 1175 (1173, 1174)
Bareither D, **4:** 2229
Barents A M C, **2:** 1139 (1136)
Bargh J, **4:** 2257 (2253); **7:** 3872 (3869), 3873 (3870)
Barham I H, **10:** 5704 (5699, 5700); **11:** 6784 (6784)
Barham J, **6:** 3638 (3635)
Barkan J, **10:** 5782
Barkan M, **1:** 198 (196), 343 (341); **11:** 6621 (6619)
Barker B, **9:** 5065 (5064)
Barker B O, **1:** 244 (240)
Barker F, **8:** 4634
Barker J, **7:** 3995 (3991, 3995)
Barker L L, **7:** 3935 (3934)
Barker P, **2:** 1011 (1008)
Barker R, **10:** 6207 (6205)
Barker R G, **1:** 230 (229); **9:** 5294 (5293)
Barker-Lunn J C, **2:** 824 (823)
Barkman B, **8:** 4940
Barlow D, **10:** 5713 (5712)
Barlow D H, **4:** 2194 (2192); **8:** 4661 (4661); **9:** 5489 (5486)
Barlow G, **1:** 570 (568)
Barlow G W, **4:** 2172 (2167)
Barlow M L, **11:** 6684
Barnard C I, **7:** 4246 (4243); **9:** 5168 (5161)
Barnard H, **5:** (2610); **6:** (3280)
Barnard J, **7:** (3843)
Barnard M M, **3:** 1548 (1545)
Barndt D, **2:** 1049; **7:** 4336 (4331, 4332)
Barnes D, **2:** 802 (800), 1098 (1095); **5:** 2536 (2533); **6:** 3209 (3206), 3311 (3308), 3416 (3412), 3442 (3440), 3458 (3456), 3638 (3635); **10:** 5961 (5959)
Barnes D L, **7:** 4293 (4291)
Barnes G T, **3:** 1449
Barnes J A, **9:** 5559 (5554, 5555)
Barnes K E, **3:** 1623 (1621)
Barnes V, **7:** 4124
Barnes W, **8:** 4936 (4932)
Barnes W S, **6:** 3453 (3448, 3449, 3451), 3480
Barnett B G, **1:** 72 (72)
Barnett J E, **10:** 5831 (5830)
Barnett L A, **8:** 4541 (4540)
Barnett M A, **8:** 4939 (4937)
Barnett S W, **7:** 3820 (3816)
Barnett V, **9:** 5081 (5077)
Barnett W S, **2:** 687 (679, 680), 1131 (1130); **3:** 1628 (1625), 1641 (1640); **4:** 2145 (2142); **5:** 2806 (2804); **8:** 4666 (4664, 4666); **11:** 6384 (6382)
Barnett-Mizhari C, **6:** 3227
Barney J, **4:** 1972 (1969, 1971)
Barnitz J G, **8:** 4939 (4937)
Barnouw V, **3:** 1252 (1247)
Barnow B S, **2:** 1093 (1090); **4:** 2150 (2147); **7:** 4200 (4197, 4199); **9:** 5372 (5368), 5385 (5382)
Barnsley G, **7:** 3936 (3933); **10:** 5673 (5673)
Barnum H N, **5:** 2945 (2944)
Barnwell D, **4:** 2363 (2360)
Barocas R, **1:** 362; **3:** 1643 (1637, 1641)
Bar-On E, **9:** 5341 (5340)
Baron G, **4:** 2166; **5:** 2954 (2952, 2954); **9:** 5168 (5162)
Baron J, **2:** 1207; **5:** 2767 (2762); **6:** 3324 (3317, 3319); **7:** 3768 (3766); **8:** 4956 (4956)
Baron J B, **1:** 193 (191); **2:** 1208; **7:** 3726 (3724); **8:** 4951
Baron J N, **4:** 2445 (2442)
Baron N, **9:** 5416 (5415)
Baron R, **10:** 6112 (6108)
Baron R M, **4:** 1877 (1874)
Baron S, **9:** 5060 (5058)
Barone T E, **3:** 1320 (1317)
Baroody A J, **6:** 3670 (3669); **11:** 6608 (6605)
Barr A, **10:** 6207 (6203)
Barr B, **1:** 594 (591)
Barr C, **3:** 1830 (1829)
Barr M J, **10:** 5805
Barr N, **10:** 5767 (5764, 5765, 5766)
Barr R, **1:** 11 (7, 8), 520 (516); **2:** 824 (821, 822, 823, 824); **4:** 1938 (1935), 1972 (1971); **5:** 2595 (2593), 2869 (2868, 2869); **7:** 3886 (3883); **8:** 4935, 4936; **9:** 5065 (5064), 5175 (5170), 5176; **10:** 5745, 5961, 6192
Barra M, **6:** 3652
Barra R, **2:** 1093 (1093)
Barraga N, **11:** 6628 (6627)
Barrass R, **6:** (3410)
Barrell G R, **6:** 3360; **9:** 5255
Barrera A, **4:** 2418 (2414)
Barrett B, **10:** 6168 (6166)
Barrett C, **8:** 4796 (4793)
Barrett D B, **9:** 5008 (4996)
Barrett E M, **7:** 4170 (4166)
Barrett I, **1:** 27

Barrett K C, **4:** 1966 (1964)
Barrett M, **4:** 2291 (2289); **6:** 3621 (3620)
Barrett M J, **4:** 2331
Barrette G T, **10:** 5713 (5708), 5713
Barrig M, **3:** 1671 (1667, 1668, 1670, 1671)
Barrington J, **3:** 1343
Barrington J M, **7:** 4111
Barro S, **2:** 711 (709)
Barro S M, **9:** 5065 (5061); **10:** 5846 (5843)
Barrón B, **5:** 2890 (2887)
Barron F, **2:** 1177 (1176)
Barron J M, **2:** 1093 (1089); **6:** 3616 (3615)
Barron J N, **4:** 2432 (2429)
Barros R F, **8:** 4751 (4745)
Barrough M N, **5:** 2799
Barrow C, **4:** 1990 (1987)
Barrow M, **3:** 1386 (1384)
Barrow P, **4:** 1990 (1987)
Barrow R, **2:** 1207 (1206); **3:** 1328 (1326, 1327), 1367 (1363); **7:** 3970 (3961); **8:** 4446 (4445, 4446), 4447; **10:** 5985 (5985)
Barrows H S, **6:** 3349 (3346)
Barry B, **4:** 2036 (2034)
Barshis D, **6:** 3631 (3630)
Bar-Simon-Tov R, **2:** 892 (890)
Barson J, **5:** 2861 (2857, 2858)
Bart W, **3:** 1513 (1510)
Barta B, **2:** 973 (970)
Bar-Tal D, **8:** 4799 (4797); **10:** 6224
Bartels J, **3:** 1567 (1565); **7:** 4220 (4218)
Barth E, **2:** 1207 (1207)
Barth H, **8:** 4419
Barth J, **2:** 770 (768)
Barth R, **10:** 6082 (6082)
Barth R P, **7:** 4081 (4079)
Barth R S, **7:** 4214 (4212)
Barthes R, **9:** 5416 (5414)
Bartholomai F, **3:** 1647 (1643)
Bartholomäi F, **4:** 1871 (1865)
Bartholomew D H, **7:** 3858 (3856)
Bartholomew D J, **5:** 2677 (2675)
Bartlett B, **1:** 400
Bartlett F, **5:** (2878)
Bartlett F C, **2:** 968 (964); **6:** 3155 (3152), 3324 (3316)
Bartlett J, **1:** 400
Bartlett M S, **2:** 631 (626, 627); **3:** 1548 (1545, 1548); **7:** 4015 (4008)
Bartlett R J, **2:** 792 (786)
Bartlett S, **6:** 3144 (3138, 3139, 3143); **10:** 5735 (5732)
Bartol C R, **3:** 1618 (1612)
Bartoli J, **7:** 4081
Barton D, **6:** 3458 (3455, 3456, 3458); **7:** 3711
Barton L, **2:** 729 (727); **3:** 1507, 1508; **4:** 1984, 2291 (2290), 2292; **6:** 3559; **10:** 5668 (5664, 5665), 6139, 6215; **11:** 6461 (6458)
Barton R F, **9:** 5475 (5472)
Barwood B, **7:** 4170 (4168)
Bascia N, **10:** 5613, 5934, 5935
Basedow J B, **3:** (1721), (1724)
Bash L, **5:** 2509; **7:** 4025 (4023); **11:** 6558
Basham R B, **4:** 1979 (1976)
Bashi J, **4:** 1934 (1929, 1931, 1933)
Basia N, **10:** 6214
Basil C, **1:** 408 (404)
Basilevsky A, **7:** 3861 (3858)
Basinger K S, **7:** 3920 (3917); **9:** 5076 (5072, 5074)
Baskett H K, **1:** 127 (124)
Bass B M, **6:** 3284 (3277, 3280)
Basset C A, **2:** 922 (918)
Bassett G W, **10:** 6227 (6226)
Bassett S, **7:** 4293 (4290, 4291, 4292)
Bassey M, **8:** 4562 (4558)
Bassi L, **7:** 4200 (4199)
Basso K H, **6:** 3452 (3446)
Basso R, **7:** 4224 (4224)
Bassok M, **2:** 838 (835); **5:** 2768 (2765); **6:** 3325 (3317); **7:** 3886 (3881); **10:** 6159 (6158)
Bastani J, **2:** 906
Bastardo P J, **4:** 1996
Bastian H G, **7:** 4025 (4023), 4030
Bastiani J, **9:** 5215 (5214)
Basu A, **10:** 5782 (5776)
Bataille L, **1:** 176; **5:** 2960 (2958); **11:** 6507
Bateman W, **11:** 6424
Bates A W, **1:** 404 (400); **3:** 1563 (1561), 1573 (1570), 1579 (1575, 1577); **4:** 1903 (1899); **5:** 2891
Bates E, **6:** 3223 (3221); **9:** 5508
Bates G C, **9:** 5338 (5335)
Bates I, **3:** 1739
Bates J E, **1:** 234 (232); **11:** 6310, 6311
Bates R J, **1:** 60 (55), 67 (61); **2:** 1203 (1199); **3:** 1774 (1772, 1773); **4:** 2165 (2162); **6:** 3284 (3280, 3282), 3528; **9:** 5030 (5024); **10:** 5606 (5599)
Bates T W, **7:** 3759 (3758)
Bateson G, **3:** 1252 (1247); **8:** 4541 (4538)
Bateson P P G, **3:** 1520 (1517)
Báthory Z, **5:** 2705 (2704), 2706
Batsche G M, **9:** 5290 (5286, 5287)
Batten H D, **10:** 5977 (5973)
Batterman N, **5:** 2916 (2913)
Battestini S, **2:** (1153)
Battista M T, **6:** 3685; **7:** 4099 (4098)
Battistich V, **8:** 4799 (4798); **10:** 6053 (6053)
Battistoni L, **5:** 3036
Bauch J P, **9:** 5268 (5265)
Baudonniere P M, **8:** 4542 (4541)
Baudrillard J, **4:** 2033 (2030)
Bauer H F, **3:** 1355 (1352)
Bauer K-O, **5:** 2480
Bauer S, **4:** 2165 (2163)
Bauer W D, **11:** 6712 (6711)
Bauernfeind R, **11:** 6511 (6508)
Bauersfeld H, **2:** 1051 (1051); **8:** 4652 (4649)
Baugh W H, **10:** 6072 (6069)
Baulac, **7:** 4099 (4097)
Baum D J, **1:** 162 (160)
Baum F E, **11:** 6437 (6433)
Baum W K, **7:** 4224, 4225
Bauman R, **6:** 3452
Bauman Z, **5:** 2586
Baumann J F, **2:** 866 (862), 867 (862); **3:** 1529 (1525)
Baumbach D J, **3:** 1398 (1397)
Baumgart M, **8:** 4816
Baumgart N, **8:** 4622 (4617, 4618, 4619, 4620, 4621)
Baumrind D, **1:** 234 (232); **2:** 705 (702); **3:** 1641 (1639); **5:** 2627 (2625)
Bauwens J, **10:** 6244 (6241)
Bawden C R, **7:** 3906
Baxter G P, **8:** 4730 (4730)
Baxter M B, **7:** 4215 (4212, 4213)
Bay E G, **11:** 6741
Baydar N, **3:** 1641 (1637, 1638, 1639)
Bayer A, **10:** 5782
Bayer A E, **11:** 6712 (6711)
Bayer E, **2:** 1121 (1119)
Bayes T, **1:** (475)
Bayles K, **1:** 234 (232)
Bayley N, **2:** 792 (787); **5:** 2812 (2812); **7:** 3706 (3702)
Bayman P, **2:** 984 (983, 984)
Bazerman C, **6:** 3219 (3217, 3218)
Beach R W, **2:** 1198; **10:** 5745 (5742), 5831 (5830); **11:** 6781
Beady C H, **4:** 1934 (1929, 1930, 1932); **9:** 5210 (5207)
Beales A C F, **9:** 5206 (5202)
Beals A R, **3:** 1729
Bean F, **8:** 4901 (4898)
Bean R, **3:** 1359 (1358)
Bean T W, **3:** 1529 (1526); **6:** 3209 (3207)
Beane J, **2:** 770 (769)
Beare H, **5:** 2508 (2504); **6:** 3496 (3494); **7:** 3840 (3837, 3839); **9:** 5281
Beaton A E, **1:** 41 (37); **5:** 3061 (3058); **6:** 3523 (3516, 3521); **7:** 3861 (3861), 3935 (3932); **8:** 4912, 4930 (4926)
Beaton A L, **4:** 2024 (2022)
Beattie J R, **10:** 5834 (5832)
Beattie N, **2:** 913 (912); **9:** 5215 (5213); **10:** 5658
Beatty P T, **8:** 4811 (4808)
Beatty R W, **4:** 2131 (2128)
Beaty E, **8:** 4429 (4425, 4429); **9:** 5411 (5408)
Beauchamp D G, **11:** 6624, 6625
Beauchamp E, **9:** 5281
Beauchamp G A, **3:** 1266 (1264), 1354 (1348)
Beauchamp L, **10:** 5995 (5994)
Beauclair P L de, **3:** (1721)
Beaumont M, **8:** 4694
Beazley K, **6:** 3459 (3456)
Beazly R M, **2:** 977 (974)
Beberman M, **4:** 2096 (2090)
Bechinger D, **1:** 553 (552)
Beck C, **8:** 4447, 4455 (4455)
Beck C M, **10:** 5804; **11:** 6580
Beck I L, **8:** 4945 (4943); **9:** 5562 (5560), 5563
Beck J A, **1:** 157 (156)
Beck R C, **7:** 3946

Beck R H, **1:** 295 (284); **3:** 1236 (1236); **7:** 3848 (3846, 3847)
Beck S J, **8:** 4791 (4788)
Becker B J, **4:** 2435 (2434); **11:** 6339 (6336)
Becker F D, **9:** 5358 (5357)
Becker G, **1:** 560 (554); **2:** 1072 (1066), 1074, 1117 (1110); **4:** 1975 (1973), 2418 (2413); **6:** 3106 (3101); **7:** 4200 (4198); **8:** 4364 (4361); **11:** 6430 (6427), 6653 (6652)
Becker G S, **1:** 111, 520 (517); **2:** 1055 (1052, 1053, 1054), 1131 (1128); **3:** 1659 (1657, 1659), 1660 (1657), 1665 (1662); **4:** 2445 (2442); **5:** 2646 (2643), 2744 (2740, 2741); **6:** 3143 (3140, 3142), 3616 (3614, 3615); **7:** 4211 (4207, 4208, 4209); **8:** 4901 (4897, 4899); **9:** 5240 (5234); **11:** 6424 (6420, 6421, 6422)
Becker H, **1:** 139 (137); **3:** (1796); **9:** 5411 (5409, 5410)
Becker H J, **2:** 984 (983), 1006 (1002, 1004), 1175 (1171); **3:** 1354 (1353); **7:** 4099 (4095, 4096); **9:** 5264 (5260); **11:** 6287 (6284, 6285, 6287)
Becker H S, **1:** 193 (190); **10:** 5613 (5611), 6126 (6123)
Becker J, **8:** 4383; **9:** 5175 (5170); **10:** 5826 (5824, 5825)
Becker J P, **6:** 3667 (3665)
Becker J V, **1:** 19 (18)
Becker M J, **7:** 3743 (3739, 3740)
Becker P, **5:** 2692 (2690)
Becker R M, **3:** 1529 (1527)
Becker W C, **1:** 486 (485); **3:** 1529 (1527); **10:** 6163 (6163)
Becker W E, **7:** 3820 (3816, 3817, 3818)
Becker-Cantarino B, **11:** 6747 (6744)
Beckerman T M, **5:** 2870 (2869)
Beckman J, **1:** 203
Beckmann J, **9:** 5403 (5402)
Beckmann P, **9:** 5416 (5415, 5416)
Beckoff M, **5:** 2684 (2684)
Bédard R, **3:** 1602
Beder H, **10:** 6058 (6056)
Bednar A K, **5:** 2874 (2871)
Bedrick D, **2:** 1139 (1136)
Bee J, **9:** 5358 (5357)
Beeby C E, **8:** 4766 (4759)
Beech J R, **1:** 376 (376); **5:** 2916
Beecher C, **11:** (6721)
Beecher M D, **4:** 2172 (2167)
Beeckman I, **3:** (1461)
Beeman W O, **5:** 2708 (2708)
Beens F, **4:** 2266 (2264)
Beentjes J W J, **1:** 570 (568)
Beer S, **10:** 5900 (5895)
Beers C D, **3:** 1809 (1808)
Beers J W, **10:** 5704 (5702), 5705
Beery R G, **1:** 32
Begab M, **7:** 3830
Begab M J, **7:** 3830
Begle E G, **4:** 2096 (2090)
Begley J, **5:** 2509 (2508)
Begley P T, **6:** 3284 (3282); **9:** 5264 (5262)
Behn R, **6:** 3608 (3603)
Behne K E, **7:** 4025 (4023)
Behr A L, **10:** 5635
Behr M, **3:** 1434; **6:** 3684 (3676), 3685 (3675)
Behrman J R, **3:** 1788 (1786); **4:** 2212 (2210), 2278 (2275, 2277, 2278), 2418 (2413); **6:** 3143 (3138, 3140, 3141, 3143), 3144 (3138, 3139, 3141, 3142, 3143); **9:** 5385
Behrmann M M, **7:** 3807; **11:** 6384 (6379)
Behymer C E, **11:** 6712 (6711)
Beicht U, **11:** 6420 (6418)
Beijderwellen W, **3:** 1579 (1577)
Beil D, **7:** 3807 (3803)
Beilin H, **8:** 4483
Beintema D J, **3:** 1520 (1518)
Beirne-Smith M, **8:** 4376
Beishuizen J J, **5:** 2767 (2762)
Beitman B P, **3:** 1619
Bejar I I, **1:** 41 (34); **7:** 4307; **8:** 4730 (4730); **11:** 6348 (6342)
Bejoint H, **4:** 2339
Belanger P, **3:** 1461
Belasco J A, **9:** 5180 (5179)
Belbase K, **1:** 254 (245, 247, 252)
Belbase L N, **5:** 2758 (2755)
Belenky M F, **1:** 162 (160); **7:** 4329 (4326); **10:** 5939 (5938), 6099 (6098); **11:** 6722 (6721)
Belfor F, **10:** 5853
Beliner D C, **3:** 1745
Bell A, **3:** (1722); **9:** 5294 (5291, 5292, 5294); **11:** (6482)
Bell B F, **10:** 5790 (5790)
Bell C, **1:** (195); **4:** 1929; **7:** 4319; **8:** 4542 (4541), 4562 (4559, 4560)
Bell C H Jr, **10:** 5900 (5900)
Bell C L G, **8:** 4601 (4599)
Bell C S, **11:** 6765 (6762)
Bell D, **4:** 2331; **7:** 3771 (3769); **11:** 6276 (6272)
Bell G, **8:** 4803
Bell J, **7:** 4171 (4163, 4166)
Bell J E, **8:** 4791
Bell K E, **10:** 6163 (6163)
Bell L, **8:** 4945 (4943); **10:** 5982, 6020
Bell N, **9:** 5507 (5505)
Bell R M, **5:** 2571 (2569)
Bell R Q, **8:** 4394 (4391)
Bell S R, **5:** 2784 (2783)
Bell T H, **11:** 6603 (6602)
Bellack A, **3:** (1288); **10:** 6168 (6165)
Bellack A A, **2:** 816 (815); **3:** 1307 (1303), 1333; **4:** 2376 (2375); **10:** 6149 (6148)
Bellack A S, **9:** 4977
Bellah R N, **4:** 2296 (2294); **10:** 5990 (5989)
Bellamy G T, **3:** 1508 (1507)
Belland J C, **7:** 3760 (3759)
Belle D, **9:** 5528 (5524)
Bellemain, **7:** 4099 (4097)
Beller A H, **4:** 2432 (2430), 2445 (2442)
Beller E K, **5:** 2806 (2805)
Beller K E, **2:** 687 (683)
Bellerate B M, **5:** 2579
Bellew R T, **3:** 1824 (1822); **4:** 2418 (2415); **9:** 5076 (5072); **11:** 6633 (6628)
Bellisle F, **8:** 4474 (4470, 4471)
Bellman B, **2:** 982 (978, 981)
Bellman L, **3:** 1750
Belloncle G, **1:** 221; **6:** 3585
Bellow R, **4:** 2286 (2283)
Bellugi U, **10:** 5690 (5687)
Belmont J M, **7:** 3768 (3767); **11:** 6456 (6454)
Belmont L, **7:** 3872 (3868, 3869)
Belsky J, **4:** 2261 (2260); **5:** 2812 (2812); **7:** 4300 (4300); **8:** (4675)
Belson W A, **1:** 570
Beltran L R, **7:** 4336 (4331)
Belyaeva A, **3:** 1252 (1250)
Bem S L, **4:** 2449 (2447)
Ben Jaballah H, **11:** 6476
Ben Salem B, **11:** 6476
Ben Salem L, **11:** 6476
Benally A, **1:** 534; **8:** 4881 (4878)
Ben-Ari R, **7:** 3970 (3967)
Benasich A A, **3:** 1642 (1637)
Benavente A, **2:** 906 (904)
Benavides A H, **1:** 535
Benavot A, **3:** 1655 (1654); **4:** 2412 (2411); **6:** 3549 (3546); **7:** 4235 (4231); **9:** 5299 (5295), 5367 (5364)
Benbow C A, **5:** 2495 (2494)
Benbow C P, **4:** 2435 (2433, 2434); **5:** 2495 (2493), 2769 (2765)
Benbrika J, **10:** 5782 (5781)
Ben-Chaim D, **5:** 2767 (2762)
Ben-David J, **10:** 5782 (5776)
Bender D, **6:** 3399
Bender M, **1:** 239
Bendix R, **7:** 3864 (3862); **9:** 5553; **10:** 6227
Bendor-Samuel D, **2:** 1160 (1154)
Bendor-Samuel J, **7:** 4132 (4125)
Benedek A, **8:** 4531 (4529)
Benedict R, **1:** 294 (290); **10:** 5590 (5587)
Benedikt E, **7:** 3925
Benejam P, **10:** 6106 (6104)
Beneke J, **6:** 3213 (3210, 3211)
Beneke W, **8:** (4495)
Benest I D, **5:** 2709 (2708)
Bengoa J M, **5:** 2575 (2573)
Bengtson V L, **5:** 2665
Bengtsson J, **4:** 2394 (2389); **8:** 4964 (4958, 4963)
Benhabib B, **4:** 2296
Benhabib S, **4:** 2033 (2030), 2296 (2295)
Benham L, **2:** 1055 (1054)
Beniger J R, **9:** 5544 (5539)
Benigni L, **9:** 5508
Benington M, **10:** 6020
Benjamin A, **5:** 3007 (3005)
Benjamin G, **8:** 4796 (4795), 4835 (4832, 4834); **10:** 5754 (5751)
Benjamin G R, **2:** 892 (891); **9:** 5215 (5215)
Benjamin L T, **4:** 1848 (1843)
Benjamin S, **6:** 3096

Benmayer R, **9:** 5510 (5508)
Benne K D, **3:** 1431
Benner D, **5:** 2579; **7:** 3924 (3922)
Bennett C, **1:** 180 (176, 177); **3:** 1642; **5:** 2937 (2935)
Bennett D S, **1:** 234 (232)
Bennett E L, **1:** 554; **5:** 2802 (2799)
Bennett G K, **11:** 6348 (6341)
Bennett J M, **6:** 3339 (3337)
Bennett J W, **1:** 294 (287)
Bennett K, **2:** 1074
Bennett K P, **10:** 5606 (5601)
Bennett L A, **4:** 2180 (2176)
Bennett N, **1:** 23; **2:** 816 (812), 831 (829, 830); **4:** 2218; **5:** 2536 (2534, 2535), 2595 (2593); **6:** 3292, 3311 (3308); **7:** 3886 (3883), 3986 (3983), 4214 (4211, 4212); **9:** 5363 (5359, 5361); **10:** 6015 (6012); **11:** 6780
Bennett R E, **8:** 4661 (4661)
Bennett S M, **4:** 2440 (2437)
Bennett S N, **2:** 831 (830); **4:** 1847 (1843); **6:** 3389 (3387); **9:** 5358 (5357), 5508; **10:** 5750 (5746)
Bennett W, **9:** (5294)
Bennett W J, **7:** 3924 (3922)
Bennion J W, **1:** 60 (53), 77 (74)
Bennis W G, **3:** 1431; **4:** 2165 (2158)
Benno R H, **11:** 6492
Benoit A, **8:** 4601 (4598)
Ben-Peretz M, **1:** 23; **3:** 1367 (1365), 1494 (1494); **6:** 3283 (3283); **10:** 5812 (5809, 5811), 5994 (5991, 5993), 6091 (6089, 6090, 6091), 6121 (6118); **11:** 6390
Ben-Porath Y S, **1:** 52 (52)
Ben-Simon A, **11:** 6340 (6334)
Benson C, **3:** 1416 (1413), 1793; **5:** 2818 (2815)
Benson C S, **2:** 1055 (1053); **5:** 2798 (2797); **6:** 3106 (3105), 3617 (3616); **9:** 5065 (5061), 5233 (5230); **10:** 5919 (5915)
Benson G M, **3:** 1567 (1566)
Benson J K, **3:** 1774 (1772); **6:** 3528
Bent D H, **7:** 4016 (4015), 4163 (4162)
Bentham J, **3:** (1294)
Bentin S, **8:** 4939 (4938)
Bentler P M, **4:** 1877 (1876, 1877), 2240 (2239), 2388 (2386); **8:** 4351 (4347), 4359 (4357)
Benton L, **1:** 103 (100, 101); **7:** 3711 (3709); **8:** 4638 (4636), 4639
Bents M, **10:** 6026 (6022)
Bents R, **10:** 6026 (6022)
Bentwich J, **5:** 3028
Bentzer F-A, **10:** 5686 (5681)
Benveniste E, **9:** 5416 (5415, 5416)
Benveniste G, **8:** 4519, 4601 (4596, 4597), 4602
Benzecri J P, **2:** 1121 (1117, 1118)
Ben-Zvi R, **8:** 4479 (4477)
Beran J, **8:** 4467
Berdasco A, **3:** 1623 (1621)
Berdie D R, **8:** 4887
Bereaud S, **9:** 5302
Bereday G Z F, **2:** 933 (924), 948, 957 (951), 1063; **5:** 2978; **8:** 4491; **9:** 5013; **11:** 6265 (6261, 6263)
Bereiter C, **2:** 677 (672), 678 (673), 838 (837), 867 (861), 1006 (1004, 1005, 1006), 1025 (1022, 1023); **5:** 2767 (2763), 2874 (2872); **6:** 3215 (3214), 3302 (3298); **7:** 3792, 4094 (4090), 4095 (4089); **11:** 6780 (6778, 6780), 6781
Berelson B, **2:** 1079 (1075, 1079); **11:** 6445 (6439)
Berends M, **1:** 12; **2:** 824 (822, 823); **9:** 5264 (5261)
Berenfeld B, **7:** 4099 (4099)
Berenson G S, **5:** 2571
Berg C A, **2:** 851, 852; **5:** 2916; **8:** 4823 (4819)
Berg D, **5:** 2852
Berg G, **7:** 4240 (4236)
Berg I, **1:** 520 (518); **3:** 1606 (1603); **9:** 5354 (5350); **11:** 6260 (6257), 6276 (6274)
Berg I E, **7:** 4211 (4210)
Berg R van den, **3:** 1278 (1274, 1278)
Berg W K, **8:** 4376 (4373, 4374)
Bergan J R, **8:** 4661 (4659)
Bergem T, **10:** 6053 (6048, 6052)
Bergeman C S, **11:** 6492 (6490)
Bergen D, **8:** 4541 (4541)
Bergendal G, **10:** 5873
Berger E H, **7:** 4301
Berger I, **7:** 3852 (3850), 3853
Berger J, **9:** 5175 (5171)
Berger J O, **9:** 5467 (5466)
Berger M, **4:** 2212 (2209); **6:** 3101
Berger M C, **11:** 6615
Berger M P F, **5:** 3061 (3058)
Berger P, **2:** 933 (925), 1072 (1071); **3:** 1347 (1344)
Berger P L, **3:** 1729 (1726); **6:** 3373 (3370)
Berger S, **6:** 3189 (3188)
Bergeron J C, **9:** 5345
Bergin C, **6:** 3452 (3448)
Bergman A, **8:** 4816 (4813, 4814)
Bergman H, **3:** 1797
Bergman K, **5:** 2623
Bergman L R, **3:** 1520; **8:** 4394 (4394), 4395; **11:** 6492
Bergman P, **11:** 6492 (6491)
Bergman R, **5:** 2861 (2860); **7:** 3991 (3989)
Bergmann B, **7:** 4200 (4199)
Bergmann B B, **2:** 692 (688)
Bergmann B R, **4:** 2445 (2442, 2443)
Bergmann H, **7:** 4124
Bergowitz M W, **5:** 2669
Bergsma H M, **11:** 6760 (6756)
Bergson H, **9:** (5052)
Bergson H L, **1:** (195), 199
Bergsten U, **6:** 3434 (3433); **7:** 4324 (4320, 4321, 4322)
Bergstrom B A, **1:** 52 (51); **5:** 2783 (2780)
Berk E, **7:** 3991
Berk L, **7:** 4050 (4047)
Berk L E, **2:** 705 (704), 867 (863)
Berk R, **5:** 3066; **7:** 3986; **11:** 6320 (6315, 6319)
Berk R A, **2:** 1189 (1185, 1188); **3:** 1431 (1427); **4:** 2131 (2129); **5:** 2595, 3043, 3050 (3043); **10:** 5725 (5722, 5724), 5726
Berke I P, **3:** 1431 (1426)
Berkeley G, **4:** 2000 (1997); **5:** (2876); **7:** 3839 (3835); **9:** 5281
Berkeley G F, **6:** 3496 (3494); **7:** 3840 (3839)
Berkenkotter C, **7:** 4094 (4089)
Berkouwer G C, **2:** 767
Berkowitz L, **1:** 570; **5:** 2532
Berkowitz M W, **1:** 380; **10:** 6168 (6167)
Berkson J, **6:** 3253 (3250)
Berlin B, **4:** 2400 (2398)
Berlin D F, **5:** 2903 (2898)
Berliner D C, **1:** 12, 23, 60, 332, 377, 520; **2:** 729, 816 (816), 1006; **3:** 1256 (1254); **4:** 2089; **5:** 2567, 2607, 2768 (2766), 2870; **6:** 3201 (3198), 3655; **8:** 4881; **9:** 5043 (5041); **10:** 5762 (5761), 5834 (5833), 6020 (6016), 6026 (6022, 6023, 6024, 6025), 6031 (6028), 6043 (6039), 6121 (6119), 6192, 6193; **11:** 6390
Berlyne D, **7:** 3946 (3943); **10:** 6223 (6221)
Berlyne D E, **2:** 969 (965); **8:** 4541 (4537)
Berman J J, **3:** 1245; **5:** 2651
Berman L M, **10:** 5817 (5816)
Berman P P, **3:** 1256 (1253, 1254), 1271 (1268, 1269), 1431 (1427); **4:** 1857 (1852, 1855); **5:** 2847 (2840, 2841); **9:** 5246 (5242, 5244)
Berman R, **8:** 4939 (4938)
Berman W, **11:** 6384 (6382)
Bernacki G, **4:** 2388 (2384)
Bernagozzi T, **9:** 4977 (4975)
Bernal J B, **7:** 4275
Bernal M E, **6:** 3261 (3260)
Bernard C, **4:** 1871 (1865)
Bernard J, **9:** 5435 (5433); **11:** 6731 (6729)
Bernard M E, **1:** 494 (491)
Bernard R, **4:** 2052 (2046)
Bernardin H J, **4:** 2131 (2128)
Bernbaum G, **10:** 6227 (6225)
Bernd O, **2:** 737 (737)
Berndt T J, **8:** 4368; **10:** 5758
Berndtsson R, **4:** 2327
Berne R, **9:** 5065 (5061)
Bernhard G, **7:** 4157 (4157)
Bernhard J G, **4:** 2171 (2169, 2171)
Bernoulli, **7:** (4158)
Berns M, **6:** 3442 (3440)
Bernsen N O, **8:** 4951
Bernstein B, **2:** (926), 1072 (1070, 1071); **3:** (1302), (1304), 1308, 1347 (1345); **4:** 1851 (1850), 2165 (2159), 2257 (2252), 2272, 2376 (2376); **5:** 2806 (2803), 2903 (2900); **6:** 3215 (3214, 3215), 3312; **9:** 5021 (5018, 5020), 5416 (5416), 5523; **10:** 6197 (6194)

Bernstein B B, **4:** 2249 (2248); **10:** 5606 (5599)
Bernstein D, **10:** 5693 (5691)
Bernstein E, **4:** 1985 (1982)
Bernstein H T, **4:** 2132 (2126)
Bernstein J G, **3:** 1619
Bernstein M, **4:** 2073 (2072), 2166 (2165); **5:** 2847 (2839, 2841)
Bernstein N, **7:** 3950 (3947, 3950)
Bernstein R J, **3:** 1524; **5:** 2585 (2585), 2586; **7:** 3925; **8:** 4455 (4453, 4454)
Bernstein S, **8:** (4815)
Berreman G D, **1:** 294 (284, 290); **4:** 2052 (2046); **9:** 5572 (5568)
Berres M, **6:** 3234 (3232)
Berruecos M P, **3:** 1402 (1399)
Berrueta-Clement J R, **2:** 687 (679, 680), 1131 (1130); **3:** 1628 (1625), 1641 (1640); **5:** 2806 (2804); **8:** 4666 (4664); **11:** 6384 (6382)
Berry A, **3:** 1694 (1693); **5:** 2945 (2943, 2944, 2945); **9:** 5240 (5235)
Berry B, **4:** 2131 (2130); **9:** 5291 (5284, 5286); **10:** 5929 (5927), 6044 (6036, 6037), 6047, 6083
Berry J W, **3:** 1240, 1241 (1239), 1252 (1246); **5:** 2651
Berry P C, **8:** 4731 (4729)
Berry W D, **8:** 4351 (4346)
Berryman S, **11:** 6415
Bertaux D, **6:** 3428; **9:** 5518
Bertenthal B, **7:** 3950
Berthe A, **2:** 913 (912)
Bertini M, **2:** 871 (870)
Bertoletti M C, **10:** 6117
Bertrand O, **2:** 1160 (1159); **4:** 2394 (2389); **11:** 6647 (6647)
Bertrand R, **5:** 2462 (2462)
Berube M R, **6:** 3196 (3195); **8:** 4586 (4585, 4586); **10:** 6078 (6077)
Berwick G, **4:** 2357 (2354, 2356)
Besant A, **5:** 2601 (2599); **11:** (6749)
Besemer S P, **2:** 1182 (1180)
Beshers J M, **9:** 5559 (5558)
Beshir M O, **10:** 5842
Besnard P, **5:** 2937
Bessant B, **10:** 6096 (6093); **11:** 6735 (6733)
Bessent A, **3:** 1386 (1384, 1385)
Bessent W, **3:** 1386 (1384, 1385)
Bessenyei I, **11:** 6647 (6641)
Bessom M E, **7:** 4026
Best D L, **7:** 3763 (3762)
Best F, **11:** 6394 (6392)
Best J H, **5:** 2618; **7:** 4225
Best K M, **6:** 3297 (3293); **8:** 4779 (4775)
Best R, **10:** 5817 (5816)
Bestor A E Jr, **3:** 1300 (1299); **8:** 4811 (4809)
Beswick D G, **1:** 322 (319, 320); **4:** 2180 (2177)
Betancourt Mejia G, **8:** (4495)
Beteille A, **9:** 5560 (5555)
Betham M T, **1:** 274 (267); **5:** 2897 (2892)
Bethel L, **10:** 5957
Bethell G, **1:** 510
Betsey C, **7:** 4200 (4199)
Betson L, **1:** 184
Bettelheim B, **6:** 3234 (3232)
Betti E, **5:** 2585 (2584)
Bettio F, **4:** 2432 (2430)
Betz M, **10:** 6227 (6226)
Betz N E, **1:** 53 (48)
Betz P, **4:** 2266 (2264)
Beukelman D, **10:** 5693 (5692)
Beukelman D R, **1:** 408 (406, 407), 409 (407)
Beukhof G, **5:** 2769 (2764); **7:** 3791
Beunen G, **8:** 4473 (4472); **10:** 5713
Bevc M, **9:** 5497 (5491)
Bever T G, **5:** 2685 (2682)
Beyer L E, **3:** 1337; **4:** 1852
Beyerbach B A, **10:** 6088 (6088)
Bhachu P, **1:** 294 (293); **7:** 3973 (3973)
Bhagwati J, **1:** 560 (560)
Bhalla A S, **4:** 1991; **11:** 6282 (6278)
Bhan S, **5:** 2759 (2754)
Bhardwaj R, **3:** 1567 (1565)
Bhatia T, **4:** 2339
Bhatt A, **2:** 906 (905, 906)
Bhatty R, **11:** 6797 (6794)
Bhola H S, **1:** 120, 135 (131), 175 (175), 176, 180 (178), 215, 221 (219); **4:** 2369; **5:** 2759, 2951 (2947); **6:** 3459 (3454); **8:** 4812; **11:** 6507 (6506)
Bhola J K, **5:** 2759
Bialystok E, **1:** 537 (536); **4:** 2345 (2345); **8:** 4939
Bianca G G, **8:** 4890 (4890)
Bianchi B D, **4:** 2452 (2451)
Bianchi L J, **4:** 2419 (2415)
Bianchi M D C, **3:** 1736
Bianchi P, **11:** 6282 (6278, 6279)
Bianchi S M, **4:** 2432 (2430)
Biarnès J, **5:** 2544
Bibby R W, **1:** 162 (160)
Bichelmeyer B, **8:** 4803 (4803)
Bickel R, **3:** 1820 (1817); **4:** 1911
Bickel W E, **4:** 2388 (2382); **8:** 4562 (4556)
Bickley V, **1:** 322
Bickman L, **11:** 6384 (6378, 6379)
Biddle B, **10:** 6043 (6036), 6207 (6204)
Biddle B J, **2:** 802 (797, 799), 816; **4:** 1840 (1836, 1837); **10:** 5758 (5756), 6132 (6127, 6128, 6130, 6131), 6239 (6236, 6237); **11:** 6797 (6796, 6797)
Biddle J, **10:** 6149 (6147, 6148)
Biddulph F, **10:** 6177 (6176)
Bidell T, **8:** 4873 (4866)
Bidell T R, **5:** 2680 (2677, 2678)
Bidwell C E, **1:** 594 (589); **2:** 1042; **4:** 1938, 2165 (2162); **5:** 2595 (2593); **6:** 3527 (3524); **8:** 4568, 4895 (4892, 4895); **9:** 5312 (5312), 5378 (5374); **10:** 5606 (5597); **11:** 6557 (6552)
Biederman I, **8:** 4939 (4938)
Bielby D D, **4:** 2445 (2442)
Bielby W T, **4:** 2432 (2429), 2445 (2442)
Bieman-Copland S, **5:** 2916 (2914)
Bienaymé A, **4:** 2385
Bierman J M, **3:** 1643 (1641)
Bierstedt R, **11:** 6575
Biervliet W E, **7:** 4155; **11:** 6451 (6445, 6450)
Biesheuvel S, **7:** 3970 (3967)
Biggs E, **6:** 3670 (3670)
Biggs J, **1:** 321 (319, 320, 321), 322 (321); **3:** 1513 (1508, 1510, 1511); **5:** 2669
Biggs J B, **1:** 193 (188, 189, 191, 192); **2:** 871 (870, 871); **6:** 3329 (3326, 3327), 3339 (3335), 3660 (3657); **8:** 4647 (4643, 4644)
Bigi L, **7:** 3788 (3785)
Bijlstra J, **7:** 4104 (4102)
Bijou S W, **1:** 497 (495); **9:** 4977; **10:** 6163
Biklen D P, **6:** 3234 (3232, 3233, 3234), 3559 (3558, 3559); **10:** 6244 (6243)
Biklen S, **11:** 6722, 6726, 6727
Biklen S K, **4:** 1958; **6:** 3284; **11:** 6722 (6722), 6726 (6723, 6724, 6725)
Biles J, **11:** 6412
Bilham T, **7:** 4171 (4163, 4166)
Bill V, **2:** 838 (836)
Billard L, **11:** 6712 (6709, 6711)
Billiet J, **9:** 5196 (5194)
Billig, **9:** (5325)
Billing M, **1:** 379 (379)
Billingsley B, **10:** 6015 (6014)
Billy J, **3:** 1676 (1672, 1673, 1674, 1675)
bin Yahya I, **4:** 2119 (2110)
Binder C, **4:** 1917 (1914)
Binder D A, **9:** 5142 (5136)
Binder M B, **11:** 6306 (6301, 6302, 6305)
Binet A, **2:** 792 (788), 846 (844); **3:** 1504 (1503), (1793); **4:** (1861), 1871 (1864, 1866, 1867, 1868); **5:** 2664 (2657), (2875), (2911), (2917), (2919); **7:** (3699), 3879 (3873); **8:** (4557); **9:** (5053), (5433), (5502); **10:** (5660), (5663)
Bingol N, **7:** 4081 (4079)
Binkley M, **5:** 2500 (2497)
Bin-Mohamed M, **3:** 1278 (1276)
Binnick R L, **10:** 5697
Binns T, **5:** 2469 (2467)
Binstock R H, **6:** 3428
Binswanger H, **4:** 2419
Bion, **7:** (4236)
Biraimah K C, **11:** 6740 (6738, 6739)
Birch D, **7:** 3942 (3937)
Birch H, **1:** 234 (232)
Birch I K F, **6:** 3360; **9:** 5255
Birch M W, **2:** 1084 (1083)
Birchenough M, **5:** 2851 (2849)
Bird G, **5:** 2993
Bird J B, **8:** 4774 (4769)
Bird M, **2:** 867 (861)
Bird R M, **8:** 4364 (4363)
Bird T, **3:** 1635 (1633); **4:** 2131 (2130); **9:** 5378 (5376); **10:** 5948 (5943, 5946)
Birdsall N, **8:** 4835
Birge L E, **6:** 3399 (3395)
Birkenhauer J, **5:** 2469 (2466, 2469)
Birks J S, **7:** 4205
Birks S, **1:** 226 (222); **11:** 6659 (6659)
Birman B, **3:** 1606 (1603); **7:** 4293 (4290)

Birnbaum A, **5:** 3054 (3052); **6:** 3253 (3250), 3523 (3521); **7:** 3706 (3701)
Birnbaum I, **2:** 977 (976)
Birnbaum M H, **9:** 4973 (4973)
Birren J E, **1:** 239; **5:** 2665; **6:** 3427 (3426), 3435; **7:** 4170 (4169); **8:** 4824
Bisanz J, **2:** 851 (847, 848, 850)
Bisconti A, **10:** 5782
Bishop A, **6:** 3459 (3457, 3458), 3638 (3635)
Bishop A J, **6:** 3452 (3450), 3652 (3650)
Bishop J, **2:** 1093 (1089, 1090, 1091), 1094 (1090), 1152 (1149); **3:** 1449, 1695 (1692, 1694), 1712 (1710); **7:** 4255 (4249, 4250, 4253, 4254), 4324 (4323); **9:** 5076 (5072); **11:** 6420 (6418), 6457
Bishop J H, **1:** 110 (107); **6:** 3616 (3615)
Bishop K K, **5:** 2812 (2811)
Bishop L, **9:** 5180 (5176)
Bishop Y M M, **6:** 3507 (3500)
Bissell H W, **8:** 4930 (4928)
Bittel L, **2:** 1094
Bitterman J, **2:** 1165
Bittner E, **6:** 3528
Bixby J, **4:** 1939 (1936); **10:** 6178 (6177)
Bizhkov G, **2:** 661 (659)
Bizzell R, **2:** 688 (682)
Bjarnasson D, **10:** 6244 (6242)
Bjerg J, **9:** 5281 (5279)
Bjerstedt AÅ, **3:** 1733; **5:** 2978
Björklund A, **4:** 2150 (2146, 2148)
Björklund D F, **2:** 705 (703, 704), 852; **7:** 3763 (3760, 3762); **9:** 5358 (5356)
Bjornemalm B, **5:** 2851 (2848)
Björnsson C H, **2:** 1079 (1077); **4:** 2024
Bjørndal I R, **7:** 4192
Black A, **9:** 5359 (5358)
Black D A, **2:** 1093 (1089); **6:** 3616 (3615)
Black D R, **11:** 6798 (6794)
Black G, **3:** 1642 (1637)
Black H, **7:** 3894 (3891, 3893, 3894)
Black J A, **9:** 5050
Black J B, **2:** 969 (967); **8:** 4942
Black K N, **9:** 5532 (5531)
Black M, **3:** 1735 (1733, 1734); **6:** 3219 (3218)
Black P, **2:** 1220 (1217); **8:** 4479 (4476, 4477); **11:** 6292 (6292)
Black R, **4:** 2007
Black S D, **2:** 982 (978)
Black T R, **8:** 4803 (4801)
Blackbourn J M, **8:** 4375 (4373)
Blackburn D J, **8:** 4811 (4807)
Blackburn M L, **6:** 3184 (3183)
Blackburn R T, **11:** 6445 (6444), 6712 (6711)
Blackburn T C, **5:** 2655 (2653)
Blackburn V, **10:** 5953 (5948), 5972 (5972)
Blackhurst A E, **7:** 3833 (3832); **10:** 5943 (5940)
Blackledge D A, **2:** 785, 1072 (1071), 1074
Blackmore J, **10:** 6072 (6068, 6070)
Blackmore K, **9:** 5281
Blackstone S W, **1:** 409
Blackwell M, **4:** 1911 (1908, 1909)
Blackwell P, **3:** 1402 (1399)
Blagg N, **2:** 846 (846), 860 (859); **3:** 1504 (1503); **9:** 5043 (5042)
Blair A G, **9:** 5013
Blair J A, **2:** 1207 (1204, 1206, 1207), 1208
Blair R C, **7:** 4162 (4162)
Blair S M, **8:** 4948
Blais J, **7:** 4324 (4321); **9:** 5563 (5562)
Blake D, **8:** 4715 (4711)
Blake E M, **3:** 1438 (1434)
Blake M E, **3:** 1460
Blake V M, **10:** 6117
Blakely R, **5:** 2897 (2892)
Blakemore A, **2:** 1093 (1089)
Blakemore K, **1:** 594 (592); **2:** 617
Blakeslee G, **2:** 982, 1012 (1008); **10:** 6008 (6007)
Blakey J, **1:** 27
Blalock A B, **11:** 6575
Blalock H M Jr, **7:** 3872 (3870); **11:** 6575 (6570)
Blanc M H A, **1:** 537
Blanchard C, **1:** 234
Blanchard D, **3:** 1778 (1776)
Blanchard J S, **7:** 3807 (3802)
Blanchard P N, **3:** 1491
Blanchard R, **1:** 234
Blanchard S, **2:** 665
Blanchard-Fields F, **8:** 4824
Blanck G, **8:** 4816 (4815)
Blanck R, **8:** 4816 (4815)
Blandford A, **1:** 347 (345, 346)
Blandow D, **11:** 6292 (6291)
Blaney N T, **2:** 1098 (1096), 1099 (1098)
Blank R K, **1:** 265 (262)
Blanken G, **6:** 3224
Blankertz H, **3:** 1300 (1290); **11:** 6684
Blasch B B, **11:** 6628
Blase J, **3:** 1775; **6:** 3284 (3280); **7:** 3826 (3821, 3822, 3823, 3824, 3825); **8:** 4586 (4583); **9:** 5065 (5061), 5181 (5179), 5272, 5273; **10:** 6062 (6060)
Blase J J, **9:** 5223 (5223)
Blashfield R K, **2:** 718 (712); **9:** 5158 (5158)
Blasi A, **7:** 3920 (3919)
Blasius J, **2:** 1036 (1036)
Blatchford P, **1:** 362 (361)
Blatt B, **3:** 1438, 1507 (1504)
Blattstein A, **10:** 6234 (6233)
Blattstein D, **10:** 6234 (6233)
Blau D, **7:** 4200 (4200)
Blau D M, **1:** 358 (355); **2:** 692 (689, 690, 691), 693
Blau F D, **1:** 358 (357); **2:** 692 (689); **4:** 2432 (2429, 2430, 2431), 2445 (2442, 2444, 2445), 2446; **5:** 2739 (2739)
Blau P, **10:** 5591 (5588), 5735 (5732, 5734)
Blau P M, **7:** 3864 (3863); **8:** 4895 (4892); **9:** 5553 (5550, 5553)
Blaug M, **1:** 135 (129), 474 (471); **2:** 1072 (1066), 1093 (1090); **3:** 1655 (1649), 1685 (1682), 1695 (1690), 1703 (1701), 1707, 1820 (1811, 1812, 1813, 1814), 1824 (1822); **5:** 2647 (2645, 2646), 2744 (2741, 2742); **6:** 3184 (3179, 3181), 3613 (3609, 3610, 3611, 3612); **8:** 4499, 4509 (4504), 4531 (4527), 4568 (4564), 4839 (4839), 4917 (4913), 4964 (4960); **9:** 5076 (5072), 5168 (5162), 5206 (5202), 5240 (5234, 5235), 5354 (5354); **10:** 5767 (5765); **11:** 6298 (6293), 6424 (6420, 6421)
Blauner R, **7:** 3848 (3841)
Blaye A, **2:** 1006 (1005); **4:** 1899 (1896); **8:** 4957 (4954)
Bledsoe J C, **9:** 5324 (5321)
Bledstein B, **11:** 6722 (6719)
Bleich D, **2:** (1194)
Bleicher J, **5:** 2586
Bleichrodt N, **11:** 6333, 6334 (6330)
Bleidick U, **10:** 5662 (5660)
Bleier R, **4:** 1851 (1851)
Blekastad M, **2:** 883
Blenkinsop J, **2:** 868 (861)
Bleuler M, **8:** 4779 (4776, 4777)
Blew P A, **8:** 4375 (4374)
Blid H, **11:** 6774 (6773)
Bliesener T, **8:** 4779 (4777)
Bligh D A, **5:** 2532 (2530)
Blinder A S, **9:** 5240
Blinkhorn S, **6:** 3523 (3521)
Blischak D M, **1:** 409 (404)
Blishen B R, **7:** 3721 (3716, 3717)
Bliss J, **2:** 988 (986); **9:** 5338 (5336)
Bloch D, **4:** 1841 (1838)
Bloch H, **7:** 3950
Blochmann E, **3:** (1722); **11:** 6747 (6745)
Block C C, **10:** 5795
Block C H, **8:** 4731 (4729)
Block J, **8:** 4394 (4392)
Block J H, **4:** 2452 (2451, 2452); **5:** 2778 (2777); **6:** 3631 (3627, 3629, 3630); **9:** 5435 (5434)
Blomeyer R L, **2:** 991 (990)
Blonskij P P, **6:** (3136)
Bloom A, **3:** (1336), 1337 (1336); **6:** 3459 (3454, 3456)
Bloom B, **3:** 1628 (1627), (1796), 1804 (1801); **6:** 3549 (3545); **7:** 3886 (3883, 3884, 3885), (4156); **8:** (4450); **9:** 5264 (5261), 5532 (5529)
Bloom B J, **11:** 6484 (6483)
Bloom B S, **1:** 41 (32), 370 (364, 367), 390 (380, 382), 396 (392); **2:** 867 (862), 957 (954), 1106 (1106); **3:** 1266 (1264), 1325 (1322), 1641 (1636), 1703 (1699); **4:** (1837), 1847 (1843, 1844), (1861), (1868), 2017 (2012), 2089 (2080), 2249 (2245), 2250, 2257 (2250, 2253, 2255, 2256); **5:** 2495, 2589 (2586), 2778 (2777), 2855 (2855), 2867 (2866), (2878); **6:** 3297 (3292), 3484, 3523 (3512, 3513, 3517), 3631 (3626, 3627, 3629, 3631); **7:** 3721 (3720), 3872 (3867); **8:** (4401), 4648, 4702 (4699), 4730 (4729), 4774 (4770), 4881 (4876); **9:** 5043 (5039), 5268, 5324 (5319, 5320), 5338; **10:** 5750

(5746), 5790 (5784), (5911), 6103 (6102, 6103); **11:** 6328 (6321), 6348 (6341, 6342, 6345)
Bloom D E, **6:** 3184 (3183)
Bloom H, **7:** 4200 (4197, 4199)
Bloom H S, **4:** 2375
Bloom J D, **11:** 6774 (6769)
Bloom K, **1:** 362
Bloom L, **6:** 3227 (3225), 3231 (3229)
Bloom P J, **3:** 1635 (1630, 1634)
Bloom S, **4:** 1972 (1968)
Bloome D, **2:** 820 (819)
Bloomfield B, **7:** 3911 (3907)
Bloomfield M, **5:** 2601 (2598)
Bloomingdale L M, **3:** 1520
Bloor M, **7:** 4319 (4319)
Blos P, **8:** (4815)
Blosser P E, **8:** 4647 (4645)
Blossfeld H-P, **9:** 5553 (5553); **10:** 5735 (5733, 5734)
Blount B G, **2:** 802
Blow F, **5:** 2623
Bluestone B, **5:** 2744 (2742)
Bluhm H P, **5:** 2831
Blum A, **1:** 244 (243); **3:** 1257 (1253, 1254); **5:** 2903 (2901, 2902); **7:** 3889 (3889); **8:** 4586 (4583, 4584, 4585, 4586)
Blum A A, **10:** 6079
Blum L A, **4:** 2296 (2294)
Blum W, **6:** 3634 (3632)
Blumberg A, **9:** 5181 (5180)
Blume S, **1:** 560 (554)
Blumenfeld P C, **9:** 5363 (5360)
Blumer H, **1:** 67 (62); **10:** 6126 (6125)
Blundell D, **9:** 5358 (5357)
Blurton-Jones N G, **4:** 2452 (2450)
Blyth A, **3:** 1461
Blyth D A, **1:** 88 (84)
Blyth J A, **1:** 93 (90); **11:** 6775
Blyth W, **3:** 1804 (1803)
Bo Yu, **11:** 6551 (6550)
Boal A, **2:** 906 (903)
Boalt G, **4:** 1864, 1872 (1869)
Boardman E, **7:** 4025 (4023)
Boas F, **1:** 294 (281); **4:** (2047); **5:** (2648); **6:** 3215 (3214), 3238 (3235)
Boaz R, **1:** 110 (105)
Bobath B, **5:** 2812 (2810)
Bobath K, **5:** 2812 (2810)
Bobbitt F, **3:** 1325 (1320), 1804 (1801); **4:** 1871 (1869)
Bobbitt J F, **3:** 1266 (1262, 1264), 1300 (1298, 1299); **5:** 2861 (2857); **9:** (5053)
Bobbitt S A, **10:** 5846
Bobillier P, **11:** 6306 (6298)
Bobrow D G, **3:** 1434
Bock D, **5:** 2596
Bock D R, **4:** 1938
Bock E, **7:** 4336
Bock J C, **1:** 135 (128); **4:** 1911, 2369; **7:** 4145 (4142, 4143)
Bock R D, **3:** 1548 (1548); **5:** 2595 (2590), 3055 (3052, 3053), 3061 (3060); **6:** 3253 (3251, 3252), 3507 (3500, 3503), 3523; **7:** 3987, 4015 (4009, 4012); **8:** 4473 (4470), 4923 (4920); **9:** 4973 (4971), 5142 (5137); **11:** 6387 (6386), 6388 (6386, 6387), 6591 (6586, 6591)
Bodmer J J, **8:** (4416)
Bodmer W F, **3:** 1647 (1646)
Boediono W, **5:** 2792
Boef-van der Meulen S, **9:** 5196 (5194)
Boehm U, **11:** 6659
Boehnlein M M, **1:** 265 (263)
Boekaerts M, **1:** 203 (200, 201, 202, 203), 204 (202); **5:** 2767 (2764); **6:** 3291 (3291); **10:** 5738 (5738)
Boekkooi-Timminga E, **2:** 998 (996); **5:** 3055 (3053)
Boeninger E, **3:** 1824 (1823)
Boer B, **9:** 5255
Boersma F J, **10:** 5826 (5823)
Boersma K Th, **3:** 1278 (1274)
Boesch E E, **5:** 2650 (2648)
Boethius of Dacia, **9:** (5124)
Boff K R, **8:** 4379
Bogart Q J, **2:** 899 (898)
Bogdan R, **3:** 1508
Bogdanor V, **5:** 2512 (2509)
Boggiano A K, **1:** 31
Boggild-Andersen B, **6:** 3224 (3219)
Boggs J, **3:** 1236 (1234)
Boggs S, **6:** 3442 (3440)
Bogin B, **1:** 294 (288); **5:** 2684 (2683, 2684)
Bohannan P J, **1:** 294 (293)
Bohrnstedt G W, **1:** 390 (384); **8:** 4351 (4347); **11:** 6328 (6327), 6576 (6574)
Boissiere M, **3:** 1784 (1782); **6:** 3184 (3179)
Bojuwoye O, **10:** 5808
Bokhari I, **7:** 4136 (4133)
Bol E, **6:** 3292
Bolam R, **1:** 72 (70), 73 (71); **10:** 5953 (5949), 5972 (5966), 5982, 6047
Bolasco S, **7:** 4006
Boldizar J P, **1:** 234 (233)
Boldt D, **1:** 553 (553)
Boles K, **10:** 6099 (6098); **11:** 6723
Bolger N, **3:** 1647; **11:** 6320 (6319)
Bolhuis S, **11:** 6437 (6436)
Boli J, **10:** 5606 (5600), 5607 (5600)
Boli J R, **2:** 933 (928)
Bolig R, **9:** 5275 (5274)
Bolino A C, **11:** 6633 (6628)
Bolk, **2:** (1008)
Boll G, **11:** 6420 (6418)
Bolleman Th G, **1:** 277
Bollen K A, **10:** 5862 (5861)
Bollen R, **5:** 2852 (2848); **10:** 5972 (5968)
Bolles R C, **4:** 2172 (2167); **8:** 4394 (4390)
Bollnow O F, **4:** 2387 (2386); **8:** 4433
Bollwark J, **11:** 6333 (6332)
Bolman L G, **4:** 2165 (2162); **6:** 3528; **9:** 5181 (5176, 5178, 5180)
Bolster A, **10:** 6207 (6205)
Boltani N, **2:** 652 (652)
Bolton E, **1:** 82 (78, 79, 80, 81, 82)
Bolton G M, **8:** 4388 (4386)
Bolus R, **8:** 4715 (4711); **9:** 5394 (5392)
Bolvin J O, **5:** 2870 (2868), (2879)
Bombi A S, **9:** 5562 (5561)
Bomstad L, **2:** 1208
Bonan J, **9:** 5185 (5183, 5184)
Bonaparte N, **8:** (4605)
Bond A L, **10:** 5738
Bond G C, **9:** 5572
Bond H M, **9:** 5572 (5569)
Bond J T, **2:** 688 (682)
Bond L, **5:** 2595 (2590); **7:** 3986 (3979); **11:** 6320 (6317), 6339 (6335)
Bond L A, **4:** 2267; **10:** 5738
Bonder G, **4:** 2412 (2409)
Bondi H, **8:** 4562 (4557)
Bondy E, **7:** 3826 (3824)
Bone M J, **8:** 4574
Bone T R, **7:** 4030
Bonet J P, **10:** (5658)
Bonett D G, **8:** 4359 (4357)
Bongaarts J, **3:** 1676 (1674)
Bonitz F, **7:** 4026 (4020)
Bonjour L, **3:** 1774 (1773)
Bonner B L, **1:** 19
Bonner J, **5:** 2874 (2871)
Bonner J T, **4:** 2172 (2168); **5:** 2684 (2681, 2683)
Bonniol J J, **6:** 3311 (3308)
Bonstrom O, **7:** 3833 (3832)
Bontempo B T, **10:** 5834 (5832, 5833)
Boocock S S, **9:** 5475 (5472)
Book C, **10:** 6214 (6209)
Bookchin M, **4:** 1851 (1851)
Booker G, **6:** 3661; **7:** 4100
Bookman A, **2:** 907
Boomer D S, **7:** 4000 (3997)
Boomsma D I, **11:** 6492 (6490)
Boonchuay T, **11:** 6377 (6371)
Boone D R, **11:** 6707 (6704, 6705)
Boone E J, **8:** 4616 (4610)
Boone R, **4:** 1957 (1956)
Boone R A, **7:** 3807 (3802)
Boonzaier D A, **10:** 5673 (5670)
Boot P A, **10:** 5643 (5637)
Boot R L, **7:** 4220
Booth A, **1:** 111; **4:** 2261; **7:** 3889 (3887)
Booth B, **2:** 988 (986, 987)
Booth C, **1:** 184 (181)
Booth M, **10:** 5985
Booth N S, **5:** 2655
Booth T, **3:** 1507 (1506); **9:** 5071; **11:** 6461
Boothby N, **8:** 4779 (4776, 4778)
Boothroyd R A, **4:** 1840 (1839); **9:** 5168 (5163, 5164)
Boothroyd W, **10:** 6004 (6000)
Bora K von, **6:** (3529)
Borasi R, **6:** 3638 (3635)
Bordia A, **1:** 176; **5:** 2758 (2756), 2759
Bordogna L, **10:** 6078 (6078)
Borg I, **4:** 2219
Borg M, **6:** 3593
Borg W, **6:** 3201 (3198)
Borg W R, **8:** 4875 (4874), 4881 (4879, 4880)
Borgatta E F, **5:** 2931; **8:** 4351, 4352; **11:** 6576
Borgatta E G, **11:** 6328

Borgatti S P, **9:** 5559 (5559)
Borgen F H, **11:** 6677 (6670, 6671)
Borgen S, **4:** 2327 (2324)
Borgström L, **3:** 1602 (1600); **11:** 6394 (6394)
Borich G, **5:** 2462 (2461); **8:** 4766; **10:** 5822 (5818, 5820, 5821), 5957 (5955)
Boriero D, **7:** 3807 (3804); **10:** 5673 (5670, 5671)
Boring E G, **3:** 1796 (1794), 1797
Boring J, **4:** 1873
Boris R B, **5:** 2855 (2855)
Borish S M, **4:** 2327
Borisoff C, **6:** 3442
Borjas G J, **4:** 2445 (2444); **5:** 2739 (2739)
Bork A, **3:** 1778 (1776); **7:** 4088 (4082); **8:** 4803 (4800); **9:** 5544 (5541)
Borko H, **3:** 1529 (1527); **10:** 6026 (6021, 6024), 6034 (6033), 6035 (6032)
Borkowski J G, **2:** 867 (866), 969 (966); **6:** 3223, 3329 (3326, 3327); **7:** 3763 (3761, 3762), 3768 (3766, 3767); **10:** 5745 (5744), 6177 (6174, 6175)
Borland J H, **5:** 2495 (2493); **9:** 5532 (5529, 5531)
Borman K M, **2:** 893 (892); **9:** 5181 (5176, 5178); **10:** 5994 (5992)
Borman W C, **11:** 6320 (6320)
Bormann E, **5:** 2532 (2530)
Borms J, **5:** 2685; **8:** 4473, 4474
Bormuth J R, **5:** 3066 (3065); **11:** 6348 (6343)
Borna E, **5:** 3036
Bornstein M H, **3:** 1643; **8:** 4383 (4381, 4383), 4542 (4540); **9:** 5518; **10:** 6202
Borofsky R, **3:** 1755 (1754)
Boruch R F, **4:** 2089 (2081, 2088), (2103); **5:** 2922 (2920); **9:** 5372 (5370, 5371)
Borus M, **11:** 6265 (6262, 6264), 6633
Borus M E, **9:** 5076 (5073, 5074, 5075)
Boruta M, **11:** 6785 (6783)
Bos H, **3:** 1821 (1811)
Boschee F, **10:** 6004 (6001)
Bosco J J, **11:** 6287 (6286)
Bose A, **3:** 1733
Boserup E, **4:** 2432 (2429)
Boshier R W, **1:** 127 (121), 162 (159), 221 (219); **3:** 1602 (1600, 1601); **4:** 2266 (2264); **7:** 4324 (4322), 4325, 4329 (4327); **8:** 4616 (4610); **11:** 6437 (6436)
Bosker R J, **4:** 1934 (1932)
Bosler U, **3:** 1778 (1776)
Bosma H, **10:** 5738
Bosman E A, **5:** 2916 (2913)
Bossert S, **9:** 5264 (5259)
Bossert S T, **2:** 820, 824 (822)
Bossing N L, **2:** 1107
Bossy R, **1:** 317 (313)
Boston J, **4:** 2292 (2290)
Boswell J, **7:** 4026 (4023)
Botel M, **7:** 4081
Both K, **7:** 4157 (4156, 4157)
Botkin D B, **4:** 1995 (1994)
Botkin J W, **6:** 3422
Botkin M, **10:** 6112 (6109)
Botkin P T, **9:** 5512 (5510)
Bott D, **10:** 5943 (5940)
Bottani N, **2:** 957 (957), 1220 (1213, 1217); **4:** 2140; **9:** 5210 (5209); **11:** 6394 (6392)
Bottari N, **5:** 2500 (2496, 2497)
Bottomore T, **10:** 5606 (5600)
Boucebi M, **10:** 5943 (5940)
Bouchard C, **8:** 4474
Bouchard D, **8:** 4642
Bouchard T J Jr, **2:** 846 (845); **5:** 2465 (2464); **6:** 3144 (3139); **8:** 4730 (4729); **11:** 6492 (6488)
Bouche D, **11:** 6741
Boucher L, **11:** 6698 (6692)
Boucher M, **7:** 4220 (4216)
Boucouvalas M, **6:** 3435
Boud D, **1:** 193 (191, 193); **4:** 2186; **6:** 3213; **9:** 5399 (5396)
Boud D J, **5:** 2773 (2773); **6:** 3204 (3203), 3349; **9:** 5338 (5335, 5336)
Boudon R, **4:** 2278 (2276); **10:** 5606 (5601), 5735 (5732)
Boulding K, **4:** 2330 (2328)
Bound J, **6:** 3184 (3183)
Bounine-Cabalé J, **4:** 2394 (2389)
Bourdieu P, **1:** 67 (62); **2:** (780), 933 (929), 1072 (1069); **3:** 1233 (1229), 1300 (1288), (1304), (1306), 1308, 1337 (1335), 1347 (1345), 1739 (1737); **4:** 2271 (2267, 2268, 2269, 2270, 2271), 2272, 2274 (2274), 2291 (2289); **5:** 2585 (2580), (2615); **6:** 3106 (3101), 3312, 3621 (3618); **9:** 5021 (5016, 5017, 5018, 5019, 5020), 5060 (5057), 5220 (5219), 5312 (5309), 5572 (5570); **10:** 5591 (5590), 5596 (5592, 5593)
Bourke S F, **1:** 41 (34); **2:** 1220 (1217); **6:** 3474 (3468, 3469); **7:** 3739, 3935 (3934); **11:** 6348 (6345), 6349 (6342)
Bousnina M, **11:** 6476
Bouting E J, **11:** 6306
Bovair K, **11:** 6461
Bovair S, **3:** 1434 (1433); **4:** 2199 (2197)
Bove M, **3:** 1406 (1405)
Boven R, **7:** 4170 (4168)
Bover W F, **8:** 4751 (4743)
Bovet M, **8:** 4482 (4481)
Bovet P, **10:** (5880)
Bovin B, **7:** 4179 (4178)
Bovy R C, **5:** 2874 (2873)
Bowden J, **1:** 322 (319, 320); **8:** 4429 (4425); **10:** 5790 (5788)
Bowe R, **6:** 3496 (3494, 3495); **7:** 3826 (3823, 3825)
Bowen H R, **1:** 520 (512, 519, 520); **9:** 5240 (5236)
Bowen J, **5:** 2972 (2969)
Bowen M, **10:** 5693 (5693)
Bower G H, **1:** 203 (200), 330 (328), 376; **2:** 984; **3:** 1245 (1241); **4:** 1980 (1978), 2281 (2280); **6:** 3324 (3315)
Bower P R, **7:** 3977 (3977)
Bower T G R, **8:** 4383 (4381)
Bowering D J, **9:** 5372 (5371)
Bowerman M, **6:** 3223 (3220, 3221)
Bowers C A, **3:** 1301 (1289), 1337 (1335); **10:** 5990 (5986, 5988), 6031
Bowers D G, **5:** 2852 (2848)
Bowers K, **4:** 1958
Bowlby J, **3:** (1639)
Bowles G, **4:** 2302; **11:** 6523, 6769
Bowles S, **1:** 294 (289); **2:** (780), 933 (925, 926, 929), 1072 (1067), 1203 (1199); **3:** 1337 (1335), 1347 (1346), 1448 (1445), 1655 (1649), 1695 (1693), 1720 (1716), 1739 (1737), 1761 (1756), 1820 (1818); **4:** 2004 (2003), 2278 (2277); **5:** 2589 (2587), 2744 (2743), 2942 (2940); **6:** 3189 (3185), (3307), 3621 (3618, 3619); **7:** 3771 (3770), 4141 (4139); **8:** 4568, 4571 (4569), 4574 (4573), 4895 (4894); **9:** 5060 (5057), 5168 (5160), 5228 (5224), 5510 (5509), 5523, 5538 (5533); **10:** 5591 (5589, 5590), 5606 (5602), 5613 (5608); **11:** 6547
Bowman B, **3:** 1635 (1631)
Bowman I, **5:** 2971 (2967); **6:** 3297 (3292)
Bowman J, **1:** 28
Bowman M, **2:** 760; **3:** 1820 (1812); **5:** 2819; **6:** 3458
Bowman M J, **1:** 254, 474 (467, 468); **3:** 1655 (1653), 1665 (1661), 1695 (1692), 1820 (1811), 1824, 1834 (1834); **4:** 2369; **5:** 2647; **7:** 4211 (4207, 4210); **8:** 4488 (4487), 4509 (4504), 4688 (4682, 4684); **9:** 5076, 5538 (5535); **10:** 5919 (5915); **11:** 6251, 6265 (6263), 6425, 6698 (6698)
Bown L, **1:** 215
Bownas D A, **11:** 6678 (6671)
Box S, **1:** 358 (357)
Boxer M, **11:** 6765 (6765)
Boxtel H W van, **5:** 2732 (2729)
Boyan N J, **1:** 60 (54), 67, 83; **3:** 1774 (1770); **4:** 1840, 1857; **5:** 2954 (2952); **6:** 3284 (3278); **7:** 4246; **9:** 5246, 5264; **11:** 6731
Boyand N, **5:** 2847
Boyce G, **6:** 3452 (3448)
Boyd D, **10:** 5991 (5988)
Boyd D R, **7:** 3925 (3921, 3923)
Boyd J R, **5:** 2870
Boyd M, **7:** 3722; **10:** 5606 (5600)
Boyd R D, **1:** 111, 127 (121); **5:** 2937 (2935); **8:** 4812
Boyd W L, **1:** 60 (54), 77 (73), 265, 594 (589); **3:** 1411 (1409, 1410), 1745 (1740), 1774; **4:** 1840 (1837, 1839), 1857 (1856), 1938 (1935), 2167 (2159); **6:** 3284 (3282), 3496 (3493, 3494), 3608 (3603, 3604, 3607); **7:** 3839 (3835), 3840; **8:** 4408 (4405, 4408), 4594 (4592, 4593), 4831, 4844 (4842), 4845; **9:** 5013, 5065 (5061), 5168 (5159, 5160, 5162), 5197, 5201, 5215 (5212), 5216 (5214), 5223 (5222), 5281; **10:** 6072; **11:** 6557 (6556), 6558 (6555), 6563 (6558, 6560)
Boyd-Barrett O, **2:** 991 (990), 1011 (1010)
Boydell D, **10:** 6004
Boydell T, **6:** 3306 (3303)
Boyden J, **3:** 1735 (1735)
Boyer C B, **1:** 88 (86); **6:** 3647

Boyer E G, **2:** 816 (812); **10:** 6112
Boyer E L, **2:** 906 (905); **3:** 1266 (1265), (1796); **9:** 5290 (5283); **11:** 6684
Boyer G, **8:** 4930
Boyer M, **7:** 3970 (3969)
Boyer N J, **9:** 5181
Boyle C, **2:** 973 (972)
Boyle C F, **2:** 1006 (1003); **6:** 3301 (3300)
Boyle M, **5:** 3020
Boyle R, **6:** 3219 (3216)
Bozeman W C, **5:** 2831
Braaksma J, **6:** 3401 (3401)
Braam J, **4:** 2267
Braaten B, **1:** 494 (493)
Braaten S, **1:** 494 (493)
Brace D L, **10:** 5834 (5832)
Bracey G W, **7:** 3726 (3724)
Brachman R J, **8:** 4722 (4719)
Bracho González T, **6:** 3261 (3258)
Bracht G, **4:** 2194 (2189)
Bracht U, **6:** 3137
Brackstone G J, **7:** 3858 (3856)
Bradburn N, **8:** 4887
Braddock J H, **1:** 11 (9); **9:** 5264 (5261)
Braddock J H II, **3:** 1485 (1483)
Braddock R, **7:** 3935 (3933); **10:** 5704 (5699)
Brademas J, **3:** (1796)
Braden B, **11:** 6625
Braden J, **9:** 4977 (4975)
Braden R A, **11:** 6624 (6622, 6623, 6624), 6625 (6623)
Bradley A, **10:** 5943 (5942)
Bradley C, **8:** 4423 (4419); **10:** 6106 (6105)
Bradley Cousin J, **5:** 2509 (2508)
Bradley F H, **8:** 4447
Bradley G W, **3:** 1485 (1483)
Bradley H, **10:** 5954 (5953), 5972 (5968, 5972)
Bradley J V, **7:** 4162 (4161)
Bradley L, **6:** 3452 (3449)
Bradley L A, **3:** 1485 (1483)
Bradley R II, **3:** 1641 (1638, 1640), 1642 (1640); **7:** 3995 (3995)
Bradley S J, **4:** 2452 (2451)
Brady M F, **6:** 3235
Brady S A, **8:** 4935 (4934), 4944 (4943)
Braga C P, **8:** 4835 (4834)
Braggett E, **5:** 2732
Bragshaw D, **2:** 770
Brah A, **10:** 5826 (5823)
Brahma D, **2:** 737 (734)
Braidwood T, **10:** (5659)
Braille L, **10:** (5659)
Braine M D S, **8:** 4956 (4951, 4953, 4954)
Brainerd C, **3:** 1513 (1508)
Brainerd C J, **2:** 856 (854); **6:** 3288 (3285); **7:** 3763 (3761), 3768
Braithwaite J, **6:** 3523 (3517)
Braithwaite R B, **9:** 5050
Brake M, **11:** 6803 (6799, 6800, 6801)
Brakke K E, **5:** 2685 (2682)
Brambring M, **8:** 4779
Brand E, **1:** 103 (101)
Brandenburg D C, **10:** 6234 (6233)
Brandhorst T, **5:** 2827
Brandon-Tuma N, **4:** 2017
Brandstädter J R, **1:** 238 (237); **8:** 4719 (4718)
Brandt D, **2:** 678 (672, 673, 674)
Brandt R, **10:** 6043 (6040)
Brandt R S, **1:** 437 (435); **2:** 893
Brandt W E, **11:** 6678 (6675, 6676)
Brandwein P F, **3:** 1544; **5:** 2589, 2903; **6:** 3416; **10:** 6043
Brann C M B, **7:** 4132 (4125)
Brannigan M, **6:** 3284
Brannon B, **7:** 3991 (3989)
Brannon J, **10:** 5690 (5688)
Branscomb A W, **9:** 5349 (5346)
Bransford J D, **2:** 838 (835), 1019; **6:** 3329 (3325, 3326, 3327), 3334 (3331, 3333), 3512 (3511); **7:** 3768 (3766), 3953; **8:** 4942 (4940); **10:** 6192 (6191)
Bransford J O, **2:** 969 (964, 965)
Branson R K, **5:** 2861 (2857, 2858, 2860); **8:** 4758 (4754, 4755, 4756, 4757)
Brant G, **2:** 1175 (1173)
Brantl G, **2:** 766 (766)
Brantlinger E, **9:** 5268 (5265, 5266, 5267, 5268)
Brantlinger E A, **6:** 3297 (3293, 3294)
Branton P, **4:** 2011 (2008, 2009)
Braskamp L A, **8:** 4751 (4745); **10:** 6224 (6223), 6234 (6233)
Brassard M R, **1:** 19
Brassinne J, **1:** 504
Brattesani K, **10:** 6112 (6109)
Brattset, **11:** 6437 (6431)
Brau M T, **10:** 5943 (5940)
Braudel F, **5:** 2623 (2622)
Braun F, **11:** 6698 (6694)
Braun H I, **5:** 2595 (2593), 3050; **6:** 3124 (3121); **9:** 5082 (5080); **11:** 6320
Braun S J, **8:** 4670 (4667, 4669)
Braungart M M, **8:** 4581 (4576, 4579)
Braungart R G, **8:** 4581 (4576, 4579)
Braverman H, **3:** 1703 (1696); **4:** 2165 (2161); **10:** 6096 (6093), 6139 (6133); **11:** 6260 (6257), 6276 (6272)
Bravi G, **5:** 2971 (2969)
Brawer F B, **2:** 900 (896, 897)
Bray M, **2:** 914 (911, 912, 913); **3:** 1416 (1415), 1655 (1652); **5:** 2512, 2642 (2640), 2643; **6:** 3544 (3540, 3543), 3545 (3543), 3593; **7:** 4136 (4133, 4134), 4141 (4140), 4235 (4233), 4236; **8:** 4707 (4704, 4705); **9:** 5168 (5162, 5165, 5166), 5240 (5240), 5251 (5247), 5294 (5291, 5292); **10:** 5753 (5752)
Bray S, **10:** 5713 (5710)
Brazelton T B, **5:** 2802 (2799); **6:** 3228
Break G F, **9:** 5240 (5237)
Brearly S, **4:** 1991 (1985)
Brecht K, **8:** 4816 (4813)
Bredberg G, **1:** 15 (13)
Bredekamp S, **5:** 2812 (2808), 2814; **9:** 5275 (5274); **11:** 6397 (6395)
Bredella L, **6:** 3443 (3440)
Bredeson P V, **7:** 4246 (4242)
Bredo E, **2:** 1203 (1199)
Breen C, **11:** 6461 (6459)
Breen E, **2:** 737 (737)
Bregman E O, **5:** 2921 (2916, 2917, 2919); **7:** 4329 (4326)
Brehm S S, **1:** 234
Brehmer I, **11:** 6747 (6747)
Breiger R L, **10:** 5735 (5732)
Brekelmans M, **10:** 5775 (5773)
Breland H M, **4:** 2024 (2021, 2023), 2180 (2179)
Brembeck C S, **4:** 2369 (2365); **7:** 4145 (4142)
Brems J, **7:** 4179 (4179)
Breneman D W, **3:** 1449; **6:** 3101; **10:** 5753 (5752)
Brennan J, **7:** 4170 (4166); **10:** 5826 (5824)
Brennan M, **1:** 48 (45)
Brennan R L, **5:** 2462 (2459, 2461); **6:** 3124 (3121); **9:** 4995 (4981); **11:** 6355 (6349, 6351)
Brennan T, **8:** 4571
Brentano F, **8:** 4433 (4430)
Bresco M, **10:** 5693 (5693)
Breslin P, **7:** 4155 (4149)
Breslow L, **2:** 851 (851); **3:** 1624
Bresnick B, **3:** 1624 (1622)
Bretherton I, **2:** 705; **6:** 3223 (3221); **8:** 4541 (4540); **9:** 5528 (5524)
Bretherton L, **9:** 5508
Breton A, **3:** 1745 (1741)
Brett M, **11:** 6523
Breuer K, **2:** 1019 (1017), 1025 (1024); **8:** 4702
Breuer T, **3:** 1553
Brewer G, **4:** 2357 (2356)
Brewer J, **11:** 6465 (6462)
Brewer M, **4:** 2302
Brewer M B, **11:** 6465 (6462)
Brewer S F, **2:** 738 (734)
Brewer W F, **6:** 3155 (3154); **7:** 3788
Brewin J, **3:** 1501 (1497)
Brewster M E, **10:** 6178 (6175)
Brezinka W, **11:** 6579 (6576, 6577)
Brezovich B, **1:** 431 (426)
Brice I, **8:** 4831
Brickell H M, **7:** 4329 (4326)
Bricker D, **5:** 2813 (2810)
Bricker W, **1:** 234 (233)
Brickman W, **9:** 5013
Brickman W W, **2:** 947 (943), 948, 957 (949); **3:** 1768 (1762); **11:** 6530
Brickner D C, **9:** 5578
Bridge R, **3:** 1386 (1383)
Bridge R G, **4:** 1938 (1934)
Bridgeman D L, **8:** 4799
Bridges D, **1:** 510; **2:** 806 (803, 804, 805); **5:** 2528 (2528); **6:** 3389 (3386)
Bridges E M, **6:** 3284 (3276, 3277, 3278, 3279, 3281)
Bridgman L, **3:** (1402), (1404)
Bridgman P W, **8:** 4634 (4633)
Briggs L J, **2:** 1170 (1166); **4:** 1898 (1892), 1928 (1927); **5:** 2861 (2858, 2860), 2862, 2867 (2866), 2874 (2872, 2873); **8:** 4783 (4781); **10:** 6192 (6188)

Briggs R, **3:** 1325 (1322)
Bright B P, **1:** 127 (125, 126)
Bright G W, **7:** 4088 (4084)
Brighton H, **7:** 4293 (4291)
Brike M, **7:** 3711
Brim O G Jr, **1:** 238 (237), 239, 362; **3:** 1641 (1636); **4:** 2261; **6:** 3288, 3427 (3425, 3426), 3428, 3434 (3429, 3431); **7:** 4296 (4295); **9:** 5518 (5513), 5528; **10:** 5591 (5587)
Brimelow P, **9:** 5065 (5062)
Brimer M A, **5:** 2642 (2641)
Brinberg D, **7:** 4006
Brindley G, **4:** 2363 (2360)
Brink T L, **9:** 5008 (5001)
Brinker R P, **5:** 2812 (2809, 2811); **11:** 6461 (6459)
Brinker-Gabler G, **11:** 6747
Brinkerhoff R O, **3:** 1490 (1489); **7:** 4059 (4057)
Brinkman P T, **2:** 1126 (1124), 1131 (1128)
Brinko K T, **10:** 6234 (6233)
Brint S, **9:** 5367 (5365)
Brinton D M, **6:** 3335
Brion P, **8:** 4796 (4794)
Briotta D A, **7:** 3810 (3808)
Brisco D B, **1:** 184
Briscoe D, **1:** 168; **8:** 4616 (4614)
Brislin R W, **11:** 6334
Brits V M, **10:** 5965
Britsch G, **1:** (341)
Brittain J, **6:** 3144 (3139); **8:** 4364 (4362)
Brittan S, **3:** 1820 (1817)
Brittingham B F, **8:** 4408 (4406); **9:** 4973
Britton B K, **8:** 4942
Britton J, **2:** 1098 (1095); **6:** 3459 (3456); **7:** 3936; **10:** 5961 (5958, 5959); **11:** 6784 (6781, 6782)
Britton J N, **7:** 3935 (3933)
Britzman D P, **10:** 6121 (6119), 6122
Brna P, **2:** 988 (987)
Broad M L, **3:** 1490 (1490)
Broadbent D E, **2:** 856 (855)
Broadfoot P, **1:** 362 (358); **2:** 1064; **3:** 1624 (1621); **7:** 3912; **8:** 4601, 4622 (4617, 4618, 4619, 4621), 4623; **9:** 5168 (5165), 5181 (5178); **10:** 5934 (5931), 6096 (6094)
Broadfoot P M, **6:** 3312 (3310, 3311); **8:** 4562 (4561)
Broady D, **4:** 2376 (2376)
Broakshine R G, **7:** 3816
Broca P, **10:** (5681)
Brock C, **2:** 640; **4:** 2291 (2288); **8:** 4601; **9:** 5008, 5013
Brock M N, **4:** 2351 (2346)
Brock T C, **9:** 5324 (5318)
Brock W H, **9:** 5327 (5324, 5325), 5328 (5325)
Brockett R, **2:** 1165
Brockett R B, **1:** 142 (140, 142)
Brockett R G, **1:** 142, 168 (163); **6:** 3434 (3434); **8:** 4736 (4731, 4734, 4735); **9:** 5399 (5395, 5396, 5397, 5398); **10:** 6058 (6054)
Brockington D, **3:** 1501
Brock-Utne B, **4:** 2423 (2419)
Broder L J, **2:** 867 (862); **8:** 4730 (4729)
Broder P K, **3:** 1441 (1439)
Broderick J S, **2:** 1107
Brodie D, **11:** 6798 (6797)
Brody G H, **6:** 3463 (3460)
Brody L, **5:** 2491 (2489)
Broeckmans J, **10:** 6034 (6033)
Broen P A, **1:** 409 (406)
Broer D P, **4:** 2212 (2211)
Brohier W G, **11:** 6628 (6625)
Brolin D E, **2:** 634 (632, 633), 635 (632)
Bromfield R, **2:** 847 (844)
Bromme R, **1:** 23; **10:** 6020, 6088 (6087); **11:** 6390
Bronfenbrenner M, **9:** 5538 (5534)
Bronfenbrenner U, **2:** 687 (678, 679), 892 (888); **3:** 1240 (1236), 1641 (1637), 1647 (1643, 1644, 1645, 1646, 1647); **4:** 2145 (2141), 2257; **5:** 2664 (2658, 2663), 2672 (2670); **7:** 4300 (4297, 4299)
Bronicki G, **10:** 6244 (6243)
Bronneman-Helmers R, **7:** 4325
Bronowski J, **6:** 3219 (3218)
Bronowski R, **6:** 3219
Bronson V, **1:** 274 (267)
Brook C G D, **8:** 4473 (4471)
Brookfield S, **1:** 135, 184 (184), 277 (275); **6:** 3434 (3428, 3434); **7:** 4185 (4181)
Brookfield S D, **1:** 152 (148), 168 (163, 164, 165, 166, 167), 277; **5:** 2532 (2530, 2531); **6:** 3349 (3346); **9:** 5399 (5395, 5398); **10:** 5596 (5594), 6058 (6054, 6055, 6056, 6057), 6202 (6200)
Brookhart S M, **10:** 6106 (6104, 6105)
Brookover W B, **4:** 1934 (1929, 1930, 1932); **9:** 5210 (5207); **10:** 5750 (5746)
Brooks A S, **1:** 280
Brooks B D, **10:** 6163 (6161)
Brooks D M, **7:** 4175 (4171, 4174); **10:** 6026 (6023)
Brooks G, **6:** 3474 (3470); **10:** 5826 (5822)
Brooks J B, **11:** 6797 (6797)
Brooks K W, **3:** 1443
Brooks L, **6:** 3442 (3439); **11:** 6678
Brooks P, **2:** 860 (859)
Brooks V D, **9:** 5577 (5575)
Brooks-Gunn J, **1:** 88 (83), 89; **2:** 705 (702); **3:** 1641 (1636, 1637, 1638, 1639, 1641), 1642 (1636, 1637, 1638, 1639, 1640, 1641); **4:** 1967, 2439; **5:** 2677 (2673), 2813 (2812); **8:** 4779 (4775, 4776, 4777, 4778); **9:** 5394 (5391, 5393), 5441 (5436)
Broom L, **7:** 3721 (3716, 3717); **8:** 4895 (4892)
Broomes D, **3:** 1599
Brophy J, **2:** 811 (807), 816 (815); **3:** 1283 (1279), 1529 (1525); **7:** 3833 (3832); **8:** 4864 (4862), 4881 (4878); **9:** 5175 (5170), 5223 (5221), 5363 (5359, 5361); **10:** 5795, 5826 (5825), 6015 (6013), 6112 (6107, 6108, 6109), 6121, 6122, 6173 (6172), 6239 (6238); **11:** 6310 (6309)
Brophy J E, **2:** 796 (794); **4:** 1847 (1846); **5:** 2767 (2766); **8:** 4881 (4880); **9:** 5264 (5259), 5363; **10:** 5762 (5761), 6020 (6016, 6018), 6031, 6088 (6086), 6121 (6119, 6120)
Brophy M, **3:** 1563 (1559), 1567 (1565)
Brose K, **8:** 4460 (4460)
Brott R, **10:** 5965 (5963)
Broudy H, **8:** 4455 (4452, 4455); **10:** 5948 (5945, 5948)
Broudy H S, **1:** 198 (196); **3:** 1354 (1351); **6:** 3201 (3197)
Broughton J M, **8:** 4383 (4381)
Brousseau G, **1:** 347 (344); **2:** 1052 (1051)
Brovey A J, **7:** 4104 (4102)
Browder D M, **8:** 4376 (4373, 4374)
Brown A, **4:** 1847 (1845); **5:** 2916 (2913); **6:** 3349, 3625 (3625); **7:** 3886 (3885); **9:** 5507 (5507); **10:** 6015 (6014); **11:** 6690
Brown A L, **1:** 5 (5), 330 (330), 374 (371, 372); **2:** 838 (835, 836, 837), 842 (839), 860 (858, 859), 867 (864), 868 (864), 969 (966, 967), 1198 (1195); **3:** 1236, 1252 (1251), 1529 (1526, 1527), 1739; **4:** 2198 (2196); **5:** 2536 (2533), 2767 (2762, 2763); **6:** 3223 (3223), 3302 (3300), 3315 (3313, 3314), 3329 (3325, 3326, 3327), 3334 (3331, 3333), 3427 (3427); **7:** 3768 (3764, 3766), 3788 (3784, 3786, 3787), 3792, 3830 (3828); **8:** 4730 (4730), 4942 (4941), 4956 (4956); **10:** 5795 (5792), 6177 (6174), 6178 (6174), 6192 (6189); **11:** 6456 (6454)
Brown B, **8:** 4568 (4563)
Brown B W, **3:** 1386 (1383); **6:** 3549 (3546); **7:** 3820 (3816, 3818)
Brown C, **2:** 1152 (1148, 1150); **3:** 1712 (1711), 1750 (1750), 1829 (1828); **4:** 2432; **5:** 2798 (2792, 2795); **6:** 3189 (3189)
Brown C C, **5:** 2779
Brown C J, **7:** 4026 (4023)
Brown D, **2:** 906 (902); **8:** 4479 (4476); **9:** 5290 (5282, 5283); **11:** 6678
Brown D J, **3:** 1411 (1408, 1409, 1410, 1411); **9:** 5185 (5183), 5307 (5304, 5306, 5307)
Brown D R, **9:** 4995 (4984)
Brown D T, **9:** 5290 (5287)
Brown F, **1:** 83 (78)
Brown G A, **1:** 27; **2:** 1194; **6:** 3209 (3208); **10:** 5977 (5974, 5975)
Brown G N, **2:** 913; **10:** 5842
Brown G W, **3:** 1520 (1519)
Brown H P, **3:** 1750 (1746)
Brown I, **3:** 1606 (1603)
Brown J, **2:** 856 (854), 1093 (1089, 1090), 1165 (1161); **6:** 3625 (3622, 3624); **7:** 3886 (3885); **10:** 6015 (6014)
Brown J A, **8:** 4730 (4730)
Brown J I, **6:** 3339 (3337); **7:** 3935 (3933)
Brown J N, **6:** 3616 (3614)
Brown J S, **1:** 347 (343), 348; **2:** 838 (837), 842 (839), 969 (967), 1007 (1003); **3:** 1252 (1251), 1529 (1526); **4:** 1899

(1895), 1917 (1917), 2281 (2281); **5:** 2773 (2770), 2867 (2865), 2884 (2882); **6:** 3301 (3299), 3344 (3341), 3345 (3342, 3344), 3660 (3658); **7:** 3792, 3953 (3953); **9:** 5232 (5229), 5363 (5360, 5362); **10:** 5795 (5794), 6177 (6174, 6177); **11:** 6456 (6454)
Brown L, **2:** 718 (715), 729 (723); **3:** 1438, 1508; **5:** 2813; **8:** 4375 (4374, 4375)
Brown L D, **3:** 1271 (1268); **7:** 4336 (4331)
Brown L M, **11:** 6726 (6724)
Brown L R, **4:** 2331
Brown M, **2:** 982, 1012 (1008); **4:** 2419 (2414); **6:** 3144 (3139); **10:** 6008 (6007)
Brown M B, **6:** 3507 (3507), 3508 (3504); **7:** 4015 (4015)
Brown M M, **1:** 234 (232)
Brown P, **1:** 594; **9:** 5060 (5058), 5117
Brown P J, **5:** 2709 (2706)
Brown R, **4:** 1990 (1987, 1990); **6:** 3224 (3221, 3223); **7:** 3768 (3765, 3767); **10:** 5596, 5606 (5599), 5690 (5687)
Brown R D, **4:** (2108); **10:** 5804 (5797)
Brown R V, **3:** 1425
Brown S, **3:** 1579 (1577); **4:** 2291 (2290); **5:** 2798 (2796), 2903; **10:** 6088 (6088), 6182 (6182)
Brown S A, **5:** 2903 (2899)
Brown S C, **3:** 1328
Brown S D, **11:** 6360 (6358)
Brown S I, **6:** 3652 (3648, 3649, 3650)
Brown S J, **5:** 2874 (2873)
Brown S R, **4:** 2194 (2190)
Brown S W, **2:** 973
Brown W, **4:** 1872 (1867)
Brown W F, **1:** 193 (187)
Browne G S, **6:** 3276
Browne M W, **7:** 4006 (4005, 4006), 4007; **8:** 4351 (4341, 4349), 4359 (4352)
Browne R K, **9:** 5060
Brownell G, **10:** 6008 (6005)
Browning G, **1:** 157 (154)
Browning K, **3:** 1624 (1623)
Brownless V, **2:** 792 (788)
Brownley J, **3:** 1402 (1400)
Brubacher J, **4:** 2387 (2386); **8:** 4455 (4452)
Brubacher J S, **10:** 5804 (5796)
Brubaker D L, **9:** 5577 (5573)
Brubaker N L, **9:** 5362 (5359, 5361)
Bruce B B, **10:** 5795 (5793, 5794), 5934
Bruce B C, **4:** 1957 (1956); **7:** 3788
Bruce E, **5:** 2827
Bruce J, **4:** 2418
Bruce K, **9:** 5181 (5178, 5179)
Bruce M G, **5:** 2514 (2514)
Bruce V, **8:** 4379
Brudner H J, **5:** 2870 (2868)
Bruggen J C van, **3:** 1278 (1273, 1277, 1278)
Bruggencate G C, **7:** 3995 (3995)
Bruininks R H, **2:** 729 (722); **3:** 1438
Brumberg S F, **9:** 5510 (5509)
Brunelli P, **1:** 362 (361)
Bruner J, **1:** 347 (344); **2:** 687 (683, 685); **3:** 1252, 1343, 1796 (1795); **4:** 1984 (1981), 2145; **5:** 2536 (2533); **6:** 3312, 3684 (3673); **7:** 3886 (3881, 3884, 3885), (4156), 4301 (4300); **8:** (4401); **9:** 5275 (5273); **10:** 6121 (6120), (6174)
Bruner J R, **4:** 1898 (1884)
Bruner J S, **3:** 1266 (1263), 1328 (1326), 1354 (1351), 1434 (1433), 1543 (1538, 1542); **4:** 1847 (1842, 1843), 2281 (2280); **5:** 2669 (2667), (2878), 2903 (2899); **6:** 3224 (3220, 3222); **7:** 4081 (4080); **8:** 4541 (4538); **9:** (5326), 5507 (5505), 5508; **10:** 5745 (5738), 5750 (5746), 6099 (6098), 6202 (6199); **11:** 6333
Brunetta R, **4:** 1976; **6:** 3617; **11:** 6420
Brunetti J, **9:** 5181 (5177)
Brunetti M, **3:** 1619
Bruno F, **3:** 1619
Bruno G, **3:** (1461)
Bruno R, **7:** 3991 (3990)
Brunstrom C K, **10:** 5901
Brunswic E, **8:** 4698 (4696, 4697)
Brunswik E, **5:** 2665
Brunt R, **4:** 1984 (1983)
Bruschini C, **3:** 1671 (1669, 1670)
Brush L R, **4:** 2435, 2436
Brush S G, **8:** 4464 (4462)
Bryan E M, **11:** 6492 (6488, 6489)
Bryan W L, **10:** 6026 (6021)
Bryant B R, **2:** 718 (715)
Bryant D, **9:** 5275 (5274)
Bryant D M, **3:** 1642 (1641)
Bryant E C, **9:** 5385 (5384)
Bryant I, **1:** 168 (166); **10:** 6058 (6056)
Bryant J, **1:** 570; **5:** 2897 (2895); **6:** 3625; **8:** 4680 (4677, 4678)
Bryant P, **6:** 3452 (3449); **8:** 4912 (4910)
Bryant S L, **7:** 3768 (3765)
Bryce J, **6:** 3356
Bryden J, **11:** 6306 (6299, 6302)
Brydon-Miller M, **7:** 4336 (4331)
Bryk A S, **1:** 11 (7), 520 (516); **2:** 677 (677), 711 (710), 834 (832, 833); **3:** 1431, 1607; **4:** 1938 (1935, 1936), 1939 (1937), 2249, 2388 (2386); **5:** 2595 (2590, 2594), 2596 (2590, 2591, 2593, 2594), 2931 (2930); **6:** 3523 (3513), 3524 (3522); **7:** 3820 (3816), 3986 (3982, 3983, 3985), 3987; **8:** 4845 (4841, 4842); **9:** 5129 (5129), 5130 (5129), 5142 (5137), 5223 (5221), 5378 (5374, 5375, 5376, 5377), 5379 (5373, 5374, 5375, 5377), 5445 (5444); **10:** 5775
Bryk T, **3:** 1513 (1512)
Bryson J M, **8:** 4509 (4503), 4601 (4600)
Bryson M, **11:** 6780
Brzezinski E J, **5:** 3043 (3037)
Buber M, **4:** (2294); **6:** 3119; **8:** (4431)
Bubner R, **5:** 2586
Buch M B, **5:** 2753; **10:** 5995 (5991)
Buchan A, **8:** 4698
Buchanan C C, **2:** 1139 (1137)
Buchanan C M, **5:** 2677 (2673)
Buchanan J, **8:** 4568 (4564), 4594 (4589)
Buchanan J M, **2:** 1072 (1066)
Buchanan N K, **5:** 2731 (2727)
Buchele R, **6:** 3189 (3187, 3188)
Buchenau A, **8:** 4419 (4419)
Buchert L, **11:** 6451
Buchman J H, **11:** 6306 (6300)
Buchman M, **10:** 5994 (5993)
Buchmann M, **3:** 1635 (1633); **10:** 5812 (5810)
Buchner E F, **7:** 3925
Buck G, **4:** 2363 (2363)
Buck G M, **9:** 5441 (5436)
Buck J N, **8:** 4791 (4791)
Buck P D, **7:** 3973 (3972)
Buckby M, **4:** 2357 (2353, 2354, 2356)
Buckle P, **4:** 2012 (2011)
Buckley F, **9:** 5559 (5556)
Bucuvalas M J, **3:** 1431 (1428)
Buddrus V, **3:** 1733
Bude E, **1:** 244 (241, 242)
Bude U, **8:** 4688 (4685, 4686); **10:** 5982 (5981)
Budetti P P, **5:** 2575 (2572)
Budgett R, **4:** 1898
Budoff M, **5:** 2767 (2762); **6:** 3315 (3313); **9:** 5070 (5068)
Buehler C, **4:** 2266 (2264)
Buffon G, **9:** (5088)
Buhain L, **8:** 4796 (4794)
Bühler C, **5:** 2664 (2656), 2692; **6:** 3427 (3426)
Bühler G, **5:** 2601 (2597, 2598, 2600); **9:** 5008 (4999)
Bühler K, **5:** (2881)
Buhrmester D, **10:** 5758 (5757)
Builis A, **6:** 3272
Bukate D, **1:** (214)
Bukowski W M, **8:** 4368 (4365, 4366, 4367)
Buktenica N A, **9:** 5290 (5290)
Bulatao R, **3:** 1676; **4:** 2412; **6:** 3106
Bulcock J W, **10:** 5762 (5761)
Bull B L, **10:** 6053 (6049), 6096 (6095), 6117 (6113)
Bull D, **8:** 4957 (4954)
Bull G L, **7:** 3807 (3802)
Bullivant B M, **9:** 5510 (5509), 5539 (5538)
Bullock A, **9:** 5185 (5184), 5307 (5307)
Bullock A B, **6:** 3209 (3205, 3206)
Bullock D, **3:** 1513 (1508, 1509, 1510, 1511, 1513); **5:** 2680 (2679)
Bullock H A, **7:** 3848 (3844)
Bullock M, **8:** 4956 (4952); **10:** 5693 (5693)
Bullough R, **2:** 796 (792); **10:** 6026 (6021)
Bulow J, **6:** 3189 (3187)
Bultmann R, **8:** 4433 (4431)
Bumfield R, **3:** 1635 (1632)
Bunch C, **11:** 6726 (6725)
Bunda M A, **4:** 2388 (2384); **8:** 4751 (4743)
Bunderson C V, **1:** 52 (51, 52), 370 (367); **2:** 998 (993); **10:** 5771 (5771)
Bunker J, **4:** 2212
Bunning R L, **7:** 4185
Bunting B, **11:** 6339 (6334, 6337, 6338)
Burbridge L, **7:** 4200 (4199)

Burbules N, **4:** 1984 (1980, 1981), 2004 (2002)
Burbules N L, **10:** 6096 (6095)
Burch P, **9:** 5268 (5265, 5267, 5268)
Burchill J, **9:** 5251 (5251)
Burchinal M R, **3:** 1643 (1640)
Burden P, **10:** 5934 (5930)
Burden P R, **10:** 5939 (5935, 5936, 5938)
Burden R, **4:** 1979 (1976); **10:** 5775 (5774)
Burdin J L, **6:** 3284
Burg S L, **5:** 2512 (2511)
Burge L, **2:** 982 (979)
Burgess D M, **5:** 2567 (2564)
Burgess E W, **11:** 6803 (6799)
Burgess R, **7:** 4319 (4317); **10:** 6215
Burgess R G, **1:** 11 (8); **4:** 2033 (2032)
Burgess S A, **2:** 737 (733)
Burgess T, **7:** 3936; **8:** 4608; **10:** 5961 (5959); **11:** 6784 (6782)
Burgman H, **4:** 2327 (2326)
Burgoyne J, **6:** 3306 (3303)
Burk F, **5:** (2774)
Burkam D T, **10:** 5607 (5604)
Burke C L, **4:** 1962 (1958, 1960); **10:** 5795 (5793)
Burke D, **2:** 893 (891)
Burke G, **2:** 1094; **3:** 1695, 1713; **4:** 1911; **6:** 3474; **10:** 5613 (5610); **11:** 6260 (6258), 6282, 6283
Burke P J, **6:** 3508 (3500); **7:** 3833 (3832)
Burke R J, **10:** 5924 (5922), 6062 (6061)
Burke W P, **9:** 5406 (5404)
Burkett D, **8:** 4751 (4743)
Burkhardt H, **3:** 1778 (1776); **6:** 3634 (3633)
Burks B S, **7:** 3872 (3870); **8:** 4351 (4339)
Burleson B R, **10:** 5617 (5617)
Burleson D L, **3:** 1796 (1796)
Burleson N, **8:** 4609
Burli A, **5:** 2910 (2908)
Burlingame M, **1:** 437 (432, 433); **9:** 5169 (5162)
Burlingham D, **8:** (4813)
Burman J H, **9:** 5572 (5569)
Burness T, **11:** 6690 (6687)
Burnett J H, **1:** 295 (288, 289, 291), 297
Burnette J, **7:** 3807 (3805)
Burnhill P, **4:** 2291 (2290)
Burnkrant R E, **1:** 389 (381)
Burns B, **8:** 4383 (4382)
Burns G P, **10:** 5804
Burns J M, **1:** 67 (65), 437 (435); **6:** 3284 (3277, 3279)
Burns M, **6:** 3670 (3669)
Burns P, **4:** 1991
Burns R, **2:** 816 (812, 813, 814, 815); **5:** 2855 (2853); **10:** 6155
Burns R B, **5:** 2778 (2776, 2777); **6:** 3631 (3627); **9:** 5043 (5038, 5041); **10:** 6239 (6238, 6239)
Burns S, **2:** 860 (859)
Burns T, **4:** 2165 (2164); **9:** 5168 (5162)
Buros O K, **11:** 6348 (6348)
Burr R L, **3:** 1624 (1621)
Burra N, **7:** 4136 (4133)
Burrell G, **1:** 67 (62); **2:** (932); **3:** 1809 (1805); **4:** 2165 (2160, 2161, 2164); **6:** 3527 (3526, 3527)
Burris B, **3:** 1774 (1772)
Burris V, **1:** 358 (357); **7:** 4255 (4250)
Burry J, **4:** 2131 (2128)
Bursch C W, **10:** 5804 (5796)
Burscheid H J, **6:** 3652 (3647, 3648, 3649, 3650)
Burstall C, **2:** 796 (795); **4:** 2345 (2344); **7:** 3726 (3724)
Burstein L, **1:** 520 (516); **3:** 1768 (1764); **4:** 2388 (2382, 2385, 2386), 2389 (2384, 2386, 2387); **5:** 2595 (2590, 2594); **7:** 3986 (3978); **10:** 6043 (6040)
Burston W H, **5:** 2623
Burstyn J N, **4:** 1957 (1955), 1958 (1954, 1955); **11:** 6765 (6761)
Burt C, **3:** (1793), (1794), (1796); **4:** (1868), 2240 (2230, 2239); **5:** (2878), (2917)
Burt C B, **6:** 3523 (3522)
Burt C L, **7:** 3879 (3873, 3875), (3931)
Burt M K, **4:** 2345 (2345)
Burt R S, **9:** 5559 (5558), 5560 (5559)
Burt V L, **9:** 5130 (5129)
Burtless G, **6:** 3184
Burton J, **1:** 198 (197)
Burton J K, **7:** 3807
Burton J M, **8:** 4388 (4384)
Burton L, **6:** 3459 (3457), 3642 (3641); **10:** 5826
Burton R D E, **5:** 2544 (2537, 2543)
Burton R R, **1:** 347 (343, 347); **4:** 2281 (2281); **8:** 4730 (4730)
Burton T L, **11:** 6797 (6795, 6797)
Buschang P H, **8:** 4473 (4472)
Bush A J, **6:** 3508 (3503)
Bush D M, **10:** 5591 (5586, 5587, 5588)
Bush G, **3:** (1358)
Bush P J, **5:** 2571 (2569)
Bush R N, **10:** 5977 (5973)
Bush T, **6:** 3528
Bush V, **5:** 2709 (2706)
Bushnell P, **7:** 4111
Busk P L, **9:** 5489 (5488)
Buss A H, **8:** 4394 (4389); **9:** 5528 (5524); **11:** 6310 (6308)
Buss D, **7:** 3889 (3886)
Busse T V, **8:** 4731 (4729)
Bussey K, **1:** 234 (230, 232); **4:** 2449 (2446)
Bustos F, **8:** 4495 (4494)
Buswell G T, **11:** 6445 (6441)
Buswinka H F, **10:** 6034 (6033)
Butcher A H, **5:** 2571 (2569)
Butcher H J, **5:** 2922
Butcher J N, **1:** 52 (51, 52)
Butcher P M, **10:** 5977 (5976)
Buthedahl P, **11:** 6420
Butler D, **6:** 3463 (3461)
Butler E W, **4:** 2266
Butler J A, **3:** 1508 (1506); **5:** 2575 (2574); **8:** 4935 (4933)
Butler K, **10:** 5693 (5692, 5693), 5694
Butler L, **6:** 3399 (3394)
Butler N R, **6:** 3523 (3512)
Butler R, **1:** 31 (31)
Butler R P, **9:** 5406 (5404)
Butt M S, **1:** 254 (246)
Butt R, **10:** 6091 (6089)
Buttedahl P, **1:** 100 (95), 120 (119), 152 (143), 180 (180); **7:** 4185 (4182)
Butterfield E C, **7:** 3768 (3767); **11:** 6456 (6454)
Butterfield H, **5:** 2607
Butterworth T, **10:** 5762 (5760)
Buttimer K J, **11:** 6798 (6796)
Buttlar L, **3:** 1589 (1587)
Button H W, **1:** 77 (73)
Butts R F, **2:** 770 (767, 769, 770); **5:** 2978; **7:** 3848 (3842, 3845), 4224 (4223)
Buunk B B, **10:** 5924 (5923)
Buvinic M, **3:** 1676
Buyse R, **4:** 1872 (1866, 1867, 1869)
Byard P J, **8:** 4473 (4469, 4470)
Bybee R W, **4:** 1995 (1994); **6:** 3416 (3411); **9:** 5327 (5325), 5345 (5344); **11:** 6292 (6291)
Byers H, **9:** 5416 (5414)
Byers M L, **11:** 6445 (6444)
Byers P, **9:** 5416 (5414)
Byers-Brown B, **10:** 5680 (5675, 5677)
Byram M, **4:** 1910 (1906)
Byrne B M, **4:** 2240 (2238); **7:** 4006 (4001); **10:** 6062 (6060)
Byrne D, **10:** 5617 (5614, 5615)
Byrne E M, **4:** 2286 (2284, 2285), 2292
Byrne R M J, **8:** 4951
Byrnes H, **4:** 2345 (2343)
Byrnes J P, **1:** 88 (85); **10:** 5745 (5744)
Byström J, **10:** 5829

Cabanus J Q, **11:** 6437 (6436)
Cabello B, **5:** 2462 (2461)
Cabezon E, **6:** 3631 (3630)
Cabral de Andrade A, **7:** 4155; **11:** 6451 (6448, 6450)
Cach J, **2:** 884
Cacioppe R, **9:** 5181 (5178, 5179)
Cadena F, **2:** 906 (903)
Cadinale L, **8:** 4881 (4878)
Cadwell C, **11:** 6310 (6309)
Caesar J, **9:** (5395)
Caffarella E P, **7:** 4325
Caffarella R S, **6:** 3434 (3434); **7:** 4325, 4329; **9:** 5399 (5396)
Cafferty T P, **8:** 4661
Caffrey J, **1:** 390 (384); **3:** 1482 (1480); **8:** 4930 (4927)
Cahen L S, **3:** 1834 (1833); **5:** 2870 (2868); **11:** 6370 (6368)
Cai J, **1:** 374 (372)
Caillods F, **3:** 1655, 1680 (1679), 1685 (1681, 1684), 1788 (1788), 1820, 1830; **5:** 2984; **7:** 4141; **8:** 4489, 4491, 4509 (4502), 4510; **9:** 5259; **11:** 6265 (6263)
Cain G G, **3:** 1707 (1705); **4:** 2445 (2442, 2444); **6:** 3189 (3186, 3187); **8:** 4845 (4840); **9:** 5372 (5368)
Cain K M, **1:** 31 (30); **9:** 5406 (5405)
Cain P, **11:** 6276 (6274)

Cain R Jr, **3:** 1643 (1639)
Cairncross D, **1:** 110 (109)
Cairnes K L, **1:** 310
Cairns B D, **1:** 234 (233)
Cairns H, **9:** 4981
Cairns L G, **1:** 486 (483)
Cairns R B, **1:** 234 (232, 233); **8:** 4394 (4390, 4392)
Cajanus, **6:** (3529)
Cake H, **4:** 2194 (2189, 2191)
Cakir A, **4:** 2011 (2010)
Calamidas A, **10:** 5924 (5923)
Calculator S N, **1:** 408 (407)
Calder I A, **1:** 193 (188)
Calderhead J, **1:** 27; **2:** 796 (792); **10:** 5812, 5985, 6058 (6054, 6055), 6088 (6088), 6092, 6122, 6183 (6180)
Calderhead T, **10:** 6096 (6094)
Calderó-Hernandez G, **7:** 4155
Calderwood A, **11:** 6712
Caldwell B J, **3:** 1411 (1410); **5:** 2508 (2504), 2509, 2672 (2670), 2852 (2849); **6:** 3496 (3491); **7:** 3840; **9:** 5185 (5183, 5184), 5217, 5308
Caldwell B M, **2:** 687 (683); **3:** 1642 (1640); **5:** 2806 (2803)
Caldwell G, **1:** 414 (411, 413), 415
Caldwell J, **1:** 474 (467); **3:** 1676 (1673, 1674, 1675)
Caldwell J C, **4:** 2418 (2417)
Caldwell N, **7:** 3861 (3858)
Caldwell O T, **9:** 5327 (5325)
Caldwell P, **4:** 2418 (2417); **11:** 6437 (6434)
Caldwell S, **10:** 6214
Calfee R C, **2:** 1006; **5:** 2767 (2762); **6:** 3655
Calhoun C J, **9:** 5510
Calhoun J F, **10:** 6062 (6061)
Calinger B J, **7:** 3726
Callahan C M, **5:** 2731 (2729)
Callahan R E, **1:** 77 (73); **2:** 1072 (1066); **4:** 2165 (2158); **7:** 4246 (4242); **9:** 5523
Callan E, **3:** 1328
Callan P M, **9:** 5317 (5316)
Callaway A, **1:** 226 (222); **4:** 2369 (2366)
Callaway H, **7:** 3852 (3849), 4336 (4332)
Callewaert G, **1:** 474 (472)
Callewaert S, **4:** 2376 (2376), 2377
Calliods F, **3:** 1829 (1825)
Calore D, **7:** 4300 (4298)
Calvin J, **6:** (3531)
Camaioni L, **6:** 3224 (3223); **9:** 5508
Cambone J, **10:** 6031 (6031)
Cambron-McCabe N, **6:** 3608
Cameron C T, **7:** 3807 (3804)
Cameron J, **3:** 1589
Cameron M, **2:** 1121 (1119)
Cameron M E, **9:** 5291 (5284, 5286)
Cameron S M, **11:** 6445 (6444)
Camilli G, **5:** 3050 (3045, 3049)
Cammish N K, **4:** 2291 (2288)
Camp B W, **3:** 1624 (1623)
Camp R, **4:** 2024
Camp R R, **3:** 1491
Campbell D, **1:** 93 (90); **2:** 645 (642), 802 (799); **8:** (4453)
Campbell D D, **7:** 4185 (4181)
Campbell D S, **10:** 5817 (5813)
Campbell D T, **2:** 1135 (1132); **3:** 1283 (1281), 1431 (1425, 1427); **4:** 1872 (1870), 1938 (1935), 2089 (2081, 2082, 2083, 2084, 2085, 2086, 2087, 2088), (2103), 2194 (2187, 2188, 2189), 2388 (2383, 2386); **6:** 3523 (3514); **7:** 4006 (4000, 4001, 4002, 4003, 4005); **8:** 4403 (4400), 4766 (4762), 4875 (4874); **9:** 5030 (5024, 5025), 5373, 5490; **11:** 6384 (6378), 6465 (6462), 6511 (6508), 6575 (6574)
Campbell F, **5:** 2806 (2804)
Campbell J, **5:** 2769 (2763); **8:** 4375 (4373)
Campbell J P, **3:** 1490 (1489); **6:** 3306 (3304, 3305)
Campbell N J, **4:** 2427 (2424)
Campbell N R, **2:** 792 (786); **7:** 3706 (3698, 3699); **9:** 5050
Campbell P B, **9:** 5076 (5072, 5074)
Campbell P H, **3:** 1406; **5:** 2813 (2808, 2809, 2811)
Campbell R, **3:** 1449; **9:** 5175 (5172)
Campbell R F, **1:** 60 (53), 77 (74); **3:** 1797
Campbell R J, **5:** 2470; **6:** 3306
Campbell S K, **9:** 5489 (5487)
Campbell T D, **9:** 5372 (5371)
Campbell W J, **9:** 5294 (5293); **10:** 6149; **11:** 6797 (6796)
Campe J H, **11:** (6745)
Campeau P L, **7:** (3758)
Campen J T, **3:** 1820 (1819); **4:** 1911
Campinos-Dubernet M, **11:** 6415
Campion J E, **8:** 4408 (4405)
Campion L E, **4:** 1898 (1885)
Campione J C, **1:** 5 (5), 374 (372); **2:** 838 (835, 836), (859); **3:** 1529 (1527); **5:** 2767 (2762, 2763); **6:** 3315 (3313), 3329 (3325, 3326, 3327), 3334 (3331, 3333); **7:** 3768 (3766), 3830 (3828); **8:** 4730 (4730); **10:** 6177 (6174); **11:** 6456 (6454)
Campos B P, **10:** 5939
Campos J J, **4:** 1966 (1964); **5:** 2802; **8:** 4383 (4380); **11:** (6308)
Campos R G, **4:** 1966 (1964)
Camstra B, **2:** 1170 (1166)
Camus A, **8:** (4431)
Canale M, **4:** 2357 (2353)
Cancro R, **7:** 3872
Candanedo A, **7:** 4275
Candler A C, **3:** 1355 (1353)
Candlin C, **6:** 3442 (3440)
Candoli I C, **9:** 5185 (5182, 5183)
Candy P C, **1:** 168 (163); **6:** 3349 (3345, 3346), 3434 (3434); **7:** 3894 (3891, 3893); **9:** 5399 (5396, 5398); **10:** 6058 (6054)
Cangelosi J S, **8:** 4408 (4406)
Canieso-Doronila M L, **8:** 4586 (4583)
Cannell J J, **7:** 3726; **8:** 4526 (4521)
Canning P M, **7:** 4296 (4295)
Cannings T R, **11:** 6603 (6602)
Cannon G, **10:** 6244 (6242)
Cannon W B, **8:** 4394 (4390)
Canon A, **9:** 5232 (5229)
Canter D, **4:** 2219; **7:** 4316; **9:** 5504
Canter L, **1:** 486 (483)
Canter M, **1:** 486 (483)
Cantor G N, **9:** 5350
Cantor L, **11:** 6684, 6690 (6689)
Cantraine G, **11:** 6307
Cao Q, **3:** 1589
Capaldi D, **1:** 234 (233)
Capecchi V, **8:** 4638 (4637)
Čapek J B, **2:** 883
Capell F J, **1:** 594 (591); **4:** 2024 (2019, 2023)
Capelle J, **8:** 4608 (4605)
Čapková D, **2:** 883
Caplan F, **8:** 4758 (4755, 4758)
Caplan G, **1:** 88
Caplan N, **3:** 1431 (1428); **4:** 1863 (1862)
Caplan R D, **10:** 6062 (6059)
Caputo J, **10:** 5925 (5920)
Carabana J, **9:** 5281 (5279)
Caradog Jones D, **7:** 3721 (3717)
Caramazza A, **10:** 5790 (5783, 5784)
Caravello-Hibbert S M, **11:** 6603 (6602)
Carbone P F, **11:** 6580
Carbonell J G, **8:** 4722 (4721)
Carbonell J R, **1:** 347 (343)
Card C, **4:** 2297
Card D, **7:** 3820 (3816); **8:** 4901 (4898, 4900), 4902 (4898)
Cardall C, **5:** 3050 (3044)
Cardinet J, **5:** 2462 (2460, 2461, 2462); **6:** 3124
Cardó A, **8:** 4415
Cardon L R, **11:** 6492 (6490)
Cardoso F H, **3:** 1712
Care N, **4:** 2036 (2034)
Carelse X F, **11:** 6292 (6288)
Carew J V, **3:** 1257 (1255)
Carey C, **6:** 3671 (3670)
Carey L M, **4:** 1928 (1927); **5:** 2861 (2860); **8:** 4751 (4743), 4783 (4781); **10:** 5900 (5899)
Carey S, **2:** 842 (839, 840, 841), 846 (845), 856 (853, 854); **3:** 1504 (1502); **5:** 2665 (2661); **6:** 3155, 3288 (3286); **8:** 4956 (4952)
Carey W B, **5:** 2575; **11:** (6308)
Carine D, **2:** 866 (862)
Carini P, **10:** 6099 (6097)
Cariño I D, **8:** 4442
Cariola P, **3:** 1593 (1591); **6:** 3256 (3254); **8:** 4495 (4492)
Carkhuff R, **5:** 3007 (3005)
Carlberg C, **10:** 5663
Carleer G, **2:** 1012
Carli L L, **9:** 5435 (5434)
Carlisle K E, **6:** 3096 (3094); **10:** 5913 (5912)
Carlisle R, **5:** 2897 (2896)
Carlsen G R, **7:** 3935 (3933)
Carlsen J C, **7:** 4026 (4023)
Carlsen W S, **8:** 4873 (4871), 4881 (4875, 4876, 4878); **10:** 6112 (6111), 6121 (6118)
Carlson B C, **2:** 635 (634)

Carlson B L, **9:** 5130 (5129)
Carlson D, **4:** 2165 (2164); **5:** 2697 (2695); **8:** 4586 (4581)
Carlson P A, **8:** 4694
Carlson R, **4:** 2331
Carlson R A, **10:** 5596 (5593)
Carlson R O, **1:** 82 (81, 82); **4:** 2166; **11:** 6731
Carlson S B, **4:** 2024 (2020)
Carlson V, **1:** 19
Carlsson G, **7:** 3864 (3862, 3863)
Carlton S T, **4:** 2024 (2020)
Carlucci C M, **7:** 3808 (3807)
Carly L, **11:** 6780 (6778)
Carmeli M, **11:** 6484 (6483)
Carmichael L, **7:** 3950
Carmines E G, **4:** 1984 (1981); **11:** 6576 (6573, 6574)
Carnahan R S, **10:** 6034 (6033)
Carnap R, **8:** 4446 (4442), (4450), (4633)
Carnegie A, **10:** (5705)
Carneiro R L, **4:** 2400 (2398)
Carnevale A P, **2:** 665 (662), 1152 (1147, 1148, 1149); **3:** 1315; **4:** 1924; **10:** 5919 (5915); **11:** 6415 (6413)
Carney M F, **9:** 5240 (5235)
Carnin D, **2:** 868 (862)
Carnine D W, **3:** 1529 (1527); **7:** 3807 (3804); **10:** 5673 (5670, 5671), 6163 (6163)
Carnoy M, **1:** 135 (128, 129, 130, 132), 296; **2:** 640, 759 (758), 760 (758), 933 (925, 929), 1072 (1067, 1068), 1074, 1135 (1134), 1146; **3:** 1655 (1649, 1654), 1680 (1677), 1685 (1681, 1683), 1695 (1691, 1692, 1693), 1712 (1710, 1711, 1712), 1713 (1710), 1720, 1788 (1786, 1788), 1789 (1788), 1810 (1808), 1820 (1810, 1818, 1819); **4:** 1910 (1904, 1905, 1910), 1911 (1904, 1905, 1908, 1909, 1910); **5:** 2607, 2697 (2696), 2744 (2740, 2743), 2798, 2942; **6:** 3106 (3103), 3184 (3184), 3189 (3188), 3549 (3548), 3621 (3619); **7:** 4141 (4140); **8:** 4509 (4505, 4508), 4568 (4564), 4571 (4569), 4839 (4836, 4838), 4902 (4898, 4899), 4917 (4914, 4915, 4916), 4918 (4913, 4914, 4916); **9:** 5076 (5072, 5074), 5539 (5533); **11:** 6260 (6257), 6282 (6278, 6279, 6280, 6281), 6283 (6280)
Caro F G, **3:** 1431 (1427); **4:** 2119 (2111); **11:** 6511
Carpenter B, **11:** 6461
Carpenter C J, **4:** 2452 (2451)
Carpenter C R, **11:** 6306 (6304)
Carpenter P, **2:** 834; **8:** 4715 (4709), 4845 (4842)
Carpenter P A, **8:** 4939 (4936)
Carpenter P G, **1:** 358 (356); **8:** 4830 (4827)
Carpenter R L, **1:** 490 (489)
Carpenter T C, **10:** 5772 (5770)
Carpenter T P, **2:** 1052 (1050); **3:** 1257 (1256); **6:** 3655 (3654), 3660 (3657, 3658, 3660), 3661, 3671 (3670), 3684 (3675); **10:** 5795 (5792, 5794), 6122 (6118)
Carper J C, **1:** 265 (264); **9:** 5008 (4998)
Carr C, **4:** 1924 (1923)
Carr D, **7:** 4050 (4046, 4047)
Carr E G, **1:** 408 (408); **6:** 3335
Carr J H, **5:** 2813 (2810), 2910 (2908)
Carr M, **2:** 867 (866), 969 (966); **10:** 5745 (5744), 5772 (5771)
Carr W, **1:** 47 (44, 46); **2:** 1203 (1199); **9:** 5030 (5024); **10:** 5985 (5984), 6219 (6218)
Carraher D W, **2:** 1052 (1050)
Carraher T N, **2:** 1052 (1050)
Carrascosa J, **10:** 6177 (6174)
Carrasquillo A, **6:** 3232
Carrea N, **10:** 6058 (6056)
Carrell P L, **8:** 4939 (4937)
Carretero M, **2:** 1006; **7:** 3791; **9:** 5562 (5560, 5561)
Carr-Hill R A, **1:** 99 (96), 100, 175 (173, 174), 474 (474); **4:** 2369 (2367)
Carriedo R, **8:** 4845 (4841)
Carrier C, **2:** 1170 (1166), 1175 (1173)
Carrier C A, **3:** 1416; **4:** 1911; **6:** 3596; **10:** 6043 (6035)
Carrier J G, **10:** 5668 (5664)
Carrier R, **3:** 1829 (1828, 1829)
Carrington B, **7:** 3978
Carrizosa S O de, **3:** 1735 (1733)
Carroll A W, **9:** 5070 (5068)
Carroll J B, **1:** 5 (2, 3), 6, 23, 389 (384), 396 (393); **2:** 957 (952, 955), 1220 (1217); **3:** 1768 (1763); **4:** 1847 (1842, 1843), 1872 (1865, 1868), 2240 (2237, 2238), 2338 (2334), 2345 (2341, 2343, 2344), 2357 (2352); **5:** 2567 (2563), 2767 (2760), 2921 (2918), 2977 (2974); **6:** 3334 (3330), 3523 (3515); **7:** 3872 (3867), 3879 (3873, 3874, 3875, 3876, 3878), 3886 (3882, 3883, 3885), 3936, 4211; **8:** (4401), 4939; **9:** 5043 (5041); **10:** 5590 (5590), 5704 (5700), 5750 (5746); **11:** 6328 (6327), 6348 (6341, 6348)
Carroll J D, **9:** 5158 (5156, 5158), 5503 (5500)
Carroll J M, **2:** 985; **5:** 2867 (2866)
Carroll T G, **7:** 3973 (3971, 3972)
Carron G, **1:** 100, 175 (172, 174), 176; **4:** 2369 (2367); **5:** 2759; **11:** 6298 (6293)
Carson C C, **7:** 3726
Carstensen L L, **1:** 239 (238)
Carta J J, **8:** 4375 (4372, 4374), 4376; **9:** 5567 (5565, 5566); **11:** 6484 (6482)
Carter B, **2:** 737 (734)
Carter C, **2:** 1031 (1028)
Carter D B, **4:** 2449 (2447, 2448); **5:** 2628
Carter J, **8:** 4661 (4658)
Carter K, **3:** 1635 (1633); **10:** 5762 (5761), 5948 (5943, 5946), 6026 (6023, 6024, 6025), 6031 (6028), 6121 (6117, 6118), 6183
Carter K R, **5:** 2495 (2493)
Carter L, **5:** 2529 (2524)
Carter L F, **6:** 3523 (3517, 3519)
Carter M, **3:** 1695 (1693)
Carter R, **2:** 1198 (1197)
Carter S, **7:** 4255 (4249, 4250, 4254)
Carter S B, **11:** (6762)
Carterette E C, **8:** 4383
Carter-Saltzman L, **5:** 2465 (2464)
Cartledge N, **4:** 1972 (1968)
Carton M, **1:** 226 (222); **3:** 1690
Cartter A M, **1:** 520 (518)
Cartwright D, **5:** 2532 (2529); **9:** 5560 (5555)
Carvalho S, **3:** 1789
Carver C S, **4:** 1979 (1978)
Casaer P, **8:** 4394, 4395
Casas Armengol M, **7:** 4220
Casassus J, **8:** 4495 (4494)
Cascante Fernández C, **1:** 47 (45), 48 (45)
Cascio W F, **2:** 1093 (1093), 1139
Case R, **2:** 856 (853), 860 (857); **4:** 1966 (1964); **5:** 2669 (2669), 2680 (2677, 2678, 2679), 2767 (2761, 2763), 2874 (2872), 2916 (2913); **6:** 3660 (3657); **8:** 4482 (4482), 4483, 4956 (4952)
Casey A, **7:** 3833 (3832); **8:** 4661 (4658)
Cash W, **3:** 1820 (1810, 1811)
Cashdan A, **6:** 3312
Cashin W E, **10:** 6234 (6230, 6234)
Cason H, **4:** 2281 (2280)
Caspar P, **7:** 4263 (4258)
Caspi A, **3:** 1647; **5:** 2916 (2914)
Caspo M, **10:** 5668 (5665)
Cass A, **5:** 2536 (2535)
Cass B, **11:** 6712 (6709)
Cass W, **10:** 6099
Cassara B, **1:** 120, 168 (166); **7:** 4336 (4331); **10:** 5596 (5592)
Casserly P L, **4:** 2435 (2433)
Cassidy A, **1:** 48 (45)
Cassidy J, **2:** 705 (701)
Cassidy T, **3:** 1829 (1828, 1829), 1830 (1825, 1826, 1827, 1829)
Cassirer E, **3:** 1464
Cassissi J E, **1:** 19 (17)
Castaldi B, **4:** 2229
Castaneda A, **2:** 872 (871)
Castaño P M, **8:** 4442
Castel R, **5:** 2523
Castelan N J, **11:** 6457
Castelijns J H M, **6:** 3315 (3315)
Castelli M C, **6:** 3224 (3223)
Castells M, **3:** 1712 (1712), 1713 (1708, 1709); **11:** 6282 (6278, 6279, 6280), 6283
Castiglione B, **8:** (4889)
Castillo A, **6:** 3256
Castine W H, **2:** 991 (990); **7:** 4104 (4102)
Castle J, **1:** 168 (167)
Castley R, **11:** 6430 (6425)
Casto G, **4:** 2145
Castro C de Moura, **4:** 1882 (1882)
Castro F, **7:** (4144)
Castro M C de, **11:** 6633 (6628)
Castrovilli M, **8:** 4811 (4807)
Caswell H L, **10:** 5817 (5813)
Caswell M, **3:** (1288)
Catalano R F, **5:** 2571 (2568)
Cataldo M F, **5:** 2571; **10:** 6164 (6161)
Catania A C, **10:** 6163 (6159)
Catanzarite L, **4:** 2432 (2431)

Cathcart H, **11:** 6523
Cattan P, **2:** 692 (690)
Cattell J M, **3:** (1794), (1795); **4:** (1841), 1872 (1866, 1867); **5:** (2875), (2877), (2911)
Cattell R B, **1:** 5 (1), 152 (147); **2:** (869); **4:** 2240 (2235, 2240), 2241; **5:** (2728), 2767 (2760), (2911), 2921 (2917); **7:** 3879 (3873, 3875, 3878, 3879), 3970 (3967); **11:** 6348 (6341)
Catterall J, **2:** 711 (707)
Catts W, **10:** 5694
Caudill W, **3:** 1240 (1238)
Cauley K, **6:** 3224 (3220)
Cauquil G, **11:** 6807 (6807)
Causey B D, **9:** 5131 (5129)
Caute D, **10:** 5782
Cavalli-Storza L L, **3:** 1647 (1646)
Cavanaugh P, **4:** 2011 (2007)
Cave E, **5:** 2508 (2505)
Cavell S, **1:** 27
Caverni J P, **8:** 4951
Cawthron E R, **8:** 4464
Cazden C B, **1:** 295 (291); **2:** 802 (799, 801); **4:** 2053; **6:** 3216, 3238 (3237), 3452 (3452); **8:** 4873; **9:** 5181, 5220, 5312 (5311), 5416, 5507 (5506), 5548 (5546); **10:** 5690 (5688), 6034 (6033), 6177 (6174), 6197 (6194, 6196)
Ceci S J, **1:** 194; **2:** 846 (846); **3:** 1647 (1644, 1645, 1646); **5:** 2916 (2914); **6:** 3288 (3286, 3287); **7:** 3763 (3761)
Cedoline A J, **10:** 5924 (5920, 5921, 5922, 5923)
Celebuski C, **2:** 711 (709)
Cell E, **6:** 3349
Centra J A, **4:** 2131 (2129); **9:** 5264 (5263); **10:** 6234 (6229, 6231, 6232)
Cercy S, **1:** 322 (319)
Cerri M, **6:** 3261
Certo N, **5:** 2907
Cervantes H T, **6:** 3232
Cervantes Saavedra M de, **6:** (3499)
Červenka J, **2:** 883
Cervero R M, **2:** 665 (662); **5:** 2689 (2686); **8:** 4736 (4735)
Cerych L, **8:** 4519; **10:** 5782
Céspedes F, **7:** 4275
Cetron M, **4:** 1857 (1855), 2330 (2329)
Cevallos E E, **6:** 3401 (3401)
GSS News, **1:** 300 (5368)
Chabay R, **4:** 2199
Chadsey-Rusch, **11:** 6461
Chadwick A, **5:** 2937 (2935); **11:** 6437, 6438 (6431), 6438
Chadwick C, **5:** 2897 (2894)
Chadwick H, **9:** 5117
Chadwick O, **2:** 1084 (1079)
Chafer L S, **2:** 767
Chaffee S, **1:** 570 (566)
Chaiklin S, **8:** 4429 (4425)
Chakela L, **7:** 3756
Chalfant A, **8:** 4715 (4709)
Chalfant J C, **8:** 4661 (4658); **10:** 6244 (6240)
Chall J S, **4:** 1962 (1962); **8:** 4945 (4944)
Chalmers A, **4:** 2194 (2186, 2194); **9:** 5031
Chalmers-Neubauer I, **2:** 806 (804)
Chalupa L M, **1:** 554
Chamberlain G, **4:** 2278 (2275, 2276, 2278); **6:** 3144 (3138, 3141, 3143)
Chamberlain M K, **11:** 6712 (6709)
Chamberlain P C, **5:** 2903 (2903)
Chamberlain S P, **9:** 5071 (5066, 5068)
Chamberlin D D, **3:** 1394 (1388)
Chambers C M, **1:** 28
Chambers D L, **1:** 41 (37)
Chambers J, **1:** 28; **2:** 1126 (1122)
Chambers J G, **9:** 5240 (5238); **10:** 6072 (6071)
Chambers M, **9:** 5318 (5314)
Chambers P, **1:** 27, 28
Chambliss J J, **10:** 5991 (5986)
Chamot A U, **6:** 3334 (3330, 3331, 3333)
Champagne A, **2:** 1031 (1030)
Champagne A B, **6:** 3205; **7:** 3726; **9:** 5327 (5325), 5338 (5337); **10:** 5790 (5785)
Champion D J, **9:** 5050
Chan A, **10:** 5782 (5782)
Chan K S, **6:** 3631 (3630)
Chanan G, **6:** 3389
Chanana K, **7:** 3973 (3973)
Chance N, **9:** 5312 (5311)
Chance P, **8:** 4730 (4729)
Chancerel J-L, **4:** 2346 (2340)
Chandler A D Jr, **3:** 1411 (1407, 1408)
Chandler D, **9:** 5544 (5542)
Chandler J, **4:** 2301 (2299); **6:** 3453 (3448, 3449, 3451), 3480; **8:** 4936 (4932)
Chandler K, **1:** 110 (104, 107)
Chandler M J, **3:** 1520 (1516, 1517); **5:** 2802 (2799); **6:** 3288 (3288); **8:** 4824; **9:** 5512 (5510)
Chandler M O, **5:** 2512 (2510); **9:** 5432 (5426); **10:** 6106 (6104)
Chandler W M, **5:** 2512
Chandra P, **10:** 5625 (5623)
Chang E, **5:** 2773 (2770)
Chang Gwang-Chol, **6:** 3160
Chang J-J, **9:** 5158 (5156, 5158)
Chang M C, **10:** 6106 (6104)
Chang Min Phang Paul, **9:** 5251 (5249)
Chang T M, **1:** 563
Chanter C, **8:** 4376 (4373)
Chao C-I, **10:** 6193 (6189)
Chapanis A, **4:** 2011 (2010)
Chapelle C, **4:** 2338 (2335), 2363 (2362)
Chapman B, **1:** 111
Chapman C A, **7:** 4081 (4078)
Chapman D, **3:** 1416, 1431, 1825, 1829 (1828, 1829); **8:** 4708; **11:** 6403
Chapman D W, **4:** 1911; **6:** 3596 (3593); **8:** 4936; **9:** 5168 (5161, 5163, 5164); **10:** 6043 (6035), 6062 (6060); **11:** 6265 (6262), 6445 (6444)
Chapman J, **3:** 1411 (1409, 1410); **4:** 1934 (1929, 1931), 2351 (2349); **6:** 3284 (3282), 3474, 3496 (3492, 3494); **7:** 3840; **9:** 5215, 5223 (5222); **10:** 6083
Chapman J C, **4:** 1872 (1867)
Chapman J D, **5:** 2508 (2507), 2509; **7:** 3839; **9:** 5181 (5179), 5308; **10:** 6083 (6081)
Chapman J E, **10:** 5673 (5669)
Chapman J W, **5:** 2910 (2908); **10:** 5826 (5823)
Chapman L J, **2:** 1079 (1078)
Chapman M, **3:** 1245 (1245); **8:** 4483, 4799 (4797, 4798, 4799)
Chapman W, **4:** 1840 (1839)
Chapuis J, **7:** 4026 (4021)
Charkin N E, **9:** 5268
Charles B, **6:** 3227
Charles C M, **1:** 486 (485, 486); **5:** 2529 (2527); **10:** 6173 (6170)
Charles D, **7:** 3830 (3829)
Charles R I, **8:** 4730 (4728)
Charlesworth R, **9:** 5567 (5563)
Charlesworth W, **4:** 2172 (2169)
Charlot B, **4:** 2385
Charmes J, **5:** 2819 (2815)
Charmot F, **9:** 5121
Charnes A, **3:** 1386 (1384, 1385)
Charness N, **5:** 2916 (2913, 2914); **7:** 3763
Charter W, **5:** 2847 (2839)
Charters A N, **1:** 120, 142 (141); **3:** 1589; **5:** 2937 (2935), 2951 (2949)
Charters W W, **3:** 1266 (1262, 1264), 1300 (1298); **4:** (1869), 2432; **5:** 2714; **10:** 6043 (6036)
Charters W W Jr, **4:** 2073 (2070); **11:** 6731
Chartrand R L, **5:** 2831 (2828)
Charvin R, **6:** 3160
Chase C I, **7:** 4293 (4292)
Chase C L, **4:** 2017 (2012)
Chase S E, **11:** 6765 (6762)
Chase W G, **2:** 842 (839); **4:** 2198 (2195); **6:** 3288 (3285); **10:** 6026 (6023)
Chase-Dunn C, **3:** 1607 (1603)
Chase-Lansdale P L, **3:** 1642 (1637, 1639)
Chatman S, **7:** 4050 (4050)
Chatterjee K, **5:** 2798 (2793)
Chatterjee S, **7:** 3986 (3984), 4015 (4009)
Chatterton J L, **2:** 991 (990)
Chau T N, **11:** 6298 (6293)
Chaudenson R, **2:** 1160
Chaudhry F, **10:** 5673 (5671)
Chaudron C, **4:** 2339 (2337); **8:** 4881 (4879)
Chauncey H, **1:** 370 (366)
Chavanne M F, **1:** 343 (342)
Chave E J, **7:** 3707 (3703)
Chazan B, **7:** 3925
Che Guevera, **2:** (1192)
Cheasty A, **3:** 1834 (1832)
Cheema G S, **3:** 1416
Cheema I, **1:** 322 (318, 319)
Cheese J, **11:** 6640 (6638)
Cheffers J, **10:** 5713 (5708)
Chelimsky E, **3:** 1406, 1431 (1425, 1428, 1429)
Chell E, **4:** 1991 (1985)
Chen C, **3:** 1240 (1239), 1241 (1238); **4:** 1903 (1901); **5:** 2627 (2627), 2628 (2626)
Chen Chia-Erh, **3:** 1573 (1570)

Chen H-T, **4:** 2089 (2088); **11:** 6384 (6378, 6379, 6381)
Chen M, **2:** 1012; **4:** 2427 (2424, 2425)
Chen X, **9:** 5528 (5527)
Chen Z, **7:** 4094 (4094)
Chené A, **2:** 906 (904)
Chene A, **9:** 5399 (5396)
Chenery H B, **3:** 1707; **5:** 2945 (2943); **8:** 4601
Cheney D L, **5:** 2685 (2682)
Cheney L V, **11:** 6370 (6369)
Cheney M S, **9:** 5151 (5143)
Cheng J J, **3:** 1421 (1421)
Cheng Kai Ming, **1:** 353; **5:** 2643; **7:** 4140 (4140)
Cheng P W, **2:** 838 (837); **8:** 4956 (4954), 4957 (4956)
Cheng Y C, **9:** 5307 (5307)
Chengelele R, **1:** 175 (173, 174)
Cheong J W, **2:** 906 (905)
Cherednikov M, **10:** 5649 (5647, 5649)
Cheren M, **6:** 3349 (3348)
Cherif M, **11:** 6653 (6648)
Cherkaoui M, **2:** 784 (777); **10:** 5606 (5601)
Cherlin A J, **2:** 711
Chernichovsky D, **3:** 1606 (1604, 1605)
Cherniss C, **10:** 5924 (5920, 5922, 5923)
Chernoff M L, **10:** 6020
Chernyshov D, **10:** 5673 (5673)
Cherry R, **11:** 6780
Cherryholmes C H, **1:** 67 (65); **2:** 933 (928, 930); **4:** 1984 (1983); **10:** 5991 (5986)
Chervin M, **2:** 906 (904)
Chess S, **1:** 234 (232); **11:** 6311 (6307, 6308, 6309)
Chesswas J, **11:** 6265 (6263, 6264)
Chester D, **4:** 2131 (2126)
Chesterfield R, **1:** 297 (286); **4:** 2045 (2044)
Chetley A, **8:** 4677 (4672)
Chetwynd S J, **8:** 4408 (4405)
Cheung K C, **6:** 3642 (3641); **7:** 3986 (3979, 3984, 3985), 4015 (4015); **8:** 4359 (4359), 4647 (4645, 4646); **9:** 5372 (5371)
Cheung P, **4:** 2257 (2255)
Chevallard Y, **6:** 3652 (3648)
Chhim S-H, **7:** 4175
Chi M T H, **1:** 374 (371); **2:** 838 (835), 842 (839), 846 (845), 856 (854), 867 (862); **3:** 1504 (1502); **4:** 2198 (2195), 2199 (2194); **5:** 2669 (2667), 2916 (2913); **6:** 3155 (3154), 3288 (3286, 3287), 3324 (3317), 3416 (3410); **7:** 3763 (3761); **8:** 4722 (4720, 4721), 4727 (4727), 4823 (4821); **10:** 5790 (5783), 6026 (6023, 6024, 6025)
Chi M T M, **3:** 1543 (1542)
Chia N, **7:** 4220 (4219)
Chiang C, **2:** 1052 (1050)
Chiappe C, **8:** 4509 (4508)
Chicago J, **5:** 2457 (2455)
Chickering A, **2:** 1165 (1161, 1162, 1163, 1164); **7:** 4329 (4326); **11:** 6551 (6548)
Chickering A W, **1:** 94; **6:** 3349 (3347); **10:** 5804 (5798), (5935), 5939
Chidiac L-M, **6:** 3356
Chieh S, **3:** 1624 (1622)
Ch'ien Mu, **2:** 1045 (1043)
Chilcott J H, **1:** 280 (278), 295 (293); **2:** 802 (799); **4:** 2249 (2248)
Child D, **8:** 4388 (4386)
Child I L, **5:** 2665 (2658)
Childs J W, **4:** 1898
Chilko D M, **9:** 5130 (5127)
Chilucos P E, **10:** 6117
Chin R, **3:** 1431; **10:** 5972 (5966)
Chinapah V, **7:** 3698, 4246 (4243); **8:** 4616 (4611)
Chiplin B, **8:** 4364 (4361); **11:** 6431 (6427)
Chipman S F, **1:** 193; **2:** 856, 868; **4:** 2435 (2432, 2434), 2436; **5:** 2767 (2762), 2769 (2762); **6:** 3288, 3297 (3296), 3324; **8:** 4730 (4728), 4731; **10:** 6192
Chipuer H M, **5:** 2465 (2464)
Chira S, **11:** 6563 (6561)
Chisholm L, **7:** 3852 (3849, 3850)
Chisholm M E, **7:** 3756 (3753)
Chisholm R M, **8:** 4536 (4533)
Chisman F P, **1:** 103; **7:** 4148 (4148), 4185 (4185); **8:** 4638 (4637)
Chiswick B R, **1:** 520 (518); **5:** 2739 (2737, 2738, 2739), 2740 (2738, 2739), 2744 (2741); **8:** 4902 (4896, 4897, 4898, 4899)
Chiswick C U, **7:** 4200 (4200)
Chitnis S, **10:** 5606 (5601)
Chittick G, **4:** 2346 (2340)
Chiu L, **2:** 737 (734)
Chizea C A, **7:** 4132
Choat E, **8:** 4680 (4679)
Choisser L, **8:** 4376 (4373, 4374)
Chomé G, **1:** 317
Chomsky N, **1:** (535); **5:** 2665 (2658), (2878); **6:** 3215 (3213), (3635); **7:** 3774 (3773); **8:** (4535); **10:** 5696 (5695)
Choppin B H, **1:** 396 (393); **4:** 2017 (2014); **5:** 2978, 3043 (3036, 3038); **7:** 4196 (4195); **8:** 4359
Choppin B J, **3:** 1482 (1478); **4:** 2180 (2177)
Chou C P, **4:** 2024 (2019, 2023)
Chou T, **2:** 635 (634)
Chrétien J P, **1:** 606
Christ E, **9:** 5403 (5402, 5403)
Christal R E, **5:** 2768 (2762), 2921 (2919); **6:** 3325 (3317, 3318, 3321)
Christensen C R, **10:** 5948 (5944)
Christensen J C, **10:** 5939 (5936)
Christensen P, **4:** 1917 (1913); **5:** 2891 (2887)
Christensen P A, **10:** 5812 (5810)
Christenson S L, **7:** 3833 (3831); **8:** 4661 (4658); **9:** 5071 (5069); **10:** 6173 (6170, 6172)
Christenson T E, **4:** 2452 (2451)
Christian-Smith L, **5:** 2457; **11:** 6726 (6726), 6727
Christie J F, **8:** 4541 (4540)
Christie J R, **9:** 5350
Christie P, **2:** 907; **7:** 3852 (3850, 3852); **10:** 5635
Christoffel P, **2:** 1152 (1147)
Christofi C, **8:** 4648
Christopher E M, **5:** 2773 (2771)
Christophersen P, **4:** 2351 (2349)
Christopherson L, **10:** 5690 (5690)
Christopherson P, **4:** 2357 (2352)
Christovich L, **2:** 1042 (1038)
Chrzastek-Spruch H M, **8:** 4473 (4472)
Chu A, **9:** 5142 (5132)
Chu D, **10:** 5783
Chu G, **5:** 2897 (2894, 2895)
Chu L, **11:** 6760 (6756)
Chu Y, **3:** 1624 (1622)
Chua T T, **5:** 2971 (2970)
Chuang D T, **3:** 1421 (1421)
Chuaprapaisilp A, **1:** 47 (46)
Chubb J E, **1:** 594 (590, 591); **3:** 1411 (1407, 1408, 1411), 1720, 1761 (1761); **5:** 2508 (2505); **6:** 3496 (3496); **7:** 3839 (3839); **8:** 4568 (4565), 4594 (4587, 4588, 4589, 4592, 4593), 4830 (4825, 4829), 4873 (4867, 4870); **9:** 5196 (5195), 5201, 5206 (5203, 5204), 5223 (5221), 5281 (5277), 5307 (5305, 5306); **11:** 6558 (6556), 6563 (6560)
Chuma P, **10:** 5808 (5805)
Chumlea W C, **8:** 4473 (4471), 4474 (4468, 4470, 4471, 4472)
Chumni W, **6:** 3684 (3683)
Chung F, **2:** 914 (911); **3:** 1567 (1565); **11:** 6256 (6252)
Chung N, **1:** 594 (593)
Chung Y-P, **3:** 1713 (1710); **5:** 2642; **8:** 4917 (4916); **9:** 5076 (5072, 5073, 5074, 5075); **11:** 6282 (6281)
Chunn E W, **9:** 5211 (5208)
Church G, **10:** 5674
Church R B, **2:** 856 (855)
Churchland P M, **9:** 5030 (5027, 5029)
Churchman C W, **6:** 3124
Churukian G A, **10:** 5965
Ciari B, **5:** (3031)
Ciavatta F M A, **6:** 3261 (3260); **11:** 6265 (6263)
Cibulka J G, **1:** 265, 594; **8:** 4845; **9:** 5013, 5216; **11:** 6558 (6555), 6563
Cicchetti D, **1:** 19; **6:** 3297
Cicero M T, **4:** (2006); **6:** (3499); **8:** (4888), (4889)
Cicourel A V, **1:** 11 (10); **4:** 2165 (2159)
Cieloha C D, **5:** 2971 (2970)
Cieślak A, **2:** 661 (656)
Ciliberti B, **6:** 3480 (3475)
Cillessen A H N, **8:** 4368 (4367)
Cin R B, **3:** 1416 (1414)
Cippolone A, **9:** 5191 (5190)
Cissé S Y, **1:** 221
Citron C C, **4:** 2452 (2451)
Civil M, **6:** 3642 (3642)
Cixous H, **5:** 2457 (2457); **9:** 5441 (5440)
Ciza J P, **7:** 4136 (4134)
Claessens A, **8:** 4473 (4472); **10:** 5713
Clancey W, **2:** 973

Clanchy M T, **6:** 3446 (3445)
Clancy J, **4:** 2249; **8:** 4895 (4893)
Clancy P, **5:** 3020
Clandinin D G, **10:** 5994 (5994)
Clandinin D J, **3:** 1320 (1317, 1319), 1334; **7:** 4050 (4047); **10:** 6043 (6037, 6038, 6040), 6091 (6089, 6091), 6099 (6097), 6121 (6119, 6120), 6183 (6181)
Claparède E, **3:** (1795); **4:** 1872 (1864, 1866, 1867); **10:** (5877), (5880)
Clapham C, **6:** 3394
Clarizio H F, **2:** 1182 (1180); **8:** 4803
Clark B, **2:** 1042 (1039); **3:** 1713; **10:** 6012 (6009)
Clark B R, **3:** 1720; **5:** 3036; **6:** 3329, 3339; **8:** 4774; **9:** 5181 (5176, 5180); **10:** 5804 (5796); **11:** 6445 (6439)
Clark C, **3:** 1494 (1492), 1635 (1631), 1804 (1802); **10:** 6207 (6206)
Clark C M, **2:** 796 (792, 793, 794); **3:** 1257 (1254, 1255, 1256); **10:** 5772 (5768), 5934 (5933), 6034 (6032, 6033), 6035 (6032, 6033), 6088 (6087, 6088), 6103 (6100), 6121 (6119), 6173 (6171), 6183 (6180)
Clark D, **4:** 2165 (2165); **5:** 2847 (2840)
Clark D H, **8:** 4531 (4527); **11:** 6633 (6628)
Clark D L, **6:** 3284 (3277); **8:** 4594 (4587); **9:** 5281 (5276); **10:** 5965 (5962)
Clark D R, **1:** 404; **11:** 6604
Clark E E, **4:** 2119 (2110, 2111)
Clark F L, **2:** 867 (863)
Clark G C, **1:** 343 (341); **3:** 1553, 1563
Clark G M, **2:** 635 (632, 633, 634)
Clark J, **5:** 2965; **8:** 4474 (4469)
Clark J L, **8:** 4881 (4876)
Clark J L D, **4:** 2345 (2343), 2351 (2348)
Clark J M, **2:** 887 (886)
Clark K B, **5:** 2672 (2670)
Clark M, **6:** 3602 (3598)
Clark M C, **1:** 168 (164)
Clark M L, **7:** 3935 (3930, 3932, 3933, 3934); **11:** 6348 (6345)
Clark M M, **3:** 1460; **7:** 4300 (4300)
Clark M P, **5:** 2672 (2670)
Clark R E, **2:** 887 (884), 888, 1019, 1170; **3:** 1573 (1571), 1579 (1577); **4:** 1898 (1891), 1911, 1911 (1904, 1909); **5:** 2874 (2872), 2897 (2894); **6:** 3306 (3304); **7:** 3743 (3739, 3740, 3742, 3743), 3753 (3744, 3745), 3760 (3757); **10:** 6008 (6005)
Clark R H, **3:** 1240 (1236, 1237, 1238)
Clark R J, **1:** 415
Clark R M, **4:** 2272 (2271)
Clark R W, **9:** 5318 (5313, 5316)
Clark S M, **7:** 4215 (4213)
Clark T, **3:** 1386 (1384, 1385)
Clark T A, **7:** 4220; **11:** 6307 (6305)
Clark W C, **8:** 4519
Clark-Baca J, **11:** 6624 (6623), 6625 (6623)
Clarke A M, **6:** 3288
Clarke B R, **5:** 2479, 2480
Clarke D B, **6:** 3288, 3634
Clarke F H, **5:** 2799
Clarke J, **11:** 6803 (6801)
Clarke J Y, **9:** 5567 (5564)
Clarke L K, **10:** 5704 (5703)
Clarke M L, **6:** 3474 (3469)
Clarke P B, **5:** 2512
Clarke R E, **4:** 1898 (1891)
Clarke S, **10:** 5961 (5959)
Clarke-Klein S, **10:** 5696 (5695)
Clarke-Stewart K A, **2:** 687 (685, 686); **3:** 1642 (1640); **4:** 2266 (2265); **5:** 2806 (2804); **7:** 4296 (4294, 4295); **8:** 4666 (4664, 4665); **11:** 6397 (6395)
Clarkson D, **2:** 640
Clatanoff W, **11:** 6638 (6636)
Claus K E, **10:** 5977 (5975)
Clausen J A, **3:** 1514, 1647 (1646); **6:** 3428 (3426)
Claussen B, **8:** 4571, 4581
Claxton G, **7:** 3788 (3785)
Clay M M, **1:** 362 (361); **7:** 3935 (3931), 4081 (4080); **8:** 4935 (4932, 4934), 4936, 4947 (4946); **10:** 5795 (5791, 5792), 5961 (5958)
Claypole W, **5:** 2544
Clayton J S, **4:** 1917 (1916); **6:** 3512
Clayton K N, **6:** 3512 (3511)
Clayton M K, **6:** 3508 (3504)
Clayton S, **7:** 3726 (3724, 3725)
Clayton-Randolph S, **7:** 3775
Clearie A F, **5:** 2572 (2569)
Cleary M J, **10:** 6004 (6000)
Clegg S, **4:** 2301 (2297); **9:** 5168 (5161)
Cleghorn A, **10:** 5762 (5761)
Cleland D, **3:** 1830 (1828)
Clement J, **8:** 4479 (4476); **10:** 5790 (5784, 5785)
Clement R, **4:** 2339 (2336)
Clement W, **6:** 3425 (3424); **11:** 6698 (6695)
Clements B S, **2:** 820; **10:** 6031 (6028)
Clements D H, **2:** 973 (971), 984 (983); **6:** 3512 (3511), 3685; **7:** 4099 (4098); **11:** 6456 (6454)
Clements D J, **7:** 4088 (4084)
Clements M A, **6:** 3638 (3635), 3652 (3648, 3650); **8:** 4647 (4643)
Clements S D, **10:** 5686 (5682)
Cleve Z J, **3:** (1724)
Cleveland M, **3:** 1602 (1601)
Cleveland N R, **10:** 5673 (5669)
Cleverly C, **2:** 785 (779)
Cliff N, **2:** 792 (789)
Clifford G, **10:** 6012 (6009)
Clifford G J, **3:** 1796 (1794, 1795); **9:** 5055 (5052); **10:** 5613 (5609); **11:** 6765 (6762, 6763)
Clifford J, **6:** 3484 (3481)
Clifford R M, **5:** 2806 (2805); **9:** 5275 (5274); **11:** 6397 (6396)
Clift J C, **10:** 5977 (5974)
Clift P, **5:** 2852 (2849); **9:** 5223 (5222); **10:** 5826 (5823)
Clift R T, **10:** 5995 (5994), 6088 (6088), 6219
Clifton J A, **1:** 294; **4:** 2052
Clifton R A, **4:** 2249; **8:** 4895 (4891, 4892, 4893, 4895); **10:** 5762 (5761), 5834 (5833)
Clignet R P, **1:** 332 (332); **2:** 933 (926, 930); **3:** 1685 (1683), 1820 (1811); **6:** 3189 (3188); **11:** 6740 (6739)
Clinchy B M, **1:** 162 (160); **7:** 4329 (4326); **10:** 5939 (5938), 6099 (6098); **11:** 6722 (6721)
Cline T, **5:** 2972
Clinkenbeard P M, **2:** 1182 (1181)
Clogg C C, **6:** 3508 (3500, 3502); **11:** 6276 (6274)
Clough B M, **7:** 4293 (4291)
Clough D B, **7:** 4293 (4291)
Clough E, **9:** 5192
Cloward R A, **11:** 6803 (6799)
Clowes M, **3:** 1778 (1776)
Clumpner J L, **2:** 729 (722)
Clune W H, **8:** 4408; **9:** 5065 (5063), 5066, 5201, 5206 (5202), 5240 (5239), 5308; **10:** 6083; **11:** 6558
Coakley C, **6:** 3442 (3439, 3441)
Coase R H, **3:** 1703 (1697); **4:** 1972 (1969)
Cobb H B, **7:** 3833 (3832)
Cobb J, **1:** 297 (290); **9:** 5572 (5569)
Cobb M V, **5:** 2921 (2916, 2917, 2919)
Cobb P, **3:** 1257 (1256); **6:** 3660 (3659), 3661, 3670 (3670), 3684 (3673); **7:** 4100; **8:** 4652 (4649), 4882 (4877)
Cobban A B, **10:** 5782 (5777)
Cocchiarella M J, **2:** 1020, 1170 (1166)
Cochran J, **4:** 1947
Cochran K F, **10:** 5999 (5999)
Cochran M M, **2:** 687 (686), 701; **3:** 1647 (1645); **7:** 4296 (4295); **9:** 5268 (5266, 5267)
Cochran P S, **7:** 3807 (3802)
Cochran W G, **1:** 390 (388); **2:** 1084 (1081); **5:** 3061 (3059); **7:** 3739 (3730, 3731), 3858, 4016 (4009); **9:** 5142 (5136), 5158 (5153)
Cochrane A, **3:** 1624 (1621)
Cochrane C B, **7:** 3925
Cochrane S H, **2:** 1055 (1053); **3:** 1665 (1663), 1676 (1672, 1673, 1674, 1675); **4:** 2412 (2411), 2418 (2415, 2417)
Cochran-Smith M, **2:** 1006 (1004, 1005); **7:** 3807 (3803), 4088 (4085), 4094 (4091); **11:** 6780 (6780)
Cock J, **7:** 3852 (3850)
Cockburn A, **1:** 23; **5:** 2536 (2534); **6:** 3311 (3308); **9:** 5363 (5359, 5361)
Cockcroft W H, **6:** 3459 (3456, 3457), 3667 (3663, 3664), 3684 (3684); **8:** 4648 (4643)
Cocking R, **6:** 3215, 3638 (3635)
Codd E F, **3:** 1394 (1388)
Codd J, **4:** 2291 (2290); **6:** 3496 (3493, 3494)
Codignola E, **5:** (3031)
Coelen C, **2:** 688 (685), 701 (696); **3:** 1636 (1634); **7:** 4300 (4298)
Coelho A M, **5:** 2684 (2682)
Coelho G V, **5:** 2978
Cofer C N, **1:** 377

Coffman W E, **4:** 2208; **5:** 3050 (3044); **7:** 3935 (3932, 3933), 4196 (4195)
Cogan J, **8:** 4601 (4596)
Cogan M L, **10:** 6004 (6002)
Coggan N, **3:** 1619
Coggins C, **4:** 2123
Cohen A, **11:** 6803 (6799)
Cohen A D, **6:** 3334 (3330)
Cohen A M, **2:** 900 (896, 897)
Cohen B, **9:** 5175 (5171)
Cohen D, **3:** 1624 (1621); **9:** 5246 (5243)
Cohen D J, **6:** 3234 (3232), 3235
Cohen D K, **1:** 12; **3:** 1257 (1256), 1337 (1335, 1336, 1337), 1431 (1426, 1427, 1428, 1429); **4:** 1864; **5:** 2672 (2670, 2671), 2673; **8:** 4519 (4515), 4604 (4603); **10:** 5953 (5952); **11:** 6538 (6531)
Cohen D R, **8:** 4526 (4523)
Cohen D S, **4:** 1980 (1976, 1977, 1978)
Cohen D V, **9:** 5379 (5374, 5376, 5377)
Cohen E, **10:** 6187 (6185, 6186)
Cohen E G, **2:** 824 (822); **3:** 1485 (1485), 1486 (1485); **5:** 2536 (2535); **8:** 4873 (4872); **9:** 5181 (5177); **10:** 6031 (6030)
Cohen I S, **8:** 4731
Cohen J, **2:** 1117 (1107, 1116); **4:** 1877 (1876), 2194 (2191, 2192, 2193); **5:** 2714 (2713), 2806, 2931 (2925, 2926); **8:** 4351 (4346); **9:** 4973 (4969, 4973); **10:** 5617 (5616), 5738 (5736), 5758 (5758), 6239 (6237)
Cohen J A, **1:** 19 (17); **8:** 4930 (4929)
Cohen L, **5:** 2462 (2462), 2783 (2781); **6:** 3224; **8:** 4383; **9:** 5240
Cohen M, **2:** 982 (981); **7:** 4094 (4089); **8:** 4388; **9:** 5168 (5162)
Cohen M D, **3:** 1745 (1741); **4:** 1934 (1930); **9:** 5181 (5176)
Cohen M R, **5:** 2714 (2710)
Cohen P, **4:** 1877 (1876); **5:** 2457 (2456), 2897 (2894), 2931 (2925, 2926); **8:** 4351 (4346); **9:** 4973 (4969, 4973); **11:** 6735 (6734), 6803 (6800)
Cohen P A, **4:** 1917 (1914); **10:** 6164 (6163), 6234 (6230, 6231, 6233); **11:** 6484 (6483)
Cohen R, **4:** 2052 (2046); **10:** 5782 (5780)
Cohen R A, **1:** 295 (289, 292)
Cohen S, **3:** 1712, 1820 (1813, 1817); **4:** 2345 (2344); **9:** 5489 (5487); **11:** 6282 (6280)
Cohen S A, **5:** 2855 (2853, 2854, 2855), 2856 (2854, 2855); **6:** 3434 (3430)
Cohen S B, **9:** 5130 (5129); **10:** 6149 (6146)
Cohen S I, **2:** 1139; **8:** 4531 (4527, 4528); **9:** 5076 (5072, 5073)
Cohen Y A, **1:** 295 (286, 288, 289, 290)
Cohler B J, **8:** 4779 (4776, 4778)
Cohn D A, **2:** 705 (701)
Cohn E, **2:** 1055, 1094 (1087, 1088, 1089, 1090), 1126 (1121, 1125); **3:** 1793, 1820 (1814, 1815, 1816); **8:** 4865; **9:** 5354 (5353), 5355 (5353)
Cohn M M, **10:** 6183
Cohn R, **5:** 2692 (2690)
Cohn S, **4:** 2432 (2431)
Cohn S J, **5:** 2495, 2731
Cohrs M, **3:** 1624 (1622)
Coie J D, **8:** 4368 (4366); **9:** 5528 (5527)
Coker H, **4:** 2131 (2128); **10:** 6020 (6018)
Coladarci T, **10:** 5772 (5770)
Colangelo N, **5:** 2491 (2488), 2732; **9:** 5532
Colardyn D, **2:** 665 (663)
Colarusso R P, **10:** 6173 (6169)
Colbert J A, **10:** 5948 (5947)
Colbert V, **3:** 1824 (1823); **8:** 4509 (4508)
Colby A, **7:** 3920 (3917, 3919)
Colchlough C, **1:** 551 (544, 551)
Colclough C, **1:** 474 (471); **6:** 3613 (3609, 3612)
Coldevin G, **4:** 1882 (1880)
Cole C L, **1:** 494 (491)
Cole H, **6:** 3393 (3393)
Cole H J, **4:** 2452 (2451)
Cole J K, **5:** 2651
Cole J R, **11:** 6712 (6711)
Cole M, **1:** 230 (229), 295 (291, 292), 297 (292), 482 (482); **2:** 1006 (1002, 1003), 1212 (1209, 1210); **3:** 1245 (1242, 1243, 1244), 1246 (1242, 1245), 1252 (1247), 1252 (1249), 1504 (1502, 1504), 1755 (1753); **4:** 1851 (1849), 1852 (1849); **5:** 2670, 2685, 2767 (2766); **6:** 3292, 3452 (3450), 3453 (3447), (3457), 3459 (3454, 3455), 3463 (3460), 3652 (3650), 3655 (3654); **7:** 3886, 3977 (3975, 3976), 4095; **9:** 5043 (5040), 5548 (5545); **11:** 6457 (6453, 6454, 6455), 6608
Cole N S, **5:** 2596 (2593); **11:** 6320 (6315, 6316, 6319), 6339 (6337), 6677 (6673)
Cole P, **4:** 2364
Cole W E, **5:** 2945 (2943)
Coleman F, **1:** 280 (278), 299 (298)
Coleman J, **2:** 892 (888), 933 (929); **4:** 2004; **8:** 4568, 4873 (4866, 4867); **9:** 5196 (5195), 5201, 5220 (5217), 5539 (5534); **10:** 5753 (5751)
Coleman J A, **8:** 4574 (4574)
Coleman J S, **1:** 520 (515, 516), 594 (589, 590); **2:** 1063 (1062), 1073 (1066), 1220 (1216, 1217); **3:** 1233 (1229), 1411 (1409, 1411), 1761 (1756), (1796); **4:** 1863 (1860, 1861), 2165 (2159, 2164), 2249, 2257 (2250, 2251, 2252), 2274 (2274), 2388 (2382); **5:** 2508 (2507), 2595 (2593); **6:** 3312 (3307), 3523 (3522); **7:** 3721 (3719), 3820 (3819); **8:** 4562 (4560), 4594 (4589), 4604 (4603), 4830 (4827, 4828), 4845 (4840, 4841, 4842, 4843), 4887 (4886), 4895 (4892, 4895); **9:** 4973 (4973), 5038 (5033), 5175 (5173), 5206 (5203, 5204), 5210 (5207), 5215 (5213, 5214), 5216 (5213, 5214), 5281 (5276), 5378 (5373, 5375), 5560 (5554); **10:** 5591 (5590), 5606 (5604, 5605), 5617 (5615), 5735 (5733), 6043 (6036); **11:** 6797 (6796)
Coleman M R, **5:** 2495 (2492)
Coleman P, **9:** 5216 (5213), 5223 (5221, 5222, 5223)
Coleman P T, **1:** (268)
Coles E K T, **5:** 2758 (2754)
Coles G, **6:** 3288, 3559 (3557); **7:** 4081 (4078)
Coles G S, **10:** 5668 (5664, 5665)
Coles M G H, **8:** 4394 (4390)
Coles R, **8:** 4581 (4579), 4780; **10:** 5817 (5817)
Colet J, **4:** (2004), (2005)
Collard S, **1:** 168 (164); **10:** 6058 (6055)
Colletta N J, **2:** 749; **4:** 2369; **11:** 6298 (6293, 6297)
Colley A M, **1:** 376; **5:** 2916
Collier B, **1:** 409 (407)
Collier J Jr, **7:** 3973 (3972)
Collier P, **2:** 1160; **11:** 6740 (6739)
Collinge J, **9:** 5216 (5213), 5223 (5221)
Collings E, **10:** 5817 (5814)
Collins A, **1:** 374 (371, 372); **2:** 838 (837), 842 (839), 969 (967), 1031 (1027, 1029); **3:** 1252 (1251), 1529 (1526); **5:** 2773 (2770), 2867 (2865), 2874 (2873), 2884 (2882); **6:** 3301 (3298, 3299), 3345 (3342, 3344), 3660 (3658); **7:** 3792, 3886 (3885), 3953 (3953); **8:** 4731 (4730); **9:** 5232 (5229), 5363 (5360, 5362); **10:** 5795 (5794), 6015 (6014), 6177 (6174, 6177); **11:** 6456 (6454)
Collins B, **4:** 2302
Collins B E, **1:** 390 (382); **11:** 6465 (6462)
Collins C, **9:** 5233; **10:** 6177 (6177)
Collins C B, **6:** 3421 (3420)
Collins G M, **6:** 3297
Collins J, **3:** 1464 (1463); **4:** 2272 (2268, 2269), 2432; **6:** 3238 (3237), 3634
Collins J B, **7:** 4324 (4322), 4329 (4327); **8:** 4616 (4610)
Collins K A, **10:** 5999
Collins L M, **2:** 677, 957, 1220 (1220); **6:** 3523 (3522); **7:** 3986, 4016; **8:** 4352
Collins M, **1:** 111, 162 (162), 168 (163); **10:** 5596 (5594), 6058 (6054, 6055)
Collins M F, **1:** 310 (307)
Collins N L, **7:** 4007
Collins R, **1:** 168 (163), 520 (517); **2:** 785 (781, 782), 1042 (1041), 1073 (1069); **7:** 3826 (3824); **8:** 4571 (4569); **10:** 5606 (5598); **11:** 6703 (6700)
Collins R A, **9:** 5307 (5306)
Collins T W, **9:** 5572 (5567, 5569)
Collins W A, **5:** 2627 (2626), 2628, 2676; **10:** 6169 (6168)
Collis B A, **2:** 977 (975), 982 (978), 991 (990), 1011 (1010), 1012 (1007); **4:** 1928, 2427 (2424); **10:** 6008 (6005, 6006); **11:** 6287 (6283, 6284)
Collis K F, **1:** 322 (321); **3:** 1513 (1508, 1510, 1511); **5:** 2669; **6:** 3660 (3657), 3661 (3658); **8:** 4647 (4643, 4644), 4648 (4644)
Collwell R J, **7:** 4030 (4030)
Colman J E, **10:** 6085 (6083)
Colmar S, **8:** 4376 (4372)
Colonius H, **2:** 792 (788)
Colorado P, **7:** 4336 (4330, 4333)
Colpaert J, **10:** 5625 (5624)

Coltham J, **8:** 4715 (4708)
Coltheart M, **8:** 4939
Colubcheck L, **2:** 893
Colvin G, **2:** 868 (862)
Colwell R J, **7:** 4026 (4023)
Comber L C, **1:** 396 (393); **2:** 1220 (1217); **3:** 1768 (1763); **4:** 2140, 2180 (2174, 2178); **6:** 3523 (3515, 3521); **7:** 3721 (3721), 3738 (3730); **8:** 4648 (4646); **9:** 5323 (5321), 5334 (5333), 5372 (5369), 5432 (5426), 5445 (5444); **11:** 6328 (6325, 6326)
Combes B, **8:** 4677 (4672)
Combs P H, **11:** 6298 (6293)
Combs R, **10:** 6112 (6110)
Comeaux M A, **10:** 6026 (6024, 6025)
Comenius J A, **2:** (776), (777), 883 (880, 881, 882, 883); **3:** (1289); **5:** (2608), (2614); **6:** (3418), (3626); **7:** (4211); **8:** (4452), 4574 (4572), (4667); **10:** (5707); **11:** (6578), (6622)
Comenius J M, **3:** (1303)
Comer J P, **4:** 2212 (2210); **5:** 2491 (2488); **7:** 3820 (3819); **8:** 4780; **10:** 5750 (5745); **11:** 6563
Comerci G D, **9:** 5435
Comfort R E, **10:** 5812 (5810)
Comings J, **3:** 1262 (1259)
Commins S K, **4:** 1840 (1838)
Commons M L, **6:** 3434 (3432), 3435; **8:** 4824
Commons M M, **10:** 5939
Compas B E, **10:** 5738 (5736, 5737)
Compte A, **2:** (776), (782); **10:** (5598)
Compton D, **4:** 2045 (2044)
Compton-Hall M, **4:** 1924
Comrey A L, **4:** 2346 (2343)
Comstock D, **7:** 4336 (4335)
Comstock G, **1:** 570 (564, 565, 566, 567, 568, 569)
Comte A, **8:** 4634 (4632); **9:** (5051), (5407)
Conant J B, **3:** (1796); **8:** 4464 (4462); **9:** 5038 (5032), 5378 (5374); **10:** (5599), 6047 (6047)
Conboy I, **4:** 1917 (1913)
Condillac E B de, **9:** (5088)
Condorcet A, **6:** (3418)
Condorcet M, **2:** (777)
Condorcet M J A N, **1:** 139 (135)
Condous J, **1:** 198 (197)
Condry J, **1:** 570 (565); **11:** 6797 (6797)
Confessore G J, **9:** 5399 (5396, 5398)
Confessore S J, **9:** 5399 (5396, 5398)
Confrey J, **6:** 3684 (3673)
Confucius, **2:** (746); **8:** (4671)
Congalton A A, **7:** 3721 (3717)
Congdon R, **9:** 5130 (5129)
Conger J J, **3:** 1240
Conklin J, **5:** 2709 (2707)
Conley J J, **9:** 5528 (5526)
Conley S C, **4:** 2165 (2163); **9:** 5181 (5176); **10:** 5934 (5934), 6062
Conlon T, **11:** 6690 (6689)
Connell D B, **5:** 2571 (2569)
Connell P J, **6:** 3224 (3223)
Connell R, **4:** 2423 (2422); **6:** (3307); **8:** 4586 (4582, 4583, 4585); **9:** 5060 (5057, 5058)
Connell R W, **1:** 358 (355); **3:** 1347 (1346), 1720 (1714, 1716); **4:** 2249 (2248), 2272 (2269, 2270, 2271); **5:** 2457 (2454); **9:** 5312 (5311); **10:** 5606 (5603), 5613 (5608), 5758 (5758), 5826 (5823), 6085 (6084), 6139 (6133, 6135, 6136, 6137); **11:** 6723, 6797 (6796)
Connell W F, **1:** 343 (340); **3:** 1300 (1300); **4:** 1872 (1871); **10:** 5704 (5697), 5826 (5823); **11:** 6797 (6796)
Connelly F M, **3:** 1266 (1263), 1271 (1267), 1320 (1317, 1319), 1334; **7:** 4050 (4047); **10:** 6043 (6035, 6037, 6040), 6091 (6089, 6091); **11:** 6328 (6326)
Connelly M F, **10:** 6121 (6119, 6120)
Connelly R, **2:** 692 (690)
Conner J, **2:** 806 (804)
Conner R E, **4:** 2089
Conner R F, **3:** 1431 (1426, 1427); **4:** 2036 (2034), 2119 (2110, 2116)
Conners C K, **7:** 4081 (4079); **9:** 5528 (5527)
Conners D A, **9:** 5359
Conners R W, **4:** 2011 (2009)
Connerton P, **2:** 1204
Connolly J, **8:** 4542
Connolly J M, **5:** 2585 (2584)
Connolly K J, **8:** 4542 (4541)
Connolly T T, **3:** 1406
Connor J M, **4:** 2452 (2451)
Connors L G, **10:** 6083 (6081)
Conoley J C, **3:** 1513, 1514; **5:** 3066 (3061, 3065); **7:** 3706 (3703)
Conrad E, **4:** 2302 (2297)
Conroy J, **6:** 3638 (3635)
Considine D M, **11:** 6625 (6623)
Conte J R, **1:** 19 (18); **4:** 2261 (2259)
Conti G J, **10:** 6058 (6056)
Converse J M, **8:** 4887 (4885); **10:** 5862 (5857)
Converse P E, **5:** 2532 (2531)
Conway C G, **10:** 6234 (6230, 6231)
Conway J A, **6:** 3284; **7:** 4240 (4238)
Conyers D, **3:** 1416 (1412)
Cook A H, **11:** 6774 (6771)
Cook D L, **8:** 4758 (4757); **11:** 6511 (6508)
Cook I D, **2:** 635 (634)
Cook J, **4:** 2302 (2297, 2298)
Cook J D, **11:** 6384
Cook K S, **2:** 1073 (1066); **5:** 2931
Cook L, **8:** 4662
Cook L K, **10:** 5745 (5741), 5831 (5831)
Cook L L, **11:** 6355 (6349, 6351)
Cook M, **10:** 5772 (5770)
Cook M A, **1:** 11 (10), 358 (357); **2:** 824 (822, 824)
Cook R F, **1:** 310 (307)
Cook S W, **1:** 389 (380, 381); **10:** 5617
Cook T, **4:** 2045 (2044), 2089 (2081); **5:** 2672 (2671); **8:** 4766
Cook T D, **2:** 1135 (1132); **3:** 1283 (1281); **4:** 1938 (1935), 2089 (2082, 2083, 2084, 2085, 2086, 2088), (2103), 2108 (2101, 2102, 2103, 2105, 2106, 2107, 2108), 2119 (2116), 2194 (2187, 2188, 2189), 2388 (2386); **8:** 4403 (4400), 4783 (4780), 4875 (4874); **9:** 5373 (5368, 5371), 5490; **11:** 6384 (6378, 6382), 6575 (6574)
Cook T H, **9:** 5030 (5024)
Cook V J, **9:** 5379 (5375)
Cook W J J, **4:** 2229
Cooke B, **7:** 4300 (4298)
Cooke B L, **10:** 6047
Cooke J, **9:** (5325)
Cooke N J, **6:** 3306 (3302, 3303)
Cooke R, **5:** 2852 (2848)
Cooke T, **6:** 3213 (3211)
Cook-Greuter S, **10:** 5939 (5937)
Cook-Gumperz J, **2:** 802 (797); **6:** 3238 (3237)
Cooksey B, **2:** 617
Cookson P, **9:** 5201
Cookson P S, **1:** 152 (150); **7:** 4220 (4218), 4324 (4320, 4321, 4324)
Cookson P W, **1:** 328; **3:** 1720 (1717)
Cookson P W Jr, **8:** 4830 (4826, 4828)
Coolahan J, **5:** 3019 (3013)
Cooley C H, **9:** 5394 (5390); **10:** 5591 (5587)
Cooley W W, **2:** 631 (629, 630); **3:** 1548 (1548), 1549 (1546, 1547, 1548); **4:** 2208 (2200), 2388 (2382); **5:** 2595 (2590), 2869 (2868); **7:** 3872 (3867), 3986 (3979); **8:** 4562 (4556), 4657 (4656), 4753 (4753); **9:** 4973 (4973), 5043 (5040), 5264 (5260)
Coombs C H, **7:** 3706 (3700), 4315 (4308, 4311); **9:** 5503 (5500); **11:** 6388 (6387)
Coombs F S, **1:** 437 (432, 433); **9:** 5169 (5162)
Coombs J, **2:** 1208
Coombs P, **1:** 135 (128); **2:** 1126 (1122), 1127 (1124); **3:** 1713 (1709), 1820 (1810, 1811, 1812, 1815, 1819); **5:** 2960 (2959), 2961 (2959)
Coombs P H, **1:** 152 (144), 474 (466, 467, 468, 472); **2:** 933 (929); **3:** 1655 (1649), **4:** 1872 (1870), 2369 (2364, 2365); **5:** 2758 (2754), 2937 (2935), 2951; **6:** 3261 (3257), 3422, 3608 (3607); **7:** 4136, 4141 (4138), 4145 (4141, 4142), 4200 (4197, 4199); **8:** 4811 (4804, 4805), 4964 (4959); **9:** 5076, 5168 (5159, 5163), 5539 (5535); **10:** 5596 (5592), 5606 (5605); **11:** 6507 (6502)
Coomes M D, **10:** 5804 (5800)
Coonan W E, **5:** 2571 (2569)
Cooney G H, **4:** 2180 (2175)
Cooney T J, **3:** 1257; **6:** 3652 (3648, 3649, 3650); **7:** 4099; **8:** 4652; **9:** 5373; **10:** 6026
Coons J E, **1:** 594 (589); **6:** 3276 (3276); **9:** 5196 (5195), 5206 (5203, 5204, 5205), 5240 (5239)
Cooper B, **3:** 1347 (1344); **9:** 5181 (5176), 5298 (5297); **10:** 6126 (6126)
Cooper B S, **1:** 77 (73), 265 (261, 262, 263); **6:** 3196 (3190, 3191, 3193, 3195),

3197; **8:** 4831; **9:** 5168 (5159, 5167), 5272 (5271, 5272); **10:** 6062
Cooper C L, **4:** 1967; **10:** 5924
Cooper C R, **2:** 733 (730); **4:** 2024
Cooper D E, **3:** 1328 (1326, 1327); **8:** 4433
Cooper D H, **5:** 2954 (2952, 2954)
Cooper H, **10:** 6112 (6107, 6108, 6109), 6240; **11:** 6390 (6389)
Cooper H M, **5:** 2631; **7:** 3783 (3775, 3776); **10:** 6103 (6101)
Cooper J, **10:** 5957 (5955)
Cooper J O, **9:** 4977
Cooper L, **2:** 1099 (1098)
Cooper L O, **6:** 3442 (3442)
Cooper M, **2:** 831 (829); **5:** 2861 (2857); **7:** 4162 (4162)
Cooper N, **7:** 4026 (4023)
Cooper P, **10:** 5826 (5822)
Cooper R, **2:** 1165 (1164)
Cooper S, **11:** 6558 (6552), 6563 (6559)
Cooper W H, **10:** 6020 (6018)
Cooper W W, **3:** 1386 (1384, 1385)
Coopersmith S, **1:** 389 (386); **9:** 5394 (5391, 5393)
Cope J, **8:** 4698 (4697)
Cope P, **11:** 6690 (6689)
Copeland A P, **2:** 867 (863)
Copeland R, **8:** 4388
Copeland W D, **6:** 3201 (3198), 3202 (3198); **10:** (6002)
Copernicus N, **6:** (3218); **9:** (5051)
Coppedge F L, **9:** 4977 (4975)
Coppi R, **7:** 4006
Coppotelli H, **8:** 4368 (4366)
Coq G, **6:** 3196 (3190)
Corazzini A J, **3:** 1449; **11:** 6633 (6628)
Corbally J E, **1:** 67; **3:** 1774, 1775 (1771, 1772); **4:** 2166, 2167; **6:** 3284
Corbett A, **2:** 973 (972)
Corbett H D, **4:** 1857 (1852, 1853, 1854, 1855); **5:** 2847 (2840); **7:** 3826 (3823, 3825); **9:** 5181 (5180)
Corbett H O, **9:** 5246 (5242)
Corbett J, **11:** 6461 (6458)
Corbetta P, **10:** 6078
Corbin J, **7:** 4319 (4318)
Corcoran T B, **8:** 4864 (4860, 4861); **10:** 5934 (5932)
Cordeiro P A, **9:** 5060 (5058, 5059)
Corder S P, **6:** 3439 (3438)
Cordray D S, **3:** 1431 (1429); **4:** 2375; **8:** 4751 (4745); **9:** 5372 (5371); **11:** 6384
Corey S, **1:** 47 (45); **10:** 6099 (6096)
Corley R, **7:** 3743 (3741)
Corley R P, **11:** 6492 (6488)
Cormier S M, **5:** 2856; **11:** 6457
Cornacchia H F, **5:** 2572
Cornavin R, **11:** 6403
Cornelius S M, **3:** 1513 (1512); **6:** 3523 (3519)
Cornelius S W, **5:** 2676 (2674), 2916 (2914)
Cornell D, **4:** 2033, 2296
Cornell D G, **5:** 2731 (2729)
Corner T, **7:** 3977 (3974)
Corner T E, **1:** 563
Corney M, **11:** 6690 (6686)
Cornia G A, **3:** 1788 (1785, 1787), 1789
Cornish G, **1:** 41 (38)
Corno L, **2:** 846 (846); **5:** 2767 (2760, 2764, 2765), 2779 (2774, 2775, 2776, 2777, 2778), 2884, 2931 (2929); **6:** 3329 (3327); **9:** 5043 (5042); **10:** 5750 (5746), 5772 (5770), 6158 (6156, 6157), 6173 (6170)
Cornu A, **6:** 3213
Cornu B, **6:** 3638 (3636)
Correa H, **7:** 3820 (3816, 3817, 3818)
Corrigan D C, **10:** 5999
Corrigan P, **11:** 6803 (6800)
Corsaro W, **9:** 5512 (5512)
Corsaro W A, **9:** 5220; **10:** 5758 (5754, 5758); **11:** 6608 (6606)
Corson D, **3:** 1739
Cortina R, **6:** 3196 (3191)
Corvalán G, **7:** 4289 (4284), 4290 (4284)
Corvalán-Vásquez O, **3:** 1593 (1592); **11:** 6451 (6451); **7:** 4155 (4151, 4152); **11:** 6265 (6262, 6263)
Corvinus M, **5:** (2698)
Corwin R, **3:** 1607
Corwin R G, **1:** 11, 310; **4:** 2165 (2162); **6:** 3527 (3524); **8:** 4568 (4562); **9:** 5181 (5176, 5178); **10:** 5606 (5599)
Coser L, **2:** (929); **5:** 2998 (2993)
Cosgrove M, **6:** 3204 (3204)
Cosin B R, **2:** 784; **10:** 5606
Cosse G B, **3:** 1746
Costa A C, **3:** 1671
Costa A L, **2:** 860 (859)
Costa P T Jr, **1:** 239 (237); **5:** 2665 (2663)
Costa P T Jr., **8:** 4823 (4823)
Costanzo W V, **7:** 4088 (4085)
Costello P, **2:** 640 (638), 906 (903)
Coster H I, **9:** 5130
Costner H L, **5:** 2931 (2922); **7:** 4007
Cota-Robles E, **2:** 711 (707)
Cotgrove S F, **3:** (1344)
Cotlear D, **1:** 254 (245, 246, 247, 252); **3:** 1707 (1704)
Cotton J W, **6:** 3155; **10:** 5745
Cotton W E, **8:** 4736 (4735)
Cougan M C, **6:** 3643 (3640, 3641)
Coulby D, **5:** 2509; **11:** 6558
Coulmas F, **6:** 3446
Coulson D B, **2:** 1189 (1188)
Coulson J E, **3:** 1486 (1484)
Coulter F, **10:** 6106 (6105)
Coulthard M, **6:** 3638 (3635)
Coulthard R M, **9:** 5416 (5415), 5508 (5506)
Council K A, **7:** 4015 (4015)
Counts F A, **10:** 6227 (6224)
Counts G, **1:** 162 (158)
Counts G S, **3:** 1266 (1263), (1299); **9:** 5523 (5522)
Courtenay B C, **4:** 2123 (2120, 2122)
Courtney D P, **10:** 5775 (5772)
Courtney S, **1:** 152 (143); **7:** 4329; **10:** 5596 (5593)
Cousin J, **8:** 4890
Cousin V, **2:** 922 (919)
Cousins J B, **6:** 3284 (3282); **9:** 5264 (5262)
Cousins M, **4:** 1984 (1983)
Couvert R, **4:** 2123 (2122)
Covington M V, **1:** 32; **2:** 1182 (1181); **4:** 1966 (1966); **8:** 4730 (4729); **11:** 6360 (6356)
Cowan C D, **9:** 5385 (5379)
Cowan E, **8:** 4779 (4777)
Cowan J, **10:** 5808
Cowan P A, **4:** 2261
Cowan R, **3:** 1589
Cowen E L, **4:** 2267 (2264)
Cowen R, **2:** 933 (925), 942
Cowie H, **5:** 2536 (2534)
Cowles S, **9:** 5394 (5390)
Cowley W H, **10:** 5804 (5796)
Cox A E, **3:** 1624 (1621)
Cox B, **6:** 3442 (3440)
Cox C B, **9:** 5582 (5578)
Cox D R, **3:** 1425; **4:** 2156 (2150, 2151); **7:** 4162 (4160); **9:** 5467 (5460, 5463, 5467)
Cox E, **9:** 5008
Cox G M, **5:** 3061 (3059); **9:** 5158 (5153)
Cox J, **2:** 649; **5:** 2869 (2868)
Cox J L, **7:** 3833 (3831)
Cox K R, **6:** 3205
Cox M J, **2:** 988 (986, 987), 1011 (1010), 1175 (1174); **7:** 4104 (4100, 4101, 4102, 4103); **8:** 4542 (4540); **10:** 6008 (6006)
Cox M L, **8:** 4803 (4800)
Cox R, **8:** 4542 (4540)
Coxon A P M, **10:** 6227 (6224)
Coyle D, **4:** 2357 (2354)
Cozad J B, **3:** 1549
Crabb G, **10:** 5621
Craelius M H, **7:** 4046
Craft M, **1:** 28
Crahay M, **2:** 1121 (1119)
Craig C, **9:** 5577 (5575)
Craig G S, **9:** 5327 (5325)
Craig J, **5:** 2607; **10:** 5957 (5954, 5955)
Craig J E, **1:** 332 (331); **3:** 1300 (1289)
Craig K, **8:** 4394
Craig R, **5:** 2689
Craig R C, **8:** 4803
Craig R L, **2:** 1094, 1139; **3:** 1491; **10:** 5730
Craik F I M, **1:** 193 (187), 239; **2:** 856; **5:** 2884 (2882); **6:** 3288 (3287)
Craik G L, **9:** 5399 (5395)
Crain R, **9:** 5233
Crain R L, **1:** 11 (8); **3:** 1486 (1484, 1485); **9:** 5379 (5375)
Cramer G, **8:** 4616 (4614)
Cramer J F, **6:** 3276
Crandall D, **3:** 1494 (1491); **5:** 2847 (2840); **10:** 5973 (5971)
Crandall J A, **6:** 3334 (3333)
Crane D, **5:** 2998 (2994)
Crane M E, **7:** 3726 (3724)
Crane S, **10:** 6062 (6060)
Cranston M, **6:** 3499
Cranton P A, **5:** 2532; **10:** 6234 (6231)
Craven M-L, **6:** 3241
Craven R G, **9:** 4977 (4976)

Cravioto J, **8:** 4473 (4469)
Crawford D W, **11:** 6621
Crawford G, **5:** 2869 (2868)
Crawford R P, **5:** 2725 (2722); **8:** 4731 (4729)
Crawford W, **6:** 3399
Creaghead N, **10:** 5693 (5692)
Crealock C, **7:** 3807 (3803)
Cree L, **6:** 3204 (3203)
Creed P, **7:** 3839 (3839)
Creemers B P M, **3:** 1315, 1431, 1746 (1741); **4:** 1934 (1929, 1931, 1932, 1933), 2119 (2110); **7:** 4236; **10:** 6035 (6033)
Cregan A, **1:** 408 (407)
Crehan E, **10:** 6214 (6214)
Crehan P, **6:** 3284 (3276, 3278, 3282)
Creighton A, **8:** 4568 (4562, 4563)
Cremer G B, **10:** 5674 (5670)
Cremer R D, **6:** 3545
Cremin A, **11:** 6547
Cremin L, **5:** (2603), 2697 (2694); **9:** 5013
Cremin L A, **3:** 1266 (1262), (1288), 1524; **5:** 2607, 2617 (2609, 2610, 2611, 2612); **7:** 3848 (3842, 3845), 4224 (4223); **9:** 5168 (5160); **10:** 5707 (5705)
Crenson M A, **5:** 2672 (2671)
Cresswell A M, **8:** 4408 (4407)
Creswell W H, **5:** 2572
Creticos P A, **8:** 4715 (4710)
Creton H A, **2:** 820 (819, 820)
Crick B, **4:** 1984 (1982)
Crick J E, **6:** 3124 (3121)
Cripe J, **5:** 2813 (2810)
Crismore A, **11:** 6370 (6369)
Crissey B L, **5:** 2672 (2671)
Crist P A, **8:** 4542 (4540)
Crites J O, **11:** 6677 (6669, 6670), 6678 (6670)
Crites S, **7:** 4050 (4047, 4048)
Criticos C, **7:** 3760 (3759)
Crittenden B, **8:** 4455 (4455)
Crittenden B S, **10:** 5804
Crnic K A, **4:** 1979 (1976)
Croce B, **1:** (195), 199
Crocker A C, **5:** 2575 (2574)
Crocker L, **10:** 6012 (6011)
Crocker L G, **9:** 5091
Crocker R K, **11:** 6328 (6326)
Crocker W J, **7:** 3935
Crockett L, **9:** 5435 (5433)
Crockett W H, **1:** 238 (237)
Croft M, **3:** 1567, 1580; **7:** 4220
Croll P, **2:** 816 (812, 813, 814, 815), 831 (829); **9:** 5070 (5067); **10:** 5686 (5683)
Croll P J, **10:** 5826 (5824)
Croll V J, **10:** 5831 (5830)
Crombie A D, **1:** 93
Crombie I M, **8:** 4536
Crome A F W, **3:** (1721)
Cromwell R L, **2:** 718 (712)
Cronbach L, **3:** 1543 (1539); **4:** 2045 (2044), (2102); **10:** 6207 (6206)
Cronbach L J, **1:** 5 (2), 41 (33), 370 (366, 368, 369), 389 (383, 387, 388), 396 (391); **3:** 1421 (1417, 1418, 1420), 1431 (1425, 1426, 1427), 1624 (1622); **4:** 1864, 1872 (1864, 1870), 2089 (2080, 2081, 2086, 2088), 2097 (2090, 2095), 2100 (2097), 2119 (2112), 2388 (2382); **5:** 2462 (2458, 2459), 2595 (2590), 2596 (2590), 2672 (2671), 2767 (2759, 2760, 2761, 2766), 2879 (2875), 2921 (2920, 2921), 2931 (2924), 3061 (3057); **6:** 3325; **7:** 3970, 3986 (3978, 3981); **8:** 4399, 4562 (4556, 4561), 4604 (4603), 4753 (4753), 4766 (4759, 4760, 4761, 4764), 4791, 4857 (4856, 4857), 4930 (4927); **9:** 4973 (4972), 4995 (4981, 4991, 4992), 5030 (5024), 5038 (5033), 5055, (5157), 5378 (5374); **10:** 6158 (6155), 6159 (6155, 6157, 6158); **11:** 6320 (6316, 6318), 6328 (6321), 6348 (6340, 6341, 6347, 6348), 6384 (6378, 6381), 6445 (6440, 6443), 6575 (6570, 6572, 6573)
Cronbach R J, **10:** 6173 (6170)
Crone C R, **11:** 6334 (6330)
Cronin J M, **8:** 4594 (4591, 4592)
Cronin K A, **11:** 6603 (6602)
Cronin M W, **11:** 6603 (6602)
Cronk C E, **8:** 4473 (4471, 4472)
Crook J H, **4:** 2172 (2168)
Crookes G, **4:** 2339 (2336, 2338)
Crooks B, **3:** 1579 (1577)
Crooks T J, **3:** 1325 (1323); **6:** 3312 (3309)
Cropley A J, **6:** 3421 (3417, 3418, 3421)
Crosbie J, **9:** 5489 (5489)
Crosbie-Burnett M, **4:** 2266 (2265)
Cross C, **4:** (1840), 2261 (2260)
Cross D, **10:** 5943 (5940)
Cross D R, **4:** 1848 (1845); **7:** 3788 (3785)
Cross F S, **5:** 2572 (2569)
Cross G, **11:** 6797 (6795, 6796)
Cross K P, **1:** 93, 94, 127 (125); **4:** 2186 (2183); **6:** 3434 (3428, 3431, 3432); **7:** 4324 (4321, 4323), 4329 (4328); **8:** 4616 (4610), 4823 (4821, 4822); **11:** 6394 (6391), 6551 (6548)
Crosse S, **11:** 6384 (6379)
Crossley R, **6:** 3234 (3233, 3234), 3235 (3232, 3233, 3234)
Crosswhite F J, **9:** 5373
Crouch C, **8:** 4568
Crouch L, **3:** 1820 (1819)
Crouter A C, **3:** 1739 (1738)
Crovitz H F, **5:** 2725 (2723)
Crow G M, **9:** 5272 (5269), 5273 (5270)
Crowell D C, **2:** 1207
Crowell R, **5:** 2856
Crowhurst M, **11:** 6781
Crowley K, **5:** 2677 (2676)
Crowson R L, **1:** 60 (54), 77 (75); **2:** 1073 (1066); **3:** 1745 (1740); **7:** 3840; **9:** 5065, 5217, 5223 (5222); **11:** 6558 (6555), 6563 (6560)
Crowther G, **6:** 3459 (3456)
Cruickshank D, **10:** 6149 (6147)
Cruickshank D R, **6:** 3202 (3198, 3199); **10:** 6149 (6147)
Cruickshank W M, **10:** 5686 (5681)
Cruikshank M, **4:** 2292 (2290)
Crum M, **3:** 1501 (1497)
Crutcher R J, **2:** 846 (845); **5:** 2665 (2658, 2661)
Crutchfield R S, **2:** 1182 (1181); **8:** 4730 (4729)
Cryer P, **6:** 3339
Crystal D, **10:** 5694
Csikszentmihalyi M, **1:** 570 (564, 566); **5:** 2631 (2630); **6:** 3288 (3288); **9:** 5528 (5524); **10:** 5758 (5757, 5758); **11:** 6797 (6794), 6798 (6794, 6796)
Cuadra E, **3:** 1834 (1831)
Cuban L, **3:** 1266 (1263), 1307 (1305); **4:** 1911 (1903, 1904, 1909), 2281 (2281); **5:** 2779 (2778); **6:** 3284, 3652 (3649); **7:** 3743, 4088 (4082); **8:** 4562 (4558); **10:** 6009, 6214 (6211); **11:** 6287 (6286), 6370 (6370), 6538 (6530, 6531, 6532)
Cubberley E P, **5:** 2607, 2617 (2609, 2610, 2611)
Cubberly E P, **11:** 6370 (6368)
Cube F von, **3:** 1300 (1291)
Cubeddu L, **3:** 1820 (1819)
Cudeck R, **6:** 3325; **7:** 3942, 4007; **9:** 5403; **10:** 6159
Cuetos F, **8:** 4939 (4938)
Cuff E, **1:** 48 (45)
Cui J P, **8:** 4796 (4793)
Culbertson J, **2:** 977 (973)
Culbertson J A, **1:** 60 (53, 55, 57), 67 (61, 63), 77 (75, 76); **2:** 977, 1012; **3:** 1774 (1769); **7:** 3808, 4104
Culbertson S A, **9:** 4977 (4975)
Cullen J G, **11:** 6425
Culler C, **11:** 6653 (6648)
Culley L, **4:** 2427
Culligan R C, **1:** 238 (237)
Cullinan B, **2:** 737 (735)
Cully K B, **9:** 5008 (4999)
Cumming A, **4:** 2364 (2360)
Cummings A L, **10:** 5939 (5937)
Cummings E M, **2:** 705 (702)
Cummings J, **9:** 5373 (5371)
Cummings L L, **3:** 1774
Cummings T C, **2:** 973; **3:** 1271
Cummings W, **1:** 11 (6), **2:** 770 (768), 1136 (1134, 1135); **6:** 3085
Cummings W K, **2:** 824 (821); **3:** 1537 (1537); **4:** 2296; **6:** 3276 (3273); **7:** 3726 (3723); **8:** 4845 (4844); **11:** 6699 (6696)
Cummins J, **1:** 534 (532), 537 (536); **2:** 718 (717); **4:** 2346 (2344); **5:** 2910; **6:** 3231 (3228, 3229, 3231), 3439 (3436); **7:** 3970 (3967); **8:** 4939 (4937)
Cunningham D, **5:** 2874 (2871)
Cunningham G K, **9:** 4995 (4995)
Cunningham J, **8:** 4661 (4658)
Cunningham L L, **1:** 77; **2:** 977, 1012; **6:** 3284; **7:** 3808, 4104; **9:** 5216; **11:** 6580
Cunningham P M, **1:** 103, 142 (140), 152, 184; **2:** 906; **3:** 1315; **6:** 3422, 3435; **7:** 4185; **8:** 4616 (4610), 4736, 4811, 4812; **9:** 5298 (5298); **10:** 6058
Cunningham W R, **1:** 238 (235)
Cuoco A, **6:** 3512
Curle A, **3:** 1733

Curran C A, **4:** 2345 (2342)
Curran J, **4:** 1991 (1987)
Curran J Blackburn R, **4:** 1991
Curry C, **10:** 5681 (5679)
Curry C A, **4:** 2427 (2424)
Curry L, **1:** 322 (319)
Curry R L, **5:** 2993
Curry T, **9:** 5013
Curti M, **5:** 2617 (2610)
Curtis M J, **5:** 2907 (2905); **8:** 4661 (4657), 4662 (4658, 4659); **9:** 5290 (5287)
Curtis R F, **11:** 6575 (6573)
Cusack S A, **4:** 2123 (2122)
Cushall M B, **7:** 4104 (4102)
Cushing K S, **10:** 5762 (5761), 6026 (6023, 6024, 6025)
Cusick P, **9:** 5175 (5173); **10:** 6103 (6101, 6102)
Cusick P A, **10:** 5818 (5815)
Custer J D, **8:** 4375 (4373)
Cutler D M, **5:** 2798 (2798)
Cutler G B Jr., **1:** 88 (84)
Cutler S, **3:** 1240
Cutler W W, **7:** 4225
Cuttance P, **3:** 1745 (1742)
Cutts N E, **9:** 5290 (5286)
Cuypers S, **8:** 4460 (4460)
Cyert R, **11:** 6277
Cyert R M, **8:** 4568 (4563); **11:** 6260 (6260), 6261, 6276 (6272, 6273)
Cygnæus U, **4:** (2387)
Cyphert F, **3:** 1443
Czerniawska O, **2:** 662
Czerniewska P, **6:** 3459 (3456)

Daa'ir S, **11:** 6515
Dagher Z R, **10:** 6149 (6144, 6145)
Dagleish M, **8:** 4542 (4539)
Dahl K, **10:** 5795 (5793)
Dahl R A, **8:** 4736 (4735)
Dahlberg G, **4:** 2376 (2376)
Dahlet P, **10:** 6117
Dahlgren J, **10:** 5808 (5807)
Dahlgren L O, **7:** 4307 (4304); **10:** 5790 (5784, 5786)
Dahllöf U, **2:** 957 (956); **4:** 2376 (2375), 2377 (2375); **7:** 3886 (3883, 3885)
Dahlman C, **3:** 1713 (1707, 1712)
Dahrendorf R, **2:** (929)
Daiker D A, **10:** 5704 (5699)
Daillak R, **3:** 1431 (1425, 1426, 1428)
Daines J M, **10:** 6202 (6198, 6201); **11:** 6437 (6433)
Dainton D, **9:** 5323 (5318)
Daiute C, **10:** 5795 (5793); **11:** 6785
Dalby D, **1:** 295 (289)
Dale E, **4:** 1898 (1883); **7:** 3753 (3744)
Dale P S, **6:** 3224 (3223)
Dale R, **3:** 1720; **5:** 2512; **8:** 4622 (4617); **9:** 5298 (5296); **11:** 6266, 6684, 6704
Dale R R, **2:** 834; **9:** 5445
Daley H, **3:** 1712 (1710); **4:** 1911 (1908, 1909, 1910); **8:** 4902 (4898, 4899)
Dalgarno G, **10:** (5658)
Dalin P, **5:** 2852 (2849, 2851); **7:** 4240 (4237, 4239); **10:** 5965, 5999
Dall'Alba G, **8:** 4429 (4425, 4429); **9:** 5411 (5408)
Dallas D, **8:** 4939 (4938)
Dallmayr F R, **5:** 2585 (2585)
d'Ally H, **4:** 2194 (2189, 2191)
Dalman V M, **10:** 6139 (6138)
Dalmases C de, **9:** 5121
D'Alonzo B J, **2:** 635 (634)
Dalton P, **7:** 4255 (4252)
Daly A, **11:** 6640
Daly J A, **9:** 5358 (5356)
Daly K, **10:** 5690 (5687, 5689)
Daly M, **4:** 2302 (2300); **10:** 5842
Dam G, **4:** 2427 (2424, 2425)
Damarin S K, **4:** 2427 (2425); **6:** 3660
Damasio A R, **6:** 3235 (3232)
D'Amato R C, **9:** 5290 (5287)
d'Amboise G, **4:** 1991 (1985)
D'Ambrosio D, **6:** 3667 (3666)
D'Ambrosio U, **6:** 3452 (3446), 3667 (3662, 3666, 3667)
Damdin D, **7:** 3905 (3895, 3900)
Damiba A, **8:** 4514 (4511, 4512)
D'Amico J, **3:** 1537 (1537)
Damico J S, **6:** 3227 (3226), 3231 (3229), 3232
D'Amico-Samuels D, **7:** 3973 (3972)
Damon A, **4:** 2012
Damon W, **3:** 1641; **7:** 3920 (3919); **8:** 4372 (4369, 4370, 4371, 4372); **9:** 5394 (5391), 5512 (5511); **10:** 5758 (5758), 6053 (6049, 6052)
Dampier P, **7:** 4185 (4183)
Dams T, **1:** 244 (242)
Dance K A, **10:** 6159 (6155)
Dancey K J, **9:** 5294 (5292)
D'Andrade R, **3:** 1240 (1237)
Dangermond J, **3:** 1829 (1829)
D'Anglejan A, **7:** 3970 (3969)
Daniel C, **9:** 5082 (5079)
Daniel D, **7:** 3807 (3802)
Daniel J, **7:** 4220
Daniel J S, **3:** 1567
Daniel N, **5:** 2869 (2868)
Daniels D, **3:** 1642 (1639); **5:** 2465 (2464); **11:** 6492 (6489, 6490)
Daniels D H, **5:** 2769 (2764)
Daniels J, **9:** 5302
Daniels P R, **5:** 2491 (2490)
Danke H L, **4:** 2229
Dannefer D, **5:** 2665 (2659)
Dannells M, **10:** 5804 (5800)
Dansereau D F, **1:** 193 (186, 187); **2:** 867 (863); **10:** 5831 (5830)
Danthine A, **11:** 6306
Dantona R, **3:** 1406
Dantonio M, **8:** 4881 (4876)
Danylewycz M, **10:** 6139 (6133, 6135)
Danzberger J, **2:** 711 (710); **6:** 3496 (3493, 3494, 3495)
d'Apollonia S, **10:** 6234 (6230)
Dar Y, **7:** 3970 (3967)
Darby J, **1:** 414 (413)
Darch C, **2:** 867 (862)
D'arcy de Oliveira M, **7:** 4336 (4331)
D'arcy de Oliveira R, **7:** 4336 (4331)
D'Arcy P, **6:** 3209 (3205, 3206, 3208)
Daresh J C, **1:** 72 (70, 72)
Darity W Jr, **4:** 2445 (2442)
Dark V, **5:** 2495 (2493)
Darkenwald G G, **1:** 152 (143, 144); **3:** 1602 (1599, 1600); **6:** 3366 (3363, 3364), 3434 (3434); **7:** 4324 (4320, 4321, 4322, 4324), 4325, 4329 (4328); **8:** 4736 (4734)
Darling C A, **4:** 2266 (2262)
Darling-Hammond L, **4:** 2131, 2132 (2126); **7:** 3821; **9:** 5196 (5194); **10:** 5929 (5926, 5927), 5935 (5933), 6020, 6043 (6035), 6044 (6036, 6037), 6047, 6083, 6106 (6104, 6105), 6187 (6187)
Darlington R, **2:** 688 (679); **3:** 1642 (1640, 1641); **7:** 3833 (3832); **11:** 6384 (6382)
Darlington R B, **2:** 631 (627); **5:** 2714 (2713); **7:** 4015 (4007); **9:** 4973 (4968, 4969), 4974, 5385 (5379); **11:** 6591 (6591)
Darrough G P, **7:** 4026 (4023)
Darvas P, **6:** 3196 (3193)
Darwin C, **2:** 767, (1177); **3:** (1520); **4:** 2172 (2167, 2168, 2170, 2171); **5:** (2655); **6:** (3218); **9:** (5424); **10:** (5659)
Darwin C R, **2:** (825); **4:** (1865), (1963); **7:** (4171); **10:** (5705); **11:** (6764)
Darwood D, **7:** 3889 (3887)
Das J P, **6:** 3435
Dasen P R, **3:** 1245 (1244), 1252 (1246); **5:** 2651
Dash M, **7:** 3905 (3895, 3900)
Datan N, **6:** 3428 (3426); **8:** 4719
Datcher-Loury L, **6:** 3106 (3105)
Datchoua Soupa C, **1:** 221 (218)
Datesman S K, **3:** 1610
Datta A, **10:** 5606 (5601)
Datta L, **4:** 2089
Datta R C, **9:** 5355 (5353, 5354)
Dauner M B, **9:** 5076 (5072, 5074)
Daurio S P, **5:** 2495 (2494), 2731 (2729, 2730)
Dave R, **4:** 2249 (2245)
Dave R H, **1:** 215, 221; **3:** 1262 (1260)
Davé R H, **4:** 2257 (2255)
Dave R H, **5:** 2758, 2759; **6:** 3421 (3418), 3422, 3585
Davenport J A, **1:** 277
Davenport S, **11:** 6558 (6556)
Davenport T R, **2:** 1064
Davenport T R H, **10:** 5635
Davey A, **9:** 5349 (5349)
Davey B, **10:** 5831 (5831)
Davey I, **11:** 6735 (6733, 6734)
Davey T, **8:** 4581 (4578)
Davico M I, **5:** 2514 (2513); **9:** 5228 (5226, 5227)
David F N, **8:** 4359
David H A, **7:** 3738 (3731); **9:** 5385
David J, **9:** 5223 (5222)
David M, **4:** 2267; **9:** 5216 (5214)
Davidson D, **9:** 5313 (5311)
Davidson D H, **2:** 1213 (1210)
Davidson E S, **4:** 1848 (1843)

Davidson J E, **5:** 2731, 2732 (2726)
Davidson J I, **2:** 973
Davidson K S, **11:** 6360 (6358)
Davidson L, **1:** 543; **11:** 6466 (6462)
Davidson R J, **4:** 1967
Davidson S, **4:** 2266 (2264)
Davidson W, **9:** 5406 (5405)
Davie R, **6:** 3523 (3512)
Davies A, **4:** 2364 (2360, 2362, 2363); **10:** 6099 (6097)
Davies B, **2:** 1127 (1124), 1198 (1198); **3:** 1411 (1408, 1409); **5:** 2457 (2453, 2454, 2455, 2457), 2458, 2500 (2498); **9:** 5302 (5301), 5308
Davies D, **2:** 892 (889); **9:** 5216 (5214), 5268 (5265, 5267, 5268)
Davies D E, **9:** 4977 (4975)
Davies D P, **8:** 4473 (4469)
Davies E, **3:** 1271 (1268)
Davies F, **8:** 4698 (4696)
Davies G, **10:** 5943
Davies I K, **2:** 969 (966); **4:** 1898 (1891); **8:** 4774 (4769), 4775
Davies J, **3:** 1619; **8:** 4803; **9:** 5355 (5350, 5351, 5354)
Davies J H, **6:** 3422
Davies J K, **5:** 2903 (2899)
Davies L, **2:** 1182 (1181); **4:** 2423 (2419, 2420, 2421, 2422); **5:** 2512; **9:** 5168 (5167); **11:** 6731 (6727, 6728)
Davies L B, **8:** 4730 (4729)
Davies M M, **8:** 4680 (4679)
Davies M W, **4:** 2432 (2431)
Davies O, **4:** 2330 (2329)
Davies R, **3:** 1733
Davies S, **2:** 977 (976)
Davies S N, **3:** 1402 (1400)
Davis A, **10:** 5994 (5994)
Davis C, **5:** 2998 (2996)
Davis C E, **9:** 5471 (5470)
Davis D A, **3:** 1755 (1753)
Davis D F, **6:** 3474 (3469); **7:** 3935 (3934); **11:** 6348 (6345)
Davis D J, **11:** 6621 (6619, 6620, 6621)
Davis E, **2:** 718 (717)
Davis F B, **7:** 3935 (3931)
Davis G, **3:** 1602 (1599), 1720 (1714), 1830 (1828)
Davis G A, **2:** 1182 (1180, 1182); **5:** 2732; **9:** 5532
Davis G B, **5:** 2831 (2828)
Davis I K, **6:** 3096 (3092)
Davis J, **4:** 2053; **9:** 5232 (5229); **10:** 5690 (5687, 5688, 5689, 5690), 5691
Davis J A, **1:** 370 (366)
Davis K, **9:** 5572 (5568)
Davis M, **7:** 4175 (4171)
Davis M A, **11:** 6360 (6356)
Davis O L, **3:** (1288)
Davis R, **3:** 1810, 1821, 1829 (1825, 1827), 1830 (1825, 1826, 1827, 1829); **8:** 4495 (4493), 4652; **9:** 5539
Davis R B, **2:** 1052; **6:** 3670 (3669, 3670), 3671 (3668, 3669, 3670), 3684 (3684)
Davis R G, **3:** 1820, 1834 (1831); **8:** 4601; **9:** 5240 (5234)
Davis S A, **1:** 11 (10)
Davis S S, **3:** 1755 (1753)
Davis W E, **2:** 711 (706, 708)
Davydov V V, **3:** 1252 (1250); **6:** 3291 (3289); **9:** 5098, 5548
Dawe L, **6:** 3638 (3637)
Dawes R M, **7:** 3706 (3700); **8:** 4923 (4918)
Dawis R V, **6:** 3315 (3312)
Dawkins D, **3:** 1720
Dawkins R, **4:** 2172 (2167)
Dawson A J, **6:** 3652
Dawson D, **4:** 2212 (2210)
Dawson D A, **9:** 5294 (5292)
Dawson G, **5:** 2681
Dawson G G, **10:** 6117 (6116)
Dawson J A, **4:** 1857
Dawson K S, **8:** 4581
Dawson M, **11:** 6712 (6709)
Dawson R E, **8:** 4581
Day C, **3:** 1271 (1267, 1270); **10:** 5972 (5971), 5982, 6092 (6090)
Day J D, **6:** 3223; **7:** 3768 (3764)
Day J E, **4:** 1847 (1845)
Day M, **1:** 198 (197), 343 (341); **2:** 1165 (1164)
Day S B, **9:** 5350
Daymont T N, **9:** 5076 (5074); **11:** 6633 (6628)
Dayton C, **2:** 1131 (1130); **3:** 1514 (1511)
Dayton C M, **2:** 831 (830)
D'Cruz J, **1:** 423
D'Cruz J V, **9:** 5544 (5541)
de Andrade A C, **11:** 6415 (6414)
de Beaugrande R, **2:** 1031 (1026)
de Beauvoir S, **8:** (4431)
De Beyer J, **10:** 5919 (5915)
De Blignières A, **8:** 4964 (4958)
De Bloois M, **2:** 649 (648)
de Bono E, **2:** 1182 (1181); **5:** 2725 (2723); **8:** 4731 (4729); **10:** 5750 (5745)
de Bruijn E, **7:** 3894 (3890, 3891, 3892, 3893)
De Castell S, **7:** 3711 (3709)
De Cillia S, **6:** 3538
De Corte E, **1:** 194, 204; **2:** 984 (983), 985, 1006 (1004, 1005); **4:** 2218; **5:** 2669, 2767 (2762), 2768, 2769, 2874 (2872), 2879 (2876, 2877), 2884 (2882); **6:** 3292 (3291), 3345 (3344), 3638 (3635), 3652, 3655 (3653, 3654), 3660 (3658, 3659), 3661; **7:** 3791, 3942; **8:** 4722; **9:** 5341 (5340, 5341), 5508; **11:** 6780
de Courtivron, **9:** 5441
De Decker B, **6:** 3213
de Falguerolles A, **6:** 3508 (3507)
de Felix J W, **5:** 2509; **6:** 3284
de Finetti B, **1:** 480 (477)
de Francis J, **6:** 3446
De Graaf N D, **4:** 2274 (2274)
De Graaf P M, **9:** 5553 (5551)
de Graaf S, **5:** 2907 (2904); **6:** 3559 (3559)
De Groof J, **1:** 504
De Groot A, **4:** 2199 (2195)
De Groot A D, **2:** 842 (839), 984 (984); **8:** 4727 (4727)
De Groot E V, **1:** 204 (202); **6:** 3329 (3328), 3345 (3344)
De Groot H, **5:** 2798 (2793); **7:** 4324 (4323)
De Gruijter D N M, **2:** 792 (788, 790, 791); **5:** 3043
de Guzman A, **8:** 4509 (4508)
De Haan R F, **5:** 2773 (2770)
De Haas J H, **8:** 4474 (4468)
De Ibarrola M, **6:** 3261 (3259, 3260)
De Jong F P C M, **7:** 3788 (3786, 3787), 3791 (3788, 3790)
De Jong M J, **4:** 1934 (1931)
de Kadt E, **2:** 1049
de Kleer J, **1:** 347 (343)
de la Rocha O, **3:** 1252 (1249)
De Lagarde J, **2:** 1121 (1117)
De Landsheere G, **1:** 152 (144), 504; **2:** 1121 (1119); **4:** 1872 (1865); **5:** 2880
De Landsheere V, **3:** 1804
De Landshere G, **4:** 2388 (2386)
de Lange J, **6:** 3670 (3670)
de Larminat P, **2:** 665
De Leeuw A C J, **3:** 1745 (1740)
de Leeuw J, **2:** 677 (677); **4:** 1877 (1876); **5:** 2596 (2590); **6:** 3508 (3507); **7:** 3986 (3984, 3985); **9:** 5159 (5158)
de Leo D, **1:** 494 (491)
de l'Epée C-M, **10:** (5659)
De Lyon H, **8:** 4586 (4584, 4585, 4586); **10:** 6139 (6134)
de Moivre, **7:** (4158)
De Moura Castro C, **6:** 3261 (3260); **11:** 6415 (6412, 6413, 6414), 6452 (6448, 6451), 6699 (6698)
De Prospero A, **9:** 5489 (5487)
De Quadros Carvalho R, **6:** 3261 (3260)
de Ribaupierre A, **5:** 2677 (2674)
de Rijke F, **9:** 5210
De Robillard D, **2:** 1160
De Saint Martin M, **9:** 5021 (5017)
de Saint Moulin L, **11:** 6814 (6809)
de Sena L, **5:** 2562
De Silva W A, **10:** 5721
de Stete M, **5:** 2852 (2848)
de Tray D, **3:** 1449
De Vellis R F, **10:** 5862 (5856)
de Viguerie, **5:** 2617 (2613)
de Villiers J G, **2:** 705 (703)
de Villiers P A, **2:** 705 (703)
De Vos A, **3:** 1240 (1238, 1239, 1240)
De Vos G A, **3:** 1240 (1238, 1239, 1240), 1241 (1238)
de Voss G, **10:** 5957 (5955)
De Vries H, **3:** 1520 (1519)
de Vries J I P, **7:** 3950 (3948)
de Vries M, **11:** 6292 (6290, 6291)
De Wit Greene A G, **5:** 2571 (2570)
de Wit T, **6:** 3256 (3255)
de Wolfe C J, **10:** 5924 (5923)
De Young D J, **3:** 1431 (1426, 1427)
Deal A G, **4:** 1980 (1976, 1978); **5:** 2813 (2810)
Deal T E, **4:** 2165 (2160, 2162); **6:** 3528;

9: 5181 (5176, 5178, 5180), 5210 (5207, 5208, 5210), 5273 (5269, 5270)
Dean C, 2: 1011 (1008); 9: 5268 (5266, 5267)
Dean E, 3: 1666; 10: 5697
Dean G, 2: 1165
Dean R S, 9: 5290 (5287)
Deane E M, 3: 1529 (1526)
Dearborn W F, 6: 3315 (3312)
Dearden R, 8: 4446 (4445, 4450)
Dearden R F, 3: 1328 (1325, 1326, 1327); 6: 3151; 8: 4447
De'Ath E, 4: 2267
Deaux K, 9: 5435 (5434)
Deay A M, 10: 5834 (5832, 5833)
DeBaggis A M, 10: 5948
DeBakey L, 4: 2131 (2127)
DeBarsyshe B D, 8: 4368 (4367)
Debeauvais M, 2: 942, 947 (945); 3: 1589; 11: 6445 (6442)
Debes J L, 11: 6625 (6622)
Debesse M, 8: 4491
Deble I, 2: 834 (834); 9: 5228 (5225)
DeBoer G E, 9: 5327 (5324)
Debus R, 1: 31 (31)
Debus R L, 9: 4977 (4976)
DeCamp Wilson R, 9: 5411 (5409)
DeCasper A J, 1: 15 (13); 5: 2802 (2801)
deCastell S, 6: 3452
DeCharms R, 7: 3942 (3940); 10: 6223 (6222)
Deci E L, 7: 3942 (3941); 11: 6798 (6794)
Decock B, 5: 2769 (2764); 7: 3942 (3940)
Decoo W, 10: 5625 (5624)
Decroly O, 4: 1872 (1867, 1869); 5: (2774)
Décroly O, 8: (4669)
DeCruyenaere M, 5: 2768 (2764)
Dede C, 7: 3995 (3992); 9: 5544 (5540)
deDenus J, 9: 5070 (5067)
Dedijer S, 1: 560 (554)
Dedrick R F, 9: 5379 (5376)
Dee Lucas D, 10: 5745 (5741)
Deem R, 4: 2292 (2290); 9: 5445
Deeming W E, 8: 4758 (4755)
DeFaire U, 11: 6492 (6489)
Deffenbacher J L, 11: 6360 (6356)
Deffenbacher K A, 5: 2879 (2875, 2877, 2878)
DeFleur M, 9: 5518 (5514)
Defoe D, 9: (5089)
Deford D, 3: 1257 (1256)
DeFord D E, 8: 4935
Deforges C, 2: 816
DeFrain J, 4: 1972 (1968)
DeFreitas G, 6: 3189 (3188)
DeFries J C, 5: 2465 (2465); 7: 3743 (3741); 10: 5680 (5680); 11: 6492 (6488, 6489, 6490)
Degen G, 7: 4263 (4262)
Degenhart R E, 3: 1381 (1377), 1589 (1585), 1768 (1763, 1764, 1765); 4: 2024, 2025, 2140 (2134); 7: 3936
Degerman A, 4: 2327
Degge R M, 11: 6621
Degler C N, 4: 2172 (2169)
deGroot A D, 10: 6026 (6023)
DeGroot E, 2: 868 (866)
Deiaco E, 4: 2394 (2389)
Deighton L C, 7: 3970 (3961); 11: 6307
Deitz S M, 9: 4977 (4975)
Dejene A, 7: 4145 (4142)
deJong T, 5: 2768 (2763)
Dejoy J K, 2: 1175 (1173)
Dejung E, 8: 4419 (4419)
Deken J E, 4: 2388 (2382)
DeKock A, 3: 1501 (1497)
del Fierro A C Jr, 10: 6139 (6138)
Del Moura Castro C, 11: 6266
Del Valle D, 3: 1671 (1670, 1671)
Delacroix J, 3: 1655 (1650)
Delamont D, 10: 5614 (5608)
Delamont S, 1: 295 (283); 2: 816 (812), 1073 (1070); 4: 2052 (2047), 2412 (2409); 7: 4319; 9: 5060, 5312 (5310, 5311); 10: 6085 (6085)
Delaney B, 9: 5379 (5377)
DeLany B, 1: 11 (10); 5: 2512 (2512)
DeLargy P F, 8: 4811 (4808)
Delay J, 8: 4423 (4419)
Delbecq A L, 3: 1443 (1443)
Delclos V R, 6: 3512 (3511)
Dele O, 8: 4514 (4513)
DeLeeuw L, 5: 2767 (2762)
Delekat F, 3: 1300 (1290)
deLemos M M, 3: 1624 (1621)
DeLeon P H, 5: 2672 (2670)
Delgado-Gaitan C, 2: 803 (799); 3: 1233; 6: 3452 (3451); 7: 3974 (3972); 9: 5220
DeLicardie E, 8: 4473 (4469)
Deliyanni-Kouimtzi K, 10: 5826 (5823)
Dell 'Orco P, 3: 1394 (1388)
della Ringa C, 11: 6420
Dell'aringa C, 4: 1976; 6: 3617
DeLoache J S, 2: 842 (839); 4: 2198 (2196); 5: 2916 (2913); 6: 3452 (3448)
DeLone R, 9: 5191 (5188)
Deloz L O, 11: 6437 (6437)
Delpit L, 10: 6099 (6098); 11: 6784 (6783)
Delquadri J C, 8: 4375 (4372, 4373, 4374), 4376 (4374)
Delucchi K, 10: 6053 (6053)
Delucchi K L, 8: 4799 (4798)
Delworth U, 10: 5804 (5798, 5799), 5805
DeLyon H, 10: 5613 (5609)
Demana F, 7: 4099 (4096)
Dembo M H, 7: 4296 (4294, 4295)
Demetriades E I, 3: 1374
Demetriou A, 2: 838; 5: 2669 (2668, 2669), 2670, 2680, 2768 (2761)
DeMets D, 7: 3858 (3857)
Demeyer-Harris C, 7: 3807 (3806)
Demick J, 2: 872 (870)
Deming B S, 11: 6425
Deming W E, 6: (3502); 9: 5130 (5126), 5142
deMontfort Supple M, 10: 5694
Dempsey J R, 3: 1642 (1640)
Dempster A P, 5: 2596 (2591); 7: 3861 (3860); 9: 5130 (5129)
Dempster F N, 7: 3763 (3760)
Demsetz H, 3: 1702 (1697); 4: 1972 (1970, 1971, 1972)
Demsky T, 1: 111; 8: 4864 (4858, 4859, 4863); 11: 6663 (6661)
Dench S, 11: 6798 (6797)
Denckla M B, 7: 4081 (4078); 8: 4936 (4934)
Denemark G W, 10: 5999
Deng Xiaoping, 3: 1300 (1293, 1294)
Dengel R E, 1: 142 (141)
Denham C, 1: 23; 5: 2714 (2709), 2779; 7: 3872 (3867), 3886; 10: 5713 (5711), 6043
Deniker P, 8: 4423 (4419)
Denison E F, 1: 520 (512); 3: 1665 (1660, 1661), 1695 (1690); 5: 2647 (2646), 2942 (2938); 11: 6653 (6652)
Denker J, 11: 6775
Denman W, 9: 5232 (5229)
Denn J, 3: 1642 (1639)
Denner P R, 2: 969 (966)
Denney D, 11: 6360 (6356)
Denney N W, 5: 2665 (2660)
Denning C, 8: 4698 (4696, 4697)
Dennis C R, 10: 5635
Dennis D, 5: 2739
Dennis J, 6: 3096 (3094)
Dennis W, 1: 497; 3: 1774
Dennison J D, 2: 900
Deno S L, 2: 718 (714), 719; 3: 1359 (1356, 1357, 1358); 9: 5071 (5067, 5068); 10: 6173 (6171)
Denscombe M, 10: 5617 (5616), 6031 (6027), 6139 (6132)
Densmore K, 10: 6096 (6095); 11: 6722 (6720)
Denson T, 8: 4751 (4743)
Dent H E, 2: 718 (716)
Dentler R A, 1: 82 (80)
Denton D E, 8: 4433 (4432)
Denton F T, 7: 3711
Denton W, 4: 2267
Denzin N K, 1: 543; 4: 2388 (2383); 11: 6465 (6462, 6463, 6464)
Deolalikar A B, 3: 1788 (1786); 4: 2418 (2413)
DePaulo B M, 9: 5435 (5434); 11: 6484 (6483)
Depoortere J, 5: 2852 (2848)
Derber S, 8: 4881 (4878)
Derlega V J, 10: 5758, 5759
Derman-Sparks L, 7: 3978
Dermen D, 7: 3706 (3705)
Dermody M, 3: 1529 (1526)
Dermutz S, 1: 432
Derr T F, 9: 4977 (4975)
Derrick R A, 4: 2310 (2302)
Derricott R, 8: 4581 (4578)
Derrida J, 1: 60 (56), (538); 8: 4642 (4641, 4642)
Derryberry D, 11: (6308)
Dershimer R A, 11: 6445 (6444)
DerSimonian R, 5: 2596; 11: 6339 (6336)
DeRuiter J A, 10: 5999 (5999)
Desai A, 6: 3616 (3615)
DeSanctis J, 9: 5246 (5243)
Desarbo W, 9: 5158 (5158)
Descartes R, 2: (776), (883); 3: 1464

(1462), (1524); **4:** 2000 (1997, 1999); **6:** (3316), (3636); **7:** (4098); **8:** (4630), (4640); **9:** (5395); **10:** (5986)
Deschamp P, **5:** 2491 (2487)
Desforges C, **1:** 23; **5:** 2536 (2534); **6:** 3311 (3308); **9:** 5363 (5359, 5361); **10:** 6015 (6012)
Deshler D D, **1:** 162 (162); **2:** 867 (863); **4:** 2123 (2120); **7:** 4185; **10:** 6178 (6175, 6177)
deSilva C R, **5:** 2758 (2755)
deSilva D, **5:** 2758 (2755)
Desiraju T, **1:** 554
Desjardins F J, **4:** 2011 (2009)
Desoran R A, **1:** 358 (355)
Dessent T, **9:** 5070 (5069, 5070)
Destine J, **11:** 6307
Detterman D K, **1:** 5 (5); **2:** 838; **5:** 2768 (2762), 2922; **11:** 6456, 6457
Dettmann D, **5:** 2491 (2488)
Deuchler G, **3:** (1722)
Deutsch M, **5:** 2503 (2501), 2504; **10:** 5617, 6223 (6220, 6221)
DeVaney A, **7:** 3760 (3757)
Devereaux M S, **1:** 157 (153); **3:** 1453 (1451, 1452); **7:** 4185
Devine J, **3:** 1703 (1698); **8:** 4939
Devins N E, **1:** 265 (264); **8:** 4845 (4844)
Devlin J, **7:** 3991
DeVos G A, **1:** 295 (292), 504
DeVoss G, **3:** 1538 (1537); **10:** 6004 (6000, 6001)
DeVries D L, **2:** 1099 (1096, 1098)
Dew K M K, **11:** 6360 (6359)
Dewe P, **10:** 6062 (6059, 6060)
Dewees A, **2:** 640 (639)
Dewey J, **1:** (195), (227), (261), 474 (465); **2:** (776), (783), (804), (919), (930), 957 (949), (1095), (1194), 1207 (1204); **3:** 1287 (1285, 1287), 1300 (1289, 1295, 1298), 1328 (1325), 1354 (1348), (1432), 1524 (1520, 1521, 1522, 1523), (1540), (1723); **4:** (1841), (1866), (1869), 1984 (1981), 2001, 2033 (2030, 2031), (2080), 2186 (2184, 2186), 2387 (2386); **5:** (2608), (2609), (2614), (2694), 2806 (2803), (2876), (2877), 2897 (2891); **6:** (3135), (3204), (3300), (3387), (3418), (3497); **7:** (3920), (3924), 4050 (4047), (4156), (4211), (4330); **8:** 4455 (4452, 4453), (4535), 4574 (4573), (4606), 4648 (4645), (4668), (4681); **9:** (5230), (5231), 5318 (5313), 5378 (5377), 5523 (5522), (5575); **10:** (5595), 5707 (5705, 5706), 5795 (5792), 5817 (5813, 5814, 5817), 5886 (5885), 5991 (5986, 5990), 6004 (6000), 6043 (6038, 6039), 6168 (6164, 6165, 6166, 6168), 6177 (6174), 6187 (6183), 6219 (6215); **11:** (6578)
Deweys J, **8:** (4481)
Dewhurst J, **4:** 1991
DeWolf M, **3:** 1778 (1778)
DeYoung A J, **1:** 244 (240)
Dhahri N, **11:** 6476
Dhakal D, **1:** 254 (245, 247, 252)
Dharmadasa K H, **2:** 1136 (1134, 1135)
Dhillon H S, **4:** 2331; **5:** 2571 (2567)
Di Chiro G, **1:** 48 (46)
Di Leonardo M, **7:** 4224 (4222)
di Sessa A, **7:** 4088 (4084)
Di Vesta F J, **3:** 1367 (1365)
Diakité S, **6:** 3585 (3579)
Diallo H A B, **5:** 2556
Diamond E E, **5:** 3050 (3043)
Diamond J, **5:** 2993; **7:** 4000 (3997)
Diamond M C, **1:** 554; **7:** 4081 (4079)
Diamond R M, **4:** 1898 (1887, 1888); **5:** 2862
Diamond S, **1:** 295 (281, 282), 296, 297 (281); **4:** 2053; **6:** 3215; **9:** 5572; **11:** 6310 (6308)
Dias S, **4:** 2052 (2050)
Díaz H, **8:** 4415
Diaz R M, **2:** 867 (863), 868 (863); **9:** 5403 (5400)
Diaz S, **3:** 1252 (1250)
Dicheva D, **2:** 977 (976)
Dichtelmiller M, **3:** 1642 (1641)
DiCiccio T J, **9:** 5471
Dick A, **2:** 816; **8:** 4372; **9:** 5043; **10:** 6053 (6051, 6053); **11:** 6580
Dick W, **4:** 1928 (1927); **5:** 2861 (2859, 2860); **7:** 3886 (3881); **8:** 4783 (4781); **10:** 5900 (5899)
Dickens C, **10:** (5814)
Dickens W, **6:** 3189 (3187, 3188)
Dickey M R, **7:** 4026 (4023)
Dickie K E, **7:** 3753 (3745)
Dickinson A K, **5:** 2623
Dickinson D, **6:** 3463 (3460)
Dickinson G, **1:** 127 (125); **11:** 6775 (6772)
Dickinson H, **9:** 5367 (5365)
Dickinson L, **6:** 3213
Dicks J E, **4:** 2351 (2350)
Dickson P W, **9:** 5508
Dickson W J, **4:** 2166 (2158)
Dickson W P, **7:** 4300 (4299, 4300), 4301 (4300)
Diderot D, **9:** (5087)
Diederich J, **3:** 1354 (1348)
Diederich P B, **4:** 2024 (2020, 2023); **9:** 5323 (5320)
Diehl-Faxson J, **6:** 3452 (3448)
Diejomaoh V P, **1:** 215; **7:** 4145 (4142)
Diener C, **1:** 31 (28, 30)
Diener C I, **2:** 867 (866)
Diener E, **4:** 1980 (1978)
Dienstbier R A, **1:** 31; **5:** 2665; **8:** 4719 (4718); **9:** 5518
Diesing P, **2:** 645 (640, 641, 642, 644)
Diesterweg F, **8:** (4418)
Dietterich T G, **8:** 4722
Diez J C, **7:** 3801
Diez M, **10:** 5957 (5955)
Digman J M, **5:** 2665 (2663); **9:** 5528 (5525, 5526, 5527); **11:** 6310 (6310)
Dijkstra S, **2:** 1026
Dike H, **4:** 1917 (1915)
Dikshit S D, **11:** 6719 (6717)
Dila K, **5:** 2972 (2969)
Dill C E, **4:** 1898
Dill D, **6:** 3202
Dillard J A, **10:** 6035 (6033)
Dillman D A, **7:** 3861 (3858)
Dillon A, **5:** 2709 (2708); **8:** 4694
Dillon D R, **2:** 806 (804)
Dillon J T, **2:** 806 (803, 804, 805); **3:** 1354; **8:** 4881 (4875, 4877); **10:** 6086 (6083)
Dillon P, **11:** 6604 (6602)
Dillon R, **1:** 194; **5:** 2921; **6:** 3325
Dillon R F, **1:** 389; **8:** 4957; **11:** 6328
DiLorenzo T M, **1:** 490 (489)
Dilthey W, **1:** (538); **3:** (1722); **4:** (1866), (2386); **5:** (2579), 2586, (2693); **8:** (4452); **9:** (5052)
Dilworth M E, **10:** 5934 (5931)
Dilworth T, **8:** (4846)
DiMaggio P, **4:** 2272 (2268, 2269)
Dimaras A, **5:** 2523
Dimmock C, **3:** 1411; **9:** 5308; **11:** 6563 (6559)
Dimondstein G, **8:** 4388 (4385)
Ding B, **8:** 4945 (4943)
Dingwall R, **10:** 6085
Dinh Te H, **7:** 4175 (4173)
Dinham S M, **10:** 6117
Diniz F, **10:** 6244 (6242)
Dinkmeyer D, **4:** 2267
Diogenes, **7:** (3707)
Dion K L, **11:** 6360 (6357)
Diorio J A, **9:** 5441 (5436)
DiPaolo M, **8:** 4950 (4949)
DiPardo A, **10:** 5795 (5791, 5793); **11:** 6784 (6783)
DiPelo G, **2:** 1182 (1182)
DiPietro J, **4:** 2452 (2450)
D'Iribarne A, **11:** 6807 (6807)
Diringer D, **1:** 295 (289); **6:** 3446 (3444)
diSessa A, **10:** 5790 (5785, 5787)
DiSilvestro F, **2:** 1165
Disinger J F, **4:** 1995
Disken M, **4:** 1954
Dissanayake E, **11:** 6618
Dittmann J, **6:** 3224
Dittmann-Kohli F, **5:** 2676 (2676)
Dittmar N, **2:** 968
DiVesta F, **1:** 322 (319)
DiVesta F J, **10:** 5831 (5830)
Dix L S, **11:** 6712 (6709)
Dixon J, **10:** 5961 (5958)
Dixon R A, **1:** 239 (238); **6:** 3288 (3288), 3428 (3427); **7:** 3768 (3766)
Dixon W J, **7:** 4015 (4015), 4162 (4162)
Djuraev R, **10:** 5649 (5647, 5649)
Dmytriw L, **10:** 5948 (5947)
Dnempova E D, **9:** 5106
Dneprov E, **10:** 5649 (5645)
Dobbert M L, **1:** 295 (285, 286, 287); **2:** 1212 (1209); **3:** 1729 (1728)
Dobbs S M, **1:** 198
Dobell A R, **9:** 5471 (5468)
Dobratz B, **4:** 1984
Dobson R B, **4:** 2257 (2254)
Dobzhansky T, **4:** 2172 (2168)
Docherty D, **8:** 4473 (4472)
Dochy F J R C, **5:** 2768 (2761); **6:** 3325 (3317); **8:** 4702 (4699, 4701, 4702)

Dockrell B, **4:** 2377
Dockrell W B, **8:** 4751 (4745)
Dockstader-Anderson K, **6:** 3452 (3448)
Doctorow M, **10:** 5831 (5830, 5831)
Dodd B G, **7:** 4307 (4307)
Dodd C, **3:** (1723)
Dodds J, **3:** 1624 (1622)
Dodds P, **10:** 5713 (5708)
Dodds T, **3:** 1573 (1568, 1570)
Dodge C, **3:** 1735 (1734)
Dodge K A, **1:** 234 (233); **8:** 4368 (4366); **9:** 5567 (5564)
Dodgson P, **4:** 1903 (1902)
Dodson D W, **10:** 5606 (5598)
Dodson J D, **6:** 3325 (3318)
Doehring D G, **7:** 4081 (4078)
Doerfert F, **3:** 1563
Doeringer P B, **3:** 1703 (1696); **4:** 1975 (1973); **5:** 2942 (2937, 2939, 2940, 2941); **6:** 3189 (3184, 3185, 3186, 3187); **7:** 4211 (4210); **8:** 4839 (4837)
Dogramact E, **11:** 6731
Doig B A, **7:** 4307 (4306); **10:** 5790 (5789)
Doig J W, **9:** 5273 (5270)
Doise W, **5:** 2536 (2535); **8:** 4372 (4371), 4482 (4482); **9:** 5548 (5546)
Dolan C V, **11:** 6492 (6490)
Dolan L, **8:** 4935 (4932, 4934)
Dolden R, **10:** 5621
Dole J, **11:** 6370 (6368)
Dole J A, **8:** 4935 (4934); **10:** 6192 (6191, 6192)
Doll E A, **9:** 5567 (5564)
Doll R C, **5:** 2773 (2770)
Dollaghan C, **1:** 408 (407)
Dollard J, **1:** (495)
Dolphin A M, **3:** 1449
Dolton P, **9:** 5355 (5353, 5354); **10:** 5846 (5844)
Domanski H, **7:** 3864 (3863)
Domingo L, **4:** 2418 (2415)
Domingo Z T, **5:** 2890 (2886), 2891
Dominice P, **10:** 5808
Domitianus T F, **8:** (4887)
Dommann F, **1:** 317 (313)
Donald J, **11:** 6769
Donaldson L, **8:** 4608
Donaldson M, **2:** 856 (852); **6:** 3288 (3285)
Donaldson T S, **10:** 5590 (5590)
Donant L, **3:** 1283 (1279), (1339)
Dondis D A, **11:** 6625 (6622)
Doneau S J, **8:** 4881 (4875)
Doney W, **3:** 1464
Donlon T F, **4:** 2180 (2174, 2176, 2177); **6:** 3523 (3515, 3521); **7:** 4000 (3999); **11:** 6355 (6354)
Donmoyer R, **2:** 892 (890); **3:** 1474 (1464)
Donnellan-Walsh A M, **1:** 490 (489); **6:** 3234 (3232), 3235 (3232)
Donnerstein E, **1:** 570 (568)
Donoghue M R, **4:** 2351 (2347)
Donohue J III, **8:** 4902 (4900)
Donovan R, **4:** 2025
Dooley A R, **10:** 5948 (5944)
Dooley P, **1:** 265 (263)
Doran R L, **4:** 2439 (2437); **5:** 2856 (2854); **8:** 4648 (4646)
Dorans N J, **2:** 1117 (1110); **5:** 3050 (3046, 3047), 3055 (3054); **11:** 6355 (6349)
Dore R, **1:** 110 (109), 520 (517); **4:** 2394 (2389); **6:** 3092; **11:** 6265 (6263), 6699 (6696, 6697)
Dore R F, **5:** 2607
Dore R J, **1:** 474 (471)
Dore R P, **4:** 1924 (1919); **5:** 2942 (2940); **8:** 4839 (4838, 4839); **11:** 6424 (6421)
Dorfman C H, **6:** 3085
Doris J, **10:** 5668 (5663, 5665)
Dormant D, **4:** 1917 (1917)
Dornbusch S M, **1:** 89, 437 (432); **3:** 1607 (1604); **5:** 2627 (2625), 2628 (2625); **8:** 4568
Dorner A H, **1:** 343 (340)
Dorner D, **3:** 1434 (1433)
Dörner D, **7:** 3788 (3786)
Dorner J, **4:** 1958
Dorr A, **6:** 3625; **7:** 3743 (3741); **8:** 4680 (4677, 4678, 4680)
Dorr-Bremme D W, **7:** 3726 (3724)
Dors H, **9:** 5196 (5193)
Dorsey B J, **5:** 2512 (2511)
Dorsey-Gaines C, **6:** 3453 (3451)
Dorson R M, **7:** 4050 (4047)
Dorsten L, **1:** 11 (7)
Doscher L, **1:** 594 (591)
Dosi G, **11:** 6282 (6278)
Doss L S, **1:** 408 (408)
Dossey J, **6:** 3684
Dossey J A, **1:** 41 (37); **9:** 5373
Dostoyevsky F, **8:** (4430)
Dougherty C, **2:** 760, 1094; **3:** 1810, 1821 (1813); **5:** 2744, 2819 (2815); **6:** 3613 (3613); **8:** 4364 (4361), 4531 (4527, 4528), 4865; **9:** 5076 (5072); **11:** 6415, 6424 (6420), 6431, 6653 (6648, 6649), 6699 (6691)
Dougherty C R S, **3:** 1448 (1445)
Doughty C, **4:** 2339 (2338)
Doughty P L, **2:** 1139 (1138)
Douglas, **10:** (5599)
Douglas C, **4:** 1911 (1908, 1909, 1910)
Douglas F D, **3:** 1398 (1398)
Douglas J D, **11:** 6465 (6464)
Douglas J W B, **6:** 3312 (3307), 3523 (3512)
Douglas L, **7:** 4225
Douglas P H, **5:** 2740
Dougna K, **11:** 6403
Dougna K D, **1:** 474 (469)
Douty A M, **11:** 6774 (6771)
Douvan E, **1:** 88 (87)
Dove L, **4:** 2423 (2420, 2421); **8:** 4586 (4582, 4584, 4585)
Dove L A, **10:** 6139 (6138)
Dove R G, **8:** 4594 (4591)
Dowden D E, **8:** 4881 (4880)
Dowdeswell W H, **9:** 5338 (5336)
Dowing C, **2:** 973
Dowling C, **2:** 977, 992; **3:** 1779; **7:** 4094; **8:** 4803; **9:** 5544
Downes B, **10:** 6244 (6240)
Downes D, **11:** 6803 (6800)
Downes T, **3:** 1398 (1395)
Downey G, **3:** 1647
Downey J, **4:** 2331
Downey J E, **11:** 6310 (6308)
Downey M T, **9:** 5562 (5561), 5577 (5576)
Downey R G, **6:** 3124 (3121)
Downing J, **1:** 175 (173); **6:** 3480 (3475); **7:** 3935 (3931); **8:** 4935 (4932)
Downs A, **8:** 4519 (4518)
Downs C, **3:** 1820 (1813, 1817); **7:** 4155 (4149)
Downs R B, **4:** 2388 (2386)
Dowsett G W, **3:** 1347 (1346); **4:** 2249 (2248), 2272 (2269, 2270, 2271); **9:** 5060 (5057, 5058), 5312 (5311); **10:** 5606 (5603), 5613 (5608), 5758 (5758)
Doyle A B, **8:** 4542
Doyle D, **1:** 265 (264)
Doyle J F, **8:** 4455 (4455)
Doyle L B, **3:** 1553
Doyle M A, **6:** 3209
Doyle W, **1:** 23; **2:** 820 (816, 817, 819, 820); **3:** 1257 (1255), 1494 (1491); **6:** 3202 (3198); **7:** 4215 (4213); **9:** 5363 (5360, 5361); **10:** 6015 (6012), 6031 (6027, 6028, 6030), 6103 (6101), 6112 (6109), 6207 (6204, 6205, 6206)
Draba R E, **5:** 3050 (3049), 3051 (3049)
Drabek A G, **7:** 4148
Drafall L E, **7:** 4026 (4023), 4030
Drake J B, **4:** 2186 (2183); **7:** 4324 (4321)
Drake K, **2:** 665 (663); **4:** 1975 (1974); **10:** 5954 (5949, 5950)
Draper J A, **1:** 158, 162 (161); **5:** 2758
Draper J F, **5:** 3050 (3044)
Draper K D, **6:** 3452 (3448)
Draper N R, **8:** 4657 (4654); **9:** 4973 (4973)
Draper S W, **3:** 1779
Drasgow F, **2:** 1117 (1110); **5:** 3055; **7:** 4000 (4000); **11:** 6334 (6331)
Dravie A, **11:** 6403
Dray W H, **8:** 4447 (4446)
Drazan R, **11:** 6647 (6641)
Drecoll F, **1:** 103 (102)
Dreeben R, **1:** 520 (516), 594 (591); **2:** 824 (821, 822, 823, 824); **4:** 1938 (1935), 1972 (1971); **5:** 2589 (2587), 2595 (2593); **7:** 3820, 3886 (3883); **9:** 5065 (5064), 5175 (5170), 5176, 5181 (5176), 5264 (5260); **10:** 5614, 6103 (6101), 6139 (6132, 6137); **11:** 6298 (6294)
Dreeler A, **7:** 4240
Dreher B, **1:** 554
Dreher M J, **2:** 824; **5:** 2651
Dreikurs R, **1:** 486 (483); **3:** (1536); **7:** 4296 (4294); **8:** 4816 (4816)
Dreitzel H P, **2:** 1204
Drenth P J D, **4:** 2257 (2254); **5:** 2879, 2884; **6:** 3292; **7:** 3970; **11:** 6333, 6334
Dressler F, **4:** 1958 (1955)

Dressler W, **2:** 1031 (1026)
Drever E, **5:** 2903 (2899)
Drews S, **8:** 4816 (4813)
Drexel I, **11:** 6272 (6269)
Dreyfus A, **1:** 244 (243); **2:** 806 (805)
Dreyfus H L, **4:** 1898 (1895); **8:** 4642; **10:** 6026 (6021)
Dreyfus S E, **4:** 1898 (1895); **10:** 6026 (6021)
Drillien C, **3:** 1624 (1621)
Drillien C M, **3:** 1647 (1644)
Driscoll M E, **8:** 4845 (4842); **9:** 5378 (5375, 5376)
Drislane F W, **7:** 4081 (4078)
Driver K, **11:** 6731 (6728, 6729)
Driver R, **2:** 991 (990); **3:** 1543 (1538, 1541, 1542); **6:** 3416; **7:** 4104 (4101); **8:** 4479 (4476, 4477), 4652 (4649, 4651); **9:** 5334 (5332), 5341 (5339), 5345 (5344), 5349 (5349), 5411 (5410); **10:** 5790 (5784); **11:** 6292 (6291)
Drǐzule M, **6:** 3272
Dronkers J, **2:** 1094 (1090, 1091, 1092); **7:** 4325 (4324); **8:** 4830 (4827); **9:** 5554 (5552, 5553); **10:** 5606 (5600)
Droogleever Fortuijn E, **3:** 1690, 1739 (1736)
Dror Y, **3:** 1431 (1425)
Drösler J, **7:** 3706 (3705)
Drossander A, **3:** (1464)
Drucker P, **8:** 4796
Drucker P F, **4:** 1924 (1923); **7:** 4155 (4154); **8:** 4519 (4515)
Drucker S M, **5:** 2709 (2706)
Drummond M, **3:** 1624 (1621)
Dryden J, **1:** (539)
Dryfoos J G, **1:** 88 (87)
Dryland A R, **11:** 6265 (6263)
Du Pisani T, **10:** 5635
Du Rietz L, **4:** 2377 (2376)
du Toit B M, **5:** 2945 (2943)
Dubar C, **4:** 1976 (1975)
Dubas J S, **9:** 5435 (5433, 5434)
Duberg B R, **6:** 3393 (3393)
Dubert A, **1:** 226 (222)
Dubes R, **2:** 831 (829)
Dubet F, **4:** 2385
Dubin F, **8:** 4939
Dubin S S, **1:** 239 (238)
Duboff B, **3:** 1406
DuBois P A, **11:** 6339 (6334)
Dubow E, **3:** 1642 (1640)
Dubreucq-Choprix F L, **5:** 2779 (2774, 2776)
Duby A, **4:** 2119 (2111); **5:** 2891
Ducci M A, **6:** 3267; **8:** 4364 (4360, 4362), 4715 (4714); **11:** 6265 (6263)
DuCette J P, **5:** 2495 (2493)
Duchacek I D, **5:** 2512 (2509)
Duchan J F, **6:** 3235 (3233)
Ducharme E R, **10:** 6012 (6009, 6010, 6011)
Duchene C, **2:** 957 (957)
Duchêne C, **2:** 1220 (1213, 1217); **5:** 2500 (2496, 2497); **11:** 6394 (6392)
Duchesne C, **2:** 652 (652)
Duckworth D, **9:** 5324 (5320)
Duckworth E, **5:** 2680 (2678); **10:** 6043 (6040), 6168 (6166)
Duclaud-Williams R, **10:** 6072 (6068), 6079 (6075)
Duda R, **4:** 2357 (2353)
Dudley B, **3:** 1563 (1559), 1567 (1565)
Dudley P, **7:** 3936 (3934)
Dudley-Marling C, **2:** 1170, 1175 (1174)
Duelli Kline R, **4:** 2302
Duerksen G L, **7:** 4026 (4023)
Duffy G G, **2:** 867 (863, 865); **3:** 1257 (1256); **8:** 4935 (4934), 4947 (4947); **9:** 5362 (5359, 5361); **10:** 6149 (6147, 6148), 6192 (6191, 6192)
Duffy T M, **4:** 1917 (1917); **5:** 2773 (2770), 2867, 2874 (2871); **8:** 4694; **10:** 5914
Dugan D J, **3:** 1449
Dugan T F, **8:** 4780
Dugas R, **3:** 1464
Dugfy H G, **5:** 2673 (2670)
Duguet P, **7:** 4088 (4085)
Duguid P, **2:** 838 (837), 842 (839); **5:** 2867 (2865), 2884 (2882); **6:** 3345 (3342, 3344); **9:** 5232 (5229); **11:** 6456 (6454)
Duguid S, **3:** 1441
Duignan P A, **7:** 3924
Duijker H C J, **5:** 2978
Duimel J, **10:** 5674 (5670)
Duisberg-Gesellschaft C, **1:** 317
Duit R, **6:** 3205; **8:** 4479, 4652; **9:** 5342 (5339)
Duke B C, **6:** 3085, 3284
Duke C, **1:** 93 (90, 91, 93), 127, 142 (141), 152 (145), 180 (177); **2:** 640; **5:** 2951 (2949); **6:** 3467; **7:** 4171; **10:** 5808 (5806); **11:** 6437 (6435)
Duke D L, **1:** 265 (263), 437; **6:** 3284 (3280, 3281); **10:** 6043 (6036)
Duke R D, **5:** 2773 (2771)
Dulay H C, **4:** 2345 (2345)
Dulbecco R, **9:** 5406
Dulberg L, **9:** 5539 (5536)
Dumais S, **8:** 4383 (4381)
Dumazedier J, **6:** 3378
Dumont R V, **9:** 5220 (5218)
Dunaway D K, **7:** 4224, 4225
Dunbar S B, **1:** 370 (370), 374 (371, 372, 373); **4:** 1848 (1847); **8:** 4623 (4619, 4622); **11:** 6320 (6315), 6349 (6343)
Duncan B, **3:** 1750 (1749); **4:** 2278 (2276, 2277), 2432 (2428)
Duncan D D, **11:** 6551
Duncan G, **2:** 1094 (1090)
Duncan G J, **2:** 1055 (1052); **3:** 1642 (1638, 1639); **6:** 3616 (3614)
Duncan J, **3:** 1642 (1637); **7:** 4275
Duncan K D, **6:** 3096 (3093)
Duncan O D, **3:** 1750 (1749); **4:** 2278 (2275, 2276, 2277), 2432 (2428); **7:** 3721 (3717, 3718), 3771 (3769, 3770), 3864 (3863); **8:** 4351 (4339, 4344), 4359, 4895 (4892); **9:** 5553 (5549); **10:** 5735 (5732, 5734)
Duncan R, **5:** 2852 (2848)
Duncan W A, **9:** 5323 (5323), 5432 (5429)
Duncan-Jones P, **7:** 3721 (3716, 3717)
Duncker K, **5:** 2884 (2881); **8:** 4727 (4722, 4724, 4726)
Dundas J, **10:** 5854
Dunette M, **2:** 1094
Dunford J E, **9:** 5252 (5249, 5250)
Dunham E A, **9:** 5544 (5540)
Dunivant N, **3:** 1441 (1438, 1439)
Dunkel H B, **5:** 2579
Dunkelberg W C, **10:** 5862 (5860)
Dunker L H, **11:** 6625
Dunkerley D, **9:** 5168 (5161)
Dunkerton J, **2:** 816 (814)
Dunkin M, **6:** 3202; **9:** 5318, 5363 (5359); **10:** 5977 (5974), 6132 (6128), 6149 (6147, 6148), 6207 (6204), 6239
Dunkin M J, **1:** 486; **2:** 802 (797, 799); **4:** 2375; **5:** 2870; **8:** 4774 (4773); **10:** 5704, 6043 (6036), 6047, 6106, 6132 (6131), 6155 (6150), 6234 (6228, 6229, 6230, 6231, 6232, 6233), 6239 (6237); **11:** 6390
Dunkle J, **11:** 6384 (6379)
Dunkley M, **11:** 6412
Dunleavy P, **3:** 1720
Dunlop D, **4:** 2212
Dunlop J T, **5:** 2942 (2941); **11:** 6277 (6272)
Dunn C, **10:** 5690 (5688), 5697 (5694)
Dunn D, **3:** 1266 (1265)
Dunn D E, **6:** 3394
Dunn G, **2:** 831 (826, 830), 1084 (1082)
Dunn J, **2:** 856 (854); **3:** 1520 (1517); **4:** 2261 (2260); **8:** 4950 (4948); **9:** 5507 (5504, 5505)
Dunn J F, **11:** 6492
Dunn J G, **6:** 3204 (3203); **9:** 5338 (5335, 5336)
Dunn K J, **5:** 2779 (2775)
Dunn L, **2:** 729 (727); **3:** 1507 (1506), 1636 (1629, 1630, 1633)
Dunn L M, **10:** 5662 (5661)
Dunn P D, **1:** 244 (242)
Dunn R S, **5:** 2779 (2775)
Dunn T, **6:** 3143 (3139)
Dunn W, **5:** 2672
Dunn W N, **3:** 1431 (1428)
Dunne E, **5:** 2536 (2535)
Dunne T T, **1:** 194 (191)
Dunnette M D, **3:** 1490; **5:** 2725; **11:** 6678 (6671)
Dunn-Rankin P, **9:** 5158 (5153, 5155)
Dunphy D C, **2:** 1079 (1076)
Dunst C J, **1:** 362 (359); **4:** 1980 (1976, 1978, 1979); **5:** 2813 (2810, 2811), 2814
Dunstan J F, **5:** 2508; **6:** 3496 (3492, 3494); **7:** 3839 (3839); **9:** 5215; **10:** 5650, 6083 (6081)
Dunstan J L, **2:** 766 (762, 764, 765)
Dupe M, **9:** 5544
Dupont B, **4:** 2423 (2420)
Duquenne V, **9:** 5560 (5559)
Duquette A, **7:** 4324 (4321)
Duraisamy P, **1:** 254 (246)

Durán R P, **2:** 718 (717); **4:** 2180 (2179); **11:** 6320 (6318)
Durand V M, **1:** 408 (408)
Durand-Prinborgne C P, **4:** 2385
Durant J, **9:** 5350 (5346)
Duranti A, **6:** 3238 (3237)
Durbridge N, **3:** 1579 (1577)
Durden W G, **5:** 2495 (2494), 2732 (2731)
Dureau F, **1:** 226 (222)
Durkheim E, **2:** 785 (777, 778, 779), (919), (928), 1073 (1065, 1066, 1070); **3:** 1347 (1344); **4:** 2165 (2159), 2274 (2273), 2400 (2397); **5:** (2605); **6:** (3136); **9:** 5050; **10:** (5587), (5596), (5597), (5598), (5606)
Durkin D, **4:** 1962 (1962); **11:** 6390 (6388)
Durkin K, **6:** 3638 (3635)
Durndell A, **4:** 2427 (2424, 2425)
Durojaiye M O A, **7:** 3978
Durovic J J, **5:** 3050 (3049)
Durra A, **6:** 3113
D'urso S, **3:** 1537, 1538
Durston S, **2:** 733 (732)
Durvy V, **5:** (2614)
Duschl R A, **6:** 3416; **8:** 4464 (4461)
Dusek J B, **10:** 5762 (5760), 6112
Duskin E, **2:** 700
Duston J, **8:** 4873 (4870)
Dutcher N, **3:** 1824 (1822); **6:** 3480 (3477)
Dutter R, **9:** 5082
Duvieusart B, **11:** 6298 (6293)
Duxbury N, **2:** 982 (978, 981)
Dwarkasing W W, **10:** 5853
Dweck C S, **1:** 31 (28, 29, 30, 31); **2:** 867 (865, 866); **5:** 2665 (2662), 2768 (2764); **7:** 3788 (3784), 3942 (3938); **9:** 5406 (5405); **10:** 5826 (5824)
Dworkin A, **3:** 1607
Dworkin A G, **10:** 5607 (5604), 5924 (5920, 5921, 5922, 5923, 5924), 6062 (6059)
Dworkin R J, **4:** 2004 (2003); **8:** 4574 (4572); **10:** 5924 (5922, 5923)
Dworkin R M, **4:** 2033 (2030)
Dwyer C, **11:** 6726 (6723, 6724)
Dwyer C A, **4:** 2131 (2128)
Dwyer D, **4:** 2418
Dwyer D C, **11:** 6608 (6607)
Dwyer F M, **2:** 887 (886)
Dwyer J, **6:** 3144 (3139)
Dwyer P, **11:** 6803 (6802)
Dwyer T, **5:** 2571 (2569)
Dyck J, **2:** 984 (983, 984)
Dyckman J, **3:** 1820 (1813, 1817)
d'Ydewalle G, **2:** 969
Dyer J, **2:** 688 (682)
Dyke W E, **6:** 3631 (3630)
Dykhuizen G, **3:** 1524
Dykman B J, **9:** 5358 (5356)
Dykstra R, **3:** 1529 (1526)
Dynneson L, **1:** 299 (298)
Dynneson T L, **1:** 280 (278)
Dyrenfurth M J, **11:** 6292 (6288)
Dyson A, **2:** 729 (729); **10:** 5696 (5696)
Dyson A H, **11:** 6784 (6781, 6782)
Dyssegaard B, **3:** 1402 (1401)
Dzvimbo P, **7:** 3960
Eads G M, **3:** 1624 (1621)
Eagersfield D, **6:** 3144 (3139)
Eagly A H, **9:** 5435 (5434)
Earles J A, **8:** 4758 (4755); **11:** 6678 (6675)
Earley P, **8:** 4408 (4404), 4864 (4860); **10:** 6047
Early M, **6:** 3443 (3440)
Eary J, **7:** 3995 (3993)
Eash M, **10:** 5886 (5886), 6117 (6116)
Easley J, **9:** 5411 (5410); **10:** 5790 (5784)
Easley J A, **8:** 4482; **9:** 5338 (5336, 5337)
Eason G, **2:** 775 (773)
Eason K D, **4:** 2011 (2008)
Eastenson A, **2:** 705 (702)
Easterby R S, **4:** 2011 (2009)
Easterlin R, **3:** 1676 (1673)
Easterly W, **4:** 2315 (2311)
Eastman P, **8:** 4509 (4505)
Easton D, **3:** 1810 (1808)
Easton J Q, **6:** 3631 (3630)
Easton P, **1:** 221; **3:** 1655 (1649), 1820 (1810); **4:** 1911; **6:** 3585
Eastwood K, **9:** 5246 (5244)
Eaton E G, **7:** 4171 (4164, 4166, 4167)
Eaton W, **8:** 4779 (4777)
Eatwell J, **3:** 1685, 1703, 1750
Ebbighausen R, **6:** 3368
Ebbinghaus H, **3:** (1793); **4:** 1872 (1866); **5:** (2875); **6:** 3325 (3316); **9:** (5407)
Ebel R L, **1:** 77; **3:** 1266; **5:** 2714; **7:** 4056 (4054), 4196 (4195), 4197; **9:** 5432; **10:** 5725 (5722), 6132; **11:** 6315 (6313, 6314)
Ebeling B, **5:** 2897 (2894)
Eberly D J, **8:** 4581 (4580)
Eberts R W, **6:** 3196 (3190); **8:** 4408 (4407); **10:** 6072 (6069, 6070, 6071)
Ebertzeder A, **1:** 317 (311)
Eccles J, **5:** 2627 (2627); **9:** 5432 (5429); **10:** 6112 (6110)
Eccles J C, **7:** 3872 (3868); **9:** 5050
Eccles J S, **4:** 2435 (2434, 2435); **5:** 2491 (2489); **10:** 5775 (5773); **11:** 6320 (6316, 6319)
Echternacht G J, **7:** 4000 (3999)
Eck J, **6:** (3529)
Eckard E W, **9:** 5572 (5569)
Eckart C, **9:** 5158 (5156)
Eckaus R S, **8:** 4917 (4914); **9:** 5240 (5235)
Eckenrode J, **3:** 1647 (1645)
Eckensberger L H, **3:** 1252 (1251); **5:** 2650 (2650), 2651 (2649)
Ecker E W, **1:** 198 (198)
Eckert P, **6:** 3238 (3236)
Eckland B K, **7:** 3872 (3870)
Eckstein M, **8:** 4526 (4521); **11:** 6266 (6263), 6699 (6698)
Eckstein M A, **2:** 933 (924), 957 (951); **3:** 1739 (1736), 1768 (1762, 1763); **8:** 4622 (4617); **10:** 5735 (5733); **11:** 6530
Eckstein O, **2:** 1131 (1127)
Eco U, **7:** 3774 (3773); **9:** 5416 (5412, 5413)
Ecob R, **4:** 1934 (1931, 1932); **5:** 2509 (2508), 2779 (2775), 2870 (2868); **7:** 3912 (3910); **9:** 5223 (5221); **11:** 6390 (6388, 6389)
Edding F, **4:** 2331
Eddinger S S, **8:** 4881 (4877)
Eddy D, **7:** 4148
Edelfelt R, **10:** 5982 (5978)
Edelfelt R A, **8:** 4568 (4562); **10:** 6047
Edelhoff C, **6:** 3442 (3440)
Edelman J M, **6:** 3368 (3367)
Edelsky C, **2:** 1198 (1197)
Edelstein W, **2:** 846 (844); **5:** 2680, 2767 (2761); **7:** 3920 (3919), 3924, 3925; **9:** 5512 (5510, 5512)
Eden D, **11:** 6511 (6509)
Eder D, **2:** 1073 (1070); **4:** 2249; **9:** 5560 (5554); **10:** 5758 (5754, 5758)
Eder R W, **4:** 2131 (2130)
Edfelt R, **6:** 3262
Edgar E, **5:** 2971 (2966); **11:** 6461 (6457)
Edgerton D, **4:** 1918 (1913)
Edgerton R B, **7:** 3830 (3828)
Edmonds J, **3:** 1530 (1526)
Edmonds R, **9:** 5210 (5207); **10:** 5750 (5746)
Edmonds R A, **10:** 6083 (6082)
Edmonds R L, **6:** 3545
Edmonds R R, **4:** 1934 (1929, 1930)
Edmundson P G, **10:** 5994 (5992, 5993)
Edquist C, **11:** 6282 (6278)
Edwards A, **7:** 3721 (3717); **8:** 4526 (4522)
Edwards A C, **3:** 1301 (1298), 1524
Edwards A D, **10:** 6197 (6194)
Edwards A L, **1:** 389 (383), 396 (392); **11:** 6388 (6386)
Edwards C H, **3:** 1529 (1527)
Edwards C P, **4:** 2449 (2447, 2448), 2452 (2449, 2450); **6:** 3228 (3225); **9:** 5528
Edwards E P, **8:** 4670 (4667, 4669)
Edwards H, **10:** 5697
Edwards J, **6:** 3204 (3203); **9:** 5338 (5336)
Edwards J A, **9:** 5560 (5558)
Edwards L N, **4:** 2212 (2210)
Edwards M, **10:** 5680 (5675, 5677), 5697
Edwards R, **2:** 1165 (1162); **6:** 3189 (3185); **7:** 4249
Edwards R C, **3:** 1703 (1697, 1698); **5:** 2942 (2938, 2940)
Edwards T, **2:** 816 (813); **8:** 4830 (4825)
Edwards V, **9:** 5216 (5214)
Edwards W, **1:** 480 (477, 479)
Edwards W L, **5:** 2955 (2953)
Eells K, **7:** 3722 (3716)
Eells W C, **11:** (6762)
Eemeren F van, **2:** 1207 (1207)
Efklides A, **2:** 838; **5:** 2669 (2668, 2669), 2670, 2680, 2768 (2761)
Efland A, **1:** 343 (339, 343); **11:** 6617 (6616)
Efron B, **4:** 2156 (2154); **5:** 2596 (2592); **9:** 5130 (5126, 5128), 5467 (5467)
Efron M, **3:** 1406
Egan D F, **3:** 1624 (1621)

Egan G, **2:** 1165; **5:** 3007 (3005); **6:** 3602 (3597)
Egan K, **6:** 3452; **7:** 3711, 4051 (4047); **8:** 4774 (4773); **9:** 5577 (5573); **10:** 5817 (5817); **11:** 6580
Egan M, **11:** 6339 (6334, 6337, 6338)
Egeland B, **8:** 4779 (4776)
Eggan D, **3:** 1755 (1754)
Eggan G, **4:** 2199 (2198)
Eggen T J H M, **4:** 2017 (2013)
Eggland S, **5:** 2689 (2685, 2686)
Eggleston E, **10:** (5814)
Eggleston J F, **2:** 816 (813, 814); **3:** 1266 (1265), 1778 (1776)
Eglen J R, **8:** 4648 (4645)
Egly M, **2:** 1160 (1159)
Egnatios E S, **10:** 5924 (5920, 5922)
Ehlers M, **3:** (1721)
Ehly S W, **11:** 6484
Ehn B, **2:** 711 (708)
Ehrenberg R G, **6:** 3101, 3184 (3179)
Ehri L C, **8:** 4945
Ehrich K, **11:** 6747 (6746)
Ehrlich I, **4:** 2212 (2211)
Ehrmann S, **2:** 973
Eiberger J, **2:** 649
Eibl-Eibesfeldt I, **4:** 2172 (2169); **5:** 2651 (2648)
Eicher J C, **2:** 1127 (1122, 1123, 1125), 1152 (1147, 1150, 1151); **3:** 1573 (1571); **4:** 1903 (1900); **5:** 2984; **9:** 5240 (5234)
Eichhorn D, **2:** 917
Eichler M, **4:** 2302 (2299)
Eichmann A, **4:** (2035), (2036)
Eichorn D, **3:** 1514 (1512)
Eichorn D H, **1:** 362 (361)
Eichorn D J, **5:** 2916 (2912)
Eichrodt W, **6:** 3119
Eickelman D, **9:** 5510 (5508)
Eide K, **6:** 3378
Eiger N, **11:** 6774 (6771, 6772), 6775 (6771)
Eignor D R, **11:** 6355 (6349, 6351)
Eimas P D, **8:** 4383 (4382)
Einberger J, **2:** 649 (646)
Einstein A, **8:** (4450); **9:** (5051)
Eiseman J, **5:** 2847 (2840)
Eisemon T, **5:** 2998 (2996)
Eisemon T E, **6:** 3480 (3479)
Eisemon T O, **1:** 254; **6:** 3550 (3546); **8:** 4688 (4686)
Eisen M, **2:** 705 (702)
Eisen Y, **6:** 3416 (3410)
Eisenberg A, **6:** 3228 (3225)
Eisenberg L, **6:** 3235 (3232)
Eisenberg N, **8:** 4799 (4797, 4798, 4799); **9:** 5528
Eisenberg T, **11:** 6484 (6483)
Eisenhart M, **4:** 2249 (2248); **9:** 5220 (5218), 5572 (5567, 5570); **10:** 6026 (6021)
Eisenhart M A, **7:** 3974 (3973); **11:** 6765 (6761)
Eisenstadt S N, **5:** 3028; **7:** 3970 (3966)
Eisenstein E, **6:** 3446 (3444)
Eisenstein M R, **4:** 2339
Eiserman W D, **3:** 1567 (1567); **8:** 4376
Eisikovits R A, **1:** 295 (284); **3:** 1236 (1236), 1729 (1728); **7:** 3848 (3846, 3847)
Eisler K, **8:** (4815)
Eisner E W, **1:** 198 (197); **3:** 1266 (1263, 1264), 1283 (1281), 1287 (1285, 1286, 1287), 1288, 1315 (1312), 1320 (1316, 1317), 1328 (1326), (1796), 1804 (1801, 1802, 1803); **4:** 2097 (2090), (2103), 2119 (2116); **5:** 2589 (2589), 2767; **7:** 4051 (4047); **9:** 4980 (4978), 5030 (5027), 5055 (5054), 5411; **10:** 6035 (6032), 6085 (6084, 6085), 6086; **11:** 6465 (6462), 6618
Eisner J P, **9:** 5406 (5405)
Eisner R, **2:** 1055 (1052)
Eisnes E, **10:** 6099
Eizenburg N, **1:** 193 (192)
Ekanayake S B, **1:** 244 (241, 242)
Ekehammer B, **5:** 2491 (2489)
Ekholm M, **3:** 1355 (1350, 1351), 1411 (1410, 1411); **5:** 2852 (2851); **6:** 3603 (3599); **8:** 4864 (4860), 4865; **9:** 5246 (5241, 5243, 5245); **10:** 5972 (5971)
Eklund S, **7:** 4179 (4178)
Ekman P, **4:** 1967; **5:** 2651 (2648); **7:** (4171)
Ekpenyong L E, **1:** 168 (164)
Ekstrand G, **7:** 3970 (3964)
Ekstrand L H, **7:** 3970 (3962, 3963, 3964, 3966, 3967, 3969)
Ekstrom R B, **3:** 1606 (1604, 1605); **7:** 3706 (3705), 3879 (3874); **9:** 5228 (5224, 5228)
Ekwall E, **7:** 3774 (3774)
El-Amine A, **6:** 3356
El Azhary S, **7:** 4206
El-Dinary P B, **7:** 3768 (3765, 3767); **10:** 6177 (6177)
El Gazali M, **5:** 3023
El-Ghannam M A, **4:** 1947
El Jack K, **4:** 2225 (2219)
El'konin D B, **2:** 1052; **5:** (2654), 2802
El-Koussy A, **4:** 1947
El-Nofely A A, **8:** 4473 (4471)
El-Sanabary N M, **3:** 1671, 1672; **4:** 2412 (2408, 2409, 2410); **11:** 6760 (6754, 6755, 6758), 6761
El Tom M E A, **6:** 3667 (3662)
Elam J, **3:** 1386 (1384, 1385)
Elam S, **3:** 1267; **11:** 6445
Elan M, **11:** 6415 (6413)
Elardo R, **3:** 1642 (1640)
Elashoff J D, **11:** 6591 (6591)
Elbaz F, **2:** 796 (792, 793); **7:** 4051 (4047); **10:** 6103 (6100, 6102), 6121 (6119, 6120)
Elbing E, **9:** 5358 (5356)
Elder G H Jr, **1:** 88 (83); **3:** 1647 (1646); **4:** 2261 (2260); **6:** 3428 (3426); **8:** 4719 (4716, 4717); **9:** 5518 (5513)
Eldering L, **1:** 295 (283); **7:** 3977 (3974, 3975)
Elen J, **5:** 2874 (2870)
Elequin E, **8:** 4442
Elgood C, **3:** 1830 (1828); **9:** 5475 (5472)
Elias J A, **8:** 4536 (4533)
Elias J L, **5:** 2737
Elias J W, **7:** 4215 (4213)
Elias L J, **1:** 111
Elias M, **11:** 6360 (6356)
Elias M J, **10:** 5738 (5738)
Elias P, **3:** 1529 (1525)
Elias S F, **7:** 4215 (4213)
Eliason S R, **6:** 3508 (3500, 3502)
Eliasson G, **2:** 1094 (1089); **11:** 6415 (6413)
Elie A, **2:** 665 (663)
Eliot C W, **3:** (1297); **10:** (5707)
Eliot G, **10:** (5705)
Eliou M, **11:** 6741
Eliseo T S, **8:** 4731 (4729)
Elizaga J C, **3:** 1671 (1670)
Elizur D, **4:** 2219; **7:** 4315 (4313), 4316 (4308, 4315)
Elkin V B, **11:** 6484 (6482)
Elkind D, **1:** 88 (85); **5:** 2680 (2677); **7:** 3774 (3773); **9:** 5275 (5274)
Elkins J, **8:** 4376
Elkjaer B, **10:** 5826 (5823)
Ellen R F, **1:** 297; **4:** 2053
Ellena W J, **2:** 816
Ellerton N F, **6:** 3638 (3635), 3652 (3648, 3650); **8:** 4647 (4643)
Ellett F S, **3:** 1283 (1280)
Ellett F S Jr., **4:** 2108 (2101, 2102, 2105)
Elley W B, **1:** 482 (482); **2:** 957 (954); **3:** 1768 (1765); **4:** 1962 (1962), 2140 (2136); **5:** 2479 (2478); **6:** 3474 (3469, 3471, 3472, 3473); **7:** 3721 (3716), 3935 (3931, 3932), 4236 (4234); **8:** 4698 (4696), 4912 (4905); **10:** 5704 (5699, 5700); **11:** 6784 (6784)
Ellgring J H, **9:** 5358 (5356)
Ellickson P E, **5:** 2571 (2569)
Ellicott R, **9:** 5544 (5542)
Ellingson R J, **1:** 15 (13)
Ellingstad V S, **9:** 5050
Ellington H I, **5:** 2773 (2771)
Elliot C, **2:** 1064; **4:** 2412, 2419
Elliot C M, **11:** 6740, 6741
Elliot D, **3:** 1494
Elliot J, **4:** 2292; **6:** 3602 (3598); **10:** 5972
Elliot M, **4:** 2131
Elliot T, **2:** 867 (866)
Elliott C, **3:** 1589; **4:** 2412
Elliott C D, **11:** 6348 (6344)
Elliott C M, **9:** 5228
Elliott D, **7:** 3858 (3856)
Elliott D L, **11:** 6371 (6367, 6368)
Elliott D M, **11:** 6797 (6797)
Elliott D S, **3:** 1441 (1439)
Elliott G, **1:** 89
Elliott J, **1:** 47 (44, 45, 46); **10:** 5972 (5969, 5970), 6099 (6097, 6098), 6219 (6216)
Elliott R F, **8:** 4839
Elliott R K, **3:** 1328 (1326)
Elliott R N, **7:** 3833 (3832)
Elliott S N, **1:** 495; **8:** 4662
Elliott-Faust D J, **7:** 3768 (3765)
Ellis A, **5:** 2714 (2710)
Ellis B B, **11:** 6333 (6330, 6332)
Ellis G, **4:** 2357 (2355)

Ellis G D, **11:** 6798 (6794)
Ellis H, **9:** (5424)
Ellis H C, **5:** 2856 (2854)
Ellis J, **3:** 1501 (1500)
Ellis R, **4:** 2339 (2333); **10:** 5977
Ellis W E, **9:** 5038
Ellison J W, **6:** 3399 (3396)
Ellison L, **3:** 1411 (1408, 1409); **5:** 2500 (2498)
Elliston F A, **8:** 4433
Ellou M, **5:** 2523
Ellson D G, **4:** 1917 (1914); **8:** 4774 (4774)
Ellsworth E, **3:** 1337 (1335); **4:** 1984 (1983); **7:** 3760 (3759); **11:** 6727
Ellwein M C, **3:** 1624 (1621); **10:** 5812 (5810)
Ellwood D, **11:** 6633
Ellwood S, **7:** 4170 (4169)
Elmandjra M, **6:** 3422
Elmore P B, **5:** 3050 (3043)
Elmore R F, **2:** 1019 (1018); **3:** 1343; **4:** 1840 (1836); **5:** 2852 (2849, 2850); **6:** 3496 (3495); **8:** 4715 (4709), 4873 (4867); **9:** 5223 (5221), 5273 (5268); **10:** 5930
Elmquist D L, **11:** 6603 (6602)
Elnahlawi A, **5:** 3023
Elsdon K T, **11:** 6437 (6433)
Elsey B, **1:** 142 (140)
Elshout-Mohr M, **10:** 6117 (6114); **11:** 6349 (6348)
Elsom-Cook M T, **1:** 347 (345, 346), 348
Elster A, **1:** 88 (86)
Elster J, **4:** 2166 (2164); **6:** 3621; **8:** 4594 (4588, 4594)
Elstgeest J, **9:** 5334 (5332, 5333)
Elvin L, **11:** 6775 (6772)
Elwood J, **10:** 5827 (5823, 5824)
Elwood J M, **11:** 6492 (6489)
Elwood P C, **8:** 4473 (4469)
Ely D P, **3:** 1800 (1799); **4:** 1898 (1889, 1891), 1903 (1903), 1924 (1920), 1928 (1925, 1927, 1928); **5:** 2861 (2859); **7:** 3743, 3753, 3756 (3753), 3760 (3757)
Ely M, **7:** 4319 (4318, 4319)
Ely M L, **8:** 4811
Elzinga A, **1:** 127 (122, 123)
Emans R, **10:** 6004 (6003)
Emanuelsson A-C, **11:** 6256 (6253)
Emanuelsson I, **5:** 2907 (2904), 2910 (2909); **6:** 3559 (3557, 3559)
Embretson S, **3:** 1513 (1511, 1513), 1514; **11:** 6320 (6316, 6319)
Emde R, **3:** 1513, 1514; **8:** 4816 (4814)
Emde R M, **1:** 362 (359)
Emde R N, **3:** 1623, 1624 (1621); **5:** 2680
Emerson H, **10:** 6112 (6109)
Emerson J M, **5:** 2529 (2525)
Emerson R W, **2:** 1073 (1066); **5:** (2609)
Emery C, **7:** 4094 (4092); **11:** 6603 (6602)
Emery F E, **10:** 5900 (5895)
Emery J C, **6:** 3596 (3593)
Emery M, **4:** 1911 (1904, 1905)
Emihovich C, **2:** 802; **3:** 1233 (1231); **6:** 3512 (3511)
Emmer E T, **2:** 820 (816, 817, 818); **10:** 6031 (6028, 6029, 6030)
Emmerson D, **10:** 5782 (5779)
Emminghaus W B, **5:** 2651 (2649)
Emmons R A, **4:** 1980 (1978)
Empress Maria Theresa, **5:** (2699)
Emrick J, **3:** 1494 (1491)
Enderby P, **1:** 408 (404), 409
Enderud H, **4:** 2166 (2163)
Endler N S, **8:** 4394 (4389); **9:** 5518; **10:** 6159 (6155)
Endreweit M E, **11:** 6287 (6283, 6284, 6285)
Eng H, **3:** (1724)
Eng S P, **9:** 5485
Engdahl H, **5:** 2586
Engel D J, **4:** 1917 (1915, 1917)
Engel F, **3:** (1773)
Engel M, **2:** 1006 (1002, 1003); **6:** 3655 (3654); **9:** 5043 (5040)
Engel R, **1:** 15 (13)
Engelhard G, **6:** 3124
Engelhardt J, **7:** 4180
Engelhart M D, **3:** 1804 (1801); **4:** 1847 (1844)
Engelkamp J, **2:** 969 (964)
Engelmann S, **6:** 3215 (3214); **10:** 5673 (5671), 6163 (6163)
Engels F, **2:** (779), 1073 (1067), (1191); **7:** (4330)
Engen E, **3:** 1402 (1399)
Engeström Y, **5:** 2689 (2688); **6:** 3292 (3291); **10:** 6202
England P, **4:** 2279 (2275); **6:** 3189; **11:** 6276
Engle P, **3:** 1628 (1627)
Engle S H, **2:** 770 (769); **4:** 1984 (1981); **9:** 5582 (5578)
Englehard G Jr, **5:** 2491 (2489)
Englemann S, **3:** (1527)
Englert C, **10:** 6015 (6014)
Englert C S, **2:** 867 (861); **11:** 6780 (6779)
Engleson D C, **4:** 1995 (1993)
English F, **3:** 1494
Englund T, **2:** 770 (769); **3:** 1307 (1303, 1304); **4:** 2377 (2376)
Engmann D, **10:** 5697 (5695)
Engs R C, **3:** 1610 (1609)
Engstrom G A, **4:** 2389 (2385)
Enna B, **9:** 5406 (5405)
Ennis E, **2:** 1208
Ennis R H, **2:** 1207 (1204, 1205, 1206); **8:** 4455 (4455), 4456 (4455), 4464 (4463, 4464); **10:** 6149 (6144)
Enns R J, **10:** 6091 (6089)
Enos J L, **3:** 1553
Enright R D, **7:** 3920 (3919)
Enslin E, **1:** 162 (160)
Entin E E, **7:** 3942 (3941)
Entwhisle D, **2:** 1073 (1070)
Entwisle B, **7:** 3986 (3980, 3982, 3986)
Entwisle D R, **4:** 2249; **5:** 2627 (2624); **11:** 6360 (6356)
Entwistle A C, **1:** 193 (189)
Entwistle B, **5:** 2596 (2590, 2591, 2594)
Entwistle H, **2:** 785 (780); **5:** 2736 (2734, 2736); **6:** 3621 (3619, 3620); **8:** 4446 (4445), 4581 (4579, 4580); **10:** 5596 (5592); **11:** 6704
Entwistle N J, **1:** 193 (188, 189, 190, 191, 192, 193), 194 (189), 322 (318, 320); **2:** 871 (870, 871), 1165; **5:** 2768 (2763), 2769 (2763), 2884 (2882); **6:** 3329 (3326, 3327), 3339 (3335, 3337, 3339); **7:** 4307; **8:** 4429 (4424, 4425); **9:** 5411 (5411); **10:** 5790, 6202 (6199)
Enzensberger H M, **5:** 2736 (2736)
Epanchin B C, **1:** 494 (492)
Epps E G, **1:** 296
Epskamp K, **2:** 907
Epstein A, **3:** 1628 (1625)
Epstein A E, **3:** 1641 (1640); **5:** 2806 (2804)
Epstein A S, **2:** 687 (679, 680), 688 (682), 1131 (1130); **8:** 4666 (4664); **11:** 6384 (6382)
Epstein C, **11:** 6722 (6719)
Epstein D, **2:** 677 (677)
Epstein E E, **2:** 640 (639)
Epstein E H, **2:** 933 (927, 932), 948 (943, 946)
Epstein I, **2:** 749
Epstein J, **2:** 867 (866)
Epstein J L, **3:** 1647 (1645); **4:** 2257 (2255); **9:** 5216 (5214), 5264 (5260), 5268 (5266), 5378 (5377); **10:** 5758 (5756, 5757), 5759
Epstein P, **1:** 295 (286); **9:** 5572 (5569)
Epstein R, **4:** 2108 (2105)
Epstein S, **9:** 5394 (5390)
Epstein W, **2:** 969 (966)
Erasmus D, **2:** (777); **4:** 2006 (2005), 2007 (2005); **6:** (3529); **8:** (4889); **9:** (5395)
Eraut M R, **2:** 977 (973, 976), 1175 (1173); **4:** 1898 (1891, 1892, 1896, 1897), 1899; **5:** 2879; **8:** 4775 (4773), 4783 (4781); **10:** 5954 (5952), 5972 (5967, 5968, 5969, 5970, 5971), 5973 (5967), 6008 (6005, 6006); **11:** 6608 (6605)
Erben M, **9:** 5367 (5365)
Erdheim M, **8:** 4816 (4815)
Ergas Y, **2:** 700 (695, 698)
Erhrlich K, **2:** 985 (984)
Eribon D, **8:** 4642
Erickson B, **2:** 807 (805)
Erickson B H, **4:** 2208
Erickson D A, **1:** 265 (260)
Erickson F D, **1:** 295 (291); **2:** 802 (797, 798, 799, 801), 820 (819); **3:** 1233 (1229, 1230); **4:** 1848 (1846), 2052 (2048, 2049, 2051, 2052); **5:** 2585 (2585); **6:** 3238 (3236); **7:** 3973 (3972); **9:** 5210 (5209), 5220 (5219), 5312 (5311); **10:** 5817 (5813)
Erickson G L, **10:** 5985
Erickson J G, **6:** 3227 (3226, 3227), 3231
Erickson L G, **10:** 5831 (5830)
Erickson M T, **10:** 5762 (5760)
Erickson P A, **1:** 280 (278), 299 (299)

Ericson B, **1:** 103 (101)
Ericsson K A, **2:** 842, 846 (845), 1177 (1177); **5:** 2665 (2658, 2661); **6:** 3288, 3339 (3338); **7:** 3768 (3767); **9:** 5411 (5409); **11:** 6456 (6454)
Erikson E, **8:** (4822); **10:** 5804 (5798), 6053 (6052), 6224 (6222)
Erikson E H, **1:** 238 (237); **5:** 2665 (2659), 2806 (2803); **6:** 3428 (3426), (3487); **8:** 4719 (4716), 4816 (4814); **9:** 5406 (5405), 5528 (5523); **10:** 5591 (5587); **11:** 6394 (6391)
Erikson F, **5:** 2884
Erikson R, **7:** 3721 (3718), 3864 (3863, 3864); **9:** 5553 (5552); **10:** 5735 (5731)
Eriksson G, **10:** 5674
Erlebacher A, **3:** 1431 (1427); **9:** 5372 (5371)
Erlich O, **5:** 2462 (2461)
Ermarth M, **5:** 2586
Ernest P, **6:** 3661
Eron L D, **1:** 234 (230), 570 (569)
Ershler J, **8:** 4542 (4541)
Erting C J, **3:** 1402 (1400)
Ervin G L, **4:** 2346
Escalona S, **11:** 6310 (6308)
Escamilla M L, **4:** 1954 (1949, 1950, 1953)
Escarabajal M C, **6:** 3660 (3659)
Escobar C M, **8:** 4666 (4664, 4666)
Esdale B, **11:** 6625 (6623)
Eshel Y, **3:** 1486 (1484); **7:** 4215 (4213)
Eshgh R, **5:** 2890 (2887)
Eskenasi A, **2:** 1175 (1174)
Eskey D E, **8:** 4939
Esland G M, **2:** 1073 (1071); **3:** (1344); **9:** 5298 (5296)
Esperandieu V, **1:** 103
Espert F, **3:** 1735 (1733, 1734)
Espin C A, **3:** 1359 (1358)
Espinada Cepeda L, **4:** 2266 (2265)
Espinet M, **10:** 6106 (6104)
Espinola B, **3:** 1735 (1733)
Espinola V, **3:** 1830 (1827)
Ess C, **5:** 2709 (2708)
Essex M J, **1:** 239 (237)
Establet R, **6:** (3307)
Estes M, **4:** 2011
Estes T H, **6:** 3209 (3207)
Estes W K, **1:** 5, 331; **6:** 3288 (3285)
Estice R M, **10:** 5795 (5792)
Estrada P, **7:** 4300 (4300)
Esty E T, **2:** 977 (974)
Etaugh C, **10:** 5826 (5823)
Ethington C A, **4:** 2412 (2410, 2411), 2435 (2432, 2433)
Ettema J S, **1:** 570 (567)
Ettinger J M, **7:** 3889
Etzioni A, **1:** 437 (434); **4:** 2166; **6:** 3527; **9:** 5168 (5160); **10:** 5613 (5611); **11:** 6722 (6720)
Etzioni-Halevy E, **2:** 785 (782)
Euclid, **3:** (1339); **6:** (3679); **8:** (4767)
Eurich N P, **1:** 94, 157 (154); **2:** 665 (662); **11:** 6551
Eurich P N, **1:** 111
Evangelou D, **1:** 230 (228, 229)
Evans A, **6:** 3602 (3598)
Evans D, **8:** 4942 (4941)
Evans D P, **8:** 4864 (4858, 4859, 4860, 4863)
Evans D R, **4:** 2369; **7:** 4136, 4145 (4143, 4144); **11:** 6501
Evans G, **3:** 1271 (1271)
Evans H, **1:** 444
Evans J, **5:** 3043 (3042); **7:** 4293 (4291), 4307 (4304, 4306)
Evans J L, **3:** 1628 (1627); **8:** 4774 (4766)
Evans J S B T, **8:** 4951
Evans M, **1:** 552
Evans M D R, **1:** 414 (410)
Evans M E, **11:** 6370 (6370)
Evans P, **11:** 6282 (6278)
Evans P L C, **5:** 2910
Evans R H, **10:** 6117 (6116)
Evans R W, **9:** 5582 (5578)
Evans T, **1:** 168; **3:** 1563 (1558)
Evans V, **3:** 1441 (1441)
Evans W, **7:** 4000 (3997)
Even R, **6:** 3671 (3670)
Evening M, **9:** 5008
Evenson R, **4:** 2419
Evered D, **9:** 5350
Everett B A, **5:** 2672 (2671)
Everett M G, **9:** 5559 (5559)
Everhart R B, **1:** 60 (54, 55); **9:** 5201, 5510 (5509); **10:** 5758 (5755, 5757, 5758)
Everitt B S, **2:** 831 (826, 827, 829, 830), 1084 (1081, 1082, 1083)
Everly H V, **1:** 274 (267)
Evers C W, **1:** 60 (55, 56); **2:** 1203 (1201, 1203); **3:** 1774 (1769, 1770, 1773, 1774); **7:** 3924 (3921, 3922); **9:** 5030 (5027, 5029)
Everson H T, **11:** 6360 (6357)
Everson M D, **2:** 687 (687)
Everston C M, **5:** 2767 (2766); **9:** 5264 (5261); **10:** 6031 (6029)
Evertson C M, **2:** 820 (816, 817, 818); **4:** 2131 (2128); **5:** 2529 (2528); **6:** 3202 (3198); **10:** 6012 (6011), 6031 (6028); **11:** 6390 (6389)
Ewan C E, **6:** 3205
Ewert G D, **2:** 1204 (1199); **3:** 1834 (1831)
Exendine L, **9:** 4977 (4975)
Extra G, **1:** 537 (537)
Eyer Widmeyer D, **11:** 6398
Eyferth K, **3:** 1647
Eyler J, **9:** 5379 (5375)
Eylon B S, **8:** 4383 (4383), 4479 (4477); **9:** 5341 (5338, 5340)
Eysenck H J, **5:** 2768 (2760); **8:** 4799 (4798); **9:** 5572 (5570)
Eysenck M W, **1:** 194; **5:** 2768 (2760); **8:** 4727
Ezzaki A, **6:** 3480 (3476)

Faaniu S, **11:** 6488
Fabes R A, **9:** 5441 (5436, 5437)
Fabre J M, **8:** 4951
Fabricus W V, **8:** 4957 (4955)
Facaoaru C, **5:** 2731 (2729)
Facco E, **1:** 554
Fafner J, **8:** 4890
Fafunwa A B, **7:** 4132 (4125)
Fagan T K, **9:** 5290 (5287)
Fagbamiye E O, **5:** 2954 (2953)
Fägerlind I, **1:** 396 (393), 474 (469); **3:** 1655 (1648, 1653), 1685 (1682); **4:** 2279 (2276, 2277); **5:** 2937 (2935); **6:** 3523 (3512), 3559 (3557); **7:** 4325 (4320, 4323), 4329 (4328); **8:** 4509 (4503), 4601 (4599), 4616 (4611); **9:** 5008 (5000, 5002), 5385 (5382)
Fagot B I, **4:** 2449 (2447), 2452 (2450, 2451); **10:** 5826 (5823)
Fahey P A, **5:** 2856 (2854)
Faiara A, **5:** 3023
Fairbairn D J, **8:** 4622 (4618, 4619, 4620)
Fairbairn W R D, **8:** (4813)
Fairbrother R W, **5:** 2903 (2903)
Fairclough N, **2:** 1198 (1196)
Fairhurst M A, **10:** 6149 (6144, 6145, 6146)
Fairley J, **11:** 6690 (6686, 6689)
Fairweather H, **9:** 5432 (5431)
Fajardo D E, **10:** 6164 (6161)
Fakhro S Q, **10:** 5673 (5671)
Falcon L M, **8:** 4895 (4891, 4892, 4893)
Falconer D S, **5:** 2465 (2464)
Fales A W, **6:** 3434 (3431); **8:** 4616 (4613), 4823 (4817)
Falk M, **6:** 3394
Falk R R, **8:** 4359
Falkner F, **1:** 88; **8:** 4473, 4474
Fallon P R, **3:** 1448 (1445)
Fals-Borda O, **1:** 47 (45); **2:** 906 (903), 1048 (1047, 1048), 1049; **7:** 4336 (4330, 4331, 4335)
Falvey M, **3:** 1406 (1405)
Falzon J, **6:** 3593
Fandal A W, **3:** 1623 (1621), 1624 (1622)
Fang J R, **6:** 3401 (3401)
Fang Y, **7:** 3848 (3847)
Fanon F, **2:** (1046)
Fansella F, **9:** 5016 (5016)
Fanso G, **2:** 617
Fantini M D, **1:** 594 (593); **2:** 892 (890); **9:** 5441 (5436); **10:** 5817 (5815)
Fantz R L, **8:** 4383 (4381)
Fapohunda E R, **4:** 2418 (2416)
Faraday M, **6:** 3219 (3216)
Farah T E, **8:** 4581 (4576)
Faraj A H, **6:** 3407; **10:** 5929 (5925)
Faraola J, **5:** 2891 (2888)
Farber B A, **10:** 5924 (5920), 6062 (6060, 6061)
Farber H S, **6:** 3616 (3614)
Farber I, **10:** 6062 (6058)
Faria L, **1:** 31 (29)
Faris A E L, **11:** 6445
Faris R, **7:** (3770)
Farkas G, **6:** 3189; **7:** 3820 (3816, 3820); **11:** 6276
Farley E, **9:** 5008 (5005)
Farley J, **11:** 6712 (6709)
Farley M, **7:** 3895
Farley P, **5:** 2572 (2570)
Farley R, **8:** 4902 (4898)
Farmer T M, **7:** 3946 (3945)
Farnan N, **6:** 3209

Farnen R F, **1:** 396 (393); **2:** 770 (768); **3:** 1769 (1763); **8:** 4571; **9:** 5582 (5581)
Farnish A M, **2:** 1099 (1096)
Farnoaga G, **4:** 2351 (2350)
Faro M J, **3:** 1504 (1502)
Farooq R A, **7:** 4270; **8:** 4873 (4869, 4871)
Farquhar R H, **1:** 73 (67, 69, 72), 77 (74, 75); **5:** 2954 (2953), 2955 (2952, 2954); **9:** 5168
Farr M J, **1:** 374; **2:** 842; **4:** 2199 (2194); **7:** 3942; **8:** 4722 (4720), 4727 (4727), 4823 (4821); **10:** 6026 (6023, 6024, 6025)
Farr R, **11:** 6370 (6368)
Farran D C, **1:** 362; **8:** 4779 (4777); **9:** 5572 (5570)
Farrar E, **1:** 12; **3:** 1607; **9:** 5191 (5190), 5246 (5243), 5379 (5374, 5376, 5377); **10:** 5818 (5816); **11:** 6538, 6726
Farrar M J, **5:** 2680 (2677, 2678, 2679)
Farrell A P, **9:** 5121
Farrell E, **10:** 5758 (5756)
Farrell G, **11:** 6628 (6626)
Farrell J P, **1:** 162 (161), 332 (331); **2:** 932 (925); **3:** 1820 (1810), 1824 (1821), 1834 (1833); **4:** 2412 (2410); **8:** 4495 (4493), 4509 (4503), 4526 (4519, 4521, 4523, 4524, 4525), 4601 (4598), 4698, 4848 (4846), 4873 (4868); **9:** 5539 (5535, 5536, 5537, 5538); **10:** 5929 (5925); **11:** 6366 (6364, 6365), 6370 (6367)
Farrow S, **4:** 2427 (2426)
Farrugia C J, **6:** 3593; **10:** 5965 (5964)
Fasching J, **2:** 807 (805)
Fass P, **10:** 5783
Fass S M, **8:** 4514 (4510), 4594 (4590)
Fatke R, **7:** 3925
Faucher T, **8:** 4779 (4777)
Fauconnet P, **2:** 785 (777)
Faulkner S L, **8:** 4864 (4858, 4860, 4861)
Faunce R C, **2:** 1107
Fauré E, **1:** 157 (157), 162 (158); **2:** 1064; **4:** 2186 (2184); **5:** 2937, 2961 (2957, 2958), 2978; **6:** 3421 (3417); **8:** 4964 (4958); **11:** 6507
Faurfelt K, **7:** 4179 (4178)
Fauvel J, **6:** 3638 (3636)
Faux J H, **9:** 5185 (5184)
Fawcett J T, **6:** 3106 (3102, 3103)
Fay A L, **2:** 984 (983, 984)
Fay B, **1:** 67 (62)
Fay C H, **8:** 4408 (4406)
Fay G, **4:** 2400 (2397)
Fay P J, **9:** 5327 (5325)
Fay W H, **6:** 3235 (3233)
Fayol H, **4:** 2166 (2158); **9:** 5168 (5161)
Fazelbhoy R S, **11:** 6628 (6626)
Feagans L, **9:** 5572 (5570)
Feagin J R, **1:** 543; **3:** 1486
Feasley C E, **11:** 6307 (6305)
Feather N T, **1:** 380; **10:** 6223 (6222)
Featherman D L, **1:** 11 (7), 89; **2:** 846; **3:** 1642 (1638), 1750 (1749); **4:** 2257, 2278 (2276, 2277); **5:** 2665; **6:** 3428 (3426); **7:** 3722, 3864 (3863), 3872; **9:** 5553 (5549, 5552, 5553); **10:** 5735 (5734)
Featherstone J, **1:** (263)
Febvre L, **8:** 4694
Fechner G T, **3:** (1793), (1794); **11:** (6385)
Fecho B, **10:** 6099 (6097)
Fecho R, **10:** 5961
Federici F, **7:** 4246 (4243)
Federico P A, **4:** 1848; **9:** 5043
Federighi P, **1:** 157 (154, 155); **6:** 3366 (3362, 3363)
Fedoruk G M, **10:** 5762 (5760)
Feeley F M, **8:** 4586 (4583, 4584, 4585, 4586)
Feeley M, **6:** 3276 (3273)
Feenberg A, **2:** 982 (978)
Feeney S, **7:** 4300 (4298)
Fehr H, **4:** 2096
Fei J C H, **3:** 1685 (1682)
Feigl H, **3:** 1774 (1769); **8:** (4450)
Feil L A, **3:** 1643 (1639)
Feiman S, **10:** 5935
Feiman-Nemser S, **2:** 796 (792, 793); **3:** 1635 (1633); **9:** 5223 (5222), 5264 (5260); **10:** 5812 (5810), 5948 (5945, 5946, 5947), 5994 (5993)
Fein G G, **3:** 1642 (1640); **7:** 4296 (4294); **8:** 4541 (4538, 4540), 4542 (4536, 4538, 4539, 4540)
Feinberg W, **2:** 1203 (1199); **10:** 5948 (5947)
Feindler E L, **3:** 1441 (1441)
Feiner S, **4:** 2412 (2409)
Feingold A, **9:** 5432 (5423, 5428, 5431)
Feingold R S, **10:** 5713
Feinman-Nemser S, **10:** 6103 (6100)
Feinstein A R, **8:** 4930 (4929)
Feistritzer E, **4:** 2131 (2126)
Feitelson D, **4:** 1962 (1958, 1962); **6:** 3452 (3449); **8:** 4945 (4944)
Feldbaum C L, **4:** 2452 (2451)
Feldhusen J F, **2:** 1182 (1178, 1181, 1182); **5:** 2495 (2493), 2731 (2726, 2727, 2728), 2732 (2730); **9:** 5532 (5529, 5530, 5531)
Feldlaufer H, **10:** 5775 (5773), 6112 (6110)
Feldman D H, **5:** 2731 (2726)
Feldman K A, **10:** 6234 (6229, 6231, 6232)
Feldman L B, **8:** 4939 (4938)
Feldman R S, **7:** 4175 (4171); **10:** 6164 (6161), 6224
Feldman S, **1:** 89; **7:** 4007; **11:** 6576 (6573)
Feldman-Summers S, **9:** 5302 (5301)
Feldstein M S, **9:** 5240 (5239)
Feldt L S, **9:** 4995 (4981)
Felix C, **10:** 5643 (5640)
Felix N, **7:** 3833 (3832)
Fellenz R A, **8:** 4736 (4734)
Fellner W, **5:** 2739
Felmlee D H, **2:** 1094 (1092)
Felsenstein J, **2:** 1084 (1081)
Felson R B, **4:** 2435 (2434)
Felterman D M, **3:** 1474
Feltovich P J, **4:** 2198 (2195); **6:** 3155 (3154); **8:** 4727 (4727); **10:** 5790 (5783)
Feltre da V, **4:** (2004)
Fend H, **10:** 5772 (5771)
Fenech J, **6:** 3593
Feniak C A, **7:** 3833 (3831, 3832)
Fenichel E S, **5:** 2812 (2807)
Fennema E, **2:** 1052 (1050); **3:** 1257 (1256); **4:** 2435 (2432, 2433, 2434); **6:** 3638, 3642 (3640), 3643, 3660 (3660), 3671 (3670); **9:** 5432 (5430); **10:** 5762 (5760), 5772 (5770), 5795 (5792, 5794), 6122 (6118)
Fennessy E, **11:** 6307 (6299)
Fenrick N, **8:** 4375 (4374, 4375)
Fensham P J, **6:** 3204 (3203); **7:** 4170 (4168); **8:** 4429 (4425), 4479 (4475); **9:** 5327 (5326), 5328, 5334 (5332), 5338 (5336), 5342 (5339, 5341), 5350
Fenske R H, **10:** 5804 (5796)
Fensom H L, **7:** 3833 (3832)
Fenson L, **8:** 4541 (4538)
Fenstermacher G D, **2:** 796 (796); **7:** 3924 (3921); **10:** 6121 (6120)
Fenton E T, **5:** 2623; **9:** 5582 (5578)
Fenton R, **2:** 868 (861)
Fenton S, **2:** 785 (777)
Fenwick J E, **5:** 2870 (2868)
Ferber M A, **1:** 358 (357); **2:** 692 (689), 1055 (1054); **4:** 2432 (2429, 2430, 2431), 2445 (2442, 2444, 2445), 2446
Ferguson A, **2:** 792 (786); **7:** 3706 (3698, 3699)
Ferguson C, **7:** 3807 (3805)
Ferguson C A, **6:** 3224 (3222)
Ferguson D, **2:** 973
Ferguson D L, **3:** 1507 (1505); **6:** 3559
Ferguson G A, **5:** 2768 (2761); **7:** 3738 (3729), 4015 (4008)
Ferguson J, **9:** 5379 (5376)
Ferguson P, **10:** 6012 (6011)
Ferguson P M, **3:** 1507 (1505)
Ferguson R F, **7:** 3820 (3816); **10:** 5846 (5845)
Ferguson T, **2:** 807 (804)
Ferguson T S, **3:** 1421 (1419)
Ferguson-Hessler M G M, **5:** 2768 (2763)
Fernandes D, **6:** 3652
Fernández B, **7:** 4275
Fernandez H, **3:** 1671 (1670)
Fernandez J A, **4:** 2059 (2058)
Fernandez M, **2:** (1140)
Fernández M, **10:** 5812 (5811)
Fernandez R R, **3:** 1607 (1603, 1605); **9:** 5216 (5214)
Fernea E W, **11:** 6760
Fernig L, **5:** 2978
Ferrara R A, **2:** 838 (835); **3:** 1252 (1251); **6:** 3329 (3325, 3326, 3327), 3334 (3331, 3333); **7:** 3768 (3766), 3830 (3828); **11:** 6456 (6454)
Ferrari M, **6:** 3652
Ferrario M, **10:** 5673 (5670)
Ferré A, **4:** 1872 (1868)
Ferre F, **8:** 4634
Ferree M, **4:** 2412 (2409)

Ferreiro E, **4:** 1962 (1960)
Ferreiro F, **6:** 3463 (3460)
Ferrell B G, **4:** 2045 (2044)
Ferrer F, **7:** (4156)
Ferretti R P, **11:** 6456 (6454)
Ferrière A, **10:** (5877)
Ferris G R, **4:** 2131 (2130)
Ferro N, **10:** 6244 (6242)
Ferster C B, **5:** 2856 (2852); **9:** 4977 (4975)
Feshbach S, **1:** 234 (232)
Fessler R, **10:** 5939 (5936)
Fest T B, **5:** 2532 (2530)
Feteris A, **2:** 992; **6:** 3096
Fetter M P, **9:** 5441 (5436)
Fetterman D M, **4:** 2045 (2043, 2044, 2045), 2046 (2043), 2052 (2049), (2103)
Feuer L, **10:** 5782 (5781)
Feuer M J, **6:** 3616 (3615)
Feuerstein P, **11:** (6309)
Feuerstein R, **2:** 860 (857, 858, 859, 860), 867 (862); **3:** 1504 (1503); **5:** 2768 (2762); **6:** 3315 (3313); **8:** 4731 (4729, 4730); **10:** 5668 (5663), 5750 (5745), 5772 (5769), 6168 (6166)
Feurzeig W, **6:** 3512
Feuser G, **10:** 6244 (6243)
Feverstein R, **3:** (1401)
Fewell J, **4:** 2292
Fey J, **6:** 3684 (3679), 3685; **7:** 4099 (4096)
Fey M, **10:** 5696 (5694)
Feyerabend P, **3:** (1770); **8:** 4634 (4631); **9:** (5028)
Fichte J G, **3:** (1721); **4:** (2386); **5:** (2576); **7:** (3924)
Fichtner B, **8:** 4419
Ficociello C, **3:** 1406
Fiddy R, **9:** 5191 (5186)
Fidell L S, **2:** 1117 (1115, 1116); **4:** 2445 (2444)
Fidler B, **11:** 6523
Field D, **6:** 3625 (3623)
Field L, **1:** 168 (163); **9:** 5399 (5398)
Field T, **7:** 4300 (4298)
Field T M, **3:** 1642 (1640); **6:** 3227 (3225)
Fielden J, **6:** 3378
Fieldhouse R, **1:** 93 (89, 91); **2:** 1194
Fielding G D, **1:** 380 (379)
Fielding J E, **3:** 1624
Fielding J L, **11:** 6465 (6462, 6463, 6464, 6465)
Fielding L, **6:** 3443 (3442); **10:** 6192 (6191)
Fielding M, **4:** 1898 (1896); **10:** 5973 (5967)
Fielding N G, **11:** 6465 (6462, 6463, 6464, 6465)
Fields A B, **10:** 5782 (5778), 5783
Fields G, **5:** 2819 (2815); **11:** 6638
Fields G S, **2:** 1131 (1128); **6:** 3184 (3181, 3182, 3184)
Fienberg S E, **6:** 3507 (3500), 3508 (3500), 3523 (3523)
Fierman J, **4:** 2432 (2431)
Fiese B H, **1:** 362 (359)
Fietze K, **11:** 6747 (6742)
Fifer W P, **5:** 2802 (2801)
Figeat M, **2:** 665 (662)
Figueres J, **2:** (1140)
Figueroa P M E, **6:** 3074
Figueroa R A, **2:** 719
Fiksdal B, **3:** 1402 (1399)
Fikumotos J S, **5:** 2673 (2670)
Filby N, **3:** 1834 (1833); **11:** 6370 (6368)
Filby N N, **1:** 23; **5:** 2870 (2868)
Filipp S H, **5:** 2665 (2663); **8:** 4719
Fillmore C, **6:** 3238 (3237)
Finch C R, **8:** 4864 (4858, 4860, 4861)
Finch J, **7:** 4319 (4317)
Fincham F D, **9:** 5406 (5405)
Findhammer W J, **7:** 3810 (3809), 4104 (4102)
Findlay J J, **3:** (1722), (1723)
Findlay M A, **5:** 2827
Fine A, **9:** 4980 (4978)
Fine G A, **10:** 5758 (5758)
Fine M, **3:** 1607 (1605); **4:** 2089 (2082); **9:** 5228 (5224, 5226, 5228), 5441 (5440); **10:** 5817 (5816); **11:** 6726 (6725, 6726)
Fineberg J, **6:** 3621
Finegold D, **9:** 5191 (5186, 5187, 5189); **11:** 6420 (6416)
Finger M, **1:** 47 (45)
Fingold D, **9:** 5191
Finifter B M, **9:** 5130 (5126)
Finitzo T, **10:** 5690 (5689)
Fink A H, **1:** 494 (493)
Fink E, **3:** 1830 (1828)
Fink M, **9:** 5367 (5366)
Finkel L, **11:** 6603 (6602)
Finks L W, **6:** 3401 (3399)
Finley E G, **5:** 2827
Finn C, **2:** 770 (769); **3:** 1367 (1362); **8:** 4594 (4587, 4589, 4591, 4592)
Finn C E, **3:** 1449; **9:** 5281 (5277); **10:** 5753 (5752)
Finn D, **11:** 6690 (6687)
Finn J D, **2:** 775 (773, 774), 834 (832); **4:** 1898 (1884, 1885, 1886, 1897), 1928 (1924), 1938 (1936); **5:** 2714 (2712); **7:** 3986 (3978), 4015 (4015); **9:** 4973 (4971); **11:** 6591 (6591)
Finn J O, **9:** 5539 (5536)
Finn P J, **5:** 3066 (3065)
Finnan C R, **3:** 1809 (1808)
Finnäs L, **7:** 4026 (4023)
Firestone W, **4:** 2046 (2043); **5:** 2847 (2840)
Firestone W A, **2:** 645 (643); **3:** 1474 (1466); **4:** 1857 (1852, 1853, 1854, 1855); **6:** 3527 (3525, 3526), 3602 (3599); **9:** 5181 (5180), 5211 (5208), 5246 (5242); **10:** 5924 (5922)
First P F, **6:** 3496; **8:** 4594, 4595
Firth R, **2:** 1212 (1209); **3:** 1755 (1754)
Fisch R, **4:** 2266 (2265)
Fischbein E, **6:** 3655 (3652), 3684 (3682)
Fischbein S, **11:** 6492 (6489, 6491)
Fischer A, **3:** (1722)
Fischer F E, **7:** 4000 (3999)
Fischer G, **3:** 1513 (1511, 1512); **8:** 4912 (4903, 4906)
Fischer K, **3:** 1513 (1508, 1509, 1510, 1511, 1513), 1647; **9:** 5008 (5006)
Fischer K W, **2:** 846 (843); **5:** 2677 (2676), 2680 (2677, 2678, 2679, 2680), 2681; **8:** 4482 (4482), 4823 (4817)
Fischer P, **7:** 4099 (4096)
Fischer S, **3:** 1449, 1750; **4:** 2315 (2311)
Fischgrund J E, **3:** 1402 (1399)
Fish M C, **4:** 2427 (2425, 2427)
Fish S, **2:** (1194); **6:** 3484 (3481, 3482)
Fishbein H D, **1:** 295 (288)
Fishbein J E, **10:** 6163 (6162)
Fishbein M, **1:** 358 (354, 356), 389 (380, 381, 382, 386); **7:** (4322); **10:** 6103 (6100)
Fisher A, **2:** 1207 (1207)
Fisher C, **1:** 23; **3:** 1257 (1254); **5:** 2567; **7:** 3886 (3883), 4215 (4212)
Fisher C J, **2:** 737 (734)
Fisher C W, **1:** 23, 377; **5:** 2768 (2766), 2779 (2775, 2776), 2870; **7:** 4215 (4213); **10:** 5834 (5833); **11:** 6390
Fisher D, **3:** 1482 (1482); **5:** 2529 (2527)
Fisher D L, **2:** 811 (810); **10:** 5775 (5773, 5774)
Fisher D M, **7:** 3950 (3948)
Fisher G, **4:** (1865); **10:** 6149 (6148)
Fisher J C, **1:** 184 (181, 183)
Fisher K, **2:** 1031 (1030); **8:** 4479
Fisher M, **10:** 6117
Fisher R, **5:** 2798 (2796); **8:** 4408 (4407)
Fisher R A, **1:** 42 (40), 389 (388); **3:** 1549 (1545, 1546); **4:** 1872 (1867), (2213); **5:** 2465 (2463), (2713), 2931 (2922); **6:** 3144 (3141), (3502); **7:** 3738 (3726, 3735, 3737), 3783 (3775), 4015 (4009); **8:** (4873); **9:** 4974 (4969), 5142 (5137), 5467 (5461)
Fisher R J, **1:** 389 (380)
Fisher R K, **6:** 3399 (3397)
Fisher S, **2:** 635 (634); **8:** 4719
Fisher W L, **3:** 1448 (1447)
Fishman A R, **6:** 3452 (3448)
Fisiak J, **6:** 3439 (3438)
Fiske D W, **4:** 2388 (2383); **7:** 4006 (4000, 4001, 4002, 4003); **11:** 6465 (6462)
Fitch A, **9:** 5294
Fitts P M, **7:** 3953 (3951, 3952)
Fitzgerald F, **11:** 6370 (6367)
Fitzgerald I, **2:** 730
Fitzgerald J, **2:** 775 (773), 1006 (1004); **10:** 5795 (5793)
FitzGerald R, **2:** 910
Fitzpatrick K, **11:** 6735 (6731)
Fitzpatrick M A, **4:** 2261 (2259)
Fitzpatrick R, **11:** 6348 (6347)
Fivush R, **2:** 705 (703)
Fizsbein A, **11:** 6599 (6593, 6599)
Flagg B N, **8:** 4803 (4801)
Flament C, **9:** 5560 (5555)
Flammer A, **5:** 2768 (2760)
Flammer M G, **2:** 892 (888)
Flanagan J C, **5:** 2870 (2868); **6:** 3096 (3094); **10:** 6168 (6165); **11:** 6348 (6341)
Flanders B, **11:** 6603 (6601)

Flanders N A, **2:** 816 (811, 813, 815); **6:** 3389 (3388); **9:** 5507 (5506)
Flap H D, **4:** 2274 (2274)
Flavell E R, **2:** 705 (703)
Flavell J H, **2:** 705 (703), 838, 846 (842), 856, 871, 969 (966); **5:** 2628, 2665 (2657), 2680 (2679), 2916; **6:** 3224, 3297 (3295), 3325 (3321), 3329; **7:** 3763 (3760, 3761), 3768 (3764), 3788 (3784, 3785), 3792; **8:** 4383, (4459), 4956, 4957; **9:** 5508, 5512 (5510), 5548
Flay B, **5:** 2571 (2569)
Flecha J, **7:** 3711 (3710)
Flechsig K H, **4:** 1898 (1896); **5:** 2862
Flechsig P, **1:** 553 (552)
Fleck M B, **1:** 362 (359)
Fleer M, **10:** 6178
Fleet J, **8:** 4942 (4941)
Fleisch B, **1:** 490 (487, 488)
Fleischmann T, **8:** 4951 (4949)
Fleishman E A, **7:** 3953 (3951); **11:** 6678 (6670, 6671)
Fleishman J A, **1:** 358 (356)
Fleming D B, **10:** 5886 (5886)
Fleming M L, **2:** 888, 1019; **4:** 2011 (2009); **7:** 3774 (3771)
Fleming T, **1:** 60 (53), 77 (74)
Flesch R F, **2:** (1077)
Fletcher B, **10:** 5738 (5736)
Fletcher C, **2:** 906 (901), 910 (907); **10:** 5596 (5594)
Fletcher J D, **5:** 2779 (2774, 2778)
Fletcher P, **6:** 3224; **10:** 5680
Fletcher-Campbell F, **8:** 4864 (4860)
Fleuret A, **11:** 6501
Fleury C, **3:** (1262)
Flew A G N, **8:** 4447
Flexner A, **5:** (2694)
Flick U, **11:** 6465 (6462, 6463, 6464)
Fliegel S, **11:** 6558 (6556)
Flinck R, **7:** 4220 (4218)
Flinders D G, **10:** 5995 (5991, 5994)
Flinders D J, **5:** 2529 (2526); **10:** 5990 (5988), 6031
Flitner W, **1:** 139 (137); **3:** (1722)
Flittner A, **7:** 3924 (3922)
Føllesdall D, **5:** 2586
Floden R E, **2:** 796 (792, 793); **3:** 1257 (1254); **9:** 5223 (5222), 5264 (5260); **10:** 5935, 6103 (6100, 6102)
Flood J, **2:** 738; **6:** 3209; **8:** 4947; **10:** 5704 (5697); **11:** 6784
Flood P K, **4:** 1934 (1929, 1930, 1932); **9:** 5210 (5207)
Flood R, **11:** 6390 (6388)
Florander J, **3:** 1266 (1263, 1265); **10:** 5643
Florencio C, **4:** 2419
Flores d'Aracais G B, **8:** 4939 (4938)
Flores P V, **7:** 4136 (4133)
Florio D H, **4:** 2131 (2129); **11:** 6384 (6379)
Florio-Ruane S, **2:** 802 (801); **3:** 1252 (1250); **10:** 5795 (5793, 5794)
Floud J, **4:** 2257 (2252), 2278; **6:** 3312 (3307); **7:** 3721 (3720); **10:** 6227 (6226)
Flouris G, **9:** 5582 (5581)
Flower L S, **2:** 867 (861); **11:** 6780 (6778), 6784 (6782)
Floyd C, **1:** 230 (228)
Fluitman F, **1:** 226 (222); **3:** 1680 (1679); **5:** 2819 (2814, 2815); **7:** 4155
Fly P K, **10:** 5795 (5793)
Flynn B S, **5:** 2571 (2570)
Flynn E A, **6:** 3209 (3208)
Flynn J R, **1:** 238 (236); **5:** 2465 (2464)
Flynn M A, **8:** 4474 (4469)
Flynn P M, **7:** 4255 (4253); **11:** 6260 (6259), 6276 (6273, 6274, 6276)
Flynn R J, **3:** 1438 (1435)
Foa L, **5:** 2862
Foa V G, **4:** 2218 (2213)
Foch T T, **1:** 88 (83)
Fodor J A, **2:** 856 (852, 853), 1025 (1022); **4:** 2400 (2397); **7:** 3879 (3877)
Fogel A, **4:** 1967
Fogelman K R, **4:** 2257 (2252); **6:** 3523 (3512); **11:** 6390 (6389)
Fogle J S, **9:** 5008 (5003)
Foks J, **7:** 4220; **9:** 5544 (5541)
Folbre N, **4:** 2418 (2414)
Folds R, **9:** 5060 (5058)
Foley B, **11:** 6558
Foley D E, **2:** 802 (800), 917 (916), 933 (930); **3:** 1233 (1229); **4:** 1851 (1850), 2272; **9:** 5060 (5059), 5313 (5311)
Foley R, **10:** 6058 (6056)
Foley W, **10:** 5957 (5954)
Folk V G, **5:** 3050 (3047)
Folkman S, **1:** 203 (201); **4:** 1980 (1977); **10:** 5738 (5736)
Follis B, **11:** 6265 (6263)
Foltz A M, **3:** 1624 (1621)
Fonacier J, **4:** 2419 (2415)
Fonda N, **11:** 6684
Fondacaro K, **10:** 5738 (5737)
Foner A, **6:** 3428
Foner N, **9:** 5510 (5508)
Fong G T, **2:** 838 (837)
Fonow M, **4:** 2302 (2297, 2298)
Fontaine A M, **1:** 31 (29)
Foot C H, **2:** 733
Foot H, **8:** 4376
Foot H C, **4:** 1899
Foote D, **5:** 2891 (2888)
Foppa K, **4:** 2172
Forbes M A, **3:** 1441
Forcucci S L, **7:** 4026
Ford A, **6:** 3559
Ford D H, **5:** 2665 (2659)
Ford G W, **6:** 3151
Ford I, **4:** 1934 (1929)
Ford J, **1:** 358 (357)
Ford J B, **10:** 5617 (5615)
Ford J K, **3:** 1490 (1490)
Ford M E, **9:** 5528 (5524, 5526)
Ford S F, **5:** 3050 (3044)
Fordam S, **9:** 5220 (5219)
Fordham P, **1:** 94; **5:** 2961 (2959); **7:** 4248 (4247); **11:** 6437 (6436)
Fordham S, **9:** 5572 (5571)
Fordyce T, **10:** 5686 (5686)
Forehand G, **3:** 1486 (1484)
Foreman D I, **5:** 3051 (3047)
Foreman E K, **9:** 5142
Forest M, **8:** 4662 (4657)
Forester A, **4:** 1924
Forester J, **8:** 4601 (4597, 4600)
Forester T, **4:** 1911
Forgas J P, **4:** 1980 (1978); **6:** 3224
Forgays D G, **4:** 1967
Form W, **11:** 6276 (6273)
Forman E, **3:** 1252; **9:** 5548 (5546)
Forman S G, **10:** 6164
Fornas J, **11:** 6803 (6802)
Forness S R, **1:** 490 (487, 488), 494 (492)
Forrest A, **10:** 5804 (5797, 5799, 5800, 5801, 5802, 5803)
Forrest L, **10:** 5804 (5798)
Forrest M, **6:** 3559 (3558)
Forrester D A R, **11:** 6425
Forrest-Pressley D L, **7:** 3768 (3765); **8:** 4942
Forret A M, **6:** 3205 (3204)
Forsfalt L, **5:** 2971 (2967, 2969)
Forsslund T, **8:** 4680 (4678)
Forster W, **8:** 4811 (4807)
Forsyth D R, **11:** 6360 (6356)
Forsyth P B, **1:** 82 (78); **6:** 3284
Forsythe C J, **10:** 5738 (5737)
Forsythe D, **9:** 5294
Forsythe K, **7:** 4220 (4217)
Forsythe R O, **5:** 2891
Fortes M, **1:** 295 (286); **2:** 1212 (1209); **3:** 1252 (1247), 1755 (1752)
Forth D, **11:** 6684
Forthofer R N, **9:** 5130 (5125), 5142 (5137)
Fosburg S, **2:** 692 (689)
Foshay A W, **2:** 957 (952), 1107 (1102); **3:** 1266 (1263), (1288), 1494, 1768 (1762, 1763); **10:** 6103 (6102); **11:** 6348 (6344)
Foshay W, **6:** 3096 (3092)
Foss B M, **5:** 2806
Fossum J A, **6:** 3197 (3190)
Foster A, **7:** 3726 (3724)
Foster D L, **5:** 2515 (2513)
Foster G E, **1:** 520 (516)
Foster J F, **7:** 3756 (3755)
Foster L, **1:** 162 (160); **7:** 4293 (4290, 4291, 4292); **10:** 5606 (5601)
Foster L E, **7:** 4170 (4166); **9:** 5060
Foster M, **3:** 1233 (1232); **6:** 3238 (3237)
Foster P, **1:** 295 (282), 332 (332); **2:** 760 (759), (1058); **3:** 1655 (1654), 1820 (1811), 1824 (1822); **4:** 1851 (1849), 2369 (2366); **8:** 4509 (4504); **9:** 5076 (5071), 5510 (5508); **11:** 6740 (6739)
Foster P J, **1:** 474 (466); **4:** 2369; **5:** 2819 (2815); **8:** 4688 (4684), 4839 (4839); **9:** 5539 (5536); **11:** 6251 (6249), 6265 (6261, 6263)
Foster R A, **4:** 2394 (2391)
Foster S, **7:** 3970
Foster W, **1:** 67 (62); **4:** 2167; **6:** 3284 (3279), 3527 (3526); **9:** 5532 (5529, 5530)
Foster W G, **1:** 358 (356)

Foster W P, **1:** 60 (55); **2:** 1204 (1199); **3:** 1774 (1772, 1773)
Foucault M, **1:** 67 (62), 162 (159); **2:** (1193); **4:** 2000 (2000); **8:** (4453), 4642 (4640, 4641); **9:** 5441 (5436, 5439, 5440); **10:** (6194)
Foulkes P, **8:** 4447 (4442)
Fourier C, **2:** (1189); **9:** (5230)
Fowler A, **5:** 2819 (2817)
Fowler C, **8:** 4388 (4384)
Fowler F J Jr, **4:** 2089 (2086); **10:** 5862 (5854)
Fowler H S, **3:** 1544 (1543)
Fowler W J, **9:** 5264 (5261)
Fowles J, **8:** 4787
Fox A A, **7:** 4081 (4079)
Fox E, **5:** 2575
Fox J, **11:** 6437 (6436)
Fox J J, **9:** 5567 (5565)
Fox J N, **9:** 5066 (5062)
Fox L H, **5:** 2491 (2489)
Fox M, **2:** (735)
Fox M F, **11:** 6712 (6711)
Fox N A, **4:** 1967
Fox R, **7:** 4336 (4335); **8:** 4383 (4381); **10:** 6234 (6233)
Fox S, **8:** 4542 (4541)
Fox T, **5:** 2972 (2970)
Fox W, **2:** 1127 (1124)
Fox W F, **9:** 5294 (5291, 5292)
Fox-Genovese E, **7:** 3852 (3849)
Foxman D, **7:** 3911 (3907); **8:** 4648 (4643, 4644)
Frager A M, **8:** 4948
Fragoudaki A, **5:** 2523
Frake C O, **2:** 802 (797)
Fraker T, **4:** 2150 (2147, 2148); **9:** 5385
Fraleigh M, **5:** 2627 (2625)
Franca V M, **8:** 4375 (4373)
Francequin-Chartier G, **2:** 665
Francis E, **2:** 807 (804)
Francis H, **9:** 5411 (5410)
Francis P, **3:** 1538
Franciscono M, **1:** 343 (340)
Frank E, **11:** 6437 (6435)
Frank F, **5:** 2831 (2831)
Frank I M, **8:** (4633)
Frank L K, **8:** 4791 (4788)
Frank M, **2:** 701
Frank O, **9:** 5560 (5558)
Franke M L, **6:** 3671 (3670)
Frankel C, **5:** 2978
Frankel J, **4:** 2388 (2386)
Frankel M R, **9:** 5130 (5125, 5126, 5127, 5128, 5129), 5142 (5136)
Frankena W, **8:** 4455 (4449)
Frankenburg W K, **3:** 1623 (1621), 1624 (1621, 1622, 1623)
Frankl V E, **5:** 2692
Franklin B, **9:** 5298 (5298)
Franklin B F, **3:** 1307 (1303)
Franklin B M, **3:** 1307 (1301, 1302, 1303, 1306, 1307), 1354 (1349)
Franklin W S, **1:** 310 (307)
Franks C M, **1:** 495
Franks J F, **6:** 3512 (3511)
Fransson A, **1:** 103 (101); **7:** 4179 (4179); **8:** 4638 (4638)
Frantz N, **4:** 1924
Franzén E, **11:** 6256 (6253)
Frary R B, **5:** 3050 (3047)
Fraser B J, **2:** 811 (807, 808, 809, 810); **3:** 1482 (1475, 1481, 1482), 1483; **4:** 2249 (2247), 2250, 2257, 2439, 2440 (2438); **5:** 2529 (2527); **6:** 3312 (3308); **7:** 3810, 4104; **8:** 4403 (4401, 4402); **9:** 5043 (5041), 5342 (5340); **10:** 5775 (5772, 5773, 5774), 6015 (6013)
Fraser B S, **11:** 6260 (6259)
Fraser C, **10:** 5690 (5687)
Fraser D M, **3:** 1266 (1263)
Fraser E, **4:** 2257 (2254)
Fraser N, **4:** 2033 (2030)
Fraser R, **3:** 1778 (1776); **7:** 4099 (4095)
Fraser S E, **11:** 6530
Frasher R, **9:** 5302 (5299)
Frasier M M, **5:** 2491 (2487), 2731 (2728)
Frasson C, **4:** 1917; **6:** 3345; **10:** 6193; **11:** 6484 (6483)
Frazer B J, **8:** 4864 (4862, 4863)
Frazer C, **10:** 5674 (5671)
Frazer M, **7:** 3839 (3839)
Frazier N, **2:** 1064; **5:** 2589 (2587)
Frechtling J A, **8:** 4622 (4620)
Frederick B C, **9:** 4974 (4972)
Frederick R, **10:** (5814)
Frederick W C, **5:** 2631 (2629)
Fredericks B, **3:** 1441 (1441)
Fredericks M, **8:** 4634 (4630); **9:** 5031
Fredericksen N, **7:** 4307
Frederiksen J, **1:** 408 (405)
Frederiksen J R, **1:** 374 (371, 372); **5:** 2768 (2762); **6:** 3325; **8:** 4731 (4730)
Frederiksen N, **1:** 60 (54), 370 (366), 374; **5:** 2767, 2768 (2762, 2765), 2769; **7:** 4170 (4163); **10:** 5772 (5769), 6192 (6189)
Fredland J E, **7:** 4200 (4200); **9:** 5076 (5074); **11:** 6633 (6628)
Fredrick W C, **11:** 6390 (6388, 6389)
Freebairn J W, **3:** 1448 (1447)
Freebody P, **2:** 1198 (1195, 1197); **9:** 5302 (5300, 5301)
Freed B F, **4:** 2339
Freed R, **3:** 1755 (1754)
Freed S, **3:** 1755 (1754)
Freedman A, **6:** 3209; **8:** 4736
Freedman D A, **4:** 1877 (1876)
Freedman K, **11:** 6617 (6617)
Freedman M, **8:** 4779 (4778)
Freedman S W, **10:** 5795 (5791, 5793), 6099 (6098); **11:** 6722 (6722), 6723, 6784 (6781, 6782, 6783), 6785 (6783)
Freeman C, **11:** 6260 (6258)
Freeman D, **3:** 1257 (1254), 1398 (1395); **5:** 2651 (2648); **10:** 6112 (6111), 6214 (6209)
Freeman D J, **10:** 6106 (6104, 6105)
Freeman E B, **9:** 5577 (5576)
Freeman H, **5:** 2847
Freeman H E, **2:** 1136 (1132); **3:** 1283 (1281); **4:** 2119 (2111), 2388 (2386); **8:** 4783 (4782); **11:** 6384 (6381)
Freeman L C, **9:** 5559 (5559), 5560 (5558)
Freeman M, **7:** 3726 (3724, 3725)
Freeman P, **3:** 1406 (1404)
Freeman R B, **1:** 520 (518); **2:** 652 (650); **3:** 1448 (1445, 1447, 1448), 1449 (1448), 1501; **6:** 3101, 3184 (3183); **7:** 4255 (4254); **8:** 4902 (4897, 4900); **9:** 5355 (5354); **10:** 6072 (6070), 6073; **11:** 6431, 6615, 6633 (6628), 6633
Freeman R D, **11:** 6628
Freeman W M, **6:** 3235 (3232)
Freeze D R, **2:** 729 (728); **5:** 2972 (2967, 2968)
Frei A, **3:** 1354 (1349)
Freiber H J, **10:** 6219 (6218)
Freilich M, **4:** 2052 (2051)
Freinet C, **5:** (3031); **8:** (4481)
Freire M, **3:** 1793
Freire P, **1:** 47 (44), 48 (45), 67 (62), (114), 135 (129, 132, 133, 134), 139 (139), 162 (161), (167), 176, (276); **2:** (635), 906 (901, 903, 904, 905), 910 (909), (926), (929), 1048 (1045, 1046, 1047), 1049, 1193 (1191, 1192, 1193), 1198 (1195, 1196); **3:** 1233 (1230), 1262 (1259, 1261), 1266 (1264), 1333 (1332, 1333), (1335), 1735 (1735); **4:** 1984 (1982), 2004, 2302 (2298); **5:** 2736 (2735, 2736), (2935), (2936); **6:** (3254), (3255), 3459 (3454, 3455, 3458); **7:** 4145 (4144), 4329 (4327), (4331); **8:** 4433 (4432), (4451), (4535), 4575 (4573); **9:** 5030 (5024), 5060 (5058); **10:** 5596 (5593, 5594), 5606 (5600), 5795 (5793), 5817 (5816), 5829, (6055), (6057), 6058 (6057), 6168 (6164, 6165, 6166, 6168)
Freize P, **2:** 1194
French E L, **10:** 5708
French F E, **3:** 1643 (1641)
French H W, **11:** 6272 (6267)
French J, **10:** 5673 (5669), 5826 (5825)
French J L, **9:** 5290 (5286)
French J R Jr., **10:** 6062 (6059)
French J W, **4:** 2024 (2020), 2240 (2240); **7:** 3706 (3705), 3879 (3874); **11:** 6678 (6675)
French L A, **6:** 3315 (3313, 3314), 3427 (3427)
French P, **10:** 5826 (5825)
French W L, **10:** 5900 (5900)
Frensch P A, **11:** 6780
Frese M, **4:** 1967
Frese W, **1:** 358
Fresko B, **11:** 6484 (6483)
Freud A, **8:** 4816 (4813, 4815)
Freud D, **5:** 2514 (2514)
Freud S, **1:** 234 (231); **3:** (1295), (1794), (1795); **4:** 1966 (1963), 2449 (2446); **5:** (2647), 2665 (2658); **7:** (3916); **8:** (4459), 4541 (4537), 4719 (4716), 4816 (4812, 4813, 4814, 4815); **10:** 5591 (5587)
Freudenberger H J, **10:** 5924 (5919, 5923), 6062 (6059)
Freudenstein R, **6:** 3213 (3211); **7:** 3970

Freudenthal H, **6:** 3661, 3684 (3682), 3685 (3676)
Freudenthal-Lutter S, **7:** (4156)
Freund J, **7:** 3826 (3822)
Frey K, **3:** 1278 (1273, 1274), 1308, 1354 (1348, 1349), 1355 (1348, 1349); **7:** 4104 (4101, 4102); **9:** 5497
Frey K S, **4:** 2449 (2447)
Freyberg P, **8:** 4479; **9:** 5335
Freyer M, **5:** 2806
Friborg G, **1:** 560 (555)
Fricke W, **11:** 6684
Friday P C, **3:** 1441
Fridrich H F, **4:** 2218
Fried M, **9:** 5572 (5568)
Fried M D, **10:** 5795 (5792)
Fried-Booth D, **6:** 3443 (3440)
Friedenthal-Hasse H, **11:** 6438
Friedkin N E, **10:** 5606 (5597)
Friedlander H, **7:** 3924 (3921)
Friedlander L, **7:** 4094 (4092)
Friedlander P, **7:** 4224 (4221)
Friedler Y, **6:** 3416 (3412); **9:** 5338 (5336, 5337)
Friedman I, **2:** 893 (891); **10:** 6062 (6060)
Friedman J, **3:** 1810 (1804)
Friedman L, **3:** 1820 (1815); **9:** 5432 (5428), 5445 (5443)
Friedman M, **1:** 594 (589); **3:** 1750 (1747), 1820 (1813); **6:** 3119; **8:** 4830 (4825); **9:** 5206 (5202, 5204, 5205), 5240 (5236, 5239)
Friedman M P, **6:** 3435; **8:** 4383
Friedman S L, **1:** 376 (375), 377
Friedmann J, **3:** 1810 (1808); **8:** 4601 (4595, 4597)
Friedrich C J, **1:** 437 (432)
Friedrich H F, **2:** 969 (966); **6:** 3292; **9:** 5508; **11:** 6780
Friedrich W N, **4:** 1980 (1976, 1977, 1978)
Friedricks A G, **6:** 3325 (3321)
Friedson E, **10:** 6096
Friel S, **9:** 5578
Friel-Patti S, **10:** 5690 (5689)
Friend J, **3:** 1573 (1572); **4:** 1911 (1906), 1918 (1913); **5:** 2891 (2887, 2888)
Friend M, **7:** 3833 (3832); **8:** 4662; **10:** 6244 (6241)
Fries C C, **6:** 3439 (3438)
Friesen D, **9:** 5181 (5176, 5178); **10:** 5924 (5920), 6062 (6059)
Friesen J, **2:** 1165
Frieze I H, **9:** 5435 (5434)
Frijda N H, **1:** 203 (199), 330 (330), 376; **5:** 2978; **8:** 4727 (4726)
Frijhoff W Th M, **4:** 2007; **5:** 2617 (2613)
Frisbie D A, **11:** 6315 (6313, 6314)
Frisch M, **9:** 5562 (5560, 5561)
Frischtak C, **3:** 1713 (1707, 1712)
Frisz R H, **10:** 5804 (5799)
Fritzell C, **9:** 5055
Fritzsche K P, **2:** 770 (768)
Fröbel F W A, **10:** (5877); **11:** (6743), (6746)
Frobenius J, **4:** (2005)
Froebel F W A, **3:** (1295); **4:** 2388 (2385); **5:** (2608); **6:** (3387); **7:** (4211); **8:** (4667), (4668)
Froebel H, **4:** 2388
Froese V, **6:** 3209 (3207), 3443 (3440)
Fröhlich M, **4:** 2357 (2357); **6:** 3334 (3330)
Fromm E, **2:** (1046); **5:** 2692 (2691); **9:** 5055; **10:** (5600)
Froomkin J T, **3:** 1784; **9:** 5240; **11:** 6277 (6272)
Frosser R C, **7:** 4136
Frost J, **3:** 1461; **8:** 4935 (4934)
Frost L A, **4:** 2435 (2433, 2434)
Frost R, **8:** 4939 (4938)
Frostig M, **10:** 5686 (5681)
Fruchter B, **9:** 5130 (5125)
Fry C L Jr, **9:** 5512 (5510)
Fry D, **2:** 737 (735)
Fry R, **1:** (195)
Frye N, **6:** 3638 (3635)
Fryer D, **11:** 6678 (6669)
Fryer M, **4:** 1911; **5:** 2890 (2887), 2891 (2889)
Fuchs D, **3:** 1359 (1356, 1358); **5:** 2779 (2777); **7:** 3807 (3805); **10:** 6173 (6171)
Fuchs L S, **3:** 1359 (1356, 1357, 1358); **5:** 2779 (2777); **7:** 3807 (3805); **10:** 6173 (6171)
Fuchs-Brüninghoff E, **3:** 1262 (1261); **8:** 4639
Führ C, **5:** 2480
Fuhrman S H, **6:** 3496 (3495); **8:** 4594; **10:** 6083
Fuhrman S I, **3:** 1343
Fujita H, **6:** 3667 (3665)
Fukász G, **2:** 661 (659)
Fulcher G, **2:** 729 (724, 728); **3:** 1507 (1506); **6:** 3559 (3559); **10:** 5668 (5665, 5666)
Fulker D W, **5:** 2465 (2465); **7:** 3743 (3741); **8:** 4799 (4798); **11:** 6492 (6488, 6490)
Fulkerson S C, **6:** 3235 (3232)
Fullan M G, **1:** 82 (79, 81); **2:** 1011 (1009, 1010); **3:** 1257 (1255), 1271 (1268), 1325 (1324), 1355 (1350, 1351), 1431 (1427), 1494 (1491, 1492, 1494); **4:** 1917 (1915), 1934 (1930, 1932), 2073 (2071), 2166 (2165); **5:** 2847 (2839, 2841, 2842, 2843, 2844, 2845, 2846), 2852 (2850, 2851); **6:** 3602 (3597, 3598, 3600, 3601); **7:** 4141, 4240 (4237); **8:** 4509 (4503), 4864 (4858); **9:** 5038 (5033), 5210 (5208, 5209), 5223 (5223), 5246 (5241, 5243); **10:** 5934 (5932, 5934), 5935, 5973 (5971), 6043 (6035, 6037), 6083 (6081, 6082), 6091 (6089), 6214 (6210, 6212, 6213)
Fuller B, **1:** 244 (241), 474 (471); **3:** 1655 (1654), 1761 (1759), 1784 (1783), 1789 (1787); **4:** 1840 (1838), 2140 (2138), 2257 (2255), 2412 (2411), 2419 (2415); **8:** 4509 (4505), 4526 (4520), 4594 (4591), 4698, 4848 (4847), 4864 (4859), 4873 (4865, 4866, 4868, 4869, 4870, 4871, 4872); **10:** 5591 (5590), 5673 (5668), 6043 (6036); **11:** 6366, 6390 (6389)
Fuller D, **7:** 3920 (3917)
Fuller D R, **1:** 408 (405), 409 (406)
Fuller F F, **10:** 6053 (6052)
Fuller W A, **9:** 5130 (5129)
Fuller W P, **3:** 1695 (1693); **7:** 4200 (4197); **9:** 5076 (5072, 5073); **11:** 6265 (6262)
Fullinwinder R K, **9:** 5582 (5578)
Fulth D, **10:** 5754 (5751)
Fulton O, **1:** 94; **7:** 4170 (4169), 4171; **11:** 6551 (6548)
Fulwiler T, **6:** 3209 (3206, 3208)
Funder D C, **10:** 5772 (5770)
Fung H C, **9:** 5532 (5530)
Funnell R, **1:** 295 (284, 285, 286); **3:** 1729 (1727)
Furey S, **1:** 103 (102)
Furinghetti F, **6:** 3652
Furlong J, **10:** 5985
Furlong M, **2:** 1011 (1010)
Furlong V J, **2:** 1073 (1070); **9:** 5060 (5058); **10:** 5957 (5956)
Furlong V T, **10:** 5995 (5993)
Furman W, **10:** 5758 (5757)
Furnham A, **10:** 6062 (6060)
Furniss W T, **2:** 834 (832)
Fürnrohr W, **5:** 2623
Furry W S, **9:** 5240 (5235)
Furst D, **11:** 6360 (6357)
Furst E, **3:** 1804 (1801)
Furst E J, **4:** 1847 (1844)
Furst N F, **2:** 816 (812, 813, 814, 815); **10:** 5713 (5708), 6149 (6148)
Furstenberg F F, **8:** 4779 (4775, 4776, 4777, 4778)
Furstenberg F F Jr., **3:** 1641 (1638), 1642 (1636, 1637, 1638, 1639, 1641); **9:** 5441 (5436)
Furth D, **2:** 900
Furth H G, **3:** 1402 (1401); **5:** 2670; **9:** 5512; **10:** 6168 (6167)
Furtwengler C B, **4:** 2131 (2126, 2129)
Fuson K C, **2:** 1052 (1049); **6:** 3660, 3661 (3659); **10:** 5745 (5741)
Futagami S, **5:** 2897
Futcher D, **2:** 1175 (1171)
Futterman A, **2:** 718 (717)

Gabbay J, **10:** 5662 (5660)
Gabel D, **2:** 811; **3:** 1482; **10:** 5775
Gaber D, **2:** 867 (865)
Gable R K, **6:** 3603 (3598)
Gadamer H-G, **3:** (1772); **5:** (2579), 2585 (2582, 2584, 2585), 2586, (2693)
Gadotti M, **1:** 135 (133); **9:** 5216 (5212)
Gadow K D, **3:** 1520 (1518)
Gadsden V, **1:** 103 (102)
Gaebler T, **9:** 5191 (5188)
Gael S, **6:** 3096
Gaertner K N, **1:** 82 (81)
Gage N L, **2:** 816; **3:** 1283, 1474 (1464), (1796); **4:** 1872, 1917, 2194; **5:** 2529, 2714, 2879 (2874, 2878), 2884 (2883); **6:** 3202 (3198), 3523; **7:** (3881);

8: 4774, 4873 (4869); **9:** 5055; **10:** 5704, 6085 (6084, 6085), 6086, 6088 (6086), 6121 (6120), 6149, 6183 (6180), 6207 (6203, 6204, 6205, 6206, 6207), 6239 (6237, 6238)
Gagel C, **11:** 6292 (6288)
Gagné E D, **6:** 3334 (3331, 3332, 3333)
Gagné F, **5:** 2731 (2726, 2728); **9:** 5532 (5529, 5531)
Gagné R M, **1:** 370; **2:** 1019, 1031 (1029, 1030), 1170 (1166); **3:** 1266 (1263), 1325 (1322), 1367, 1513 (1508), 1543 (1538); **4:** 1848 (1842, 1844), 1898 (1892), 1928 (1927), 2100; **5:** 2862, 2867, 2874 (2872, 2873), 2879 (2878, 2879), 2903 (2899), (2920); **6:** 3345 (3341); **7:** 3760 (3757, 3758), 3886 (3881); **8:** 4766, 4774 (4770), 4775 (4769), 4783 (4780, 4781); **9:** 5275 (5273); **10:** 5913 (5911, 5913), 6192 (6188), 6202
Gagnon P, **11:** 6370 (6369)
Gahfar S, **7:** 4206
Gail A J, **4:** 2007
Gaile G L, **3:** 1553
Gailîte G, **6:** 3272
Gaillard A W K, **8:** 4394 (4390)
Gainer L J, **2:** 665 (662), 1152 (1147, 1148, 1149); **11:** 6415 (6413)
Gajaanayake J, **5:** 2758 (2755)
Gajardo M, **1:** 180 (177); **3:** 1820 (1818); **6:** 3256 (3254)
Galabawa J C J, **2:** 914 (912)
Galaburda A M, **7:** 4081 (4078); **10:** 5680 (5679)
Galambos N L, **1:** 88
Galanter E, **3:** 1434 (1432)
Galassi J P, **11:** 6360 (6359)
Galassi M D, **11:** 6360 (6359)
Galba S S, **8:** (4887)
Galbraith J K, **3:** 1720 (1714, 1715, 1719)
Galbraith J R, **9:** 5264 (5259)
Galbraith M W, **3:** 1315 (1309); **7:** 4185; **8:** 4736 (4735), 4864 (4863); **10:** 6058 (6054)
Galbraith R C, **7:** 3872 (3870)
Galda K, **4:** 1911 (1906); **5:** 2891 (2887, 2888)
Galda L, **2:** 737 (735)
Galen, **9:** (5122)
Galileo G, **3:** (1254), (1461); **8:** (4462); **9:** (5051)
Gall J P, **5:** 2529 (2528); **8:** 4881 (4877)
Gall M D, **3:** 1283 (1279); **5:** 2529 (2528); **6:** 3202 (3198); **8:** 4875 (4874), 4881 (4876, 4877, 4879, 4880)
Gall R S, **7:** 3807 (3803)
Gallagher D G, **10:** 6072 (6071)
Gallagher J J, **3:** 1642; **5:** 2495 (2492, 2493), 2672, 2673, 2731 (2730), 2813 (2809); **9:** 5181 (5177), 5206, 5512; **10:** 6015 (6014)
Gallagher M, **2:** 1160 (1157)
Gallagher P, **2:** 900
Gallagher P A, **10:** 6031 (6030)
Gallaire H, **3:** 1394 (1388)
Gallart M-A, **1:** 100 (96); **6:** 3261 (3257, 3258, 3259, 3260), 3267; **11:** 6265 (6263), 6272 (6270)
Gallaudet T H, **10:** (5659)
Gallia A, **5:** 2623
Gallimore R, **2:** 803 (799), 867 (865); **3:** 1236 (1234, 1236); **6:** 3312 (3308, 3309), 3453 (3452)
Gallini J, **2:** 1031 (1026)
Gallistel C R, **2:** 705 (703); **8:** 4957 (4952)
Galloway D, **4:** 1934 (1932)
Galloway J, **9:** 5275 (5274)
Galluzzo G R, **10:** 5957 (5954, 5955, 5956), 5999 (5998)
Galotti K M, **8:** 4957 (4955)
Gal'perin P Y, **5:** 2884 (2881); **6:** 3292 (3291), (3344); **7:** 3886 (3885)
Galton F, **3:** 1796 (1793, 1794); **4:** 1872 (1865, 1867), 1873, (2168); **5:** (2875); **7:** (3699), (3873); **9:** (5053)
Galton M J, **2:** 816 (812, 813, 814, 815), 831 (829); **3:** 1461; **9:** 5294 (5293); **10:** 5826 (5824)
Galtung J, **3:** 1733 (1730); **9:** 5055
Galvin P, **7:** 3821 (3819)
Gam P, **7:** 4180
Gamble H, **9:** 5255
Gamby G, **8:** 4935 (4931, 4933)
Gamel N M, **1:** 490 (487)
Games P A, **8:** 4351 (4340)
Gammage P, **1:** 27
Gamoran A, **1:** 11 (6, 7, 8, 10), 12; **2:** 824 (822, 823), 825 (821, 822, 823, 824); **3:** 1320 (1318); **8:** 4881 (4877); **9:** 5176 (5170), 5264 (5260, 5261), 5379 (5377); **10:** 6015 (6014)
Gamradt J K, **3:** 1729 (1728)
Gamson Z F, **4:** 2186 (2185)
Gandhi M K, **1:** (132); **3:** (1687); **5:** 2753, (2755); **7:** (4135); **8:** (4809)
Gangolly J S, **5:** 2798 (2793)
Ganiel U, **8:** 4479 (4478)
Gannicott K, **8:** 4489
Ganor M, **7:** 4220 (4219)
Ganss G E, **9:** 5121
Gant W L, **3:** 1443
Gants J, **7:** 4240
Ganzeboom H B G, **7:** 3864 (3864); **10:** 5735 (5731, 5732)
Gao F, **3:** 1567 (1565)
Garb G, **7:** 4148
Garbarino J, **1:** 362 (359)
Garber H L, **7:** 3830
Garberg R, **8:** 4751 (4745)
Garbutcheon-Singh M, **1:** 48 (46)
Garcia Garrido J L, **2:** 1064
Garcia O, **1:** 534
Garcia S B, **6:** 3232 (3229, 3230)
Garcia W, **3:** 1789
Garcia-Blanco A M, **2:** 906 (901), 907
Garden R A, **2:** 957 (954); **3:** 1768 (1764); **4:** 2140 (2137, 2139); **6:** 3643, 3668; **10:** 6155 (6150)
Gardiner L, **11:** 6735 (6731, 6732)
Gardiner P, **1:** 409 (406)
Gardner D P, **9:** 5281 (5276); **10:** 6083 (6079)
Gardner H, **1:** 152 (147), 343 (343); **4:** 1848, 1939 (1936); **5:** 2669 (2668), 2670, 2731 (2726), 2732 (2726), 2879 (2875, 2878), 2921 (2918); **6:** 3301 (3301); **7:** 3743 (3739, 3743), 3879 (3873, 3876, 3877, 3878); **8:** 4727 (4726); **10:** 5817 (5816), 6178 (6177); **11:** 6617 (6617), 6618
Gardner J R, **4:** 2427 (2424)
Gardner M, **3:** 1529; **10:** 6177, 6178
Gardner M K, **5:** 2874 (2873)
Gardner P L, **9:** 5323 (5318, 5319, 5320, 5321)
Gardner R, **1:** 322 (318); **10:** 6067
Gardner R C, **1:** 537 (536); **4:** 2339 (2335, 2336), 2346 (2343, 2344)
Gardner R W, **2:** 871 (869)
Gardner W, **5:** 2906 (2905)
Gardner W D, **9:** 5201
Gardner W E, **10:** 5957
Gardner W R, **11:** 6339
Garen J, **4:** 2279 (2275)
Garet M, **1:** 11 (10)
Garet M S, **5:** 2672 (2670); **8:** 4604 (4603); **9:** 5379 (5377)
Garfield E, **5:** 2998 (2995)
Garfinkel A, **10:** 6149 (6144)
Garfinkel H, **2:** 803 (797), (926), 1073 (1071); **9:** 5416 (5412); **10:** 5591 (5588)
Garfinkel I, **2:** 693 (690); **3:** 1642 (1639)
Garfinkle R J, **5:** 2867 (2867)
Gargi, **11:** (6748)
Garin E, **4:** 2007 (2004)
Garland C W, **5:** 2813 (2809)
Garland J, **10:** 6227 (6226)
Garman M, **6:** 3224
Garmezy N, **3:** 1642 (1637); **4:** 1980 (1976); **5:** 2802 (2799); **6:** 3297 (3293); **8:** 4779 (4775, 4777), 4780; **9:** 5528 (5527)
Garms W I, **9:** 5307 (5306)
Garner J F, **6:** 3276 (3273, 3275)
Garner M, **7:** 3970
Garner R, **2:** 1025 (1022); **6:** 3339 (3338); **7:** 3788 (3784, 3785, 3786); **10:** 5795 (5794)
Garrard J, **9:** 5334 (5332)
Garrett A W, **9:** 5582 (5582)
Garrett N, **7:** 4095
Garrick N, **4:** 2357 (2352)
Garrido C, **7:** 4275
Garrison D R, **1:** 127 (124); **3:** 1579 (1578), 1602 (1600, 1601); **7:** 4220 (4219)
Garrod A, **5:** 2669 (2668)
Garrod S C, **8:** 4942 (4941)
Garry A, **10:** 5808
Gartner A, **2:** 700, 711 (710), 729 (728); **3:** 1508; **5:** 2907 (2905), 2971 (2966); **6:** 3559 (3557); **8:** 4372 (4370), 4661 (4658), 4935 (4933); **9:** 5071; **10:** 6244 (6242, 6243); **11:** 6484 (6482)
Gartside P, **7:** 3889
Garvey B, **9:** 5252 (5247)
Garvey C, **8:** 4541 (4540); **9:** 5508

Garwood S F, **9:** 5359 (5357)
Gary G, **7:** 3991
Garza T J, **9:** 5358 (5356)
Garzarolli, **11:** 6515
Gaskins I, **2:** 867 (866)
Gaskins I W, **8:** 4956 (4956)
Gaspar J, **8:** 4630
Gassendi P, **3:** (1461)
Gastright J F, **5:** 2870 (2869)
Gatawa B S M, **3:** 1563 (1559); **11:** 6821
Gate A, **4:** (1861)
Gates A I, **7:** 3935 (3930); **10:** 5745 (5738)
Gati I, **11:** 6678 (6674)
Gatta L A, **9:** 5323 (5321)
Gattegno C, **4:** 2346 (2342)
Gattringer H, **9:** 5216 (5213)
Gattullo M, **5:** 3036
Gatz M, **11:** 6492 (6489)
Gaudig H, **6:** (3136)
Gaudry E, **11:** 6360 (6356, 6358)
Gaul C A, **8:** 4473 (4472)
Gaur A, **1:** 483; **6:** 3446 (3444)
Gauthier G, **6:** 3345; **10:** 6193; **11:** 6484 (6483)
Gauthier J, **4:** 1917
Gauthier R, **4:** 2452 (2450)
Gaventa J, **1:** 47 (45); **2:** 906 (906); **7:** 4336 (4330, 4335)
Gavin W J, **3:** 1602
Gay B M, **3:** 1538 (1537)
Gay G, **9:** 5577 (5576)
Gay J, **1:** 295 (291, 292); **2:** 1212 (1209); **3:** 1246 (1245), 1252 (1247), 1755 (1753); **4:** 1851 (1849), 1852 (1849); **5:** 2685; **6:** 3452 (3450), (3457)
Gayeski D M, **5:** 2897 (2896); **7:** 3995 (3991, 3992), 3996 (3993); **8:** 4803 (4800); **10:** 5913 (5913)
Gayfer M, **11:** 6719
Gayle M, **4:** 1857 (1855)
Gaylord-Ross R, **11:** 6461 (6459)
Gaynor C, **4:** 2286 (2285)
Gaza T, **4:** (2005)
Gaziel H H, **6:** 3197 (3190)
Gazzaniga M S, **2:** 846; **3:** 1504; **5:** 2665; **7:** 3774 (3774)
Gbikpi-Benissan F, **11:** 6403
Gearhart M, **6:** 3453 (3449); **7:** 3726 (3724)
Gearing F O, **1:** 295 (282, 283, 285, 286), 296, 297 (281); **2:** 1212 (1209); **3:** (1727); **4:** 2053; **6:** 3215; **9:** 5572 (5569)
Geber B, **2:** 1152 (1148); **7:** 3996 (3993)
Gecas V, **10:** 5591 (5586, 5587, 5588, 5589)
Geddes M, **6:** 3213
Gee J P, **2:** 802 (800), 1198 (1197, 1198)
Geer B, **1:** 193 (190); **9:** 5411 (5409, 5410); **10:** 6126 (6123), 6227 (6227)
Geertz C, **3:** 1695; **5:** (2605); **9:** 5210 (5209, 5210), 5313 (5309); **11:** 6465 (6463)
Gegenheimer L, **8:** 4779 (4776, 4777)
Gehin J-P, **2:** 665 (662)
Gehring T, **3:** 1441 (1440)
Gehrke N J, **6:** 3655 (3653); **9:** 5318 (5315, 5316, 5317)
Geibenk G, **10:** 5690 (5687, 5689)
Geiger R, **8:** 4796 (4794, 4796); **10:** 5753 (5751)
Geißler K, **11:** 6660
Geis G L, **6:** 3306 (3303)
Geisler-Brenstein E, **1:** 322 (319)
Geisser S, **6:** 3508 (3504); **8:** 4359 (4356)
Geiwitz J, **1:** 239
Gelatt H B, **2:** 1165 (1163)
Gelb I J, **1:** 483; **6:** 3446 (3444)
Gelb S A, **2:** 718 (717)
Gelfand D, **8:** 4383
Geller E S, **9:** 4977 (4976)
Geller P E, **2:** 1102
Gelles R J, **1:** 19 (16); **4:** 2261 (2259)
Gellner E, **5:** 2623 (2622); **8:** 4446 (4446), 4455 (4455); **9:** 4980 (4979), 5050
Gelman R, **2:** 705 (703), 842 (840, 841), 856; **5:** 2768 (2762); **8:** 4957 (4952)
Gelman S A, **2:** 838, 842 (840); **8:** 4957 (4952)
Gelpi E, **6:** 3421 (3417, 3419)
Genberg V, **3:** 1553 (1550, 1552)
Genby D, **4:** 2212
Gendler T, **1:** 520 (516)
Genemans L, **9:** 5246
Genesee F, **6:** 3335 (3333)
Genghis Khan, **7:** (3895), (3897)
Gengler C, **6:** 3538
Genishi C, **8:** 4950 (4949)
Gennaoui A, **7:** 4246 (4243); **10:** 5895
Gennari P, **5:** 2779 (2776, 2777)
Genova W J, **3:** 1486 (1485)
Genovesi G, **5:** 3036
Gensheimer L K, **8:** 4779 (4776, 4778)
Gentile G, **5:** (3029)
Gentle J E, **9:** 5082 (5079)
Gentle P, **10:** 5713 (5710)
Gentner D R, **8:** 4727 (4724), 4957 (4955); **9:** 5342 (5339, 5340); **10:** 5790
Gentry J R, **9:** 5475; **10:** 5704 (5702, 5703)
George C, **5:** 2515 (2514)
George D, **5:** 2731 (2728)
George J, **9:** 5180 (5176), 5275 (5274)
George L K, **1:** 239 (237)
George W C, **5:** 2495, 2731
Gephart W J, **4:** 2108 (2103); **10:** 5957 (5954)
Geppert U, **4:** 1966 (1965)
Gerace Larufa F, **7:** 4336 (4331)
Gerald D, **8:** 4788
Gerber M M, **3:** 1441 (1440, 1441); **6:** 3559 (3558)
Gerber R, **5:** 2469, 2470
Gerber S, **1:** 408 (407)
Gerbing D W, **11:** 6384 (6381, 6382)
Gerdes P, **6:** 3452 (3451)
Gere A R, **6:** 3209; **10:** 5795 (5793)
Gergen K J, **1:** 380; **9:** 5350 (5349), 5441 (5436)
Gerin-Lajoie D, **4:** 2052 (2051)
Gerlach V S, **5:** 2861 (2857, 2859); **7:** 3760 (3757)
Gerlach-Downie S, **2:** 693 (690, 691)
Gerlack K, **3:** 1750
Germain R, **1:** 19
German D J, **10:** 5680 (5675)
Germe J F, **5:** 2942 (2939)
Gerritz K, **11:** 6320 (6316, 6319)
Gerry M, **5:** 2907 (2906); **11:** 6461 (6460)
Gershaw N J, **9:** 5567 (5566)
Gershon R C, **5:** 2783 (2780)
Gersten R, **2:** 866 (862), 868 (862); **3:** 1529 (1527); **8:** 4947 (4946)
Gerstle J E, **10:** 5607
Gerth H H, **2:** 785; **4:** 2249 (2248)
Gertler P, **3:** 1449 (1448); **4:** 2315 (2314); **6:** 3106 (3104, 3105)
Gerty C, **1:** 474
Gertzog W A, **8:** 4652 (4651); **10:** 5790 (5784)
Gerver E, **1:** 111; **11:** 6731 (6729)
Gery G J, **5:** 2861 (2860, 2861); **6:** 3306 (3305); **8:** 4758 (4757)
Geschka H, **5:** 2725 (2722, 2723, 2724)
Geschwind N, **7:** 4081 (4078)
Gesell A L, **5:** 2665 (2664), 2680 (2677); **7:** 3950 (3947); **9:** (5273)
Geske T G, **2:** 1056, 1094 (1087, 1088, 1090), 1126 (1121, 1125); **3:** 1784 (1779), 1793; **4:** 2212; **6:** 3106
Gesner J M, **3:** (1721)
Getson P R, **5:** 3050 (3044, 3049)
Gettinger M, **8:** 4864 (4862)
Getzels J W, **2:** 1182 (1178); **3:** 1774 (1770); **4:** 1840 (1837), 2166 (2160); **5:** 2589 (2587), 2714 (2710); **8:** (4561), 4791 (4791); **9:** 5168 (5162), 5358 (5358)
Geuze R H, **3:** 1520 (1519)
Gewirth A, **7:** 3925
Gewirtz G L, **10:** 6169
Gewirtz J L, **9:** 5512, 5518
Gewirtz S, **8:** 4830 (4825)
Ghafoor A, **7:** 4270; **8:** 4708 (4703, 4705)
Ghani Z, **10:** 5999 (5997)
Ghanim M, **11:** 6793
Ghatak R, **3:** 1607 (1604)
Ghatala E S, **7:** 3768 (3767)
Ghesquiere P, **4:** 2266 (2264)
Ghesquière T, **10:** 5713
Ghez R C, **3:** 1660 (1657)
Ghurye S G, **9:** 4974
Giaconia R M, **7:** 4215 (4212, 4214); **10:** 6239 (6235, 6236, 6237, 6238)
Giacquinta J B, **4:** 2073 (2072), 2166 (2165); **5:** 2847 (2839, 2841)
Gianotten V, **6:** 3256 (3255)
Giardina M, **5:** 2773
Giarelli J M, **4:** 2033; **10:** 5991 (5986)
Gibb A, **4:** 1991 (1985, 1989)
Gibb C, **9:** 4977 (4976)
Gibb S, **1:** 89
Gibbons A, **2:** 1031 (1030)
Gibbons F X, **1:** 234
Gibbons J D, **2:** 792 (787, 789)
Gibbons R, **6:** 3253 (3252)
Gibbs B, **9:** 5399 (5396)
Gibbs G, **1:** 193 (185, 189, 190, 191); **6:** 3349 (3346, 3347)

Gibbs G I, **9:** 5475 (5472, 5473)
Gibbs J, **1:** 380 (378)
Gibbs J C, **7:** 3920 (3917)
Gibbs N, **4:** 2330 (2330)
Gibbs R, **9:** 5192
Giblin P, **4:** 2266 (2266)
Gibson C, **10:** 5808
Gibson C C, **1:** 168 (166)
Gibson E J, **8:** 4383 (4380)
Gibson F W, **10:** 5725 (5725)
Gibson J J, **7:** 3950 (3947); **8:** 4379 (4378, 4379)
Gibson K R, **1:** 88
Gibson M A, **1:** 295 (291, 293), 296, 297; **2:** 933 (930); **3:** (1228); **7:** 3974 (3971); **9:** 5220 (5219), 5510 (5509)
Gibson M R, **1:** 27
Gibson R, **1:** 47 (46)
Gibson R L, **9:** 5290 (5283)
Gibson S, **11:** 6438 (6437)
Gick M L, **5:** 2856 (2854); **11:** 6456 (6454), 6608
Gickling E, **2:** 719
Giddens A, **1:** 67 (61, 62); **4:** 1984 (1983); **6:** 3373 (3369); **9:** 5030 (5025), 5038 (5033), 5060 (5059), 5210 (5209), 5313 (5309); **10:** 5596 (5594, 5595)
Giddings F H, **7:** 3848 (3841)
Giddings G J, **2:** 811 (809); **4:** 2440; **10:** 5775 (5774)
Gideonse H D, **1:** 28; **10:** 5929 (5928), 5957 (5956), 5965
Gideppe, **2:** 1160 (1155, 1156, 1157, 1159)
Giele J Z, **4:** 2446
Gielen K, **1:** 73; **9:** 5246 (5242, 5244)
Giere R, **3:** 1543; **6:** 3416
Giere U, **3:** 1262 (1260)
Giesecke H, **8:** 4461 (4458)
Giesen B, **2:** 933
Gifford A, **11:** 6538 (6534)
Gifford B, **2:** 867 (866); **6:** 3301
Gifford B R, **1:** 5; **7:** 3726; **11:** 6260 (6258)
Gilbert G, **10:** 5713 (5710)
Gilbert J K, **4:** 1848 (1845)
Gilbert P H, **2:** 1198 (1194, 1195, 1197)
Gilbert R, **2:** 770 (767); **3:** 1347 (1344); **4:** 1984 (1982)
Gilbert T, **6:** 3096 (3093)
Gilbreth F B, **5:** (2878)
Gilbreth L, **5:** (2878)
Gilding K R, **4:** 2180 (2177)
Giles M B, **5:** 3050 (3047)
Gilhooly K J, **8:** 4728
Gill M, **8:** 4791 (4790)
Gill W M, **7:** 4215 (4213, 4214); **9:** 5359 (5358)
Gillespie J A, **5:** 2736; **8:** 4581 (4576, 4579)
Gillespie R, **9:** 5233
Gillett M, **3:** 1635 (1631)
Gillette A, **8:** 4337
Gilley J W, **5:** 2689 (2685, 2686)
Gilliam M E, **4:** 2351 (2349)
Gilligan C, **1:** 162 (160); **4:** 2296 (2294, 2295), 2439 (2437); **7:** 3920 (3918); **9:** 5435 (5433); **10:** 5804 (5798), 5939 (5936, 5937), 5991 (5990), 6053 (6049), 6214 (6209); **11:** 6723 (6721), 6726 (6724, 6725)
Gilligan C J, **4:** 2033 (2030, 2031)
Gilligan S G, **1:** 330 (328)
Gilliland R J, **2:** 900
Gilliom M, **6:** 3202 (3198, 3200)
Gillion K L, **4:** 2310
Gillis J J, **10:** 5680 (5680)
Gillmore G M, **10:** 6234 (6229, 6230)
Gilly M, **8:** 4957 (4954)
Gilmore G, **1:** 32 (30)
Gilmore G M, **5:** 2462 (2461)
Gilmore P, **1:** 296; **4:** 2052; **6:** 3453, 3459
Gilmore S, **10:** 5977 (5974)
Gil-Perez D, **10:** 6177 (6174)
Gilroy P, **1:** 28
Ginagreco M F, **5:** 2814 (2809)
Giner S, **10:** 5607
Ginner T, **10:** 5829
Ginott H G, **7:** 4296 (4294)
Ginsberg H, **10:** 6168 (6165)
Ginsberg L H, **8:** 4719
Ginsberg R, **4:** 2131 (2130)
Ginsburg A, **9:** 5066 (5062)
Ginsburg A L, **5:** 2491 (2487)
Ginsburg H P, **6:** 3670 (3669); **11:** 6334 (6332), 6608 (6605)
Ginsburg M B, **2:** 933; **4:** 1910 (1906, 1910); **5:** 2512 (2510); **8:** 4509 (4505), 4586 (4582, 4583, 4584, 4585, 4586); **10:** 5995 (5994), 6043 (6038); **11:** 6558 (6552), 6563 (6559), 6741
Gintis H, **1:** 294 (289); **2:** (780), 933 (925, 926, 929), 1072 (1067), 1073 (1067), 1203 (1199); **3:** 1337 (1335), 1347 (1346), 1655 (1649), 1695 (1693), 1720 (1716), 1739 (1737); **4:** 2004 (2003); **5:** 2589 (2587), 2744, 2942 (2940); **6:** 3189 (3185), (3307), 3621 (3618, 3619); **7:** 3771 (3770); **8:** 4568, 4571 (4569), 4574 (4573), 4895 (4894); **9:** 5060 (5057), 5168 (5160), 5228 (5224), 5510 (5509), 5523, 5538 (5533); **10:** 5591 (5589, 5590), 5606 (5602), 5613 (5608); **11:** 6547
Ginzberg E, **3:** 1641, 1642
Giovannoni J, **1:** 19 (15)
Giovenco A, **2:** 868 (863)
Gipps C V, **6:** 3474; **7:** 3911 (3908, 3911), 3912 (3907, 3908); **8:** 4935 (4933)
Girard A, **4:** 2257 (2252)
Girard D, **4:** 2346 (2340)
Girard D L, **5:** 2879 (2879)
Giraud B, **9:** 5259
Girgus J S, **9:** 5406 (5404, 5405)
Girling R, **8:** 4902 (4898)
Girotto V, **8:** 4957 (4954)
Giroux H A, **2:** 906 (900), (926), 1072, 1073 (1067, 1068), 1204 (1199, 1200); **3:** 1233 (1232), 1266 (1263), 1315, 1333 (1332, 1333), 1337 (1334, 1335), 1347 (1346), 1720 (1717); **4:** 1984 (1982, 1983), 2249 (2249), 2291 (2289); **5:** 2589; **6:** 3621 (3619, 3620); **7:** 4336 (4335); **8:** 4586 (4582), 4895 (4894); **9:** 5060 (5057, 5058), 5210 (5209); **10:** 5606 (5602), 6197 (6194); **11:** 6563 (6561)
Githiora W, **5:** 2891 (2885, 2886)
Gitlin A, **6:** 3602 (3598); **10:** 6139 (6136, 6137)
Gitlin T, **10:** 5783
Gittell M, **1:** 594 (593)
Giurescu D, **9:** 5087
Givner C, **7:** 3808 (3806)
Givon H, **9:** 5363 (5362)
Gjengset G T, **2:** 737 (734)
Gjerde C, **2:** 645 (642)
Gjesme T, **11:** 6360 (6358)
Gjinushi S, **1:** 260
Gladieux L, **10:** 5767 (5766), 5768
Gladwin C H, **3:** 1474
Glaesel B, **8:** 4935 (4931, 4933)
Glantz F, **2:** 688 (685), 701 (696); **3:** 1636 (1634); **7:** 4300 (4298)
Glas C A W, **7:** 4307 (4306)
Glas D, **6:** 3213
Glaser B G, **2:** 645 (641, 644); **4:** (2299), (2301), 2374 (2373)
Glaser E M, **2:** 1207 (1204)
Glaser G C, **3:** 1421 (1417, 1420)
Glaser R, **1:** 5 (3), 6 (3), 193 (191), 370 (368), 374 (371, 372); **2:** 838 (835), 842 (839), 847, 856, 868, 1031 (1030), 1189 (1183); **3:** 1504 (1502), 1513 (1509, 1510, 1513); **4:** 1848 (1843, 1845), 1872, 1898 (1885), 1899 (1884), 2198 (2195), 2199 (2194); **5:** 2767 (2762), 2768 (2762, 2765), 2769 (2762), 2861 (2857), 2874 (2871), 2879 (2874, 2878, 2879), 2884, 2921; **6:** 3155 (3154), 3292, 3297 (3296), 3324 (3317), 3325 (3317), 3345 (3344); **7:** 3726 (3725), 3788, 3886 (3881), 3942; **8:** (4401), 4722 (4720), 4727 (4727), 4730 (4728), 4731, 4774 (4766), 4775, 4823 (4821); **9:** 5043 (5040), 5363 (5360, 5361, 5362), 5563 (5562); **10:** 5745 (5738), 5750 (5746), 5762, 5790 (5783), 6026 (6023, 6024, 6025), 6159 (6156, 6157, 6158), 6192; **11:** 6608
Glaser W A, **1:** 560 (555)
Glasgow Z, **5:** 2862 (2857, 2860)
Glass D V, **7:** 3864 (3862, 3863)
Glass G V, **1:** 594 (590); **2:** 775 (771, 773), 1127 (1126), 1136 (1134, 1135); **3:** 1784 (1780), 1834 (1833); **4:** (1861), 1911 (1907, 1909), 2194 (2189); **5:** 2714 (2713); **6:** 3373 (3372); **7:** 3783 (3775, 3776, 3777, 3778, 3779, 3780, 3782, 3783), 3784 (3777, 3778, 3782), 3821 (3816, 3817); **8:** 4562 (4559), 4652 (4651), 4873; **9:** 5201, 5373 (5368), 5489 (5487, 5488); **10:** 5725 (5721, 5722), 6239 (6236, 6237); **11:** 6339 (6336), 6591 (6590, 6591)
Glass J, **10:** 5924
Glass L, **7:** 4081 (4079)
Glasser W, **1:** 486 (483); **3:** (1536); **8:** 4758; **10:** (6030), 6103 (6102)
Glassman R B, **6:** 3527 (3524, 3526)
Glathorn A A, **1:** 296; **4:** 2052

Glatter R, **1:** 73 (67, 69, 72); **3:** 1579 (1575); **5:** 2954 (2953, 2954); **6:** 3528; **9:** 5246 (5242, 5244)
Glatthorn A A, **3:** 1278 (1272, 1274); **10:** 5935 (5931, 5932, 5933)
Glaubman R, **7:** 4215 (4212, 4213, 4214)
Glauser B, **3:** 1735 (1733)
Glauser M J, **3:** 1553
Glavich M K, **9:** 5008 (5003)
Glavin J P, **9:** 5070 (5068), 5071 (5068)
Glaze A J, **2:** 1161
Glazer J, **9:** 5567 (5563)
Glazer M, **10:** 5783; **11:** 6723 (6719)
Glazer N, **6:** 3238 (3235)
Glazer N N, **8:** 4433 (4432)
Glazer R, **4:** 2345
Glazewski B, **1:** 362 (359)
Gleason D, **3:** 1406
Gleason M, **7:** 3807 (3804); **10:** 5673 (5670, 5671)
Gleditsch M, **1:** 175 (171)
Gleeson V, **9:** 5255
Gleick J, **10:** 5991 (5986)
Gleitman L R, **6:** 3223; **8:** 4945 (4943)
Glenberg A M, **2:** 969 (966)
Glendenning F, **10:** 5596 (5596); **11:** 6395 (6391)
Glendinning F, **7:** 4249
Glenn C L, **1:** 594 (591); **2:** 711 (706); **8:** 4830, 4831; **9:** 5197 (5193, 5195)
Glenn J, **10:** 6178 (6177)
Glenn J III, **4:** 1939 (1936)
Glennen S, **10:** 5674
Glennon T, **2:** 693 (690)
Gleser C C, **1:** 5 (2)
Gleser G C, **1:** 41 (33); **5:** 2462 (2458, 2459), 3061 (3057); **8:** 4753 (4753), 4857 (4856, 4857); **9:** 4995 (4981)
Glesne C, **7:** 4319 (4317)
Glewwe P, **3:** 1449 (1448); **4:** 2315 (2314), 2418 (2415); **6:** 3106 (3101, 3102, 3104, 3105)
Glick B, **1:** 494
Glick H A, **6:** 3616 (3615)
Glick J A, **1:** 295 (291); **3:** 1252 (1247); **4:** 1851 (1849); **5:** 2685
Glickman C D, **10:** 5934 (5933), 5935 (5930, 5933), 6004 (6002)
Gliedman J, **3:** 1507 (1506)
Gliessman D H, **6:** 3202 (3199, 3200); **8:** 4881 (4880); **10:** 5948 (5946)
Glisan E, **6:** 3443 (3441, 3442)
Glissov P, **4:** 2427 (2424, 2425)
Globerson T, **2:** 871 (870), 888 (885); **5:** 2536 (2535), 2669 (2669), 2769 (2764); **6:** 3625 (3623); **7:** 3942 (3937); **8:** 4383; **9:** 5363 (5362); **11:** 6457 (6454)
Gloeckner G, **7:** 3889
Glover J, **3:** 1513, 1514; **9:** 5318 (5314)
Glover J A, **2:** 820, 1182; **4:** 1848; **5:** 2880; **8:** 4731; **9:** 4977
Glover R W, **1:** 310 (307)
Gluck S B, **7:** 4051 (4048)
Glueckauf R L, **4:** 1877 (1874)
Glynn A, **9:** 5359 (5356)
Glynn R J, **9:** 5385
Glynn T, **6:** 3463 (3461, 3462); **8:** 4376 (4373); **10:** 6031 (6030)
Gmelch W, **10:** 6062 (6058)
Gmelin W, **3:** 1557
Gnezda M T, **9:** 5275 (5274)
Goddard H H, **2:** 718 (717)
Goddard N, **6:** 3459 (3456)
Goddard R W, **1:** 184 (181)
Goddard T, **1:** 158 (155)
Godel K, **8:** (4633)
Godfrey C, **2:** 1094
Godfrey K, **9:** 5082 (5080)
Godfrey M, **3:** 1685 (1681); **8:** 4531 (4529); **9:** 5076 (5072); **11:** 6265 (6262), 6633 (6628), 6638 (6635)
Godoy-Kain P, **4:** 1911; **5:** 2891 (2889)
Godshalk F I, **7:** 3935 (3932, 3933), 4196 (4195)
Godwin D, **10:** 5887
Goedegebuure L, **3:** 1720 (1718)
Goel P, **6:** 3508
Goelenboth F, **1:** 244 (241)
Goelman H, **2:** 687 (686); **6:** 3452; **7:** 4301 (4297)
Goertz M E, **3:** 1606 (1604, 1605); **9:** 5191, 5228 (5224, 5228)
Goethe J W von, **6:** (3136); **10:** (5814)
Goetz C G, **3:** 1618 (1611)
Goetz E T, **1:** 193, 194 (186, 187); **6:** 3339; **7:** 3768 (3765)
Goetz J P, **4:** 2046 (2044), 2052 (2047, 2048, 2050, 2051); **11:** 6726 (6725)
Goetz L, **3:** 1406 (1403)
Goetz P W, **3:** 1367
Goetze M, **7:** 4026 (4023)
Goffinet S, **1:** 103
Goffman E, **1:** 93 (93); **2:** 1073 (1071); **10:** 5591 (5587), 5668 (5665)
Goffree F, **6:** 3435, 3661 (3659)
Goh K S, **9:** 5485 (5484)
Golby M, **3:** 1328
Gold R L, **7:** 4319 (4316)
Goldberg F, **8:** 4479, 4652
Goldberg H, **4:** 2046 (2044)
Goldberg J E, **6:** 3235 (3233)
Goldberg L R, **11:** 6310 (6310)
Goldberg M S, **4:** 2445 (2442, 2444)
Goldberg S, **3:** 1642
Goldberg V, **5:** 2942 (2940)
Goldberger A, **6:** 3144 (3140)
Goldberger A J, **8:** 4351, 4359
Goldberger A S, **8:** 4845 (4840)
Goldberger N, **1:** 162 (160); **10:** 5939 (5938); **11:** 6722 (6721)
Goldberger N R, **7:** 4329 (4326); **10:** 6099 (6098)
Goldchstein M, **1:** 194 (192)
Golden M, **5:** 2806 (2804)
Goldenberg C, **3:** 1236 (1236)
Goldenberg E P, **6:** 3512
Goldfarb R, **11:** 6638, 6653 (6649, 6651)
Goldfried M R, **8:** 4791 (4789)
Goldhammer R, **10:** 6004 (6002)
Goldin G, **11:** 6608
Goldin L, **10:** 6112 (6110, 6111)
Golding J, **6:** 3523 (3512)
Goldin-Meadow S, **2:** 856 (855)
Goldman B, **4:** 2331
Goldman J, **8:** 4779 (4776, 4778)
Goldman S, **9:** 5210 (5209); **11:** 6608 (6607)
Goldman S R, **1:** 5 (5); **6:** 3325 (3321); **8:** 4730 (4730)
Goldminz E, **3:** 1544 (1538, 1542)
Goldring E B, **2:** 893 (888, 889), 1073 (1066); **9:** 5216 (5213, 5214), 5273 (5269, 5270, 5271, 5272), 5308 (5303)
Goldschmidt D, **10:** 5606 (5601)
Goldsmith H H, **11:** 6310 (6308)
Goldsmith J, **4:** 2423 (2420)
Goldsteen K, **4:** 2261 (2259)
Goldstein A P, **1:** 494; **9:** 5567 (5566)
Goldstein B, **3:** 1739 (1737)
Goldstein D, **8:** 4957
Goldstein H, **3:** 1300 (1296); **4:** 1934 (1932), 1938 (1937), 2180 (2177), 2257 (2252); **5:** 2596 (2590, 2592, 2594, 2595), 3043 (3038); **6:** 3523 (3512, 3513, 3521, 3522); **7:** 3706 (3706), 3738 (3738), 3858 (3857), 3912 (3907, 3910, 3911), 3986 (3982, 3984), 4015 (4009, 4012); **8:** 4623 (4620, 4621), 4845 (4842); **9:** 5142 (5137); **10:** 5735 (5734), 5826 (5824); **11:** 6260 (6259)
Goldstein H I, **9:** 5130 (5129)
Goldstein I L, **3:** 1490 (1489); **6:** 3306 (3302, 3304)
Goldstein K, **10:** 5686 (5681)
Goldstein R, **4:** 2156 (2156)
Goldstein S, **6:** 3360; **9:** 5255
Goldstein Z, **4:** 1962 (1958, 1962); **5:** 2462 (2460); **6:** 3452 (3449); **10:** 6062 (6059)
Goldstone B P, **2:** 737 (736)
Goldthorpe J H, **6:** 3312; **7:** 3721 (3717, 3718), 3864 (3863, 3864); **9:** 5553 (5549, 5552); **10:** 5735 (5731)
Goldwaite D, **6:** 3202 (3198)
Golemi B, **1:** 260
Golinkoff R M, **6:** 3224 (3219, 3220)
Gollwitzer P M, **10:** 6053
Goltz G L, **11:** 6384 (6379)
Golumb C, **1:** 343 (342)
Gomes da Costa A C, **3:** 1735 (1735)
Gomez H, **5:** 2769 (2762)
Gómez Campo V M, **6:** 3261 (3260)
Gomez Millas J, **8:** (4495)
Gonçalves C, **10:** 5713 (5709)
Goncu A, **8:** 4542 (4539)
Gonon P, **6:** 3137
Gonzales A, **8:** 4442
Gonzalez J, **7:** 3996 (3995)
González L E, **6:** 3261
Gonzalez M, **8:** 4951
González R, **10:** 5812 (5811)
Gonzalez-Mena J, **11:** 6398
Gooch S, **11:** 6360 (6358)
Good C V, **1:** 389 (380); **7:** 3970 (3961); **9:** 5275 (5273)
Good R, **3:** 1359 (1357), 1635 (1632)
Good T L, **2:** 811 (807), 816 (815); **3:** 1257 (1255), 1529 (1525); **4:** 1847 (1846); **5:** 2870 (2869); **6:** 3655 (3654);

8: 4864 (4862), 4881 (4878, 4880); **9:** 5223 (5221), 5264 (5259); **10:** 5826 (5825), 6015 (6013), 6020 (6016, 6018), 6031, 6112 (6107, 6108, 6109), 6121 (6119, 6120), 6173 (6172); **11:** 6310 (6309)
Goodacre C, **8:** 4694
Goodale J G, **5:** 3007
Goodall J van Lawick, **5:** 2684 (2682)
Goodchild F, **8:** 4942 (4941)
Goode W T, **3:** (1723)
Goodenough D, **3:** 1241 (1239)
Goodenough D R, **2:** 872 (868)
Goodenough F, **4:** 2452 (2450)
Goodenough F L, **2:** 705 (701)
Goodenough W H, **3:** 1729 (1726); **7:** 3974 (3971); **9:** 5210 (5209), 5220 (5218), 5313 (5309)
Goodenow R, **5:** 2607
Gooderham P N, **7:** 4179 (4178); **10:** 5808 (5805)
Goodey J, **6:** 3528
Goodlad J H, **9:** 5223 (5221, 5223)
Goodlad J I, **1:** 230 (227, 228); **2:** 1107; **3:** 1266 (1263, 1264, 1265), 1271 (1267, 1268, 1269), 1315 (1310), 1325 (1323), 1333 (1329, 1332), 1343, 1355 (1349), 1486, 1494 (1491, 1492), (1796); **4:** 2388 (2382, 2386), 2389; **5:** 2697 (2695), 2847 (2839); **7:** 4157 (4156); **8:** 4568 (4567); **9:** 5210 (5209), 5318 (5315), 5379 (5374, 5377), 5582 (5579); **10:** 5795 (5791), 5991 (5989), 6012 (6009), 6053, 6062 (6060), 6092 (6089), 6096, 6103, 6168 (6165); **11:** 6580
Goodlad J L, **2:** 796; **10:** 5999
Goodlad J T, **2:** 807 (804)
Goodlad S, **5:** 2773 (2770, 2771)
Goodman D R, **8:** 4482 (4482)
Goodman G, **7:** 4293
Goodman G S, **5:** 2802
Goodman I F, **6:** 3453 (3448, 3449, 3451), 3480; **8:** 4936 (4932)
Goodman J, **10:** 5995 (5993), 6004
Goodman J C, **6:** 3224
Goodman K, **4:** 1962 (1962); **10:** 5961 (5958)
Goodman K S, **8:** 4939, 4945 (4944)
Goodman L A, **6:** 3508 (3500, 3502, 3507); **7:** 3864 (3863); **9:** 5559 (5558), 5560 (5557)
Goodman N, **9:** 4980 (4977, 4978), 5416 (5415)
Goodman P, **8:** 4964 (4960)
Goodman S, **1:** 265
Goodman Y M, **7:** 4081 (4080)
Goodnight J H, **11:** 6591 (6591)
Goodnow J J, **4:** 2281 (2280); **5:** 2627 (2626)
Goodnow J T, **10:** 6202 (6199)
Goodrich C A, **10:** 6117
Goodson I F, **1:** 244; **3:** 1307 (1301, 1302, 1304, 1305, 1306, 1307), 1325 (1320); **8:** 4594 (4591); **9:** 5013, 5298 (5296, 5297, 5298), 5327 (5324); **10:** 5613 (5611), 6139 (6132)
Goodson L A, **3:** 1315 (1313); **4:** 1898 (1888); **5:** 2861 (2860), 2874 (2873)
Goodson N D L, **3:** 1490 (1487)
Goodstein L P, **10:** 5913 (5913)
Goodwin C, **6:** 3238 (3237)
Goodwin D A, **10:** 5919 (5914); **11:** 6538
Goodwin M H, **6:** 3238 (3237)
Goody J, **1:** 295 (289); **4:** 1852 (1849); **6:** 3446 (3446), 3452 (3447, 3448), 3459 (3454)
Goodyear P, **1:** 348
Gooler D D, **4:** 1924 (1921, 1922); **5:** 2831
Gopinathan S, **2:** 770 (768); **4:** 2296; **5:** 2998 (2996); **8:** 4442, 4845 (4844), 4848 (4847)
Goransson L, **1:** 157 (155), 162 (160)
Gorbachev M, **9:** (5099), (5102)
Gorden R L, **5:** 3007
Gordon A J, **10:** 5591 (5587)
Gordon C, **2:** 1194
Gordon C W, **4:** 2166 (2157, 2159)
Gordon D, **2:** 1152 (1149); **3:** 1328 (1327), 1820 (1818); **5:** 2589 (2587, 2588), 2744 (2743); **6:** 3189 (3185); **10:** 6092 (6090)
Gordon D F, **3:** 1703 (1697)
Gordon E, **2:** 693; **3:** 1257
Gordon E W, **2:** 820; **3:** 1233; **7:** 4300, 4301
Gordon H W, **10:** 5680 (5679)
Gordon I J, **2:** 893 (888)
Gordon J, **2:** 1094; **11:** 6669
Gordon L, **3:** 1720 (1717)
Gordon L C, **6:** 3224 (3220)
Gordon L D, **11:** 6765 (6763)
Gordon L R, **11:** 6461 (6457, 6459)
Gordon P, **5:** 2618; **9:** 5252 (5249)
Gordon R, **3:** 1739 (1738)
Gordon T, **3:** (1536); **8:** 4461 (4457)
Gordon V N, **3:** 1602 (1602)
Gordon W J J, **5:** 2725 (2723)
Gore J M, **2:** 1198 (1196); **10:** 6219 (6218); **11:** 6727 (6725)
Gore K, **7:** 3807 (3804)
Gore S, **3:** 1647 (1645)
Gore T, **10:** 6048
Gorelick S, **11:** 6276 (6274)
Gorham A, **11:** 6266
Goris A, **9:** 5510 (5508)
Gorman K, **4:** 2412 (2411)
Gorman T, **10:** 5826 (5822); **11:** 6784 (6784)
Gorman T P, **1:** 176; **3:** 1768 (1765); **4:** 2024 (2020), 2025, 2140 (2134); **7:** 3936
Gorman W, **2:** 784 (776)
Gormley W T Jr, **5:** 2672 (2671); **8:** 4830 (4825), 4835
Górowska-Fells M, **10:** 5613 (5610)
Gorsuch R L, **4:** 2241
Gorter R, **2:** 1107; **3:** 1266, 1278 (1273)
Gorth W P, **10:** 6020
Gosden P H J H, **1:** 28
Goslin D A, **2:** 1073 (1065); **3:** 1241; **5:** 2665 (2658), 2681; **10:** 5591
Gospodinoff K, **2:** 802 (801); **9:** 5313 (5311)
Gossett W S, **4:** (1867)
Goswami U, **8:** 4957 (4955, 4956)
Gotovos A, **5:** 2523
Gotshalk D W, **1:** (195), 199
Gott S, **7:** 3726 (3725)
Göttert R, **7:** 4220 (4218)
Gottfredson G D, **11:** 6678 (6674)
Gottfredson L S, **11:** 6678 (6673, 6675)
Gottfried A W, **3:** 1642 (1640); **5:** 2813 (2812)
Gottlieb G, **1:** 15 (12); **5:** 2802; **8:** 4394 (4392)
Gottlieb J, **2:** 729 (727); **9:** 5070 (5068)
Gottman J M, **9:** 5489 (5487, 5488, 5489), 5490, 5560 (5558); **10:** 5758, 5759
Gottschall E M, **8:** 4694
Gough H G, **1:** 239 (237)
Gough P B, **8:** 4945
Gouhier R, **9:** 5090 (5090)
Gould K H, **4:** 2296 (2295)
Gould S J, **2:** 718 (717); **4:** 2172 (2168); **10:** 5826 (5824)
Gould W T S, **9:** 5259
Gouldner A, **5:** 2998 (2994)
Gouldner A W, **9:** 5175 (5174)
Goulet D, **4:** 1911; **5:** 2736 (2735)
Goulet L R, **5:** 2665
Goulet R, **2:** 846; **5:** 2665
Gourlay N, **11:** 6591 (6591)
Govier T, **2:** 1207 (1206)
Govinda R, **10:** 5995 (5991)
Gowin D B, **2:** 1031 (1026, 1027, 1028, 1029, 1030); **6:** 3349; **8:** 4652 (4649, 4652); **10:** 5831 (5830)
Gowing M K, **6:** 3306 (3302)
Goy R W, **9:** 5435 (5434)
Gozo K, **11:** 6403
Grabe W, **8:** 4939
Graber J A, **1:** 88 (84)
Grabowski B L, **11:** 6603 (6601)
Grabowski G, **3:** 1449
Grabowski R, **1:** 254 (245, 247, 252)
Grabowski S M, **11:** 6437
Grace G, **8:** 4586 (4582, 4583, 4584, 4585, 4586); **10:** 6079, 6139 (6133, 6137, 6138)
Graciani M S S, **2:** 910 (909)
Graczyk S L, **9:** 5185 (5184, 5185)
Graden J L, **5:** 2907 (2905); **7:** 3833 (3832); **8:** 4661, 4662 (4657, 4658, 4659); **9:** 5071 (5069)
Gradous D B, **2:** 1139; **6:** 3096 (3095)
Graesser A C, **2:** 969 (967)
Graetz B, **8:** 4830 (4826, 4827)
Graff H, **6:** 3459 (3454), 3531; **8:** 4639
Graff H G, **5:** 2759
Graff H J, **1:** 135 (131, 132), 175 (169)
Grafton A, **4:** 2007 (2004)
Graham A, **6:** 3209 (3207)
Graham B, **7:** 4170 (4166, 4167, 4168)
Graham G, **10:** 5713 (5711)
Graham J, **7:** 3889 (3888)
Graham J W, **7:** 4007
Graham K, **8:** 4447 (4443); **10:** 6197 (6195, 6196)

Graham P, **4:** (1839)
Graham P A, **2:** 834 (832); **6:** 3238 (3235); **10:** 6106 (6105); **11:** 6765 (6764)
Graham S, **2:** 867 (861); **7:** 3807 (3803); **10:** 6224 (6222)
Graham T B, **10:** 6202 (6198, 6201); **11:** 6437 (6433)
Grahame P R, **9:** 5060 (5058, 5059)
Grajia M L, **3:** 1529 (1526)
Gramlich E, **8:** 4715 (4709)
Gramsci A, **2:** (780), (1047), 1073 (1067), (1191), (1192); **5:** 2736 (2732, 2734, 2735); **6:** 3621 (3618, 3619); **10:** (5592, 6055)
Gran B, **10:** 5954 (5952)
Grandjean E, **4:** 2011, 2012
Grandstaff M, **4:** 2369 (2365)
Grandy J, **4:** 2439 (2437)
Granger B, **10:** 5817 (5817)
Granger L, **10:** 5817 (5817)
Granheim M, **3:** 1804 (1803); **4:** 2377
Grant C, **3:** 1337
Grant C A, **7:** 3974 (3973), 3978 (3975)
Grant D R B, **3:** 1635 (1630)
Grant G, **2:** 1006; **3:** 1343, 1486; **4:** 1939; **6:** 3655; **8:** 4873; **9:** 5043, 5379 (5375, 5376, 5377, 5378), 5432, 5441, 5445; **10:** 5934, 5948, 6178, 6219
Grant J H, **3:** 1449 (1445, 1446)
Grant J W, **7:** 4026 (4023), 4030
Grant L, **11:** 6726 (6725)
Grant M, **1:** 362 (358)
Grant R, **10:** 5613 (5611)
Grant S, **3:** 1449 (1446); **5:** 2897 (2893)
Grant W, **11:** 6608 (6607)
Grantham-McGregor S, **5:** 2575 (2572)
Grapin P, **11:** 6807 (6805)
Gräsel, **6:** 3306 (3304)
Gräser H, **8:** 4719
Grass R T, **5:** 2575
Grasso J T, **11:** 6633 (6628), 6704 (6700)
Grattan C H, **1:** 120 (111, 112, 116); **11:** 6437 (6431)
Gratz R K, **6:** 3209 (3208)
Gratzer D, **7:** 4030 (4027)
Graubard A, **1:** 265 (263)
Graue M E, **10:** 5812 (5810)
Graves D, **11:** 6781
Graves N, **10:** 6187 (6185)
Graves N B, **8:** 4799 (4798)
Graves N J, **1:** 28; **5:** 2469 (2467, 2468)
Graves T, **10:** 6187 (6185)
Graves T D, **8:** 4799 (4798)
Gray C, **4:** 1991
Gray E, **6:** 3638 (3637)
Gray H, **7:** 4240 (4238)
Gray J, **4:** 1938 (1934)
Gray J A, **11:** (6308)
Gray M A, **5:** 2692 (2690)
Gray M J, **6:** 3096 (3093)
Gray O P, **8:** 4473 (4469)
Gray P, **7:** 3970 (3966)
Gray W S, **1:** 175 (174); **6:** 3480 (3453, 3474)
Grayson D, **7:** 4007 (4003, 4005)
Graziani L J, **1:** 15 (13)
Greaney V, **4:** 2257 (2252)
Gredler M B, **4:** 1924
Greeley A M, **8:** 4830 (4828), 4845 (4840, 4841)
Green A, **2:** 1074 (1070)
Green B F, **5:** 3050 (3047); **9:** 5158 (5154); **10:** 5790 (5783, 5784)
Green B F Jr, **7:** 3726
Green B L, **2:** 705 (704)
Green C W, **5:** 2623
Green D R, **5:** 3050 (3044)
Green F, **5:** 2744
Green F L, **2:** 705 (703)
Green J, **3:** 1233 (1227, 1230), 1257 (1256); **4:** 2052 (2048, 2050); **6:** 3227
Green J A, **6:** 3508 (3500)
Green J E, **7:** 4293 (4291)
Green J L, **2:** 820 (818, 819); **10:** 6197 (6195, 6196), 6235 (6234), 6239 (6237)
Green K R, **6:** 3453 (3447)
Green L W, **5:** 2571 (2567), 2572
Green P, **4:** 2338 (2335)
Green P E, **9:** 4974 (4967)
Green P R, **8:** 4379
Green P S, **4:** 2357 (2353)
Green S F, **7:** 4099 (4096)
Green T F, **4:** 2001, 2033 (2031); **10:** 5900 (5900), 5991; **11:** 6580
Green T H, **8:** (4450)
Greenacre M J, **2:** 1084 (1082)
Greenberg B S, **1:** 570 (565)
Greenberg D F, **6:** 3523 (3514)
Greenberg J, **6:** 3276 (3273)
Greenberg J B, **1:** 534 (534)
Greenberg K H, **2:** 860 (859)
Greenberg K L, **4:** 2025
Greenberg M T, **3:** 1402 (1401); **4:** 1979 (1976)
Greenberger M, **2:** 649; **5:** 2672 (2671)
Greenblat C S, **3:** 1830 (1828); **5:** 2773 (2771); **9:** 5475 (5472)
Greene D, **1:** 31 (30); **4:** 2281 (2280); **7:** 3942 (3941)
Greene J C, **3:** 1283 (1281)
Greene K, **6:** 3463 (3461)
Greene M, **1:** 198 (195); **4:** 2033 (2031); **8:** (4430), 4433; **11:** 6726 (6725)
Greene T R, **9:** 5563 (5562)
Greenfield L, **5:** 2998
Greenfield P M, **1:** 570; **2:** 888; **3:** 1252 (1246); **6:** 3215, (3451), 3625; **11:** 6333 (6329)
Greenfield T B, **1:** 60 (54), 67 (61, 63), 77 (76); **3:** 1774 (1770, 1771), 1775; **4:** 2166 (2161); **6:** 3284 (3278, 3280, 3281, 3282), 3528; **9:** 5168 (5161, 5162)
Greenfield W D, **6:** 3284 (3277); **7:** 3826 (3822, 3823, 3825); **9:** 5181 (5180)
Greenglass E R, **10:** 5924 (5922), 6062 (6061)
Greengross S, **7:** 4170 (4170)
Greenhalgh J, **9:** 5185 (5183)
Greenhalgh S, **4:** 2418 (2416)
Greenhill L P, **11:** 6306 (6304)
Greenland J, **4:** 2423 (2420); **10:** 5973 (5966)
Greenland T, **1:** 607
Greenleaf C, **11:** 6784 (6783)
Greeno J G, **1:** 5 (4); **2:** 838 (837), 1031 (1027); **4:** 1848 (1842, 1843); **5:** 2768 (2762); **6:** 3655 (3653, 3654); **8:** 4727 (4726); **10:** 5887, 6026 (6023); **11:** 6456 (6454, 6455)
Greenspan S, **1:** 362; **3:** 1643 (1637, 1641); **8:** 4816
Greenwald A G, **9:** 5324 (5318), 5394
Greenwald J, **3:** 1328
Greenwood C R, **8:** 4375 (4372, 4373, 4374), 4376; **9:** 5567 (5563, 5565); **10:** 6163 (6162); **11:** 6484 (6482)
Greenwood G E, **10:** 5948 (5946)
Greenwood J, **4:** 2302 (2298)
Greenwood S, **8:** 4694
Greer B, **2:** 1006 (1004); **5:** 2884; **6:** 3652, 3655 (3654)
Greer D, **8:** 4542 (4541)
Greer J T, **8:** 4408 (4405, 4406, 4407)
Greer M, **7:** 3756; **8:** 4758 (4756, 4757)
Greer R D, **8:** 4376 (4373)
Greer S, **3:** 1643 (1639); **11:** 6575 (6569)
Greer W D, **1:** 198 (197), 343 (341)
Gregg L W, **2:** 867; **11:** 6784
Gregg R T, **1:** 60 (53), 77 (75)
Gregory I, **10:** 5977 (5976)
Gregory R L, **8:** 4379 (4378)
Gregory T B, **9:** 5294
Gregson A, **8:** 4864 (4858, 4860, 4861)
Greig S, **3:** 1501; **4:** 1852 (1850)
Greinert W D, **11:** 6452 (6449)
Grenfell J, **4:** 1934 (1929)
Gresham F M, **1:** 495
Gress J S, **3:** 1307
Greszco K, **7:** 3807 (3802)
Grewe W, **1:** 238 (237)
Grey-Johnson C, **11:** 6256 (6255)
Gribble H, **1:** 415 (411)
Gribble J, **8:** 4447 (4445)
Grice H P, **4:** 2364 (2358)
Griffey D C, **10:** 6026 (6023)
Griffin A, **7:** 4171 (4163, 4165, 4166)
Griffin C, **10:** 5596 (5593), 6058 (6055)
Griffin D R, **10:** 5991 (5986)
Griffin G, **3:** 1635 (1633); **10:** 5613 (5611, 5612), 5812, 5935, 6169
Griffin G A, **10:** 5973 (5967)
Griffin H, **8:** 4680 (4679)
Griffin J, **10:** 5826 (5823)
Griffin J A, **2:** 977 (976)
Griffin P, **1:** 230 (229); **3:** 1252 (1250), 1504 (1502, 1504); **5:** 2642 (2641), 2670; **6:** 3652 (3650); **9:** 5548 (5545); **10:** 5713 (5710)
Griffin P E, **7:** 4307 (4306)
Griffin R E, **11:** 6625 (6624)
Griffin S, **5:** 2680 (2677, 2678, 2679)
Griffin V, **6:** 3213
Griffin W J, **10:** 5704 (5700)
Griffith B C, **3:** 1553
Griffith C R, **9:** 5359 (5357)
Griffith J, **9:** 5066 (5064)
Griffith J E, **7:** 3711
Griffith W S, **8:** 4736 (4735)
Griffiths D A, **9:** 5471 (5469)

Griffiths D E, **1:** 60 (54, 57), 67 (61), 77 (75), 82 (78); **3:** 1774 (1769); **4:** 1898 (1887), 2165, 2166 (2161, 2162); **6:** 3284
Griffiths R, **4:** 2339 (2335); **10:** 5977 (5974, 5975)
Griffiths V L, **10:** 5843,
Griggs C, **11:** 6775
Griliches Z, **1:** 254; **3:** 1449 (1446), 1665 (1665), 1750 (1749); **4:** 2278 (2275, 2276, 2278), 2279 (2278); **6:** 3144 (3138, 3141, 3143)
Grim J, **5:** 2813
Grimes B A, **4:** 2346 (2340)
Grimes J, **1:** 490 (487, 488); **9:** 5290
Grimes P W, **10:** 6072 (6071)
Grimm H, **6:** 3224 (3220, 3222, 3223)
Grimmett P P, **3:** 1635 (1632); **10:** 5985, 6004 (6000), 6214 (6214), 6219 (6217)
Grimshaw A D, **11:** 6608 (6604)
Grimshaw P, **11:** 6735
Grimshaw W J, **6:** 3197 (3195)
Grindal B, **2:** 1212 (1209); **3:** 1755 (1753)
Grinder R E, **4:** 1848 (1841); **5:** 2495 (2492)
Grindle M, **3:** 1825
Grise P J, **5:** 2891
Grissmer D W, **10:** 5846 (5845)
Grissom J B, **5:** 2515 (2513); **9:** 5228 (5226)
Grobman A B, **3:** 1257 (1253, 1254)
Grochelewsky K, **7:** 3920 (3918)
Groever Z, **2:** 907
Gromoll E W, **9:** 5562 (5560)
Gronau R, **4:** 2279 (2276); **6:** 3106 (3101, 3103)
Gronlund N E, **5:** 3066 (3061); **8:** 4753 (4752), 4930 (4928); **10:** 5617 (5615, 5616); **11:** 6315 (6314)
Gronn P C, **1:** 67 (63); **4:** 2166 (2161); **6:** 3284 (3280, 3282); **7:** 3826 (3825); **9:** 5313 (5312)
Groom J M, **8:** 4375 (4373)
Groombridge J, **7:** 4249
Groot W, **7:** 4324 (4323), 4325; **9:** 5355 (5352)
Grootaert C, **2:** 1160 (1156, 1157), 1161; **3:** 1680 (1677, 1678); **5:** 2819 (2815); **9:** 5076 (5072, 5073, 5074)
Grootendorst R, **2:** 1207 (1207)
Grootings P, **1:** 310 (306); **11:** 6452 (6448), 6647 (6641, 6642, 6643, 6647), 6669 (6665)
Grosjean F, **6:** 3227 (3225)
Gross A L, **3:** 1421 (1419, 1421); **4:** 2427 (2425, 2427)
Gross E, **4:** 2432 (2430)
Gross H, **8:** 4935 (4933)
Gross L S, **11:** 6307 (6300, 6305)
Gross M U M, **9:** 5532 (5528, 5529, 5530, 5531)
Gross N, **4:** 2073 (2072), 2166 (2165); **5:** 2847 (2839, 2841); **10:** 6132 (6131); **11:** 6765 (6762)
Gross R, **1:** 162
Gross R T, **3:** 1642 (1639)
Grossi M C, **2:** 746; **3:** 1834 (1831)
Grossman H J, **7:** 3830 (3826)
Grossman J B, **5:** 2740
Grossman M, **2:** 1055 (1053); **4:** 2212 (2209, 2210)
Grossman P L, **10:** 5812 (5810), 5961 (5960), 6122, 6183 (6182)
Grossmann K, **4:** 1967; **5:** 2651 (2649)
Grosz B J, **8:** 4942 (4941)
Grotberg E H, **3:** 1623 (1622); **7:** 4296 (4294)
Grotelueschen A D, **4:** 2123 (2120)
Grottkau B J, **10:** 6106 (6105, 6106)
Grouws D A, **2:** 1006, 1052; **3:** 1257; **5:** 2870 (2869); **6:** 3643, 3647, 3652 (3647, 3648, 3649, 3650), 3655 (3652), 3667 (3667), 3685; **7:** 4100; **8:** 4652; **10:** 5795, 6026
Grovdahl E C, **8:** 4803 (4802)
Grove R, **3:** 1325 (1323)
Groves R M, **10:** 5862 (5854)
Grubb N, **5:** 2672 (2671); **11:** 6282 (6281)
Grubb R, **4:** 1918 (1913)
Grubb W, **4:** 1911
Grubb W N, **3:** 1739 (1736); **11:** 6266, 6538 (6530, 6531)
Grubel H, **1:** 560 (554, 556)
Gruber H, **1:** 431 (426)
Gruber K H, **1:** 431 (430)
Gruca J, **4:** 2412 (2410)
Gruder C L, **4:** 2108 (2108)
Grue-Sørensen K, **3:** (1724)
Grugeon D, **1:** 564; **4:** 2186 (2185)
Grugeon E, **7:** 3977 (3977)
Grumet M, **11:** 6723 (6721, 6722), 6726 (6724), 6735 (6733)
Grumet M R, **7:** 4051 (4047)
Grunberger R, **9:** 5013
Grundin H U, **11:** 6445 (6440)
Grundtvig N F S, **1:** 139 (136, 137, 138); **2:** (908); **3:** (1457); **4:** (2324), (2325), (2326); **5:** (2734), (2735); **7:** (4175); **10:** (6055)
Gruneberg M M, **2:** 969; **4:** 2011 (2011); **7:** 3768
Grüner G, **11:** 6647 (6642)
Grüner G, **11:** 6684
Grunewald K, **10:** 6244 (6242, 6243)
Grunwald B, **1:** 486 (483)
Grunwell P, **10:** 5680, 5696 (5695), 5697
Grusec J E, **9:** 5528
Grusky D B, **9:** 5553 (5549)
Gruvaeus, **4:** (2233)
Gruver G W, **7:** 3820 (3816, 3817, 3818)
Gryskiewicz N D, **2:** 1182 (1180)
Gryskiewicz S S, **5:** 2725
Gstettner P, **1:** 431 (431)
Guba E G, **1:** 77 (74); **2:** 645 (644); **3:** 1283 (1282), 1287 (1285), 1474 (1474), 1475, 1774 (1770), 1820 (1818); **4:** 2036, 2089 (2087), (2103), 2119 (2112, 2116), 2166 (2160), 2374 (2370, 2372), 2375; **7:** 4051 (4050), 4059 (4057), 4319 (4316, 4318, 4319); **8:** 4634 (4630); **9:** 4980 (4977, 4978), 5030 (5022, 5023, 5025, 5027), 5055, 5168 (5162); **10:** 5957 (5954); **11:** 6445, 6465 (6462), 6466 (6464, 6465)
Gubb J, **11:** 6784 (6784)
Guberman S R, **6:** 3453 (3449)
Guckenberg T, **11:** 6456 (6454)
Gudmundsdottir S, **10:** 6121 (6118, 6119), 6183 (6454)
Guehenno J, **9:** 5091
Guenthner F, **4:** 2364
Guenthner-Reutter M, **4:** 2364
Guðmundsson G, **5:** 2721
Guerney B, **4:** 2266 (2266)
Guerney L, **1:** 88 (85)
Guerrero J S, **8:** 4442
Guesne E, **8:** 4479; **9:** 5334 (5332), 5341 (5339)
Guess D, **3:** 1406 (1403, 1405)
Guetzkow H, **5:** 2978
Gugler J, **5:** 2945 (2943, 2945)
Guglielmino L M, **9:** 5399 (5395, 5398)
Gugnani H R, **11:** 6719 (6717)
Guiang A M, **8:** 4796 (4794)
Guichard O, **4:** (2054)
Guida G, **10:** 5914
Guidici E, **4:** 2011 (2010)
Guilford J P, **2:** 1182 (1180); **4:** 1872 (1869), 2241; **5:** 2768 (2760), 2773 (2770), (2911), (2917); **6:** 3124 (3121); **7:** 3738 (3727, 3732), 3872 (3868), 3879 (3873, 3874); **8:** 4727 (4723), 4923 (4919, 4922), 4930 (4924, 4927, 4929); **9:** 5130 (5125); **11:** 6349 (6341)
Guillon R, **11:** 6272 (6268, 6269)
Guinagh B J, **7:** 4296 (4295)
Guiton G, **1:** 11 (9, 10)
Gulick L, **4:** 2166 (2158); **9:** 5168 (5161)
Gulko J, **4:** 2452 (2450)
Gullichsen A, **7:** 4180
Gulliksen H, **1:** 42 (33); **2:** 792 (786); **5:** 3061 (3057); **7:** 3706 (3700, 3702); **8:** 4930 (4927); **9:** 5158 (5153)
Gullo D F, **2:** 973 (971), 984 (983); **11:** 6456 (6454)
Gulpen E, **10:** 5853
Guluma E L, **6:** 3394
Gumbert E B, **10:** 5965
Gump P V, **9:** 5294 (5293); **10:** 6207 (6205)
Gumperz J J, **2:** 802 (798); **6:** 3213 (3210), 3227 (3226), 3238 (3236, 3237)
Gunawardena C, **4:** 2423 (2419, 2420, 2421, 2422); **10:** 5721
Gunawardena G B, **10:** 5721
Gundem B B, **3:** 1307 (1304, 1307), 1308 (1304, 1305, 1307)
Gunderson M, **4:** 2446
Gunew S, **4:** 1984 (1983)
Günler C, **7:** 3925
Gunnar M R, **9:** 5394, 5528
Gunnarsson L, **3:** 1647 (1645); **5:** 2806 (2804)
Gunnerson L, **2:** 688 (686)
Gunstone R F, **6:** 3205; **8:** 4479 (4477); **9:** 5338 (5337); **10:** 5790 (5785)
Gunter B, **5:** 2897 (2895)
Gunther P, **6:** 3235

Guntrip H, **8:** (4813)
Gunz H, **9:** 5475 (5475)
Guo G, **3:** 1642 (1641)
Guo Hanye, **3:** 1301 (1293)
Guo S, **8:** 4473 (4469, 4471), 4474 (4470, 4471, 4472)
Gupta A F, **9:** 5302 (5300, 5301)
Gupta H, **8:** 4812 (4805)
Gupta H C, **1:** 100 (94)
Guralnick M J, **3:** 1642; **8:** 4375 (4373); **9:** 5567 (5564, 5565)
Gurgsdies E, **10:** 5873
Gurin A, **10:** 5948
Gurowitz W D, **10:** 5804 (5798, 5801, 5802, 5803)
Gurriaran J, **8:** 4495 (4494)
Gurtner J L, **2:** 1006 (1002, 1003, 1004); **7:** 3744
Gurugé A, **1:** 581 (581)
Gurwitsch A, **8:** 4429 (4427)
Gusene E, **6:** 3416
Guskey T R, **3:** 1635 (1632); **5:** 2779 (2777); **6:** 3631 (3625, 3627, 3628, 3630); **10:** 5973
Guskin S L, **6:** 3297 (3293, 3294)
Gustad J W, **1:** 358 (355)
Gustafson D H, **3:** 1443 (1443)
Gustafson K, **5:** 2861 (2858, 2859, 2860, 2861); **8:** 4758; **10:** 5625 (5625)
Gustafson K L, **3:** 1315 (1313)
Gustafson S, **2:** 1055 (1053, 1054)
Gustafsson C, **4:** 2377 (2376)
Gustafsson I, **3:** 1690 (1685); **4:** 2369 (2366)
Gustafsson J-E, **4:** (2240); **5:** 2768 (2760, 2761), 2769 (2761); **7:** 3879 (3875, 3878); **10:** 6159 (6158); **11:** 6492 (6489)
Gustafsson S, **2:** 692 (690); **8:** 4666 (4663, 4664)
Gustavsen B, **6:** 3602 (3601); **11:** 6647 (6642)
Gustman A L, **11:** 6633 (6628)
Gutek G L, **8:** 4670 (4667, 4669)
Guterman E, **2:** 888 (885); **11:** 6457 (6454)
Guthke J, **6:** 3315 (3313); **10:** 5772 (5769)
Guthrie G, **9:** 5313
Guthrie G P, **4:** 2052
Guthrie J, **7:** 3774; **9:** 5379 (5374); **10:** 5831
Guthrie J T, **6:** 3334 (3331, 3333); **7:** 3711 (3710), 3768; **10:** 6177, 6178
Guthrie J W, **5:** 2500 (2497, 2498); **6:** 3608; **9:** 5216 (5212), 5307 (5306); **10:** 6012 (6009)
Guthrie P G, **1:** 534 (533)
Gutierez Lopez F, **8:** 4473 (4472)
Gutierrez R, **1:** 230 (229); **7:** 4157 (4157)
Gutierrez-Clellen V, **6:** 3227 (3226)
Gutkin J, **8:** 4947 (4946)
Gutkin T B, **2:** 998, 1189; **8:** 4661 (4659), 4662
Gutknecht D B, **4:** 2266
Gutman A, **8:** 4575 (4572)
Gutmann A, **3:** 1328 (1327); **4:** 2004; **8:** 4594 (4593)
Guttenplan S, **9:** 5030
Guttentag M, **3:** 1431; **4:** 2037, 2119; **11:** 6424
Guttman L, **1:** 389 (384), 390 (382, 384, 385); **3:** 1514 (1510); **4:** 2218 (2213, 2214, 2217, 2218), 2219; **5:** 2680 (2678, 2680); **7:** 3706 (3703), 3879 (3876, 3878), 4315 (4308, 4314); **9:** 5503 (5497, 5498, 5500, 5503); **11:** 6388 (6387)
Guy R, **9:** 5252 (5248)
Guyton E, **10:** 5812, 6004 (6001)
Guzdial M, **2:** 973 (972)
Guzzetti B J, **8:** 4652 (4651)
Gwalla-Ogisi N, **5:** 2971 (2969)
Gwartney J D, **6:** 3425 (3425)
Gwei S N, **2:** 617
Gyampong A O, **3:** 1386 (1383)
Gyimah-Brempong K, **3:** 1386 (1383)

Ha P, **3:** 1534 (1531)
Haaften A W van, **8:** 4461
Haan B J, **5:** 2709 (2706)
Haan N S, **7:** 3920 (3918)
Haas C, **11:** 6780 (6778)
Haas N S, **6:** 3474; **11:** 6339 (6338)
Haavelsrod M, **3:** 1733
Habberman M, **10:** 5995
Haber L, **3:** 1534 (1530)
Haber R, **11:** 6360 (6356)
Haber R N, **7:** 3774 (3774)
Haberman M, **8:** 4947; **10:** 5948, 5965, 5994, 5995 (5992), 6004; **11:** 6558 (6554)
Haberman S J, **6:** 3508 (3500, 3502, 3507)
Habermas J, **1:** 47 (45), 48 (43, 45), 67 (62, 63), (164); **2:** (926), (929), (930), 1204 (1199, 1200, 1201, 1202, 1203); **3:** (1347), 1774 (1772, 1773); **4:** 2033 (2030), 2291 (2289); **5:** 2585 (2585), 2586; **6:** 3368 (3367), 3373 (3370); **7:** 3924 (3920, 3921, 3922, 3924), 3925 (3922), (4331); **8:** 4455 (4453, 4454), 4461 (4459), 4642 (4641); **9:** 5030 (5022, 5023), (5052), (5054), 5055, 5523; **10:** 5596 (5594), (5984), 6219; **11:** 6579 (6579)
Habermas L, **2:** (780)
Habicht J-P, **3:** 1252 (1248); **8:** 4474 (4472)
Hablé R, **5:** 2457 (2455)
Habte A, **4:** 1840 (1838); **8:** 4594 (4591)
Haby R, **2:** 1064
Hack W G, **1:** 77; **9:** 5185 (5182, 5183)
Hacker B J, **5:** 2813 (2810)
Hacker W J, **9:** 5489 (5488)
Hackett R, **1:** 265 (262)
Haddad W D, **3:** 1655 (1649, 1654), 1789 (1788); **6:** 3550 (3546); **7:** 4141 (4140); **8:** 4526 (4525); **9:** 5076 (5072); **11:** 6298 (6293)
Hadden J K, **9:** 5008 (5003)
Haddon A C, **4:** (2047)
Hade D D, **2:** 977 (974)
Hadley M, **2:** 1012 (1009); **7:** 4100 (4096); **11:** 6287 (6284, 6285, 6286, 6287)
Haebara T, **11:** 6355 (6353)
Haeckel E H P A, **10:** (5707)
Haefele D, **6:** 3202 (3198, 3199)
Haenel E, **10:** 5754 (5751)
Haenen J P P, **6:** 3292
Haenszel W, **5:** 3050 (3046)
Haertel E, **3:** 1514 (1511)
Haertel E D, **8:** 4830, 4831
Haertel E H, **2:** 811 (809); **8:** 4844, 4845 (4841); **9:** 5373 (5368); **10:** 5775 (5772, 5773), 6020 (6017)
Haertel G D, **2:** 811 (809); **3:** 1483 (1475); **4:** 1848 (1841), 2108, 2109; **5:** 2879 (2875, 2879), 2910, 2931 (2926); **7:** 3788 (3787); **8:** 4403 (4401), 4404 (4402), 4702 (4699); **9:** 5043 (5040); **10:** 5750 (5747), 5775 (5772, 5773), 5817 (5816)
Hafner A, **2:** 711 (709); **10:** 5846
Haft H, **3:** 1278 (1273, 1274), 1308 (1302, 1304, 1305, 1306, 1307), 1355 (1348, 1349); **9:** 5497
Hagan N, **7:** 4185
Hagan R, **4:** 2452 (2450)
Hagen B, **7:** 3807 (3805)
Hagen E, **3:** 1672; **7:** 4196 (4195)
Hagen E P, **8:** 4930 (4924); **9:** 4995 (4995)
Hagen J W, **1:** 89; **7:** 3763, 3768
Hagenaars J A, **6:** 3508 (3506); **10:** 5735 (5734)
Hagestad G O, **6:** 3428 (3426, 3427)
Haggard E A, **7:** 4015 (4009); **9:** 5142 (5139)
Hagger H, **10:** 6088 (6088)
Haggis S, **9:** 5327 (5325)
Hägglund S, **6:** 3602 (3600)
Hagman J D, **5:** 2856; **11:** 6457
Hagtvet K A, **4:** 2244 (2244); **10:** 5738
Hahn A, **2:** 711 (710)
Hahn C H, **8:** 4845 (4844)
Hahn H, **2:** 982 (981)
Hahn K, **5:** (2957); **8:** (4633)
Hahn M E, **11:** 6492
Hahnel R, **3:** 1819 (1818)
Haidara B, **1:** 215 (211, 212)
Haider G, **3:** 1355 (1353); **9:** 5216 (5215)
Haig-Brown C, **4:** 1852 (1849)
Haight W, **5:** 2596
Hailey J, **4:** 1991 (1988)
Haiman F S, **5:** 2532 (2531)
Haith M M, **5:** 2802
Hajjar H, **8:** 4698 (4696, 4697); **10:** 5834 (5832)
Hajzler D J, **1:** 494 (491)
Hake B J, **1:** 127 (121, 124, 125)
Haken H, **7:** 3950 (3947)
Haket L, **8:** 4688; **11:** 6451 (6450), 6452 (6450)
Hakim C, **9:** 5373
Hakkarainen P, **6:** 3292
Hakstian A R, **7:** 4000 (3999)
Hakuta K, **1:** 534, 537 (536); **2:** 842; **4:** 2199; **5:** 2656
Haladyna T J, **5:** 3043 (3036), 3066 (3065); **9:** 5324 (5321)
Haladyna T M, **6:** 3474; **7:** 4197; **11:** 6339 (6338)

Halász G, **5:** 2706 (2699, 2703)
Halasz G, **11:** 6647 (6647), 6648 (6641, 6647)
Halász L, **8:** 4429 (4426)
Haldane E S, **3:** 1464 (1462, 1463)
Haldane-Lutterodt C, **8:** 4514 (4511)
Hale D, **10:** 5681 (5679)
Hale G, **6:** 3625
Haley-Oliphant A, **10:** 6035 (6033)
Halisch F, **7:** 3942 (3937)
Hall A R, **3:** 1464 (1462)
Hall B, **7:** 4336 (4330, 4331); **8:** 4337
Hall B L, **5:** 2937 (2935, 2936), 2951 (2946), 2961 (2958)
Hall D, **10:** 5680
Hall D E, **11:** 6712 (6711)
Hall E, **1:** 162 (160); **4:** 2412 (2409)
Hall E T, **4:** 1852 (1850); **7:** 3970 (3964), 4175; **8:** 4526 (4521)
Hall G, **8:** 4715 (4708, 4709); **9:** 5246 (5244); **10:** 5957 (5955)
Hall G E, **1:** 73 (70, 72); **3:** 1271 (1268)
Hall G S, **3:** 1301 (1297), (1723), 1796 (1793, 1794, 1795); **4:** (1841), (1843), (1864), (1866), (1868); **5:** (2877); **11:** (6795)
Hall J, **2:** 1011 (1010); **7:** 3721 (3717), 3894 (3891, 3893, 3894)
Hall J W, **11:** 6551
Hall K A, **2:** 1170 (1167)
Hall N, **6:** 3459 (3456)
Hall R H, **9:** 5181 (5176, 5177)
Hall R P, **11:** 6608 (6604)
Hall R V, **8:** 4375 (4372, 4373, 4374), 4376 (4374); **9:** 4977 (4974); **11:** 6484 (6482)
Hall S, **2:** 1194; **4:** 1984; **8:** (4668); **9:** 5060 (5057); **10:** (5705); **11:** 6803 (6801)
Hall V, **1:** 73 (69), 83 (80); **10:** 6047
Hall V C, **10:** 6193 (6191)
Hall W C, **10:** 6072 (6071)
Hall W S, **10:** 5621
Hallack J, **5:** 2961 (2958)
Hallahan D P, **5:** 2906 (2905); **6:** 3297 (3295); **10:** 5662 (5659, 5661)
Hallak J, **2:** 1126 (1122), 1127 (1124); **3:** 1680 (1679), 1685 (1681, 1684), 1789 (1788), 1830 (1829); **4:** 2229 (2226, 2228); **7:** 4141 (4138); **8:** 4491; **9:** 5076, 5168 (5159, 5164, 5165, 5167), 5259; **11:** 6530
Hallam R N, **9:** 5577 (5576)
Hallden O, **9:** 5562 (5560)
Halle M, **10:** 5696 (5695)
Hallenbeck W C, **1:** 120, 127; **7:** 4185, 4329; **11:** 6438
Haller A O, **1:** 358 (357); **10:** 5606 (5600)
Haller E J, **1:** 11 (10); **2:** 825 (822); **4:** 2033 (2032); **9:** 5066 (5064, 5065), 5264 (5261)
Haller O, **9:** 5176 (5172)
Halliday M, **6:** 3638 (3636)
Halliday M A K, **2:** 1079 (1078); **3:** 1402 (1399); **6:** 3443 (3441)
Hallinan M T, **1:** 11 (7), 12 (9); **2:** 825 (822), 825 (822, 824); **3:** 1257; **5:** 2769 (2766); **8:** 4895 (4892, 4895); **9:** 5175 (5173, 5174, 5175), 5176 (5175), 5379, 5560 (5554); **10:** 5617 (5615, 5617), 5759, 5924
Hallinger P, **1:** 72 (69, 70, 71, 72), 73 (69, 72), 77; **4:** 1934 (1932); **9:** 5264 (5261, 5263), 5308 (5307)
Halliwell M D, **5:** 2910 (2908)
Halls W D, **2:** 922 (918), 933, 958, 1063 (1057); **4:** 2331; **5:** 2978 (2977); **8:** 4608 (4605); **9:** 5252 (5248); **11:** 6523
Halmos P, **10:** 6096
Halner A, **5:** 2515 (2513)
Halperin M, **7:** 3858 (3857)
Halpern D F, **8:** 4727 (4723)
Halpern R, **3:** 1628 (1625)
Halpern S A, **11:** 6445 (6439)
Halpin A W, **1:** 60 (53); **3:** 1482 (1477), 1774 (1769, 1770); **4:** 2166 (2160); **6:** 3284 (3279, 3280)
Halsey A H, **2:** 933 (926), 1074; **4:** 2257 (2251, 2252), 2278; **6:** 3215, (3307), 3312 (3307); **7:** 3721; **8:** 4562 (4560), 4831; **9:** 5553 (5551); **10:** 5606, 5607 (5598, 5599, 5600), 6227
Halstead D, **3:** 1589
Halstedt E, **8:** 4359
Halverson C F, **4:** 2449 (2447); **5:** 2665 (2663); **11:** 6310 (6310)
Halverson P, **3:** 1367 (1360)
Halvorsen T, **11:** 6699
Ham M, **6:** 3661 (3659)
Ham S H, **4:** 1995 (1992)
Hamadache A, **1:** 176, 221; **4:** 2369
Hamaker C, **6:** 3661 (3659); **8:** 4881 (4877); **10:** 6192 (6191)
Hamann J G, **8:** (4430)
Hamann M S, **2:** 851 (849)
Hamayan E V, **6:** 3227, 3231, 3232
Hamayer U, **9:** 5246 (5241, 5245)
Hambey D, **5:** 2813 (2811)
Hambleton R K, **1:** 42 (36), 52 (50); **2:** 998 (994), 1189 (1185, 1188, 1189); **3:** 1421 (1418); **5:** 3043 (3037, 3039, 3041), 3055; **6:** 3253 (3248, 3250); **7:** 4000 (3998, 3999), 4056 (4055, 4056); **10:** 5725 (5722, 5723, 5724, 5725); **11:** 6333 (6329, 6332), 6334
Hambleton R L, **11:** 6355
Hamblin A C, **3:** 1491
Hamblin C L, **2:** 1207 (1204)
Hamer A W, **4:** 1980 (1976, 1978)
Hamerle A, **10:** 5735 (5734)
Hamermesh D S, **8:** 4839
Hamermesh S, **3:** 1449 (1445, 1446)
Hamers J F, **1:** 537
Hamers J H M, **6:** 3315 (3313, 3314, 3315)
Hameyer U, **3:** 1278 (1273, 1274, 1278), 1308, 1343, 1355 (1348, 1349, 1350), 1553 (1550); **5:** 2852 (2850); **6:** 3602 (3598, 3601); **8:** 4865; **9:** 5246 (5241, 5243), 5497
Hamidi A S, **9:** 5151 (5147, 5150)
Hamill P V V, **8:** 4474 (4470)
Hamilton D, **2:** 645, 816 (812); **3:** 1287 (1285); **4:** 2037, 2073 (2072), (2103), 2377
Hamilton D L, **9:** 5518
Hamilton E, **9:** 4981
Hamilton M, **1:** 94; **6:** 3458 (3455, 3458); **7:** 4171; **11:** 6551 (6548)
Hamilton M E, **7:** 3711
Hamilton S F, **1:** 310 (309); **2:** 711 (710), 825 (821); **3:** 1739 (1738); **9:** 5264 (5261)
Hamilton V, **1:** 376
Hamilton-Pennell C, **6:** 3399 (3394)
Hamlett C L, **3:** 1359 (1358); **7:** 3807 (3805)
Hamm C, **7:** 3925
Hammer B, **3:** (1724)
Hammer M, **7:** 4316; **10:** 5759
Hammersley J M, **9:** 5471 (5468)
Hammersley M, **2:** 1073 (1070), 1074; **4:** 2052 (2048); **7:** 4319 (4316); **9:** 5312 (5310, 5311), 5313 (5311), 5411; **10:** 6085, 6127; **11:** 6465 (6463)
Hammill D D, **2:** 718 (715); **7:** 4081 (4077)
Hammink K, **1:** 103 (100, 101); **3:** 1262 (1261)
Hammitte D J, **8:** 4661 (4661)
Hammod R, **1:** 450
Hammond D, **6:** 3349 (3346)
Hammond K M, **2:** 820 (817, 818, 820); **10:** 6035 (6033), 6122 (6119)
Hammond M, **1:** 168 (163)
Hammond N, **5:** 2709 (2707)
Hammond R, **10:** 5957 (5954)
Hampel F R, **9:** 5082 (5078, 5079)
Hampton R, **5:** 2575 (2573)
Hamreus D, **5:** 2861 (2858)
Han H S, **1:** 495; **6:** 3228 (3226); **10:** 6244 (6243)
Han W S, **1:** 358 (355)
Hanaway J, **5:** 2798
Hancock G, **11:** 6488
Hand D J, **2:** 831 (829)
Handay G, **1:** 48 (45)
Handel G, **8:** 4581
Handley H M, **7:** 4293 (4291, 4292)
Handscombe D C, **9:** 5471 (5468)
Handy C, **9:** 5168 (5161)
Hanely P E, **10:** 5925 (5923)
Haney C A, **10:** 5924 (5922, 5923)
Haney R E, **9:** 5324 (5320)
Haney W, **11:** 6339 (6334)
Hanke U, **10:** 5713
Hanley T V, **1:** 490 (487); **7:** 3807 (3806)
Hanmer J, **9:** 5441 (5437, 5440)
Hanna G, **4:** 2435 (2432, 2434); **6:** 3339 (3337)
Hanna G E, **11:** 6445 (6444)
Hanna G S, **9:** 5389 (5387); **10:** 6234 (6233)
Hanna J, **4:** 2046 (2044)
Hanna J L, **8:** 4388 (4384); **9:** 5510 (5508, 5509)
Hanna P, **7:** 3936 (3933); **9:** (5573)
Hanna P R, **10:** 5817 (5814)
Hanna W J, **9:** 5510 (5509)
Hannafin M J, **2:** 1170
Hannan A, **3:** 1271 (1271)
Hannan D F, **5:** 3020

Hannan M T, **2:** 957 (951)
Hannaway J, **2:** 824; **3:** 1486; **7:** 3840; **8:** 4568 (4564, 4565), 4873; **9:** 5065
Hannay L, **10:** 6092 (6090)
Hannifin M J, **5:** 2862; **7:** 3743 (3739, 3743)
Hanninen G, **10:** 6026 (6025)
Hannum W H, **8:** 4758; **10:** 5913 (5910, 5912)
Hanoch G, **8:** 4918 (4914)
Hans N, **1:** (331); **2:** (923), 957 (951)
Hansell S, **1:** 12 (7); **8:** 4715 (4711), 4796 (4794)
Hanselmann H, **1:** 277 (275)
Hansen A J, **10:** 5948 (5944)
Hansen B K, **7:** 4179 (4179)
Hansen C, **8:** 4758; **11:** 6678 (6672, 6673, 6677)
Hansen D A, **10:** 5607 (5598)
Hansen D J, **1:** 19 (18)
Hansen D N, **1:** 52 (49)
Hansen E, **6:** 3224 (3219); **11:** 6603 (6602)
Hansen H, **2:** 1208
Hansen I V, **8:** 4831
Hansen J, **3:** 1449 (1448); **10:** 5767 (5766); **11:** 6461 (6460)
Hansen J F, **1:** 295 (287)
Hansen M, **8:** 4935 (4931, 4933)
Hansen M H, **5:** 3061 (3055); **9:** 5142 (5136, 5140)
Hansen R, **7:** 4000 (3999)
Hansen W L, **3:** 1449 (1447); **11:** 6298
Hansen-Strain L, **1:** 322 (318)
Hansford K, **7:** 4132 (4125)
Hansome M, **11:** 6775
Hanson, **8:** (4632)
Hanson B A, **11:** 6355 (6352)
Hanson D, **10:** 6126 (6124)
Hanson D J, **3:** 1610 (1608)
Hanson E M, **1:** 594 (592); **3:** 1411 (1407), 1830 (1827); **4:** 2166 (2163); **5:** 2512 (2510, 2511); **6:** 3596 (3593); **8:** 4601 (4595); **9:** 5168 (5167); **10:** 6096 (6095)
Hanson G R, **10:** 5804 (5798, 5799), 5805
Hanson J R, **11:** 6625 (6623)
Hanson M J, **2:** 914 (913); **5:** 2813 (2806, 2807); **11:** 6599
Hanson M K, **9:** 5307 (5306)
Hanson N R, **6:** 3219 (3218); **9:** 5050
Hanson S L, **5:** 2491 (2487)
Hansot E, **5:** 2618 (2614); **9:** 5445; **11:** 6765 (6761, 6763)
Hanushek A E, **6:** 3106 (3101); **9:** 5240 (5235)
Hanushek E A, **1:** 594 (589); **2:** 775 (771, 772, 775), 1094 (1085), 1127 (1121), 1136 (1134); **3:** 1386 (1383), 1425, 1761 (1756, 1757, 1759, 1761), 1762 (1761), 1784 (1779, 1780, 1782, 1783), 1820 (1815); **4:** 2156 (2153); **5:** 2508 (2507), 2891 (2889); **6:** 3550 (3545); **7:** 3821 (3816, 3820); **8:** 4568 (4563), 4873 (4865, 4868, 4869), 4902 (4897, 4898); **10:** 5750 (5749), 5846 (5844), 5954 (5949), 6073 (6069); **11:** 6298 (6294)
Hany E A, **5:** 2731 (2729), 2732 (2726)
Haq K, **11:** 6415
Haq M N, **7:** 4136 (4133)
Haq S, **7:** 4270
Haran H H, **7:** 3706 (3705)
Harary F, **9:** 5559 (5556), 5560 (5555)
Harasim L M, **2:** 982 (978, 979, 980, 981); **3:** 1579 (1576)
Harber C, **2:** 770; **7:** 3977 (3974, 3977)
Harber C R, **3:** 1655 (1652)
Harberger A C, **5:** 2647 (2644)
Harbin G L, **5:** 2813 (2809)
Harbison C, **11:** 6277 (6272)
Harbison F H, **3:** 1820 (1811, 1812); **5:** 2978 (2977)
Harbison R, **8:** 4873 (4868, 4869)
Harbison R W, **3:** 1761 (1757), 1784 (1783); **10:** 5846 (5844)
Harby M H, **11:** 6761
Hardick E, **10:** 5690 (5687, 5688, 5689, 5690), 5691
Hardie C D, **8:** 4455 (4450, 4454)
Harding A, **4:** 2357 (2355)
Harding S, **4:** 2302 (2297, 2299, 2300); **10:** 6099 (6098)
Hardman M L, **11:** 6461 (6457, 6459, 6460)
Hardy C, **8:** 4602
Hare R H, **7:** (3920)
Hare R M, **4:** 2004 (2003)
Hare V C, **8:** 4823 (4821); **10:** 5745 (5740, 5741), 6192 (6188)
Hare W, **8:** 4447
Harel I, **2:** 973 (971, 972), 1006; **6:** 3302 (3300), 3512 (3511)
Harel K, **10:** 6112 (6109)
Harel S, **3:** 1624 (1621)
Harf J, **3:** 1501 (1497)
Hargis C H, **3:** 1607 (1604)
Hargreaves A, **3:** 1271 (1267); **5:** 2847 (2843); **6:** 3602 (3598, 3602); **7:** 3826 (3823); **9:** 5060 (5057, 5059), 5273 (5269), 5411 (5408); **10:** 5614, 5934, 5935 (5932), 6085, 6126 (6125), 6214 (6208, 6212, 6213)
Hargreaves D, **4:** 1934 (1930, 1932, 1933); **7:** 3889 (3886); **10:** 6214 (6209); **11:** 6803 (6800)
Hargreaves D H, **1:** 11 (7, 8); **2:** 645 (642), 820 (817, 818, 819), 918, 1073 (1070); **3:** 1507 (1506); **4:** 2166 (2159); **5:** 2852 (2850); **6:** 3602 (3597, 3600); **10:** 5617 (5615), 6085 (6084)
Hargreaves M, **4:** 2345 (2344)
Hari M, **5:** 2813 (2810)
Haring K A, **5:** 2906 (2905)
Haring N, **5:** 2907
Haring N G, **3:** 1359 (1356); **5:** 2906 (2905)
Haring T G, **9:** 4977 (4975), 5567 (5563)
Harker J O, **2:** 820 (819); **10:** 6197
Harker R K, **4:** 2272; **9:** 5021
Harlan S L, **4:** 2286 (2281, 2282, 2283)
Harlen W, **2:** 1220 (1217); **3:** 1494 (1493); **9:** 5334 (5329, 5332, 5333), 5335 (5330)
Harley B, **4:** 2346 (2344)
Harlow J G, **1:** 77 (76)
Harman D, **1:** 103; **6:** 3446 (3445); **7:** 4148 (4147)
Harman G S, **6:** 3496 (3494); **7:** 3840 (3834, 3837, 3839); **9:** 5168 (5162), 5281
Harman H H, **2:** 1117 (1109); **4:** 2240 (2239); **7:** 3706 (3705), 3879 (3874)
Harman K, **10:** 5606 (5601)
Harmon G, **5:** 2508 (2504)
Harmon L W, **4:** 2183 (2181); **11:** 6320 (6318)
Harmon R, **3:** 1513, 1514
Harmon R J, **5:** 2680
Harms T, **5:** 2806 (2805); **11:** 6397 (6396)
Harnack R K, **5:** 2532 (2530)
Harney K, **1:** 317
Harnisch D L, **4:** 2140 (2137); **7:** 4000 (4000)
Harnischfeger A, **1:** 23, 377 (376); **4:** 1848 (1843); **7:** 3872 (3867), 3886 (3883)
Harnish D, **5:** 3050 (3049)
Harnishfeger K K, **2:** 705 (704)
Härnqvist K, **11:** 6445 (6438)
Haroutunian-Gordon S, **2:** 807 (804); **8:** 4536 (4534)
Harper A E, **6:** 3124 (3121, 3123)
Harper F, **1:** 362 (361)
Harper G F, **8:** 4376 (4373, 4374), 4881 (4880)
Harper M, **4:** 1991 (1986, 1989, 1990)
Harper W, **8:** (4809)
Harré H R, **4:** (2297)
Harré R, **2:** 1026 (1022)
Harrell F E, **4:** 2156 (2156); **9:** 5471 (5470)
Harries-Jenkins G, **1:** 93
Harrigan P J, **5:** 2607
Harrington C, **1:** 295 (290)
Harrington P, **4:** 2388 (2384)
Harris C, **10:** 6208
Harris C R, **9:** 5532 (5530)
Harris C W, **2:** 677, 678; **5:** 2773 (2770); **10:** 5704
Harris D, **1:** 409 (407); **3:** 1543 (1538, 1539, 1543), 1563 (1557), 1579 (1577), 1733; **4:** 2186 (2184)
Harris F C, **9:** 5475 (5473)
Harris I B, **10:** 6117 (6116)
Harris J, **1:** 374 (373); **3:** 1685 (1682); **7:** 4307
Harris J A, **5:** 2684 (2682)
Harris J C, **6:** 3235 (3233)
Harris J R, **3:** 1685 (1682)
Harris K, **2:** 737 (734); **3:** 1328 (1326, 1327); **8:** 4455 (4455); **10:** 5831, 6139 (6134)
Harris K C, **10:** 5943 (5942)
Harris K R, **2:** 867 (861, 863); **6:** 3334 (3331, 3333); **7:** 3768; **10:** 6177, 6178
Harris L J, **11:** 6390 (6389)
Harris M, **6:** 3634
Harris N D C, **9:** 5338 (5336)
Harris P, **8:** 4956 (4952); **9:** 5512 (5512); **11:** 6437 (6433)

Harris P O L, **9:** 5512
Harris R, **6:** 3446 (3444); **7:** 3894 (3891, 3893)
Harris R J, **2:** 1117 (1116); **4:** 2339; **11:** 6591 (6591)
Harris S, **7:** 4255 (4254)
Harris T L, **10:** 5704 (5698)
Harris T O, **3:** 1520 (1519)
Harris W J A, **8:** 4608
Harris W M Jr, **6:** 3416 (3413, 3415)
Harris W T, **3:** (1296), (1297)
Harris W V, **6:** 3446 (3444)
Harrison B, **5:** 2744; **7:** 4201 (4197)
Harrison C, **4:** 2357 (2354)
Harrison E F, **3:** 1425
Harrison F I, **5:** 2714 (2710)
Harrison J, **7:** 4215 (4212, 4213, 4214)
Harrison J E, **5:** (2614)
Harrison M, **3:** 1271 (1268)
Harrop J W, **9:** 5489 (5488), 5490 (5488)
Harrop L, **2:** 816 (813)
Harry B, **5:** 2813 (2806, 2807, 2809)
Harry K, **1:** 564; **3:** 1563; **4:** 2266; **7:** 4220, 4248 (4247)
Harry T, **11:** 6461 (6459)
Harste J C, **4:** 1962 (1958, 1960); **10:** 5795 (5793)
Hart A W, **8:** 4408 (4408)
Hart C H, **10:** 5617 (5617)
Hart C W M, **2:** 1213 (1209)
Hart D, **9:** 5394 (5391)
Hart D J, **4:** 2011 (2010)
Hart D K, **4:** 2033 (2032)
Hart K, **6:** 3685 (3675, 3677)
Hart L, **11:** 6731 (6729)
Hart L E, **6:** 3642 (3639, 3640)
Hart M M S, **3:** 1529 (1526)
Hart M U, **10:** 5596 (5594)
Hart P, **4:** 1995 (1994)
Hart R, **2:** 982 (978)
Hart S N, **1:** 19; **2:** 711 (706, 710)
Hart W O, **6:** 3276 (3273, 3275)
Harter N, **10:** 6026 (6021)
Harter S, **1:** 31 (30), 88 (87); **9:** 5394 (5391)
Hartigan J A, **2:** 831 (826); **11:** 6678 (6677)
Hartley D, **4:** 2166 (2159)
Hartley E R, **5:** 2672
Hartley H J, **1:** 60 (54)
Hartley H O, **7:** 3738 (3731)
Hartley J, **2:** 969 (966); **8:** 4694, 4774 (4771), 4775
Hartley W, **2:** 1099 (1098)
Hartman D, **6:** 3119
Hartman E E, **9:** 5008 (4997)
Hartman J, **8:** 4474 (4470)
Hartman J A, **1:** 230 (228, 229)
Hartman M, **3:** 1315 (1309)
Hartman R W, **10:** 5767 (5766)
Hartman W T, **2:** 1135 (1132); **9:** 5065 (5061), 5185 (5182, 5183, 5185)
Hartmann H, **2:** 693; **4:** 2291 (2289); **6:** 3189 (3188); **8:** (4813)
Hartmann H I, **4:** 2286 (2281, 2282), 2432 (2428), 2445 (2442)
Hartmann J, **11:** 6808
Hartnett A, **11:** 6704
Hartog J, **7:** 4324 (4323); **9:** 5355 (5352, 5354); **11:** 6260 (6257)
Hartog P, **7:** (3932)
Hartree A, **10:** 6058 (6054)
Hartshorne H, **1:** 380 (379)
Hartsock N, **9:** 5441 (5438, 5439, 5440)
Hartup W H, **5:** 2665
Hartup W W, **1:** 234 (230); **2:** 705 (702); **4:** 2449 (2448); **8:** 4368 (4365, 4367), 4372 (4369), 4542 (4541); **9:** 5507, 5548, 5567 (5563, 5564)
Hartweck A, **8:** 4935 (4933)
Hartwell P, **10:** 5704 (5698, 5699, 5702)
Hartzler J S, **6:** 3634
Harvey B, **6:** 3512
Harvey F A, **7:** 4104 (4102)
Harvey J, **7:** 4099
Harvey J H, **11:** 6360
Harvey J T, **5:** 2515 (2513)
Harvighurst R J, **9:** 5572 (5567, 5569)
Harwood K, **2:** 737 (735)
Hasan R, **2:** 1079 (1078); **4:** 1984 (1982)
Hasazi S B, **11:** 6461 (6457, 6459)
Hashimoto M, **5:** 2798 (2792), 2942 (2940); **10:** 5919 (5915)
Hashmi A, **5:** 2740 (2739)
Hashweh M Z, **10:** 6121 (6118)
Hasibuan S, **8:** 4531 (4527)
Haskell J F, **5:** 2870
Haskell T, **11:** 6723
Haskins R, **5:** 2672, 2673, 2806 (2804); **6:** 3463; **9:** 5206; **11:** 6563
Hasrat B J, **1:** 531
Hassall D, **1:** 27
Hassard J, **9:** 5345 (5344)
Hasselbring T S, **7:** 3807 (3803, 3804)
Hassell D, **2:** 988 (986)
Haste H, **5:** 2536 (2533); **6:** 3312 (3307)
Hasting S C, **3:** 1619
Hastings J F, **11:** 6328 (6321)
Hastings J T, **1:** 41 (32); **2:** 957 (954); **4:** 2089 (2080); **6:** 3484; **8:** 4648, 4774 (4770); **9:** 5338; **10:** 5790 (5784)
Hastings N, **7:** 3942
Hastings T J, **1:** 370 (364); **11:** 6348 (6342)
Hatano G, **2:** 842 (839); **4:** 2199 (2194, 2196); **6:** 3302 (3298); **7:** 3768 (3764)
Hatch E M, **4:** 2339 (2337)
Hatch J A, **2:** 1073 (1071)
Hatcher R, **10:** 5827 (5825)
Hatfield L L, **7:** 4100 (4098); **8:** 4648
Hathaway W E, **2:** 1175 (1173); **4:** 2388 (2382)
Hativa N, **2:** 1001 (1001); **11:** 6287 (6285, 6286, 6287)
Hatt H, **3:** 1343
Hatt P K, **7:** 3771
Hatta M, **10:** (5779)
Hattie J, **10:** 6015 (6013)
Hattie J A, **8:** 4403 (4401, 4402), 4864 (4862, 4863); **9:** 5043 (5041)
Hau K, **1:** 31 (30)
Haub C, **3:** 1452 (1450)
Haubrich H, **5:** 2469 (2466, 2468, 2469), 2470
Hauer J, **5:** 2596
Hauert C A, **5:** 2680
Haug F, **5:** 2457 (2455)
Haug M R, **7:** 3721 (3716)
Hauge T, **9:** 5246 (5245)
Hause J, **4:** 2279 (2275)
Hausen K, **11:** 6747 (6745)
Hauser P, **11:** 6575 (6569)
Hauser R M, **1:** 358 (356, 357); **3:** 1642 (1638); **4:** 2257 (2252, 2254), 2279 (2277); **6:** 3144 (3138); **7:** 3722, 3864 (3863, 3864), 3872; **8:** 4351 (4343, 4345), 4359 (4355); **9:** 5175 (5172), 5553 (5549, 5551, 5552, 5553); **10:** 5606, 5607 (5600), 5735 (5734)
Hauser T S, **10:** 5606
Hauser-Cram P, **3:** 1643 (1640); **5:** 2813 (2812)
Hauspie R, **8:** 4473, 4474
Haussler P, **3:** 1257 (1253)
Hautecoeur, **3:** 1262
Haüy V, **10:** (5659)
Havelock E A, **6:** 3446 (3443), (3447)
Havelock R G, **3:** 1553 (1550)
Haveman R H, **2:** 1056, 1131 (1128); **3:** 1820 (1815); **4:** 2212 (2210)
Havemann J, **5:** 2512 (2509)
Havertape J, **2:** 719
Havighurst R J, **3:** 1315 (1311), 1486 (1484); **4:** 1872 (1864); **6:** 3428 (3427), 3435 (3431); **7:** 4329 (4326); **8:** 4719 (4716); **9:** 5528 (5525); **10:** 5613 (5610), (5935), 6053 (6052), 6227 (6226); **11:** 6395 (6391), 6798 (6794)
Havnevik K J, **4:** 1840 (1838)
Hawes H, **2:** 733 (731); **10:** 5973 (5971)
Hawes H R, **6:** 3385
Hawk D, **10:** 5957 (5955)
Hawke G, **10:** 6026 (6023)
Hawke S, **9:** 5578 (5574)
Hawkesworth M, **4:** 2302 (2300)
Hawking S W, **9:** 5334 (5330)
Hawkins A, **10:** 6026 (6023, 6024)
Hawkins A J, **4:** 2266 (2265)
Hawkins A M, **11:** 6638 (6636)
Hawkins E M, **8:** 4351, 4359
Hawkins E W, **4:** 2357 (2353, 2354)
Hawkins H, **4:** 2229 (2227)
Hawkins J, **2:** 973 (971, 972), 1012 (1008); **7:** 4104 (4102)
Hawkins J D, **5:** 2571 (2568)
Hawkins J N, **7:** 3848 (3847); **11:** 6563 (6559, 6561)
Hawkins K, **11:** 6704 (6700)
Hawkins L S, **11:** 6538 (6530)
Hawkins S A, **6:** 3685 (3682)
Hawkridge D, **1:** 404; **2:** 977 (975), 991 (991), 1011 (1008, 1010), 1127 (1122, 1125), 1152 (1147, 1150, 1151); **3:** 1573 (1570, 1571, 1572); **4:** 1898 (1892, 1894), 1903 (1899, 1900, 1901), 1928 (1925, 1928), 1929; **5:** 2891 (2885), 2897; **7:** 4088 (4085), 4100
Hawley K, **10:** 5804 (5801)

Hawley W, **10:** 6012 (6011)
Hawley W D, **3:** 1486 (1485); **9:** 5379; **10:** 5965 (5962)
Haworth J, **4:** 1991 (1985)
Hay R A, **9:** 5490
Hayami Y, **1:** 254
Hayashi T, **5:** 2651 (2649)
Hayden A H, **5:** 2813 (2810), 2971 (2966)
Hayden M, **2:** 834
Hayduk L, **2:** 1073 (1070)
Hayduk L A, **4:** 2249; **8:** 4351 (4341); **11:** 6360 (6356), 6384 (6381)
Hayek F A von, **3:** (1569)
Hayes C, **11:** 6684
Hayes C D, **2:** 692 (689, 690, 691, 692), 700 (696); **3:** 1642 (1640)
Hayes E, **10:** 6058 (6055)
Hayes E R, **6:** 3435 (3429); **7:** 4324 (4322), 4329
Hayes J, **1:** 321 (319)
Hayes J R, **2:** 867 (861); **6:** 3288 (3285); **11:** 6457 (6453), 6780 (6778), 6784 (6782)
Hayes M J, **8:** 4811 (4808)
Hayes S C, **1:** 497 (496)
Haymann F, **9:** 5216 (5212)
Haynes M E, **8:** 4758
Hays F B, **8:** 4864 (4858, 4859, 4860, 4863)
Hays W L, **2:** 1117 (1111); **6:** 3508 (3500); **7:** 3738 (3729), 4162 (4159)
Haythorn W W, **5:** 2529 (2524)
Hayward B J, **3:** 1534 (1531); **11:** 6538 (6535)
Hayward F H, **3:** (1723)
Hayward S, **4:** 1966 (1964)
Haywood H C, **2:** 860 (859); **3:** 1402; **6:** 3228 (3226); **7:** 3830
Haywood M C, **7:** 3830
Hazaleus S L, **11:** 6360 (6356)
Hazan C, **5:** 2802
Hazary S C, **10:** 5783
Hazlewood A, **11:** 6424 (6420)
Hazlewood D G, **6:** 3634
Hazzard A P, **1:** 19 (19)
Head B F, **11:** 6515
Head G E, **2:** 1139 (1137)
Head J, **10:** (5681)
Healey R M, **9:** 5013
Healy M J R, **9:** 5467 (5466)
Healy P, **9:** 5302 (5299)
Heap N W, **11:** 6307 (6303)
Hearold S, **1:** 570 (569)
Hearshaw L S, **3:** 1796 (1794)
Heater D, **2:** 770 (767); **3:** 1501 (1496); **5:** 2736; **8:** 4581 (4576, 4578, 4579)
Heath A F, **4:** 2257 (2251, 2252); **8:** 4831; **9:** 5553 (5551); **10:** 5607 (5598, 5600)
Heath R A, **2:** 792; **7:** 3706
Heath R B, **1:** 389
Heath R W, **11:** 6349 (6343)
Heath S B, **1:** 244 (240); **2:** 802 (800), 917 (916); **3:** 1233 (1227), 1236 (1234, 1235), 1246 (1243); **4:** 2052 (2050), 2272 (2269); **6:** 3227 (3226), 3452 (3447, 3448, 3449, 3451), 3459 (3454, 3455); **10:** 5795 (5794); **11:** 6780 (6779), 6784 (6782), 6785 (6783)
Heatherington M, **9:** 5567
Hebbelinck M, **8:** 4473, 4474
Hebdige D, **11:** 6803 (6801)
Hechinger F, **8:** 4715 (4709); **11:** 6397 (6396)
Hechter M, **2:** 1073 (1066)
Heck G, **3:** 1733
Heckel H, **6:** 3276 (3274)
Heckhausen H, **1:** 377 (375); **4:** 1966 (1965); **5:** 2665 (2662); **7:** 3771 (3770), 3942 (3937); **10:** 6053, 6159 (6158)
Heckhausen J, **6:** 3428 (3427)
Heckman J J, **4:** 2279 (2276); **6:** 3189 (3188); **7:** 3858 (3857); **8:** 4902 (4900); **9:** 5385 (5383, 5384), 5467
Heckman S, **4:** 2302 (2299)
Heclo H, **5:** 2512 (2509)
Hedegaard M, **6:** 3292
Hedge R, **9:** 5192
Hedges L V, **4:** 1938 (1938); **5:** 2931 (2929); **7:** 3783 (3776, 3777, 3778, 3780, 3781, 3782), 4215 (4212, 4214); **9:** 5264 (5261), 5373 (5368); **10:** 6239 (6235, 6236, 6237, 6238), 6240
Hedman B, **11:** 6712 (6709)
Heegaard F, **3:** 1829 (1826)
Heene J, **4:** 2011
Heer D M, **4:** 2257 (2251, 2253)
Heerman B, **11:** 6307
Hees R, **7:** 4282
Heese C, **10:** 5635
Hegarty P, **7:** 4214 (4211, 4212)
Hegarty S, **2:** 729 (720, 722, 725, 728); **5:** 2907 (2905), 2910, 2972 (2966, 2968, 2970); **6:** 3315 (3314); **10:** 5943
Hegarty-Hazel E, **6:** 3204 (3203), 3205 (3202, 3203); **9:** 5338 (5335, 5336, 5337)
Hegde M N, **6:** 3227 (3226)
Hegel G W F, **3:** (1721); **4:** (1981); **7:** (3921); **8:** (4430), (4431), (4451), (4452), (4453)
Hegelheimer A, **8:** 4364
Hehir T, **10:** 5668
Heibert A, **4:** 1962 (1962)
Heibert E H, **4:** 1962 (1962); **6:** 3631 (3630)
Heid H, **10:** 6053 (6049)
Heid M K, **6:** 3685 (3679); **7:** 4099 (4096)
Heidegger M, **3:** (1524), (1772); **5:** (2579), 2586; **8:** 4433 (4430, 4431, 4432, 4433), (4453); **9:** 5055; **11:** 6465 (6462)
Heidenheimer A J, **4:** 1840 (1835); **5:** 2512 (2509)
Heider F, **10:** 6224 (6222)
Heider K, **1:** 280
Heidt E U, **2:** 888 (884); **7:** 3760 (3757)
Heigl-Evers A, **8:** 4816
Heijeler R, **7:** 3810 (3809), 4104 (4102)
Heikkinen S, **2:** 746, 1146 (1141); **7:** 4290 (4284); **11:** 6599 (6593, 6594)
Heiland H, **4:** 2388 (2386, 2387)
Heimann P, **3:** 1301 (1291)
Heimlich E P, **7:** 4175 (4174)
Heimstra N W, **9:** 5050
Hein C, **3:** 1671 (1666), 1672; **4:** 2431 (2430), 2432
Hein D D, **10:** 6004 (6001)
Hein K, **1:** 88 (86)
Heinich R, **2:** 888 (884); **4:** 1898 (1886, 1887, 1893), 1917 (1916), 1918, 1928 (1927); **5:** 2861 (2859); **7:** 3753; **11:** 6625 (6622)
Heinicke S, **10:** (5659)
Heining-Boynton A L, **4:** 2351 (2348)
Heinze-Fry W, **2:** 1031 (1028)
Heise D R, **1:** 390 (384); **7:** 3987; **8:** 4351 (4339, 4344, 4345, 4347); **11:** 6576 (6574)
Heise K, **11:** 6328 (6327)
Heisel B E, **7:** 3768 (3765)
Heisler D W, **3:** 1452 (1450)
Heiss A M, **11:** 6445 (6441)
Helander M, **2:** 984, 985; **3:** 1779
Helbing N, **4:** 2449 (2447), 2452 (2450)
Held D, **1:** 60; **2:** 1204
Helgren D M, **5:** 2469 (2468)
Hell P, **10:** 5686 (5683)
Hellemans M, **8:** 4461
Heller A, **1:** 380 (377)
Heller K A, **2:** 729 (725); **5:** 2495 (2492), 2731 (2726, 2728), 2732 (2726, 2729); **7:** 3830 (3828), 3833 (3831)
Heller M, **10:** 6043
Heller P, **11:** 6638 (6634)
Heller P S, **3:** 1834 (1832); **5:** 2993
Heller V, **6:** 3276
Hellinckx W, **4:** 2266 (2264)
Hellmuth J, **3:** 1431; **9:** 5372
Hellriegel D, **8:** 4519 (4518)
Hellyn J, **5:** 2852 (2848)
Helm V M, **2:** 893 (889); **4:** 2132 (2124, 2131)
Helmer O, **3:** 1443 (1441); **4:** 2330 (2328); **8:** 4787 (4783)
Helmke A, **1:** 203 (202), 204 (200); **2:** 846 (846); **3:** 1504 (1503, 1504); **9:** 5043 (5041), 5394 (5392, 5393); **10:** 5772 (5768, 5770, 5771), 6173 (6172)
Helmreich E C, **9:** 5013
Helmstad G, **8:** 4429 (4429)
Helmstetter E, **3:** 1406 (1405)
Helson R, **4:** 2435 (2435)
Helvétius C A, **5:** (2608)
Helwig C C, **5:** 2669 (2668); **9:** 5512 (5512)
Helwig J T, **7:** 4015 (4015)
Hembree R, **1:** 203 (200); **4:** 1966 (1963, 1965, 1966); **6:** 3643 (3639); **11:** 6360 (6357, 6358)
Hempel C G, **8:** (4450), (4633); **9:** 5050
Hemphill J K, **1:** 60 (54)
Hemphill L, **6:** 3453 (3448, 3449, 3451), 3480; **8:** 4936 (4932)
Hemwall M, **4:** 2046 (2044)
Henchelwood J, **10:** 5686 (5681)
Henchey N, **4:** 2331
Hencley S P, **1:** 77
Hendershot G E, **10:** 5674
Henderson A, **4:** 2257
Henderson A M, **6:** 3373 (3370)

Henderson C R Jr., **3:** 1647 (1645)
Henderson E H, **10:** 5704, 5705
Henderson J, **2:** 760; **11:** 6282 (6278)
Henderson L, **8:** 4939 (4938)
Henderson L W, **3:** 1624 (1623)
Henderson R A, **5:** 2972 (2970)
Hendersson N D, **11:** 6492
Hendrick C, **4:** 2449; **9:** 5441
Hendrick I G, **10:** 5783
Hendricks M, **4:** 2089, 2119 (2110, 2116)
Hendricks W E, **4:** 2432 (2429, 2430)
Hendrickson J M, **9:** 5567 (5564, 5565)
Hendrix J, **2:** 807 (805)
Hendry L B, **11:** 6798 (6794, 6796, 6797)
Hene B, **2:** 737 (737)
Henige D, **7:** 4224 (4222)
Henkel M, **4:** 1864; **8:** 4556 (4550, 4552)
Henkelman J, **7:** 4240 (4238)
Henn R, **8:** 4359
Henning-Stout M, **8:** 4661 (4659)
Henri F, **7:** 4220
Henri V, **4:** 1871 (1866)
Henricksson B, **11:** 6803 (6802)
Henriot-van Zanten A, **1:** 295 (283); **2:** 917 (917), 918
Henriques N, **3:** 1671
Henry J, **1:** 295 (283, 285, 291); **2:** 1213 (1209); **4:** 2052 (2047)
Henry M, **11:** 6735
Henry N B, **5:** 2773, 2903; **9:** 5327 (5326); **10:** 5745
Henry N W, **8:** 4912
Henson K T, **3:** 1544
Henson T, **1:** 175 (171)
Henstock T F, **9:** 5185 (5185)
Hentges K, **3:** 1443
Hentschke G C, **9:** 5185 (5183)
Heon M, **5:** 2544 (2541)
Herath J P, **10:** 5721
Herbart J F, **1:** (262), (274); **3:** (1289), (1290), (1298), (1303), (1721), (1722), (1723); **4:** (1865); **5:** 2578 (2578), (2608); **6:** (3626); **8:** (4452), 4461; **11:** (6308)
Herbert J, **9:** 5453 (5452)
Herbert-Jackson E, **5:** 2806 (2804)
Herbst J, **10:** 5613 (5609, 5611)
Herbst P G, **7:** 3706 (3706)
Herdt G H, **3:** 1233, 1246; **5:** 2685; **6:** 3227
Hergert L F, **10:** 6092 (6090)
Herget D E, **8:** 4464
Herick A, **7:** 4016 (4013)
Heritage J, **9:** 5416 (5412)
Herman B, **4:** 2296 (2293, 2294)
Herman J, **9:** 5441 (5436)
Herman J L, **5:** 2462 (2461); **7:** 3726 (3724)
Herman K L, **8:** 4779 (4775)
Herman R, **7:** 4215 (4213)
Herman W E, **11:** 6360 (6358)
Hernandez H, **1:** 280; **7:** 3974 (3972)
Hernando A, **5:** 2470
Hernes T, **11:** 6461 (6457)
Hernstein R J, **2:** 718 (717); **8:** 4727
Herodotus, **8:** (4575)
Heron A, **3:** 1245 (1244), 1252 (1246)
Heron E W, **8:** 4791
Heron T E, **9:** 4977 (4974); **10:** 5943 (5942)
Herrick V E, **3:** 1266 (1264)
Herrington M, **10:** 6126 (6124)
Herriott R E, **2:** 645 (643); **3:** 1474 (1466); **4:** 2046 (2043); **6:** 3527 (3525, 3526); **9:** 5211 (5208)
Herrlin A, **3:** (1724)
Herrmann B A, **10:** 6149 (6147, 6148)
Herrmann U, **8:** 4461 (4458)
Herrnstadt I, **11:** 6276 (6273)
Herrnstein R J, **7:** 3771 (3770); **9:** 5572 (5570)
Herschbach D R, **8:** 4864 (4858, 4859, 4860, 4863)
Herscovics N, **9:** 5345
Hersen M, **1:** 19 (17, 18); **3:** 1641; **4:** 2194 (2192); **8:** 4661 (4661); **9:** 4977, 5489 (5486); **10:** 5713 (5712)
Hersh R H, **1:** 380 (379)
Hershberger S, **11:** 6492 (6489)
Hershenson D B, **2:** 635 (633)
Hershfield A, **3:** 1567; **7:** 4220
Hershkowitz R, **6:** 3685 (3680)
Herskovits M J, **3:** 1729 (1724), 1755 (1752)
Hertenberg R, **3:** 1628 (1625)
Hertlein F, **7:** 3833 (3832)
Hertz B, **11:** 6761
Hertzig M E, **3:** 1520 (1515)
Hertz-Lazarowitz R, **5:** 2504, 2529 (2527), 2536 (2535); **10:** 6187 (6184, 6186)
Hertzog C, **7:** 3768 (3766)
Herz E J, **9:** 5441 (5436, 5437)
Herzberg F, **4:** 1972 (1968)
Herzenberg S, **11:** 6283 (6281)
Herzmark G, **8:** 4542 (4539)
Herzog A R, **1:** 239 (237)
Herzog D B, **3:** 1619 (1611)
Herzog J D, **1:** 295 (283, 288); **5:** 2684 (2684)
Herzog W, **5:** 2692 (2691); **7:** 3925 (3924)
Heschel A J, **6:** 3120
Heshusius L, **2:** 645; **3:** 1359 (1356, 1357); **9:** 5030 (5023, 5025, 5026), 5056
Hesiod, **11:** (6742)
Hesketh J, **2:** 831 (830); **6:** 3389 (3387); **7:** 3986 (3983)
Heslop Y, **1:** 414 (411, 413)
Hess A Jr, **3:** 1411 (1408, 1410)
Hess G A Jr, **9:** 5273 (5269, 5270, 5271, 5272)
Hess R, **4:** 2412 (2411)
Hess R D, **4:** 2140 (2138); **5:** 2627 (2624, 2625); **6:** 3238 (3235), 3312 (3310); **7:** 4300 (4299, 4300), 4301 (4300); **9:** 5216 (5213); **10:** 5591 (5590)
Hess T M, **5:** 2916
Hesse H, **10:** 5817 (5817)
Hesse M, **9:** 5030 (5027)
Hesse M B, **6:** 3219 (3218)
Hesselink J R, **1:** 553 (553)
Hessels M G P, **6:** 3315 (3314)
Hester M, **10:** 5808 (5807)
Hester S K, **2:** 820 (817, 818, 819)
Hesterly W S, **4:** 1972 (1969)
Hetherington E M, **1:** 234; **3:** 1642; **8:** 4542 (4540); **9:** 5406, 5528
Hetherington M, **4:** 2261
Hethy A, **11:** 6648 (6641)
Hethy L, **8:** 4531 (4529); **11:** 6647 (6642), 6648 (6641)
Hettich W, **2:** 1055 (1054)
Hettmansperger T P, **9:** 5082 (5080)
Hetzel B S, **5:** 2567 (2565), 2571
Hetzer H, **5:** 2664 (2656)
Heward C M, **8:** 4935 (4933); **9:** 5327 (5324)
Heward W L, **5:** 2972 (2966); **9:** 4977
Hewer S, **4:** 2357 (2354)
Hewett D, **4:** 2357 (2355)
Hewett E L, **1:** 295 (281, 291)
Hewison J, **6:** 3463 (3461, 3462)
Hewitt J K, **11:** 6492
Hewitt J P, **6:** 3435 (3433)
Hewitt R, **6:** 3238 (3236)
Hewlett S A, **6:** 3608 (3604)
Hewson P W, **8:** 4652 (4651); **10:** 5790 (5784)
Hewton E, **3:** 1789 (1784); **4:** 1898 (1892); **6:** 3608; **10:** 5973 (5971)
Heydebrand W, **3:** 1774 (1772)
Heyman G D, **1:** 31 (30)
Heyman R, **2:** 933 (926, 930)
Heymans P G, **3:** 1315 (1311)
Heyneman S P, **1:** 244 (241), 474 (470); **2:** 957 (955), 1127 (1126); **3:** 1789; **4:** 1840 (1835, 1839), 2257 (2254); **5:** 2500 (2499), 2891 (2888); **6:** 3480 (3479), 3608 (3603, 3606, 3607); **7:** 3721 (3720); **8:** 4495 (4494), 4509 (4500), 4698, 4848 (4846), 4873 (4868, 4869); **9:** 5240 (5235), 5539 (5536, 5537); **11:** 6366 (6364, 6365), 6370 (6367)
Heyns B, **10:** 5924 (5923)
Heyworth-Dunne J, **11:** 6760 (6755)
Heyzer N, **4:** 2423
Hickcox E S, **10:** 6043 (6037)
Hickey J, **7:** 3925 (3923)
Hickman J A, **2:** 737 (735); **5:** 2907 (2904)
Hickman M, **8:** 4951
Hickman R D, **9:** 5130 (5129)
Hicks D, **3:** 1402 (1402)
Hicks F, **6:** 3373 (3370)
Hicks L, **4:** 1984 (1984)
Hicks N, **3:** 1666 (1663)
Hicks R D, **8:** 4948
Hickson D J, **10:** 6096 (6092)
Hidalgo J, **7:** 4155 (4149)
Hidi S, **5:** 2768 (2764), 2769 (2764); **10:** 6192 (6191); **11:** 6780 (6779)
Hidiroglou M A, **9:** 5130 (5129)
Hiebert B, **10:** 6062 (6058)
Hiebert E H, **1:** 11 (8), 23; **10:** 5795 (5791); **11:** 6780 (6779)
Hiebert J, **1:** 348; **3:** 1434 (1432); **6:** 3660 (3659), 3685 (3675)
Hiebert M B, **6:** 3096 (3095, 3096)
Hiemstra R, **1:** 168 (163); **5:** 2773 (2771,

2773); **6:** 3434 (3434), 3435 (3428, 3433); **8:** 4616 (4613); **9:** 5399 (5395, 5396, 5397, 5398); **10:** 6058 (6054), 6202
Høien T, **10:** 5680 (5678)
Hieronymus A N, **11:** 6349 (6342), 6355 (6354)
Higgenbotham H, **1:** 494 (491)
Higginbotham-Wheat N, **5:** 2870 (2868)
Higgins A, **1:** 380 (379); **7:** 3920 (3919)
Higgins E T, **2:** 838 (837); **7:** 3942; **9:** 5507 (5505), 5512 (5511)
Higgins J J, **7:** 4162 (4162)
Higgins P J, **1:** 280 (278), 299 (298), 300; **7:** 3974 (3972)
Higgins R, **11:** 6307 (6299)
Higuchi Y, **1:** 111
Hilgard E R, **3:** 1245 (1241); **4:** 1898 (1885), 1899; **6:** 3324 (3315); **7:** 3886 (3881); **9:** 5043 (5040); **10:** 5745
Hill A, **1:** 570 (568); **11:** 6760 (6755)
Hill A C, **7:** 3848 (3846); **11:** 6558 (6553)
Hill A D, **5:** 2469 (2466, 2467, 2468)
Hill B K, **2:** 729 (722), 730 (722); **3:** 1438 (1436)
Hill C R, **6:** 3106 (3104)
Hill D, **5:** 2509 (2504)
Hill E, **3:** 1406 (1405)
Hill F M, **10:** (5659)
Hill F W, **9:** 5185 (5182)
Hill M A, **4:** 2418 (2415, 2416, 2417), 2419; **11:** 6740
Hill M L, **11:** 6461 (6459)
Hill N, **10:** 5808
Hill P T, **1:** 520 (516); **9:** 5185 (5183, 5184)
Hill P W, **4:** 2240 (2238)
Hill S, **1:** 110 (105)
Hill W, **3:** 1804 (1801)
Hill W F, **5:** 2532
Hill W H, **4:** 1847 (1844)
Hill-Burnett J, **3:** (1727)
Hilleard F M, **7:** 4293
Hiller J, **10:** 6149 (6148)
Hillgarten W, **10:** 6234 (6231)
Hilliard A G, **7:** 3977 (3975, 3976)
Hillman D J, **3:** 1394 (1388)
Hillocks G Jr, **10:** 5704 (5698, 5699, 5700, 5701); **11:** 6777 (6777), 6785
Hills C, **4:** 2292
Hills J R, **1:** 370 (366); **5:** 3050 (3049)
Hills P J, **1:** 193 (185), 194
Hills R J, **1:** 60 (54)
Hills S N, **1:** 310 (307)
Hilsendager S, **8:** 4388 (4385)
Hilton M, **1:** 111
Hiltz S R, **2:** 982 (978, 979, 980, 981)
Himes J H, **8:** 4473 (4470), 4474 (4470, 4472)
Himmelfarb H S, **9:** 5008 (4997)
Himmelstrup P, **6:** 3378
Himmelweit H T, **1:** 570 (564, 565)
Hince K, **10:** 6079 (6076)
Hinchcliffe J K, **3:** 1810; **8:** 4509 (4504, 4505)
Hinchliffe K, **1:** 552 (550), 560 (554); **2:** 1055 (1053); **3:** 1449 (1445), 1707 (1703, 1704), 1789 (1787), 1820 (1811, 1818), 1821 (1813); **6:** 3613 (3611, 3613); **8:** 4531 (4527, 4528); **9:** 5076 (5072, 5074)
Hind I W, **9:** 5294
Hinde J, **5:** 2595 (2590, 2593); **7:** 3986 (3983)
Hinde R A, **3:** 1520, 1642 (1637); **4:** 2261; **8:** 4368 (4365), 4372; **9:** 5507 (5504)
Hindley C B, **7:** 3706 (3702)
Hindmarsh J H, **1:** 415 (414)
Hinds E, **7:** 4220 (4215)
Hinds J O, **9:** 5268
Hindson C, **2:** 785
Hindson C E, **6:** 3148
Hines J M, **4:** 1995 (1992)
Hinkley D V, **9:** 5467 (5463)
Hinnekint H, **11:** 6437 (6435)
Hinnersmann H, **5:** 2495 (2492)
Hinojosa R, **3:** 1712 (1710); **8:** 4902 (4898, 4899)
Hinrichs J R, **3:** 1490 (1489)
Hinshelwood J, **7:** (4078)
Hinton F, **1:** 415 (410)
Hinton J, **2:** 893 (890)
Hinton T, **8:** 4803 (4801)
Hinzer H, **2:** 907
Hipgrave R, **5:** 2831 (2828)
Hippocrates, **9:** (5122)
Hirsch C R, **6:** 3685 (3683); **7:** 4099
Hirsch E C, **10:** 5961 (5959)
Hirsch E D, **3:** (1336); **5:** 2585 (2584), 2697 (2696)
Hirsch E D Jr, **2:** 1107 (1105, 1106); **4:** 1852 (1850); **6:** 3459 (3454)
Hirsch G, **9:** 5090 (5090)
Hirschen W, **3:** 1567 (1566)
Hirschfeld L, **2:** 838
Hirschheim R, **3:** 1830 (1829)
Hirschhorn L, **9:** 5232 (5230); **11:** 6276 (6276)
Hirschman A, **1:** 594 (589)
Hirschman A O, **7:** 4155 (4154); **10:** 6073 (6070)
Hirschman C, **8:** 4895 (4891, 4892, 4893)
Hirschman O, **6:** 3106 (3103)
Hirschorn L, **7:** 4255 (4253)
Hirsh E D, **3:** 1337 (1336)
Hirsh-Pasek K, **6:** 3224 (3219, 3220)
Hirst A, **7:** 4099
Hirst B, **5:** 2773 (2770, 2771)
Hirst K, **7:** 4099
Hirst P H, **3:** 1328 (1325, 1326, 1327); **8:** 4447 (4445, 4446), 4455 (4447, 4450, 4455); **9:** 5416 (5414); **10:** 5957 (5956), 5985 (5984), 5995 (5993)
Hirstein J J, **6:** 3667 (3663)
Hiscox M D, **5:** 3043 (3037)
Hiskett M, **2:** 913; **10:** 5842
Hitch C J, **2:** 1135 (1132)
Hitchens D, **11:** 6640
Hitchens H, **10:** 5886
Hively W, **5:** 3066 (3063)
Hjelmslev L, **9:** 5416 (5413, 5414)
Hlynka D, **7:** 3760 (3759)
Ho K, **1:** 52 (51)
Ho Ming Ng, **4:** 2423 (2419)
Ho P T, **2:** 1042 (1038)
Hoachlander E G, **11:** 6538 (6534)
Hoad P, **10:** 6127 (6125)
Hoad S, **8:** 4388 (4384, 4385)
Hoadley-Maidment E, **6:** 3213 (3211)
Hoaglin D C, **4:** 2208; **9:** 5082
Hoare Q, **2:** 1193 (1191); **7:** 4336 (4333, 4335)
Hoban C F Jr, **4:** 1899 (1887); **7:** 3753 (3744)
Hobart D, **8:** 4680 (4679)
Hobbes T, **3:** (1461); **6:** (3497); **7:** (3920); **9:** (5088)
Hobbles T, **6:** (3316)
Hobbs G, **9:** 5130 (5127)
Hobbs N, **2:** 718
Hobson C J, **10:** 5725 (5725)
Hocevar D, **2:** 1182 (1179, 1180); **4:** 2241 (2239); **7:** 4006 (4006); **10:** 6234 (6229)
Hochapfel G, **8:** 4816 (4815)
Hochschild J, **8:** 4595 (4587, 4588, 4589, 4590)
Hock E, **3:** 1642 (1639)
Hockey G R, **8:** 4394 (4390)
Hocking K, **10:** 6099 (6097)
Hocutt A M, **7:** 3833 (3831)
Hodge M, **9:** 5350
Hodge R W, **10:** 6227 (6224)
Hodges R E, **10:** 5704 (5698, 5702, 5703)
Hodgkinson C, **1:** 60 (55), 72 (72); **3:** 1774 (1771); **4:** 2166 (2164); **6:** 3284 (3277, 3278, 3280, 3281, 3282)
Hodgkinson H L, **2:** 711 (708, 709); **4:** 2257 (2251)
Hodgkinson V, **4:** 2212 (2210)
Hodgson D, **4:** 2150
Hodgson L, **2:** 766 (765)
Hodgson V, **8:** 4429 (4425)
Hodgson V E, **3:** 1563 (1557); **7:** 4220
Hodkinson P, **7:** 3894 (3891, 3893)
Hodson B, **10:** 5696 (5695), 5697 (5694, 5695)
Hodson H V, **2:** 942
Hoeffding W, **9:** 4974
Hoeffer T, **2:** 892 (888)
Hoem J M, **9:** 5467 (5460)
Hoemann H W, **8:** 4383
Hoenack S A, **3:** 1449; **7:** 3821 (3816, 3819)
Hoetker J, **10:** 6197 (6195)
Hofer M, **8:** 4951 (4949)
Hoff Wilson J, **5:** 2457 (2454)
Höffe O, **7:** 3925 (3921, 3922)
Hoffer T, **1:** 520 (516), 594 (590); **5:** 2595 (2593); **8:** 4568, 4830 (4827, 4828), 4845 (4840, 4841, 4842, 4843), 4887 (4886); **9:** 5196 (5195), 5206 (5203, 5204), 5378 (5375); **10:** 5606 (5604), 5735 (5733), 5753 (5751)
Hofferth S L, **2:** 692 (690, 691)
Hoff-Ginsberg E, **6:** 3224 (3219)
Hoffman A, **11:** 6452 (6447)
Hoffman D, **2:** 1093 (1089)
Hoffman D D, **4:** 1995

Hoffman J M L, **8:** 4751 (4745)
Hoffman M, **2:** 860 (858, 859); **3:** 1504 (1503); **10:** 5618 (5614, 5615)
Hoffman M B, **2:** 867 (862); **6:** 3315 (3313); **8:** 4731 (4729)
Hoffman M L, **7:** 3920 (3919); **8:** 4799 (4797, 4798); **9:** 5512 (5510), 5528 (5524)
Hoffman N, **10:** 5613 (5609); **11:** 6723 (6721)
Hoffman R R, **5:** 2879 (2875, 2877, 2878)
Hoffman S, **6:** 3616 (3614)
Hoffman W L, **1:** 553 (553)
Hoffmann B, **7:** 4197
Hoffmann D, **7:** 3925 (3924)
Hoffmann E, **4:** 2388 (2387)
Hoffmann S, **8:** 4816 (4815)
Hoffwenius P, **3:** (1464)
Hofman H-G, **11:** 6647 (6641)
Hofmeister A, **10:** 5673 (5670, 5671), 6163 (6163)
Hofstadter R, **10:** 5708
Hofstaetter P R, **5:** 2916 (2911)
Hofstee W K B, **3:** 1431 (1429); **7:** 4056 (4055)
Hofstein A, **10:** 5994
Hogan D, **3:** 1739 (1736); **11:** 6266 (6263)
Hogan M, **4:** 2364 (2363)
Hogan P, **10:** 5994 (5994), 6099 (6097)
Hogarty P, **3:** 1514 (1512)
Hogarty P S, **1:** 362 (361); **5:** 2916 (2912); **7:** 3706 (3702)
Hogbin I, **3:** 1755 (1754)
Hoge J, **2:** 770 (770)
Hoge R D, **10:** 5772 (5770)
Hogg R V, **9:** 5082 (5077, 5078, 5081)
Hoggart R, **5:** 2736 (2735)
Höghielm R, **3:** 1602 (1601); **7:** 4179 (4179)
Hogue L, **11:** 6603 (6602)
Hohn D, **8:** 4467 (4466)
Hojsholt-Poulson L, **3:** 1778 (1776); **10:** 5622
Hokenstad M C, **1:** 494 (493)
Holahan C J, **4:** 1980 (1978)
Holborn P, **10:** 6043 (6038)
Holbrook J, **5:** 2642 (2641)
Holdaway D, **6:** 3463 (3459)
Holden D J, **7:** 3768 (3764)
Holden K, **8:** 4788
Holec H, **6:** 3213, 3349 (3347, 3348)
Holland D C, **7:** 3974 (3973); **9:** 5220 (5218), 5572 (5567, 5570); **11:** 6765 (6761)
Holland J, **9:** 5441 (5437, 5438)
Holland J G, **8:** 4774 (4768, 4770)
Holland J H, **8:** 4722 (4720, 4721), 4951
Holland J L, **1:** 358 (357); **10:** 5804 (5798); **11:** 6678 (6670, 6674, 6676)
Holland P B, **8:** 4845 (4841, 4842); **9:** 5378 (5374, 5375, 5377)
Holland P W, **5:** 3050 (3046); **6:** 3507 (3500); **11:** 6355 (6349)
Holland R, **1:** 494 (491)
Holland W, **3:** 1624 (1621)
Hollaway S D, **4:** 2140 (2138)
Holliday A, **6:** 3213 (3211)
Holliday S G, **8:** 4824
Hollingshead A B, **9:** 5175 (5173), 5220 (5217), 5313 (5311), 5572 (5569); **10:** 5617 (5616)
Hollingsworth L S, **9:** (5433)
Hollingsworth S, **3:** 1257 (1256); **8:** 4947 (4946, 4947); **10:** 6099 (6098)
Hollingworth L S, **9:** 5532 (5529, 5530)
Hollingworth S, **10:** 6183 (6180)
Hollins M, **11:** 6628
Hollis M, **4:** 2388 (2386)
Hollister L E, **3:** 1619 (1611)
Hollister R, **3:** 1810 (1807), 1821 (1813); **6:** 3613 (3613); **8:** 4531 (4527, 4528)
Hollos M, **3:** 1755 (1753)
Holloway M, **2:** 1175 (1171, 1172)
Holloway S D, **4:** 2140, 2412 (2411); **5:** 2627 (2624); **7:** 4300 (4299, 4300), 4301 (4300); **8:** 4873 (4869); **10:** 5591 (5590)
Holly D, **5:** 2697 (2693)
Holly M L, **10:** 5939
Holm A E, **4:** 1995 (1994)
Holm J L, **9:** 5008 (5000)
Holm K A, **1:** 280
Holm S, **2:** 1037 (1034)
Holman M, **6:** 3394
Holmberg B, **3:** 1563 (1557, 1559), 1579 (1578); **7:** 4220 (4218, 4219); **9:** 5367 (5366); **10:** 5596
Holmes B, **1:** 474 (470); **2:** 933 (927, 930), 957 (949); **3:** 1257 (1254), 1589; **5:** 2544 (2541, 2542); **6:** 3421 (3419); **8:** 4499, 4964 (4959, 4960); **10:** 5929 (5925)
Holmes C T, **5:** 2515 (2513, 2514); **7:** 4157 (4157)
Holmes D, **1:** 494 (493); **9:** 5567 (5566)
Holmes E, **3:** (1295)
Holmes J, **7:** 4336 (4331)
Holmes M, **2:** 1107 (1103); **8:** 4526; **9:** 5264, 5539; **10:** 5929
Holmes O W, **10:** (5705), (5707)
Holmes T R, **1:** 494 (493)
Holmstrom R W, **7:** 4081
Holst C, **8:** 4912 (4911)
Holsti O R, **2:** 1079 (1075, 1078)
Holt D, **7:** 3858 (3856, 3857); **9:** 5130 (5125), 5142 (5137), 5467 (5460); **10:** 5862 (5858)
Holt J, **1:** 265 (260); **9:** 5475 (5474); **10:** (5815)
Holt M, **11:** 6704
Holt M E, **4:** 2123 (2120, 2122)
Holt M M, **9:** 5130 (5129)
Holt W, **4:** 2452 (2451)
Holte R, **9:** 5117
Holtom D C, **9:** 5453 (5450)
Holton G, **9:** 5349 (5347)
Holtzman W H, **1:** 193 (187); **2:** 729 (725), 998; **4:** 1872 (1870); **7:** 3830 (3828), 3833 (3831); **8:** 4791
Holubec E, **5:** 2504 (2501); **10:** 6224 (6221)
Holvast A, **2:** 820 (819)
Holyoak K J, **5:** 2856 (2854); **8:** 4722 (4720, 4721), 4951, 4956 (4954), 4957 (4956); **11:** 6456 (6454), 6608
Holzer F, **2:** 1220 (1217); **6:** 3474 (3468, 3469); **7:** 3935 (3934); **11:** 6348 (6345)
Holzman P S, **1:** 322 (318); **2:** 871 (869)
Holzman W H, **6:** 3297 (3294)
Homang R T, **5:** 2767 (2762)
Homans G C, **9:** 5175 (5173); **10:** 5591 (5588)
Home K R, **9:** 5055
Homer, **9:** (5117), (5121), (5122)
Homme L E, **8:** 4774 (4766)
Honey P, **1:** 322 (319)
Honeywell L, **2:** 1182 (1180)
Honig A S, **5:** 2806 (2803, 2804); **7:** 4296 (4295)
Honig B, **9:** 5201 (5198)
Honig E, **2:** 738 (736)
Honigmann J J, **1:** 295; **4:** 2400
Honzik M P, **6:** 3428 (3426)
Hoock J, **3:** 1553
Hood L, **1:** 296 (283); **11:** 6608
Hood P, **11:** 6461 (6460)
Hoogerwerf A, **3:** 1431 (1429)
Hooke R, **5:** 3061 (3060); **6:** (3218)
Hooker C A, **9:** 5030 (5022)
Hooker D, **1:** 15 (12)
Hooker R, **6:** (3499)
Hooks B, **2:** 1194; **7:** 4336 (4333); **11:** 6768 (6768)
Hooper E, **2:** 1175 (1173)
Hooper K, **2:** 1012
Hooper S R, **7:** 3743 (3739, 3743), 3830
Hoopers W, **11:** 6452 (6450)
Hoopes D, **3:** 1589
Hoopes K, **3:** 1589
Hoot J L, **5:** 2813 (2807)
Hoover C, **5:** 2827
Hoover H D, **5:** 3050 (3044); **8:** 4623 (4617); **11:** 6355 (6349, 6350, 6354)
Hoover S M, **9:** 5532 (5529)
Hooymayers H P, **2:** 820 (819, 820); **10:** 5775 (5773)
Hope K, **4:** 1877 (1876); **7:** 3721 (3717); **9:** 5553 (5549)
Hopes C, **1:** 72 (68, 69), 82 (78, 79, 80), 83 (78, 79, 80, 81)
Hopf C, **6:** 3276 (3275)
Hopfenberg W S, **1:** 520 (516)
Hopkin A, **3:** 1501 (1498)
Hopkins C, **9:** 5233
Hopkins D, **4:** 1934 (1930, 1932, 1933); **5:** 2852 (2848, 2850, 2851); **6:** 3602 (3597, 3600); **8:** 4568 (4562, 4563, 4566, 4567); **9:** 5223, 5224, 5246 (5244); **10:** 5972 (5968), 5982, 6099 (6097)
Hopkins F S, **8:** 4787 (4783)
Hopkins K, **4:** 2145 (2144)
Hopkins K D, **5:** 2714 (2713); **11:** 6591 (6590, 6591)
Hopkins L T, **3:** 1287 (1287); **10:** 5817 (5813)
Hopkins P G H, **1:** 180 (178)
Hopkins T K, **3:** 1449; **4:** 2432
Hopmann S, **3:** 1278 (1273), 1308 (1302,

1304, 1305, 1306, 1307), 1355 (1349); **10:** 6121 (6119)
Hopp C, **4:** 2435 (2433, 2434)
Hoppe R A, **9:** 5518
Hopper E, **2:** 1074; **9:** 5168 (5160)
Hoppers W, **1:** 226 (222); **3:** 1690 (1688), 1739 (1736), 1789 (1787); **4:** 2369 (2366); **8:** 4688; **11:** 6256 (6252), 6452 (6446)
Hops H, **9:** 5567 (5563, 5565)
Horace Q H F, **6:** (3499)
Horckheimer M, **9:** (5052)
Hord S M, **1:** 73; **3:** 1271 (1268); **4:** 2073 (2073); **9:** 5246 (5242, 5244); **10:** 5957 (5955)
Hore T, **7:** 4170 (4163, 4164, 4166, 4168), 4171 (4164, 4166, 4167); **11:** 6551 (6548)
Horio T, **6:** 3360; **9:** 5255
Horkheimer M, **2:** (930); **7:** (4335); **8:** (4453); **10:** (5600)
Hörmann H, **2:** 969 (964)
Horn J, **3:** 1514 (1512); **5:** (2911)
Horn J L, **1:** 239 (235); **2:** 677, 957, 1220 (1220); **5:** 2768 (2761), 2921 (2917); **6:** 3523 (3522); **7:** 3879 (3873, 3875, 3878, 3879), 3986, 4016; **8:** 4352
Horn L, **11:** 6538 (6534)
Horn R, **2:** 1146; **9:** 5228 (5225, 5227); **11:** 6431 (6428)
Horn R E, **10:** 5900 (5899)
Hornberger N H, **1:** 534; **2:** 802 (799)
Horne D, **10:** 5686 (5681)
Hornell E, **4:** 2394 (2389)
Hörner H, **10:** 5873
Hornig L S, **11:** 6712 (6709)
Hornik R, **4:** 1911; **5:** 2897 (2892)
Horowitz F D, **1:** 234; **3:** 1520; **5:** 2491, 2672 (2670), 2802; **8:** 4779 (4775); **9:** 5532
Horowitz G, **9:** 5441 (5440)
Horowitz H L, **10:** 5782 (5776); **11:** 6765 (6763)
Horowitz I L, **5:** 2998 (2994)
Horowitz M, **11:** 6276 (6273)
Horrocks G, **4:** 2364 (2360)
Horsnell P, **2:** 1160; **11:** 6740 (6739)
Horst P, **2:** 631 (630); **11:** 6678 (6675)
Horstkemper M, **11:** 6747 (6747)
Hort B, **4:** 2452 (2450)
Hortin J A, **11:** 6624 (6622)
Horton A, **10:** 5973 (5967)
Horton B D, **7:** 4336 (4331)
Horton D, **1:** 295 (287)
Horton G, **1:** 494 (493)
Horton J, **4:** 2432 (2431)
Horton L, **10:** (6055)
Horton M, **1:** 48 (45), 135 (129); **10:** 6127 (6125)
Horton R, **9:** 5567 (5566)
Horton S V, **7:** 3807 (3802)
Horvath A, **3:** 1337 (1335)
Horváth A, **5:** 2706
Horwitz P, **10:** 5790 (5784)
Horwitz R A, **7:** 4215 (4212); **10:** 6239 (6238)
Hosenfeld C, **6:** 3334 (3330)
Hosford P, **10:** 6043
Hoskin M, **4:** 1984 (1981)
Hosokawa M, **3:** 1443
Hospers J, **3:** 1367 (1360); **8:** 4447
Hossler D, **10:** 5804 (5800, 5803)
Hostetler J A, **1:** 295 (291); **2:** 917 (914); **4:** 2052 (2050)
Hotchkiss L, **1:** 11 (7); **7:** 3820 (3816, 3820)
Hotelling H, **2:** 631 (626); **3:** (1545), (1548); **4:** (2230)
Hotta T, **5:** 2993 (2992)
Hotz V J, **6:** 3189 (3188)
Hough J E, **2:** 816
Hough J R, **10:** 5873
Hough L N, **5:** 2725
Houghton H, **2:** 1170
Houghton H A, **2:** 888; **11:** 6370
Houghton S, **1:** 490 (488)
Houghton V, **6:** 3421 (3417, 3418)
Houle C O, **1:** 127 (120, 121), 152 (147); **5:** 2532, (2936); **7:** 4185 (4180, 4184), 4324 (4322), 4329 (4326, 4327); **9:** 5399 (5395); **10:** 5596 (5595); **11:** 6437 (6431, 6434)
Hounsell D, **10:** 5790
Hounsell D J, **1:** 193, 194 (189), 322; **2:** 1165; **5:** 2769 (2763); **7:** 4307; **8:** 4429 (4424, 4425); **9:** 5411 (5410); **10:** 5790, 6202 (6199)
Hourcade J J, **10:** 6244 (6241)
House E R, **3:** 1283 (1280), 1553; **4:** 2036 (2034, 2035), 2037, 2108 (2101, 2102, 2103, 2104, 2105), 2119 (2115, 2118); **8:** 4766; **9:** 5030 (5023)
Housego B E J, **1:** 28; **10:** 5812 (5810)
Housego I E, **5:** 2954 (2953); **9:** 5168
Houser J E, **4:** 2281 (2280)
Housner L D, **10:** 6026 (6023)
Houston N R, **10:** 5957, 6106
Houston R, **10:** 6155
Houston W R, **6:** 3202; **7:** 3833 (3832); **8:** 4947; **9:** 5318, 5345; **10:** 5585, 5812, 5934, 5939, 5943, 5948, 5965, 5994, 5995 (5992), 5999, 6012, 6043 (6035, 6037), 6048, 6088 (6088), 6121, 6219; **11:** 6621
Hout M, **7:** 3864 (3863, 3864)
Houtkoop M, **7:** 4325
Houtkoop W, **1:** 152 (149); **3:** 1602; **7:** 4324 (4320), 4330; **10:** 5643 (5640)
Houtveen T, **9:** 5224 (5223)
Houtz J C, **2:** 1182 (1181)
Hovell M F, **10:** 6164 (6161)
Howard A, **1:** 296 (293); **3:** 1756 (1754)
Howard G S, **10:** 6234 (6230, 6231)
Howard J, **10:** 5954 (5953)
Howard K W, **7:** 4329 (4326)
Howard M, **4:** 2180 (2175)
Howard R A, **9:** 5560 (5558)
Howard R J, **5:** 2586
Howard-Merriam K, **11:** 6761
Howe A, **5:** 2773
Howe B, **3:** 1610
Howe D S, **8:** 4388
Howe H Jr, **3:** (1796)
Howe K, **4:** 2249 (2248)
Howe K R, **4:** 2037 (2035), 2119 (2116)
Howe L W, **10:** 6053 (6052)
Howe M J A, **6:** 3288 (3285, 3286)
Howe M L, **2:** 705
Howe S G, **3:** 1406 (1404); **10:** (5659); **11:** 6628 (6626)
Howe W G, **4:** (2233)
Howell C T, **9:** 5528 (5527)
Howell D R, **11:** 6260 (6260)
Howell F M, **1:** 358
Howell J, **10:** 5697
Howell K W, **3:** 1359 (1356)
Howell W C, **6:** 3306 (3302, 3303)
Howells J, **4:** 2331
Howells R A, **9:** 5294 (5293)
Howes C, **2:** 688 (685, 686), 693 (689, 690, 691); **3:** 1635 (1634), 1636 (1634), 1642 (1640), 1643 (1639); **8:** 4542 (4539); **11:** 6397 (6396), 6398 (6395, 6396, 6397)
Howey K R, **10:** 5957, 6012 (6009)
Howieson C, **7:** 3894 (3892, 3893)
Howlett J, **1:** 198 (197)
Howley A A, **5:** 2495 (2492)
Howley C B, **5:** 2495 (2492)
Howley E, **5:** 2628 (2626)
Howlin P, **3:** 1520 (1515); **6:** 3224 (3223)
Howsam R B, **10:** 5999, 6048
Howson A G, **6:** 3647
Howson G, **6:** 3646 (3643, 3644, 3645, 3646), 3652 (3647), 3661
Hox J, **5:** 2596
Hoxeng J, **7:** 4148 (4147)
Hoy D C, **5:** 2585 (2584); **8:** 4642
Hoy W K, **1:** 437 (432); **3:** 1774 (1769, 1770); **4:** 1972 (1967); **9:** 5379 (5376); **10:** 5613 (5612)
Hoyer W J, **8:** 4823 (4818, 4820, 4821, 4823)
Hoyle E, **1:** 72 (69), 83; **4:** 1934 (1929), 2165, 2166 (2160), 2167, 2423 (2422); **7:** 3826 (3821, 3822, 3824), 4246 (4244); **9:** 5066 (5061); **10:** 5873, 6096 (6092, 6094), 6214 (6212), 6227 (6227)
Hoyles C, **2:** 807 (805), 991 (990), 1175 (1173); **4:** 1899 (1895, 1897), 2427; **6:** 3652 (3649); **7:** 4099 (4098); **11:** 6608 (6605)
Hoyos V, **7:** 4136 (4133)
Hoyt D P, **10:** 6234 (6233)
Hoyt J D, **6:** 3325 (3321)
Hoytink H, **3:** 1514 (1513)
Hrago M F, **1:** 139
Hård H S, **7:** 4179 (4179)
Hrubec Z, **4:** 2278 (2275, 2277, 2278); **6:** 3143 (3138, 3140, 3141, 3143)
Hryniuk S, **8:** 4895 (4895)
Hsu T-C, **2:** 998 (992); **5:** 2784 (2780)
Hu S, **1:** 495; **2:** 760; **6:** 3228 (3226); **10:** 6244 (6243)
Hu T-W, **9:** 5240 (5235); **11:** 6633 (6628)
Hu Y, **2:** 631 (629, 630)
Hua H, **8:** 4873 (4868, 4869, 4870)
Huaco G A, **9:** 5572
Huang A, **10:** 5693 (5693)
Huba G J, **1:** 88 (87)
Hubbard G, **11:** 6621 (6619)

Hubel D H, **1:** 553 (553); **5:** 2802 (2799)
Huber D M, **1:** 400
Huber P J, **9:** 5082 (5077, 5078, 5079, 5080)
Huberman A M, **2:** 645 (644); **3:** 1343, 1474 (1464, 1465, 1466, 1467, 1469, 1470, 1471, 1472, 1474), 1553 (1552); **4:** 1857 (1853, 1855); **6:** 3602 (3600, 3601); **10:** 6239 (6237)
Huberman M, **3:** 1431 (1427), 1553 (1550); **4:** 1899 (1889); **5:** 2847 (2840, 2841), 2874 (2872); **9:** 5030 (5025), 5246 (5242, 5243); **10:** 5935 (5931), 5939 (5935), 5973 (5972), 6214 (6210)
Hubert J A, **10:** 6062 (6061)
Hubler O, **3:** 1750 (1749)
Huckfeldt V E, **3:** 1443 (1441, 1442)
Huczynski A, **2:** 942
Hudak M, **1:** 322 (318)
Hudén T, **6:** 3398
Hudgins B B, **10:** 6149 (6144, 6145, 6146)
Hudgins H C, **6:** 3276 (3273, 3274, 3275)
Hudson B M, **3:** 1557, 1810 (1804)
Hudson J, **7:** 3768 (3764)
Hudson J A, **2:** 705 (703)
Hudson L, **2:** 871 (869, 871); **10:** 5846 (5845)
Huebner K M, **10:** 5943 (5939)
Huebner L A, **10:** 5804 (5798)
Huelskamp R M, **7:** 3726
Huesmann L R, **1:** 234 (230), 570 (569)
Huff C R, **5:** 2529 (2527)
Hüfner K, **5:** 2480; **8:** 4499
Hughes C, **8:** 4945 (4943)
Hughes D, **7:** 4111
Hughes E, **9:** 5411 (5409, 5410); **10:** 6126 (6123)
Hughes E C, **1:** 193 (190); **10:** 5948
Hughes H, **7:** 3852 (3850)
Hughes J A, **10:** 6183 (6181)
Hughes M G, **1:** 67, 73 (67, 69, 72), 77; **3:** 1774; **4:** 2166 (2162); **5:** 2954 (2952, 2953), 2955 (2952, 2954); **6:** 3463 (3459, 3460); **7:** 4246 (4240); **9:** 5168, 5168 (5159, 5161)
Hughes P, **10:** 5935
Hughes R, **7:** 4301 (4297, 4298); **10:** 5804 (5800, 5801)
Hughes V, **10:** 5826 (5823)
Hugill B, **6:** 3671 (3668)
Hui P K F, **6:** 3545 (3543, 3544)
Huinink J J, **6:** 3428 (3427); **9:** 5553 (5551)
Huitema B E, **9:** 5489 (5488)
Hula R, **2:** 700
Hulbert C M, **7:** 4293
Hulin C L, **5:** 3055; **11:** 6333 (6333), 6334 (6331)
Huling-Austin L, **10:** 6047
Hull C H, **7:** 4016 (4015), 4163 (4162)
Hull C L, **1:** (495)
Hull J, **9:** 5008 (5007)
Hull M, **11:** 6461 (6457, 6459)
Hull R, **3:** 1635 (1632); **7:** 4319 (4318); **9:** 5475
Hull T E, **9:** 5471 (5468)
Hullin R, **3:** 1606 (1603)
Hulmes E, **4:** 1852 (1850)
Hulsebosch P L, **9:** 5216 (5214)
Hulstijn J H, **4:** 2339 (2332, 2338)
Hult S, **7:** 4094 (4092)
Hultin M, **3:** 1680; **11:** 6699 (6698)
Hultinger E-S, **11:** 6395
Hultsch D F, **1:** 239 (238); **6:** 3288 (3288); **9:** 5528 (5525)
Hultsman J T, **11:** 6798 (6794)
Hultvist E, **11:** 6461 (6460)
Hum D P J, **7:** 3861 (3858)
Human P G, **2:** 1052 (1051); **6:** 3661 (3660)
Humboldt W von, **3:** (1290), (1721)
Hume D, **4:** 2000 (1997); **6:** (3316); **8:** (4631); **9:** (5088)
Humes L, **10:** 5690 (5690)
Hummel J W, **7:** 3808 (3806)
Hummell T, **10:** 5957 (5956)
Hummel-Rossi B, **5:** 2768 (2766)
Hummert M L, **1:** 238 (237)
Humphrey G, **8:** 4727 (4726)
Humphrey J, **4:** 2432 (2431); **11:** 6265 (6263)
Humphrey T, **1:** 15 (12)
Humphreys G W, **8:** 4379
Humphreys L G, **7:** 3706 (3705)
Humphreys P, **7:** 4081 (4078)
Humphries S, **7:** 4224 (4223)
Humrich E, **9:** 5432 (5423)
Hundeide K, **2:** 860 (860)
Hungerford H R, **4:** 1995 (1992, 1993)
Hungerford T, **9:** 5355 (5352)
Hungtington G E, **4:** 2052 (2050)
Hunkins F P, **3:** 1315 (1310)
Hunsberger M, **8:** 4947 (4947)
Hunsley J, **11:** 6360 (6359)
Hunt A, **11:** 6292 (6291)
Hunt B D, **2:** 785, 1072 (1071), 1074
Hunt D E, **5:** 2779 (2774, 2775); **10:** (5930), 5939 (5937), 6168 (6166, 6167, 6168)
Hunt D W, **10:** 6047 (6047)
Hunt E B, **1:** 5 (3), 295 (289); **5:** 2921 (2918)
Hunt F, **2:** 738 (734); **9:** 5168 (5166)
Hunt J, **10:** 5697 (5696), 6224 (6221)
Hunt J M, **7:** 4301 (4299); **8:** 4394 (4389); **9:** 5518
Hunt J Mc, **9:** 5572 (5570)
Hunt J McV, **3:** 1628 (1627); **5:** 2806 (2803)
Hunt J V, **3:** 1642 (1636)
Hunt K W, **10:** 5704 (5700)
Hunt R, **1:** 295 (289)
Hunt S, **10:** 6164 (6162)
Hunt T C, **1:** 265; **9:** 5008 (4998)
Hunter A, **11:** 6465 (6462)
Hunter B, **2:** 973 (970), 977 (974, 975), 982 (978), 1011 (1007, 1010), 1031 (1026); **11:** 6370 (6369)
Hunter C S, **1:** 103; **7:** 4148 (4147)
Hunter C St J, **1:** 180 (177); **6:** 3446 (3445)
Hunter J, **7:** 4255 (4250)
Hunter J E, **2:** 1139; **7:** 3783 (3776, 3778, 3779, 3780, 3781, 3782, 3783), 3784 (3776, 3779); **10:** 6240; **11:** 6678 (6670, 6675)
Hunter M, **3:** 1529 (1525); **4:** 2131 (2126, 2129); **10:** 6043 (6039)
Hunter M M, **11:** 6307 (6305)
Hunter R F, **7:** 4255 (4250)
Hunter S, **8:** 4824
Hunting G, **8:** 4531; **11:** 6638 (6635)
Hunting R, **6:** 3639
Hunting W, **4:** 2012
Huntington G E, **1:** 295 (291); **2:** 917 (914)
Huntington S, **1:** 135 (130)
Huntley I, **6:** 3634 (3632)
Huntze S L, **1:** 490 (487)
Hurd P D, **9:** 5328 (5324)
Hurley D, **4:** 1991
Hurley K, **7:** 3807 (3804)
Hurn C J, **2:** 1073 (1066, 1067), 1074; **8:** 4895 (4891, 4894)
Hurrelmann K, **8:** 4779
Hurst P, **3:** 1589; **4:** 1966 (1964); **5:** 2965
Hurt J, **11:** 6735
Hurtle S C, **2:** 984 (984)
Hurwitz A, **1:** 198 (197), 199, 343
Hurwitz E, **8:** 4788 (4783)
Hurwitz W N, **5:** 3061 (3055); **9:** 5142 (5136, 5140)
Husain S S, **9:** 5008 (4998, 5001)
Husband W B, **5:** 2512 (2511)
Husein M G, **6:** 3177
Husek T R, **2:** 1189 (1183)
Husén T, **1:** 94, 127, 139 (139), 152 (144), 158, 176, 184, 396 (393); **2:** 640, 645, 662, 711 (710), 775 (770), 910, 933 (925, 930), 947, 958, 1052, 1063 (1057), 1107, 1220 (1217); **3:** 1257, 1266, 1283, 1308, 1315, 1325, 1374, 1443, 1474 (1465), 1483, 1494, 1573, 1589, 1593, 1655, 1720, (1724), 1768 (1763), 1789, 1796 (1796); **4:** 1840 (1835, 1836, 1837), 1863 (1858, 1859, 1863), 1864, 1872 (1865, 1869, 1871), 1947, 2140 (2133, 2137), 2180 (2174, 2178), 2258, 2331, 2375; **5:** 2470, 2779, 2856 (2853), 2978 (2975, 2977), 3011; **6:** 3144, 3204, 3205, 3312 (3307), 3373 (3369), 3389, 3416, 3421 (3418), 3435, 3474, 3523 (3512), 3559 (3557), 3585, 3642, 3685; **7:** 3721 (3718), 3771 (3769, 3771), 3840 (3838), 3848, 3935, 3970, 3986 (3979), 4016, 4054, 4100; **8:** 4351 (4347), 4388, 4514, 4526, 4536, 4556 (4550, 4551, 4552, 4554), 4616 (4615), 4811, 4812, 4823, 4881, 4964; **9:** 5030 (5022, 5024, 5025), 5038 (5033), 5055, 5130, 5142, 5216, 5268, 5324, 5335, 5373 (5369), 5385, 5432; **10:** 5591, 5607, 5745, 5750 (5745), 5795, 5873, 5895, 5929, 5948 (5943), 5977, 6015, 6067 (6066), 6155, 6178, 6239; **11:** 6287, 6298 (6293), 6328 (6325), 6339, 6340, 6384, 6395, 6507 (6506), 6523, 6530, 6653, 6660, 6678, 6704
Huss J, **2:** (880)
Hussain A, **4:** 1984 (1983)

Hussain F, **4:** 2423 (2421); **11:** 6761
Hussain S A, **5:** 2753
Hussar W, **8:** 4788
Husserl E G A, **2:** (1070), 1073 (1071); **8:** (4427), 4433 (4430, 4431), (4453); **9:** (5052); **10:** (5588)
Hustler D, **1:** 48 (45)
Huston A C, **3:** 1642 (1639, 1640); **4:** 2449 (2446, 2447, 2448), 2452 (2450, 2451); **6:** 3625 (3623)
Huston-Stein, **8:** 4542 (4541)
Huszczo G E, **3:** 1491
Hutchings C H, **11:** 6360 (6356)
Hutchins R M, **5:** (2614); **6:** 3151 (3150); **8:** 4509
Hutchins T T, **8:** 4881 (4880)
Hutchinson C, **7:** 4307
Hutchinson D, **7:** 3911 (3907)
Hutchinson E, **7:** 4170 (4166)
Hutchinson E M, **8:** 4812 (4804)
Hutchinson T P, **2:** 792 (788)
Huttenlocher J E, **5:** 2596
Hutto N, **1:** 244 (240)
Huxley T H, **10:** (5705)
Huynh C-L, **11:** 6511 (6509)
Huynh H, **3:** 1421 (1420); **7:** 3706 (3702, 3703), 4056 (4055); **9:** 5082 (5079, 5080)
Hyams B K, **5:** 2617 (2615); **7:** 4224 (4223)
Hyde G D, **4:** 1947
Hyde J C, **9:** 5432 (5428)
Hyde J E, **4:** 2302 (2298, 2299)
Hyde J S, **4:** 2435 (2432, 2433, 2434), 2439 (2436, 2437); **5:** 2665 (2663); **9:** 5432 (5423, 5426, 5427, 5428), 5435 (5433), 5445
Hyde K A L, **4:** 2286 (2283), 2412 (2408); **11:** 6740 (6738)
Hyland A M, **11:** 6678 (6674)
Hylland A, **8:** 4594
Hyltenstam K, **4:** 2339 (2332, 2334)
Hylton J, **7:** 4026 (4022)
Hyman H H, **9:** 5373 (5368); **11:** 6579 (6577)
Hyman I A, **3:** 1537 (1536)
Hyman J, **11:** 6690 (6688)
Hyman J S, **5:** 2855 (2853), 2856 (2854, 2855); **6:** 3434 (3430)
Hyman R, **10:** 6168 (6165)
Hyman R T, **2:** 816 (815); **4:** 2376 (2375); **5:** 2532; **10:** 6149 (6148)
Hymes D, **1:** 296 (287, 291); **2:** 802 (798), 831; **4:** 2052 (2049), 2053; **6:** 3215 (3214), 3216, 3238 (3236, 3237); **9:** 5220, 5416
Hymes J L Jr, **5:** 2813 (2807)
Hynd G W, **7:** 3830; **10:** 5680
Hynds S, **2:** 1198; **6:** 3442, 3443; **10:** 5745 (5742); **11:** 6781
Høyrup J, **6:** 3646 (3643), 3647 (3643)
Høyrup S, **7:** 4179 (4178)

Iacona C M, **1:** 77 (74)
Iadicola P, **3:** 1486 (1485)
Iannaccone L, **9:** 5181 (5176, 5179)
Ianni F A J, **1:** 294, 296 (288); **9:** 5510
Iannotti R J, **2:** 705 (702)
Ibe-Bassey G S, **7:** 3760 (3759)
Ibraham M, **7:** 4205
Ibrahim M A, **11:** 6390 (6389)
Ibser M H, **10:** 5919 (5915)
Ichilov O, **3:** 1655 (1652); **8:** 4571 (4569, 4571), 4581 (4578); **9:** 5367
Ichniowski C, **10:** 6073
Ickes W, **11:** 6360
Idol L, **3:** 1252; **5:** 2884; **6:** 3329, 3334, 3335; **8:** 4731; **10:** 5831 (5830), 6244 (6240, 6241, 6242)
Idol-Maestas L, **3:** 1359 (1356); **7:** 3833 (3832)
Idrus R, **10:** 5808 (5806)
Iglesias A, **5:** 2813 (2810); **6:** 3227 (3226)
Igoe A, **4:** 1928 (1928)
Iguiniz J, **3:** 1671
Igwe S O, **2:** 914 (912); **3:** 1416 (1414)
Iinuma T, **6:** 3247
Ikeda H, **2:** 792 (790)
Ilboudo P T, **1:** 221 (218)
Ilg F L, **5:** 2665 (2664); **9:** 5275 (5274)
Il-hwan C, **7:** 4246 (4243)
Illback R J, **8:** 4661 (4661)
Illich I, **1:** (138), 474 (466); **2:** 1073 (1067); **5:** 2589 (2587); **6:** 3421 (3419); **8:** (4430), (4451), 4575 (4574); **9:** 5201
Ilomo C S, **8:** 4698 (4697)
Ilyas T H, **8:** 4485
Imahashi M, **9:** 5255
Imel S, **1:** 142 (139, 140, 141)
Imeson R, **2:** 1165 (1163)
Imhoof M, **4:** 1911, 1917 (1913); **5:** 2891 (2887, 2889)
Immegart G L, **6:** 3284 (3278, 3281)
Immelmann K, **4:** 2172 (2167)
Immergart G L, **3:** 1774 (1770); **4:** 2167
Impara J C, **8:** 4751 (4743)
Impey L, **8:** 4912 (4910)
Inabr J, **10:** 5762 (5761)
Inagaki K, **2:** 842 (839); **4:** 2199 (2196); **6:** 3302 (3298)
Inagamov T, **10:** 5649 (5647, 5649)
Inbar D E, **1:** 265 (261); **3:** 1810; **6:** 3284 (3280, 3283); **9:** 5216 (5212), 5367 (5364, 5366)
Inbar J, **11:** 6511 (6509)
Ing P S, **10:** 5680 (5680)
Ingekamp K, **8:** 4622 (4618)
Ingels S, **2:** 711 (709)
Ingenkamp K, **5:** 2479 (2478), 2480 (2478)
Ingersoll F, **7:** 4225
Ingersoll J, **7:** 4225
Ingle H T, **7:** 3970 (3960); **11:** 6608 (6605)
Inglehart R, **1:** 380 (377)
Inglis C, **1:** 296 (283); **8:** 4489
Ingraham B, **7:** 4094 (4092); **11:** 6603 (6602)
Ingram D E, **4:** 2346 (2340), 2357 (2352, 2354); **10:** 5694, 5697 (5695, 5696)
Inhelder B, **2:** 857 (853); **3:** 1434 (1433); **5:** 2655 (2655), 2680 (2678); **6:** 3671 (3669), 3685 (3677, 3682, 3683); **8:** 4455 (4453), 4482 (4481), 4483, 4957 (4951, 4952, 4954)
Inkeles A, **3:** 1655 (1650), 1695 (1691); **5:** 2798 (2792); **11:** 6282 (6280)
Inkeles T, **2:** 957 (956)
Inkis R, **6:** 3272
Inman R P, **8:** 4787 (4786)
Innes J, **3:** 1830 (1829)
Innes R, **7:** 3894 (3890)
Innis H, **1:** 162 (159)
Inoki I, **6:** 3616 (3616)
Inoki T, **9:** 5232 (5230)
Inoue K, **11:** 6699 (6696, 6697)
Inouye D K, **1:** 52 (51, 52), 370 (367); **2:** 998 (993); **10:** 5771 (5771)
Instance D, **10:** 6047
Intriligator B, **4:** 2423 (2422)
Inverarity J, **3:** 1607 (1603)
Iozzi L A, **4:** 1995 (1992), 1996
Iram Y, **11:** 6265 (6263)
Iran-Nejad A, **10:** 5745 (5741)
Iredale R, **5:** 2965
Ireson J, **5:** 2910
Ireton H, **3:** 1624 (1621, 1622)
Iriarte N, **4:** 2257
Ironside D, **1:** 100 (95), 120 (119), 152 (143), 180 (180); **2:** 1165 (1162); **11:** 6420
Ironson G H, **5:** 3050 (3045, 3049)
Irvin L, **1:** 142 (141); **8:** 4736 (4732, 4734)
Irvine J J, **10:** 5762 (5760)
Irvine J T, **11:** 6334 (6329)
Irvine J W, **11:** 6484 (6483)
Irvine P, **5:** 2907 (2904); **10:** 5662 (5659, 5660)
Irving J C, **7:** 3721 (3716)
Irwin J W, **6:** 3209
Irwin R B, **11:** 6628 (6626)
Isaac S, **4:** 2089 (2082, 2086, 2087)
Isaacs M, **9:** 5359 (5357)
Isaksen S, **2:** 1182 (1181)
Isango I W, **11:** 6814 (6811, 6813)
Isenbarger K U, **9:** 5328 (5325)
Ishii S, **7:** 4175 (4172)
Ishikawa T, **6:** 3092
Ishler M, **10:** 6047
Islam M, **9:** 5228 (5227)
Iso-Ahola S E, **11:** 6798 (6794, 6796)
Isocrates, **5:** (2693)
Israel A, **8:** 4419, 4519
Israeli E, **1:** 157 (154), 162 (160)
Israelsson A M, **9:** 5432 (5425)
Isralowitz R E, **3:** 1610 (1608)
Issa M A, **7:** 4205
Istance D, **6:** 3399 (3395); **7:** 4263 (4257, 4262), 4325, 4329; **8:** 4616; **10:** 5643; **11:** 6761
Itard J M G, **7:** (3913); **10:** (5658), (5659)
Iuppa N V, **7:** 3991; **11:** 6603 (6601)
Ivanic R, **6:** 3458 (3456)
Iventosch L, **7:** 4307
Iverson B K, **4:** 2258
Iverson R L, **11:** 6707 (6704)
Iwanicki E F, **4:** 2132 (2125); **6:** 3603

(3598); **10:** 5924 (5922), 5925 (5920), 6062 (6059, 6060, 6061)
Iwánska A, **3:** 1266 (1262)
Iwata M, **3:** 1441 (1441)
Iwawaki S, **5:** 2651
Iyer K B, **5:** 2601 (2598)
Izard C E, **4:** 1966 (1963, 1964); **8:** 4799
Izard E, **9:** 5406

Jabre B, **1:** 221
Jack D, **7:** 4336 (4332)
Jack R, **4:** 2296 (2295)
Jackiw N, **7:** 4099 (4097)
Jacklin C N, **1:** 234 (230); **2:** 705 (702); **4:** 2449, 2452 (2450); **9:** 5432 (5424, 5427, 5428), 5435 (5433, 5434), 5445 (5443); **10:** 5826 (5822, 5824)
Jackman, **9:** (5325)
Jackson B, **2:** 825 (821), 917 (916); **4:** 2272 (2269, 2270, 2271)
Jackson C M, **5:** 2684 (2682)
Jackson D, **9:** 4977 (4974)
Jackson D N, **4:** 1877 (1874)
Jackson E F, **11:** 6575 (6573)
Jackson G A, **3:** 1425
Jackson G B, **7:** 3783 (3775, 3776, 3778, 3779, 3780, 3781, 3782, 3783); **10:** 6239 (6236)
Jackson J A, **10:** 6086, 6096, 6099 (6098); **11:** 6723
Jackson J E, **3:** 1425; **4:** 2156 (2153)
Jackson J W, **1:** 19
Jackson K, **2:** 906 (901, 902), 1193 (1192)
Jackson M, **8:** 4956 (4952)
Jackson N E, **5:** 2732 (2729)
Jackson P, **1:** 11; **3:** 1334, 1337 (1334), 1774 (1771); **6:** 3661; **10:** 5924 (5922), 6096 (6094)
Jackson P A, **3:** 1325
Jackson P H, **1:** 480; **4:** 2183 (2182); **5:** 2596 (2591, 2593); **8:** 4536
Jackson P W, **2:** 796 (792, 794), 802 (798), 825; **3:** 1257, 1266 (1263), 1315 (1309), 1320 (1316, 1317), 1343, 1355 (1354), 1494; **4:** 2166 (2163); **5:** 2589 (2586, 2588); **6:** 3483, 3484; **9:** 5038 (5034), 5411 (5408); **10:** 5817, 6085 (6084), 6224 (6219); **11:** 6777
Jackson S E, **10:** 5924 (5923), 5925 (5919), 6062 (6060), 5738
Jackson T, **2:** 1139; **7:** 4336 (4331)
Jacob E, **1:** 295, 296; **2:** 802 (800); **3:** 1233 (1228, 1230), 1252 (1248, 1250), 1253; **4:** 2052 (2046); **9:** 5312, 5313 (5310)
Jacobowitz S, **4:** 2212 (2209)
Jacobs F, **1:** 362 (359, 361)
Jacobs H H, **4:** 1924 (1919)
Jacobs J A, **4:** 2432 (2429), 2435 (2434)
Jacobs S, **11:** 6608 (6605)
Jacobs S S, **7:** 4000 (3999)
Jacobs T O, **8:** 4887
Jacobsen B, **7:** 4180
Jacobsen K M, **7:** 4179 (4179), 4180
Jacobsen L, **2:** 1074 (1070)
Jacobsen S, **4:** 1939 (1936)
Jacobson D, **4:** 2218 (2216)
Jacobson L, **10:** 5762 (5759, 5760), 6112 (6106, 6107), 6224 (6220); **11:** 6511 (6509)
Jacobson S L, **6:** 3284; **8:** 4408 (4404, 4406)
Jacobson W J, **4:** 2439 (2437); **5:** 2856 (2854)
Jacobson-Widding A, **3:** 1240
Jacobsson S, **11:** 6282 (6278)
Jacobvitz D, **8:** 4423 (4421), 4779 (4776)
Jacoby H, **6:** 3106 (3101, 3102, 3105)
Jacoby S M, **5:** 2942 (2938)
Jacques M, **2:** 1194; **4:** 1984
Jaederholm G A, **3:** (1724)
Jaeger A, **7:** 4240 (4239)
Jaeger R M, **1:** 370 (364, 366, 368); **7:** 4319; **8:** 4622 (4617); **9:** 5055, 5142; **10:** 5725 (5725); **11:** 6328 (6321)
Jaffe A J, **11:** 6277 (6272)
Jäger A O, **5:** 2768 (2760)
Jäger R S, **5:** 2479 (2478), 2480 (2478); **10:** 5772 (5771)
Jaggar A, **6:** 3443
Jaggar A M, **4:** 2296 (2293)
Jahnke H N, **6:** 3660 (3656)
Jahoda G, **5:** 2651 (2649); **9:** 5577 (5576)
Jahoda M, **10:** 5617
Jaikumar R, **11:** 6260 (6259), 6277 (6275, 6276)
Jain A K, **2:** 831 (829)
Jain S, **5:** 2891 (2886)
Jakobson R, **6:** 3224 (3219); **9:** 5416 (5413); **10:** 5697 (5695)
Jakubs D, **6:** 3401 (3401)
Jalaluddin A K, **7:** 4140 (4140)
Jalil N, **4:** 1857 (1856); **8:** 4601 (4597)
Jallade J-P, **10:** 5767 (5767); **11:** 6265 (6263), 6669 (6664), 6807 (6806), 6808
Jamal A M, **9:** 5151 (5144)
Jamal V, **8:** 4839 (4839)
Jambyn Batmonh, **7:** (3896)
James D, **11:** 6719
James E, **1:** 265 (260, 261); **8:** 4796 (4795), 4830 (4825, 4826, 4828), 4835 (4831, 4832, 4833, 4834, 4835); **9:** 5206 (5202); **10:** 5753 (5751), 5754 (5751)
James F, **11:** 6558 (6553)
James J, **11:** 6282 (6278)
James L R, **8:** 4351 (4346)
James M, **8:** 4622 (4618)
James R, **7:** 3889 (3888)
James R J, **3:** 1619
James T, **1:** 265; **8:** 4830, 4831, 4844, 4845; **9:** 5196, 5206 (5202); **10:** 5754 (5751)
James W, **1:** 377 (374); **3:** (1296), 1524 (1521, 1524), (1794), (1795); **4:** (1841), (2030), 1863 (1857), (1865); **5:** (2876), (2877); **9:** 5055 (5051, 5052, 5053), 5394 (5390); **10:** (5705), 6085 (6083), 6169 (6164, 6167)
Jameson F, **8:** (4639)
Jameson K P, **1:** 254 (247)
Jameson M, **7:** 4094 (4090)
James-Reid O, **3:** 1599
Jamieson I M, **3:** 1739 (1736, 1737, 1738)
Jamieson M, **4:** 2345 (2344)
Jamieson S, **1:** 27
Jamison D T, **1:** 254 (244, 245, 246, 247, 252, 253), 474 (467), 563; **2:** 1127 (1124, 1125, 1126), 1135 (1134); **3:** 1266 (1263), 1573 (1572), 1655 (1649), 1666 (1665), 1695 (1693, 1694), 1707 (1704), 1762 (1757), 1784; **4:** 1911 (1907, 1908), 2418 (2414); **5:** 2744, 2891 (2888, 2889), 2945 (2944); **6:** 3480 (3479); **7:** 4145 (4143); **8:** 4848 (4846), 4873 (4868, 4869); **9:** 5240
Jamison P J, **7:** 3808 (3807)
Jamous H, **10:** 6085 (6085)
Jan J E, **11:** 6628
Jangira N K, **5:** 2972 (2969)
Janke R, **2:** 1099 (1098)
Janne H, **4:** (2054)
Janos P M, **9:** 5532 (5529, 5530, 5531)
Janowitz M, **8:** 4581 (4576, 4580)
Janowski A, **8:** 4549
Jansen J, **4:** 2291 (2290); **8:** 4586 (4582, 4585), 4688; **9:** 5246 (5241)
Jansen M, **3:** 1460, 1461; **8:** 4935 (4931, 4933)
Jansen P G W, **4:** 2017 (2012)
Jansen W J, **4:** 2212 (2211)
Janssen K N, **1:** 494 (493)
Janssen S, **10:** 6053 (6052)
Janssens V, **6:** 3660 (3658)
Jansson T, **2:** 692 (692)
Jantzi D, **9:** 5216 (5213)
Januszewski A, **9:** 5544 (5540)
Jaques-Dalcroze E, **7:** 4026 (4019)
Jarausch K, **8:** 4586 (4582, 4583, 4584, 4585, 4586)
Jardine D W, **9:** 5060 (5058, 5059)
Jardine L, **4:** 2007 (2004)
Jares X R, **3:** 1733
Jarjoura D, **11:** 6355 (6351)
Jarousse J P, **1:** 598; **2:** 1055 (1052); **11:** 6403
Jarrar S A, **1:** 328 (323, 325, 327); **9:** 5582 (5579)
Jarrell R H, **9:** 5532 (5529)
Jarvella R J, **6:** 3224
Jarvis P, **1:** 142 (140), 152 (143), 162, 163, 168 (165, 167), 277; **3:** 1315 (1311); **5:** 2937 (2935); **6:** 3421 (3417), 3422; **7:** 4180, 4185, 4263, 4329; **10:** 5596 (5593, 5594, 5595); **11:** 6437, 6438 (6431, 6434, 6437)
Jarvis P E, **9:** 5512 (5510)
Jasman A, **2:** 816 (813)
Jason H, **8:** 4930 (4925, 4928)
Jaspers K, **8:** 4433 (4430, 4431)
Jastrzab J, **11:** 6538 (6536)
Jatoi H, **3:** 1829 (1828)
Jaworski B, **1:** 404; **6:** 3671 (3669)
Jaworski J, **4:** 1903 (1899, 1901); **7:** 4088 (4085), 4100
Jay A, **6:** 3373 (3371)
Jay T B, **2:** 977 (974)
Jayaram N, **10:** 5783
Jayaratne T E, **4:** 2302

Jayasuriya J E, **10:** 5721
Jayatilleke K N, **1:** 581 (579)
Jayaweera S, **10:** 5721; **11:** 6719 (6714), 6761
Jeavons T, **8:** 4694
Jecchinis C, **6:** 3197 (3192)
Jefferson F E, **1:** 244 (240)
Jefferson T, **9:** 5060 (5057); **11:** 6803 (6801)
Jeffries R, **8:** 4731 (4729)
Jehng J C, **2:** 888 (885); **11:** 6603
Jellinek M S, **3:** 1619 (1611)
Jellison J A, **7:** 4026 (4023)
Jelsma O, **7:** 3953 (3953)
Jencks C S, **1:** 358 (357), 520 (517); **2:** 1063 (1062); **3:** 1707 (1703), 1750 (1750); **4:** 2279 (2276, 2277); **6:** 3144 (3138, 3139, 3141, 3143), (3307); **7:** 3721 (3719); **8:** 4845 (4841), 4896 (4892, 4893); **9:** 5206 (5202), 5281 (5276), 5539 (5537), 5553 (5551); **10:** 5591 (5590), 5735 (5732), 6043 (6036); **11:** 6558 (6553)
Jenkins D, **2:** 645; **3:** 1287 (1285)
Jenkins E, **2:** 852 (848); **8:** 4464 (4462); **9:** 5299 (5297), 5349 (5349), 5350
Jenkins E W, **5:** 2903; **9:** 5328 (5324, 5326)
Jenkins H O, **7:** 4246 (4241, 4244, 4245)
Jenkins J, **3:** 1563, 1573; **4:** 1903 (1900); **10:** 5690 (5689); **11:** 6821
Jenkins J G, **7:** 4016 (4015), 4163 (4162)
Jenkins J J, **7:** 3768 (3764)
Jenkins J R, **6:** 3297 (3293, 3295); **7:** 3833 (3831); **8:** 4376; **9:** 5070 (5068); **10:** 6173 (6169, 6170)
Jenkins L B, **1:** 42 (37); **6:** 3474 (3471), 3523 (3515); **7:** 3725 (3724); **9:** 5432 (5426)
Jenkins L M, **8:** 4376
Jenkins R, **9:** 5572 (5570)
Jenkins S, **10:** 6062 (6061)
Jenne M, **10:** 5606 (5601)
Jenness D, **1:** 280 (278); **5:** 2623; **8:** 4571 (4571)
Jennings A, **8:** 4473 (4471)
Jennings B, **6:** 3366 (3361); **10:** 5991 (5986)
Jennings D E, **6:** 3508 (3504)
Jennings E M, **1:** 482
Jennings K D, **8:** 4542 (4540)
Jennings Z, **3:** 1690 (1686, 1688, 1689, 1690)
Jennings-Wray Z D, **11:** 6452 (6448)
Jennrich R I, **4:** 2240 (2238)
Jens K G, **5:** 2813 (2810)
Jensema C, **5:** 2910 (2908)
Jensen A, **7:** (3770)
Jensen A R, **2:** 718 (717); **3:** 1233 (1227); **5:** (2917); **6:** 3215 (3213)
Jensen G E, **1:** 120, 127 (121, 123); **7:** 4185; **11:** 6438
Jensen J, **3:** 1672; **11:** 6784
Jensen J M, **8:** 4947; **10:** 5704 (5697)
Jensen L C, **6:** 3202 (3198); **7:** 3925
Jensen M, **8:** 4731 (4729)
Jensen M R, **5:** 2768 (2762)
Jensen T S, **6:** 3224 (3219)
Jenson W R, **10:** 6164
Jeppesen M, **3:** 1501 (1496)
Jeppson E S, **5:** 2813 (2811)
Jepson N, **1:** 94
Jerison H S, **5:** 2684 (2681)
Jernigan T L, **1:** 553 (553)
Jesperson O, **4:** (2340)
Jessell T M, **1:** 553 (552)
Jesson D, **3:** 1386 (1384)
Jessop B, **3:** 1720 (1715)
Jessop D Y, **8:** 4779 (4776, 4778)
Jessor R, **1:** 358 (355)
Jessup D K, **6:** 3197 (3195)
Jessup F W, **6:** 3421 (3418)
Jessup G, **3:** 1739 (1737); **7:** 3894 (3891); **11:** 6669 (6667)
Jester R E, **7:** 4296 (4295)
Jeunehomme L, **4:** 1872 (1869)
Jimenez E, **2:** 834 (833); **3:** 1449 (1448), 1789 (1788), 1793; **4:** 1840 (1838, 1839), 2315 (2313, 2314, 2315), 2316 (2314), 2418 (2415, 2418); **7:** 4201 (4197, 4199); **8:** 4595 (4592), 4707 (4706), 4835 (4834), 4845 (4843); **9:** 5076 (5073); **10:** 5754 (5751, 5752), 5768 (5765)
Joblin D, **6:** 3421 (3418)
Joffe C E, **7:** 4301 (4298)
Joffe L, **8:** 4648 (4643)
Johansen G, **2:** 1031 (1028)
Johansson B, **10:** 5790 (5784, 5785, 5786)
Johansson C, **5:** 2813 (2811)
Johansson E, **5:** 2607; **6:** 3531
Johansson G, **8:** 4379 (4379)
Johansson R E A, **1:** 581 (579)
John E G, **3:** 1354 (1354)
John G, **4:** 2357 (2352)
John O P, **11:** 6310 (6310)
John P D, **10:** 6088 (6088)
John V, **6:** 3216, 3238; **9:** 5220
John V P, **1:** 295 (291); **4:** 2053; **9:** 5416
Johnson A, **1:** 215
Johnson A E, **9:** 5130 (5129)
Johnson B J, **5:** 2813 (2811)
Johnson C H Jr, **7:** 3925 (3922)
Johnson C J, **7:** 3768 (3765)
Johnson C M, **7:** 4282
Johnson D, **2:** 893 (890, 891); **9:** 5216 (5214), 5217; **10:** 6117 (6113), 6187 (6186)
Johnson D L, **3:** 1355 (1353)
Johnson D W, **2:** 991 (990), 1099 (1097, 1098); **3:** 1486 (1485); **5:** 2503 (2502, 2503), 2504 (2501), 2536 (2534), 2907 (2906); **6:** 3297 (3293); **10:** 6163 (6162), 6164, 6224 (6220, 6221, 6222)
Johnson E, **7:** 3861 (3861)
Johnson G, **3:** 1449 (1445); **6:** 3184 (3183)
Johnson I, **6:** 3235 (3233)
Johnson J, **7:** 4293 (4291, 4292); **10:** 6004 (6001)
Johnson J E, **5:** 2813 (2808); **7:** 4301 (4299); **8:** 4542 (4541)
Johnson J J, **1:** (537)
Johnson J K, **4:** 1928 (1927)
Johnson J L, **2:** 718 (716)
Johnson J M, **10:** 5834 (5833)
Johnson J R, **11:** 6292 (6288)
Johnson K, **5:** 2862
Johnson L, **4:** (2080); **11:** 6735 (6734)
Johnson L J, **5:** 2491 (2490); **8:** 4661 (4659, 4661), 4662 (4657, 4658, 4661)
Johnson L V, **1:** 486 (483)
Johnson M Jr, **3:** 1278, 1334 (1331, 1332); **6:** 3428; **7:** 3935 (3931), 4051 (4047)
Johnson M B, **5:** 2922 (2917)
Johnson M C, **3:** 1381 (1378)
Johnson N B, **1:** 296 (289)
Johnson N L, **8:** 4912 (4912); **9:** 5082
Johnson R E, **3:** 1402 (1400); **11:** 6461 (6457, 6459)
Johnson R H, **2:** 1207 (1204, 1206, 1207), 1208
Johnson R T, **1:** 415 (410); **2:** 991 (990), 1099 (1097, 1098), 1194; **3:** 1386 (1382), 1486 (1485); **5:** 2503 (2502, 2503), 2504 (2501), 2536 (2534), 2907 (2906); **6:** 3297 (3293); **9:** 5544 (5542); **10:** 6163 (6162), 6164, 6187 (6186), 6224 (6220, 6221, 6222)
Johnson R W, **3:** 1416 (1412)
Johnson S, **1:** (195); **5:** 2462 (2462); **9:** 5567 (5565); **10:** 6183
Johnson S F, **10:** 5939 (5936)
Johnson S M, **6:** 3197 (3195); **10:** 5613 (5612), 5846 (5843), 5935 (5932), 6079, 6083 (6080)
Johnson V R, **9:** 5268 (5265, 5268)
Johnson W, **6:** 3101
Johnson-Laird P N, **2:** 856 (852); **6:** 3155 (3153); **8:** 4722 (4719), 4942 (4941), 4951, 4957 (4954)
Johnson-Martin N M, **5:** 2813 (2810)
John-Steiner V, **3:** 1252 (1248); **5:** 2495; **7:** 4095
Johnston A, **1:** 175 (173, 174), 474; **3:** 1262 (1259); **5:** 2758 (2757, 2758); **6:** 3467
Johnston B, **1:** (270)
Johnston B F, **8:** 4519
Johnston F E, **8:** 4473 (4469, 4470)
Johnston G, **4:** 2423 (2423)
Johnston J, **1:** 570 (567); **7:** 3986 (3985); **8:** 4352 (4344); **11:** 6797 (6795)
Johnston J M, **10:** 6164 (6161)
Johnston J R V, **5:** 2827
Johnston J W, **3:** 1315
Johnston M, **4:** 2364 (2360, 2362); **10:** 5939 (5936)
Johnston P, **2:** 1198; **9:** 5071
Johnston P A, **8:** 4935 (4933)
Johnston P J, **8:** 4936
Johnston T, **8:** 4609
Johnston V M, **2:** 1175 (1174)
Johnston W B, **4:** 1924; **11:** 6260 (6257, 6258)
Johnstone D B, **10:** 5754 (5753), 5767 (5763, 5766, 5767)
Johnstone J N, **4:** 2257 (2255); **7:** 3738 (3733, 3734)
Johnstone J W, **8:** 4616 (4614)
Johnstone J W C, **1:** 158 (153)

Joillet L, **6:** 3660 (3658)
Jolayemi E T, **6:** 3508 (3504)
Jolley M, **10:** 5973 (5971)
Jolly A, **5:** 2684 (2682, 2683); **6:** 3613 (3612)
Jolly R, **3:** 1789
Jonas H, **10:** 6053 (6048)
Jonassen D H, **2:** 888, 1012 (1008), 1170 (1166, 1169); **4:** 1917 (1917); **5:** 2709 (2707), 2773 (2770), 2867, 2874; **7:** 3946; **8:** 4803 (4802); **10:** 5913 (5910, 5912), 5914; **11:** 6603
Jónasson J T, **5:** 2721
Jonathan R, **7:** 3894 (3892); **11:** 6704
Jonçich G, **4:** 1872 (1867)
Joncich G, **5:** 2880
Jones A, **6:** 3496 (3493, 3494)
Jones B, **4:** 2331, 2357 (2356)
Jones B F, **2:** 1031 (1026); **3:** 1252; **5:** 2884; **6:** 3329, 3334, 3335; **8:** 4731
Jones B S, **5:** 2532 (2530)
Jones C, **5:** 2897 (2895)
Jones C L, **10:** 6227 (6224)
Jones D, **2:** 1052, 1193; **3:** 1257; **6:** 3652 (3648, 3649, 3650); **8:** 4652; **10:** 6026 (6021)
Jones D H, **5:** 2595 (2593)
Jones D P, **4:** 2229
Jones E, **2:** (1190); **3:** (1794); **4:** 1928 (1928); **10:** 6112 (6107)
Jones E D, **5:** 2732 (2731); **9:** 5532 (5531)
Jones E E, **3:** 1240
Jones F L, **7:** 3721 (3716, 3717); **8:** 4895 (4892); **9:** 5553 (5552)
Jones F R, **7:** 4094 (4093)
Jones G, **7:** 4094 (4092, 4093)
Jones G K, **9:** 5130 (5129)
Jones G R, **4:** 1972 (1971)
Jones H, **11:** 6735 (6732, 6734, 6735)
Jones H C, **4:** 2059
Jones I, **2:** 1152 (1147, 1149); **11:** 6640
Jones J, **5:** 2847 (2839)
Jones J D, **1:** 12 (7, 8)
Jones J E, **4:** 2073 (2070)
Jones J M, **3:** 1486 (1485)
Jones K, **8:** 4601 (4598); **9:** 5475 (5472)
Jones L B, **6:** 3602 (3600)
Jones L S, **10:** 6031
Jones L V, **10:** 6169 (6165); **11:** 6388 (6386, 6387)
Jones M, **5:** 2862 (2860); **6:** 3345; **10:** 6193
Jones M E, **2:** 816 (813, 814)
Jones M G, **9:** 5359 (5357)
Jones M K, **5:** 2503; **8:** 4803 (4800)
Jones N, **10:** 5943, 6031 (6028)
Jones P, **10:** 5693 (5693)
Jones P D, **4:** 2331
Jones P E, **10:** 5977 (5974)
Jones P S, **6:** 3685 (3674)
Jones P W, **5:** 2937 (2932, 2935); **8:** 4830 (4825); **11:** 6507 (6506)
Jones R E, **10:** 6099 (6097)
Jones R L, **2:** 718, 719; **10:** 5783
Jones R M, **8:** 4722 (4721)
Jones R R, **9:** 5489 (5487), 5490
Jones S, **7:** 3711 (3710)
Jones T J, **7:** 3848 (3841, 3842, 3843)
Jones V, **6:** 3235 (3232); **10:** 5826 (5825)
Jones V F, **10:** 6031
Jones W, **4:** 2331; **11:** 6677 (6676)
Jónsdóttir G A, **5:** 2721
Jonson R, **10:** 6117 (6113)
Jontiez P L, **3:** 1733
Joo K K, **5:** 2891 (2886)
Joram E, **11:** 6780
Jordan B, **1:** 310 (306)
Jordan C, **1:** 295, 296; **2:** 802 (800), 867 (865); **3:** 1233 (1228, 1230), 1236 (1234, 1236); **4:** 2052 (2049, 2050); **6:** 3453 (3452); **9:** 5312, 5313
Jordan D K, **3:** 1729 (1726)
Jordan J R, **3:** 1623 (1621)
Jordan R, **1:** 494 (492); **3:** 1501 (1496)
Jordan R R, **8:** 4940
Jordan S, **7:** 3894 (3890, 3893)
Jordell K O, **10:** 5961
Jöreskog K G, **1:** 390 (384, 388); **2:** 1117 (1110), 1220 (1219); **3:** 1514 (1512); **4:** 2140 (2137), 2241 (2233, 2235, 2236, 2238, 2239), 2388 (2386); **7:** 3879 (3875), 4006 (4003), 4015 (4008, 4009, 4011); **8:** 4352 (4341, 4342, 4347, 4349, 4351), 4359 (4352), 4930 (4930); **9:** 5130 (5129), 5467 (5467); **11:** 6334 (6333), 6492 (6490), 6576 (6574)
Jorgensen C, **9:** 5389 (5387)
Jorgenson D W, **3:** 1666
Jörgenson T O, **10:** 6244 (6243)
Jose P E, **2:** 738 (734)
Jose R T, **11:** 6628
Joseph E C, **4:** 1917 (1915)
Joseph G, **10:** 5762 (5760)
Joseph G G, **6:** 3647
Joseph L E, **4:** 1852
Joshi R M, **8:** 4935 (4934)
Jourard S M, **5:** 2692
Jourdan M, **1:** 184; **6:** 3421 (3417)
Jovanovic B, **6:** 3616 (3614); **9:** 5355 (5354)
Joy L A, **4:** 2266 (2264)
Joyce B, **1:** 72 (70); **5:** 2847 (2845, 2846), 2852 (2850); **7:** 3886 (3881); **9:** 5318 (5314); **10:** 5934, 5973 (5968, 5969), 5982, 6012 (6009), 6169 (6167)
Joyce B R, **3:** 1635 (1632); **5:** 2779; **10:** 5812 (5809), 6043 (6039), 6192 (6188, 6190)
Joyce T, **4:** 2212 (2209, 2210)
Jozefowicz J, **11:** 6647 (6647)
Jozefzoon E O J, **2:** 1107
Juarbe A, **9:** 5510 (5508)
Juárez M, **6:** 3231 (3230)
Judd C, **3:** 1386 (1383), (1793), (1794), (1795); **5:** (2877)
Judd C H, **4:** (1864), (1869); **9:** 5055 (5053)
Judd C M, **4:** 1938 (1934); **8:** 4657 (4654)
Judd D, **11:** 6558 (6553)
Judge H, **10:** 6012 (6010)
Judges A V, **8:** 4455 (4452)
Judy J E, **2:** 1026; **6:** 3329 (3327)
Julian E R, **4:** 2017 (2012); **7:** 4307 (4306)
Jullien M-A, **2:** 922 (919), (923); **4:** 1872 (1868)
Jumper S R, **5:** 2469 (2468)
June L, **11:** 6798 (6797)
Jung C G, **2:** (868); **3:** (1360); **6:** 3428 (3426); **8:** (4822), 4857 (4855)
Jung H, **1:** 553 (552)
Jung J H, **11:** 6707 (6705)
Jung R K, **9:** 5281 (5276)
Jung U O H, **6:** 3241
Jungck S, **7:** 4088 (4082); **9:** 5180 (5180); **10:** 6214 (6209)
Jungeblut A, **1:** 103; **6:** 3480 (3478); **7:** 3711 (3710); **8:** 4638 (4635); **11:** 6339 (6335, 6336)
Junger-Tas J, **3:** 1441 (1439)
Jurado J, **3:** 1671 (1669)
Jusczyk P W, **6:** 3224 (3220, 3222); **8:** 4383 (4382)
Jussim L, **10:** 5762 (5761), 6112 (6107, 6108, 6109)
Just M A, **8:** 4939 (4936)
Juster F T, **2:** 1055; **4:** 2212; **5:** 2631 (2629); **11:** 6615
Juster T, **2:** 1073 (1066)
Jüttner E, **10:** 5873
Juul K D, **1:** 494 (491); **5:** 2972 (2969)
Juvenal D J J, **6:** (3499); **8:** (4887)

Kaas J H, **5:** 2684 (2681)
Kabacoff R I, **3:** 1624 (1621)
Kabayashi, **6:** 3228
Kabeer M, **11:** 6719
Kabir M, **9:** 5228 (5227)
Kabwasa N O, **8:** 4616 (4613)
Kaczala C M, **9:** 5432 (5429)
Kaczor S, **11:** 6648 (6641)
Kádaár-Fülöp J, **4:** 2400 (2400); **11:** 6777 (6775, 6776)
Kaeley G, **10:** 5808
Kaeser S, **3:** 1538 (1537)
Kaess W, **10:** 6149 (6148)
Kaestle C F, **4:** 1840 (1839, 1840); **5:** 2607, 2617 (2612); **7:** 3711
Kafka F, **8:** (4426), 4433 (4430, 4432)
Kafle B D, **7:** 4067
Kafry D, **10:** 5925 (5920), 6062 (6060)
Kagan D M, **10:** 5812 (5810), 6088, 6183, 6219 (6216)
Kagan J, **3:** 1240, 1641 (1636); **5:** 2669; **6:** 3427 (3425); **8:** 4799; **9:** 5512
Kagan S, **2:** 693 (690); **3:** 1240 (1240)
Kagan S L, **5:** 2672 (2671), 2673; **7:** 4301
Kahane E, **9:** 5180
Kahane R, **11:** 6265 (6262)
Kahi A, **6:** 3356
Kahl J A, **5:** 2931 (2927)
Kahle J B, **2:** 811 (810), 1031 (1028); **4:** 2439 (2438), 2440 (2438); **9:** 5328 (5326), 5342 (5340); **10:** 5775 (5774)
Kahler D, **3:** 1262 (1259)
Kahn A, **5:** 2672 (2671)

Kahn A J, **2:** 693 (688, 689), 700 (694, 695, 696, 698, 699, 700)
Kahn D, **1:** 265 (261, 262)
Kahn L M, **2:** 1213 (1212); **4:** 2445 (2444, 2445)
Kahn R L, **10:** 5924 (5920, 5921), 6062 (6060)
Kahne H, **4:** 2446
Kahneman D, **1:** 377 (375)
Kahr A S, **3:** 1425
Kail R V, **1:** 6 (4), 15; **2:** 851 (847, 848, 850, 851); **7:** 3763, 3768
Kain J F, **3:** 1761 (1756)
Kainja C, **9:** 5228 (5225, 5227)
Kairamo K, **1:** 184 (181, 182)
Kaiser F J, **4:** 2024 (2020)
Kaiser H F, **1:** 390 (384); **3:** 1482 (1480); **4:** 2241 (2238); **8:** 4930 (4927)
Kaiser H J, **7:** 4026 (4023), 4030
Kaiser L, **6:** 3538
Kaiserman P, **7:** 3889 (3889)
Kakalik J W, **9:** 5240 (5235)
Kakwani N C, **3:** 1789 (1787); **5:** 2744
Kalaja M, **7:** 4094 (4092)
Kalantzis M, **1:** 534 (533)
Kalbach W E, **5:** 2740
Kalbfleisch J D, **4:** 2156 (2151)
Kale J, **2:** 617
Kalekin-Fishman D, **10:** 5924 (5921)
Kalinowski A, **4:** 2258
Kalirajan K P, **1:** 254 (246)
Kallaway P, **7:** 3852 (3850)
Kalleberg A L, **2:** 1094 (1091)
Kallen D B P, **3:** 1431, 1746; **4:** 1863 (1859), 2394 (2388, 2389); **8:** 4556, 4964
Kallenbach W W, **6:** 3202 (3198)
Kallós D, **4:** 2377 (2376)
Kalmanson B, **1:** 362 (359)
Kalmykova Z I, **6:** 3315 (3312)
Kalsbeek W D, **9:** 5130 (5127)
Kalton G, **7:** 3858; **9:** 5142 (5141)
Kaltsounis B, **2:** 1182 (1180)
Kaltsounis T, **9:** 5582 (5582)
Kaluba H, **1:** 474 (469)
Kaluba L H, **2:** 914 (912); **3:** 1416 (1415)
Kalupahana D J, **1:** 581 (578, 579)
Kalverboer A F, **3:** 1520 (1517, 1518, 1519)
Kam K W, **9:** 5485 (5484)
Kameenui E J, **2:** 867 (862), 868 (862)
Kamen L P, **9:** 5406 (5404)
Kamenetsky C, **2:** 738 (736)
Kamens D H, **9:** 5299 (5295)
Kamerman S B, **2:** 693 (688, 689), 700 (694, 695, 696, 698, 699, 700), 701; **11:** 6563 (6560, 6561)
Kamfwa F, **10:** 5808 (5806)
Kamhi A, **10:** 5694
Kamii C, **6:** 3671 (3670)
Kamil M L, **2:** 824; **8:** 4935, 4936; **10:** 5745, 5961, 6192
Kamin L, **10:** 5668 (5663)
Kaminski J, **11:** 6339 (6338)
Kaminsky J, **5:** 2856 (2854, 2855)
Kamp M van der, **3:** 1602
Kampe K, **6:** 3247
Kamper G, **3:** 1262 (1261)
Kamps D, **8:** 4375 (4374), 4376 (4374)
Kamradt E M, **5:** 2867 (2866)
Kamradt T F, **5:** 2867 (2866)
Kamvnema A, **10:** 5808
Kana D, **6:** 3550 (3546)
Kanawaty G, **5:** 3003; **11:** 6452 (6448, 6451)
Kanbur R, **2:** 1161; **3:** 1685 (1681)
Kandel D, **1:** 88 (86); **10:** 5758 (5757)
Kandel E R, **1:** 553
Kandel I L, **1:** (331); **2:** (923), 923 (920), 957 (951); **9:** 5168 (5160, 5165)
Kando T M, **11:** 6798 (6795)
Kane M T, **4:** 1857; **5:** 2462 (2461), 2847; **10:** 6234 (6229, 6230)
Kané O, **1:** 221 (218)
Kaneko M, **9:** 5255
Kanevsky L, **10:** 5673 (5670)
Kanfer F H, **9:** 5403 (5400)
Kanfer R, **1:** 377 (375); **5:** 2768 (2763); **6:** 3325 (3317); **7:** 3942; **9:** 5403; **10:** 6159
Kang J, **4:** 2212 (2211)
Kang S J, **2:** 1094 (1090); **5:** 2596 (2594); **6:** 3603 (3599)
Kangas K A, **1:** 409 (405)
Kaniel S, **5:** 2768 (2762)
Kann U, **1:** 552 (551)
Kanner L, **6:** 3235 (3232)
Kansen P, **6:** 3389
Kansup W, **7:** 4000 (3999)
Kant E, **6:** (3316)
Kant I, **3:** (1524), (1721); **4:** (1865), 2000 (1997), (2293), (2294), (2295); **5:** 2578 (2575, 2576); **7:** 3925 (3920, 3922, 3923, 3924); **8:** (4452), (4453), 4461 (4458), (4640); **9:** (5027); **11:** (6380), (6578)
Kant L, **4:** 2292 (2290)
Kanter J, **3:** 1830 (1828)
Kanter R 1977, **4:** 2445 (2444)
Kanter R M, **10:** 5591 (5589); **11:** 6731 (6730)
Kanters M A, **11:** 6798 (6795, 6796)
Kanthak L M, **1:** 437 (436)
Kantor H, **11:** 6538
Kantor J R, **1:** 497 (495)
Kantor R N, **11:** 6370 (6369)
Kantowski M G, **8:** 4648 (4644)
Kao R C, **7:** 4315 (4308, 4311)
Kapferer J L, **3:** 1271 (1271)
Kapisovsky P M, **2:** 982; **7:** 4099
Kaplan A, **1:** 396 (391); **2:** 645 (641, 645), 957 (949); **3:** 1474 (1465); **7:** 3872 (3865, 3866); **8:** 4766 (4762); **9:** 5050; **11:** 6328 (6328), 6576 (6570)
Kaplan B, **7:** 3861 (3861); **8:** 4395 (4392)
Kaplan C A, **1:** 331 (328)
Kaplan D, **4:** 2241 (2239)
Kaplan F, **3:** 1507 (1504); **10:** 5668
Kaplan H B, **10:** 5924 (5923)
Kaplan H S, **5:** 2692
Kaplan M, **11:** 6558 (6553)
Kaplan M S, **1:** 19 (18)
Kaplan N, **2:** 705 (701); **11:** 6445 (6444)
Kaplan R B, **2:** 1160
Kaplan R E, **7:** 4336 (4331)
Kaplan R J, **11:** 6608 (6605)
Kaplinsky M, **11:** 6416
Kapp A, **1:** (274)
Kaput J J, **2:** 1006 (1002, 1003, 1004, 1006); **7:** 4099 (4096), 4100
Karabel J, **2:** 933 (926), 1074; **4:** 2257; **9:** 5367 (5365); **10:** 5606, 5607 (5599, 5600)
Karageorgis A G, **3:** 1374
Karas H, **9:** 5268
Karat J, **8:** 4803
Kareland L, **2:** 738 (737)
Karier C, **3:** 1348 (1347)
Kariya T, **1:** 11 (6); **2:** 825 (821); **5:** 2942 (2939)
Karlan G R, **1:** 409 (404, 407)
Karle W, **10:** 5735 (5732, 5734)
Karlin L, **10:** 6143 (6141)
Karlson H C, **1:** 19
Karlsson M, **1:** 474 (469)
Karmann G, **5:** 2692 (2691)
Karmel P H, **8:** 4562 (4559)
Karmiloff-Smith A, **2:** 856 (855); **5:** 2669 (2669); **6:** 3224 (3221)
Karnes M B, **4:** 2145; **5:** 2491 (2490)
Karoly L, **1:** 11 (9, 10)
Karplus R, **6:** 3685 (3677)
Karve D K, **11:** (6749)
Karweit N I, **1:** 520 (515); **2:** 1099 (1098); **4:** 2388 (2382); **5:** 2870 (2869); **8:** 4873 (4870), 4935; **9:** 5378; **10:** 5758, 5759
Karweit N L, **2:** 1220 (1217); **8:** 4935 (4932, 4934); **9:** 5071; **10:** 5862 (5854)
Karylowski J, **8:** 4799
Kasakow N, **7:** 4094 (4091)
Kasarda A J, **3:** 1394 (1388)
Kasarda J D, **3:** 1676 (1672, 1673, 1674, 1675); **5:** 2595 (2593); **9:** 5378 (5374); **11:** 6557 (6552)
Kaser J S, **7:** 3726 (3724)
Kashima Y, **5:** 2651
Kashiwagi K, **4:** 2140 (2138), 2412 (2411); **10:** 5591 (5590)
Kashy D A, **7:** 4006 (4003, 4006)
Kasl E S, **2:** 1152 (1147, 1150); **11:** 6424
Kaslow N J, **9:** 5406 (5404, 5405)
Kasper H, **10:** 6073 (6069)
Kass H, **9:** 5334 (5332); **11:** 6328 (6326)
Kassam Y, **1:** 175 (170); **7:** 4336 (4335)
Kassin S M, **1:** 234
Kast M, **4:** 1954 (1948, 1949, 1950)
Kasten A S, **2:** 649 (646)
Kastenbaum M, **6:** 3660 (3659)
Kastoor B, **2:** 1208 (1206)
Kasworm, **11:** 6551 (6548)
Katak R, **5:** 2891 (2887)
Katchadourian H A, **1:** 88 (84, 85); **9:** 5441 (5436, 5438)
Kathuri N J, **1:** 474 (470)
Katoda H, **10:** 5663 (5660)
Katriel P, **6:** 3638 (3637)
Katunzi N, **4:** 2423 (2419)
Katz B M, **7:** 4162 (4161)
Katz D, **3:** (1724), (1794)
Katz E, **5:** 2897 (2892); **6:** 3616 (3615); **8:** 4364 (4361); **9:** 5355 (5353); **11:** 6430 (6427)
Katz F E, **4:** 2166 (2162); **6:** 3527 (3524)
Katz I, **1:** 296 (292)

Katz J, **2:** (944), (945); **10:** 5691, 5804 (5798)
Katz J J, **4:** 2400 (2397)
Katz L, **3:** 1750 (1750); **4:** 2452; **8:** 4939 (4938); **10:** 5812, 5957 (5955); **11:** 6397 (6396)
Katz L F, **5:** 2798 (2798)
Katz L G, **1:** 230 (228, 229); **3:** 1635 (1629, 1631); **8:** 4670, 4677 (4675); **10:** 5948, 5957 (5956), 5994, 5995 (5994)
Katz M B, **5:** 2607, 2617 (2612); **6:** 3496 (3494)
Katz P A, **3:** 1486
Katz W, **10:** 5681 (5679)
Katzko M W, **5:** 2495
Katzman N, **1:** 570 (566)
Kauffman J M, **1:** 494 (493); **5:** 2906 (2905); **6:** 3297 (3295), 3559 (3558); **10:** 5662 (5659, 5661), 5663
Kaufman D, **3:** 1579 (1574)
Kaufman J, **1:** 19 (17)
Kaufman J E, **11:** 6798 (6794)
Kaufman K L, **1:** 19
Kaufman L, **8:** 4379
Kaufman P W, **10:** 5613 (5609); **11:** 6765 (6762)
Kaufman R, **6:** 3096 (3092); **11:** 6276 (6273)
Kaufman R A, **7:** 4059 (4057); **8:** 4758 (4754, 4755, 4756)
Kaufman R L, **6:** 3508 (3502)
Kaufmann I, **9:** 5359 (5356)
Kaufmann W E, **7:** 4081 (4078)
Kaupp P A, **1:** 280
Kausler D H, **7:** 3763
Kavale K, **10:** 5663
Kavanagh J F, **1:** 175; **6:** 3224; **10:** 5681, 5694
Kavanaugh J, **10:** 5691
Kawaikita J, **3:** 1830 (1828)
Kawakami A J, **10:** 5795 (5792)
Kawanobe S, **8:** 4616 (4613, 4615)
Kay A, **7:** 4220
Kay E, **1:** 110 (105)
Kay P, **4:** 2400 (2398)
Kay R S, **10:** 6047
Kay S, **1:** 332 (331)
Kaye A, **2:** 1012 (1008); **3:** 1563 (1561), 1579 (1576); **4:** 2266; **5:** 2897 (2894); **7:** 4220, 4248 (4247)
Kaye T, **2:** 982 (978)
Kay-Shuttleworth J, **5:** (2608)
Kazamias A, **5:** 2523
Kazamias A M, **11:** 6760 (6754)
Kazanas H C, **5:** 2689 (2687); **6:** 3096 (3092)
Kazdin A E, **3:** 1441; **6:** 3297; **8:** 4368; **9:** 4977 (4976); **10:** 6164
Kazepides A, **7:** 3925
Kazlauskas E J, **9:** 5185 (5185)
Kazuk E, **3:** 1624 (1622)
Kealiinohomoku J, **8:** 4388 (4385)
Keane A, **8:** 4623 (4620)
Keane K, **3:** 1402 (1401)
Keane M J, **9:** 5294
Keane M T, **8:** 4951
Keane P, **7:** 4185
Kearsley G, **2:** 1011 (1010), 1139; **10:** 5625 (5624)
Keasey C B, **9:** 5512
Keating D P, **1:** 88 (85), 194
Keating P, **3:** 1486
Keating P J, **4:** 2389
Keats D M, **5:** 3007 (3004); **10:** 5758 (5756), 6132 (6130); **11:** 6797 (6796, 6797)
Keats J A, **1:** 42 (35), 389; **2:** 792 (786, 787, 788, 789, 790, 791); **7:** 3706 (3699, 3702, 3703); **10:** 5758 (5756), 6132 (6130); **11:** 6797 (6796, 6797)
Kebanuv P K, **3:** 1642 (1638, 1639)
Kedar-Cabelli S, **8:** 4722 (4721)
Kedar-Voivodas G, **4:** 2452 (2451)
Keddie N, **1:** 11 (8); **2:** 1073 (1071, 1072); **3:** (1344); **5:** 2736 (2733)
Keefe J W, **5:** 2768 (2763)
Keegan D J, **1:** 563; **3:** 1563 (1557), 1573 (1568), 1579; **4:** 1903 (1900); **7:** 4220 (4219); **9:** 5367 (5366); **10:** 5596; **11:** 6307 (6302)
Keegler B, **4:** 1841 (1838)
Keehn M M, **1:** 180 (177)
Keely C B, **1:** 162 (160)
Keen P G W, **5:** 2831 (2828)
Keen T R, **9:** 5016
Keenan E, **4:** 2364 (2359)
Keens W, **8:** 4388 (4387)
Keeps E J, **6:** 3096 (3093)
Keesing R, **3:** (1728)
Keetman G, **7:** 4027
Keeton M T, **4:** 2186
Keeves J P, **1:** 41 (34), 42 (38), 152, 370 (369), 390 (381, 387), 396 (393, 394, 395), 423; **2:** 631 (630), 645, 957 (950, 953, 954, 955, 956), 1220 (1217); **3:** 1474 (1465), 1482 (1477, 1479), 1483, 1768 (1763, 1764, 1767); **4:** 1872 (1865), 2140 (2137, 2139), 2180 (2174, 2176, 2178, 2179), 2249 (2245), 2250, 2439 (2437), 2440 (2437); **5:** 2931 (2930); **6:** 3373 (3372), 3474 (3468, 3469), 3523 (3515, 3516, 3521); **7:** 3721 (3717, 3720, 3721), 3722 (3720), 3738 (3730), 3739, 3986 (3979, 3982, 3984, 3985), 4006, 4015 (4015), 4016 (4012, 4013, 4015); **8:** 4352 (4339), 4359 (4353, 4357, 4359), 4479 (4475), 4648 (4646), 4753 (4752); **9:** 5030 (5024, 5025), 5031, 5055 (5054), 5201, 5323 (5321), 5324 (5320, 5321, 5322, 5323), 5334 (5333), 5335, 5342 (5340), 5372 (5369, 5371), 5373 (5369, 5371), 5385 (5380), 5432 (5423, 5424, 5425, 5426, 5427, 5430), 5445 (5444); **10:** 5607 (5601, 5603), 5735 (5733), 5862 (5855, 5857); **11:** 6328 (6322, 6325, 6326), 6349 (6342), 6355 (6354)
Kegan R, **10:** 5939 (5937), 6053 (6052), 6169 (6167)
Kehm B, **5:** 2479 (2474)
Kehoe A B, **1:** 280 (278)
Kehoe E, **2:** 1042 (1038)
Kehrer B, **4:** 2212
Keil F C, **2:** 842 (839), 856 (853, 854); **5:** 2916 (2913); **8:** 4957 (4952, 4956)
Keilitz I, **3:** 1441 (1438, 1439)
Keirns J, **11:** 6608 (6607)
Keitel C, **6:** 3646 (3644, 3645), 3647, 3671 (3668)
Keith A B, **5:** 2601
Keith D, **9:** 5406 (5406); **11:** 6797 (6797)
Keith P M, **4:** 2166 (2165); **5:** 2847 (2839)
Keith S, **3:** 1283 (1279)
Keith T Z, **5:** 2631; **8:** 4845 (4840)
Kell A, **1:** 317 (311)
Kellaghan T, **4:** 2250, 2257 (2250, 2252, 2253, 2255, 2256); **9:** 5268; **11:** 6320 (6319), 6563 (6562)
Keller E A, **4:** 1995 (1994)
Keller E F, **4:** 2439 (2437, 2438)
Keller F, **4:** 1848 (1844)
Keller F S, **5:** 2773 (2772, 2776); **8:** 4774 (4773); **10:** 6164 (6163); **11:** 6484 (6483)
Keller H, **3:** (1402); **6:** 3224
Keller J M, **2:** 1170 (1169); **7:** 3946 (3943, 3944, 3945, 3946); **8:** 4823 (4822)
Keller M, **2:** 846 (844); **7:** 3920 (3919); **9:** 5512 (5510, 5512)
Keller R, **8:** 4722 (4721)
Kellerman B, **10:** 5939
Kelley C, **6:** 3106 (3105)
Kelley G P, **9:** 5539
Kelley H H, **5:** 2532 (2531)
Kelley M L, **8:** 4881 (4879, 4880)
Kelley M R, **11:** 6277 (6275, 6276)
Kelley T L, **2:** 792 (786); **4:** (2230); **5:** (2917)
Kellmer-Pringle M L, **11:** 6360 (6358)
Kells H R, **1:** 28
Kelly A, **4:** 2292 (2287, 2288), 2412 (2409); **9:** 5302 (5300, 5301), 5328 (5326), 5432 (5425)
Kelly D H, **3:** 1589 (1587)
Kelly D M, **8:** 4791 (4788); **9:** 5228 (5224)
Kelly E F, **1:** 327 (326); **4:** (2103)
Kelly F, **11:** 6735 (6731, 6733)
Kelly G, **2:** 1064; **3:** 1589 (1586, 1587); **4:** 1851 (1849, 1850), 2412, 2419; **7:** 3852, 3853; **8:** 4509, 4586 (4583, 4584, 4585); **11:** 6723
Kelly G A, **8:** 4652 (4649); **9:** 5016 (5013)
Kelly G P, **2:** 933 (926, 929); **4:** 2286 (2282); **8:** 4698; **9:** 5060, 5228; **11:** 6366, 6371, 6740, 6741
Kelly J, **4:** 2131 (2128)
Kelly J R, **11:** 6798 (6794)
Kelly K, **7:** 3711 (3710)
Kelly L G, **4:** 2346 (2341)
Kelly M, **7:** 4220 (4219)
Kelly M J, **4:** 1840 (1839)
Kelly P, **3:** 1553 (1549, 1552)
Kelly R A, **4:** 2364 (2360)
Kelly T, **1:** 120; **8:** 4736 (4731); **11:** 6438 (6431), 6638, 6653 (6648, 6649, 6651)
Kelly V, **11:** 6292 (6289)
Kelman H C, **5:** 2978
Kelsall H M, **10:** 6132 (6130, 6131)
Kelsall R K, **10:** 6132 (6130, 6131)
Kemeny J G, **9:** 5560 (5558)
Kemmerer F, **2:** 914; **3:** 1416 (1415); **4:** 1911 (1906, 1907, 1910); **5:** 2891 (2888); **7:** 3821 (3816); **10:** 5954 (5951)
Kemmis S, **1:** 47 (44, 46), 48 (42, 43, 46);

2: 645 (641, 644), 991 (990), 1203 (1199); **6:** 3373 (3370); **9:** 5030 (5024); **10:** 5985 (5984), 6099 (6097), 6219 (6218)
Kemna H J M I, **4:** 2212 (2209)
Kemp J, **5:** 2861 (2859)
Kempa R F, **8:** 4648 (4645); **9:** 5324 (5320)
Kemper D, **10:** 5948 (5947)
Kemper H C G, **8:** 4473 (4472)
Kempf W, **3:** 1513, 1514
Kemple J J, **4:** 2156 (2154); **10:** 5846 (5844, 5845), 6106 (6104, 6105, 6106)
Kendall M G, **2:** 792 (787, 789); **3:** 1549 (1545, 1546); **7:** 3739 (3734), 4163 (4158, 4159); **9:** 5130 (5128)
Kendall P L, **10:** 6127 (6122, 6123)
Kendrick C F W, **3:** 1501 (1499)
Kendrick J W, **1:** 520; **2:** 1055 (1052); **3:** 1665; **5:** 2647
Kendrick W, **4:** 2351
Kenen P, **3:** 1789
Keniston K, **10:** 5782 (5781)
Kenkel D, **4:** 2212 (2209, 2210)
Kennan B, **10:** 5994 (5994)
Kennard B, **10:** 6099 (6097)
Kennard M A, **1:** 553 (552)
Kennedy C E, **8:** 4616 (4613)
Kennedy C H, **9:** 4977 (4975)
Kennedy E, **1:** 234 (232)
Kennedy J, **10:** 6149 (6147)
Kennedy J G, **10:** 5707 (5705)
Kennedy J J, **6:** 3508 (3500, 3501, 3502, 3503, 3504, 3505, 3506, 3507)
Kennedy M, **3:** 1529 (1527); **6:** 3596 (3593)
Kennedy M I, **4:** 2225 (2224)
Kennedy M M, **6:** 3602 (3597); **10:** 5995 (5992)
Kennedy P J, **2:** 900 (899)
Kennedy R E, **1:** 89; **9:** 5435 (5433, 5435)
Kennedy R F, **4:** (2111)
Kennedy S, **8:** 4408 (4404)
Kennedy W, **9:** 5130 (5129)
Kennedy W A, **9:** 5071 (5068)
Kenney M J, **6:** 3685 (3683)
Kennington T, **3:** 1386 (1384)
Kenny A, **9:** 5124
Kenny A M, **9:** 5441 (5436)
Kenny D A, **4:** 1877 (1874); **7:** 4006 (4003, 4006)
Kent A, **2:** 988; **8:** 4736
Kent D, **8:** 4376 (4373)
Kent G H, **8:** 4791 (4790)
Kent R, **6:** 3227; **8:** 4473 (4471)
Kent R N, **4:** 2452 (2451)
Kenway J, **5:** 2457 (2455); **11:** 6727 (6726)
Kenworthy L S, **5:** 2623 (2621)
Kenyon G M, **5:** 2665 (2659)
Keogh B, **10:** 5831 (5829)
Keogh B K, **6:** 3297 (3295); **7:** 3833 (3831); **10:** 5686 (5683); **11:** 6310 (6308, 6309)
Keogh R, **1:** 193 (191); **4:** 2186; **6:** 3349
Kephart N C, **10:** 5686 (5681)
Kepner H S, **9:** 5302 (5300)
Kercher M H, **7:** 3808 (3807)
Kerchner C T, **1:** 437 (435); **6:** 3197 (3192); **8:** 4831; **9:** 5201; **10:** 6079 (6077)
Kerckhoff A C, **1:** 11 (7), 358 (356); **2:** 825 (821); **6:** 3527; **9:** 5176 (5170), 5553; **10:** 5591 (5590), 5607
Kerek A, **10:** 5704 (5699)
Kerensky V M, **2:** 906 (900, 901)
Kergomard P, **8:** (4669)
Kerkhoff W, **10:** 5686 (5683)
Kerlinger F, **3:** 1655; **8:** 4766 (4762)
Kerlinger F N, **2:** 631; **4:** 1872 (1870); **5:** 2714 (2710); **7:** 4211; **8:** 4754 (4752), 4857 (4855, 4857), 4930 (4926); **9:** 4974 (4969, 4973), 5030 (5023)
Kerlinger F R, **2:** 1079 (1075, 1076)
Kermond B M, **7:** 4171 (4164, 4166, 4167)
Kern B, **11:** 6747 (6745)
Kern H, **11:** 6747 (6745)
Kernberg O F, **8:** (4813)
Kerr C, **8:** 4839 (4837); **11:** 6277 (6272)
Kerr D, **10:** 5613 (5612)
Kerr J F, **9:** 5299
Kerr M M, **8:** 4375 (4373); **10:** 6031 (6028)
Kerr S, **2:** 973 (970)
Kerrins J A, **10:** 6026
Kerry T, **6:** 3389 (3387)
Kerschensteiner G, **1:** 343 (339); **3:** (1722); **6:** 3137 (3133, 3135, 3137); **8:** (4681); **9:** (5230), (5231); **11:** 6659 (6654)
Kerschensteiner M, **6:** 3137
Kerschensteiner R, **11:** (6694)
Kersh B Y, **11:** 6511 (6510)
Kersh M, **4:** 1924 (1919)
Kershaw J A, **10:** 5846
Kerstiens L, **7:** 3925
Kerzner-Lipsky D, **10:** 6244 (6242, 6243)
Keskassa B, **1:** 348 (346)
Kessel F S, **6:** 3224
Kesselring T, **7:** 3925 (3921)
Kessels J W M, **6:** 3096 (3092, 3094, 3095)
Kessen W, **1:** 362; **2:** 838, 856; **3:** 1253
Kessler R C, **6:** 3523 (3514); **8:** 4719
Kessler S, **3:** 1347 (1346); **4:** 2249 (2248), 2272 (2269, 2270, 2271); **9:** 5060 (5057, 5058), 5312 (5311); **10:** 5606 (5603), 5613 (5608), 5758 (5758)
Kestelyn C, **1:** 103
Ketterlinus R, **8:** 4394
Keursten J J H, **7:** 4088 (4085)
Keursten P, **2:** 991 (990), 1011 (1009, 1010); **3:** 1494 (1493); **4:** 1918 (1915)
Keutner T, **5:** 2585 (2584)
Key E, **3:** (1722)
Key M R, **7:** 4175 (4171)
Keynes J M, **3:** (1697)
Keyser D, **1:** 322
Kfir D, **7:** 3852 (3849)
Khader F, **11:** 6515
Khalifa M, **1:** 139 (137)
Khalique C M, **6:** 3643 (3641)
Khan L S, **1:** 296 (293)
Khan M S, **9:** 5008
Khan S, **4:** 2418 (2417)
Khandker S R, **1:** 254 (246)
Khattab H A S, **11:** 6761
Khawaja S, **11:** 6760 (6755)
Khisty L, **6:** 3638 (3637)
Khlebnikova A, **10:** 5649 (5646)
Khleif B, **1:** 296 (289)
Khoo S T, **7:** 4307 (4306)
Ki Un Hahn, **1:** 139 (137)
Kibby M R, **5:** 2709 (2708)
Kibler D, **11:** 6608 (6604)
Kickert W J M, **3:** 1745 (1740)
Kicklighter R H, **3:** 1359 (1358); **7:** 3830 (3828)
Kidchanapanish S, **2:** 1127 (1123); **8:** 4708 (4704, 4705); **9:** 5241 (5234, 5240)
Kidd D, **3:** 1756 (1752)
Kidd G, **11:** 6678 (6676)
Kidd J R, **1:** 120 (113), 152 (151), 158 (153), 180 (176, 177); **5:** 2758, 2759, 2937 (2935), 2951 (2946), 2961 (2958); **7:** 4185; **8:** 4616 (4610), 4736, 4812 (4809)
Kidd R F, **11:** 6360
Kidder L H, **7:** 4006
Kiecolt K J, **3:** 1381; **9:** 5373
Kiefer N, **4:** 2212 (2211); **7:** 4201 (4199); **9:** 5385
Kiely G L, **1:** 53 (48, 49, 51)
Kieran C, **6:** 3652
Kieras D E, **3:** 1434 (1433); **4:** 2199 (2197)
Kierkegaard S, **8:** 4433 (4430, 4431, 4432), (4453), 4536 (4535)
Kiernan W E, **3:** 1508
Kieser A, **3:** 1745 (1741)
Kieslar E R, **3:** 1543, 1544
Kiesler C A, **1:** 390 (382)
Kiesler S B, **8:** 4604 (4603); **9:** 5038 (5034)
Kiesling H J, **10:** 5590 (5590)
Kieviet F K, **10:** 5995 (5991)
Kiewra K, **1:** 193 (187)
Kifer E, **6:** 3643 (3640, 3641, 3642)
Kight H R, **7:** 4206
Kiker B F, **2:** 1094 (1089); **9:** 5354 (5353)
Kiker K, **9:** 5355 (5353)
Kilburg D, **10:** 5694
Kilgore B S, **1:** 520 (516)
Kilgore S, **1:** 594 (590); **8:** 4568, 4830 (4827, 4828), 4845 (4840, 4841, 4843); **10:** 5753 (5751)
Kilgore S B, **5:** 2595 (2593); **6:** 3297 (3293); **8:** 4845 (4841)
Kili S, **8:** 4571
Killen J D, **5:** 2571 (2569)
Killen M, **5:** 2669 (2668); **8:** 4372 (4371); **9:** 5512 (5512)
Killmer S, **2:** 687; **7:** 4296
Kilminster S, **7:** 4170 (4166)
Kilpatrick J, **4:** 2199 (2198); **6:** 3638, 3646 (3644, 3645), 3647 (3646), 3652 (3647, 3648, 3649, 3650), 3655, 3667 (3666), 3671, 3685
Kilpatrick W H, **1:** 265 (263); **3:** (1521); **5:** 2589 (2588); **7:** (4156); **9:** (5575); **10:** 5817 (5813)
Kim H, **2:** 982 (978); **6:** 3631 (3630)
Kim J O, **4:** 2241
Kim Jong Il, **6:** 3160 (3156)
Kim K S, **2:** 677 (677)
Kim L, **11:** 6282 (6278), 6551 (6548)
Kim M S, **6:** 3661 (3659)
Kimball M M, **4:** 2435 (2434), 2449 (2448)
Kimball S T, **1:** 295, 296 (283, 289), 297; **2:** 918; **4:** (2047)

Kimbell R, **11:** 6292 (6289)
Kimberling W J, **10:** 5680 (5680)
Kimbrough R B, **1:** 437 (432)
Kimchee R, **2:** 851 (848)
Kimura D, **9:** 5432 (5429)
King A, **10:** 5831 (5831), 6015 (6014); **11:** 6266
King A D, **7:** 4296 (4294)
King B, **3:** 1563 (1558)
King C, **2:** 645; **3:** 1287 (1285)
King E, **4:** 2418 (2415, 2416, 2417); **8:** 4835 (4834); **10:** 5606 (5601); **11:** 6760 (6755)
King E J, **2:** 957 (951)
King E M, **4:** 2286 (2283), 2418 (2415, 2417), 2419; **11:** 6740
King F J, **2:** 991 (990), 1175 (1174); **7:** 4104 (4102)
King G, **4:** 1984 (1981)
King J, **4:** 2225 (2220)
King J A, **4:** (2108)
King J E, **3:** (1232)
King J M, **11:** 6603 (6600)
King K, **1:** 226 (222), 474 (474); **3:** 1501 (1495), 1557, 1685, 1690 (1690), 1694; **4:** 2145 (2142); **5:** 2965; **6:** 3189; **7:** 4211 (4211); **8:** 4364, 4531, 4604 (4602), 4666, 4715 (4714); **9:** 5349 (5348); **11:** 6265 (6262, 6263), 6452 (6448)
King K J, **3:** 1681; **11:** 6251 (6245, 6248, 6251)
King M, **2:** 918; **3:** 1394 (1388)
King M C, **4:** 2432 (2429, 2430)
King P M, **1:** 168 (165); **6:** 3435 (3428)
King R, **2:** 785 (781); **3:** 1348 (1345), 1720
King R A, **10:** 5999 (5999)
King R P, **3:** 1359 (1357)
King T, **2:** 1131; **3:** 1655, 1665, 1666; **9:** 5240
King W, **3:** 1830 (1828)
Kingsbury G G, **1:** 52 (48, 49, 50, 51, 52), 53 (50)
Kingsley C, **3:** (1299); **7:** (3843)
Kingston P W, **8:** 4830
Kini A S, **2:** 1170 (1168)
Kinnaman D E, **7:** 4100
Kinnear T C, **5:** 2931 (2923)
Kinney D K, **7:** 4170 (4169)
Kinsella V, **4:** 2351
Kinsey A C, **8:** 4887 (4883)
Kintgen E R, **6:** 3452
Kintsch W, **2:** 1006 (1003, 1004); **4:** 2199 (2197); **8:** 4942 (4940, 4941)
Kintzer F C, **2:** 900 (895)
Kirby B, **10:** 5713 (5710)
Kirby J, **1:** 322 (319)
Kirby J R, **7:** 3788
Kirby S, **9:** 5196 (5194)
Kirby S N, **10:** 5846 (5845)
Kirchofer J, **6:** 3334 (3330)
Kirdar U, **11:** 6415
Kirk D L, **9:** 5255
Kirk J, **2:** 738 (734); **9:** 5544
Kirk U, **10:** 5680
Kirkpatrick D, **2:** 1094 (1084); **5:** 2689 (2686)
Kirkwood A, **3:** 1579 (1577)
Kirkwood C, **3:** 1262 (1259); **6:** 3459 (3455)
Kirkwood G, **3:** 1262 (1259); **6:** 3459 (3455)
Kirn J R, **1:** 554
Kirp D L, **2:** 1042 (1038); **6:** 3276 (3274), 3360; **8:** 4595 (4590, 4591); **10:** 5929 (5926)
Kirsch D, **2:** 738 (733)
Kirsch I S, **1:** 103; **6:** 3480 (3478); **7:** 3711 (3710); **8:** 4638 (4635)
Kirschenbaum H, **10:** 6053 (6052)
Kirsh I S, **7:** 3711 (3710)
Kirst M W, **1:** 594 (590); **3:** 1334 (1331); **6:** 3496 (3493, 3494, 3495); **7:** 3840 (3835); **8:** 4602; **9:** 5066 (5062), 5216 (5213, 5214), 5281 (5276)
Kirton M J, **2:** 1182 (1180)
Kirwan B, **6:** 3096
Kiselev B G, **7:** 3756 (3755)
Kiselev N V, **10:** 5649 (5648)
Kish L D, **2:** 1220 (1214, 1215); **5:** 3061 (3055); **7:** 3739 (3737), 3858; **9:** 5130 (5124, 5125, 5126, 5127, 5128), 5142 (5131, 5133, 5135, 5136, 5137, 5138, 5139, 5140); **10:** 5862 (5854, 5855, 5857)
Kishchuk N, **3:** 1610 (1610)
Kishor S, **4:** 2432 (2430)
Kisker E, **2:** 693 (691)
Kispala A, **10:** 5826 (5822)
Kiss S, **11:** 6292 (6291)
Kissock C, **10:** 5965
Kistiakowsky V, **2:** 834 (832)
Kita B, **4:** 1962 (1962)
Kitayama S, **5:** 2651 (2650)
Kitchener K S, **1:** 168 (165); **6:** 3435 (3428)
Kitsuse J I, **1:** 11 (10)
Kitsuse J J, **4:** 2165 (2159)
Kittay E F, **4:** 2297; **10:** 5991 (5990)
Ki-Zerbo J, **1:** 221
Kjellan G B, **11:** 6461 (6460)
Kjellgren A M, **9:** 5302 (5300)
Kjerland L, **5:** 2814
Klabbers B, **3:** 1830 (1828)
Klabbers J, **3:** 1830 (1825)
Klafki W, **1:** 48 (45); **3:** 1301 (1291), 1355 (1351, 1352); **7:** 3925 (3922); **8:** 4419
Klahr D, **2:** 842, 851 (848), 852, 856 (852), 1026 (1022); **8:** 4722 (4720); **10:** 5887
Klare G R, **2:** 1079 (1077)
Klassen D L, **2:** 977 (974)
Klasson M, **1:** 127 (124); **7:** 4180
Klatt H, **7:** 4081
Klatzky R, **6:** 3155; **10:** 5745
Klauer K C, **1:** 380 (379); **7:** 3886 (3881)
Klauer K J, **4:** 2218 (2218); **5:** 2768 (2762); **9:** 5503 (5503)
Klaus J, **10:** 5674 (5670)
Klaus R, **3:** 1810
Klausmeier H J, **1:** 230 (228); **5:** 2870 (2868)
Klauss R, **3:** 1501
Klebanov P K, **3:** 1642 (1637, 1641)
Klee H D, **4:** 1903 (1902)
Klees S J, **2:** 1127 (1124), 1135 (1134), 1136 (1134); **3:** 1655 (1649), 1810, 1820 (1810, 1813, 1814, 1816, 1817, 1818, 1819); **4:** 1841 (1839), 1911 (1904, 1905, 1910); **5:** 2744, 2891 (2888); **8:** 4509 (4505); **11:** 6265 (6263)
Kleffner F R, **10:** 5680 (5677)
Kleiber D, **11:** 6798 (6794, 6796)
Kleiman A B, **8:** 4881 (4877)
Kleiman M A R, **3:** 1619 (1618)
Klein D M, **10:** 5924
Klein F, **3:** 1325 (1323)
Klein G, **1:** 322 (318)
Klein G D, **6:** 3480 (3476)
Klein G S, **2:** 871 (869)
Klein H, **3:** 1830 (1829)
Klein H E, **10:** 5948
Klein J, **4:** 1928 (1928)
Klein K, **4:** 2131 (2129)
Klein L W, **11:** 6355 (6351)
Klein M, **3:** 1494 (1491, 1492); **5:** 2847 (2839)
Klein M F, **3:** 1266 (1263, 1264), 1271 (1267), 1283 (1279), 1301 (1288), 1337; **4:** 2388 (2382)
Klein M P, **3:** 1338
Klein P A, **6:** 3634
Klein P S, **2:** 860 (860)
Klein R D, **4:** 2302; **11:** 6768 (6766, 6767), 6769
Klein R E, **3:** 1252 (1248)
Klein S, **4:** 2412; **8:** 4873 (4869); **9:** 5432 (5423, 5425, 5428), 5445; **11:** 6726, 6727 (6725)
Klein S G, **10:** 5919 (5915)
Klein Z, **3:** 1486 (1484); **7:** 4215 (4213)
Kleinbauer W E, **11:** 6621
Kleinberger A F, **9:** 5013
Kleine-Kracht P, **7:** 3826 (3823)
Kleinen G, **7:** 4026 (4023)
Kleiner M M, **10:** 6073 (6071)
Kleinfeld J, **7:** 4175; **10:** 5948 (5944, 5946)
Kleinginna A M, **4:** 1966 (1963)
Kleinginna P R, **4:** 1966 (1963)
Kleinmuntz B, **4:** 2199
Kleinschmidt E, **4:** 2357 (2353)
Klemish J, **7:** 4026 (4022)
Klemm K, **5:** 2480
Klemme H, **8:** 4375 (4374, 4375)
Klepp K I, **5:** 2571 (2571), 2572 (2569)
Klepper W M, **10:** 5804 (5799)
Klerman G L, **3:** 1619
Klerman J A, **2:** 693 (690)
Klevins C S, **4:** 2123; **6:** 3421 (3419)
Kliebard H M, **2:** 816 (815), 1107 (1106); **3:** 1266 (1265), 1301 (1300), 1308 (1301, 1303, 1305, 1306), 1333, 1343, 1355 (1349); **4:** 2376 (2375); **7:** 3848; **9:** 5299 (5295, 5297); **10:** 5817 (5813), 6149 (6148), 6168 (6165)
Kliegl R, **5:** 2676 (2676), 2916 (2915); **6:** 3428 (3427); **7:** 3763 (3762, 3763)
Klieme E, **4:** 2435 (2433, 2434)
Klimt F, **8:** 4473
Kline F M, **10:** 6178 (6175, 6177)
Klineberg O, **5:** 2978; **10:** 5782 (5781)
Klink G, **8:** 4419
Klink J, **8:** 4419
Klinteberg B, **8:** 4394 (4390)
Klinzig H G, **10:** 5995 (5991, 5993)
Klinzing D G, **3:** 1636 (1632)

Klinzing H G, **8:** 4881 (4876, 4878, 4879, 4880)
Klinzing-Eurich G, **8:** 4881 (4876, 4878, 4879)
Kliss B, **3:** 1425
Klitgaard R E, **10:** 5846 (5843, 5845)
Klivington K A, **1:** 376 (375), 377
Kloosterman P, **6:** 3643 (3640, 3641)
Klopfer B, **8:** 4791 (4788)
Klopfer L E, **2:** 1031 (1030); **3:** 1529; **7:** 3792; **8:** 4648 (4646); **9:** 5324 (5319, 5320), 5327 (5325), 5338 (5335, 5336); **10:** 5790 (5785)
Klopper D L, **4:** 2427 (2424, 2425, 2426)
Kloprogge J J J, **1:** 295; **3:** 1431, 1746; **7:** 3977 (3974, 3975)
Klovdahl A S, **9:** 5560 (5555, 5557); **10:** 5617 (5617)
Kluckhohn C, **9:** 5210 (5208)
Klüppelholz W, **7:** 4026 (4023)
Kluwe R H, **3:** 1514 (1511); **5:** 2665; **6:** 3349, 3435; **7:** 3942
Knapp C A, **1:** 194
Knapp M R, **9:** 5232 (5231)
Knapp M S, **3:** 1809 (1808); **4:** 1848 (1847); **6:** 3655 (3653); **8:** 4935
Knapp T, **5:** 3061 (3058)
Knapp T J, **2:** 851
Knapp T R, **2:** 1117 (1116); **4:** 2388 (2385, 2386)
Knasel E G, **7:** 4249 (4246)
Knefelkamp L, **10:** 5805
Kneller G F, **1:** 296 (282, 283); **2:** 1213; **3:** 1338
Knerr C S, **4:** 1972 (1968)
Knezevich S J, **3:** 1810 (1807)
Kniep W, **3:** 1501 (1497)
Knight B J, **3:** 1411 (1408, 1409, 1410), 1660 (1659)
Knight C, **5:** 2680 (2679, 2680); **9:** 5168 (5160)
Knight D L, **5:** 3050 (3044, 3049)
Knight F W, **5:** 2544
Knight J B, **3:** 1411, 1695 (1693), 1707, 1713 (1710), 1784 (1782); **6:** 3184 (3179, 3182, 3184), 3550 (3549); **8:** 4839, 4873 (4868), 4918 (4916); **11:** 6282 (6280)
Knight L W, **11:** 6731 (6729)
Knight R, **2:** 770 (769)
Knight R S, **7:** 3925
Knight S K, **9:** 5318 (5315)
Knights D, **3:** 1703
Knights S, **7:** 4170 (4166)
Knirk F G, **4:** 1898
Knitzer J, **1:** 490 (487, 488), 494 (492)
Knoblock P, **6:** 3234 (3232)
Knock G H, **10:** 5804 (5797)
Knoell D M, **11:** 6445 (6441)
Knoff H M, **9:** 5290 (5286, 5287)
Knoke D, **6:** 3508 (3500); **9:** 5560 (5558)
Knoll J H, **1:** 120; **2:** 640, 661; **6:** 3366 (3363); **10:** 5643 (5635)
Knoll P, **1:** 280
Knopf M, **6:** 3428 (3427); **7:** 3763 (3762)
Knott A E, **6:** 3360; **9:** 5255
Knotterus J D, **2:** 1094 (1088)
Knowles A, **3:** 1589
Knowles A S, **1:** 111
Knowles E S, **9:** 5359 (5357)
Knowles J, **10:** 6214 (6210)
Knowles M, **1:** 94, 152 (144, 148); **5:** (2936); **6:** 3435 (3434); **10:** 6202 (6198)
Knowles M S, **1:** 120 (117), 277 (275, 276); **4:** 2369 (2365); **5:** 2773 (2770, 2771); **6:** 3421 (3419); **8:** 4616 (4610), 4736 (4731); **9:** 5399 (5395); **10:** 5596 (5595), 6058 (6054)
Knowlton H E, **2:** 635 (632)
Knox A, **1:** 127 (123, 126); **2:** 1165 (1164)
Knox A B, **4:** 2123; **6:** 3421 (3419); **7:** 4185; **8:** 4812 (4806), 4823 (4818); **10:** 5808 (5807)
Knox J, **6:** (3531)
Knudsen G, **3:** 1402 (1399)
Knuth D E, **9:** 5471 (5468)
Knuttgen H G, **8:** 4468
Kobasa S C, **8:** 4719 (4718)
Kobasigawa A, **7:** 3768 (3766)
Kobayashi V N, **2:** 1207; **4:** 1903 (1903)
Köbbel I, **4:** 2266 (2265)
Kobrak F, **5:** 2998
Koch G G, **8:** 4930 (4929)
Koch S, **5:** 2692
Koch W R, **7:** 4307 (4307)
Kochan T A, **6:** 3197 (3190)
Kochanek T T, **3:** 1624 (1621)
Kochen M, **3:** 1830 (1829); **9:** 5560
Kochman T, **1:** 296 (291)
Koczor M L, **5:** 2856 (2854)
Kodaira S, **5:** 2897 (2895)
Kodaira S I, **5:** 2891 (2885, 2886); **8:** 4680 (4678, 4679)
Kodaira S M, **1:** 563 (561)
Kodály Z, **7:** 4026
Koedinger K R, **4:** 2199 (2198)
Koehler M S, **6:** 3643 (3640)
Koehler V R, **10:** 6004 (6001)
Koehn L R, **9:** 5302 (5300)
Koelling C H, **10:** 5834 (5832, 5833)
Koenig W, **10:** 5735 (5732, 5734)
Koerner J, **10:** 6012 (6009, 6010)
Koerner M E, **10:** 5812 (5811)
Koeske R D, **2:** 867 (862)
Koestler A, **5:** 2903 (2899); **8:** 4455
Koetting J R, **9:** 5544 (5540)
Kofele-Kale N, **2:** 617
Köferl P, **4:** 2089 (2082)
Koffka K, **5:** (2876), (2877), (2880); **6:** (3316)
Koffman G, **11:** 6603 (6600)
Kofsky E, **3:** 1514 (1510)
Kogan K, **3:** 1411 (1408)
Kogan M, **3:** 1720 (1718); **4:** 1840 (1835, 1836, 1837), 1863 (1858, 1863), 1864, 1872 (1871); **6:** 3373; **7:** 3840 (3838); **8:** 4499, 4556 (4550, 4552), 4562 (4559), 4602; **9:** 5038 (5033); **10:** 5873; **11:** 6530
Kogan M C, **8:** 4608
Kogan N, **1:** 239 (237); **2:** 871 (869, 870), 1183 (1180); **5:** 2773 (2770); **9:** 4974 (4972)
Kohl H, **10:** (5815)
Kohlberg L, **1:** 380 (377, 379); **4:** 2033, 2296 (2292); **5:** (2650), 2665 (2662, 2663, 2664), (2668); **6:** 3435; **7:** 3920 (3916, 3917, 3918, 3919), 3925 (3921, 3923); **8:** 4455 (4453), (4458), (4459); **10:** 5804 (5798), 6053 (6049, 6051, 6052), 6169 (6164, 6165, 6166, 6167, 6168), 6197 (6194); **11:** 6579 (6577, 6578)
Kohlberg L A, **4:** 2449 (2446, 2447); **5:** 2681 (2677, 2678)
Kohler M C, **11:** 6484 (6482)
Köhler W, **5:** (2876), (2880); **6:** (3316); **8:** 4372 (4370)
Kohli M, **6:** 3428 (3427)
Kohn A, **5:** 2504
Kohn M, **5:** 2942
Kohn M G, **3:** 1449
Kohn M L, **4:** 2257 (2252); **6:** 3428 (3426); **10:** 5591 (5589)
Köhnlein W, **3:** 1355 (1352)
Kohnstamm G A, **5:** 2665 (2663); **11:** 6310 (6309, 6310), 6311
Kohut H, **8:** 4816 (4815)
Koike K, **5:** 2798 (2792, 2796), 2942 (2939, 2940); **6:** 3616 (3616); **9:** 5232 (5230); **11:** 6420 (6419)
Koizumi T, **3:** 1449
Kolb B, **1:** 553 (552, 553)
Kolb D, **1:** 322 (318); **5:** (2935), (2936)
Kolb D A, **1:** 72 (70); **4:** 2186 (2184); **6:** 3435 (3428, 3430, 3431); **9:** 5475
Kolbe L J, **5:** 2571 (2568, 2569), 2572 (2569); **9:** 5290 (5284)
Kold C, **4:** (2324)
Kolen M J, **8:** 4623 (4617); **11:** 6355 (6349, 6350, 6351, 6352, 6354)
Kolping A, **1:** (137)
Kolstad A, **2:** 711 (709)
Kolstoe O P, **2:** 635 (633, 634)
Koluchova J, **6:** 3288 (3285)
Kolvin I, **7:** 4293
Komatsu L K, **8:** 4957 (4955)
Komba D, **3:** 1690 (1688, 1689); **11:** 6452 (6446)
Komenan A G, **2:** 1160 (1157)
Kominski R, **7:** 4255 (4252)
Komisar B P, **8:** 4455 (4454)
Kommers P A M, **2:** 1012 (1008); **5:** 2709
Komocar J, **11:** 6334 (6331)
Komorowska H, **8:** 4549
Komoski P K, **2:** 1001 (1001); **10:** 6117 (6113)
Komulainen E, **6:** 3389
Konar V, **3:** 1406 (1403)
Kong S L, **7:** 3970 (3967, 3969)
Koniarski C, **10:** 6164 (6162)
König H, **4:** 2388 (2386)
König I, **10:** 5644
Koning J de, **4:** 2150 (2149)
Kontogiannopoulou-Polydorides G, **5:** 2523 (2513, 2514)
Kontos S, **2:** 688 (686); **7:** 4301 (4298)
Kooi S W, **9:** 5216 (5212)
Kool S, **9:** 5281
Kopp C B, **1:** 362 (361); **9:** 5403 (5400, 5402)
Kopp T, **2:** 1170 (1169)
Koran J J, **10:** 5977 (5974)

Koran M L, **10:** 5977 (5974)
Korb R, **1:** 110 (104, 107)
Korchin S, **3:** 1240
Körgesaar J L, **10:** 5663
Korhonen L, **3:** 1602
Korinek L, **6:** 3297 (3294); **7:** 3833 (3831)
Körkel J, **2:** 706 (704); **5:** 2916 (2914); **7:** 3763, 3768 (3764)
Korman N, **4:** 1864; **8:** 4556 (4550, 4552)
Kornadt H J, **5:** 2651 (2649)
Kornblau B W, **11:** (6309)
Korner P, **3:** 1789
Kornhuber H H, **1:** 553 (552)
Korol A G, **8:** 4608 (4605)
Korten D C, **3:** 1501, 1810; **5:** 2937 (2936); **7:** 4148; **8:** 4519 (4515, 4518)
Korthagen F, **3:** 1635 (1633); **10:** 6219 (6218)
Korzenik D, **1:** 343 (342)
Koshel P, **8:** 4715 (4709)
Koskinen P S, **11:** 6484 (6483, 6484)
Koss M, **4:** 2150 (2149)
Kosse G B, **3:** 1431; **4:** 1863 (1859)
Kosslyn S M, **2:** 1031 (1026); **6:** 3155
Kosters M H, **11:** 6615
Kota J, **8:** 4670
Kotecha P, **7:** 3853 (3850, 3851)
Kotnik N, **9:** 5497 (5495)
Kotovsky K, **5:** 2732 (2727)
Kotte D, **9:** 5324 (5323), 5432 (5423, 5424, 5425, 5427, 5430); **10:** 5607 (5603)
Kottkamp R B, **10:** 6183, 6219 (6218)
Kotz S, **8:** 4912 (4912); **9:** 5082
Kotze P, **10:** 5674 (5673)
Koul B N, **3:** 1563, 1573; **4:** 1903 (1900); **11:** 6821
Koumi J, **1:** 404 (400)
Kounin J S, **1:** 486 (483); **3:** 1537 (1537); **6:** 3389 (3387); **10:** 6031 (6029)
Kourany J, **9:** 4980 (4979)
Kourlsky M, **9:** (5577)
Kourvetaris G, **4:** 1984
Koury M, **8:** 4376 (4373, 4374)
Koutroukis T, **6:** 3197 (3192)
Kovacs M, **9:** 5406
Kowalski J P, **10:** 6020 (6018)
Kowalski T, **9:** 5318 (5313, 5314, 5317)
Koyré A, **3:** 1464
Kozakiewicz M, **8:** 4595 (4588, 4592)
Koziol S M, **6:** 3209 (3207)
Kozma R B, **2:** 888 (884); **3:** 1573 (1572); **4:** 1911; **6:** 3625 (3623); **7:** 3743 (3739, 3742, 3743), 3753 (3745); **10:** 5673 (5671), 5674 (5673)
Kozol J, **1:** 265 (260); **2:** 711; **11:** 6547, 6558 (6555), 6563 (6559)
Kraan R J, **4:** 2331
Kraat A W, **1:** 408, 409 (407)
Krabbe E, **2:** 1207 (1207)
Krabbe M A, **10:** 6026 (6023)
Krabbendam H, **11:** 6292
Kraemer H C, **3:** 1642 (1639); **4:** 2194 (2192); **5:** 2714 (2713); **7:** 3783 (3778)
Kraemer R-D, **7:** 4026 (4023), 4030 (4029)
Kraevskij V V, **3:** 1328 (1327)
Krafchik M, **7:** 4248 (4248)
Kraft R H, **3:** 1820 (1819)
Krainer K, **6:** 3671 (3670)
Krais B, **10:** 5643 (5637)
Krajcik J, **2:** 1031 (1029)
Krajnc A, **1:** 277 (276)
Kramer J J, **7:** 3706 (3703)
Kramer M S, **8:** 4930 (4929)
Kramer R, **7:** 3914; **10:** 6012 (6009, 6010)
Kramlinger T, **6:** 3096 (3094); **10:** 5914 (5912)
Krampen G, **1:** 238 (237)
Krams M, **10:** 6164 (6162)
Krane J, **10:** 6244 (6242)
Kranjc A, **1:** 127 (121, 126); **11:** 6719 (6715, 6716)
Krantz D H, **7:** 4006
Krantz G C, **2:** 729 (722)
Krantz J, **8:** 4408 (4408)
Krantz P J, **8:** 4376 (4374)
Krantz S E, **4:** 1980 (1978)
Kranz J, **9:** 5308 (5306, 5307); **11:** 6558 (6555)
Krapf G, **3:** 1402 (1401)
Krapp A, **5:** 2769 (2764)
Krappman L, **8:** 4372 (4371, 4372)
Krappmann L, **9:** 5512 (5511)
Krashen S D, **4:** 2346 (2342, 2345), 2357 (2353); **6:** 3213, 3231 (3231), 3334 (3330), 3399 (3395)
Kraska K, **6:** 3325 (3321); **9:** 5403 (5401, 5402, 5403); **10:** 6159 (6158)
Krasnagor N, **5:** 2571
Krasnegor N A, **3:** 1643
Krasnow J H, **9:** 5268
Krathwohl D R, **1:** 390 (380, 382), 396 (392); **3:** 1804 (1801); **4:** 1847 (1844), 2017 (2012); **5:** 2867 (2866); **9:** 5324 (5319, 5320); **11:** 6328 (6321), 6445 (6440)
Kratochwill T R, **6:** 3523 (3517, 3520); **8:** 4661 (4659), 4662; **9:** 4977 (4974), 5489, 5490
Kraus V, **8:** 4896 (4893, 4894)
Krause Eheart B, **11:** 6397 (6397), 6398 (6396)
Krause G, **8:** 4474 (4469)
Krause O, **6:** 3261 (3257)
Krause R, **8:** 4816 (4814)
Krauss E S, **10:** 5783
Krauss M W, **1:** 362 (359, 361); **5:** 2813 (2812)
Krausz M, **9:** 4980 (4978, 4980)
Kraut A G, **3:** 1504
Krauth J, **2:** 1037 (1036)
Krebs B L, **7:** 4026 (4023)
Kreft I G G, **2:** 677 (677); **5:** 2596 (2590); **7:** 3986 (3984, 3985)
Kreft W, **8:** 4639
Kregel J, **11:** 6461 (6459)
Kreipe R E, **9:** 5435
Kreitlow B W, **7:** 4185; **8:** 4736
Krell D F, **8:** 4433
Kremer-Hayon L, **10:** 6062 (6059)
Krendl K, **6:** 3625 (3623)
Krepelka E J, **8:** 4731 (4729)
Kreppner K, **4:** 2261; **9:** 5512
Kress G, **2:** 1198 (1196)
Kretzmann N, **9:** 5124
Kreuter M W, **5:** 2572
Krewer B, **3:** 1252 (1246)
Krewski D, **7:** 3858
Kridel C, **3:** 1301 (1288, 1300); **10:** 5817
Krigel C, **3:** 1308
Krimerman L, **8:** 4455 (4455)
Krishnan Namboodiri N, **9:** 5130
Kristeva J, **5:** 2457 (2457)
Kritz M M, **1:** 162 (160)
Kroeber A L, **2:** 1073; **9:** 5210 (5208)
Krohne H W, **9:** 5406
Krol R A, **3:** 1486 (1483)
Kroll B M, **6:** 3452
Kroll J, **10:** 5804 (5802)
Kron F W, **10:** 6043 (6037)
Kronick R F, **3:** 1607 (1604)
Kropotkin P, **8:** 4575 (4573)
Kropp U, **8:** 4639
Kropveld P, **10:** 6244 (6242)
Kroth R, **10:** 5943 (5942)
Krowitz A, **8:** 4383 (4380)
Krueger A, **6:** 3184 (3179); **7:** 3820 (3816); **8:** 4901 (4898, 4900), 4902 (4898); **11:** 6653 (6653)
Krueger A O, **3:** 1666 (1663, 1664); **4:** 1841 (1838); **5:** 2993 (2990, 2991); **11:** 6638
Krueger J, **9:** 5211 (5208)
Krug D, **9:** 5318 (5314)
Krüger A, **2:** 906, 907, 910 (908)
Kruger A C, **8:** 4372 (4371)
Kruidenier B G, **4:** 2339 (2336)
Kruiger T, **2:** 1207 (1207)
Krulik S, **8:** 4648 (4643)
Krumbholtz J D, **9:** 5043
Krumboltz J, **10:** 6223
Krumm V, **2:** 893 (890); **3:** 1355 (1353); **9:** 5216 (5213, 5215)
Krupa S V, **5:** 2567
Krupp J A, **6:** 3435; **10:** 6214 (6210)
Kruppenbach S E, **4:** 2286 (2285)
Krupskaya N K, **8:** (4605)
Krus D, **3:** 1513 (1510)
Kruskal J B, **9:** 5158 (5157), 5503 (5497, 5498)
Kruskal W H, **7:** 3722
Krutetskii V A, **6:** 3671 (3669); **8:** 4648 (4643)
Krymkowski D H, **8:** 4896 (4892)
Kubey R W, **1:** 570 (564, 566); **11:** 6798 (6795, 6797)
Kubicek H, **3:** 1745 (1741)
Kubinger K D, **4:** 2017 (2012)
Kubiszyn T, **10:** 5822 (5818, 5820, 5821)
Küchenhoff H, **2:** 1037 (1033)
Kuder G F, **9:** 4995 (4991, 4992)
Kudjoh A, **11:** 6403
Kuebart F, **9:** 5497
Kuebert F, **3:** 1343
Kugel R, **3:** 1507; **10:** 5663
Kugler B, **7:** 4201 (4197, 4199); **8:** 4364 (4360); **9:** 5076 (5073, 5074)
Kuh G D, **1:** 77 (74); **10:** 5804 (5798, 5799, 5800, 5801, 5802, 5803), 5805, 5808
Kuhara-Kojima K, **7:** 3768 (3764)
Kuhl J, **1:** 31 (29), 203 (203); **5:** 2768 (2764);

6: 3325 (3321); 7: 3942 (3937, 3938); 9: 5403 (5400, 5401, 5402, 5403); 10: 6159 (6158)
Kuhl P, 6: 3224
Kuhlenkamp D, 6: 3425
Kuhn A, 8: 4581 (4578)
Kühn A D, 4: 2327
Kuhn D, 5: 2681; 7: 3920 (3918); 8: 4372, 4951 (4949), 4957 (4953); 10: 6178 (6176)
Kuhn T, 10: 6207 (6202, 6203, 6204, 6206, 6207)
Kuhn T S, 1: 60 (56); 3: 1348 (1344), (1540), (1770); 4: (1870), 2000 (1998); 6: 3671 (3669); 8: (4632), (4649), (4651); 9: 4980 (4977, 4978, 4979), 5030 (5025, 5026), 5050, 5055 (5051), 5334 (5330)
Kühnen H, 11: 6699 (6695)
Kukla I, 3: 1406
Kuklinski J H, 9: 5560 (5558)
Kularatna N G, 2: 1136 (1134, 1135)
Kulich J, 1: 127 (123, 124), 180 (176, 177), 563; 2: 661 (657); 5: 2937 (2935); 9: 5098; 11: 6551 (6550)
Kulick E, 5: 3050 (3046)
Kulick J, 5: 2759
Kulik C, 9: 5264 (5261)
Kulik C C, 1: 230 (228); 5: 2779 (2775); 6: 3631 (3625, 3630); 7: 3783 (3776, 3779, 3782), 4104 (4101); 11: 6339 (6336), 6484 (6483)
Kulik C E, 5: 2779 (2777)
Kulik C-L C, 2: 1006 (1003), 1170 (1169); 4: 1917 (1914); 9: 5043 (5042); 10: 6164 (6163); 11: 11 (7), 6307 (6301)
Kulik J, 1: 11 (7), 230 (228); 5: 2897 (2894); 7: (3758); 9: 5264 (5261)
Kulik J A, 2: 1002 (999), 1006 (1003), 1170 (1169); 4: 1917 (1914); 5: 2779 (2774, 2775, 2776, 2777); 6: 3631 (3625, 3630); 7: 3783 (3776, 3779, 3782), 4104 (4101); 9: 5043 (5042); 10: 6164 (6163), 6173 (6169); 11: 6339 (6336), 6484 (6483)
Kulik J E, 11: 6307 (6301)
Külpe O, 5: (2881)
Kumagai K, 7: 4100
Kumar K, 5: 2759
Kumar R, 2: 1127 (1124)
Kümmel, 1: 317 (311)
Kummer R, 2: 1025 (1024)
Kunkle J F, 4: 2351 (2348)
Kunzel K, 1: 180 (177)
Künzli R, 3: 1355 (1348, 1349, 1353)
Kuo Chieh-ming, 2: 1045
Kupfersmid J H, 5: 2669 (2668)
Kupisiewicz C, 6: 3608 (3605)
Küpper L, 6: 3334 (3330, 3333)
Kurachi A, 10: 5957 (5955)
Kurian G, 6: 3407
Kurian G T, 1: 184 (181, 182), 328; 3: 1589; 10: 5929 (5925)
Kurita J A, 7: 3768 (3765)
Kurland D M, 2: 973 (971, 972), 985 (983), 1012 (1008, 1010); 6: 3425; 7: 4088 (4084); 8: 4803 (4800); 11: 6457 (6453)
Kurland L C, 2: 1012 (1010)
Kurland N D, 10: 5954 (5951)
Kuroda Y, 8: 4581 (4576)
Kurth M, 10: 6073 (6071)
Kurtines W M, 9: 5512, 5518; 10: 6169
Kurt-Schai R, 10: 6053 (6052)
Kurtz B E, 10: 5772 (5771)
Kurucz R, 8: 4670 (4667)
Kusche C, 3: 1402 (1401)
Kushton J, 4: 2249
Kutner M A, 1: 103 (102)
Kutscha G, 1: 317
Kuttner B, 9: 5539 (5538)
Kuttner R, 3: 1820 (1819)
Kuzmich J, 7: 4025 (4023)
Kuznets S, 3: 1750 (1747)
Kwamena-Po M A, 5: 2486
Kwee H, 10: 5674 (5670)
Kweka A N, 1: 175 (173, 174)
Kwiatkowski J, 10: 5697 (5695)
Kwong J Y S, 9: 5216 (5212), 5281
Kyburg H E, 1: 480; 8: 4464
Kyle D W, 11: 6370 (6368)
Kyle J, 3: 1635 (1632)
Kyle N, 11: 6735 (6734)
Kyle R M J, 8: 4864 (4858, 4860)
Kyle W C, 6: 3416 (3412)
Kyllonen P C, 4: 2219 (2218); 5: 2768 (2762, 2763), 2921 (2919, 2920); 6: 3325 (3317, 3318, 3319, 3321); 7: 3879 (3876, 3878)
Kymlicka W, 4: 2004 (2004)
Kyriacou C, 1: 490 (487); 6: 3312 (3308); 10: 5924 (5920, 5921, 5922), 6062 (6060)
Kyvik S, 2: 900 (899)

La Bar C, 2: 1208
La Belle T J, 1: 135 (127, 129, 131, 133), 296 (291); 2: 1048 (1047, 1048), 1049; 3: 1486 (1483); 4: 2369; 6: 3256 (3253, 3254), 3262; 7: 4145 (4142, 4143, 4144, 4145); 9: 5367 (5366); 10: 5596 (5592, 5594); 11: 6282
La Bruyère J de, 6: (3499)
La Forme C, 5: 2813 (2811)
La Freniere P, 4: 2452 (2450)
La Vigna G W, 1: 490 (489)
Laagland E F, 7: 3995 (3995)
Laan S, 1: 374 (373); 7: 4307
Labaki B, 6: 3356
Laband D N, 6: 3101
Labaree D F, 10: 5991 (5989)
Labaw P J, 8: 4887
Laboa J M, 4: 2266, 2267
Laborde C, 6: 3638 (3635), 3652
Laborde J-M, 7: 4099 (4097)
Labouvie-Vief G, 1: 239 (235); 6: 3288 (3288); 8: 4824
Labov W, 4: 2257 (2252); 6: 3215 (3214), 3238 (3236)
Labrecque M F, 11: 6741
Labregère A, 5: 2910 (2907, 2908, 2909)
Labrousse A, 2: 618
Lacey A R, 8: 4447 (4443), 4634 (4630)
Lacey C, 1: 11 (7, 8), 296 (283); 2: 917 (916); 3: 1501; 4: 2166 (2159); 5: 3043; 9: 5313 (5311); 10: 6086 (6084), 6126 (6125), 6127 (6125)
Lachenmeyer C W, 9: 5050
Lachman M F, 1: 239 (237)
Laciura J, 6: 3334 (3330)
LaCrosse I, 5: 2665 (2663)
Lacy L, 11: 6625 (6623)
Ladd E C, 10: 5782 (5781)
Ladd G W, 8: 4368; 10: 5617 (5617), 5758
Ladenburg T, 9: 5578
Lado R, 6: 3439 (3438)
Ladson-Billings G, 3: (1232)
Laertius D, 8: (4532)
Laewen H J, 5: 2806 (2805)
Laferrière T, 1: 28
Lafleur C D, 6: 3373 (3371)
Lagerspetz K, 8: 4429
Lagerweij N, 9: 5246 (5245)
Lagos R, 3: 1824 (1822)
Lahey B B, 6: 3297; 8: 4368
Lahey L L, 10: 5939 (5937)
Lahey M A, 6: 3124 (3121), 3227, 3231 (3229); 10: 5680 (5675)
Lahm E A, 7: 3807 (3802)
Laird N M, 5: 2596 (2591); 7: 3861 (3860); 9: 5130 (5129), 5385; 11: 6339 (6336)
Laird S, 11: 6723 (6722)
Lajoie S P, 3: 1513 (1509, 1510, 1513); 4: 2199 (2198); 5: 2768 (2762)
Lakatos I, 4: 2000 (1998); 9: 5030; 10: 6207 (6206)
Lakeyard B B, 3: 1441
Lakil R, 10: 6149
Lakin K C, 2: 730 (722); 3: 1438 (1434, 1435, 1436); 7: 3833 (3831)
Lakomski G, 1: 60 (55, 56); 2: 1203 (1201, 1203); 3: 1774 (1769, 1770, 1773, 1774); 4: 2302 (2300, 2301); 5: 2589 (2587); 8: 4634 (4630); 9: 5030 (5029)
Lal S, 3: 1628 (1625)
Lalik R V, 10: 6219 (6217)
Lalkhen Y, 5: 2910 (2908)
Lallez R, 2: 618
Lally J R, 5: 2806 (2803, 2804); 7: 4296 (4295)
Lalonde R J, 4: 2150 (2147)
Lam Y, 3: 1602 (1600)
Lam Y Y, 9: 5359 (5357)
Lamb C E, 10: 6004 (6001)
Lamb D, 2: 1160 (1153)
Lamb H, 10: 5704 (5699, 5700); 11: 6784 (6784)
Lamb M, 4: 2145 (2144); 8: 4394, 4666 (4664), 4677 (4676)
Lamb M E, 3: 1236, 1739; 6: 3224; 8: 4383, 4542; 9: 5518
Lamb S, 5: 2669; 9: 5512
Lambert D, 8: 4375 (4373)
Lambert L, 9: 5318 (5316)
Lambert N M, 9: 5359 (5358)
Lambert P, 2: 906 (903)
Lambert R, 8: 4830 (4828)
Lambert R D, 4: 2346 (2340)
Lambert T, 11: 6461 (6460)
Lambert W E, 1: 537 (536); 4: 2346 (2344); 7: 3970 (3969)
Lambiri-Dimaki T, 5: 2523
Lamborn S D, 5: 2628 (2625), 2677 (2676)
Lamm Z, 6: 3151 (3151); 7: 3886 (3881)

Lamon S J, 4: 2435 (2432); 6: 3660
Lamont M, 4: 2272
Lamoure J, 11: 6807 (6805)
Lampert M L, 2: 1052 (1051); 6: 3302 (3298), 3655 (3654); 7: 4099 (4097); 9: 5363 (5361, 5362); 10: 5795 (5791, 5793), 6035 (6033), 6099 (6097), 6121 (6119)
Lancaster C S, 5: 2685 (2684)
Lancaster J, 3: (1722); 11: (6482)
Lancaster J B, 5: 2685 (2684)
Lancaster S, 11: 6712 (6711)
Lance K C, 6: 3399 (3394)
Lancey D, 5: 2607
Lancy D F, 6: 3452 (3448, 3450), 3453
Land K C, 8: 4352 (4339)
Landau M, 6: 3684, 3685
Landau S, 2: 867 (863)
Landau W M, 10: 5680 (5677)
Landberg I, 6: 3224 (3220)
Lander R, 3: 1411 (1407); 6: 3602 (3600); 9: 5246 (5245)
Landis R J, 8: 4930 (4929)
Lando M, 2: 1055 (1053)
Landow G P, 5: 2709 (2707)
Landquist J, 3: (1724); 9: 5055
Landry M, 5: 2965
Landsheere G de, 9: 5055
Landsman T, 5: 2692
Landsmann L T, 11: 6456
Lane F C, 3: 1655
Lane H, 3: (1295)
Lane J H, 9: 5185
Lane J-E, 6: 3197 (3196)
Lane S, 1: 374 (373); 3: 1359 (1358)
Lanford A G, 10: 5614 (5609)
Lang K, 6: 3189 (3187, 3188)
Lang Malliou K, 3: 1354 (1349)
Langdell C C, 10: (5944)
Langdon H, 10: 5694
Lange D, 4: 1857 (1855)
Lange G, 7: 3768 (3767)
Lange K, 8: 4383 (4382)
Lange P C, 5: 2870; 8: 4774 (4772)
Lange R R, 8: 4803 (4802)
Langefors B, 3: 1394 (1388)
Langeheine R, 4: 2017; 6: 3631 (3630)
Langenbach M, 3: 1602
Langer A, 8: 4383 (4380)
Langer E, 8: 4824
Langer E J, 11: 6456 (6455)
Langer J A, 5: 2665 (2664); 6: 3209 (3208), 3484 (3481, 3482); 7: 3725 (3724), 3920 (3918); 10: 5961; 11: 6777 (6776), 6780 (6779, 6780), 6785 (6783)
Langer P, 8: 4881 (4879, 4880)
Langer R M H, 1: 415 (413)
Langerman S, 2: 892 (890)
Langeveld M, 8: 4461 (4456)
Langford G, 10: 6096 (6095)
Langford P, 1: 423
Langley D, 8: 4479 (4478)
Langley P, 2: 842, 852, 1026 (1022); 8: 4722 (4720, 4721)
Langlois J H, 1: 234 (232)
Langmuir C R, 3: 1549 (1544)
Langsted O, 2: 701
Lanier J E, 10: 6012 (6009, 6010), 6103 (6101), 6106 (6105)
Lanier V, 1: 199 (195)
Lankshear C, 2: 1198 (1196)
Lanman B A, 7: 4225 (4224)
Lanouette J, 1: 280
Lanphier C M, 9: 5372 (5370)
Lansing M, 6: 3235 (3232, 3233)
Lantz O, 3: 1266 (1263)
Lanzetta J, 5: 2529 (2524)
Laor T, 10: 5618 (5614, 5615)
Laosa L M, 1: 362 (361); 3: 1643; 4: 2257, 2258; 7: 4301 (4299)
Lapco A, 9: 4977 (4976)
Lapkin S, 4: 2346 (2344), 2351 (2350)
Laplace P S, 1: (476)
Laplanche J, 8: 4816
LaPlante M P, 10: 5674
Lapointe A E, 1: 42 (37); 3: 1768 (1765); 4: 2140 (2136), 2439 (2436); 6: 3550 (3546); 7: 4053 (4053); 9: 5334 (5333), 5342 (5340), 5432 (5426), 5497 (5496); 11: 6334 (6332)
Lapp D, 1: 239 (238); 6: 3209; 8: 4947; 10: 5704 (5697); 11: 6784
Lappalainen A, 4: 2323
Lappan G, 5: 2767 (2762)
Lapsley D K, 7: 3920 (3919)
Laqueur T W, 5: 2607
Laqueur W, 10: 5783
Lareau A, 4: 2249 (2248), 2272 (2269, 2270, 2271); 9: 5216 (5215), 5313 (5312)
Large J A, 7: 3889 (3886)
Laridon P E, 4: 1903 (1902)
Larke P J, 10: 6106 (6105, 6106)
Larkin A I, 6: 3373 (3372); 7: 3986 (3982, 3984)
Larkin J H, 2: 867 (862); 3: 1529 (1526); 4: 2199 (2195, 2196); 8: 4479, 4727 (4727); 9: 5342 (5339); 10: 5745 (5741), 5790 (5783)
Larkin K C, 11: 6360 (6358)
Larner M B, 3: 1647 (1645); 4: 2145 (2144); 5: 2813 (2812)
Larntz K, 2: 1084 (1081)
LaRocque L, 9: 5223 (5221, 5222, 5223)
Larroyo F, 7: 3801
Larsen I B, 10: 6008 (6007)
Larsen S C, 7: 4081 (4077); 11: 6484
Larsen W A, 4: 2208 (2203)
Larsen-Freeman D, 4: 2339 (2336); 6: 3213 (3210)
Larson C W, 1: 28
Larson K A, 3: 1441 (1439, 1440, 1441)
Larson M S, 10: 6096 (6093), 6227 (6225); 11: 6723 (6719)
Larson R, 5: 2631 (2630); 6: 3288 (3288); 9: 5528 (5524); 10: 5758 (5757, 5758); 11: 6798 (6794, 6795, 6796, 6797)
Larson S, 10: 6214 (6212)
Larson S A, 3: 1438 (1435)
Larson-Shapiro N, 10: 5745 (5742)
Larsson S, 1: 103 (101); 7: 4179 (4179), 4180; 8: 4616, 4638 (4638); 10: 5829
Lasagna L, 3: 1619 (1611)
Laserna C, 8: 4873 (4866)
Laska J A, 3: 1635 (1631)
Lasker B, 2: 807 (804)
Lasker H M, 7: 4329 (4326)
Lasley T J, 3: 1538 (1537), 1635 (1632)
Lasser C, 11: 6765
Lassila O, 7: 4094 (4092)
Lassnigg L, 1: 431 (426)
Lasswell H, 8: 4556 (4550)
Last J M, 5: 2571
Latapí P, 6: 3256 (3254); 7: 3801
Latchem C R, 9: 5544 (5543)
Latham G P, 6: 3306 (3304)
Latham R, 11: 6707 (6706)
Lather P, 2: 933 (928, 930); 4: 2302 (2298)
Lattes Z R D, 3: 1671 (1667, 1668, 1669), 1672 (1668)
Latukefu S, 3: 1655 (1652)
Latus T, 10: 5668
Lau L J, 1: 254 (244, 245, 246, 247, 252, 253), 474 (467); 3: 1386 (1383), 1655 (1649), 1666 (1665), 1695 (1693, 1694), 1707 (1704), 1762 (1757); 4: 2418 (2414); 7: 4145 (4143)
Lau L L, 5: 2945 (2944)
Laubach F C, 1: 175 (174), (214); 3: (1259); 5: (2932)
Laudan L, 8: 4634 (4631); 9: 5030 (5029)
Lauder H, 1: 594; 4: 2292 (2290); 7: 4111
Laughlin J E, 9: 4974 (4972)
Lauglo J, 1: 244, 317; 3: 1416 (1413), 1690 (1686, 1687, 1689), 1739 (1736); 5: 2512; 6: 3261; 8: 4586 (4585); 9: 5076, 5168 (5159, 5165); 10: 6067 (6065); 11: 6256 (6253, 6254, 6255), 6265 (6262, 6263), 6266, 6699 (6690, 6691)
Laumann E O, 9: 5503 (5501, 5502), 5559 (5558)
Lauper G, 3: 1355 (1354)
Laurie A, 10: (5814)
Laurie S S, 3: (1723)
Laurillard D, 7: 3991; 8: 4429 (4425, 4429)
Laurillard L M, 2: 988 (986)
Lauritzen P, 7: 4296 (4294, 4295)
Laursen B, 2: 705 (702)
Lauterbach R, 3: 1355 (1352); 6: 3602 (3598)
Lauterbach U, 1: 317 (312, 314)
Lautrey J, 8: 4482 (4482)
Lautsch E, 2: 1036 (1036)
Lauwerys J A, 2: 1063; 8: 4491
Laux L, 9: 5406
Lauzon A C, 11: 6307 (6304)
Lavatelli C S, 5: 2665; 10: 6197
Lave C A, 3: 1425
Lave J, 1: 230 (229); 3: 1233 (1230), 1246, 1252 (1248, 1249, 1251), 1252 (1248), 1253; 5: 2685 (2684); 6: 3302 (3299), 3452 (3450, 3451); 8: 4727 (4726); 9: 5232 (5229), 5349 (5349); 11: 6456 (6454)
Lave L, 3: 1624
Laver J, 4: 2364 (2359)
Laville C, 9: 5577 (5576)
Lavoie D, 3: 1820 (1813)
Lavoisier A, 6: 3219 (3217)
Law B, 8: 4623 (4618, 4619)
Law M, 1: 168 (164); 10: 6058 (6055)

Lawler E E, **4:** 2165 (2163); **7:** 3826 (3823); **9:** 5175, 5180 (5176)
Lawler M, **2:** 1198 (1196)
Lawler R W, **6:** 3512
Lawless P, **11:** 6557
Lawley D N, **4:** 2241 (2233, 2235); **6:** 3253 (3248); **7:** 4016 (4009)
Lawlor H, **2:** 640
Lawlor S, **6:** 3459 (3454, 3456)
Lawn M A, **6:** 3197 (3191); **8:** 4586 (4582, 4583, 4584, 4585, 4586), 4601; **10:** 6072, 6079, 6096 (6093), 6139 (6133, 6135, 6138)
Lawrence E, **4:** 2388 (2386); **8:** 4670 (4668)
Lawrence P J, **2:** 816 (815); **10:** 6149 (6148)
Lawrence P R, **4:** 2166 (2164); **8:** 4519 (4516)
Lawry J R, **5:** 2779 (2774, 2776)
Lawson A, **3:** 1544 (1540, 1541); **6:** 3416
Lawson A E, **8:** 4479 (4476), 4652 (4649, 4652)
Lawson E N, **11:** 6765 (6761)
Lawson K H, **5:** 2737
Lawson L, **7:** 3774 (3774)
Lawson M J, **1:** 358; **7:** 3788 (3784, 3787)
Lawton D, **3:** 1301 (1295), 1720 (1717); **5:** 3043; **9:** 5252 (5249), 5523; **11:** 6558
Lawton S, **3:** 1720 (1717, 1718); **9:** 5201 (5197); **10:** 5613 (5611)
Lawton S B, **3:** 1607 (1604); **10:** 6043 (6037)
Lawton S C, **7:** 3768 (3764)
Lawton T A, **6:** 3474 (3473)
Lay W A, **3:** (1722), (1724); **4:** 1872 (1864, 1866)
Layard P R G, **3:** 1448 (1445); **6:** 3184 (3179, 3181)
Layard R, **1:** 520 (518); **2:** 1094 (1090); **3:** 1750; **4:** 2445; **5:** 2942; **6:** 3106; **9:** 5355 (5352, 5353)
Layne A, **1:** 465 (464)
Layton D, **1:** 244; **5:** 2903; **9:** 5299 (5297), 5328 (5324, 5325, 5326, 5327), 5338 (5335, 5338), 5349 (5349), 5350; **11:** 6251 (6248), 6292 (6292)
Lazar I, **2:** 688 (679); **3:** 1642 (1640, 1641); **5:** 2672 (2670); **7:** 3833 (3832); **11:** 6384 (6382)
Lazarini F, **9:** 5497
Lazarsfeld P F, **7:** 4315; **8:** 4912; **11:** 6445 (6441)
Lazarsfeld S, **3:** 1514
Lazaruk W A, **2:** 893 (892)
Lazarus R S, **1:** 203 (201), 221 (217); **4:** 1980 (1977); **10:** 5738 (5736)
Lazear E P, **2:** 1055 (1053); **3:** 1703 (1698), 1750 (1750); **5:** 2798 (2793); **6:** 3616 (3614); **11:** 6638 (6636)
Lazerson M, **11:** 6538 (6530, 6531)
Le Boterf G, **1:** 227 (222)
Le Guen M, **7:** 3912 (3906, 3907)
Le Métais J, **10:** 6047
Le Roux A A, **7:** 3889 (3888)
Lê Thành Khôi, **8:** 4491
Le Vine R, **4:** 2412 (2411)
Le Vine V T, **2:** 618
Leach R J, **7:** 3970 (3964)
Leacock E B, **1:** 296 (286, 290); **2:** 917 (916); **9:** 5572 (5569)
Leal Filho W D S, **5:** 2562 (2559)
Lealand G, **6:** 3496 (3496)
Leamer E, **3:** 1820 (1815)
Leap W, **7:** 3974 (3972)
Leary D E, **5:** 2880
Leatt D, **7:** 4240 (4239)
Leavey M B, **2:** 1099 (1096, 1098)
Leavitt H B, **10:** 5812 (5808), 5965, 6106 (6104)
Leavitt H J, **5:** 2529 (2524)
Leavitt R, **11:** 6397 (6397), 6398
LeBlanc P E, **7:** 4081 (4079)
Lebovici S, **1:** 88
Lecaros C, **3:** 1695 (1693)
Lechte R, **4:** 2423 (2421)
LeClair C, **4:** 2351 (2348)
Leclerc G, **9:** 5197 (5195)
Leclercq D, **4:** 2011
Leclercq J-M, **11:** 6265 (6262, 6264)
LeCompte M D, **1:** 296 (289); **2:** 1074; **3:** 1253, 1607; **4:** 2046 (2044), 2052 (2047, 2048, 2050, 2051); **10:** 5606 (5601), 5607 (5604), 5924 (5920, 5921, 5922, 5923); **11:** 6466
Lecours A R, **1:** 15 (13)
Leder G C, **6:** 3643 (3639, 3640, 3642), 3652 (3649)
Lederman A, **1:** 198 (197)
Lederman N G, **10:** 6178 (6176, 6177)
Ledolter J, **8:** 4788
Ledoux N, **10:** 5738 (5736, 5737)
Leduc-Fayette D, **9:** 5090 (5090)
Lee B, **4:** 1917 (1915)
Lee D, **1:** 296 (291)
Lee E S, **9:** 5130 (5125), 5142 (5137)
Lee Eun-Jin, **4:** 2432 (2431)
Lee H R, **1:** (267)
Lee J A, **1:** 127 (124)
Lee J W, **1:** 110 (108, 110)
Lee K H, **1:** 474 (466)
Lee L, **6:** 3638 (3635); **9:** 5445
Lee M K, **5:** 2643
Lee M L, **11:** 6633 (6628)
Lee M W, **3:** 1643 (1640)
Lee P C, **4:** 2452 (2451)
Lee P J, **5:** 2623
Lee P S C, **9:** 5490 (5488)
Lee R D, **3:** 1676; **4:** 2412; **6:** 3106; **11:** 6615
Lee S, **3:** 1240 (1239), 1241 (1238)
Lee S-Y, **3:** 1768 (1765); **4:** 2140 (2132, 2137, 2138); **5:** 2628 (2625, 2627)
Lee V E, **1:** 11 (7), 520 (516); **2:** 834 (832, 833); **4:** 1938 (1935); **5:** 2596 (2594), 2813 (2812), 2931 (2930); **8:** 4845 (4841, 4842); **9:** 5378 (5374, 5375, 5377), 5379 (5373, 5374, 5375, 5376, 5377), 5445 (5444); **10:** 5607 (5604)
Lee Y, **1:** 110 (108, 110), 296 (293)
Leeb-Lundberg K, **4:** 2388
Leech R, **9:** 5567 (5565)
Leekam S R, **2:** 857 (854)
Leenders F J, **3:** 1553 (1551)
Leeper H A, **11:** 6707 (6704)
Lees D, **8:** 4364 (4361); **11:** 6431 (6427)
Lees J, **10:** 5680 (5676)
Lees S, **5:** 2457 (2454); **10:** 5826 (5824, 5825, 5826)
Leestma R, **6:** 3085, 3312; **10:** 5991 (5987)
Leeuwen S van, **2:** 1094 (1090, 1091, 1092)
Lefebvre J, **2:** 1121
Lefevre J, **8:** 4473 (4472)
Leff G, **9:** 5124
Leffert N, **8:** 4423 (4421)
Lefkowitz B, **2:** 711 (710)
Lefkowitz M R, **11:** 6712 (6711)
Lefranc R, **9:** 5544 (5543)
Léger A, **2:** 917 (917)
Legg B H, **4:** 2266 (2264)
Leggatt T, **10:** 6096
Legge A H, **5:** 2567
Legge C D, **11:** 6438 (6432)
Legge D L, **1:** 184; **5:** 2532; **11:** 6438 (6433)
Leggett E L, **1:** 31 (28, 29, 31); **2:** 867 (865, 866); **5:** 2768 (2764)
Legrand L, **4:** 2385
Legresley K, **1:** 409 (407)
Legters N, **3:** 1607 (1605, 1606)
Lehmacher W, **2:** 1037 (1036)
Lehman D R, **2:** 838 (837); **8:** 4951 (4950)
Lehman I I, **7:** 4000 (3997, 3998)
Lehman J, **2:** 1031 (1028)
Lehman R H, **11:** 6265 (6262)
Lehmann I J, **11:** 6315 (6313)
Lehmann R, **3:** 1768 (1764, 1765)
Lehmann R H, **4:** 2024 (2020, 2022, 2024); **11:** 6266 (6262)
Lehming R, **2:** 942; **4:** 1857; **5:** 2847
Lehr U, **8:** 4719 (4716)
Lehrer R, **2:** 984 (983); **11:** 6456 (6454)
Lehtinen E, **2:** 969 (966)
Lehtinen L E, **10:** 5686 (5681)
Lehtisalo L, **4:** 2324
Lehtisalo T, **7:** 4094 (4092)
Lehtonen H, **7:** 4180
Lehtonen J, **6:** 3439 (3438)
Leibenstein H, **3:** 1676 (1673)
Leiblum M D, **10:** 5622
Leibniz G W von, **6:** (3316, 3680)
Leibowitz A, **2:** 693 (690), 1055 (1053); **6:** 3106 (3105)
Leicester M, **11:** 6719 (6715)
Leichenke S, **11:** 6461 (6457)
Leiderman P H, **5:** 2627 (2625); **6:** 3227
Leigh D, **1:** 158 (154)
Leigh D E, **1:** 310 (307)
Leigh J, **11:** 6798 (6796)
Leigh J E, **7:** 4081 (4077)
Leigh J H, **5:** 2931 (2923)
Leigh J P, **4:** 2212 (2209)
Leighten P, **4:** 2199 (2197)
Leighton L, **11:** 6638 (6635)
Leiman J M, **4:** 2241 (2239)
Leinbach M D, **4:** 2449 (2447), 2452 (2450, 2451)
Leinhardt G, **2:** 820 (817, 818, 820); **4:** 2073 (2073), 2208 (2200); **5:** 2869 (2868), 2870 (2869); **6:** 3389 (3386); **9:** 5264 (5260), 5562 (5561); **10:** 6026 (6023), 6035 (6033),

6122 (6117, 6118, 6119), 6183; **11:** 6608 (6605)
Leinhardt S, **4:** 2156, 2208 (2203); **5:** 2596; **7:** 3986
Leinhardt S L, **9:** 5560
Leinwand G, **5:** 2623 (2623)
Leirman W, **1:** 139 (135), 504, 563; **2:** 640; **5:** 2759
Leis P, **3:** 1755 (1753), 1756 (1753)
Leisch-Kriesl, **11:** 6747 (6742)
Leiser D, **9:** 5563
Leitenberg H, **4:** 2100 (2098)
Leithwood K A, **1:** 73 (69, 72); **4:** 2073 (2071), 2074 (2070, 2073); **5:** 2509 (2508); **6:** 3284 (3282), 3602 (3600); **9:** 5216 (5213), 5264 (5262, 5263), 5539; **10:** 5929, 5935 (5930, 5932), 6043 (6037)
Leitner E, **9:** 5497
Leler H, **6:** 3463 (3462)
Leleux S A, **7:** 4293
Lemaitre M J, **2:** 746
Leman J, **1:** 296 (283)
Lemann N, **8:** 4830 (4829)
LeMay M, **7:** 4081 (4078)
Lemel H, **5:** 2945 (2943)
Lemennicier B, **2:** 1055 (1052, 1054)
Lemert C C, **2:** 1073 (1071)
Lemert E, **2:** 1073 (1070)
Lemeshow S, **9:** 5142
Lemke J L, **6:** 3219 (3218); **10:** 6197
LeMon R, **4:** 1911 (1908, 1909, 1910)
Lempert R O, **8:** 4951 (4950)
Lempert W, **1:** 310 (308)
Lemyre L, **3:** 1520 (1519)
Lenglet F, **5:** 2897 (2893)
Lengrand P, **1:** 100 (95), 120 (119), 152 (143), 180 (180); **6:** 3421 (3417, 3418, 3419), 3422; **11:** 6420
Lenhardt G, **10:** 5607 (5605)
Lenhart V, **11:** 6699 (6695)
Lenin V I, **6:** 3621 (3617); **7:** (3847); **8:** (4605); **9:** (5092)
Lenk C, **2:** 982 (981)
Lennenberg E H, **6:** 3215 (3213)
Lennerstrand G, **10:** 5680, 5681
Lens W, **5:** 2768 (2764), 2769 (2764); **7:** 3942 (3940, 3941)
Lenskyj H, **9:** 5441 (5439)
Lensmire T J, **10:** 5795 (5794)
Lent R M, **2:** 1139 (1137, 1138)
Lent R W, **11:** 6360 (6358)
Lentz B F, **6:** 3101
Lentz R, **7:** 3774 (3773)
Lenz B, **2:** 867 (863)
Lenzen D, **7:** 3924; **10:** 5662; **11:** 6684
Leo J, **11:** 6576 (6574)
Leonard J E, **11:** 6707 (6704)
Leonard L B, **6:** 3224 (3222, 3223)
Leonard R, **1:** 239; **3:** 1635 (1632)
Leonard V W, **5:** 2512 (2511)
Leonardi R, **10:** 6078
Leonardi R L, **5:** 2697 (2696)
Leone C M, **5:** 2631 (2629, 2630); **11:** 6390 (6388)
Leong C K, **8:** 4935 (4932)
Leonhard C, **7:** 4026 (4023); **8:** 4388
Leont'ev A N, **3:** 1252 (1248, 1249)
Leontief W W, **4:** (1864), (1869); **11:** 6260 (6259)
Leontiev A N, **5:** (2882); **9:** 5403 (5400)
Leontiev W, **6:** (3289)
Leontyev A N, **9:** 5548
Leopold A, **4:** 1995 (1992)
Lepenies W, **4:** 2172
Lepetit B, **3:** 1553
Leplin J, **9:** 4980 (4979)
Lepper M R, **1:** 31 (30); **2:** 1006 (1002, 1003, 1004); **4:** 2281 (2280); **5:** 2768 (2763); **7:** 3744, 3942 (3939, 3941)
Leprince F, **11:** 6398 (6396)
Lerchalolarn C, **4:** 1917 (1915)
LeRiche L W, **9:** 5577 (5573)
Lerman D, **11:** 6360 (6356)
Lerman R I, **1:** 310 (309)
Lerner D, **3:** 1655 (1650); **8:** 4556 (4550)
Lerner I Y, **3:** 1328 (1327)
Lerner J V, **11:** 6310 (6308)
Lerner J W, **7:** 3808 (3807)
Lerner M J, **5:** 2665 (2663); **8:** 4719
Lerner R M, **1:** 88 (83, 84, 85), 89; **2:** 846; **4:** 1967, 2261, 2439; **5:** 2665 (2659), 2677; **6:** 3428; **8:** 4824; **9:** 5406, 5512; **11:** 6310 (6308)
Leron U, **6:** 3512 (3511)
Lesgold A M, **1:** 374; **2:** 1001 (1001), 1012 (1008); **3:** 1513 (1509, 1510, 1513); **4:** 2199 (2198); **5:** 2767, 2768 (2762, 2765), 2769, 3325 (3317); **6:** 3660; **7:** 3726 (3725), 3774 (3773), 3788, 3942; **10:** 6026 (6023)
Lesh R, **6:** 3684 (3676), 3685 (3675)
Leshin C, **5:** 2862; **10:** 5913 (5911)
Lesko N, **3:** 1607 (1603, 1605); **8:** 4845 (4841); **9:** 5216 (5214); **11:** 6727 (6726)
Leslie A M, **2:** 856 (854)
Leslie J, **2:** 1055 (1053); **3:** 1628 (1627)
Leslie L L, **2:** 1126 (1124), 1131 (1128)
Lesourne J, **4:** 2331, 2385
Lesser G, **5:** 2897 (2895)
Lesser R, **10:** 5693 (5692, 5693)
Lester B M, **5:** 2802 (2799)
Lester N B, **10:** 5961
Leu D J, **1:** 77; **4:** 2229
Leune J, **9:** 5246
Leung J, **5:** 2643 (2637)
Leung J P, **6:** 3512 (3511)
Leung K, **5:** 2651
Leushina A M, **5:** 2768 (2762)
Levacic R, **9:** 5185 (5184), 5216 (5211, 5212)
Levasseur J, **5:** 2515 (2513)
Levelt W J M, **6:** 3224, 3428 (3426)
Levenson S, **4:** 2351
Lever J, **4:** 2296 (2293)
Leveson I, **4:** 2212 (2209)
Levesque H J, **8:** 4722 (4719)
Levett J, **3:** 1398 (1395)
Levhari D, **2:** 1056; **7:** 4324 (4323)
Levie W H, **2:** 888; **4:** 2011 (2009); **7:** 3753 (3745), 3760 (3757, 3758), 3774 (3771, 3773)
Levien R E, **3:** 1394 (1388)
Levin H M, **1:** 265, 296 (286), 520 (516); **2:** 711 (710), 760 (758), 775 (772, 775), 1072 (1067, 1068), 1073 (1066), 1074, 1094 (1089), 1127 (1121, 1125, 1126), 1131 (1127, 1129, 1130), 1135 (1132, 1133, 1134), 1136 (1134, 1135), 1152; **3:** 1655 (1649), 1671 (1669, 1670), 1685, 1695 (1691), 1713 (1709, 1711), 1761 (1756), 1784 (1779, 1780, 1781), 1789 (1784), 1820 (1818, 1819); **4:** 1863 (1858), 1911 (1904, 1905, 1907, 1908, 1909, 1910), (2102); **5:** 2744 (2743), 2942; **6:** 3106 (3103, 3105), 3189, 3368 (3367), 3425 (3423, 3424), 3550 (3545, 3546), 3621 (3619); **7:** 3821 (3816, 3819), 4255 (4250), 4263 (4261); **8:** 4364 (4362), 4509 (4505), 4568 (4562, 4563, 4564), 4571 (4569), 4707 (4706), 4830, 4831, 4844, 4845, 4964 (4961); **9:** 5038 (5038), 5066 (5063), 5076 (5074), 5196, 5206 (5202, 5203, 5204), 5240 (5235, 5236, 5238, 5239, 5240), 5539 (5533); **10:** 5754 (5751), 5954 (5949); **11:** 6260 (6257, 6258, 6259), 6261 (6257), 6277 (6273), 6282 (6282), 6283 (6279), 6283, 6424 (6422, 6424), 6563 (6562)
Levin J A, **2:** 982 (978), 1175 (1173); **6:** 3302; **11:** 6785 (6783)
Levin J R, **1:** 194 (191); **2:** 888; **6:** 3508 (3503); **7:** 3768 (3765, 3766), 3774 (3773), 3920
Levin L, **4:** 2357 (2353)
Levin M R, **2:** 1073 (1066); **6:** 3421 (3418)
Levin S, **6:** 3625 (3623)
Levin T, **2:** 1175 (1173)
Levinas E, **8:** (4459)
Levine A, **10:** 5782 (5778)
Levine C, **7:** 3925 (3921, 3923)
Levine D, **1:** 296; **5:** 2856 (2853)
Levine D K, **3:** 1745 (1741)
Levine D M, **8:** 4574
Levine D U, **3:** 1486 (1484); **6:** 3631 (3627); **10:** 5613 (5610), 6227 (6226)
Levine D W, **9:** 5359 (5357)
Levine H, **2:** 1165 (1162)
Levine H A, **11:** 6775 (6770)
Levine H G, **2:** 645 (644)
Levine J, **5:** 2532 (2529, 2531)
Levine J M, **2:** 838 (837); **6:** 3297; **9:** 5507; **10:** 6088
Levine K, **8:** 4639; **10:** 5596 (5593)
Levine M, **4:** (2103); **9:** 5191, 5318 (5315); **10:** 5935
Levine M D, **2:** 868 (861)
Levine M L, **5:** 2575
Levine M V, **7:** 4000 (4000)
Levine R, **3:** 1628 (1627), 1676 (1675, 1676); **8:** 4873 (4866)
LeVine R A, **1:** 296 (287, 292); **3:** 1240 (1237, 1238); **7:** 4301; **9:** 5510 (5509)
Levine S, **10:** 5939 (5936)
Levinsohn H, **7:** 4316 (4314)
Levinson D J, **6:** 3428 (3426); **10:** 5939 (5935)
Levis D S, **10:** 5977 (5975), 6106 (6105)
Levi-Strauss C, **2:** 1073 (1071)
Levitas M, **2:** 1073 (1067)
Leviton L C, **4:** 2089 (2088), 2108 (2101, 2102, 2103, 2106, 2107, 2108); **8:** 4783 (4780); **11:** 6384
Levitsky J, **4:** 1991 (1985, 1986)

Levitt C, **10:** 5782 (5780)
Levitz R, **3:** 1602
Levstik L, **9:** 5577 (5576)
Levstik L S, **9:** 5562 (5561), 5577 (5576)
Levy D, **8:** 4835 (4832, 4833, 4834); **10:** 5754 (5751), 5782 (5779)
Levy D C, **1:** 265; **8:** 4830, 4831
Levy G D, **4:** 2449 (2447)
Levy J, **2:** 811 (809); **6:** 3538
Levy M E, **5:** 2945 (2944)
Levy M R, **1:** 570
Levy P, **11:** 6360 (6358)
Levy P S, **9:** 5142
Levy S, **4:** 2218 (2218); **7:** 3879 (3876); **9:** 5503 (5503)
Levy V M, **7:** 3920 (3919)
Levy-Garboua L, **2:** 1055 (1052), 1152
Levy-Leblond J-M, **9:** 5349 (5348)
Lewenstein B V, **9:** 5349 (5347)
Lewin A Y, **3:** 1386 (1382)
Lewin H, **3:** 1671 (1670)
Lewin H M, **8:** 4964
Lewin K, **1:** 48 (44); **2:** 811 (807); **3:** (1536), 1647 (1645), 1789 (1788); **4:** (1861); **5:** 2529 (2523, 2524), 2773 (2771); **7:** (3937), 4329 (4327); **8:** 4394 (4392); **9:** 5281; **10:** 6099 (6096), 6224 (6220)
Lewin K M, **6:** 3608 (3603, 3605, 3606, 3607); **8:** 4514 (4512); **10:** 5973
Lewis A, **1:** 296 (284); **2:** 1213 (1211)
Lewis A B, **10:** 5831 (5831)
Lewis A J, **3:** 1315 (1312); **7:** 4249
Lewis C, **8:** 4359 (4357), 4873 (4870)
Lewis D, **5:** 2509 (2508), 2779 (2775), 2870 (2868); **6:** (3457); **7:** 3912 (3910); **9:** 5223 (5221); **11:** 6390 (6388, 6389)
Lewis E G, **1:** 396 (393); **3:** 1768 (1763); **4:** 2357 (2352); **5:** 2978 (2974); **6:** 3439 (3436)
Lewis E L, **4:** 2439 (2437); **9:** 5342 (5339, 5340)
Lewis G E, **8:** 4940
Lewis G K, **1:** 444
Lewis H D, **9:** 5169 (5160), 5252 (5248)
Lewis H W, **4:** 2331
Lewis I, **1:** 48 (46)
Lewis J, **8:** 4479 (4475)
Lewis J F, **3:** 1619
Lewis J R, **9:** 5294
Lewis L, **8:** 4571 (4569)
Lewis L S, **8:** 4830
Lewis M, **1:** 234; **2:** 705 (702), 973 (972); **3:** 1520 (1514); **4:** 1966 (1964), 1967 (1964); **5:** 2769 (2760); **6:** 3625; **7:** 4301 (4298); **9:** 5394 (5391, 5393); **10:** 6159 (6155); **11:** 6633 (6628)
Lewis M W, **2:** 838 (835)
Lewis O, **2:** 917 (916); **6:** 3238 (3235)
Lewis P, **10:** 6085
Lewis R, **1:** 348; **2:** 988; **3:** 1579 (1576), 1778; **4:** 2186 (2184, 2185); **7:** 4016 (4012); **10:** 5625 (5624), 6008 (6005)
Lewis R B, **2:** 718 (712, 714, 715), 719; **11:** 6315 (6313, 6314)
Lewis S G, **9:** 5228 (5225, 5227)
Lewis T, **9:** 5081 (5077); **11:** 6292 (6288, 6291)
Lewis W A, **3:** 1685 (1682)
Lewontin R C, **2:** 1084 (1081)
Lewy A, **1:** 244; **2:** 1107; **3:** 1271 (1269), 1272, 1278 (1274), 1307, 1308, 1325, 1355 (1351), 1367; **4:** 2218 (2218), 2435 (2434); **5:** 2856 (2853); **6:** 3647; **7:** 4060, 4316 (4315); **8:** 4388, 4751 (4745); **10:** 5817, 5995, 6092
Leyser Y, **4:** 1980 (1978, 1979)
Lezotte L W, **3:** 1745 (1741); **4:** 1934 (1930, 1932); **10:** 5750 (5746)
L'Hommedieu R, **10:** 6234 (6233)
Li C, **7:** 4088 (4085)
Li Jian, **2:** 755
Li K T, **4:** 1924 (1918)
Li L, **4:** 2183
Li W L, **11:** 6633 (6628)
Li Z, **5:** 2862 (2860); **8:** 4803 (4800)
Liang Cheng-t'ing, **2:** 1045 (1043, 1045)
Liao Y-K C, **7:** 4088 (4084)
Liaw F R, **3:** 1624 (1623), 1642 (1641); **5:** 2813 (2812)
Liben L S, **4:** 2449
Liberman A M, **8:** 4945 (4944)
Liberman I Y, **8:** 4945 (4944)
Liberoff M, **1:** 409 (404)
Licata J, **3:** 1537 (1537)
Licht B G, **10:** 5826 (5824)
Lichtenberg J, **8:** 4816 (4814)
Lichtenstein P, **11:** 6492 (6489, 6491)
Lichtenstein R, **3:** 1624 (1621, 1622)
Lichtner M, **1:** 180 (177); **5:** 2937 (2936); **10:** 5596 (5596)
Lickona T, **1:** 380
Liddel C, **8:** 4680 (4680)
Liddell S K, **3:** 1402 (1400)
Lidstone J, **5:** 2469 (2468, 2469), 2470
Lidz C S, **1:** 5 (5); **2:** 860 (859); **3:** 1402; **5:** 2767, 2768 (2762); **6:** 3315 (3314); **8:** 4730
Lieb-Brilhart B, **7:** 3935 (3935)
Liebenstein H, **3:** 1746 (1741)
Lieber J, **7:** 3808 (3802)
Lieberman A, **1:** 23; **3:** 1278 (1278), 1494 (1492); **5:** 2714 (2709), 2779; **6:** 3603 (3602); **7:** 3872 (3867), 3886; **8:** 4661 (4661); **9:** 5246 (5241); **10:** 5713 (5711), 5929, 5935 (5932), 6043 (6039), 6099, 6187
Lieberman R, **2:** 806 (805)
Liebert R M, **9:** 5050; **11:** 6360 (6356)
Liebeskind J, **4:** 1972 (1969)
Liebig, **9:** (5335)
Liebknecht W, **1:** 139 (136)
Liebman A, **10:** 5783
Liebman E, **9:** 5130 (5129)
Liebow E B, **9:** 5560 (5557)
Liebowitz J, **4:** 1924; **11:** 6307 (6299)
Liell P, **6:** 3360; **9:** 5255
Lien I-n, **10:** 5694
Lienert G A, **2:** 1037 (1031, 1033, 1036)
Liepa G U, **5:** 2567
Lietard B, **5:** 2937
Liétard F, **2:** 665 (663)
Lietz P, **1:** 396 (393); **2:** 957 (956)
Liew-On M, **7:** 3791 (3790)
Ligappa S, **7:** 4124
Light J, **1:** 409 (407, 408)
Light L L, **7:** 3763 (3762)
Light P, **4:** 1899 (1896); **8:** 4957 (4954); **9:** 5548 (5547)
Light R J, **2:** 688 (686); **4:** 2375; **10:** 6239 (6236), 6240
Lightfoot M, **3:** 1739 (1738)
Lightfoot S, **9:** 5210 (5209)
Lightfoot S L, **3:** 1257 (1255), 1320 (1319); **9:** 5379 (5376, 5377); **10:** 6086 (6085)
Lighthall F F, **11:** 6360 (6358)
Liker J D, **4:** 2261 (2260)
Likert R A, **1:** 390 (382), 396 (392); **7:** 3706 (3703); **8:** 4519 (4516), 4923 (4918, 4921); **9:** 5158 (5153)
Liljefors R, **6:** 3559 (3557)
Lillard L A, **2:** 1094 (1090), 1152; **4:** 2418 (2417), 2419; **6:** 3616 (3615)
Lillis K M, **1:** 244, 317; **2:** 914 (911, 912); **3:** 1416, 1690 (1687, 1689), 1739 (1736); **6:** 3261; **7:** 4141 (4140); **8:** 4688, 4707 (4704, 4705); **9:** 5240 (5240); **10:** 5753, 6067; **11:** 6256, 6265 (6262), 6266 (6263), 6699 (6691)
Lilly M S, **7:** 3833 (3832)
Lilyquist J M, **6:** 3096
Lima A K, **7:** 3821 (3816, 3820)
Limage L, **1:** 103 (101, 102); **8:** 4639
Limberg J W, **9:** 5013
Lin A, **10:** 5674 (5671)
Lin C, **1:** 570 (565)
Lin F L, **6:** 3685 (3678)
Lin H T, **2:** 1182 (1182)
Lin J, **2:** 635 (634); **10:** 5782 (5782)
Lin N, **9:** 5539 (5537)
Lin P, **7:** 4099 (4098)
Lin Y G, **2:** 969 (966)
Lin Z, **7:** 4088 (4085)
Linacre J M, **5:** 3055 (3053); **6:** 3124 (3122); **7:** 4307 (4306); **8:** 4923 (4923)
Linberg L, **8:** 4568
Lincoln J R, **2:** 1094 (1091)
Lincoln L S, **11:** 6465 (6462)
Lincoln Y S, **2:** 645 (644); **3:** 1283 (1282), 1287 (1285), 1474 (1474), 1820 (1818); **4:** 2089 (2087), (2103), 2119 (2112, 2116), 2374 (2372), 2375; **7:** 4051 (4050), 4059 (4057), 4319 (4316, 4318, 4319); **9:** 4980 (4977, 4978), 5030 (5022, 5023, 5025, 5027); **11:** 6466 (6464, 6465)
Lind A, **1:** 175 (171, 172, 173, 174), 215, 474 (468); **3:** 1262 (1259); **5:** 2758 (2757, 2758); **6:** 3467
Lind G, **7:** 3920 (3918)
Lindauer D L, **3:** 1707 (1703); **11:** 6638 (6635)
Lindbeck A, **5:** 2942
Lindberg K J, **5:** 2689 (2687)
Lindberg L N, **6:** 3368
Lindberg U, **11:** 6803 (6802)
Lindberg W, **2:** 1102 (1100)
Lindblom C E, **3:** (1427), 1431 (1426); **4:** 1864; **5:** 2672 (2671); **8:** 4519 (4515)

Lindborg R, **3:** 1464 (1463)
Linde S G, **7:** 3970 (3969)
Lindelow J, **9:** 5308 (5304)
Lindeman E C L, **1:** 142 (140), 168 (164), 277 (275)
Linder C J, **8:** 4429 (4429)
Lindert P, **6:** 3144 (3139)
Lindgren A, **2:** (737)
Lindgren B W, **3:** 1421 (1419)
Lindgren G, **11:** 6492 (6491)
Lindguist H M, **1:** 296 (282)
Lindholm S, **9:** 5055
Lindle J, **9:** 5216 (5214)
Lindley D V, **1:** 480; **3:** 1421 (1420); **5:** 2596 (2590, 2591); **9:** 5130 (5129)
Lindman H, **1:** 480 (477, 479)
Lindover D L, **8:** 4839 (4838, 4839)
Lindquist E F, **1:** 42 (33), 370 (363); **4:** 2079; **5:** 2931 (2923); **9:** 4995 (4981); **11:** 6349 (6340, 6342)
Lindquist M M, **1:** 41 (37); **6:** 3685 (3680)
Lindsay B, **8:** 4947 (4945); **11:** 6621 (6618)
Lindsay D, **5:** 2998
Lindsay M, **10:** 5957 (5956)
Lindsay P, **11:** 6798 (6797)
Lindsey G, **1:** 358
Lindsey G, **9:** 5158
Lindvall C M, **4:** 1848 (1843); **5:** 2870 (2868)
Lindzey G, **2:** 1079; **3:** 1797; **5:** 2665, 3061; **8:** 4727, 4791 (4788); **9:** 5130; **10:** 5617 (5614, 5615)
Lines P, **2:** 893 (889)
Lingoes J C, **9:** 5503 (5497, 5499, 5500)
Link C, **2:** 1012 (1008); **10:** 6008 (6007)
Linke R, **1:** 358
Linn M C, **2:** 867 (862), 984, 985 (983), 1006; **3:** 1529 (1526); **4:** 2435 (2434), 2439 (2436, 2437); **5:** 2491 (2489), 2665 (2663); **7:** 3810 (3809), 4104 (4100, 4101, 4102, 4103); **8:** 4479 (4478), 4722, 4751 (4743), 4957 (4953, 4956); **9:** 5341 (5338, 5340, 5341), 5342 (5339, 5340), 5432 (5423, 5426, 5427, 5428), 5435 (5433), 5445
Linn P, **1:** 157 (154)
Linn R L, **1:** 52, 370 (363, 369, 370), 374 (371, 372, 373); **2:** 677 (672, 673), 998; **4:** 1848 (1847), 2183, 2241 (2238); **5:** 2769, 2921, 3050 (3049); **7:** 3726 (3724), 4000 (4000); **8:** 4622, 4623 (4619, 4622), 4648, 4731 (4730), 4751 (4743, 4747); **9:** 4995; **10:** 5772, 6159, 6173; **11:** 6315 (6314), 6320 (6315), 6328, 6339, 6349 (6340, 6343), 6355, 6677
Linsker R, **7:** 3950 (3948)
Linstone H, **3:** 1443 (1442), 1830 (1828)
Lintner M, **10:** 6008 (6005, 6006)
Linton H, **1:** 322 (318)
Linton H B, **2:** 871 (869)
Linton R, **10:** (6127)
Linz D, **1:** 570 (568)
Lion A, **1:** 103
Lionis C, **5:** 2571 (2569)
Lipham J M, **1:** 77
Lipka J M, **3:** 1236 (1235)
Lipman M, **1:** 28, 199 (197); **2:** 868 (862), 1207 (1205, 1206, 1207); **5:** (2695)
Lipman P, **9:** 5060 (5059)
Lipman-Blumen J, **4:** 2412 (2407)
Lippitt P, **11:** (6482)
Lippitt R, **5:** 2529 (2524); **7:** (4236); **11:** (6482)
Lips H M, **4:** 2427 (2424, 2425)
Lipset S M, **7:** 3864 (3862); **9:** 5553 (5552); **10:** 5782 (5781), 5783, 6227
Lipsey M, **4:** 2194 (2189, 2190, 2191, 2192, 2193, 2194), 2375
Lipsey M W, **11:** 6384 (6379)
Lipsitt L P, **3:** 1624 (1621); **5:** 2664 (2660), 2802 (2800, 2801); **6:** 3297, 3427 (3426); **8:** 4383, 4719 (4716)
Lipsky D K, **2:** 711 (710), 729 (728); **3:** 1508; **5:** 2907 (2905), 2971 (2966); **6:** 3559 (3557); **8:** 4661 (4658), 4935 (4933); **9:** 5071
Lipsky M, **10:** 5668 (5666), 6139
Lipsmeier A, **1:** 317; **11:** 6659 (6658), 6684
Lipson M, **9:** 5363
Lipson M Y, **6:** 3329 (3327)
Lipton G C, **4:** 2351 (2346, 2350)
Lipton M, **5:** 2993
Liska A E, **1:** 358 (356)
Liss M B, **4:** 2452
Lissak M, **5:** 3028
Lissitz R W, **2:** 796 (795); **11:** 6355 (6349)
Lister I, **2:** 770 (767); **8:** 4571 (4569); **9:** 5582 (5578); **10:** 5585 (5583, 5585)
Liston D P, **1:** 48 (45); **2:** 785; **3:** 1636 (1633); **4:** 2004; **9:** 5539 (5533); **10:** 5585 (5584), 6044 (6038), 6219
Litchfield B C, **11:** 6603 (6602)
Litherland R A, **4:** 1995 (1992)
Litowitz B E, **2:** 868 (863)
Litt M D, **10:** 5924 (5921)
Litt T, **3:** (1722); **8:** 4419 (4419)
Litterer J A, **3:** 1774 (1770)
Little D, **6:** 3213
Little J, **10:** 6012 (6009, 6010)
Little J W, **3:** 1635 (1633); **6:** 3602 (3597); **9:** 5246 (5242), 5264 (5260), 5378 (5376); **10:** 5935 (5930, 5932), 6047, 6103 (6101), 6106 (6105), 6214 (6214)
Little K, **2:** 1213 (1209); **3:** 1756 (1753)
Little R D, **7:** 4200 (4200); **9:** 5076 (5074); **11:** 6633 (6628)
Little R J A, **7:** 3858 (3857), 3861 (3858, 3861)
Little T, **1:** 158 (154)
Littlefield J, **2:** 984 (983); **6:** 3512 (3511)
Littlejohn G, **9:** 5216
Littler C R, **3:** 1703 (1696); **11:** 6277 (6273)
Littman R A, **1:** 234 (233)
Litwak E, **4:** 2166 (2162); **9:** 5217
Litwin G H, **9:** 5211
Liu Huozi, **2:** 755
Liu I-Shêng, **2:** 1045
Liu M, **1:** 374 (373); **10:** 5674 (5668, 5673)
Liu Pak Wai, **3:** 1685 (1683)
Liu S C, **10:** 5782 (5780)
Liu T, **7:** 3853 (3849)
Livećka E, **1:** 127 (123, 124); **2:** 662 (659)
Liveright A A, **1:** 111 (104), 120, 127, 215; **7:** 4185; **11:** 6438
Livermon B J, **8:** 4935 (4932, 4934)
Livingston C, **10:** 6026 (6024), 6034 (6033)
Livingston S A, **7:** 4056 (4055); **9:** 5475 (5472, 5473, 5474); **10:** 5725 (5723), 5726 (5722, 5724)
Livingstone M S, **7:** 4081 (4078)
Livingstone Sir R, **1:** 139 (138)
Lizarzaburu A, **8:** 4415
Lizaur M P, **7:** 3801
Ljung B-O, **9:** 5432 (5429); **11:** 6492 (6491)
Llach J J, **1:** 338
LLamas I, **3:** 1685 (1681, 1682, 1683)
Llanddowror G J, **11:** (6431)
Lloreda P, **5:** 2769 (2762)
Llorens M, **9:** 4977 (4976)
Lloyd B, **4:** 2423 (2420)
Lloyd C, **3:** 1257 (1256); **8:** 4948 (4946)
Lloyd C B, **2:** 693
Lloyd D I, **8:** 4447
Lloyd J W, **10:** 5686 (5684), 6173 (6169)
Lloyd L L, **1:** 408 (405), 409 (404, 405, 406, 407)
Lloyd P, **1:** 226 (222)
Lloyd S, **7:** 3833 (3832)
Lloyd-Jones R, **4:** 2024, 2024 (2021); **7:** 3935 (3933); **10:** 5704 (5699)
Lloyd-Smith M, **8:** 4935 (4933)
Lloyd-Still J D, **5:** 2575 (2573)
Loadman W, **10:** 5958 (5955)
Lobban G, **9:** 5302 (5299, 5300)
Lobes D, **2:** 1165
Lobo E S, **3:** 1671 (1667, 1668)
Lobo J, **3:** 1685 (1683); **5:** 2744 (2740, 2743)
Locheed M, **8:** 4845 (4843)
Lochhead J, **2:** 868 (862); **4:** 2281 (2280); **11:** 6457
Lockard D, **5:** 2903 (2903)
Locke D, **8:** 4376 (4374)
Locke E A, **2:** 1094 (1093); **3:** 1325 (1322); **4:** 1972 (1968)
Locke J, **2:** (776); **3:** (1289); **4:** 2000 (1997); **5:** (2608), (2876); **6:** (3316), 3499 (3497, 3498, 3499), **7:** (3920), (3924); **8:** 4455 (4451, 4452), (4535), 4575 (4572), (4631); **9:** (5088), (5229); **10:** 5694; **11:** (6578)
Locke L, **8:** 4467 (4467); **10:** 5713 (5708)
Locke M, **9:** 5169 (5160)
Locke P, **8:** 4375 (4374)
Lockhard J D, **9:** 5328 (5326)
Lockhart R S, **1:** 193 (187); **5:** 2884 (2882); **6:** 3288 (3287)
Lockheed M E, **1:** 254 (244, 245, 246, 247, 252, 253), 474 (471); **2:** 775 (771), 824, 834 (833), 977 (974), 1136 (1134); **3:** 1486, 1655 (1649), 1666 (1665), 1695 (1693), 1707 (1704), 1762 (1761), 1784 (1782, 1783), 1789 (1788), 1824 (1823), 1834 (1831); **4:** 1841 (1838), 1910, 1911 (1904, 1905, 1907), 1938 (1937), 2257 (2255), 2316 (2314), 2418 (2415, 2418), 2419 (2415); **5:** 2891 (2889), 2993 (2991); **6:** 3297 (3292); **7:** 4145 (4143); **8:** 4526 (4524), 4698 (4694, 4696, 4697), 4707 (4706), 4835 (4834), 4845 (4843), 4848 (4847), 4864

(4859), 4873 (4865, 4868, 4869, 4870); **9:** 5169 (5159, 5162, 5164), 5228 (5225, 5226, 5227), 5240 (5240), 5252 (5247), 5539 (5535, 5536, 5538); **10:** 5750 (5749), 5754 (5751), 5929 (5925); **11:** 6298 (6293), 6663 (6660, 6663)
Lodewijks H, **1:** 194; **5:** 2669, 2767, 2768, 2769, 2884; **6:** 3345; **7:** 3791, 3942
Lodewijks J G L C, **7:** 3791 (3789)
Lodola M, **10:** 5673 (5670)
Loeb M B, **4:** 1872 (1864); **9:** 5572 (5567, 5569)
Loeber H B, **7:** 4325 (4321, 4322)
Loeber R, **8:** 4368 (4367)
Loeber-Pautsch U, **7:** 4325 (4321, 4322)
Loebestein A, **1:** 103
Loef M, **2:** 1052 (1050); **3:** 1257 (1256)
Loehlin J C, **5:** 2465 (2464)
Loesch L C, **4:** 2131 (2130)
Loesch T, **10:** 6058 (6056)
Loevinger J, **10:** 5939 (5937)
Loewenberg-Ball D L, **10:** 5995 (5992)
Loewenstein M A, **2:** 1093 (1089); **6:** 3616 (3615)
Löfgren H, **7:** 3970 (3969)
Lofland J, **7:** 4319 (4317)
Lofland L H, **7:** 4319 (4317)
Löfstedt J-I, **3:** 1690 (1687)
Lofti A, **3:** 1655 (1651)
Logan D, **4:** 2199 (2198)
Logan J R, **11:** 6558
Logan L, **1:** 423
Logue M E, **11:** 6398 (6396)
Lohaus A, **4:** 2449 (2447)
Lohman D F, **1:** 5 (3), 152 (147), 374 (371); **4:** 1848 (1843, 1847); **5:** 2768 (2762, 2763), 2769 (2761, 2762), 2921 (2918), 2922; **6:** 3435 (3430, 3431); **10:** 6159 (6158)
Lohman T G, **8:** 4474
Lohmöller J B, **8:** 4359 (4353)
Lohnes P R, **2:** 631 (629, 630); **3:** 1548 (1548), 1549 (1546, 1547, 1548); **4:** 2244 (2242, 2244), 2245; **7:** 3872 (3867); **8:** 4657 (4656); **9:** 4973 (4973), 5373 (5371)
Lohse B, **6:** 3531
Lokan J J, **4:** 2132; **11:** 6678 (6675)
Lomax D E, **10:** 5954
Lombard A D, **7:** 4296 (4294, 4295), 4301 (4298)
Lombard P, **9:** (5123)
Lombardo M M, **4:** 2166; **6:** 3284
Lombardo V S, **7:** 4293 (4290, 4291)
Lomotey K, **6:** 3284
Lompscher J, **6:** 3292 (3289); **9:** 5548
London J, **6:** 3378 (3376)
London M, **11:** 6425
London P, **1:** 198 (197)
London S H, **11:** 6774, 6775
Long B C, **10:** 5924 (5920)
Long D H, **10:** 5991 (5990)
Long H B, **1:** 127 (124, 125); **6:** 3421 (3419); **8:** 4736 (4731, 4734, 4735); **9:** 5399 (5395, 5396, 5398); **10:** 6058
Long J M, **5:** 2529 (2527)
Long M, **6:** 3213 (3210)
Long M H, **1:** 537 (535); **4:** 2339 (2334, 2336, 2337, 2338)
Longford N T, **4:** 1933 (1929, 1932), 1938 (1937); **5:** 2595 (2590, 2593), 2596 (2590, 2592, 2594, 2595); **7:** 3986 (3979, 3982, 3983), 4015 (4012); **8:** 4873 (4869); **9:** 5130 (5129)
Longino H E, **4:** 2439 (2438)
Longobardi E, **6:** 3224 (3223)
Lonner N, **8:** 4394 (4394)
Lonner W, **5:** 2651
Lonner W J, **11:** 6334 (6329)
Loomer B M, **10:** 5704 (5704)
Loomis C P, **10:** 5617 (5615)
Loontjens A, **1:** 103
Loop L, **4:** 1911 (1908, 1909, 1910)
Loose G, **11:** 6266 (6263)
Lopez M A, **10:** 5674 (5673)
Lopez V, **10:** 5808 (5806)
Lopez-Schubert A L, **3:** 1301 (1300); **10:** 5817 (5813)
Lorch E, **6:** 3625 (3623)
Lord B, **4:** 2004 (2002)
Lord C A, **1:** 194
Lord F M, **1:** 52 (48, 49, 50); **2:** 677 (673), 792 (786, 788, 789, 790), 998 (993, 994); **5:** 3043 (3041), 3050 (3048), 3055 (3051, 3053, 3054), 3061 (3057, 3058); **6:** 3253 (3248, 3250), 3523 (3521); **7:** 3706 (3701, 3702, 3703), 4000 (3996, 3997, 3998); **8:** 4912 (4906, 4907); **11:** 6328 (6326), 6355 (6350, 6352, 6353)
Lorenz K, **1:** 234 (231); **4:** 2172 (2169)
Lorfing I, **1:** 328
Lorimer R J, **9:** 5130 (5125), 5142 (5137)
Lorsch J W, **4:** 2166 (2164); **8:** 4519 (4516)
Lortie D C, **2:** 796 (792, 793); **3:** 1271 (1268); **4:** 2166 (2162, 2163); **6:** 3527 (3524); **9:** 5181 (5178), 5379 (5377); **10:** 5613 (5611, 5612), 5995 (5993), 6073 (6070), 6092 (6089, 6091), 6096, 6103 (6101), 6132 (6129), 6139, 6214 (6209); **11:** 6723 (6720)
Lortie J, **5:** 2847 (2844)
Losche G, **6:** 3235 (3232)
Lösel F, **4:** 2089 (2082, 2086); **8:** 4779 (4777)
Lotto L S, **6:** 3284 (3277)
Lotto S, **5:** 2847 (2840)
Louat F F, **3:** 1666 (1665)
Loucks S, **3:** 1494 (1492); **10:** 5973 (5971)
Loucks-Horsley S, **9:** 5246 (5243, 5245); **10:** 5939, 6092 (6090)
Louden W, **10:** 6214 (6208, 6210)
Loughran E L, **7:** 4145
Louis K S, **2:** 645 (643); **5:** 2847 (2840, 2842, 2844, 2845); **6:** 3602 (3597, 3598, 3599, 3601); **9:** 5181 (5178), 5210 (5208, 5209), 5246 (5242, 5243), 5246 (5242, 5243, 5244, 5245); **10:** 5935 (5931), 5973 (5971)
Louis-Guerin L, **10:** 5782 (5781)
Louks K, **4:** 1991 (1988, 1990)
Lourde A, **7:** 4336 (4332); **10:** 6099 (6098)
Lourie S, **1:** 474 (473); **2:** 1146 (1141); **3:** 1789, 1824 (1821), 1830 (1829); **8:** 4495 (4494)
Loury G, **4:** 2274 (2274)
Loutfi M F, **11:** 6719 (6714)
Louviere J J, **3:** 1421 (1419)
Lovano-Kerr J, **11:** 6621 (6621)
Lovatt T, **5:** 2736 (2733, 2734)
Love C, **7:** 3889
Love E, **6:** 3638
Lovel H, **2:** 733 (731)
Lovelace E A, **8:** 4824
Loveless D, **5:** 2856 (2854); **6:** 3434 (3430)
Lovell K, **6:** 3685 (3677)
Lovell M, **3:** 1820 (1815)
Loveluck C, **9:** 5475 (5475)
Loveridge R, **8:** 4839 (4836)
Lovett D L, **5:** 2906 (2905)
Lovett T, **2:** 907, 1193 (1192), 1194; **5:** 2736 (2734); **7:** 4248 (4247), 4249 (4247); **10:** 5596 (5594)
Lovibond S H, **1:** 389; **2:** 792; **7:** 3706
Lovinger L, **9:** 5567 (5563)
Lovis F, **2:** 977, 988; **3:** 1779; **10:** 5625
Lovitt T C, **7:** 3807 (3802)
Lovitts B E, **7:** 3726
Low B, **11:** 6412
Low H, **1:** 234 (232)
Low P S, **10:** 5591 (5589)
Low-Beer A, **10:** 5707 (5705, 5706, 5707)
Lowe J, **1:** 111, 120, 152 (151), 180 (178); **3:** 1343; **5:** 2937 (2931), 2951, 2961 (2959); **6:** 3366 (3364), 3378 (3374); **7:** 3840 (3834); **8:** 4812 (4810), 4964 (4963); **11:** 6507 (6504)
Lowe R, **3:** (1294)
Löwel S, **1:** 554
Lowell E L, **3:** 1240 (1236, 1237, 1238), 1406
Lowell J, **7:** (3843)
Lowenbraun S, **3:** 1402 (1400)
Lowenfeld V, **1:** 343 (340)
Lowman R L, **11:** 6678 (6671, 6672, 6675)
Lowry W H, **10:** 5674 (5671)
Lowyck J, **5:** 2874 (2870); **10:** 5914
Loxley W A, **2:** 760, 957 (955); **3:** 1784 (1781); **4:** 2257 (2254); **6:** 3262 (3257); **7:** 3721 (3720); **8:** 4688 (4687), 4845 (4843), 4873 (4868); **9:** 5240 (5235), 5539 (5536); **11:** 6256 (6254, 6255), 6266 (6263), 6633 (6628), 6664 (6663)
Loyd B H, **5:** 2731 (2729)
Loyd R J, **2:** 635 (632)
Loyola, **9:** 5121 (5118, 5119)
Lozanov G, **4:** 2346 (2342)
Lu M-Y, **4:** 1917 (1915)
Lu S, **3:** 1624 (1622)
Luangpraseut K, **7:** 4175
Lubart T I, **5:** 2732 (2726)
Lubeck S, **6:** 3452 (3451)
Lubetsky M J, **1:** 19 (18)
Lubke M, **10:** 5673 (5671)
Lucas A, **9:** 5349 (5348)
Lucas C J, **1:** 328 (323); **8:** 4455 (4448)
Lucas D, **5:** 2910
Lucas J, **4:** 1984 (1982); **11:** 6608 (6607)
Lucas R E B, **3:** 1695 (1693), 1707 (1705); **4:** 2279 (2275); **11:** 6298 (6293)
Lucas S, **7:** 4170 (4166)
Luce R D, **2:** 792 (786); **3:** 1425; **6:** 3124 (3122); **7:** 3706 (3700), 4006; **8:** 4727

Luce S C, **8:** 4375 (4374)
Luchins A S, **8:** 4727 (4724)
Luckasson R, **7:** 3830 (3826); **11:** 6461
Luckmann T, **2:** 933 (925), 1072 (1071); **3:** 1347 (1344), 1729 (1726); **6:** 3373 (3370)
Ludlow B L, **11:** 6461
Lueders-Salmon E, **9:** 5181 (5177)
Luehrmann A, **2:** 973 (969), 977 (974), (1008)
Luey B, **5:** 2998
Lugthart E, **4:** 1934 (1931)
Luhmann N, **8:** 4461 (4458)
Luhmer K, **1:** 139 (137); **8:** 4845 (4844)
Luijkx R, **7:** 3864 (3864); **10:** 5735 (5731)
Lukacs L, **9:** 5121
Lukacs P, **11:** 6648 (6641, 6647)
Lukatela G, **8:** 4939 (4938)
Luke A, **2:** 1198 (1195, 1196, 1197); **6:** 3452; **7:** 3711 (3709); **9:** 5302 (5300)
Luke C, **2:** 1198 (1196); **8:** 4680 (4677); **11:** 6727 (6725)
Lukes S, **2:** 785, 1042 (1041)
Lulat Y G M, **8:** 4688 (4683)
Lummis M, **3:** 1240 (1239), 1768 (1765); **5:** 2628 (2627)
Lumms T, **7:** 4225 (4221)
Lumsdaine A A, **4:** 1898, 1899 (1884, 1885, 1890); **5:** 2861 (2857), (2879); **8:** 4774, 4775
Lumsden C J, **4:** 2172 (2167, 2168)
Lumsden J, **7:** 3706 (3702)
Lumumba-Kasongo T, **11:** 6740 (6738), 6741
Luna E, **8:** 4835 (4834), 4845 (4843)
Lunacharsky A V, **3:** 1538
Lund B, **7:** 4059 (4059)
Lund D, **9:** 4977 (4974)
Lundberg G, **9:** 5055 (5052)
Lundberg I, **3:** 1461; **8:** 4935 (4934); **10:** 5680 (5678), 5681; **11:** 6777
Lundberg L-J, **6:** 3224 (3220)
Lundberg S, **4:** 2377
Lundgren U P, **3:** 1308 (1304), 1355 (1348), 1804 (1803); **4:** 2376 (2376), 2377 (2375, 2376); **5:** 2870 (2868); **6:** 3389 (3386); **7:** 3886 (3883); **10:** 6088 (6087), 6149 (6148)
Lundin R, **9:** 5545
Lundin S, **5:** 3066 (3063)
Lundquist O F, **7:** 4179 (4178)
Lundsteen S, **6:** 3443 (3441, 3442)
Lunetta V N, **9:** 5345 (5343, 5344)
Lunnenborg C E, **1:** 390 (388)
Lunnenborg P W, **1:** 390 (388)
Lunsford A A, **6:** 3452
Lunz M E, **1:** 52 (51); **5:** 2783 (2780); **6:** 3124 (3122)
Lunzer E A, **8:** 4957
Luria A R, **2:** 868 (863); **3:** 1246 (1243, 1244); **4:** (1864), (1869); **6:** (3289); **9:** (5400), 5548 (5545); **11:** 6457 (6454, 6455)
Lüscher K, **4:** 2266 (2265)
Luster T, **3:** 1642 (1640)
Lusterman S, **2:** 1152
Luther A C, **2:** 649
Luther M, **6:** 3531; **8:** (4889); **11:** (6744)
Lutonsky L, **9:** 5318 (5314)
Lutrell W, **7:** 4329 (4326)
Lüttinger P, **10:** 5735 (5732, 5734)
Luttringer J M, **1:** 111 (110)
Lutz B, **11:** 6266 (6263)
Lutz F W, **1:** 60; **10:** 6062 (6061)
Luvia A R, **3:** (1248)
Lyall A, **5:** 2623
Lybarger M B, **7:** 3848 (3842)
Lybeck L, **8:** 4429 (4426); **10:** 5790 (5785)
Lycette M A, **2:** 834 (834)
Lykken D T, **2:** 846 (845); **6:** 3144 (3139); **11:** 6492 (6488)
Lyle J, **1:** 570 (564, 565)
Lyman H B, **10:** 5822
Lynas W, **5:** 2910 (2908)
Lynch A Q, **1:** 94; **2:** 1165 (1161, 1162, 1163, 1164); **6:** 3349 (3347); **11:** 6551 (6548)
Lynch D J, **10:** 5886 (5885)
Lynch E W, **5:** 2813 (2806, 2807)
Lynch J, **1:** 28; **7:** 3977 (3975, 3976); **8:** 4526
Lynch J K, **7:** 4099 (4096)
Lynch K, **3:** 1348 (1347)
Lynch L, **1:** 310; **11:** 6420 (6418)
Lynch L M, **6:** 3616 (3615); **10:** 5919 (5915)
Lynch M D, **10:** 5925 (5921, 5922)
Lynch O M, **9:** 5510 (5509)
Lynch P D, **3:** 1810
Lynch R H, **1:** 534; **8:** 4881 (4878)
Lynch S W, **3:** 1443
Lynch-Brown C, **2:** 738 (734)
Lynd R, **1:** 296 (286)
Lynd S, **1:** 296 (286)
Lynn J, **6:** 3373 (3371)
Lynn L E Jr, **11:** 6558 (6553)
Lynn M L, **9:** 5008 (5007)
Lynne H, **3:** 1271 (1267, 1270)
Lyon S, **10:** 5948 (5946)
Lyons C A, **8:** 4935 (4932, 4934)
Lyons J, **4:** 2364
Lyons N, **10:** 5939 (5937)
Lyotard J-F, **4:** 2000 (2000), 2033 (2030); **8:** (4453), 4642 (4639, 4640)
Lysakowski R, **5:** 2856 (2854)
Lysynchuk L, **4:** 2194 (2189, 2191)
Lytle S L, **2:** 1198 (1198); **10:** 5961
Lytton H, **9:** 5528

Maass G, **3:** 1789
Mabawonku A F, **1:** 226 (222, 224)
Mac an Ghaill M, **1:** 265 (263); **9:** 5060 (5058)
McAdoo H P, **1:** 296; **5:** 2628
McAdoo J L, **5:** 2628
McAleese R, **4:** 1928 (1925); **5:** 2709
McAllister A, **5:** 2572 (2569)
McAlpin A, **10:** 5625 (5623)
McAlpine A, **10:** 6088 (6088)
McAnany E G, **1:** 563; **2:** 1127 (1122, 1125), 1136 (1134), 1152 (1147, 1150, 1151); **3:** 1573 (1571); **4:** 1903 (1900), 1911; **5:** 2891, 2891 (2884), 2897 (2892, 2893)
McAnarney E R, **9:** 5435
McAninch A R, **10:** 5948 (5944)
McArdle J J, **2:** 677 (677); **3:** 1514 (1512)
MacArthur C A, **7:** 3807 (3803)
Macaulay C, **9:** 5197 (5194)
McAulay J D, **9:** 5578 (5573)
Macauley J T, **7:** 4132 (4125)
McBeath C, **9:** 5544
McBee S, **5:** 2998 (2994)
Macbeth A, **2:** 893 (890); **9:** 5197 (5194)
McBride J R, **1:** 52 (50, 51), 53 (50)
McBride S, **10:** 5831 (5831)
McBryde B, **4:** 2180 (2176)
McBurney P J, **11:** 6638 (6636)
McCafferty I, **5:** 2572 (2567)
McCain L J, **8:** 4875 (4874)
McCall G J, **7:** 4319 (4316)
McCall J, **7:** 4030
McCall M W, **4:** 2166
McCall M W Jr., **6:** 3284
McCall R, **3:** 1514 (1512)
McCall R B, **1:** 362 (361); **5:** 2916 (2912); **7:** 3706 (3702); **8:** 4474 (4470)
McCall W A, **4:** 1872 (1867)
McCallister W J, **5:** 2617 (2608)
MacCallum J A, **10:** 5939 (5936)
McCammon R, **8:** 4474 (4472)
McCamus D R, **4:** 2331
McCandless B R, **5:** 2802 (2799, 2800)
McCann S J, **10:** 5745
McCarthey S J, **5:** 2529 (2528)
McCarthy C, **4:** 2250
McCarthy C R, **3:** 1337 (1335)
McCarthy Gallagher J, **8:** 4482
McCarthy J, **3:** 1635 (1632); **11:** 6760 (6755)
McCarthy M, **7:** 3978
McCarthy M M, **1:** 77 (74)
McCarthy P J, **9:** 5130 (5126, 5127)
McCarthy T A, **2:** 1204 (1201, 1203); **5:** 2585 (2585)
McCartney K, **2:** 688 (686); **3:** 1643 (1636); **5:** 2628 (2626); **7:** 4296 (4295, 4296)
McCarty T L, **1:** 534; **8:** 4881 (4878)
McCaskill D, **7:** 4336 (4331)
McCaslin M, **6:** 3655 (3654)
McCaul E J, **2:** 711 (706, 708)
McChesney I, **10:** 5625 (5623)
Macchiarola F J, **2:** 700
McChord W, **3:** 1402 (1402)
McClannahan L E, **8:** 4376 (4374)
McClearn G E, **3:** 1647; **11:** 6492 (6488, 6489, 6490, 6491)
McCleary R, **9:** 5490
McCleary W, **4:** 2316 (2314)
McCleland K, **11:** 6808
McClellan J E, **8:** 4455 (4454)
McClelland C E, **10:** 6079 (6073)
McClelland D C, **1:** 296 (292); **3:** 1240 (1236, 1238, 1239); **4:** 1991 (1986); **5:** 2651 (2648); **7:** 3946 (3943); **10:** 6224 (6222)
McClelland G H, **8:** 4657 (4654)
McClelland J, **8:** 4939 (4936)
McClelland J A G, **5:** 2642 (2641); **7:** 4236 (4231)
McClelland J L, **2:** 856 (853), 857 (853); **6:** 3155
McClelland V A, **1:** 28
McClintic S, **1:** 32 (30)

McClintock C, **3:** 1283 (1281); **11:** 6384 (6379)
McClintock E, **11:** 6608
McCloskey M, **10:** 5790 (5783, 5784, 5785)
McCloskey O S A, **10:** 6183
McClung M S, **11:** 6328 (6321)
McClure M W, **8:** 4595 (4594)
McClurg P A, **7:** 4094 (4091)
McClusky H Y, **7:** 4329 (4327); **8:** 4736 (4734, 4735)
Maccoby E E, **1:** 234 (230); **2:** 705 (702); **3:** 1642 (1639, 1640); **4:** 2449, 2452 (2449, 2450, 2451); **5:** 2628 (2624), 2672 (2671); **9:** 5432 (5424, 5427, 5428), 5435 (5433, 5434), 5445 (5443)
Maccoby E M, **10:** 5826 (5822, 5824)
McCollum P, **2:** 1213 (1210)
McCombs B L, **4:** 1848 (1846); **5:** 2769 (2764); **7:** 3946 (3943)
McCombs M, **1:** 570 (566)
McConaghy J, **2:** 738 (735)
McConkey R, **10:** 5943 (5942)
McConnell S R, **9:** 5567 (5563, 5564, 5565, 5566, 5567)
McConnell T R, **11:** 6445 (6441)
McConville C, **11:** 6735
McCord J, **1:** 234 (232)
McCorkell V, **5:** 2972 (2967, 2968)
McCormick C B, **2:** 867; **5:** 2814 (2807)
McCormick C G, **7:** 3768 (3765)
McCormick C H, **7:** 4059 (4057)
McCormick E J, **6:** 3096
McCormick K, **1:** 162 (161); **11:** 6699 (6696, 6697)
McCormick M C, **3:** 1642 (1637)
McCormick P, **8:** 4433
McCormick R, **4:** 1903 (1901); **5:** 2852 (2849)
McCormick S, **3:** 1779 (1778); **8:** 4947
McCrae R R, **1:** 239 (237); **5:** 2665 (2663); **8:** 4823 (4823)
McCready E B, **7:** 4081 (4078)
McCreary E K, **11:** 6307 (6303)
MacCrimmon K R, **5:** 2725 (2721)
McCulley G A, **6:** 3209 (3208)
McCulloch G, **9:** 5299 (5297)
McCullough J S, **3:** 1416 (1412); **6:** 3508 (3501, 3503, 3506)
McCune L, **1:** 362 (359); **8:** 4542 (4538)
McCune S D, **8:** 4601 (4600)
McCune S K, **9:** 5399 (5398)
McCurdy D W, **2:** 803 (797); **4:** 2053; **9:** 5220 (5218)
McCutcheon G, **3:** 1271 (1267, 1270), 1287 (1286); **10:** 6088 (6087), 6092 (6090), 6183 (6178, 6180); **11:** 6370 (6368, 6369)
McDaniel E, **8:** 4882 (4878)
McDermott J, **2:** 867 (862); **4:** 2199 (2195, 2196); **9:** 5342 (5339)
McDermott L C, **8:** 4479 (4475); **9:** 5342 (5339); **10:** 5790 (5785)
McDermott R P, **1:** 296 (283, 289); **2:** 802 (801), 1073 (1070); **4:** 2052 (2049, 2050); **6:** 3238 (3236), 3453 (3449), 3459 (3456); **9:** 5210 (5209), 5220 (5219), 5313 (5311); **11:** 6608 (6604)
McDevitt T M, **7:** 4301 (4300)
McDiarmid G W, **9:** 5363 (5360); **10:** 5995 (5992), 6106 (6104, 6105)
McDill E L, **1:** 11 (10); **2:** 711 (707, 708, 709); **3:** 1607 (1605, 1606)
MacDonald B, **2:** 645; **3:** 1257 (1253, 1254, 1256), 1287 (1285); **4:** 2037 (2036), (2103)
McDonald D, **4:** 1972 (1968)
McDonald F J, **3:** 1529 (1525); **10:** 5977 (5974, 5975)
McDonald G, **6:** 3496 (3496)
MacDonald G, **9:** 5355 (5350, 5351, 5354)
MacDonald J B, **3:** 1266 (1264)
MacDonald K B, **4:** 2172 (2168)
McDonald P J, **9:** 5359 (5357)
McDonald R, **7:** 4170 (4166)
MacDonald R E, **10:** 6149 (6144, 6145, 6146)
McDonald R P, **2:** 792 (788, 791); **4:** 2241 (2238, 2239); **5:** 2596 (2595); **6:** 3253 (3252); **7:** 3706 (3706), 4006 (4002), 4007; **8:** 4359 (4357)
MacDonald S, **1:** 343 (339, 342)
Macdonald-Ross M, **8:** 4694
McDonnell J, **11:** 6461 (6457, 6459, 6460)
McDonnell L M, **4:** 2388 (2384); **6:** 3197 (3195); **10:** 5930
McDonnell P, **7:** 3721 (3716, 3717); **8:** 4895 (4892)
McDonough D, **8:** 4383 (4382)
McDonough S H, **4:** 2339
McDougall A, **2:** 973, 977, 992; **3:** 1779; **7:** 4094; **8:** 4803; **9:** 5544
McDowall D, **9:** 5490
McDowell L, **7:** 3853 (3849)
Mace D R, **4:** 2266 (2264)
Mace J, **7:** 4263 (4262); **8:** 4964
Mace T, **10:** 5625 (5624)
McEachern A W, **10:** 6132 (6131)
Macedo D, **1:** 135 (129, 132, 133, 134); **2:** 1198 (1195); **6:** 3459 (3454)
McElroy M B, **4:** 2419 (2414)
McElroy W, **7:** 4293 (4291)
McEvoy M A, **9:** 5567 (5563, 5564, 5565, 5566, 5567)
McEwan H, **10:** 6117 (6113)
McEwen A, **4:** 2427 (2424)
McEwen B S, **9:** 5435 (5434)
McEwen E, **11:** 6735
McFadden C P, **8:** 4464; **9:** 5328
McFadden D, **3:** 1425
McFarland D, **9:** 5175 (5175)
McFarland L, **9:** 5191 (5189)
McFarland R A, **4:** 2012
MacFarlane K, **1:** 19
McFarlane S C, **11:** 6707 (6704, 6705)
McGaghie W, **8:** 4623 (4617)
Mcgarry J, **8:** 4964
McGaw B, **3:** 1514 (1511); **4:** 2240 (2238); **6:** 3474 (3473); **7:** 3783 (3775, 3776, 3777, 3778, 3779, 3780, 3782, 3783), 3784 (3778); **9:** 5038 (5033, 5036, 5037), 5373 (5368, 5371); **10:** 6239 (6236, 6237); **11:** 6339 (6336)
McGeary M G H, **11:** 6558 (6553)
McGechan S, **7:** 4059 (4059)
McGee M G, **1:** 5 (3)
McGeevor P, **10:** 5826 (5824)
McGill I, **4:** 2186 (2184)
McGill R, **4:** 2208 (2203)
McGill-Franzen A M, **2:** 868 (865); **8:** 4935 (4931, 4933, 4935); **9:** 5070 (5069), 5071 (5069)
McGillicuddy-DeLisi A V, **4:** 2257 (2252); **7:** 4301 (4299)
McGilly K, **1:** 5 (5)
McGinn N F, **2:** 1042 (1040); **3:** 1411 (1407), 1810 (1807), 1820 (1818), 1824 (1821, 1822), 1834 (1831); **4:** 1857 (1856); **6:** 3608 (3606, 3607); **8:** 4495 (4493), 4509 (4503, 4506), 4595 (4589), 4601 (4598, 4599), 4601 (4597)
McGinnis E, **9:** 5567 (5566)
McGinnis M, **10:** 5680 (5677)
McGoldrick J A, **7:** 3768 (3765)
McGonigel M J, **5:** 2813 (2809)
McGough R L, **8:** 4864 (4860)
McGrath E J, **4:** 2351 (2347); **5:** 2572 (2570); **9:** 5050; **10:** 5862 (5855)
McGraw M B, **5:** 2802 (2800); **7:** 3950 (3947)
McGregor A L, **9:** 5544 (5543)
McGregor D M, **3:** (1537); **4:** 2166 (2158)
McGroarty M, **6:** 3334 (3331)
McGue M, **2:** 846 (845); **5:** 2465 (2464); **6:** 3144 (3139); **11:** 6492 (6488)
McGuffey W H, **4:** (2111)
McGuffy C W, **4:** 2229; **9:** 5185 (5182)
McGuigan F J, **7:** 3775
McGuinness P J, **4:** 2435 (2435)
McGuire C B, **3:** 1821 (1817)
McGuire J, **10:** 5834 (5833)
McGuire J W, **5:** 2725
McGuire K, **9:** 5191 (5187, 5188, 5190)
McGuire M F, **5:** 2965
McGuire W J, **1:** 358 (354), 390 (381)
McGuire W T, **1:** (378)
McGurk H, **8:** 4368
Mach E, **8:** 4464 (4462)
Mac-Harg R, **2:** 1031 (1028)
Macharia D, **11:** 6719 (6718)
Machiavelli N, **8:** 4509 (4506), (4597)
Machlup F, **5:** 2998 (2997); **9:** 5355 (5353); **11:** 6424 (6421, 6423)
McHugh E L, **5:** 2655 (2653)
McHugh M C, **9:** 5435 (5434)
Machugh R, **10:** 6214
McIlroy J A, **1:** 93 (91, 92), 94; **11:** 6775 (6772)
McInerney J D, **6:** 3416 (3410)
McInnis J, **3:** 1406
McIntosh D M, **4:** 2180 (2173)
McIntosh J, **3:** 1685 (1681)
McIntosh P, **10:** 6099 (6098)
McIntosh R, **1:** 495
MacIntyre A, **1:** 67 (62, 65); **4:** 2033 (2030, 2032); **7:** 4051 (4047); **8:** 4447 (4443)
McIntyre D, **10:** 5668 (5664, 5665), 6088 (6088), 6127 (6123), 6182 (6182)
McIntyre D I, **5:** 2903 (2899); **10:** 5977 (5974, 5975, 5976)
McIntyre D J, **6:** 3202 (3197); **10:** 5812
McIntyre T, **10:** 6062 (6061)

MacIver D, **1:** 32; **2:** 706 (704)
MacIver D J, **5:** 2769 (2764)
Mack D E, **10:** 5804 (5801)
Mack D P, **9:** 5038
McKay A, **5:** 2769 (2762); **8:** 4666 (4665)
Mackay A F, **8:** 4736
McKay G, **4:** 2267
Mackay H, **1:** 83 (80)
McKay H, **5:** 2769 (2762); **8:** 4666 (4665)
Mackay L D, **9:** 5324 (5318, 5319), 5345 (5343)
Mackay R, **8:** 4940
McKeachie W J, **1:** 194 (191); **2:** 969 (966); **8:** 4803 (4800); **10:** 6235 (6233)
McKean J W, **9:** 5082 (5080)
McKean R N, **2:** 1135 (1132); **10:** 5846
McKee P, **3:** 1359 (1358); **7:** 3830 (3828)
McKeithen K B, **2:** 984 (984)
McKenna D, **7:** 3833 (3832)
Mackenzie A M, **10:** 6202 (6198)
McKenzie B, **4:** 2267
Mackenzie D, **4:** 2331
Mackenzie D E, **9:** 5223 (5221, 5222)
McKenzie G R, **8:** 4881 (4879)
McKenzie P, **1:** 423; **4:** 2132
McKenzie P A, **6:** 3373 (3372); **9:** 5066 (5064, 5065)
MacKenzie R, **1:** 280 (278, 279), 299 (299)
McKenzie R B, **7:** 3821 (3816, 3817)
McKenzie R D, **11:** 6803 (6799)
MacKenzie S, **2:** 1175 (1173)
McKeon B, **8:** 4857 (4857)
McKeon R, **10:** 5995 (5994)
McKeown M G, **9:** 5562 (5560), 5563
MacKeracher D, **1:** 158 (154, 156)
McKernan J, **1:** 48 (45); **10:** 6099 (6097)
Mackett M, **5:** 2831 (2831)
McKey R H, **2:** 688 (680, 681); **3:** 1642 (1641); **4:** 2145 (2142); **7:** 4301 (4299)
McKibbin M, **10:** 6169 (6167)
Mackie M, **10:** 6132 (6130)
Mackie R, **2:** 1048 (1046)
Mackie S L, **4:** 2037 (2033)
McKillip J, **8:** 4751 (4745)
McKim R H, **11:** 6625 (6622)
McKinlay P, **7:** 4111
McKinley R L, **5:** 3043 (3041); **6:** 3253 (3252)
McKinna C, **3:** 1537 (1536)
McKinney J D, **1:** 362
Mackinnon A, **11:** 6735 (6731, 6732)
MacKinnon A M, **10:** 6219 (6217)
MacKinnon C A, **6:** 3621 (3620); **9:** 5441 (5437, 5438)
Mackinnon D, **11:** 6523
MacKinnon G E, **4:** 1963; **8:** 4912, 4942
Macklin E D, **4:** 2266 (2263)
McKnight C, **5:** 2709 (2708); **8:** 4694
McKnight C C, **1:** 11 (9); **2:** 775 (771); **4:** 1938 (1935); **9:** 5373 (5369); **11:** 6328 (6325)
McKusick V A, **5:** 2465 (2463)
McLagan P A, **2:** 1139 (1136); **3:** 1490 (1487, 1488); **5:** 2689 (2686)
McLanahan S, **3:** 1642 (1639)
McLaren D J, **4:** 2331
McLaren I A, **7:** 4111
McLaren J, **11:** 6780 (6779)
MacLaren M D, **9:** 5471 (5468)
McLaren P, **2:** 1072, 1073 (1068), 1074; **3:** 1337 (1334); **4:** 1984 (1982, 1983); **8:** 4642; **10:** 5817 (5816)
McLaughlin A, **7:** 4200 (4199)
McLaughlin B, **1:** 537; **4:** 2339 (2338); **6:** 3334 (3333); **8:** 4939 (4938)
McLaughlin D H, **3:** 1431 (1429)
McLaughlin H J, **10:** 6053 (6048)
McLaughlin J P, **4:** 2199 (2197)
McLaughlin M, **4:** 2100; **5:** 2673, 2847 (2840, 2841); **8:** 4568 (4565), 4875; **9:** 5216 (5214), 5223 (5221, 5222, 5223), 5246 (5242, 5244); **10:** 6214 (6213)
McLaughlin M E, **7:** 4000 (4000)
McLaughlin M W, **3:** 1256 (1253, 1254), 1257 (1253, 1254), 1271 (1268, 1269), 1431 (1427); **4:** 1841 (1837), 1857 (1852, 1855), 2037, 2089, 2108, 2132 (2126); **6:** 3602 (3599); **7:** 4215 (4213); **8:** 4715 (4709), 4783; **9:** 5066 (5063), 5216 (5213, 5215), 5223 (5222); **10:** 5613, 5934, 5935 (5931), 6083 (6082); **11:** 6563 (6561, 6562), 6580
McLaughlin P, **2:** 1002
McLaughlin S D, **1:** 227 (222)
MacLaughlin S D, **3:** 1680 (1679)
McLaughlin T F, **9:** 4977 (4975), 5359 (5356)
MacLean H, **1:** 162 (161); **8:** 4526 (4524)
McLean L, **7:** 3912 (3906, 3911); **8:** 4526 (4521)
McLean L D, **8:** 4623 (4619)
McLean M, **3:** 1416 (1413), 1589; **5:** 2512
Maclean M, **6:** 3452 (3449)
Mclean M, **9:** 5168 (5159, 5165), 5216 (5211); **11:** 6558, 6563
Maclean R, **1:** 423; **10:** 6047
McLean R S, **2:** 1006 (1004, 1006); **11:** 6781
McLeish J A B, **8:** 4812 (4806); **10:** 5808 (5807)
MacLennan D, **7:** 3711 (3709)
MacLennan S, **10:** 5995 (5992, 5993)
McLeod A, **7:** 3936; **10:** 5961 (5959); **11:** 6784 (6782, 6783)
McLeod B, **6:** 3334 (3333); **8:** 4939 (4938)
McLeod D A, **6:** 3643 (3639, 3640, 3641, 3642)
McLeod D B, **1:** 204 (199, 201); **6:** 3642, 3643, 3655 (3653)
MacLeod F, **9:** 5216 (5214)
McLeod F, **9:** 5268
McLeod G R, **6:** 3202 (3198)
MacLeod G R, **10:** 5977 (5974, 5975, 5976)
McLeod J, **1:** 158 (154)
MacLeod J, **4:** 2272 (2268, 2269, 2270, 2271)
McLeod M A, **10:** 6035 (6033)
McLeod S A, **1:** 358 (357)
Macload H, **4:** 2427 (2424, 2425)
McLoughlin C S, **10:** 5939
McLoughlin J A, **2:** 718 (712, 714, 715), 719; **7:** 3833 (3832); **11:** 6315 (6313, 6314)
McLoyd V, **3:** 1642 (1639, 1640)
McLuhan M, **1:** 162 (159), 482 (480); **5:** 2897; **6:** 3446 (3444)
MacLure M, **6:** 3443 (3439); **8:** 4930 (4929); **10:** 5826 (5822)
Maclure S, **6:** 3496 (3493, 3494); **9:** 5013
McMahon A, **1:** 72 (69), 73 (71), 83; **4:** 1934 (1929), 2165, 2423 (2422); **10:** 5982
McMahon H, **2:** 888 (885); **4:** 1903 (1899, 1901); **7:** 4088 (4085), 4100
McMahon R J, **9:** 5567
McMahon S, **5:** 2529 (2528)
McMahon W J, **4:** 2212; **5:** 2792; **11:** 6266 (6263)
McMahon W W, **2:** 1055 (1052, 1053, 1054), 1056; **3:** 1793; **6:** 3106
McManamon F P, **1:** 280
McManana J, **7:** 4293 (4291)
McManus P, **5:** 2575 (2572)
McMeckin R, **4:** 1841 (1838)
McMeeking S, **8:** 4622 (4618)
MacMillan D L, **7:** 3830 (3830)
McMillan J H, **11:** 6360 (6356)
McMillan M, **9:** 5233
Macmillan R, **10:** 6214 (6213)
McMorris R F, **4:** 2183
McMorrow J F, **10:** 6083 (6081)
McMurchy M, **5:** 2457 (2455)
McMurray C A, **10:** 6004
McMurry C, **9:** 5578 (5573)
McNab A S, **5:** 2827
McNabb R, **9:** 5191 (5186)
McNair J, **10:** 5658; **11:** 6461 (6459)
McNally D, **9:** 5338
McNamara D, **10:** 5995 (5991)
Macnamara J, **4:** 2257 (2253)
McNamara T C, **4:** 2364 (2360), 2388 (2382)
McNamara T P, **10:** 6192 (6191)
McNaughton S S, **6:** 3463 (3461, 3462); **8:** 4376 (4373)
McNay I, **8:** 4601; **9:** 5169 (5160)
McNeal E, **6:** 3670 (3670)
McNeil B J, **11:** 6603 (6602)
McNeil D R, **4:** 2208; **9:** 5082 (5080)
McNeil J D, **3:** 1283 (1279), 1315 (1312)
McNeil L, **3:** 1257 (1255); **10:** 5817 (5816)
McNeil L M, **9:** 5264 (5263); **10:** 6083 (6080)
McNeil M, **10:** 6244 (6243)
McNeill D, **9:** 5416 (5415)
McNemar Q, **1:** 5 (2); **2:** 1084 (1082), 1117 (1109, 1111); **7:** 3879 (3874)
McNergney R F, **10:** 5965 (5962)
McNutt G, **7:** 3833 (3832), 4081 (4077)
Maconachie M, **7:** 3853 (3851)
McPartland J M, **1:** 11 (8), 520 (515); **3:** 1486 (1484), 1607 (1605, 1606)
McPeck J, **2:** 1207 (1205, 1206, 1207)
McPhee J, **9:** 5181 (5180)
McPherson A, **4:** 2291 (2290); **10:** 5735 (5733)
MacPherson C B, **9:** 5523
McPherson M, **3:** 1449 (1447)
McPherson R B, **1:** 77 (75); **9:** 5223 (5222)
Macpherson R J S, **7:** 3840 (3839), 3924
McRae D, **10:** 6083 (6081)
MacRae D, **11:** 6563
MacRae D Jr, **4:** 1841 (1835)

Macrae J W, **5:** 2806 (2804)
Mcrae S, **11:** 6808 (6806)
Macready G B, **2:** 831 (830); **3:** 1514 (1511)
McReynolds L, **10:** 5697 (5695)
Macridis R C, **5:** 2512 (2511)
McRobbie A, **9:** 5060 (5057); **11:** 6727 (6726)
MacRobbie A, **11:** 6803 (6801)
McRobbie C J, **2:** 811 (809); **10:** 5775 (5774)
McRoberts H A, **7:** 3722 (3718)
McSweeney M, **7:** (4161), 4162 (4161), 4163 (4159, 4160, 4161, 4162)
McTaggart R, **1:** 47, 48 (42, 43, 46)
McTaggert R, **10:** 6099 (6097)
McTeague F, **6:** 3209 (3207)
Macurdy T, **3:** 1660 (1656, 1657)
McVey S, **8:** 4848
McWhorter L, **9:** 5441 (5440)
McWilliam H O A, **5:** 2486
McWilliams B J, **10:** 5693 (5693); **11:** 6707 (6706, 6707)
Madaus C F, **9:** 5334 (5334)
Madaus G F, **1:** 41 (32), 520 (515); **2:** 957 (954); **3:** 1283; **4:** 2017 (2012), 2079, 2089 (2080), 2108, 2131 (2128), 2374; **6:** 3484; **7:** 3726 (3723, 3724); **8:** 4648, 4766, 4774 (4770); **9:** 5338; **10:** 5790 (5784); **11:** 6328 (6321), 6348 (6342), 6563 (6562)
Madaus G T, **1:** 370 (364)
Maddaus J, **2:** 893 (891)
Madden N A, **2:** 711 (710), 1099 (1096, 1098); **5:** 2910 (2908); **8:** 4935, 4935 (4932, 4934); **9:** 5071
Maddirala J, **10:** 6062 (6061)
Maddock J, **2:** 785
Maddock T, **3:** 1775
Maddux C D, **3:** 1355 (1353)
Madeira F, **3:** 1672 (1668)
Madeja S S, **1:** 198
Madelin A, **9:** 5197 (5195)
Mader W M, **1:** 127 (121, 122, 123, 124, 125)
Mades G G, **8:** 4688 (4682, 4683, 4684, 4685, 4686, 4687)
Madey D L, **4:** 2119 (2116)
Madigan K, **2:** 665
Madow W G, **5:** 3061 (3055); **7:** 3858 (3855, 3857); **9:** 4974, 5142 (5136, 5140)
Madrazo C V, **3:** 1624 (1622)
Madron T W, **7:** 3816
Madsen C H, **1:** 486 (485)
Madsen C K, **7:** 4030
Madsen M, **3:** 1240 (1238, 1239, 1240)
Madsen R, **10:** 5990 (5989)
Maehr M L, **1:** 32 (30); **2:** 868 (866); **4:** 2440 (2437); **9:** 5432; **10:** 6224 (6223)
Maeroff G I, **11:** 6563 (6559, 6561)
Maes S, **10:** 5738
Magabe M, **11:** 6814 (6809, 6810)
Magallon P, **10:** 5674 (5670)
Magat R, **1:** 594 (593)
Magendzo S, **2:** 1049
Mager A, **7:** 3853 (3850)
Mager K S, **1:** (274)
Mager R, **5:** 2862 (2857)
Mager R F, **3:** 1266 (1264), 1804 (1801); **4:** 1848 (1844); **5:** 2862 (2857, 2879); **6:** 3096 (3093); **8:** 4774 (4769); **10:** 6035 (6032), 6164 (6161)
Magidson J, **9:** 5373 (5368)
Magnen A, **3:** 1824 (1822)
Magnusson D, **1:** 89 (83, 87); **3:** 1520 (1516); **5:** 2665 (2659); **6:** 3428; **8:** 4394 (4389, 4390, 4392, 4393, 4394), 4395 (4390, 4391); **10:** 6159 (6155); **11:** 6492
Magone M, **1:** 374 (372)
Magsino R F, **10:** 5613
Magstadt T M, **5:** 2512 (2509)
Maguire M J, **3:** 1739 (1737)
Maguire P, **2:** 907; **7:** 4336 (4330, 4332)
Mahalanobis P C, **9:** 5130 (5126)
Mahanjan V, **3:** 1553
Mahapatra M, **9:** 5512 (5512)
Mahard R E, **3:** 1486 (1484, 1485); **9:** 5379 (5375)
Maheady L, **8:** 4375 (4372, 4374), 4376 (4373, 4374), 4881 (4880)
Maher C A, **2:** 1052; **6:** 3670 (3670), 3671 (3668, 3669, 3670), 3684 (3684); **8:** 4652, 4661 (4661); **9:** 5021; **10:** 6164; **11:** 6484
Maher F, **4:** 1984 (1983)
Mahfoudh D, **11:** 6476
Mahl G F, **2:** 1079 (1075)
Mählck L, **1:** 474 (469); **3:** 1416, 1825; **6:** 3597; **8:** 4510; **9:** 5169 (5162); **11:** 6403
Mahler M, **8:** 4816 (4813, 4814)
Mahr C A, **6:** 3684
Mahrouse M E, **4:** 1947
Maier S F, **9:** 5406 (5404)
Maijling M R, **7:** 3996 (3995)
Main M, **2:** 705 (701); **4:** 2172 (2167)
Mair J, **9:** 5016 (5016)
Maithreyi, **11:** (6748)
Maitland-Gholson J, **11:** 6621 (6619)
Majhanovich S, **4:** 2351 (2349)
Majnarich B, **2:** 1165
Majone G, **5:** 2847 (2847)
Majoribanks K, **5:** 2491 (2487)
Major-Kingsley S, **7:** 3833 (3831); **10:** 5686 (5683)
Makarenko A S, **3:** 1538; **8:** (4451); **9:** (5229)
Maker C J, **5:** 2491 (2490)
Maker J, **5:** 2491 (2487, 2490)
Makonda A, **7:** 4236 (4232)
Makonnen E, **3:** 1789 (1787)
Makrakis V, **2:** 1006 (1002)
Makrinioti D, **5:** 2523 (2514)
Maksakovsky V, **5:** 2470 (2468)
Malaguzzi L, **5:** (2805)
Malan T, **8:** 4514 (4512)
Malanowski J, **10:** 6062 (6061)
Malara N A, **6:** 3652
Malatesha R N, **5:** 2767
Malatesta C Z, **4:** 1966 (1963, 1964)
Malcarne V L, **10:** 5738 (5737)
Malcher W, **11:** 6420 (6418)
Maldonado C, **1:** 227 (222); **3:** 1680 (1678)
Maldonado-Colón E, **6:** 3232 (3228)
Male G A, **1:** 184 (182); **7:** 3848 (3844, 3845)
Male M, **7:** 3808 (3804, 3805, 3806)
Malen B, **1:** 594 (593); **3:** 1343, 1411 (1410); **5:** 2799; **8:** 4408 (4408), 4594; **9:** 5308 (5306, 5307); **10:** 6083; **11:** 6558 (6555)
Maley D, **5:** 2903 (2900); **10:** 5674 (5673)
Malherbe E G, **10:** 5635
Malik A, **8:** 4873 (4869, 4871)
Malina R M, **8:** 4473 (4472), 4474
Malinowski B, **1:** 296 (281, 291); **4:** (2043), 2052 (2047); **5:** 2651 (2647), 2655 (2653)
Maliţa M, **9:** 5087
Maliyamkono T L, **2:** 893 (892)
Malizia G, **5:** 3036
Malkova Z A, **2:** 1064
Mallasi I, **10:** 5843
Mallea J R, **3:** 1768 (1763); **10:** 5735 (5733)
Mallette B, **8:** 4376 (4374), 4881 (4880)
Mallick K, **7:** 3978
Mallick S, **8:** 4408 (4405)
Mallinson G G, **9:** 5328 (5326)
Mallinson V, **2:** 957 (951); **9:** 5169 (5160)
Malmberg A C, **10:** 6008 (6007)
Malmi R A, **5:** 2922 (2920)
Malmquist E, **1:** 103; **11:** 6445 (6440)
Malone T W, **2:** 1170 (1169); **7:** 3942 (3939)
Malouf D, **7:** 3808 (3807)
Malpica C, **8:** 4415
Maltby G P, **2:** 718 (717)
Maltzman I, **6:** 3292; **7:** 3886
Mamon J, **5:** 2572 (2568)
Manatt R P, **4:** 2131 (2126, 2129)
Mandal A C, **4:** 2011 (2009)
Mandelbaum D G, **3:** 1729; **4:** 1852; **6:** 3238 (3235)
Mandell L, **2:** 1055 (1054)
Mandl H, **2:** 888, 968 (967), 969 (966), 984, 985, 1006, 1012 (1008); **4:** 2218; **5:** 2651, 2709, 2768, 2773 (2770); **6:** 3292, 3306 (3304), 3325 (3317), 3660; **8:** 4722; **9:** 5341 (5340, 5341), 5508; **11:** 6780
Mandler G, **1:** 204 (199); **6:** 3643 (3641); **8:** 4727 (4726); **11:** 6360 (6356)
Mandler J M, **2:** 856 (855, 856); **8:** 4727 (4726)
Mane S, **9:** 5518 (5514)
Mangieri J, **10:** 5795
Mangiola L, **11:** 6785 (6783)
Mangione J, **2:** 907
Mangione P L, **5:** 2806 (2803, 2804); **7:** 4296 (4295)
Mangubhai F, **4:** 2310; **8:** 4698 (4696)
Mangum S, **2:** 1152 (1150)
Manheimer R J, **8:** 4433
Manirabona G, **6:** 3550 (3546)
Manley F, **2:** 893 (891), (907)
Manley-Casimir M E, **8:** 4680 (4677)
Mann A, **1:** 139 (137)
Mann A P, **10:** 5901
Mann C W, **4:** 2310
Mann D, **8:** 4604 (4604)
Mann H, **4:** (2080), (2111); **5:** (2608); **8:** (4827); **11:** (6721)
Mann H B, **9:** 4974
Mann J S, **3:** 1287 (1285)
Mann L, **5:** 2907; **8:** 4936; **10:** 5662, 5663, 5686

Mann L D, **4:** 1996
Mann S J, **3:** 1563 (1557); **7:** 4220
Mannarino A P, **1:** 19 (17)
Mannell R C, **11:** 6798 (6794)
Mannheim K, **2:** 785 (782, 783); **3:** (1344); **10:** 5591 (5587)
Manning B H, **4:** 1848 (1846)
Manning P R, **4:** 2131 (2127)
Manning S, **7:** 3894 (3890, 3893)
Mansbridge A, **5:** (2735)
Mansell J, **8:** 4623 (4618, 4621)
Manser M, **4:** 2419 (2414)
Mansfield R S, **8:** 4731 (4729)
Manski C F, **3:** 1425, 1449; **10:** 5846 (5844)
Mantel N, **5:** 3050 (3046)
Mantl W, **1:** 432
Manu G, **4:** 1991 (1989)
Manzer R A, **10:** 6079 (6074, 6075)
Mao B J, **5:** 2595 (2590); **7:** 3986 (3979)
Mao Tse-Tung, **2:** (1192); **6:** 3621 (3617); **7:** (3847)
Mao Zedong, **3:** 1301 (1292, 1293)
Maple S, **4:** 2412 (2410)
Maqsud M, **6:** 3643 (3641)
Marans R W, **4:** 2225 (2220)
Marascuilo L A, **6:** 3508 (3503); **7:** 4163 (4159, 4160, 4161, 4162); **9:** 5489 (5488)
Marbe K, **5:** (2875)
Marble R P, **1:** 254 (246, 247)
Marcelino E, **2:** 910 (909)
Marcelissen F H G, **10:** 5924 (5923)
March C, **3:** 1553 (1550); **4:** 1857
March J, **8:** 4568 (4563); **9:** 5168 (5162)
March J G, **1:** 594; **3:** 1425, 1745 (1741); **4:** 1934 (1930), 2165, 2166 (2163), 2167; **5:** 2798 (2793); **6:** 3527 (3524, 3525); **8:** 4519 (4515, 4518); **9:** 5181 (5176), 5312, 5313 (5308), 5378
March L, **1:** 120 (115)
Marchman V A, **9:** 5363 (5359)
Marconnit G D, **3:** 1355
Marcoulides G A, **5:** 2462 (2460); **11:** 6307 (6301)
Marcus J, **1:** 296 (289); **3:** 1774
Marcus S, **10:** 5674 (5673)
Marcuse H, **2:** (780, 929); **8:** (4454)
Marcuse J, **10:** (5600)
Marder C, **11:** 6538 (6536)
Marder J V, **5:** 2827
Mare R D, **1:** 11 (7, 10); **9:** 5553 (5553)
Marechal J, **5:** 2470 (2467)
Marecki S, **7:** 4289 (4284)
Marenbach D, **6:** 3549 (3548); **8:** 4917 (4915, 4916); **11:** 6282 (6280)
Marentič Požarnik B, **9:** 5497 (5495)
Maretzki T, **5:** 2685
Marfo K, **6:** 3227
Margalit M, **4:** 1980 (1976, 1977, 1978, 1979); **7:** 3808 (3806)
Marge M, **5:** 2972 (2966, 2969); **7:** 3935 (3934)
Marginson S, **9:** 5308 (5305)
Marglin S, **3:** 1703 (1696)
Margolis J, **9:** 4980 (4979, 4980)
Mariage T V, **2:** 867 (861)
Marien M M, **4:** 2331
Mariet F, **2:** 1127 (1122, 1125); **3:** 1573 (1571); **4:** 1903 (1900)
Marin A, **1:** 135 (130); **11:** 6298 (6293)
Maritain J, **8:** 4455 (4449)
Marja T, **1:** 168 (165)
Marjomaki V, **10:** 5808 (5807)
Marjoribanks K, **3:** 1482, 1483; **4:** 2249 (2245), 2250, 2257 (2251, 2255), 2258; **5:** 2628 (2624), 2931 (2926); **6:** 3523 (3519); **9:** 4974 (4972), 5060 (5057); **10:** 5607 (5597, 5599)
Mark A J, **7:** 4175 (4174)
Mark H T, **3:** (1723)
Mark J H, **10:** 5924 (5923)
Mark M, **4:** 2108
Mark M L, **7:** 4027
Mark M M, **3:** 1283; **5:** 2672 (2671), 2673
Market R W, **5:** 2870 (2868)
Markewich T S, **6:** 3508 (3507)
Markle S M, **5:** 3066 (3065); **8:** 4774 (4770, 4771); **10:** 6164
Marklund S, **8:** 4751 (4745); **10:** 5873; **11:** 6699 (6692)
Markman E M, **2:** 838, 856, 871; **5:** 2628, 2916; **6:** 3224 (3220), 3329; **7:** 3768; **8:** 4383, 4956, 4957 (4955); **9:** 5512
Markou G, **3:** 1375
Markova A K, **9:** 5548; **11:** 6777 (6775)
Markovits H, **8:** 4957 (4955)
Marks C, **10:** 5831 (5830, 5831)
Marks E, **6:** 3508 (3500); **9:** 5441
Marks I M, **4:** 1967 (1965)
Marks L, **6:** 3621
Marks S, **7:** 3853 (3850)
Markus G B, **7:** 3873 (3869)
Markus H, **7:** 3873 (3869); **9:** 5394 (5393); **10:** 6112 (6107)
Markus H R, **5:** 2651 (2650)
Markus R L, **1:** 239 (237)
Marland M, **2:** 977 (975); **6:** 3209 (3205, 3206); **7:** 3826 (3824); **8:** 4698 (4696); **10:** 5826
Marland P, **10:** 6183 (6182)
Marland S P, **5:** (2492), 2779 (2774)
Marler P, **5:** 2685 (2682)
Marliave R, **1:** 23
Marlowe H A, **9:** 5528
Marolla F A, **7:** 3872 (3868, 3869)
Maron M E, **3:** 1394 (1388)
Marotto R, **4:** 2046 (2044)
Marquardt D W, **8:** 4758; **9:** 4974 (4972)
Marques A H O, **8:** 4630
Marrett C B, **6:** 3642; **9:** 5175, 5176
Marrin Y, **5:** 2972 (2969)
Marriott S A, **1:** 93 (90, 92); **3:** 1441 (1441)
Marris P, **4:** 1967 (1964)
Marris R, **3:** 1666 (1663)
Marrou H-I, **6:** 3647 (3644); **9:** 5117
Marrow A J, **10:** 6062
Marsagli G, **9:** 5471 (5468)
Marsden D, **2:** 917 (916); **4:** 1976 (1973), 2272 (2269, 2270, 2271); **5:** 2942; **6:** 3189 (3188)
Marsden P V, **9:** 5560 (5556, 5557, 5558)
Marsden W E, **5:** 2469 (2469), 2470 (2467), 2607
Marsh C, **3:** 1271 (1267, 1270); **4:** 1857; **5:** 2642; **6:** 3545; **7:** 4236; **10:** 6092 (6090)
Marsh D D, **8:** 4751 (4743); **10:** 6053 (6052)
Marsh D T, **10:** 5650
Marsh H W, **1:** 193 (191); **4:** 2241 (2238, 2239); **7:** 4006 (4002, 4003, 4006), 4007 (4003, 4005); **8:** 4359 (4357); **9:** 4977 (4976), 5394 (5393); **10:** 6234 (6228, 6229, 6230, 6231, 6232, 6233)
Marshalek B, **4:** 2219 (2218); **5:** 2921 (2920); **7:** 3879 (3876, 3878)
Marshall A, **6:** (3097)
Marshall C, **1:** 67 (62, 64), 83 (78); **2:** 645; **6:** 3284 (3277); **7:** 3826 (3822, 3824, 3825), 4319 (4316, 4317, 4318); **9:** 5273 (5269); **11:** 6731 (6728)
Marshall D G, **9:** 5294
Marshall E K, **10:** 5854
Marshall G, **6:** 3213
Marshall H, **9:** 5394 (5392); **10:** 6112 (6109)
Marshall H H, **7:** 4215 (4212); **10:** 6183
Marshall J, **8:** 4461, 4642; **10:** 5924
Marshall J C, **6:** 3224
Marshall J D, **3:** 1325, 1337; **10:** 6106 (6105)
Marshall R, **1:** 310 (307)
Marshall S, **3:** 1257 (1255), 1381 (1377)
Marshall S P, **4:** 2435 (2433, 2434); **6:** 3335 (3331), 3660 (3659)
Marshall W A, **1:** 88 (84, 85)
Marsick V J, **2:** 1165 (1164); **6:** 3349 (3348), 3422, 3435 (3433); **9:** 5399; **10:** 5596 (5594), 6058 (6055)
Marston D, **7:** 3833 (3832)
Martendale C J, **4:** 2186 (2183)
Martenot M, **7:** 4027
Martin A, **10:** 5680
Martin B, **1:** 234 (232); **9:** 5441 (5437, 5439)
Martin B L, **5:** 2867 (2866)
Martin C, **7:** 4301 (4299)
Martin C E, **8:** 4887 (4883)
Martin C L, **4:** 2449 (2447)
Martin D, **1:** 176, 221; **2:** 991 (990)
Martin E, **1:** 194 (192); **5:** 2457 (2456)
Martin F M, **6:** 3312 (3307)
Martin H J, **8:** 4694
Martin I, **2:** 906 (902)
Martin J, **4:** 1984 (1982); **11:** 6723 (6721)
Martin J A, **3:** 1642 (1639, 1640)
Martin J R, **3:** 1328; **4:** 2033 (2031); **5:** 2589 (2586); **10:** 5985 (5982), 5995 (5991); **11:** 6579 (6578), 6727 (6724)
Martin J T, **1:** 52 (50, 51)
Martin L, **7:** 4307 (4306)
Martin L G, **1:** 168, 184 (181, 183); **3:** 1602 (1601); **8:** 4616 (4614)
Martin M, **1:** 408 (405); **2:** 893 (891); **5:** 2998
Martin M W, **11:** 6287 (6283, 6284, 6285)
Martin N C, **6:** 3209 (3205, 3206, 3208); **7:** 3935, 3936 (3933); **10:** 5961 (5959); **11:** 6784 (6782)
Martin N G, **11:** 6492 (6490)
Martin R, **4:** 2427 (2424, 2425)
Martin R M, **8:** 4447 (4443)

Martin R P, **1:** 362 (360, 361); **5:** 2665 (2663); **11:** 6310 (6308, 6309, 6310)
Martin S, **7:** 3894 (3891, 3893, 3894)
Martin T P, **11:** 6765 (6764)
Martindale C J, **7:** 4324 (4321)
Martindale D, **1:** 60 (57)
Martinellini A, **5:** 3036 (3032)
Martinez M, **2:** 738
Martinez M L, **3:** 1735 (1733, 1734)
Martinez Paz F, **1:** 338
Martington M, **1:** 560 (560)
Martino A M, **6:** 3670 (3670)
Martinos H, **11:** 6807 (6806)
Martins Z, **7:** 3960
Martlew M, **7:** 4095
Marton F, **1:** 193, 194 (189), 322 (319, 320, 321); **2:** 871 (870), 969 (965), 1165; **3:** 1514 (1509); **5:** 2769 (2763), 2884 (2882); **6:** 3329 (3326, 3327), 3602 (3597); **7:** 4307; **8:** 4429 (4424, 4425, 4426, 4427, 4429), 4652 (4649, 4650); **9:** 5411 (5408); **10:** 5790 (5784, 5785, 5786); **11:** 6699
Martorell R, **8:** 4474 (4472)
Maruyama G, **6:** 3297 (3293)
Marvani M, **4:** 2286 (2282)
Marx E, **9:** 5246 (5241, 5242); **11:** 6398 (6396)
Marx F, **3:** 1635 (1634)
Marx K, **2:** 785 (779), (1067), 1073 (1067), (1191), (1199), (1200), (1201), (1202); **3:** (1695), (1696), (1699); **5:** (2605), (2735); **6:** 3621 (3618), 3622; **7:** (3716), (3847), (4330); **8:** (4430), (4453), (4573), (4605), (4642); **9:** (5052); **10:** (5589), (5596), (5597), (5598), (5730)
Marx R W, **10:** 5745 (5743), 6035 (6032, 6033), 6193 (6188), 6208 (6206)
Maryanski A, **2:** 1074 (1065)
Masemann V L, **2:** 933 (924, 927); **4:** 1852 (1850)
Masia B B, **1:** 390 (380, 382), 396 (392); **5:** 2867 (2866); **9:** 5324 (5319, 5320); **11:** 6328 (6321)
Masic S B, **9:** 5532 (5528, 5530)
Masilela P, **8:** 4680 (4680)
Maslach C, **10:** 5924 (5920, 5923), 5925 (5919, 5922), 6062 (6059)
Maslankowski W, **11:** 6659
Maslow A H, **1:** (276); **3:** (1363); **4:** 1972 (1967); **5:** 2692 (2690, 2691), (2936); **7:** 4329 (4326, 4327); **8:** (4822); **10:** 6202 (6198)
Mason B J, **7:** 3833
Mason D, **10:** 6112 (6110)
Mason E F, **5:** 2571 (2569)
Mason G, **3:** 1739 (1736); **11:** 6640
Mason G E, **7:** 3807 (3802)
Mason H, **10:** 5943 (5942)
Mason J, **2:** 802 (800); **6:** 3459 (3457); **7:** 3889 (3887)
Mason J M, **2:** 825 (821); **8:** 4881 (4878)
Mason K O, **3:** 1676 (1673, 1674, 1675)
Mason R, **1:** 343 (341); **2:** 982 (978, 979, 981), 1012 (1008); **3:** 1563 (1561), 1579 (1576); **7:** 4094
Mason T R, **4:** 2229
Mason W, **3:** 1750 (1749)
Mason W M, **5:** 2596 (2590, 2591, 2594, 2595); **6:** 3523 (3523); **7:** 3722 (3719), 3986 (3980, 3982, 3986), 3987 (3986)
Mason W S, **10:** 6132 (6131)
Masri M, **6:** 3113
Massad C E, **1:** 396 (393); **3:** 1768 (1763); **4:** 2357 (2352); **5:** 2978 (2974); **8:** 4940
Masschelein J, **8:** 4461 (4459); **10:** 6197
Massey C R, **1:** 12 (7)
Massialas B G, **1:** 328 (323, 325, 327); **6:** 3407; **9:** 5582 (5578, 5579, 5580, 5581); **10:** 5782 (5782)
Massy W, **8:** 4568 (4562, 4563, 4566, 4567)
Mastain R, **10:** 5965 (5963)
Masten A S, **6:** 3297 (3293); **8:** 4779 (4775, 4777)
Masten C L, **2:** 1131 (1130)
Masten W G, **5:** 2491 (2487)
Masterman L, **5:** 2897
Masterman M, **9:** 5030 (5025)
Masters G N, **1:** 390 (385, 387); **3:** 1514 (1511); **4:** 2017 (2012, 2016), 2180 (2177); **5:** 2784 (2781), 3043 (3042), 3055 (3052); **6:** 3253 (3251, 3252), 3474 (3469); **7:** 4307 (4304, 4305, 4306); **8:** 4754 (4752), 4923 (4921); **10:** 5790 (5788), 5791 (5788); **11:** 6355 (6354)
Masters G R, **9:** 5324 (5320)
Masters J C, **6:** 3228 (3226)
Masters J R, **1:** 390 (387)
Masterton M, **11:** 6461
Masuda Y, **4:** 1911 (1903), 2331
Matarazzo J D, **1:** 239 (236)
Matas J A, **1:** 409 (407)
Matheny A P, **11:** 6311
Matheny A P Jr, **11:** 6492 (6491)
Matheson K A, **11:** 6307 (6303, 6305)
Mathew A, **5:** 2759
Mathews D A, **9:** 5201
Mathews J C, **4:** 2180 (2178, 2179)
Mathews M, **9:** 5013
Mathias H, **4:** 1898
Mathijsen A, **10:** 5854
Mathinos D L, **11:** 6370 (6370)
Mathy-Laikko P, **1:** 409 (407)
Matila J P, **3:** 1449 (1447)
Matilla J, **4:** 2279 (2275)
Matos J F, **6:** 3652; **7:** (4098)
Matras M A, **7:** 4099 (4096)
Matson J L, **1:** 490 (489)
Matsushita T, **1:** 353
Matsuzawa T, **5:** 2685 (2682)
Matt S R, **11:** 6603 (6600)
Mattes L, **6:** 3231 (3230)
Matthay E R, **4:** 2131 (2130)
Mattheier K J, **2:** 968
Matthew M, **3:** 1599
Matthews D A, **1:** 594 (590)
Matthews J, **11:** 6735 (6733)
Matthews K M, **7:** 4157 (4157)
Matthews M R, **6:** 3416; **8:** 4464 (4461, 4464)
Mattil E L, **1:** 198, 343
Mattimore-Knudson R, **7:** 4059 (4057)
Mattingly I W, **4:** 1962 (1958)
Mattingly P H, **10:** 6012 (6009)
Mattison R E, **7:** 3830
Mattson A, **1:** 234 (232)
Mattson D, **7:** 4000 (3997)
Mattsson I, **5:** 2714 (2712)
Matus Lazo R, **2:** 640
Matwana M, **2:** 907
Matza D, **11:** 6803 (6799)
Matzner E, **11:** 6260 (6258)
Mau T, **4:** 1995 (1994)
Mauermann L, **7:** 3925 (3923)
Maughan B, **3:** 1538; **4:** 1934 (1933), 2166 (2164); **5:** 2589 (2588); **8:** 4779 (4777), 4873 (4870); **9:** 5211 (5207, 5209), 5224 (5221), 5264 (5262), 5379 (5375); **10:** 5750 (5746), 6083 (6082)
Maurer H, **8:** 4694
Maurer R E, **10:** 6031 (6030)
Maurer R G, **6:** 3235 (3232)
Maurice M, **4:** 1976 (1973); **5:** 2942 (2939, 2941); **11:** 6420 (6419)
Maurolico F, **3:** (1462)
Mausner B, **4:** 1972 (1968)
Mauss M, **2:** 1073 (1070)
Maxson P, **4:** 2266 (2266)
Maxwell G, **5:** 3066 (3063)
Maxwell J A, **11:** 6466 (6462)
Maxwell M, **1:** 194 (185, 186)
Maxwell S E, **1:** 5 (3); **10:** 6234 (6230, 6231)
May L S, **3:** 1491
May M A, **1:** 380 (379)
May W T, **10:** 6004 (6002, 6003)
Mayberry P W, **8:** 4751 (4745)
Mayberry W, **8:** 4542 (4540)
Maybury R H, **9:** 5328 (5326)
Mayer E, **3:** 1720 (1719)
Mayer G R, **1:** 486; **10:** 5762 (5760), 6164 (6160, 6162)
Mayer H, **3:** 1672
Mayer K-M, **10:** 5735 (5734)
Mayer K-U, **6:** 3428 (3427)
Mayer P, **9:** 5220 (5217)
Mayer R E, **1:** 194 (187), 322 (319); **2:** 984 (983, 984), 985, 1031 (1026); **4:** 2281 (2279, 2280, 2281); **5:** 2665 (2664), 2769 (2762), 2884 (2882); **6:** 3329 (3326), 3335 (3329, 3331); **7:** 3925 (3923); **8:** 4727 (4723, 4725, 4726, 4727), 4731 (4728); **10:** 5745 (5741, 5742), 5831 (5829, 5830, 5831), 6192 (6191); **11:** 6456
Mayer R H, **10:** 5919 (5914)
Mayes J T, **2:** 1012 (1008); **5:** 2709 (2708)
Mayeske G W, **2:** 631 (629); **8:** 4930; **9:** 4974 (4973)
Mayhall W F, **9:** 5070 (5068)
Mayher J S, **10:** 5961
Mayhew K C, **3:** 1301 (1298), 1524
Maynard A K, **10:** 5767 (5765)
Maynard E J, **5:** 2571 (2569)
Maynard R, **2:** 693 (691); **4:** 2150 (2147, 2148); **9:** 5385
Maynes D D, **1:** 52 (51)
Maynes M J, **5:** 2607
Mayntz R, **6:** 3368 (3367)
Mayo E, **4:** 2166 (2158); **9:** 5169 (5161)

Mayo J, **2:** 1136 (1134); **4:** 1911 (1904, 1905, 1906, 1908); **5:** 2897 (2892)
Mayo M, **2:** 1193
Mayor F, **5:** 2951 (2947)
Mayr E, **4:** 2172 (2167)
Mays F B, **3:** 1266 (1264)
Mayston D, **3:** 1386 (1384)
Mazrui A A, **5:** 2998 (2995)
Mazur P J, **10:** 5925 (5921, 5922)
Mazurier M, **1:** 294 (283); **5:** 2514 (2514)
Mazzolenis A, **5:** 2562
Mbilinyi M, **11:** 6719 (6715, 6716)
Mbithi P M, **2:** 914 (911)
Meacham A W, **4:** 2331
Meacham J A, **3:** 1253
Meacock P, **5:** 2491 (2487)
Mead G H, **2:** 838 (837), (929), (930), 1073 (1070); **3:** (1521), (1524); **6:** (3308); **7:** (4330); **9:** 5512 (5510); **10:** 5591 (5587), (5594), (6127)
Mead M, **1:** 296 (283); **2:** 1213 (1209); **3:** 1729 (1724), 1756 (1754); **4:** 2052 (2047); **5:** 2651 (2648); **8:** (4459); **10:** 5591 (5587)
Mead N A, **3:** 1768 (1765); **4:** 2140 (2136), 2439 (2436); **6:** 3550 (3546); **7:** 4053 (4053); **9:** 5334 (5333), 5342 (5340), 5432 (5426), 5497 (5496); **11:** 6334 (6332)
Mead R J, **5:** 3051 (3049)
Meadow K, **3:** 1402 (1401)
Meadows D, **3:** 1830 (1828)
Meadows J, **8:** 4479 (4477)
Meager N, **8:** 4531 (4527)
Means B, **4:** 1848 (1847)
Means M L, **8:** 4951 (4949); **9:** 5563 (5562)
Meara H, **10:** 5834 (5832, 5833)
Measor L, **7:** 3826 (3825); **9:** 5313 (5312), 5411 (5410)
Mebrahtu T, **3:** 1501
Mechanic D, **10:** 5606
Meckel H C, **10:** 5704 (5699, 5700)
Mecklenburger J, **8:** 4715 (4709)
Mecklenburger J A, **9:** 5544 (5541)
Medawar P B, **3:** (1540); **6:** 3219 (3217)
Medin D L, **6:** 3155 (3152)
Medina L M, **3:** 1735 (1734)
Medina N J, **8:** 4623 (4619)
Medley D M, **2:** 816 (813, 814); **4:** 2131 (2128); **10:** 5957 (5954), 6020 (6018), 6043 (6035, 6036)
Medoff J L, **2:** 652 (650); **3:** 1750 (1750); **10:** 6072 (6070)
Medrich E A, **7:** 3711
Medway F J, **8:** 4661 (4659); **11:** 6484 (6482, 6483)
Meece J L, **9:** 5432 (5429); **10:** 5775 (5772)
Meehl P E, **11:** 6575 (6570, 6572, 6573)
Meek M, **6:** 3459 (3456)
Meek V L, **3:** 1720 (1718, 1719)
Meeker M, **2:** 1182 (1180); **7:** 3722 (3716)
Meeker R, **2:** 1182 (1180)
Meeks B N, **2:** 1175 (1171)
Meeks S, **1:** 239 (238)
Meerman J, **8:** 4707 (4704)
Meesook O A, **3:** 1606 (1604, 1605), 1707 (1703); **8:** 4839 (4838, 4839); **11:** 6638 (6635)
Megarry J, **5:** 2773 (2771); **8:** 4562 (4558); **9:** 5432 (5423), 5475; **10:** 5873, 6096
Megarty J, **7:** 3895
Meghnagi S, **11:** 6266 (6262, 6264)
Mehan H, **1:** 296 (290); **2:** 802 (799, 801), 803 (799), 982 (978), 1073 (1071); **4:** 2052 (2051); **6:** 3215 (3215), 3238 (3237); **8:** 4896 (4894, 4895), 4935 (4933); **9:** 5313 (5310, 5311); **10:** 5795 (5791), 6035 (6033)
Mehaut P, **4:** 1976 (1973); **11:** 6272 (6269), 6452 (6448)
Mehler B, **2:** 718 (717)
Mehlhorn G, **9:** 5532 (5531)
Mehlick L, **8:** 4519
Mehlinger H D, **8:** 4581
Mehmet O, **8:** 4531 (4530)
Mehra K, **4:** 2418 (2417)
Mehrens W A, **2:** 1182 (1180); **5:** 2856 (2854, 2855); **7:** 4000 (3997, 3998); **8:** 4803; **11:** 6315 (6313), 6339 (6338)
Mehriz Z, **11:** 6761
Mehta G R, **2:** 1084 (1081)
Mehtäläinen J, **6:** 3213 (3211)
Meichenbaum D, **2:** 868 (863); **9:** 5403 (5400)
Meidinger E E, **9:** 5490
Meihls J L, **8:** 4935 (4933)
Meijer A, **1:** 553 (553)
Meijer C J W, **2:** 729 (723); **5:** 2910 (2908)
Meijer H, **5:** 2470 (2468)
Meijer K, **11:** 6669 (6668)
Meijer M, **10:** 5854
Meijnen G W, **10:** 5606 (5600)
Meiklejohn J M D, **3:** (1723)
Meiland M, **9:** 4980 (4978)
Meili R, **5:** 2769 (2760)
Meisels S J, **1:** 362 (358, 359, 361); **3:** 1624 (1621, 1622, 1623), 1642 (1641); **5:** 2814; **8:** 4779; **9:** 5275 (5274)
Meister A, **8:** 4736 (4735)
Meister C, **10:** 6015 (6013, 6014)
Meister G R, **2:** 1127 (1126), 1136 (1134, 1135); **3:** 1784 (1780); **4:** 1911 (1907, 1909); **7:** 3821 (3816); **11:** 6287 (6283)
Meister-Steiner B, **1:** 431 (431)
Mejding J, **3:** 1461
Mejía B, **7:** 4275
Mekete B, **4:** 2043
Melamed L, **4:** 2194 (2190)
Melanchthon P, **4:** (2004); **6:** (3529), (3530)
Melhuish E C, **4:** 2145 (2144); **8:** 4677 (4675); **11:** 6398 (6397)
Melican G, **10:** 5726 (5725)
Mellenbergh G J, **3:** 1421 (1420, 1421); **5:** 3050 (3045, 3046), 3051 (3046); **6:** 3508 (3507); **10:** 5726 (5723)
Mellin-Olsen S, **3:** 1236 (1233, 1235); **6:** 3459 (3457, 3458)
Mellon J, **10:** 5704 (5701)
Mellor F J, **2:** 820 (817, 818, 819)
Mellor J W, **1:** 244
Mellor R W, **9:** 5130 (5129)
Mellor W, **4:** 1934 (1931)
Mellor W L, **8:** 4489
Melmed A, **5:** 2897
Melnick S A, **6:** 3603 (3598)
Melo A, **2:** 906 (904)
Melosh B, **11:** 6723 (6720)
Melton A W, **4:** 1899 (1885); **5:** (2920)
Meltsner A J, **8:** 4556 (4551, 4552)
Meltzer A, **11:** 6415 (6413)
Meltzer L J, **2:** 868 (861)
Meltzoff A, **5:** 2802 (2800)
Melzer A M, **9:** 5090 (5090)
Memmi A, **2:** (1046)
Menacker J, **8:** 4788 (4783); **9:** 5216 (5211); **11:** 6563 (6560, 6561, 6562)
Menard, **10:** 5862 (5855)
Menck P, **8:** 4419
Mendeleyev D L, **2:** (825)
Mendenhall W, **5:** 2714 (2713); **9:** 5142; **11:** 6591 (6591)
Mendes de Oliviera M E, **2:** 1094 (1089); **9:** 5354, 5355 (5353)
Mendez E G, **3:** 1736
Mendicati T N, **6:** 3661
Mendicutti T N, **7:** 4100
Mendiola H, **2:** 1146 (1142)
Mendoza A, **2:** 738 (734)
Menges R J, **5:** 2879 (2879); **6:** 3339; **10:** 6234 (6233)
Menke J, **3:** 1438 (1436)
Menke R, **3:** 1402 (1399)
Menlo A, **9:** 5181 (5177, 5178); **10:** 5925 (5921)
Menter I, **11:** 6558 (6556)
Menyuk P, **6:** 3224 (3219, 3221)
Mercante V, **4:** (1866)
Mercer J R, **2:** 1073 (1070); **3:** 1486 (1485); **6:** 3297 (3294); **10:** 5668 (5664, 5665)
Mercer N, **10:** 6197 (6194)
Mercier R, **9:** 5091 (5090)
Meredith K, **1:** 390 (388)
Meredith P, **9:** 5441 (5436, 5437)
Meredith W, **3:** 1514 (1512)
Merelman R, **4:** 1984 (1981)
Merenheimo J, **5:** 2495 (2493)
Mergendoller J R, **1:** 23; **9:** 5363 (5359, 5360)
Meriwether C, **3:** 1301 (1296)
Merluzzi F, **4:** 2011 (2010)
Merrett P, **1:** 490 (488, 489)
Merriam S B, **1:** 103, 142 (140), 152 (143), 184; **2:** 906; **3:** 1315 (1309); **5:** 2737; **6:** 3366 (3363, 3364), 3422, 3434 (3434), 3435; **7:** 4185 (4181), 4324 (4320, 4321, 4324), 4329 (4328); **8:** 4616 (4610), 4736 (4734), 4811, 4812; **9:** 5399 (5396); **10:** 6058
Merrick D, **3:** 1680 (1679)
Merrill M A, **1:** 53 (49); **11:** 6315 (6315)
Merrill M D, **2:** 1020, 1026, 1031 (1030), 1170 (1166, 1168); **5:** 2862 (2860), 2884; **8:** 4803 (4800); **10:** 5913 (5911, 5912); **11:** 6765 (6761)
Merrill P F, **10:** 5913 (5911)
Merriman H, **10:** 5957 (5954)
Merritt J E, **2:** 738
Merritt R, **5:** 2697 (2696)

Merritt S, **2:** 973 (970)
Merryfield M M, **2:** 770 (768); **9:** 5582 (5579); **10:** 5585 (5583)
Merseth K K, **10:** 5948 (5944, 5945, 5946, 5947), 6088 (6088)
Mertens D, **11:** 6633 (6628)
Mertens G B, **10:** 6117
Mertens T, **2:** 807 (805)
Mertens W, **8:** 4816
Merton R H, **2:** (777), 1073 (1071)
Merton R K, **10:** 6127 (6122, 6123); **11:** 6511 (6509)
Mervis R C, **5:** 2575 (2574)
Merwin J C, **8:** 4751 (4743)
Meshcheryakov A, **3:** 1406
Meslin G, **3:** 1347 (1345)
Messaâdi M, **11:** 6476
Messara A N, **6:** 3356
Messenger R C, **7:** 4016 (4011)
Messer S B, **6:** 3325 (3319)
Messick B M, **6:** 3453 (3447)
Messick S, **1:** 362 (360), 374 (372, 373); **2:** 729 (725), 871 (869, 870), 872 (869, 870); **3:** 1624 (1622); **7:** 3706, 3830 (3828), 3833 (3831); **8:** 4648 (4647); **11:** 6320 (6316), 6339 (6335, 6336, 6337)
Messick S M, **5:** 3061 (3058)
Mestre J, **6:** 3638 (3635)
Met M, **4:** 2351 (2350); **6:** 3335 (3333)
Metcalf D H, **3:** 1695 (1692); **4:** 2212 (2210); **6:** 3267; **8:** 4531; **9:** 5076 (5072)
Metcalf E, **2:** 738 (737)
Metcalf K K, **6:** 3202 (3198); **10:** 6149 (6147)
Metcalf L E, **10:** 6149 (6144, 6145)
Metfessel N S, **4:** 2089 (2080)
Metge J, **10:** 6178 (6173)
Mettelin P, **5:** 2819 (2814)
Mettem P, **8:** 4376 (4373)
Metz H C, **6:** 3407; **9:** 5013
Metz M, **9:** 5210 (5209); **10:** 5613 (5608), 6214 (6213)
Metz M H, **1:** 12
Metzler H, **11:** 6461 (6459)
Meumann E, **3:** (1722), (1723), (1794); **4:** 1872 (1864, 1866, 1869); **9:** 5055 (5053)
Meuwissen I, **11:** 6712 (6711)
Meux M O, **2:** 816 (815); **10:** 6149 (6147, 6148)
Mevarech Z R, **6:** 3631 (3629, 3630); **7:** 3970 (3967)
Meyenn R J, **9:** 5060 (5058)
Meyer D K, **6:** 3339 (3337)
Meyer H J, **4:** 2166 (2162); **9:** 5217
Meyer J, **2:** 770 (768), 933 (928); **3:** 1607 (1603), 1655 (1652); **8:** 4568 (4562, 4563); **9:** 5181 (5177, 5180); **11:** 6558 (6554)
Meyer J F, **4:** 2296 (2295)
Meyer J H F, **1:** 193 (191), 194 (190, 191)
Meyer J W, **2:** 957 (951), 1042 (1038), 1073 (1069); **4:** 1938 (1935), 2166 (2162); **6:** 3368 (3367), 3428 (3427), 3527 (3525); **9:** 5246 (5243), 5299 (5295); **10:** 5607 (5600)
Meyer L, **2:** 729 (723)
Meyer L A, **8:** 4947 (4946)
Meyer L H, **3:** 1438, 1508; **5:** 2813
Meyer M, **2:** 1208; **6:** 3625
Meyer M R, **6:** 3643 (3640)
Meyer M W, **3:** 1774 (1770)
Meyer R, **5:** 2681 (2677); **9:** 5345 (5343); **11:** 6538 (6535)
Meyer R H, **11:** 6633 (6628)
Meyer-Probst B, **8:** 4395 (4390)
Meyers A V, **7:** 3808 (3806); **9:** 5441 (5436)
Meyers C S, **2:** 792 (786)
Meyers D T, **4:** 2297; **10:** 5991 (5990)
Meyers E D Jr, **8:** 4474 (4470)
Meyers P, **8:** 4586 (4585)
Meyrowitz N, **5:** 2709 (2706)
Mezirow J, **1:** 135 (133), 168 (164), 277 (276); **2:** 1204 (1199); **6:** 3349 (3345)
Mezirow J A, **10:** 5596 (5594)
Mezirow J M, **10:** 6058 (6055)
Mialaret G, **8:** 4491
Micceri T, **2:** 1175 (1173, 1174); **8:** 4881 (4876); **9:** 5471 (5470)
Michael I, **6:** 3096 (3092)
Michael R T, **2:** 1055 (1052, 1053, 1054); **4:** 2212
Michael W B, **4:** 2089 (2080, 2082, 2086, 2087)
Michaelis J W, **9:** 5578 (5573)
Michaels S, **2:** 802 (801); **6:** 3238 (3237), 3452 (3449)
Michalopoulos C, **2:** 693 (690); **4:** 1841 (1838); **5:** 2993 (2991)
Michalos A C, **2:** 1094 (1093)
Michel A, **9:** 5302 (5300, 5301)
Michels K M, **9:** 4995 (4984)
Michener B, **1:** 296 (284)
Micheva P, **2:** 661 (659)
Mickelson N I, **10:** 5613 (5612)
Middelton J, **3:** 1416 (1412, 1413)
Middelton S, **4:** 1984 (1982, 1983)
Middleton J, **1:** 111, 295, 296 (283); **2:** 760 (758), 933 (929), 1152, 1212, 1213; **3:** 1252, 1713 (1710, 1711), 1825 (1822), 1830 (1829); **4:** 1910, 1911 (1904, 1905, 1907), 2052 (2047); **5:** 3003 (3001); **8:** 4510, 4519 (4515), 4601 (4596, 4597, 4599), 4864 (4858, 4859, 4863); **9:** 5076 (5071, 5072); **10:** 5919; **11:** 6266 (6262, 6263), 6282 (6281), 6431 (6430), 6452 (6449), 6638 (6633), 6663 (6660, 6661, 6662, 6663)
Middleton K, **5:** 2572
Middleton N, **7:** 3906
Middleton S, **4:** 2292 (2290); **6:** 3496 (3493, 3494); **10:** 6139 (6138); **11:** 6723, 6727 (6724)
Midgley C, **2:** 868 (866); **10:** 5775 (5773), 6112 (6110)
Midgley M, **3:** 1367 (1362, 1363)
Midwinter E C, **1:** 94; **2:** (1192); **4:** 2249 (2249); **7:** 4170 (4170), 4171
Miel A, **10:** 6187 (6183)
Mies M, **4:** 2302 (2297, 2298)
Mieszalski S, **6:** 3608 (3605)
Mieszkowski B, **8:** 4787
Mifflen F J, **10:** 5607 (5601)
Mifflen S C, **10:** 5607 (5601)
Migniudo F W, **10:** 5613 (5609)
Migniuolo F W, **8:** 4586 (4584, 4585, 4586); **11:** 6730 (6729)
Mihály O, **5:** 2706
Mikl-Horke G, **11:** 6684
Miklos E, **1:** 77 (74, 75), 83 (78, 80, 82)
Mikulecky L, **1:** 111; **6:** 3209 (3207); **7:** 3711 (3710)
Milbank J E, **4:** 2145; **8:** 4666 (4665)
Milburn G, **7:** 3970 (3961); **8:** 4447
Miles A, **1:** 162 (160)
Miles J, **7:** 3706 (3702), 4293 (4292)
Miles M, **2:** 729 (723, 727); **5:** 2847 (2840, 2841), 2852 (2848); **7:** 4293; **8:** 4509 (4503); **9:** 5030 (5025), 5246 (5241, 5242, 5243, 5245); **10:** 5973 (5972), 6224 (6220)
Miles M B, **2:** 645 (644), 1011 (1009, 1010); **3:** 1343, 1355 (1351), 1411 (1410, 1411), 1474 (1464, 1465, 1466, 1467, 1469, 1470, 1471, 1472, 1474); **4:** 1857 (1853, 1855), 1898, 2166 (2165); **5:** 2847 (2840, 2844, 2845); **6:** 3602 (3597, 3599, 3600, 3601), 3603 (3599, 3602); **7:** 4240 (4237), 4293 (4290); **8:** 4865; **9:** 5210 (5208, 5209), 5246 (5242, 5243, 5245); **10:** 6239 (6237)
Miles R F, **4:** 1899
Miles S, **10:** 5957 (5956), 5995 (5993)
Miles T, **10:** 5680 (5678)
Milgate M, **3:** 1685, 1750
Milgram N A, **9:** 5532 (5530)
Milgram R M, **2:** 1182 (1180); **9:** 5532 (5530)
Milheim W D, **5:** 2870 (2868)
Miliband R, **6:** 3621 (3619)
Milkman M I, **10:** 6073 (6070)
Mill J, **3:** (1294); **5:** (2876)
Mill J S, **2:** (804); **3:** (1540); **5:** (2608); **6:** (3316); **7:** (3924); **8:** (4452), (4453), 4536 (4535); **9:** (5051); **10:** (5705); **11:** (6578)
Millar R, **3:** 1543; **6:** 3219; **11:** 6292 (6291)
Millar R H, **9:** 5328 (5326)
Millar T B, **7:** 4171
Miller A, **3:** 1624 (1621), 1739 (1737, 1738); **7:** 4170 (4166); **8:** 4816 (4815); **9:** 5232 (5231); **10:** 5939 (5937), 6169 (6167)
Miller C J, **1:** 494 (493); **6:** 3227 (3227); **8:** 4951 (4948, 4950); **10:** 5943 (5942)
Miller D C, **7:** 3722 (3717, 3719); **10:** 5862 (5854)
Miller D L, **10:** 6192 (6191)
Miller D R, **5:** 2512 (2510); **6:** 3184
Miller E, **7:** 3830 (3829)
Miller E L, **6:** 3074
Miller G A, **1:** 331 (329); **2:** 856 (852); **3:** 1434 (1432)
Miller G E, **2:** 867, 868 (863); **3:** 1233 (1231); **6:** 3512 (3511); **7:** 3768 (3765); **10:** 6178 (6175)
Miller H, **11:** 6558 (6556), 6690 (6689)
Miller H L, **7:** 4329 (4327)
Miller J, **3:** 1337 (1336); **6:** 3224
Miller J A, **8:** 4948; **11:** 6484 (6484)
Miller J D, **9:** 5349 (5348)
Miller J G, **9:** 5512 (5512)
Miller J P, **1:** 380 (379); **3:** 1315 (1312), (1721)
Miller L B, **2:** 688 (682); **8:** 4661 (4661);

9: 5246 (5241); **10:** 5935 (5932), 6099; **11:** 6625
Miller L S, **3:** 1449
Miller L W, **11:** 6625
Miller M, **4:** 1924; **8:** 4951 (4948); **11:** 6282 (6278), 6283 (6278)
Miller N, **1:** 390 (382); **3:** 1486 (1484); **5:** 2504, 2529
Miller N B, **8:** 4359
Miller N H, **1:** (495)
Miller P, **7:** 4301; **9:** 5394 (5390); **11:** 6735 (6733)
Miller P A, **8:** 4799 (4798)
Miller P D, **4:** 1962 (1962)
Miller P H, **2:** 705 (704); **7:** 3788 (3785)
Miller P W, **3:** 1449 (1447); **5:** 2740 (2739); **9:** 5355 (5352)
Miller R, **2:** 867 (862); **3:** 1504 (1503); **4:** (1865); **7:** 3996 (3993)
Miller R A, **3:** 1750 (1748)
Miller R C, **9:** 5008 (4999)
Miller R L, **2:** 649 (646)
Miller S, **1:** 234; **5:** 2628 (2626); **8:** 4634 (4630)
Miller S I, **9:** 5031
Miller S M, **3:** 1520 (1514); **7:** 3864 (3862)
Miller T, **3:** 1386 (1383)
Miller T K, **10:** 5804 (5797)
Miller V, **2:** 640, 1048 (1046); **5:** 2961 (2957)
Miller-Jacobs H H, **8:** 4803 (4801, 4803)
Millerson G, **1:** 404
Millham S, **8:** 4830 (4828)
Milligan G, **2:** 831 (829)
Millikan R H, **5:** 2508 (2504)
Millins P K C, **7:** 4171 (4166)
Millman J, **2:** (1183); **4:** 2131 (2129); **5:** 3043 (3036, 3038, 3039), 3066; **7:** 3821; **10:** 5935 (5933), 6020, 6043 (6035)
Millot B, **3:** 1834 (1834); **5:** 2993 (2989); **6:** 3550 (3548)
Millroy W L, **3:** 1253; **6:** 3452 (3451); **11:** 6466
Mills A J, **4:** 2286 (2284)
Mills C J, **5:** 2495 (2494), 2732 (2731)
Mills C N, **10:** 5726 (5725)
Mills C W, **1:** 543 (538); **2:** 785; **4:** 2249 (2248)
Mills H, **2:** 1175 (1173)
Mills J M, **2:** 1220 (1217); **6:** 3474 (3468, 3469)
Millsap M A, **11:** 6538 (6536)
Millsap R E, **7:** 4007; **11:** 6360 (6357)
Millwood R, **3:** 1779 (1778); **10:** 5625 (5622, 5624)
Milman D, **6:** 3360; **9:** 5255
Milner D, **10:** 5826 (5823)
Milofsky C, **10:** 5668 (5664, 5665, 5666)
Milson J L, **5:** 2903 (2898)
Milton G, **3:** 1367 (1363)
Milton G A, **9:** 5518
Milton J, **2:** (776)
Min F B M, **2:** 988 (985); **7:** 3996 (3995)
Min W, **2:** 760 (759); **3:** 1695 (1693); **9:** 5076 (5072, 5073, 5074, 5075); **11:** 6633 (6628, 6630, 6631)
Mincer J, **1:** 111 (107); **2:** 1056, 1094 (1090, 1091, 1092); **3:** 1660 (1657, 1658, 1659); **4:** 2279 (2275); **5:** 2744 (2741), 2942 (2937); **6:** 3425, 3617 (3614); **7:** 4201 (4198), 4211 (4207, 4208, 4210), 4324 (4323); **8:** 4364 (4363), 4918 (4914); **9:** 5355 (5351); **11:** 6424 (6420, 6421), 6638 (6635)
Minden G von, **8:** 4816 (4813)
Mines R A, **6:** 3435 (3428)
Mingat A, **1:** 598; **4:** 2316 (2311); **8:** 4509 (4504); **11:** 6403
Minhas R, **10:** 5826 (5823)
Minick N, **3:** 1252, 1253 (1249)
Minker J, **3:** 1394 (1388)
Minkowski A, **1:** 15
Minkowski M, **1:** 15 (12)
Minor B B, **3:** 1800; **4:** 1928 (1927, 1928); **7:** 3753
Minsky M, **6:** 3512
Minton H L, **2:** 718 (716, 717)
Mintz S L, **10:** 6035
Mintzberg H, **3:** 1411 (1407, 1408), 1746 (1741); **4:** 1934 (1930); **6:** 3284 (3277, 3281)
Mintzes J J, **2:** 1031 (1029); **10:** 5790 (5790)
Minuchin P P, **4:** 2449 (2448); **9:** 5528 (5527)
Mirabito M M, **4:** 1958 (1956)
Miracle A W, **2:** 825 (822)
Miramontes O B, **4:** 2037 (2035)
Miranda E, **10:** 5613
Miranda G V, **3:** 1672 (1667, 1669, 1670, 1671)
Mircea M, **6:** 3422
Mirenda P, **1:** 408 (406, 407); **6:** 3235 (3232, 3233); **10:** 5693 (5692)
Mirkin P K, **3:** 1359 (1356)
Miron G, **10:** 5663 (5660)
Mirowsky J, **4:** 2261 (2259)
Mirvis P, **5:** 2852
Mirza Zada A K, **1:** 210
Mischel H N, **1:** 380 (377); **9:** 5403 (5400)
Mischel W, **1:** 380 (377); **4:** 2449 (2446); **9:** 5403 (5400)
Misener B, **11:** 6307 (6303)
Miserandino A, **10:** 5939 (5936)
Mishan E J, **2:** 1131 (1127, 1128)
Misiak H, **5:** 2692 (2689)
Misja V, **1:** 260
Miskel C G, **1:** 437 (432); **3:** 1774 (1769, 1770); **4:** 1972 (1967, 1968)
Mislevy R J, **1:** 374 (373); **5:** 3055 (3053), 3061 (3060); **7:** 3861 (3861), 3862 (3861), 4307
Mislevy R M, **3:** 1514 (1511); **5:** 3061 (3060)
Misra L, **11:** 6753 (6748, 6749)
Misra V S, **6:** 3124 (3121, 3123)
Mistry V, **3:** 1636
Misurcova V, **8:** 4670
Mitchell A, **3:** 1635 (1634)
Mitchell B, **6:** 3284; **9:** 5216; **11:** 6580
Mitchell B G, **5:** 2495 (2492, 2494)
Mitchell B R, **3:** 1589 (1585)
Mitchell D C, **8:** 4939 (4938)
Mitchell D E, **1:** 437 (432, 433, 434, 435); **6:** 3197 (3192); **7:** 3826 (3822, 3824, 3825); **9:** 5181 (5176, 5177), 5191, 5308 (5307); **10:** 6079 (6077)
Mitchell I J, **8:** 4652 (4652); **9:** 5327 (5326)
Mitchell J, **11:** 6608 (6604)
Mitchell J C, **9:** 5560 (5554)
Mitchell J G, **1:** 437 (435)
Mitchell J V, **10:** 6020
Mitchell M H, **9:** 5290 (5283)
Mitchell R, **8:** 4623 (4619, 4621, 4622)
Mitchell S M, **9:** 5210 (5207)
Mitchell T K, **9:** 5181 (5176, 5177)
Mitchell T M, **8:** 4722 (4721)
Mitman A, **5:** 2931 (2929)
Mitman A L Packer M J, **9:** 5363 (5359)
Mitter W, **4:** 1872; **5:** 2479 (2477); **6:** 3608 (3605); **7:** 3978; **8:** 4499, 4623 (4618); **11:** 6648 (6641)
Mitterand F, **5:** (2537)
Mitterer J O, **8:** 4912 (4910)
Mittler P, **10:** 5943
Mitzel H, **6:** 3202; **10:** 6208 (6203)
Mitzel H E, **1:** 60, 77, 389; **2:** 816 (813, 814), 1220; **4:** 2119, 2281; **5:** 2779; **7:** 3925, 3970, 4016; **9:** 5432, 5435; **10:** 5862, 6043, 6173
Miura S, **1:** 353; **6:** 3078
Miwa T, **6:** 3667 (3665)
Mizen P, **3:** 1739 (1738)
Mkandawire D, **2:** 914 (912)
Mmanga W R, **6:** 3564
Mmari G, **6:** 3638 (3636, 3637)
Mmari G R V, **11:** 6266 (6262)
Moberg D O, **9:** 5008 (5007)
Möbus M, **11:** 6272, 6669 (6664)
Mocellin R, **8:** 4473
Mock E, **1:** 139 (137)
Mocker D W, **9:** 5399 (5395, 5398)
Modell J, **3:** 1647 (1646)
Modgil C, **1:** 380; **5:** 2921; **7:** 3978; **8:** 4526
Modgil S, **1:** 380; **5:** 2921; **7:** 3978; **8:** 4526
Modiano N, **3:** 1756 (1755)
Modolo M A, **5:** 2572 (2568)
Modra H, **1:** 168 (167); **11:** 6727 (6726)
Modrein M J, **1:** 494
Moe T, **1:** 594 (590, 591); **8:** 4568 (4565); **11:** 6558 (6556)
Moe T E, **9:** 5307 (5305, 5306)
Moe T M, **3:** 1411 (1407, 1408, 1411), 1720; **5:** 2508 (2505); **6:** 3496 (3496); **7:** 3839 (3839); **8:** 4594 (4587, 4588, 4589, 4592, 4593), 4830 (4825, 4829), 4873 (4867, 4870); **9:** 5196 (5195), 5201, 5206 (5203, 5204), 5223 (5221), 5281 (5277); **11:** 6563 (6560)
Moerk E L, **6:** 3224 (3222)
Moffett J, **11:** 6785 (6781)
Moffitt R, **4:** 2150
Mogami H S, **1:** 28
Moglen H, **6:** 3452
Mohadjer L, **7:** 3711
Mohamed A L, **1:** 244 (241)
Mohamed F E, **11:** 6760 (6759)
Mohan B A, **4:** 2339; **6:** 3334 (3333), 3443
Mohan R, **8:** 4918 (4916)
Mohanty C, **10:** 5957 (5955)
Mohatt G, **2:** 802 (801); **4:** 2052 (2049); **9:** 5220 (5219)
Möhle H, **5:** 2480 (2474)

Mohle H, **10:** 5808
Mohr C, **9:** 5489 (5486)
Mohr L B, **7:** 3872 (3866)
Mohrman A, **5:** 2852 (2848)
Mohrman S, **5:** 2852 (2848)
Moi T, **5:** 2457 (2454)
Moisan C, **10:** 5953 (5948), 5972 (5972)
Mok A L, **8:** 4839 (4836)
Mokros J R, **7:** 3810 (3809), 4104 (4101)
Molenaar I W, **3:** 1421 (1420), 1514 (1513)
Molenaar P, **5:** 2681 (2679, 2680)
Molenaar P C M, **11:** 6492 (6490)
Molenda M, **4:** 1918, 1928 (1927); **5:** 2861 (2859); **7:** 3753; **11:** 6625 (6622)
Moles O C, **2:** 820; **10:** 6031
Molina C G, **6:** 3261 (3260)
Moll L C, **1:** 534 (532, 534); **3:** 1252 (1250); **4:** 2052 (2050); **9:** 5403
Moll L S, **9:** 5548
Mollenhauer K, **7:** 3924, 3925 (3924); **8:** 4461 (4459)
Mollenkopf W G, **7:** 3706 (3702)
Moller L, **4:** 2452 (2450)
Molnar A, **10:** 5887
Molnar S, **9:** 5181 (5177)
Molutsi P P, **3:** 1416 (1415)
Molyneux G, **7:** 3889 (3889)
Monahan W G, **1:** 437
Monard G, **1:** 504
Monge P R, **9:** 5560 (5558)
Moniot H, **5:** 2623
Monk C C, **7:** 4293 (4291, 4292)
Monk D, **10:** 5613
Monk D H, **4:** 1972 (1969, 1970); **7:** 3820, 3821 (3816, 3817, 3818, 3819); **9:** 5065, 5066 (5063, 5064, 5065), 5185, 5240 (5233), 5264 (5261), 5294; **11:** 6390 (6389)
Mönks F J, **5:** 2495 (2493), 2731, 2732 (2729)
Monnet J, **4:** (2053), (2057)
Monroe P, **11:** 6370
Monroe W S, **11:** 6349 (6340)
Monson D, **2:** 738
Montada L, **5:** 2665 (2663), 2806; **8:** 4719
Montagu A, **3:** 1538 (1534)
Montague E J, **10:** 6004 (6001)
Montague W E, **4:** 1848; **9:** 5043; **11:** 6603 (6603)
Montaigne M, **2:** (777)
Montaigne M E de, **10:** (5707)
Montandon C, **2:** 802; **9:** 5268
Montaperto R, **2:** 760
Monteiro K P, **1:** 330 (328)
Montello P A, **8:** 4408 (4405, 4406, 4407)
Montemayor R, **2:** 705 (702)
Montenegro X, **2:** 1127 (1126); **8:** 4848 (4846)
Montepare J M, **1:** 239 (237)
Montero-Sieburth M, **10:** 5834 (5832)
Montesquieu C L de, **9:** (5088)
Montessori M, **1:** (227); **3:** (1432), (1528); **5:** (2494), (2608), (2731), (3031); **6:** (3387), (3497); **7:** 3914 (3913, 3914); **8:** (4481), (4669); **10:** 5663 (5659), (5877), 6224; **11:** (6308)
Montgomery D J, **4:** 2074 (2070, 2073); **5:** 2942; **10:** 5686 (5683, 5684)
Montigny G, **7:** 3711 (3710)
Montoya A, **11:** 6283 (6278)
Montoya C R, **8:** 4751 (4749)
Montrichard R, **2:** 910 (908)
Moo G, **7:** 4240 (4238)
Moock P R, **1:** 254 (245, 246, 252); **3:** 1386 (1383), 1680 (1677, 1678), 1695 (1693); **4:** 1938 (1934); **9:** 5076 (5072); **11:** 6633 (6628)
Mood A M, **2:** 631 (629)
Mook D A, **9:** 5043 (5039)
Mookerji R K, **11:** 6753 (6748, 6749)
Moon B, **3:** 1343; **9:** 5299 (5297)
Moon R, **7:** 3889
Moonen J C M M, **2:** 991 (990), 1012 (1007, 1010); **3:** 1421, 1779 (1776); **8:** 4803 (4800); **10:** 6008 (6006)
Mooney J A, **1:** 53 (49)
Moore A, **1:** 296 (286, 289, 293)
Moore B, **8:** 4799 (4798)
Moore B G, **4:** 2427 (2424, 2425)
Moore C A, **3:** 1491
Moore C M, **3:** 1443
Moore C N, **2:** 738 (736)
Moore D, **7:** 3861 (3858); **11:** 6558 (6556)
Moore D R, **9:** 5066 (5063)
Moore D W, **9:** 5359 (5356)
Moore G, **2:** 1165
Moore G A B, **11:** 6307 (6302, 6304, 6305)
Moore G E, **3:** 1464; **8:** 4447 (4442, 4444)
Moore G F, **6:** 3120
Moore H, **3:** 1486 (1485)
Moore J, **8:** 4376
Moore J F, **7:** 4329 (4326)
Moore J H, **4:** 2389
Moore J L, **2:** 838 (837); **11:** 6456 (6454, 6455)
Moore M G, **1:** 564; **3:** 1563 (1558), 1567 (1566, 1567), 1573 (1571); **7:** 4220; **8:** 4383 (4381); **11:** 6307 (6302)
Moore M K, **5:** 2802 (2800)
Moore O K, **1:** 244 (240); **4:** 1899 (1895)
Moore P, **1:** 322 (319); **10:** 5607
Moore R, **3:** 1739 (1737); **8:** 4715 (4711), 4796 (4794)
Moore T, **5:** 2861 (2860); **7:** 3991 (3989)
Moore W E, **9:** 5572 (5568)
Moorehouse M, **3:** 1647
Moores D, **3:** 1402 (1400)
Moorhouse J, **9:** 5544 (5542)
Moors K F, **8:** 4536
Moos B S, **4:** 1980 (1978)
Moos R, **4:** 1980 (1978)
Moos R H, **2:** 811 (807, 808, 809); **4:** 1980 (1978), 2249 (2247); **10:** 5775 (5772, 5773)
Moos R M, **3:** 1482 (1481, 1482)
Moosbrucker M, **9:** 5216 (5215)
Morales Gómez D A, **1:** 135 (132, 133), 332 (332); **5:** 2965; **6:** 3261, 3597; **8:** 4602
Moran P, **9:** 5060 (5058)
Moreland R, **5:** 2532 (2529, 2531)
Morenberg M, **10:** 5704 (5699)
Moreno F J, **6:** 3368 (3367)
Moreno J L, **9:** 5560 (5554); **10:** 5617 (5614, 5615)
Moreno L, **10:** 5607
Moreno V, **1:** 322 (319)
Morentz J W, **5:** 2831 (2828)
Morero J, **10:** (6127)
Morf H, **8:** 4419 (4419)
Morgaine C A, **4:** 2267 (2265)
Morgan A, **1:** 193 (189)
Morgan C, **1:** 83 (79, 80); **10:** 6214
Morgan G, **1:** 42 (33, 34), 67 (62); **2:** (932); **3:** 1809 (1805); **4:** 2165 (2160, 2161, 2164), 2167; **6:** 3527 (3526, 3527); **9:** 5181 (5180), 5313 (5308); **11:** 6355 (6354)
Morgan J, **4:** 2364
Morgan J L, **5:** 2814 (2807); **6:** 3224 (3222)
Morgan J N, **7:** 4016 (4011)
Morgan M J, **1:** 570 (567); **2:** 733; **3:** 1690, 1739 (1736); **4:** 1899; **8:** 4376; **9:** 5518 (5514); **11:** 6798 (6797)
Morgan N, **8:** 4881 (4875)
Morgan P, **3:** 1642 (1637, 1638)
Morgan R M, **5:** 2897 (2894); **8:** 4758 (4754)
Morgan S, **11:** 6735 (6734)
Morgan S P, **8:** 4779 (4775, 4776, 4777, 4778)
Morganstein D, **9:** 5142 (5132)
Morgen S, **2:** 907; **7:** 3974 (3972); **9:** 5510 (5508)
Morgenstern B L, **4:** 1958 (1956)
Morgenstern C, **1:** 396 (395); **9:** 5324 (5323); **10:** 5735 (5733)
Morholt E, **6:** 3416
Morick H, **8:** 4634 (4632)
Morin P, **1:** 564
Morine-Dershimer G, **10:** 6035 (6032), 6088 (6086)
Moris J, **8:** 4688
Morissey C T, **7:** 4225 (4224)
Morlan J, **4:** 1917 (1915)
Morlan J E, **4:** 1917 (1915)
Morley D, **2:** 733 (731)
Morocco C C, **7:** 3808 (3806)
Moroney M, **9:** 5567 (5565)
Moroney R M, **5:** 2672 (2671)
Moro'oka K, **1:** 158 (157); **6:** 3078; **8:** 4812 (4810)
Morphet E, **10:** 5972
Morrell R, **7:** 3853 (3850, 3852)
Morrill R, **3:** 1553
Morris C, **3:** 1524; **5:** 2596 (2591, 2592)
Morris C N, **11:** 6355 (6350)
Morris C R, **5:** 2500 (2496)
Morris C W, **2:** 1073 (1070)
Morris E D, **4:** 2452
Morris G B, **6:** 3284 (3276, 3277)
Morris G S, **3:** (1520)
Morris H, **2:** (907)
Morris H L, **11:** 6707 (6706, 6707)
Morris I, **10:** 6086 (6083)
Morris J E, **10:** 5834 (5832)
Morris L W, **11:** 6360 (6356)
Morris M, **4:** 2024
Morris P, **3:** 1337 (1335); **4:** 1857; **5:** 2642 (2637), 2643; **6:** 3545; **7:** 4236
Morris P E, **2:** 969; **7:** 3768
Morris R, **9:** 5334 (5328)

Morris S, **10:** 6004 (6001)
Morris V C, **2:** 1073 (1066); **8:** 4433
Morriseau V, **3:** (1402)
Morrison A, **7:** 4088 (4083); **10:** 6127 (6123)
Morrison E J, **11:** 6348 (6347)
Morrison F J, **1:** 194
Morrison G R, **7:** 3743 (3739, 3743)
Morrison G S, **5:** 2813 (2808)
Morrison H C, **1:** 23
Morrison J E, **6:** 3096
Morrissett I, **9:** 5578 (5574)
Morrissey M, **5:** 2470 (2468)
Morrow G, **3:** 1607 (1603)
Morrow L, **7:** 4301 (4300)
Morse W C, **1:** 495
Morsy Z, **9:** 5233
Mortimer P, **5:** 2589 (2588)
Mortimer R G, **10:** 6143 (6141)
Mortimore J, **8:** 4408 (4404)
Mortimore P, **1:** 390 (381, 389); **3:** 1538; **4:** 1934 (1931, 1932), 2166 (2164); **5:** 2509 (2508), 2779 (2775), 2870 (2868); **7:** 3912 (3910); **8:** 4408 (4404), 4623 (4620), 4779 (4777), 4873 (4870); **9:** 5211 (5207, 5209), 5223 (5221), 5224 (5221), 5264 (5262), 5379 (5375); **10:** 5750 (5746), 6083 (6082); **11:** 6390 (6388, 6389)
Mosback, **10:** 5886 (5884)
Moscati R, **5:** 3036
Mosco V, **9:** 5544 (5543)
Mosenthal P B, **2:** 824; **7:** 3711 (3710); **8:** 4935, 4936; **10:** 5961, 6192
Moser C A, **7:** 3858; **9:** 5142
Moser J M, **6:** 3660 (3657, 3658), 3661; **10:** 5795 (5792)
Moser J P, **10:** 5795
Moses D, **9:** 5070 (5067); **10:** 5686 (5683), 5943
Moses K D, **4:** 1918 (1913)
Moses Y T, **1:** 280; **7:** 3974 (3972)
Mosha H F, **2:** 906 (904)
Mosher A, **1:** 244 (241)
Mosher R L, **6:** 3276 (3275); **7:** 3925; **10:** 6004 (6002)
Moshman D, **8:** 4957 (4955)
Mosier C I, **8:** 4657 (4653)
Mosier N R, **2:** 1094
Moskovitz S, **8:** 4779 (4776, 4777, 4778)
Moskowitz J H, **9:** 5066 (5062)
Mosley J, **1:** 494 (491)
Moss A J, **10:** 5674
Moss G D, **3:** 1398 (1395)
Moss P, **2:** 701 (694, 695, 698, 699); **4:** 2145 (2144); **8:** 4677 (4675); **9:** 5066 (5064); **11:** 6398 (6397)
Moss P A, **11:** 6320 (6315, 6316, 6319), 6677 (6673)
Moss R, **5:** 2897 (2895)
Mossel P, **4:** 2279 (2277)
Mossenson L, **1:** 374 (373); **7:** 4307
Mosteller F M, **3:** 1761; **4:** 2208; **5:** 3061 (3057); **9:** 5082, 5130 (5127), 5572 (5570)
Mothobi B D, **11:** 6821
Mott C S, **2:** (907)
Mott F L, **3:** 1642 (1639)
Mottahar M, **11:** 6793
Motulsky A G, **5:** 2465 (2463)
Motyka C, **2:** 1102 (1101)
Mouffe C, **2:** 1073 (1067)
Moulton J, **5:** 2891 (2888); **7:** 4145 (4143)
Moultrie R, **8:** 4661 (4658); **10:** 6244 (6240)
Mounier J, **9:** 5091 (5090)
Mounts N, **5:** 2628 (2625)
Moura Castro C, **5:** 3003; **11:** 6265 (6263)
Mourell M P, **10:** 5591 (5589)
Moursund D, **2:** 973 (969)
Mowat F, **4:** 2331
Mowery D C, **11:** 6260 (6260), 6261, 6276 (6272, 6273), 6277
Moxon D, **3:** 1501 (1499)
Moynihan D P, **1:** 520 (515); **3:** 1761; **6:** 3238 (3235); **9:** 5572 (5570)
Mpogolo Z J, **1:** 215 (212, 213)
Mroz T, **3:** 1660 (1656, 1657)
Mtewa M, **11:** 6741
M'Timkulu D, **5:** 2655 (2653)
Muchinsky P M, **11:** 6678 (6674)
Mueller B, **2:** 1079 (1075)
Mueller C W, **4:** 2241
Mueller D J, **7:** 4293 (4292)
Mueller E, **3:** 1676 (1673)
Mueller H, **8:** 4581
Mueller R O, **3:** 1549
Mueller V D, **9:** 5185
Mueller-Vollmer K, **5:** 2586
Mufti A G, **7:** 4270
Mugny A, **9:** 5548 (5546)
Mugny G, **5:** 2536 (2535); **8:** 4372 (4371), 4482 (4482)
Mugridge I, **3:** 1567; **7:** 4220
Muhammad A, **4:** 2432
Muir W, **10:** 6008 (6005)
Mukherjee D, **4:** 1991 (1986); **8:** 4473 (4472), 4474 (4470, 4471)
Mukhopadhyay C C, **1:** 280; **7:** 3974 (3972)
Mulcahy D G, **3:** 1343; **5:** 3020
Mulcaster R, **5:** (2608)
Mulder M, **2:** 1139 (1136, 1138); **3:** 1355 (1352), 1490 (1487), 1491; **4:** 1976 (1973); **6:** 3306; **7:** 3889
Muldowney M, **4:** 1991 (1985)
Mulhall M G, **1:** 338
Mulhern G, **5:** 2884
Mulholland M, **3:** 1406 (1405)
Mulier S, **11:** 6814 (6812)
Mulier V, **11:** 6814 (6812)
Mullen J A, **1:** 490 (488)
Mullen M A, **10:** 5804 (5799)
Mullenax P B, **9:** 5232 (5230)
Müller D K, **5:** 2617 (2613); **10:** 5735
Müller F M, **9:** 5008
Müller G E, **3:** (1793), (1794)
Muller H, **6:** 3124 (3123)
Muller M, **5:** 2601
Muller M M, **1:** 194 (190)
Müller W, **10:** 5735 (5732, 5734)
Mulligan J G, **7:** 3821 (3816, 3818)
Mullinax M F, **9:** 5232 (5229)
Mullis I V S, **1:** 41 (37), 42 (37); **4:** 2024 (2021); **6:** 3474 (3471), 3523 (3515); **7:** 3725 (3724); **9:** 5432 (5426)
Mulopo M M, **3:** 1544 (1543)
Mulryan C, **6:** 3655 (3654)
Mumford A, **1:** 322 (319); **6:** 3349 (3348)
Mumme D L, **5:** 2768 (2763)
Mumme J, **6:** 3671 (3670)
Munby H, **3:** 1257 (1256); **10:** 6122 (6119), 6183 (6179, 6181)
Münch J, **11:** 6659 (6655)
Munch R, **2:** 933
Munck I M E, **1:** 396 (393); **4:** 2140 (2137); **8:** 4887 (4886); **11:** 6328 (6327)
Mundel D S, **3:** 1449
Mungall C, **4:** 2331
Munger B, **8:** 4715 (4710)
Munn P, **8:** 4950 (4948)
Munoz B, **2:** 906 (901), 907
Múñoz-Repiso M, **10:** 5658
Munro D, **2:** 792 (788)
Munroe R H, **4:** 2449 (2447); **5:** 2651
Munroe R L, **4:** 2449 (2447); **5:** 2651
Munsey B, **7:** 3925
Munske B, **3:** 1733
Munson R G, **1:** 490 (487)
Münsterberg H, **5:** (2877), (2878)
Muraki E, **6:** 3253 (3252); **7:** 3862 (3861), 4307
Muraskin L D, **10:** 5919 (5914); **11:** 6538 (6536)
Murchison C A, **1:** 379, 389; **3:** 1647, 1796 (1794)
Murdoch J P, **10:** 5853 (5853)
Murgatroyd S J, **2:** 1165 (1161, 1162, 1163, 1164); **4:** 1934 (1933)
Muriel M, **5:** 2831
Murnane R J, **3:** 1762 (1759); **4:** 2156 (2154); **7:** 3821 (3816, 3817, 3820); **8:** 4526 (4523), 4568, 4830 (4828), 4831; **10:** 5846 (5844, 5845), 6106 (6104, 6105, 6106)
Murphy G L, **6:** 3155 (3152)
Murphy J, **1:** 73 (69, 72), 77 (74, 75, 76); **5:** 2852 (2849); **6:** 3284 (3278, 3279, 3283); **9:** 5206 (5203), 5264 (5261, 5263), 5281, 5308 (5307); **10:** 6187 (6187)
Murphy J F, **4:** 1934 (1932)
Murphy J J, **8:** 4890
Murphy J T, **2:** 711 (706, 708); **6:** 3496 (3495); **8:** 4556 (4555)
Murphy J W, **10:** 5925 (5922)
Murphy K M, **1:** 520 (517, 518); **3:** 1713 (1710); **6:** 3101; **8:** 4902 (4900), 4918 (4916); **11:** 6615
Murphy M J, **8:** 4408 (4407)
Murphy R, **2:** 785; **3:** 1624 (1621), 1784 (1782); **7:** 3912; **8:** 4622, 4623 (4618); **10:** 5607
Murphy R T, **11:** 6511 (6508)
Murphy S, **4:** 2024 (2019, 2022)
Murphy S B, **10:** 6219 (6217)
Murphy T F, **8:** 4433
Murray C, **10:** 6043
Murray F B, **8:** 4372 (4371)
Murray H, **6:** 3661 (3660)
Murray H A, **2:** 811 (807); **3:** 1240 (1239), 1482 (1476); **4:** 2249 (2245); **8:** 4395 (4392)

Murray H G, **10:** 5939 (5937), 6235 (6231, 6233)
Murray H T, **8:** 4774 (4773)
Murray J, **1:** 317; **2:** 738 (736); **6:** 3209 (3207), 3625 (3622)
Murray J C, **2:** 1052 (1051)
Murray M, **8:** 4964 (4961)
Murray-Lasso M, **2:** 1012 (1009)
Murray-Seegert C, **1:** 494 (493); **8:** 4935 (4933); **10:** 6244 (6243)
Murray-Smith S, **11:** 6735
Murrell P, **3:** (1232)
Mursi A, **11:** 6515
Mursi M M, **8:** 4485
Murstein B I, **8:** 4791
Murtaugh M, **3:** 1252 (1249)
Murthy K D, **1:** 554
Murwin S W, **11:** 6603 (6600)
Muse I D, **1:** 72 (72)
Musella D F, **1:** 83 (80); **7:** 4215 (4213); **9:** 5264, 5539; **10:** 6043 (6037)
Musgrave A, **4:** 2000; **9:** 5030; **10:** 6207
Musgrave B S, **1:** 377
Musgrave P, **2:** 910 (910)
Musgrave P B, **9:** 5240 (5236, 5237, 5238)
Musgrave P W, **1:** 358 (357); **3:** 1348 (1344); **4:** 2272; **8:** 4455; **9:** 5299 (5298); **10:** 5591 (5586, 5587, 5588, 5590), 5607 (5599), 5613 (5609)
Musgrave R A, **9:** 5240 (5236, 5237, 5238)
Musgrove F, **1:** 296 (291); **9:** 5169 (5161), 5299 (5296); **11:** 6798 (6795)
Musgrove P, **3:** 1680 (1677, 1678)
Mushkin S J, **4:** 2212; **6:** 3425; **8:** 4964
Musick J S, **8:** 4779 (4776, 4778)
Musonda D, **2:** 1031 (1029, 1030)
Mussella D F, **1:** 83 (80); **7:** 4215 (4213); **9:** 5264, 5539; **10:** 5929
Mussen L P H, **3:** 1642
Mussen P, **3:** 1246, 1624; **8:** 4799
Mussen P H, **1:** 88, 234; **2:** 852, 871; **3:** 1240; **4:** 2449; **5:** 2628, 2802; **8:** 4368, 4394, 4395, 4483, 4542, 4799 (4797, 4798, 4799); **9:** 5394, 5512
Mussen P T, **6:** 3334
Mustafa S, **11:** 6515
Mustapha K, **7:** 4336 (4335)
Muta H, **1:** 563 (562)
Muthén B O, **2:** 677 (677), 957 (954); **4:** 2241 (2239), 2388 (2386); **5:** 2596 (2595); **6:** 3523 (3513, 3522); **7:** 3986 (3986), 4016 (4012); **8:** 4352 (4341, 4347, 4349, 4351), 4359 (4352, 4358), 4930 (4930)
Muthukrishna N, **10:** 6177 (6174, 6175)
Muthull E T, **1:** 338
Muyanda-Mutebi P, **2:** 770 (768); **9:** 5582 (5579); **10:** 5585 (5583)
Mveng E, **2:** 618
Mwirial J, **1:** 175 (172, 174)
Mworoha E, **1:** 607
Myeni A D, **5:** 2572 (2570)
Myers B L, **7:** 3774 (3774)
Myers C A, **3:** 1820 (1811, 1812); **5:** 2978 (2977); **11:** 6277 (6272)
Myers E D, **6:** 3647 (3644)
Myers M, **7:** 3788 (3785); **8:** 4947 (4946)
Myers R G, **3:** 1628 (1625), 1629, 1824 (1821, 1823); **4:** 2145 (2142); **8:** 4604 (4602), 4666, 4677 (4672, 4673)
Myers S A, **11:** 6621 (6619)
Myers W E, **3:** 1735 (1733, 1734)
Myklebust H, **3:** 1402 (1401); **7:** 3774
Myles J, **11:** 6277 (6274)
Myrdal A, **8:** 4670 (4669)
Myrdal G, **5:** 2758 (2754), 2978; **8:** 4902 (4899); **9:** 5050, 5055 (5053), 5572 (5569)
Mys A A, **10:** 5854

Nabuzoka D, **9:** 5567 (5564)
Naccarato R W, **5:** 2462 (2461); **10:** 6234 (6229, 6230)
Nachmias C, **9:** 5050
Nachmias D, **9:** 5050
Nadel S F, **2:** 1213 (1209); **3:** 1756 (1752)
Nader L, **5:** 2685
Nadin M, **9:** 5416 (5415, 5416)
Nadiri M I, **3:** 1666
Nadler L, **2:** 1139 (1136); **3:** 1315 (1313), 1490 (1486); **5:** 2689 (2685, 2686); **6:** 3096 (3092)
Nadler Z, **5:** 2689 (2685)
Nafpaktitis M, **10:** 5762 (5760)
Nafstad A, **3:** 1406
Nag M, **4:** 2419 (2417)
Nagai J, **8:** 4581 (4579)
Nagai K, **9:** 5255
Nagaoka K, **7:** 3946 (3945)
Nagel E, **9:** 5050
Nagel J, **6:** 3256
Nagel K, **11:** 6371
Nagel R N, **3:** 1549; **11:** 6310 (6309)
Nagel S S, **4:** 1841 (1835); **5:** 2672 (2671)
Nagel T, **4:** 2004 (2001)
Nagle A, **7:** 4155 (4151)
Nagler M, **5:** 2813 (2807)
Nagy J, **5:** 2706 (2704)
Nahm M C, **3:** 1367 (1365)
Nahrgang C L, **6:** 3209 (3208)
Naik C, **7:** 4136 (4133)
Naik J P, **5:** 2753
Naiman A, **2:** 1175 (1171)
Naiman D W, **7:** 3808 (3803)
Naiman N, **4:** 2357 (2357); **6:** 3334 (3330)
Naish M, **5:** 2470 (2466, 2468); **11:** 6704
Naito M, **2:** 705 (704)
Najat A, **11:** 6515
Nakadak N, **11:** 6780
Nakamura G V, **7:** 3768 (3765)
Nakamura M, **1:** 353
Nakane C, **6:** 3086
Nakano T, **5:** 2891 (2886)
Nakayama S, **9:** 5578 (5575, 5576)
Nakib Y, **3:** 1820 (1819)
Nakken H, **3:** 1520
Nakosteen M, **6:** 3647
Nam C B, **7:** 3722 (3717)
Nam Y-S, **3:** 1713 (1710); **8:** 4918 (4916, 4917); **11:** 6283 (6280)
Namboodiri K, **3:** 1607
Namuddu K, **2:** 733 (732)
Nanda H, **1:** 41 (33); **5:** 2462 (2458, 2459), 3061 (3057); **9:** 4995 (4981)
Nanda S, **1:** 299 (299)
Napier D, **9:** (5157)
Napitupulu W P, **6:** 3467
Närman A, **9:** 5076; **10:** 6067 (6065); **11:** 6256 (6253, 6254, 6255)
Narot R E, **3:** 1486 (1485)
Narroll R, **4:** 2052 (2046)
Nasaw D, **4:** 2272 (2269)
Nash A, **11:** 6775 (6772)
Nash C, **4:** 1898 (1896); **5:** 2491 (2487)
Nash M, **3:** 1756 (1754)
Nash R J, **2:** 1074 (1070); **8:** 4489; **10:** 6012 (6011), 6053 (6048, 6049, 6052)
Nash S C, **10:** 5826 (5823)
Nashihara H, **10:** 5674 (5670)
Nashinosono H, **3:** 1398 (1395)
Naso B, **7:** 4081 (4079)
Nassif P, **4:** 2131
Nasson B, **8:** 4595 (4588, 4591, 4593)
Natarella M A, **2:** 737 (734)
Nathan G, **7:** 3858 (3857)
Nathan J A, **3:** 1655 (1651, 1652); **9:** 5197, 5206 (5202)
Nathan L E, **3:** 1381; **9:** 5373
Nathan M, **11:** 6678 (6674)
Nathanson J H, **10:** 5674 (5668, 5669)
Nation D, **1:** 168
Natorp P, **3:** (1722); **8:** 4419 (4419)
Natriello G, **2:** 711 (707, 708, 709); **3:** 1606 (1603, 1606), 1607 (1604, 1605, 1606)
Nauck-Börner C, **7:** 4026 (4023)
Naumann J, **5:** 2480
Nava M, **11:** 6803 (6801)
Navaratnam K K, **11:** 6677 (6676)
Navka M, **5:** 2884
Navon D, **11:** 6287 (6285, 6287)
Nawtry F A, **4:** 2331
Nayar D P, **5:** 2758 (2755)
Nayar P K B, **10:** 5606
Nayar U, **4:** 2423 (2421)
Naylor F, **11:** 6678 (6676)
Ndimurukundo N, **1:** 607
Ndong B, **1:** 221 (220)
Neal C J, **9:** 5403 (5400)
Neale D C, **10:** 6122 (6118), 6239 (6238)
Neale J M, **9:** 5050
Neale M C, **8:** 4799 (4798); **11:** 6492 (6490)
Neave G R, **4:** 2059; **5:** 2479, 2480, 3036; **6:** 3329, 3339; **7:** 4171 (4168); **8:** 4774; **10:** 5954 (5948); **11:** 6266 (6263)
Nebhut D H, **2:** 1055 (1052)
Neches R, **2:** 842, 852, 1026 (1022); **8:** 4722 (4720)
Nedelsky L, **7:** 4056 (4054); **10:** 5726 (5722)
Needels M, **8:** 4873 (4869)
Needham J, **6:** 3446 (3444)
Needham R M, **2:** 831 (831)
Needleman H L, **5:** 2567 (2565)
Neice D, **8:** 4638 (4635)
Neiderer H, **8:** 4479
Neidermeyer F C, **5:** 2856 (2852, 2853)
Neil M W, **10:** 5901 (5895, 5900)
Neill A S, **1:** (261), 265 (264); **5:** (2608), 2692 (2691); **7:** 3925 (3923); **8:** (4451), (4535)
Neill D M, **8:** 4623 (4619)

Neill G W, **7:** 3808 (3807)
Neill S B, **7:** 3808 (3807), 4175 (4171, 4172)
Neilsen L, **8:** 4948 (4947)
Neilson D, **10:** 5674 (5671)
Neisser U, **2:** 969 (964); **11:** 6558
Nelder J A, **7:** 4015 (4015)
Nelkin D, **9:** 5350
Nelleman G, **7:** 3970 (3967)
Nelli E, **10:** 5957 (5955)
Nelson C, **9:** 5290 (5288)
Nelson C E, **3:** 1431 (1428)
Nelson C M, **1:** 490 (489), 494 (493); **3:** 1441 (1438, 1440); **10:** 6031 (6028)
Nelson C O, **7:** 4059 (4057)
Nelson D J, **7:** 4026 (4023)
Nelson G D, **5:** 2572 (2569)
Nelson H B, **9:** 5328 (5326)
Nelson H D, **6:** 3394
Nelson K R, **7:** 3768 (3764); **10:** 6026 (6024, 6025); **11:** 6603 (6602)
Nelson L, **4:** 2302 (2300, 2301); **5:** 2897 (2892); **8:** 4536 (4533); **10:** 6047
Nelson L M, **1:** 274 (267)
Nelson M R, **1:** 280 (278)
Nelson R P, **5:** 2575 (2574)
Nelson R R, **5:** 2673 (2671); **7:** 3821 (3816, 3820)
Nelson S, **9:** 5406 (5405)
Nelson V, **4:** 2278 (2277)
Nenniger P, **5:** 2769 (2764)
Nerlove S B, **3:** 1252 (1248); **9:** 5158 (5152, 5157)
Nesbit W C, **5:** 2972 (2969)
Nesbitt P, **1:** 103
Nesher P, **6:** 3638 (3637), 3652 (3647, 3648, 3649, 3650), 3655, 3661 (3658), 3685; **10:** 5790 (5784)
Nespor J, **10:** 6086
Ness E, **7:** 3970 (3961), 4192
Nesselroade J R, **3:** 1513 (1512); **4:** 1877; **5:** 2665, 2676 (2673, 2674, 2675, 2676); **6:** 3523 (3513, 3514, 3519, 3522); **11:** 6492 (6488, 6489, 6491)
Netley R, **11:** 6608 (6605)
Nettleton G, **4:** 1910, 1911 (1904, 1905, 1906, 1907, 1908)
Netzer R, **9:** 5240
Neubauer C, **9:** 5216 (5213)
Neubauer E, **9:** 5216 (5213)
Neubourg C de, **4:** 2150
Neuchterlein K H, **6:** 3297
Neufeld J, **10:** 6215 (6209)
Neufeld R W J, **10:** 6159 (6155)
Neugarten B L, **6:** 3428 (3426, 3427); **10:** (5935)
Neuhaus J, **5:** 2514 (2514)
Neulinger J, **11:** 6798 (6794)
Neuman D, **8:** 4429 (4425, 4426)
Neuman S, **6:** 3625; **9:** 5076 (5072, 5074)
Neuman S B, **1:** 570 (568)
Neumann P H, **11:** 6366
Neumann S, **11:** 6266 (6262)
Neumark D, **6:** 3144 (3139)
Neurath K, **9:** (5051)
Neurath O, **8:** (4633)
Nevera E, **8:** 4796 (4794)
Nevermann K, **6:** 3276 (3275)
Nevin A, **7:** 3833 (3832); **10:** 6244 (6241, 6242, 6243)
Nevo D, **5:** 2491 (2487); **7:** 4060; **8:** 4751 (4745)
New D A, **2:** 711 (706)
New P K, **9:** 5290 (5290)
New R, **7:** 4301 (4297)
Newacheck P W, **5:** 2575 (2572)
Newberg D, **8:** 4844
Newberger E H, **5:** 2575 (2573)
Newburger H B, **3:** 1449 (1447)
Newcomb A F, **8:** 4368 (4365, 4366, 4367)
Newcomb T M, **5:** 2532 (2531), 2672
Newell A, **1:** 409 (407); **2:** 851 (847); **5:** 2725 (2722), (2919); **8:** 4722 (4719, 4720, 4721), 4727 (4723, 4725); **10:** 5745 (5740), 6026 (6023); **11:** 6608 (6607)
Newell I J, **1:** 77 (74)
Newell L J, **1:** 60 (53), 77 (74)
Newfarmer R, **3:** 1713 (1711)
Newfield J, **10:** 5886 (5886)
Newhouse J, **7:** 3833 (3832)
Newlon J H, **1:** 77 (74)
Newman D, **1:** 230 (229); **3:** 1252 (1250), 1504 (1502, 1504); **5:** 2670, 2867 (2864); **6:** 3652 (3650); **8:** 4429 (4425); **9:** 5548 (5545)
Newman D L, **4:** (2108)
Newman J D, **10:** 6099 (6098)
Newman J H, **2:** (776)
Newman J M, **4:** 1962 (1961)
Newman M, **5:** 2572
Newman P, **3:** 1685, 1750; **10:** 5693 (5692)
Newman R, **10:** 6112 (6110, 6111)
Newman S, **6:** 3301 (3299); **7:** 3886 (3885); **10:** 6015 (6014); **11:** 6633 (6628)
Newman S E, **2:** 969 (967); **3:** 1252 (1251), 1529 (1526); **5:** 2773 (2770), 2874 (2873), 2884; **7:** 3792, 3953 (3953); **9:** 5363 (5360, 5362); **10:** 5795 (5794), 6177 (6174, 6177)
Newman W B, **8:** 4751 (4743)
Newmann F, **4:** 1984 (1981)
Newmann F M, **9:** 5379 (5376, 5378)
Newmeyer F H, **6:** 3439
Newstrom J W, **6:** 3096
Newton A, **10:** 5929 (5927)
Newton B, **6:** 3209 (3205, 3206, 3208)
Newton D E, **9:** 5345 (5343)
Newton I, **3:** (1462); **6:** (3680); **9:** (5051); **10:** (5986)
Newton J, **5:** 2567
Newton L, **10:** 5690 (5688)
Newton R G, **2:** 631 (629)
Newton-Smith W, **9:** 4980 (4978, 4979, 4980)
Ng C T, **4:** 2011 (2009)
Ng D, **11:** 6798 (6797)
Ng E K L, **7:** 4094 (4088, 4090)
Ng L N, **2:** 1042 (1039)
Ngara E, **11:** 6256 (6252)
Ngatara L A, **4:** 1903 (1902)
Ngondo S, **11:** 6814 (6809)
Nhavoto A, **7:** 3960
Niall B, **2:** 738 (735)
Nias D K B, **8:** 4799 (4798)
Nias J, **4:** 2166 (2163); **6:** 3603 (3599); **10:** 6215 (6209, 6210, 6212)
Nibbrig B, **11:** 6684
Nice D, **9:** 5255
Nicholas E J, **9:** 5169 (5160)
Nicholi A M Jr, **3:** 1619
Nicholls J, **10:** 5826 (5824)
Nicholls J G, **1:** 31 (28, 30), 204 (201, 202); **2:** 868 (866); **3:** 1529 (1527, 1529); **7:** 3788 (3784); **9:** 5406 (5405)
Nichols D G, **4:** 1918 (1914)
Nichols R C, **5:** 2465 (2464)
Nicholson L, **8:** 4642
Nicholson L J, **9:** 5441
Nickell S J, **6:** 3617 (3614)
Nickerson C J, **5:** 2572
Nickerson M, **10:** 5795 (5793)
Nickerson R S, **1:** 194 (191); **2:** 868 (861), 985 (983); **5:** 2769 (2762); **8:** 4731 (4730); **10:** 6169 (6165)
Nickles T, **4:** 2302 (2300, 2301)
Nickolai-Mays S, **10:** 6106 (6105, 6106)
Nickse R, **6:** 3463 (3461)
Nicolae V, **6:** 3366 (3364)
Nicolayev J, **7:** 3925 (3921)
Niculescu A, **9:** 5087
Nides M A, **4:** 2389 (2385)
Nie H, **8:** 4945 (4943)
Nie N H, **7:** 4016 (4015), 4163 (4162)
Niedderer H, **8:** 4652
Niederer J, **8:** (4416), (4418)
Niedermeyer F C, **10:** 5887 (5885)
Niehues N, **6:** 3276 (3273, 3274, 3275)
Niekus Moor C, **11:** 6747 (6744)
Nielsen D, **2:** 1136 (1134, 1135)
Nielsen H, **8:** 4464
Nielsen H D, **10:** 5954 (5950)
Nielsen J, **5:** 2709 (2706)
Nielson H D, **8:** 4442
Nielson J M, **7:** 4336
Niemec R, **4:** 1911 (1908, 1909)
Niemi P, **8:** 4429
Niemic R, **2:** 1139
Niemiec R P, **2:** 991 (990); **7:** 4088 (4084), 4104 (4101); **9:** 5043 (5040)
Niemz G, **5:** 2470 (2467)
Nienhuis E, **8:** 4803 (4800)
Nies A C M, **3:** 1278 (1274)
Nietzche F W, **8:** (4430), (4453), (4641)
Nihan G, **1:** 227 (222)
Nihlen A S, **2:** 933 (926, 929)
Niimi A, **4:** 1980 (1978)
Nijhof W J, **3:** 1315 (1313, 1314)
Nikhilananda S, **5:** 2601 (2597, 2598), 2655 (2652)
Nikken P, **8:** 4680
Nikolov R, **2:** 977 (976)
Niles J A, **10:** 6149, 6219 (6217)
Nilsson B, **4:** 2376 (2376)
Nilsson L, **11:** 6699 (6691, 6692)
Nimmer D, **2:** 1102 (1101)
Nimmer M B, **2:** 1102 (1101)
Ninio A, **6:** (3448); **7:** 4301 (4300)
Ninomiya A, **9:** 5181 (5178); **10:** 6062 (6060)

Nirje B, **3:** (1435), 1507 (1505); **10:** 5663 (5662)
Nisan M, **7:** 3920 (3919)
Nisbet J, **1:** 162 (161), 194 (185); **3:** 1343; **8:** 4562 (4558, 4561), 4604 (4602, 4603)
Nisbet R A, **1:** 437 (432); **2:** 785 (776)
Nisbet S, **7:** 3895; **8:** 4562 (4558)
Nisbett R, **2:** 1207 (1207)
Nisbett R E, **1:** 31 (30); **2:** 838 (837); **4:** 2281 (2280); **8:** 4722 (4720, 4721), 4951 (4950), 4957 (4956); **9:** 5411 (5409)
Nishimoto M, **5:** 2897 (2892)
Nishinosono H, **2:** 973 (970)
Niskanen W A, **3:** 1746 (1741); **8:** 4568 (4564)
Niss M, **6:** 3634 (3632)
Nitko A J, **1:** 370 (367); **5:** 2784 (2780); **10:** 5772 (5770), 6173 (6171); **11:** 6349 (6341)
Nitsch K E, **3:** 1438 (1435)
Nitsch W, **10:** 5782 (5776)
Nivedita Sister, **11:** (6749)
Nix D, **2:** 888 (885), 973; **11:** 6603
Nixon J, **1:** 48 (45)
Nixon M, **1:** 77 (74)
Nixon R, **8:** 4715 (4709)
Nizam J, **6:** 3356
Nkinyangi J A, **3:** 1557; **8:** 4601 (4598, 4599)
Nkomo M, **7:** 3853 (3850)
Noah H J, **1:** 152 (150); **2:** 933 (924), 957 (951); **3:** 1739 (1736), 1768 (1763); **8:** 4526 (4521), 4622 (4617); **9:** 5181 (5177); **10:** 5735 (5733); **11:** 6266 (6262, 6263), 6452 (6449), 6530, 6699 (6698)
Noam G, **7:** 3920
Noble D, **11:** 6277 (6272)
Noble G, **8:** 4680 (4679); **10:** 6227 (6225)
Noble K B, **6:** 3394
Noblitt G W, **9:** 5572 (5567, 5569)
Noda T, **2:** 1152 (1148)
Noddings N, **1:** 67 (64); **2:** 1052; **4:** 2004, 2033 (2030, 2031), 2296 (2294, 2295), 2297 (2295); **6:** 3684; **8:** 4652; **10:** 5818 (5816), 5939 (5937), 5995 (5991, 5994); **11:** 6723 (6721, 6722)
Noel E, **4:** 2059
Noel L, **3:** 1602
Noel M, **7:** 3833 (3832)
Noell J, **8:** 4845 (4840)
Noelting G, **6:** 3685 (3677)
Noffke S E, **1:** 48 (45)
Nohda N, **7:** 4099 (4098)
Nohl H, **3:** (1291), (1722)
Nolan S B, **11:** 6339 (6338)
Nolen L L, **5:** 2856 (2855)
Nolen S B, **2:** 868 (866); **6:** 3474
Nolen-Hoeksema S, **9:** 5406 (5404, 5405)
Noll I, **11:** 6420 (6418)
Nolte E, **7:** 4026, 4030
Nonomuva C, **10:** 5697
Noonan R D, **4:** 2140; **8:** 4359 (4353)
Noor Azmi I, **10:** 5973 (5972)
Nopakun O, **2:** 906 (905)
Nordhaug O, **7:** 4179 (4178), 4180, 4325, 4329 (4326)
Nordkvelle Y, **3:** 1501 (1496)
Nordlund D J, **3:** 1549
Nordstrom G Z, **11:** 6618 (6616)
Noreen E W, **9:** 5471
Norman C A, **10:** 5762 (5760)
Norman D A, **3:** 1779; **6:** 3155 (3154); **10:** 5745 (5744), 5831 (5829)
Norman L, **7:** 3889 (3888)
Norman R Z, **9:** 5560 (5555)
Norris C, **8:** 4642 (4641)
Norris D, **9:** 5544 (5542)
Norris R C, **10:** 5704 (5700)
Norris S, **2:** 1208
North B, **4:** 2363 (2361, 2362), 2364; **5:** 2784
North C C, **7:** 3771
North L, **4:** 1954
Northern J, **10:** 5691 (5687)
Northfield J R, **1:** 28
Northway M L, **10:** 5617 (5614, 5615)
Norton D, **7:** 4171 (4170)
Norton M S, **8:** 4408 (4405, 4406, 4407)
Norton T M, **2:** 785 (779)
Norusis M J, **1:** 390 (383); **3:** 1381 (1378); **7:** 3862 (3859), 4016 (4008, 4009, 4015)
Norwich B, **5:** 2910 (2908)
Nosanchuk T A, **4:** 2208
Noshpitz J D, **7:** 4081
Noss A, **3:** 1789 (1786)
Noss R, **2:** 991 (990); **4:** 1899 (1895, 1897); **6:** 3652 (3649)
Nothdurft W E, **1:** 310 (309); **4:** 1924 (1919)
Nott D, **10:** 6004 (6000, 6001)
Nottebohm F, **1:** 554
Nourot P M, **5:** 2813 (2808)
Novak J D, **2:** 1031 (1026, 1027, 1028, 1029, 1030); **6:** 3205, 3349; **8:** 4652 (4649, 4652), 4774 (4773); **9:** 5334 (5330), 5338 (5337, 5338); **10:** 5831 (5830)
Novalis H, **4:** (2386)
Novick M R, **1:** 480; **2:** 792 (790), 1189 (1188); **3:** 1421 (1418, 1419, 1420, 1421); **4:** 2183 (2182); **5:** 2596 (2591, 2593), 3055, 3061 (3057); **6:** 3253 (3248); **7:** 3706 (3702); **8:** 4912 (4906); **10:** 5725 (5723); **11:** 6320 (6317)
Novick P, **5:** 2607
Novick S, **6:** 3661 (3657)
Novikov L, **4:** 1872 (1870)
Novlick M R, **7:** 3706
Nowak J, **2:** 661 (656)
Nowak S, **4:** 1877 (1873); **7:** 3996 (3993)
Nowakowski J, **4:** 2388 (2384); **5:** 2831 (2831)
Nowell-Smith G, **2:** 1193 (1191); **7:** 4336 (4333, 4335)
Nowotny H, **9:** 5349 (5347)
Noyelle T, **1:** 103 (100, 101), 111, 184; **4:** 2394 (2389); **7:** 3711 (3709); **8:** 4638 (4636), 4639 (4636)
Nozick R, **4:** 2004 (2002); **8:** 4575 (4572); **9:** 5201 (5198, 5199)
Ntebe G, **1:** 221 (218)
Ntiri D W, **11:** 6719 (6717)
Nturibi D N, **4:** 2123 (2121)
Nuakey Y, **11:** 6403
Nübold P, **4:** 2357 (2353)
Nucci L, **4:** 2297 (2293)
Nugent J K, **5:** 2802 (2799)
Nuissl E, **7:** 4263 (4262)
Nunan D, **4:** 2364
Nunes T, **6:** 3655 (3654); **7:** 4100 (4097)
Nunn P, **3:** (1723)
Nunnally J C, **8:** 4754 (4752), 4857 (4857), 4930 (4924, 4927); **9:** 5324 (5320)
Nunner-Winkler G, **7:** 3919 (3919), 3920 (3918), 3924, 3925
Nunnery M Y, **1:** 437 (432)
Nurhadi M, **3:** 1829 (1826)
Nurullah S, **5:** 2753
Nusbaum H C, **6:** 3224
Nus'hi F, **8:** 4485 (4483)
Nuss E M, **10:** 5804 (5800, 5801, 5802, 5803)
Nussbaum J, **6:** 3661 (3657)
Nussbaum M C, **4:** 2297 (2295)
Nutbeam D, **5:** 2572 (2568, 2570)
Nuthall G A, **2:** 816 (815), 1121 (1119); **6:** 3345 (3344); **7:** 3886 (3881); **8:** 4882 (4879); **10:** 6149 (6148)
Nuttall D L, **3:** 1746 (1742); **4:** 1934 (1932), 2140 (2139), 2180; **5:** 2852 (2849); **6:** 3596 (3594); **7:** 3726 (3725), 3911, 3912 (3911); **8:** 4622 (4618), 4623 (4620, 4621)
Nutter N, **10:** 5957 (5955)
Nuttin J, **5:** 2769 (2764); **7:** 3942 (3941)
Nwa-Chil C C, **9:** 5510 (5509)
Nwaerondu N G, **5:** 2891 (2885)
Nwagwu N, **8:** 4586 (4584, 4585, 4586)
Nyamaa D, **7:** 3905 (3895, 3900)
Nyamete A, **1:** 254; **8:** 4688
Nyberg D, **4:** 1984 (1984)
Nyerere J K, **1:** (212), 474 (466); **3:** 1690 (1687); **4:** 1857 (1853)
Nyhan B, **6:** 3306 (3303)
Nyirenda S, **9:** 5228 (5225, 5227)
Nyirongo R, **4:** 2257 (2255), 2419 (2415); **8:** 4873 (4868, 4869)
Nylen C, **11:** 6731 (6729)
Nystrand M, **8:** 4881 (4877); **9:** 5176 (5170); **11:** 6780 (6779)
Nystrand R O, **1:** 77
Nyström K, **1:** 474 (469); **10:** 5721
Nystrom M, **10:** 6015 (6014)
Nziramasanga C T, **10:** 5585 (5584)
Nzuzi P L, **11:** 6814 (6812)

Ó Buachalla S, **5:** 3020
Oakes J, **1:** 11 (6, 8, 9, 10), 520 (515); **2:** 825 (821, 822, 823, 824), 1074 (1068); **3:** 1320 (1318); **4:** 2388 (2384), 2389 (2382); **5:** 2779 (2775); **7:** 4157 (4157); **9:** 5066 (5064), 5071 (5069), 5176 (5170), 5367 (5365); **10:** 6103 (6101), 6215 (6213), 6219
Oakeshott M, **2:** 1165 (1163, 1164)
Oakhill J, **8:** 4957 (4954)
Oakland T, **1:** 495; **6:** 3228 (3226), 3297; **8:** 4661 (4658); **10:** 6244 (6243)
Oakman R L, **4:** 1958 (1957)
Oates M J, **2:** 834 (832)
Oates W E, **9:** 5241 (5239)
Obebe B, **10:** 5585 (5584)
Obemeata J O, **9:** 5389 (5387)
Oberg A A, **6:** 3452

Oberlin J F, **8:** (4667)
Oberlin S, **2:** 649
Obiakor F E, **2:** 718 (716, 717)
Oborne D J, **4:** 2011 (2010, 2011), 2012
O'Brien D G, **2:** 806 (804); **8:** 4948 (4947)
O'Brien D P, **8:** 4956 (4951, 4954)
O'Brien M, **4:** 2452 (2450); **5:** 2491, 2672 (2670); **9:** 5532
O'Brien U, **10:** 5754 (5753)
Obrzut J E, **10:** 5680
Obstfeld L S, **9:** 5441 (5436)
Ocho L O, **5:** 2954 (2953)
Ochoa A, **2:** 770 (769); **4:** 1984 (1981)
Ochoa A S, **9:** 5582 (5580)
Ochs E, **6:** 3227 (3225); **11:** 6608
Ochse R, **2:** 1177
Ochsner N L, **1:** 521 (513); **6:** 3508 (3507)
O'Connell E J, **7:** 4006 (4003, 4005)
O'Connor A C, **1:** 139
O'Connor C, **6:** 3301
O'Connor D J, **8:** 4455 (4450, 4451, 4455)
O'Connor K, **6:** 3238 (3237)
O'Connor L, **7:** 4296 (4296)
O'Connor M, **2:** 867 (866); **9:** 5350
O'Connor M C, **1:** 5; **7:** 3726
O'Connor N, **6:** 3435
Oda D S, **9:** 5291 (5284)
Odaet C F, **11:** 6501
O'Day J, **3:** 1343; **5:** 2799 (2797); **10:** 5954 (5952), 6083 (6080)
Odden A, **2:** 775 (774, 775); **6:** 3608; **9:** 5066 (5063)
O'Dell F, **3:** 1739 (1737); **11:** 6266 (6262)
Odell L, **4:** 2024
Odell S J, **10:** 6047
Oden M H, **4:** 2436 (2435); **5:** 2491 (2488)
Oden S, **9:** 5567 (5566)
Ödman P-J, **5:** 2586
Odom S, **4:** 2145
Odom S L, **9:** 5567 (5563, 5564, 5565, 5566, 5567)
O'Donnell A M, **1:** 52 (50)
O'Donnell J M, **6:** 3434 (3434); **9:** 5399 (5396)
O'Donnell M, **1:** 162 (161)
O'Donnell R C, **10:** 5704 (5700)
Odor J P, **1:** 193 (192)
Oehler J S Jr, **5:** 2697 (2694)
Oelkers J, **8:** 4419
Oerter R, **5:** 2806
O'Farrell B, **4:** 2445 (2444, 2445)
Offe C, **1:** 135 (131), 317 (311); **6:** 3368 (3367), 3621 (3619); **8:** 4568 (4562, 4564)
Offer D, **1:** 88 (84, 86)
Offermann L R, **6:** 3306 (3302)
Offord K P, **1:** 238 (237)
Ogarev E I, **9:** 5098
Ogawa R T, **1:** 594 (593); **3:** 1411 (1410); **8:** 4408 (4408); **9:** 5308 (5306, 5307); **11:** 6558 (6555)
Ogborn J, **2:** 988 (986)
Ogborn J M, **9:** 5338 (5335, 5336, 5337)
Ogbu J U, **1:** 295 (291, 293), 296 (283, 287, 289, 290, 291, 292, 293, 294), 297; **2:** 718 (716, 717), 802 (799, 801), 917 (916), 933 (930), 1213 (1211); **3:** 1233 (1228, 1232); **4:** 2052 (2048, 2049, 2050); **6:** 3215 (3215), 3227 (3226), 3452 (3451), 3480 (3476); **7:** 3974 (3971, 3972); **9:** 5220 (5219), 5313 (5311), 5510 (5509), 5572 (5567, 5568, 5569, 5570, 5571); **10:** 5607 (5603), 5925 (5922); **11:** 6558 (6554), 6563 (6561)
Ogbu S M, **2:** 1160 (1157)
Ogbue R M, **2:** 718 (717)
Ogburn W F, **3:** (1342)
Ogden C, **9:** 5130 (5129)
Ogilvie D M, **2:** 1079 (1076)
Ogle D S, **6:** 3335
Oglesby K L, **11:** 6719 (6714, 6715, 6716)
Ogunniyi M B, **9:** 5350 (5348)
Oguthorpe R, **5:** 2972 (2969)
O'Hara D J, **2:** 1055 (1053)
O'Hare F, **10:** 5704 (5701)
O'Hear A, **3:** 1328; **10:** 5985 (5983, 5984)
Ohlenforf G, **9:** 5176 (5172)
Ohliger J, **6:** 3421 (3419)
Ohlin L E, **11:** 6803 (6799)
Ohlsson S, **3:** 1434 (1432, 1433); **5:** 2769 (2763)
Öhlund U, **4:** 2377
Öhman A, **3:** 1520 (1516); **8:** 4395 (4391)
Oi W Y, **7:** 4211 (4209)
Oishi S, **2:** 1099 (1098)
Oja S N, **1:** 48 (45); **10:** 5939 (5938), 6099 (6097)
Okafor R C, **7:** 4026 (4019), 4030 (4027)
Okagaki L, **5:** 2628
Okamoto K, **3:** 1343
Okamura J, **2:** 907
Okasaki A, **1:** 343 (342)
Okato T, **9:** 5181 (5178); **10:** 6062 (6060)
Oke E, **2:** 868 (864)
Okebukola P, **2:** 1031 (1028)
Okedara J T, **1:** 215 (210, 213)
O'Keefe D, **3:** 1501 (1500)
O'Keefe P, **9:** 5318 (5315, 5316)
O'Keefe W M, **5:** 2725 (2722)
Okeem E O, **1:** 215
Okimoto D, **3:** 1713 (1712)
Okin S M, **4:** 2004, 2297 (2295)
Okner B A, **9:** 5241 (5237)
Okoye M, **2:** 914
Okpala J, **5:** 2470 (2466, 2468, 2469)
Oksala K J, **3:** (1724)
Okun A M, **3:** 1703 (1698)
Okun M A, **1:** 239 (237)
Olaitan S O, **1:** 244 (240, 241)
Olbrechts-Tyteca L, **2:** 1207 (1204); **8:** 4536 (4533)
Olby R C, **9:** 5350
Oldenberg H, **5:** 2601 (2597, 2600, 2601); **9:** 5008 (4999)
Oldham E E, **4:** 2435 (2435)
Oldham J, **3:** 1739 (1737)
Oldham V, **8:** 4479 (4476)
Oldroyd D, **10:** 6047
Olds D, **9:** 5359 (5357)
Olds H F, **4:** 2166
O'Leary B, **3:** 1720
O'Leary D D M, **1:** 553 (552)
O'Leary K D, **4:** 2452 (2451)
Olechowski R, **10:** 6053
Olenick M, **2:** 688 (686)
Oley E, **5:** 2827
Olgren C H, **3:** 1579 (1576)
Oliner P M, **8:** 4799 (4798)
Oliner S P, **8:** 4799 (4798)
Olivarez A, **10:** 5686 (5686)
Olive J, **7:** 4099 (4098), 4100 (4095, 4098)
Oliveira J B A, **2:** 1011 (1010); **4:** 1903 (1902), 1911 (1904, 1907, 1908); **8:** 4526 (4519); **11:** 6266, 6272 (6268), 6415 (6414), 6416
Oliver A, **3:** 1367 (1361, 1366)
Oliver D, **2:** 1084 (1081); **4:** 1984 (1981)
Oliver L, **2:** 906 (904)
Oliver L M, **8:** 4957 (4956)
Oliver L P, **10:** 5829
Oliver M, **5:** 2457 (2455); **6:** 3559 (3557)
Oliveros A, **8:** 4586 (4583, 4584)
Olivia P F, **3:** 1315 (1310), 1367 (1361)
Olivier A I, **2:** 1052 (1051); **6:** 3661 (3660)
Olivier W P, **7:** 4094 (4088)
Olkiewicz E, **7:** 3970
Olkin I O, **4:** 1938 (1938); **7:** 3783 (3776, 3781, 3782), 3784 (3775); **9:** 4974, 5082; **10:** 6240
Oller J W Jr, **6:** 3231 (3229, 3230); **7:** 3936
Ollman B, **2:** 785 (779), 933, 1072
Olmedo E L, **11:** 6334 (6333)
Olmstead B, **9:** 5318 (5314)
Olmstead P S, **9:** 5471 (5468)
Olmsted P P, **2:** 701 (695, 696); **5:** 2813 (2807); **7:** 4301; **8:** 4677 (4674)
Olmsted P S, **5:** 2480
Olneck M R, **4:** 2279 (2275, 2277); **6:** 3144 (3138, 3143); **7:** 3978 (3974, 3975, 3976)
Olofsson B, **8:** 4395 (4393)
Olofsson L, **7:** 4179 (4178)
O'Loughlin M, **8:** 4957 (4953)
Olsen J, **9:** 5168 (5162)
Olsen J B, **1:** 52 (51, 52); **2:** 998 (993); **10:** 5771 (5771)
Olsen J K, **10:** 6117
Olsen J P, **1:** 370 (367); **3:** 1745 (1741); **4:** 1934 (1930), 2166 (2163); **6:** 3527 (3524, 3525); **9:** 5313 (5308)
Olsen L K, **5:** 2572
Olsen O, **11:** 6699
Olsen R J, **4:** 2156 (2154); **10:** 5846 (5844, 5845), 6106 (6104, 6105, 6106)
Olsen S E, **10:** 5913 (5913)
Olsen T, **9:** 5246 (5242)
Olson C, **11:** 6511 (6508)
Olson D R, **3:** 1246 (1242); **6:** 3446 (3444), 3452 (3447), 3459 (3454); **7:** 3753; **8:** 4956 (4952); **9:** 5512, 5548
Olson F I, **11:** 6558 (6555)
Olson G M, **5:** 2874
Olson J, **2:** 991 (990), 1175 (1172); **5:** 2768; **6:** 3652 (3649); **10:** 5713
Olson J K, **3:** 1257 (1256)
Olson L, **4:** 1918 (1915, 1916)
Olson M H, **3:** 1830 (1828); **5:** 2831 (2828); **8:** 4595 (4589)
Olson R K, **8:** 4912 (4910)
Olson R L, **4:** 2331
Olson R W C, **5:** 2725

Olson W C, **2:** 816 (811)
Olsson N G, **10:** 6235 (6234)
Olsson O, **8:** (4809); **10:** (5828)
Olsson R, **4:** 2331
Olsson U, **2:** 1117 (1110)
Olszewski-Kubilius P, **5:** 2491 (2486)
Olton R M, **2:** 1182 (1181); **8:** 4730 (4729)
Olver R R, **3:** 1252 (1246); **11:** 6333
Olweus D, **1:** 234 (230, 232, 233); **4:** 1877 (1877); **8:** 4368 (4365, 4368); **9:** 5528 (5526)
Olzak S, **8:** 4896 (4894)
O'Malley J M, **6:** 3334 (3330, 3331, 3333)
O'Malley P M, **5:** 2931 (2924, 2925); **11:** 6797 (6795)
Omanson S F, **5:** 2769 (2762)
O'Mara F E O, **4:** 2345 (2343)
Omari I M, **4:** 2257 (2254)
Omark D R, **6:** 3227 (3227), 3231 (3230)
Omelich C L, **11:** 6360 (6356)
Omori-Gordon H P, **7:** 3833 (3831)
Omori-Gordon L, **10:** 5686 (5683)
O'Neal E C, **4:** 2452 (2451); **9:** 5359 (5357)
O'Neal S, **3:** 1636 (1633); **10:** 6004 (6000)
O'Neil H F, **2:** 968; **5:** 3066 (3061, 3065)
O'Neil H F Jr., **9:** 5233
O'Neill B, **2:** 888 (885)
O'Neill M, **7:** 4148
Ong W J, **2:** 1160 (1153); **6:** 3446 (3444), 3459 (3454)
Oni B, **11:** 6653 (6648)
Ono S, **9:** 5453 (5450)
Onushkin V G, **9:** 5098
Oosterbeek H, **7:** 4324 (4323); **9:** 5355 (5352); **11:** 6260 (6257)
Openshaw D, **8:** 4774 (4769)
Opie I, **10:** 5817 (5815)
Opie P, **10:** 5817 (5815)
Oppenheim A N, **1:** 390 (381, 383, 384, 386), 396 (393), 570 (564, 565); **3:** 1769 (1763); **7:** 3722 (3717); **8:** 4791, 4887; **9:** 5016, 5324 (5319), 5582 (5581)
Oppenheim N, **2:** 770 (768)
Oppenheim R, **6:** 3235 (3233)
Opper S, **5:** 2642 (2638), 2643 (2641); **7:** 3848, 3970; **10:** 6168 (6165)
Oppler S H, **11:** 6320 (6320)
Oppong C, **3:** 1676 (1674); **4:** 2419 (2416)
Opwis K, **8:** 4722
O'Quin K, **2:** 1182 (1180)
Orasanu J, **2:** 969; **8:** 4942
Orazen P, **4:** 2279 (2275)
Ore O, **9:** 5560 (5555)
Orefice P, **7:** 4336 (4331)
O'Reilly D, **7:** 4220 (4215)
O'Reilly K, **5:** 2897 (2896); **9:** 5563 (5561)
Orff C, **7:** 4027
Orff G, **7:** 4027
Orgee A, **2:** 1220 (1217)
Ori H R, **3:** 1315 (1312)
Orivel F, **2:** 1127 (1122, 1125), 1152 (1147, 1150, 1151); **3:** 1573 (1568, 1569, 1571, 1572); **4:** 1903 (1900), 1911 (1907, 1908); **5:** 2984, 2993 (2989); **11:** 6298 (6293), 6664 (6660)
Orland M E, **3:** 1486 (1484)
Orlansky M D, **5:** 2972 (2966)
Ormerod M B, **9:** 5324 (5320)
Ormian C, **5:** 3028
Ormiston G, **5:** 2586
Ornstein A C, **3:** 1315 (1310)
Ornstein P A, **7:** 3763 (3762), 3768 (3764)
Oros E, **5:** 2890 (2887)
Orozco G, **3:** 1824 (1822)
Orpwood G, **9:** 5334 (5328)
Orr D P, **9:** 5435
Orr D W, **10:** 5991 (5990)
Orr E, **6:** 3638 (3637)
Orr L, **4:** 2180 (2177)
Orr M T, **9:** 5441 (5436)
Orris M J, **8:** 4751 (4747)
Orsolini M, **8:** 4951 (4949); **9:** 5507 (5506)
Ortar G R, **11:** 6339 (6337)
Ortega y Gasset J, **2:** (903); **10:** 5613
Ortiz A A, **6:** 3232 (3228, 3229, 3230, 3231)
Ortiz F I, **1:** 67 (62, 64), 83 (78); **9:** 5181 (5176, 5177); **11:** 6731 (6728)
Ortiz R M, **3:** 1735 (1733)
Ortner D J, **5:** 2685
Ortner G E, **7:** 4220
Orton S T, **10:** 5686 (5681)
Ortony A, **2:** 856; **6:** 3155; **8:** 4957; **10:** 5745 (5742); **11:** 6456, 6457
Orum A M, **1:** 543
Ory J C, **10:** 6234 (6233)
Osawa K, **4:** 2199 (2194)
Osborn A E, **8:** 4731 (4729)
Osborn A F, **4:** 2145; **5:** 2725 (2722); **8:** 4666 (4665)
Osborn J, **9:** 5363 (5359); **11:** 6370 (6368)
Osborn M, **6:** 3312 (3310, 3311); **9:** 5181 (5178); **10:** 5934 (5931), 6096 (6094)
Osborne A, **10:** 6183 (6182)
Osborne A R, **6:** 3685 (3674)
Osborne B, **3:** 1236 (1236)
Osborne C W, **2:** 1016 (1012); **3:** 1800 (1798, 1799); **4:** 1882 (1879)
Osborne D, **1:** 238 (237); **9:** 5191 (5188)
Osborne J, **8:** 4479 (4477)
Osborne R, **6:** 3204 (3204)
Osborne R J, **4:** 1848 (1845); **8:** 4479; **9:** 5335; **10:** 5790 (5784, 5785)
Osbourne C W, **7:** 4088 (4085)
Osbourne R, **10:** 6177 (6176)
Osburn D D, **9:** 5294 (5291)
Oscanyan F S, **2:** 868 (862), 1207 (1207)
Oser F K, **1:** 380 (378); **2:** 816; **5:** 2669; **7:** 3920 (3919), 3925 (3922, 3923); **8:** 4372, 4461 (4458); **9:** 5043; **10:** 5939 (5936), 6053 (6048, 6049, 6050, 6051, 6052, 6053), 6168, 6169 (6167, 6168); **11:** 6580
Osgood C E, **1:** 390 (381, 382, 387); **2:** 1079 (1075); **9:** 5158 (5154)
Osguthorpe R T, **8:** 4375 (4373), 4376 (4372, 4373)
O'Shaughnessy R, **5:** 2972 (2969)
O'Shaughnessy T, **4:** 2412 (2408)
O'Shea T, **2:** 1170
Osheba I T, **4:** 2418 (2417)
Osherson D N, **2:** 842; **8:** 4722, 4727 (4726), 4957 (4955)
Osin L, **2:** 1012 (1010); **6:** 3480 (3479)
Osipow S H, **11:** 6677, 6678 (6672)
Osofsky J D, **1:** 362; **3:** 1642 (1639); **4:** 1966, 1967; **5:** 2802
Ossandón C J, **4:** 2123 (2122)
Osser H, **6:** 3216 (3214)
Ostendorf F, **11:** 6310 (6310)
Osteria T, **2:** 907
Osterlind J J, **3:** 1443
Osterlind S J, **5:** 2462 (2462); **11:** 6320 (6315)
Osterman P, **5:** 2942 (2939, 2940); **6:** 3189 (3187); **11:** 6277 (6275)
Osterwalder F, **8:** 4419
Ostling R N, **9:** 5008 (4996, 4997)
Ostrom T M, **9:** 5324 (5318)
Osuala J, **3:** 1567 (1565)
O'Sullivan D, **5:** 2736, 2737 (2733), 3020
O'Sullivan P J, **9:** 5071 (5069)
Oswald H, **4:** 2249 (2248)
Oswald P, **1:** 265 (263)
Oswald W D, **1:** 239
Oswalt W H, **5:** 2655 (2654)
Ota C C, **2:** 914
Otaala B, **1:** 552
Otis A S, **4:** 1872 (1867)
Otis-Wilborn A K, **10:** 6106 (6105)
O'Toole B, **5:** 2972 (2966, 2969)
O'Toole J, **2:** 1074 (1066)
O'Toole R, **6:** 3373
Otsuki S, **1:** 348
Ott L, **5:** 2714 (2713); **9:** 5142
Ott M D, **6:** 3508 (3507)
Ott R, **1:** 343
Otten R, **1:** 204 (202)
Ottenberg S, **3:** 1756 (1753)
Otterburg S, **9:** 5191 (5189)
Otto G, **1:** 343 (341); **3:** 1301 (1291)
Otto H J, **7:** 4293 (4290)
Otto L B, **1:** 358 (357)
Ottoson D, **5:** 2978
Ouane A, **1:** 221 (218); **3:** 1262 (1260); **5:** 2758, 2759; **6:** 3585 (3578, 3582), 3586
Ouchi W G, **4:** 1972 (1969, 1971), 2166 (2160); **6:** 3527 (3525); **9:** 5211 (5207)
Oud M, **6:** 3213
Oudin X, **1:** 226 (222); **3:** 1680 (1679)
Ousmane D A, **7:** 3691
Ousten J, **8:** 4779 (4777)
Ouston J, **4:** 1934 (1933), 2166 (2164); **5:** 2589 (2588); **9:** 5211 (5207, 5209), 5224 (5221), 5264 (5262), 5379 (5375); **10:** 5750 (5746)
Outson J, **3:** 1538
Outston J, **10:** 6083 (6082)
Over J, **11:** 6712 (6711)
Over R, **11:** 6712 (6711)
Overall C, **9:** 5441 (5438)
Overall J E, **7:** 4163 (4160)
Overbeek B, **3:** 1520 (1519)
Overholt W, **8:** 4787 (4783)
Overly N V, **5:** 2589
Overman S E, **9:** 5030 (5024, 5025)
Overmier J B, **9:** 5406 (5404)
Overton W F, **1:** 88 (85); **5:** 2665 (2658, 2659); **8:** 4956, 4957 (4954, 4956); **9:** 5512
Owen C F, **7:** 3706 (3702)
Owen D B, **4:** 2183

Owen R, **1:** 280 (278); **5:** (2608), (2610); **8:** (4667); **9:** (5229)
Owen R J, **1:** 52 (50); **2:** 998 (994)
Owen S V, **9:** 5490 (5488)
Owen T, **7:** 4094 (4089); **11:** 6307 (6303)
Owens E, **4:** 2369 (2366)
Owens T R, **4:** (2103)
Owings J A, **2:** 711 (709); **10:** 5846
Owston R D, **2:** 1170, 1175 (1174)
Oxenham J, **1:** 135 (131), 175 (173); **6:** 3459 (3453), 3480; **10:** 5607 (5603); **11:** 6266 (6263), 6699 (6698), 6704 (6700)
Oxford R L, **6:** 3334 (3330, 3333)
Oxley B, **9:** 5358 (5357)
Oxtoby R, **11:** 6266 (6263)
Oyeneye O, **1:** 227 (222)
Oyserman D, **10:** 6112 (6107)
Ozbay F, **11:** 6760 (6758)
Ozer E M, **4:** 1980 (1979)
Ozga J T, **4:** 2166 (2161); **8:** 4586 (4582, 4583, 4584, 4585, 4586), 4601; **9:** 5169 (5160); **10:** 6079 (6074), 6096 (6093), 6139 (6133, 6135)
Ozigi A O L, **7:** 4132

Paananen M, **10:** 5713 (5709, 5710)
Pace C R, **3:** 1482 (1476, 1482); **4:** 2097 (2093); **10:** 5957 (5955)
Pachaka L, **5:** 2972 (2969)
Pachociński R, **2:** 661 (657, 659, 660)
Pacione M, **5:** 2945
Packer A E, **4:** 1924; **11:** 6260 (6257, 6258)
Packwood W T, **10:** 5804 (5799)
Padberg R, **4:** 2007
Paddock J T, **10:** 5925 (5922)
Paden E, **10:** 5696 (5696), 5697 (5694, 5695)
Padilla K A, **2:** 868 (863)
Padilla R V, **1:** 535
Padron Y N, **6:** 3334 (3331)
Padua J, **7:** 3801
Pagaard P E, **3:** 1461
Pagano J, **11:** 6723 (6721)
Pagano M, **2:** 1084 (1081)
Page B, **4:** 2357 (2355)
Page E B, **7:** 3935 (3933); **8:** 4845 (4840)
Page G T, **7:** 3970 (3962); **10:** 5901 (5895)
Page J K, **7:** 3991 (3988)
Page R N, **1:** 11 (6, 8, 10); **2:** 824, 825 (821, 822, 823, 824); **3:** 1320 (1318); **9:** 5211 (5209); **10:** 5613 (5608), 5817 (5816)
Paget K, **11:** 6310 (6309)
Pagiannis G, **4:** 1911 (1908, 1909, 1910)
Pahl R H, **9:** 5582 (5581)
Paik I W, **2:** 1131 (1130)
Paikoff R L, **5:** 2677 (2673)
Pain A, **11:** 6452
Painchaud G, **7:** 4324 (4321)
Paine L, **10:** 6106 (6104)
Paine L W, **5:** 2512 (2512)
Paine N, **6:** 3435 (3434)
Paine W S, **10:** 5925, 6062
Painter S L, **4:** 2266 (2264)
Paisley W, **2:** 1012
Paivio A U, **2:** 887 (886); **7:** 3768 (3765), 3774 (3774)
Palaemon R, **8:** (4887)
Palanki A, **9:** 5268 (5267)
Paley V G, **10:** (5815)
Palfrey J S, **5:** 2575 (2574, 2575)
Palincsar A, **6:** 3625 (3625); **7:** 3886 (3885); **10:** 6015 (6014)
Palincsar A M, **2:** 969 (967); **8:** 4942 (4941); **9:** 5507
Palincsar A S, **1:** 374 (371); **2:** 867 (864), 868 (864); **3:** 1252 (1251), 1529 (1526); **5:** 2536 (2533); **6:** 3223 (3223), 3297 (3295), 3302 (3300), 3334 (3331, 3333), 3335; **7:** 3788 (3787), 3792; **8:** 4881 (4878); **10:** 5745 (5744), 5795 (5792), 6178 (6174), 6192 (6189); **11:** 6456 (6454)
Pallak M S, **5:** 2672 (2670)
Pallas A, **3:** 1606 (1606), 1607 (1604, 1605, 1606)
Pallas A M, **2:** 711 (707, 708, 709); **8:** 4844 (4840, 4841); **9:** 5211 (5208)
Palme M, **7:** 3960
Palmer D G, **1:** 322 (319); **4:** 2180 (2178)
Palmer D J, **10:** 5686 (5686)
Palmer D R, **6:** 3339 (3337)
Palmer E, **8:** 4680
Palmer H E, **4:** 2346 (2340, 2342)
Palmer I, **10:** 6079
Palmer J L, **2:** 692 (689, 690, 691, 692), 700 (696); **3:** 1642 (1640)
Palmer P, **8:** 4680 (4677)
Palmer R E, **5:** 2585 (2579, 2581, 2583); **9:** 5055
Palmer S E, **2:** 851 (848)
Palmer W J, **7:** 3816
Pals N, **4:** 1899 (1883)
Palti H, **1:** 553 (553)
Paludi M A, **11:** 6712 (6711)
Pancrazio S B, **8:** 4595 (4591)
Pandit HN, **5:** 2486
Pánek J, **2:** 883
Panelas T, **11:** 6798 (6795, 6797)
Pang Hwan Ju, **6:** 3160
Pang K C, **10:** 6047
Panhelainen M, **11:** 6551
Pankhurst R, **4:** 2043
Pankowski M L, **5:** 2532 (2531)
Pankratius W, **2:** 1031 (1028)
Pankratz R S, **10:** 5957 (5956), 5999 (5998)
Pant Y R, **7:** 4067
Pantin G, **2:** (908)
Panton L, **1:** 409 (406, 407)
Pantzar E, **1:** 127 (124); **7:** 4180
Panyan M V, **7:** 3808 (3806)
Paolisso M, **3:** 1628 (1627)
Paolitto D P, **11:** 6484 (6482)
Paolucci-Whitcomb P, **7:** 3833 (3832); **10:** 6244 (6241, 6242)
Paour J L, **2:** 860 (858)
Papagiannis G J, **1:** 135 (128); **3:** 1820 (1817); **4:** 1911, 2369; **7:** 4145 (4142, 4143), 4201 (4197)
Papakonstantinou P, **5:** 2523
Papandropoulou I, **4:** 1962 (1960)
Papanek H, **4:** 2419 (2417)
Papastavrou A S, **3:** 1375
Papert S, **2:** 888 (885), 973 (969, 970, 971, 972), 988 (986), 991 (991), 1006 (1004, 1005), 1012 (1008); **4:** 1899 (1896); **6:** 3459 (3458), 3512 (3509, 3510, 3511); **7:** 4088 (4082, 4084)
Papousek H, **5:** 2802 (2800)
Papoušek H, **6:** 3224 (3222)
Papoušek M, **6:** 3224 (3222)
Pappas C C, **9:** 5577 (5576)
Pappi F U, **9:** 5503 (5501, 5502)
Paqueo V, **8:** 4835 (4834), 4845 (4843); **10:** 5754 (5751)
Paquet P, **1:** 180
Paracone C, **11:** 6416
Paradise L V, **8:** 4881 (4876)
Parajuli P, **1:** 162 (160)
Paramskas D, **6:** 3241
Parasher S V, **4:** 2351 (2347)
Paraskevopoulos J, **7:** 4301 (4299)
Parcel T, **11:** 6276 (6273)
Paredes R, **3:** 1680 (1677)
Parekh A J, **7:** 4081 (4079)
Parelius A P, **10:** 5613 (5609, 5612)
Parelius R J, **10:** 5613 (5609, 5612)
Parer M S, **3:** 1563 (1560)
Parham I A, **1:** 239 (237)
Parich R, **9:** 5211 (5208)
Paris S, **2:** 868 (864)
Paris S G, **4:** 1848 (1845); **5:** 2874; **6:** 3329 (3327), 3334 (3332), 3474 (3473); **7:** 3788 (3785); **10:** 5745 (5744)
Pařízková J, **8:** 4474 (4471)
Park H J, **9:** 5130 (5129)
Park O, **2:** 1020
Park P, **7:** 4336 (4331, 4335)
Park P B, **1:** 82 (79, 81)
Park R E, **1:** (537); **11:** 6803 (6799)
Park W H, **3:** 1553
Parkay F W, **1:** 73 (70, 72); **10:** 5948 (5946)
Parke R D, **1:** 234 (230, 232, 233); **3:** 1647 (1646); **5:** 2627, 2628 (2624, 2625)
Parker B J, **3:** 1589 (1587)
Parker C A, **10:** 5805
Parker E B, **1:** 570 (564, 565)
Parker F, **3:** 1589 (1587)
Parker F L, **7:** 4301 (4299)
Parker J G, **8:** 4368 (4365); **10:** 5759
Parker J S, **8:** 4698
Parker L, **3:** 1579 (1576)
Parker R, **3:** 1359 (1358); **6:** 3209 (3205, 3206, 3208)
Parker R N, **1:** 358 (357)
Parker S, **3:** 1643 (1639); **4:** 2249
Parker W C, **10:** 5585
Parker W R, **4:** 2351 (2348)
Parkes C M, **4:** 1967 (1964)
Parkes D, **3:** 1739; **11:** 6669
Parkhurst H, **5:** (2731), 2773 (2770); **7:** (4156)
Parkinson K J, **2:** 1107
Parkinson M, **11:** 6558 (6553)
Parkyn G W, **4:** 2180 (2176, 2177)
Parlee M, **4:** 2302 (2298)
Parlett M R, **2:** 645; **3:** 1287 (1285); **4:** (2103)
Parlier M, **2:** 665 (663)
Parmenter T R, **2:** 635 (634)

Parmentier R, **1:** 194; **5:** 2669, 2767, 2768, 2769, 2884; **6:** 3345; **7:** 3791, 3942
Parmer P, **7:** 3852 (3849)
Parnes H, **3:** 1820 (1811); **8:** 4531 (4526)
Parnes H S, **1:** 358 (355)
Parnes P, **1:** 409 (407)
Parnes S J, **2:** 1182 (1181)
Parreño A, **10:** 5674 (5670)
Parrinder G, **5:** 2656
Parry G, **2:** 665
Parry T S, **4:** 2339; **6:** 3334
Parry-Jones W L, **3:** 1538 (1537)
Parseghian P E, **6:** 3325 (3321)
Parsons C K, **2:** 645 (642); **5:** 3055
Parsons D O, **6:** 3617 (3615); **11:** 6424 (6421)
Parsons G, **10:** 5995 (5994)
Parsons J E, **9:** 5432 (5429), 5507 (5505)
Parsons M J, **11:** 6618
Parsons P, **1:** 194 (191)
Parsons T, **1:** 296 (289), 437 (433); **2:** 785 (781), (929), 1074 (1065, 1066); **3:** 1774 (1770); **4:** 2166 (2156); **5:** 2529 (2524), (2605); **6:** 3276 (3272), 3373 (3370); **9:** 5176 (5173); **10:** (5587), 6132 (6130)
Parsonson K, **8:** 4895 (4895)
Partington J A, **6:** 3360; **9:** 5255
Partridge D, **3:** 1779 (1775)
Partridge P H, **7:** 3840 (3838)
Pascal A, **3:** 1486 (1484); **6:** 3197 (3195)
Pascal B, **8:** (4430)
Pascarella E T, **1:** 520 (519); **3:** 1602; **4:** 2412 (2410)
Paschal R A, **5:** 2631 (2628, 2629); **8:** 4403 (4401)
Paschen H, **8:** 4419
Pascoe C E, **10:** (5814)
Pascual-Leone J, **2:** 856 (853); **8:** 4482 (4482)
Pashigan B P, **3:** 1449 (1447)
Pashigian P, **6:** 3101
Pasigna A, **4:** 1918 (1913)
Pask G, **1:** 194 (188, 189, 190), 322 (318, 320); **2:** 872 (870, 871); **5:** 2769 (2763); **10:** 5901 (5895), 6202 (6199)
Pasnak R, **2:** 705
Passeron C, **6:** 3106 (3101)
Passeron J-C, **1:** 67 (62); **2:** 933 (929), 1072 (1069); **3:** 1233 (1229), 1300 (1288), (1304), (1306), 1308, 1337 (1335), 1347 (1345), 1739 (1737); **4:** 2271 (2267, 2268, 2269), 2291 (2289); **5:** 2585 (2580); **6:** 3621 (3618); **9:** 5021 (5016, 5017, 5018, 5019, 5020), 5060 (5057), 5312 (5309), 5572 (5570); **10:** 5591 (5590), 5596 (5592)
Passmore J, **2:** 1207 (1204)
Passow A H, **3:** 1524, 1768 (1763); **5:** 2731, 2732 (2729), 2972 (2970, 2971); **10:** 5735 (5733)
Pasteur L, **6:** (3218)
Pastore J, **3:** 1680 (1677)
Pasurka C, **1:** 254 (247)
Patai D, **7:** 4051 (4048)
Patching W, **2:** 868 (862)
Pate R, **8:** 4467 (4466)
Patel N R, **2:** 1084 (1081)
Pateman T, **8:** 4446
Paterson C, **1:** 111
Paterson D G, **5:** 2684 (2682)
Paterson L, **11:** 6690 (6689)
Paterson R K, **2:** 807 (803)
Paterson R W K, **1:** 120 (114); **3:** 1315
Patnaik P B, **7:** 3739 (3731)
Patočka J, **2:** 883
Patrick C, **10:** 5617 (5616)
Patrick H, **2:** 816 (814, 815); **9:** 5294 (5293)
Patrick J, **2:** 770 (770); **6:** 3096 (3092, 3093, 3094, 3095)
Patrick J J, **8:** 4581 (4577)
Patry J-L, **2:** 816; **3:** 1355 (1354); **8:** 4372; **9:** 5043; **10:** 6053 (6051, 6053); **11:** 6580
Pattanayak D P, **7:** 3974 (3973)
Pattee L, **8:** 4368 (4365, 4366, 4367)
Patten O T, **7:** 4240 (4236)
Patterson C H, **5:** 2692 (2690)
Patterson F, **4:** 2292
Patterson G R, **1:** 234 (232, 233, 234); **4:** 2452 (2451); **8:** 4368 (4367)
Patterson J H, **7:** 3808 (3804)
Patterson J M, **8:** 4779 (4775, 4776, 4778)
Patterson L, **10:** 6012 (6011)
Patterson L R, **2:** 1102 (1100)
Patterson R K W, **5:** 2737
Pattison P, **4:** 2357 (2352)
Patton J, **5:** 2491 (2486, 2487)
Patton M Q, **3:** 1283 (1281, 1283), 1431 (1425, 1426, 1428); **4:** 2046 (2044), 2089 (2087, 2088), (2102), (2108), 2123 (2121); **11:** 6384 (6378), 6466 (6464, 6465)
Patty M, **9:** 5228 (5226)
Paukert L, **4:** 2286 (2282)
Paukku P, **10:** 5713 (5709, 5710)
Paul A A, **8:** 4474 (4469)
Paul B, **1:** 89
Paul C, **3:** 1501 (1497)
Paul III, **9:** (5118)
Paul J L, **1:** 494 (492)
Paul R, **2:** 1207 (1205, 1206); **6:** 3224 (3220, 3222), 3234 (3232), 3235 (3232)
Paul R H, **4:** 2186
Paul S, **3:** 1820 (1816)
Paulet R, **2:** 1165 (1161, 1164)
Paulsen A, **8:** 4707 (4703)
Paulsen F, **3:** (1722), (1723)
Paulsen M F, **11:** 6307 (6302, 6303)
Paulston C B, **1:** 534 (532, 533)
Paulston R G, **2:** 933 (927, 928, 929, 930, 932), 1042 (1038); **4:** 2327, 2369 (2366); **7:** 4145 (4142)
Pauly M, **4:** 2212 (2209)
Pauwels A, **9:** 5302
Pavalko R M, **8:** 4736 (4734)
Pavan B N, **1:** 230 (228, 229); **7:** 4157 (4157); **10:** 5935 (5933)
Pavitt K, **11:** 6283 (6278)
Pavlov I P, **1:** (495); **4:** (1869); **5:** (2875), (2880); **6:** (3316); **10:** (5705); **11:** (6308)
Paxman B, **8:** 4698 (4696)
Paxton P, **6:** (3499)
Payan R, **6:** 3232 (3228)
Payer L, **8:** 4423 (4419)
Payne D A, **4:** 2183
Payne J, **2:** 1165; **3:** (1722)
Payne M A, **9:** 5268; **10:** 6062 (6060)
Payne R, **6:** 3209 (3207)
Payne S L, **8:** 4887
Payner B, **8:** 4902 (4900)
Pea R, **2:** 973 (971, 972)
Pea R D, **2:** 985 (983), 991 (990), 1012 (1008); **7:** 4088 (4084); **11:** 6287, 6457 (6453)
Pea R W, **2:** 838 (837)
Peabody E P, **4:** (2385), 2388; **8:** (4668)
Peacock D, **1:** 28
Peacock J L, **3:** 1729 (1726); **9:** 5510 (5508)
Peaker G F, **1:** 396; **2:** 631 (629), 1220 (1216); **3:** 1482, 1768 (1763); **4:** 2180 (2177), 2257 (2254); **6:** 3524 (3519); **7:** 3872 (3870), 3986 (3979, 3980), 4016 (4009); **8:** 4352 (4339), 4359 (4353), 4873 (4866, 4867), 4930 (4926); **9:** 5130 (5125, 5126, 5127), 5142 (5138, 5139); **11:** 6328 (6326)
Peaker G P, **7:** 3739 (3731)
Peal E, **1:** 537 (536)
Pearce D, **2:** 693; **11:** 6366 (6362)
Pearce F, **2:** 785 (776)
Pearce G, **10:** 5995 (5993)
Pearl A, **4:** 2440 (2438); **5:** 2806; **10:** 6149 (6146)
Pearlman K, **2:** 1139
Pearson A, **10:** 5985
Pearson A M, **5:** 2910 (2908)
Pearson C S, **11:** 6765
Pearson D P, **6:** 3443 (3442); **11:** 6370 (6369)
Pearson K, **3:** (1545), (1793); **4:** 1872 (1867), (2230); **6:** (3499); **7:** 3706 (3702), 3858 (3854), (3873); **9:** 5055 (5051, 5053), (5424)
Pearson L B, **5:** 2978
Pearson M R, **7:** 4282
Pearson P D, **2:** 824, 868 (866), 1198; **8:** 4935 (4934), 4936, 4942; **10:** 5961, 6192 (6191, 6192)
Pearson R W, **9:** 5372 (5370)
Pease-Alvarez L, **1:** 534 (533, 534)
Peaslee A, **3:** 1695 (1691, 1692)
Peatling J H, **9:** 5008 (5007)
Peay L, **7:** 4301 (4299)
Pechman J A, **4:** 2432; **6:** 3189 (3189); **9:** 5241 (5237)
Peck B T, **10:** 5613 (5610, 5611)
Peck C A, **2:** 729 (723); **3:** 1438, 1508; **5:** 2813
Peck E, **9:** 5232 (5229)
Peck K L, **2:** 1170; **5:** 2862
Peck L, **5:** 2779
Peck R F, **3:** 1636 (1632); **10:** 6234 (6233), 6235 (6234)
Pedersen F A, **3:** 1643 (1639)
Pedersen N L, **11:** 6492 (6488, 6489, 6490, 6491)
Pedhazur E J, **2:** 631; **4:** 1877 (1873), 2140 (2137); **5:** 2931 (2922, 2923); **7:** 3986 (3981); **8:** 4352 (4344), 4657 (4655, 4656), 4779 (4777), 4930 (4926); **9:** 4974 (4969, 4973)

Pedler M, **6:** 3306 (3303)
Pedler P, **4:** 2017 (2013)
Pedro E, **4:** 2377 (2376)
Pedro-Carroll J A, **4:** 2267 (2264)
Pédron G, **8:** 4474 (4470)
Peek R P, **4:** 1958 (1954)
Peel D A, **8:** 4788
Peel J D Y, **2:** 785 (782)
Peel R, **5:** 2656
Peers R, **11:** 6438
Peet R C, **4:** 2419 (2417)
Peeters A L, **8:** 4680
Peeters J, **4:** 2267
Pegg J E, **10:** 5977 (5974, 5976)
Pehrsson R, **2:** 738 (733)
Peil M, **1:** 227 (222)
Peirce C S, **3:** 1524 (1521, 1522, 1524); **9:** 5416 (5411, 5412)
Peisner E, **9:** 5275 (5274)
Pekrun R, **4:** 1967 (1963, 1966); **9:** 5394 (5392)
Peled E, **2:** 1012 (1009)
Peled Z, **2:** 1012 (1009)
Pelgrum H, **8:** 4352
Pelgrum W, **10:** 6008 (6005, 6006)
Pelgrum W J, **2:** 957, 977 (975, 976), 985 (983), 991 (991), 1006 (1002), 1012 (1008, 1009); **3:** 1746 (1742), 1768 (1764); **4:** 1918 (1915, 1916, 1917), 1934 (1932), 2427 (2424, 2425); **7:** 3810 (3808), 4088 (4084, 4085), 4104 (4102); **11:** 6287 (6283, 6284, 6285, 6286)
Pellegrini D, **1:** 239 (238)
Pellegrino J W, **1:** 5 (4, 5), 6 (3, 4); **5:** 2921; **6:** 3325 (3321)
Pellens K, **5:** 2623
Pellerey M, **6:** 3652 (3647)
Pelligrini A D, **6:** 3463 (3460)
Pelligrini D, **3:** 1643 (1640)
Peloille B, **10:** 6085 (6085)
Pelosi J, **7:** 3833 (3831)
Pelton J, **3:** 1580 (1576)
Pelzman F, **6:** 3399 (3395)
Pemberton C, **11:** 6398 (6396)
Peña E, **6:** 3227 (3226)
Penalver L M, **3:** 1567 (1564)
Pencavel J, **3:** 1660 (1656, 1657)
Pence A R, **2:** 687 (686); **3:** 1647 (1645); **7:** 4301 (4297)
Pendarvis E D, **5:** 2495 (2492)
Penfold D, **3:** (1228)
Penick J E, **9:** 5345 (5343, 5344)
Penn D M, **10:** 6053 (6052)
Penna A N, **3:** 1333
Penna Firme T, **3:** 1735 (1733, 1734, 1735)
Pennington B F, **10:** 5680 (5680)
Pennock G, **11:** 6511 (6508)
Pennock J R, **8:** 4581 (4575)
Pennycuick D, **8:** 4623 (4621)
Pennypacker H, **10:** 6164 (6161)
Penrod S, **1:** 570 (568)
Penrose P, **1:** 510
Pépin L, **6:** 3197 (3190, 3191); **10:** 6073 (6068), 6079 (6077)
Peplau L, **4:** 2302 (2297)
Pepler D J, **1:** 234 (233); **8:** 4368, 4542 (4539)
Pepper A D, **11:** 6424 (6422)
Pepper F, **1:** 486 (483)
Pepper S, **9:** 5281
Pera M, **4:** 2302
Percival F, **5:** 2773 (2771)
Percy K, **10:** 5596 (5596); **11:** 6395 (6391)
Pereire J, **10:** (5659)
Perelman C, **2:** 1207 (1204); **8:** 4536 (4533)
Perelman L J, **4:** 1924 (1923); **5:** 2867 (2864)
Perelman P F, **5:** 2972 (2970)
Perera D A, **1:** 221; **3:** 1262 (1260); **5:** 2758, 2759; **6:** 3585
Perera S M D, **7:** 4136 (4133)
Pérez Cordoba R, **2:** 1146
Perfetti C, **7:** 3774 (3773)
Perfetti C A, **1:** 6 (3); **5:** 2769 (2762); **8:** 4940, 4945 (4942, 4943, 4944)
Periera M E, **5:** 2685 (2682)
Perkin H, **10:** 6096 (6093)
Perkins D N, **2:** 868 (861, 865), 985 (983), 1207 (1207); **4:** 1848 (1845); **5:** 2769 (2762), 2867 (2865); **6:** 3625 (3623), 3655 (3653); **7:** 3791 (3790); **8:** 4652 (4650), 4951 (4948, 4949); **9:** 5563; **10:** 5745 (5741, 5744); **11:** 6457 (6453, 6454, 6455, 6456)
Perkins W H, **9:** 5328 (5326)
Perl S, **10:** 5961
Perleth C, **5:** 2732 (2726)
Perlman M, **4:** 2212
Perlman R, **9:** 5355 (5354)
Perlmutter M, **1:** 89, 234; **3:** 1643; **5:** 2806; **7:** 3763 (3760), 3768; **8:** 4368, 4542; **9:** 5406, 5567
Perloff E, **4:** 2036
Perloff R, **4:** 2036, 2089
Perls F S, **5:** 2692 (2690)
Perner J, **2:** 856 (854, 856), 857 (854, 856); **9:** 5512 (5511)
Perraton H, **2:** 1127 (1124); **3:** 1573 (1568, 1570); **4:** 1903 (1899), 1911
Perren G E, **4:** 2357 (2354)
Perrenoud P, **2:** 802 (799)
Perret J F, **9:** 5507 (5505)
Perret-Clermont A N, **5:** 2536 (2535); **8:** 4372, 4482 (4482); **9:** 5507 (5504, 5505, 5507), 5548 (5546)
Perriman H R, **8:** 4455
Perrin D G, **4:** 1898 (1885)
Perrin D W, **4:** 2183 (2183)
Perrot D, **5:** 2623 (2622)
Perrot J, **6:** 3550 (3547)
Perrott C, **10:** 6197
Perrow C, **2:** 1042 (1041); **4:** 2166 (2164)
Perry A D, **6:** 3124 (3122)
Perry C L, **5:** 2572 (2567, 2569, 2570); **10:** 6073 (6069)
Perry D G, **1:** 234 (230, 232, 233)
Perry E, **5:** 2529 (2526)
Perry J D, **5:** 2874 (2871)
Perry L C, **1:** 234 (232, 233)
Perry M, **3:** 1246 (1245)
Perry P J C, **11:** 6690 (6685)
Perry R B, **3:** 1524
Perry R P, **8:** 4895 (4895)
Perry S, **2:** 906 (906)
Perry W, **1:** 564; **3:** 1580 (1575); **4:** 2330 (2330); **7:** 4220
Perry W G, **1:** 194 (186); **9:** 5411 (5409), 5475 (5474); **10:** 5939 (5938)
Perry W Jr., **10:** 5804 (5798)
Persaud G, **6:** 3074
Persell C H, **8:** 4830 (4826, 4828); **11:** 6712 (6711)
Pershkin A, **9:** 5411
Persianis P, **3:** 1375
Persius A P F, **6:** (3499)
Persky B, **2:** 893
Peruniak G S, **4:** 2186 (2185)
Pervin L A, **5:** 2769 (2760); **8:** 4394, 4395 (4388); **10:** 6159 (6155)
Peschar J L, **7:** 4324; **10:** 5735 (5734)
Peshkin A, **1:** 296 (291); **2:** 917 (915), 1213 (1209); **3:** 1288, 1320 (1316); **7:** 4319 (4317); **10:** 5817 (5815), 6086
Peskova J, **2:** 884
Pesmazoglou S, **5:** 2523
Pesola C A, **4:** 2351 (2346)
Pestalozzi J H, **1:** (262); **3:** (1289), (1290), (1295), (1303), (1699), (1721); **4:** (1865), (2386), (2387); **5:** (2608); **6:** (3136), (3497), (3499), (3626); **7:** (4211); **8:** (4452), (4667), (4681); **9:** (5230); **10:** (5874)
Petch A, **1:** 594 (591); **9:** 5196 (5194); **11:** 6557 (6556)
Petch R, **4:** 1898 (1897)
Peter L J, **9:** 5475
Peters D D, **9:** 5567
Peters D F, **11:** 6798 (6797)
Peters D L, **3:** 1635, 1636 (1629, 1632, 1633)
Peters J, **1:** 162, 163
Peters J M, **1:** 142; **7:** 4185; **8:** 4812
Peters M, **8:** 4642
Peters M E, **3:** 1599
Peters O, **3:** 1563, 1573 (1568), 1579 (1575); **7:** 4220 (4219); **10:** 5596 (5594)
Peters R, **1:** 127 (122)
Peters R S, **2:** 1207, 1208 (1206); **3:** 1328 (1326, 1327), 1367; **4:** 2033; **8:** 4447 (4445, 4446), 4455 (4447, 4450, 4455), 4456, 4575 (4574); **9:** 5416
Peters T, **4:** 1934 (1929, 1931, 1933); **5:** 2847 (2845); **7:** 4236; **10:** 6053 (6052)
Peters T J, **6:** 3496 (3495); **7:** 4246 (4244); **8:** 4758 (4754); **9:** 5211 (5207)
Petersen A C, **1:** 88 (83, 84), 89; **4:** 2435 (2434), 2439; **5:** 2491 (2489), 2677; **9:** 5432 (5423, 5424, 5428, 5429), 5435 (5433, 5434, 5435); **10:** 5826
Petersen B T, **6:** 3209 (3208)
Petersen N S, **3:** 1421 (1419, 1421); **8:** 4623 (4617); **11:** 6355 (6349, 6350, 6354)
Petersen O, **8:** 4935 (4934)
Petersen O P, **3:** 1461
Petersen P, **1:** (227), (228); **3:** (1722); **7:** (4156)
Petersen R C, **8:** 4831
Peterson A C, **4:** 1967
Peterson A D C, **5:** 2957, 2978
Peterson C, **3:** 1425; **9:** 5406 (5404, 5405)

Peterson D A, **1:** 152 (147, 150); **6:** 3435 (3429, 3432)
Peterson D C, **7:** 3833 (3831)
Peterson D L, **6:** 3297 (3293, 3295)
Peterson D R, **8:** 4395 (4391)
Peterson D W, **9:** 5290 (5286, 5287); **11:** 6484 (6484)
Peterson G W, **11:** 6798 (6797)
Peterson J, **4:** 2418 (2415); **10:** 6112 (6110)
Peterson J E, **7:** 4206
Peterson K D, **1:** 73 (70); **9:** 5264 (5263), 5273 (5269, 5270)
Peterson M R, **8:** 4383
Peterson N G, **11:** 6678 (6671)
Peterson P, **3:** 1257, 1494 (1492), 1804 (1802); **5:** 2769 (2766); **9:** 5176; **10:** 6207 (6206)
Peterson P E, **7:** 3722 (3720); **11:** 6558 (6553)
Peterson P L, **1:** 12; **2:** 796 (792, 793, 794), 825, 1052 (1050); **3:** 1257 (1254, 1255, 1256); **6:** 3642 (3640); **9:** 5176; **10:** 5762 (5760), 5772 (5768, 5770), 5795 (5792, 5794), 6026 (6024, 6025), 6035 (6032, 6033), 6088, 6103 (6100), 6121 (6119), 6122 (6118), 6173 (6171), 6183 (6180), 6239 (6238)
Peterson R A, **3:** 1553; **6:** 3096
Peterson R E, **10:** 5643
Peterson R W, **1:** 376 (375), 377; **6:** 3685 (3677)
Peterson S, **3:** 1494 (1491)
Peterssen P, **5:** (2731)
Petillon H, **5:** 2479 (2478)
Petkov I, **2:** 661 (659)
Petree D L, **10:** 6073 (6071)
Petrei A H, **1:** 338
Petri H L, **7:** 3946 (3943)
Petrie H, **3:** 1607; **11:** 6726
Petrie H G, **8:** 4698; **10:** 5818 (5816); **11:** 6371
Petrinovich L, **4:** 2172 (2167)
Petroni F A, **9:** 5572 (5571)
Petrosko J, **2:** 1182 (1180)
Petruchenia J, **2:** 906
Petry C, **2:** 910 (908)
Pettersen K, **11:** 6731
Pettersson R, **7:** 3774 (3772, 3773, 3774)
Pettersson S, **4:** 2377 (2376)
Pettigrew T F, **3:** 1486 (1484); **5:** 2672 (2671); **8:** 4896 (4891, 4892)
Pettinger R, **4:** 2267 (2265)
Pettini A, **5:** (3031)
Pettito L A, **5:** 2685 (2682)
Pettitt G A, **3:** 1729 (1725)
Petty M, **1:** 338
Peukert H, **7:** 3924 (3922); **8:** 4461 (4459)
Peverly S T, **6:** 3339 (3337)
Pevsner N, **1:** 343 (339)
Peyton R B, **4:** 1995 (1992)
Pezeshkpour P, **11:** 6777 (6776)
Pezzullo T R, **8:** 4408 (4406); **9:** 4973
Pfaffmann C, **5:** 2802 (2800)
Pfeffer J, **4:** 2167; **6:** 3284 (3279); **7:** 3826 (3823)
Pfeffer L, **9:** 5013
Pfeifer R, **3:** 1690 (1686, 1690); **11:** 6452 (6447)
Pfeiffer H, **5:** 2480
Pfeiffer R S, **6:** 3602 (3599); **9:** 5223 (5222)
Pfennig R, **1:** (341)
Pfirrmann M, **3:** 1262 (1261)
Pfister G, **11:** 6747 (6747)
Pfleiderer J, **4:** 2439
Pfæler D, **4:** 2388
Pfundt H, **9:** 5342 (5339)
Phares V, **10:** 5738 (5736, 5737)
Pheasant S T, **4:** 2011 (2009)
Phelan P, **6:** 3209 (3208)
Phelan T, **6:** 3144 (3139)
Phelps E, **8:** 4372 (4369, 4370, 4371, 4372); **10:** 5758 (5758)
Phelps E S, **4:** 2445 (2444)
Phelps R, **2:** 982 (981)
Phenix P H, **3:** 1328 (1326), 1355 (1348, 1351), 1367 (1361, 1362); **6:** 3151
Phi Delta Kappan, **9:** 5268
Philip of Macedon, **8:** (4888)
Philipp E, **5:** 2529 (2526); **7:** 4240 (4239)
Philippi D L, **5:** 2655 (2652)
Philips B, **3:** 1762 (1759)
Philips D, **6:** 3496 (3496)
Philips D C, **4:** 2108
Philips S U, **2:** 803 (801), 917 (916); **4:** 2053 (2050); **6:** 3216 (3215); **7:** 4175 (4172, 4173); **9:** 5220 (5219), 5572 (5571)
Phillipps R W, **5:** 2856 (2853)
Phillips C B, **3:** 1636 (1633)
Phillips C E, **8:** 4715 (4709)
Phillips C J, **7:** 4171 (4166)
Phillips D A, **2:** 687, 688 (685, 686), 693 (689, 690, 691); **3:** 1636 (1634), 1643 (1639); **4:** 2100, 2145; **11:** 6397, 6398 (6395, 6396, 6397)
Phillips D C, **2:** 1031 (1027, 1030); **4:** 2037, 2089, 2108; **7:** 3925 (3921, 3924); **8:** 4455 (4452, 4455), 4536 (4532, 4535), 4634 (4630, 4632, 4634), 4783, 4875; **9:** 4980 (4978), 4981 (4978, 4979, 4980), 5030 (5022, 5027), 5031, 5055 (5054); **10:** 5708; **11:** 6579 (6577, 6579), 6580
Phillips D H, **3:** 1642 (1639)
Phillips G W, **3:** 1768 (1765); **4:** 2140 (2136), 2439 (2436); **6:** 3550 (3546); **7:** 4053 (4053); **9:** 5342 (5340), 5432 (5426)
Phillips J, **2:** 1152
Phillips J M, **1:** 254 (246, 247)
Phillips L D, **1:** 480; **7:** 4006 (4006)
Phillips P, **10:** 5674 (5668, 5673)
Phillips S U, **3:** 1233 (1227); **6:** 3227 (3226), 3238 (3236)
Phillips T, **6:** 3443
Phillips W E, **10:** 5977 (5974)
Phillipson R, **6:** 3439 (3436)
Phiri S, **11:** 6719
Phoenix A, **10:** 5826 (5823)
Phonekeo K, **6:** 3247
Piaget J, **1:** (113), (147), 570 (567); **2:** 705 (703), 838 (835), (841), (843), (850), 857 (852, 853, 854, 855), 860 (857, 858, 859), 1052; **3:** 1246 (1244, 1245), 1434 (1433), 1504 (1502), (1508), (1509), (1795); **4:** 1848 (1843), 1872 (1864, 1866, 1870), 2297 (2292, 2293); **5:** (2534), (2649), (2650), 2655 (2655), 2665 (2658, 2659, 2661, 2662), (2666), (2678), (2679), 2680 (2678), 2802 (2800, 2801), (2803), (2876), (2878), 2884 (2881), (2899), (2912), (2915), (3003); **6:** (3154), (3204), (3221), 3325 (3317), (3431), (3487), (3511), 3671 (3669), (3680), 3685 (3677, 3682, 3683); **7:** 3920 (3916, 3917), (3921), 3950 (3947, 3949), (4211); **8:** 4372 (4369), 4455 (4453), (4459), (4464), 4482 (4479, 4480, 4482), 4483 (4479, 4480, 4481, 4482), (4535), 4542 (4537), 4823 (4818, 4819), 4957 (4951, 4952, 4954); **9:** 5275 (5273), (5326), (5332), (5433), 5508 (5507), (5510), 5548 (5545); **10:** 5591 (5587), (5881), 5939 (5937), 6053 (6052), 6169 (6164, 6165, 6166, 6167, 6168), (6174), 6197 (6194), 6224 (6221)
Piatelli-Palmarini M, **6:** 3224
Pica T, **4:** 2339 (2332)
Pichert J W, **7:** 3768 (3766)
Piciga D, **9:** 5497 (5493)
Pick A D, **1:** 234; **5:** 2627
Pickar J, **6:** 3228
Pickard A, **10:** 5995 (5993)
Pickard D, **4:** 1924
Pickard L, **1:** 127 (121)
Pickering J, **10:** 5674 (5671)
Pickles A, **4:** 1934 (1933); **8:** 4395 (4391, 4393)
Picón C, **6:** 3256; **7:** 4275
Picot B, **9:** 5308 (5303)
Picus L O, **7:** 3821 (3819); **9:** 5185 (5185)
Pidgeon D A, **3:** 1768 (1762); **9:** 5389 (5388)
Piedermann M, **4:** 2012
Piehl E, **1:** 158 (155)
Pieke F N, **2:** 1213 (1211)
Piele P K, **1:** 77 (75); **6:** 3284
Pienemann M, **4:** 2339 (2333), 2364 (2360, 2362)
Piepho H E, **6:** 3443 (3440)
Pierce C, **2:** (1202)
Pierce J, **2:** 1031 (1026)
Pierce J L, **8:** 4896 (4893, 4894)
Pierce L C, **5:** 2500 (2498); **6:** 3196 (3190); **9:** 5307 (5306)
Piercy F P, **4:** 2261 (2261)
Piéron H, **4:** (1868)
Piéron M, **10:** 5713 (5708, 5709, 5710, 5712)
Pierrehumbert B, **8:** 4677 (4675)
Piersel W, **8:** 4661 (4659)
Piestrup A, **6:** 3238 (3236)
Pieters J P M, **2:** 992, 998; **6:** 3096 (3092); **8:** 4702
Pigelet J L, **11:** 6272 (6269)
Pigge F, **10:** 5957 (5956)
Piggins D, **2:** 1165 (1162)
Pigott T D, **6:** 3631 (3625, 3630)
Pijl S J, **2:** 729 (723); **5:** 2910 (2908)
Pike G, **3:** 1501; **4:** 1852 (1850)
Pikowsky B, **8:** 4951 (4949)
Pile W, **8:** 4562 (4560)
Pilecki F J, **3:** 1774 (1770)

Pillemer D B, **7:** 3872 (3866); **10:** 6240
Pilot A, **6:** 3401 (3401)
Piltz A, **9:** 5124
Pimm D, **6:** 3638 (3635)
Pimsleur P, **4:** 2346 (2343)
Pinar W F, **3:** 1266 (1264), 1301 (1289), 1333, 1337 (1335), 1338; **5:** 2697 (2695); **7:** 4051 (4047)
Pinborg J, **9:** 5124
Pincus J, **10:** 5590 (5590)
Pine F, **8:** 4816 (4813, 4814)
Pine J, **8:** 4730 (4730)
Pineau G, **6:** 3421 (3419)
Pineo P C, **7:** 3711, 3722 (3717, 3718)
Pinera S, **8:** 4666 (4665)
Pines A, **10:** 5925 (5920, 5922), 6062 (6060)
Pines L A, **10:** 5790
Pink W T, **2:** 893 (892)
Pinker S, **8:** 4945 (4942)
Pinnegar P, **10:** 6026 (6023)
Pinnegar S, **10:** 5762 (5761), 6183
Pinnell G S, **3:** 1538 (1537); **6:** 3443 (3441); **8:** 4935; **10:** 5795 (5792)
Pinochet A, **7:** (4142)
Pintrich P R, **1:** 204 (202); **2:** 868 (866), 969 (966); **6:** 3329 (3328), 3339 (3335), 3345 (3344)
Piolat A, **2:** 1006 (1005)
Piore M J, **3:** 1703 (1696), 1713 (1708); **4:** 1975 (1973); **5:** 2942 (2940, 2941); **6:** 3189 (3184, 3185, 3186, 3187, 3188); **7:** 4211 (4210); **8:** 4639 (4636), 4839 (4837)
Piotrkowski C S, **7:** 4301 (4299)
Pious C G, **6:** 3297 (3293, 3295); **7:** 3833 (3831)
Pipe P, **6:** 3096 (3093)
Piper D W, **4:** 2291
Pipho C, **3:** 1337 (1336)
Pipp S, **3:** 1513 (1508, 1509, 1510, 1511, 1513); **5:** 2680 (2679)
Pires B V, **6:** 3545 (3539)
Pires E, **8:** 4622 (4617)
Pirie S, **6:** 3638 (3635)
Pisoni D B, **11:** 6457
Pissarides C A, **3:** 1449
Pissart F, **11:** 6807 (6805)
Pita de Melo A M, **9:** 5228 (5224, 5227)
Pitcher G D, **10:** 6031
Piternick A B, **4:** 1958 (1955)
Pitman M A, **3:** 1729 (1728); **4:** 2045, 2046 (2043); **11:** 6466 (6462)
Pitman T, **1:** 31
Pitner N J, **9:** 5181 (5178), 5223 (5222)
Pitt J, **4:** 2302
Pittman J, **3:** 1257 (1253)
Pitts-Conway V, **11:** 6461 (6459)
Pizzamiglio L, **2:** 871 (870)
Plake B S, **1:** 53 (51); **5:** 3050 (3044); **10:** 5725 (5725), 6020; **11:** 6677, 6678
Plamenatz J V, **5:** 2737
Plancke R L, **2:** 948
Plank D N, **2:** 933 (929); **4:** 1841 (1839); **6:** 3608; **7:** 3960; **8:** 4595 (4588, 4590, 4592, 4593); **11:** 6563 (6559, 6560, 6561, 6562)
Plant M, **11:** 6615
Plas J M, **1:** 494 (492)
Plaschka G, **4:** 1991 (1987)
Plaskow M, **3:** 1278 (1275)
Platek R, **7:** 3858
Plato, **1:** (195), (274); **2:** (776), (804); **3:** (1338), (1520); **4:** 2001 (1996); **5:** (2608), (2693); **6:** (3418); **7:** (3920), (3924); **8:** (4442), (4444), 4456 (4448, 4449, 4452), (4460), 4536 (4532, 4533, 4534, 4535), 4575 (4572), (4575), (4596), (4641), (4667), (4671), (4888), (4889); **9:** 4981 (4978), (5122), (5395), (5412); **10:** (6173); **11:** (6578), (6622), (6742)
Platsidou M, **5:** 2669 (2668, 2669)
Platt G, **2:** 1074 (1065)
Platt J, **4:** 2330 (2328)
Platt J J, **3:** 1441
Platt J R, **5:** 2714 (2710)
Plattor E, **6:** 3443 (3440)
Playko M A, **1:** 72 (70, 72)
Pleines J E, **8:** 4461 (4458)
Plekker S J, **10:** 5635
Plemons J K, **9:** 5528 (5525)
Plewis I, **1:** 362 (361); **2:** 678 (673); **4:** 1938 (1935)
Pliny the Younger, **8:** (4887)
Ploman E W, **1:** 162; **8:** 4526
Plomin R, **1:** 234 (232); **2:** 846 (845); **3:** 1642 (1639), 1647; **4:** 2249 (2247), 2261 (2258); **5:** 2465 (2463, 2464, 2465), 2665 (2660); **7:** 3743 (3741); **8:** 4394 (4389); **10:** 6159; **11:** 6310 (6308), 6492 (6488, 6489, 6490, 6491)
Plomp T, **2:** 957, 977 (973, 974, 975, 976, 977), 985 (983), 991 (990, 991), 992, 1002, 1006 (1002), 1011 (1009, 1010), 1012 (1008, 1009, 1010); **3:** 1315, 1421, 1494 (1493), 1768 (1764), 1779; **4:** 1899 (1883), 1918 (1915, 1916, 1917), 1924 (1920), 2427 (2424, 2425); **5:** 2862 (2857); **6:** 3096; **7:** 3810 (3808), 4088 (4083, 4084, 4085), 4104 (4102); **8:** 4352, 4803; **10:** 6008 (6005, 6006); **11:** 6287 (6283, 6284, 6285, 6286)
Ploog D, **4:** 2172
Plotke H, **6:** 3276 (3273, 3275)
Plotnicov L, **9:** 5572 (5568)
Plötzner R, **8:** 4722 (4721)
Plouffe S, **1:** 299 (299)
Ploug Olsen T, **5:** 2852 (2851)
Plumer D, **6:** 3216 (3214)
Plutarch, **4:** (2006)
Pocklington K, **5:** 2910; **10:** 5957 (5956), 5995 (5993)
Podell D M, **10:** 5674 (5671)
Podeschi R, **1:** 168 (166)
Pöggeler F, **1:** 139 (135, 138), 152 (145), 277 (275, 276), 504; **7:** 3925
Poggio G F B, **8:** (4889)
Pogrow S, **3:** 1784 (1779); **10:** 5674 (5671)
Pogrund B, **10:** 5843
Poignant R, **11:** 6684
Polachek S, **1:** 111 (107); **4:** 2279 (2275)
Poland S, **10:** 6031
Polanyi M, **3:** 1434 (1432); **4:** (1870); **10:** 5745 (5740)
Polgar S, **9:** 5220 (5218)
Polirstok S R, **8:** 4376 (4372, 4373)
Politz A, **7:** 3858 (3856)
Politzer R L, **6:** 3334 (3331)
Polkinghorne D E, **7:** 4051 (4046)
Pollack J M, **3:** 1606 (1604, 1605); **5:** 2862; **9:** 5228 (5224, 5228)
Pollack M, **4:** 2440 (2438)
Pollack R A, **10:** 5674 (5668)
Pollack S, **11:** 6726 (6725)
Pollak R A, **3:** 1676 (1673); **4:** 2278 (2277); **6:** 3144 (3142)
Pollard A, **2:** 1074 (1070, 1071); **10:** 6219 (6218)
Pollard D, **4:** 1958; **11:** 6726 (6725), 6727
Pollard J, **11:** 6384 (6379)
Pollard L A, **11:** 6765 (6762, 6763)
Pollard S J, **6:** 3148
Pollen P, **10:** 5854
Pollitt A, **7:** 4307
Pollitt D, **5:** 2567 (2565)
Pollitt E, **3:** 1628 (1626, 1627); **4:** 1852 (1850), 2258; **5:** 2567; **8:** 4677 (4676)
Pollock G, **8:** 4816
Pollock J, **10:** 5913 (5911)
Pollock L A, **5:** 2618
Pollock M, **5:** 2572
Polsgrove L, **1:** 494 (493)
Polsky R, **5:** 2897 (2893)
Polson C, **2:** 1165 (1162)
Polson P, **8:** 4731 (4729)
Pólturzycki J, **2:** 661 (659, 660)
Polya G, **6:** (3632); **8:** 4648 (4643), 4727 (4723); **10:** 6026 (6022)
Pomeroy S B, **11:** 6747 (6742)
Pomeroy W B, **8:** 4887 (4883)
Pomfret A, **3:** 1257 (1255), 1431 (1427), 1494 (1492)
Ponce de Leon P, **10:** (5658)
Poncelet M, **11:** 6807 (6805)
Pond L, **1:** 194 (186)
Ponder G A, **3:** 1494 (1491)
Ponder P, **3:** 1406 (1405)
Pondy L R, **4:** 2166 (2164)
Pönisch H, **6:** 3213 (3211)
Pons M M, **6:** 3335 (3332)
Pontalis J B, **8:** 4816
Ponte J P, **6:** 3652; **7:** 4100 (4097)
Pontecorvo C, **8:** 4951 (4949); **9:** 5507 (5506), 5508 (5507), 5562 (5561)
Ponti C R, **5:** 2907 (2905); **8:** 4662 (4658, 4659)
Pool I D S, **2:** 1079
Poole K P, **6:** 3360; **9:** 5255
Poole M E, **1:** 358 (356); **11:** 6798 (6794, 6796)
Poon L W, **1:** 239; **8:** 4824
Poortinga Y H, **5:** 2651; **11:** 6320 (6316), 6334 (6329, 6330, 6332)
Pope M, **2:** 1006; **7:** 3791; **9:** 5562
Pope M L, **9:** 5016
Popham J W, **10:** 6035 (6032)
Popham W J, **2:** 1189 (1183, 1185); **3:** 1266 (1264), 1804; **4:** 2097 (2089), 2108 (2104); **5:** 3043 (3036); **7:** 3726 (3722, 3723); **8:** 4766 (4759); **10:** 5726 (5721, 5722),

5822, 5887, 5957 (5954, 5955); **11:** 6339 (6338)
Popkewitz T, **9:** 5030 (5022); **11:** 6722
Popkewitz T L, **5:** 2779 (2776)
Popkewitz T S, **1:** 127 (125); **3:** 1308 (1305, 1306); **9:** 5299 (5298); **10:** 5614, 6086
Poplack S, **6:** 3227 (3225)
Popp M, **9:** 5359 (5357)
Popper K R, **2:** 645 (641), (924); **3:** (1540); **4:** (1870), 2001 (1998); **5:** 2714 (2710); **7:** 3872 (3868); **8:** 4456 (4448), (4632), (4633), (4874); **9:** (4979), 5050, 5335 (5330), (5461); **11:** 6579 (6576, 6577)
Popper S H, **6:** 3284
Popping R, **10:** 5735 (5734)
Poppleton P, **10:** 5925 (5921, 5923, 5924), 6139 (6138)
Porcher L, **4:** 2357 (2354); **6:** 3213 (3210)
Porges S W, **3:** 1520 (1518)
Portal C, **9:** 5563
Portecarero, **7:** 3721 (3718)
Porter A, **3:** 1257 (1254); **4:** 1984 (1981, 1982); **8:** 4571 (4569); **10:** 6112 (6111); **11:** 6390 (6388)
Porter A C, **7:** 3725 (3724)
Porter A T, **9:** 5460
Porter G L, **3:** 1508; **6:** 3559 (3558)
Porter J, **7:** 3722 (3717, 3718)
Porter L W, **4:** 1972 (1967)
Porter M, **3:** 1713 (1708)
Porter M E, **4:** 2394 (2389)
Porter P, **3:** 1720 (1715, 1716)
Porter R J, **6:** 3297; **8:** 4424
Porter R L, **3:** 1411
Portes A, **1:** 358 (357); **6:** 3189 (3188); **8:** 4638, 4896 (4892)
Portocarero L, **10:** 5735 (5731)
Portwood D, **7:** 4249 (4248)
Posch P, **1:** 47 (45), 431 (431), 432 (431); **4:** 1995 (1991); **9:** 5246 (5242); **10:** 6099 (6097)
Posey L, **2:** 1020, 1026
Posner G J, **3:** 1334; **8:** 4652 (4651); **10:** 5790 (5784), 5887
Posner M I, **1:** 331 (328), 377 (375); **7:** 3953 (3951, 3952); **8:** 4722
Post D, **1:** 358 (357); **2:** 1042 (1038, 1041)
Post T A, **4:** 2199 (2196, 2197)
Post T R, **6:** 3684 (3676)
Poster C D, **2:** 906, 907 (908), 910; **6:** 3603 (3598); **10:** 5972, 6020
Poster D, **6:** 3603 (3598); **10:** 6020
Postiglione G A, **5:** 2643 (2637)
Postlethwait S N, **8:** 4774 (4773)
Postlethwaite T N, **1:** 127, 152 (144), 158, 176, 184, 390 (381), 396 (393); **2:** 640, 645, 662, 775 (770, 772), 910, 947, 957 (953, 954), 1052, 1107; **3:** 1257, 1266, 1283, 1308, 1315, 1325, 1374, 1443, 1482 (1478), 1494, 1573, 1589, 1593, 1655, 1720, 1768 (1762, 1764), 1789; **4:** 1841 (1835, 1836, 1837), 1934 (1929), 1947, 2140 (2134, 2137, 2139), 2180 (2174), 2310, 2375, 2440 (2437); **5:** 2470, 2631 (2629), 2779, 2856 (2853), 2978, 2989 (2988), 3011; **6:** 3204, 3205, 3389, 3398, 3399 (3395), 3416, 3421, 3435, 3474, 3585, 3642, 3685; **7:** 3722 (3721), 3840, 3935, 3970, 4016, 4054, 4100, 4236 (4234); **8:** 4359, 4388, 4514, 4526, 4536, 4811, 4812, 4823, 4881, 4964; **9:** 5142 (5131), 5216, 5324 (5322), 5335 (5333), 5373 (5369), 5385 (5380), 5432; **10:** 5591, 5607, 5643, 5745, 5795, 5862 (5855), 5895, 5929, 5948 (5943), 5977, 6015, 6155 (6154), 6178, 6239; **11:** 6287, 6339, 6340, 6384, 6390 (6389), 6395, 6445, 6507, 6653, 6678, 6777
Postman N, **5:** 2897 (2896); **6:** 3151 (3151); **7:** 3775 (3774)
Pott D, **10:** 5866
Potter D A, **9:** 5264 (5263)
Potts G R, **11:** 6457
Potts M, **2:** 867 (863)
Potts P, **9:** 5071; **11:** 6461
Pouissant A, **1:** 296 (292)
Poulantzas N A, **3:** 1720 (1715); **6:** 3622
Poulos G, **3:** 1607 (1604)
Poulton G, **7:** 4248 (4247)
Pouncy H, **1:** 310 (309)
Pounder D G, **8:** 4408 (4405, 4406)
Pourtois J P, **4:** 2267
Powell A, **1:** 12; **10:** 6012 (6009)
Powell A G, **9:** 5379 (5374, 5376, 5377); **11:** 6538
Powell B, **9:** 5385 (5382)
Powell C, **4:** 2292; **5:** 2575 (2572)
Powell D R, **3:** 1636 (1629, 1630, 1633); **7:** 4296 (4295, 4296), 4300, 4301 (4296, 4297)
Powell G E, **8:** 4408 (4405)
Powell J, **7:** 3996 (3993); **11:** 6370 (6368)
Powell J P, **7:** 4170 (4166, 4168)
Powell J S, **5:** 2916 (2911)
Powell M, **10:** 6043 (6036)
Powell S, **1:** 494 (492); **7:** 4056 (4056); **10:** 5725 (5722, 5724)
Power C N, **6:** 3204 (3203); **7:** 3912 (3906, 3911); **9:** 5338 (5336), 5338 (5337); **10:** 6149 (6148)
Power E, **5:** 2575
Power F C, **1:** 380 (379); **7:** 3920 (3919)
Powers A R, **7:** 3833 (3832)
Powers D E, **7:** 3935 (3935); **11:** 6339 (6336, 6337, 6338)
Powers D P, **1:** 495; **3:** 1402 (1399)
Powers M G, **7:** 3722 (3717)
Powers T F, **11:** 6704 (6700)
Powles M, **7:** 4171 (4166)
Powlishta K, **4:** 2452 (2450)
Poyen J, **4:** 2351 (2350)
Pozo J I, **2:** 1006; **9:** 5562 (5560, 5561)
Pozo M, **7:** 3791
Prader A, **5:** 2685 (2683); **8:** 4474 (4471, 4472)
Pradervand P, **3:** 1501 (1495, 1498, 1499)
Prais S J, **4:** 2394 (2391); **6:** 3092; **11:** 6420 (6419), 6638 (6636), 6640
Prakash B, **8:** 4488 (4487)
Prakasha V, **7:** 4136 (4135)
Prasiidananda A, **4:** 2331
Prater D, **2:** 1031 (1028)
Pratt D, **1:** 230 (227, 229); **7:** 4157 (4157)
Pratt D D, **1:** 120 (117), 168 (166); **10:** 6058 (6055, 6056), 6202 (6198)
Pratt J, **8:** 4608
Pratt S, **9:** 5169 (5162)
Pratte R, **2:** 770 (767, 769, 770)
Pratzner F C, **1:** 310; **3:** 1449
Prawat R S, **3:** 1504 (1503); **10:** 5745 (5741)
Prawatt R, **7:** 3791 (3790)
Prawda J, **6:** 3608 (3606, 3607); **8:** 4495 (4494); **9:** 5169 (5166, 5167)
Prechtl H F R, **3:** 1520 (1518); **7:** 3950 (3948)
Prediger D J, **11:** 6678 (6675, 6676)
Preissle J, **3:** 1253; **11:** 6466
Preiswerk R, **5:** 2623 (2622)
Premfors R, **1:** 127 (120, 126)
Prentice A, **10:** 5613 (5609), 6139 (6133, 6135); **11:** 6727 (6724), 6765 (6761, 6762, 6764)
Prentice R L, **4:** 2156 (2151)
Prenzel M, **6:** 3306 (3304)
Prescott C, **11:** 6307 (6306)
Prescott D R, **10:** 6004 (6001)
Presley R, **11:** 6310 (6309)
Press S J, **3:** 1425
Presseisen B Z, **8:** 4957
Presser H B, **4:** 2432 (2430)
Presser R C, **7:** 4145 (4142)
Presser S, **8:** 4887 (4885); **10:** 5862 (5857)
Pressley M, **1:** 194 (191); **2:** 867; **3:** 1529 (1526); **4:** 2194 (2189, 2191), 2281 (2280); **6:** 3329 (3326, 3327), 3334 (3331, 3333), 3335; **7:** 3763 (3760, 3761, 3762), 3768 (3765, 3766, 3767), 3920; **8:** 4942 (4941); **10:** 5831 (5829, 5830, 5831), 6177 (6177), 6178 (6175)
Pressman J L, **8:** 4519 (4515)
Prest A R, **10:** 5768 (5765)
Preston D R, **4:** 2339 (2332)
Preusker K, **1:** (137)
Preuss-Lausitz U, **10:** 6244 (6243)
Prewitt K, **8:** 4581; **9:** 5350 (5348)
Preyer W, **4:** (1864), (1865)
Pribram K H, **3:** 1434 (1432)
Price B, **7:** 3986 (3984), 4015 (4009)
Price E, **11:** 6784 (6784)
Price G G, **7:** 4300 (4299, 4300), 4301 (4300)
Price J L, **10:** 5925 (5923)
Price K, **11:** 6579 (6578)
Price L A, **7:** 3879 (3874)
Price L M, **7:** 3833 (3832)
Price M, **2:** 860 (860)
Price R, **8:** 4394
Price R F, **2:** 1064; **8:** 4608 (4606)
Price R G, **3:** 1690, 1739 (1737)
Price R H, **8:** 4394, 4719; **11:** 6266 (6263)
Price-Williams D, **3:** 1240 (1239)
Prick L G M, **10:** 6000
Pridham B R, **11:** 6793
Priest R F, **9:** 5406 (5404)
Prillaman D, **5:** 2491 (2486, 2487)
Prince G M, **5:** 2725 (2723)
Prince J S, **10:** 5804 (5797)
Pring R, **3:** 1328 (1326)
Pringle I, **6:** 3209

Pringle M L K, **9:** 5532 (5530)
Pringle R, **7:** 3853 (3849)
Prins D J, **10:** 5804 (5796, 5798, 5801, 5802, 5803)
Prinsloo J, **7:** 3760 (3759)
Prior M R, **1:** 553 (553); **6:** 3235 (3232); **7:** 4081
Pritchard W H, **2:** 1175 (1173, 1174)
Pritzel M, **1:** 554 (552)
Prizant B M, **6:** 3235 (3232, 3233)
Probald F, **5:** 2470 (2468)
Probst P, **6:** 3459 (3454)
Procter T B, **9:** 5532 (5531)
Proctor C H, **10:** 5617 (5615)
Proctor C P, **10:** 5826 (5823)
Prokop C M, **9:** 5181 (5176, 5178); **10:** 5924 (5920), 6062 (6059)
Pronovost G, **10:** 5834 (5833)
Propper C, **2:** 1094
Propst S, **4:** 1980 (1976, 1978)
Prosser C, **3:** (1299); **11:** 6538 (6530)
Prosser M, **1:** 322 (321)
Prosser M T, **6:** 3205 (3203)
Prosser R, **4:** 1934 (1932); **5:** 2961 (2959)
Prosser R C, **1:** 152 (144); **4:** 2369 (2365); **6:** 3261 (3257)
Prosser R J, **7:** 4094 (4090)
Prost A, **4:** 2385
Proudhon P-J, **8:** 4575 (4573)
Prouty R W, **3:** 1438 (1434); **6:** 3550 (3546)
Provence S, **1:** 362 (359, 361); **3:** 1624 (1621, 1622)
Provenzo E F, **10:** 6183
Provus M M, **1:** 230 (228); **4:** (2102); **10:** 5957 (5954)
Prucha J, **6:** 3608 (3605)
Prunty J J, **2:** 1204 (1199)
Pruzek R M, **9:** 4974 (4972)
Pryor B W, **7:** 4325 (4322, 4323, 4324)
Pryzwansky W B, **9:** 5290 (5287), 5291 (5286, 5289)
Psacharopoulos G, **1:** 135 (129, 130), 423, 520 (518), 560 (554); **2:** 760 (759), 1055 (1053), 1094 (1090, 1092), 1127 (1124, 1125), 1131 (1128, 1129, 1131); **3:** 1449 (1445), 1655 (1648, 1649, 1653, 1654), 1660 (1659), 1666 (1661, 1662), 1685 (1684), 1707 (1703), 1740, 1784 (1781), 1789 (1787, 1788), 1793, 1810, 1820 (1810, 1818, 1819), 1821 (1813), 1834 (1831); **4:** 1911, 2316 (2314), 2419 (2414); **5:** 2523, 2647 (2644, 2645, 2646), 2744, 2942 (2940), 2945 (2944, 2945), 2993; **6:** 3074, 3262 (3257), 3613 (3610, 3613); **7:** 4201 (4200), 4236; **8:** 4488, 4489, 4509 (4505), 4526 (4522), 4531 (4527, 4528, 4529), 4595 (4587), 4601 (4596), 4688 (4682, 4687), 4707 (4705), 4839 (4837), 4845 (4843), 4902, 4918 (4915, 4916); **9:** 5076 (5072, 5073, 5074), 5169 (5162, 5166, 5167), 5241 (5234, 5239), 5355 (5352, 5353); **10:** 5754 (5751, 5752), 5768 (5765); **11:** 6256 (6254, 6255), 6260 (6260), 6266 (6263), 6298 (6293, 6294, 6295), 6599 (6593, 6599), 6633 (6628), 6664 (6663)
Ptolemy, **9:** (5122)
Ptolemy C, **9:** (5051)
Puchner L, **6:** 3480 (3475)
Pudasaini S P, **1:** 254 (245, 247, 252)
Pufall P B, **8:** 4483
Pufendorf S, **6:** (3499)
Pugach M C, **8:** 4661 (4659, 4661), 4662 (4657, 4658, 4661); **9:** 5071 (5070); **10:** 6088 (6088), 6219
Pugh G, **4:** 2267
Pugh R C, **2:** 631 (629, 630); **6:** 3202 (3199, 3200); **8:** 4881 (4880)
Pugno L, **6:** 3151
Pühler S, **7:** 4325 (4321, 4322)
Puig de la Bellacasa R, **1:** 408 (405)
Pulakos E D, **11:** 6320 (6320)
Pulkkis A, **5:** 2689 (2688)
Pullin D C, **10:** 5818 (5815)
Pullis M E, **11:** 6310 (6309)
Punch K F, **4:** 2166 (2158)
Punch M, **4:** 2033
Punsalmaagiin Ochirbat, **7:** (3896)
Puntasen A, **2:** 910 (908)
Purcell-Gates V, **6:** 3453 (3447, 3449, 3451)
Purdy M, **6:** 3442
Puri M L, **7:** 4163 (4161)
Purkey C, **5:** 2509 (2507)
Purkey S C, **9:** 5379 (5373); **10:** 5750 (5746); **11:** 6558 (6554)
Puro P, **2:** 820 (819)
Purpel D E, **3:** 1307, 1337 (1334); **5:** 2589; **6:** 3276 (3275); **10:** 5991 (5989), 6004 (6002)
Purves A C, **1:** 396 (393), 482 (482), 483; **2:** 738 (734), 958, 1107; **3:** 1278 (1277), 1355 (1349), 1768 (1763, 1764, 1765); **4:** 2024 (2018, 2019, 2020), 2025, 2140 (2134); **5:** 2697, 2856 (2853); **6:** 3483 (3481), 3484 (3481, 3483); **7:** 3726 (3724), 3936, 4196 (4195); **10:** 5750 (5749), 6155; **11:** 6390, 6777 (6776, 6777)
Purvis J, **11:** 6765
Puryear J M, **7:** 4201 (4197); **9:** 5076 (5073, 5074, 5075); **11:** 6266 (6263)
Pusch M D, **7:** 3970 (3962)
Pusci L, **6:** 3593
Pusey M R, **6:** 3373 (3370)
Putnam H, **9:** 4981 (4978, 4979)
Putnam R T, **10:** 6088 (6087), 6122 (6119)
Pütz W, **7:** 4026 (4023)
Pyart B, **7:** 3889 (3888)
Pyart S, **7:** 3889 (3888)
Pyke L, **9:** 5544 (5542)
Pyl S J, **5:** 2907 (2904); **6:** 3559 (3559)
Pylyshyn Z W, **2:** 856 (853); **8:** 4722 (4719)
Pysh M V, **8:** 4661 (4658); **10:** 6244 (6240)
Pythagoras, **8:** (4767); **11:** (6622)

Qadhafi M, **6:** 3407 (3402, 3405)
Qiwei M A, **8:** 4468
Quade D, **7:** 4163 (4161)
Quadling D A, **6:** 3668
Quaine A, **2:** 1170 (1168)
Quandt S, **5:** 2623
Quantz R A, **7:** 4225 (4222, 4223)
Quay H C, **9:** 5070 (5068), 5071 (5068), 5528 (5527)
Quellmalz E S, **4:** 2024 (2019, 2023)
Quenouille M H, **9:** 5130 (5127)
Quetelet A, **4:** (1867)
Quicke J C, **11:** 6484 (6483)
Quigley A, **9:** 5060 (5058)
Quigley B A, **7:** 4329 (4326)
Quigley J M, **2:** 1094 (1085)
Quillian M R, **2:** 1031 (1027, 1029)
Quine W V O, **3:** 1475, 1774 (1773); **4:** (2300); **9:** 4981 (4980), 5030 (5027, 5028, 5029)
Quinlan M, **10:** 5827 (5823, 5824)
Quinn B, **2:** 1136 (1134)
Quinn C N, **2:** 982 (978)
Quinn D W, **3:** 1567 (1567)
Quinn N, **6:** 3453 (3450); **9:** 5220 (5218)
Quinn R, **6:** 3227 (3226)
Quinn R P, **10:** 5924 (5920, 5921), 6062 (6060)
Quinn W, **2:** 910 (907)
Quintanilla S A R, **6:** 3434 (3433)
Quintilian M F, **4:** (2006); **8:** 4890 (4888); **11:** (6412), (6482)
Quirk T J, **10:** 6020 (6017)
Quist R D, **1:** 409 (404, 405)
Quitmann H, **5:** 2692 (2690, 2691)
Quittner A L, **4:** 1877 (1874)
Quyine W V, **9:** 5050
Qvistgaard J, **4:** 2357

Raaheim K, **1:** 194 (184)
Raapke H D, **4:** 2267
Raaum O, **4:** 1976 (1974)
Raban C, **11:** 6557
Rabehl G, **5:** 3066 (3063)
Rabelais F, **8:** (4889); **10:** (5814)
Rabin A I, **8:** 4791
Rabinow P, **3:** 1774 (1772); **5:** 2586; **8:** 4642
Rabukawaqa E, **4:** 2310
Rachlin M, **11:** 6775
Racino J A, **3:** 1508
Rackliffe G, **10:** 6149 (6147, 6148)
Rada R D, **2:** 1074 (1066)
Radcliff D, **4:** 2369 (2364)
Rade L, **6:** 3685
Rademacher C, **11:** 6798 (6794)
Radev R, **2:** 1175 (1174); **10:** 5625 (5624)
Radford J, **1:** 194 (184); **5:** 2495
Radford W C, **9:** 5038 (5032)
Radice G L, **5:** (3031)
Radin N, **9:** 5291 (5287)
Radke-Yarrow M, **8:** 4799 (4797, 4798, 4799)
Radley G W, **9:** 5475 (5474)
Radner R, **3:** 1449, 1784, 1821 (1817); **9:** 5240
Raffe D, **7:** 3895 (3894); **8:** 4562 (4559, 4560); **9:** 5367 (5364); **11:** 6690 (6686)
Ragan W B, **9:** 5578 (5573)
Raggatt P, **11:** 6699 (6694, 6695)
Raghavan K, **9:** 5563 (5562)
Raghu R, **11:** 6558 (6552), 6563 (6559)
Ragin C, **3:** 1655 (1650)
Ragosta M, **3:** 1486 (1484)
Ragozin A S, **4:** 1979 (1976)
Ragsdale R G, **2:** 1012

Rahman M A, **1:** 47 (45); **2:** 906 (903), 1049; **7:** 4336 (4330)
Rahnema M, **7:** 4336 (4334)
Raiffa H, **3:** 1425
Rainbow B, **7:** 4027
Rainbow E, **7:** 4026 (4022)
Rainforth B, **5:** 2814 (2809)
Raisian J, **5:** 2942 (2940)
Raivola R, **4:** 2324
Raizen S A, **7:** 3726 (3724); **8:** 4479 (4475); **9:** 5232 (5229); **11:** 6415 (6412)
Raj D, **9:** 5142
Rajan M S, **1:** 563 (563)
Rajangu V, **4:** 2029
Rajaoson, **6:** 3556
Rajaratnam N, **1:** 41 (33); **5:** 2462 (2458, 2459), 3061 (3057); **9:** 4995 (4981)
Raju N, **5:** 3050 (3048)
Rakel R E, **3:** 1618, 1619
Rakhyoot A M, **7:** 4206
Rakic P, **7:** 3950
Ralston A, **6:** 3685 (3683)
Ram R, **1:** 254 (246); **5:** 2744 (2742)
Rama G, **2:** 1042 (1042); **6:** 3262 (3258, 3261)
Ramachandran K, **7:** 4140 (4140)
Ramanaiah N, **1:** 322 (319)
Ramasut A, **10:** 5943 (5941)
Ramazanoglu C, **9:** 5441 (5437, 5438)
Rambaran R, **10:** 5834 (5833)
Ramberg M, **3:** 1779 (1776)
Ramdas L, **1:** 162 (160); **11:** 6719
Ramdoyal R D, **7:** 3698
Ramesar E D, **2:** 640
Ramey C T, **3:** 1642 (1641), 1643 (1640); **5:** 2806 (2804)
Ramirez B A, **6:** 3232
Ramirez F O, **2:** 933 (928); **10:** 5607 (5600)
Ramírez J, **6:** 3267
Ramírez M, **2:** 872 (871); **3:** 1240 (1239)
Ramo S, **4:** 1899 (1887)
Ramos F V, **8:** (4438)
Ramos P, **5:** 2562 (2559)
Ramos-Ford V, **5:** 2732 (2726)
Ramp E A, **10:** 6164
Rampaul W E, **2:** 729 (728); **5:** 2972 (2967, 2968, 2969, 2970)
Rampton A, **11:** 6523 (6522)
Ramsay P, **9:** 5268 (5265, 5266, 5267)
Ramsay P D K, **3:** 1411 (1409); **4:** 1934 (1929)
Ramsden P, **1:** 193 (188, 190), 194 (189, 192), 322 (318, 319, 320); **8:** 4429; **9:** 5411 (5410); **10:** 5790 (5788)
Ramsey E, **8:** 4368 (4367)
Ramsey F P, **1:** 480 (477)
Ramsey G, **9:** 5544 (5540)
Ramsey J M, **4:** 1995 (1993)
Ramsey P D K, **3:** 1320 (1318)
Ramsland S E, **8:** 4376 (4374)
Ranaweera A M, **3:** 1262 (1260), 1367 (1360, 1366); **7:** 4136 (4133)
Rand D C, **4:** 2296 (2295)
Rand P, **5:** 2769 (2764); **7:** 3942 (3940)
Rand Y, **2:** 860 (858, 859), 867 (862); **3:** 1504 (1503); **5:** 2768 (2762); **6:** 3315 (3313); **8:** 4731 (4729)
Randahl G J, **11:** 6678 (6675)
Randall P E, **9:** 4977 (4976)
Randle L, **7:** 4248 (4247)
Raney L, **3:** 1824 (1822)
Ranftl-Guggenberger D, **11:** 6731
Rang A, **8:** 4419 (4419)
Rang M, **3:** 1301 (1290)
Rangel J, **6:** 3545
Ranis G, **3:** 1685 (1682); **11:** 6638
Rankin E F Jr, **10:** 6132 (6131); **11:** 6349 (6343)
Ransley W, **3:** 1553 (1551)
Ransom E, **9:** 5217
Ransom K, **8:** 4881 (4878)
Ranson S, **8:** 4601 (4598)
Rantanen J, **10:** 5621
Rao A N, **1:** 244
Rao C R, **3:** 1549 (1545, 1546); **8:** 4912 (4902)
Rao J N K, **7:** 3858 (3856); **9:** 5130 (5128)
Rao M J M, **9:** 5355 (5353, 5354)
Rao T, **4:** 1991 (1986)
Rao V K R V, **5:** 2758 (2758)
Rapaport D, **8:** 4791 (4790)
Rapaport M, **4:** 1958
Raphael T E, **8:** 4881 (4880); **10:** 5795 (5793), 6015 (6014)
Raphael T M, **2:** 867 (861)
Rapin I, **10:** 5680 (5675, 5676, 5677)
Rapoport A, **9:** 5056
Rapple B A, **9:** 5206 (5202)
Rasbash J, **4:** 1934 (1932)
Rasch G, **1:** 52 (50); **2:** 792 (786), 998 (994); **3:** 1514 (1510); **4:** 2017 (2012); **6:** 3253 (3250); **7:** 3707 (3700, 3702); **8:** 4912 (4902, 4904, 4906), 4913 (4902, 4904, 4905); **11:** 6388 (6387)
Rasch J, **1:** 432 (431)
Rasch M, **2:** 1019 (1018), 1026 (1021, 1022); **5:** 2874 (2872)
Rasera J-B, **5:** 2993 (2989); **6:** 3556
Rasmussen D, **4:** 2033 (2030)
Rasmussen E T, **3:** (1724)
Rasmussen S, **7:** 4100 (4098)
Rasmussen V, **10:** (5913)
Rasmusson R, **2:** 914 (911)
Rasp A, **3:** 1443
Rassekh S, **2:** 1107 (1106); **3:** 1278 (1277), 1355 (1351), 1367 (1361, 1362, 1363); **8:** 4812
Ratcliff B, **8:** 4803 (4801)
Rathbone C J, **7:** 4214 (4212)
Raths J D, **10:** 5812, 5948, 5957 (5955, 5956), 5994, 5995 (5994)
Ratke W, **3:** (1289, 1303)
Ratoosh P, **6:** 3124
Rattansi A, **2:** 1194; **11:** 6769
Ratzeberu F H, **10:** 5686 (5681)
Ratzlaff H C, **3:** 1635 (1632); **10:** 6004 (6000)
Rauch J M, **1:** 88 (87)
Raudenbush S W, **1:** 520 (516), 521 (516); **2:** 677 (677); **3:** 1513 (1512); **4:** 1938 (1936), 1939 (1934, 1937), 2388 (2386); **5:** 2595 (2590, 2594), 2596 (2590, 2591, 2593, 2594, 2595), 2931 (2930); **6:** 3523 (3513), 3524 (3522), 3603 (3599); **7:** 3820 (3816), 3986 (3982, 3983, 3985), 3987; **8:** 4845 (4841), 4873; **9:** 5129 (5129), 5130 (5129), 5142 (5137), 5223 (5221); **10:** 5762 (5761), 5775, 5862 (5861)
Raul B M, **7:** 3801
Raul C R, **7:** 3801
Raum O, **3:** 1756 (1752)
Rausch H, **1:** 390
Rausser G, **5:** 2965
Raven B H, **5:** (2918)
Raven J, **6:** 3312 (3311)
Ravid G, **9:** 5399 (5398)
Ravitch D, **2:** 1175 (1172); **3:** 1367 (1362); **5:** 2617 (2612); **8:** 4595 (4590); **9:** 5523
Raviv A, **9:** 5359 (5358)
Rawley C, **3:** 1829 (1828)
Rawlins G J E, **8:** 4694
Rawlins W K, **10:** 5759
Rawls J, **4:** 2004 (2003), 2033 (2030), 2037 (2035), 2297 (2292, 2293, 2294, 2295); **6:** 3144 (3142); **7:** 3771 (3771), 3925 (3920, 3921, 3924); **8:** 4575 (4572, 4574); **9:** 5201 (5198), 5523
Ray B, **1:** 265 (265)
Ray J, **10:** 6091 (6089)
Ray J R, **9:** 5185 (5182, 5183)
Rayborn R, **7:** 3833 (3832)
Raymond M, **11:** 6798 (6797)
Raymond M D, **10:** 6091 (6089)
Rayner K, **8:** 4939; **10:** 5680 (5679)
Rayner M, **8:** 4830 (4826)
Raynor J O, **7:** 3942 (3941)
Raywid M A, **1:** 265 (262), 594 (591); **4:** 2033 (2031); **9:** 5197
Razel M, **8:** 4383 (4383)
Razik T, **7:** 4206
Read A, **8:** 4698 (4696)
Read C, **4:** 1962 (1960); **8:** 4945 (4943); **10:** 5704 (5702)
Read G H, **2:** 948 (943, 945); **9:** 5013
Read H, **1:** 343 (340)
Read J, **5:** 2813 (2810)
Read M, **1:** 296 (281); **3:** 1756 (1753)
Read P B, **9:** 5406
Read T, **8:** 4698
Readance J E, **2:** 803; **3:** 1529 (1526); **6:** 3209 (3207); **10:** 5795
Reader G G, **10:** 6127 (6122, 6123)
Reagan B, **3:** 1386 (1384)
Reason J, **8:** 4719
Reason P, **7:** 4336
Rebell M A, **4:** 2131 (2128)
Reber A S, **2:** 857 (855); **8:** 4945
Recchia S, **1:** 32 (30)
Reckase M D, **2:** 998 (993); **3:** 1421 (1421); **5:** 2784 (2780), 3043 (3041); **6:** 3253 (3252)
Rečnik F, **9:** 5497
Record R, **6:** (3636)
Reddi U V, **9:** 5544 (5542)
Reddy C, **3:** 1672
Reddy G Ram, **3:** 1563 (1559)
Reddy K B, **7:** 4329 (4328)

Reddy P H, **4:** 2418 (2417)
Reddy T R, **9:** 5399
Reder L M, **10:** 6192 (6191)
Reder M, **8:** 4839 (4837)
Reder S, **6:** 3453 (3447)
Redfern A, **9:** 5216 (5214)
Redfern B, **1:** 199 (195, 198)
Redfield D L, **10:** 6239 (6238)
Redfield R, **3:** 1756 (1755)
Redjali S M, **5:** 3011
Redmond P, **5:** 2910
Ree H, **2:** 910 (907)
Ree M J, **8:** 4758 (4755); **11:** 6678 (6675)
Reed C E, **7:** 3936
Reed D, **2:** 907
Reed D B, **6:** 3284 (3277)
Reed E, **6:** 3144 (3139)
Reed E S, **7:** 3950 (3950)
Reed H, **7:** 4145 (4145)
Reed H J, **3:** 1252 (1248)
Reed M, **10:** 5674 (5668, 5673)
Reed R J, **1:** 594; **11:** 6558, 6563 (6559, 6560)
Reed S, **2:** 711 (708); **6:** 3144 (3139)
Reed W M, **2:** 1026 (1025); **7:** 3807
Reed-Danahay D, **2:** 917 (915); **4:** 2272 (2268)
Rees A, **4:** 2445
Rees C R, **10:** 5713
Rees E T, **2:** 842 (839); **3:** 1434 (1432, 1433); **5:** 2669 (2667); **6:** 3324 (3317)
Rees J, **3:** 1520 (1517)
Reese E P, **10:** 6164 (6161)
Reese H W, **1:** 330; **2:** 705, 851; **4:** 2449; **5:** 2664 (2660), 2665 (2658, 2659), 2676 (2673, 2674, 2675, 2676); **6:** 3297, 3427 (3426); **7:** 3763; **8:** 4719 (4716); **9:** 5518 (5517)
Reeve R A, **11:** 6456 (6454)
Reeve V L, **2:** 649 (646)
Reeves D J, **4:** 2244 (2244)
Reeves T C, **5:** 2861 (2861); **8:** 4803 (4800); **10:** 5625 (5625); **11:** 6603 (6601)
Regan C, **3:** 1501
Regehr W, **3:** 1599
Regel O, **3:** 1655 (1649, 1654), 1789 (1788); **7:** 4141 (4140)
Register C A, **10:** 6072 (6071)
Rego M, **7:** 3960
Rehberg R A, **8:** 4896 (4894); **11:** 6798 (6796)
Rehn G, **6:** 3425 (3423); **8:** 4964 (4959)
Reich L, **3:** 1252 (1246)
Reich M, **1:** 135 (130); **3:** 1703 (1696, 1698), 1712 (1711); **5:** 2798 (2792); **6:** 3189 (3185, 3186, 3188); **8:** 4902 (4899)
Reich R B, **5:** 2867 (2865); **8:** 4519 (4514)
Reichardt C S, **4:** 2045 (2044), 2089 (2081), 2119 (2116)
Reichenbach H, **8:** (4633)
Reichle J, **1:** 408 (408)
Reichler R J, **6:** 3235 (3232, 3233)
Reid B J, **5:** 2971 (2969)
Reid E H E, **3:** 1599
Reid H P, **7:** 3833 (3831); **10:** 5686 (5683)
Reid I, **8:** 4830 (4826)
Reid M, **10:** 6085 (6085)
Reid N A, **7:** 3935 (3931, 3932)
Reid W A, **3:** 1266 (1265), 1271 (1270), 1272, 1308 (1306), 1355 (1348, 1349); **4:** 2073; **10:** 6092
Reif F, **3:** 1529 (1526); **10:** 5831; **11:** 6416
Reigeluth C M, **2:** 969 (965), 1170 (1166); **4:** 1918 (1914); **5:** 2862 (2860), 2867 (2864, 2866, 2867), 2874 (2870), 2884; **6:** 3301; **7:** 3946; **8:** 4823; **10:** 5901 (5900), 5913 (5911, 5912, 5913), 6192 (6188), 6193 (6189)
Reiger K, **11:** 6735 (6733)
Reil M, **7:** 4094 (4089); **11:** 6785 (6783)
Reilly M E, **11:** 6678 (6670, 6671)
Reimann P, **2:** 838 (835)
Reimer B, **1:** 199 (196); **7:** 4026 (4023)
Reimer E W, **1:** (262), 474 (466)
Reimerink B, **7:** 3996 (3995)
Reimers F, **2:** 1146; **3:** 1789 (1787, 1788), 1830 (1826); **5:** 2993 (2990); **6:** 3608 (3603, 3604, 3605); **8:** 4601 (4597, 4598); **11:** 6599
Rein M, **3:** 1431 (1427); **4:** 1864, 2046 (2044); **8:** 4562 (4558, 4561)
Rein N, **10:** 5674 (5671)
Rein W, **3:** (1290); **9:** 5043 (5038)
Reineke R A, **4:** 2131 (2124); **8:** 4751 (4750)
Reinharz S, **1:** 543; **4:** 2302 (2297); **11:** 6466 (6462)
Reinisch J M, **1:** 234 (232)
Reis H T, **9:** 5358 (5356)
Reis J, **9:** 5539 (5536)
Reis J S, **9:** 5441 (5436, 5437)
Reis S M, **5:** 2732 (2726, 2728)
Reischauer E, **3:** 1501
Reischauer R, **10:** 5768 (5764)
Reische D L, **8:** 4581 (4578)
Reise S P, **1:** 53 (51)
Reisel E, **9:** 5359 (5358)
Reiser B J, **1:** 347 (343); **2:** 1006 (1003); **6:** 3301 (3300)
Reiser R A, **5:** 2861 (2859); **7:** 3760 (3757, 3758); **8:** 4783 (4780)
Reisman J, **2:** 1042 (1038)
Reiss A J, **4:** 2278; **7:** 3721, 3771; **9:** 5553
Reissman F, **11:** 6484 (6482)
Reister G, **8:** 4779 (4776, 4777)
Reitman J S, **2:** 984 (984)
Reitz A L, **8:** 4375 (4373)
Rekkedal T, **3:** 1567 (1565)
Remy R C, **3:** 1655 (1651, 1652); **8:** 4581 (4576, 4577)
Renaud A J, **7:** 4293 (4291)
Renaud G, **5:** 2957
Rende R, **4:** 2261 (2258)
Renner G, **1:** 238 (237); **8:** 4719 (4718)
Renner J W, **3:** 1544 (1540, 1541); **6:** 3416; **8:** 4479 (4476), 4652 (4649, 4652); **10:** 6169 (6166)
Renninger K A, **5:** 2769 (2764)
Renou L, **5:** 2601 (2597, 2598, 2599), 2656 (2652)
Rensch E S, **10:** 5853 (5853)
Renshaw P D, **8:** 4368 (4365)
Renshon S A, **3:** 1655 (1651); **8:** 4581 (4579)
Renson R, **8:** 4473 (4472)
Renström L, **8:** 4429 (4425, 4429)
Rentel V, **6:** 3202 (3198)
Rentiers K A, **2:** 868 (863)
Rentz A L, **10:** 5804 (5799, 5802), 5805
Renwick M, **9:** 5275 (5274)
Renzulli J S, **5:** 2732 (2726, 2728, 2729); **9:** 5532 (5529)
Repp A, **8:** 4423 (4423)
Repucci N D, **9:** 5406 (5405), 5441 (5436)
Reschly D J, **1:** 390 (388); **3:** 1359 (1358); **6:** 3297 (3293, 3294); **7:** 3830 (3826, 3827, 3828, 3830)
Resh N, **7:** 3970 (3967)
Reskin B F, **4:** 2286 (2281, 2282), 2432 (2428, 2431), 2445
Resnick D P, **4:** 1848 (1847); **7:** 3726 (3724)
Resnick L B, **1:** 194 (191), 374; **2:** 838 (836, 837), 867, 969, 1025; **3:** 1252, 1504, 1529 (1528); **4:** 1848 (1847); **5:** 2768, 2769 (2762), 2773, 2874 (2873), 2879 (2875, 2879), 2884; **6:** 3292 (3291), 3301, 3302 (3297, 3301), 3306, 3345 (3340); **7:** 3726 (3724), 3788, 3792, 3886, 3953; **8:** 4483 (4482), 4951; **9:** 5233 (5229), 5342 (5339, 5340, 5341), 5345 (5344), 5363, 5507; **10:** 5795 (5794), 5822 (5821), 6015 (6014), 6177
Rest J R, **7:** 3920 (3917, 3918, 3919); **10:** 5939 (5936), 6169 (6166, 6167, 6168)
Reutter E E Jr, **6:** 3360; **9:** 5255
Revelle W, **6:** 3325 (3319)
Rey A, **2:** (858)
Reybrouck A, **10:** 5713
Reyes A, **8:** 4364 (4360)
Reyes L H, **6:** 3643 (3639, 3640)
Reyes P, **9:** 5181
Reykowski J, **8:** 4799
Reymond H, **8:** 4408 (4405)
Reynolds A, **3:** 1537 (1536); **8:** 4864 (4860, 4862, 4863); **11:** 6608 (6604)
Reynolds A J, **11:** 6384 (6378, 6379, 6382, 6383), 6390 (6389)
Reynolds B P, **7:** 4293 (4290, 4291)
Reynolds C R, **2:** 1182, 1189; **5:** 2907; **8:** 4623 (4618), 4662, 4936; **10:** 5662
Reynolds D, **3:** 1746; **4:** 1934 (1929, 1931, 1933); **5:** 2509 (2508)
Reynolds H T, **6:** 3508 (3500)
Reynolds J, **1:** (195)
Reynolds M C, **1:** 490; **2:** 711 (710), 729 (723, 724, 728), 730 (724), 802; **3:** 1402, 1443 (1442), 1534 (1534), 1804; **5:** 2731, 2813, 2907 (2905); **6:** 3297 (3293), 3559 (3557), 3560 (3557, 3559); **7:** 3830 (3830), 3833 (3831); **8:** 4936 (4931, 4933); **9:** 5363; **10:** 5686, 5745, 5943 (5941), 5999, 6173, 6244 (6241, 6243); **11:** 6461
Reynolds R E, **7:** 3768 (3765)
Reynolds-Myers P, **7:** 3775 (3774)
Reys R E, **8:** 4648 (4643)
Rezmovic E L, **4:** 2074 (2072)
Reznick L, **6:** 3634
Rhee T Y, **11:** 6628 (6626)
Rheingold H L, **5:** 2802 (2801)
Rhenius D, **7:** 3788

Rhodes E C, **3:** 1386 (1384, 1385); **7:** (3932)
Rhodes N C, **4:** 2351 (2348, 2350)
Rhodes S C, **7:** 3935 (3934)
Rhodes V, **2:** 1011 (1010); **10:** 6008 (6006)
Rhody T, **8:** 4881 (4876, 4879)
Rhys S, **2:** 1165 (1161, 1162, 1163, 1164)
Riach P A, **4:** 2445 (2444)
Ribar D C, **2:** 693 (690)
Ribbins P, **1:** 73 (67, 69, 72); **3:** 1775; **4:** 2166; **5:** 2954 (2953, 2954); **9:** 5168 (5159)
Ribe H, **3:** 1789
Ribeiro L, **8:** 4698 (4697)
Ribich F, **1:** 322 (319)
Ribich T I, **2:** 1131 (1128)
Ricciuti H, **5:** 2672 (2670)
Rice C, **10:** 5817 (5814)
Rice D, **3:** 1406 (1403)
Rice J, **4:** (2080)
Rice J M, **3:** 1530 (1525); **4:** 1872 (1864, 1866, 1868)
Rice L, **10:** 5768 (5766)
Rice M J, **1:** 280 (278), 299 (298)
Rice P, **1:** 299 (299)
Rice T, **10:** 5817 (5814)
Rice W K, **5:** 2515 (2513)
Rich A, **11:** 6769
Rich J, **4:** 2445 (2444)
Rich J M, **10:** 5991
Rich R F, **9:** 5038 (5033)
Rich W D, **3:** 1441 (1439)
Rich Y, **7:** 3970 (3967)
Richard A H, **5:** 2740
Richard K, **2:** 906
Richards F A, **6:** 3434 (3432), 3435; **8:** 4824
Richards I A, **1:** (195); **6:** 3484 (3482)
Richards M H, **5:** 2631 (2629, 2630); **11:** 6390 (6388)
Richards S B, **3:** 1359 (1356, 1358)
Richardson A, **2:** 766 (765)
Richardson B, **9:** 5268
Richardson C P, **7:** 4026 (4023)
Richardson E, **4:** 2166 (2165)
Richardson G, **11:** 6398 (6396)
Richardson J, **5:** 2709 (2708); **8:** 4694
Richardson J G, **4:** 2271; **10:** 5591, 5668
Richardson J T E, **1:** 194
Richardson K, **6:** 3421
Richardson M E, **1:** 94
Richardson M W, **9:** 4995 (4991, 4992)
Richardson P, **6:** 3366 (3363)
Richardson R, **3:** 1501 (1494); **10:** 5939 (5937)
Richardson S, **7:** 3830 (3828)
Richardson V, **3:** 1257 (1256); **8:** 4948 (4946); **10:** 5762 (5761)
Richardson W, **4:** 2119 (2110); **9:** 5191 (5187, 5189)
Richardson-Koehler V, **3:** 1635; **10:** 5925 (5922)
Richaudeau F, **8:** 4698
Richert A E, **10:** 5812 (5810), 5948 (5947), 5985 (5984), 6092 (6089), 6122 (6117)
Riches C, **6:** 3528
Richey R, **5:** 2862
Richler D, **3:** 1508; **6:** 3559 (3558)
Richmond J B, **5:** 2806 (2803)
Richmond M, **2:** 640 (637)
Richmond P, **5:** 2903
Richmond P A, **7:** 3833
Richmond S, **1:** 199 (196)
Richmond W K, **8:** 4608
Richter D, **7:** 4163 (4161)
Richter I, **6:** 3276 (3275), 3360; **9:** 5255
Richter J, **3:** 1643 (1640)
Richter L, **6:** 3613 (3613)
Richter M N Jr, **3:** 1333 (1329, 1332)
Richterich R, **4:** 2346 (2340); **6:** 3213
Rickards J P, **2:** 969 (966)
Rickards T, **5:** 2725 (2723, 2724)
Rickards W, **10:** 5957 (5955)
Rickert H, **6:** (3137); **9:** (5052)
Ricks D M, **5:** 2665 (2663); **6:** 3235 (3233)
Ricoeur P, **5:** 2585 (2583, 2584), 2586; **7:** 4051 (4047)
Riddell C, **4:** 2150 (2147)
Riddell S, **4:** 2291 (2290), 2292 (2288, 2289)
Rideout W M Jr, **8:** 4601 (4598)
Ridge B, **1:** 234 (232)
Ridge J M, **4:** 2257 (2251, 2252); **8:** 4831; **9:** 5553 (5551); **10:** 5607 (5598, 5600)
Riding R, **1:** 322 (318, 319); **6:** 3593
Ridings J M, **8:** 4751 (4743)
Ridler G E, **9:** 5185 (5183)
Ridley-Johnson R, **7:** 3950 (3948)
Rieben L, **8:** 4945 (4943, 4944)
Rieber L P, **2:** 1170 (1168)
Rieber R W, **9:** 5416
Riecke R D, **6:** 3443 (3439)
Rieder H, **10:** 5713
Riedmiller S, **8:** 4688 (4682, 4683, 4684, 4685, 4686, 4687)
Riegel K F, **1:** (276); **3:** 1253
Riel M, **2:** 982 (978, 981); **7:** 4094 (4089); **9:** 5544 (5541)
Riely F Z, **1:** 244
Riesbeck C, **6:** 3345
Rieser J, **2:** 1019
Riessman F, **5:** 2806; **8:** 4372 (4370)
Riew J, **9:** 5294 (5291)
Rif A, **8:** 4468
Rife F, **10:** 5713
Riggar T F, **10:** 5925 (5920)
Riggs F, **3:** 1824 (1821)
Righa K, **1:** 175 (172, 174)
Riis V, **9:** 5432 (5425)
Rikers J A H N, **2:** 998 (997)
Rikowski G, **3:** 1739 (1738)
Riley D, **3:** 1647 (1645), 1779 (1778); **4:** 2119 (2110)
Riley E P, **1:** 15 (14)
Riley J, **9:** 5355 (5350, 5353)
Riley M W, **6:** 3428 (3426)
Riley P, **4:** 2357 (2353); **6:** 3349
Rimé B, **7:** 4175 (4171)
Rimland B, **6:** 3235 (3232)
Rimm S B, **2:** 1182 (1180)
Rinaldi R, **3:** 1655 (1649, 1654), 1789 (1788); **7:** 4141 (4140); **9:** 5076 (5072)
Rindskopf D, **3:** 1514 (1511)
Rinehart S C, **10:** 5831 (5830)
Ringenbach S, **2:** 1182 (1181)
Ringer F, **5:** 2617 (2613); **10:** 5735
Ringstaff C, **11:** 6608 (6607)
Rink D F T, **7:** 3925
Rink J, **8:** 4467 (4467)
Rinneberg K-J, **1:** 317 (311)
Riordan C, **2:** 834 (832)
Ripich D N, **6:** 3227
Rippa S A, **8:** 4731 (4728)
Rippberger S, **2:** 933 (932)
Rippey R M, **4:** (2103)
Ripple R E, **5:** 2884
Rips L R, **6:** 3155 (3152)
Riquelme G, **7:** 4155
Risager K, **4:** 2351 (2349)
Risatti H, **11:** 6621
Rischmiller S, **6:** 3204 (3203)
Riseborough G F, **10:** 6139 (6138)
Riskin E, **4:** 2440 (2438)
Risley T R, **10:** 6164 (6161)
Rist R C, **1:** 11 (9); **2:** 825 (822), 1074 (1070); **4:** 2053 (2049); **5:** 2978 (2973); **7:** 3848 (3845), 3970 (3967); **11:** 6511 (6509)
Ritchie S M, **10:** 6183 (6179)
Ritchie W, **4:** 2339
Ritmeester J W, **8:** 4473 (4472)
Ritter P, **3:** 1607 (1604); **5:** 2627 (2625)
Ritzen J M M, **2:** 1093, 1094; **4:** 2212 (2211); **6:** 3425, 3616, 3617 (3615); **7:** 4325 (4320, 4323); **9:** 5233, 5246; **10:** 5919
Ritzer G, **2:** 1073
Riu F, **9:** 5197 (5192)
Rivarola D M, **7:** 4290 (4284)
Rivarola M M, **7:** 4290 (4284)
Rivera C, **3:** 1252
Rivera J, **3:** 1593 (1592)
Rivera Pizarro J, **7:** 4290
Rivera R, **8:** 4616 (4614)
Rivera W M, **6:** 3367
Rivero J, **2:** 640
Rivers W, **4:** 2346 (2341, 2342)
Rivers W M, **6:** 3241 (3240)
Rivest L P, **8:** 4542
Riviera R J, **1:** 158 (153)
Riviere A, **10:** 5658
Rivkin M, **8:** 4542
Rivlin A M, **2:** 688 (682)
Rivlin L G, **9:** 5359
Rizo F M, **3:** 1474 (1464); **9:** 5056
Rizvi F, **7:** 3978 (3975)
Rizzo D, **9:** 5445 (5441)
Rønning J, **9:** 5567 (5564)
Roach P B, **4:** 1996
Robb R, **9:** 5385 (5383, 5384)
Robbins A, **4:** 2046 (2043)
Robbins A M, **10:** 5691 (5687, 5688)
Robbins D, **9:** 5021
Robbins N, **3:** 1406 (1403, 1404), 1407
Robbins P, **2:** 988 (986, 987)
Robbins S P, **10:** 5591 (5589)
Robert J I, **1:** 296
Roberts A, **7:** 4225
Roberts B, **4:** 2412 (2409)
Roberts D, **1:** 570 (566); **5:** 2627 (2625)

Roberts D J, **3:** 1619 (1612)
Roberts D M, **7:** 4000 (3999)
Roberts F K, **11:** 6628 (6626)
Roberts H, **7:** 4185 (4182), 4319
Roberts H W, **8:** 4812 (4809); **10:** 5808 (5806)
Roberts I, **7:** 3895 (3890)
Roberts J, **8:** 4474 (4470); **10:** 5691 (5689)
Roberts J I, **1:** 295, 296, 297 (282, 283, 284, 285, 288); **2:** 1212, 1213
Roberts J M, **3:** 1252 (1248)
Roberts K, **3:** 1607 (1604); **11:** 6798 (6795, 6797)
Roberts N, **2:** 982, 1012 (1008); **9:** 5578; **10:** 6008 (6007)
Roberts N C, **9:** 5246 (5243)
Roberts T A, **4:** 2266 (2265)
Roberts T D, **2:** 1160 (1155, 1156, 1158)
Robertson B A, **8:** 4824 (4820)
Robertson C, **4:** 2412 (2408); **7:** 3853 (3851)
Robertson I T, **4:** 1967
Robertson L C, **2:** 851
Robin D, **8:** 4865; **9:** 5246 (5241, 5243)
Robins K, **4:** 1911
Robins L N, **4:** 2212 (2210)
Robins P K, **2:** 693 (690)
Robinsohn S B, **3:** 1355 (1348, 1351)
Robinson E, **8:** 4608 (4605)
Robinson F P, **1:** 194 (186)
Robinson G E, **2:** 775 (771, 773)
Robinson G L N, **7:** 3970 (3965)
Robinson H A, **2:** 738 (733)
Robinson H J, **5:** 2806
Robinson J, **1:** 404, 564; **2:** 687 (686), 1213 (1211); **3:** 1580 (1575); **4:** 1903 (1899); **5:** 2891 (2885), 2897; **6:** 3378; **9:** 5475
Robinson J C, **2:** 914 (912); **9:** 5216 (5212)
Robinson J P, **1:** 570 (564)
Robinson J T, **9:** 5338 (5336)
Robinson K, **8:** 4388 (4384, 4385)
Robinson M, **5:** 2732
Robinson N M, **2:** 729 (727); **4:** 1979 (1976); **5:** 2806; **9:** 5532 (5529, 5530, 5531)
Robinson P, **7:** 4171 (4168)
Robinson R, **11:** 6625 (6623)
Robinson R J, **5:** 2802
Robinson S, **1:** 28; **6:** 3443 (3441, 3442)
Robinson S B, **3:** 1257, 1301 (1289)
Robinson V M, **6:** 3463 (3462); **8:** 4376 (4373); **9:** 5224 (5222)
Robinson W P, **6:** 3297 (3294); **9:** 5508
Robinson W S, **5:** 2596 (2590); **7:** 3986 (3978)
Robitaille D F, **2:** 957 (954); **3:** 1768 (1764); **4:** 2140 (2137); **6:** 3643 (3640, 3641, 3642), 3668; **10:** 6155 (6150)
Roblyer M D, **2:** 991 (990), 1170 (1167, 1169), 1175 (1174); **7:** 4104 (4102); **8:** 4803 (4800)
Robottom I, **4:** 1995 (1994)
Robotton J, **5:** 2544
Robson C, **10:** 5943
Robson G, **5:** 2491 (2487)
Robson M, **10:** 6088 (6088), 6183
Roby P, **11:** 6712 (6711)
Rocco P L, **1:** 494 (491)
Roche A F, **8:** 4473 (4469, 4470, 4471, 4472), 4474 (4468, 4469, 4470, 4471, 4472, 4473)
Rochon J, **9:** 5130 (5127)
Rock D A, **3:** 1486 (1484), 1606 (1604, 1605); **4:** 2435 (2433); **9:** 5228 (5224, 5228)
Rock I, **8:** 4379 (4378)
Rockhill K, **1:** 93 (89, 90, 91)
Rocklin T, **1:** 52 (50)
Rockwell R C, **7:** 3862 (3860)
Rodd A, **3:** 1784 (1783)
Rodd J, **11:** 6608 (6605)
Rode C, **11:** 6659 (6659)
Roder-Gordon C, **10:** 6244 (6243)
Roderick G W, **1:** 93 (90); **5:** 2532; **7:** 4171 (4163, 4166); **11:** 6684
Rodger A, **4:** 2011 (2007)
Rodgers G, **11:** 6615
Rodgers R, **10:** 5805 (5798)
Rodgers-Jenkinson F, **10:** 6062 (6060)
Rodin J, **1:** 239 (237)
Rodney W, **8:** 4638 (4635)
Rodrigues de Oliveira T, **8:** 4751 (4745)
Rodriguez C M, **11:** 6360 (6357)
Rodríguez E, **6:** 3256
Rodriguez G, **11:** 6307 (6303)
Rodriguez L, **7:** 4136 (4133)
Rodriguez N, **11:** 6599
Rodriguez R, **10:** (5813), (5815)
Roe A, **11:** 6678 (6672, 6674)
Roe H, **1:** 490 (487)
Roebke C, **10:** 6244 (6243)
Roede M J, **8:** 4474 (4472)
Roeder M, **6:** 3389 (3386)
Roehler L R, **2:** 867 (865); **3:** 1257 (1256); **8:** 4935 (4934); **9:** 5318 (5316); **10:** 6149 (6147, 6148), 6192 (6191, 6192)
Roell S, **10:** 5854
Roelofs J J, **5:** 2732 (2729)
Roessler R T, **2:** 635 (632)
Roethlisberger F I, **4:** 2166 (2158)
Rogers A, **5:** 2937 (2935); **10:** 6202
Rogers C, **1:** 152 (148); **8:** 4461 (4457); **10:** 5596 (5594)
Rogers C C, **2:** 711 (708)
Rogers C R, **1:** 194 (191), (276); **5:** 2692 (2690, 2691); **7:** 4215 (4212); **10:** 5805 (5797, 5798), (6054), 6202 (6198)
Rogers D, **1:** 594 (593); **10:** 6053 (6050, 6052)
Rogers D C, **10:** 5768 (5766)
Rogers D E, **3:** 1641, 1642
Rogers E M, **1:** 254 (252); **3:** 1416 (1414), 1494 (1491), 1553 (1550); **9:** 5246 (5243), 5518 (5514); **11:** 6283 (6278)
Rogers H J, **1:** 42 (36); **5:** 3043 (3037, 3039, 3041), 3050 (3047); **7:** 4000; **11:** 6333 (6332)
Rogers J, **2:** 973 (970); **5:** 2532
Rogers K L, **7:** 4225 (4224)
Rogers K W, **10:** 5826 (5823); **11:** 6797 (6796)
Rogers L T, **7:** 3810 (3808)
Rogers P J, **5:** 2623
Rogers T, **6:** 3484; **8:** 4881 (4877); **11:** 6370 (6368)
Rogin L, **11:** 6775
Rogoff B, **1:** 230 (229); **2:** 705 (705), 838 (838), 851 (850); **3:** 1236, 1246, 1252, 1253, 1504, 1739; **4:** 2452 (2449); **5:** 2685 (2684); **8:** 4727 (4726); **9:** 5508 (5504)
Rogoff N, **7:** 3864 (3862)
Rogosa D R, **2:** 678 (672, 673, 674, 676); **3:** 1514 (1512); **4:** 1877 (1876); **5:** 2596 (2590)
Rogozinski J T, **10:** 5831 (5830)
Rohde-Dachser C, **8:** 4816 (4814)
Rohlen T P, **1:** 11 (6); **2:** 1213 (1211); **9:** 5181 (5177, 5178), 5220 (5217)
Rohlfes J, **5:** 2623 (2618)
Rohner R P, **8:** 4799 (4797, 4798)
Rohrkemper M M, **10:** 6088 (6086)
Röhrs H U I, **3:** 1301 (1290); **11:** 6699
Rohwer W D Jr, **1:** 194 (184, 188, 191)
Roi H de, **3:** (1464)
Roid G H, **2:** 998 (992, 997), 1182 (1180); **5:** 3043 (3036), 3066; **7:** 4197
Rojas Y, **2:** 1146
Rokeach M, **1:** 380 (379); **9:** 5324 (5322)
Rolandelli D R, **8:** 4680 (4678)
Roland-Lévy C, **9:** 5563
Roldan A H, **9:** 5532
Rolf J, **6:** 3297
Rolff H-G, **5:** 2480, 2529 (2526), 2852 (2849, 2851); **7:** 4240 (4239)
Rolland-Cachera M-F, **8:** 4474 (4469, 4470, 4471)
Rollett B A, **5:** 2769 (2764); **7:** 3942 (3937)
Romaguera P, **3:** 1680 (1677)
Romain R, **3:** 1825 (1823, 1824); **8:** 4688 (4681)
Romaine S, **1:** 537
Roman L, **11:** 6727 (6726)
Roman L G, **1:** 543
Romanes G, **5:** (2875)
Romano J P, **9:** 5471
Romberg T A, **6:** 3643, 3655 (3654), 3660, 3661 (3658); **7:** 4099 (4096); **8:** 4648 (4644); **10:** 5795 (5792)
Romenets V A, **10:** 5887 (5885)
Romer P M, **2:** 1094 (1089); **3:** 1666 (1665)
Romijn H, **4:** 1991 (1986)
Romiszowski A J, **1:** 404; **3:** 1315 (1313), 1490 (1487, 1488), 1491; **4:** 1899 (1891), 1976 (1973); **5:** 2773 (2770, 2771, 2772), 2862 (2857); **6:** 3096 (3092, 3093, 3094), 3306 (3302); **7:** 3760 (3757, 3758, 3759), 3953 (3951, 3952), 3991 (3987), 4249; **8:** 4783 (4781); **9:** 5544 (5541); **10:** 5901 (5895, 5900)
Romney A K, **9:** 5158 (5152, 5157), 5560
Romney L C, **4:** 2229
Romski M A, **1:** 408 (407)
Ronchetti E M, **9:** 5082 (5078, 5079)
Rondinelli D A, **2:** 933 (929); **3:** 1416 (1412, 1413, 1414), 1825 (1822), 1830 (1829); **5:** 2512 (2509, 2511); **8:** 4510, 4519 (4515, 4518), 4601 (4596, 4597, 4599)
Ronen M, **8:** 4479 (4478)
Ronge B, **4:** (2386), (2387)
Roning L U, **7:** 4293 (4291, 4292)
Ronnen S, **2:** 942

Ronning R R, **2:** 820, 1182; **3:** 1513, 1514; **4:** 1848; **5:** 2880; **8:** 4731; **9:** 4977
Rönnqvist L, **7:** 3950 (3948, 3949)
Rontopoulou J L, **11:** 6807 (6807)
Roodin P A, **5:** 2677 (2674); **8:** 4823 (4818, 4820, 4821, 4823)
Roopnarine J L, **5:** 2628, 2813 (2808); **8:** 4542
Roos P A, **4:** 2432 (2431)
Roosa M W, **8:** 4779 (4776, 4778)
Root S J, **1:** 415
Roper B L, **1:** 52 (52)
Ropiequet S, **2:** 649
Rorschach H, **8:** 4791
Rorty R, **2:** (930); **3:** 1524 (1524); **4:** 2001 (2000), 2033 (2030); **5:** 2585 (2585); **8:** 4456 (4448, 4453); **9:** (4977), (4978)
Rosaen C, **2:** 803 (800)
Rosanoff A J, **8:** 4791 (4790)
Roschelle J, **11:** 6608 (6607)
Rose E J B, **7:** 3848 (3844)
Rose G, **7:** 4163 (4161)
Rose H, **9:** 5349 (5347)
Rose J, **4:** 1976 (1974)
Rose L H, **2:** 1182 (1182)
Rose M, **4:** 2272 (2269); **6:** 3452; **10:** (5815)
Rose M A, **8:** 4642 (4639)
Rose R, **6:** 3368 (3367)
Rose S, **3:** 1520 (1517)
Rose T L, **10:** 5834 (5832)
Rose-Ackerman S, **8:** 4835 (4833)
Rosegrant T, **5:** 2812 (2808), 2814
Rosemberg F K, **3:** 1672 (1670); **9:** 4977 (4976)
Rosen B C, **1:** 297 (292); **3:** 1240 (1237)
Rosen G D, **7:** 4081 (4078)
Rosen G F, **10:** 5680 (5679)
Rosen H, **1:** 310; **7:** 3935 (3933), 3936; **10:** 5961 (5959); **11:** 6784 (6782)
Rosen R, **3:** 1449
Rosen S, **3:** 1449, 1695 (1692), 1750 (1747, 1748, 1749, 1750); **4:** 2279 (2275); **6:** 3101, 3144 (3140); **9:** 5328 (5325); **11:** 6424 (6421), 6615
Rosen W G, **6:** 3416
Rosenau P, **4:** 2302 (2297)
Rosenbach W, **7:** 4240 (4238)
Rosenbaum J E, **1:** 11 (6, 7), 12; **2:** 825 (821, 822, 824); **5:** 2942 (2939)
Rosenbaum L K, **7:** 4301 (4299)
Rosenbaum M, **7:** 4081 (4079)
Rosenbaum P, **9:** 5385 (5384)
Rosenberg B, **5:** 2596 (2590)
Rosenberg D, **3:** 1779 (1778)
Rosenberg K C, **7:** 3753
Rosenberg M, **9:** 5394 (5391, 5392); **10:** 5591; **11:** 6576 (6570, 6572)
Rosenberg N, **11:** 6283 (6278)
Rosenberg S, **6:** 3189 (3187, 3188), 3224; **7:** 4095
Rosenberger M, **10:** 6244
Rosenblatt L, **2:** 738 (734), (1194); **6:** 3484 (3481, 3482); **10:** 5961 (5959)
Rosenblum S H, **5:** 2532, 2847 (2840, 2842); **9:** 5246 (5242, 5243); **10:** 5924 (5922)
Rosenbusch M H, **4:** 2351 (2349, 2350)
Rosencranz H A, **10:** 6132 (6131)
Rosendaal B, **5:** 2862
Rosenfeld D, **2:** 1099 (1098)
Rosenfeld G, **2:** 917 (916); **4:** 2053 (2049)
Rosenfield P, **9:** 5359 (5358)
Rosengart G, **1:** 474 (471); **5:** 2562 (2560)
Rosengren K E, **1:** 570 (564, 568)
Rosenholtz S J, **1:** 230 (229); **4:** 1939 (1935); **5:** 2509 (2508), 2847 (2843); **9:** 5181 (5176, 5177, 5178, 5179), 5224 (5221, 5222), 5264 (5263), 5379 (5373); **10:** 5935 (5932), 6103 (6101), 6215 (6208, 6214)
Rosenquist J, **5:** 2910 (2909)
Rosenshine B V, **2:** 811 (807), 816 (812, 813, 814, 815); **3:** 1530 (1525, 1526); **4:** 2132 (2129); **8:** 4864 (4863), 4881 (4877, 4879, 4880); **10:** 5713 (5708), 6015 (6013, 6014), 6088 (6086), 6143 (6141), 6149 (6148), 6192 (6188), 6193, 6239 (6237)
Rosenstiel A, **1:** 297 (288)
Rosenstock-Huessy E, **1:** (136), (274)
Rosenthal A S, **8:** 4586 (4584); **9:** 5066 (5062)
Rosenthal E, **8:** 4896 (4894)
Rosenthal L S, **7:** 3816
Rosenthal M, **11:** 6398 (6396)
Rosenthal R A, **2:** 1074 (1070); **7:** 3783 (3775), 3784 (3775, 3776, 3777, 3779, 3781, 3782); **9:** 5411 (5407), 5435 (5434); **10:** 5762 (5759, 5760), 5924 (5920, 5921), 6062 (6060), 6112 (6106, 6107, 6109), 6224 (6220), 6239 (6236); **11:** 6511 (6509)
Rosenthal T L, **9:** 5518 (5514)
Rosenzweig F, **8:** (4431), (4432)
Rosenzweig L W, **9:** 5577 (5576), 5578 (5577)
Rosenzweig M R, **1:** 88, 554 (553); **4:** 2419 (2413); **5:** 2802 (2799)
Roser N, **2:** 738
Rosier J C, **10:** 5674 (5670)
Rosier M J, **2:** 957 (950, 955); **3:** 1768 (1764); **4:** 2140, 2440 (2437); **7:** 4307 (4306); **8:** 4479 (4475); **9:** 5342 (5340), 5350 (5348); **10:** 5790 (5789), 5862 (5855); **11:** 6328 (6325)
Rosinski R R, **8:** 4383
Roskam E E, **4:** 2017 (2012); **9:** 5503 (5500)
Roske M, **7:** 4030
Rösler H-D, **8:** 4395 (4390)
Rosnay J de, **8:** 4803 (4800)
Rosney B, **11:** 6628 (6626)
Rosnow R L, **9:** 5411 (5407)
Rosow J M, **4:** 1976 (1975); **6:** 3197 (3193); **10:** 6083 (6080)
Ross B, **3:** 1514 (1512)
Ross C E, **4:** 2261 (2259)
Ross D, **10:** 5977 (5974)
Ross D D, **7:** 3826 (3824); **10:** 6106 (6104, 6105)
Ross D H, **2:** 729 (720); **5:** 2972 (2966)
Ross E D, **4:** 2388 (2386); **8:** 4670 (4668)
Ross G R T, **3:** 1464 (1462, 1463)
Ross H P, **3:** 1563
Ross H S, **8:** 4368; **10:** 5759
Ross J, **10:** 5713 (5710)
Ross K, **1:** 474 (469)
Ross K N, **3:** 1394 (1394); **6:** 3399 (3395), 3597; **7:** 3722 (3721), 3739 (3734), 4016 (4013); **8:** 4510, 4519; **9:** 5130 (5125, 5126), 5142 (5131, 5138, 5139), 5169 (5162), 5385 (5380)
Ross L, **2:** 1207 (1207); **3:** 1431 (1427); **8:** 4957; **9:** 5508, 5512
Ross M S, **8:** 4803 (4802)
Ross P A, **9:** 4977 (4975)
Ross S, **4:** 2339 (2337); **7:** 3707 (3700); **10:** 5977 (5974)
Ross S M, **7:** 3743 (3739, 3743)
Rossbach H-G, **5:** 2480 (2474); **7:** 4301 (4299)
Rosseel P, **6:** 3213
Rossell C H, **2:** 1074 (1066); **9:** 5379
Rosser P, **4:** 2435 (2434)
Rossett A, **6:** 3096 (3092, 3093, 3094)
Ross-Gordon J M, **1:** 168 (166), 184; **8:** 4616 (4614)
Rossi A S, **11:** 6712, 6765 (6761)
Rossi P, **4:** (2088); **10:** 6227 (6224)
Rossi P H, **2:** 1136 (1132); **3:** 1283 (1281), 1431 (1427); **4:** (2103), 2119 (2111), 2388 (2386); **5:** 2672 (2670); **7:** 3861; **8:** 4751 (4737, 4745), 4783 (4782), 4830 (4828); **10:** 5862 (5860); **11:** 6384 (6378, 6379, 6381)
Rossi R J, **3:** 1431 (1429)
Rossiter M W, **4:** 2440 (2437); **11:** 6765 (6763)
Rosskopf M F, **6:** 3685
Rossman F, **4:** 1962 (1961)
Rossman G B, **7:** 4319 (4316, 4317, 4318); **9:** 5181 (5180)
Rossman M H, **7:** 4185
Rossman T, **6:** 3334 (3333)
Rossmiller R A, **1:** 230 (228); **3:** 1784 (1779); **7:** 3821 (3816); **8:** 4865
Rost D H, **10:** 5738 (5737)
Rost J C, **3:** 1514 (1511); **4:** 2017; **6:** 3284 (3277, 3278)
Roszak T, **7:** 4088 (4082)
Rotering-Steinberg S, **9:** 5216
Roth C E, **4:** 1995 (1991)
Roth E M, **10:** 5914 (5912)
Roth G, **2:** 785
Roth G L, **4:** 1924 (1921, 1922)
Roth J, **7:** 4059 (4057)
Roth J L, **6:** 3474 (3473)
Roth J P, **2:** 649
Roth K J, **7:** 4104 (4101)
Roth L, **3:** 1354
Roth R, **3:** 1636 (1633)
Roth R E, **4:** 1995 (1994)
Roth S, **10:** 5738 (5736)
Roth W, **3:** 1507 (1506)
Rothbart M K, **11:** 6310 (6308), 6311
Rothcrug P, **4:** 2331
Rothenberg J, **7:** 4215 (4214)
Rothery A, **6:** 3638 (3637)
Rothkopf E Z, **2:** 969 (965); **4:** 1939, 2194; **6:** 3453; **9:** 5224; **10:** 6169
Rothman R, **5:** 2798 (2792)
Rothrock D, **5:** 2779 (2774)
Rothschild J, **6:** 3368 (3367)

Rothschild N, **11:** 6798 (6797)
Rothwell R, **11:** 6260 (6259)
Rothwell W J, **5:** 2689 (2685, 2687); **6:** 3096 (3092)
Rottenberg S, **11:** 6638
Rouet J-F, **5:** 2709 (2707)
Roug L, **6:** 3224 (3220)
Rouin C C, **3:** 1406
Rourke B, **7:** 4081 (4078)
Rouse M J, **11:** 6461 (6458), 6621 (6619)
Rousseau E W, **10:** 6239 (6238)
Rousseau J-J, **1:** (261), (262); **2:** (776), (777); **3:** (1289), (1290), (1295), (1520), (1538), (1720), (1721), (1795); **4:** (2386); **5:** 2579 (2576), (2608); **6:** (3497), (3499); **7:** 3925 (3922, 3923, 3924), (4211); **8:** (4416), (4535), (4680), 4456 (4452), 4575 (4573), (4640), (4667); **9:** 5091 (5087, 5088, 5089, 5090), (5229); **10:** (5707), (5874); **11:** (6578), 6747 (6745), (6795)
Rousseeuw P J, **9:** 5082 (5078, 5079)
Rovee-Collier C, **5:** 2802 (2800, 2801)
Rovine M J, **5:** 2465 (2464), 2677 (2674, 2675)
Rowan B, **2:** 825 (822); **4:** 2166 (2162); **5:** 2596 (2594); **6:** 3527 (3525), 3603 (3599); **8:** 4873 (4870); **9:** 5181 (5177, 5180), 5246 (5243); **11:** 6558 (6554)
Rowan J, **7:** 4336
Rowden D, **8:** 4616 (4610)
Rowe H, **8:** 4647
Rowe M B, **9:** 5338
Rowe R, **11:** 6785 (6783)
Rowell J A, **8:** 4464 (4463)
Rowell S, **4:** 2357 (2355)
Rowitz L, **2:** 1073
Rowland E J, **9:** 5324 (5320)
Rowland G, **5:** 2874 (2873)
Rowley G L, **5:** 2462 (2459, 2462); **7:** 4000 (3997)
Rowley G R, **2:** 1189 (1188)
Rowley J D, **6:** 3416 (3413)
Rowley J E, **3:** 1553 (1550)
Rowntree D, **4:** 1899 (1890, 1892); **7:** 3760 (3757, 3758)
Rowse J 1987, **7:** 3820 (3816, 3818)
Roy A, **2:** 893 (892); **10:** 5834 (5832)
Roy A K, **9:** 5560 (5558)
Roy H, **2:** 738 (735)
Roy R R M, **11:** (6749)
Roy-Pernot M-P, **8:** 4474 (4470)
Rozada Martínez J, **1:** 48 (45)
Rozin P, **8:** 4945 (4943)
Rørdam T, **2:** 910 (908); **4:** 2327
Rubba P A, **4:** 1995 (1994)
Ruben B D, **9:** 5560
Rubenson K, **1:** 93 (90); **2:** 906 (900), 1094 (1093); **3:** 1602 (1601); **5:** 2951 (2949); **7:** 4179 (4178, 4179), 4249 (4247, 4248), 4325 (4321, 4322, 4323, 4324), 4329 (4325, 4326, 4327); **8:** 4616 (4611, 4612); **11:** 6394, 6551 (6548)
Ruberto A, **5:** 3036
Rubin A, **10:** 5795 (5793, 5794)
Rubin D, **1:** 239; **6:** 3442, 3443; **10:** 6112 (6109)
Rubin D B, **5:** 2595 (2593), 2596 (2591, 2592, 2593); **7:** 3784 (3777), 3858 (3857), 3861 (3858, 3860, 3861), 3862 (3858, 3860, 3861); **9:** 5130 (5129), 5385 (5384); **11:** 6355 (6349), 6511 (6509)
Rubin D C, **8:** 4824; **9:** 5435
Rubin H, **4:** (2233)
Rubin J, **6:** 3334 (3330), 3335
Rubin K H, **1:** 234 (233); **8:** 4368, 4542 (4536, 4538, 4539, 4540); **9:** 5528 (5525, 5527); **10:** 5759
Rubin L J, **10:** 6086 (6084)
Rubin Z, **10:** 5759
Rubinger R, **9:** 5281
Rubinson R, **3:** 1655 (1652); **5:** 2942 (2940)
Rubinstein R Y, **9:** 5471
Rubison L G, **5:** 2572 (2567)
Ruble D N, **9:** 5507
Rübsamen H, **3:** 1262 (1261)
Rubtsov V, **9:** 5548 (5546, 5547)
Rudbeck O, **3:** (1464)
Ruddick R, **4:** 2297 (2294)
Ruddle K, **1:** 297 (286)
Ruddock R, **4:** 2123 (2120, 2122)
Rudduck J, **3:** 1271, 1272, 1553 (1549, 1552); **5:** 2536 (2534); **10:** 6092
Rudin H, **2:** 618
Rudinger G, **3:** 1520, 1647; **8:** 4395; **11:** 6492
Rudman H C, **1:** 77
Rudner L M, **5:** 3050 (3044, 3045, 3048, 3049); **7:** 3726 (3724)
Rudnitsky A N, **3:** 1334; **10:** 5887
Rudolph F, **10:** 5805 (5796)
Rudolph J D, **9:** 5013
Rudy W, **10:** 5804 (5796)
Rueda R, **2:** 718 (717)
Ruehl S, **11:** 6704 (6700)
Rueter H H, **2:** 984 (984)
Ruffman T, **2:** 857 (854)
Rugg H O, **3:** 1266 (1262, 1263), 1301 (1299); **9:** (5298), (5575); **10:** 5817 (5813); **11:** (6367)
Rugh A, **8:** 4873 (4869, 4871)
Ruijs A, **11:** 6731 (6727, 6728)
Ruijssenaars A J J M, **6:** 3315 (3313, 3314, 3315)
Ruiz D G, **8:** 4415
Ruiz R, **1:** 408 (404); **10:** 6163
Rule J B, **4:** 1864
Rulon P J, **3:** 1549 (1544)
Rumain B, **8:** 4956 (4953, 4954)
Rumbaugh D, **5:** 2685 (2682)
Rumberger R W, **1:** 521 (517, 519); **2:** 1055 (1052), 1094; **3:** 1607 (1604, 1606), 1695, 1713 (1709, 1711); **4:** 1911 (1908, 1909); **6:** 3189 (3188); **7:** 4255 (4250, 4253); **8:** 4902 (4898); **9:** 5076 (5074), 5228 (5225, 5226, 5227), 5367 (5365); **10:** 5607 (5604); **11:** 6260 (6257, 6258, 6259), 6277 (6273), 6282, 6283 (6279), 6633 (6628)
Rumble G, **4:** 2186 (2184); **5:** 2897 (2894); **7:** 4220 (4219)
Rumelhart D E, **2:** 856 (853), 857 (853); **6:** 3155 (3154); **8:** 4722 (4719), 4939 (4936); **10:** 5745 (5744)
Rumney S, **10:** 5812 (5809, 5811)
Runco M A, **2:** 1182
Rundell C R, **5:** 2773 (2773)
Runkel P J, **5:** 2529 (2525, 2526), 2852 (2848); **7:** 4240 (4236, 4237); **9:** 5050; **10:** 5862 (5855)
Ruopp R, **2:** 688 (685), 701 (696)
Rüppell H, **5:** 2495 (2492)
Ruppert D, **9:** 5082 (5080)
Rury J L, **5:** 2607; **10:** 5613 (5609, 5610); **11:** 6558
Rusch F R, **11:** 6461 (6459)
Rusell J D, **11:** 6625 (6622)
Rush J C, **11:** 6621 (6621)
Rushby N, **4:** 1898; **7:** 3991 (3987), 4088 (4083); **8:** 4803 (4800)
Rushcamp S, **9:** 5318 (5316)
Rushton J P, **8:** 4799 (4798)
Rusimbi M, **1:** 175 (173, 174)
Rusk R R, **5:** 2617 (2608); **8:** 4670 (4667)
Rusnell D, **1:** 127 (125)
Russel P, **4:** 1954
Russel R, **1:** 318
Russell B, **2:** (776); **3:** 1464; **8:** 4447 (4442, 4443, 4444), 4456 (4450, 4451, 4452, 4453); **10:** 6183 (6179)
Russell D, **11:** 6360 (6356)
Russell D E H, **10:** 6139 (6138)
Russell D W, **10:** 5925 (5921, 5922, 5923)
Russell G, **1:** 358 (355)
Russell J D, **4:** 1918, 1928 (1927); **5:** 2861 (2859); **7:** 3753
Russell J T, **3:** 1421 (1417)
Russell P, **7:** 4282
Russell R, **7:** 3895 (3891, 3892)
Russell S J, **7:** 3808 (3802, 3804, 3806)
Russell T, **9:** 5335 (5330); **10:** 6183 (6179, 6181)
Rust K, **9:** 5130 (5127, 5129), 5142 (5136)
Rust V D, **1:** 184 (182, 183), 594 (592); **2:** 711 (706), 933 (925, 928, 930); **5:** 2852 (2849); **7:** 4192, 4240 (4237, 4239); **9:** 5281; **10:** 5965, 5999
Rust W B, **5:** 2697 (2697)
Rustin R, **3:** 1394
Rutenfranz J, **8:** 4473
Ruth L, **4:** 2024 (2019, 2022)
Rutherford R B Jr, **1:** 490 (489); **3:** 1441 (1438, 1440)
Rutherford W, **1:** 73 (69)
Rutledge M M, **8:** 4474 (4469)
Rutt T, **7:** 4157 (4156)
Ruttan V W, **1:** 254; **4:** 1841 (1838); **5:** 2965, 2993 (2991)
Rutter M, **3:** 1643 (1640)
Rutter M J, **1:** 494 (491); **3:** 1266 (1265), 1520 (1514, 1515), 1538, 1642 (1637); **4:** 1934 (1929, 1931, 1933), 1980, 2166 (2164), 2261 (2260); **5:** 2589 (2588), 2802 (2799); **6:** 3224 (3223), 3235 (3232), 3297 (3293); **8:** 4395 (4391, 4393), 4779 (4777), 4780, 4873 (4870); **9:** 5211 (5207, 5209), 5224 (5221), 5264 (5262), 5379 (5375), 5406, 5528 (5527); **10:** 5750 (5746), 6083 (6082)
Rutter R, **2:** 711 (710); **3:** 1607 (1603, 1605)

Rutter R A, **9:** 5216 (5214); **10:** 5935 (5932); **11:** 6558 (6554)
Ruus V, **4:** 2029
Ruvinsky L I, **9:** 5399 (5396)
Rwehera M, **1:** 606 (601)
Ryan C, **10:** 5972
Ryan C M, **4:** 2266 (2264)
Ryan D, **7:** 3886 (3881); **8:** 4873 (4869, 4871); **10:** 6173 (6172)
Ryan D W, **1:** 389 (381, 389); **2:** 775 (772); **3:** 1482 (1475), 1768 (1764); **4:** 2140 (2135); **5:** 2778 (2774), 2869 (2868, 2869); **7:** 4236; **10:** 5861 (5856), 6043 (6036, 6040), 6155 (6150, 6151, 6152, 6153); **11:** 6390 (6388, 6389)
Ryan E B, **10:** 5831 (5830)
Ryan J, **4:** 1852 (1850)
Ryan J W, **1:** 175 (173), 176
Ryan K, **10:** 5977 (5973, 5974, 5975)
Ryan M, **4:** 2435 (2433, 2434)
Ryan M P, **10:** 6117
Ryan P, **1:** 103 (100), 111 (104, 109); **2:** 1094 (1089), 1152; **5:** 2942; **6:** 3189 (3188); **9:** 5191 (5186), 5302 (5299); **10:** 5954 (5949); **11:** 6420 (6416, 6418), 6690 (6687)
Ryan R, **11:** 6798 (6794)
Ryan R M, **7:** 3942 (3941)
Ryan T A, **5:** 2714 (2713)
Ryans D G, **3:** 1636 (1631)
Ryba R, **2:** 948; **6:** 3421 (3419); **8:** 4964 (4959, 4960)
Rybash J M, **8:** 4823 (4818, 4820, 4821, 4823)
Rybash J W, **5:** 2677 (2674)
Rydell P J, **6:** 3235 (3233)
Ryerson E, **5:** (2608); **8:** (4500)
Ryff C D, **1:** 239 (237); **9:** 5518 (5513)
Ryle G, **3:** 1434 (1432); **8:** 4447 (4442, 4444), 4456 (4450); **11:** 6438 (6434)
Rynders J E, **2:** 860 (858)
Ryoo J, **3:** 1713 (1710)
Ryoo J-K, **8:** 4918 (4916, 4917); **11:** 6283 (6280)
Rytina N, **4:** 2432 (2430), 2445 (2440)
Rzepski B R, **9:** 5291 (5289)

Saad A M, **7:** 3946 (3944)
Saal F E, **6:** 3124 (3121)
Saari H, **4:** 2024 (2018, 2019, 2020); **11:** 6777 (6776)
Saarni C, **4:** 1967 (1964)
Sabar N, **3:** 1271 (1267), 1272, 1494 (1492); **10:** 6092 (6090)
Sabaroche H, **3:** 1599
Sabatier P, **8:** 4519; **10:** 5782
Sabatino D A, **9:** 5071 (5068); **10:** 5663, 5686
Sabel C, **3:** 1713 (1708); **8:** 4639 (4636)
Sabers D, **1:** 390 (388); **10:** 5762 (5761), 6026 (6023, 6024, 6025)
Sabot H R, **3:** 1660 (1659)
Sabot R H, **3:** 1685 (1682), 1695 (1693), 1707, 1713 (1710), 1784 (1782); **5:** 2945 (2943, 2944, 2945); **6:** 3184 (3182, 3184), 3184 (3179), 3550 (3549); **8:** 4835, 4839, 4844 (4843), 4873 (4868), 4918 (4916); **11:** 6282 (6280)
Sacca K, **8:** 4881 (4880)
Sachs A, **5:** 2457 (2454)
Sachs P, **11:** 6416
Sachs S, **4:** 1928 (1927)
Sack R, **3:** 1695 (1693)
Sackney L, **4:** 1934 (1929, 1931)
Sacré Cœur M-A du, **11:** 6741 (6737)
Saddlemire G L, **10:** 5804 (5799), 5805
Sadiman A S, **9:** 5544 (5542)
Sadke M, **2:** 1064
Sadker D, **8:** 4873 (4869); **9:** 5432 (5423, 5425, 5428), 5445 (5442, 5443)
Sadker M, **5:** 2589 (2587); **8:** 4873 (4869); **9:** 5432 (5423, 5425, 5428), 5445 (5442, 5443)
Sadler M E, **1:** (331); **2:** 923 (919), (923); **3:** (1723)
Sadovnik A R, **1:** 328; **9:** 5201
Sadowy P G, **10:** 5705 (5701)
Sáenz A, **1:** 135 (131)
Saettler L P, **3:** 1800 (1798)
Saettler P, **4:** 1899 (1883), 1929; **10:** 6008 (6005)
Safa H I, **3:** 1672 (1668)
Saffiotti H I B, **3:** 1672 (1669)
Saffle M, **7:** 4026 (4023)
Safo E, **9:** 5389 (5387)
Safran N, **9:** 5013
Safran S P, **5:** 2972 (2969)
Sagar H A, **9:** 5379 (5375)
Sage D D, **7:** 3833 (3832)
Sager C, **5:** 2692
Saha L J, **1:** 358 (355, 356, 357), 474 (469); **2:** 785 (783); **3:** 1655 (1648, 1653, 1654), 1685 (1682); **4:** 2250; **5:** 2937 (2935); **7:** 3722 (3720); **9:** 5201, 5367 (5365); **10:** 5607 (5599, 5600, 5601), 5735 (5733)
Sahasrabudhe A, **11:** 6719 (6718)
Sahm W B, **4:** 2449 (2447), 2452 (2450)
Sahn D E, **5:** 2945 (2943)
Sahota G S, **5:** 2744
Sai F T, **4:** 2418 (2415)
Saigh P A, **10:** 6164 (6162)
Sailor W, **5:** 2907 (2906); **11:** 6461 (6457)
Saily M, **1:** 230 (228)
Sainato D, **9:** 5567 (5565, 5566)
Saint W S, **8:** 4698 (4696)
Saiyidain K G, **5:** 2753
Sajavaara K, **6:** 3439 (3438)
Sakamoto T, **1:** 563 (562); **4:** 1899 (1883)
Sakamoto Y, **6:** 3508 (3504)
Sako M, **4:** 1924 (1919); **6:** 3078, 3092; **11:** 6424 (6421), 6699 (6696, 6697)
Saks D H, **3:** 1386 (1383); **6:** 3549 (3546); **7:** 3820 (3816); **8:** 4568 (4563)
Salaman G, **7:** 3826 (3822, 3824)
Salame B, **3:** 1681
Salapatek P, **6:** 3224; **8:** 4383
Salazar E, **8:** (4624)
Sales G C, **2:** 1175 (1173); **11:** 6603 (6602)
Salgado J, **2:** 640
Salganik L, **2:** 711 (709)
Salih K, **11:** 6283 (6278)
Salili F, **1:** 31 (30), 32 (30)
Salinger G L, **8:** 4479 (4476); **9:** 5342 (5340)
Salisbury C L, **5:** 2814 (2807)
Salisbury D, **5:** 2862
Salisbury D F, **9:** 5043 (5042)
Salisbury R H, **6:** 3276 (3273)
Säljö R, **1:** 194 (189), 322 (319, 321); **2:** 871 (870); **3:** 1246; **5:** 2884 (2882); **7:** 3788 (3784); **8:** 4429 (4425), 4951 (4949); **9:** 5411; **10:** 5790 (5784)
Sallee, **7:** 4111
Sallis J, **5:** 2509 (2505); **7:** 3840
Sallis R, **6:** 3325 (3321)
Salmi J, **4:** 1924 (1919); **10:** 5808 (5806, 5807)
Salmon D, **5:** 2773 (2770)
Salmon R G, **10:** 5613 (5611)
Salomé B, **3:** 1681; **5:** 2819 (2814)
Salomon G, **1:** 570 (566); **2:** 645 (641), 838, 888 (885, 886, 887), 985 (983), 1006 (1002, 1004, 1005), 1175 (1174); **4:** 1898 (1891), 1899 (1891); **5:** 2536 (2535), 2769 (2764), 2897 (2895); **6:** 3625 (3623), 3652 (3651); **7:** 3743 (3739, 3740, 3741, 3742, 3743), 3753 (3745), 3760 (3757, 3758, 3759), 3791 (3790), 3942 (3937); **9:** 5031, 5363 (5362), 5548 (5547); **10:** 5745 (5744), 6053 (6051); **11:** 6457 (6453, 6454, 6455, 6456)
Salomon O, **4:** (2387)
Salop J, **6:** 3617 (3614)
Salop S C, **6:** 3617 (3614)
Salter B, **4:** 1984 (1982); **8:** 4601 (4598)
Salter C, **5:** 2470 (2468)
Salthouse T A, **5:** 2677 (2674, 2676), 2916 (2913); **6:** 3428 (3426); **7:** 3763 (3763); **8:** 4823 (4819), 4824
Salton G, **3:** 1394 (1388)
Saltzman G M, **10:** 6073 (6068)
Saltzstein H D, **7:** 3920 (3919)
Saluri D, **3:** 1602
Salvia J, **2:** 718 (712, 714, 715, 716); **10:** 6173 (6169, 6170); **11:** 6315 (6314)
Salyer K M, **7:** 4081
Salzberg C L, **10:** 6163 (6163)
Salzinger K, **7:** 4316
Salzinger S, **10:** 5759
Samejima F, **3:** 1514 (1511); **5:** 3055 (3052); **6:** 3253 (3251); **8:** 4923 (4920)
Sameroff A J, **1:** 362 (359); **3:** 1520 (1516, 1517), 1643 (1637, 1639, 1640, 1641); **5:** 2802 (2799); **8:** 4395 (4392)
Samet J, **2:** 857 (853)
Samir A, **6:** 3407
Sammons P, **1:** 390 (381, 389); **4:** 1934 (1931, 1932); **5:** 2509 (2508), 2779 (2775), 2870 (2868); **7:** 3912 (3910); **9:** 5223 (5221); **11:** 6390 (6388, 6389)
Samoff J, **1:** 135 (128, 132); **2:** 759 (758), 933 (929); **3:** 1416, 1810 (1808); **4:** 1841 (1838), 1857 (1853); **5:** 2697 (2696), 2965; **8:** 4835 (4834)
Sampath S, **2:** 1170 (1168)
Sampson A, **8:** 4830 (4827)
Sampson G, **6:** 3446 (3443)
Sampson P F, **4:** 2240 (2238)
Samson G E, **8:** 4882 (4876)
Samuda R J, **2:** 718 (716, 717), 719 (716); **7:** 3970 (3967, 3969)
Samuel J, **8:** 4595 (4588, 4591, 4593)
Samuel L, **9:** 5060 (5058)

Samuel R, **7:** 4224, 4225 (4222)
Sanches M, **2:** 802
Sancilio L, **11:** 6456 (6454)
Sand A, **8:** 4473, 4474
Sand G, **3:** (1345)
Sanday P R, **2:** 802; **4:** 2053 (2049)
Sandeen A, **10:** 5805
Sandefur J T, **10:** 5957 (5955)
Sandel M, **4:** 2033
Sandelbach N B, **10:** 6035 (6033)
Sander B, **6:** 3597 (3594); **7:** 4246 (4242); **8:** 4495 (4494)
Sander C L, **3:** (1724)
Sanders A F, **3:** 1520 (1518)
Sanders D C, **7:** 4293 (4290)
Sanders D P, **9:** 5038 (5034); **10:** 6183 (6178, 6180)
Sanders H T, **11:** 6558 (6553)
Sanders J B, **6:** 3360; **9:** 5255
Sanders J R, **3:** 1283 (1280, 1281, 1282); **4:** 2097 (2089), 2109 (2101, 2102, 2104, 2105), 2119 (2110, 2111, 2113, 2114, 2115, 2117, 2118); **8:** 4766; **11:** 6445 (6444)
Sanders J S, **4:** 2427 (2425, 2427)
Sanders M P M, **5:** 2732 (2729)
Sanders N, **7:** 3726 (3724)
Sanders P F, **5:** 2462 (2460)
Sanders R, **8:** 4479 (4475)
Sanders R D, **5:** 2945 (2943)
Sanders R J, **5:** 2685 (2682)
Sanderson D A, **4:** 2357 (2353)
Sandholtz J H, **11:** 6608 (6607)
Sandler B R, **11:** 6712 (6709)
Sandström C I, **3:** 1796 (1794)
Sanford A J, **8:** 4942 (4941)
Sanford J P, **5:** 2529 (2528); **10:** 6031 (6028); **11:** 6390 (6389)
Sanford N, **1:** 48 (47); **10:** 5805 (5798); **11:** 6684
Sangaré A K, **1:** 226 (222); **5:** 2819 (2814, 2815)
Sanghatana S S, **5:** 2457 (2456)
Sangster S, **7:** 4293 (4292)
Sanguinetty J, **2:** 1146; **3:** 1789 (1787); **5:** 2891 (2888)
Sansregret M, **4:** 2186
Santos J dos, **5:** 2562 (2560)
Santos R R, **8:** 4751 (4745)
Santrock J W, **5:** 2677 (2674)
Sanyal B C, **4:** 1947; **10:** 5843
Sapier L, **6:** 3216
Sapir E H, **3:** 1729 (1725, 1727); **6:** 3216 (3214)
Sapon S, **4:** 2338 (2334)
Sapp G L, **7:** 3920
Sapsford D, **9:** 5191
Sara N G, **6:** 3284 (3280, 3283)
Saraceno C, **2:** 701 (695)
Sarachek D, **4:** 2212 (2209)
Saracho O N, **3:** 1635, 1636 (1629, 1630, 1633, 1635)
Saraf S N, **5:** 2759
Sarah E, **4:** 2292
Saran R, **1:** 72
Sarason I G, **4:** 1967; **11:** 6315 (6314), 6360
Sarason S B, **2:** 803 (798); **3:** 1257, 1797 (1795); **4:** 2388 (2388); **5:** 2847 (2839), 2852 (2848); **9:** 5211 (5209, 5210), 5313 (5310); **10:** 5668 (5663, 5665), 5901 (5900), 5925 (5920), 6103 (6100), 6187 (6183, 6187), 6215 (6211, 6213); **11:** 6360 (6356, 6358)
Saraswati D, **11:** (6749)
Saravia-Shore M, **1:** 535; **7:** 3973 (3972)
Sarbin T R, **3:** 1240; **7:** 4050, 4051
Saretsky G, **11:** 6511 (6509)
Sargant N, **6:** 3378; **11:** 6719 (6714)
Sargent L, **4:** 2291
Sarig G, **4:** 2364 (2360)
Sarigiani P A, **9:** 5435 (5433, 5435)
Sarnacki R E, **11:** 6340 (6335)
Sarnat L, **2:** 687 (687)
Sarno R A, **9:** 5008 (5002)
Sarnoff I, **11:** 6360 (6358)
Sarros A M, **10:** 5925 (5921)
Sarros J C, **9:** 5181 (5176, 5178); **10:** 5924 (5920), 5925 (5921), 6062 (6059)
Sartorius R, **5:** 2965
Sartre J-P, **8:** 4433 (4429, 4430, 4431, 4432), (4641)
Sarup M, **2:** 785, 1074 (1067); **10:** 5826 (5822)
Saso M, **5:** 2798 (2792, 2796)
Sass Z, **4:** 1934 (1929, 1931, 1933)
Satin A, **7:** 3711 (3710)
Sato A, **10:** 5995 (5991, 5992)
Sato C J, **4:** 2339 (2337)
Sato I S, **2:** 1182
Sato J, **10:** 5735 (5733)
Sato N, **9:** 5216 (5213, 5215); **10:** 6083 (6082); **11:** 6563 (6561, 6562)
Sato R, **3:** 1449
Sato T, **7:** 4000 (3999)
Satterfiel T H, **7:** 4293 (4292)
Sattler J M, **11:** 6315 (6315)
Sauer E, **1:** 553 (552)
Saul A, **3:** 1821 (1818)
Saunders M M, **5:** 2806
Saupe J L, **4:** 2183 (2183)
Saur R, **9:** 5359 (5357)
Saussure F de, **2:** 1074 (1070, 1071); **9:** 5416 (5411, 5413)
Sautter R C, **2:** 711 (708)
Sautu R, **3:** 1672 (1667, 1669)
Savage C W, **8:** 4634
Savage L J, **1:** 480 (477, 479)
Savage M, **2:** 733 (732)
Savage T, **10:** 5957
Savage-Rumbaugh S, **5:** 2685 (2682)
Savali I, **1:** (270)
Savenye W, **4:** 1928 (1928)
Saver K, **10:** 6244 (6240)
Savicevic D M, **1:** 168 (165), 277 (274)
Savićević D M, **2:** 662 (658)
Saville-Troike M, **6:** 3227 (3226)
Savin-Williams R C, **8:** 4799 (4797)
Sawin C R, **4:** 2131 (2124); **8:** 4751 (4750)
Sawin M M, **4:** 2267 (2264)
Sawinski Z, **7:** 3864 (3863)
Sawyer W D M, **2:** 1012 (1007)
Sawzin S A, **11:** 6425
Saxe D W, **10:** 5585 (5583)
Saxe G B, **2:** 1052; **3:** 1246; **6:** 3453 (3449, 3450)
Saxe L, **4:** 2089 (2082); **10:** 6224
Saxena S, **1:** 254
Saxl E, **6:** 3603 (3602)
Saxonhouse G R, **3:** 1666 (1665)
Saxton J, **8:** 4881 (4875)
Saydawi A, **1:** 450
Sayer A G, **2:** 678 (677)
Sayer J, **10:** 5943
Sayers J H, **2:** 649 (646)
Sayers R, **9:** 5328 (5326)
Saylor J G, **3:** 1315 (1312); **7:** 4249
Sayre W C, **1:** 297 (289)
Scales P, **9:** 5441 (5436)
Scandlen G B, **3:** 1416 (1414)
Scane J, **10:** 6043
Scanlan C L, **7:** 4325, 4329 (4328)
Scanlon D, **2:** 1064
Scanlon E, **2:** 991 (990), 1011 (1010); **7:** 4104 (4101); **10:** 5625 (5625)
Scanlon J W, **5:** 2673 (2670)
Scannell D P, **10:** 5929 (5928)
Scannell M M, **10:** 5929 (5927), 5930
Scarborough D L, **8:** 4945
Scarborough H, **10:** 5680 (5678)
Scardamalia M, **2:** 838 (837), 1006 (1004, 1005, 1006), 1025 (1023); **6:** 3302 (3298); **7:** 3792, 4094 (4090), 4095 (4089); **11:** 6780 (6778, 6780), 6781
Scarella R, **6:** 3213
Scarpitti F R, **3:** 1610
Scarr S, **2:** 688 (686), 706 (701), 846 (845); **3:** 1643 (1636); **4:** 2279 (2278); **5:** 2465 (2464), 2665 (2660); **7:** 4296 (4295, 4296)
Scarr-Salapatck S, **6:** 3144 (3140)
Scarth J, **10:** 6139 (6135)
Schaaf D, **8:** 4758 (4754)
Schaars F, **10:** 5674 (5673)
Schachar, **1:** 139 (136)
Schack G D, **5:** 2495 (2492)
Schaefer U, **6:** 3608; **8:** 4499
Schaeffer-Simmern H, **1:** (340)
Schafer R, **8:** 4791 (4790)
Schäfer U, **11:** 6648 (6641)
Schafer W D, **2:** 796 (795)
Schafer W E, **11:** 6798 (6796)
Schaffer G L, **9:** 5291 (5288)
Schaffer H R, **6:** 3288 (3285)
Schaffner B, **8:** 4541
Schaie K W, **1:** 238, 239 (235, 236, 237, 238); **5:** 2677 (2674, 2675, 2676), 2916 (2915); **6:** 3428, 3435, 3524 (3515, 3518, 3519); **8:** 4824; **11:** 6394 (6391)
Schaie W, **3:** 1647 (1646); **10:** 6026
Schaitmann G W, **3:** 1733
Schaller K, **2:** 884; **3:** 1301 (1290)
Schallert D L, **7:** 3768 (3765); **8:** 4823 (4821); **10:** 5745 (5740, 5741), 6192 (6188)
Schalling D, **1:** 234 (232)
Schalock R L, **3:** 1508; **11:** 6461 (6460)
Schank R C, **6:** 3155, 3345
Schaps E, **8:** 4799 (4798); **10:** 6053 (6053)
Schardein J L, **1:** 15 (13)
Scharf P, **7:** 3925 (3923)
Scharmann L C, **6:** 3416 (3413, 3415)

Schattschneider E E, **4:** 1841 (1837)
Schaude G R, **5:** 2725 (2722, 2723, 2724)
Schawlow A T, **6:** 3235 (3233)
Schawlow L, **6:** 3235 (3233)
Scheaffer R L, **9:** 5142
Schecter S R, **10:** 6099 (6097)
Scheele B, **2:** 969 (968)
Scheerenberger R C, **2:** 730; **10:** 6244 (6243)
Scheerens J, **3:** 1431 (1426, 1427, 1429, 1430), 1746 (1741, 1742); **4:** 1934 (1932); **8:** 4751 (4745)
Scheffé H, **11:** 6591 (6591)
Scheffler I, **2:** 1208 (1204, 1206); **3:** 1367 (1361, 1363), 1524; **4:** 2001; **6:** 3151; **8:** 4447 (4445), 4456 (4447, 4450, 4455), 4464 (4463), 4575 (4574); **9:** 4981 (4979, 4980)
Scheffler L, **10:** 5991 (5990)
Schefft B K, **9:** 5403 (5400)
Schegloff E A, **2:** 1074 (1071)
Scheibe K, **3:** 1240
Schein E H, **9:** 5273 (5270)
Scheinkein J, **4:** 2364 (2359)
Scheirer M A, **4:** 2074 (2072); **11:** 6384 (6378)
Scheler M F, **4:** 1979 (1978)
Schellhaas H, **4:** 2150 (2148)
Schelling F W J, **3:** (1721); **8:** (4418)
Schelsky H, **2:** (1062); **7:** (3769)
Schemerhorn R A, **1:** (533)
Schempp P, **10:** 5713 (5712)
Schenk S M, **1:** 194 (189)
Schensul J J, **7:** 3973 (3971, 3972)
Scherer K R, **4:** 1966, 1967 (1963)
Schermer F J, **10:** 5738 (5737)
Scherz Z, **9:** 5341 (5340)
Scheu J A, **9:** 5363 (5362)
Scheuneman J D, **5:** 3050 (3044, 3045, 3047); **11:** 6320 (6316, 6319)
Scheurman G, **1:** 152 (147); **6:** 3435 (3430, 3431)
Schibeci R A, **9:** 5324 (5320, 5322)
Schickendanz J A, **2:** 893 (888); **4:** 1962 (1958, 1959, 1960, 1962)
Schiefelbein E, **2:** 746, 1146 (1141); **3:** 1593 (1592), 1810 (1807), 1820 (1818), 1824 (1821), 1825 (1823, 1824), 1830 (1826, 1827), 1834 (1831, 1832, 1833, 1834); **4:** 2412 (2410); **5:** 2512 (2511); **7:** 4289 (4284), 4290 (4284); **8:** 4415 (4414), 4495 (4493, 4494, 4495), 4509 (4503, 4506, 4507, 4508), 4526 (4523), 4601 (4598), 4707 (4703), 4873 (4868); **9:** 5241 (5234, 5240), 5539 (5536, 5537, 5538); **11:** 6266 (6261, 6263), 6298 (6293), 6599 (6593, 6594)
Schiefelbein L, **9:** 5268 (5265)
Schiefelbein S, **9:** 5539 (5536, 5537)
Schiefelbusch R, **6:** 3228
Schiefele U, **1:** 204 (201, 202); **6:** 3345 (3344)
Schieffelin B, **6:** 3228 (3225), 3453, 3459; **11:** 6608
Schifter D, **6:** 3671 (3669)
Schijf H, **8:** 4830 (4827)
Schild E O, **9:** 5475 (5472)
Schildkamp-Kündiger E, **4:** 2435, 2436 (2433)
Schiller F, **8:** 4542 (4536)
Schiller H A, **11:** 6625 (6623)
Schillinger, **4:** 2229
Schindele R, **5:** 2972 (2970)
Schlaefli A, **1:** 380 (378)
Schlechty P C, **6:** 3603 (3599, 3601); **9:** 5246 (5241), 5273 (5268, 5269); **10:** 5613 (5612), 6043 (6042)
Schlechty P S, **10:** 6106 (6104)
Schleicher A, **1:** 42 (38), 370 (369); **3:** 1381 (1379); **5:** 2989 (2988)
Schleiermacher F E D, **3:** (1290), (1291), (1303), (1721); **4:** (2386); **5:** (2579), (2581)
Schlerdren A, **11:** 6355 (6354)
Schlesinger A, **7:** 3970 (3966)
Schlesinger B, **4:** 2199 (2198)
Schlesinger I M, **4:** 2218 (2216, 2218); **9:** 5503 (5500, 5503)
Schleyper Y G M, **4:** 2427 (2424, 2425, 2426)
Schlick M, **8:** (4633)
Schlicksupp H, **5:** 2725 (2722, 2723)
Schliemann A D, **2:** 1052 (1050); **8:** 4951 (4949)
Schlossberg N K, **1:** 94; **2:** 1165 (1161, 1162, 1163); **6:** 3349 (3347); **11:** 6551 (6548)
Schlösser M, **11:** 6659 (6654)
Schlosser R W, **1:** 408 (405)
Schlossman S L, **7:** 4296 (4294, 4295)
Schlucter M D, **5:** 2572 (2569)
Schlüter A, **1:** 317
Schmalt H D, **10:** 6159 (6158)
Schmeck R, **1:** 322 (319)
Schmeck R B, **6:** 3329
Schmeck R R, **1:** 194 (188), 389; **2:** 872 (870), 969; **5:** 2769 (2763); **11:** 6328
Schmelkes S, **2:** 640; **7:** 4155 (4150, 4154)
Schmid J, **4:** 2241 (2239); **8:** (4416)
Schmidbauer W, **8:** 4816 (4815)
Schmidt F L, **2:** 1139; **7:** 3783 (3776, 3778, 3779, 3780, 3781, 3782, 3783), 3784 (3776, 3779); **10:** 6240
Schmidt G L, **4:** 1972 (1968)
Schmidt H, **11:** 6699 (6695)
Schmidt H D, **5:** 2677 (2674)
Schmidt J, **6:** 3224 (3219)
Schmidt J A, **4:** 2199 (2197)
Schmidt L R, **10:** 5738
Schmidt P, **3:** 1553
Schmidt R A, **7:** 3953 (3952)
Schmidt R E, **9:** 5359 (5356)
Schmidt R W, **4:** 2339 (2336, 2338)
Schmidt W, **3:** 1257 (1254)
Schmidt W H, **5:** 2596 (2595); **9:** 5275 (5274)
Schmieder A, **4:** 1995 (1992)
Schmitt A P, **11:** 6334 (6330)
Schmitt G, **9:** 5008 (5001)
Schmitt N, **7:** 4007
Schmitt S A, **1:** 480
Schmitz-Scherzer R, **1:** 239 (236)
Schmuck R A, **4:** 2423 (2422), 2432; **5:** 2529 (2524, 2525, 2526, 2527, 2528), 2852 (2848); **7:** 3946 (3943), 4240 (4236, 4237, 4239); **10:** 6187 (6185); **11:** 6731
Schmuller A M, **9:** 5043 (5039)
Schneevoigt N, **7:** 4263 (4257); **11:** 6775 (6774)
Schneewind K A, **4:** 2261 (2261)
Schneider B, **2:** 711 (709)
Schneider F, **3:** (1722)
Schneider F H, **11:** 6775 (6770)
Schneider F W, **2:** 718 (716, 717)
Schneider G, **5:** 2623
Schneider G E, **1:** 554 (552)
Schneider G T, **9:** 5181 (5179)
Schneider K, **10:** 6159 (6158)
Schneider W, **1:** 390 (389); **2:** 706 (704); **4:** 2199 (2198); **5:** 2769 (2761), 2916 (2914); **6:** 3302 (3300), 3329 (3326, 3327), 3428 (3427); **7:** 3763 (3760, 3761, 3762), 3768 (3764, 3765, 3766); **8:** 4395 (4393); **10:** 6159 (6158)
Schnell D, **9:** 5130 (5129)
Schnell S V, **1:** 380 (378)
Schniedewind N, **11:** 6768 (6766)
Schnur E, **5:** 2813 (2812)
Schober K, **11:** 6699 (6695)
Schoenberger E, **3:** 1820 (1813, 1817)
Schoenfeld A H, **6:** 3302 (3299), 3643, 3655 (3653), 3661 (3658); **7:** 3788 (3786); **10:** 5795 (5793); **11:** 6608 (6604, 6607)
Schoenfeldt E, **11:** 6699 (6694)
Schoenmaker J, **2:** 1012 (1010); **3:** 1779 (1776); **8:** 4803 (4800)
Schoer L, **7:** 3935 (3933); **10:** 5704 (5699)
Schofer G, **2:** 738 (733)
Schofield B, **4:** 2292
Schofield C I, **2:** 767
Schofield J W, **3:** 1486 (1484, 1485); **9:** 5379 (5375)
Schofield N, **1:** 322 (319)
Schofield W N, **6:** 3463 (3461, 3462)
Scholem G G, **6:** 3120
Schöler W, **9:** 5328 (5324)
Scholl G T, **11:** 6628
Scholnick E, **8:** 4957 (4956)
Scholten J, **8:** 4803 (4800)
Scholz C, **7:** 3816
Schommer M, **1:** 362 (361)
Schön D A, **1:** 48 (45), 73 (70); **2:** 796 (792); **3:** 1320; **4:** 1899 (1892); **5:** 2773 (2770); **6:** 3219 (3218); **7:** 4050, 4246 (4245); **8:** 4562 (4558, 4561), 4803 (4802); **10:** 5585 (5584), 5961 (5960), 5985 (5984), 6026 (6022), 6043 (6038, 6040), 6088 (6087), 6219 (6215, 6218); **11:** 6292 (6288), 6395 (6394)
Schönbach K-H, **11:** 6699 (6695)
Schönebaum H, **8:** 4419 (4419)
Schonell F J, **7:** 3935 (3931)
Schonemann P H, **9:** 5504 (5501)
Schonfeld W A, **1:** 88 (84)
Schonfield D, **8:** 4824 (4820)
Schonmann S, **10:** 6092 (6090)
Schooler C, **1:** 239 (237); **6:** 3428 (3426); **8:** 4824; **10:** 5591 (5589), 6026
Schoonever R A, **7:** 3775
Schoonman W, **5:** 2784
Schopler E, **1:** 494 (491); **6:** 3235 (3232, 3233)

Schoppa L J, **8:** 4595 (4588, 4589, 4591, 4592, 4593), 4602; **9:** 5191 (5187)
Schorr D, **5:** 2813 (2808)
Schorr K E, **8:** 4461 (4458)
Schorr L B, **2:** 711 (710); **3:** 1643 (1641); **5:** 2813 (2808)
Schrader F-W, **1:** 204 (200); **2:** 846 (846); **3:** 1504 (1503, 1504); **9:** 5043 (5041); **10:** 5772 (5768, 5770, 5771), 6173 (6172)
Schrader R M, **9:** 5082 (5080)
Schrader W B, **4:** 2183; **7:** 4000 (3997), 4170 (4163)
Schrag F, **2:** 933 (926); **8:** 4634 (4630)
Schramm W L, **1:** 274 (267), 563 (562), 570 (564, 565); **3:** 1580 (1579); **4:** 1911 (1904); **5:** 2891, 2897 (2892, 2894, 2895); **8:** 4774 (4772)
Schras G A, **10:** 5939 (5936)
Schratz M, **1:** 431 (430), 432 (426); **2:** 803 (799)
Schreibstein A R, **4:** 2351 (2350)
Schreier E, **7:** 3808 (3806)
Schreiner R, **10:** 5705 (5701)
Schrettenbrunner H L, **5:** 2470 (2468)
Schriever S W, **5:** 2491 (2487, 2490)
Schriewer J, **1:** 317 (311); **2:** 933; **11:** 6684
Schrift A, **5:** 2586
Schrijvers J, **5:** 2862
Schriver K A, **11:** 6780 (6778)
Schröder E, **2:** 846 (844)
Schrodt P A, **7:** 3816
Schroeder F J, **3:** 1449 (1447)
Schroeder W L, **8:** 4812 (4804)
Schroeter D, **10:** 6112 (6110)
Schrooten H, **2:** 984 (983), 1006 (1005)
Schroyer G, **7:** 4240 (4238)
Schründer A, **10:** 5662
Schubert A, **6:** 3234 (3233, 3234)
Schubert N A, **7:** 4215 (4212, 4213)
Schubert W H, **3:** 1266 (1262), 1278 (1274), 1301 (1300), 1308 (1302, 1303, 1305), 1325 (1325), 1334, 1337 (1334); **4:** 1848 (1842); **10:** 5817 (5813, 5815), 5818 (5816)
Schubring G, **6:** 3647
Schuder T, **10:** 6177 (6177)
Schuele C, **10:** 5691 (5689)
Schuemer R, **7:** 4220 (4218)
Schuetze H G, **1:** 564
Schug M C, **9:** 5563 (5562)
Schuh J H, **10:** 5805 (5800), 5808
Schulenberg W, **4:** 2267; **7:** 4325 (4321, 4322)
Schuler A L, **6:** 3235 (3232, 3233)
Schuler R A, **10:** 6062 (6060)
Schuler R S, **10:** 5924 (5923)
Schuller T, **8:** 4616 (4615), 4964; **11:** 6395 (6391)
Schulman L, **10:** 6117 (6113)
Schulman P, **9:** 5406 (5404, 5406)
Schulte A C, **1:** 322 (319); **6:** 3339 (3337)
Schultz D, **11:** 6775 (6770)
Schultz K, **2:** 1198 (1198)
Schultz L H, **5:** 2681 (2678)
Schultz T, **1:** 560 (554); **2:** 1074 (1066); **11:** 6283 (6280)
Schultz T P, **3:** 1707; **4:** 2419 (2413); **5:** 2945 (2944); **11:** 6638
Schultz T W, **1:** 254 (245, 252), 521 (512, 517); **2:** 933 (929), 1055 (1052, 1054), 1056; **3:** 1666 (1662), 1676, 1695 (1690, 1691); **5:** 2500 (2496), 2647 (2643, 2646); **6:** 3101, 3106
Schultze W, **5:** 2978
Schulz E M, **5:** 2515 (2513)
Schulz T W, **9:** 5523
Schulz W, **3:** 1301 (1291); **11:** 6699 (6695)
Schulze K G, **10:** 6149 (6146)
Schumaker J B, **2:** 867 (863); **10:** 6164 (6161), 6178 (6175, 6177)
Schunk D H, **1:** 204, 377 (376); **6:** 3297 (3295), 3329 (3325), 3340 (3335), 3345; **10:** 5745, 5775 (5772)
Schurig M, **3:** 1733
Schurr J, **3:** 1301 (1290)
Schuttenberg E, **10:** 6012 (6011)
Schutz A, **2:** 1074 (1070, 1071); **3:** (1344); **8:** (4430); **10:** (5588), 5973 (5969)
Schutz H G, **7:** 4329
Schutz W, **5:** 2529 (2524)
Schütze H E, **1:** 94; **7:** 4263 (4257, 4262)
Schütze H G, **1:** 180 (178); **6:** 3399 (3395), 3425 (3422); **7:** 4263 (4261), 4325; **8:** 4364, 4616, 4964 (4961); **10:** 5643; **11:** 6551 (6548)
Schutze H J, **5:** 2951 (2949)
Schuyten M C, **4:** 1872 (1866, 1867)
Schvader-Breymann H, **4:** (2385)
Schwab J J, **1:** 48 (45); **3:** 1267 (1263, 1264, 1265), 1271 (1268), 1320 (1316, 1317), 1334 (1329, 1330, 1331, 1332), 1355 (1348), 1544 (1539, 1540, 1541), 1804 (1801); **4:** 1848 (1842); **5:** 2589 (2587), 2903 (2898, 2899); **6:** 3416 (3414); **10:** 5818 (5815), 5887 (5885), 6043 (6041), 6092 (6091), 6099 (6097)
Schwab R L, **10:** 5924 (5923), 5925 (5920), 6062 (6059, 6060, 6061)
Schwabe H, **3:** 1647 (1643)
Schwadron A A, **7:** 4026 (4023)
Schwartz A, **3:** 1681; **5:** 2740, 2819 (2814); **11:** 6452 (6448)
Schwartz B, **2:** 665 (663); **4:** 1976 (1973); **6:** 3422; **8:** 4964 (4958); **11:** 6452 (6448)
Schwartz F, **2:** 825 (822, 824)
Schwartz I S, **8:** 4375 (4374)
Schwartz J, **7:** 4100 (4097)
Schwartz J H, **1:** 553
Schwartz P, **4:** 2331
Schwartz R D, **11:** 6511 (6508)
Schwartz T, **3:** 1729 (1726)
Schwartzman S, **3:** 1713 (1712)
Schwarz G, **6:** 3508 (3504)
Schwarz H, **4:** 2357
Schwarz J C, **7:** 4301 (4298)
Schwarzenberger R L E, **6:** 3638 (3635)
Schwarzer R, **9:** 5518; **10:** 5772
Schwarzwald J, **10:** 5618 (5614, 5615)
Schweinhart L J, **2:** 687 (679, 680), 688 (679, 680, 681), 1131 (1130); **3:** 1628 (1625), 1641 (1640), 1825 (1824); **4:** 1841 (1837), 2145 (2144); **5:** 2806 (2804), 2813 (2812); **6:** 3524 (3517); **7:** 4301 (4298); **8:** 4666 (4664); **11:** 6384 (6382)
Schweitzer J, **2:** 662; **4:** 1934 (1929, 1930, 1932); **10:** 5919 (5915)
Schweitzer J H, **9:** 5210 (5207)
Schweitzer W, **2:** 766 (765)
Schwenkmezger P, **10:** 5738
Schwerin J B, **2:** 649 (646)
Schwier R, **5:** 2897 (2895, 2896); **7:** 3996
Schwieso J, **7:** 3942
Schwille J, **2:** 770 (768); **3:** 1257 (1254, 1255), 1381 (1377), 1655 (1651); **6:** 3550 (3546)
Scollon R, **2:** 803 (800); **6:** 3453 (3449)
Scollon S B K, **6:** 3453 (3449)
Scott A M E, **1:** 560 (554, 556); **3:** 1672 (1668, 1671); **4:** 2432 (2430)
Scott B C E, **5:** 2769 (2763); **10:** 6202 (6199)
Scott D, **11:** 6798 (6797)
Scott E L, **11:** 6712 (6709, 6710, 6711)
Scott E M, **4:** 2145
Scott E P, **11:** 6628
Scott G, **7:** 4111
Scott J, **9:** 5560 (5558)
Scott J A, **10:** 5795 (5791)
Scott J J, **10:** 6244
Scott J R, **11:** 6484 (6482)
Scott K P, **4:** 2412 (2409); **9:** 5302 (5301), 5445 (5442), 5578
Scott M, **2:** 1094
Scott Morton M S, **5:** 2831 (2828)
Scott P A, **4:** 2435 (2434)
Scott P H, **8:** 4479 (4477), 4652
Scott R, **9:** 5043 (5040)
Scott R R, **3:** 1486 (1484)
Scott S, **7:** 4319 (4317); **9:** 5441 (5437, 5438)
Scott T, **2:** 1006 (1002, 1003); **6:** 3655 (3654)
Scott W A, **2:** 816 (813); **10:** 6227 (6226)
Scott W R, **1:** 437 (432); **3:** 1774 (1770); **4:** 2166 (2157); **8:** 4568 (4562, 4563)
Scott-Hodgetts R, **10:** 5826 (5824)
Scott-Jones D, **4:** 2258; **7:** 3722 (3719), 3872 (3870)
Scott-Jones P, **9:** 5264 (5260)
Scovel T, **4:** 2339 (2334, 2335)
Scribner S, **1:** 295 (291), 297 (292), 482 (482); **2:** 1212 (1210); **3:** 1246 (1242), 1252; **6:** 3453 (3447), 3459 (3454, 3455), 3463 (3460); **7:** 4095; **11:** 6416, 6457 (6453, 6454, 6455)
Scrimshaw P, **9:** 5294
Scriven M, **1:** 370 (364); **2:** 1208 (1204); **3:** 1283 (1281, 1282), 1367 (1359); **4:** 1848 (1844), 2037, 2074 (2070), 2079, (2088), 2097 (2092, 2094), 2100 (2097, 2098), 2108 (2102, 2103, 2105, 2107, 2108), 2119 (2109, 2110, 2111, 2112, 2115, 2118), 2132 (2125, 2126), 2374 (2370, 2371); **5:** (2879); **7:** 3833 (3832), 4059 (4057); **8:** 4634 (4633), 4766 (4761, 4764), 4783 (4780, 4781); **11:** 6511 (6510)
Scruggs T E, **8:** 4376 (4372)
Scrupski A, **1:** 295
Scruton R, **3:** 1501 (1500)
Scrutton D, **5:** 2812, 2813
Sczcepanski J, **11:** 6648 (6641)

Seadon T, **10:** 5995 (5992, 5993)
Sealand N, **3:** 1642 (1637)
Seammon R E, **5:** 2684 (2682)
Search P, **5:** 2773 (2770)
Searle B, **3:** 1573 (1572); **4:** 1911 (1906), 1918 (1913); **5:** 2891 (2887, 2888); **8:** 4698 (4696); **11:** 6366 (6361, 6362, 6363)
Sears J T, **3:** 1325, 1337; **10:** 6106 (6105)
Sears R R, **1:** 497 (495)
Seashore C E, **5:** (2878)
Seashore H G, **11:** 6348 (6341)
Sebba G, **3:** 1464
Sebba J, **10:** 5943
Sebeok T A, **7:** 4175
Sebesta S, **2:** 738
Secada W G, **6:** 3652 (3650); **7:** 4099; **11:** 6617
Sechrest L, **1:** 390 (385, 386); **11:** 6511 (6508)
Secord P F, **4:** (2297)
Secord W, **10:** 5693 (5692)
Sederberg C H, **7:** 4215 (4213); **9:** 5185 (5183)
Sedlak M W, **10:** 5818 (5815)
See K O, **8:** 4896 (4891, 4895)
Seeborg M, **7:** 4201 (4199)
Seel N M, **2:** 888 (886)
Seeley D, **2:** 893 (888)
Seeley K, **9:** 5532 (5529, 5530)
Seels B, **5:** 2862 (2857, 2860)
Seeman M, **10:** 5925 (5921)
Seetharamu A S, **3:** 1607 (1604)
Seffrin J, **5:** 2572
Segal J W, **1:** 193; **2:** 856, 868; **5:** 2767 (2762), 2769 (2762); **6:** 3288, 3297 (3296), 3324; **8:** 4730 (4728), 4731, 4951 (4948); **9:** 5563; **10:** 6192
Segal N L, **2:** 846 (845); **11:** 6492 (6488)
Segall M H, **5:** 2651
Segalowitz N, **8:** 4939 (4938)
Segar J, **7:** 3853 (3850)
Segebarth K, **1:** 194 (192)
Séguin E, **7:** (3913); **10:** (5659)
Seibel C, **5:** 2515 (2513)
Seidel J F, **5:** 2567 (2564)
Seidel R J, **2:** 973, 1011
Seidman S A, **4:** 1918 (1916)
Seifer R, **1:** 362; **3:** 1643 (1637, 1640, 1641)
Seifert R V, **10:** 6079 (6076)
Seifert T, **9:** 5216 (5213)
Seiffge-Krenke I, **10:** 5738 (5737)
Seifman E, **2:** 760
Seiford L M, **3:** 1387 (1384)
Seigfried C, **4:** 2302 (2300)
Seipp P, **6:** 3276 (3274)
Seitz F, **10:** 6117 (6114, 6116)
Seitz P, **11:** 6633 (6628)
Seitz V, **7:** 4301 (4299)
Sekowski A, **5:** 2495 (2492)
Selander S, **4:** 2377 (2376)
Selby D, **3:** 1501; **4:** 1852 (1850)
Selby J G, **7:** 4225 (4223)
Selden W K, **1:** 28
Self J A, **1:** 348; **2:** 1170; **3:** 1779; **4:** 1899 (1895); **10:** 6193 (6192)
Selfe C L, **6:** 3209 (3208)
Selig R O, **1:** 280, 299, 300; **7:** 3974 (3972)
Seligman M E P, **7:** 3942 (3940), 3946; **9:** 5406 (5404, 5405, 5406), 5407
Seligman P F, **7:** 3810 (3808)
Seligson M, **3:** 1635 (1634)
Selim M A, **3:** 1544 (1543)
Selinker L L, **6:** 3439 (3439)
Selleck R J W, **8:** 4715 (4708); **10:** 5708, 6139 (6133); **11:** 6735 (6734)
Seller M, **7:** 3853 (3850)
Seller W, **3:** 1315 (1312)
Sellers S, **5:** 2457
Sellier F, **4:** 1976 (1973); **5:** 2942 (2939, 2941); **11:** 6420 (6419)
Sellin B, **4:** 2070 (2065); **9:** 5191 (5190)
Sellin N, **5:** 2931 (2930); **7:** 3986 (3979, 3984, 3985), 4015 (4015); **8:** 4359 (4353, 4357); **9:** 5372 (5371), 5373 (5371)
Selltiz C A, **1:** 389 (380, 381)
Selman G, **7:** 4185 (4183); **8:** (4459)
Selman R L, **5:** 2681 (2678); **9:** 5512 (5510, 5511); **10:** 6053 (6052, 6053)
Selmes I P, **9:** 5363 (5360, 5361)
Selowsky M, **3:** 1666 (1662); **4:** 2145; **8:** 4666 (4665)
Seltzer M, **5:** 2596; **9:** 5130 (5129)
Selvin M, **1:** 11 (9, 10)
Selz O, **5:** (2876), 2884 (2881)
Selznick P, **4:** 2166 (2157)
Semel S F, **1:** 328
Semeonoff B, **8:** 4791
Semin G R, **9:** 5350 (5349)
Semmel M I, **2:** 729 (727); **6:** 3559 (3558); **7:** 3808 (3802)
Sempé G, **8:** 4474 (4470)
Sempé M, **8:** 4474 (4470, 4471)
Semple C, **6:** 3458 (3458)
Sen A, **4:** 2419 (2413, 2416); **7:** 3739 (3734)
Åsén G, **4:** 2377 (2376)
Sen P K, **7:** 4163 (4161)
Sendov B, **2:** 1175 (1172)
Sendova E, **2:** 977 (976)
Senga-Nsilazolo V, **7:** 4236 (4232)
Senge P M, **4:** 1924 (1923); **5:** 2689 (2687); **6:** 3306 (3303)
Senghaas D, **3:** 1733 (1730)
Sennett R, **1:** 297 (290); **9:** 5572 (5569)
Sension D, **5:** 3066 (3063)
Seo G-H, **1:** 495; **6:** 3228 (3226); **10:** 6244 (6243)
Sepulveda Lagos J, **4:** 2267 (2262)
Sepulveda-Stuardo M A, **8:** 4848 (4846); **11:** 6366, 6370 (6367)
Serbin L A, **4:** 2449 (2449), 2452 (2450, 2451)
Seregny S, **8:** 4586 (4585)
Sergeant J A, **3:** 1520 (1518); **5:** 2879, 2884; **6:** 3292
Sergent F, **5:** 2984, 2993 (2989); **11:** 6664 (6660)
Sergiovanni T J, **1:** 67, 437 (432, 433); **3:** 1774 (1771), 1775 (1771, 1772); **4:** 1972 (1968), 2166, 2167, 2389; **6:** 3284 (3278); **7:** 4246 (4244); **9:** 5169 (5162); **10:** 5991, 6004 (6003)
Sernhede O, **11:** 6803 (6802)
Serra L, **1:** 48 (45)
Servaes J, **7:** 3760 (3759)
Servan-Schreiber J J, **7:** 4088 (4082)
Sethuraman S V, **5:** 2819 (2814)
Setsaas R, **7:** 4180
Sevcik R A, **1:** 408 (407); **5:** 2685 (2682)
Sever R, **9:** 5367 (5366)
Severijnen, **10:** 5674 (5673)
Severin T, **7:** 3906
Sevestre P, **11:** 6669 (6664)
Sevigny M J, **11:** 6621
Sevón G, **9:** 5563
Sewart D, **3:** 1563, 1579; **7:** 4220 (4218); **9:** 5367 (5366); **10:** 5596
Sewel S, **9:** 5201
Sewell G T, **11:** 6370 (6369)
Sewell W, **6:** 3144 (3138); **9:** 5176 (5172)
Sewell W H, **1:** 358 (356, 357); **4:** 2257 (2252, 2254); **7:** 3872; **9:** 5553 (5551); **10:** 5607 (5600)
Sewell W M, **7:** 3722
Sexton P, **9:** 5572 (5569)
Sexton S, **9:** 5273 (5272)
Sexton V S, **5:** 2692 (2689)
Seybold J, **4:** 1958 (1955)
Seyer P, **7:** 4095 (4091)
Seyfarth R M, **5:** 2685 (2682)
Seyle H, **10:** 6062 (6058)
Shachar C, **2:** 1099 (1095, 1098)
Shachar H, **5:** 2536 (2534); **10:** 6187 (6186)
Shadish W R, **11:** 6384 (6378, 6382)
Shadish W R Jr, **4:** 2089 (2088), 2108 (2101, 2102, 2103, 2105, 2106, 2107, 2108); **8:** 4783 (4780)
Shadur M A, **11:** 6638 (6636)
Shaeffer S, **2:** 914; **3:** 1557, 1825 (1822); **4:** 1852 (1849); **8:** 4526 (4525), 4601 (4598, 4599)
Shafer G, **9:** 5467 (5466)
Shafer S M, **4:** 1857 (1853)
Shaffer D R, **1:** 380 (378), 390 (381, 382); **2:** 706 (702); **3:** 1520; **9:** 5324 (5319)
Shaffer J B P, **5:** 2692 (2689, 2690, 2691)
Shaffer J P, **6:** 3508 (3500)
Shafi M, **1:** 210
Shafriri N, **10:** 6092 (6090)
Shafto M G, **1:** 374; **5:** 2767, 2768 (2762, 2765), 2769
Shah A B, **5:** 2759 (2754)
Shah B V, **9:** 5130 (5129)
Shaiken H, **11:** 6283 (6281)
Shaikh I, **11:** 6753 (6751)
Shake M C, **10:** 5762 (5760)
Shakeshaft C, **1:** 67 (62), 437 (436); **11:** 6726 (6723), 6731 (6727, 6728, 6729, 6730)
Shakotko R A, **4:** 2212 (2210); **6:** 3616 (3614)
Shalaby A, **11:** 6760 (6754)
Shames G, **10:** 5691, 5693
Shan S-J, **6:** 3459 (3457, 3458)
Shanas E, **6:** 3428
Shand R T, **1:** 254 (246)
Shane H, **2:** 1175 (1172)
Shane H C, **1:** 409 (405)
Shane H G, **5:** 2773 (2770); **10:** 6103

Shank A, **2:** 1073 (1066)
Shank P C, **7:** 4293 (4291)
Shanker A, **6:** 3197 (3191); **10:** 6043 (6037), 6096 (6093)
Shankweiler D P, **8:** 4935 (4934), 4944 (4943)
Shanner W M, **5:** 2870 (2868)
Shannon C E, **2:** 1079 (1075)
Shannon P, **2:** 737 (734), 1198; **11:** 6371
Shannon S M, **1:** 534 (534)
Shantz C U, **1:** 234; **9:** 5512 (5510); **10:** 5758 (5758)
Shapin S, **9:** 5350 (5349)
Shapira A, **3:** 1240 (1238, 1239)
Shapira R, **2:** 893 (889); **7:** 3852 (3849); **8:** 4571 (4571); **9:** 5216 (5212, 5213, 5214), 5367 (5365, 5366); **11:** 6287 (6285, 6287)
Shapira Y, **3:** 1624 (1621)
Shapiro B J, **1:** 389 (381, 389); **2:** 775 (772); **3:** 1482 (1475); **4:** 2140 (2135); **5:** 2778 (2774), 2869 (2868, 2869); **7:** 3886 (3881), 4236; **8:** 4873 (4869, 4871); **10:** 5861 (5856), 6155 (6150, 6151, 6152, 6153), 6173 (6172); **11:** 6390 (6388, 6389)
Shapiro C, **3:** 1703 (1698)
Shapiro D, **1:** 266 (263)
Shapiro E K, **4:** 2449 (2448); **9:** 5528 (5527)
Shapiro E S, **9:** 4977 (4975); **10:** 6173 (6170, 6171)
Shapiro F, **7:** 3905 (3897)
Shapiro H, **3:** 1624 (1622)
Shapiro R J, **3:** 1768 (1764)
Shapiro S, **2:** 1204 (1199); **3:** 1642 (1637, 1639), 1720; **6:** 3621 (3619); **10:** 5607 (5602)
Shapiro T, **3:** 1520 (1515)
Shaplin J J, **4:** 2166
Shapovalenko S G, **2:** 1064
Shapson S M, **2:** 775 (773)
Sharabi H, **1:** 328
Sharan M, **1:** 111
Sharan S, **2:** 1099 (1095, 1097, 1098); **3:** 1486; **5:** 2504, 2536 (2533, 2534); **8:** (4369); **10:** 6187 (6183, 6184, 6185)
Sharan Y, **2:** 1099 (1097); **10:** 6187 (6183, 6185)
Sharko J, **8:** 4473 (4469)
Sharma D V, **5:** 2759
Sharma J C, **11:** 6492 (6491)
Sharon D, **5:** 2897 (2893)
Sharp A M, **1:** 199 (197); **2:** 868 (862), 1207 (1207)
Sharp D W, **1:** 295 (291); **3:** 1252 (1247); **4:** 1851 (1849); **5:** 2685
Sharp L, **4:** 2388 (2386); **10:** 6112 (6109)
Sharp R, **2:** 785 (783), 1074 (1070)
Sharpe D, **11:** 6511 (6509)
Sharpe T, **10:** 6026 (6023, 6024)
Sharpes D K, **10:** 6043 (6035, 6042)
Sharples M, **8:** 4694
Sharpless R, **7:** 4225 (4221, 4222)
Sharpley A M, **11:** 6484 (6483)
Sharpley C F, **9:** 5489 (5486, 5487, 5488, 5489); **11:** 6484 (6483)
Shatz M, **6:** 3224 (3221)
Shaughnessy J M, **6:** 3685 (3682); **9:** 5324 (5321)
Shaunnessey M, **5:** 2870 (2869)
Shavelson R J, **1:** 42 (33), 370 (368); **3:** 1257 (1255, 1256); **4:** 1863 (1863), 2240 (2238), 2388 (2384); **5:** 2462 (2459, 2461, 2462), 2714 (2713); **6:** 3124; **7:** 3726 (3724), 4006 (4001); **8:** 4730 (4730); **9:** 5394 (5392); **10:** 5772 (5768), 6035 (6032), 6043 (6040), 6088 (6086), 6173 (6172); **11:** 6591 (6591)
Shaver D, **3:** 1534 (1531)
Shaver J, **2:** 770 (769); **4:** 1984 (1981); **10:** 5585
Shaver J P, **9:** 5562, 5563, 5582 (5580)
Shaver J R, **1:** 280
Shaver P, **4:** 2449; **9:** 5441
Shavit R, **9:** 5367 (5365)
Shavit Y, **1:** 11 (7); **2:** 825 (821); **8:** 4896 (4893, 4894); **9:** 5553 (5553); **10:** 5735 (5733)
Shavlik J W, **8:** 4722
Shaw E, **1:** 15
Shaw G B, **8:** (4605)
Shaw G K, **10:** 5767
Shaw J, **4:** 2292 (2291)
Shaw J G, **2:** 851 (847)
Shaw M E, **1:** 390 (383); **5:** 2529 (2523, 2524, 2527); **7:** 3707 (3703)
Shaw M L G, **9:** 5016
Shaw R, **4:** 2369 (2366); **7:** 3953
Shaw S, **7:** 4095 (4092)
Shaw W E, **4:** 1918 (1913)
Shawcross V, **4:** 2423 (2420)
Shayer M, **2:** 838; **5:** 2669 (2667), 2670, 2680; **8:** 4478 (4476)
Shea C M, **9:** 5180
Shea J R, **11:** 6633 (6628), 6704 (6700)
Shea S L, **8:** 4383 (4381)
Shearer A, **3:** 1507
Shearer D, **5:** 2813 (2810)
Shearer M, **5:** 2813 (2810)
Shearon R W, **8:** 4616 (4610)
Shears B, **6:** 3560 (3559)
Sheather S J, **9:** 5082 (5079, 5081)
Sheckley B C, **11:** 6307 (6301)
Shedd J B, **1:** 437 (435)
Shedd J D, **10:** 5805
Sheehan K M, **5:** 3055 (3053); **7:** 3861 (3861)
Sheehan R, **1:** 362 (361); **4:** 2266 (2266)
Sheen R, **4:** 2339 (2335)
Sheets C, **7:** 4099 (4096)
Sheets R, **8:** 4715 (4710)
Sheffield J R, **1:** 215; **4:** 2369; **7:** 4145 (4142); **8:** 4688
Sheffield P W, **5:** 2827
Sheick J A, **1:** 239 (238)
Sheingold K, **2:** 973, 991 (990), 1012 (1009); **7:** 4100 (4096), 4104 (4102); **11:** 6287 (6283, 6284, 6285, 6286, 6287)
Sheldon S, **6:** 3209 (3207)
Sheldrake P, **10:** 6085 (6085)
Shellard J S, **4:** 1863 (1860)
Shelley, **8:** (4641)
Shelton M, **6:** 3660
Shelton R L, **11:** 6707 (6706, 6707)
Shelton T L, **5:** 2813 (2811)
Shemilt D, **9:** 5563 (5561)
Shen B, **9:** 5350 (5346, 5347)
Shepard L A, **3:** 1359 (1358), 1624 (1621); **5:** 2515 (2513, 2514), 3050 (3045, 3049); **7:** 3726 (3724); **9:** 5228 (5225, 5226), 5275 (5274); **10:** 5726 (5722); **11:** 6320 (6318), 6563 (6561)
Shepard R N, **9:** 5158 (5152, 5157), 5503 (5498, 5502)
Shepard T H, **1:** 15 (13)
Shephard R J, **8:** 4474
Shepherd R B, **5:** 2813 (2810)
Shepp B E, **8:** 4383 (4382)
Sheppard R W, **4:** 1924 (1923)
Sher J P, **9:** 5233 (5230)
Sheriffs A C, **7:** 4000 (3997)
Sherington G, **8:** 4831
Sherman A, **4:** 2004 (2002)
Sherman C, **2:** 649; **7:** 3991
Sherman G D, **10:** 5680 (5679)
Sherman G F, **7:** 4081 (4078)
Sherman H J, **3:** 1703 (1699)
Sherman J, **7:** 4336; **9:** 5066 (5062)
Sherman J A, **9:** 5432 (5424, 5428, 5430, 5431); **10:** 6164 (6161)
Sherman J D, **9:** 5241 (5236)
Sherman J G, **5:** 2773 (2772); **8:** 4774 (4773)
Sherraden M W, **8:** 4581 (4580)
Sherratt W J, **8:** 4464 (4462)
Sherrill L, **8:** 4956 (4952)
Sherrod L R, **6:** 3428 (3426); **8:** 4719
Sherwin R, **9:** 5385
Sherwood B A, **10:** 5887 (5886)
Sherwood R, **2:** 1019
Sherzer J, **6:** 3452
Sheu T, **2:** 635 (634)
Shiang C P, **8:** 4882 (4878)
Shiefelbein E, **8:** 4495 (4493)
Shields P M, **8:** 4935
Shields S A, **9:** 5435 (5433)
Shiffrin R M, **6:** 3302 (3300)
Shigemasu K, **5:** 2596
Shigematsu A, **7:** 3946 (3945)
Shih Y F, **7:** 4100
Shillcock R, **6:** 3209 (3208)
Shilling C, **3:** 1739 (1738); **10:** 5607 (5602)
Shillingford D, **3:** 1599
Shils E, **5:** 2998 (2996); **8:** 4830 (4827); **10:** 5782 (5776)
Shils E A, **2:** 1074 (1065)
Shimahara N K, **1:** 295, 297 (293); **2:** 1213 (1208, 1210, 1212); **10:** 5991 (5990); **11:** 6699 (6696)
Shimizu H, **6:** 3228 (3225)
Shimmin H S, **4:** 2449 (2447)
Shimoni R, **7:** 4301 (4298)
Shimron J S, **5:** 2779 (2776), 2870 (2868)
Shinkfield A J, **4:** 2089 (2080)
Shinn M R, **2:** 718, 719 (714); **3:** 1359 (1357); **8:** 4375; **10:** 5686 (5684), 6031 (6028)
Shinohara M, **5:** 2972 (2970)
Shinzawa M, **8:** 4796 (4794)
Shipman M D, **10:** 6127 (6124)

Shipman V, **6:** 3238 (3235)
Shiqi H, **2:** 900 (898)
Shire B, **6:** 3638 (3635)
Shirk Li, **6:** 3484 (3481)
Shiva V, **7:** 4336 (4333)
Shizukurshi K, **10:** 5674 (5670)
Shlanka D, **2:** 738 (735)
Shlapentokh V, **10:** 5758 (5755, 5757)
Shlechter T M, **7:** 3743
Shneiderman B, **2:** 1170
Shoben E, **3:** 1514 (1512)
Shockey J W, **11:** 6276 (6274)
Shockley R J, **9:** 5185 (5183)
Shoemaker D, **4:** 2097 (2092)
Shoemaker F F, **1:** 254 (252); **3:** 1494 (1491)
Shonkoff J P, **1:** 362; **3:** 1624 (1621), 1643 (1640); **5:** 2813 (2812), 2814; **8:** 4779
Shor I, **4:** 1984 (1982); **8:** 4575 (4573); **10:** 5607 (5602), 6058 (6057)
Shores J H, **3:** 1267 (1264); **10:** 5818 (5813, 5814)
Shores R E, **9:** 5567 (5564, 5565, 5566)
Shorish M M, **5:** 2512 (2511)
Short A H, **9:** 5475 (5473)
Short E C, **3:** 1271 (1269), 1320 (1316), 1325 (1323), 1355; **4:** 2389
Short E J, **10:** 5831 (5830)
Short J, **3:** 1501 (1497, 1498)
Short J L, **8:** 4779 (4776, 4778)
Short R, **3:** 1514 (1512)
Short R H, **10:** 5745
Shortall S, **5:** 3020
Short' ind M, **9:** 5350
Sho .ani Y, **2:** 635 (634)
Shotland L, **4:** 2108
Shotland R L, **3:** 1283; **5:** 2672 (2671), 2673
Shoven B, **4:** 2315 (2311, 2312)
Showers B, **1:** 72 (70); **3:** 1635 (1632); **5:** 2847 (2845, 2846), 2852 (2850); **10:** 5973 (5968, 5969), 5982, 6192 (6188, 6190)
Shrager J, **2:** 852 (848)
Shrewsbury C M, **11:** 6768 (6767)
Shriberg L, **10:** 5697 (5695)
Shrigley R L, **3:** 1544 (1543)
Shriver B, **5:** 2529 (2524)
Shuard H, **6:** 3638 (3637)
Shubik M, **3:** 1830 (1828)
Shucksmith J, **1:** 194 (185)
Shuell T J, **2:** 1019 (1018); **4:** 1848 (1842, 1843, 1845); **6:** 3306 (3303), 3345 (3340, 3341, 3342, 3344); **10:** 6026 (6021)
Shukla S, **5:** 2897 (2893)
Shulman J H, **10:** 5948 (5947), 6122
Shulman L S, **3:** 1257, 1355, 1504 (1503), 1543, 1544 (1538, 1539, 1541, 1542), 1636 (1632); **4:** 1848 (1842, 1844), 2001, 2033, 2132 (2125, 2130); **5:** 2769, 2778, 2874 (2871, 2873); **6:** 3652 (3651); **8:** 4464 (4463), 4948 (4946); **9:** 5030 (5022, 5024), 5056, 5411 (5408); **10:** 5613, 5887 (5884), 5948 (5943, 5944, 5945, 5947), 5957 (5955), 5961 (5959), 5985 (5984), 5995 (5992, 5993), 5999 (5999), 6015 (6014), 6043 (6039), 6092 (6089), 6099, 6122 (6117, 6118, 6120), 6183 (6182), 6208 (6203, 6204, 6206); **11:** 6320 (6316), 6580
Shulte A P, **6:** 3685 (3680)
Shultz D, **5:** 2880
Shultz J, **2:** 820 (819); **4:** 2052 (2051); **10:** 5817 (5813)
Shultz T R, **8:** 4957 (4952)
Shumaker A, **9:** (5575); **10:** 5817 (5813)
Shuman A, **6:** 3459 (3455)
Shuman B A, **6:** 3399 (3395)
Shuman H H, **3:** 1642 (1640)
Shuman R B, **8:** 4388 (4386)
Shumway-Cook A, **7:** 3950
Shure M B, **3:** 1441
Shurston P W, **9:** 5169 (5162)
Shute R, **2:** 733
Shute R H, **4:** 1899; **8:** 4376
Shute R W, **9:** 5168 (5159, 5167), 5272 (5271, 5272)
Shute V J, **5:** 2921 (2920); **6:** 3325; **9:** 5563 (5562)
Shuttleworth D E, **2:** 910 (908)
Shweder R A, **3:** 1233, 1246; **5:** 2651 (2648), 2685; **6:** 3227; **9:** 5512 (5512)
Shye S, **4:** 2218 (2213, 2214, 2215, 2216, 2217, 2218), 2219 (2213, 2218); **7:** 4316 (4308, 4310, 4311, 4315); **9:** 5503 (5498, 5500, 5501, 5503), 5504 (5498, 5500, 5501, 5503)
Shymansky J A, **6:** 3416 (3412)
Shyu S, **2:** 635 (634)
Sia A H, **4:** 1995 (1993)
Siaciwena M C, **3:** 1567 (1565)
Siann G, **4:** 2427 (2424, 2425)
Sibayan B, **8:** 4442
Sicard R A, **10:** (5659)
Sichel B A, **4:** 2033 (2031)
Sichel W, **2:** 1074 (1066)
Siddiqui D, **3:** 1589
Sidnell R, **7:** 4026 (4023)
Sidner C L, **8:** 4942 (4941)
Siebens A, **10:** 5673 (5669)
Sieber J E, **4:** 2033 (2032), 2037 (2034)
Sieber R T, **10:** 5591 (5587)
Sieber S D, **11:** 6445 (6441)
Siebert H, **1:** 139 (136)
Siebold T, **3:** 1789
Siedentop D, **8:** 4467 (4467); **10:** 5713 (5710, 5712), (6002)
Siegel A E, **1:** 362
Siegel A G, **3:** 1624
Siegel B, **2:** 918
Siegel B N, **3:** 1449
Siegel G M, **1:** 409 (406)
Siegel H, **2:** 1208 (1205, 1206); **9:** 4981 (4978, 4980)
Siegel I E, **3:** 1643
Siegel M, **6:** 3638 (3635)
Siegel P M, **7:** 3722 (3717)
Siegel S, **4:** 2194 (2191); **7:** 4163 (4160)
Siegerist E, **7:** 4325 (4323)
Siegler I C, **1:** 239 (235, 237)
Siegler R S, **2:** 842, 846, 852 (848), 856, 867; **3:** 1504 (1503), 1514 (1512); **4:** 2198, 2199; **5:** 2665 (2661), 2677 (2676), 2732 (2727), 2769 (2763), 2916; **6:** 3288; **7:** 3763 (3760); **11:** 6608 (6604)
Sierpinska A, **6:** 3652 (3648)
Sierra F B, **7:** 3801
Sierra J B, **7:** 3801
Siervogel R M, **8:** 4473 (4470, 4471), 4474 (4470, 4471, 4472)
Sierwald W, **5:** 2732 (2726)
Sifuna D, **11:** 6256 (6255)
Sigel I, **10:** 6015 (6014)
Sigel I E, **3:** 1643 (1639); **4:** 2257, 2258; **6:** 3463 (3460); **7:** 4301 (4299); **9:** 5528 (5525)
Sigel L S, **3:** 1643 (1639)
Sigel R S, **4:** 1984 (1981); **8:** 4581
Sigmon S B, **7:** 4081
Signorella M L, **4:** 2449
Signorielli N, **1:** 570 (567); **9:** 5518 (5514)
Sigsworth A, **9:** 5294 (5291, 5292, 5294)
Siimaste E, **4:** 2029
Sijtsma K, **6:** 3315 (3314)
Sikes J, **2:** 1098 (1096), 1099 (1098); **10:** 5826 (5824)
Sikes P, **7:** 3826 (3825); **9:** 5313 (5312)
Sikes W, **7:** 4240
Sikorski M F, **7:** 4088 (4084)
Sikula G, **10:** 5994, 5995 (5992)
Sikula J, **9:** 5318 (5315); **10:** 5948, 5965, 6048
Sikula T, **8:** 4947
Silber K, **6:** 3096 (3092)
Silberberg M, **6:** 3235 (3232)
Silberberg N, **6:** 3235 (3232)
Silbereisen R K, **1:** 89; **3:** 1647
Silberman C E, **7:** 4215
Silberstein J, **8:** 4479 (4477)
Silberstein M, **10:** 5948 (5946), 5995 (5993), 6091 (6089), 6092 (6090)
Sillari J, **1:** 362 (359)
Silliman E, **10:** 5694
Sills D, **7:** 3826
Silva L M, **3:** 1672 (1669)
Silver E A, **1:** 374 (372); **4:** 2199 (2198); **6:** 3335 (3331), 3684 (3676); **8:** 4730 (4728)
Silver H, **5:** 2618
Silver H F, **11:** 6625 (6623)
Silver P F, **1:** 77 (74, 75)
Silverman D, **11:** 6466 (6464)
Silverman H A, **11:** 6438 (6432)
Silverman J, **5:** 2697 (2693, 2694)
Silverman R, **5:** 2998 (2996); **10:** 5948 (5946)
Silverman R J, **4:** 1958 (1957)
Silverman S, **8:** 4467 (4467); **10:** 5713 (5708, 5711)
Silvern L C, **2:** 846 (843); **5:** 2862 (2857, 2858); **8:** 4823 (4817)
Silverstein C D, **9:** 5441 (5436)
Silvestre J-J, **4:** 1924 (1919), 1976 (1973); **5:** 2942 (2939, 2941); **11:** 6420 (6419)
Sim W K, **9:** 5485 (5484)
Sima M, **7:** 4030 (4027)
Simkins T, **1:** 73 (67, 69, 72); **5:** 2954 (2953, 2954); **7:** 4145 (4142)
Simmel E C, **9:** 5518
Simmel G, **2:** (929); **6:** (3136); **8:** (4448)
Simmel M, **11:** 6747 (6746)

Simmons B J, **10:** 5834 (5832)
Simmons D, **4:** 2423 (2421)
Simmons G, **2:** 868 (865)
Simmons J, **3:** 1820; **11:** 6298 (6293)
Simmons J L, **7:** 4319 (4316)
Simmons J M, **10:** 5939 (5938)
Simmons R, **4:** 1848 (1845); **8:** 4652 (4650); **10:** 5745 (5741, 5744)
Simmons R G, **1:** 88 (84); **10:** 5591 (5586, 5587, 5588)
Simmons W, **7:** 3858 (3856)
Simms M, **7:** 4200 (4199)
Simon A, **2:** 816 (812); **10:** 6112
Simon A B, **10:** 6053 (6052)
Simon A H, **9:** 5169 (5161)
Simon B, **2:** 816 (814), 831 (829), 1194; **5:** 2607, 2617 (2610, 2613, 2616), 2737 (2733), 2802; **8:** 4562, 4715 (4708); **9:** 5216 (5211); **10:** 5735, 5826 (5824)
Simon D P, **2:** 867 (862); **4:** 2199 (2195, 2196); **9:** 5342 (5339)
Simon E, **4:** 2046 (2044), 2327 (2326)
Simon H, **1:** 67 (61); **2:** 867 (862); **11:** 6416, 6608 (6607)
Simon H A, **1:** 331 (328); **2:** 842 (839), 851 (847); **3:** 1431 (1426), 1775 (1769); **4:** 2166 (2163), 2167, 2198 (2195), 2199 (2195, 2196); **5:** 2725 (2722), 2798 (2793), 2831 (2828), 2867 (2863), (2878), (2919), 2942; **6:** 3288 (3285), 3339 (3338); **7:** 3768 (3767), 3788 (3784); **8:** 4519 (4515, 4518), 4722 (4720), 4727 (4723, 4725, 4726), 4803 (4801); **9:** 5342 (5339), 5411 (5409); **10:** 6026 (6023); **11:** 6457 (6453)
Simon H S, **4:** 2208 (2200)
Simon L H, **9:** 5577 (5573)
Simon M, **6:** 3671 (3669)
Simon R, **4:** 1984 (1983); **7:** 4336 (4335)
Simon R J, **10:** 5607 (5599)
Simon T, **2:** 792 (788), 846 (844); **3:** 1504 (1503); **4:** 1871 (1864, 1866, 1868), 1872 (1866); **5:** 2664 (2657), (2911); **7:** 3879 (3873)
Simonen M, **3:** 1793
Simonoff J, **6:** 3508 (3507)
Simons G, **7:** 4026 (4023)
Simons H, **2:** 645; **3:** 1288; **10:** 5972, 6099 (6097)
Simons H D, **6:** 3216 (3214, 3215)
Simons P R J, **5:** 2769 (2764); **7:** 3791 (3788, 3789, 3790); **8:** 4702
Simons R-J, **2:** 1006; **9:** 5562
Simonson H P, **2:** 766 (763)
Simonson R, **6:** 3484 (3483)
Simonton D K, **6:** 3288 (3285)
Simpson A W, **10:** 5762 (5760)
Simpson C, **1:** 230 (229)
Simpson E, **7:** 4329 (4326)
Simpson E L, **5:** 2692 (2690); **7:** 3920 (3918)
Simpson J, **4:** 2331
Simpson J A, **8:** 4812 (4810)
Simpson R, **10:** 5693 (5693), 6117
Sims A, **1:** 158 (155)
Sinatra R, **6:** 3209; **7:** 3775 (3773, 3774); **11:** 6625 (6623)
Sinclair A, **6:** 3224
Sinclair B, **4:** 2357 (2355)
Sinclair C, **1:** 226 (222); **11:** 6653 (6648), 6659 (6659)
Sinclair E, **1:** 490 (487)
Sinclair H, **4:** 1962 (1960); **6:** 3685 (3673); **8:** 4482 (4481)
Sinclair J M, **9:** 5508 (5506)
Sinclair J McH, **9:** 5416 (5415)
Sinclair J N, **6:** 3638 (3635)
Sinclair K, **10:** 5674 (5673)
Sinclair K E, **10:** 5826 (5823); **11:** 6797 (6796)
Sinclair M E, **3:** 1690 (1689); **8:** 4688 (4684); **9:** 5233 (5232)
Sinclair R L, **2:** 892, 893; **10:** 5817 (5815)
Sincoff J B, **5:** 2916 (2912)
Sindelar P T, **9:** 5071 (5067, 5068)
Sindell P S, **1:** 297 (282)
Singer B, **9:** 5467
Singer D G, **8:** 4542 (4541)
Singer H, **8:** 4812 (4807)
Singer H W, **5:** 2993 (2990)
Singer J, **9:** 5441 (5439, 5440)
Singer J D, **3:** 1508 (1506); **4:** 2156 (2150, 2152, 2154, 2155); **8:** 4935 (4933); **10:** 5846 (5844, 5845), 6106 (6104, 6105, 6106)
Singer J L, **8:** 4542 (4541)
Singer M, **3:** 1610 (1608)
Singer P, **3:** 1672 (1668)
Singer R N, **7:** 3953
Singer W, **1:** 554; **7:** 3950 (3948)
Singh A, **5:** 2753
Singh B, **7:** 4000 (3998)
Singh I B, **11:** 6307 (6299)
Singh J, **10:** 6164 (6161)
Singh M, **9:** 5358 (5357)
Singh N, **8:** 4423 (4423)
Singh N N, **10:** 6164 (6161)
Singh R D, **1:** 254 (246)
Singhal R P, **10:** 5721
Singleton J, **1:** 297 (283, 284); **2:** 1213 (1210); **4:** 2053 (2050)
Singleton W T, **10:** 5901 (5895)
Singley M K, **8:** 4731 (4729)
Singule C, **2:** (944)
Sinisterra L, **5:** 2769 (2762)
Sinnott J D, **6:** 3434 (3432); **8:** 4824
Sinnott L T, **5:** 3050 (3044)
Sinofsky E R, **2:** 1102 (1099, 1101)
Sinyor R, **6:** 3241
Siow A, **6:** 3101
Siqueland E R, **8:** 4383 (4382)
Sirbu M, **3:** 1449 (1447)
Siring E, **7:** 3858 (3857)
Sirota R, **1:** 294 (283); **5:** 2514 (2514)
Sirotkin K A, **6:** 3655 (3653)
Sirotnik K, **4:** 2388 (2382, 2385, 2386), 2389 (2382, 2384, 2385, 2386, 2387, 2388); **5:** 2529 (2525), 3061 (3056, 3060); **8:** 4882 (4876, 4879); **9:** 5318 (5315); **10:** 5991, 5995 (5992, 5994), 5999, 6012 (6009), 6053, 6096, 6219; **11:** 6580
Sisco B, **5:** 2773 (2771, 2773); **6:** 3435 (3433); **9:** 5399 (5397); **10:** 6202
Sisson de Castro M L, **1:** 83 (79)
Sisson G R, **11:** 6425
Sitko M, **7:** 3807 (3803)
Sitoi A, **7:** 3960
Siwitibau S, **4:** 2423 (2421)
Sixma H, **9:** 5553 (5549)
Sizer T R, **3:** 1267 (1265), 1301 (1296), 1337 (1336), 1804 (1803); **5:** 2697 (2693); **9:** 5206 (5202), 5211 (5209), 5224 (5221); **10:** 5991, 6083 (6080)
Sjoberg G, **1:** 543; **4:** 2037 (2036)
Sjöstedt B, **8:** 4509 (4503), 4601 (4599)
Skagen A, **8:** 4639
Skaggs G, **11:** 6355 (6349)
Skalka J, **2:** 662 (659)
Skallist I, **3:** 1402 (1399)
Skatershchikov V K, **1:** 343 (340)
Skau K G, **9:** 5578 (5575)
Skeel D J, **9:** 5578 (5573, 5574, 5577)
Skeels H M, **5:** 2465 (2465); **7:** 3707 (3703)
Skehan P, **4:** 2339 (2334, 2335), 2346 (2343, 2344), 2364 (2361, 2362)
Skellam J G, **9:** 5471 (5469)
Skelton M, **7:** 4319 (4318)
Skilbeck M, **2:** 1107 (1103); **3:** 1271 (1267, 1268), 1278, 1328, 1343; **10:** 6092 (6090)
Skinner A F, **3:** 1636 (1631)
Skinner B F, **1:** 486 (483), 497 (495), (535); **3:** (1536), 1797 (1795); **4:** 1848 (1843, 1844), 1899 (1885), 2281 (2279, 2280); **5:** 2665 (2657, 2664), 2709 (2706), 2856 (2852), 2867, 2874 (2871), 2884 (2880); **6:** (3316), (3340); **7:** (3938); **8:** 4395 (4390), 4456 (4453), 4634 (4633), 4774 (4767, 4768, 4771); **9:** 4977 (4974), 5043 (5040), (5487); **10:** 5991 (5987), 6164 (6159, 6161), 6202 (6198, 6199)
Skinner B P, **5:** (2875), (2876), (2878)
Skinner C J, **9:** 5130 (5125), 5142 (5137); **10:** 5862 (5858)
Skinner E A, **9:** 5528 (5525)
Skinner R R, **5:** 2903 (2903)
Skinner W, **10:** 5948 (5944)
Skodak M, **5:** 2465 (2465); **7:** 3707 (3703)
Skoog G, **11:** 6370 (6367)
Skorov G, **6:** 3184 (3179)
Skov P, **3:** 1266 (1263, 1265)
Skowronek H, **6:** 3224; **8:** 4779
Skrtic T M, **1:** 494 (494); **2:** 729 (721, 724, 728); **4:** 2089 (2087); **6:** 3559 (3557); **8:** 4935 (4934); **11:** 6461 (6458)
Skull J, **1:** 198 (197)
Skurnik L S, **9:** 5389 (5387)
Skutnabb-Kangas T, **6:** 3439 (3436)
Slaby R G, **1:** 234 (230, 232, 233); **4:** 2449 (2447)
Slade K, **8:** 4796 (4793)
Slakter M J, **7:** 4000 (3997)
Slater M, **11:** 6723 (6719)
Slater P, **3:** 1549 (1545)
Slater R O, **9:** 5273 (5270)
Slater W H, **2:** 824
Slaughter D T, **7:** 4301 (4299)
Slaughter S, **4:** 2412
Slavenburg J H, **8:** 4935 (4933)
Slavet J S, **6:** 3421 (3418)
Slavin R E, **1:** 11 (6, 7), 12 (7), 230 (229); **2:** 711 (710), 775 (772, 775), 825 (821, 824),

846 (846), 1099 (1095, 1096, 1097, 1098); **3:** 1257 (1255), 1486 (1484, 1485), 1504 (1504); **4:** 1918 (1914); **5:** 2504, 2532, 2536 (2533, 2534), 2779 (2774, 2777), 2910 (2908); **6:** 3373 (3372), 3631 (3630); **7:** 3821 (3819), 3942 (3939), 4157 (4157); **8:** 4372 (4369), 4873 (4872), 4935 (4932, 4934); **9:** 5043 (5042), 5071, 5176 (5170, 5171), 5264 (5261); **10:** 6031 (6028), 6149 (6147), 6239 (6237)
Slavin S, **10:** 6187
Slavings R, **10:** 6112 (6109)
Slawson D, **1:** 52 (51)
Sleeman D H, **1:** 347, 348; **2:** 985 (983), 1007 (1003); **4:** 1899 (1895)
Sleeter C E, **3:** 1233 (1231, 1232); **7:** 3974 (3973), 3978 (3975); **8:** 4936 (4931); **11:** 6727 (6725)
Sleezer C M, **2:** 1139 (1138)
Slentz K, **5:** 2813 (2810)
Slevin J, **6:** 3452
Slichter S H, **5:** 2942 (2938)
Slinde J A, **2:** 677 (672, 673)
Sloan D, **7:** 3924, 4088 (4082)
Sloan K, **4:** 2257 (2250, 2253, 2255, 2256); **9:** 5268
Sloane H N, **10:** 6164
Sloane J, **6:** 3463 (3460)
Sloane K, **4:** 2258
Slobasky R, **7:** 3861 (3858)
Slocum J W Jr, **8:** 4519 (4518)
Slomkowski C, **2:** 856 (854)
Slowey M, **1:** 93 (90), 94, 180; **5:** 2951 (2949); **7:** 4171; **11:** 6394, 6551 (6548)
Sluckin A, **1:** 230 (229)
Slumstrup F, **4:** 2327 (2324)
Sly C, **4:** 1995 (1993)
Smagorinsky P, **10:** 5795 (5793)
Smallwood W N, **6:** 3096 (3095, 3096)
Smart B, **9:** 5216
Smart D, **7:** 3840; **8:** 4408 (4405); **9:** 5168 (5159, 5160, 5162); **10:** 6072
Smart J, **10:** 6234
Smart K F, **11:** 6266
Smart W D, **1:** 28
Smelser N J, **1:** 59, 60 (54, 57); **2:** 933; **8:** 4896; **10:** 5606
Smeyers P, **8:** 4461 (4460)
Smilansky M, **5:** 2491 (2487)
Smiles S, **9:** 5399 (5395)
Smiley S S, **7:** 3768 (3764)
Smircich L, **3:** 1775 (1771)
Smit C A, **6:** 3096 (3094, 3095)
Smith A, **2:** (776), 1074 (1066); **3:** (1295), 1538, (1698); **4:** 2046 (2043); **5:** (2643); **8:** 4873 (4870); **9:** 5211 (5207, 5209); **10:** 5750 (5746)
Smith A F M, **5:** 2596 (2590, 2591); **9:** 5130 (5129)
Smith B, **3:** (1723); **9:** 5181 (5178)
Smith B A, **6:** 3602 (3598)
Smith B E, **2:** 906 (906)
Smith B H, **5:** 2685 (2683)
Smith B O, **2:** 816 (815); **3:** 1267 (1264), 1367 (1360); **8:** 4456 (4455); **10:** 5818 (5813, 5814), 5999, 6149 (6146, 6147, 6148)
Smith C, **5:** 2572 (2570); **8:** 4736
Smith C B, **6:** 3209 (3207)
Smith C R, **1:** 490 (487, 488)
Smith D, **2:** 820 (819); **3:** 1695 (1691); **7:** 4336 (4332); **10:** 6219; **11:** 6282 (6280), 6366 (6362), 6608 (6605), 6723 (6721)
Smith D A, **10:** 6122 (6117, 6118, 6119)
Smith D C, **4:** 1924 (1923); **10:** 6020, 6122 (6118), 6239 (6238)
Smith D H, **3:** 1655 (1650)
Smith D Jr, **6:** 3241 (3239)
Smith D M, **11:** 6798 (6796)
Smith D R, **2:** 838 (837); **11:** 6456 (6454, 6455)
Smith E, **4:** 1958 (1956); **8:** 4766
Smith E E, **2:** 842, 868 (861), 985 (983); **5:** 2769 (2762); **6:** 3155; **8:** 4722, 4727 (4726), 4951 (4950)
Smith E L, **6:** 3416 (3410); **10:** 6035 (6033)
Smith E R, **4:** 2089 (2080)
Smith F, **6:** 3452; **8:** 4939; **10:** 6168 (6165)
Smith F L, **2:** 816 (815); **4:** 2376 (2375); **10:** 6149 (6148)
Smith G, **6:** 3205; **9:** 5060 (5059)
Smith G A, **3:** 1607 (1603, 1605); **9:** 5216 (5214)
Smith G K, **9:** 5294
Smith G P, **10:** 5846 (5845)
Smith H, **4:** 2257 (2255); **8:** 4657 (4654); **9:** 4973 (4973); **10:** 6099 (6097)
Smith H A, **7:** 4175 (4171)
Smith H L, **11:** 6277 (6274)
Smith H W, **9:** 5071 (5068)
Smith I D, **1:** 358
Smith J, **1:** 358 (355); **2:** 807 (805), 842, 1177 (1177); **4:** 2432; **5:** 2916 (2915); **6:** 3284, 3288, 3428 (3427), 3435 (3432); **7:** 3763 (3762); **8:** 4376 (4373, 4374), 4823 (4819), 4902 (4900); **11:** 6456 (6454)
Smith J B, **9:** 5379 (5373, 5374, 5376)
Smith J E, **1:** 168 (167)
Smith J K, **2:** 645; **3:** 1775; **6:** 3284 (3280); **9:** 5030 (5023, 5025, 5026), 5056
Smith J P, **4:** 2445 (2441); **11:** 6608 (6604)
Smith J S, **11:** 6292
Smith K C, **1:** 280 (279)
Smith L, **5:** 2847 (2839)
Smith L B, **8:** 4383 (4382)
Smith L E, **5:** 2773 (2771)
Smith L M, **1:** 543; **4:** 2166 (2165)
Smith M, **3:** 1834 (1833); **4:** 2194 (2189, 2191); **5:** 2509 (2507); **7:** 3821 (3817), 4163 (4161); **8:** 4479 (4477); **10:** 5704 (5698, 5699, 5700)
Smith M E, **2:** 1139 (1137, 1138); **3:** 1491; **6:** 3306
Smith M F, **8:** 4803 (4801)
Smith M L, **2:** 775 (771, 773); **3:** 1624 (1621); **5:** 2515 (2513, 2514); **6:** 3373 (3372); **7:** 3783 (3775, 3776, 3777, 3778, 3779, 3780, 3782, 3783), 3784 (3777, 3782); **9:** 5228 (5225), 5275 (5274), 5373 (5368); **11:** 6340 (6335)
Smith M S, **2:** 688 (682), 1079 (1076); **3:** 1343; **5:** 2799 (2797); **7:** 3808 (3804); **9:** 5066 (5062), 5379 (5373); **10:** 5750 (5746), 5954 (5952), 6083 (6080)
Smith M U, **8:** 4727 (4726)
Smith N L, **4:** 2108 (2101, 2105, 2108); **8:** 4783
Smith N W, **1:** 497
Smith P, **3:** 1386 (1384), 1655 (1652); **7:** 4220 (4219)
Smith P A, **7:** 3810 (3808)
Smith P D, **4:** 2357 (2353)
Smith P K, **4:** 2452 (2450, 2451); **8:** 4542 (4539, 4541)
Smith P L, **5:** 2462 (2459)
Smith P V, **10:** 6239 (6236)
Smith R, **1:** 295 (284, 285, 286); **3:** 1619 (1612), 1729 (1727); **6:** 3184 (3179); **10:** 5625 (5625)
Smith R A, **3:** 1537, 1538
Smith R C, **7:** 4225 (4222)
Smith R J, **11:** 6360 (6358, 6359)
Smith R M, **1:** 168 (165); **6:** 3349 (3346), 3435 (3431); **7:** 4185; **8:** 4616 (4610), 4736, 4812; **9:** 5399 (5398); **10:** 6058 (6054)
Smith R S, **1:** 89 (88); **3:** 1520 (1517), 1643 (1637, 1641); **8:** 4779 (4775, 4776, 4777, 4778)
Smith S C, **6:** 3284; **10:** 6244
Smith S D, **10:** 5680 (5680)
Smith S G, **10:** 5887 (5886)
Smith S L, **2:** 626 (624); **6:** 3209 (3207); **10:** 6244
Smith T, **6:** 3339 (3338); **7:** 4301 (4297)
Smith T M F, **9:** 5130 (5125), 5142 (5137), 5467 (5460); **10:** 5862 (5858)
Smith T W, **8:** 4896 (4891)
Smith V, **6:** 3399 (3395)
Smith W, **10:** 5808 (5807), 6106 (6104, 6105)
Smith W A, **2:** 1048 (1047)
Smith W F, **6:** 3241; **7:** 4095 (4092)
Smith-Burke M T, **6:** 3443
Smith-Davis J, **7:** 3833 (3832)
Smithers A, **7:** 4171 (4163, 4165, 4166, 4168)
Smith-Hefner N J, **1:** 534 (533)
Smoker P, **3:** 1733
Smokler H E, **1:** 480
Smolicz J J, **7:** 3970 (3964)
Smollar J, **10:** 5758 (5757)
Smooha S, **8:** 4896 (4893, 4894)
Smoski W, **10:** 5691 (5690)
Smothergill N L, **9:** 5548
Smull M W, **3:** 1508 (1507)
Smulyan L, **1:** 48 (45); **10:** 5939, 6099 (6097)
Smuts B B, **5:** 2685
Smylie M A, **2:** 820 (818)
Smyth G, **10:** 5995
Smyth J, **6:** 3602 (3598); **9:** 5308; **10:** 5935 (5933), 6043 (6040), 6219 (6217)
Smyth M, **10:** 5995
Smythe J, **10:** 6043; **11:** 6723
Smythe W J, **11:** 6390 (6389)
Smythies J R, **5:** 2903; **8:** 4455
Snapp M, **2:** 1098 (1096)
Snarey J R, **7:** 3920 (3917, 3918)
Sneddon D G, **4:** 1934 (1929)

Snedecor G W, **1:** 390 (388); **7:** 3739 (3730, 3731), 4016 (4009)
Snee R D, **9:** 4974 (4972)
Snelbecker G E, **5:** 2867 (2863)
Snell J L, **9:** 5560 (5558)
Snell R, **3:** 1563 (1557); **7:** 4220
Snell W van R, **3:** (1462)
Snellings E C, **7:** 3821 (3816, 3817)
Snodgrass D R, **9:** 5539 (5538)
Snoek J D, **10:** 5924 (5920, 5921)
Snoek J K, **10:** 6062 (6060)
Snook I, **7:** 3886 (3881); **8:** 4447 (4445), 4456 (4455)
Snook R K, **8:** 4775 (4773)
Snow C E, **6:** 3224 (3222), 3453 (3448, 3449, 3451), 3480; **8:** 4936 (4932); **10:** 5694; **11:** 6511 (6508)
Snow C P, **3:** 1367 (1363); **5:** 2697; **9:** 5038 (5032)
Snow M A, **4:** 2351 (2346); **6:** 3335 (3333)
Snow R, **8:** 4766; **10:** 6207 (6206)
Snow R E, **1:** 5 (2), 6 (2), 370 (366), 374 (371); **2:** 846 (846); **4:** 1848 (1843, 1847), 2219 (2218); **5:** 2714 (2711), 2767 (2760, 2761, 2765, 2766), 2769 (2760, 2761, 2762, 2763, 2764, 2765, 2766), 2779 (2774, 2775, 2776, 2777, 2778), 2879 (2875, 2877), 2884 (2883), 2921 (2917, 2918, 2920, 2921), 2931 (2924, 2929, 2930); **6:** 3315 (3314), 3325 (3317), 3435 (3430); **7:** 3879 (3876, 3878), 3942 (3937); **9:** 5043 (5041, 5042), 5504 (5503); **10:** 5750 (5746), 5762 (5759), 5772 (5770), (6024), 6158 (6156, 6157), 6159 (6155, 6156, 6157, 6158), 6173 (6170), 6193 (6188); **11:** 6320 (6316, 6319), 6445 (6444)
Snow R F, **3:** 1421 (1418)
Snower D, **5:** 2942
Snowling M J, **7:** 4081; **8:** 4913 (4910); **10:** 5680, 5681
Snyder B R, **5:** 2589 (2587)
Snyder C Jr, **8:** 4873 (4869, 4871)
Snyder J C, **5:** 2575 (2573)
Snyder K J, **9:** 5211 (5207)
Snyder L, **2:** 1019 (1018); **6:** 3223 (3221)
Snyder M, **9:** 5518 (5515)
Snyderman B, **4:** 1972 (1968)
Soar R S, **4:** 2131 (2128); **10:** 6020 (6018)
Sobel I, **2:** 1074 (1066)
Sobel M E, **7:** 3864 (3863)
Sockett H, **10:** 6099 (6097)
Socrates, **4:** (2111); **7:** (3924); **8:** (4432), (4449), (4452), (4532), (4533), (4534), (4535); **9:** (5395), (5412); **11:** (6622)
Soden K von, **11:** 6747 (6746)
Soder R, **2:** 796; **10:** 5991, 5999, 6012 (6009), 6053, 6096; **11:** 6580
Sodian B, **2:** 857 (854); **7:** 3920 (3918); **8:** 4957 (4955)
Soete L, **11:** 6260 (6258)
Sofield C, **4:** 2423 (2421)
Soh K C, **9:** 5485 (5484)
Sohngen B, **4:** 1924 (1919)
Soisson J-P, **11:** 6669
Sojka G, **4:** 2330 (2328)
Sokoloff D R, **2:** 1012 (1008); **7:** 3810 (3809); **8:** 4479 (4478)
Sokolov E N, **1:** 377 (375)
Sokoya J A F, **7:** 4132 (4125)
Sola P, **9:** 5180
Solana F, **7:** 3801
Solarczyk-Ambrozik E, **2:** 662 (661)
Soldatova G, **3:** 1252 (1250)
Soled S W, **6:** 3631 (3629)
Soliman A M, **10:** 5808
Solimano G, **7:** 4155 (4149)
Solinger J W, **6:** 3422
Šoljan N N, **9:** 5497 (5495)
Solmon L C, **1:** 520, 521 (513, 517, 518)
Solo R A, **9:** 5206
Solomon B, **2:** 868 (861)
Solomon B M, **11:** 6765 (6761)
Solomon C, **6:** 3512
Solomon D, **8:** 4799 (4798); **10:** 6053 (6053)
Solomon D J, **4:** 2183 (2183)
Solomon J, **9:** 5328 (5326), 5350 (5347)
Solomon L C, **2:** 1055 (1053)
Solomon R P, **1:** 297 (293)
Solon G, **6:** 3144 (3139); **9:** 5355 (5352)
Solono C H, **5:** 2769 (2765)
Soloveitchik J B, **6:** 3120
Solow R M, **3:** 1820; **9:** 5240
Soloway E, **2:** 973, 985 (983, 984)
Soltis J F, **3:** 1328 (1327), 1334; **4:** 2033 (2032); **8:** 4447 (4445), 4456 (4449); **9:** 5056; **10:** 5948 (5947), 5985 (5985), 5991 (5988, 5990), 6043; **11:** 6579 (6579), 6580
Soltys M J, **5:** 3055 (3053)
Soltz V, **7:** 4296 (4294); **8:** 4816 (4816)
Somazzi I, **11:** 6747 (6744)
Somekh B, **1:** 431 (431)
Somers G G, **11:** 6425
Somerset H C A, **2:** 733 (731)
Somerville M, **5:** 2457 (2456); **11:** 6735 (6734)
Somerville S C, **8:** 4957 (4954)
Sommer D, **2:** 701
Sommer R, **5:** 2529 (2524); **9:** 5358 (5357), 5359 (5357)
Sommers N I, **11:** 6785 (6783)
Somon A, **8:** 4930
Sonesson G, **9:** 5416 (5415)
Song M J, **11:** 6334 (6332)
Song Y, **2:** 948
Songe A H, **6:** 3401 (3401)
Songer N B, **4:** 2439 (2437); **7:** 3810 (3809), 4104 (4101, 4102, 4103); **8:** 4479 (4478); **9:** 5342 (5339, 5340)
Sonquist J A, **7:** 4016 (4011); **10:** 5862 (5860)
Soo Pong C, **8:** 4388 (4384)
Soon L Y, **7:** 4201 (4200)
Sophasan K, **11:** 6307 (6306)
Sophian C, **2:** 852; **8:** 4957 (4954, 4955)
Sörbom D, **1:** 390 (384, 388); **2:** 1117 (1110), 1220 (1219); **3:** 1514 (1512); **4:** 2140 (2137), 2241 (2239); **7:** 3879 (3875), 4015 (4008, 4011); **8:** 4352 (4341, 4342, 4347, 4349, 4351), 4359 (4352), 4930 (4930); **9:** 5130 (5129), 5373 (5371); **11:** 6334 (6333)
Sørensen A B, **1:** 11 (7), 12 (9); **2:** 825 (822, 824); **6:** 3428 (3426); **8:** 4719; **9:** 5175 (5173), 5176 (5175), 5379 (5375)
Sorhuus E, **11:** 6731 (6729)
Soriyan M A, **9:** 5389 (5388)
Sork T J, **5:** 2532
Sorokin P A, **2:** 1042 (1040); **7:** 3864 (3862)
Sorrentino R M, **7:** 3942
Sosinsky B, **4:** 1958 (1956)
Soskice D, **1:** 310 (308); **6:** 3617 (3616); **11:** 6420 (6416, 6419)
Sosnowski T, **4:** 1967
Sostek A M, **3:** 1642; **6:** 3227
Söter A, **6:** 3484
Soto H de, **5:** 2819 (2814)
Souberman E, **3:** 1252 (1248); **7:** 4095
Souder W E, **5:** 2725 (2722)
Southall C, **7:** 3889 (3887)
Southall I, **2:** (735)
Southern W T, **5:** 2732 (2731); **9:** 5532 (5531)
Southgate D D, **4:** 1995
Southworth G, **4:** 2166 (2163)
Southworth L E, **3:** 1624 (1621)
Souza P R, **3:** 1680 (1677)
Sowards J K, **4:** 2007
Sowder J, **6:** 3685 (3675)
Sowell E J, **1:** 553 (553); **3:** 1434 (1433)
Soysal Y N, **10:** 5607 (5600)
Spache G D, **2:** (1077)
Spada H, **3:** 1513, 1514 (1511); **8:** 4722 (4721)
Spadavecchio V N, **3:** 1394 (1388)
Spade J Z, **1:** 12 (7, 8)
Spady W G, **1:** 437 (432, 433, 434); **9:** 5176 (5172); **11:** 6798 (6795, 6796)
Spae J J, **9:** 5453 (5451)
Spaeth M, **2:** 1055
Spahr F, **10:** 5691 (5689)
Spain P L, **5:** 2891
Spalding D, **7:** 3935 (3931)
Spalter-Roth R, **2:** 693
Span P, **1:** 194; **5:** 2669, 2767, 2768, 2769, 2884; **6:** 3345, 3661; **7:** 3791, 3942; **10:** 5674 (5672)
Spang-Hanssen H, **4:** 2357
Spaniol L, **10:** 5925 (5920)
Sparkes A W, **7:** 3826 (3822, 3823, 3825); **8:** 4447 (4443)
Spaulding C L, **7:** 3946
Spaulding S, **4:** 2123 (2120); **7:** 3905 (3895)
Spaull A D, **5:** 2607; **6:** 3197 (3191, 3193); **10:** 6072 (6068, 6070), 6079 (6073, 6074, 6076, 6078), 6096 (6093)
Spavold J, **3:** 1398 (1397)
Speak G, **2:** 1160 (1156)
Spear G E, **9:** 5399 (5395, 5398)
Spear N S, **1:** 15
Spearman C, **3:** (1793); **4:** 1872 (1867, 1868), 2241 (2230, 2231); **5:** (2726), (2911); **6:** 3253 (3247); **7:** 3707 (3699, 3704, 3705), 3880 (3873, 3874, 3875, 3878, 3879); **9:** (5502)
Spearman C E, **1:** 6 (4); **5:** (2875), (2878), (2917); **9:** (4981); **11:** 6349 (6347)
Spearritt D S, **4:** 2241 (2238); **7:** 3706, 3935 (3931, 3933); **8:** 4923; **11:** 6355
Spears A E, **7:** 3889
Specht D A, **7:** 3986 (3981); **8:** 4352 (4344)
Spedding C R W, **1:** 244

Speed T J, **9:** 5475 (5473)
Speedie S M, **2:** 1182 (1181)
Spekman N J, **8:** 4779 (4775)
Spelke E S, **2:** 857 (853); **8:** 4383, 4957 (4952)
Spelman E, **11:** 6769 (6768)
Spence D, **1:** 322 (318); **2:** 871 (869)
Spence J T, **3:** 1240 (1237); **5:** 2627; **9:** 5432; **11:** 6320
Spence M, **3:** 1750 (1748); **6:** 3617 (3614); **9:** 5355 (5350, 5351, 5354)
Spence M J, **1:** 15 (13)
Spencer B, **1:** 93 (91, 92)
Spencer B G, **7:** 3711
Spencer C D, **7:** 3810 (3808)
Spencer D A, **10:** 5614 (5608, 5609, 5611, 5612)
Spencer H, **2:** 785 (782), 1074 (1065); **5:** 2665 (2656); **6:** 3151 (3149); **7:** (3841), (3924); **8:** (4452); **9:** (5424); **10:** 5708 (5706, 5707)
Spencer K, **2:** 888; **7:** 3744
Spencer K K, **8:** 4779 (4776, 4778)
Spencer L M, **2:** 1094
Spencer L M Jr, **2:** 1139 (1138)
Spender D, **4:** 2292 (2289, 2291); **7:** 4336 (4332); **10:** 5827 (5822)
Spener D, **1:** 534 (533)
Spenner K I, **11:** 6261 (6257, 6258, 6259), 6277 (6273, 6274, 6275), 6283 (6279)
Speranza F, **6:** 3652
Sperber D, **4:** 2364 (2358); **9:** 5416 (5414)
Sperle D H, **10:** 5948 (5944)
Sperling M, **11:** 6785 (6783)
Sperna-Weiland J, **4:** 2007
Sperry R, **7:** 3775 (3774)
Spicuzza R J, **9:** 5567 (5564, 5565)
Spiecker B, **8:** 4461 (4460)
Spiegelman R G, **4:** 2212 (2211)
Spielberger C D, **9:** 5233; **10:** 5772; **11:** 6360 (6356, 6357, 6358)
Spielberger D, **2:** 968
Spies R, **3:** 1449
Spiker C C, **5:** 2802 (2799, 2800)
Spiker D, **3:** 1642 (1639, 1641)
Spillane J P, **3:** 1337 (1335, 1336, 1337), 1431 (1429)
Spindler G, **2:** 917
Spindler G D, **1:** 295, 296, 297 (281, 282, 283, 285, 286, 288, 291); **2:** 802, 917 (915), 918 (915), 933 (930), 1073, 1212, 1213 (1208, 1209, 1210, 1212); **3:** 1233, 1729 (1724, 1727, 1728); **4:** 1872 (1871), 2046, 2052, 2053 (2048, 2051); **6:** 3238; **7:** 3974 (3972); **9:** 5220, 5312, 5313 (5311), 5572
Spindler L, **1:** 297 (286); **2:** 918 (915), 933 (930), 1073, 1213 (1210); **3:** 1729 (1727, 1728); **7:** 3974 (3972); **9:** 5220, 5312, 5313 (5311)
Spinelli F M, **6:** 3227
Spinks J M, **3:** 1411 (1410); **5:** 2509, 2852 (2849); **6:** 3496 (3491); **7:** 3840; **9:** 5185 (5183, 5184), 5217, 5308
Spiro R J, **2:** 888 (885), 973; **7:** 3788; **8:** 4942 (4940); **11:** 6603 (6603)
Spitholt W E, **2:** 1139 (1136)
Spitz R A, **5:** 2672 (2670), 2806 (2803); **8:** (4813)
Spivak G, **3:** 1441
Splaine J, **5:** 2897 (2896)
Spodek B, **3:** 1635, 1636 (1629, 1630, 1635); **5:** 2672, 2806; **8:** 4670 (4669, 4670)
Spoehr K T, **4:** 2199 (2197)
Spohrer J C, **2:** 985 (983)
Spolsky B, **4:** 2339 (2335), 2346 (2341, 2342); **6:** 3439 (3435, 3436, 3437)
Spotted-Bear A, **9:** 5066 (5064)
Spradley J P, **1:** 297 (284); **2:** 803 (797); **4:** 2053 (2048, 2051); **9:** 5220 (5218)
Sprafkin R P, **9:** 5567 (5566)
Spranger E, **3:** (1722); **6:** (3136); **8:** 4419 (4419)
Spranges M, **10:** 6117 (6114)
Sprat T, **6:** 3219 (3217)
Spratt F, **11:** 6621
Spratt J E, **3:** 1820 (1819); **6:** 3453 (3447), 3480 (3476); **9:** 5228 (5225, 5227)
Spreckelsen K, **3:** 1355 (1352)
Sprenger C J A, **9:** 5560 (5559)
Sprenkle D H, **4:** 2261 (2261), 2266 (2266)
Spring J, **7:** 3848 (3844)
Spring J H, **5:** 2617 (2612)
Springfield S, **9:** 5281 (5276)
Sprinthall N A, **10:** 5935 (5931), 6169 (6165, 6168); **11:** 6484 (6482)
Sprinthall R C, **10:** 6169 (6165)
Sprung B, **4:** 2452 (2451)
Spuck D W, **1:** 77; **5:** 2831
Spurgeon P, **6:** 3096 (3092)
Spurrell D J, **2:** 631 (629)
Spychiger M, **3:** 1355 (1354)
Squire J, **11:** 6784
Squire J J, **6:** 3463
Squire J R, **6:** 3484 (3481); **8:** 4947; **10:** 5704 (5697)
Squire L, **3:** 1707 (1706), 1821 (1816); **8:** 4839 (4838)
Squires D, **3:** 1778 (1776), 1779 (1778); **5:** 2855 (2853); **10:** 5625 (5622, 5624)
Squires G, **2:** 665 (663), 900; **7:** 3895 (3892); **11:** 6684, 6808
Squires G D, **11:** 6558 (6553)
Srebalus D J, **9:** 5290 (5282, 5283)
Srinivas M N, **9:** 5560 (5555)
Srinivasan L, **2:** 1048 (1046)
Srinivasan T N, **3:** 1707
Srivastava A B L, **7:** 3711
Srivastava H S, **5:** 2753
Sroufe L A, **1:** 234 (232); **3:** 1520 (1514, 1515), 1643 (1640); **4:** 1967; **8:** 4423 (4421), 4542 (4540), 4779 (4776); **9:** 5394, 5528 (5525)
St Augustine, **2:** (776); **5:** (2608); **7:** (3924); **8:** (4535); **9:** 5117 (5115, 5116, 5117); **11:** (6578), (6742)
St Ignatius, **9:** 5121 (5118, 5119)
St Jerome, **11:** (6743)
St John E P, **2:** 1131 (1130)
St John L, **2:** 733 (730)
St John N H, **3:** 1486 (1483)
St Thomas Aquinas, **11:** (6742)
Staab C, **6:** 3443 (3441)
Staaf R I, **7:** 3821 (3816)
Stables K, **11:** 6292 (6289)
Stacey B, **8:** 4581
Stacey J, **4:** 2302 (2299); **9:** 5302
Stacey K, **6:** 3459 (3457)
Stacey M, **9:** 5268
Stacey N, **1:** 111 (107, 109)
Stack E M, **6:** 3241
Stackhouse J, **10:** 5680 (5677, 5678)
Stadler P, **8:** 4419 (4419)
Stafford F, **2:** 692 (690), 1094 (1090); **8:** 4666 (4663, 4664)
Stafford F P, **5:** 2631 (2629); **6:** 3106 (3104)
Stage C, **9:** 5445
Stage F, **4:** 2412 (2410)
Stager D, **10:** 5754 (5752)
Stahel W A, **9:** 5082 (5078, 5079)
Stahl I, **3:** 1830 (1828)
Stahl R J, **1:** 280 (278)
Stahl S A, **4:** 1962 (1962); **10:** 5831 (5830)
Stahnke M, **5:** 2806 (2805)
Stainback S, **2:** 711 (710), 729 (724, 727); **5:** 2907 (2905); **6:** 3559 (3558); **8:** 4662 (4657); **10:** 6244
Stake R, **4:** (2088); **5:** 2697 (2695); **7:** 3889 (3889); **8:** 4634 (4634), 4751 (4743); **10:** 5957 (5954)
Stake R E, **2:** 645 (642); **3:** 1283 (1281, 1282), 1287 (1285), 1367 (1359); **4:** 2097 (2089), 2108 (2101, 2102, 2104), 2119 (2111, 2116), 2374 (2370, 2371); **8:** 4783 (4780); **9:** 5338 (5336, 5337); **11:** 6384 (6378)
Staley E, **11:** 6424 (6420)
Stalin J, **7:** (3847)
Stalker G M, **4:** 2165 (2164); **9:** 5168 (5162)
Stallings J A, **9:** 5318 (5313, 5314, 5317)
Stamas S, **5:** 2862 (2860)
Stamm C, **10:** 5795 (5793)
Stammers R B, **6:** 3096 (3093)
Stamp R M, **8:** 4509
Stampe D, **10:** 5697 (5695)
Stanback T, **8:** 4638 (4636)
Stanchev I, **2:** 1175 (1172)
Standing E M, **7:** 3914
Standing G, **11:** 6277 (6272)
Standish P, **8:** 4461
Stanford R, **7:** 4132 (4125)
Stangvik G, **5:** 2907 (2905); **6:** 3559 (3558); **10:** 5663 (5662)
Stanhope R, **8:** 4473 (4471)
Stanic G M A, **6:** 3647
Stankiewicz M, **1:** 343 (339)
Stankov L, **7:** 3879 (3875)
Stankovski M, **7:** 3970
Stanley Hall G, **3:** (1520)
Stanley J C, **3:** 1283 (1281); **4:** 1872 (1870), 2089 (2081, 2082, 2083, 2084, 2087, 2088), 2194 (2187, 2188, 2189), 2346 (2340), 2435 (2433, 2434); **5:** 2495, 2731, 2732 (2730, 2731), 2769 (2765); **6:** 3523 (3514); **8:** 4766 (4762), 4875 (4874)
Stanley L, **4:** 2302; **5:** 2457 (2455)
Stanley W C, **5:** 2769 (2765)

Stanley W O, **3:** 1267 (1264); **10:** 5818 (5813, 5814)
Stanne M B, **2:** 991 (990)
Stanovich K E, **8:** 4936 (4931); **10:** 5681 (5678, 5680)
Stansfield C W, **4:** 2339; **6:** 3334
Stanworth J, **4:** 1991 (1987)
Stanworth M, **4:** 2292 (2287, 2289, 2291); **10:** 5827 (5825)
Stanyon J, **2:** 1220 (1217); **6:** 3474 (3468, 3469)
Stapleton D C, **3:** 1449 (1447)
Stapp W B, **4:** 1995 (1991), 1996
Star S, **3:** 1514
Stariha W E, **8:** 4403 (4401)
Staris A, **6:** 3272
Stark J A, **11:** 6461 (6460)
Starko A J, **5:** 2495 (2492)
Stärk-Rötters D, **11:** 6669 (6666)
Starlin C, **8:** 4376 (4375)
Starobinski J, **9:** 5091
Starr L, **11:** 6265 (6262)
Starr M, **2:** 1031 (1029); **11:** 6438 (6431)
Start K B, **9:** 5532 (5531)
Stassinet G, **2:** 665
Statham J, **11:** 6523
Stattin H, **1:** 89 (83, 87); **8:** 4394 (4390), 4395 (4390)
Staub E, **8:** 4799
Staudte R G, **9:** 5082 (5079, 5081)
Staupitz J von, **6:** (3528), (3529)
Stavy R, **6:** 3416 (3410)
Staw B M, **3:** 1774
Stead T, **6:** 3458 (3458)
Steadman S, **5:** 2851 (2849); **10:** 5973 (5967)
Stebbins G L, **4:** 2172 (2168)
Steckelberg A L, **7:** 4293 (4291, 4292)
Stecker P M, **7:** 3807 (3805)
Stedman L C, **7:** 3711
Steedman C, **10:** 6139 (6136)
Steedman H, **11:** 6638 (6636), 6640
Steeh C G, **7:** 3858
Steele R G D, **7:** 4163 (4161)
Steelman L C, **9:** 5385 (5382)
Steen L A, **6:** 3661 (3655), 3685 (3680); **7:** 4100 (4096)
Steens G, **8:** 4473 (4472)
Stefanou S E, **1:** 254
Steffe L P, **2:** 1052; **6:** 3684, 3685 (3672); **7:** 4100 (4095); **8:** 4652 (4649)
Stegö N E, **1:** 73; **9:** 5246 (5242, 5244)
Steier F, **3:** 1789 (1787); **5:** 2993; **9:** 5076 (5074)
Steigelbauer S, **4:** 1934 (1930, 1932)
Steiger J H, **9:** 5504 (5501)
Steigler J, **10:** 6103 (6100)
Stein C, **9:** 4974 (4972)
Stein M I, **5:** 2725
Stein N, **8:** 4951 (4948, 4950); **11:** 6727 (6726)
Stein P, **10:** 6026 (6024, 6025)
Stein R, **8:** 4779 (4776, 4778)
Steinbach R, **1:** 73 (72)
Steinberg C, **1:** 176 (173)
Steinberg E R, **2:** 867, 1170 (1167); **11:** 6784
Steinberg L, **1:** 53 (49), 89 (85); **5:** 2628 (2625)
Steinberg L D, **3:** 1739 (1738); **5:** 2812 (2812)
Steinberg L S, **4:** 2436 (2434); **11:** 6321 (6317)
Steinberg M S, **6:** 3205 (3204); **10:** 5782 (5779)
Steinberg R J, **4:** 2286 (2281, 2282, 2283); **5:** 2628
Steinberg Z, **1:** 490 (487, 488)
Steinbrenner K, **7:** 4016 (4015), 4163 (4162)
Steiner H G, **4:** 2435; **6:** 3667
Steiner P O, **9:** 5240
Steiner R, **1:** (261)
Steinkamp M W, **4:** 2440 (2437); **9:** 5432; **11:** 6398 (6396)
Steinmeier T L, **11:** 6633 (6628)
Steinmetz S K, **4:** 2266
Stelcner M, **3:** 1680 (1677, 1678)
Stendler F, **5:** 2665; **10:** 6197
Stenhouse L A, **1:** 48 (44, 45); **2:** 645 (642); **3:** 1267 (1264), 1320 (1319), 1474 (1466); **10:** 6099 (6096)
Stenlund V, **9:** 5180 (5178)
Stensland P G, **8:** 4812 (4808)
Stenson N, **8:** 4844
Stensvold M, **2:** 1031 (1028)
Stenzel N, **4:** (2103)
Stepan A, **8:** 4595
Stephan C, **1:** 234 (232); **2:** 1098 (1096)
Stephan E G, **3:** 1486
Stephan F F, **6:** (3502)
Stephan S, **2:** 1099 (1098)
Stephan W G, **3:** 1486
Stephens D, **5:** 2512
Stephens J T, **5:** 2971 (2969)
Stephens M D, **1:** 93 (90); **5:** 2532, 2937 (2932); **10:** 6202; **11:** 6684
Stephens R, **5:** 2972 (2969)
Stephenson J B, **9:** 5232 (5229)
Stephenson T, **7:** 3826 (3824)
Stephenson W, **8:** 4857 (4855, 4856)
Stepick C D, **8:** 4473 (4472)
Sterba J P, **4:** 2004
Sterberg R J, **10:** 5762
Stergar E, **9:** 5497 (5496)
Stern B, **11:** 6394 (6392)
Stern D, **2:** 917, 1093, 1094, 1131 (1130); **3:** 1712 (1711); **5:** 2798 (2792); **6:** 3425, 3616, 3617 (3615, 3616); **8:** 4816 (4814); **9:** 5233 (5230); **10:** 5919
Stern G, **4:** 2097 (2093)
Stern G G, **2:** 811 (807); **3:** 1482 (1476, 1482)
Stern H H, **4:** 2351 (2347, 2348), 2357 (2354, 2356, 2357); **6:** 3334 (3330)
Stern J D, **3:** 1746 (1742); **5:** 2512 (2510); **9:** 5432 (5426)
Stern J P, **10:** 6106 (6104)
Stern M R, **1:** 94
Stern P, **3:** 1257 (1255, 1256); **10:** 5772 (5768), 6173 (6172)
Stern W, **2:** 846 (844); **5:** 2665 (2657), (2917); **8:** 4395 (4392)
Sternberg K, **4:** 2145 (2144); **8:** 4666 (4664)
Sternberg K J, **3:** 1643 (1640)
Sternberg R J, **1:** 5 (5), 6, 152 (147), 193 (191), 239, 377; **2:** 838, 842, 846 (845), 847, 851, 852, 856, 1177, 1178, 1207, 1208 (1206); **5:** 2731, 2732 (2726, 2727), 2767 (2762), 2768 (2762), 2769 (2762), 2884, 2916 (2911, 2912), 2921 (2918), 2922; **6:** 3315 (3313, 3314), 3324, 3325; **7:** 3788 (3785), 3830, 3879, 3880 (3873, 3876, 3877, 3878); **8:** 4727 (4725, 4726), 4823, 4824 (4818, 4819), 4951 (4950), 4956, 4957; **9:** 5043, 5504, 5563; **10:** 5831 (5829, 5830), 5914 (5913), 6159 (6158); **11:** 6456, 6457, 6780
Sternberg S J, **4:** 2219
Sternglanz S H, **4:** 2449 (2449), 2452 (2451)
Stettbacher H, **8:** 4419 (4419)
Stevens A, **10:** 5790
Stevens A L, **6:** 3301 (3298); **8:** 4727; **9:** 5342 (5339, 5340)
Stevens D, **10:** 6015 (6014)
Stevens J, **10:** 5862 (5860)
Stevens J H, **7:** 4296 (4295)
Stevens R, **2:** 811 (807); **3:** 1530 (1525); **8:** 4864 (4863); **10:** 5948 (5944), 6143 (6141)
Stevens R J, **2:** 1099 (1096)
Stevens R P, **6:** 3385
Stevens S, **4:** 1934 (1929)
Stevens S S, **6:** 3124 (3120); **7:** 3707 (3700); **11:** 6576 (6569)
Stevenson D, **2:** 711 (709); **5:** 2628 (2626)
Stevenson D L, **4:** 2249 (2248)
Stevenson H W, **1:** 32 (29, 31), 353, 362; **2:** 842; **3:** 1240 (1239), 1241 (1238), 1624, 1647 (1645), 1768 (1765); **4:** 2140 (2132, 2137, 2138), 2199; **5:** 2628 (2625, 2626, 2627), 2656, 2870 (2868), 2874; **6:** 3446 (3443); **8:** 4873 (4866), 4936 (4932); **9:** 5363 (5361, 5362); **10:** 5750 (5749), 5795 (5792), 6083 (6080, 6081), 6103 (6100); **11:** 6390 (6388, 6389)
Stevenson J C, **7:** 3889
Stevenson K R, **9:** 5185
Stevenson M, **8:** 4623 (4618, 4621)
Stevenson Z, **9:** 5211 (5208)
Stevenson-Hinde J, **3:** 1642 (1637); **4:** 1967 (1964), 2261; **8:** 4372; **9:** 5507 (5504)
Steves J, **7:** 3808 (3806)
Stevick E W, **4:** 2346 (2342)
Steward F H, **9:** 5220 (5217)
Stewart A J, **3:** 1241 (1236, 1237)
Stewart B, **10:** 5693 (5692, 5693)
Stewart C, **11:** 6798 (6797)
Stewart D M, **6:** 3643
Stewart D W, **9:** 5373
Stewart F, **3:** 1789
Stewart J, **2:** 1031 (1030)
Stewart J F, **7:** 3820 (3816)
Stewart J P, **9:** 5359 (5356)
Stewart L, **10:** 5826 (5822)
Stewart M, **8:** 4423 (4421)
Stewart M I, **2:** 705 (702)
Stewart R A, **8:** 4408 (4405), 4948 (4947)

Stewart S R, **11:** 6780 (6779)
Stewart T F M, **4:** 2011 (2010)
Stewart V L, **3:** 1441
Stewart W A C, **2:** 785 (782, 783)
Stewin L L, **10:** 5745
Steyer R, **4:** 1877 (1876)
Stibbs J H, **10:** 5805 (5798)
Sticht T G, **9:** 5233 (5229)
Stiefel L, **9:** 5065 (5061)
Stiegelbauer S, **5:** 2847 (2839, 2841, 2842, 2846); **6:** 3602 (3597, 3598, 3600, 3601); **7:** 4141; **9:** 5246 (5241, 5243); **10:** 6083 (6081, 6082), 6214 (6210, 6213)
Stiegler J W, **5:** 2685
Stier W F, **8:** 4468
Stierer B, **8:** 4622 (4618)
Stiggins R J, **3:** 1359 (1358); **10:** 6043 (6036)
Stigler J W, **1:** 353; **3:** 1233, 1241 (1238), 1246 (1245), 1647 (1645); **4:** 2140 (2132, 2137); **5:** 2628, 2870 (2868); **6:** 3227, 3453 (3450), 3661 (3659); **8:** 4873 (4866); **9:** 5363 (5361, 5362); **10:** 5750 (5749), 5795 (5792), 6083 (6080, 6081); **11:** 6390 (6388, 6389)
Stigler L W, **3:** 1768 (1765)
Stiglitz J E, **3:** 1703 (1698); **9:** 5355 (5350, 5351)
Stika C, **3:** 1402 (1401)
Stillman A, **1:** 82 (78, 79, 80, 81, 82)
Stimpson C, **11:** 6727 (6723)
Stinchcombe A L, **3:** 1607 (1604); **9:** 5560 (5557)
Stinson A, **7:** 4336 (4331)
Stipek D J, **1:** 32 (30); **2:** 706 (704); **5:** 2769 (2764); **7:** 3942, 3947; **9:** 5394 (5392); **10:** 5772 (5770), 6103 (6100); **11:** 6360 (6359)
Stiratelli R, **5:** 2596
Stires L K, **9:** 5359 (5357)
Stirner M, **8:** 4575 (4573)
Stirner P, **4:** 2394 (2391)
Stites R, **11:** 6563 (6559, 6561)
Stobart G, **10:** 5827 (5823, 5824); **11:** 6384 (6379)
Stock B, **6:** 3446 (3445), (3447)
Stock H, **1:** 139 (136)
Stock W, **9:** 5264 (5261), 5373 (5368)
Stockdill S H, **8:** 4751 (4745)
Stocker C, **4:** 2261 (2260)
Stockford L, **8:** 4930 (4928)
Stocking M L, **11:** 6355 (6353)
Stockley D, **1:** 162 (160); **7:** 4293 (4290, 4291, 4292)
Stockwell R P, **4:** 2346 (2343)
Stoddart T, **9:** 5318 (5315, 5316); **10:** 6215 (6210)
Stodolsky S S, **1:** 23; **2:** 796 (793), 807 (804); **5:** 2870 (2868); **9:** 5176 (5171); **10:** 5762 (5760), 5935 (5933), 6043 (6040); **11:** 6370 (6369)
Stoel W G R, **3:** 1746 (1742)
Stoel-Gammon C, **10:** 5697 (5694)
Stoikov V, **6:** 3425 (3423)
Stokes D E, **8:** 4352 (4339)
Stokes K E, **9:** 5008 (5002)
Stokey E, **3:** 1425
Stokie M D, **3:** 1567 (1564)
Stokking K M, **3:** 1278 (1274, 1278), 1553 (1550, 1551); **9:** 5246 (5241, 5245)
Stokman F N, **9:** 5560 (5559)
Stokols D, **10:** 6207
Stolberg A L, **4:** 2267
Stoll C S, **9:** 5475 (5472, 5473, 5474)
Stoll L, **1:** 390 (381, 389); **4:** 1934 (1931, 1932); **5:** 2509 (2508), 2779 (2775), 2870 (2868); **7:** 3912 (3910); **9:** 5223 (5221); **11:** 6390 (6388, 6389)
Stolnitz J, **1:** 199 (198)
Stolovitsch H D, **6:** 3096 (3093)
Stoltman J, **5:** 2470 (2468)
Stolurow L M, **9:** 5043 (5041)
Stolze B, **11:** 6747 (6746)
Stone A, **4:** 2427; **10:** 6072 (6069)
Stone A P, **10:** 6117 (6114)
Stone C, **1:** 374 (373)
Stone C A, **2:** 998 (996); **3:** 1252
Stone C N, **11:** 6558 (6553)
Stone D B, **5:** 2572 (2567)
Stone E J, **5:** 2572 (2567, 2568, 2570)
Stone J, **9:** 5233
Stone J A, **8:** 4408 (4407); **10:** 6072 (6069, 6070, 6071)
Stone J R, **10:** 5808 (5807)
Stone L, **5:** 2607, 2617 (2613, 2615)
Stone M H, **3:** 1514 (1510, 1513); **4:** 2017 (2012); **5:** 2784 (2781), 3043 (3041); **8:** 4359 (4356); **10:** 5827 (5823); **11:** 6349 (6348), 6355 (6353)
Stone P G, **1:** 280 (278, 279), 299 (299)
Stone P J, **2:** 1079 (1076)
Stone V I, **3:** 1735 (1733, 1734, 1735)
Stonehill R M, **5:** 2827
Stonequist E V, **7:** 3970 (3966)
Stoner G, **8:** 4375; **10:** 6031 (6028)
Stones E, **10:** 6004 (6001)
Storandt M, **8:** 4823, 4824
Storck I F, **3:** 1438
Storey E, **1:** 294, 296 (288)
Storm M, **3:** 1501 (1495); **5:** 2470 (2467)
Stotsky S L, **10:** 5704 (5701)
Stott F M, **8:** 4779 (4776, 4778)
Stoudt W H, **4:** 2012
Stouffer A, **11:** 6388
Stouffer S A, **3:** 1514; **6:** 3634; **7:** 4315
Stout R T, **1:** 82 (78); **6:** 3284
Stouthamer-Loeber M, **1:** 234 (232)
Stover G, **5:** 2855 (2854)
Stow S, **4:** 2131 (2126, 2129)
Stowasser R, **6:** 3647
Strachan D, **9:** 5197 (5194)
Strachey J, **4:** 2449
Straf M L, **7:** 3783, 3784 (3783)
Strain P S, **5:** 2814 (2807, 2808); **8:** 4375; **9:** 5567 (5564, 5565, 5566)
Strang D, **8:** 4568 (4562, 4563)
Straszheim M, **8:** 4787
Stratford R, **5:** 2529 (2526); **7:** 4240 (4239)
Stratmann K, **1:** 317 (311); **11:** 6659 (6654), 6684
Straton R B, **8:** 4751 (4745)
Stratta L, **7:** 3936 (3934)
Stratton P, **5:** 2802
Straus J P, **10:** 5635
Straus M A, **1:** 19 (16)
Strauss A, **4:** 2302 (2299, 2301); **7:** 4319 (4318); **10:** 5596 (5594)
Strauss A A, **10:** 5686 (5681)
Strauss A L, **2:** 645 (641, 644); **4:** 2194 (2186), 2374 (2373); **7:** 3826 (3822, 3825); **11:** 6576 (6574)
Strauss H, **7:** 4215 (4214)
Strauss J S, **2:** 718 (712)
Strauss W, **7:** 3925 (3924)
Straw B, **7:** 3986
Straw S B, **10:** 5705 (5701)
Strayer F F, **4:** 2452 (2450)
Strayer J, **9:** 5528
Streeck W, **6:** 3617 (3616); **11:** 6292 (6288)
Streefland L, **6:** 3661, 3685 (3678)
Streeker-Seeborg I, **7:** 4201 (4199)
Street B, **6:** 3446 (3445), 3459 (3454, 3455, 3457)
Street S, **2:** 1042 (1040); **3:** 1411 (1407), 1824 (1822); **6:** 3608 (3606, 3607); **8:** 4509 (4503), 4595 (4589), 4601 (4599)
Streeten P, **3:** 1672; **8:** 4839 (4838)
Streibel M J, **5:** 2773 (2770), 2874 (2871)
Streifer P, **4:** 2132 (2125)
Streissguth A P, **5:** 2567 (2564)
Streit R, **7:** 4100
Strelau J, **11:** 6310 (6308), 6311 (6308)
Stremel-Campbell K, **3:** 1406 (1403)
Strenio J L F, **5:** 2596 (2591)
Stretton K, **8:** 4375 (4374)
Streumer J N, **3:** 1315 (1310, 1313, 1314)
Streumer W, **7:** 3895 (3892)
Stricker G, **8:** 4791 (4789)
Stricker H, **9:** 5532 (5528, 5531)
Stricker K, **11:** 6747
Strickland B, **5:** 2813 (2811)
Strickland D, **4:** 1962 (1962)
Striebel M, **9:** 5544 (5540)
Strike K A, **4:** 2004, 2033 (2032); **8:** 4652 (4651); **10:** 5790 (5784), 5887, 5991 (5988, 5990), 6053 (6048); **11:** 6579 (6579), 6580
Striley J S, **7:** 3810 (3809), 4104 (4102)
Stringfield S, **4:** 1934 (1929, 1932)
Striniste N A, **8:** 4542 (4541)
Strittmatter P, **2:** 888 (886); **7:** 3743 (3741), 3753 (3744)
Strober M H, **2:** 693 (690, 691, 692); **4:** 2432 (2428, 2431); **7:** 4201 (4199); **10:** 5614 (5609)
Strodtbeck F L, **3:** 1240 (1236)
Ströhlein G, **7:** 4220 (4218)
Strom S, **10:** 5957 (5956)
Strömdahl H, **8:** 4429 (4426)
Strommen M P, **9:** 5008 (5007)
Stromquist M, **11:** 6719
Stromquist N P, **1:** 135 (132), 176 (174); **2:** 933 (929); **3:** 1655 (1653); **4:** 2412 (2407, 2410); **7:** 4141 (4138); **9:** 5228 (5226, 5227)
Strömquist S, **2:** 692 (692)
Stromsdorfer E W, **9:** 5240 (5235); **11:** 6425, 6633 (6628)
Strong A H, **2:** 766 (761, 762, 764)
Strong E K Jr, **11:** 6678 (6670)

Strong R W, **11:** 6625 (6623)
Stronge J H, **4:** 2132 (2124, 2131)
Stroobant R E, **10:** 5826 (5823); **11:** 6797 (6796)
Stroomberg H, **6:** 3435
Stroud A, **6:** 3496 (3494)
Strouse J, **9:** 5441 (5436, 5437)
Strube G, **8:** 4722
Strudwick J, **8:** 4595 (4592)
Struening E L, **3:** 1431; **4:** 2037, 2119; **11:** 6424
Struhsaker T T, **5:** 2685
Strukhoff R, **2:** 649 (646)
Strumwasser K P, **10:** 5943 (5939)
Strunk G, **4:** 2267 (2264)
Struve H, **6:** 3652 (3647, 3648, 3649, 3650)
Strykowski B, **8:** 4882 (4876)
Stuart A, **7:** 3739 (3734), 4162 (4160); **9:** 5130 (5128), 5142
Stuart J, **1:** (137)
Stuart J S, **10:** 5973 (5970)
Stubblefield H W, **7:** 4185
Stubbs M, **6:** 3638 (3638); **9:** 5313 (5311); **10:** 5614 (5608)
Stucker J, **8:** 4715 (4708)
Stuckless E R, **3:** 1402 (1402)
Studstill J, **4:** 2046 (2044)
Stueart R D, **11:** 6306
Stufflebeam D L, **3:** 1283 (1282), 1431 (1425); **4:** 2037 (2034), 2079, 2089 (2080), 2108, 2109 (2102, 2104), 2119 (2111), 2374, 2375 (2370); **7:** 4059 (4057); **8:** 4751 (4745), 4766; **10:** 5957 (5954); **11:** 6384
Stukát K-G, **8:** 4670 (4670); **10:** 5663 (5662)
Stults D M, **7:** 4007
Sturm J, **4:** (2004)
Sturman A, **2:** 645 (641, 642); **6:** 3373 (3372), 3527 (3525), 3528; **10:** 5591 (5590)
Sturni-Bossart G, **5:** 2910 (2908)
Sturtridge G, **6:** 3213
Style E, **10:** 6099 (6098)
Stynen J, **11:** 6307 (6301)
Su W H, **3:** 1421 (1419, 1421)
Suarcs F, **3:** 1671 (1669)
Suárez F, **3:** (1463)
Suarez T M, **3:** 1325 (1321); **7:** 4060 (4057)
Suarez-Berenguela R, **3:** 1707 (1704)
Suárez-Orozco M M, **1:** 297 (293); **2:** 1213 (1212); **3:** 1233 (1228), 1240 (1240), 1241 (1238, 1239), 1486 (1483); **7:** 3974 (3973)
Subbarao K, **3:** 1824 (1822)
Subelman I, **8:** 4482 (4482)
Subirats A, **10:** 5812 (5811)
Subirats M, **10:** 5607 (5601)
Subkoviak M J, **5:** 3050 (3045, 3049); **6:** 3507 (3507)
Subotnik R, **5:** 2732 (2726)
Subsaeng P, **11:** 6638 (6635)
Suchman E A, **3:** 1431 (1425); **4:** (2103); **6:** 3373 (3369)
Suchman F, **3:** 1514
Suchman J R, **3:** (1540)
Suchting W A, **8:** 4464
Suci G J, **1:** 390 (381, 382); **9:** 5158 (5154)
Sudaprasert K, **6:** 3247
Sudman S, **2:** 1055; **8:** 4887; **9:** 5142 (5140), 5560 (5557)
Suebsaeng P, **3:** 1707 (1703); **8:** 4839 (4838, 4839)
Suen H K, **9:** 5489 (5488), 5490 (5488)
Suezaki F, **1:** 353
Sugai G, **8:** 4376 (4373), 4661 (4658)
Sugano T, **3:** 1713
Sugar M, **9:** 5435
Sugarman B, **8:** 4456 (4455)
Sugarman S, **1:** 594 (589); **6:** 3276 (3276); **9:** 5196 (5195)
Sugarman S D, **9:** 5206 (5203, 5204, 5205), 5240 (5239)
Sugrue B M, **7:** 3743 (3739, 3740, 3742, 3743)
Suh S, **2:** 770 (768)
Suhadolnik D, **3:** 1490 (1487, 1488)
Suhor C, **6:** 3443
Suite A, **9:** 5358 (5356)
Suitor J H, **9:** 5066 (5062)
Sukarno, **10:** (5779)
Sukhatme B V, **9:** 5142
Sukhatme P V, **9:** 5142
Sukhatme S, **9:** 5142
Sukhbaatar D, **7:** (3895)
Sulimov E F, **6:** 3621 (3617)
Sullivan A, **3:** (1402)
Sullivan E, **8:** 4455 (4455)
Sullivan E V, **5:** 2779 (2775); **6:** 3512 (3511); **10:** 5804
Sullivan G, **9:** 5130 (5129)
Sullivan H, **4:** 1928 (1928); **8:** 4803 (4802)
Sullivan H S, **10:** 5758 (5757)
Sullivan J A, **11:** 6576 (6573)
Sullivan J L, **7:** 4007
Sullivan J W, **3:** 1623, 1624, 1624 (1621)
Sullivan M G, **3:** 1607 (1604); **6:** 3197 (3193); **11:** 6735 (6734)
Sullivan T, **3:** 1602 (1600); **11:** 6437 (6433)
Sullivan W M, **3:** 1774 (1772); **5:** 2586; **10:** 5990 (5989)
Sully J, **4:** (1864)
Suls J, **9:** 5394; **10:** 5738 (5736)
Sultana R, **6:** 3593; **8:** 4586 (4582, 4585)
Sulzbacher S I, **4:** 2281 (2280)
Sulzby E, **4:** 1963 (1961); **6:** 3453, 3463 (3460, 3461); **7:** 4301; **10:** 5961 (5959)
Sulzer B, **1:** 486; **10:** 6164 (6162)
Sulzer-Azaroff B, **10:** 6164 (6160, 6161, 6162)
Sumarah J, **5:** 2972 (2970)
Sumathipala K H M, **10:** 5721
Summer R J, **6:** 3373 (3371)
Summers A A, **4:** 1972 (1971)
Summers E G, **5:** 2827
Summers J A, **10:** 6244 (6243)
Summers L, **6:** 3189 (3187)
Sumner D L, **9:** 5460
Sun Y, **9:** 5528 (5527)
Sundel M, **8:** 4824
Sundgren G, **4:** 2327 (2326)
Sundland D, **8:** 4857 (4857)
Sung Y W, **5:** 2643
Super D E, **2:** 957 (956); **11:** 6678 (6669, 6670)
Superka D P, **9:** 5578 (5574)
Suppe F, **9:** 5030 (5026); **10:** 6207
Suppes P, **1:** 5; **2:** 1007 (1003), (1008); **3:** 1266 (1263), 1573 (1572); **4:** 1840, 1864, 1872 (1864), 1918 (1913), 2119 (2112); **5:** 2891 (2887); **7:** 4006, 4088 (4082, 4083); **8:** 4562 (4556, 4561), 4604 (4603), 4766 (4760); **9:** 5038 (5033, 5035); **11:** 6445 (6440)
Supple M de M, **10:** 5681 (5678)
Supplee P L, **5:** 2495
Suransky V P, **10:** 5818 (5816)
Surgue B, **2:** 1175 (1173)
Surhomme M, **5:** 2544
Suryadi A, **8:** 4835 (4834)
Susanne C, **8:** 4473, 4474
Susman E J, **9:** 5435 (5434)
Sussman L, **3:** 1810 (1809)
Sussman M B, **4:** 2266
Süssmuth H, **5:** 2623
Sutaria M C, **8:** 4442
Sutcliffe J, **10:** 5924 (5920, 5922)
Sutcliffe J M, **9:** 5008
Suter D, **5:** 2491 (2488)
Suter L, **10:** 5846 (5843)
Sutherland D I M, **1:** 28
Sutherland D S, **4:** 1995 (1992)
Sutherland M, **2:** 1064
Sutherland N, **5:** 2617 (2613)
Sutherland R, **2:** 991 (990); **7:** 4099 (4098)
Suttner M, **1:** 176 (173)
Sutton A, **3:** 1461; **5:** 2814 (2810); **6:** 3315 (3313)
Sutton C R, **6:** 3219 (3216, 3217)
Sutton R E, **4:** 1911 (1909), 2427 (2423, 2424); **10:** 6012 (6011)
Sutton S, **7:** 4316
Sutton-Smith B, **7:** 4051 (4047)
Suzallo H, **10:** 5607 (5597)
Suzuki H, **6:** 3092
Suzuki K, **2:** 1170 (1169); **7:** 3946 (3944, 3946)
Suzuki S, **7:** 4027
Svalastoga K, **7:** 3864 (3862)
Svanberg Hård H, **4:** 2327 (2327)
Svatos M, **2:** 884
Svenningson L, **1:** 560 (554)
Svenningsson L, **11:** 6395
Svensen A, **2:** 738 (737)
Svensson H, **10:** 5674 (5670)
Svensson L, **1:** 194 (191); **8:** 4429 (4426); **10:** 5790 (5784, 5785, 5786)
Svensson N-E, **4:** 1872 (1869)
Svik G, **10:** 6053
Svinicki M D, **6:** 3339 (3337)
Swadener E B, **5:** 2814 (2811)
Swafford J O, **9:** 5373
Swain M, **4:** 2339, 2346 (2344), 2351 (2350), 2357 (2353); **7:** 3970 (3967)
Swallow J, **2:** 1006 (1004, 1006); **11:** 6781
Swaminathan H, **1:** 42 (36), 52 (50); **2:** 998 (994), 1189 (1188); **5:** 3043 (3037, 3039, 3041), 3050 (3047), 3055; **6:** 3253 (3248, 3250); **7:** 4000, 4056 (4055); **11:** 6333 (6332)
Swaminathan M, **8:** 4677 (4676)
Swan M, **7:** 3936 (3933)

Swan W, **5:** 2814 (2807)
Swann C E, **9:** 5008 (5003)
Swann W, **11:** 6461
Swanson A D, **3:** 1411 (1408)
Swanson G E, **5:** 2672
Swanson H L, **5:** 2495 (2493); **10:** 5686 (5682, 5684), 5831 (5829)
Swanson J, **5:** 2769 (2762, 2765, 2766); **7:** 3942 (3937); **10:** 6159 (6158)
Swanson J L, **11:** 6678 (6675)
Swanson J M, **3:** 1520
Swanson R A, **2:** 1139 (1138); **6:** 3096 (3095); **11:** 6425
Swanston M, **8:** 4379
Swanstrom T, **11:** 6558
Swantz M L, **5:** 2737 (2735)
Swanwick K, **11:** 6618
Swarthout D, **9:** 5363 (5360)
Swartland J R, **3:** 1416 (1415)
Swartz E, **7:** 3978
Swartz J, **11:** 6538 (6536)
Swartz J B, **9:** 5544 (5540)
Swartz J D, **8:** 4791
Swartz M J, **3:** 1729 (1726)
Swartz R J, **2:** 1208 (1207)
Swartz S S, **7:** 3807 (3803)
Sweeney J A C, **9:** 5582 (5582)
Sweet H, **4:** 2346 (2340, 2341)
Sweet R, **3:** 1579; **8:** 4796 (4793); **11:** 6306 (6305)
Sweeting A E, **5:** 2642 (2637), 2643 (2637)
Sweetland R, **1:** 322
Sweetnam P M, **8:** 4473 (4469)
Sweitzer M, **7:** 4296 (4294, 4295)
Swenson W M, **1:** 238 (237)
Swetz F, **6:** 3459 (3458), 3634
Swick K J, **2:** 1175 (1173); **10:** 5925 (5923)
Swider A, **10:** 5990 (5989)
Swidler A, **4:** 2167 (2163)
Swift A, **3:** 1735 (1733, 1735)
Swift D F, **10:** 5607 (5601)
Swift J, **7:** 3978
Swift L F, **10:** 6149 (6145)
Swinbourne E, **1:** 157, 158, 162 (161), 414, 415
Swinburn E, **6:** 3366
Swindell R F, **1:** 162 (160)
Swineford F, **7:** 3935 (3932, 3933), 4196 (4195)
Swinton S S, **11:** 6339 (6336)
Switzer K A, **4:** 1996
Sybouts W, **1:** 83 (80)
Sydney A, **6:** (3499)
Syed S, **4:** 2418 (2415)
Sykes G, **3:** 1257; **4:** 2033; **10:** 5613, 5614 (5612), 5948 (5943, 5946), 6096 (6093), 6099, 6219 (6218); **11:** 6580
Sykes R C, **8:** 4473 (4470)
Sykes R M, **7:** 3768
Sykes R N, **2:** 969
Symeonides K, **11:** 6438 (6436)
Symons S, **7:** 3768 (3765)
Sympson J B, **6:** 3253 (3252)
Syrquin M, **5:** 2945 (2943)
Sysko L, **7:** 4300 (4298)
Szanton E, **10:** 5693 (5693)
Szebenyi P, **5:** 2706 (2704); **8:** 4499
Szreter R, **5:** 2618
Szulc H, **10:** 5617 (5616)
Szyliowicz J S, **11:** 6760 (6754, 6755)

Taba H, **3:** 1267 (1264), 1334 (1329, 1330, 1331, 1332); **4:** 1848 (1843); **10:** 5818 (5813)
Tabachnick B G, **2:** 1117 (1115, 1116)
Tabachnick B R, **5:** 2779 (2776); **10:** 5948, 6086, 6127 (6126), 6219 (6218)
Tabachnick R, **10:** 5961 (5960)
Tabachnik R B, **3:** 1272 (1271)
Taback S, **6:** 3685
Tabberer R, **1:** 194 (192)
Tabler M, **2:** 1175 (1172)
Tachibana Y, **5:** 2651 (2649)
Tachibanaki T, **3:** 1750 (1749)
Tacitus P, **8:** (4887)
Taçon P, **3:** 1735 (1733, 1734, 1735)
Taft H L, **11:** 6355 (6351)
Taft R, **1:** 389; **2:** 792; **7:** 3706
Tagg E D, **2:** 977, 988, 1012 (1008); **3:** 1778, 1779; **10:** 5625, 6008 (6005)
Tagg W, **10:** 5622
Tagiuri R, **9:** 5211 (5207)
Tait A, **11:** 6638 (6634)
Tait H, **1:** 193 (190, 191, 193); **6:** 3339 (3337)
Taiwo C O, **7:** 4132
Takács D V, **4:** 2400 (2397)
Takahashi C, **8:** 4473 (4470)
Takai T, **7:** 3946 (3945)
Takaki R, **7:** 3848 (3841)
Takala S, **4:** 2024 (2020), 2025; **6:** 3213 (3211); **7:** 3726 (3724), 3936 (3933)
Takane Y, **9:** 5159 (5158)
Takanishi R, **5:** 2672 (2670)
Takens R J, **5:** 2884; **6:** 3292
Takeuchi Y, **11:** 6699 (6696)
Talabi J K, **11:** 6608 (6605)
Talbert J, **8:** 4568 (4565); **10:** 6214
Talbert J E, **10:** 5613, 5934, 5935 (5931)
Tall A Y, **6:** 3113
Tall D O, **6:** 3685 (3681)
Tall G, **5:** 2903 (2898)
Tallal P A, **1:** 553 (553); **6:** 3224 (3223); **10:** 5681 (5679)
Tallmadge G K, **1:** 490 (487)
Talmage H, **4:** 2119 (2111); **5:** 2870
Talyzina N, **7:** 3886 (3885)
Tamagnini G, **5:** (3031)
Tambashe B, **11:** 6814 (6809)
Tamblyn R M, **6:** 3349 (3346)
Tamez E, **9:** 5008 (5006)
Tamir D, **3:** 1624 (1621)
Tamir P, **2:** 1175 (1173); **3:** 1283 (1279), 1325 (1321), 1544 (1538, 1539, 1541, 1542); **6:** 3205 (3203), 3415 (3410), 3416 (3408, 3412, 3415); **8:** 4648 (4646); **9:** 5328 (5326), 5338 (5336, 5337), 5345 (5343, 5344); **10:** 5948 (5946), 5957 (5956), 5994
Tamis-LeMonda C S, **8:** 4542 (4540)
Tamsky B F, **1:** 239 (238)
Tan H W, **1:** 111; **2:** 1094 (1090), 1152; **4:** 2419; **6:** 3616 (3615)
Tan J-P, **3:** 1789 (1788), 1793; **4:** 2316 (2311, 2314); **8:** 4364 (4361), 4509 (4504), 4707 (4705); **10:** 5754 (5752), 5768 (5765); **11:** 6431
Tan Shiow Ling, **5:** 2972 (2970)
Tanabe S, **11:** 6563 (6560, 6561, 6562)
Tanaka-Matsumi J, **1:** 494 (491)
Tancred P, **4:** 2286 (2284)
Tandon B B, **5:** 2740
Tandon R, **1:** 48 (45); **7:** 4336 (4330); **8:** 4337
Tandon Y, **11:** 6256 (6253)
Tang G, **6:** 3443 (3440)
Tanguy L, **2:** 665 (662)
Tangyong A F, **10:** 5973 (5971), 5982 (5979)
Tankonogaya E P, **9:** 5098
Tann S, **10:** 6219 (6218)
Tannahill J, **10:** 5691 (5690)
Tannatt L M, **10:** 5772 (5770)
Tannen D, **6:** 3238; **8:** 4945 (4942)
Tannen M B, **9:** 5076 (5072, 5073, 5074); **11:** 6633 (6628)
Tannenbaum A J, **3:** 1402 (1401); **5:** 2732 (2726, 2727); **9:** 5532 (5528, 5529, 5530)
Tannenbaum P H, **1:** 390 (381, 382); **9:** 5158 (5154)
Tannenbaum R L, **9:** 5406 (5404, 5405)
Tannenbaum S I, **6:** 3306 (3304, 3305)
Tanner D, **3:** 1301 (1300), 1308 (1303, 1305, 1306), 1334
Tanner D K, **9:** 5363 (5362)
Tanner J M, **1:** 88 (84, 85), 89 (83, 84, 85); **2:** 706 (701); **8:** 4473, 4474; **9:** 5060 (5058)
Tanner L N, **3:** (1288), 1301 (1300), 1308 (1301, 1302, 1303, 1305, 1306), 1334; **9:** 5334
Tannery P, **3:** 1464 (1462, 1463)
Tannhausser M T, **10:** 5686 (5681)
Tansey P J, **9:** 5475 (5472)
Tanz C, **9:** 5417 (5413)
Taoklam W, **2:** 1127 (1123); **8:** 4708 (4703, 4706, 4707)
Tapiola K, **4:** 2394 (2389)
Tapper T, **4:** 1984 (1982); **8:** 4601 (4598)
Tapsoba S, **8:** 4514 (4510, 4513)
Tar Z, **3:** 1774
Tarnopol L, **7:** 4081
Tarnopol M, **7:** 4081
Tarone E, **4:** 2339 (2332)
Tarr E R, **11:** 6774, 6775
Tarrant J M, **8:** 4581 (4575, 4576, 4578)
Tarrow N B, **2:** 948 (943); **4:** 1852
Tarule J M, **1:** 162 (160); **7:** 4329 (4326); **10:** 5939 (5938), 6099 (6098); **11:** 6722 (6721)
Tarvin W L, **10:** 5929 (5925)
Tasman A, **4:** (2302)
Tason M, **3:** 1810
Tasso C, **10:** 5914
Tatarunis A M, **7:** 4026
Tate C N, **7:** 3816
Tate R L, **7:** 3987 (3984)
Tatsuno S M, **5:** 2725 (2723, 2724)
Tatsuoka M M, **2:** 631 (628); **3:** 1549 (1544, 1545, 1546); **5:** 2931 (2925); **7:** 3872 (3866, 3868), 4016 (4008); **9:** 4974 (4967, 4971)
Tatto M T, **2:** 1136 (1134, 1135); **10:** 5954 (5950)

Tatur M, **11:** 6648 (6641)
Taubman P, **1:** 520, 521 (517); **3:** 1750 (1750); **4:** 2278 (2275, 2277, 2278), 2279 (2275, 2276, 2277, 2278); **6:** 3143 (3138, 3140, 3141, 3143), 3144 (3138, 3139, 3140, 3141, 3142, 3143); **9:** 5355 (5353); **11:** 6615
Taueber R C, **3:** 1431 (1430), 1746 (1742, 1745)
Taumab P, **6:** 3144 (3140)
Tausworthe R C, **7:** 3816
Tawfi M N, **11:** 6627 (6626)
Tawfik W A, **8:** 4473 (4471)
Tawney D A, **2:** 645 (644)
Tawney R H, **5:** 2737 (2733, 2735); **10:** (6055)
Taxel J, **3:** (1346), (1347)
Tayler C A, **6:** 3297 (3294)
Taylor A E, **8:** 4456 (4448, 4451)
Taylor B, **1:** 88 (83); **10:** 6015 (6014)
Taylor B M, **10:** 5831 (5830)
Taylor C, **3:** (1770), (1772); **4:** 2388 (2386); **5:** 2586 (2583, 2584, 2585)
Taylor C W, **2:** 1177 (1176)
Taylor D, **6:** 3453 (3447, 3451), 3459 (3456)
Taylor D A, **3:** 1486
Taylor D C, **3:** 1416 (1415)
Taylor D S, **3:** 1729 (1728)
Taylor D T, **8:** 4731 (4729)
Taylor E, **1:** 193 (189); **4:** 2423 (2419, 2420)
Taylor F, **9:** (5053)
Taylor F W, **1:** 67 (61); **3:** (1299); **4:** 2167 (2157); **5:** (2878); **7:** (3951), (4236); **9:** 5169 (5160)
Taylor G, **4:** 1899 (1889), 2364 (2361); **6:** 3360; **7:** 4240 (4237)
Taylor H C, **3:** 1421 (1417)
Taylor I A, **2:** 1182
Taylor J C, **3:** 1573 (1572)
Taylor J L, **9:** 5475 (5472)
Taylor J M, **4:** 2296
Taylor L, **4:** 1963 (1959)
Taylor M, **1:** 158; **3:** 1543 (1538, 1539, 1543); **5:** 2491 (2487)
Taylor M C, **1:** 103, 162 (161)
Taylor M J, **9:** 5008
Taylor O, **6:** 3227, 3228 (3227)
Taylor P C, **10:** 5775 (5774)
Taylor P H, **3:** 1278; **10:** 6035 (6032)
Taylor P M, **4:** 2266
Taylor R, **1:** 93 (89, 91); **2:** 973, 1007 (1002); **3:** 1449; **8:** 4647 (4645, 4646); **10:** 5674 (5672)
Taylor R E, **1:** 310
Taylor R L, **3:** 1359 (1356, 1358)
Taylor R N, **5:** 2725 (2721)
Taylor R P, **2:** 991 (990), 1012 (1008); **3:** 1779
Taylor S, **4:** 1984 (1984); **11:** 6735
Taylor S C, **10:** 6178 (6176, 6177)
Taylor S J, **2:** 729 (723); **3:** 1508; **6:** 3559 (3558)
Taylor W, **1:** 28; **4:** 2166; **5:** 2954 (2953); **7:** 3840 (3834); **8:** 4562 (4556, 4561); **9:** 5168 (5162); **11:** 6445
Taylor W D, **9:** 5544 (5540)
Taylor W L, **7:** 3936 (3931); **11:** 6349 (6342)
Teale W H, **6:** 3453 (3449), 3463 (3460, 3461); **7:** 4301 (4300); **10:** 5961 (5959)
Teasdale J D, **7:** 3942 (3940); **9:** 5406 (5404, 5405)
Teasley S D, **2:** 838 (837); **6:** 3302; **9:** 5507
Teather D C B, **7:** 4170
Teberosky A, **4:** 1962 (1960); **6:** 3463 (3460)
Teddlie C, **4:** 1934 (1929, 1932); **9:** 5281 (5276)
Tedesco J C, **8:** 4495 (4494)
Tehranian M, **9:** 5544 (5539)
Teichler U, **5:** 2479 (2474)
Teichmann H, **8:** 4395 (4390)
Teifel V, **6:** 3401 (3401)
Teikari V, **5:** 2689 (2688)
Teitlebaum K, **10:** 6139 (6133)
Teixeira M, **6:** 3545
Telama R, **10:** 5713 (5709, 5710)
Telem M, **3:** 1830 (1829); **5:** 2831 (2828, 2829, 2830, 2831)
Teles L, **2:** 982 (978, 979, 980, 981)
Telhaug A O, **7:** 4192
Tell G S, **5:** 2572 (2569)
Tellegen A, **2:** 846 (845); **6:** 3144 (3139); **8:** 4779 (4775, 4777); **11:** 6492 (6488)
Teller J, **6:** 3671
Telschow R L, **10:** 5924 (5922, 5923)
Temo S, **1:** 260
Temple D, **11:** 6712 (6709)
Temple L, **4:** 2427 (2424, 2425)
Templeton S, **4:** 1962
Templin M, **10:** 5697 (5694)
Templin T, **10:** 5713 (5712)
Temu E B, **3:** 1690 (1689)
ten Brummelhuis A C A, **2:** 957 (954); **8:** 4352 (4351)
Ten Have T T, **1:** 277 (275, 277); **3:** 1624 (1623)
Tendler J, **4:** 1991 (1989)
Tenenbaum G, **11:** 6360 (6357)
Tenent M, **7:** 4329
Tennant M, **1:** 168 (168); **10:** 6058 (6054)
Tennyson R D, **2:** 1019 (1017, 1018), 1020, 1026 (1021, 1022), 1170 (1166), **5:** 2874 (2872); **8:** 4783 (4780), 4803 (4802)
Tenzer N, **4:** 2385
Tepperman L, **10:** 5607 (5600)
Ter Maat J, **7:** 3861 (3858)
Terakawa T, **9:** 5328 (5325)
Terenzine P T, **1:** 520 (519)
Terkla D G, **5:** 2942 (2941)
Terleckyj N E, **2:** 1055; **4:** 2212, 2279
Terlouw C, **4:** 2119 (2110)
Terman L M, **1:** 53 (49); **4:** (1841), 2436 (2435); **5:** 2491 (2488), (2492), (2726), (2878), (2917); **9:** (5433); **11:** 6315 (6315)
Terrace H S, **5:** 2685 (2682)
Terrana T, **4:** 2011 (2010)
Terrell F, **6:** 3228 (3225)
Terrell J U, **5:** 2656
Terrell S L, **6:** 3228 (3225)
Terrell T, **6:** 3231 (3231)
Terrell T D, **4:** 2346 (2343)
Terrot N, **4:** 1976 (1972)
Terry C, **2:** 1031 (1028)
Terry D V, **5:** 2813 (2809)
Tesla C, **2:** 856 (854)
Tesolowski D G, **4:** 1924 (1922)
Tesser A, **1:** 380 (378), 390 (381, 382); **9:** 5324 (5319)
Tessier A, **5:** 2814 (2807)
Tessmer M, **10:** 5913 (5910, 5912)
Tetlock P E, **1:** 380 (379)
Tétreau B, **11:** 6678 (6672)
Tetzlaff R, **3:** 1789
Thagard P R, **4:** 2302 (2301); **8:** 4722 (4720, 4721), 4951
Thaiss C, **6:** 3443
Thaler R, **4:** 2279 (2275)
Thandika M, **8:** 4514 (4513)
Tharp R G, **2:** 803 (799), 867 (865), 868 (865); **3:** 1236 (1234, 1236); **6:** 3312 (3308, 3309)
Thatcher D C, **9:** 5475
Thatcher M, **6:** (3206)
Thatcher R W, **5:** 2681 (2680)
Thaubault R, **5:** 2607
Thayer D T, **5:** 2595 (2593), 2596 (2591, 2593), 3050 (3046)
Thayer N H, **7:** 3775
Theil H, **3:** 1425
Thein T M, **9:** 5228 (5227)
Thelen E, **4:** 1967; **7:** 3950 (3948)
Thelen H A, **9:** 5168 (5162); **10:** 6187 (6183)
Theman J, **8:** 4429 (4425)
Theobald M R, **10:** 5613 (5609), 6139 (6133); **11:** 6727 (6724), 6735 (6732)
Theodorou E, **2:** 820 (819)
Theodossin E F, **7:** 3895 (3890, 3892)
Théry B, **1:** 180 (178, 179)
Theunissen T J J M, **2:** 998 (996); **5:** 2462 (2460)
Thiagarajan S, **4:** 1918 (1913); **8:** 4774 (4774); **10:** 6043 (6042)
Thias H, **6:** 3184 (3184); **8:** 4918 (4913, 4914, 4916)
Thibadeau G, **7:** 4215 (4211)
Thibaut J W, **5:** 2532 (2531)
Thiemann S, **4:** 2194 (2192); **5:** 2714 (2713)
Thies-Sprinthall L T, **10:** 5935 (5931), 6169 (6168)
Thijssen J A, **3:** 1315 (1313, 1314)
Thirkell B, **9:** 5359 (5356)
Thissen D, **1:** 53 (49); **8:** 4473 (4470), 4474 (4468, 4471)
Thistlewood D, **1:** 343 (341)
Thobani M, **1:** 474 (468)
Thögersen S, **3:** 1690 (1686, 1687)
Thoma S J, **7:** 3920 (3918)
Thomae H, **1:** 239 (236); **5:** 2665 (2662); **8:** 4719 (4716)
Thomas A Jr, **9:** 5151
Thomas A M, **1:** 127 (126), 135 (131), 158 (153, 154, 155, 156, 157), 162 (159, 161), 234 (232); **5:** 2650; **6:** 3367; **8:** 4526 (4524), 4639 (4638); **9:** 5290; **10:** 5596 (5593); **11:** 6311 (6307, 6308, 6309)
Thomas A R, **5:** 2954 (2953)
Thomas B, **4:** 2440 (2438)
Thomas C A, **8:** 4774 (4769)

Thomas D, **4:** 1979 (1976), 2419; **8:** 4857 (4857)
Thomas D R, **1:** 486 (485)
Thomas E J, **2:** 1194; **10:** 6132
Thomas G, **7:** 4293 (4291); **9:** 5185 (5184), 5216 (5211, 5212), 5350 (5346)
Thomas G M, **10:** 5607 (5600)
Thomas H, **4:** 2166; **9:** 5168 (5159), 5185 (5184), 5307 (5307)
Thomas J, **4:** 2267 (2262)
Thomas J A, **7:** 3820, 3821 (3816); **11:** 6298 (6294)
Thomas J B, **7:** 3970 (3962); **10:** 5901 (5895), 5999 (5996)
Thomas J E, **1:** 142 (140); **2:** 1194; **6:** 3078, 3422
Thomas J P, **8:** 4379
Thomas J W, **1:** 194 (188)
Thomas M A, **9:** 5240 (5235)
Thomas M R, **8:** 4408 (4404, 4405)
Thomas M W, **10:** 6096 (6092)
Thomas N, **2:** 1165
Thomas P, **5:** 2601 (2599)
Thomas P R, **1:** 194 (188, 190)
Thomas R, **2:** 1165 (1164)
Thomas R C, **8:** 4601
Thomas R K, **1:** 297 (291, 293)
Thomas R M, **1:** 274 (267, 268), 497; **2:** 948 (943), 958; **4:** 1857 (1854), 1903 (1903), 2310; **5:** 2656 (2654), 2773 (2770); **6:** 3368; **7:** 4236 (4230, 4233); **8:** 4595, 4601 (4596), 4604, 4812 (4808); **10:** 6103 (6100)
Thomas S, **5:** 2965
Thomas S C, **7:** 4215 (4212)
Thomas S J, **10:** 5939 (5936)
Thomas S M, **5:** 2773 (2770)
Thomas T, **1:** 199 (196)
Thomas V G, **4:** 2435 (2432), 2436
Thomas W I, **2:** 785 (784); **11:** 6466 (6463)
Thomason T C, **7:** 4296 (4295)
Thomassen P A, **11:** 6492 (6489)
Thompson A, **3:** 1257 (1256); **6:** 3643 (3642)
Thompson A R, **10:** 6067 (6063, 6066)
Thompson B, **2:** 631; **9:** 5082; **10:** 5939 (5937)
Thompson C, **1:** 199 (198), 510
Thompson E P, **2:** 1194; **5:** 2737 (2735)
Thompson G, **5:** 2891 (2885)
Thompson G F, **11:** 6704 (6700)
Thompson G G, **1:** 537 (535)
Thompson H B, **5:** 2680 (2677); **9:** (5433)
Thompson I, **7:** 3858 (3857)
Thompson J, **1:** 93 (91); **2:** 1194; **5:** 2870 (2868); **7:** 4249
Thompson J B, **2:** 1204; **5:** 2586
Thompson J D, **3:** 1746 (1741)
Thompson J L, **5:** 2736, 2737 (2733); **8:** 4788; **10:** 5596 (5592)
Thompson M, **2:** 1031 (1026); **3:** 1402 (1400)
Thompson M M, **11:** 6307 (6302)
Thompson M S, **4:** 2249
Thompson N, **2:** 906; **10:** 5596 (5594)
Thompson P, **7:** 4224, 4225 (4222); **10:** 6139
Thompson R, **7:** 4225
Thompson S, **1:** 193 (193); **2:** 730
Thompson T, **7:** 3848 (3842)
Thompson T J, **7:** 4145
Thompson-Hoffman S, **3:** 1438
Thomsen P, **8:** 4464
Thomson G, **3:** (1793)
Thomson G H, **4:** 1872 (1867), (2230)
Thomson M, **10:** 5680, 5681
Thonhauser J, **1:** 432 (423, 431)
Thönnissen M, **10:** 5674 (5670)
Thor O C, **5:** 2891 (2886)
Thoresen C E, **10:** 5977
Thorgood N, **3:** 1386 (1384)
Thorkildsen R, **10:** 5674 (5671)
Thorkildsen R J, **10:** 5673 (5670)
Thorndike E L, **1:** (122), (495); **2:** (1077); **3:** 1301 (1296), (1793), (1794), (1795); **4:** (1841), (1861), 1872 (1864, 1867, 1868, 1869), 2281 (2279); **5:** (2876), (2877), (2878), (2880), 2921 (2916, 2917, 2919); **6:** (3316), (3340); **7:** 4329 (4326); **8:** 4731 (4729); **9:** 5055 (5052, 5053), (5424), (5564); **11:** 6457 (6453, 6455)
Thorndike R L, **1:** 3 (33, 35), 41, 42 (33, 38, 40), 370 (363), 390 (383), 396 (393); **2:** 678 (673), 957 (954), 1117 (1110); **3:** 1768 (1767), 1769 (1763); **6:** 3524 (3520, 3521); **7:** 3936 (3931, 3932), 4000 (3996, 3997), 4056, 4196 (4195); **8:** (4557), 4657 (4655, 4656), 4753, 4930 (4924); **9:** 4995 (4983, 4991, 4993, 4994, 4995), 5324 (5319); **10:** 5725; **11:** 6328, 6348, 6349 (6340, 6348), 6355, 6511 (6509), 6575
Thorndike R M, **2:** 631 (630), 1117 (1109, 1111, 1115, 1116, 1117); **8:** 4930 (4928); **9:** 4995 (4995)
Thorne B, **10:** 5948 (5944)
Thorne J, **3:** 1534 (1531)
Thornieporth G, **11:** 6748
Thornley J, **5:** 2457 (2455)
Thornton R K, **2:** 1012 (1008); **7:** 3810 (3808, 3809); **8:** 4479 (4478)
Thornton S J, **10:** 5995 (5991, 5994)
Thorpe J S, **8:** 4791
Thorpe L P, **9:** 5043 (5039)
Thorpe M, **1:** 564; **4:** 2186 (2185)
Thorpe M E, **11:** 6461 (6459)
Thorpe R, **2:** 906 (902)
Thousand J, **10:** 6244 (6242, 6243)
Thrall G I, **3:** 1553
Thrasher F M, **11:** 6803 (6799)
Throsby C D, **10:** 5754 (5753)
Thucydides, **2:** (804)
Thum Y M, **2:** 711 (710); **3:** 1607; **4:** 2249
Thurber F, **9:** 5291 (5284, 5286)
Thurlow M L, **2:** 719 (712); **9:** 5071 (5069); **10:** 5686 (5683)
Thurow L C, **3:** 1695 (1693), 1707 (1705), 1821 (1816, 1819); **6:** 3184 (3182); **9:** 5355 (5350); **10:** 5735 (5732); **11:** 6261 (6257)
Thurston P W, **1:** 437 (432, 433); **9:** 5211
Thurstone L L, **1:** 390 (382, 385), 396 (392); **2:** 792 (788), 847 (845), 872 (869); **4:** 1872 (1867), 2241 (2230, 2231, 2233, 2234, 2236); **5:** (2911), (2917); **6:** 3325 (3320); **7:** 3707 (3699, 3702, 3703, 3704), 3880 (3873, 3874, 3875, 3876, 3878); **8:** 4923 (4918, 4919, 4922); **9:** 5435 (5433); **11:** 6349 (6341), 6388 (6385, 6386, 6387)
Thurstone T G, **7:** 3880 (3874, 3875)
Thut I N, **8:** 4509 (4500)
Thyssen S, **1:** 317
Tibble J W, **8:** 4456 (4455); **10:** 5985 (5983)
Tiberghien A, **6:** 3416; **8:** 4479; **9:** 5334 (5332), 5341 (5339)
Tibi C, **9:** 5066 (5062, 5063)
Tibshurani R, **9:** 5130 (5128)
Tiburcio L, **7:** 4246 (4243)
Tickton S G, **4:** 1899 (1889)
Tidball M E, **2:** 834 (832); **11:** 6712 (6709)
Tidwell D, **3:** 1257 (1256); **8:** 4948 (4946)
Tidwell M, **2:** 933 (930)
Tiedeman D V, **3:** 1381 (1377), 1549 (1544)
Tiedeman J, **5:** 2769 (2763)
Tiedge J, **1:** 139
Tiefer L, **9:** 5441 (5436)
Tiegerman E, **10:** 5693 (5691)
Tiemann P W, **5:** 3066 (3065)
Tienda M, **8:** 4901 (4898)
Tiene D, **5:** 2897 (2895)
Tierney A J, **5:** 2685 (2681)
Tierney R J, **9:** 5363
Tietze W, **5:** 2480 (2474); **7:** 4301 (4299); **8:** 4666 (4663, 4664)
Tiffin J, **4:** 1918 (1916)
Tighe M A, **6:** 3209 (3207)
Tight M, **1:** 94, 277; **2:** 1165
Tijiboy J A, **3:** 1735 (1733, 1734, 1735)
Tilak J B G, **2:** 1127 (1123); **3:** 1666, 1789 (1787); **5:** 2759 (2754); **6:** 3608 (3604); **8:** 4707 (4703); **11:** 6266 (6263)
Tillema H H, **9:** 5043 (5041)
Tillermans T, **5:** 2813 (2810)
Tillich P, **8:** (4431)
Tillman M, **5:** 2861 (2860); **8:** 4758
Tillmann K-J, **5:** 2480 (2473); **8:** 4461 (4458)
Tilson T, **4:** 1911; **5:** 2891 (2889)
Tilton J W, **7:** 4329 (4326)
Timar J, **2:** 1160 (1159)
Timar T B, **10:** 5929 (5926)
Timiras P S, **5:** 2685 (2682)
Timm M A, **9:** 5567 (5566)
Timm N H, **3:** 1549 (1544)
Timmermann D, **6:** 3425 (3422, 3423, 3424)
Timpane P M, **2:** 688 (682); **8:** 4604 (4602)
Timpano D M, **11:** 6731 (6729)
Tinbergen J, **3:** 1449 (1445), 1821 (1811)
Tinbergen N, **4:** 2172 (2169)
Tindal G, **3:** 1359 (1358)
Tindall B A, **1:** 297 (285)
Tindimubona A, **2:** 982 (978, 981)
Tingey C, **5:** 2567 (2564)
Tinker B, **7:** 3810 (3808)
Tinker R F, **2:** 982; **7:** 3810 (3809), 4099, 4100 (4099), 4104 (4101); **8:** 4479 (4477, 4478); **11:** 6603 (6601, 6602)
Tinning R, **10:** 5713 (5712)
Tinsley J D, **2:** 1012 (1008); **8:** 4803 (4800)

Tinto V, **3:** 1602 (1601)
Tippett D C, **10:** 5673 (5669)
Tipton S, **10:** 5990 (5989)
Tirado Mejia A, **2:** 880
Tirmazi I, **7:** 4136 (4133)
Tirre W C, **6:** 3325 (3319)
Tisak J, **3:** 1514 (1512)
Tisher R P, **8:** 4881; **9:** 5324; **10:** 5795 (5791), 5965, 5994, 5995 (5991, 5993), 6149 (6148)
Tissot P, **5:** 2856
Titchener E B, **5:** (2876), (2877)
Titmus C J, **1:** 94, 100 (95), 120 (112, 113, 116, 119), 127 (122, 124), 142 (140), 152 (143, 151), 158 (153), 180 (177, 180), 277; **2:** 661, 1094; **3:** 1315 (1315); **4:** 2123; **5:** 2937 (2936), 2951 (2949); **6:** 3366, 3422, 3467; **7:** 4325; **8:** 4616 (4610), 4812; **9:** 5098; **10:** 5808; **11:** 6266 (6263), 6420, 6437, 6719
Titone R, **4:** 2351 (2347)
Tittle C K, **1:** 370 (368); **9:** 5240; **11:** 6321 (6316, 6318), 6678 (6669)
Titulaer J, **8:** 4803 (4800)
Tizard B, **3:** 1520 (1517); **6:** 3463 (3459, 3460)
Tizard J, **6:** 3463 (3461, 3462)
Tjon H, **10:** 5853
Tjossem T, **5:** 2813, 2814 (2808)
Tlili B, **11:** 6476
To D, **1:** 111 (107, 109)
Tobach E, **1:** 15; **7:** 4163 (4161)
Tobias S, **11:** 6360 (6356)
Tobin A, **9:** 5228 (5226)
Tobin D, **5:** 2491 (2489)
Tobin J, **9:** 5313 (5311)
Tobin J J, **2:** 1213 (1210)
Tobin K, **2:** 811 (807, 810); **4:** 2249 (2247), 2439, 2440 (2438); **9:** 5181 (5177), 5342 (5340); **10:** 5775 (5774), 6183 (6179, 6181)
Tobin K G, **8:** 4882 (4879)
Tobin-Richards M H, **9:** 5435 (5433)
Tochter K D, **7:** 4163 (4160)
Todaro M P, **3:** 1655 (1648), 1685 (1682); **5:** 2945 (2943, 2945)
Todd F, **5:** 2536 (2533)
Todd N, **9:** 5567 (5565)
Todd N M, **9:** 5567 (5563)
Todd R, **11:** 6292 (6291)
Todd T A, **4:** 2369
Todesco A, **4:** 2357 (2357); **6:** 3334 (3330)
Todis B, **1:** 494 (493); **9:** 5567 (5566)
Toebes J, **5:** 2623 (2623)
Toffler A, **5:** 2867 (2865); **7:** 4088 (4082)
Togerson W S, **11:** 6388 (6386)
Tokens R J, **5:** 2879
Tokman V, **3:** 1680 (1677), 1681
Toledo A, **3:** 1685 (1683); **5:** 2744 (2740, 2743)
Toles R E, **5:** 2515 (2513)
Toll C M, **2:** 738 (736)
Tollison R D, **5:** 2567
Tolman E C, **5:** (2877)
Tolsma D D, **5:** 2571 (2567)
Tolstoy L N, **1:** (195); **5:** (2608)
Tom A R, **10:** 5995 (5993)
Tom D, **10:** 6112 (6108)
Tom D Y H, **10:** 6103 (6101)
Tomada Y, **2:** 770 (768); **4:** 2296
Tomasello M, **8:** 4372 (4371)
Tomasi S M, **1:** 162 (160)
Tomera A N, **4:** 1995 (1992, 1993)
Tomes N, **6:** 3143 (3142)
Tomiak J J, **5:** 2618 (2613)
Tomic W, **1:** 390 (389); **5:** 2779 (2778); **6:** 3096
Tomich E, **10:** 6132 (6131)
Tomkins G S, **9:** 5299 (5298)
Tomlinson H, **8:** 4623 (4618)
Tomlinson J, **6:** 3602 (3598); **11:** 6523
Tomlinson S, **2:** 730 (728); **3:** 1233 (1228); **4:** 2292 (2289); **5:** 2567 (2566), 2656 (2654); **7:** 3978 (3974); **10:** 5668 (5664, 5665)
Tomlinson T M, **2:** 775 (771, 774)
Tomm W, **4:** 2302
Tomoda Y, **2:** 770 (768); **8:** 4845 (4844)
Toner B B, **11:** 6360 (6357)
Tong R, **5:** 2458
Tonick I J, **4:** 2449 (2449), 2452 (2451)
Tonigan R F, **9:** 5294
Tönnies F, **5:** (2605)
Toombs W, **7:** 3840
Toomey D M, **6:** 3463 (3460, 3461, 3462)
Top B L, **8:** 4376 (4373)
Topel R, **4:** 2279 (2275); **6:** 3617 (3614)
Topping D M, **2:** 1207
Topping K, **6:** 3463 (3461, 3462); **8:** 4376 (4373); **9:** 5268 (5265)
Torbert W R, **4:** 2186; **6:** 3435 (3429)
Törestad B, **3:** 1520; **8:** 4394 (4393), 4395 (4391); **11:** 6492
Torgesen J K, **8:** 4945 (4943)
Törmäkangas K, **4:** 2024 (2022)
Torney J V, **1:** 396 (393); **2:** 770 (768); **3:** 1769 (1763); **8:** 4581; **9:** 5582 (5581)
Torney-Purta J, **2:** 770 (767, 768); **3:** 1655 (1651); **8:** 4845 (4844); **9:** 5563 (5562); **10:** 5585
Torper U, **4:** 2377 (2376)
Torrance E P, **2:** 1182 (1178, 1180, 1181); **5:** 2491 (2487)
Torrance H, **3:** 1624 (1621); **7:** 3912
Torrance N, **6:** 3446 (3444)
Torrance R, **8:** 4622, 4623 (4618)
Torrence E P, **10:** 6143 (6143)
Torres C A, **1:** 135 (128, 129, 130, 132, 133), 176 (170), 332 (332); **2:** 640 (637, 639), 1048 (1047), 1146; **3:** 1720 (1715), 1788 (1788); **5:** 2697 (2696), 2961 (2960); **7:** 3960, 4145 (4145); **8:** 4602; **9:** 5367 (5366)
Torruellas R M, **9:** 5510 (5508)
Totten W F, **2:** 893 (891)
Tough A M, **4:** 2186 (2185); **6:** 3378 (3376), 3421 (3418); **7:** 4329 (4325); **9:** 5399 (5395, 5396); **10:** 6202 (6200)
Tough J, **6:** 3443
Toulmin S E, **2:** 1208 (1204); **4:** 2001 (1999); **9:** 5335 (5330)
Touraine A, **4:** 1985 (1983); **10:** 5783
Touré A, **1:** 474 (469)
Tourneur Y, **5:** 2462 (2460, 2461, 2462); **6:** 3124
Tousignant M, **10:** 5713 (5710)
Touwen B C L, **3:** 1520 (1518)
Towne B, **8:** 4474 (4472)
Townsend Coles E K, **1:** 552; **8:** 4812 (4804)
Townsend J, **2:** 760; **7:** 4206
Townsend M A R, **7:** 3768 (3764)
Townsend M L, **10:** 5924 (5921)
Toye J, **5:** 2993
Trabasso T R, **4:** 2281 (2280); **8:** 4383
Tracey W R, **3:** 1491; **6:** 3096 (3092, 3094, 3095); **8:** 4865 (4861)
Trachman R, **9:** 5191
Trafford V, **1:** 72
Trahan M, **11:** 6678 (6672)
Traill R, **10:** 5977 (5974)
Trankell A, **5:** 2586 (2584)
Trapp E C, **3:** (1721), (1724)
Trask A E, **11:** 6765 (6762)
Tratnik M, **9:** 5497 (5495)
Traub R E, **2:** 1189 (1188); **7:** 4000 (3997, 3998, 3999), 4215 (4212, 4213)
Trautner H M, **4:** 2449 (2447), 2452 (2450)
Travers J R, **2:** 688 (685, 686), 701 (696); **3:** 1636 (1634)
Travers K J, **3:** 1769 (1764); **4:** 2140; **6:** 3668 (3663, 3667), 3685 (3674); **9:** 5373; **10:** 6155 (6150); **11:** 6328 (6325)
Travers R, **2:** 687; **7:** 3753, 3886; **10:** 5713
Travers R M W, **2:** 816; **3:** 1544, 1636; **4:** 1899 (1884); **9:** 5043, 5181; **10:** 6086 (6083), 6139
Treagust D F, **2:** 811 (809)
Trecker J L, **9:** 5302 (5300)
Treffers A, **2:** 1052 (1050); **6:** 3655 (3654), 3661 (3656, 3659)
Treffinger D J, **2:** 1182 (1178, 1180, 1181)
Treffry J, **3:** 1406
Trehub S, **1:** 239
Treiman D J, **4:** 2445 (2442); **7:** 3722 (3718), 3864 (3864); **9:** 5553 (5549); **10:** 5735 (5731, 5734), 6227 (6224, 6225); **11:** 6276 (6274)
Treiman R, **8:** 4945
Tremblay A S, **9:** 5567 (5564, 5565)
Trend M G, **11:** 6466 (6465)
Tress B, **1:** 553 (553)
Tress W, **8:** 4779 (4776, 4777)
Trester D J, **5:** 2827
Treu T, **6:** 3197 (3192)
Treuner P, **4:** 2043
Triandis H C, **3:** 1245, 1252; **5:** 2651 (2650); **8:** 4394; **9:** 5324 (5318)
Tribe L H, **10:** 5991 (5986)
Tribe M A, **8:** 4775 (4773)
Trickett E J, **2:** 811 (807, 809); **10:** 5775 (5772)
Trickett E M, **3:** 1482 (1481, 1482)
Trickett P, **5:** 2673 (2671)
Trieschmann M, **7:** 3808 (3807)
Trigwell K, **1:** 322 (321)
Trilling L, **5:** 2697 (2693)
Trim J L M, **4:** 2346 (2340)
Tripier M, **2:** 917 (917)

Tripp D H, **2:** 646, 1107 (1103); **10:** 6058 (6056)
Tripp S D, **8:** 4803 (4801, 4803)
Trismen D M, **7:** 4307 (4305)
Trivellato U, **5:** 3036
Trivette C M, **1:** 362 (359); **4:** 1980 (1976, 1978, 1979); **5:** 2813 (2810, 2811)
Trochim W, **2:** 1031 (1027)
Trollip S R, **2:** 1011 (1008), 1170 (1166, 1168, 1169); **7:** 4094 (4093)
Trombulak S, **6:** 3209 (3207)
Trommsdorff G, **5:** 2651 (2649, 2650)
Trompf G W, **10:** 5708
Tropp A, **10:** 6139
Trost G, **5:** 2480 (2478); **11:** 6340 (6334)
Trotter A, **7:** 3808 (3805); **10:** 5834 (5832, 5833)
Trotter B B, **4:** 2266 (2264)
Trousson R, **9:** 5091
Troutman A C, **10:** 6164
Troutner L, **8:** (4430)
Trow M, **3:** 1720 (1718); **11:** 6511 (6508)
Trowbridge D E, **10:** 5790 (5785, 5790)
Trowbridge M H, **4:** 2281 (2280)
Trowbridge N, **2:** 1121 (1119)
Troyer M, **6:** 3202 (3199); **10:** 5957 (5955)
Troyna B, **7:** 3978; **10:** 5827 (5825)
Trudeau L, **4:** 2435 (2434)
Trueba H T, **2:** 803 (799); **3:** 1233; **4:** 2052; **6:** 3227; **7:** 3974 (3972); **9:** 5220, 5313
Truman H S, **4:** (1860)
Trumbull D J, **10:** 6086 (6084)
Trumbull W N, **4:** 2212 (2211)
Truscott K, **7:** 3853 (3850, 3851, 3852)
Truss T J, **6:** 3224; **10:** 5681
Trusty F M, **4:** 1972 (1968)
Truxaw C, **11:** 6608 (6604)
Trybus R, **5:** 2910 (2908)
Tryon G, **11:** 6360 (6356)
Tsai S L, **4:** 2140 (2137)
Tsang M C, **2:** 760 (755, 758, 759), 1127 (1121, 1123, 1124, 1126), 1152 (1147, 1150); **4:** 1911 (1908); **6:** 3550 (3546); **8:** 4707 (4706), 4708 (4703, 4704, 4705, 4706, 4707); **9:** 5066 (5063), 5076 (5071, 5072, 5073, 5074, 5075), 5241 (5234, 5240); **11:** 6261 (6257), 6633 (6628, 6629, 6630, 6631, 6632)
Tsang Mun, **7:** 4255 (4250)
Tsang T, **3:** 1624 (1622)
Tsao Y C, **8:** 4939 (4938)
Tset G, **3:** 1347 (1345)
Tshibangu T, **11:** 6814 (6809)
Tsoi S C, **7:** 3986 (3979, 3984, 3985), 4015 (4015); **9:** 5372 (5371)
Tsoukalas K, **5:** 2523
Tøsse S, **7:** 4180
Tsugawa T, **10:** 6099 (6098)
Tsukada M, **9:** 5367 (5365); **11:** 6699 (6696)
Tsurumi E P, **2:** 1042 (1039)
Tsutakawa R K, **5:** 3055 (3053)
Tuana N, **4:** 2302
Tubbs S L, **10:** 5901 (5899)
Tubesing D A, **10:** 5925 (5923)
Tubesing N L, **10:** 5925 (5923)
Tucker G R, **4:** 2351 (2348); **7:** 3970 (3969)
Tucker J, **4:** 2351 (2349)
Tucker J A, **2:** 730 (725); **3:** 1359 (1356), 1636 (1632); **7:** 3833 (3831, 3832)
Tucker J L, **8:** 4581
Tucker L R, **8:** 4359 (4357); **9:** 5158 (5153)
Tucker R N, **7:** 3995 (3991, 3995), 3996; **10:** 6008 (6006)
Tuden A, **9:** 5572 (5568)
Tudor R, **7:** 4319 (4318)
Tueros M, **3:** 1680 (1677, 1678), 1695 (1693), 1713 (1711)
Tufte E, **7:** 3775 (3772)
Tugendhat E, **7:** 3925 (3921)
Tuijnman A C, **1:** 152 (146), 168 (168), 184; **2:** 652 (652), 711 (710), 957 (954, 957), 958, 1063 (1057), 1094 (1090, 1091, 1093), 1220 (1213, 1217); **3:** 1315, 1695 (1694); **4:** 1976 (1975), 2279 (2276, 2277), 2331; **5:** 2500 (2496, 2497), 2978 (2977); **6:** 3366, 3422 (3418, 3420), 3425, 3435, 3524 (3512), 3617 (3615); **7:** 3711 (3709), 4179 (4178), 4180, 4325 (4320, 4321, 4322, 4323, 4324), 4329 (4326, 4328); **8:** 4339, 4351 (4347), 4352 (4351), 4616 (4611, 4614), 4639 (4637), 4812 (4810), 4964 (4958, 4959, 4963); **9:** 5385 (5382), 5553 (5552); **10:** 5596 (5593), 5607 (5600), 5643 (5638), 5750 (5745); **11:** 6394 (6392), 6395, 6507 (6506), 6523
Tukey J W, **2:** 792 (786); **4:** 2208 (2199, 2203); **5:** 3061 (3057); **7:** 3706 (3700); **8:** 4352 (4341), 4359 (4356); **9:** 5082 (5077, 5078), 5130 (5126, 5127)
Tulasiewicz W, **8:** 4601; **9:** 5008, 5013; **10:** 6042 (6037), 6043
Tullberg A, **8:** 4429 (4426)
Tulley M, **11:** 6370 (6368)
Tullgren R, **10:** 6026 (6023)
Tulloch S, **9:** 5008 (5006)
Tullock G, **8:** 4568 (4564), 4594 (4589)
Tulving E, **2:** 857 (855, 856); **6:** 3288 (3287)
Tuma D T, **10:** 5831; **11:** 6416
Tuma J E, **11:** 6538 (6534)
Tuma N B, **9:** 5082
Tuman M, **8:** 4694
Tumin M M, **9:** 5572 (5568)
Tung C P, **1:** 353
Tunks T W, **7:** 4026 (4023)
Tuomisto J, **1:** 127 (124); **7:** 4180
Tupou I, **11:** (6405)
Turbay K, **11:** 6272 (6270)
Turiansky K, **3:** 1406 (1405)
Turiel E, **1:** 380 (378); **5:** 2669 (2668); **7:** 3920 (3916, 3918, 3919); **9:** 5512 (5510, 5511, 5512)
Turk D C, **10:** 5924 (5921)
Turkle S, **6:** 3512 (3510, 3511)
Turky A, **7:** 4206
Turnbull A P, **10:** 6244 (6242, 6243); **11:** 6461
Turnbull G H, **2:** 884
Turnbull H, **10:** 6244 (6243)
Turnbull P, **8:** 4526 (4522)
Turner B, **2:** 770
Turner C F, **8:** 4604 (4603)
Turner C M D, **3:** 1553 (1550)
Turner D A, **2:** 933 (929)
Turner F J, **10:** (6144)
Turner G, **2:** 1073 (1070)
Turner J, **7:** 4046
Turner J C, **6:** 3474 (3473)
Turner J D, **4:** 2249
Turner J H, **2:** 1074 (1064, 1065); **10:** 5707 (5705)
Turner J L, **4:** 2218 (2213)
Turner M J, **8:** 4581 (4576, 4577, 4579)
Turner P, **7:** 4301 (4297)
Turner R H, **1:** 358 (355); **2:** 1074 (1065); **5:** 2532 (2531); **6:** 3528; **10:** 5591
Turner R R, **5:** 2571 (2569)
Turner T, **3:** 1599; **7:** 4293 (4292); **10:** 5745 (5742)
Turner V, **1:** (539)
Turner V W, **7:** 3826 (3825)
Turney C, **9:** 5318 (5314); **10:** 5977 (5974), 6004
Turnham D, **3:** 1681; **5:** 2819 (2814)
Turoff M, **2:** 982 (978, 979, 980); **3:** 1443 (1442), 1830 (1828)
Turrentine E, **7:** 4026 (4022)
Turvey M T, **7:** 3953 (3952); **8:** 4939 (4938)
Tuthill D, **9:** 5056
Tutken H, **3:** 1257 (1253)
Tuttle D W, **11:** 6628
Tversky A, **7:** 3706 (3700)
Twa J, **10:** 6004 (6000)
Tweedie J, **1:** 594 (591); **9:** 5196 (5194); **11:** 6557 (6556)
Twigger D, **8:** 4479 (4478)
Twining J, **7:** 3895
Twitchell K S, **9:** 5151 (5144)
Twose N, **10:** 5843
Twyman J P, **10:** 6132 (6131)
Tyack D B, **1:** 67 (61); **3:** 1301 (1296), 1343; **4:** 2432 (2431); **5:** 2607, 2618 (2612, 2614); **7:** 3848 (3842); **9:** 5201, 5445; **11:** 6547, 6765 (6761, 6763)
Tyack T B, **11:** 6538
Tye K A, **3:** 1266 (1263), 1494 (1491, 1492); **4:** 2388 (2382)
Tykociner J T, **3:** 1355 (1348, 1351)
Tyler I K, **5:** 2891 (2890)
Tyler L E, **9:** 5432 (5424, 5425, 5427)
Tyler L L, **3:** 1283 (1279)
Tyler R W, **1:** 370 (363, 365); **2:** 893 (889), 1107; **3:** 1266 (1264), 1267 (1263, 1264), 1283 (1280), 1334 (1329, 1330, 1331, 1332), 1355 (1348), 1367 (1360), 1797 (1793, 1796), 1804 (1801, 1802, 1803); **4:** 1848, 1872 (1868), 2074, 2079, 2089 (2080), 2100, (2102); **5:** 2862 (2857); **7:** 3726 (3722, 3723), 4054 (4051); **8:** 4766 (4765); **9:** 5038 (5034); **10:** (5815), 5887 (5883), 6035 (6032), 6099 (6097), 6169 (6165)
Tyler S, **3:** 1252 (1247)
Tyler W B, **4:** 2167; **6:** 3527 (3526); **9:** 5181 (5177)
Tylor E B, **3:** 1729 (1725), 1756 (1751)
Tynan T, **1:** 409 (406)
Tyre C, **6:** 3463 (3462)
Tyson L, **5:** 2891 (2888); **11:** 6282 (6280)
Tzannatos Z, **4:** 2419 (2414); **9:** 5191
Tzelgov J, **7:** 4016 (4013)

Tzeng O C S, **1:** 19
Tzinner A E, **4:** 2219 (2213)
Tzuriel D, **3:** 1402; **5:** 2768 (2762); **6:** 3228

Uberto F, **11:** 6416
Udinsky B F, **3:** 1443
Udo R K, **8:** 4609
Ueberschlag G, **4:** 2327
Ueckert H, **7:** 3788
Ueda K, **9:** 5453 (5450)
Uemura K, **4:** 1980 (1978)
Ueno H, **11:** 6618 (6616)
Ufermann K, **5:** 2480 (2474); **7:** 4301 (4299); **8:** 4666 (4663)
Uhl N P, **3:** 1443
Ukeje B O, **5:** 2954 (2953)
Ukobizoba F, **6:** 3550 (3546)
Ulich R, **5:** 2618 (2608, 2609); **8:** 4456 (4451), 4677
Ullian J S, **3:** 1475; **9:** 5050
Ulmer G, **1:** (541)
Ultee W C, **9:** 5553 (5549)
Umar A M, **10:** 6164 (6162)
Umar J, **5:** 3043 (3037, 3041)
Underhill N, **7:** 3936 (3934)
Underhill O E, **9:** 5328 (5324)
Underwood B J, **1:** 377 (374); **5:** 2922 (2920); **8:** 4799 (4798)
Underwood G, **2:** 992
Underwood J D M, **2:** 992; **3:** 1398 (1395); **7:** 3820, 3821; **9:** 5065, 5066, 5185
Undheim J O, **5:** 2769 (2761); **7:** 3880 (3874, 3875)
Unterkircher L, **7:** 3920
Unwin D, **4:** 1928 (1925)
Upadhayay M P, **9:** 5544 (5542)
Updyke J F, **8:** 4661 (4659)
Upshur C C, **5:** 2813 (2812)
Upton G J G, **2:** 729; **5:** 2972 (2970); **6:** 3508 (3500); **10:** 5942, 5943
Urbach E E, **6:** 3120
Urban K K, **2:** 1182 (1181)
Urban W J, **6:** 3197 (3193); **10:** 6079 (6074)
Uri N D, **11:** 6633 (6628)
Urlings M, **4:** 2427 (2424, 2425)
Urquhart A H, **8:** 4939
Urquidi V I, **7:** 3802
Urry J, **1:** 297 (284); **4:** 2053 (2047)
Urwick L, **4:** 2166 (2158); **9:** 5168 (5161)
Urwin S, **10:** 5680 (5676)
Ury W, **8:** 4408 (4407)
Usdan M, **6:** 3496 (3493, 3494, 3495)
Useem E, **8:** 4568
Ushadevi M S, **3:** 1607 (1604)
Usher R S, **1:** 168 (166); **10:** 6058 (6056)
Ushiwata G, **10:** 5995 (5991, 5992)
Usiskin Z, **3:** 1514 (1508, 1510)
Uthmann K J, **11:** 6452 (6448)
Utley C A, **6:** 3228 (3226)
Uttal D, **3:** 1240 (1239); **5:** 2627 (2627), 2628 (2626)
Uyeda S, **9:** 5030

Vacc N A, **4:** 2131 (2130)
Vacca R S, **6:** 3276 (3273, 3274, 3275)
Vaccarro L, **2:** 1048 (1048)
Vachon R, **8:** 4957 (4955)
Vaessen W, **3:** 1520 (1519)
Vähäpassi A, **4:** 2024 (2019)
Vaherava T, **7:** 4180
Vaid J, **8:** 4939; **10:** 5694
Vaideanu G, **2:** 1107 (1106); **3:** 1278 (1277), 1355 (1351), 1367 (1361, 1362, 1363)
Văideanu G, **9:** 5087
Vail S C, **8:** 4848 (4847), 4864 (4859)
Vakatale T, **4:** 2310
Valdés G, **11:** 6785 (6782)
Vale C D, **1:** 53 (51); **5:** 2784 (2780), 3055 (3053)
Valencia S, **2:** 868 (866)
Valentine C A, **1:** 297 (281, 283); **4:** 2053 (2048)
Valentine C W, **4:** 2180 (2174)
Valentine J W, **4:** 2172 (2168)
Valentine T, **7:** 4324 (4321), 4325, 4329
Valerien J, **8:** 4698 (4696, 4697)
Vallance E, **3:** 1266 (1263), 1315 (1312); **5:** 2589 (2588); **10:** 6035 (6032)
Valli L, **1:** 11 (8, 10); **2:** 824; **3:** (1346); **10:** 5995 (5993)
Valo M, **5:** 2544 (2542)
Valtin R, **8:** 4936 (4932)
Valverde L A, **1:** 83 (78)
Van Adams A, **2:** 760 (758); **3:** 1713 (1710, 1711); **5:** 3003 (3001); **11:** 6282 (6281), 6653 (6649, 6651)
van Aken M A G, **9:** 5394 (5393), 5528 (5526)
van Balkom H, **1:** 409 (404)
van Bemmelen S, **4:** 2412 (2410)
van Boxtel H W, **5:** 2495
Van Bruggen J C, **3:** 1355 (1353)
Van Calster K, **5:** 2769 (2764); **7:** 3942 (3941)
Van Crombrugge H, **4:** 2267 (2264)
Van Daalen H, **5:** 2767 (2762)
Van Daalen-Kapteiins M, **10:** 6117 (6114)
Van Daele H, **2:** 948
Van de Geer J P, **2:** 631 (627, 630); **7:** 4016 (4013)
Van de Graaf J H, **6:** 3276 (3273, 3275)
van de Grift W, **9:** 5224 (5223)
Van de Velde J, **11:** 6292 (6290)
Van de Ven A H, **3:** 1443 (1443)
van de Ven P H, **6:** 3484 (3481); **11:** 6777 (6776)
van de Vijver F J R, **11:** 6320 (6316), 6334 (6329, 6330, 6332)
van de Wolde J, **2:** 977 (973, 974); **7:** 4088 (4083, 4085)
Van Dellen T, **3:** 1520 (1519)
van den Akker J, **2:** 991 (990), 1011 (1009, 1010); **3:** 1494 (1493); **4:** 1918 (1915); **7:** 4088 (4085)
Van den Berg G, **3:** 1431 (1429)
van den Berg R, **3:** 1553 (1550); **9:** 5246 (5241, 5245)
van den Dunghen E, **11:** 6731
van den Eiden P, **5:** 2596
Van den Heede R, **4:** 2267
van Der Berg-Eldering L, **9:** 5210
van der Flier H, **4:** 2257 (2254); **5:** 3051 (3046)
van der Gaag J, **3:** 1789 (1787); **4:** 2212; **5:** 2744
van der Heijden P G M, **6:** 3508 (3507)
van der Kamp L J T, **2:** 792 (788, 790, 791); **5:** 3043; **11:** 6320
Van der Kamp M, **1:** 152 (149), 168 (168); **3:** 1315; **6:** 3349, 3366, 3435 (3430, 3434); **7:** 4325 (4321), 4330; **8:** 4339, 4616 (4614), 4812, 4964
van der Lem T, **3:** 1402 (1399)
van der Linden N J, **7:** 4056 (4055)
van der Linden W J, **2:** 998 (993, 995, 996), 1189 (1188); **3:** 1421 (1418, 1420, 1421); **4:** 2017 (2013); **5:** 3043 (3037), 3055 (3053), 3061 (3058); **10:** 5726 (5723)
Van der Maas H, **5:** 2681 (2679, 2680)
van der Mast C, **3:** 1779 (1776)
van der Meer Q L T, **3:** 1797
Van der Meere J J, **3:** 1520 (1518)
van der Ploeg H M, **10:** 5772
Van der Sijde P C, **1:** 390 (389); **2:** 1026; **3:** 1491; **4:** 1976 (1973); **5:** 2779 (2778); **6:** 3306
van der Sijde P D, **9:** 5211 (5207)
van der Tak H, **3:** 1821 (1816)
van der Vegt R, **1:** 73 (69)
van der Voort T H A, **1:** 570 (568); **6:** 3625 (3624); **7:** 3743 (3741)
van der Waerden, **7:** (4159)
Van Der Zee H, **6:** 3435 (3434)
Van Dijk J, **3:** 1406 (1404, 1405)
van Dijk T A, **2:** 969 (967); **4:** 2199 (2197); **8:** 4942 (4940, 4941)
van Dyck J, **3:** 1449
Van Dyke D C, **7:** 4081 (4079)
van Eck M, **9:** 5197 (5194)
van Ek J A, **4:** 2346 (2340), 2351 (2348)
van Els T J M, **4:** 2346 (2340)
Van Elsen E, **10:** 5625 (5624)
Van Enckevort G, **1:** 277 (274), 564
Van Essen G, **6:** 3661 (3659)
Van Evra J, **1:** 570
Van Galen J, **2:** 893 (890)
van Geel T, **9:** 5013
Van Geert P, **5:** 2681 (2679, 2680)
Van Gelder T, **2:** 857 (853)
van Gemert G H, **3:** 1520
Van Gendt R, **8:** 4499
van Gennip J, **9:** 5246 (5242)
Van Gent B, **1:** 277 (275, 276)
Van Grafhorst H, **6:** 3661 (3659)
Van Haecht A, **1:** 504
Van Hasselt V B, **1:** 19 (17); **3:** 1641
Van Herpen M, **3:** 1746 (1742)
van Hest E, **6:** 3213
van Hiele P M, **6:** 3685 (3680); **7:** 4100 (4098)
Van Horn R, **7:** 4095 (4092); **11:** 6603 (6602)
van Hout Wolters B H A M, **2:** 1026; **6:** 3661
Van Ijzendoorn H W, **8:** 4368 (4367)
van Kemenade J A, **9:** 5246; **10:** 5853 (5853)

van Laarhoven P, **8:** 4830 (4827)
van Leest P F, **11:** 6334 (6330)
Van Leeuwen S, **7:** 4325 (4324); **9:** 5554 (5552)
van Lieshout C F M, **5:** 2884 (2883); **8:** 4368 (4367)
Van Loon-Vervoorn W A, **6:** 3315
Van Luit J E H, **6:** 3315 (3314)
Van Maanen J, **4:** 2053; **7:** 4051 (4047)
Van Manen M, **1:** 48 (45); **2:** 1204 (1199); **10:** 5818 (5816), 6219 (6216)
van Marwijk-Kooy L, **9:** 5197 (5195)
Van Mater Stone G, **6:** 3329 (3325, 3326), 3340 (3335)
van Merrienboer J J G, **2:** 985 (983)
Van Oers B, **6:** 3292 (3291)
Van Overwalle F, **1:** 194 (192)
Van Parreren C F, **5:** (2877); **6:** 3315
Van Parys M, **5:** 2680 (2679, 2680)
van Patten J, **5:** 2862 (2860); **10:** 6193 (6189)
van Praagh G, **8:** 4648 (4645)
Van Rensburg P, **3:** 1690 (1689); **9:** 5233; **11:** 6256 (6252), 6266 (6262)
Van Rijswijk F, **7:** 3791 (3789)
Van Riper C, **10:** 5697 (5694)
Van Rompaey S E, **9:** 5553 (5549)
Van Rossum E J, **1:** 194 (189)
van Schaick Zillesen P G, **2:** 988 (985); **7:** 3996 (3995), 4104 (4100)
van Seventer C W, **8:** 4751 (4745)
Van Sickle R L, **3:** 1367 (1363, 1364)
Van Tasell D J, **10:** 5691 (5688)
Van Theil C C, **5:** 3043 (3042)
Van Till W, **3:** 1367 (1362)
Van Tongeren P, **3:** 1501 (1496)
Van Velzen D, **10:** 5925 (5921, 5922, 5923)
Van Velzen W G, **8:** 4865; **9:** 5246 (5241, 5243); **10:** 5973 (5971)
van Vliet M, **4:** 2412 (2410)
Van Vught F, **8:** 4519
van Weering B, **2:** 977 (976, 977)
Van Weert T J, **8:** 4803 (4800)
van Wieringen A M L, **1:** 73; **4:** 1934 (1929)
van Wieringen J C, **8:** 4474 (4468, 4472)
Van Woerden J A, **10:** 5674 (5670)
Van Woerden W M, **10:** 5948 (5944)
Vance V S, **10:** 5613 (5612), 6106 (6104)
Vandemeulebroecke L, **4:** 2267 (2264)
Vandenberg B, **8:** 4542 (4536, 4538, 4539, 4540)
Vandenberg D, **4:** 2033 (2031); **8:** 4433 (4430)
Vandenberghe P, **1:** 504
Vandenberghe R, **3:** 1355 (1351), 1411 (1410, 1411); **6:** 3603 (3599); **9:** 5246 (5243, 5245), 5308 (5303)
VandenBos G R, **8:** 4823, 4824
Vander Ven K, **3:** 1636 (1630)
Vandergrift L, **6:** 3335 (3330)
Vanderheiden G C, **1:** 409 (404, 405, 407)
Vanderheiden M, **6:** 3213
Vanderlinden J, **11:** 6814
Vaney V, **4:** 1872 (1866)
Vanfossen B E, **1:** 12 (7, 8)
VanGundy A B, **5:** 2725 (2721, 2722, 2723, 2724)
Vanheerwynghels A, **1:** 503
Vanier J, **1:** 162 (159)
Vanlehn K, **1:** 348 (347); **8:** 4722 (4720, 4721)
VanMondfrans A, **2:** 1136 (1134)
Vann R J, **6:** 3335 (3330)
VanTassel-Baska J L, **5:** 2491 (2486, 2487); **9:** 5532 (5529, 5530)
Varapipatana K, **2:** (904)
Varavarn K, **1:** 158 (154); **4:** 2123 (2122)
Varenne H, **6:** 3453 (3449), 3459 (3456); **9:** 5313 (5311)
Vargas R, **8:** 4415
Vargas V, **3:** 1671 (1669)
Varma V P, **1:** 28
Varstala V, **10:** 5713 (5709, 5710)
Vartiainen E, **5:** 2572 (2570)
Vartiainen T, **5:** 2689 (2688)
Vasa S F, **7:** 4293 (4291, 4292)
Vasquez J Z, **2:** 1042 (1040)
Vasquez O A, **1:** 534 (534)
Vasta R, **1:** 497; **2:** 851; **3:** 1647; **6:** 3329; **7:** 3763
Vaughan J L, **6:** 3209 (3207)
Vaughan P, **2:** 665 (663)
Vaughn C, **3:** 1241 (1238, 1240)
Vaughn S, **1:** 495
Vaughn V L, **5:** 2495 (2493), 2732 (2730)
Vaught R S, **9:** 5489 (5487), 5490
Vaux A, **4:** 1980 (1978)
Vazquez J Z, **7:** 3802
Veale D, **9:** 5206 (5202)
Veale J R, **5:** 3051 (3047)
Veblen T, **2:** 785 (783)
Vecoli R J, **7:** 3970 (3963)
Vedder P, **10:** 6173
Veeman F C, **8:** 4812 (4807)
Veenman S A M, **9:** 5043 (5041); **10:** 6047, 6169 (6167)
Veeraraghavan J, **8:** 4488 (4487)
Vejsiu Y, **1:** 260
Velasquez A G, **7:** 3970 (3960)
Velazco J, **3:** (1821)
Veldhuis G H, **7:** 3809 (3809)
Velez E, **2:** 1094 (1090, 1092), 1146; **7:** 4201 (4200)
Velez W, **1:** 12 (7)
Velez-Ibañez C G, **1:** 534 (534)
Velicer W F, **9:** 5489 (5488), 5490 (5488)
Vélis J-P, **1:** 180 (177, 178)
Velis J-P, **7:** 3711
Vella C, **10:** 5674 (5671)
Vellar O D, **5:** 2572 (2569)
Velleman P F, **4:** 2208
Velloso J, **3:** 1685 (1683); **5:** 2744 (2740, 2743); **7:** 4100 (4097)
Vellutino F R, **7:** 4081 (4078); **8:** 4936 (4934); **10:** 5681 (5679)
Venezky R L, **1:** 175; **2:** 1012 (1010); **6:** 3480 (3475, 3479)
Veraart P W V, **9:** 5197 (5194)
Verba S, **3:** 1654 (1650)
Verbrugge H P, **8:** 4474 (4468)
Verdier E, **11:** 6272
Verduin J R, **7:** 4220
Verduin J R Jr, **11:** 6307 (6305)
Vergidis D, **11:** 6438 (6434, 6436)
Vergnaud G, **3:** 1434 (1433); **6:** 3660, 3661 (3658), 3685 (3676)
Verhelst N D, **3:** 1514 (1511); **7:** 4307 (4306)
Verhelst T, **6:** 3459 (3455)
Verhine R E, **7:** 3960, 4145 (4143); **9:** 5228 (5224, 5227); **11:** 6265 (6262), 6266 (6262)
Verhoeven J C, **1:** 504
Verhoeven L, **1:** 537 (537)
Verhoeven W F J, **3:** 1315 (1312)
Verkaik A, **4:** 2150 (2149)
Verkerk G, **7:** 3810 (3809), 4104 (4102)
Verma A, **3:** 1636
Verma G K, **7:** 3978 (3974, 3977)
Vermeulen C J A J, **3:** 1746 (1742); **4:** 1934 (1932); **9:** 5211 (5207)
Vermunt J D H M, **5:** 2874 (2873); **7:** 3788 (3784, 3787), 3791 (3789)
Verner C, **3:** 1602 (1599); **11:** 6775 (6772)
Vernoff E, **2:** 933, 1072
Vernon P E, **1:** 6 (1); **2:** 1182 (1178); **4:** 2241 (2239); **5:** (2911), (2917); **7:** 3706 (3704), 3872 (3868), 3880 (3873, 3875, 3876, 3878, 3879), 3936 (3930, 3932); **9:** 5389 (5388); **11:** 6340 (6338), 6349 (6341, 6347), 6678 (6674)
Vernon-Jackson H O, **2:** 618
Veronese G, **4:** (2004)
Verry D, **2:** 1127 (1124)
Verschaffel L, **2:** 984 (983), 985, 1006 (1004, 1005); **5:** 2767 (2762), 2884; **6:** 3655 (3654), 3660 (3658, 3659), 3661 (3658); **8:** 4722; **9:** 5341 (5340, 5341)
Verschoor A, **2:** 998 (996)
Verschuur R, **8:** 4473 (4472)
Vershaffel L, **6:** 3652
Verspoor A M, **1:** 474 (471); **2:** 775 (771), 933 (929); **3:** 1416 (1412, 1413), 1762 (1761), 1784 (1782, 1783), 1789 (1788), 1824 (1823), 1825 (1822), 1830 (1829), 1834 (1831); **5:** 2993 (2991); **6:** 3297 (3292); **8:** 4510, 4519 (4515), 4526 (4524), 4601 (4596, 4597, 4599), 4698 (4694, 4696, 4697), 4865 (4858, 4860), 4873 (4865, 4868, 4870); **9:** 5169 (5159, 5162, 5164), 5228 (5225, 5226, 5227), 5252 (5247), 5539 (5535, 5536, 5538); **10:** 5929 (5925); **11:** 6298 (6293), 6663 (6660, 6663)
Verstegen D A, **7:** 3821; **9:** 5240
Vertecchi B, **3:** 1567 (1565); **5:** 3036; **7:** 4220
Vesey G, **8:** 4447 (4442)
Vespasian T F V, **8:** (4887)
Vessey I, **2:** 985 (984)
Vetter B M, **11:** 6712 (6711)
Vetter L, **4:** 2286 (2284)
Veysey L R, **5:** 2978 (2976)
Vickers M, **10:** 5919 (5915)
Vickery G, **4:** 2394 (2389)
Victor N, **2:** 1037 (1032)
Vidal A, **3:** 1830 (1829)
Vidyasagar I, **11:** (6749)
Viederman S, **8:** 4609

Viennot L, **10:** 5790 (5785)
Vietorisz T, **7:** 4201 (4197)
Vietze P, **6:** 3227
Vigil J D, **5:** 2529 (2527)
Vigliani E, **4:** 2011
Vigorito J, **8:** 4383 (4382)
Vijn P, **3:** 1421 (1420)
Vijverberg W, **3:** 1680 (1677, 1678)
Vilberg W, **2:** 984 (983, 984)
Villa R, **10:** 6244 (6242)
Villar L M, **10:** 6219
Villegas A M, **1:** 12 (9, 10)
Villegas-Reimers E, **11:** 6599
Villet J, **2:** 665 (662)
Villeval M C L, **4:** 1976 (1974)
Villiger D, **1:** 317 (313)
Vince P, **1:** 570 (564, 565)
Vincent J, **8:** (4809)
Vincent L J, **5:** 2814 (2807)
Vincent M L, **5:** 2572 (2569)
Vincent T, **4:** 1898 (1894)
Vinovskis M A, **5:** 2607, 2617 (2612)
Vio Grossi F, **6:** 3256; **7:** 4336 (4334, 4335)
Virgil P V M, **9:** (5117), (5122)
Virochsiri X, **4:** 2225 (2220)
Visalberghi A, **5:** 3036
Viscusi W, **4:** 2279 (2275)
Vishwanath, **6:** 3160
Visscher A J, **5:** 2831
Visser G H A, **7:** 3950 (3948)
Visser J, **7:** 3946 (3945)
Vitrier J, **4:** (2004)
Vitz P C, **11:** 6370 (6369)
Vives J L, **4:** (2004); **5:** (2608)
Vlcek C W, **7:** 3756 (3754)
Voelker A M, **9:** 5328 (5324)
Vogel E F, **10:** 5758 (5757)
Vogel F, **5:** 2465 (2463)
Vogt E M, **5:** 2673 (2670)
Vogt L A, **3:** 1236 (1234, 1236)
Voisin M, **11:** 6807 (6805)
Volbeck M, **3:** 1746
Volk T L, **4:** 1995 (1993)
Volker P A, **3:** 1449 (1447); **9:** 5355 (5352)
Volkmann H, **5:** 2470 (2467, 2468)
Volman M, **4:** 2427 (2424, 2425)
Voltaire F M A de, **9:** (5087)
Volterra V, **6:** 3224 (3223); **9:** 5508
Voltz D, **7:** 3833 (3832)
von Bertalanffy L, **3:** 1775 (1770); **4:** 1899 (1887)
von Borries B, **5:** 2623
von Borstel F, **9:** 5233 (5229, 5231, 5232)
von Cranach M, **4:** 2172
von Daalen-Kapteijns M M, **11:** 6349 (6348)
von der Malsburg C, **7:** 3950 (3948)
von Euler C, **10:** 5680, 5681
Von Eye A, **4:** 1877; **5:** 2677 (2674, 2675); **6:** 3508 (3507)
von Frisch K, **4:** (2169)
von Gilardi R, **11:** 6699 (6695)
von Glaserfeld E, **2:** 1052 (1049, 1050); **6:** 3416, 3685 (3672); **8:** 4652 (4649); **9:** 5345 (5344)
von Hentig H, **3:** (1796)
von Hofsten C, **7:** 3950 (3948, 3949)
von Humboldt W, **5:** (2610)
Von Marenholz-Bülow B, **4:** (2385), (2386)
von Moltke K, **7:** 4263 (4257); **11:** 6775 (6774)
Von Neumann J, **9:** 5471 (5468)
von Olberg H J, **6:** 3137
von Ranke L, **5:** 2623 (2618)
Von Recum H, **2:** 933 (928, 930)
von Rosenstiel L, **4:** 2261
von Tetzchner S, **1:** 408 (405)
von Werder L, **1:** 139 (137)
von Zuben M V, **8:** 4542 (4540)
Vong C S, **6:** 3545
Vonk J H C, **10:** 5939 (5936)
Voogel A, **2:** 1170; **6:** 3306 (3304)
Vooglaid Y, **1:** 168 (165)
Voogt J, **2:** 1175 (1173); **3:** 1494 (1493); **4:** 2427 (2424, 2425); **5:** 2852 (2849); **7:** 3810 (3808), 4104 (4102); **9:** 5247 (5244)
Vooijs M W, **6:** 3625 (3624); **7:** 3743 (3741)
Voorbach J T, **10:** 6000
Vopp R, **3:** 1636 (1634)
Vorbeck M, **3:** 1431
Vorhees C V, **1:** 15 (14)
Vos A J, **10:** 5965
Vos H J, **3:** 1421 (1418)
Vosniadou S, **6:** 3155 (3154); **8:** 4957; **11:** 6456, 6457
Voss H L, **3:** 1441 (1439)
Voss J F, **4:** 2199 (2196, 2197); **8:** 4951 (4948, 4949); **9:** 5563 (5562)
Votaw D F, **7:** 4000 (3997)
Vrignaud P, **2:** 665
Vrijens J, **10:** 5713 (5710)
Vroom V H, **4:** 1972 (1968)
Vrooman J C, **9:** 5554 (5553)
Vucinich A, **5:** 2998 (2994)
Vulfson B L, **2:** 1064
Vulliamy G, **4:** 1934 (1931); **8:** 4688 (4687); **10:** 5973 (5970)
Vuyk R, **8:** 4483
Vye N, **2:** 1019
Vygotsky L S, **1:** 6 (5), (287), 374 (372); **2:** 803 (799, 800), 838 (835, 837), 857 (852), 860 (857, 858, 859), 868 (863), 1052 (1050); **3:** 1233 (1230), 1246 (1243), 1252 (1246, 1248), 1504 (1502); **4:** 1848 (1842, 1846), (1850), 1872 (1864, 1869), 1899 (1897); **5:** 2536 (2533), (2654), (2669), (2875), (2876), 2681 (2679); 2884 (2881), (2914); **6:** (3289), (3308), 3315 (3313), (3340), (3342), (3344), (3511); 3463 (3460); **7:** 4081, 4095 (4090); **8:** 4372 (4370, 4481), 4542, (4535), (4537); **9:** 5275 (5274), (5400), 5508 (5507), 5548 (5545); **10:** 5795 (5792), 6015 (6014), 6112 (6108), 6169 (6164, 6165, 6166, 6167), 6178 (6174); 6197 (6193, 6194); **11:** 6785 (6783)

Wachs H, **5:** 2670
Wachs T D, **1:** 362 (361); **8:** 4383 (4383); **10:** 6159
Wachs T O, **11:** 6492
Wachtel G F, **6:** 3224 (3220)
Wachter K W, **7:** 3783, 3784 (3783)
Wachter M L, **3:** 1676 (1673); **5:** 2942; **6:** 3189 (3186)
Wachterhauser B, **5:** 2586
Wacker A, **11:** 6684
Wacker D P, **8:** 4376 (4373, 4374)
Wacker S, **10:** 5924 (5920, 5922)
Wacquant L J D, **9:** 5021
Waddington C H, **3:** 1520 (1517)
Wade B, **7:** 4214 (4211, 4212)
Wade M G, **7:** 3950
Wade N J, **8:** 4379
Wadycki W J, **5:** 2945 (2944)
Wafelbakker F, **8:** 4474 (4468)
Wagatsuma H, **3:** 1241 (1238)
Wagen H C, **3:** 1746
Wagenaar H C, **3:** 1431; **4:** 1863 (1859)
Wagenaar J, **11:** 6437 (6436)
Wagenaar T, **3:** 1607; **10:** 5606 (5601)
Wagenschein M, **2:** 969 (965)
Wager S, **2:** 1170
Wager W W, **2:** 1170 (1166); **4:** 1928 (1927); **5:** 2862, 2867, 2874 (2872, 2873); **10:** 6192 (6188)
Waggoner M D, **2:** 982
Wagner A C, **1:** 180; **4:** 1911 (1906, 1907, 1910); **10:** 5954 (5951), 5977 (5974)
Wagner A P, **2:** 1055 (1053)
Wagner B J, **8:** 4388 (4386); **11:** 6785 (6781)
Wagner B M, **4:** 2267; **10:** 5738 (5737)
Wagner D A, **1:** 175, 215, 482 (482); **3:** 1655 (1651); **6:** 3453 (3447), 3480 (3475, 3476, 3478); **7:** 3711; **8:** 4936
Wagner I, **7:** 3920
Wagner K, **11:** 6640
Wagner L, **1:** 94; **5:** 2575; **7:** 4171, 4220 (4219); **11:** 6551 (6548)
Wagner M, **3:** 1534 (1531); **11:** 6260 (6258), 6461 (6457)
Wagner R K, **1:** 239; **5:** 2916; **8:** 4824 (4818), 4945 (4943)
Wagner S, **1:** 103 (100)
Wagner W W, **8:** 4783 (4781)
Wagoner S, **6:** 3339 (3338)
Wagstaff A, **3:** 1387 (1383)
Wahgudi R, **10:** 5973 (5971)
Wahlen K, **9:** 5512 (5510)
Wahlgren B, **1:** 127 (124); **7:** 4179 (4178, 4179), 4180
Wahrhaftig A L, **1:** 297 (291, 293)
Wain K, **6:** 3422, 3593
Wainer H, **1:** 53 (48, 49, 51); **2:** 998 (993); **4:** 2436 (2434); **5:** 3050, 3061 (3056); **8:** 4474 (4471); **9:** 4974 (4972), 5385 (5382, 5383); **11:** 6320, 6321 (6317), 6334 (6332)
Wainerman C, **3:** 1672 (1668)
Waissman F, **8:** (4633)
Waite L J, **2:** 693 (690)
Waite R R, **11:** 6360 (6358)
Waits B K, **7:** 4099 (4096)
Wake C, **2:** 665
Wakeford J, **9:** 5216
Walberg H J, **1:** 490, 520; **2:** 631 (627), 711 (710), 729 (724, 728), 730 (724), 811 (807, 808, 809), 893 (890), 991 (990); **3:** 1387 (1382), 1402, 1431, 1482 (1478),

1483 (1475), 1486 (1485), 1534 (1534); **4:** 1848 (1841, 1843), 1911 (1908, 1909), 1918 (1912), 2108, 2109, 2140 (2137), 2249 (2247), 2250, 2257, 2258; **5:** 2631 (2628, 2629, 2630), 2731, 2778, 2779, 2799 (2792), 2813, 2856 (2854), 2879 (2875, 2879), 2903 (2900), 2907 (2905), 2910, 2931 (2926); **6:** 3297 (3293), 3312, 3496, 3559 (3557), 3560 (3557, 3559), 3631 (3630); **7:** 3788 (3787), 3810, 3830 (3830), 3833 (3831), 3886 (3881), 4015 (4007), 4088 (4084), 4104 (4101), 4215 (4212); **8:** 4403 (4400, 4401, 4402), 4404 (4401, 4402), 4594, 4595, 4666, 4702 (4699), 4708, 4766, 4864 (4862, 4863), 4873, 4882 (4876), 4936 (4931, 4933); **9:** 5043 (5040, 5041), 5197, 5201, 5264 (5261), 5323 (5318), 5373 (5367, 5368, 5371, 5372); **10:** 5686, 5745, 5750 (5747), 5775 (5772, 5773), 5943, 5991 (5987), 6015 (6013), 6117, 6169 (6166), 6173 (6172), 6239 (6236, 6237, 6238, 6239), 6244; **11:** 6384 (6378, 6379, 6382), 6390 (6388, 6389), 6461, 6558
Walberg J, **6:** 3085
Walberg M J, **10:** 5991
Walbesser H H Jr, **8:** 4648 (4645)
Walby S, **4:** 2432; **11:** 6768
Walczyk J J, **10:** 6193 (6191)
Wald H, **3:** 1690 (1686, 1690); **11:** 6452 (6447)
Waldmann M, **2:** 847 (844)
Waldron M, **2:** 1165
Wales T J, **1:** 521 (517); **4:** 2278 (2275, 2277, 2278); **6:** 3143 (3138, 3140, 3141, 3143), 3144 (3138, 3141, 3143); **9:** 5355 (5353); **11:** 6615
Walford G, **1:** 265, 266 (264); **3:** 1720 (1717); **8:** 4562, 4830 (4825, 4827), 4831, 4845 (4842); **9:** 5013, 5201 (5197), 5206 (5202); **11:** 6558 (6556), 6690 (6689), 6704
Walford R, **9:** 5475 (5472)
Walk R D, **8:** 4383 (4380)
Walker A, **9:** 5302 (5299)
Walker A D, **11:** 6625
Walker C, **7:** 3852
Walker C E, **1:** 19
Walker C H, **8:** 4702 (4700)
Walker D, **1:** 193 (191); **2:** 1107 (1105); **3:** 1278 (1274), 1325, 1494 (1492, 1493), 1804 (1802, 1803); **4:** 2186; **6:** 3349; **8:** 4376 (4374)
Walker D A, **1:** 396 (393, 394); **3:** 1381 (1377), 1769 (1763); **4:** 2140 (2132, 2137), 2180 (2174); **7:** 3722 (3720); **9:** 5385 (5381, 5384), 5432 (5426)
Walker D F, **2:** 1012 (1010); **3:** 1334 (1330, 1331), 1355 (1352); **4:** 2073; **6:** 3512 (3511); **7:** 4104 (4103); **10:** 5818 (5815)
Walker D W, **9:** 5544 (5542)
Walker H M, **1:** 494 (493); **8:** 4375; **9:** 5567 (5563, 5564, 5565, 5566); **10:** 6031 (6028)
Walker J, **11:** 6803 (6801, 6802)
Walker J C, **6:** 3621 (3620); **9:** 5030 (5027, 5029, 5030), 5060 (5058, 5059), 5539 (5538)
Walker J R, **2:** 693 (690)
Walker K, **10:** 5783
Walker L, **10:** 6169 (6166)
Walker L J, **7:** 3920 (3917, 3918)
Walker P, **7:** 4171 (4166)
Walker R, **2:** 816 (812, 813); **3:** 1257 (1253, 1254, 1256); **10:** 5613 (5611)
Walker S, **4:** 2291, 2292; **6:** 3227, 3484 (3483); **10:** 6139, 6215
Walker V S, **9:** 5071 (5068)
Walker W G, **1:** 73 (67, 69, 72), 77 (73, 74); **5:** 2954 (2952, 2954), 2955 (2952, 2954); **6:** 3284 (3276)
Walkerdine V, **4:** 2292 (2287); **5:** 2457 (2453, 2454), 2458; **6:** 3639 (3636)
Walkers S, **4:** 1984
Walkin L, **10:** 6202
Wall C A, **9:** 5328 (5324)
Wall W D, **4:** 1864
Wallace A F C, **3:** 1729 (1726, 1727)
Wallace J, **2:** 1031 (1029)
Wallace L, **9:** 5142 (5132)
Wallace M, **1:** 73 (69, 70); **4:** 2012 (2011); **11:** 6276 (6273)
Wallace M J Jr, **8:** 4409 (4406)
Wallace R, **7:** 4201
Wallace R B, **5:** 2571
Wallace S, **1:** 534; **8:** 4881 (4878)
Wallace T, **2:** 893 (890)
Wallach J, **5:** 3028
Wallach M A, **2:** 1183 (1180); **5:** 2773 (2770); **9:** 4974 (4972)
Wallat C, **2:** 820 (819); **4:** 2052 (2048, 2050); **6:** 3227; **10:** 6197
Wallenborn M, **11:** 6660
Waller M I, **7:** 4000 (3999)
Waller N G, **1:** 53 (51)
Waller R, **8:** 4694
Waller T G, **4:** 1963; **8:** 4912, 4942
Waller W, **2:** 785 (783), 1074 (1066); **4:** 2167 (2159); **7:** (4298); **9:** 5211 (5207), 5313 (5312), 5379 (5377), 5411 (5408); **10:** 5614 (5612), 6086 (6084), 6103 (6101), 6132 (6130), 6139 (6132, 6133), 6227 (6227)
Wallerstein I, **7:** 4081 (4080)
Wallerstein N, **4:** 1985 (1982)
Wallesch C-W, **6:** 3224
Wallis L W, **8:** 4694
Walmsley S, **6:** 3484 (3482)
Walp T, **6:** 3484 (3482)
Walsh B, **8:** 4394
Walsh C E, **9:** 5510
Walsh D J, **3:** 1624 (1621); **11:** 6558 (6554)
Walsh J E, **5:** 2596
Walsh J J, **8:** 4791 (4791)
Walsh L H, **4:** 2131 (2124); **8:** 4751 (4750)
Walsh W B, **10:** 5805 (5798); **11:** 6677, 6678 (6672)
Walstad W B, **9:** 5563 (5562)
Walt D, **7:** 4088 (4084)
Walter R J, **10:** 5782 (5778, 5779)
Walters P, **7:** 4240 (4238)
Walters R H, **1:** 497 (495); **9:** 5518 (5515)
Walters S, **2:** 907
Walther G, **6:** 3652 (3647, 3648, 3649, 3650)
Walton D N, **2:** 1208 (1207)
Walton W T, **5:** 2910 (2909)
Wandall J, **7:** 4179 (4178)
Wandersee J, **2:** 1031 (1029)
Wang B L C, **4:** 2419 (2418); **9:** 5228 (5227)
Wang C, **4:** 1958 (1955)
Wang J, **2:** 749
Wang M C, **1:** 490; **2:** 711 (710), 729 (724, 728), 730 (724); **3:** 1402, 1534 (1534); **4:** 1848 (1843, 1847); **5:** 2731, 2778, 2779 (2776, 2777), 2813, 2907 (2905), 2910 (2908); **6:** 3297 (3293, 3295), 3339 (3337), 3559 (3557), 3560 (3557, 3559); **7:** 3788 (3787), 3830 (3830), 3833 (3831), 3886 (3881); **8:** 4404 (4402), 4936 (4931, 4933); **9:** 5071 (5068); **10:** 5686, 5745 (5744), 5750 (5746, 5747), 5943, 6088, 6173, 6239 (6239), 6244 (6241); **11:** 6384 (6379), 6461
Wang N, **1:** 374 (372)
Wang R I H, **3:** 1619
Wang T, **3:** 1624 (1622)
Waniewicz I, **1:** 158 (153)
Wankowski J, **1:** 194 (184)
Wanna J, **3:** 1720 (1714)
Wanner E, **6:** 3223
Wansart W, **10:** 6015 (6014)
Waples D, **10:** 6043 (6036)
Wapner S, **2:** 871 (870), 872 (870); **8:** 4395 (4392)
Ward F C, **5:** 2978
Ward J G, **7:** 3821; **9:** 5240; **11:** 6558
Ward J V, **4:** 2296
Ward L E, **9:** 5379 (5375)
Ward L F, **5:** (2875)
Ward M, **3:** 1406 (1403); **4:** 2445 (2441)
Ward P, **7:** 4170 (4166)
Ward S M, **7:** 3830 (3827, 3828)
Warden J, **2:** 907 (902)
Wardrop J C, **8:** 4751 (4743)
Ware J H, **5:** 2596
Wargo M J, **8:** 4751 (4743)
Warhurst J, **3:** 1720 (1714)
Waring M, **9:** 5328 (5324, 5326)
Warke S, **7:** 4248 (4248)
Warman J, **11:** 6283 (6278)
Warner J E, **1:** 19 (18)
Warner Schaie K, **7:** 4170 (4169)
Warner W L, **1:** 297 (286, 290, 293); **4:** 1872 (1864); **7:** 3722 (3716); **9:** 5572 (5567, 5569)
Warnock G J, **8:** 4447 (4443)
Warnock H M, **5:** 2972 (2966)
Warnock M, **5:** 2910 (2907); **7:** 3833 (3832)
Warren B M, **5:** 2768 (2762)
Warren D, **8:** 4587 (4584, 4585, 4586); **10:** 5613, 5614 (5609), 6012 (6009), 6139 (6135)
Warren D H, **8:** 4383; **11:** 6628 (6626)
Warren R D, **7:** 3986 (3981)
Warren R L, **2:** 918, 1213 (1210); **4:** 2053 (2049)
Warren Piper D, **1:** 194
Warshauer M, **6:** 3634
Wartenweiler F, **1:** 139 (137)
Warwick D, **3:** 1810 (1807), 1821 (1818, 1819), 1824 (1821), 1825 (1822); **7:** 3889 (3887); **8:** 4495 (4493), 4509 (4506), 4601 (4595, 4597, 4598)
Warwick J, **4:** 2286 (2285)
Wasden F, **7:** 3889

Wasem J, **11:** 6699 (6695)
Washburn S L, **1:** 297 (288); **5:** 2685 (2684)
Washburne C W, **5:** 2779 (2774); **7:** (4156)
Washington K, **10:** 6112 (6110)
Washington R O, **9:** 5290 (5288, 5289)
Wasik B A, **1:** 362; **3:** 1624 (1621)
Wasik B H, **10:** 6163 (6162)
Wasserman E, **5:** 2669 (2668); **7:** 3925 (3923)
Wasserman S S, **4:** 2208 (2203)
Wasson P, **1:** 409 (406)
Watanabe T, **2:** 1152 (1148)
Waterman R H, **9:** 5211 (5207); **10:** 6053 (6052)
Waterman R H Jr, **6:** 3496 (3495); **7:** 4246 (4244)
Waters A, **6:** 3213
Waters E, **2:** 705; **9:** 5528 (5525)
Waterston S, **1:** 193 (188, 189)
Wati R, **3:** 1628 (1625)
Watkins B, **6:** 3625 (3623)
Watkins B A, **8:** 4542 (4541)
Watkins C L, **4:** 1917 (1914)
Watkins J E, **4:** (2328)
Watkins P, **3:** 1412 (1409), 1739 (1738); **6:** 3284; **9:** 5273 (5269, 5270, 5271), 5544 (5540)
Watkins W H, **7:** 3848 (3841, 3843)
Watson C, **11:** 6370 (6370)
Watson D, **10:** 5625 (5623)
Watson D A, **11:** 6628 (6625)
Watson D M, **2:** 988, 991 (990); **3:** 1779 (1777, 1778)
Watson F, **5:** 2891 (2887); **9:** 5299 (5296)
Watson F G, **9:** 5345 (5343)
Watson J, **6:** 3416 (3413); **10:** (5659)
Watson J B, **1:** 497 (495), (535); **5:** 2665 (2657, 2664), (2875), (2876), (2877), (2878)
Watson K, **3:** 1501 (1495); **5:** 2937; **9:** 5169 (5164)
Watson K W, **7:** 3935 (3934)
Watson L, **1:** 73 (67, 69, 72); **5:** 2954 (2953, 2954)
Watson M, **10:** 6053 (6053)
Watson M S, **8:** 4799 (4798)
Watson N, **10:** 6043
Watson R 1990, **1:** 404
Watt A J, **2:** 1107 (1103)
Wattanawaha N, **8:** 4707 (4706), 4835 (4834), 4845 (4843); **10:** 5754 (5751)
Wattenberg R, **6:** 3197 (3193)
Watts A F, **9:** 5389 (5388)
Watts A G, **3:** 1739 (1737, 1738); **7:** 4249 (4246); **9:** 5232 (5231); **11:** 6704 (6700)
Watts E S, **5:** 2684, 2685
Watts H, **1:** 404
Watts J 1990, **2:** 907 (903)
Watts S M, **1:** 12 (9, 10)
Waugh M, **2:** 1175 (1173)
Wax M L, **1:** 295, 296, 297 (281, 283, 284, 286); **4:** 2053; **6:** 3215; **9:** 5220 (5218), 5510 (5508)
Wax R H, **4:** 2053; **9:** 5220 (5218)
Waxman H C, **5:** 2509, 2779 (2776, 2777); **6:** 3284, 3334 (3331); **8:** 4403, 4404, 4873; **10:** 5745, 6015, 6219 (6218), 6239 (6236, 6238)
Wayson W, **3:** 1538 (1537)
Waywood A, **6:** 3639 (3635)
Weade R, **10:** 6197 (6195, 6196)
Wearne D, **6:** 3660 (3659)
Weatherburn C E, **7:** 3739 (3736)
Weatherley R, **10:** 5668 (5666)
Weaver W T, **2:** 1079 (1075); **3:** 1443 (1442)
Webb E J, **11:** 6511 (6508)
Webb J, **10:** 6053 (6050, 6052)
Webb L, **1:** 103 (102)
Webb L D, **8:** 4408 (4405, 4406, 4407); **9:** 5185
Webb M, **2:** 988 (986, 987)
Webb N, **4:** 2388 (2382); **5:** 2596 (2590); **7:** 3986 (3981)
Webb N M, **1:** 42 (33), 370 (368); **5:** 2462 (2459, 2461, 2462), 2536 (2534, 2535), 2769 (2766); **6:** 3124; **10:** 6043 (6040)
Webb R, **8:** 4873 (4872); **10:** 5973 (5970), 6214 (6208, 6211, 6214)
Webber L S, **1:** 5 (5)
Weber D, **2:** 1152 (1148)
Weber E, **3:** 1355 (1354); **4:** 2388 (2386); **8:** 4670 (4668)
Weber E H, **11:** (6385)
Weber F, **4:** 2089 (2082)
Weber J, **10:** 5691 (5688)
Weber L, **7:** 4215
Weber M, **1:** 437 (433, 436), 594 (589); **2:** 785 (781), (929), (1067), 1074 (1068), (1199); **3:** 1241 (1237), 1775 (1772); **4:** 2167 (2157), (2248); **5:** (2605); **6:** 3368 (3367); **7:** (3716), (4242); **8:** (4555); **9:** 5050, (5161), 5169 (5161); **10:** (5588), (5596), (5597), (5598), (5730)
Weber R, **10:** 5762 (5760)
Weber R P, **2:** 1079 (1075)
Webster C, **2:** 884; **10:** 5662 (5660)
Webster D, **9:** 5008 (5007)
Webster F, **4:** 1911; **11:** 6492 (6489)
Webster G, **10:** 5713 (5711)
Webster H, **2:** 678 (673)
Webster W J, **4:** 2109 (2102, 2104); **11:** 6381
Wechsler D, **7:** 3707 (3702)
Weddle P, **2:** 1208
Wedell E G, **3:** 1579 (1575)
Wedell G, **5:** 2897 (2892)
Wedell K, **5:** 2910, 2971 (2967)
Wedell N, **5:** 2971 (2967)
Wedenberg E, **1:** 15 (13)
Weeden W J, **7:** 4282 (4276)
Weedon C, **5:** 2458
Weeks J, **8:** 4839 (4839); **9:** 5441 (5436, 5437)
Weeks S, **7:** 4282
Weffort F, **8:** 4595 (4588, 4594)
Wehby J H, **9:** 5567 (5565)
Wehing R S, **10:** 5745 (5744)
Wehlage G G, **2:** 711 (710); **3:** 1607 (1603, 1605); **5:** 2779 (2776); **9:** 5060 (5059), 5216 (5214)
Wehle G, **6:** 3137
Wehman P H, **11:** 6461 (6459)
Wei L J, **9:** 5385 (5379)
Weick K E, **2:** 910 (907, 910); **3:** 1746 (1741); **4:** 1934 (1930), 2167 (2161, 2162); **6:** 3527 (3524, 3526); **9:** 5247 (5242), 5313 (5312)
Weidenhammer B, **8:** 4816
Weidman C, **2:** 820 (817, 818, 820); **10:** 6122 (6119)
Weigand H, **6:** 3685 (3683)
Weikart D, **8:** 4677 (4674)
Weikart D P, **2:** 687 (679, 680), 688 (679, 680, 681, 682), 701 (695, 696), 1131 (1130); **3:** 1628 (1625), 1641 (1640), 1825 (1824); **4:** 1841 (1837), 2145 (2144); **5:** 2480, 2806 (2804), 2813 (2807, 2812); **6:** 3524 (3517); **7:** 4301 (4298); **8:** 4666 (4664); **11:** 6384 (6382)
Weil M, **7:** 3886 (3881); **9:** 5318; **10:** 6043 (6039), 6192 (6188, 6190)
Weil S W, **4:** 2186 (2184)
Weiler D, **9:** 5206 (5203)
Weiler H N, **2:** 933 (929), 1204 (1199); **3:** 1343, 1412 (1408, 1410), 1416 (1413), 1431 (1429), 1655 (1649), 1810, 1821; **4:** 1852 (1851); **6:** 3368 (3368); **8:** 4499, 4509 (4504), 4514 (4512), 4595 (4588), 4604 (4602); **9:** 5181 (5177), 5216 (5212); **10:** 5607; **11:** 6298 (6293)
Weiler K, **8:** 4587 (4582, 4585); **10:** 6139 (6134); **11:** 6723, 6765 (6761)
Weiler W C, **3:** 1449
Weinberg M, **3:** 1486 (1483)
Weinberg P D, **11:** 6266 (6262)
Weinberg R, **4:** 2279 (2278)
Weinberg R A, **3:** 1643 (1636)
Weinberg R B, **9:** 5528
Weinberg S F, **10:** 6020 (6017)
Weinberg S L, **2:** 631 (627); **7:** 4015 (4007)
Weindling D, **8:** 4408 (4404)
Weiner B, **1:** 204 (201); **4:** 1848 (1842, 1846), 1967 (1963); **5:** 2879 (2879); **6:** 3329 (3328); **7:** 3942 (3940), 3947; **8:** 4824 (4821); **10:** 6224 (6222); **11:** 6360 (6356)
Weiner B A, **6:** 3297 (3295)
Weiner F, **10:** 5697 (5695)
Weiner G, **4:** 2291, 2292 (2287); **7:** 3852 (3849, 3850); **10:** 5826 (5823), 5827, 6099 (6098)
Weiner H, **9:** 5385
Weiner I B, **8:** 4791 (4789)
Weiner R, **4:** 2291 (2290)
Weiner S P, **11:** 6333 (6330)
Weinert F E, **1:** 204 (200), 390 (389); **2:** 706 (704), 847 (844, 846); **3:** 1504 (1503, 1504); **5:** 2665, 2669 (2666), 2769 (2761), 2884 (2882), 2916 (2914); **6:** 3349, 3428 (3426, 3427), 3435; **7:** 3763 (3760), 3768 (3764), 3942 (3939); **8:** 4395 (4393), 4702 (4699, 4700), 4719; **9:** 5043 (5041); **10:** 5772 (5768), 6053, 6159 (6158)
Weinert S, **2:** 857 (855)
Weingarten G, **11:** 6360 (6357)
Weingartner C, **6:** 3151 (3151)
Weinman J, **10:** 5738
Weinrach S G, **11:** 6678 (6675)
Weinraub M, **7:** 4301 (4298)
Weinreich U, **1:** 537 (536)

Weinrib A, **4:** 2351 (2348)
Weinrott M M, **9:** 5489 (5487), 5490
Weinstein C E, **1:** 193, 194 (186, 187, 192), 322 (319); **2:** 969 (966); **6:** 3329 (3325, 3326), 3335 (3329, 3331), 3339 (3337), 3340 (3335); **10:** 5745 (5742), 5831 (5829)
Weinstein C S, **9:** 5264 (5262), 5359; **10:** 5812 (5810)
Weinstein F, **3:** 1713
Weinstein M, **2:** 1208 (1206)
Weinstein R, **10:** 6112 (6109, 6110, 6111)
Weinstein R S, **9:** 5394 (5392)
Weinstein T, **5:** 2631 (2628, 2629), 2931 (2926); **8:** 4403 (4401), 4702 (4699), 4882 (4876); **9:** 5043 (5040)
Weinstock H, **8:** 4803 (4800)
Weinstock R, **7:** 4171 (4169)
Weintraub J K, **4:** 1979 (1978)
Weintraub M, **3:** 1619 (1611)
Weintraub S, **6:** 3297
Weir C, **4:** 2364 (2363)
Weir S, **7:** 4088 (4084)
Weis L, **2:** 918, 933 (930), 1074 (1072); **3:** 1607; **4:** 2004 (2003); **8:** 4698; **9:** 5060 (5057, 5059), 5572 (5570); **10:** 5818 (5816); **11:** 6371, 6726
Weisberg A, **2:** 1131 (1130)
Weisberg H I, **5:** 2596 (2591)
Weisberg R W, **8:** 4731 (4729)
Weisbord M, **7:** 4240 (4239)
Weisbrod B A, **2:** 1056; **4:** 2212 (2210); **9:** 5241 (5236); **11:** 6298
Weisgerber R A, **4:** 1898, 1899 (1890); **8:** 4775 (4773)
Weishaupt H, **6:** 3608 (3604)
Weismantel L, **1:** (341)
Weisner T S, **6:** 3453 (3452)
Weiss A, **9:** 5355 (5354); **10:** 5691 (5689)
Weiss B, **2:** 847 (844)
Weiss C H, **3:** 1431 (1425, 1426, 1427, 1428), 1746 (1740); **4:** 1841 (1835, 1836, 1837), 1864 (1862), 2037 (2036), 2046, (2088), (2103), (2108), 2119 (2112); **5:** 2672 (2670), 2673; **6:** 3373 (3369); **8:** 4556 (4550, 4554), 4562 (4559, 4560), 4604 (4604); **9:** 5038; **11:** 6384 (6379)
Weiss D J, **1:** 52 (48), 53 (48, 49, 50, 51); **2:** 998 (993); **3:** 1421; **4:** 2017 (2012); **5:** 2784 (2780), 3055; **6:** 3253
Weiss J, **7:** 4215 (4212, 4213)
Weiss J A, **5:** 2673
Weiss L, **3:** (1346), 1347 (1346)
Weiss M, **6:** 3608 (3604); **8:** 4499; **11:** 6648 (6641)
Weiss R S, **3:** 1431 (1427); **4:** 2046 (2044)
Weiss Y, **2:** 1056; **3:** 1750 (1747); **4:** 2279 (2275); **7:** 4324 (4323)
Weissflog I, **7:** 3894 (3890, 3893)
Weisskopf T E, **3:** 1820 (1818); **5:** 2744
Weisskopf-Joelson E, **8:** 4731 (4729)
Weistein C S, **9:** 5359 (5355)
Weisz J R, **2:** 847 (844)
Weitz B O, **4:** 2024 (2020)
Weitzman E D, **1:** 15 (13)
Weitzman L, **9:** 5445 (5441)
Weitzman M, **4:** 2212 (2210); **5:** 2567 (2563)
Weizenbaum J, **7:** 4088 (4082)
Welborn L, **6:** 3399 (3394)
Welch B L, **9:** 5471 (5471)
Welch F, **1:** 254 (245), 520 (517, 518); **2:** 1055 (1054); **3:** 1449 (1445), 1666 (1665), 1695 (1691, 1693), 1713 (1710), 1762 (1757); **6:** 3101; **7:** 4201 (4199); **8:** 4902 (4897, 4898, 4900), 4918 (4916); **11:** 6283 (6280), 6615
Welch W W, **2:** 811 (807); **8:** 4403 (4401, 4402), 4648 (4645), 4864 (4862, 4863); **9:** 5043 (5041), 5324 (5318, 5321), 5338 (5336); **10:** 5775 (5772, 5773), 6015 (6013)
Weldon W, **8:** 4788 (4783)
Welle Donker-Gimbrere M, **1:** 409 (404)
Weller P, **3:** 1720 (1714)
Wellingham A, **2:** 906 (906)
Wellings A, **7:** 4325
Wellings J, **1:** 157, 158, 162 (161), 414, 415; **6:** 3366
Wellings P A, **2:** 914 (912)
Wellington J J, **3:** 1544 (1538, 1539, 1543), 1779
Wellington R, **4:** 2389 (2387)
Wellman C, **7:** 3925 (3922)
Wellman H M, **2:** 842 (840); **7:** 3763 (3761); **8:** 4957 (4952, 4955); **9:** 5512 (5511)
Wellmer A, **7:** 3925 (3921)
Wells A, **1:** 103
Wells B, **10:** 5680 (5678)
Wells C, **3:** 1778 (1776)
Wells G, **6:** 3443 (3441), 3463 (3460); **9:** 5508 (5506)
Wells I, **6:** 3463 (3461, 3462)
Wells R, **2:** 982 (981)
Wells S, **2:** 1127 (1124), 1135 (1134); **3:** 1266 (1263); **4:** 1911 (1904, 1905, 1910); **5:** 2891 (2888)
Wells W, **7:** 4301 (4298)
Welsch H, **4:** 1991 (1987)
Welsh A R, **2:** 933 (929)
Welsh B L, **9:** 5290 (5288, 5289), 5291 (5287)
Welsh R L, **11:** 6628
Welsh W W, **11:** 6390 (6389)
Weltens B, **1:** 537 (537)
Welton M, **1:** 135 (129, 132); **2:** 907
Welty D A, **7:** 4293 (4291)
Welty W M, **10:** 5948 (5946)
Wendel F C, **1:** 83 (80)
Wendelin K H, **2:** 738 (733)
Wenden A, **6:** 3335 (3330)
Wender K F, **8:** 4722
Wenestram C G, **2:** 969 (965); **8:** 4429 (4425)
Wenger E, **1:** 348; **2:** 1007 (1003), 1012 (1008); **3:** 1233 (1230); **6:** 3302 (3299); **8:** 4722; **9:** 5232 (5229); **11:** 6608 (6604)
Wenkert R, **6:** 3378 (3376)
Wennås O, **4:** 2377 (2376)
Wentworth W M, **10:** 5591 (5586)
Wenzel H J, **8:** 4688 (4685)
Wenzel J, **11:** 6659 (6658)
Wepner S B, **7:** 3808 (3803, 3806)
Werdelin I, **9:** 5334 (5328)
Werebe M J G, **8:** 4542 (4541)
Werker J, **1:** 15 (13)
Werle F O C, **1:** 83 (79)
Werner C, **11:** 6747
Werner D, **2:** 730 (728)
Werner E E, **1:** 89 (88), 362; **3:** 1520 (1517), 1643 (1637, 1641); **6:** 3228 (3225); **8:** 4779 (4775, 4776, 4777, 4778); **10:** 5686 (5685)
Werner H, **5:** 2665 (2656); **10:** 5644
Werner H-J, **7:** 3925
Wernicke C, **10:** (5681)
Werry B, **10:** 6155 (6151)
Werry J S, **9:** 5070 (5068), 5071 (5068)
Wersch J, **2:** 860
Wertheimer B M, **11:** 6775
Wertheimer M, **5:** (2876), 2884 (2880); **6:** (3316); **8:** 4727 (4723, 4724)
Werthein J, **3:** 1821 (1818)
Werts C E, **4:** 2241 (2238)
Wertsch J V, **2:** 1026; **3:** 1233, 1246 (1243), 1252, 1253 (1249, 1250); **9:** 5548 (5545); **10:** 6035 (6033)
Wesche M B, **6:** 3335
Wesman A G, **11:** 6348 (6341)
Wesselingh AA, **7:** 4324
Wesselman R, **10:** 6149 (6147)
Wesson C L, **3:** 1359 (1357); **9:** 5071 (5070)
West E G, **9:** 5206 (5202, 5204), 5241 (5239)
West G, **6:** 3261
West J, **1:** 110 (104, 107); **7:** 3711; **10:** 5691 (5688)
West J F, **10:** 6244 (6240, 6242)
West K, **3:** 1676 (1672, 1673, 1674, 1675)
West L, **9:** 5334 (5332); **11:** 6551 (6548)
West L H T, **7:** 4170 (4163, 4164, 4166), 4171 (4164, 4166, 4167); **10:** 5790
West M, **7:** 4301
West P, **11:** 6265 (6263)
West R, **3:** 1328
West R P, **10:** 6163 (6163)
West S G, **5:** 2931 (2927); **9:** 4974
Westborg J, **4:** 1991 (1988)
Westbrook R B, **10:** 5818 (5813)
Westbury I, **2:** 1107 (1106); **3:** 1278 (1277), 1320, 1355 (1349), 1494 (1492), 1769 (1764); **4:** 2140; **5:** 2697 (2694); **6:** 3668 (3663, 3667), 3685 (3674); **10:** 6155 (6150); **11:** 6334 (6332)
Westerhof K, **10:** 6035 (6033)
Western J S, **1:** 358 (356)
Westgaard O, **6:** 3096 (3092)
Westgate D, **2:** 816 (813)
Westgeest R, **10:** 5674 (5670)
Westin B, **2:** 738
Westkott M, **11:** 6769 (6766)
Westoby A, **4:** 2167
Weston P, **1:** 362 (360); **6:** 3311
Westphal B, **7:** 4026
Westwood S, **2:** 1193 (1192), 1194
Wettstein E, **1:** 317 (313)
Wetzel G, **3:** 1355 (1353)
Wexler P, **2:** 770 (767); **3:** 1337 (1335), 1348 (1347); **9:** 5523
Wexley K N, **3:** 1490 (1489); **6:** 3306 (3304)
Weyhing R S, **2:** 867 (866), 969 (966)

Whaley K, **5:** 2814 (2811)
Whalley J, **4:** 2315 (2311, 2312), 2316 (2315); **8:** 4364 (4361, 4362)
Whalley P, **8:** 4694
Whang K, **1:** 110 (108, 110)
Whatley M H, **7:** 3760 (3759)
Wheatley A, **8:** 4623 (4618)
Wheatley M, **11:** 6731 (6730)
Wheatly G, **6:** 3660 (3659)
Wheeler B G, **9:** 5008 (5005)
Wheeler C W, **10:** 5818 (5815)
Wheeler D, **3:** 1666 (1663)
Wheeler L J, **8:** 4936 (4932)
Wheeler S, **6:** 3427 (3426), 3434 (3429, 3431); **10:** 5591 (5587)
Wheeler T, **11:** 6292 (6289)
Wheldall K, **1:** 490 (488, 489), 494 (491); **8:** 4376 (4372, 4373); **9:** 5359 (5357); **10:** 6031 (6030)
Whimbey A, **2:** 868 (862)
Whipple G M, **5:** 2779 (2774); **7:** 4300; **8:** 4948 (4945)
Whishaw I Q, **1:** 553 (552, 553)
Whisler J S, **5:** 2769 (2764)
Whitaker D P, **6:** 3247
Whitaker J, **8:** 4542 (4541)
Whitaker U, **4:** 2186
White B, **4:** 2419 (2417)
White B L, **6:** 3288 (3285)
White B Y, **6:** 3325; **10:** 5790 (5784, 5785, 5787)
White C, **7:** 3853 (3850)
White C C, **3:** 1438 (1434)
White D, **1:** 474 (470); **9:** 5291 (5284)
White D R, **9:** 5560
White D S, **6:** 3608 (3607)
White E E, **8:** 4616 (4610)
White G, **8:** 4587 (4585)
White J, **1:** 244 (241, 243); **3:** 1328 (1326, 1327), 1337 (1335, 1336); **10:** 5826 (5822)
White J J, **9:** 5582 (5579)
White J P, **8:** 4447 (4445)
White J W, **10:** 5995 (5993)
White K R, **4:** 2145 (2142), 2257 (2251, 2252, 2255); **5:** 2814 (2812); **11:** 6384 (6382)
White L, **1:** 537 (535); **4:** 2339 (2333, 2338)
White L A, **11:** 6320 (6320)
White M, **2:** 738 (736); **6:** 3086, 3312 (3310); **9:** 5281; **11:** 6808 (6806)
White M I, **9:** 5510 (5509)
White O R, **3:** 1359 (1356); **9:** 5490 (5487)
White P, **3:** 1431 (1425, 1426, 1428); **4:** 2297 (2296)
White P A, **3:** 1486 (1483)
White R, **1:** 322 (321); **3:** 1501; **8:** 4479 (4477); **10:** 5790 (5785), 5834 (5832)
White R K, **5:** 2529 (2524)
White R T, **3:** 1514 (1509); **6:** 3416 (3411, 3412); **8:** 4775 (4769); **9:** 5324 (5319); **10:** 6178 (6174, 6176)
White R W, **7:** 3947
White V J, **3:** 1573 (1572)
Whitebook M, **2:** 693 (689, 690, 691); **3:** 1636 (1634); **11:** 6398 (6395, 6396, 6397)
Whitehead A N, **1:** (195); **2:** (776); **3:** 1343; **6:** 3151 (3150); **8:** (4532)
Whitehead C W, **4:** 2310
Whitehead J, **1:** 48 (45)
Whitehead R G, **8:** 4474 (4469)
Whitehouse D, **6:** 3235 (3233)
Whitehurst G, **6:** 3329
Whitely S E, **6:** 3315 (3312)
Whiteside C, **11:** 6625 (6624)
Whiteside J A, **11:** 6625 (6624)
Whiteside T, **10:** 6227 (6225)
Whiteside-Taylor K, **7:** 4301 (4298, 4299)
Whiting B, **3:** 1253 (1247)
Whiting B B, **1:** 89, 230 (229); **4:** 2449 (2447, 2448), 2452 (2449, 2450); **5:** 2651 (2649, 2650), 2685; **6:** 3228 (3225); **8:** 4799 (4798); **9:** 5528
Whiting C S, **5:** 2725 (2723)
Whiting H T R, **7:** 3950
Whiting J, **3:** 1756 (1754)
Whiting J W M, **1:** 89, 230 (229), 297 (283); **5:** 2651 (2649, 2650), 2685; **8:** 4799 (4798)
Whitla D K, **7:** 3872, 4015
Whitley B E, **9:** 5435 (5434)
Whitlock M S, **5:** 2495 (2493)
Whitlock Q, **2:** 1011 (1008)
Whitmarsh G, **8:** 4571 (4569)
Whitmore J R, **5:** 2491 (2488, 2490); **9:** 5532 (5530, 5531)
Whitney D R, **1:** 370 (366); **4:** 2183 (2183)
Whitson J A, **3:** 1720 (1715, 1716); **6:** 3360
Whitt E J, **10:** 5805, 5808
Whittaker A K, **7:** 3726 (3724)
Whitten P, **9:** 5206 (5202)
Whittington D, **10:** 5977
Whittrock M C, **8:** 4864; **10:** 5887
Whitty G, **3:** 1348 (1347); **6:** 3496; **8:** 4830 (4825), 4831; **9:** 5299; **11:** 6557 (6556), 6558 (6556), 6563 (6559, 6560, 6561, 6562)
Wholey J S, **5:** 2673 (2670); **11:** 6384 (6379), 6385
Wholey K, **7:** 3807 (3804)
Wholey S S, **4:** (2103)
Whorf B, **6:** 3216 (3214)
Whybrew W E, **7:** 4026 (4023)
Whyte J, **4:** 2292 (2290); **9:** 5432 (5425), 5445; **10:** 5681 (5678, 5679)
Whyte W F, **2:** 918 (916); **7:** 4319 (4319); **11:** 6803 (6799)
Wiatrowski M D, **1:** 12 (7)
Wichit S, **1:** 563 (562)
Wick J W, **9:** 5324 (5321)
Wickelgren W A, **1:** 331 (329)
Wicker A W, **1:** 390 (386)
Wickert R, **1:** 415 (410)
Wickman E K, **1:** 490 (488)
Widaman K F, **7:** 4007 (4003)
Widdowson F, **10:** 6139 (6134)
Wideen M F, **8:** 4881; **9:** 5224; **10:** 5965, 5973, 5982, 5994, 5995 (5991), 6043 (6038)
Wideman C, **10:** 6035 (6033)
Widick C, **10:** 5805
Wieberdink L, **5:** 2572 (2567)
Wiechmann J, **6:** 3602 (3598)
Wiedeburg F A, **3:** (1721)
Wiedenbeck S, **2:** 985 (984)
Wieder A, **7:** 4225
Wiederhold-Fritz S, **11:** 6420 (6418)
Wiederholt J L, **9:** 5071 (5066, 5068); **10:** 5663, 5686 (5681)
Wiegand J, **5:** 2495 (2492)
Wiegand P, **5:** 2470 (2468)
Wielemans W, **1:** 504
Wiemann, **11:** 6452 (6449)
Wiener H, **4:** 2025
Wiersma W, **5:** 2779 (2776)
Wiesel T N, **5:** 2802 (2799)
Wieser K, **10:** 5873
Wiess L, **10:** 6139
Wigdor A K, **7:** 3726; **11:** 6339, 6678 (6677)
Wigger L, **8:** 4419
Wiggin K D, **4:** (2385)
Wiggins G, **8:** 4731 (4730)
Wiggins T, **7:** 4246 (4242)
Wigginton E, **3:** 1267 (1264); **7:** 4051 (4047); **9:** 5233 (5231); **10:** 6099 (6097)
Wigley T M L, **4:** 2331
Wiig E, **10:** 5691, 5693
Wijerathna H S, **7:** 4136 (4133)
Wijn M, **5:** 3051 (3046)
Wijnroks L, **3:** 1520 (1519)
Wilbur F, **9:** 5318 (5316)
Wilcox B, **11:** 6461 (6459)
Wilcox K, **4:** 1972 (1968), 2053 (2049)
Wilcox K A, **1:** 297 (286, 289, 290)
Wilcox R A, **9:** 5159 (5156)
Wilcox R C, **1:** 358 (355)
Wilcox R R, **2:** 792 (788); **9:** 5471 (5470, 5471)
Wilcoxon F, **9:** 5159 (5156)
Wilczenski F L, **10:** 6164 (6161)
Wildavsky A B, **4:** 1841 (1836); **5:** 2847 (2847); **7:** 3826 (3823); **8:** 4519 (4515), 4604 (4604)
Wilde J A, **4:** 1841 (1835)
Wildemeersch D, **10:** 6202 (6199)
Wildemuth B M, **8:** 4751 (4743)
Wilderson F, **2:** 1099 (1098)
Wildman T, **3:** 1529 (1527); **10:** 6015 (6014)
Wilen W W, **2:** 807 (804); **5:** 2528, 2529 (2528); **8:** 4881; **9:** 5582 (5579)
Wilensky H A L, **10:** 5596 (5595)
Wiles K, **9:** 5355 (5352)
Wiley D E, **1:** 23, 377 (376), 390 (381); **2:** 775 (772), 957 (953, 954); **3:** 1768 (1764); **4:** 1848 (1843), 2140 (2134, 2137, 2139), 2180 (2174), 2440 (2437); **5:** 2631 (2629); **7:** 3872 (3867), 3886 (3883), 4236 (4234); **9:** 5324 (5322), 5335 (5333), 5373 (5369), 5385 (5380); **10:** 5862 (5855), 6159; **11:** 6445 (6444)
Wilhelm T, **6:** 3138
Wilkening F, **8:** 4383 (4382)
Wilkerson L C, **1:** 12
Wilkes C, **9:** 5021
Wilkins A L, **4:** 2166 (2160)
Wilkins D A, **4:** 2346 (2342)
Wilkins M, **10:** 5985
Wilkinson A, **6:** 3443; **7:** 3936 (3933, 3934)
Wilkinson A C, **2:** 969 (966)
Wilkinson B, **1:** 23; **5:** 2536 (2534); **6:** 3311 (3308); **9:** 5363 (5359, 5361)

Wilkinson C, **2:** 825; **5:** 2508
Wilkinson F, **6:** 3189 (3188)
Wilkinson G L, **7:** 3753
Wilkinson I A G, **10:** 5795 (5791)
Wilkinson L, **3:** 1257; **10:** 5694
Wilkinson L C, **2:** 820; **5:** 2769 (2766); **6:** 3642; **8:** 4950; **9:** 5175, 5176, 5508 (5506)
Wilkinson S, **4:** 2302 (2297)
Wilkof N J, **3:** 1320
Wilks S S, **5:** 3061 (3056, 3058)
Wilks Y, **3:** 1779 (1775)
Will G, **2:** 893 (889)
Will M, **2:** 730 (724, 725, 727); **9:** 5071 (5069); **11:** 6461 (6457)
Willbrand M L, **6:** 3443 (3439)
Willeke M J, **4:** 2131 (2124); **8:** 4751 (4750)
Willems G M, **4:** 2357
Willer B, **2:** 693 (690)
Willer D, **2:** 1074 (1066)
Willerman M, **2:** 1031 (1028); **10:** 5834 (5833)
Willett J B, **2:** 678 (672, 673, 674, 676, 677); **4:** 1939 (1936), 2156 (2150, 2152, 2154, 2155), 2194 (2193); **5:** 2681 (2680); **10:** 5846 (5844, 5845), 6106 (6104, 6105, 6106)
Williams A, **5:** 2993 (2992)
Williams B I, **7:** 3833
Williams C, **1:** 444
Williams D, **10:** 5948
Williams D D, **3:** 1567 (1567)
Williams D L, **9:** 5268
Williams D V, **7:** 3996 (3993)
Williams E A, **9:** 5490
Williams E J, **3:** 1549 (1545, 1546)
Williams F, **6:** 3215, 3216 (3213, 3214)
Williams G, **1:** 94; **8:** 4526 (4522); **10:** 5754 (5751, 5753)
Williams J E, **4:** 2109 (2105)
Williams J W, **9:** 5577 (5573)
Williams L R, **5:** 2814 (2811)
Williams M, **9:** 5030 (5027)
Williams N, **8:** 4456 (4455)
Williams P, **2:** 730, 914; **10:** 5754 (5753)
Williams P D, **3:** 1624 (1622)
Williams R, **1:** 11 (7); **2:** 825 (821); **3:** 1348 (1346), 1501; **6:** 3597, 3621 (3619); **8:** 4830 (4826), 4939 (4938); **9:** 5175 (5173), 5299 (5297); **10:** (6055)
Williams R C, **4:** 2388 (2382), 2389
Williams R G, **5:** 3066 (3065)
Williams T, **3:** 1756 (1754); **8:** 4830 (4827), 4845 (4842), 4895 (4892, 4893)
Williams T H, **4:** 2249; **7:** 3872 (3870, 3871)
Williams T I, **9:** 5328
Williams T M, **1:** 570 (564, 568); **4:** 2266 (2264), 2449
Williams T Mc, **8:** 4680 (4677)
Williams T R, **1:** 82 (79, 81); **4:** 2053 (2047)
Williams W G, **5:** 2495 (2492, 2494)
Williams W H, **9:** 5142
Williamson B, **5:** 2697 (2696)
Williamson E G, **10:** 5805 (5797)
Williamson G M, **10:** 5705 (5703)
Williamson N, **4:** 1911 (1908, 1909, 1910)
Williamson O, **4:** 1972 (1969, 1971); **5:** 2799 (2793)
Williamson O E, **5:** 2942 (2937)
Williamson S, **2:** 834 (832)
Willig A C, **6:** 3232 (3231)
Willims E P, **1:** 390
Willinsky J, **2:** 1198 (1194); **6:** 3459 (3454, 3456), 3484; **11:** 6778
Willis G, **3:** 1287 (1285, 1287); **4:** (2103); **5:** 2697 (2695); **10:** 5818 (5816)
Willis G B, **10:** 5745 (5741)
Willis J, **2:** 1012 (1009)
Willis P E, **1:** 60 (55); **2:** 918 (916); **3:** 1233 (1229), 1337 (1335), 1739 (1737); **4:** 2272 (2268, 2269, 2270); **5:** 2589 (2588); **6:** 3238 (3236), 3621 (3620); **9:** 5060 (5057, 5059), 5061 (5057), 5211 (5209), 5220 (5219), 5313 (5311), 5411 (5408), 5510 (5509), 5539 (5538), 5572 (5570); **10:** 5818 (5816); **11:** 6558 (6554), 6803 (6801)
Willis R J, **3:** 1449; **5:** 2942 (2937); **6:** 3101; **9:** 5385
Willis S, **5:** 2457 (2455); **6:** 3459 (3456); **11:** 6727 (6726)
Willis S L, **1:** 239 (235, 236, 238); **5:** 2677 (2676), 2916 (2915)
Willits F K, **11:** 6798 (6796, 6797)
Willits P P, **3:** 1359 (1356, 1358)
Willits W L, **11:** 6798 (6796)
Willmot H, **3:** 1703
Willms D, **8:** 4845 (4840, 4841)
Willms J D, **4:** 1938, 1939 (1934, 1935, 1936, 1937); **5:** 2596 (2590, 2593, 2594); **7:** 3987; **8:** 4831 (4827), 4873; **10:** 5735 (5733), 5862 (5861)
Willower D J, **1:** 60 (54, 55, 56, 59); **3:** 1537 (1537); **4:** 2167 (2159, 2161)
Willows D M, **2:** 888, 1170; **11:** 6370 (6370)
Willrock M, **1:** 322
Wills S, **10:** 5625 (5622); **11:** 6712 (6709)
Willson V L, **9:** 5489 (5488); **10:** 5686 (5686)
Wilms J D, **1:** 521 (516)
Wilms W W, **8:** 4715 (4710, 4711, 4712), 4796 (4792, 4793, 4794); **11:** 6699 (6696)
Wilson A, **3:** 1793; **9:** 5394 (5390)
Wilson A L, **1:** 168 (164)
Wilson B, **1:** 239, 343 (343); **6:** 3652 (3647); **9:** 5328 (5326); **11:** 6580, 6618 (6617), 6803 (6801, 6802)
Wilson B A, **8:** 4824
Wilson B L, **6:** 3527 (3526); **8:** 4864 (4860, 4861); **9:** 5211 (5208)
Wilson C O, **4:** 2172 (2167, 2168)
Wilson D, **1:** 158 (155, 156), 162 (161); **4:** 2364 (2358); **9:** 5416 (5414)
Wilson D L, **1:** 12 (7)
Wilson D M, **4:** 2435 (2434), 2436
Wilson D N, **2:** 948; **4:** 2229 (2228); **8:** 4526 (4524), 4601 (4598); **11:** 6266 (6262, 6263)
Wilson E K, **2:** 785 (778)
Wilson E O, **4:** 2172 (2170); **5:** 2656 (2655)
Wilson F R, **11:** 6741
Wilson H A, **1:** 52; **2:** 1011 (1008)
Wilson H C, **1:** 297 (286, 287, 288, 289)
Wilson I, **1:** 120 (115)
Wilson J, **2:** 1031 (1028); **3:** 1779 (1778); **4:** 1924, 2004; **8:** 4447 (4445), 4456 (4450, 4455); **10:** 5972
Wilson J D, **1:** 193 (188); **8:** 4509 (4500)
Wilson J F, **11:** 6774, 6775
Wilson J Q, **8:** 4556 (4554)
Wilson K L, **8:** 4896 (4892)
Wilson L, **6:** 3334 (3330)
Wilson L R, **4:** 2183 (2183)
Wilson M, **1:** 42 (37), 343 (343), 390 (385), 396 (395); **3:** 1421, 1513 (1511), 1514 (1510, 1511, 1512, 1513); **5:** 2523, 2783; **6:** 3124 (3123); **7:** 4016 (4013), 4307 (4305, 4306); **9:** 5131 (5129), 5324 (5319); **11:** 6618 (6617)
Wilson N, **10:** 5625 (5623), 5961
Wilson R J, **9:** 5560 (5555)
Wilson R M, **11:** 6484 (6483, 6484)
Wilson R S, **5:** 2465 (2465); **11:** 6492 (6491)
Wilson S, **2:** 645 (641, 644); **3:** 1425
Wilson S M, **10:** 5985 (5984), 6092 (6089), 6122 (6117, 6118)
Wilson W, **2:** (1039); **7:** (4245), 4246 (4245)
Wilson W C, **5:** 2907 (2906)
Wilson W J, **2:** 692; **4:** 2212 (2211); **5:** 2942; **8:** 4896 (4891, 4895)
Wilt M E, **6:** 3443
Wiltshire D, **10:** 5708 (5706)
Wilturner L T, **4:** 1980 (1976, 1977, 1978)
Wiman R V, **7:** 3756 (3754)
Wimmer H, **8:** 4957 (4955)
Wimpelberg K, **2:** 807 (804)
Wimpelberg R K, **1:** 72 (69, 70, 72); **9:** 5281 (5276)
Wimsatt W, **4:** 2302 (2301)
Winchester I, **6:** 3416
Wincor R, **2:** 1102 (1102)
Windahl S, **1:** 570 (564, 568)
Windelband W, **9:** (5052)
Winden van F, **9:** 5355 (5353)
Winders R, **3:** 1580 (1576); **8:** 4803
Windham D M, **2:** 1042; **3:** 1386, 1416 (1412, 1414), 1810, 1820, 1821 (1812, 1813, 1818); **4:** 1938; **6:** 3578, 3597 (3595); **8:** 4509 (4504), 4568, 4708 (4706), 4936 (4931); **9:** 5168 (5161); **10:** 5607 (5605); **11:** 6265 (6262), 6298 (6293)
Windmayer S M, **6:** 3227 (3225)
Windmuller J P, **7:** 4263 (4261)
Windschuttle E, **11:** 6735 (6732)
Windsor J, **1:** 409 (404, 405)
Windsor K, **4:** 2287 (2285)
Wineburg S S, **7:** 4175 (4172); **9:** 5563 (5561); **10:** 6092 (6089), 6122 (6118); **11:** 6511 (6509)
Winegarden C R, **5:** 2744 (2741)
Winer B J, **9:** 4974 (4969), 4995 (4984)
Wines R, **1:** 41 (38)
Wing L, **6:** 3235 (3232, 3233)
Winger M, **4:** 1924 (1922)
Wingersky M S, **5:** 3043 (3041), 3055 (3053); **11:** 6355 (6353)
Winitzky N, **6:** 3202 (3198); **9:** 5318 (5315, 5316)
Winkler A, **11:** 6712 (6709)

Winkler D, **4:** 2316 (2311); **8:** 4836 (4832, 4834)
Winkler M, **5:** 2692 (2691)
Winkler R L, **1:** 480
Winn M, **6:** 3625 (3622)
Winn W D, **2:** 1020; **5:** 2874 (2872); **7:** 3743 (3742)
Winne P H, **6:** 3345; **10:** 5745 (5739, 5741, 5743), 6193 (6188, 6189, 6192), 6208 (6206), 6240 (6238)
Winnicott D W, **8:** (4813)
Winnubst J A M, **10:** 5924 (5923)
Winograd P, **6:** 3334 (3332); **9:** 5363
Winograd T W, **3:** 1434 (1432, 1433)
Winstead B A, **10:** 5758, 5759
Winston B, **5:** 2470 (2468)
Winston C, **7:** 4255
Winston P H, **2:** 857 (852)
Winston R, **2:** 1165
Winter C, **3:** 1461
Winter D, **4:** 1991 (1986)
Winter P D, **9:** 5467 (5460)
Winter R, **1:** 48 (45); **10:** 6099 (6098)
Wintrobe R, **3:** 1745 (1741)
Wiratchai N, **2:** 824 (822, 823); **7:** 3886 (3883)
Wirszup I, **7:** 4100
Wirt F M, **2:** 1042 (1038); **3:** 1486 (1483); **7:** 3840 (3835, 3837), 4246 (4241); **8:** 4408 (4404), 4602
Wirt J G, **10:** 5919 (5914); **11:** 6538 (6535)
Wirth A, **3:** 1524
Wisdom J, **8:** 4447 (4442)
Wise A, **3:** 1412 (1407); **9:** 5318 (5316)
Wise A E, **4:** 2132 (2126); **6:** 3360; **10:** 6044 (6036, 6037), 6047
Wise D A, **10:** 5846; **11:** 6633 (6628)
Wise E, **9:** 5255
Wise J H, **3:** 1537 (1536)
Wise L L, **4:** 2436 (2433); **9:** 5131 (5127)
Wise S, **4:** 2302; **5:** 2457 (2455)
Wise S L, **1:** 53 (51); **2:** 998; **10:** 6020
Wiseman D, **10:** 6106 (6105)
Wiseman D L, **9:** 5318 (5315)
Wiseman S, **7:** 3936 (3933)
Wisenbaker J M, **4:** 1934 (1929, 1930, 1932); **9:** 5210 (5207)
Wishnia J, **10:** 6079 (6073)
Wishnick T K, **5:** 2856 (2854)
Wiske M S, **3:** 1624 (1623); **11:** 6287 (6286)
Wisler C F, **2:** 631 (629)
Wisner A, **4:** 2012 (2008)
Wisniewski R, **10:** 6012 (6009, 6011)
Wiśniewski W, **10:** 5614 (5611)
Wiss C, **4:** 2351 (2350)
Wissing J, **11:** 6659 (6657)
Wissoker D A, **2:** 692 (690, 691)
Wit G de, **9:** 5355 (5353)
Witherell C, **10:** 5818 (5816), 5939 (5937)
Withers G A, **3:** 1448 (1447)
Withers H L, **3:** (1723)
Withnall A M E, **7:** 4249 (4247); **8:** 4616 (4613)
Witkin B R, **7:** 4060 (4057, 4059)
Witkin H A, **2:** 872 (868); **3:** 1241 (1239)
Witle S, **11:** 6780
Witmer D, **1:** 521 (518)
Witnov S J, **10:** 5591 (5588)
Witszup Z, **6:** 3671
Witt J C, **1:** 495; **3:** 1513, 1514; **11:** 6484 (6484), 6678
Witt P W F, **4:** 1899 (1889)
Witte J F, **1:** 594 (591); **8:** 4408, 4887 (4886); **9:** 5065 (5063), 5066, 5201, 5206 (5202, 5203, 5204), 5308; **10:** 6083; **11:** 6558 (6554)
Wittebols J H, **2:** 775 (771, 773)
Wittels N E, **4:** 2011 (2011)
Witten B J, **10:** 6020 (6017)
Wittenborn J R, **8:** 4857 (4855)
Wittgenstein L, **3:** (1524); **4:** 2001 (1999), 2377 (2375); **5:** (2579); **6:** 3155 (3152); **7:** (3920); **8:** 4447 (4442, 4444), 4456 (4448, 4450, 4452), 4461 (4460), 4634 (4633), (4640); **9:** 4981 (4978)
Wittich C, **2:** 785
Wittig B A, **5:** 2806
Wittig M A, **9:** 5432 (5428, 5429); **10:** 5826
Wittmann W W, **4:** 2089 (2082, 2086)
Wittner J, **7:** 4336 (4332)
Witton E, **6:** 3373 (3371)
Wittrock M C, **1:** 23, 377 (376); **2:** 796 (792), 802, 811, 816, 820, 846, 888; **3:** 1257, 1387, 1494, 1529, 1530, 1544 (1538, 1539), 1804; **4:** 1847, 1848, 1898; **5:** 2585, 2767, 2779, 2874, (2879), 2884; **6:** 3329, 3335, 3655; **7:** 3726, 3743, 3753, 3760, 3792, 3924; **8:** 4403, 4864, 4881; **9:** 5030, 5043, 5223, 5264, 5373, 5411, 5507, 5563; **10:** 5745 (5739), 5750, 5772, 5775 (5772), 5790 (5784, 5785), 5831 (5830, 5831), 6012, 6015, 6020, 6031, 6034, 6043, 6088, 6103, 6106, 6117, 6121, 6143, 6155, 6158, 6169, 6173, 6178 (6173, 6176), 6183, 6207, 6208, 6239; **11:** 6384, 6511 (6510), 6604 (6602)
Wivatchai N, **5:** 2869 (2868, 2869)
Wixson K K, **6:** 3329 (3327); **8:** 4882 (4877); **9:** 5363
Wlodkowski R J, **7:** 3946 (3943)
Wodtke K H, **1:** 362 (361)
Woelfel J, **3:** 1830 (1828)
Woelfel N, **5:** 2891 (2890)
Wohlwill J F, **5:** 2665 (2659), 2680 (2679)
Wolcott H F, **1:** 60 (55), 297 (284); **3:** 1729 (1726, 1727, 1728), 1756 (1755), 1775 (1771); **4:** (2043), 2053 (2050, 2051); **7:** 3974 (3972), 4319 (4316); **9:** 5220 (5219), 5313 (5312); **10:** 6086 (6085)
Wold D, **8:** 4359 (4355)
Wold H, **4:** 2140 (2137); **8:** 4359 (4352, 4353, 4356, 4357)
Wolery M, **1:** 362 (360, 361); **5:** 2814 (2808)
Wolf B, **5:** 2479 (2478)
Wolf D, **4:** 1939 (1936); **10:** 6178 (6177)
Wolf D P, **1:** 199 (198); **7:** 3726 (3724); **11:** 6785 (6784)
Wolf E, **4:** 2440 (2438)
Wolf J, **5:** 2491 (2488)
Wolf R L, **3:** 1283 (1282); **4:** (2103)
Wolf R M, **1:** 396 (392); **3:** 1483 (1477); **4:** 2089 (2083, 2084), 2249 (2245); **8:** 4887 (4886); **11:** 6328 (6326)
Wolfe A, **4:** 1985 (1982); **6:** 3368 (3367)
Wolfe B L, **2:** 1056; **3:** 1820 (1815); **4:** 1972 (1971), 2212 (2210); **6:** 3144 (3139, 3143)
Wolfe D A, **1:** 19 (16), 20
Wolfe D M, **10:** 5924 (5920, 5921), 6062 (6060)
Wolfe R, **2:** 1131 (1128)
Wolfendale S, **6:** 3463 (3461, 3462)
Wolfensberger W, **3:** 1438 (1435), 1507, 1508 (1505); **10:** 5663 (5662)
Wolff E N, **11:** 6260 (6260)
Wolff L, **2:** 1127 (1123), 1146; **8:** 4708 (4703); **9:** 5241 (5240)
Wolfgang A, **2:** 802; **7:** 4175
Wolfle L, **4:** 2412 (2411)
Wolford B I, **1:** 494 (493); **3:** 1441 (1438, 1440)
Wolfram S, **6:** 3685 (3681)
Wolfram W, **6:** 3228 (3225)
Wolgast E H, **4:** 2297 (2293)
Wolleat P E, **9:** 5432 (5430)
Wolman B B, **5:** 2665, 2921, 2922
Wolmark J, **11:** 6731
Wolpert R L, **9:** 5467 (5466)
Wolpin K I, **9:** 5355 (5353)
Wolstenholme F, **7:** 4293
Wolter K H, **5:** 3061 (3057)
Wolter K M, **9:** 5131 (5125), 5142 (5136)
Wolterhoff B, **1:** 139
Wolters C, **1:** 89
Wolters M A, **6:** 3292
Woltz D J, **5:** 2768 (2763)
Wolvin A, **6:** 3442 (3439, 3441)
Womack S T, **7:** 4293 (4291); **10:** 6012 (6011)
Wonderly D, **5:** 2669 (2668)
Wong A, **3:** 1602 (1600)
Wong B Y L, **2:** 868 (861); **8:** 4882 (4878)
Wong D B, **7:** 3925
Wong G Y, **5:** 2596 (2590, 2591, 2594, 2595); **7:** 3986 (3980, 3982, 3986), 3987 (3986)
Wong K K, **1:** 594 (589, 591); **7:** 3826 (3823); **11:** 6558, 6563
Wong R, **2:** 868 (861); **5:** 2642; **7:** 4325 (4323)
Wong R S-K, **9:** 5553 (5551)
Wong S Y, **1:** 353
Wong Y C, **9:** 5076
Wongbundhit Y, **7:** 3987 (3984)
Wonnacott C A, **8:** 4881 (4880)
Woock R, **11:** 6803 (6802)
Wood A, **10:** 5617 (5616)
Wood A E, **9:** 5510 (5508)
Wood A W, **7:** 4145 (4142)
Wood B S, **6:** 3443 (3441)
Wood C, **11:** 6538 (6536)
Wood D J, **3:** 1402 (1401)
Wood F H, **1:** 490 (487, 488)
Wood G, **3:** 1337 (1336)
Wood J E Jr, **1:** 265
Wood J M, **9:** 5252 (5247)
Wood P, **10:** 6062 (6061)
Wood P D P, **8:** 4473 (4469)

Wood R, **7:** 3912 (3906, 3911), 4000 (3998), 4196 (4195); **8:** 4623 (4618)
Wood R C, **9:** 5185
Wood R H, **3:** 1655 (1651)
Wood S, **6:** 3560 (3559); **11:** 6261 (6257), 6277 (6272, 6273)
Wood S F, **9:** 5082 (5079)
Wood T, **2:** 1052; **3:** 1257 (1256); **6:** 3660 (3659), 3670 (3670), 3684, 3685; **8:** 4882 (4877)
Woodall T D, **7:** 3726
Woodcock R W, **5:** 2922 (2917)
Woodhall M, **2:** 652 (652), 1131 (1128, 1129, 1131); **3:** 1655 (1648); **5:** 2647 (2646), 2744; **6:** 3184 (3179, 3181), 3613 (3610); **8:** 4531 (4528), 4707 (4705); **10:** 5754 (5753), 5767, 5768 (5763, 5765, 5766, 5767); **11:** 6298 (6294)
Woodhead M, **1:** 239; **3:** 1643 (1640)
Woodley A, **1:** 94; **7:** 4171; **11:** 6551 (6548)
Woodley K K, **3:** 1530 (1526)
Wood-Robinson C, **6:** 3416 (3409, 3410)
Woodrow H, **1:** 6 (2); **5:** (2919)
Woodrow M, **7:** 4171 (4166)
Woodruff C, **8:** 4474 (4469)
Woodruff D S, **7:** 4170 (4169)
Woodruff E, **2:** 1006 (1004, 1006)
Woodruff R A, **9:** 5131 (5129)
Woods D D, **10:** 5914 (5912)
Woods J, **2:** 1208 (1207); **8:** 4447 (4446)
Woods M, **5:** 2725 (2723)
Woods P, **2:** 893 (891), 1073, 1074 (1070, 1071); **4:** 2053 (2047); **7:** 3826 (3825), 3977 (3977); **9:** 5060, 5313 (5311, 5312), 5411 (5408); **10:** 5614 (5608), 6126, 6127 (6125), 6139 (6133), 6214, 6215 (6210)
Woodward A, **3:** 1494; **11:** 6370 (6369, 6370), 6371 (6367, 6368)
Woodward J, **3:** 1529 (1527)
Woodward V A, **4:** 1962 (1958, 1960); **10:** 5795 (5793)
Woodward W H, **4:** 2007
Woodworth R S, **1:** 396; **3:** 1301 (1296); **5:** (2878); **8:** 4731 (4729); **9:** (5053); **11:** 6457 (6453)
Woody T, **11:** 6765 (6764)
Woodyard E, **5:** 2921 (2916, 2917, 2919); **7:** 4329 (4326)
Woolever R M, **9:** 5578
Wooley H T, **9:** (5433)
Woolf M, **7:** 4293 (4290, 4291, 4292)
Woolf V, **4:** (2292)
Woolfe R, **2:** 1165 (1161, 1162, 1163, 1164)
Woolfolk A E, **7:** 4175 (4171, 4174)
Woolhouse J, **9:** 5192 (5187)
Woolhouse R S, **6:** 3499
Woollacott M, **7:** 3950
Woolner P, **4:** 1924 (1923); **5:** 2689 (2687)
Woolnough B E, **8:** 4648 (4645); **9:** 5299 (5297), 5328 (5324)
Woolsey S, **5:** 2673 (2671)
Word E, **2:** 775 (774)
Worden R L, **7:** 3906
Work W C, **8:** 4779 (4777)
Working R, **4:** 2388 (2384)
Worpole K, **10:** 6139 (6138)
Worrall N, **9:** 5359 (5356)
Worsham M E, **2:** 820; **10:** 6031 (6028)
Worsley A, **5:** 2571 (2569)
Worster-Drought C, **10:** 5681 (5676)
Worswick G D N, **11:** 6640
Worth A G, **9:** 5523
Worth M, **6:** 3213
Worth V, **7:** 4220 (4215)
Worthen B R, **2:** 1136 (1134); **3:** 1283 (1280, 1281, 1282); **4:** 2097 (2089), 2109 (2101, 2102, 2104, 2105, 2108), 2119 (2110, 2111, 2113, 2114, 2115, 2117, 2118); **8:** 4766; **11:** 6445 (6443)
Worthke W, **4:** 2089 (2088)
Wortman C B, **8:** 4719; **9:** 5406
Wortman P M, **4:** 2089 (2081); **9:** 5372 (5371)
Wosniak A, **11:** 6292 (6289)
Wothke W, **7:** 4007 (4003, 4006)
Woyach R B, **4:** 1995 (1994)
Woytanowitz G M, **1:** 94
Wozniak G, **4:** 2212 (2211)
Wozniak R H, **3:** 1647
Wragg E C, **2:** 1121 (1119); **6:** 3389 (3386, 3388); **10:** 5977 (5975), 6020
Wragg T, **10:** 5834 (5832, 5833)
Wrangham R W, **5:** 2685
Wren T E, **7:** 3920, 3925 (3921)
Wright B D, **1:** 52 (51); **3:** 1514 (1510, 1513); **4:** 2017 (2012, 2016); **5:** 2783 (2780), 2784 (2781, 2783), 3043 (3041), 3051 (3049), 3055 (3053); **6:** 3124 (3122); **7:** 4307 (4304, 4305, 4306); **8:** 4923 (4921); **10:** 5668 (5665), 5791 (5788); **11:** 6349 (6348), 6355 (6353), 6604 (6602)
Wright C, **4:** 1991 (1986); **10:** 5827 (5824)
Wright C A, **11:** 6266
Wright C A H, **2:** 645 (642)
Wright C J, **8:** 4882 (4879)
Wright C R, **11:** 6579 (6577)
Wright E, **2:** 991 (990)
Wright E N, **2:** 775 (773)
Wright G H von, **9:** 5056
Wright H F, **1:** 230 (229)
Wright I, **2:** 1208
Wright J, **6:** 3625 (3623); **7:** 3889 (3887)
Wright J C, **11:** 6538 (6530)
Wright J D, **5:** 2672 (2670); **7:** 3861; **10:** 5862 (5860)
Wright J M, **1:** 390 (383); **7:** 3707 (3703)
Wright J W, **9:** 5512 (5510)
Wright N D, **4:** 2033 (2032)
Wright P, **4:** 2012 (2009, 2010)
Wright R, **10:** 6132 (6130)
Wright R D, **5:** 2942
Wright S, **8:** 4352 (4339)
Wright S R, **4:** 2119 (2111)
Wright T L, **1:** 239 (238); **11:** 6360 (6358, 6359)
Wrightson P, **2:** (735)
Wringe C, **3:** 1328 (1326); **11:** 6580 (6578)
Writer J, **3:** 1406 (1405)
Wrong D H, **10:** 6127 (6123)
Wronski S, **2:** 770
Wrzesniewski K, **4:** 1967
Wu A, **4:** 2440 (2438)
Wu C C, **1:** 254
Wu C F J, **9:** 5130 (5128)
Wu D, **9:** 5313 (5311)
Wu D Y H, **2:** 1213 (1210)
Wu L L, **9:** 5082 (5077, 5081)
Wubbels T, **2:** 811 (809), 820 (819, 820); **10:** 5775 (5773), 5812 (5812)
Wulf C, **3:** 1733
Wulf K M, **9:** 5359 (5357)
Wulfemeyer K T, **2:** 1079 (1075)
Wulfing I, **2:** 738 (737)
Wundt W M, **3:** (1722), (1723); **4:** (1864), (1865), (1866), (1867); **5:** (2647), 2665 (2656), (2875), (2876), (2877), (2917); **6:** (3316); **9:** (5053)
Wunsch J, **8:** 4514 (4513)
Wunt W, **3:** 1797 (1793, 1794)
Wurf E, **9:** 5394 (5393)
Wurgaft J, **7:** 4155 (4149, 4154)
Wurzburg G K, **4:** 2394 (2389); **8:** 4964 (4963)
Wyatt D H, **7:** 4095 (4091)
Wyatt T, **5:** 2500 (2497)
Wyckoff D C, **9:** 5008 (5006)
Wykstra R A, **11:** 6425
Wylie I, **4:** 2292 (2290)
Wylie L, **1:** 297 (281); **2:** 918 (915); **9:** 5313 (5311)
Wylie R C, **9:** 5394 (5390)
Wyllie M, **10:** 5704 (5699, 5700); **11:** 6784 (6784)
Wyn J, **11:** 6803 (6801, 6802)
Wyndhamna J, **8:** 4951 (4949)
Wyner N B, **9:** 5211 (5209); **10:** 6187
Wynn D, **9:** 5324 (5321)
Wynn R, **7:** 4301 (4298)
Wynne B, **9:** 5350 (5349)

Xanthopoulos J A, **9:** 5130 (5129)
Xenophon, **2:** (804); **11:** (6742)
Xerri C, **6:** 3593
Xie Y, **7:** 3864 (3863)
Xu H, **9:** 5281
Xu H Y, **2:** 749
Xue Muqiao, **2:** 755

Yackel E, **3:** 1257 (1256); **6:** 3660 (3659), 3670 (3670); **8:** 4882 (4877)
Yacoub S A, **10:** 5843
Yaden D, **4:** 1962
Yager R E, **9:** 5324 (5321), 5345 (5343, 5344, 5345)
Yahouza I, **7:** 4124
Yaici L, **10:** 5843
Yakimanskaya I S, **5:** 2769 (2762)
Yakovlev P I, **1:** 15 (13)
Yakuba Yu, **10:** 5649 (5647)
Yalow E, **5:** 2921 (2917, 2921)
Yamada T, **4:** 2212 (2211)
Yamamoto K, **3:** 1514 (1511)
Yamauchi H, **5:** 2651 (2649)
Yamauchi Y, **7:** 3947
Yan Xu Hong, **11:** 6551 (6550)
Yanagisawa S, **8:** 4473 (4470)
Yandila C D, **1:** 244 (241)
Yankelovitch N, **5:** 2709 (2706)

Yano Y, **4:** 2339 (2337)
Yanok J, **2:** 730 (721)
Yao T, **5:** 2784 (2780)
Yap J Y C, **9:** 5485
Yap L, **5:** 2945 (2944)
Yarbrough C, **3:** 1252 (1248)
Yarger S, **10:** 6012 (6009)
Yarmol-Franko K, **5:** 2961 (2959)
Yarnit M, **7:** 4263 (4262)
Yates A, **9:** 5389 (5388)
Yates B A, **11:** 6741 (6737)
Yates C, **8:** 4478 (4476)
Yates F, **1:** 42 (40), 389 (388); **7:** 3858, 4015 (4009); **9:** 5142
Yates F A, **7:** 3768 (3764)
Yates J R, **6:** 3232 (3230, 3231)
Yates J W, **10:** 6004 (6001)
Yates L, **4:** 2292 (2291); **7:** 3853 (3849, 3850); **11:** 6727 (6726)
Yat-ming J L, **7:** 4236 (4234)
Yauger D, **9:** 5539 (5537)
Yavas M, **10:** 5697
Yazdani N, **2:** 1175 (1171)
Yazykova V S, **9:** 5098
Yeager K E, **2:** 693 (690, 691, 692)
Yeakey C, **4:** 2423 (2423)
Yeazell M I, **10:** 5939 (5936)
Yee A H, **6:** 3545; **10:** 6004 (6001)
Yellen J L, **3:** 1703
Yelon S, **5:** 2856 (2853)
Yeloushan, **4:** 2427 (2424)
Yembe O W, **2:** 617, 618
Yen W, **11:** 6355 (6354)
Yeoh O C, **9:** 5485
Yeoman L, **2:** 834 (834)
Yeomans A R J, **9:** 5544 (5541)
Yeomans R, **4:** 2166 (2163)
Yerkes R M, **5:** (2878); **6:** 3325 (3318)
Yerushalmy M, **7:** 4100 (4097)
Yesavage J A, **1:** 239 (238)
Yeung W Y W A, **4:** 1857 (1854)
Yi L, **7:** 4006 (4005)
Yifhar Y, **5:** 3028
Yin A L S, **9:** 5302 (5300, 5301)
Yinger J M, **8:** 4896 (4891)
Yinger M, **3:** 1240
Yinger R J, **10:** 6034 (6032, 6033), 6035 (6032, 6033), 6088 (6087)
Yip H K, **11:** 6298 (6297)
Yip J S K, **9:** 5485 (5484)
Yip L, **2:** 1079 (1075, 1076); **9:** 5302 (5300)
Yip Y H, **8:** 4531 (4530)
Yip Y S W, **9:** 5485
Ylieff Y, **1:** 504
Yli-Luoma P V J, **2:** 958 (954)
Yodder J H, **1:** 552
Yoder C P, **1:** 280
Yoder D, **6:** 3227
Yogev A, **1:** 12 (7); **8:** 4571 (4571); **9:** 5367 (5366)
Yoloye E A, **3:** 1278 (1274, 1277); **7:** 4132; **9:** 5389 (5387)
Yonas A, **8:** 4383 (4381)
Yonge G D, **1:** 277
York H, **5:** 2907
York J, **5:** 2814 (2809)
Yorkston K M, **1:** 408 (407)
Youdi R V, **6:** 3613 (3611); **8:** 4531 (4527)
Young A, **6:** 3209 (3206, 3208)
Young B, **2:** 733 (732)
Young C, **2:** 910 (907)
Young D, **6:** 3202 (3198); **9:** 5433 (5430)
Young D R, **5:** 2673 (2671)
Young F W, **9:** 5159 (5158)
Young G, **9:** 5158 (5156)
Young I M, **9:** 5441
Young J H, **10:** 6092 (6091)
Young J I, **6:** 3202 (3198)
Young K E, **1:** 28
Young K R, **10:** 6164
Young M F D, **1:** 11; **2:** 785 (783), 1073, 1074 (1071); **3:** 1308, 1334 (1330, 1333), 1337 (1335), 1347, 1348 (1343, 1344, 1345), 1563 (1559); **5:** 2903; **6:** 3151, 3621 (3618); **7:** 3771 (3769); **9:** 5298, 5299 (5297), 5318 (5316), 5554 (5550); **10:** 5607 (5600); **11:** 6395 (6391)
Young M J, **10:** 5943 (5940)
Young M L, **11:** 6283 (6278)
Young P, **6:** 3463 (3462)
Young R, **10:** 6163 (6163)
Young R E, **2:** 1204 (1199); **6:** 3373; **10:** 6197 (6196)
Young R L, **6:** 3373
Youngblade L, **2:** 856 (854)
Youngday D J, **3:** 1449 (1447)
Youngman F, **1:** 135 (129, 132); **10:** 5596 (5592)
Youniss J, **8:** 4372 (4369, 4371); **9:** 5512 (5511); **10:** 5758 (5757)
Youssef N H, **3:** 1676; **11:** 6760 (6758)
Youtz R, **3:** 1655 (1650)
Yrjola P, **11:** 6438 (6433, 6435, 6436)
Ysseldyke J E, **2:** 718 (712, 714, 715, 716), 719 (712, 714, 715, 716); **6:** 3297 (3294); **7:** 3833 (3831), 4081; **8:** 4936 (4931); **9:** 5071 (5069); **10:** 5686 (5683), 6173 (6169, 6170, 6172); **11:** 6315 (6314)
Yu B, **2:** 749
Yu L, **2:** 998 (992)
Yudof M G, **6:** 3276 (3274), 3360; **9:** 5255
Yuen K, **9:** 5471 (5470)
Yuille J C, **7:** 3774
Yukl G, **6:** 3306 (3304, 3305)
Yule G, **6:** 3209 (3208)
Yule G U, **4:** 1872 (1867)
Yule W, **2:** 1084 (1079); **3:** 1520 (1515); **6:** 3224
Yusofzia Aziz Ahmand, **1:** 210
Yusuf S, **7:** 3906
Yuval-Davis N, **7:** 3852 (3849); **9:** 5216

Zaal J N, **2:** 998; **3:** 1421; **11:** 6334
Zabalza A, **3:** 1449 (1447); **6:** 3262; **8:** 4526 (4522); **9:** 5076 (5072, 5073)
Zabarah M A, **11:** 6794
Zachariah M, **1:** 135 (132, 133); **2:** 1049; **3:** 1501 (1495, 1497), 1690 (1688); **4:** 1841 (1837); **11:** 6452 (6447)
Zafar F, **11:** 6760 (6755)
Zagar D, **8:** 4939 (4938)
Zager R, **4:** 1976 (1975); **6:** 3197 (3193); **10:** 6083 (6080)
Zahn K G, **5:** 2870 (2869)
Zahn-Waxler C, **2:** 705 (702); **8:** 4799 (4797, 4798, 4799)
Zahorik J A, **10:** 5887, 6015 (6014), 6035 (6032, 6033)
Zainu'ddin A, **11:** 6735 (6731, 6732, 6734)
Zajda J, **9:** 5539 (5538); **11:** 6266 (6262)
Zajochowski R, **8:** 4942 (4941)
Zajonc R B, **4:** 2257 (2253); **5:** 2665 (2662); **7:** 3872 (3869), 3873 (3869, 3870); **8:** 4799
Zaki M, **8:** 4708 (4703, 4705)
Zammit S J, **3:** 1491
Zammuner V L, **4:** 2449 (2447); **8:** 4951 (4949)
Zampieri P, **1:** 554
Zanardi L, **1:** 554
Zandberg T, **3:** 1520
Zander A, **5:** 2532 (2529, 2530, 2531)
Zane N, **11:** 6726 (6726)
Zane T, **10:** 5674 (5671)
Zanga J R, **9:** 5291 (5284)
Zanna M P, **5:** 2768
Zappin M, **10:** 5697
Zappolo A, **2:** 730 (722); **3:** 1438 (1436)
Zara A R, **1:** 52 (49, 50, 51)
Zaragoza N, **1:** 495
Zarcadoolas C, **3:** 1402 (1399)
Zarembka P, **3:** 1425
Zarifian P, **11:** 6272 (6268)
Zarkin G A, **3:** 1449 (1447); **6:** 3101
Zaslow M E, **2:** 692 (689, 690, 691, 692), 700 (696); **3:** 1642 (1640), 1643 (1639); **8:** 4666 (4665)
Zavaloni M, **10:** 5782 (5781)
Zax M, **1:** 362; **3:** 1643 (1637, 1641)
Zeanah C, **3:** 1642
Zecha G, **11:** 6580 (6577)
Zeckhauser R, **3:** 1425
Zegarra H, **11:** 6558 (6552), 6563 (6559)
Zegeye A, **7:** 4201 (4199)
Zegveld W, **11:** 6260 (6259)
Zeichner K M, **1:** 48 (45); **3:** 1636 (1632, 1633); **8:** 4948 (4945); **10:** 5585 (5584), 5948, 5961 (5960), 6044 (6038), 6048, 6099 (6098), 6127 (6126), 6219 (6218)
Zeigler H, **2:** 1042 (1038); **8:** 4587 (4582, 4585, 4586)
Zeitsman A, **8:** 4479 (4476)
Zeitz C M, **4:** 2199 (2197)
Zeizinger H, **6:** 3276
Zelditch M Jr, **9:** 5175 (5171)
Zelenak B S, **3:** 1315 (1309); **7:** 4185; **8:** 4736 (4735)
Zeller N, **4:** 2375 (2374)
Zeller R A, **11:** 6576 (6573, 6574)
Zellermayer M, **9:** 5363 (5362)
Zelli A, **1:** 234 (230)
Zellner A, **6:** 3508
Zelniker T, **2:** 871 (870); **5:** 2669; **8:** 4383
Zeman B R, **9:** 5358 (5356)
Zemke R, **6:** 3096 (3094); **8:** 4758 (4754); **10:** 5914 (5912)
Zenger T R, **4:** 1972 (1969)
Zetterberg H L, **9:** 5553 (5552)

Zetterström K, **6:** 3393 (3393)
Zevin J, **9:** 5582 (5581)
Zhang J, **1:** 244 (240)
Zhang X D, **10:** 6202
Zhang Y, **8:** 4945 (4943)
Zhao A X, **10:** 6202 (6200)
Zhongyuan W U, **8:** 4468
Zhou Tianxing, **11:** 6452 (6450)
Ziderman A, **2:** 760 (758), 1152; **3:** 1713 (1710, 1711); **4:** 2316 (2315); **5:** 3003 (3001); **6:** 3616 (3615); **8:** 4364 (4361, 4362), 4519 (4515), 4531 (4529); **9:** 5076 (5072, 5073, 5074, 5075), 5355 (5353); **10:** 5767 (5766, 5767), 5919; **11:** 6266 (6262), 6282 (6281), 6424 (6424), 6430 (6427), 6431 (6428, 6430), 6633 (6628), 6638 (6633), 6663 (6660, 6661, 6662, 6663)
Ziedler D L, **10:** 6178 (6176, 6177)
Ziegler E F, **8:** 4467 (4465)
Ziegler R W, **5:** 2725
Ziegler S, **2:** 1099 (1098)
Ziegler W L, **4:** 2331
Ziehe T, **11:** (6802)
Ziehen J, **3:** (1722)
Zieky M J, **7:** 4056 (4055); **10:** 5726 (5722, 5724)
Zielinska K, **11:** 6647 (6641)
Zigerell J, **1:** 564
Zigler E F, **1:** 19 (17); **2:** 693, 701; **3:** 1643 (1640); **4:** 2145; **5:** 2665 (2658), 2673 (2671); **7:** 4300, 4301 (4297); **11:** 6384 (6382)
Zigmond N, **4:** 2208 (2200)
Zill N, **2:** 711 (708)
Ziller T, **3:** (1290)
Ziman J, **6:** 3205 (3203)
Zimbalist A, **11:** 6261 (6257)
Zimmer J, **2:** 910
Zimmer J M, **10:** 5591 (5588)
Zimmerer L K, **4:** 2440 (2437)
Zimmerman B J, **1:** 377 (376); **6:** 3297 (3295), 3329 (3325, 3326), 3335 (3332), 3340 (3335), 3345; **7:** 3788 (3785); **9:** 5518 (5514); **10:** 5745 (5743, 5744), 5750 (5745)
Zimmerman J, **3:** 1441 (1439)
Zimmerman M P, **7:** 4026 (4023)
Zimmermann E, **3:** 1355 (1354)
Zimowski M, **2:** 678 (672, 673, 674)
Zimpher N L, **10:** 5929 (5926, 5928), 5958 (5955), 6004 (6002), 6012 (6009), 6106 (6104, 6105)
Zinchenko V P, **9:** 5098
Zinck R A, **2:** 738 (733)
Zins J E, **5:** 2907 (2905); **8:** 4661 (4657), 4662 (4658, 4659); **9:** 5290 (5287); **11:** 6484
Ziolkowski U, **11:** 6684
Zipfel G, **11:** 6747 (6746)
Zissman S B, **7:** 3753 (3744)
Zloczower A, **10:** 5782 (5776)
Zlotlow S, **11:** 6360 (6356)
Zlotnik M, **10:** 6012 (6011)
Znaniecki F, **2:** 785 (784); **11:** 6466 (6463)
Zodhiates P P, **9:** 5211
Zoellick B, **2:** 649
Zohar A, **2:** 1175 (1173); **6:** 3416 (3412)
Zollers N J, **10:** 6244 (6241)
Zorfass J, **7:** 3808 (3806)
Zsigmond Z, **3:** 1453 (1451, 1452)
Zuber-Skerritt O, **2:** 1019
Zuboff S, **4:** 1958 (1955); **9:** 5233 (5230); **11:** 6416
Zubrzycki J, **7:** 3721 (3717)
Zuccarello M, **1:** 554
Zucchermaglio C, **9:** 5562 (5561)
Zuck L, **9:** 5210
Zucker K J, **4:** 2452 (2451)
Zuckerman B, **3:** 1643 (1639)
Zuckerman H, **1:** 60 (58); **11:** 6712 (6709)
Zuckerman J V, **10:** 6143 (6141)
Zuckerman M, **7:** 3947
Zukas M, **3:** 1602; **10:** 6058
Zuliani A, **5:** 3036
Zumwalt K, **3:** 1804 (1802)
Zuñiga L, **7:** 4290 (4284)
Zutavern M, **10:** 5939 (5936)
Zutell J, **8:** 4947; **10:** 5705 (5702)
Zvobgo R J, **11:** 6821
Zvulun E, **7:** 4316 (4308)
Zwaenepoel P P, **1:** 244
Zwarts M A, **2:** 998 (993); **5:** 3043 (3042)
Zwick R, **7:** 3861 (3861); **11:** 6355 (6351, 6354)
Zwicker T, **9:** 5216 (5215)
Zwingli U, **6:** (3531)
Zygmunt C, **4:** 1976 (1974)
Zymelman M, **2:** 1152; **3:** 1830 (1827); **8:** 4531; **11:** 6266 (6263), 6638 (6635)
Zytowski D G, **11:** 6321 (6318)

SUBJECT INDEX

The Subject Index has been compiled as a guide to the reader who is interested in locating all the references to a particular subject area within this *Encyclopedia*.

Every effort has been made to index as comprehensively as possible, and to standardize the terms used in the index. Given the diverse nature of the field and the varied use of terms throughout the international community, synonyms and foreign language terms have been included with appropriate cross-references. As a general rule, the selection of preferred terms has followed the recommendations given in the *Thesaurus of ERIC Descriptors, 12th Edition* 1990, Oryx Press, Phoenix, Arizona, ISBN 0-89774-561-2. Foreign language terms are given in italics.

The index entries are presented in word-by-word alphabetical sequence in which a group of letters followed by a space is filed before the same group of letters followed by a letter; for example, "Art therapy" is filed before "Articulation (education)." The index is arranged in set-out style, with a maximum of three levels of heading, and location references refer to volume number (in bold) and page number (separated by a colon); major coverage of a subject is indicated by bold, italicized page numbers; for example:

"Courseware
and computer literacy courses **5**: 1234
design **5**: ***1212–1223***"

"*See*" cross-references direct the user to the preferred term; for example:

"Learning time
See Time on task"

"*See also*" cross-references provide the user with guideposts to terms of related interest, from the broader term to the narrower, and appear at the end of the main heading to which they refer; for example:

"Curriculum
See also
Core curriculum
Hidden curriculum
Modular curriculum
Student-centered curriculum"

A List of Foreign Terms and a List of Abbreviations and Acronyms are provided at the end of this index for quick and easy access to the terms used within the index.

Ability
and academic achievement
interaction effects **5:** 2926
and aptitude **1:** ***1–6***
definitions of **1:** 146
computer-assisted testing
algorithm for **5:** 2781
and computerized adaptive testing **2:** 993
conceptions of **1:** 201
Confucian theory **2:** 1044
and contingency tables
item bias procedures **5:** 3045
distinguished from aptitude **6:** 3312
and earnings **3:** 1659, 1704; **5:** 2645
effects of television viewing on **1:** 568
and energy expenditure **1:** 201, 202
achievement need **1:** 29
parent attitudes **5:** 2627
estimation of
and computer-assisted testing **5:** 2780
and maximum likelihood statistics **4:** 2014
individual differences **1:** ***1–6***, 375
and intelligence tests **7:** 3769
and item response theory **4:** 2012
and item sampling **5:** 3056
and learning **5:** 2760
measurement of **7:** 3700, 3702, 3878
and performance
in instructional alignment **5:** 2855
sex differences in
origins of **9:** 5428
taxonomy of factors **5:** 2760
testing
and Bayesian statistics **1:** 477
tests of
characteristics **11:** 6341
types of **1:** 146
vs. cognitive style **2:** 869
See also
Academic ability
Aptitude
Cognitive ability
Gifted
Spatial ability
Talent
Verbal ability
Ability grouping **1:** ***6–12***; **2:** ***821–825***
academic achievement **2:** 824; **9:** 5170
and academically gifted **9:** 5531
classroom research **2:** 822

and classrooms
interpersonal relationships **1:** 8
criticisms of
de facto segregation **2:** 824
learning theories **2:** 824
and curriculum **1:** 7
educational objectives **2:** 823
educational experience **2:** 822
and educational opportunities **1:** 7
effect on friendship **1:** 7
effect on student attitudes **1:** 7
flexible progression **2:** 823
gifted **5:** 2494
homogeneous grouping **5:** 2730
impact on achievement **1:** 6
and individual differences **5:** 2766
influence on educational attainment **1:** 7
instructional effectiveness **5:** 2774
interaction
and academic achievement **5:** 2535
interpersonal relationship **2:** 824
learning theories **2:** 821
outcomes of education **9:** 5261
educational and sociological research **1:** 6
and school dynamics **9:** 5169
and secondary education
China, People's Republic of **2:** 756
social influences **2:** 822
and special education placement **6:** 3293
steering group learning model **7:** 3883
student attitudes **2:** 824
teachers
and instruction **1:** 8
and youth subcultures **11:** 6800
Ability identification
autism **6:** ***3232–3235***
Abitur **1:** 182; **10:** 5637
Absenteeism
See Attendance
Employee absenteeism
Abstract reasoning **8:** 4723, ***4948–4951***
abstraction
and transfer of training **11:** 6454, 6455
analytic philosophy **8:** 4443
and reflection **8:** 4449
concept of **8:** 4948
and critical thinking **2:** 1205
culture
and cognitive development **3:** 1244
formal and informal **8:** 4948
mathematics skills
history of **6:** 3644
See also
Reasoning
Abstracting
systems
Latin America **3:** 1590
Abstracts
production of
and policy formation **3:** 1590
Academic ability
and item response theory
equated scores **11:** 6352
sex differences
and outcomes of education **9:** 5427
and social mobility **9:** 5551
studies
and selection bias **9:** 5381
teachers' beliefs **10:** 6101
vs. academic achievement
and learning disabilities **10:** 5682
Academic achievement
and ability
interaction effects **5:** 2926
and ability grouping **2:** 824; **9:** 5170
and age **6:** 3285
and apprenticeships
Africa **1:** 223
and aptitude
interaction effects **5:** 2923
and attendance **11:** 6389
and birth order
confluence model **7:** 3869
and certification **8:** 4617
charting **10:** ***5783–5791***
collecting observations **10:** 5787
examples **10:** 5788
and child care occupations **2:** 689
and class size **8:** 4868
classroom environment
and group unity **5:** 2527
coeducation vs. single sex schools **2:** ***831–834***
and collective bargaining **10:** 6069
and community involvement **6:** 3105
compared with energy expenditure **10:** 5820
cooperative learning
teamwork **2:** 1095
cross-national model **2:** 956
and cultural capital **9:** 5019
culture and cognition approach **3:** 1230
and curriculum development
evaluation **5:** 2497
decline
and teacher role **10:** 6079
and earnings differentials
cost per unit comparison **8:** 4567
and educational benefits **1:** 510, 516
and educational environment **8:** 4860
and educational quality **8:** 4866, 4868
and educational resources **3:** 1779
and educational technology
studies **4:** 1912
effect of institutional values on **8:** 4563
effect of unions on **10:** 6070
and effective schools research **9:** 5377
effects of educational resources on **7:** 3817
and employment level **3:** 1748; **7:** 3716, 3720
and equal education **9:** 5536
and ethnicity **8:** 4892
and factor analysis **4:** 2234
factors affecting **9:** 5260; **10:** 6069
research **9:** 5041
and family attitudes **9:** 5017
and family characteristics **4:** ***2250–2258***, ***2267–2272***
and family environment **5:** ***2624–2628***
female blacks
South Africa **7:** 3851
and generalizability theory **5:** 2460
and health
adolescents **5:** 2568
and hierarchical linear models **5:** 2590
homework **11:** 6389
influences **10:** 6172
and information technology
in science education **7:** 4101
and institutional autonomy
studies **1:** 590
international studies
comparative analysis **3:** ***1762–1769***
historical background **3:** 1762
and item characteristic curves **5:** 3040
and item writing techniques **5:** 3061
and kinship studies **6:** 3138
and learning motivation **7:** 3936
and learning processes
research **10:** 5747
mainstreaming **5:** 2908
measures
comparative analysis **1:** 470
constructing **10:** 5787
minority students
and desegregation **3:** 1483
and network learning **2:** 981
and open plan schools
research synthesis **10:** 6238
ordered outcome categories
construction of **10:** 5786
and parent child relationship **5:** 2625
and partial order scalogram analysis **7:** 4313
and peer groups **9:** 5171
and performance contracts **8:** 4708
prediction of **7:** 3874
and preschool education **11:** 6560
benefits **8:** 4664
and preschool evaluation **4:** 2142, 2143
and productivity **3:** 1694; **11:** 6629
public schools vs. private schools **8:** 4839
and questioning techniques
problems **8:** 4876
research synthesis **10:** 6238
regular and special education relationship **9:** 5068
and school administration
research **5:** 2507
and school-based management **3:** 1410
and school climate **9:** 5208
and school effectiveness **5:** 2508; **8:** 4870
and school organization **5:** 2505
and school self-evaluation **5:** 2850
and school size **9:** 5293
and schools
effects on **10:** 5589

and science
attitudes toward **9:** 5321
and selection tests **4:** 2172
models **4:** 2173
and self-efficacy
of teachers **8:** 4565
and self-motivation **9:** 5400
sex differences **5:** 2489; **10:** 5824
affective factors **6:** 3640
comparative area studies **9:** 5426
research **9:** 5423, 5425
and single sex schools **2:** 832
social background
measurement **7:** 3720
and social class **6:** 3307
stress variables **10:** 5736
and student evaluation **7:** 4234
studies
and analysis of variance methods **11:** 6586
surveys
data collection **2:** 1217
and teacher characteristics **8:** 4869
and teacher education **10:** 6036
and teacher effectiveness **8:** 4872
and teacher expectations of students **10:** 6106
teacher guidance **10:** 6032
and teacher indirectness
research synthesis **10:** 6237
of teachers **10:** 6226
teachers' beliefs **10:** 6100
and teaching skills **8:** 4869
and television viewing **1:** 568; **7:** 3741
and test anxiety **4:** 1965
and textbooks
role of **11:** 6367
and time factors (learning) **6:** 3547; **11:** 6389
and time on task **8:** 4870; **11:** 6389
and visual literacy **11:** 6623
vs. academic ability
and learning disabilities **10:** 5682
vs. employment opportunities
in demand occupations **11:** 6258
See also
Educational attainment
Academic aptitude
and achievement **1:** 2
evaluation **1:** 119
and student needs **10:** 5769
individualized instruction **5:** 2775
instructional effectiveness **5:** 2775
tests **1:** 1
Academic education
core curriculum **2:** 1103
teacher commitment to **10:** 6209
and teacher evaluation **10:** 6040
and textbook preparation **11:** 6364
and track system (education) **7:** 4231
and vocational education for development **3:** 1654
vs. vocational education
and primary school agriculture **8:** 4684
United States **11:** 6531, 6534
Academic failure
adolescents
and drug abuse **5:** 2568
and cost effectiveness **3:** 1791
and dropouts **9:** 5224
ethnography of **2:** 800
future directions **2:** 802
strengths and limitations **2:** 801
grade repetition **5:** ***2512–2515***
and grade repetition rate **9:** 5226
minority groups
and anthropological linguistics **6:** 3235
See also
Reading failure
Academic freedom
and curriculum **6:** 3358
and educational administration **6:** 3273
See also
Institutional autonomy
Intellectual freedom
Academic journals
See Scholarly journals
Academic learning time **1:** ***20–23***
academic achievement **1:** 22
applications **1:** 20
fundamental concepts of **1:** 20
success rate **1:** 21
task analysis **1:** 23
teacher student relationship **1:** 23
See also
Time on task
Academic libraries
educational resources **6:** 3397
and printed materials **8:** 4697
Academic persistence
and institutional characteristics **3:** 1605
in primary education
developing nations **9:** 5535
Academic rank (professional)
equal opportunities **11:** ***6709–6712***
females **11:** ***6709–6712***
teacher salaries **11:** 6711
tenure **11:** 6709
publications
sex bias **11:** 6711
teacher evaluation
sex discrimination **11:** 6711
Academic records
disadvantages of **8:** 4620
historical background **8:** 4618
and negotiation **8:** 4620
recording problems **8:** 4620
records of personal achievement **8:** 4618
types of **8:** 4619
uses of **8:** 4620
Academic standards
and public examinations **4:** 2173
Academically gifted
characteristics of **9:** 5529, 5531
and educational technology
research **10:** 5672
and friendship choice **9:** 5530
future research **9:** 5531
motivation **9:** 5529
theories of **9:** 5529
and peer acceptance **9:** 5530, 5531
peer relationship **9:** 5530
programs for **9:** 5531
recreational preferences **9:** 5530
self-concept **9:** 5529
social–emotional development of **9:** ***5528–5532***
See also
Gifted
Academy of Pedagogical Sciences (APS) (former Soviet Union) **2:** 938; **9:** 5096, 5097
Acceleration (education)
for the gifted **5:** 2493, 2729; **9:** 5531
high risk students **2:** 710
Access to education
adult education
financial support **10:** 5806
adults **4:** 2393, 2394; **7:** 4321
affirmative action **8:** 4611
Europe **10:** 5643
higher education **1:** 178; **7:** 4166, 4169
universal **8:** 4960
university education **11:** 6548
children with disabilities **2:** 720
deafness and **3:** 1399
developing nations
sex bias **1:** 468
in disadvantaged environments **7:** 4134
and economic change **5:** 2505
educational media **7:** 3758
and educational technology **9:** 5542
employees to continuing **4:** 1975
equal education **9:** 5535
interpretations **4:** 2001
secondary education **9:** 5388
females **4:** 2407
and educational research **11:** 6725
francophone Africa **11:** 6738
Islamic culture **11:** 6756, 6757
and liberal feminist theory **5:** 2453
and mass media **4:** 1894
nonformal education
comparative analysis **7:** 4133
and multishift schooling **7:** 4133
and paid educational leave **7:** 4262
racial factors
anthropological research **9:** 5569
secondary education
and school mapping **9:** 5256
universal **6:** 3418, 3420
See also
Equal education
Access to postsecondary education
Albania **1:** 257
Mongolia **7:** 3905
Accessibility (for disabled)
education work relationship **11:** 6457, 6460

Accountability
  assessment
    criticisms of **6:** 3473
  and curriculum development **9:** 5520
  and educational planning **7:** 4057, 4058
  and evaluation **4:** 2100, 2374, 2381
  evaluation procedures
    and data envelopment analysis **3:** 1386
  and governance **5:** 2510
    of teacher education **10:** 5964
  and institutional self-evaluation
    United States **4:** 2381
  and international education indicators **5:** 2989
  and management information systems **6:** 3593
  and monitoring national standards **7:** 3906, 3911
  and performance contracts **8:** 4709
  of principals
    scope **9:** 5272
  and program evaluation **4:** 2070
  and school administration **9:** 5166
  school effectiveness **3:** 1386; **4:** 2381
  and school failure **1:** 128
  and school self-evaluation **5:** 2848
  skill development
    funds **11:** 6651
  and state departments of education **7:** 3834
  teachers
    vs. professionalism **1:** 435
  urban schools **11:** 6561
  See also
    Relevance (education)
Accreditation (teacher education institutions) **1:** ***24–28***
  Australia **1:** 24, 25
  Botswana **1:** 24, 26
  Canada **1:** 24, 26
  criteria **1:** 25, 27
  England and Wales **1:** 24, 26
  formative evaluation **1:** 27
  input output analysis **1:** 26
  issues **1:** 26
  Scotland **1:** 25, 26
  standardization **1:** 27
  summative evaluation **1:** 27
  United States **1:** 25, 26
Accreditation Commission (UK) **2:** 664
Acculturation **7:** 3966
  immigrants
    United States **7:** 3844; **9:** 5509
  and intelligence **8:** 4818
  and peer groups **9:** 5218
  relationship with social mobility **9:** 5219
  television viewing **9:** 5514
  and women's education
    French West Africa **11:** 6736
  See also
    Social integration
Achievement
  attitudes and **1:** 390
  and class size **6:** 3372
  and conformity **5:** 2764
  cross-national comparison
    evaluation of **4:** ***2132–2140***
  and emotional development **4:** 1965
  emotions related to **4:** 1965
  and improvement
    grading **10:** 5820
  instructional strategies
    equalizing **3:** 1504
  psychological patterns **9:** 5404
  and self-motivation **5:** 2764
  sex differences **9:** 5433
  and sociometric techniques **10:** 5616
  See also
    Academic achievement
    High achievement
    Low achievement
Achievement gains
  and grading **10:** 5820
  measurement
    joint production model **6:** 3103
  and undereducation **7:** 4254
Achievement need
  and affiliation need **3:** ***1236–1241***
  anthropological approach **3:** ***1236–1241***
  Atkinson's theory **7:** 3939
  and behavioral objectives **1:** 28
  causal attribution approach **1:** 30
  characteristics of **3:** 1236
  cross-cultural studies **1:** 30; **3:** 1238; **5:** 2648
  cultural context **3:** 1238
  cultural differences in **1:** 292
  development of **1:** ***28–32***
  and field dependence independence **3:** 1239
  goals approach **1:** 28, 31
  hypothesis testing
    and smallest space analysis **9:** 5501
  intrinsic motivation approach **1:** 26, 31
  and parent attitudes **3:** 1237
  social behavior **9:** 5525
  and test anxiety **7:** 3939, 3940; **11:** 6358
  theory of **10:** 6221
    application **10:** 6222
  training
    and entrepreneurship **4:** 1985
Achievement tests **1:** 1
  characteristics of **11:** 6341
  classical test theory **1:** 33
  computer-assisted **10:** 5787
  and conceptual understanding **10:** 5785
  conventional **10:** 5784
  and hearing impairments **3:** 1401
  historical background **1:** 32
  historical development **4:** 1868
  item response theory **1:** 33
  item sampling theory **1:** 33
  and learning disabilities
    diagnosis of **10:** 5683
  limitations **10:** 5783
  and longitudinal studies **6:** 3515
  matrix sampling **1:** 373
  and moderation procedures **4:** 2176
  national schemes **11:** 6561
  and objective tests **7:** 4193
  and prediction **8:** 4654
  psychometric bases of **1:** 32
  purpose of **1:** 32
  and questioning techniques **8:** 4876
  scales **1:** ***32–42***
    age **1:** 36, 40
    grade **1:** 36, 40
    item response theory **1:** 36, 41
    mastery **1:** 34
    naturally occurring distributions **1:** 36
    normal score distributions **1:** 35
    p-values **1:** 34
    Rasch **1:** 37
    raw score **1:** 34
    rectangular score distributions **1:** 35
    standard score **1:** 34
    stanine **1:** 35
    sten **1:** 36
    types of **1:** 34
  scaling **1:** 38
    area conversions **1:** 39
    linear score conversions **1:** 39
  and screening hypothesis **9:** 5351
  secondary education
    selection **9:** 5387
  and student needs
    diagnosis of **10:** 5769
  and teacher effectiveness **8:** 4521
  and test bias **11:** 6318
    studies **11:** 6319
  and test coaching **11:** 6336
  United States **7:** 4053
  and validity **11:** 6321
  See also
    Criterion referenced tests
    Domain referenced tests
    Mastery tests
    Norm referenced tests
Acoustical environment
  for classrooms **1:** 399
  educational facilities **4:** 2221
Acoustics
  and audio media **1:** 396
Acquired Immune Deficiency Syndrome (AIDS)
  and child mental retardation **5:** 2564
  drug therapy
    in schools **8:** 4420
  education about **4:** 2330
  and population education **8:** 4608
  and visual impairments **11:** 6625
Acting
  educational programs **8:** ***4384–4388***
  and teaching **10:** 6084
Action learning
  See Experiential learning

Action research **1:** ***42–48***; **2:** 1048;
6: 3369
and administrator education
inservice **1:** 70
and case studies **2:** 642
criticisms of **1:** 46; **8:** 4560
definition of **1:** 42
and epistemology **9:** 5024
ethnography as **4:** 2049
fallacies **1:** 47
inservice teacher education **10:** 5969
international perspectives **1:** 44
key features of **1:** 43
mathematics education **6:** 3651
periodicals **1:** 43
processes **1:** 42
and science education **8:** 4477
semantics **1:** 46
shortcomings of **1:** 46
and teacher education **10:** 5984
and teaching **6:** 3598
See also
Participatory research
Action theory
and functionalism
universities **2:** 1065
Activism
and adult education **1:** 131;
2: ***1189–1194***
and adult educators **10:** 6055
high school students
and nationalism **10:** 5779
student characteristics **10:** 5781
student organizations **10:** 5778
students **10:** ***5775–5783***
historical perspectives **10:** 5778
ideological variations **10:** 5780
Latin America **10:** 5779
and nationalism **10:** 5779, 5780
sociological generalizations
10: 5781
United States **10:** 5779
teachers **8:** 4585; **10:** 6138
unions **10:** 6076
factors affecting **10:** 6076
uses of **10:** 6076
Activities Index
and descriptive scales **3:** 1476
Activity learning
See Experiential learning
Adaptive behavior (of disabled)
mild mental retardation **7:** 3829
Adaptive instruction
See Adaptive teaching
Adaptive Learning Environments
Model (ALEM)
instructional effectiveness **5:** 2777
Adaptive teaching
characteristics of **9:** 5042
and learning theories **10:** 5746
Adaptive testing **1:** ***48–53***
applications **1:** 51
approaches **1:** 48
Bayesian procedure **1:** 50
in the classroom **5:** 2779
computerized **1:** 50; **2:** 992
item response theory models **2:** 993
potential problems with **1:** 51
rules for **2:** 994
conditions for **2:** 993
and courseware design **2:** 1169
and decision theory **3:** 1419
definition of **1:** 48
flexilevel **2:** 993
future trends **1:** 52
information functions **5:** 3054
initial items **1:** 49
item banks
computer software **5:** 3042
prestructured **1:** 49
unstructured **1:** 49
and item response theory **1:** 48, 49;
5: 3054
maximum information procedure
1: 50
measurement efficiency **1:** 50
precision **1:** 50
principles of **1:** 49
self-adapted testing **1:** 50
and sequential approach compared
1: 48
testlets **1:** 49
two-stage **1:** 49; **2:** 993
Addition
learning strategies **6:** 3657
Adjudicated youth
See Delinquency, juvenile justice
Adjustment (to environment)
and achievement need **1:** 30
adult strategies **8:** 4819, 4822
evolutionary processes **4:** 2168
individual development **6:** ***3425–3428***
and social cognition **9:** ***5513–5518***
infant behavior
reflexes **5:** 2800
and mental health **11:** 6309
personality development **8:** 4390
visual perception **8:** ***4376–4379***
Administration
and anti-administration **1:** 66
databases
and management information
systems **6:** 3594
and educational objectives **8:** 4564
educational technology
occupations **4:** 1926
of labor
strategies **3:** 1696
research
unified theory **1:** 61, 65
See also
Educational administration
Administrative organization
and authority
theories of **1:** 433
centralization vs. decentralization
8: 4565
and state departments of education
7: 3833, 3836
See also
Power structure
Administrative principles
ethics of **4:** 2032
and humanism **3:** 1771
and logical empiricism **3:** 1769
and organizational theory **3:** 1771
and values in decision making **3:** 1771
Administrator attitudes
effect of unions on **10:** 6070
and management information systems
6: 3594
Administrator characteristics **1:** 66;
9: 5160
and inservice education **1:** 68
and recruitment **1:** 78
state departments of education
7: 3837
Administrator education
faculty composition **1:** 74
inservice **1:** ***67–73***
methods **1:** 70
preservice **1:** ***73–77***, 81
behavioral science era (1947–1985)
1: 74
and critical theory **1:** 76
dialectic era **1:** 76
future trends **1:** 76
prescriptive era (1900–1946) **1:** 73
program content **1:** 73, 75
program structure **1:** 74
Administrator evaluation
assessment centers **1:** 80
in education **4:** ***2123–2132***
Administrator preparation
See Administrator education
Administrator role **1:** 67
media programs **7:** 3753
Administrator selection
assessment centers **1:** 80
and careers **1:** ***78–83***
criteria **1:** 79
processes **1:** 79
proposals **1:** 80
shortcomings **1:** 80
Administrator teacher relationship
See Teacher administrator
relationship
Administrators
and micropolitics **7:** 3824
needs
and inservice education **1:** 68
occupational mobility
state departments of education
7: 3837
recruitment
factors influencing **1:** 78
processes **1:** 78
source of candidates **1:** 78
training
for special education **10:** 5941
Admission criteria
adult students
higher education **7:** 4165
universities **11:** 6548
and advanced placement **5:** 2765
and expectancy tables **4:** 2181
recurrent education **8:** 4958

Admission tests (higher education)
See College entrance examinations
Admissions officers
and college students **10:** 5799
Adolescent development **1:** ***83–89***
biological influences **1:** 84
biology **5:** 2683
and cognitive development **1:** 84
context effect **1:** 83, 87
developmental stages
puberty **1:** 84
family influence **1:** 85
identity and role diffusion **8:** 4716
individual differences **1:** 84, 88
Judaic theory **6:** 3115
parent influence **1:** 85, 87
peer influence **1:** 85, 87
and personal autonomy **1:** 85
physical development
body composition **8:** 4471
body height **8:** 4471
determinants **8:** 4472
menstruation **1:** 84
and physical fitness **8:** 4472
sex differences **8:** 4471
sexual development **8:** 4470
social influences **1:** 85, 87
stress variables **1:** 85
Adolescent literature
reading interests **2:** 734
Adolescents
academic achievement
and health **5:** 2568
academic failure
and drug abuse **5:** 2568
behavior problems
context effect **1:** 87
drinking **1:** 86
drugs use **1:** 86
friendship
and social values **1:** 85
mental health
sex differences **9:** 5435
mortality rate **5:** 2567
self-actualization **1:** 88
sexuality **1:** 86
and sex education **9:** 5437
smoking **1:** 86
social problems **1:** 86
Adopted children
genetic factors in cognitive development **5:** 2465
Adoption
quantitative genetic studies **5:** 2464
Adoption (ideas)
and educational change **6:** 3599
Adult basic education **1:** 90, ***100–103***, 116; **6:** 3420
Anglophone Africa **1:** ***210–215***
Arab nations **1:** 322
Australia **1:** 410
Canada **1:** 102
and curriculum-based assessment **3:** 1358
definition **1:** 100
developing nations **6:** 3362
and the disadvantaged **1:** 91
distance education **3:** 1571
Europe **7:** 4247
dropout research **3:** 1600, 1601
and economic development **1:** 129
females
Islamic culture **11:** 6757
Francophone Africa **1:** 216
future directions **1:** 102
international **5:** 2935
international education
conferences **5:** 2957, 2958
Latin America **6:** 3254
legislation **6:** 3363, 3366
Netherlands **10:** 5640
Nicaragua **2:** 637, 638
participants **1:** 100
Portugal **10:** 5641
provision **8:** 4805
Sweden **10:** 5638
and UNESCO **11:** 6501, 6505
United Kingdom **10:** 5639
United States **1:** 102; **8:** 4637
women's education **11:** 6713
work-related **1:** 103, 110
See also
Basic education
Adult development **1:** 113; **8:** 4817
aging and compensation **6:** 3427
and aging (individuals) **1:** ***234–239***
cognitive development **1:** 235
age differences **1:** 235
and cognitive factors **1:** 147
age related **1:** 147
and concept of adulthood **8:** 4457
developmental stages
expectation **6:** 3427
ego psychology **8:** 4822
and role of education **8:** 4456
teacher education **10:** ***5935–5939***
theory and counseling **2:** 1163
Adult education
administration **1:** 153
Afghanistan **1:** 206
Albania **1:** 257
Anglophone Africa **1:** ***210–215***
Antigua and Barbuda **1:** 302, 305
Arab nations **1:** ***322–328***
Asia **1:** ***348–353***
Australia **1:** ***409–415***
Austria **1:** 426
Caribbean **2:** ***635–640***
Central America **2:** ***635–640***
Central and Eastern Europe **11:** 6645
certification **2:** ***662–665***
China, People's Republic of **1:** 348, 350; **2:** ***746–749***
classical concept of **1:** 112
clinical models **1:** 134
colleges
United Kingdom **11:** 6689
communication problems **1:** 119
communicative competence (languages) **6:** ***3209–3213***
and communism **2:** 657, 1191
community approach **2:** 1191
community colleges **2:** ***900–907***
comparative analysis **1:** ***176–180***
conferences **1:** 176
development **1:** 176
forms of study **1:** 177
international studies **1:** 176, 178, 179
objectives **1:** 177
organizations **1:** 176
publications **1:** 176
topics **1:** 178
comparative research **1:** 150; **5:** 2935
compensatory education **2:** 636
and compulsory education **1:** 154
concepts of **1:** ***111–120***, 127, 143; **4:** 2388; **8:** 4610
consciousness raising **2:** 637, ***1045–1049***
continuation students **1:** ***181–184***
criteria for **1:** 119
critical approaches **2:** ***1189–1194***
Cuba **3:** 1224
as cultural politics **1:** 133, 134
curriculum **3:** ***1308–1315***
definitions of **1:** 104, 128, 143, 153; **10:** 5591
boundary problems **10:** 5635
for statutory purposes **6:** 3361
UNESCO **1:** 89, 113, 143; **11:** 6502
demand for **4:** ***2388–2394***; **8:** 4962
demand and supply
evaluation of **1:** 150
and democracy **1:** 136
departments **1:** 125, 126
and dependency theory **1:** 132
and deschooling of society **1:** 138
for development **5:** 2946
and development
clinical models **1:** 134
political mobilization **1:** 131
role in **1:** ***127–135***; **5:** 2934, 2935
development aid in **1:** 132
disadvantaged **1:** 112
discipline of **1:** 118, ***120–127***, 144
debate on **1:** 120
development **1:** 122
and distance education **1:** ***561–564***; **3:** ***1557–1563***, 1564; **10:** 5594
diversity of forms **1:** 115
dropouts **3:** ***1599–1602***
Eastern Europe **2:** ***656–662***
ecological issues **2:** 1193
economic impact **2:** ***1084–1094***
economic and labor market functions **1:** 146
and educational opportunities **8:** 4611
emancipatory **1:** 139; **2:** 1190; **7:** 4326; **10:** 6055
for development **1:** 129
Freire's views **1:** 133
and employment policy **4:** ***1972–1976***
ethnocentrism in **1:** 166
Europe **2:** ***656–662***
evaluation **4:** ***2119–2123***
public policies **4:** 1974
expenditure **8:** 4962

experiential learning **4:** ***2183–2186***
females **4:** 2411; **11:** ***6712–6719***
developed nations **11:** 6713
developing nations **11:** 6714
evaluation studies **11:** 6718
field of study **1:** 143
financial support **1:** 146, 153, 156; **6:** 3365
business investment **4:** 2392, 2393
price and cost distortion **4:** 2392
social investment **4:** 2393, 2394
supply and demand **4:** ***2388–2394***
foreign students **8:** 4607
formal **10:** 5592
functions of **10:** 5592
studies **10:** 5593
France **10:** 5636
Francophone Africa **1:** ***215–221***
functions of **1:** 128
general education **1:** 89, 91, 146
Germany **10:** 5636
Ghana **5:** 2482
government involvement **6:** 3361
Greece **10:** 5641
growth of **1:** 113, 118
and higher education **1:** ***89–94***
history of **1:** 112, ***135–139***
content **1:** 138
educational associations **1:** 136
institutions **1:** 137
legislation **1:** 136
political factors **1:** 135
political power **1:** 136
scientific **1:** 136
teaching methods **1:** 138
and vocational education **1:** 138
and ideology
political dogma **2:** 639
ideology in **1:** 114, 123; **2:** ***1189–1194***; **5:** ***2732–2737***, 2934
independent study **9:** ***5394–5399***
India **5:** 2748, ***2753–2759***
informal **10:** 5594
information sources **1:** ***139–142***
information transfer **5:** 2949
institutions **1:** 110, 122
quality control **4:** 1974
instrumentalism **5:** 2732
interdisciplinary approach **1:** 121, 126
intergovernmental cooperation **5:** 2933
intergovernmental organizations **1:** 151
Israel **1:** 136; **5:** 3026
Italy **10:** 5642
Japan **6:** ***3074–3078***
and labor market **1:** ***103–111***; **2:** ***1084–1094***; **4:** ***1972–1976***
Latin America **6:** ***3253–3256***
leadership and **5:** 2735
learning strategies **6:** ***3345–3349***
Lebanon **6:** 3353
legislation **1:** 153, 154; **6:** ***3360–3367***; **8:** 4960
definition **6:** 3361
France **7:** 4258
history **6:** 3361
impact **6:** 3363
international aspects **6:** 3361
research **6:** 3366
and leisure time **6:** ***3373–3378***
Lesotho **6:** 3382
liberal concept of **1:** 112, 118
lifelong learning **1:** 144, 145; **6:** 3417, 3419; **8:** 4615
links with youth education **11:** 6393
and Marxism **2:** 1191
measurement **7:** ***3707–3711***
direct **7:** 3707, 3709
indirect **7:** 3707, 3709
international comparative research **7:** 3710
prospects and future strategies **7:** 3710
reasons for **7:** 3707
terminological diversity **7:** 3708
variations in **7:** 3708
via administrative systems **7:** 3707
media support
future strategies **1:** 563
motivation **1:** 115; **7:** ***4325–4330***; **8:** 4821
females **11:** 6714, 6717
multicultural education **8:** 4614
Myanmar **7:** 4035
for national development **1:** ***127–135***
national studies **1:** 151
Nepal **7:** 4064
Netherlands **7:** 4072; **10:** 5639
and new technology **1:** 110
New Zealand **1:** ***409–415***
Nigeria **7:** 4128
nonformal education **10:** 5593
international conferences **5:** 2959
nongovernmental organizations **1:** 132, 151; **5:** 2932; **7:** **4146–4148**
Nordic countries **7:** ***4175–4180***
North America **7:** ***4180–4185***
Norway **7:** 4189
objectives of **1:** 145
open education **4:** ***2183–2186***; **6:** 3434
open universities **11:** 6549, 6550
outreach programs **7:** ***4246–4249***
overview **1:** ***143–152***
paid educational leave **6:** 3362
participation **1:** 104, 131, 149; **8:** ***4610–4616***
age differences **1:** 104; **7:** 4321
age groups **8:** 4612
antecedent factors **7:** ***4319–4325***
and characteristics of provision **7:** 4321
cost effectiveness **7:** 4323
deterrents to **7:** 4321, 4328
economic factors **2:** 1148; **7:** 4323
and educational attainment **1:** 107; **8:** 4614
and employment level **8:** 4614
ethnicity **8:** 4614
extent of **8:** 4612
factors influencing **8:** 4610
females **11:** 6713
growth in **1:** 110
horizontal elaboration **1:** 154
ISSTAL model **7:** 4324
and leisure time **6:** 3375
models of **7:** 4323
motivation **7:** 4322, ***4325–4330***; **8:** 4615
and nonparticipation **8:** 4610
obligatory **6:** 3362
older adults **6:** 3376
political factors **7:** 4327
and provider organizations **7:** 4327
psychological factors **7:** 4321
racial differences **1:** 107
rates **1:** 104; **4:** 2388
research **7:** ***4319–4325***; **8:** 4610
resource conversion theory **7:** 4328
sex differences **1:** 107; **7:** 4321, 4326; **8:** 4614
and social context **7:** 4326
sociological factors **7:** 4320
studies **10:** 5593
Sweden **11:** 6392
and unemployment **6:** 3377
variation in levels **7:** 4325
vertical elaboration **1:** 154
paternalism **1:** 134
and performance contracts **5:** 2771
philosophical characterization **1:** 144
philosophical values **8:** 4735
planning public policy for **1:** ***152–158***
background **1:** 153
policies **1:** 146
and learning **1:** 157
and literacy curriculum **3:** 1258
political aspects **1:** ***127–135***
and political context **10:** 5635
political economy of **1:** 128, 131
political motivation **1:** 116; **2:** ***1189–1194***
political socialization **8:** 4580
politics **6:** 3361, 3365
polytechnics **8:** ***4604–4608***
and popular education **1:** 145; **2:** 1192
Portugal **10:** 5640
practice of **1:** 123
principles **1:** ***111–120***, 127
conflicts **1:** 117
Euro-American **1:** 113, 118
private provision **1:** 115
professional associations **8:** ***4731–4736***
professionalization **1:** 277; **5:** 2936; **8:** 4735; **10:** 5595
and curriculum design **3:** 1309
higher education **1:** 112
and political issues **5:** 2950, 2951
scientification **1:** 123, 126
and teacher education **11:** 6437
United States **1:** 122
providers **1:** 108; **4:** 2392; **8:** ***4803–4812***; **10:** 5592
classification of institutional **8:** 4804

formal and public **8:** 4805
governmental **1:** 110; **6:** 3364
ineffective **4:** 2392
nonformal public **8:** 4807
nonformal self-supporting **8:** 4808
nongovernmental **6:** 3364
nonschool-based **1:** 108
profitmaking **6:** ***3614–3617***; **8:** 4810
public private partnerships **8:** 4338
purposes of **1:** 115
school-based **1:** 108
support services **6:** 3365
types of **1:** 114, 149
typologies **8:** 4804
provision
long range planning **4:** 2330
psychology **8:** ***4816–4824***
public awareness of needs **8:** 4734
purposes **1:** ***111–120***
and curriculum content **3:** 1311
individual and collective **1:** 117
typology of **1:** 116
radical **10:** 5594
rate of return **1:** 130
reform strategies **1:** ***158–163***
background **1:** 158
definitions **1:** 159
and disadvantaged **1:** 159
and life events **1:** 159
and social change **1:** 161
regional studies **1:** 151
remedial **5:** 2736
research **1:** 121
by country **1:** 124
and employment **1:** 161
and health promotion **1:** 161
international development patterns **1:** 122
and literacy **1:** 161
and practice **1:** 126
quality **1:** 125
role of national and international organizations **1:** 123
resource allocation **4:** 2393
responsibility for payment for **1:** 117
role of
minority groups **10:** 5592
scholarship and **1:** 126
and school education
comparison of **10:** 5591
self-supporting students **4:** 2394
social acceptability **1:** 115
for social change **1:** 122, 145; **10:** 6055
social class and **2:** 1190; **5:** 2733
and social outcomes **4:** 2393
social role **1:** 121
and socialism **2:** 1189, 1193
sociocultural
Europe **10:** 5643
sociology of **10:** ***5591–5596***
models **10:** 5593
theories of **10:** 5595
Southern and Western Europe **10:** ***5635–5644***
Soviet Union (former) **9:** ***5091–5098***
state and class conflict **2:** 1190
statistical data **1:** ***94–100***; **7:** 3707
structures **1:** 114
student support systems **1:** 148; **10:** ***5805–5808***
supply of **4:** ***2388–2394***
Swaziland **10:** 5864
Sweden **8:** 4611; **10:** 5637, 5869
Tanzania **10:** 5905
target groups **8:** 4610
teaching methods **10:** ***6198–6202***
telecommunications **1:** ***561–564***
terminology **1:** 119
themes and theories **1:** 145
training concepts and statistics **11:** ***6416–6420***
and training markets **1:** ***103–111***
trends **1:** 110; **10:** 5596; **11:** 6393
in provision **8:** 4810, 4958
Tunisia **11:** 6471
types of **10:** 5592
Uganda **11:** 6498
and UNESCO **11:** ***6501–6507***
United Kingdom **10:** 5638; **11:** 6518
United States **11:** 6543
universities **1:** 89, 92; **11:** ***6547–6551***
uses of term **1:** 89, 143, 144; **5:** 2931; **6:** 3419
and continuing education **1:** 118
and the Enlightenment **1:** 111
national equivalents **1:** 112, 118
utilitarianism **5:** 2732
viability of universal **5:** 2734, 2735
vocabulary
international studies **1:** 180
and vocational education **1:** 112, 146
in socialist societies **11:** 6642
work-related issues **1:** 123; **6:** 3376
Yemen **11:** 6791
See also
Adult students
Andragogy
Community colleges
Community education
Continuing education
Distance education
Family life education
Independent study
International adult education
Lifelong learning
Migrant adult education
Nonformal education
Paid educational leave
Proprietary schools
Women's education
Adult Education Association of the United States **7:** 4181
Adult education centers
Soviet Union (former) **9:** 5096
Adult Education Research Conference (US) **7:** 4184; **8:** 4732
Adult educators
and adult literacy campaigns **3:** 1258
authenticity **10:** 6057
continuation students **1:** 183
credibility **10:** 6057
cross-cultural studies **1:** 177
cultural awareness **1:** 166
and curriculum design **3:** 1309
ethnicity
and multicultural education **1:** 166
and independent study **10:** 6054
inservice teacher education **10:** 6057
and learning strategies **6:** 3345; **10:** 6054
lobbying **5:** 2949
and political issues **1:** 91
professional development **5:** 2950; **10:** 6057
international organizations **5:** 2950
role as facilitators **1:** 148
teacher certification **11:** 6432, 6436
teacher education **11:** ***6431–6438***
curriculum competencies **11:** 6434
degree courses **11:** 6435
form and structure **11:** 6433
Francophone Africa **1:** 219
history **11:** 6431
trends **11:** 6437
United Kingdom **11:** 6431
workshops on program planning **11:** 6434
teacher qualifications **11:** 6436
teaching role **10:** ***6054–6058***
as critical animator **10:** 6055
as facilitator **10:** 6054
teaching styles **10:** ***6054–6058***
cognitive style **10:** 6056
concept of **10:** 6055
critical reflection on **10:** 6055
research **10:** 6056
theory practice relationship **1:** 166
types of **10:** 5591
Adult farmer education
China, People's Republic of **2:** 748
government support **10:** 5806
history of **1:** 136
Adult learning **1:** 147, ***163–168***; **6:** ***3428–3435***; **8:** 4818
anxiety in **6:** 3432
approaches **1:** 189
cognitive ability **6:** 3429
cognitive science approach **8:** 4820
cognitive style **1:** 189; **6:** 3430
computer assisted instruction **6:** 3433
concepts of **1:** 188
conditions for **6:** 3431
cross-cultural studies **1:** 166, 167
developmental tasks **6:** 3431
differences from child learning **1:** 276
distance education **1:** 166
effectiveness **6:** ***3345–3349***
facilitation of **1:** 148
factors influencing **6:** 3431
future research **8:** 4823
and genetic epistemology **8:** 4819
in groups **5:** ***2529–2532***
affective and cognitive objectives **5:** 2530
history of **1:** 138
improving **1:** 191, 193
independent study **9:** ***5394–5399***

international studies **5:** 2949
individual differences **10:** 6198, 6200
individualized instruction **6:** 3433
influences of academic context **1:** 190
information processing approach **8:** 4820
issues in understanding **1:** 163
lack of interest in organized **6:** 3377
learning strategies **1:** ***184–194***
statistical analysis **1:** 185, 188
motivation **1:** 188; **6:** 3432; **7:** 4322, 4326; **10:** 6199
older adults
anxiety in **1:** 238
characteristics of **1:** 238
opportunities
demand and supply **1:** 148
orientations in **1:** 189; **7:** 4327
and psychometrics **8:** 4818
research **1:** 122, 163, 188
research proposals **1:** 167
sex differences **1:** 167
socialization **6:** 3429
studies **10:** 5594
study skills **1:** ***184–194***
and teaching
Nordic countries **7:** 4179
teaching methods
choice of **10:** 6198
trends **1:** 166
See also
Adult education
Andragogy
Lifelong learning
Adult literacy **6:** ***3453–3459***
and adult education
social functions of **10:** 5593
Australia **1:** 414
benefits of **1:** 170
and community education **2:** 909
curriculum **3:** ***1257–1262***
developed nations **1:** ***100–103***
developing nations **2:** 1046
educational finance
measurement of **3:** 1790
Francophone Africa **1:** 216
illiteracy
and family educational programs **6:** 3461
instructional materials **3:** ***1257–1262***
developed nations **3:** 1260
developing nations **3:** 1260
international cooperation **5:** 2935
for liberation **2:** 1046
measurement **6:** 3477
motivation **1:** 173
New Zealand **1:** 414
and phoneme grapheme correspondence **8:** 4943
scientific **9:** 5348
second stage **8:** ***4634–4639***
concepts and policies **8:** ***4634–4639***
and UNESCO **11:** 6501
teaching methods **3:** 1258
Laubach method **3:** 1259
learner centeredness **3:** 1259
and UNESCO **11:** 6503, 6504
valorization of **1:** 173
See also
Adult basic education
Functional literacy
Illiteracy
Literacy education
Adult Literacy and Basic Skills Unit (ALBSU) (UK) **1:** 102; **7:** 4147
Adult literacy programs **1:** 96; **6:** 3420
apperception–interaction method **2:** 1046
campaign series **1:** 171
design and implementation **1:** 173
developing nations **1:** ***169–176***
evaluation **4:** 2122
language of instruction **1:** 173
literacy teachers **1:** 174
mass campaigns **1:** 170, 171
objectives and strategies **1:** 170
orientations of **3:** 1257
outreach **7:** 4247
Philippines **2:** 1046
psychosocial method **2:** 1046
public **1:** 101
selective small-scale **1:** 171
strategies for organizing **1:** 170
Thailand **2:** 1046
time factor **1:** 173
Turkey **2:** 1046
United States **2:** 1046
volunteer and community-based **1:** 102
Adult programs
policies for **1:** 155
Adult Reading and Literacy Assistance Association Federation
New Zealand **1:** 414
Adult secondary education
See Continuation students, adult education
Adult secondary schools **1:** 183
Adult students
academic achievements **7:** 4166
Australia **7:** ***4163–4171***
characteristics of **7:** 4164; **8:** 4863; **10:** 6200
classification of **7:** 4164, 4165
definitions of **1:** 153
disadvantaged **7:** 4166
dropout prevention **3:** 1601
dropout rate **7:** 4166
educational counseling **2:** ***1161–1165***
employer attitudes to **7:** 4168
employment level **7:** 4167
equal education **7:** 4166
females **7:** 4164, 4166, 4168
financial support **7:** 4168
higher education **7:** ***4163–4171***
access to **7:** 4166, 4169
admission criteria **7:** 4165
individual development **7:** 4167
institutional responses **7:** 4169
interpersonal relationships **7:** 4167
minority groups **7:** 4166
nontraditional students **7:** ***4163–4171***
outcomes of education **7:** 4167
part-time students **7:** ***4163–4171***
and population trends **7:** 4169
and social mobility **7:** 4164
socioeconomic status **7:** 4164, 4165, 4168
United Kingdom **7:** ***4163–4171***
Adult vocational education **1:** 116; **6:** 3416, 3417; **8:** 4338
China, People's Republic of **2:** ***746–749***
and continuing education **6:** 3418, 3420
European Community **4:** ***2059–2063***
cross-national comparisons **4:** 1973
Eastern Europe **2:** 658
and employment policy **4:** ***1972–1976***
Europe **2:** 658; **10:** 5642
financial support **4:** 1973
France **10:** 5636
and general education **1:** 119; **6:** 3376
Germany **1:** 112
Greece **10:** 5641
international studies
comparative analysis **1:** 178
Japan **6:** ***3074–3078***
and labor force development **5:** 2686
legislation and finance **6:** 3365
measurement **7:** ***3711–3715***
Netherlands **10:** 5640
part-time **6:** 3416, 3417
Portugal **10:** 5641
post experience **1:** 91
rate of return to **4:** 2391; **6:** ***3614–3617***
research **11:** ***6416–6420***
rights to continuing
Europe **4:** 2060
Soviet Union (former) **9:** 5094
and training markets **1:** ***103–111***
United Kingdom **10:** 5639, 5807
United States **1:** 112
See also
Industrial training
Job training
Retraining
Adulthood
conceptions of **1:** 113
cultural differences in **5:** 2935
Adults
and child behavior
attribution theory **9:** 5405
definition of **1:** 143
education for illiterate and undereducated **6:** 3420
hearing impairments
and speech and language handicaps **10:** 5689
socialization
participant observation **10:** 6123
special needs students
adult education **8:** 4612
technical education

and educational technology
4: ***1918–1924***, ***1922***
See also
Adulthood
Advanced placement
and admission criteria **5:** 2765
Advantaged children
preschool education
long term benefits **8:** 4665
Advertising
See Television commercials
Advisory Committee for the Supply and Training of Teachers (ACSTT) **11:** 6433
Advisory committees
on governance of teacher education **10:** 5963
Aesthetic education **1:** ***194–199***; **5:** 2695
art education **1:** 338, 339
child's readiness for **1:** 197
choices of emphasis **1:** 198
cultural diversity **1:** 197
interest group responses **1:** 196
meaning and usage of term **1:** 196
portfolio method **1:** 198
preferences in **11:** 6617
Taiwan **1:** 342
theoretical background **1:** 195
theories of **1:** 195
valuation theory **1:** 195
visual arts **1:** 195
See also
Art education
Aesthetic values
art expression **1:** 198
Aesthetics
and philosophy **1:** 194
Affective behavior
and attitudes **1:** 381
cognitive development
and early moral development **7:** 3918
cognitive psychological explanations **6:** 3641
and consumption benefits **2:** 1054
and curriculum objectives **3:** 1699
effect on learning **1:** ***199–204***; **6:** 3318
heuristic model **1:** 201
emotional development **4:** ***1963–1967***
emotional responses **6:** 3639
and mathematics education **6:** ***3639–3643***
and science education **9:** 5319
Affective education
See Humanistic education
Affective learning
See Humanistic education
Affective measures
and interaction effects **5:** 2927
in science education **9:** 5320
Affective objectives
and religious education **9:** 5000
Affiliation need
and achievement need **3:** ***1236–1241***
Affirmative action
effect on earnings
United States **8:** 4900
Afghanistan
adult education
nonformal education **1:** 206
curriculum development **1:** 207
educational change **1:** 208
educational research **1:** 208
government school relationship
financial support **1:** 204
school administration **1:** 207
language **1:** 204
preschool education **1:** 206
primary education **1:** 206
secondary education **1:** 206
system of education **1:** ***204–210***
degrees and qualifications **1:** 206
educational objectives **1:** 205, 206
enrollment **1:** 206
major problems **1:** 204, 209
teacher education **1:** 206
teacher recruitment **1:** 207
teaching methodology **1:** 207
Afikpo
ethnography of **3:** 1753
Africa
adult education and missionaries **1:** 128
apprentices **1:** 223
apprenticeships
occupational categories **1:** 222
traditional **1:** ***221–227***
basic education **1:** 465, 466
civic education **2:** 768
community colleges **2:** 896
correspondence schools **3:** 1565
curriculum development **8:** 4681
economic change
and debt **3:** 1708
education and fertility **3:** 1672
educational administration **7:** 4243
educational expenditures
comparative area studies **5:** 2981
educational history **2:** 1060
educational radio **5:** 2885
educational research
action research **1:** 45
educational technology
video equipment **4:** 1902
equal education **11:** 6736, 6739
financial support
international **5:** 2989, 2991
labor force planning **6:** 3609
evaluations **6:** 3612
population
school age **3:** 1450
primary education
equal education **9:** 5386
primary school agriculture **8:** ***4680–4688***
public sector earnings **8:** 4839
racial segregation
in schools **8:** 4681
secondary education
diversified **11:** 6254
interviews **9:** 5387
selection **9:** 5386
secondary school curriculum
citizenship education **9:** 5579
social studies **10:** 5584
trends **9:** 5582
special needs students
educational diagnosis **2:** 717
teacher strikes **6:** 3193
technical assistance **11:** 6658
vocational education **11:** 6245
and educational planning **11:** 6255
international aid **11:** 6660, 6661
International Labour Organization programs **5:** 3002
women's education
and family financial resources **4:** 2416
See also
Anglophone Africa
East Africa
Francophone Africa
South Africa
Sub-Saharan Africa
West Africa
African Association for Literacy and Adult Education (AALAE) **5:** 2932; **8:** 4732
African Curriculum Organization (ACO) **3:** 1276
After school education
measurement-driven curriculum
Japan **7:** 3722
Age
and academic achievement **6:** 3285
earnings and on-the-job training **6:** 3614, 3615
effect on learning strategies **6:** 3287
effects on labor force participation
females **3:** 1669
and participation in adult education **1:** 104
Age differences
and attitude measures
science education **9:** 5322
teachers **10:** 5610
and youth culture **11:** 6802
Age–earnings profiles
characteristics of **3:** 1656
cross-sectional studies
human capital theory **3:** 1657
earnings differentials **3:** 1658
and education **3:** 1656; **6:** 3100
and employment level **4:** 2275
interpretation of **3:** 1656
research methodologies
synthetic cohort **3:** 1656
and sex bias **4:** 2441
and vocational education **3:** 1710
Age grade placement **1:** ***227–230***
compared with nongraded instructional grouping **7:** 4157
cross-cultural studies **9:** 5217
historical background **1:** 227
and school organization **9:** 5217
Age grouping
See Age grade placement

Age groups
and vocational education
Western Europe **11:** 6666
Agence de Coopération Culturelle et Technique (ACCT) (France)
educational technology
activities **4:** 1879
Agency for Instructional Television (AIT) **5:** 2893
Aggression **1:** ***230–234***
biological influences **1:** 232
in children
antisocial behavior **8:** 4798
hostility **1:** 230
intervention programs **1:** 233
and parent attitudes **1:** 232
cross-cultural studies **5:** 2649
developmental patterns **1:** 230
changes in form and elicitors of **1:** 230
sex differences **1:** 230
ethological theory **1:** 231
family influences **1:** 232
mass media influence **1:** 233
and peace education **3:** 1730
peer influence **1:** 233
peer relationship **8:** 4365, 4368
psychoanalytic theory **1:** 231
and rejection
by peer group **1:** 233
sex differences **9:** 5434
social cognitive theory **1:** 231, 233
socialization and **1:** 232
stability of **1:** 230
and violent entertainment **1:** 569
Aging (individuals)
and adult development **1:** ***234–239***
biological differences **8:** 4817
and cognition **8:** 4819
and deafness **8:** 4818
and knowledge utilization **8:** 4821
and labor force development **5:** 2688
and locus of control **1:** 237
memory and **8:** 4820
and nervous system **8:** 4818
and physical fitness **8:** 4818
research **1:** 234
and responses **8:** 4818
and self-concept **1:** 237
and social change **6:** 3426
and vision **8:** 4818
Agricultural education **1:** ***240–244***
agricultural literacy **1:** 243
agriculture in the classroom programs
United States **1:** 243
international aid
for vocational education **11:** 6663
rehabilitation and compensation programs
for the disadvantaged **1:** 244
and rural education **1:** 240
vocational education **1:** 241
decision-making skills **1:** 243
developed nations **1:** 242
developing nations **1:** 241
objectives **1:** 241
problems in **1:** 243
secondary schools **1:** 242
Agricultural extension agents
See Rural extension agents
Agricultural extension
See Rural extension
Agricultural production
in input output analysis measurement **3:** 1757
Agricultural productivity
and education **1:** ***244–254***; **5:** 2944
allocative effect **1:** 245, 252
empirical research **1:** 245
of farmers **3:** 1691, 1692; **6:** 3100
worker effect **1:** 245, 252
Agriculture
impact on society
educational programs **1:** 243
labor force participation
females **3:** 1667
occupational segregation in **4:** 2429
and primary education
Africa **8:** ***4680–4688***
teaching science through **1:** 243
and vocational education
Soviet Union (former) **10:** 5644, 5648
Aid agencies
and adult education **5:** 2948, 2950
educational policy
problems **4:** 1839
studies **4:** 1838
and educational research **5:** 2964
leadership training **1:** 69
and official development assistance **5:** 2961
policies **5:** 2964
role of **5:** 2962
and small business training **4:** 1988
See also
Donors
International aid
AIDS (disease)
See Acquired Immune Deficiency Syndrome (AIDS)
Air conditioning
educational facilities **4:** 2221
Alaska
evaluation studies **4:** 2117
Albania
adult education
nonformal education **1:** 257
curriculum development **1:** 258
educational research **1:** 259
ethnic groups **1:** 254
government school relationship
school administration **1:** 257
illiteracy **2:** 657
language **1:** 254
law
and education **1:** 258
literacy campaign **2:** 658
postsecondary education **1:** 256
preschool education **1:** 257
primary education **1:** 256
private education **1:** 258
secondary education **1:** 256
vocational education **1:** 257
special education **1:** 257
system of education **1:** ***254–260***
degrees and qualifications **1:** 259
educational objectives **1:** 255
enrollment **1:** 255
historical background **1:** 255
major problems **1:** 259
teacher education **1:** 258
teacher recruitment
women **1:** 258
technical education **1:** 257
Alcohol abuse
history of **3:** 1608
and resilience **8:** 4778
Algebra
computer-assisted instruction **7:** 4096
early history of
instruction **6:** 3643
high school curriculum **6:** 3678
learning strategies **6:** 3658
technology and research **6:** 3678
thinking skills **6:** 3678
Algorithms **6:** 3669
computation **6:** 3673
for computer-assisted testing **5:** 2781
PROX **5:** 2781
construction of
and computer literacy **2:** 975
and Galois lattice method **4:** 2398, 2399
relational
and idea generation **5:** 2723
Alienation
in secondary schools **9:** 5378
All India Association for Educational Technology (AIAET) **3:** 1798
Allergy
effect on learning **5:** 2565
Allocated time
See Time management
Allocation of resources
See Resource allocation
Alpha coefficient **5:** 2645
and earnings differentials **3:** 1659
Alphabets **1:** 481
written language
writing readiness **4:** 1959
Alternation education **8:** 4337, ***4957–4965***
benefits of **8:** 4962
impact **8:** 4962
use of term **1:** 119; **8:** 4961
Alternative communication
speech handicaps **1:** ***404–409***
definition **1:** 404
Alternative programs
See Nontraditional education
Alternative schools
See Nontraditional education
Alternative teacher certification **10:** 5927, 5929, 5961
issues and trends **10:** 5927
regional **10:** 5927
Altruism
children
moral development **8:** 4798

cross-cultural studies **5:** 2649
and feminism **4:** 2294
young children **8:** 4797
and moral development **7:** 3918
Ambition
See Aspiration
American Anthropological Association **1:** 281, 282, 283; **7:** 3972
Council on Anthropology and Education **1:** 279; **7:** 3972
curriculum study project **1:** 279
and feminism **7:** 3972
and teaching of anthropology **1:** 298; **7:** 3972
teaching task force **1:** 279
American Association for Adult and Continuing Education **1:** 145; **7:** 4148, 4181; **8:** 4731, 4732, 4733, 4734
financial support **8:** 4734
publications **8:** 4734
American Association of Colleges for Teacher Education (AACTE)
general education **3:** 1631
study of teacher educators **10:** 6009
American Association for Counseling and Development (AACD)
See American Counseling Association (ACA)
American Association on Mental Retardation (AAMR)
classification scheme **7:** 3826
American Association of School Librarians (AASL) **3:** 1798
American Association of School Personnel Administrators **8:** 4746
American Association of Secondary School Principals **8:** 4746
American Association of State Colleges and Universities (AASCU)
educational planning **3:** 1828
American College Testing (ACT)
and equated scores **11:** 6354
American Counseling Association (ACA)
standards **9:** 5283
American Educational Research Association (AERA) **1:** 145; **4:** 1863; **7:** 4051, 4052
curriculum research **3:** 1265
and educational administration
international **5:** 2952
educational researchers **11:** 6438, 6443, 6444
Test Standards **8:** 4737
American Federation of Teachers **8:** 4746
American Library Association (ALA) **6:** 3401
American Lyceum **8:** 4732, 4733
American Psychological Association (APA)
and school psychologists **9:** 5286
Test Standards **8:** 4737, 4743
American Samoa
educational television **4:** 1904
large-scale projects **5:** 2892
language **1:** 266
religious education **9:** 4998
system of education **1:** ***266–274***
educational objectives **1:** 266, 267
structure **1:** 268
American sign language **3:** 1400
American Society for Training and Development **7:** 4181
human resource wheel **3:** 1487
labor force development study **5:** 2686
Amish
literacy **6:** 3448
Analog models **7:** 3866
example **7:** 3867
Analysis
See Evaluation methods
Analysis of covariance (ANCOVA) **11:** ***6586–6591***
applications **11:** 6590
assumptions underlying **11:** 6590
and change
measurement of **2:** 677
computer software **11:** 6590, 6591
and experimental studies **4:** 2190
models **11:** 6589
and nonparametric statistics **7:** 4161
one-way
statistical power of **4:** 2191
procedures **11:** 6589
Analysis of variance (ANOVA) **11:** ***6586–6591***
applications **11:** 6586
assumptions underlying **11:** 6590
computer software **11:** 6591
and effect size **7:** 3782
estimation of effects **11:** 6588
examples **11:** 6586, 6587, 6588
and exploratory data analysis **4:** 2205
function **11:** 6586
and generalizability theory **5:** 2458
and interaction **11:** 6587
and interaction effects **5:** 2925
and item sampling **5:** 3057
models **11:** 6586
and multiple regression analysis **9:** 4969
one-way
and intraclass correlation coefficients **7:** 3736
statistical power of **4:** 2191
procedures **11:** 6586
and reliability **9:** 4984, 4989
three-way analysis **9:** 4986
and robustness (statistics) **9:** 5080
statistical significance **11:** 6588
two-way **11:** 6588
uses of **11:** 6586
Analytic philosophy **8:** ***4442–4447***
achievements of **8:** 4446
clarification of concepts **8:** 4449, 4454
criticism of **8:** 4443
development of **8:** 4442
and philosophy of education **8:** 4449, 4454, 4574
Anarchism
and philosophy of education **8:** 4573
Ancillary school services
and related services personnel **9:** 5289
Andragogy **1:** 117, 121, ***274–277***
andragogical cycle **1:** 276
compared with pedagogy **1:** 276, 277
concept of **1:** 275; **10:** 5595
and continuing education **1:** 92
definition **1:** 144
derivation of word **1:** 274
and experiential learning **1:** 164
future of **1:** 277
history **1:** 274
and ideologies **5:** 2733, 2735
independent study **9:** 5395
normative theory **1:** 275
objectives **1:** 274
origins of **1:** 274
as a specific approach **1:** 276
and teacher role **10:** 6054
uses of term **1:** 274
varieties of **1:** 275
Andragology **1:** 275
Androgyny
individual psychology **4:** 2446
Anemia
effect on learning **5:** 2565
Anger
effect on performance **1:** 200
Anglophone Africa
adult education **1:** ***210–215***
concept of **1:** 210
enrollment rate **1:** 214
Animation socio-culturelle
Africa **1:** 216, 217
Anorexia nervosa **3:** 1516
Anthropological linguistics **1:** 297, 299; **6:** ***3235–3238***
Anthropology
applied
in education **1:** 289
and bilingual education **1:** ***531–535***
cultural **1:** 297
cultural context
and cognitive processes **3:** 1247
and cultural transmission **3:** ***1724–1729***, ***1726***
data collection **4:** 2047, 2048
definitions **1:** 297
development of field studies **4:** 2047
evolution of education studies **1:** 288
and development of written language **1:** 289
and literacy **1:** 289
and socialization **1:** 288
and sociocultural patterns **1:** 288
in high schools
Canada **1:** 298
future trends **1:** 299
United States **1:** 298
holistic tradition **2:** 914
inservice teacher education

United States **1:** 298
multicultural education **7:** ***3971–3974***
future research **7:** 3973
and oral history
relationships **7:** 4221
study of literacy **6:** ***3446–3453***
study of numeracy **6:** ***3446–3453***
and teacher education **7:** 3973
teaching of **1:** ***277–280***
current status in schools **1:** 278
and curriculum development **1:** 278
disciplinary support **1:** 279
future prospects **1:** 279
high schools **1:** 278, ***297–300***
historical background **1:** 278
and multicultural education **1:** 278
in public schools **1:** 281, 293
See also
Ethnography
Anthropology of education
historical background **1:** 280
history and overview **1:** ***280–297***
Anthropometry
See Body size
Anti poverty programs
See Poverty programs
Antigonish Movement
Canada **2:** 1190; **7:** 4182
Antigua and Barbuda
curriculum development **1:** 304
educational change **1:** 305
educational research **1:** 304
government school relationship
school administration **1:** 303
language **1:** 300
postsecondary education **1:** 301
preschool education **1:** 302
primary education **1:** 301
secondary education **1:** 301
special education **1:** 302
student evaluation **1:** 304
system of education **1:** ***300–306***
educational objectives **1:** 300
major problems **1:** 305
structure **1:** 301
teacher education **1:** 303
teacher recruitment **1:** 303
teaching methodology **1:** 304
technical education **1:** 302
vocational education **1:** 302, 305
Antisocial behavior
aggression **1:** ***230–234***; **3:** 1516
behavior disorders **1:** ***490–495***
behavior modification **1:** 491
decriminalization of delinquency **3:** 1438
peer relationship **8:** 4365, 4368
sociobiological approach **4:** 2171
special programs for **1:** 488
and violent entertainment **1:** 569
Anxiety **3:** 1516
in adult learning **6:** 3432
and aptitude treatment interaction **10:** 6158
disorders
drug therapy for **8:** 4422
effect on learning **1:** 199
and eye contact
in classrooms **7:** 4173
in interviews **5:** 3004
Speilberger's theory of **11:** 6356
and stress management **10:** 5737
See also
Mathematics anxiety
Stress (psychological)
Test anxiety
Applied music
music education **7:** 4017
Appraisal
See Evaluation
Apprenticeship proposals
apprentices **1:** 225
masters **1:** 226
United States
costs and benefits to apprentices **1:** 309
costs and benefits to employers **1:** 309
costs and benefits to society **1:** 309
youth
United States **1:** 309
Apprenticeships **1:** 105, 108; **4:** 1975; **5:** 2938
and academic achievement
Africa **1:** 223
and alternation education **8:** 4961
and alternative training **1:** 312
apprentices
Africa **1:** 223
characteristics of **1:** 310, 312, 316; **7:** 4206
Colombia **10:** 6064
as a component of school education **9:** 5230
construction industry **11:** 6636
contractual conditions
Africa **1:** 224
cost effectiveness of **9:** 5072, 5073; **11:** 6695
costs **11:** 6418
in developed nations **1:** 312
in developing nations **1:** 315; **11:** 6657
dropouts
Africa **1:** 223
economic and political background **11:** 6654
economics of **1:** ***306–310***
and educational technology **4:** 1918
effect of economic crisis on
German Democratic Republic (former) **11:** 6656
enrollment rate
Germany, Federal Republic of (former) **11:** 6654
finance
Africa **1:** 224
and financing lifelong learning **6:** 3424
in former COMECON nations **1:** 314
and general education
Germany, Federal Republic of (former) **11:** 6654
Germany **1:** 108, 306, 307; **6:** 3616; **11:** 6419
costs and benefits to apprentices **1:** 308
costs and benefits to employers **1:** 308
costs and benefits to society **1:** 308
Germany, Federal Republic of (former) **11:** 6638, 6653, 6664, 6693
historical background **1:** ***310–318***, 310; **11:** 6681
Germany **1:** 311
and imperialism
Germany, Federal Republic of (former) **11:** 6654
instructional innovation
Germany, Federal Republic of (former) **11:** 6656
learning processes
Africa **1:** 224
main features of **1:** 306
modular programs
United Kingdom **11:** 6685
and national training agencies
Latin America **6:** 3263
occupational categories
Africa **1:** 222
open enrollment
Germany, Federal Republic of (former) **11:** 6655
Poland **11:** 6643
and productivity **4:** 2366
and school business partnerships **9:** 5186
and school business relationship **8:** 4337
selection
factors affecting **11:** 6694
and skill development **3:** 1242
Soviet Union (former) **9:** 5094
Sweden **11:** 6691
and technical education
Germany **11:** 6269
technological advancement
Germany, Federal Republic of (former) **11:** 6656
traditional
Africa **1:** ***221–227***
characteristics of **1:** 224
policy issues **1:** 225
training costs
Germany **2:** 1149
United Kingdom **2:** 1149
and training standards **6:** 3616
and unions **1:** 108
United Kingdom **11:** 6638
United States **1:** 109
costs and benefits to apprentices **1:** 307
costs and benefits to employers **1:** 307
costs and benefits to society **1:** 307
United States and Germany
comparison of **1:** 306
West Africa **11:** 6247

Western Europe **11:** 6664
See also
Vocational education
Approaches to Study Inventory (ASI) (UK) **1:** 320
Approved programs (validated)
See Validated programs
Aptitude **6:** ***3312–3315***
and academic achievement
interaction effects **5:** 2923
and achievement **1:** 1
cognitive psychological approaches **1:** 2
concept of **6:** 3312
definitions of **11:** 6670
distinguished from ability **6:** 3312
future research **1:** 5
grading according to **10:** 5819
individual differences **1:** ***1–6***
and educational improvement **5:** ***2759–2769***
learning
definition of **11:** 6341
learning factors in **8:** 4400, 4402
research issues **6:** 3313
sociology **6:** 3307
and Sternberg's triarchic theory **6:** 3313
theories of **1:** 1
research **11:** 6671
and time on task **7:** 3882
and Vygotsky's zone of proximal development **6:** 3313
See also
Academic aptitude
Aptitude tests **1:** 1
basic format **6:** 3313
characteristics of **11:** 6341
content of **6:** 3314
and curriculum **6:** 3314, 3315
development of **5:** 2875
history of educational research **4:** 1865
in job selection **3:** 1701
measurement of change **6:** 3314
and moderation procedures **4:** 2176
and objective tests **7:** 4193
predictive measurement **6:** ***3312–3315***
research trends **6:** 3314
secondary education
selection **9:** 5387
sex differences in **9:** 5428
use of **6:** 3314
validity of **6:** 3314
See also
Academic aptitude, tests
Differential aptitude tests
Scholastic Aptitude Test (SAT)
School readiness tests
Aptitude treatment interaction (ATI) **1:** 2; **5:** 2875, 2883, 2929
and cognitive development **10:** 6165
definitions of **10:** 6155
statistical **10:** 6156
substantive **10:** 6155
diagnostic teaching **10:** 6170
evaluation **10:** 6157
future research **10:** 6158
hierarchical levels **5:** 2929
instructional effectiveness **10:** 6170
and instructional systems
examples **10:** 6157
and media research **7:** 3742
methodology **10:** 6156
model
teaching **10:** ***6155–6159***
and placement **3:** 1418
research
problems **10:** 6156, 6157
Arab Bureau of Education for the Gulf States
objectives **8:** 4483
Arab League Educational, Cultural and Scientific Organization (ALECSO) **1:** 323; **2:** 1061; **8:** 4732
Arab Literacy Organization (ARLO) **1:** 323; **5:** 2932
Arab nations
adult education **1:** ***322–328***
cooperative programs **1:** 327
financial support **1:** 326
history and objectives **1:** 322
institutional arrangements and program development **1:** 326
participation **1:** 326
trends and policy implications **1:** 326
basic education **1:** 465, 466
characteristics of **8:** 4483
citizenship education **9:** 5579
education and fertility **3:** 1672
educational administration **7:** 4243
educational history **2:** 1061
educational planning **8:** ***4483–4485***
characteristics of **8:** 4484
limitations **8:** 4484
illiteracy
eradication programs **1:** 323, 327
literacy **1:** 323
population growth **1:** 322
vocational education
International Labour Organization programs **5:** 3002
women's education **1:** 327
Arab Organization of Education, Culture, and Science (AOECS)
objectives **8:** 4483
Arabic
computer software
special needs students **10:** 5671
Arbeit und Leben
and labor education **11:** 6771
Arbeitsschulen **6:** 3133, 3135
and citizenship education **6:** 3135
Archaeology **1:** 297, 299
and discriminant analysis **3:** 1545
promotion of school programs
Europe **1:** 279
teaching of
comparative studies **1:** 278
in high schools **1:** 278
Architectural design *See* Building design
Area
conversions
and achievement tests **1:** 39
Area studies
case study approach **1:** 332
comparative education **1:** ***331–332***
educational development approach **1:** 331
international education **1:** ***331–332***
international studies **5:** 2976
use of term **1:** 331
Argentina
adult education **1:** 336; **6:** 3253
cultural influences **1:** 332
curriculum development **1:** 337
educational research **1:** 337
government school relationship
financial support **1:** 334
school administration **1:** 336
labor education **1:** 129
labor force participation
females **3:** 1669
and industrial development **3:** 1668
labor market analysis
informal sector **3:** 1680
postsecondary education **1:** 335
preschool education **1:** 334
primary education **1:** 334
private education **1:** 334
secondary education **1:** 334
special education **1:** 335
structure of government **1:** 333
student evaluation **1:** 337
system of education **1:** ***332–338***
educational objectives **1:** 334
enrollment **1:** 334
major problems **1:** 337
structure **1:** 334
teacher recruitment **1:** 336
technical education **1:** 335
universities
and research training **11:** 6280
vocational education
apprenticeships **11:** 6659
historical background **6:** 3257
technical **6:** 3258
Argumentation *See* Persuasive discourse
Arithmetic
basic skills **6:** 3456
computation **6:** 3673
curriculum development **6:** 3672
elementary schools
history of **6:** 3644
mathematics curriculum **6:** 3673
mathematics instruction **6:** 3673
place value
instructional materials **6:** 3659
symbols **6:** 3659
skills
cognitive development **2:** 848
See also
Addition
Subtraction
Armed forces
adult education in **8:** 4807

Armed Services Vocational Aptitude Battery (ASVAB)
and vocational evaluation **11:** 6671
Arousal patterns
effect on learning **1:** 199
learning processes **6:** 3432
Art
and cultural pluralism
anthropological perspective **7:** 3972
philosophy of **1:** 195
Art appreciation **11:** 6617
Art criticism **1:** 196; **11:** 6617
Art education
aesthetic education
interdisciplinary approach **1:** 196
as a school subject **1:** 196
structural modes of analysis **1:** 196
and Bauhaus **1:** 340
clinical psychology **11:** 6616
cognitive psychology **11:** 6616
cultural differences **11:** 6616
curriculum reform
Germany **6:** 3135
developing nations **1:** 342
developmental psychology **11:** 6616
discipline-based
teacher education **11:** 6619, 6620
United States **1:** 197, 341
educational programs **1:** ***338–343***
England and Wales **1:** 341
France **1:** 341
Froebelian kindergarten **1:** 339
Germany **1:** 341
historical background **11:** 6616
historical development **1:** 339
and ideology
Soviet Union (former) **1:** 340
and intellectual disciplines **1:** 196
Japan **1:** 342
and mass media **11:** 6616
and progressive education **1:** 340
psychological frameworks **11:** 6616
in public schools **11:** 6616
research **1:** 342
role of aesthetic education in **1:** 197
secondary schools **1:** 340
in United States **1:** 340
Waldorf education **1:** 341
Art expression
cultural influences **11:** 6617
self-expression **1:** 339, 340
Art history **1:** 196, 340
Art teachers
specialists
teacher education **11:** 6618, 6620
Art therapy **11:** 6616
gifted **5:** 2491
Articulation (education)
of education, training, and work
Latin America **6:** ***3256–3262***
Articulation (speech)
assessment
phoneme-oriented **10:** 5694
therapy **10:** 5694
Articulation impairments **10:** ***5694–5697***
and hearing impairments **10:** 5688
incidence of **10:** 5692
and speech handicaps **10:** 5691
See also
Cleft palate
Stuttering
Artificial intelligence
computer software **5:** 2919
and declarative and procedural knowledge **3:** 1432, 1433
definition **1:** 344
and instructional design **1:** ***343–348***
uses in **1:** 346
models
Sierra **1:** 347
and teaching models **1:** 345
Artistic talent
See Talent
Artists
teachers as **10:** ***6083–6086***
Arts centers
and adult education **8:** 4807
Asia
adult education **1:** ***348–353***
characteristics of **1:** 349, 352
and credentials **1:** 350, 353
East **1:** 348
and economic development **1:** 353
financial support **1:** 350, 352
objectives **1:** 349, 353
provision **1:** 348, 351
Southeast **1:** 351
automation
and effects on skills **11:** 6279
basic education **1:** 465, 466
civic education **2:** 768
distance education **1:** 562
earnings differentials
and education **3:** 1712
education and fertility **3:** 1672
educational choice
sex bias **4:** 2413
educational development **8:** 4485
patterns of **8:** 4487
educational facilities planning **8:** 4485
educational history **2:** 1061
educational indicators **5:** 2988
educational planning **8:** ***4485–4489***
changes in scope **8:** 4487
and educational technology **8:** 4488
experiences **8:** 4486
future trends **8:** 4488
origins **8:** 4485
problems **8:** 4486
regional initiatives **8:** 4486
educational radio **5:** 2886
educational research
action research **1:** 45
literacy education **6:** ***3463–3467***
teacher rights
denial of **6:** 3191
technical assistance **11:** 6657
technical education
and paraprofessional personnel **11:** 6269
vocational education
International Labour Organization programs **5:** 3002
training with production **11:** 6448
Asia and Pacific Program of Educational Innovation for Development (APEID) **8:** 4486
Asian Association of Open Universities (AAOU) **1:** 563; **7:** 4216
development of **3:** 1581
objectives **3:** 1581
Asian Development Bank
distance education program **5:** 2934
Asian South Pacific Bureau of Adult Education (ASPBAE) **5:** 2932; **6:** 3464; **8:** 4732
Aspiration
causal variations **1:** 357
compared with expectation **1:** 355
and educational attainment **1:** 356
future research **1:** 357
sex differences **4:** 2410
student interpretation of **1:** 356
of students **1:** ***354–358***
Soviet Union (former) **10:** 5648
See also
Occupational aspiration
Parent aspiration
Assertiveness
children
prosocial behavior **8:** 4798
Assessment
criterion-referenced
See Criterion-referenced tests
early childhood education **1:** ***358–362***
and learning **1:** ***370–374***
performance
and educational assessment **1:** 369
grading **10:** 5821
teacher education **10:** 5955
special needs students
cultural differences **2:** 717
See also
Evaluation
Measurement
Testing
Assessment centers (personnel)
administrator selection **1:** 80
and evaluation of principals **4:** 2130
France **2:** 663
in teacher development
United States **4:** 2128
Assessment of Performance Unit (APU) (UK) **7:** 3907
curriculum coverage **7:** 3907
and mathematics **8:** 4644
monitoring standards **7:** 3907, 3911
oracy testing **6:** 3470
and science **8:** 4645
and science education **9:** 5330
Assignments
completion of
social contexts **9:** 5361
and teacher assistance **9:** 5361
criticisms of **9:** 5360
future trends **9:** 5362

issues **9:** 5360
supervision of **9:** ***5359–5363***
types of **9:** 5359
and understanding **9:** 5360
See also
Homework
Seatwork
Assistive devices (for disabled)
and educational technology **10:** 5668
See also
Communication aids (for disabled)
Assistive technology
access to **10:** 5669
applications **10:** 5669
definition of **10:** 5668
funding **10:** 5669
and special needs students **10:** 5669
Association for Community-based Education (US) **2:** 901; **7:** 4147
Association for Computing Machinery (US)
computer science courses **2:** 970
Association for Continuing Higher Education (ACHE) (US) **8:** 4731, 4732
Association for Educational Communications and Technology (AECT) (US) **3:** 1797, 1798; **4:** 1925
ethics
code of **4:** 1927
instructional development **5:** 2858
Association for Educational Training and Technology (AETT) (UK) **3:** 1797
Association of European Correspondence Schools (AECS) **7:** 4216
objectives **3:** 1582
Association for the Higher Education of Working Men (UK) **8:** 4732, 4733
Association for Moral Education
and cultural pluralism **10:** 5990
Association Nationale pour la Formation Professionelle des Adultes (France) **1:** 182
Association for Persons with Severe Handicaps, The (TASH) **3:** 1505
Association of School Business Officials (ASBO) (US)
guidelines **9:** 5182
survey **9:** 5182
Association of South East Asian Nations (ASEAN)
adult education programs **6:** 3464
Association for Supervision and Curriculum Development (ASCD) (US) **3:** 1360
Association of Tutors in Adult Education (UK)
courses **11:** 6432
Association for World Education **5:** 2932
Associative learning **6:** 3316, 3319
mammalian foundations **5:** 2681
measurement of **6:** 3316
and memory **7:** 3765
problem-solving **8:** 4726
At risk persons
adolescents **1:** 87
definitions **2:** 706
global approach **2:** 706
high risk students **2:** ***706–711***
ATD Fourth World Movement **1:** 102
Athletic coaches
behavior **10:** 5709
preparation
descriptive studies **10:** 5711
Athletics
and physical education **8:** 4466
Attachment behavior
and aggression
developmental patterns **1:** 232
to child caregiver
and emotional development **4:** 1966
cross-cultural studies **5:** 2649
mother–infant
and day care **5:** 2804
reactive attachment disorder **3:** 1516
Attainment
See Educational attainment
Attendance
and academic achievement **11:** 6389
diversity of
and organizational effectiveness **9:** 5374
and dropouts **3:** 1602
female blacks
South Africa **7:** 3851
and human capital theory
parental attitudes **6:** 3102
and school organization **7:** 4233
See also
Teacher attendance
Attendance patterns
and educational history **5:** 2606
and truancy **3:** 1603
vocational education
Japan **6:** 3089
Attendance records
and dropout rate **3:** 1603
Attention **1:** ***374–377***
and ability
individual differences **1:** 375
in cognitive science **1:** 374
concept formation
cognitive system model **2:** 1018
conceptual models **1:** 375
definition **1:** 374
empirical educational research **1:** 371, 375
future research trends **1:** 376
involuntary arousal **1:** 375
and learning **1:** 328, 330
measurement **1:** 375
and motivation **1:** 374, 375; **7:** 3944
and neurophysiology **1:** 375
in observational learning **9:** 5514
role in short term memory **1:** 375
selective strategies **1:** 375, 376
and television viewing
children and youth **1:** 566
voluntary **1:** 375
Attention control
age effects **6:** 3287
in learning **6:** 3318
metacognition **7:** 3785
self efficacy
and academic achievement **1:** 376
Attention deficit disorders **1:** 375
hyperactivity **3:** 1516, 1517; **8:** 4419, 4420
and drug use **3:** 1611
and personality **11:** 6309
and minimal brain dysfunction **1:** 491
Attitude change
consciousness raising **1:** 379
measurement **1:** 381
toward science **9:** 5318
Attitude measures **1:** ***380–390***
and acquiescence **1:** 388
attitudinal items
construction of **1:** 383
and behavioral measures **1:** 385
comparative analysis **1:** ***390–396***
validity **1:** 391
cross-cultural studies **1:** 391
choice of item format **1:** 391
construct validity **1:** 395
degree of internalization **1:** 392
problems with **1:** 391
response style (tests) **1:** 391
specification of dimensions **1:** 391
cultural differences **1:** 395
development of **7:** 3703
external validity **1:** 387
and facet theory **4:** 2214
future of **1:** 389
Guttman scales **1:** 382, 384, 387, 392
item response theory **1:** 395
mathematics education
sex differences in **9:** 5430
methods **9:** 5319
multidimensional **6:** 3639
and partial credit model **7:** 4304
and path analysis **8:** 4355
problems in **1:** 388
projective methods **1:** 386
and psychological response **1:** 386
Rasch **1:** 387
reliability **1:** 386
responses
nature of **1:** 382
scales
construction of **1:** 383
testing properties of **1:** 383
in science education **9:** 5319
scores
distribution of **1:** 388
self-reports **1:** 382
and social desirability **1:** 388
structural equation model **1:** 395
studies **1:** 389
technical quality of **1:** 386
and test translation **11:** ***6328–6334***

problems **11:** 6330
training **11:** 6330
Thurstone scales **1:** 382, 387; **11:** 6386, 6387
visual representation **1:** 381
vs. descriptive scales **3:** 1482
See also
Likert scales
Semantic differential
Attitude scales
See Attitude measures
Attitudes
academic
to collaborative research **7:** 4334
and adult education participation **7:** 4322
capitalism **1:** 129
change across lifespan **8:** 4823
components of **1:** 354
affective **1:** 354
cognitive **1:** 354
conative **1:** 354, 356
consistency of **1:** 381
correspondence with behavior **1:** 354, 356
cross-national comparison
evaluation of **4:** ***2132–2140***
definitions of **1:** 378, 380; **9:** 5318
developing nations **1:** 129
development in adults **8:** 4822
direction of **1:** 381
and educational research
oral history approach **7:** 4223
emotional component of **1:** 381
in evaluation studies **4:** 2094
as hypothetical constructs **1:** 387
and instructional design theory **5:** 2866
intensity of **1:** 381
interaction effects **5:** 2926
measurement of **1:** ***380–390***
and surveys **10:** 5856
and motivation **1:** 354
positive
and individual development **9:** 5404
relationship with achievement **1:** 390
sex differences in
and outcomes of education **9:** 5429
systems approach **1:** 378
targets of **1:** 381
and values **1:** ***377–380***
Attribution theory **4:** 1963
in education **10:** 6222
and learning motivation **7:** 3939
and mathematics anxiety **11:** 6359
and psychological impact of life events **8:** 4718
self-concept **9:** ***5403–5407***
sex differences **9:** 5443
and social cognition **9:** 5511
and test anxiety **11:** 6356
Audience analysis
and content analysis **2:** 1075
and narrative inquiry **7:** 4050
Audience response
mass media
studies **1:** 564
Audiences
of credentials **8:** 4617
for scholarly journals **5:** 2996
Audio equipment
acoustic characteristics of **1:** 397
consoles **1:** 399
in education **1:** 396; **7:** 3748
and educational research **11:** 6605
loudspeakers **1:** 399
microphones **1:** 398
mixers **1:** 399
Audio media
applications **7:** 3749
audiotape recorders
digital **1:** 398
and audiovisual instruction **1:** 401
characteristics of **7:** 3748
classroom use of **1:** 399
in education **7:** 3744
educational role of **7:** ***3744–3753***
optical disks **1:** 397
production of **1:** ***396–400***
recordings **1:** 399
sound quality in **1:** 396
speech and music **1:** 400
types of **7:** 3748
Audiodisks
analog **1:** 396
characteristics of **7:** 3749
digital **1:** 397
and language laboratories **6:** 3238
Audiolingual methods
foreign language instruction **4:** 2341, 2353
Audiotape cassettes
characteristics of **7:** 3750
digital (R-DAT) **1:** 398
uses in education **1:** 401
Audiotape recorders **7:** 3749
digital **1:** 398
multitrack **1:** 399
Audiotape recordings
analog **1:** 396
characteristics of **7:** 3749
digital **1:** 397
in educational research **11:** ***6604–6608***
analytic issues **11:** 6607
settings for **11:** 6606
techniques **11:** 6606
uses **11:** 6604
validity **11:** 6607
mixing process **1:** 399
open reel
characteristics of **7:** 3750
technical considerations **11:** 6605
Audiovisual aids
adult education **10:** 6201
in education **1:** 400; **4:** 1904
educational role of **7:** ***3744–3753***
theoretical bases **7:** 3744
foreign language instruction **4:** 2353
and message design **7:** 3772
and programmed instruction **8:** 4773
sound/slide programs
applications **7:** 3751
characteristics of **7:** 3750
teacher education curriculum **10:** 6005
technical characteristics of **1:** 401
types of **7:** 3746, 3750
in education **4:** 1913
use of **4:** 1883
and verbal learning **7:** 3744
Audiovisual communications
and distance education
United States **3:** 1566
Audiovisual coordinators
role of **4:** 1883
Audiovisual instruction
and educational technology **4:** 1883, 1891
program production **1:** ***400–404***
facilities for **1:** 403
and teaching machines **4:** 1884
Audiovisual materials
See Audiovisual aids
Audiovisual media
See Audiovisual aids
Audiovisual programs
See Audiovisual instruction
Auditory perception
infants **8:** 4382
language processing **8:** 4382
and intelligence **5:** 2760
Auditory stimuli
responses by fetus to **1:** 13
and smallest space analysis **9:** 5501
and test bias **11:** 6319
Auditory training
deaf–blind children **3:** 1404
Augmentative and alternative communication **1:** ***404–409***
aided and unaided approaches **1:** 404
autism **6:** 3232
and communicative competence **1:** 408
consequences of using **1:** 407
multimodal approach **1:** 407
needs assessment **1:** 405
potential users **1:** 405
selection techniques **1:** 405
symbols **1:** 405
system selection **1:** 407
transmission techniques **1:** 405
Augmentative communication
deaf–blind children **3:** 1404
speech handicaps **1:** ***404–409***
definition **1:** 404
Australia **2:** 895, 896
academically gifted
research **9:** 5530
adult basic education **1:** 101, 410
adult education **1:** ***409–415***, 418
community provision **1:** 411
general education **1:** 410
government departments and agencies **1:** 411
institutions **1:** 411
labor market organizations **1:** 412
participation **1:** 107, 410
private sector provision **1:** 412
public provision **1:** 411

status **1:** 410
adult vocational education **1:** 411
career education and disabilities **2:** 633
citizenship education
and citizen participation **4:** 1982
civic education **2:** 767
class size **6:** 3371
community education **1:** ***409–415***; **2:** 902
computer-managed learning **2:** 1000
computer uses in education
organizations for **2:** 1015
courseware
design training **10:** 5622
curriculum-based assessment **3:** 1357
curriculum development **1:** 420
distance education
in schools **3:** 1564
educational administration
theories of **1:** 61
educational change **1:** 422
educational finance
and unions **5:** 2507
educational history **2:** 1062
educational policy
effect of unions on **10:** 6070
teacher role in **10:** 6080
educational radio
interactive programs **4:** 1913
educational research **1:** 422
action research **1:** 44
and databases **3:** 1394
essay tests **4:** 2014
interaction effects **5:** 2927
priorities **9:** 5032, 5036, 5037
vocational interests **11:** 6676
educational technology
role of **9:** 5542
rural areas **9:** 5542
employment policy and on-the-job training **6:** 3616
equal education
and governance **5:** 2504
ethnic groups **1:** 415
family environment
studies **4:** 2245
females
equal opportunities **4:** 2291
gifted disadvantaged **5:** 2487
governance
schools **6:** 3494
government school relationship **1:** 416
financial support **1:** 419
school administration **1:** 419
higher education
and student fees **10:** 5751
history of women's education **11:** ***6731–6735***
immigrants
educational attainment **8:** 4893
labor force surveys **11:** 6416, 6417, 6418
labor relations
in education **6:** 3193
leadership
research **6:** 3282
theories of **6:** 3280
national surveys **2:** 650
competence **6:** 3468
nontraditional students
higher education **7:** ***4163–4171***
occupations
classification of **7:** 3717
on-the-job training **4:** 1975
postsecondary education **1:** 417
preschool education **1:** 416
primary education **1:** 416
principals
role of **9:** 5269, 5270
private education **1:** 419
public schools vs. private schools **8:** 4842
school-based management **5:** 2507, 2849; **9:** 5303, 5304
characteristics of **9:** 5184
school choice **8:** 4825
school health education **5:** 2571
school reform
influences on **9:** 5278
school size
and resource allocation **9:** 5065
science and society
integrated curriculum **8:** 4475
second chance education
research **9:** 5365
secondary education **1:** 417
vocational education **1:** 418
social class
conflict **9:** 5311
sociology of education
development of **10:** 5599
special education **1:** 418
teams **10:** 6243
state departments of education **7:** 3836
and educational change **7:** 3839
role of Directors General **7:** 3837
student evaluation **1:** 421
student loan programs **10:** 5764
system of education **1:** ***415–423***
degrees and qualifications **1:** 420
educational objectives **1:** 416, 421
enrollment **1:** 416
historical background **1:** 415
major problems **1:** 422
structure **1:** 416
teacher education
accreditation **1:** 24, 25
teacher militancy **6:** 3191
teacher participation
decision making **9:** 5179
teacher persistence
barriers to **9:** 5178
teacher recruitment **1:** 420
teacher salaries
and legitimatory research **6:** 3371
teaching methods debate **6:** 3454
technical education **1:** 417
technical and further education colleges **4:** 2391; **8:** 4338
termination of national monitoring of standards **7:** 3911
test anxiety
studies **11:** 6358
training legislation **7:** 3711
training statistics **7:** 3712
unions **10:** 6068
state incorporation **10:** 6074
writing tests
and partial credit model **7:** 4306
youth culture
research **11:** 6801
Australian Aborigines
location system **6:** 3457
women's education **11:** 6734
Australian Association for Adult and Community Education **1:** 410
Australian Broadcasting Corporation (ABC)
educational radio **5:** 2885, 2886
Australian Council for Educational Research (ACER) **2:** 939
Basic Skills Testing Program **6:** 3469
tests **5:** 2927
Australian Education Council
Staffing and Resources Study **6:** 3372
Australian Education Index (AEI)
contact details **5:** 2826
scope **5:** 2825
Australian literature
children's literature
portrayal of Aborigines **2:** 736
Australian Science Education Project (ASEP) **8:** 4476; **10:** 5773
Australian Society for Educational Technology (ASET) **3:** 1798
Australian and South Pacific External Studies Association **7:** 4216
Austria
adult education
financial support **6:** 3365
nonformal education. **1:** 426
apprenticeships **1:** 314
computer uses in education
organizations for **2:** 1015
curriculum development **1:** 428
educational change **1:** 430
educational finance
and school organization **7:** 4231
educational research **1:** 430
government school relationship
financial support **1:** 427
school administration **1:** 426
law
and education **1:** 426
parent participation
legislation **9:** 5213
research **9:** 5215
postsecondary education **1:** 425; **2:** 895
preschool education **1:** 425; **8:** 4669
primary education **1:** 424
secondary education **1:** 424
vocational education **1:** 424, 426
special education **1:** 425
system of education **1:** ***423–432***

educational objectives 1: 423, 428
enrollment 1: 423
major problems 1: 424, 425, 426, 431
structure 1: 423
teacher education 1: 425
teacher recruitment 1: 428
teaching methodology 1: 428
technical education 1: 426
vocational education 11: 6682
Authoring aids (programming)
for courseware design 10: 5622–5625
analysis procedures 10: 5623
evaluation procedures 10: 5623
future trends 10: 5624
languages 10: 5623
problems 10: 5624
systems 10: 5623
uses 10: 5622, 5624
and language laboratories 6: 3240
and models 2: 986
and multimedia systems 7: 3988, 3995
characteristics of 7: 3989
needs 10: 5624
for test item writing 2: 997
types of 10: 5622
Authoritarianism
and civic education 2: 768
and governance 5: 2511
Authority
contemporary issues 1: 434
modes of 1: 433
nature of 1: 432
persuasion and exchange 1: 433
in organizations
educational 1: 432–437
theories of 1: 432
Authority structure
See Power structure
Authors
cooperation
and printing 8: 4690
and copyrights 2: 1100, 1101
Autism 3: 1515
ability identification 6: 3232–3235
alternative communication methods 6: 3232
biophysical approach 1: 491
characteristic behavior 6: 3232
communication disorders 6: 3232–3235
communication problems
speech handicaps 6: 3232
drug therapy for 8: 4422
facilitated communication training 6: 3233
interpersonal relationship
social reinforcement approach 9: 5506
language handicaps 6: 3232–3235
mainstreaming 6: 3232
reading skills
early reading 6: 3233
reinforcement 9: 4976
social cognition
impairment 6: 3232
teaching methods 6: 3232
word recognition skills 6: 3232
writing skills 6: 3233
Autobiographies
and biographical research 1: 539
educational history in 3: 1793–1797
and narrative inquiry 7: 4047, 4048
and student experience 10: 5814
See also
Biographies
Autodidaxy
See Independent study
Autoinstructional aids
early developments 8: 4768
See also
Teaching machines
Automatic interaction detection (AID) 5: 2924
and multivariate analysis 7: 4011
Automation
and skill development 10: 5917
Autonomous learning
See Independent study
Awareness
See Perception

Baby boomers 1: 235
and educational planning 3: 1452
Baccalauréat 1: 182
and technical education 11: 6269
Back to Basics Movement (US) 6: 3454, 3456
and intellectual disciplines 9: 5295
mathematics education 6: 3646
Bahamas
curriculum development 1: 443
educational change 1: 441
ethnic groups 1: 439
government school relationship
school administration 1: 442
postsecondary education 1: 442
private education 1: 441
secondary education
vocational education 1: 441
structure of government 1: 440
student evaluation 1: 443
system of education 1: 439–444
educational objectives 1: 440
major problems 1: 444
structure 1: 441
teacher education 1: 443
technical education 1: 442
Bahrain
curriculum development 1: 448
educational change 1: 449
educational research 1: 449
educational technology
special needs students 10: 5671
enrollment rates 9: 5536
government school relationship
financial support 1: 448
school administration 1: 447
literacy 1: 447
nonformal education 1: 447
postsecondary education 1: 446
preschool education 1: 446
private education 1: 445
special education 1: 447
student evaluation 1: 449
system of education 1: 444–450
educational objectives 1: 445
major problems 1: 450
structure 1: 446
teacher education 1: 448
technical education 1: 447
Bangladesh
adult education programs 5: 2756
Campaign for Popular Education 7: 4148
Dhaka Asania Mission 7: 4146, 4148
dropout rate
and sex differences 9: 5227
educational change 1: 456
educational radio 5: 2886
Gonoshahajjo Sangstha 7: 4146
government school relationship
financial support 1: 455
school administration 1: 454
literacy rates 5: 2753
mass literacy program 5: 2754, 2756
nonformal education 7: 4133
postsecondary education 1: 452
preschool education 1: 452
primary education 1: 451; 5: 2753
Rural Advancement Committee 7: 4146, 4148
secondary education 1: 451
student evaluation 1: 456
system of education 1: 450–457
degrees and qualifications 1: 453
educational objectives 1: 450
major problems 1: 457
structure 1: 451
teacher education 1: 455
teacher recruitment
women 1: 456
technical education 1: 453
women's education 11: 6755
barriers to 4: 2417
Barbados
adult education 1: 461
curriculum development 1: 462
educational change 1: 464
educational research 1: 464
government school relationship
financial support 1: 461, 463, 464
school administration 1: 461
law 1: 464
nonformal education 1: 460
postsecondary education 1: 459, 464
preschool education 1: 460
secondary education 1: 459, 464
special education 1: 460
structure of government 1: 458
system of education 1: 458–465
educational objectives 1: 458
enrollment 1: 459
major problems 1: 463, 464
structure 1: 459
teacher education 1: 462
technical education 1: 460
Basal reading
sex bias in 9: 5299, 5441

BASIC (programming language) **2:** 970
and computer literacy
curricula **2:** 974
and computer simulation **2:** 985
Basic education
comparative analysis
international studies **1:** ***465–475***
content of curriculum **1:** 472
cross-national comparison
equivalence problem **1:** 469
definition **1:** 465
efficiency and equity **1:** 472
financial support **1:** 473
international support agencies **1:** 473
issues of control
developing nations **1:** 473
and national development **1:** 467
policy issues **1:** 472
use of term **1:** 465
See also
Adult basic education
Primary education
Basic factor model
See Factor analysis, basic factor model
Basic skills
changing concept of **1:** 110
literacy
curriculum **3:** 1736
nonformal education
comparative analysis **7:** ***4132–4136***
tests
characteristics of **11:** 6342
and vocational education **11:** 6413
Bauhaus
and art education **1:** 340
Bayesian statistics **1:** ***475–480***
and achievement tests **1:** 33
and adaptive testing **1:** 50; **2:** 994
applications **1:** 479
Bayes' theorem **1:** 475
criteria for use of **1:** 475
and decision theory **3:** 1419
examples **1:** 477
and expectancy tables **4:** 2182
and hierarchical linear models
5: 2591, 2592; **7:** 3982
problems with **1:** 479
and statistical significance **9:** 5466
Beginning reading
alphabets
letter names **8:** 4944
developmental stages theory **8:** 4943
and grapheme systems **1:** ***480–483***
learning and instruction **8:** ***4942–4945***
oral preparation
and cultural differences **6:** 3449
phoneme grapheme correspondence
4: 1959; **8:** 4943
phonemic segmentation **4:** 1960
age effects **4:** 1960
skill development
contribution of story reading
4: 1961
vocabulary development **8:** 4944
Beginning teacher induction
10: ***6044–6048***
and adult educators **10:** 6057
apprenticeship model **10:** 5983
Beginning teachers
peer evaluation **4:** 2129
probationary period **3:** 1721
conformity **10:** 6124
teacher education programs
10: ***5995–6000***
teacher evaluation **3:** 1254
teacher orientation **10:** 6045
time management **3:** 1255
Behavior
assessment
Q-methodology **8:** 4855
and attitudes **1:** 382
and brain development **1:** ***552–554***
and educational history **5:** 2606
and human factors engineering
4: 2009
individual
and group dynamics **11:** 6629
intellectual
and reproduction theory **9:** 5019
and interpersonal competence
9: 5563, 5565
measurement
and attitude measures **1:** 385
and surveys **10:** 5856
and moral development **7:** 3915
nonverbal
in classrooms **7:** ***4171–4175***
organizational
and school culture **9:** 5209
research
and videotape recordings **11:** 6607
and role theory
in schools **10:** 6220
samples
and reliability **9:** 4984
and school culture
concept of **9:** 5209
vocational education
curriculum development **11:** 6667
Behavior analysis
of migration **5:** 2944
Behavior chaining **10:** 6160
Behavior change
and behavioral theories
of teaching **10:** 6159
and innovation
implementation of **4:** 2071
and television viewing **1:** 569
Behavior development
emotional development
individual differences **4:** 1964
See also
Individual development
Behavior disorders **3:** 1516
antisocial behavior **1:** ***490–495***
assessment **1:** 492
behavioral approach **1:** 489, 491
biophysical approach **1:** 490
collaborative approaches **1:** 493
curriculum issues **1:** 493
definitional issues **1:** 492
ecological approach **1:** 492
and educational practice **1:** 492
placement issues **1:** 492
psychoeducational approach **1:** 491
regular and special education
relationship **1:** 492
and biochemistry **1:** 491
cognitive–emotional interventions
1: 489, 491
cognitive restructuring **1:** 492
description and classification **1:** 487
Diagnostic and Statistical Manual of
Mental Disorders (DSM III-R)
1: 487
drug therapy for
teacher role in **8:** 4420
and education work relationship
1: 493
educational interventions **1:** 488
emotional disturbances **1:** ***486–490***
identification and placement **1:** 487
incidence estimates
United States **1:** 488
International Classification of
Diseases **1:** 487
oppositional defiant disorder **3:** 1516
regular education initiative
United States **1:** 492
role of genetics **1:** 491
and social problems **1:** 494
stereotype/habit disorder **3:** 1516
teacher education **1:** 493
use of term **1:** 486
See also
Behavior problems
Behavior modification
antisocial behavior **1:** 491
autism **6:** 3232
in children **8:** 4419
contingency management
negative reinforcement **1:** 485
positive reinforcement **1:** 484
punishment **1:** 485
response cost **1:** 485
social reinforcement **1:** 484
timeout **1:** 485
token reinforcement **1:** 485
criticisms of **1:** 486, 496
diminishing behavior **10:** 6160
discipline **3:** 1536
emotional disturbances **1:** 489
to increase attention **1:** 376
operant conditioning
and language **1:** 496
planning of **1:** 483
program evaluation **1:** 486
and programmed instruction **8:** 4767, 4770
research
theory practice relationship **9:** 4976
schedules of reinforcement **1:** 485
self-control
and learning **1:** 203
teacher role **1:** 483, 484
and test anxiety **11:** 6357

Behavior patterns
and interests **11:** 6669
Behavior problems
antisocial behavior
disruptive **3:** 1516
attention deficit disorders **9:** 5527
crime **3:** 1535
discipline **3:** ***1534–1538***
externalizing **9:** 5527
incidence in schools
United States **3:** 1536
internalizing **9:** 5527
modification **1:** 484
and peer relationship **9:** 5527
and self-control **9:** 5402
social development **9:** 5527
teacher response **10:** 6030
intervention **10:** 6030
reality therapy **10:** 6030
theories of
and discipline **3:** 1535
See also
Antisocial behavior
Attention deficit disorders
Hyperactivity
Behavior rating scales
and drug therapy **8:** 4421
Behavior theories
chaining **10:** 6160
diminishing behavior **10:** 6160
and learning theories **9:** 5040
maintenance **10:** 6161
measurement
and generalizability theory **5:** 2458
shaping **10:** 6160
stimulus control **10:** 6160
of teaching **10:** ***6159–6164***
transfer **10:** 6161
See also
Attribution theory
Mediation theory
Behavioral instruction
individualized **10:** 6162
programs **10:** 6161
group management **10:** 6162
peer teaching **10:** 6162
precision teaching **10:** 6163
programmed instruction **10:** 6162
social skills training **10:** 6162
token economies **10:** 6162
Behavioral objectives **7:** 3938
and achievement tests **10:** 5784
cognitive strategies **2:** 1021
contextual skills **2:** 1021
creative processes **2:** 1021
and criterion referenced tests **2:** 1184
and educational objectives **10:** 6161
intellectual skills **2:** 1021
and learning modules **7:** 3891
and programmed instruction **8:** 4769
time factors (learning) **2:** 1021
verbal information **2:** 1021
Behavioral psychology
See Behavioral sciences, psychology
Behavioral science research
and administrator education
preservice **1:** 74
and educational research **10:** 6160
methodology **9:** 5044
and personnel management **8:** 4404
prediction **9:** 4976
and resilience **8:** 4775
and single case research **9:** 5487
use of terms **9:** 5044
Behavioral sciences
ambiguities in **9:** 5044
experiments **9:** 5047
and facet theory **4:** 2213
interpretation
and explanations **9:** 5049
levels of **9:** 5046
operationism **9:** 5044
psychology
and instructional design **5:** 2858
semantics
problems **9:** 5044
and twin studies **11:** 6489
Behaviorism **1:** ***495–497***
and adult education models **1:** 134
behavior analysis theory **1:** 495
developmental principles **1:** 495
influence of **1:** 496
research methods **1:** 496
culture and learning **3:** 1241
and educational research **9:** 5054
feedback
in learning and instruction **4:** 2279
and history of instructional psychology **5:** 2876
humanistic psychology view of **5:** 2689
individual development **5:** 2657, 2658
and industrial training **6:** 3303
and instructional psychology **5:** 2871
interbehavioral psychology **1:** 497
learning theories **5:** 2880; **6:** 3316
Skinner's **5:** 2880
Thorndike's **5:** 2880
and logical positivism
educational research **8:** 4633
teacher attitudes toward **1:** 483
United States **6:** 3340
Watson's contribution **1:** 495
Behaviorist psychology
See Behaviorism
Belgium
adult basic education **1:** 101
apprenticeships **1:** 312
computer uses in education
organizations for **2:** 1015
curriculum development **1:** 502
educational research **1:** 503
ethnic groups **1:** 498
government school relationship
financial support **1:** 502
school administration **1:** 501
law
and education **1:** 498
nonformal education **1:** 501
preschool education **1:** 500; **2:** 695; **8:** 4669
school choice
research **9:** 5194
special preschool education **1:** 500
system of education **1:** ***497–504***
educational objectives **1:** 498
enrollment **1:** 503
historical background **1:** 498
structure **1:** 499
teacher recruitment
women **1:** 502
Beliefs
about origins of human race
religious factors **5:** 2651
cultural differences
and scientific attitudes **5:** 2654
cultural influences
individual development **5:** ***2651–2656***
and discipline **3:** 1537
evaluation **10:** 6100
influence on learning **1:** 200
sex differences **5:** 2627
and learning
Mandler's theory of mind and emotion **6:** 3641
mathematics education **6:** 3639, 3641
metacognitive **7:** 3784
religious factors
individual development **5:** ***2651–2656***
and scientific attitudes **5:** 2654, 2655
Belize
curriculum development **1:** 508
educational change **1:** 509
ethnic groups **1:** 504
government school relationship
financial support **1:** 507
school administration **1:** 506
language **1:** 506
law
and education **1:** 505
religious cultural groups **1:** 504
secondary education **1:** 505
vocational education **1:** 506
special education **1:** 506
student evaluation **1:** 508
system of education **1:** ***504–510***
degrees and qualifications **1:** 504
enrollment **1:** 505
major problems **1:** 509
structure **1:** 505
teacher education **1:** 507
technical education **1:** 506
Bell–Doksum test
nonparametric statistics **7:** 4160
Benefits of education
See Educational benefits
Benin
curriculum development **1:** 524
educational change **1:** 521, 522, 524
government school relationship
financial support **1:** 523
school administration **1:** 523

postsecondary education **1:** 523
secondary education **1:** 522
vocational education **1:** 523, 524
system of education **1:** ***521–525***
degrees and qualifications **1:** 524
educational objectives **1:** 521
enrollment **1:** 522
historical background **1:** 521
structure **1:** 522
teacher education **1:** 523
vocational education
training with production **11:** 6447
women's education **11:** 6737
Berechtigungswesen **11:** 6742
Berne Convention for the Protection of Literary and Artistic Works **2:** 1100, 1101
Berufliches Gymnasium
vocational education
Germany, Federal Republic of (former) **11:** 6655
Berufsaufbauschulen
vocational education
Germany, Federal Republic of (former) **11:** 6655
Berufsfachschulen
vocational education
Germany, Federal Republic of (former) **11:** 6655
Berufsschulen **1:** 182
vocational education
Germany, Federal Republic of (former) **11:** 6655
Bhutan
curriculum development **1:** 530
government school relationship
financial support **1:** 529
school administration **1:** 528
language **1:** 525, 526
postsecondary education **1:** 528
primary education **1:** 527
structure of government **1:** 525
student evaluation **1:** 527, 530
system of education **1:** ***525–531***
educational objectives **1:** 526
enrollment **1:** 527
major problems **1:** 531
structure **1:** 526
teacher education **1:** 529, 531
teacher recruitment **1:** 525, 526, 529
technical education **1:** 528
Bias
in interviews **5:** 3006
measurement
and generalizability theory **5:** 2459
in standard estimates
unobserved variables **6:** 3142
Biblical literature
and individual development
Christian theory **2:** 760
Luther's translation of New Testament **6:** 3529
and models of Christianity **2:** 764
moral education
Saint Augustine **9:** 5116
Bibliographic databases
and management information systems **6:** 3594
online systems **5:** 2823
Bibliographies
and documentation systems
Latin America **3:** 1591
Bibliography of Education Theses in Australia (BETA) **5:** 2825
Biculturalism
and second language learning **6:** 3210
Bilingual education
and academic achievement
effect of comparative analysis on **3:** 1832
additive **1:** 532
anthropological perspectives **1:** ***531–535***
and assimilation **1:** 532, 533
background **1:** 531
and colonialism **4:** 2347
cross-cultural studies **1:** 532
and cultural deficit model **1:** 532
and cultural differences **3:** 1231
and dominant language **4:** 2268
ethnography **1:** 532, 534
evaluation research **1:** 532, 534
minority group languages as instructional resources **1:** 534
objectives of **1:** 531
and parents' attitudes **1:** 533
program development
research **1:** 533
research **1:** 532
transitional **1:** 532, 533
See also
Second languages
Bilingual students
communication disorders
6: ***3228–3232***
language handicaps **6:** ***3228–3232***
choice of language of instruction **6:** 3230
cultural differences **6:** 3230
eligibility for referral to special education **6:** 3230
intervention **6:** 3230
reciprocal teaching **6:** 3231
teacher education **6:** 3231
teaching methods **6:** 3231
Bilingual teachers
and minority group socialization
curriculum research **1:** 534
Bilingualism **1:** ***535–537***; **4:** 2340
advantages of **7:** 3967
attitude and motivation **1:** 536
compound **1:** 536
coordinate **1:** 536
development of **1:** 535
and social cognition **1:** 535
and different orthographic systems **1:** 482
diglossia **6:** 3436
effect on cognitive processes **1:** 536
evaluation of prior learning **6:** 3230
individual differences **1:** 536
and language maintenance **1:** 531
and language skill attrition **1:** 537
memory organization in **1:** 536
sociolinguistic circumstances **1:** 535
and test translation **11:** 6331
Binary variables
Galois lattice method **4:** 2395
Binet intelligence tests **1:** 49; **7:** 3699
Binomial error models **7:** 3702
and classical test theory **2:** 789
Biographical research
conventions **1:** 539
criticisms of **1:** 539
definitions of **1:** 537
epiphanies **1:** 539
historical development **1:** 537
interpretive view **1:** 538
life stories **1:** 541
lives **1:** 539
representation of **1:** 541
methods **1:** ***537–543***
personal experience narratives **1:** 541
personal writing **1:** 542
self-stories **1:** 541
subject of **1:** 538
terms for **1:** 538
Biographies
and biographical research **1:** 539
educational history **5:** 2614
educational history in **3:** ***1793–1797***
and narrative inquiry **7:** 4048
and oral history **7:** 4223
and research triangulation **11:** 6463
and student experience **10:** 5814
See also
Autobiographies
Biological influences
on human learning **5:** ***2681–2685***
on individual development **6:** 3513
and panel studies **6:** 3518
Biological sciences
concept teaching **6:** 3408
critical thinking
and computer use **6:** 3412
curriculum **6:** 3408
age differences **6:** 3408
definition **6:** 3407
fields of study **6:** 3408
and scientific literacy **6:** 3409
secondary school science
6: ***3407–3416***
curriculum **6:** 3413
developments and trends **6:** 3408
microcomputers **6:** 3412
sex differences **6:** 3410
students' misconceptions **6:** 3409
teaching methods **6:** 3409
writing skills **6:** 3411
Biology
curriculum
scope and relationship to other fields of study **6:** 3408
and human factors engineering **4:** 2007
molecular **6:** 3413

sex differences **9:** 5434
testing in **4:** 2075
Biomechanics
and human factors engineering **4:** 2009, 2010
Birth defects
See Congenital impairments
Birth order
and academic achievement **4:** 2253
and family size
relationships **7:** 3868
and intellectual development
confluence model **7:** 3868
Birth rate
decline in **3:** 1450
and education
developed nations **3:** 1673
developing nations **3:** 1672
and educational attainment **3:** ***1672–1676***
effect of female education on **4:** 2411
and female enrollment rate **4:** 2415
literacy and **3:** 1663
See also
Population trends
Birth weight
and child development **3:** 1639
physical development **8:** 4468
Bivariate analysis
and surveys **10:** 5860
Bivariate correlations
See Correlation, bivariate
Black attitudes
females
and feminism **11:** 6768
Black education
United States **8:** 4900
Black power
and adult education **2:** 1192
Black stereotypes
socialization **10:** 5823
Black students
academic achievement
effect of unions on **10:** 6071
resistance **9:** 5570
and teacher education **10:** 5845
Black studies
and feminism **2:** 1192
Blackboards
See Chalkboards
Blacks
educationally disadvantaged females
South Africa **7:** ***3848–3853***
females in coeducation
South Africa **7:** 3851
Blacky Pictures **8:** 4790
Blindness
and assistive technology **10:** 5670
computer software **10:** 5670
braille **10:** 5659; **11:** 6626
history of education **11:** 6626
incidence **11:** 6625
mainstreaming **11:** 6626
social attitudes
negative attitudes **11:** 6627
special education for **10:** 5659
Bloom Taxonomy of Educational Objectives
and tests **11:** 6341
Blue collar occupations
and employment level **7:** 3716
and incidence of training **1:** 107
and white collar occupations
demarcation **7:** 3770
Boarding schools
enrollment influences **7:** 4232
full-time
and religious education **9:** 4997
Boards of education **6:** ***3491–3496***
and educational innovation
implementation of **5:** 2842
and parent participation **5:** 2507
and syllabi **10:** 5883
Body composition
assessment of physical development **8:** 4468
Body Mass Index (BMI) **8:** 4468, 4470
Body image
and aging (individuals) **1:** 237
Body language
in classrooms
cultural differences **7:** 4172
research **7:** 4172
Body size
and human factors engineering **4:** 2009, 2010
Bolivia
educational radio **4:** 1906
interactive **5:** 2887
Book development councils
policies of
developing nations **8:** 4848
Books
access to
and literacy testing **6:** 3472
bindings **8:** 4693, 4695
durability **8:** 4693
ease of handling **8:** 4693
functions of **8:** 4696
legibility **8:** 4693
vs. television
children and youth **1:** 565
See also
Printed materials
Textbooks
Workbooks
Bootstrap procedure
compared with t-test **9:** 5470
and sampling errors **9:** 5128
and simulation **9:** 5469
Boston Compact (US)
school business partnerships **9:** 5188
Botswana
adult education
nonformal education **1:** 547
classroom techniques **8:** 4871
computer uses in education **4:** 1901
curriculum development **1:** 549
educational change **1:** 551
educational radio **5:** 2885
educational research **1:** 550
evaluation of national literacy program **4:** 2121
government school relationship
school administration **1:** 548
inservice teacher education
and curriculum development **10:** 6067
language **1:** 543
postsecondary education **1:** 546
preschool education **1:** 546
primary education **1:** 545
private education **1:** 545
schools
decentralization **3:** 1415
science achievement
sex differences in **9:** 5429
science education
attitudes toward **9:** 5323
secondary education **1:** 545
special education **1:** 546
system of education **1:** ***543–552***
educational objectives **1:** 544
enrollment **1:** 545
major problems **1:** 551
structure **1:** 544
teacher education
accreditation **1:** 24, 26
teacher recruitment **1:** 549
teaching methodology **1:** 549
technical education **11:** 6253
vocational education **9:** 5074
apprenticeships **11:** 6658
historical background **11:** 6252
vocational training centers **11:** 6253
Youth Brigade Movement **4:** 2366
Braille **10:** 5659; **11:** 6626
and assistive technology **10:** 5670
Brain
development
in enriched environment **1:** 553
and human behavior **1:** ***552–554***
and interactions with environment **1:** 552
in mammals **1:** 552
sex differences **9:** 5434
stimulation
influence of environment **1:** 552
Brain damage
See Neurological impairments
Brain drain
benefits of **1:** 559
developing nations **1:** 471, 554, 557
and modernization **3:** 1651
economics of **1:** ***554–561***
and educational finance **1:** 558
externalities **1:** 559
measurement of **1:** 555
motivation **1:** 555
nonmarginal flows **1:** 559
output effects
long-term **1:** 556
short-term **1:** 556
policy recommendations **1:** 560
welfare effects
internationalist model **1:** 557

nationalist model **1:** 557
taxes and services **1:** 558
See also
Migration
Brain hemisphere functions
and learning disabilities **10:** 5681
and sex differences **9:** 5429
Brain imaging techniques
and neuropsychological tests **1:** 553
Brainstorming **6:** 3298
and courseware design **2:** 1166
and problem-solving **8:** 4729
vs. brainwriting
and idea generation **5:** 2722, 2723
Branching **4:** 1844
fixed
and adaptive testing **1:** 49
and programmed instruction
frame design **8:** 4770
Brazil
adult education
legislation **6:** 3363
SENAI model **6:** 3254
community education **2:** 909
consciousness raising **2:** 1046
cooperative education **7:** 4138
cooperative education facilities **2:** 1147
dropout rate **9:** 5226, 5227
education system
and females **3:** 1670
educational administration
administrator selection **1:** 79
educational benefits
higher education **1:** 519
educational reform
Educação para Todos 1985 **11:** 6560
employment opportunities
and social discrimination **3:** 1679
evaluation standards **8:** 4745
governance
and exploitation **8:** 4590
income distribution **5:** 2743
individualized instruction **5:** 2772
labor education **1:** 129
labor force participation
females **3:** 1667
mathematics programs **6:** 3666
national training agencies
creation of **6:** 3262
occupational segregation
and sex bias **4:** 2431
production
technology transfer models **11:** 6278
public vs. private sector earnings comparison **8:** 4837
social mobility
labor market analysis **3:** 1677
study circles **2:** 904
teacher education
by distance learning **4:** 1907
unemployment
factors affecting **3:** 1669
universities and research training **11:** 6280
vocational education **7:** 4206; **9:** 5073, 5074
national training agencies **6:** 3257
technical **6:** 3259
training with production **11:** 6448
vocational schools
resources **6:** 3259
Breastfeeding
education and **3:** 1674
and infant behavior **5:** 2801
Bristol Bay Curriculum Project (BBCP) Alaska **3:** 1235
British Association for the Advancement of Science (BAAS)
measurement techniques **7:** 3699
British Broadcasting Corporation (BBC)
adult education **1:** 561
adult literacy program **1:** 101, 102
educational radio **5:** 2885
educational technology
and satellites **4:** 1881
and educational television **5:** 2895
British Council
educational technology
activities **4:** 1879
British Education Index (BEI)
contact details **5:** 2826
scope **5:** 2824
British Education Theses Index (BETI) **5:** 2824
British Educational Management and Administration Society (BEMAS) **5:** 2953
British National Bibliography (BNB) **5:** 2824
British Standing Conference on University Teaching and Research in Educationof Adults **8:** 4732
Broadcast communications
See Telecommunications
Broadcast education
adult education **1:** ***561–564***
compared with conventional instruction **1:** 561
interactive communication
electronic media **1:** 563
See also
Distance education
Broadcast television
and learning **6:** 3299
Broadcasting
effects on children and youth **1:** ***564–570***
Brunei Darussalam
adult education
nonformal education **1:** 575
computer uses in education **4:** 1901
cultural influences **1:** 573
curriculum development **1:** 576
educational change **1:** 576
language **1:** 571
postsecondary education **1:** 573
special education **1:** 574
system of education **1:** ***570–577***
educational objectives **1:** 571
major problems **1:** 577
structure **1:** 572
teacher education **1:** 576
teacher recruitment **1:** 575
Bryn Mawr School for Women Workers (US) **11:** 6770, 6771
Buddhism
empiricism **1:** 577
individual development **1:** ***577–581***
educational implications of theory **1:** 581
goal of **1:** 579, 580
influences on **1:** 580
individual differences **1:** 581
individualized instruction **1:** 581
influence on Shinto **9:** 5450
intellectual freedom
personal autonomy **1:** 581
karma **1:** 578
moral development **1:** 581
motivation and the learning process **1:** 580
nirvana **1:** 578, 579
and personality development **1:** 578
rebirth **1:** 578
relationship with Hinduism **1:** 577
sankhara **1:** 579
vinnana **1:** 579
Budgeting
and policy analysis **8:** 4552
retrenchment
and participative decision-making **5:** 2797
school
approaches **9:** 5183
definition **9:** 5182
site-based **9:** 5183
and school administration **9:** ***5181–5186***
and school-based management **3:** 1409
See also
Program budgeting
Budgets
educational
and teachers **8:** 4520
and media program administration **7:** 3754
school
preparation of **9:** 5183
Building design
educational facilities **4:** 2221
factors **4:** 2223
Bulgaria
adult education
history **2:** 656, 658, 659
nonformal education **1:** 585
computer literacy
courses **2:** 975
curriculum development **1:** 587
educational change **1:** 588
educational research **1:** 587
ethnic groups **1:** 582

government school relationship
school administration **1:** 585
illiteracy **2:** 657
language **1:** 582
occupational segregation **4:** 2430
postsecondary education **1:** 584
primary education **1:** 583
secondary education
vocational education **1:** 584
special education **1:** 584
structure of government **1:** 582
system of education **1:** ***581–588***
degrees and qualifications **1:** 587
educational objectives **1:** 583
historical background **1:** 582
teacher recruitment
women **1:** 586
technical education **1:** 584
vocational education **10:** 5915
Bulimia **3:** 1516
Bulletin boards
and computer networks **2:** 978
and copyrights **2:** 1102
Bullock Report 1975 (UK)
language across the curriculum
6: 3205, 3206
Bullying
See Aggression, peer relationship
Bureaucracy
and compliance (psychology) **6:** 3525
and critical theory **1:** 63
distrust of **1:** 589
in elementary schools **6:** 3525
and organizations (groups) **9:** 5161
as a rational organization model
6: 3524
and school-based management **1:** 592
and school effectiveness **1:** ***589–594***
school choice approach **1:** 589
and school organization **4:** 2157;
7: 4242
and urban schools **11:** 6554
vs. autonomy **4:** 2162
and Weber's sociology of education
2: 781
See also
Administrative organization
Burkina Faso
adult education
nonformal education **1:** 596
curriculum development **1:** 597
distance education **1:** 218
educational change **1:** 597
educational planning **8:** 4511
educational reform **8:** 4511
government school relationship
school administration **1:** 597
language **1:** 595
postsecondary education **1:** 596
preschool education **1:** 596
primary education **1:** 595
printed materials
provision **8:** 4697
public sector employment **8:** 4838
secondary education **1:** 596
system of education **1:** ***594–598***
educational objectives **1:** 595
enrollment **1:** 596
major problems **1:** 598
teacher recruitment **1:** 597
youth training schemes **1:** 218
Burma
See Myanmar
Burnout
assessment
Maslach Burnout Inventory
10: 5919
concept of **10:** 5919
human services **10:** 6059
psychological patterns **10:** 6059
and sociology of education **10:** 5604
stages in **10:** 5920
See also
Teacher burnout
Burundi
adult education **1:** 218
nonformal education **1:** 602
curriculum development **1:** 604
distance education **1:** 218
educational change **1:** 606
educational research **1:** 606
ethnic groups **1:** 598
government school relationship
school administration **1:** 602
language **1:** 598
nonformal education **7:** 4134
postsecondary education **1:** 602
primary education **1:** 600
primary school agriculture
tests **8:** 4686
secondary education **1:** 601
structure of government **1:** 598
system of education **1:** ***598–607***
degrees and qualifications **1:** 605
educational objectives **1:** 600
major problems **1:** 606
structure **1:** 600
teacher recruitment **1:** 603
Business
case methods **10:** 5944
competition
and labor force development
4: 1918
and educational finance
tax allocation **8:** ***4359–4364***
and educational television **5:** 2894
links with initial and adult education
8: ***4337–4339***
and multimedia systems **7:** 3995
objectives and labor force
development **5:** 2687
and organizational development
7: 4236
plans
development of **4:** 1986
projections
and educational statistics **8:** 4783
and training
factors affecting **11:** 6635
training courses
cost effectiveness of **2:** 1136
Business education
and national training agencies
Latin America **6:** 3266
and self-employment **11:** 6250
Business school partnerships
See School business partnerships
Business skills
training programs **4:** 1986

Cable television
and educational television **5:** 2896
Calculators
mathematical applications **6:** 3632
in mathematics education **6:** 3649;
7: 4096
Calculus
and analysis **6:** 3680
and computers **6:** 3681
curriculum **6:** 3681
history of instruction **6:** 3645
California Psychological Inventory
8: 4396, 4397
California Test of Personality (CTP)
8: 4397
Camcorders
See Video equipment
Cameroon
adult education **1:** 218
nonformal education **2:** 613
curriculum development **2:** 615
educational research **2:** 616
government school relationship
financial support **2:** 613
school administration **2:** 613
language **2:** 609
postsecondary education **2:** 612
preschool education **2:** 612
primary education **2:** 611
private education **2:** 613
secondary education
vocational education **2:** 611
segmentation theory
studies **3:** 1683
special education **2:** 612
structure of government **2:** 611
system of education **2:** ***609–618***
degrees and qualifications **2:** 616
educational change **2:** 617
educational objectives **2:** 610
major problems **2:** 617
structure **2:** 611
teacher education programs
work experience programs **10:** 6066
teacher recruitment **2:** 614
teaching methodology **2:** 615
technical education
coordination of **10:** 6064
Campus 2000 network
United Kingdom **10:** 6008
Canada
adult basic education **1:** 101, 102
adult education
finance **1:** 156
legislation **6:** 3361
nonformal education **2:** 621
participation rates **1:** 104

provision **7:** 4181, 4182
research **1:** 124
surveys **7:** 3713
adult literacy services **1:** 102
adult literacy surveys **7:** 3710
apprenticeship survey **7:** 3714
assistive technology
access to **10:** 5669
attendance
and dropouts **3:** 1604
brain drain **1:** 556, 560
community colleges **2:** 895
community development programs **2:** 905
computer conferencing
applications **11:** 6303
computer mediated writing **11:** 6303
computer uses in education
organizations for **2:** 1015
continuing education expenditure **2:** 1148
curriculum
historical background **9:** 5298
curriculum-based assessment **3:** 1357
curriculum development **2:** 614
development education **3:** 1496
distance education
in schools **3:** 1564
educational change
studies **6:** 3600
educational research **2:** 616
action research **1:** 45
educational technology
simulation **4:** 1914
elementary school teachers
studies **10:** 6212
ethnic groups **2:** 618, 621
family environment
research **7:** 3871
foreign language instruction **4:** 2354
French language instruction **4:** 2349, 2350
further education councils **7:** 4181
government school relationship
school administration **2:** 613
human resources training and development survey **7:** 3714
institutional support for independent study **9:** 5395
labor education **1:** 129; **11:** 6772
labor force surveys **11:** 6416
labor relations
in education **6:** 3194
language **2:** 618
leadership
research **6:** 3282
theories of **6:** 3280
literacy levels **1:** 131
literacy movement **7:** 4148; **8:** 4637
literacy skills survey (1989) **6:** 3478; **8:** 4635
minority groups and social change
ethnography **2:** 1212
multicultural education **7:** 3969
multimedia systems
French language instruction **7:** 3995
occupations
classification of **7:** 3717
paid educational leave **7:** 4257
parent participation
research **9:** 5213
performance contracts
historical background **8:** 4709
postsecondary education **2:** 620
preschool education **2:** 621
primary education **2:** 619
primary schools
social studies in **9:** 5575
racial discrimination
and education **9:** 5227
school-based management **9:** 5303, 5304
studies **9:** 5183
school health education **5:** 2571
school size
studies **9:** 5292
science education **8:** 4461, 4462
secondary education **2:** 620
structure of government **2:** 618
student loan programs **10:** 5766
student teaching
field experience programs **10:** 5809
study circles **10:** 5829
system of education **2:** ***618–626***
degrees and qualifications **2:** 614, 615
educational objectives **2:** 619
major problems **2:** 616
structure **2:** 619
teacher burnout
research **9:** 5178
teacher education
accreditation **1:** 24, 26
teacher militancy **6:** 3192
teacher recruitment **2:** 614
teacher student relationship
research **10:** 5761
teaching methodology **2:** 615
teaching methods debate **6:** 3454
teleclassrooms **11:** 6304
teleconferencing **11:** 6305
training statistics **7:** 3713, 3714
tuition fees **10:** 5752
unions
participation in literacy programs **8:** 4637
state incorporation **10:** 6074
university adult education **11:** 6549, 6551
videotex
applications **11:** 6305
vocational education **8:** 4793
worker-teachers **7:** 4182
See also
North America
Canadian Association for Adult Education (CAAE) **7:** 4181
Canadian Association for the Study of Adult Education (CASAE) **7:** 4184
Canadian Education Index (CEI)
contact details **5:** 2827
document delivery **5:** 2825
scope **5:** 2825
Canadian International Development Agency (CIDA) **5:** 2826
special education **5:** 2967
Cancer
drug therapy
in schools **8:** 4420
Canonical analysis **2:** ***626–631***
applications **2:** 626, 630
developments **2:** 630
and factor analysis **2:** 627
and multiple regression analysis **2:** 627
and multivariate analysis **7:** 4010
pictorial representation **2:** 627
redundancy
measures **2:** 629
partitioning of **2:** 629
significance testing **2:** 630
structure coefficients **2:** 628
transformation weights **2:** 628
variance considerations **2:** 629
See also
Multivariate analysis
Canonical correlation
coefficient **2:** 627
See also
Multivariate analysis
Capital
deficient accumulation of
and labor markets **3:** 1682
definition of **4:** 2267
dominant **4:** 2268, 2269
forms of
and values **4:** 2267
substitution for labor **11:** 6634
See also
Cultural capital
Social capital
Capital expenditures
definition of **9:** 5233
in education **8:** 4702
Capital–labor substitution
and education **3:** 1445
Capitalism
and adult education **1:** 128; **2:** 1191, 1193
and critical theory **10:** 5600
dominance of science **2:** 1199
and formal adult education **10:** 5592
and hidden curriculum **8:** 4582
and ideological basis of power **3:** 1714
individual attitudes **1:** 129
Marxism
and employment contracts **3:** 1696
and the state **6:** 3618
and Marxist educational thought **6:** 3617
and popular education **2:** 1048
and social reproduction **5:** 2612
and socialist feminism **5:** 2456
and sociology of education **10:** 5608

state **6:** 3618
vertical organization
and education **7:** 3770
Capitalist nations
educational planning
history of **8:** 4490, 4500
and legitimacy **6:** 3367
role of education in **5:** 2743
Cardiovascular system
health promotion programs **5:** 2569
Career awareness
and small business training **4:** 1985
Career choice
and apprenticeships
Africa **1:** 222, 223
factors affecting
teaching **10:** 5844
females **4:** 2410
Germany, Federal Republic of (former) **11:** 6654
Career counseling **5:** 2685
college students **10:** 5802
and test bias **11:** 6318
use of computers **2:** 1164
Career development
career education **2:** 632, 633
and special education students **2:** 633
college students **10:** 5802
and discriminant analysis **3:** 1544, 1548
and instructional program divisions **6:** 3098
and labor force development **5:** 2685
teachers
factors affecting **10:** 6210
Career education **3:** 1736
curriculum in schools **2:** 631
and disabilities **2:** ***631–635***
Australia **2:** 633
barriers to implementation **2:** 632
Europe **2:** 633
historical development **2:** 631
Israel **2:** 634
life centered model **2:** 632, 633, 634
school-based model **2:** 633
Taiwan **2:** 634
theory of work adjustment **2:** 632
and special education **2:** 631
Career guidance
computer-assisted testing in **11:** 6673
Career ladders
and personnel management **8:** 4407
and teacher evaluation **4:** 2126, 2129
and teacher salaries **10:** 6081
Career planning
career pathing **5:** 2685
theoretical perspectives **1:** 356
Careers
educational administration
comparative area studies **1:** 81
and selection **1:** ***78–83***
Caribbean
adult education **2:** ***635–640***
popular education **2:** 635
educational radio **5:** 2886
science curriculum **3:** 1253
vocational education
education with production **3:** 1688
International Labour Organization programs **5:** 3002
training with production **11:** 6448
Caribbean Regional Council for Adult Education (CARCAE) **5:** 2932; **8:** 4733
Caring
feminist ethics of **4:** 2292, 2294, 2295; **11:** 6721
and school organization **4:** 2295
moral development **10:** 5936
Carl D Perkins Vocational Education Act 1984 (US) **11:** 6533
1990 Amendments **11:** 6537
reauthorization of 1990 **11:** 6536
Carnegie Corporation **7:** 4183
Carnegie Forum on Education
teacher education curriculum **10:** 5994
Carnegie Task Force **9:** 5315
Case studies
and biographical research **1:** 539
and data analysis **3:** 1466
procedural stages **3:** 1468
methods **2:** ***640–646***
criticisms of **2:** 642, 644
data collection **2:** 643
deduction vs. patterns **2:** 641
ethics of **2:** 645
holistic approach **2:** 640
types of **2:** 642
and micropolitics research **7:** 3825
theories
development of **2:** 641
See also
Longitudinal studies
Single case research
Categorical data
See Nominal data
Categorization
See Classification
Catholic educators
Saint Ignatius Loyola **9:** ***5118–5121***
Catholic schools
and academic achievement **1:** 516; **8:** 4840, 4841
black females in
South Africa **7:** 3850
convents
history of women's education **11:** 6743
educational research
criticisms of **8:** 4840
effective schools research **1:** 590; **8:** 4841, 4843
studies **9:** 5377
females
Australia **11:** 6735
organization of **8:** 4841
political education in **8:** 4570
and school choice **9:** 5193, 5195
single sex schools
United States **2:** 832
social stratification in **10:** 5733
vs. public schools
school organization **9:** 5375
Catholicism
and adult education
Central and Eastern Europe **2:** 660
Latin America **6:** 3253
and Nazism **9:** 5009
state church relationship **5:** 2511
Catholics
and political education **8:** 4570
Causal attributions
See Attribution theory
Causal models **7:** 3870
analysis **3:** 1381
and attitude measures
science education **9:** 5322
and cross-sectional studies **2:** 1219
and data analysis **3:** 1471
in evaluation **11:** 6379
example **7:** 3870
and longitudinal studies **6:** 3522
and mediation theory **4:** 1875
semantics **4:** 1876
and status attainment **10:** 5600
and time **6:** 3514
CD-ROMs
See Optical data disks, CD-ROMs
CEDEFOP
See European Centre for the Development of Vocational Training (CEDEFOP)
Censorship
and curriculum **6:** 3358
instructional materials **6:** 3359
teaching methods **6:** 3359
and textbooks **11:** 6367
Census figures
and adult education measurement **7:** 3709
data collection **2:** 649
and databases **3:** 1394
and national survey data **2:** ***649–653***
occupations **7:** 3717
and projections **8:** 4784
publication of **2:** 650
and surveys **10:** 5854
uses and limitations **2:** 650
See also
National surveys
Center for the Advanced Study of Educational Administration (CASEA) (US)
and organizational development **7:** 4237
Center for Civic Education (US)
CIVITAS curriculum **2:** 769
Center for Research and Pedagogical Applications (CRAPEL) (France) **6:** 3347
Central African Republic
adult education
nonformal education **2:** 654
ethnic groups **2:** 653

government school relationship
financial support **2:** 655
school administration **2:** 655
language **2:** 654
preschool education **2:** 654
system of education **2:** ***653–656***
degrees and qualifications **2:** 656
educational objectives **2:** 653
enrollment **2:** 653
major problems **2:** 656
structure **2:** 654
teacher recruitment **2:** 655
Central America
adult education **2:** ***635–640***
popular education **2:** 635
educational research
action research **1:** 45
public education finance
effect of economic adjustment on **3:** 1787
Central and Eastern Europe
women's education **11:** 6714
Central Europe
apprenticeships **1:** 314
educational planning
and educational change **8:** 4498
social stratification
research **10:** 5734
vocational education
future trends **11:** 6647
historical background **11:** 6641
and international co-operation **11:** 6645
problems **11:** 6645
vocational education and training **11:** ***6641–6648***
Centralization
advantages **3:** 1413
and curriculum development **5:** 2497
and decentralization **3:** 1407
educational administration
rationale for **6:** 3272
and educational change **5:** 2506
and educational planning **8:** 4496, 4503
sub-Saharan Africa **8:** 4512
and educational quality **8:** 4872
and educational reform **9:** 5277
and governance **6:** 3491; **8:** 4590
and school administration **6:** 3494; **9:** 5165
and school-based management **9:** 5211, 5305
and school inspectors **9:** 5247
and school organization **7:** 4242
and school as workplace **9:** 5176
and selection
secondary education **9:** 5389
and state departments of education **7:** 3835, 3838
and vocational education
Eastern and Central Europe **11:** 6643
vs. decentralization **3:** 1412
and educational administration **8:** 4565
and educational equity (finance) **3:** 1791
and educational planning **8:** 4498
See also
Decentralization
Centre for Contemporary Cultural Studies (CCCS) (UK) **11:** 6800
Centre for Educational Research and Innovation (CERI) **2:** 942; **7:** 4226
access to education
equal education **7:** 4226
comparative data **3:** 1586
educational facilities
special needs students **7:** 4226
International Indicators Project **5:** 2986
recurrent education **8:** 4958, 4959, 4962
teacher education **10:** 5963
Centre d'Enseignement par Correspondance (France) **1:** 182
Centre International d'Etudes Pédagogiques (*CIEP*) (France) **2:** 938
Centre National D'Enseignement à Distance (France) **8:** 4806
Centre for Policy Studies
United Kingdom
numeracy concern **6:** 3456
Centro de Cooperación Regional para la Educación de Adultos en América Latina y el Caribe **5:** 2932
Centro de Investigación y Desarrollo de la Educación (*CIDE*) (Chile)
abstracting systems **3:** 1590
Centro Europeo Dell'Educazione (*CEDE*) (Italy) **2:** 940
Centroid method of factor analysis
See Factor analysis
Cerebral palsy
incidence of **10:** 5692
special education **10:** 5661
Certification
adult education **2:** ***662–665***
challenges to conventional approaches **2:** 662
integrated approaches to **2:** 664
and validation **2:** 662
and criterion referenced tests **2:** 1188
definition of **8:** 4617
and lifelong learning **2:** 662
mandatory recertification **6:** 3362
prevocational education **3:** 1737
and public examinations **4:** 2172
purposes of **8:** 4617
of secondary school completion **1:** 181
student evaluation **8:** ***4617–4623***
See also
Credentials
Teacher certification
Ceylon
See Sri Lanka
Chad
curriculum development **2:** 669
educational research **2:** 670
enrollment rates **9:** 5536
government school relationship
school administration **2:** 668
language **2:** 666
structure of government **2:** 666
system of education **2:** ***665–670***
educational objectives **2:** 666
major problems **2:** 670
structure **2:** 667
teacher recruitment **2:** 668
teaching methodology **2:** 669
Chagga
ethnography of **3:** 1752
Chalkboards
characteristics of **10:** 5729
production of **10:** 5726
Change
analysis of
and experimental studies **4:** 2193
measurement of **2:** ***671–678***
background to **2:** 671
choice of model **2:** 675
and individual development **2:** 672
and longitudinal studies **6:** 3520
methods **2:** 674
statistical analysis **2:** 676
traditional methods **2:** 671
univariate models of
and longitudinal studies **6:** 3521
Change management **6:** ***3597–3603***
Change strategies
and networks
characteristics **6:** 3601
and nonformal education **7:** 4143
in schools **6:** 3599
Character
See Personality
Charitable trusts
See Trusts (financial)
Charity schools **8:** 4827
Charts
characteristics of **10:** 5729
and concept maps **2:** 1026
production of **10:** 5726
Chautauqua Movement **7:** 4182, 4183; **8:** 4808; **11:** 6773
Cheating
in tests **11:** 6314
Chemicals
producing congenital impairment **1:** 13
Chemistry
curriculum development **8:** 4477
Chi square
and configural frequency analysis **2:** 1033, 1035
and contingency tables
item bias procedures **5:** 3045
and path analysis **8:** 4344
and small expected frequencies **2:** 1081
and structural equation models **8:** 4350

test of independence
and contingency tables **2:** 1080
tests
and contingency table analysis **7:** 4011
and factor analysis **4:** 2238
hypothesis testing **6:** 3499
and log-linear models **6:** 3502
and logit models **6:** 3505
and nonparametric statistics **7:** 4159
and statistical significance **9:** 5462
values
and classical test theory **2:** 790
Chicago Comparative Education Center **2:** 935
Chicago, University of (US)
social ecology school **11:** 6799
Child abuse **1:** ***15–20***
assessment and intervention **1:** 17
causes **1:** 16
data collection **1:** 16
definitions of **1:** 15
effects **1:** 17
epidemiology **1:** 16
etiology **5:** 2573
and family violence **4:** 2259
homeless children **3:** 1733, 1734
incidence
United States **1:** 16
international comparative analysis **1:** 16
and parent child relationship **1:** 16
prevention programs **1:** 19
psychotherapy **1:** 18
reports of **1:** 16
and resilience **8:** 4776
runaways **3:** 1734
screening and identification **1:** 18
violence **1:** 16
See also
Child neglect
Physical abuse, of children
Sexual abuse, of children
Child advocacy
homeless children **3:** 1734
Child care
See Child rearing
Day care
Child care centers
See Day care centers
Child care occupations
day care **2:** 689
earnings differentials
determinants of **2:** 689
and elasticity of supply **2:** 690
and racial segregation **2:** 689
turnover rate **2:** 690
Child care policies
See Day care, policies
Child care services
See Day care, services
Child caregivers **5:** 2808
compared with parents **2:** 686
day care
effect on quality of **2:** 691
and resilience **8:** 4777
Child centered instruction
reform pedagogy movement **8:** 4457
and teacher education **10:** 5982
Child costs
See Expenditure per student
Child development **2:** ***701–706***
attitudes and motivation **1:** 355
biology **5:** 2683
child language **2:** 702
and cognitive ability
Montessori method **7:** 3912
cognitive development **2:** 703
cultural context **2:** 704
and domain-specific knowledge **3:** 1502
learning processes **2:** 703
learning strategies **2:** 704
memory **2:** 703
problem-solving **2:** 704
symbolic learning **2:** 703
cognitive processes
age differences **2:** 704
cumulative risk model **3:** 1641
developmental continuity **5:** 2678
individual differences **5:** 2678
developmental disabilities
classification **3:** 1515
developmental stages
characteristics **5:** 2678
synchrony in **5:** 2679
and visual impairments **11:** 6626
early experience **3:** ***1636–1643***
ecological model **3:** 1637
education and quality of **4:** 2210
and educational policy studies **4:** 1837
effect of change on **3:** 1637
emotional development **2:** 701
and expert novice differences **2:** 839
and family characteristics **3:** 1637
and family environment **5:** 2624
family influence **4:** ***2258–2261***
family system model **3:** 1637
and friendship **10:** 5757
influence of interpersonal relationships **9:** 5546
and interpersonal competence **9:** 5563
measurement of early **1:** ***358–362***
metacognition **2:** 704
parent influence **2:** 701
parent role
zone of proximal development **6:** 3460
peer relationship **2:** 702
physical development **2:** 701
motor development **2:** 701
preschool education
benefits **8:** 4664
prosocial behavior **8:** ***4796–4799***
risk and vulnerability model **3:** 1637
self-concept **2:** 702
skill development
generalization **5:** 2679
social development **2:** 701
studies in preschool teacher education **3:** 1632, 1633
talent identification **5:** 2729
Vygotsky's zone of proximal development **5:** 2679
See also
Infants
Piagetian theory
Child Development Associate (CDA) program (US) **3:** 1633
Child health
nutrition
global approach **2:** 706
Child labor
and primary school agriculture
Africa **8:** 4686
Child language **2:** 702
and caregiver speech **6:** 3222
cognitive development
schemata **2:** 703
development of grammar **6:** 3220
and grammatical acceptability **6:** 3221
interpersonal communication **6:** 3221
metalinguistics **6:** 3221
and parent child relationship **6:** 3222
second language learning **2:** 703
semantics **2:** 703
verbal development
developmental stages **6:** 3219
Child maltreatment
See Child abuse
Child neglect **1:** 15
assessment and treatment **1:** 18
causes **1:** 17
effects **1:** 17
etiology **5:** 2573
and social adjustment **8:** 4366
Child parent relationship
See Parent child relationship
Child protective service agencies
child abuse **1:** 18
Child psychology
and developmental psychology **5:** 2656
educational research **4:** 1864
individual development **5:** 2647
research **6:** 3426
Child rearing
by children **2:** ***730–733***
cultural differences **5:** 2806, 2807
and educational theories **8:** 4457
effect on child development **3:** 1640
ethnography **2:** 1209
family environment **5:** 2625
and individual development
Christian theory **2:** 766
Confucian theory **2:** 1045
Hindu theory **5:** 2600
Islamic theory **5:** 3022
leaves of absence policies **2:** 697
parent insurance benefit **2:** 697
Locke's theories **6:** 3497
parent role
and day care centers **2:** 686
preschool children
day care policies **2:** 699

parental benefits **2:** 698
preschool education **2:** ***678–688***
and social capital **4:** 2272
standards
and definitions of child abuse **1:** 15
Child role
transformation of
factors **10:** 5794
Child-to-child programs
developing nations **2:** 730, 731
innovations deriving from **2:** 732
Child welfare
public interests in
preschool education **8:** 4662
Childhood **2:** ***701–706***
anthropological perspective **2:** 705
Judaic view of **6:** 3114
nature of
and existential phenomenology **8:** 4432
Childhood interests
and television viewing **1:** 564
Children
aggression **2:** 702
biographies of
and curriculum **10:** 5816
characteristics of
and preschool education **8:** 4663
as child caregivers **2:** ***730–733***
cognitive development
and concept formation **2:** 853
and theory of mind **2:** 854, 856
and deafness **10:** 5687
drug therapy in **8:** ***4419–4424***
economic utility **3:** 1673
effects of broadcasting and technology on **1:** ***564–570***
empathy **2:** 702
helping relationship **2:** 702
as income providers
and earnings differentials **6:** 3102
intellectual development **5:** 2911, 2912, 2913
language acquisition
and speech handicaps **10:** 5696
language handicaps
specific **10:** ***5674–5681***
and partial hearing **10:** 5689
physical development **8:** 4470
body composition **8:** 4470
body height **8:** 4470
determinants **8:** 4470
maturity indicators **8:** 4470
and physical fitness **8:** 4470
problems
teams for **10:** 6240
prosocial behavior **2:** 702
as teachers of younger children **2:** 731
voice disorders in **11:** ***6704–6707***
writing for children **2:** 732
Children's Apperception Test (CAT) **8:** 4790
Children's art **1:** 339
developmental stages **1:** 342
and peace **1:** 340
Children's games
sex differences
and moral development **4:** 2293
Children's literature **2:** ***733–738***
literary genres **2:** 733
research
Australia **2:** 735
Canada **2:** 735
Germany **2:** 736
Scandinavia **2:** 737
United Kingdom **2:** 736
responses to **2:** 734
age differences **2:** 735
ethnographic studies **2:** 735
sex bias in **9:** 5442
Children's Personality Questionnaire (CPQ) **8:** 4398
Children's rights **2:** 706, 710
and corporal punishment **3:** 1536
and the curriculum **6:** 3359
homeless children **3:** 1734
Children's Television Workshop (CTW) (US)
and educational television **5:** 2893
Chile
adult education **6:** 3253
nonformal education **2:** 741
curriculum development **2:** 743
educational change **2:** 739; **8:** 4493
and educational planning **8:** 4507
slow political consensus building **8:** 4508
educational planning **3:** 1818; **8:** 4493
abstract production **3:** 1590
equal education **8:** 4598
implementation problems **3:** 1821
educational research **2:** 745
enrollment rates **9:** 5536
folk schools **2:** 904
government school relationship
financial support **2:** 742
school administration **2:** 742
learning workshops program **2:** 1048
private education
grants **3:** 1824
school support **3:** 1827
special education **2:** 741
student evaluation **2:** 744
study circles **2:** 904
system of education **2:** ***738–746***
degrees and qualifications **2:** 744
educational objectives **2:** 739
enrollment **2:** 740, 741
major problems **2:** 745
structure **2:** 740
teacher recruitment **2:** 743
teaching methodology **2:** 743
technical education **2:** 741
vocational education **9:** 5074
apprenticeships **11:** 6659
for the disadvantaged **7:** 4151
training with production **11:** 6451
China Association for Adult Education **2:** 748
China (Imperial)
examinations
and conflict **2:** 1038
China, People's Republic of (PRC)
adult education **1:** 348, 350; **2:** ***746–749***
achievements **2:** 748
administration **2:** 748
concepts and principles **2:** 746
degree education **2:** 747
functions **2:** 747
history **2:** 746
legislation **6:** 3363, 3364
nonformal education **2:** 752
policy **2:** 749
research **2:** 749
for socialism **1:** 132
systems and forms **2:** 747
target population **2:** 747
civic education **2:** 768
community colleges **2:** 895, 898
comparative achievement data **4:** 2137
computer uses in education **4:** 1902
organizations for **2:** 1015
Cultural Revolution **3:** 1292
effect on vocational education **2:** 757
curriculum
urban schools **11:** 6561
curriculum development **2:** 753
curriculum history **3:** 1291
and disengagement theory **9:** 5227
distance education **4:** 1901
in schools **3:** 1565
educational change **2:** 754
educational demand
studies **8:** 4704
educational finance studies
private vs. public resources **8:** 4703, 4704
educational history **2:** 1061
educational planning
and politics **3:** 1808
educational policy
and governance **5:** 2512
educational reform
implementation **4:** 1854
educational research **2:** 754
elementary literacy schools **2:** 747
enrollment rate
vocational education **2:** 757
ethnic groups **2:** 750
farms into educational units **4:** 2366
female enrollment rate **4:** 2408
general education
and vocational education **2:** 756
government school relationship
financial support **2:** 752
school administration **2:** 752
Han language education **7:** 3847
index of segregation **4:** 2430
industrial productivity **3:** 1693
influence of Dewey's democratic ideas **3:** 1524

literacy campaigns **1:** 171; **7:** 4146, 4148
minority group education **7:** 3847
national development
and vocational education **2:** 758
nonformal education for social change **1:** 132
political education **3:** 1292, 1293, 1294
polytechnical education **8:** 4605
preschool education **2:** 751
primary education
financial support **2:** 1150; **7:** 4140
production
technology transfer models **11:** 6278
school-based management
recentralization **9:** 5212
school organization
curriculum design **7:** 4233
schools into production units **4:** 2366
secondary education
and vocational education **2:** 756
selective colleges
key schools **3:** 1293
Social Education Department **2:** 747
special education **2:** 751
structure of government **2:** 750
syllabi
and conflict **10:** 5884
system of education **2:** ***750–755***
degrees and qualifications **2:** 754
educational objectives **2:** 750
major problems **2:** 755
structure **2:** 750
teacher education **2:** 753
teacher recruitment **2:** 753
technical education **2:** 751
technology transfer **11:** 6278
television universities **1:** 563; **4:** 1902
test anxiety
studies **11:** 6357
textbooks
provision **11:** 6361
universities
adult education **11:** 6550
and research training **11:** 6280
vocational education **2:** ***746–749***; **9:** 5073, 5075; **11:** 6245
case studies **11:** 6630, 6632
education with production **3:** 1686
historical background **2:** 756
international perspectives **2:** 758
and modernization policy **11:** 6632
reforms **2:** 755
strategies for **2:** 757, 759
training with production **11:** 6447, 6450
vocational schools **8:** 4794, 4795
development of **2:** 756
quality of **2:** 758
vocationalizing education **2:** ***755–760***
youth unemployment
and vocational education **2:** 759
China, Republic of
See Taiwan
Chinese
in Hong Kong education **2:** 1039
Chinese National Institute for Educational Research (CNIER) **2:** 940
Christianity
beliefs about origin of man **5:** 2652
conservative model **2:** 765
death **2:** 763, 764
and Erasmus' educational theories **4:** 2006
and history of women's education **11:** 6742
francophone Africa **11:** 6737
individual development **2:** ***760–767***
childrearing implications of theory **2:** 766
developmental stages **2:** 763
educational implications of theory **2:** 766
influences on **2:** 764
length of **2:** 763
motivation **2:** 766
objectives **2:** 762
intention **2:** 764
liberal model **2:** 765
mainstream model **2:** 765
missionary schools
Egypt **11:** 6754
Turkey **11:** 6754
moral development **2:** 760, 762
origin of the soul **2:** 761
personality development **2:** 761
and philosophy of education
Saint Augustine on **9:** ***5115–5117***
Reformation theology **6:** 3529
and religious education
objectives **9:** 4998
Chronemics
See Time management
Chronic illness
and health promotion **5:** 2567
and resilience **8:** 4778
Chronicles
and narrative inquiry **7:** 4048
Church state relationship
See State church relationship
Cities
See Municipalities
Citizen participation **2:** 901
democratic values **4:** 1981
and individual power **4:** 1981
preschool education **7:** 4296
Citizenship
and adult education **1:** 128
education and improvement of **4:** 2210
and postmodernism **2:** 767
traditional conceptions of **2:** 767
Citizenship education **1:** 91
Australia **4:** 1982
and community education **2:** 900
democratic values **8:** 4576, 4577
geography instruction **5:** 2466
global approaches **8:** 4581
homeless children **3:** ***1733–1736***
for immigrants and minority groups
United States **7:** 3843
indigenous populations
United States **7:** 3842
objectives **9:** 5579
and participation **1:** 131
and political education **8:** 4568
and politicization of curriculum **5:** 2467
and social studies **10:** 5583
and sociology of education **10:** 5604
and teacher education **10:** 5982, 5984, 5985
United States **8:** 4578
and vocational schools
Germany **6:** 3134
See also
Civic education
Political education
Citizenship responsibility
education and **3:** 1651
and humanities education **5:** 2695
philosophy of education
Herbart's views **5:** 2576
City and Guilds of London Institute (UK)
adult educators
teacher education **11:** 6432
City Technology Colleges (CTC) (UK) **1:** 264
Civic education **2:** ***767–770***
Asia **2:** 768
attitudes and achievement
cross-cultural studies **1:** 393
Australia **2:** 767
China, People's Republic of **2:** 768
Eastern Europe **2:** 768
Germany **7:** 4259
Germany, Federal Republic of (former) **2:** 767
holistic approach **2:** 769
implicit curriculum **2:** 768
Japan **2:** 768
Korea, Republic of **2:** 768
Latin America **2:** 768
regional and national differences **2:** 767
Soviet Union (former) **2:** 768
Sub-Saharan Africa **2:** 768
Sweden **2:** 767
textbooks
United States **2:** 769
United Kingdom **2:** 767
Western civilization **2:** 768
Western Europe **2:** 767
See also
Citizenship education
Civil liberties
and adult education **1:** 134; **2:** 1190; **5:** 2934; **6:** 3362, 3365
and literacy **1:** 169, 170, 175
and moral philosophy **4:** 2030
and program evaluation **4:** 2034
and school choice **8:** 4830; **9:** 5199
UNESCO educational program **11:** 6502, 6504

Civil rights
  and adult education **2:** 1192
  and citizenship **2:** 768
  and curriculum **6:** 3359
  and disabilities **3:** 1506
  and mainstreaming **6:** 3556, 3557
  and multicultural education **7:** 3975
  and special education **10:** 5661, 5662
  United States **8:** 4896, 4900
  See also
    Equal education
    Social equality
Civil rights legislation
  and occupational tests **11:** 6677
  and school law **9:** 5254
Clans
  school organization
    and control **6:** 3525
Class activities
  knowledge acquisition **10:** 6013
  and teacher behavior **10:** 6013
  teacher student relationship **10:** 6028
  thinking tasks **10:** 6013
    and teacher behavior **10:** 6014
  types of **10:** 6012
Class organization
  anthropological research **2:** 798
  computer uses in education
    sex fairness **4:** 2424
  group dynamics **5:** 2527
  grouping (instructional purposes)
    and cooperative learning **9:** 5546
  mainstreaming
    individualized instruction **5:** 2909
  planning of **10:** 6029
    managerial behavior **10:** 6029
  seating arrangement **9:** ***5355–5359***
  and semiotics **9:** 5415
  social rules
    and educational quality **8:** 4871
    research **8:** 4871
  and teacher knowledge **10:** 6119
  teacher role
    small group instruction **10:** 6027
Class size
  and academic achievement **2:** 771; **6:** 3372; **8:** 4868
    effects on **7:** 3817
    research **2:** 772, 773
  cost effectiveness
    production function approach **2:** 772
  and descriptive scales **3:** 1478
  developing nations
    input output analysis **3:** 1760
  ecological approach
    research problems **2:** 772
  and educational finance **9:** 5235
  educational statistics
    and input output analysis **3:** 1758
  and legitimatory research **6:** 3371
  measurement techniques **2:** 771
  and outcomes of education **9:** 5261
  and population trends **3:** 1452
  research **2:** 771
    comparative analysis **2:** 771
    Project STAR **2:** 773
  and school mapping **9:** 5258
  and school organization **7:** 4232
  See also
    Small classes
    Teacher student ratio
Classical test theory **2:** ***785–792***
  and achievement tests **1:** 33
  generalized hypergeometric distribution **2:** 789
  historical background **2:** 785
  item difficulty **2:** 791
  item homogeneity **2:** 788
  and latent trait measurement models **6:** 3248
  and meta analysis **7:** 3779
  ordinal true score theory **2:** 789
  strong true score theory **2:** 789
    future use of **2:** 791
    robustness in **2:** 790
  weak true scores theory **2:** 786
Classification **2:** 1017
  and cluster analysis **2:** 825, 830
  cognitive development
    and literacy **3:** 1244
  and contingency tables **2:** 1081
  and data analysis **3:** 1471
  and decision theory **3:** 1418, 1419
  and discriminant analysis **3:** 1544, 1545
  learning strategies
    memory **7:** 3762
  and models of intelligence **7:** 3876, 3878
  and scientific attitudes **5:** 2654
  of skill development **10:** ***5914–5919***
Classroom Action Research Network (CARN) **1:** 45
Classroom communication
  communication skills **9:** 5506
  communicative competence **6:** 3237
  discourse analysis **2:** 798; **6:** 3237
    and decision-making **6:** 3237
    IRF (initiation, response, feedback) sequence **6:** 3635
    literacy studies **6:** 3237
  discourse modes
    and cultural differences **6:** 3237
  as a discourse process **6:** 3236
  ethnography **2:** 798; **3:** 1234
  and foreign language learning **4:** 2337
  and hearing impairments **10:** 5688
  hidden curriculum **5:** 2587
  initiation response evaluation structure **2:** 799
  international studies
    comparative analysis **10:** 6153
  interpersonal competence **9:** 5506
  language patterns **10:** 6195
    educational effectiveness **10:** 6196
    student role **10:** 6195
    teacher student relationship **10:** 6195
  language usage
    anthropological studies **2:** 798, 800
  microethnographic studies **2:** 1210; **3:** 1233
  research **2:** 818; **10:** 6196
  routines
    systems approach **2:** 819
  rules
    context effect **2:** 819
  and semiotics **9:** 5414
  sex bias in **9:** 5443
  and small group instruction **10:** 6185
  social control **10:** 6194
  sociolinguistic approach **2:** 798; **9:** 5506
    disadvantaged children **6:** 3215
  teacher student relationship **2:** 1210
  and writing skills **11:** 6779
Classroom design
  educational facilities **4:** 2221, 2223
  flexible facilities
    teacher attitudes toward **7:** 4212
  open education
    student development **7:** 4212
    teaching methods **7:** 4212
  and personal space **7:** 4172
  for small group instruction **10:** 6185
  student development **9:** 5355
  See also
    Class organization
    Seating arrangement
Classroom environment **2:** ***807–811***
  and action research **1:** 43
  anthropological studies **2:** ***796–803***
    future trends **2:** 802
  assessment of
    and multilevel analysis **7:** 3978
  audio equipment
    placement of **1:** 400
  co-operation
    and cognitive development **1:** 371
  and computer uses in education **11:** 6284
  cross-cultural studies **2:** 798, 800
  cultural differences
    and peer influence **9:** 5218
  and descriptive scales **3:** 1475
  and environmental measures **4:** ***2245–2250***
  evaluation
    alpha press **2:** 807
    beta press **2:** 807
  evaluation methods **2:** ***807–811***
    higher education **2:** 809
    questionnaires **2:** 807
    science laboratories **2:** 809
  factors in learning **8:** 4400, 4401, 4402
  group unity
    and academic achievement **5:** 2527
  improvement
    Classroom Environment Scale **2:** 810
  interaction
    cognitive processes **10:** 6033
  and learning factors **10:** 5747
  and learning theories **10:** 5746
  measures

and descriptive scales **3:** 1481
and multiple regression analysis **9:** 4972
and nonverbal communication **7:** 4174
and outcomes of education **9:** 5262
studies **10:** 5773
paradigm of **10:** 6205
perceptual measures of **4:** 2247
questionnaires
Classroom Environment Scale **2:** 807
Learning Environment Inventory **2:** 807
My Class Inventory **2:** 807
teacher student relationship **2:** 809
research **4:** 2132
affective objectives **2:** 809
cognitive objectives **2:** 809
room acoustics **1:** 399
and school organization **7:** 4228
and student attitudes **2:** 810; **4:** 2247; **10:** 5773
and student behavior **8:** 4871; **10:** 5791
and teacher behavior **10:** 5791
and teacher expectations of students **6:** 3309
teacher role **10:** 6027
teachers
coping strategies **6:** 3309
political attitudes **8:** 4582
and visual aids **10:** 5729
Classroom Environment Scale (CES) **2:** 809; **3:** 1481; **4:** 2247; **10:** 5772
explanatory power of **3:** 1482
Classroom furniture design
educational facilities **4:** 2221
Classroom management
See Classroom techniques
Classroom observation techniques **2:** 807, ***811–816***
audiotape recordings
interaction process analysis **2:** 815
cluster analysis
validity **2:** 813
coding
time sampling **2:** 814
data collection
electronic equipment **2:** 812
disabilities
and interpersonal competence **9:** 5564
electronic equipment
criticism of **2:** 812
Flanders Interaction Analysis System **2:** 807
interaction **2:** 811
international studies
comparative analysis **10:** 6151
micro vs. macro aspects **10:** 6012
and mild disabilities **8:** 4933
naturalistic observation **2:** 812
Observation Schedule and Record **2:** 807
and small group instruction **10:** 6186
structured observation **2:** 811
characteristics of **2:** 812
history of **2:** 811
and student evaluations of teacher effectiveness **10:** 6231
teacher effectiveness **8:** 4521
teacher evaluation **4:** 2128
teacher role
naturalistic observation **2:** 794
teaching methods
early childhood education **3:** 1632
videotape recordings
interaction process analysis **2:** 815
vs. descriptive scales **3:** 1475
See also
Student behavior
Classroom research
designs **4:** 2193
instructional effectiveness **2:** 815
interaction process analysis **2:** 814
lesson structure **6:** ***3385–3389***
observation instruments
validity **2:** 813
observers
training of **2:** 813
reliability
testing for **2:** 813
routines **2:** 817
rules **2:** 817
teacher development **2:** 816
teacher evaluation **2:** 816
Classroom tasks
See Class activities
Classroom techniques
computers
research studies **7:** 4096
in science education **7:** 4102
and educational quality
vocational education **8:** 4863
group dynamics **5:** 2527
for individual testing **5:** ***2779–2784***
and innovation
implementation of **5:** 2839
and instructional design models **5:** 2859
and learning factors **10:** 5747, 5748
and lesson structure **6:** 3387
and microcomputer-based laboratories **7:** 3808
routines **2:** 817
rules **2:** 817, 818
standards
effect of unions on **10:** 6071
and teacher knowledge **10:** 6118
types of **10:** 6120
and teaching guides **10:** 6113
See also
Discipline
Reinforcement
Classrooms
audio media in **1:** 396, 399
behavior standards **5:** 2525
and computer networks **2:** 978
nonverbal behavior in **7:** ***4171–4175***
peer groups **8:** 4365
and school dynamics **9:** ***5169–5176***
student attitudes to **10:** ***5772–5775***
student role in **10:** ***5791–5796***
traditional
tasks in **10:** 5791
Cleft palate
incidence of **10:** 5692; **11:** 6705
and resonance problems **11:** 6705
treatment of **11:** 6706
types of **11:** 6706
See also
Articulation impairments
Climate control
educational facilities **4:** 2220
Clinical psychology
and educational history **3:** 1795
Clinical research
interviews for **5:** ***3003–3007***
bias in **5:** 3006
factors affecting **5:** 3004
types of **5:** 3003
Clinical supervision (of teachers)
teacher evaluation **4:** 2126, 2129
teacher improvement **10:** 5933
Closed tests
characteristics of **11:** 6342
Cloze procedure
characteristics of **11:** 6342, 6346
and content analysis **2:** 1075
and foreign language testing **4:** 2362
and projective measures **8:** 4790
and readability formulas **7:** 3931
Sentence Completion Test (SCT) **10:** 5937
and text analysis **2:** 1078
Cluster analysis **2:** ***825–831***
agglomerative hierarchical methods **2:** 827
distance and similarity measures **2:** 826
evaluation **2:** 830
and international education indicators **5:** 2988
k-means iterative reallocation methods **2:** 828
latent class analysis **2:** 830
mixture method **2:** 829
and multivariate analysis **7:** 4010
numerical methods **2:** 825
ratio of homogeneity **7:** 3737
uses of **7:** 3738
and scaling **9:** 5154
and variation measures **7:** 3734
Cluster grouping
analysis of **2:** 825
numerical methods **2:** 825
Coaching
See Tutoring
Coaching for tests
See Test coaching
Coalition of Adult Education Organizations (CAEO) **7:** 4181
Coalition of Essential Schools (US) **5:** 2693
Cobb–Douglas production function
and education **1:** 245

Cocaine
drug abuse
effect on learning **3:** 1618
Cochran Q test
nonparametric statistics **7:** 4161
Cockcroft Report 1982 (UK)
Mathematics Counts
mathematics education **6:** 3663
Codes of ethics
in evaluation **4:** 2034
for teachers **11:** 6579
Coding
data organization **3:** 1378
educational surveys
and microcomputers **7:** 3814
of essay tests **4:** 2021
meta analysis **7:** 3780
problem-solving research
and videotape recordings **11:** 6604
reliability checks **3:** 1469
and semiotics **9:** 5413
and surveys **10:** 5859
techniques
contrast coding **9:** 4971
and data analysis **3:** 1468
effect coding **9:** 4971
and regression analysis **9:** 4970
videotape recordings
and educational research **11:** 6607
Coeducation
curriculum
sex bias **4:** 2291
educational history
Germany **11:** 6747
higher education
North America **11:** 6761
Islamic culture **11:** 6759
and sex discrimination **4:** 2421
sex segregated classes
developing nations **2:** 831
vs. single sex schools **2:** ***831–834***; **4:** 2410; **9:** 5444
Coefficient of correlation
See Correlation, coefficients of
Cognition
cross-cultural studies **1:** 291
See also
Culture and cognition approach
Cognitive ability
and adult education participation **7:** 4322
adult learning **6:** 3429
and aging (individuals) **1:** 235; **8:** 4819
cognitive development
individual differences **3:** 1503; **5:** 2761
and congenital impairments **11:** 6706
constructs
and aptitude treatment interaction **10:** 6158
cultural differences **3:** 1230
anthropological perspective **3:** ***1246–1253***
interdisciplinary approach **3:** 1247
psychological research **3:** 1246
domains of specialization **8:** 4821
dynamic assessment
and deafness **3:** 1401
general and specific **5:** 2669
generation gap
cohort analysis **1:** 236
genetic determinants **2:** 845
individual differences **2:** 844
age differences **1:** 236
stability of **3:** 1504
and intelligence **5:** 2911
models of **7:** 3873
and interpersonal relationships **2:** 838
maintenance
and aging (individuals) **1:** 236
measurement of **7:** 3878
adults **8:** 4818
preschool children **8:** 4951, 4952
and preschool education **2:** 680
reasoning
logical thinking **8:** 4952
sex differences **9:** 5433
and structural equation models **8:** 4347
tests
and error of measurement **9:** 4994
See also
Intelligence
Thinking skills
Cognitive anthropology
See Ethnography
Cognitive conflict
See Cognitive dissonance
Cognitive development **5:** 2658, 2661
acceleration of **10:** 6166
and acquisition of expertise **2:** ***838–842***
adult development
teachers **10:** 5937
in adults **8:** 4819
encapsulation model **8:** 4823
Piagetian theory **8:** 4818, 4819
in children
and parent education **7:** 4294
children's theories **2:** 853
theory of mind **2:** 854, 856
cognitive ability
individual differences **3:** 1503; **5:** 2761
cognitive apprenticeship model **5:** 2882; **6:** 3299, 3344; **7:** 3885
and computer-assisted instruction **2:** 990
concept formation **10:** 6188
and conflict resolution **5:** 2534
connectionist paradigm **2:** 853
contextual approach **2:** 850
contextual influences
ethnography **3:** 1248, 1249, 1251
cross-cultural studies **3:** ***1241–1246***; **4:** 1849; **5:** 2649
and cultural deficit theory **3:** 1246
cultural historical school **3:** 1243, 1248, 1249; **6:** 3289
face to face interactions **3:** 1250
formative experiments **3:** 1249, 1251
interpsychological studies **3:** 1248, 1249
intrapsychological studies **3:** 1248, 1249
cultural influences on **3:** 1242
culture and evolution **4:** 2167
and curriculum **10:** 5816
and dropouts **3:** 1606
during childhood and adolescence **5:** 2683
and educational practices **5:** 2666
and educational technology **4:** 1896
effect of literacy on **3:** 1242, 1243
and emotional development **4:** 1963, 1964
and energy expenditure **2:** 850
and expertise **2:** 836
educational implications **2:** 841
genetic factors
adopted children **5:** 2465
twins **5:** 2465
grouping (instructional purposes)
cooperative learning **5:** 2533
individual differences **2:** ***842–847***
in content-specific knowledge **2:** 845
determinants of **2:** 845
developmental rate **2:** 843
and educational practices **2:** 846
environmental factors **2:** 846
predictive measurement **2:** 844
role of school **2:** 846
types of **2:** 843
infants **5:** 2799
influence of domain-specific knowledge on **3:** 1502
influence of instruction on **3:** 1502, 1503
influence of learning on **3:** ***1501–1504***
information processing approach **2:** ***847–852***; **5:** 2661
assumptions **2:** 847
developmental stages **2:** 849
thinking skills **2:** 848
instructional design model **2:** 1020
and interpersonal relationship **2:** 1051; **9:** 5507
intra individual differences
developmental stages **2:** 843
and knowledge **6:** 3150, 3151
and learning **10:** 6165
and learning strategies **3:** 1502
mass media role in **2:** 885
mastery learning research **5:** 2662
maturity (individuals) **3:** 1501, 1503
measurement of
dynamic model **6:** 3313
Saltus model **3:** 1512
measurement techniques **7:** 3702
academic learning time **1:** 20
memory **7:** ***3760–3763***
memory systems **2:** 1020
methods
characteristics of **10:** 6168

and moral development **5:** 2662
and motivation **5:** 2662
parent student relationship
helping relationship **5:** 2626
and perceptual development **8:** 4380, 4382
and personality development **5:** 2662
Piagetian theory **2:** 850; **3:** 1244, 1502; **5:** 2649; **6:** 3340
psycholinguistics **10:** 6194
sex differences **9:** 5433
and play **8:** 4539
and pre-existence of concepts **2:** 853
prerequisites for **3:** 1501
problems **10:** 6167
psychometric approach **5:** 2657
reasoning
in children **8:** ***4951–4957***
social cognition **3:** 1502
and social development **9:** 5505
social rules **8:** 4871
sociocultural influences **3:** 1250
and sociometric techniques **10:** 5617
and specific life experiences
ethnography **3:** 1248
stimulation programs **3:** 1503
teacher role **10:** 6051, 6194
and teaching methods **5:** 2666
and television viewing **1:** 566
theoretical problems **2:** ***852–857***
theories of **2:** 842
revision **10:** 6166
and teaching **10:** ***6164–6169***
and thinking skills **3:** 1503
and use of educational media **7:** 3742
and values education **1:** 377
Vygotsky's zone of proximal development **3:** 1230, 1502; **5:** 2533, 2881; **6:** 3308, 3313
definitions of **3:** 1248; **9:** 5545
determinants of **3:** 1251
and dynamic assessment **1:** 372
and learning activity **5:** 2876; **6:** 3290
and learning theories **9:** 5546
See also
Intellectual development
Perceptual development
Cognitive dissonance **8:** 4651
and moral development **7:** 3918
Cognitive knowledge
See Cognitive structures
Cognitive linguistics
reading comprehension **8:** 4942
Cognitive measurement **1:** ***370–374***
and factor analysis **4:** 2240
and multiple regression analysis **9:** 4972
and multivariate analysis **7:** 3704
test validity
evaluation criteria **1:** 372
See also
Intelligence tests
Cognitive objectives
anticipatory outcomes **9:** 5515
and religious education **9:** 5000
Cognitive processes
abstract reasoning **6:** 3291
in adults **8:** 4818
and artificial intelligence **5:** 2919
and associative learning **2:** 849
classificatory behavior
discrimination learning **2:** 1017, 1018
generalization **2:** 1017, 1018
cognitive control **1:** 203
comprehension
effort after meaning **2:** 964
computer simulation **8:** ***4719–4722***
concept formation **2:** ***1016–1020***
connectionism **6:** 3153
cultural differences
intracultural comparisons **3:** 1246
and multiple literacies **3:** 1230
development of consciousness **2:** 855
Dewey on **3:** 1522
direct instruction **3:** 1526
and discrimination learning **2:** 849
and educational media **7:** 3745
ethnography **3:** 1247
executive functions **1:** 330
experimental introspection theory **5:** 2881
expert performance
protocol analysis **2:** 839
expertise **4:** ***2194–2199***
formal operational **8:** 4820
and generalization **2:** 849
guiding of
and study habits **10:** 5830
and heuristics **10:** 6174, 6175
implications for curriculum development **4:** 1844
information processing approach **2:** 847; **4:** 1843; **5:** 2875; **6:** 3317, 3328
and intellectual development **5:** 2913
and study habits **10:** 5829
instruction **10:** ***6187–6193***
and instructional tasks **10:** 5742
and intelligence **5:** 2918
and knowledge
theories of **10:** 5740
and knowledge acquisition **2:** 840
knowledge dependent **2:** 835
and learning **2:** ***835–838***; **10:** ***5738–5745***
learning strategies **5:** 2882; **6:** 3328
older adults **1:** 236, 237, 238
levels of consciousness **2:** 1047
measurement **1:** 319
and memory **8:** 4820
research **7:** 3765
metacognition **2:** 966; **7:** ***3784–3788***
models **1:** 319
postformal/dialectical **8:** 4819, 4820, 4823
encapsulation model **8:** 4823
problem-solving **8:** 4724
and radical constructivism **2:** 1049
reading comprehension **10:** 6191
and realist constructivism **2:** 1049
reasoning **8:** 4952
role of meaning in **3:** 1250
schematic anticipation theory **5:** 2881
and school dynamics **9:** 5169
and social learning theories **1:** 495
and student characteristics **10:** 5740
and task analysis **10:** 5743, 5911
theories
and second language learning **6:** 3332
thinking skills **8:** ***4722–4728***
types of **8:** 4819
use of tools in **2:** 837
See also
Creative thinking
Critical thinking
Learning processes
Memory
Metacognition
Perception
Problem-solving
Social cognition
Cognitive psychology **4:** 1843, 1844; **5:** 2882
content and process analysis **5:** 2762
definitions of learning **6:** 3341
feedback
in learning and instruction **4:** 2280
and heuristics **10:** 6174
implications for testing **1:** 371
information processing approach **2:** 852
and instructional design **5:** 2871
and instructional psychology **5:** 2878
and learning processes
research **10:** 5783
and learning strategies **1:** 187
second language learning **6:** 3331
and learning theories **6:** 3317, 3340, 3341
and models of learning **7:** 3881
problem-solving **8:** 4726
and psychometrics **1:** ***370–374***
standard model of cognition **1:** ***328–331***
Cognitive restructuring **2:** ***857–861***; **4:** 1992; **6:** 3154
age differences **8:** 4952
attribution retraining **6:** 3295
behavior disorders **1:** 492
cognitive strategy instruction **2:** 862
domain-specific **6:** 3154
and dynamic assessment **2:** 859
educational programs **2:** 859
COGNET program **2:** 859
instrumental enrichment **2:** 859, 862
Feuerstein's mediated learning experience model **2:** 858
global **6:** 3154
and knowledge acquisition **2:** 840
in long term memory **8:** 4701
and parent education **2:** 860
Piagetian theory **2:** 857
publications and associations **2:** 860

radical **6:** 3154
and science education **9:** 5332
Vygotsky's theory **2:** 858
weak **6:** 3154
Cognitive skills
See Thinking skills
Cognitive strategies
for children
to reduce aggression **1:** 233
and expertise **2:** 835
See also
Learning strategies
Cognitive strategy instruction
2: ***861–868***
cultural differences **2:** 865
definition of **2:** 861
direct explanation **2:** 863
direct instruction **2:** 862
informed strategies for learning
2: 864
and learning motivation **2:** 865
and portfolio assessment **2:** 866
reading instruction **2:** 863
reciprocal teaching **2:** 864
special education
historical development **2:** 861
reading **2:** 862
special needs students **6:** 3296
strategies intervention model **2:** 863
and teacher support **2:** 866
and thinking skills **2:** 865
types of knowledge in **2:** 861, 865
Cognitive structures **1:** ***328–331***; **8:** 4820
analysis of **5:** 2882
conceptual change **6:** 3154
enrichment **6:** 3154
constructivist **3:** 1541
and curriculum objectives **3:** 1699
and developmental stages **5:** 2669
domain specific **2:** 851
and educational strategies **5:** 2668
enculturation
and realist constructivism **2:** 1050
evaluation of
pre-instructional **2:** 1025
extent
experts **4:** 2195
and Galois lattice method **4:** 2395, 2398
individual differences
and learning **6:** 3287
intra individual **2:** 844
and language **6:** 3214
and learning **6:** 3317
learning processes **2:** 839, 840
and memory **7:** 3761
organization
experts **4:** 2194
preconceptions and misconceptions
about **8:** 4650
and prior learning **6:** 3327
schemata (cognition) **6:** 3152
semantic network **6:** 3152
and teacher behavior **10:** 6014
theories of **6:** 3153
time factors (learning) **2:** 836
types of knowledge **4:** 1844
Cognitive style **6:** 3319
adult learning **6:** 3430
attention control
individual differences **2:** 870
classification **2:** 870
cognitive psychology
Gestalt psychology **2:** 869
concept formation **2:** 870
concepts of **2:** 868
historical development **2:** 868
conceptual tempo **2:** 870
convergent thinking **2:** 870
core conceptualization **2:** 869
cultural differences **2:** 836; **6:** 3310
Embedded Figures Test **4:** 2335
field dependence independence
2: 868, 870; **3:** 1239
foreign language learning **4:** 2334
historical background **1:** 318
individual differences **5:** 2763
and individual psychology **2:** 868
information processing approach
2: 870
in learning **2:** ***868–872***
and learning strategies **6:** 3327, 3346
and memory **7:** 3765
nature and measurement of
1: ***318–322***
perception
discrimination learning **2:** 870
and psychoanalysis
ego development **2:** 869
and reading processes **8:** 4937
and teaching methods **2:** 871; **5:** 2669
and teaching styles
adult education **10:** 6056
types of **1:** 318
vs. ability **2:** 869
vs. learning strategies **2:** 869
Cognitive tests
preference
characteristics of **11:** 6343
Cognitive theory
See Epistemology
Cognitively Guided Instruction (CGI)
and student role **10:** 5792, 5794
Coherence
sense of **4:** 1976
in families with disabled children
4: 1977, 1978
mothers compared with fathers
4: 1978
Coherence justification
feminist approach **4:** 2300, 2301
Cohesion (written composition)
and text analysis **2:** 1078
Cohort analysis
by age
and educational equity (finance)
3: 1792
and longitudinal studies **6:** 3518
Cohort effects
See Vintage effects
Coleman Report 1966 (US)
input output analysis **3:** 1756
Collaboration
See Cooperation
Collaborative demonstration
See Demonstrations (educational), co-operation
Collective bargaining **10:** 6068
and academic achievement **10:** 6069
empirical research **10:** 6070
and education
effects on **8:** 4407
and labor relations **6:** 3192
and paid educational leave
7: ***4257–4263***
and personnel management **8:** 4407
and teacher associations **6:** 3191
teachers **6:** 3275
and unions **10:** 6076
See also
Unions
Collective settlements
and education
Soviet Union (former) **10:** 5646
College Characteristics Index
and descriptive scales **3:** 1476
College credits
vocational education
learning modules **7:** 3892
College entrance examinations
models for **11:** 6317
and test bias **11:** 6317
College graduates
and educational development
studies **6:** 3183
College housing **10:** 5800
College life
studies
and self-report **9:** 5409
College programs
problem-solving **8:** 4729
College registrars
See Registrars (school)
College role
in participatory research **7:** 4333
College unions
See Student unions
Colleges
professional autonomy
and governance of teacher
education **10:** 5963
Colleges of education
See Schools of education
Colleges of technology
See Technical institutes
Collegiality
contrived
and teacher cultures **10:** 6214
and prereferral intervention **8:** 4659
and principals
role of **9:** 5269, 5271
and school organization **4:** 2163
teacher improvement **10:** 5933
Colombia
adult education
nonformal education **2:** 876
apprenticeships **10:** 6064
curriculum development **2:** 878

early intervention
nutrition programs **3:** 1626
educational change **2:** 879
educational finance
and tax allocation **8:** 4363
educational planning
Escuela Nueva **8:** 4507
implementation problems **3:** 1823
educational radio **4:** 1906
educational research **2:** 879
educational television **4:** 1904
large-scale projects **5:** 2892
ethnic groups **2:** 872
government school relationship
financial support **2:** 877
school administration **2:** 876
inservice teacher education
technical education **10:** 6066
job training **7:** 4197
labor education
empirical research findings **3:** 1684
language **2:** 872
nonformal education **7:** 4133
popular education **1:** 133
postsecondary education **2:** 875
preschool education **2:** 875
primary distance education **3:** 1559
primary education **2:** 874
public vs. private sector earnings comparison **8:** 4837
returns to education **5:** 2644; **8:** 4916
school enterprise
rural development program **9:** 5230
secondary education **2:** 875
structure of government **2:** 872
student loan programs **10:** 5764
system of education **2:** ***872–880***
degrees and qualifications **2:** 879
educational objectives **2:** 873
major problems **2:** 880
structure **2:** 873
teacher education **2:** 877
teaching methodology **2:** 878
technical education **2:** 875
and paraprofessional personnel **11:** 6270
vocational education **2:** 875; **7:** 4206; **9:** 5073, 5074
comprehensive schools **6:** 3257
technical **6:** 3259
Colonialism
and basic education **1:** 465
and education
Hong Kong **2:** 1039
Taiwan **2:** 1039
and educational change **4:** 1849
and educational development
sub-Saharan Africa **8:** 4510
and educational planning
Latin America **8:** 4492
effects on developing nations **8:** 4680
and history of women's education
francophone Africa **11:** 6736
racial discrimination
and sexual discrimination **7:** 3849
and school organization **7:** 4243
and social change
educational anthropology **9:** 5508
and Western civilization
ethnocentrism **9:** 5508
and women's education
India **11:** 6748
COMETT **4:** 2055, 2061; **5:** 2976; **7:** 3968
Commercial television
educational impact of **5:** 2895
Commission of the European Communities
career education program **2:** 633
studies
and learning disabilities **10:** 5683
Commissions on education
international education **5:** 2957
Commitment
teachers
career-continuance **10:** 6210
professional **10:** 6209
vocational **10:** 6209
Common factor model
See Factor analysis, common factor model
Commonplaces of education
and curriculum planning **3:** 1330
Commonwealth Association for the Education and Training of Adults (CAETA) **5:** 2932, 2948; **8:** 4732
Commonwealth Council for Educational Administration (CCEA)
activities of **5:** 2952
Commonwealth Foundation **5:** 2933
Commonwealth of Learning (COL) **5:** 2934
educational technology
activities **4:** 1879
objectives **3:** 1581
purpose **3:** 1581
Commonwealth Secretariat
distance education
activities **4:** 1879
Human Resources Development Group **5:** 2933
nonformal education forum **5:** 2933
Communicable diseases
effect on learning **5:** 2565
and health education **5:** 2567
Communication
demonstrations (educational) **10:** 6140
and human factors engineering **4:** 2009
and infology **7:** 3772
and interaction (Habermas) **2:** 1201
and language **4:** 2358
and learning **6:** 3298
Communication aids (for disabled)
autism
facilitated communication training **6:** 3233
deafness **3:** 1399
Communication apprehension
classroom environment
and foreign language learning **4:** 2335
Communication disorders
autism **6:** ***3232–3235***
bilingual students **6:** ***3228–3232***
and communication problems **6:** ***3225–3228***
intervention **6:** 3227
prevalence of **11:** 6704
speech handicaps
augmentative and alternative communication **1:** ***404–409***
and speech perception **10:** 5688
See also
Hearing impairments
Language handicaps
Speech handicaps
Communication problems
and communication disorders **6:** ***3225–3228***
language acquisition
deaf blind children **3:** 1403
Communication research
and cultural differences **6:** 3210
representativeness and voice **6:** 3636
Communication skills **1:** 96; **9:** ***5504–5508***
daily living skills
assessment of bilingual students **6:** 3229
definition of **9:** 5504
and language acquisition **9:** 5505
literacy and work **8:** 4636
and social development **9:** 5505
sociolinguistic approach **9:** 5506
vocational education
curriculum development **11:** 6667
Communications
educational implication of **9:** 5539
and educational planning **11:** 6297
model
and educational technology **4:** 1893
Communications media
See Mass media
Communications satellites
characteristics of **11:** 6300
and copyright **2:** 1102
and distance education
China, People's Republic of **3:** 1565
United States **3:** 1566
in education **4:** 1913
and educational technology **4:** 1881
and educational television **5:** 2893
Communicative action
communicative competence
critical theory **2:** 1202
critique of Habermas' views **4:** 2030
and educational administration **3:** 1773
and pedagogy
Habermas **8:** 4459
Communicative competence (languages)
adult education **6:** ***3209–3213***
and augmentative and alternative

communication **1:** 408
interpersonal **1:** 408
linguistic **1:** 408
cultural differences
and academic achievement **3:** 1228
empirical research **4:** 2363
foreign language instruction **4:** 2341, 2353
and foreign language testing
characteristics **4:** 2359
and job training **6:** ***3209–3213***
language of mathematics **6:** 3638
language tests
children **6:** 3226
and linguistic competence **6:** 3236
programs
ICONS project (US) **6:** 3212
and second language learning **6:** 3436
teacher education
and cultural pluralism **10:** 5990
Communism
and adult education **2:** 1191
Central and Eastern Europe **2:** 657
and Marxist educational thought
6: 3617
Communitarianism
communities and **4:** 2029
and individual freedom **4:** 2031
and liberalism **4:** 2031
and moral philosophy **4:** 2030
Community
definitions of **2:** 901
and educational assessment
reports **1:** 365
literacies **6:** 3456
resistance
and adult education **1:** 129
Community-based education (CBE)
2: 901, 903, 906; **8:** 4339
adult literacy programs **1:** 102
for adults **7:** 4147
Canada **1:** 102
and community education
United States **2:** 900
Community centers
adult education
Australia **1:** 411
Community characteristics
and learning factors **10:** 5748, 5749
Community colleges **2:** ***893–900***
admission criteria **2:** 894
adult basic education **2:** 895
adult education **2:** ***900–907***
Canada **1:** 102; **2:** 895
China, People's Republic of **2:** 895, 898
curriculum **2:** 897
development **2:** 894
distance education **2:** 895
enrollment **2:** 896
faculty and staff **2:** 897
fees **2:** 894
finance and facilities **2:** 897
goals and functions **2:** 895
lifelong learning **2:** 893, 895
New Zealand **2:** 895, 898
Norway **2:** 895, 899
open education **2:** 895
organization **2:** 895
scope and definition **2:** 893
students **2:** 896
Sweden **2:** 895
trends and issues **2:** 899
United States **2:** ***893–900***; **4:** 2388, 2391; **6:** 3418
student support systems **10:** 5806
universities
links with **2:** 899
use of term **2:** 893
vocational education **2:** 895
Community development **2:** 904; **6:** 3420
and adult education **2:** 1191
Malaysia **6:** 3464
and community education **2:** ***900–907***
definition of **2:** 904
evaluation **2:** 1048
Latin America **6:** 3254
and private organizations **7:** 4153
use of term **1:** 119
Community education **1:** 129; **2:** ***907–910***
and adult literacy **2:** 909
Australia **1:** ***409–415***
and community development
2: ***900–907***
and computer networks **2:** 978
and conflict theories **2:** 900
definition of **2:** 907
in developing nations **2:** 908
and functionalist theories **2:** 900
goals and ideology **2:** 902
historical background **2:** 907
international development **2:** 907
management of **2:** 910
as a process **2:** 902
radical model **2:** 902
reformist model **2:** 902
social change model **2:** 902
universal model **2:** 902
programs
financing **2:** 902
and public schools **8:** 4808
United Kingdom **2:** 901, 902
uses of term **1:** 119; **2:** 901
Community Education Development Centre (CEDC) (UK) **2:** 902
Community health services
mental health programs **3:** 1436
Community involvement
and academic achievement **6:** 3105
and decentralization **3:** 1414
and disabilities **11:** 6458
in education
and private resources **8:** 4704
in educational planning **8:** 4600
sub-Saharan Africa **8:** 4513
and school effectiveness **9:** 5375
in school organization **9:** 5213
Community organizations
North America **7:** 4146
Community Programme (CP) (UK)
vocational education **11:** 6688
Community role
in education **8:** 4593
and educational innovation
implementation of **5:** 2842
Community school relationship
See School community relationship
Community schools **2:** ***907–910***; **8:** 4827
and community involvement in curriculum **2:** 891
developing nations **2:** 891
United States **2:** 900
village colleges **2:** 907
Community services
delivery systems
and school-based management
9: 5305
Community support
educational finance **2:** ***910–914***; **4:** 2315
fund raising methods **2:** 911
and inequalities **2:** 912
potential **2:** 911
vs. central control **2:** 912
and educational improvement **9:** 5243
and educational quality **2:** 912
families with disabled children
4: 1978
Israel **4:** 1978
Community surveys
of learning needs **6:** 3377
Comoros
occupational segregation **4:** 2430
Compact discs (CD)
See Optical discs
Comparable worth
in education **8:** 4406
screening hypothesis **9:** 5352
Comparative analysis
educational research **2:** ***958–964***
impact on educational policy
3: ***1830–1835***
meta analysis **3:** 1834
student evaluation **8:** 4621
trend analysis **3:** 1833
vocational education **11:** ***6690–6699***
Comparative area studies
in education **4:** 1835
educational finance **5:** 2979
effect of economic adjustment on
3: 1787
Germany and United Kingdom
vocational education and training
11: ***6638–6640***
labor force planning **6:** 3610, 3612
literacy **6:** 3472
and national surveys **2:** 652
policy formation **2:** 1124
private education **8:** 4833
public expenditures **2:** 1123
science
attitudes toward **9:** 5321
vocational education
Latin America **6:** 3258
Comparative education **2:** 948
adult education **1:** 150
area studies **1:** ***331–332***

bibliographies **3:** 1587
course content **2:** 920
cross-cultural studies **2:** 919
cross-sectional studies **2:** 953
data collection **2:** 953
sampling **2:** 953, 956
descriptive studies **2:** 950
development education **3:** ***1494–1501***
developmental studies **2:** 951
doctoral dissertations **3:** 1587
documentation **3:** ***1584–1589***
status and prospects **3:** 1587
ecological approach **2:** 927
educational anthropology **2:** 919
educational policy
research **11:** 6524
ethnography **2:** 926, 930
evaluation of cross-national studies
4: ***2132–2140***
evolutionary and functionalist
perspectives **2:** 923
functionalism **2:** 923, 928
historical background **3:** 1723
historical development **2:** 918
humanism **2:** 926, 929, 930, 948
hypothesis testing **2:** 924
information sources **3:** ***1584–1589***
databases **3:** 1587
direct publication **3:** 1586
information centers **3:** 1584, 1586
information networks **3:** 1587
national databases **3:** 1586
professional associations **3:** 1587
input output utilization model **2:** 956
institutions **2:** 920
and international education
2: ***918–923***, 925; **5:** 2972, 2973
methodology **2:** 919, 922, 923,
948–958
neo-Marxian **2:** 925, 929
organizations and institutions
2: ***933–942***
multinational **2:** 921
regional **2:** 921
survey **2:** 935
origins of **2:** 919
overview **2:** ***918–923***
paradigms and theories **2:** ***923–933***
phenomenography **2:** 930
policy-oriented and discipline-
oriented studies **2:** 949
postmodernism **2:** 930
professional associations **2:** 920,
942–948
qualitative or quantitative approaches
2: 949
quantification **2:** 954
reference materials **3:** 1586
relationships and processes **2:** 950,
952
role of social sciences **2:** 920, 922,
923
scholarly journals **2:** 920, 921;
3: 1586
scientific methodology **2:** 924, 948,
949
statistical analysis **2:** ***958–964***
statistical data
international and regional sources
2: 958
international standardization
2: 958, 959
national sources **2:** 958
structural equation models
LISREL **2:** 954
types of research **2:** 950
in universities
Europe **2:** 921
United States **2:** 921
use of term **1:** 331
Comparative Education Society (US)
See Comparative and International
EducationSociety (CIES) (US)
Comparative Education Society in
Europe (CESE) **2:** 921, 944
conferences **2:** 945
membership **2:** 944
objectives **2:** 944
Comparative and International
Education Society (CIES) (US)
2: 920, 943, 945
conferences **2:** 943
membership **2:** 943
objectives **2:** 943
publications **2:** 943, 947
Comparative religion
See Religion studies
Compensation (remuneration)
external equity **8:** 4406
internal equity **8:** 4406
and personnel management **8:** 4406
Compensatory education **1:** 116;
8: 4958
adult education **2:** 636
and educational philosophy of justice
8: 4574
evaluation
and test bias **11:** 6318
high risk students **2:** 709
history of women's education
Australia **11:** 6731
legitimacy of **1:** 129
and literacy **6:** 3451
rationale of **8:** 4931
research **8:** 4933
Competence
distinguished from performance
3: 1728
evaluation of stages in development
of **4:** 2198
individual differences
research on expertise **2:** 839
and intelligence
in adulthood **8:** 4819
labor force
and technical education **4:** 1919
needs
and training investment **2:** 1137
perceptions of
and self-esteem theory **10:** 6222
and self-motivation **7:** 3939, 3940
of teachers **10:** 6021
and testing **6:** 3468
Competency-based education
and administrator education
inservice **1:** 71
for adults **1:** 183, 184; **8:** 4806
elements of
and teaching guides **10:** 6113
and learning modules **7:** 3890
and nonformal education **4:** 2365
objectives **11:** 6776, 6777
testing
and accountability **7:** 3725
and vocational education **11:** 6250
Competency-based teacher education
10: 6016
curriculum **10:** 5993
Competition
and co-operation
sociobiological approach **4:** 2170
and development strategies **11:** 6633
and governance **8:** 4592
and investment in education
differentiation **6:** 3548
and performance
learning **6:** 3301
performance factors **5:** 2501
and school choice **9:** 5202
and social interdependence theory
10: 6220
Complementary education
See Literacy education
Complex covariance component models
See Hierarchical linear models (HLM)
Compliance (psychology)
social behavior **9:** 5525
Componential analysis **5:** 2918;
10: 5913
Composite Development Index (CDI)
and literacy testing **6:** 3472
Composition (literary)
See Writing (composition)
Comprehension
cloze procedure **2:** 1078
constructive theory **2:** 964
context effort **2:** 965
educational objectives
teacher guidance **2:** 965
and human factors engineering
4: 2009
influences
cognitive processes **2:** 964
learning processes **2:** 964, 965
and rote learning **8:** 4724
social context
reciprocal teaching **2:** 967
situated learning **2:** 967
teaching methods **2:** ***964–969***
adjunct questions **2:** 965
advance organizers **2:** 965
educational effectiveness **2:** 966
elaboration theory **2:** 965
examples **2:** 965
inquiry-oriented teaching **2:** 965
testing of
application **2:** 968
cloze procedure **2:** 968

free recall **2:** 967
questioning techniques **2:** 967
structure displays **2:** 968
summarizing **2:** 967
thinking aloud **2:** 967
and text analysis **2:** 1077
See also
Reading comprehension
Comprehensive colleges
teacher education programs **10:** 5996
Comprehensive Employment and Training Act (CETA) (US)
evaluation studies **4:** 2147
impact on earnings **7:** 4197
Comprehensive schools
vocational education
Sweden **11:** 6691
Western Europe **11:** 6664
Compulsory education
and adult education **1:** 154, 158
ages for
Europe **9:** 5386
duration of **4:** 2173; **11:** 6393
comparative analysis **2:** 959
legislation **6:** 3358
and educational planning
socialist nations **8:** 4497
legislation **6:** 3362
limitations of **4:** 2364
teacher role in **9:** 5020
and vocational education
Japan **6:** 3086
in vocational schools
Germany **1:** 311
women's education
Australia **11:** 6733
Computation **6:** 3673
and affective behavior **6:** 3640
sex differences **4:** 2433
testing **4:** 2075
Computer adaptive testing
See Computer-assisted testing
Computer applications
See Computer oriented programs
Computer-assisted design
and desktop publishing **4:** 1956
Computer-assisted instruction (CAI) **2:** ***988–992***, 1003, 1007; **8:** 4774
adult learning **6:** 3433
attributes of **2:** 991
classification
by software type **2:** 988
by usage **2:** 989
cognitive development **10:** 6191
compared with conventional instruction **7:** 3740
and computer-managed learning **2:** 999
and cooperative learning **9:** 5547
courseware design **2:** 1165; **10:** 5624
criticism of **4:** 1909
developing nations **4:** 1900
disabled children
parents as teachers **4:** 1979
planned support by parents **4:** 1979
and distance education **3:** 1561; **9:** 5396; **11:** 6301
applications **11:** 6304
and drills (practice) **7:** 4082
economics of **4:** 1908
educational change
and cost effectiveness studies **2:** 1135
evidence of use **2:** 990, 991
expert systems **2:** 1003
evaluation studies **2:** 1003
independent study **5:** 2770; **9:** 5395, 5396
individualized instruction **4:** 1844
interaction
and courseware design **2:** 1168
and international organizations **4:** 1881
and literacy education **6:** 3479
and management information systems **5:** 2829
media research **7:** 3739
and multimedia systems **7:** 3992
in physical sciences
secondary school programs **8:** 4478
programmed tutoring **8:** 4721
explanation in **10:** 6146
research studies **7:** 4083
role of **2:** 991
in science education **7:** 4101
special needs students **7:** ***3802–3808***; **10:** 5671
and vocational education **4:** 1922
writing (composition) **11:** 6783
See also
Computer-assisted learning (CAL)
Computer managed learning (CML)
Computer-assisted learning (CAL) **2:** ***988–992***, ***1002–1007***
and computer-assisted instruction **2:** 1003
criticisms of **2:** 1003, 1004
drills (practice) **2:** 1003
research on effects of **2:** 1003
See also
Computer-assisted instruction (CAI)
Computer managed learning (CML)
Computer-assisted manufacturing
Anglo–German comparisons **11:** 6640
Computer-assisted testing
for academic achievement **10:** 5787
adaptive testing **2:** 992
algorithms for **5:** 2781
applications **2:** 992
automated test design **2:** 996
in career guidance **11:** 6673
in the classroom **5:** ***2779–2784***
computer software for **5:** 2780
and criterion referenced tests **7:** 3703
for diagnosis **5:** 2782
in education **2:** ***992–998***
for essays **4:** 2020
feedback of results **5:** 2781
item banks **2:** 994, 995
and item sampling **5:** 3056, 3057
and mastery tests **5:** 2782
multimedia technology **2:** 997
and partial credit model **7:** 4306
personality inventories **8:** 4399
speeding up item presentation **5:** 2782
and student development **5:** 2783
and test anxiety **5:** 2782
test items
construction of **5:** 2780
and vocational evaluation **11:** 6676
Computer-based instruction
See Computer-assisted instruction (CAI)
Computer conferencing
applications **11:** 6302
asynchronous nature of **11:** 6299
characteristics of **11:** 6299
systems **11:** 6299
See also
Teleconferencing
Computer equipment
See Hardware (computers)
Computer games **9:** 5474
and computer-assisted instruction **2:** 989
See also
Real time games
Computer Intensive Algebra Curriculum (US) **7:** 4096
Computer as Lab Partner Curriculum (CLP) **7:** 3809
Computer literacy **2:** 969, ***973–977***
courses
algorithmic oriented **2:** 975
application oriented **2:** 974
information oriented **2:** 975
mixed approach **2:** 976
negative aspects **2:** 975
objectives of **2:** 974, 975
as cultural capital **3:** 1231
curricula **2:** 974
and curriculum theory **3:** 1353
definitions of **2:** 973
developing nations **4:** 1900
historical background **2:** 974
integrated curricula **2:** 975, 976
programming **2:** 974, ***982–985***
cognitive effects hypothesis **2:** 1005
research studies **7:** 4084
sex fairness **4:** ***2423–2427***
in teacher education **10:** 6005
Computer-managed instruction
See Computer-managed learning (CML)
Computer-managed learning (CML) **2:** ***998–1002***
development of **2:** 1001
growth and evolution of **2:** 999
international applications of **2:** 999
nature and origins of **2:** 999
and proprietary software **2:** 1001
research and evaluation **2:** 1001
studies **2:** 1001
See also
Computer-assisted instruction (CAI)
Computer-assisted learning (CAL)

Computer networks
background **2:** 978
and computer-managed learning **2:** 999
courseware
licensing issues **10:** 5619
and distance education **3:** 1576
in education **2:** 1011
for education **2:** ***977–982***
research directions **2:** 981
and educational research **7:** 3811
dissemination of **3:** 1554
and electronic publishing **4:** 1955
and global education **2:** 981
international
and educational media organizations **3:** 1798
and knowledge transmission **5:** 2994
and language education **7:** 4089
learning circles **7:** 4089
and mathematics education
and co-operation **7:** 4099
microcomputers **7:** 3813
and multimedia systems **7:** 3992
and network learning
approaches **2:** 980
and outcomes of education **2:** 980
and printing **8:** 4690
theoretical framework **2:** 979
Computer oriented programs **2:** 969, 970
Computer printers
laser
and document production **8:** 4690
microcomputers **7:** 3812
Computer programming
See Programming
Computer programs
See Computer software
Computer science
curriculum **2:** 969
as a profession **2:** 970
Computer science education **2:** 1008
curricular approaches **2:** ***969–973***
primary education **2:** 970
secondary education **2:** 970
Computer simulation **9:** 5474
cognitive processes **8:** ***4719–4722***
and computer-assisted instruction **2:** 988
curriculum examples **2:** 987
definition of **2:** 985
design **2:** 985
in education **2:** 985
educational environment **4:** 1895
laboratory training
teacher education **6:** 3200
and language education **7:** 4093
and learning **6:** 3300
and modeling **2:** ***985–988***
in physical sciences
secondary school programs **8:** 4478
role in instruction **2:** 1173
and science education **7:** 4100
and technical education **4:** 1922
Computer software **2:** 982
for achievement tests
LOGIST **1:** 37
for adaptive testing **1:** 52
for analysis of covariance **11:** 6590, 6591
for analysis of variance **11:** 6591
and artificial intelligence **1:** 344
and assistive technology **10:** 5670
authoring aids (programming) **2:** 986
business
uses in education **10:** 5618
for career guidance **11:** 6673
for cluster analysis **2:** 825
commercial
production models **3:** 1775
compatibility **3:** 1776
for computer-assisted instruction **2:** 988
for computer-assisted testing **5:** 2780
and computer-managed learning **2:** 999
and copyright **2:** 1102; **10:** 5620
for criterion referenced tests **7:** 3703
for data banks **3:** 1379
databases **3:** 1387, 1392
for discriminant analysis **3:** 1544, 1546
for educational planning **11:** 6296
educational technology
maintenance of **4:** 1916
for exploratory data analysis **4:** 2208
for factor analysis **4:** 2238, 2239
for factorial modeling **4:** 2242
file servers
and electronic publishing **4:** 1955
general purpose
for computer-assisted instruction **2:** 989
and models **2:** 986
for generalizability theory **6:** 3121
hypermedia **2:** 885; **5:** 2861; **7:** 4092
hypertext **5:** 2706
illegal copying of **10:** 5620
for integrated activities
features of **2:** 999
integrated learning systems
and vocational education **4:** 1921
interactive
and educational technology **4:** 1895
for interactive video **11:** 6600
for item banks **5:** 3042
and item bias procedures **5:** 3048
for item response theory **5:** 3053
and language education
simulations **7:** 4093
for language laboratories **6:** 3240
for latent variable path analysis **8:** 4353
in libraries **6:** 3396
for log-linear models **6:** 3500, 3502
for logit models **6:** 3503
for management information systems **6:** 3593
and material development **8:** 4800
for mathematics education
geometry **7:** 4097
types of **7:** 4095
for mediated educational environments **2:** 885
for microcomputer-based laboratories **7:** 3808
microcomputers **7:** 3812
operating systems (OS) **7:** 3812
for models **2:** 986
applications **2:** 987
for multivariate analysis **7:** 4014
for nonparametric statistics **7:** 4162
for partial credit model **7:** 4306
for partial order scalogram analysis **7:** 4308, 4310, 4313
for path analysis **8:** 4349, 4351
in physical sciences
secondary school programs **8:** 4477, 4478
and piracy **2:** 1009
for printing **8:** 4689
for project management **8:** 4758
protection systems **10:** 5620
prototypes
and courseware development **3:** 1778
publishing **10:** ***5618–5622***
development **10:** 5618
future trends **10:** 5621
historical background **10:** 5618
licensing **10:** 5619
networks **10:** 5620
production **10:** 5619
telesoftware **10:** 5621
versions **10:** 5620
for regression analysis **9:** 4973
for robustness (statistics) **9:** 5079
for sampling errors
balanced repeated replication **9:** 5127
jackknife procedure **9:** 5127
Taylor's series approximations **9:** 5129
for scaling methods **9:** 5153
for school administration **9:** 5184
school surveys of **3:** 1395
science education
research studies **7:** 4102
for simulations
applications **2:** 987
THESIS **2:** 985
for smallest space analysis **9:** 5497, 5499
for social networks **9:** 5558
for sociometric techniques **10:** 5617
specific purpose
for computer-assisted instruction **2:** 989
for statistical analysis **2:** 677; **4:** 2387
Statistical Analysis System (SAS) **9:** 5156, 5158
task analysis
SNOWMAN (System for Knowledge Management) **10:** 5913

teacher use of **11:** 6284
telecommunications **7:** 4090
for test coaching **11:** 6337
for text analysis **2:** 1077
for time series analysis **9:** 5488
for typographic design **8:** 4691
for videotape recordings
coding **11:** 6607
for word processing **7:** 4090
See also
Courseware
Computer software development **2:** 983; **3:** 1775
and computer literacy **2:** 975
courseware **10:** 5618
LOGO **2:** 971
and prototyping **8:** 4801
Computer software evaluation
courseware
See Courseware, evaluation
Computer system design
for multimedia applications **2:** 648
and school administration **9:** 5185
Computer technology
See Computers
Computer tutoring systems
See Programmed tutoring
Computer uses in education **2:** 970, ***1007–1012***; **4:** 1908
academically gifted **10:** 5672
access to **10:** 5668
administration **5:** 2828
and assignments **9:** 5362
barriers to **11:** 6286
behavioral instruction **10:** 6163
classification of types **2:** 1002
and classroom environment **11:** 6284
in classroom instruction **11:** 6283
classroom techniques
research studies **7:** 4096
and computer-assisted instruction **2:** 988
and computer literacy **2:** 975
computer networks **2:** 978
criticism of **4:** 1909
and cultural differences **3:** 1231
databases **3:** 1395
desktop publishing **4:** 1956
developing nations
examples **4:** 1901
educational planning **3:** 1827
models **3:** 1828
educational research **9:** 5034
and educational technology **4:** 1895
effects on learning **2:** ***1002–1007***
cognitive residue **2:** 1002, 1004
and equal education **4:** ***2423–2427***
Europe **7:** 3739
extent of
in classrooms **11:** 6285
females
organizational issues **4:** 2424
functionality
by rationale **2:** 1008
by type **2:** 1007
future research **11:** 6287
hypertext **5:** ***2706–2709***
impact on curriculum **4:** 2330
influences on **9:** 5540
and information networks
international **5:** 2997
and information technology **7:** 4082
integration **2:** 1011
International Association for the Evaluation of Educational Achievement survey **2:** 1002
language education **7:** 4088
language laboratories **6:** 3240
learner-oriented **2:** 1007
and learning theories **9:** 5040
LOGO **6:** ***3508–3512***
management information systems **6:** 3595
mathematical applications **6:** 3632
mathematics education **7:** 4096
future trends **7:** 4098
mathematics instruction **6:** 3647, 3649
and media programs **7:** 3755
microcomputer-based laboratories **7:** 3808
microcomputers **7:** 3813
models for **2:** 1009
multimedia systems **7:** 3987, ***3991–3996***
North America **7:** 3739
objective tests **7:** 4196
optical data disks
digital video interactive (DVI) **2:** 647
optical disks **2:** ***646–649***
organizations **2:** ***1012–1016***
listing **2:** 1013
selection procedures **2:** 1012
periodicals **2:** ***1012–1016***
listing **2:** 1013
selection procedures **2:** 1012
physical sciences
secondary school programs **8:** 4477
priorities
clarification of **2:** 1011
promotion of **11:** 6286
and questioning techniques **8:** 4878
rationales for **4:** 1900
realizing the potential of **2:** 1009, 1010
research findings **4:** 1920
school administration **9:** 5184
for school mapping **9:** 5258
science education **7:** 4100
research studies **7:** 4102
sex fairness **4:** 2425
Computer Equity Expert Project (US) **4:** 2426
curriculum development **4:** 2425
school organization **4:** 2426
Scottish Women into the Computing Habit (SWITCH) **4:** 2426
teaching methods **4:** 2426
Technika 10 (Netherlands) **4:** 2426
software
production of **3:** ***1775–1779***
studies **11:** 6283
teacher attitude
sex bias **4:** 2425
teacher-oriented **2:** 1008
and teacher role **11:** 6283
trends **2:** 1010
tutoring **11:** 6483
types of **4:** 1913
United Kingdom **11:** 6689
visual aids **10:** 5729
vocational education **4:** 1922
Computers
access to
sex differences **4:** 2424
and adaptive testing **1:** 50
and artificial intelligence **1:** 344
and assistive technology **10:** 5669
in career counseling **2:** 1164
characteristics of
and educational testing **2:** 992
communication with
and LOGO **6:** 3510
and concepts of numeracy **6:** 3458
in curriculum-based assessment **3:** 1358
customized
for multimedia applications **2:** 648
definition of **2:** 1007
and historical research **5:** 2604
in home management **2:** 1054
and information retrieval systems **5:** 2821
and interaction research **5:** 2924
and interactive video **11:** 6600
and item banks **2:** 995; **5:** 3037
in item response theory **5:** 3053
and job skill requirements **11:** 6259
as learning tools **2:** 1004
in libraries **6:** 3396
and multivariate analysis **7:** 4007
per student **11:** 6284
and prediction **8:** 4656
and printing **8:** 4688, 4689
and questionnaires
coding schemes **8:** 4886
and random number generation **9:** 5468
in schools
introduction of **7:** 3994
location of **11:** 6284
in special education **10:** 5662
specialists
teacher role **10:** 6007
and survey data **2:** 650
in surveys **10:** 5859
use in content analysis **2:** 1076, 1079
use in text analysis **2:** 1077
and vintage effects **11:** 6614

See also
Mainframe computers
Microcomputers
Computers in the Curriculum (CIC) Project (UK)
characteristics of **3:** 1776
and courseware production **3:** 1778
development issues **3:** 1777
procedures **3:** 1777
software production model **3:** 1776
Comrey Personality Scale **8:** 4398
Concept formation **2:** ***1020–1026***; **6:** 3322; **8:** 4648
abstract reasoning
in children **2:** 1017
affective variables **2:** 1019
behavioral objectives **2:** 1020
classification **2:** 1017
cognitive development **8:** 4651
individual differences **6:** 3286
cognitive restructuring **8:** 4651
complex-dynamic strategies **2:** 1024
and concept maps **2:** 1027
connectionist learning **2:** 853
contextual knowledge
and long term memory **2:** 1018
decomposition into perceptual features **2:** 852
and educational objectives **10:** 6167
educational strategies **2:** 1023
evaluation of
during instruction **2:** 1025
postinstructional **2:** 1025
expository strategies
instructional variables **2:** 1023
external sources **2:** 1017
frameworks
and descriptive data analysis **3:** 1466
innateness theories **2:** 853
internal sources **2:** 1017
and laboratory packages **6:** 3203
language of thought theory (Fodor) **2:** 852
compositionality feature **2:** 852, 853
practice strategies
instructional variables **2:** 1023
preinstructional **8:** ***4648–4652***
problem-oriented strategies **2:** 1024
and science education **9:** 5330
self-directed experiences **2:** 1024
computer-assisted instruction **2:** 1025
teachers **10:** 6180
Concept maps **2:** ***1026–1031***
characteristics of **2:** 1027
criticisms of **2:** 1027
and descriptive data analysis **3:** 1466
functions of **2:** 1027
hierarchical structure of **2:** 1029
hypertext **5:** 2707
Novak's **2:** 1027
scoring **2:** 1030
studies in the use of **2:** 1028
Concept teaching **2:** ***1020–1026***
behavioral objectives **2:** 1021
explanation **10:** ***6143–6149***
Concepts
acquisition of
and hypothesis testing **2:** 853
information processing approach **2:** 852
classical view **6:** 3152
classification of **6:** 3152
definition of **2:** 1016
learning capability
teachers **10:** 6166
nature of **2:** 1016
prototype view **6:** 3152
understanding of
charting procedure **10:** 5786
tests for **10:** 5783, 5785
Conceptual frameworks
See Concept formation, frameworks
Conceptual knowledge
See Declarative knowledge
Conceptual tempo **2:** 870; **6:** 3319
and minimal brain dysfunction **1:** 491
Conceptual understanding
See Concepts, understanding of
Concurrent validity **11:** 6571
and classical test theory **2:** 787
Conditioning **1:** 495
behavior modification **1:** 495
and moral development **7:** 3915
and programmed instruction **8:** 4767
Conferences
and educational research
dissemination of **3:** 1555
international education **5:** ***2957–2961***
specialized **5:** 2958
writing
and student role **10:** 5793
Confidence
See Self-esteem
Confidence interval (statistics)
and Bayesian statistics **1:** 476
and correlation **2:** 1112
Confidence testing
and classical test theory **2:** 791
and guessing (tests) **7:** 3999
Confidentiality
and computerized educational research **4:** 2387
information systems **11:** 6297
and social background measurement **7:** 3718
Configural frequency analysis (CFA) **2:** ***1031–1037***
alpha adjustment **2:** 1033
example **2:** 1035
Krauth's test **2:** 1033
Kristof's test **2:** 1033
Lienert's test **2:** 1033
and log-linear models **6:** 3507
and multivariate analysis **7:** 4012
relation to other methods **2:** 1036
special applications **2:** 1035
types of **2:** 1032, 1035
Confirmatory factor analysis (CFA)
See Factor analysis, confirmatory
Conflict
and adult education **10:** 5593
causes of **2:** 1037
and educational administration **7:** 3835
in educational organizations
examples **2:** 1039
in educational planning **8:** 4598
management of **2:** ***1037–1042***
procedures for **10:** 6221
in organizations
and micropolitics **7:** 3821, 3823
origins of **2:** 1037
and principals
role of **9:** 5269
responses to **2:** 1038
in schools
and youth subcultures **11:** 6800
student behavior
in schools **10:** 5758
types of **2:** 1038
within friendship **10:** 5758
Conflict resolution
playground programs **5:** 2525
Conflict theory **2:** 1066
comparative education **2:** 929
and dominant ideologies **2:** 1067, 1068
Durkheim's sociology **2:** 778
in education **10:** 6221
and hidden curriculum **2:** 1067
Marxist sociology **2:** 779, 1067
and role of intellectuals **2:** 1067
and social reproduction **2:** 1067
and teacher role **10:** 5608
Weberian **2:** 1068
Confluent education
See Humanistic education
Conformity
and achievement **5:** 2764
in schools
and social mobility **9:** 5219
sex differences **9:** 5434
Confucianism
ability and effort **2:** 1044
and achievement need **3:** 1238, 1239
adult education and **1:** 348
individual development **2:** ***1042–1045***
childrearing implications of theory **2:** 1045
educational implications of theory **2:** 1045
influences on **2:** 1043, 1045
objectives **2:** 1043
individual differences **2:** 1043, 1044
influence on Shinto **9:** 5450
jen **2:** 1043
learning processes **2:** 1044
learning theory **2:** 1043
moral development **2:** 1043
moral education
and civic education **2:** 768

personality development **2:** 1042
and school reform **9:** 5280
social mobility and education **1:** 349
Congenital impairments **1:** 553
anoxia during birth **1:** 553
and cognitive ability **11:** 6706
Downs syndrome **1:** 553
effect on learning **5:** 2564
fetus
prenatal influences **1:** ***12–15***
fragile-X syndrome **1:** 553
malformations and their causes **1:** 13
See also
Cerebral palsy
Downs syndrome
Conscientization
See Consciousness raising
Consciousness raising **2:** ***1045–1049***
and adult education **1:** 132; **2:** 637, ***1045–1049***
and curriculum planning **3:** 1332
and feminism **4:** 2298; **5:** 2456
Freire's concept of **1:** 172; **2:** 1046; **3:** 1259; **6:** 3455, 3458
and concept of dialog **8:** 4432
and curriculum politics **3:** 1335
and empowerment **4:** 1982
in Latin America **6:** 3254
and literacy **6:** 3455
and mobilization **2:** ***1045–1049***
and nonformal education **7:** 4144
and popular education **1:** 133
popular theater **2:** 903
praxis
and liberation **2:** 1046, 1047
and psychology of oppression **2:** 1046
for social change **2:** 1048
Consejo de Educación de Adultos de América Latina (CEAAL) **5:** 2932; **8:** 4733
Conservation education
environmental education **4:** 1992, 1993
Conservatism
authoritarian
and governance **5:** 2511
and educational planning **3:** 1817
and educational quality **5:** 2504
Conservatoire National des Arts et Métiers **1:** 182
Constitutional history
and religion **9:** 5012
religious education **9:** 5012
Constitutional law
school law
and educational planning **9:** 5253
Construct validity **1:** 387; **11:** 6572
and aptitude treatment interaction **10:** 6155
of causes of effects **4:** 2084
and classical test theory **2:** 787
and essay tests **4:** 2023
establishment of **11:** 6572
and experimental studies **4:** 2188
and factorial modeling **4:** 2241
and foreign language testing **4:** 2361
interpretations of **11:** 6573
and student evaluations of teacher effectiveness **10:** 6230
and test bias **11:** 6316
Construction industry
job training **11:** 6636
Construction programs
international aid
for vocational education **11:** 6661
Constructivism
cognitive development **2:** 835
learning environments **2:** 835
developmental psychology **5:** 2666
dialectic method **4:** 2372
and dualism **2:** 1049, 1050, 1051
and educational administration **1:** 62
and educational environment **10:** 5774
and educational media **7:** 3745
educational research
preconceptions and misconceptions **8:** 4649
epistemology **4:** 2372
and fourth generation evaluation **4:** 2088, 2372
hermeneutic method **4:** 2372
and instructional design **5:** 2861
instructional implications **2:** 1049
and instructional psychology **5:** 2871
learning and **2:** ***1049–1052***; **6:** ***3297–3302***
learning theories **6:** 3210, 3669
and task analysis **10:** 5913
and LOGO **6:** 3511
and mathematics learning **6:** 3653
methodology **4:** 2372
ontology **4:** 2372
and physical sciences
secondary school programs **8:** 4476
radical **2:** 1050
realist **2:** 1049
research trends **2:** 1051
and science education **9:** 5329, 5332
and science instruction **9:** 5344
sex education **9:** 5436
Foucault's view **9:** 5436, 5439
sexuality **11:** 6725, 6726
and teaching methods **10:** 6014
teaching methods
and cognitive conflict **8:** 4651
See also
Interpretive sociology
Constructivist Learning Environment Survey (CLES) **10:** 5774
Constructs
classification of **9:** 5015
eliciting
procedures **9:** 5014
and repertory grid technique **9:** 5014
Consultants
characteristics of **7:** 4236
educational
and media program administration **7:** 3754
and organizational development in education **7:** ***4236–4240***
and prereferral intervention **8:** 4659
Consultation programs
and prereferral intervention **8:** 4659
regular and special education relationship **10:** 6241
teams **10:** 6242
Consumer behavior
See Consumer economics
Consumer economics
and adult education **8:** 4810
education and efficiency of choice **4:** 2210
theory of consumer behavior
consumption benefits **2:** 1053
Consumer education
consumption benefits
and education **2:** 1052
Consumer electronics
and technology transfer **11:** 6277
Consumption
and investment
brain drain **1:** 558
Consumption benefits
of education **2:** ***1052–1056***
affective behavior **2:** 1054
and rate of return **8:** 4913
expected
and education **2:** 1053
theory of consumer behavior **2:** 1053
Content analysis
definitions of **2:** 1075
language communication model **2:** 1075
methods **2:** 1076
and narrative inquiry **7:** 4049
periodicals
and teachers as artists **10:** 6084
and student evaluations of educational quality **10:** 6229
task analysis **10:** 5911
and text analysis **2:** ***1074–1079***
See also
Text analysis
Content area reading **6:** 3207
Content validity **1:** 387; **11:** 6570
and classical test theory **2:** 787
in cross-national comparison tests **4:** 2133
and essay tests **4:** 2023
and personality inventories **8:** 4396, 4397
and test bias **11:** 6316
Context effect
and adaptive testing **1:** 51
and peer influence **9:** 5172
and questioning techniques **8:** 4876, 4877
and vocational education **11:** 6412
Contingency contracts
See Contingency management

Contingency management
  feedback in **4:** 2280
Contingency tables **2:** ***1079–1084***
  chi square
    test of independence **2:** 1080
  configural frequency analysis
    2: ***1031–1037***
  and correspondence analysis **2:** 1082, 1117
  derived **2:** 1034
  and expectancy tables **4:** 2180
  independent classifications **2:** 1080
  and item bias **5:** 3045
  log-linear models **2:** 1083
  and log-linear models **6:** 3499
  matched samples **2:** 1082
  multidimensional **2:** 1081, 1083; **6:** 3500
  and multivariate analysis **7:** 4011
  and nonparametric statistics **7:** 4159
  and rating scales **8:** 4918
  three-dimensional **2:** 1079, 1083
  two-dimensional **2:** 1079, 1083, 1117
Continuation students
  adult education **1:** ***181–184***
    access **1:** 183
    financial support **1:** 184
    France **1:** 182
    Germany **1:** 182
    methods and materials **1:** 183
    nature and scope of provision **1:** 181; **8:** 4806
    trends and issues **1:** 183
    United Kingdom **1:** 181
    United States **1:** 181
  adult educators **1:** 183
Continuing education **6:** ***3416–3422***
  administrative organization **1:** 92
  benefits **2:** 1085
  compared with lifelong learning **6:** 3420
  concept of **6:** 3418, 3420
  as criticism of conventional education **6:** 3419
  and cultural reproduction theory **2:** 1088
  curriculum design **1:** 92
  definitions **1:** 90
  developed nations
    costs **2:** ***1146–1152***
  distance education **3:** 1559
  and earnings differentials **2:** 1090
    and age **2:** 1090
  economic theories of **2:** 1087
  economies of scale **2:** 1150
  employment
    sex differences **2:** 1092
  and employment level **2:** 1091
  evaluation research **2:** 1084
  financial support **1:** 92
  functions of **1:** 128; **6:** 3417
  and higher education **1:** ***89–94***
  and human capital theory **2:** 1087
  individual rate of return **2:** 1090
  input output analysis **2:** 1085
  job matching theory **2:** 1087, 1091
  and job satisfaction **2:** 1093
  and occupational mobility **2:** 1091
  and overschooling **2:** 1087
  Oxford University Symposium **6:** 3418, 3420
  participation in
    and needs for **6:** 3420
  and productivity **2:** 1087, 1088
  professional associations **8:** ***4731–4736***
  and quality of life **2:** 1092
  reasons for participation **8:** 4821
  research **1:** 92
  and screening hypothesis **2:** 1087
  social–psychological effects **2:** 1092
  and social reproduction **2:** 1092
  social returns **2:** 1090
  and social stratification **2:** 1087
  sociological theories of **2:** 1087
  Soviet Union (former) **9:** 5095
  studies
    and selection bias **9:** 5382
  teacher education **1:** 92
  teaching methods **1:** 92
  and technology **2:** 1089
  training concepts and statistics **11:** ***6416–6420***
  translation of concepts **6:** 3417, 3418
  trends in **1:** 93
  and unemployment incidence **2:** 1091
  UNESCO definition **6:** 3463
  United Kingdom **1:** 89, 91, 92
  United States **1:** 89
  use of term **1:** 118; **6:** 3416, 3418, 3420
  women's education **11:** 6714
Continuing education units **2:** 663
Continuing professional education
  See Professional continuing education
Continuous education
  See Lifelong learning
Continuous progress plan
  nongraded instructional grouping **7:** 4155
Contraception
  and education **3:** 1674
  and female sexuality **9:** 5438
Contract learning
  See Performance contracts
Contracts
  implicit
    employer employee relationship **3:** 1697
Contrastive linguistics
  and error analysis (language) **6:** 3438
  and second language learning **6:** 3438
Control
  See Locus of control
Control groups
  composition of
    and metacognition research **7:** 3790
Controversial issues (course content)
  and social studies
    research **9:** 5581
Conventional instruction
  compared with informal and nonformal education **4:** 2368
  and curriculum development **9:** 5520
  decomposition method **4:** 2197
  formal education
    definition **4:** 2364
  intellectual disciplines **9:** 5295
  and social reproduction **6:** 3419
  vs. information technology **7:** 4083
  vs. multimedia systems **7:** 3993, 3994
  vs. small group instruction **10:** 6186
  See also
    Formal education
Convergent thinking **8:** 4723
Conversation
  and nonformal education **7:** 4142
Cooperating teachers **10:** 5809
  attitudes to student teachers **10:** 6000
  incentives **10:** 6001
  results of feedback **10:** 5810
  selection **10:** 6001
  teacher education for **10:** 6000, 6001
  and teacher supervision **10:** 6000
  universities **10:** 5960
Cooperation
  and action research **1:** 42
  between school districts
    benefits **7:** 3819
  and educational change **6:** 3602
  and educational improvement **9:** 5244
  with labor force
    strategies **5:** 2742
  and microeconomics **7:** 3818
  and micropolitics **7:** 3822
  and participative decision-making **5:** 2796
  problem-solving
    and videotape recordings **11:** 6604
  and program implementation **4:** 2073; **5:** 2844
  and small group instruction **10:** 6185
  and social interdependence theory **10:** 6220
  and teacher cultures **10:** 6213
Cooperative education
  and apprenticeships **1:** 312
  and core curriculum **2:** 1104
  and desktop publishing **4:** 1956
  and experiential learning **4:** 2185
  Korea **11:** 6657
  vocational education
    and productivity **11:** 6629
  workers and **1:** 132
Cooperative Education Data Collection and Reporting (CEDCAR) (US)
  standards **8:** 4737
Cooperative extension
  See Extension education
Cooperative learning **2:** ***1094–1099***; **5:** 2528; **9:** ***5545–5548***
  academic achievement **2:** 1097
    teamwork **2:** 1095
  and behavioral instruction **10:** 6162
  children **2:** 730

and computer-assisted instruction
2: 990
gifted **5:** 2730
group investigation **8:** 4369
grouping (instructional purposes)
5: ***2532–2536***
individual development
self-concept **5:** 2503
individual differences **5:** 2766
instructional effectiveness **5:** 2502
integrated activities
jigsaw method **2:** 1096; **8:** 4369
reading **2:** 1096
writing (composition) **2:** 1096
interpersonal relationship **5:** 2501, 2502
learning activities **9:** 5546
mastery learning **6:** 3628
and microcomputer-based laboratories **7:** 3809
and multimedia systems **7:** 3992
and network learning **2:** 980
and peer relationship **8:** 4369, 4370
peer teaching **9:** 5546
performance factors
instructional effectiveness **5:** 2503
and questioning techniques **8:** 4880
regular and special education relationship **5:** 2906
and school desegregation **3:** 1485
self-esteem **2:** 1098
small group instruction **2:** 1051
language teaching **6:** 3440
socio-economic status **2:** 1098
special needs students
microcomputers **7:** 3804
student participation **5:** 2535
student teams achievement divisions **8:** 4369
and study skills training **1:** 187
teamwork **2:** 1095
use of competition **8:** 4369
Cooperative planning
teacher improvement **10:** 5933
Cooperative teaching
See Team teaching
Cooperatives
and adult education **8:** 4810
Soviet Union (former) **10:** 5646
Coordination (psychomotor)
See Psychomotor skills
Coping
control of context **10:** 5737
crises
effectiveness of methods **8:** 4718
definition of **10:** 5736
health
and personality development **10:** 5737
and learning **10:** ***5735–5738***
life events **8:** ***4715–4719***
protective factors **8:** 4718
risk factors **8:** 4717
older adults **1:** 237
for parents of disabled children **4:** 1977
affective behavior **4:** 1977
problem-solving **10:** 5736, 5737
psychological patterns **10:** 5736
self-control
and learning **1:** 203
strategies for
teachers **10:** 6211
stress management **10:** ***5735–5738***
Copying (reproduction)
See Reprography
Copyrights **2:** ***1099–1102***
acts for
general provisions **2:** 1100
and desktop publishing **4:** 1955
educational issues **2:** 1101
electronic media **10:** 5620
and electronic publishing **4:** 1955
historical background **2:** 1099
infringement
and reprography **5:** 2997
international agreements **2:** 1100
and moral rights **2:** 1100
and multimedia systems **7:** 3990
scope **2:** 1100
and textbook publication **11:** 6365
Core curriculum **2:** ***1102–1107***
and changing interests of students **2:** 1103
cultural differences and **3:** 1231
and curriculum theory **3:** 1352
debate over composition **2:** 1103
defining the core **2:** 1105
cultural literacy approach **2:** 1105
subject structure **2:** 1105
and differing course content **2:** 1103
essential components **2:** 1104
Hungary **3:** 1335
national programs
and curriculum policies **3:** 1335
national systems **2:** 1103
and new intellectual disciplines **2:** 1103
pressures for inclusion **2:** 1104
significance for schools **2:** 1106
and social studies **2:** 769
student projects
teaching methods **5:** 2694
use of term **2:** 1102
Cornell University (US)
science education programs **2:** 1026
Corporal punishment
alternatives to **3:** 1536
and children's rights **3:** 1536
Corporate colleges
See Corporate education
Corporate education **11:** 6393
industrial training **6:** 3304
job analysis in **6:** ***3092–3096***
mass media role in **2:** 884
United States **11:** 6551
Corporate training
See Industrial training
Correctional education
definition of **3:** 1440
delinquency and **3:** 1440
special education **3:** 1440
functional curriculum **3:** 1441
social cognitive problem-solving training **3:** 1441
trends in **3:** 1441
vocational education **3:** 1440
Correctional Education Association **3:** 1440
Correctional institutions
adult education in **8:** 4807
delinquency and **3:** 1440
Correctional rehabilitation
delinquency and **3:** 1440
and educational change **1:** 159
Correlation **4:** 2385
attenuation of
and reliability **9:** 4994
bipartial **2:** 1113
biserial **2:** 1110
bivariate **2:** 1109
in classical test theory **2:** 786
coefficients of **2:** 1107
biserial-phi **2:** 1110
and discriminant analysis **3:** 1546
and essay tests **4:** 2022
and factor analysis **4:** 2231
and factorial modeling **4:** 2242
interclass **7:** 3735
intraclass **7:** 3735; **9:** 5138
and meta analysis **7:** 3779
and nonparametric statistics **7:** 4158
and prediction **8:** 4654
product–moment **2:** 1109; **8:** 4753
and regression analysis **9:** 4967
and single case research **9:** 5488
and surveys **10:** 5860
testing differences between **2:** 1111
tetrachoric **2:** 1110
and composite variables **2:** 1107
in confirmatory factor analysis **7:** 4003
and construct validity **11:** 6573
in cross-national comparisons **4:** 2136, 2137
cross-validation **2:** 1116
decomposition of
and path analysis **8:** 4343
and difference scores **2:** 672
ecological
and multilevel analysis **7:** 3978
and educational history **5:** 2605
in educational research **7:** 3705
fourfold point **2:** 1109
genotype-environment
twin studies **11:** 6489
and hypothesis testing **5:** 2712
intraclass
and clustering **7:** 3735
uses of **7:** 3738
and item sampling **5:** 3057
mathematical definition of **2:** 1107
and matrices **2:** 1114
factor analysis **4:** 2230
and missing scores **7:** 3859
and models of intelligence **7:** 3874
moderating effects in **4:** 1874

and moderation procedures **4:** 2175
multidimensional scaling
unfolding analysis **1:** 190
multiple **2:** 1113
asymmetry of **2:** 1114
statistical significance **2:** 1114
stepwise analysis **2:** 1115
in multitrait multimethod techniques **7:** 4001
and multivariate analysis **2:** 1115
partial **2:** 1112, 1113
higher order **2:** 1113
statistical significance **2:** 1113
personal biserial **7:** 3999
point biserial **2:** 1109
polyserial
and multivariate analysis **7:** 4008
and predictive validity **11:** 6571
procedures **2:** ***1107–1117***, ***1117***
product–moment **2:** 1108
estimates **2:** 1110
and Q-methodology **8:** 4855
rank
and cognitive ability **7:** 3873
and employment level **7:** 3716
in nonparametric statistics **7:** 4158
Rasch measurement models **6:** 3123
in scaling methods **9:** 5155
and standard deviation estimates **7:** 3730
ratios
and clustering **7:** 3734
and reliability **9:** 4982
semipartial **2:** 1112, 1113
set **2:** 1107, 1116
Spearman rank-order **2:** 1109
and Thurstone scales **11:** 6385
Correlation coefficients
See Correlation, coefficients of
Correspondence analysis
and contingency tables **2:** 1082, 1117
and factor analysis **2:** 1121
hyperplane representation **2:** 1118
and log-linear models **6:** 3507
and multivariate analysis **7:** 4011
nominal data
use with **2:** 1117
procedure **2:** 1117
of qualitative data **2:** ***1117–1121***
reciprocal analysis
procedure **2:** 1118
studies
teacher behavior **2:** 1119
Correspondence argument
See Hidden curriculum
Correspondence courses
See Correspondence study
Correspondence schools
Africa **3:** 1565
distance education **3:** 1558
United States **3:** 1566
Correspondence study
Asia **1:** 350
and distance education **3:** 1563
France **1:** 182
historical background **3:** 1574
Japan **1:** 109; **6:** 3077
Soviet Union (former) **9:** 5093, 5095
United States **4:** 2185
Correspondence theory
education work relationship **6:** 3185
CoRT thinking program **8:** 4729
and creativity training **2:** 1181
Cosmology
Cartesian **3:** 1461
Cost analysis
See Cost effectiveness
Cost benefit analysis
See Cost effectiveness
Cost effectiveness
of apprenticeships **11:** 6695
assessment **2:** 1132
barriers to
technical and sociopolitical **2:** 1122
behavioral studies **2:** 1123
benefits and costs combined **2:** 1129
compared with cost benefit analysis **2:** 1127, 1131
and educational finance **3:** 1790
input output analysis **2:** 1125
of computers
in education **4:** 1908
continuing education **2:** 1147, 1150
planning and management **2:** 1151
and cost benefits **2:** 1136
distance education **4:** 1907
in education **2:** ***1131–1136***, 1146
basic concepts **2:** ***1127–1131***
developing nations **3:** 1665
and educational choice **4:** 2413
and educational efficiency **3:** 1780
and educational objectives **2:** 1137
and educational planning **3:** 1813; **8:** 4504
criticisms of **3:** 1815
models **3:** 1806
educational radio **4:** 1905
and educational reform
implementation of **4:** 1856
educational technology **4:** 1903
educational television **4:** 1904
elements of **2:** 1136
human capital **5:** ***2643–2647***
intervention cost
defined **2:** 1132
of job training **3:** 1679; **7:** 4197
Colombia **7:** 4197
India **7:** 4197
measurement
ingredients approach **2:** 1128, 1132
resource recovery approach **2:** 1127
techniques **2:** 1132
units **2:** 1133
measurement problems **2:** 1128
methodological issues **2:** 1122
nonformal education **2:** 1147, 1149; **7:** 4139
internal efficiency **2:** 1149
on-the-job training **6:** 3615, 3616
policy formation
determinants of **3:** 1791
and policy formation
in education **2:** ***1121–1127***
feasibility studies **2:** 1122
of preschool education **8:** 4663
studies **8:** 4665
and productivity **2:** 1121
and program effectiveness **2:** 1131
and small business training **4:** 1989
studies **2:** 1130, 1134
classification **2:** 1121, 1126
of training courses **2:** ***1136–1139***
calculation **2:** 1138
factors **2:** 1137
models for **2:** 1138
problem-solving strategy **2:** 1138
vocational education
learning modules **7:** 3892
vocational education and training
developing nations **11:** ***6648–6653***
See also
Rate of return
Cost indexes
national-effort **2:** 1123
use in social studies
criticisms of **3:** 1815
Costa Rica
curriculum development **2:** 1144
educational change **2:** 1145
educational research **2:** 1144
government school relationship
financial support **2:** 1143
school administration **2:** 1143
postsecondary education **2:** 1142
preschool education **2:** 1142
primary education **2:** 1141
public education finance
effect of economic adjustment on **3:** 1787
secondary education **2:** 1142
special education **2:** 1142
system of education **2:** ***1139–1146***
degrees and qualifications **2:** 1144
educational objectives **2:** 1140
historical background **2:** 1140
major problems **2:** 1145
structure **2:** 1141
teacher recruitment **2:** 1144
technical education **2:** 1143
Costs
continuing education
classification **2:** 1147
cross-national comparison **2:** 1147
developed nations **2:** ***1146–1152***
problems in estimating **2:** 1147
reduction **2:** 1151
size of **2:** 1147
of education
private **8:** 4913
educational
patterns **2:** 1146
nonformal education
marginality **7:** 4139
patterns and efficiency **7:** 4137
reductions **7:** 4138
on-the-job training **6:** 3615
recovery of

through school enterprise **9:** 5229
training courses
factors **2:** 1137
See also
Opportunity cost
Private costs
Social costs
Total costs
Unit costs
Côte d'Ivoire
adult education **1:** 218, 220
curriculum development **2:** 1158
educational change **2:** 1159
educational television **4:** 1902, 1904
large-scale projects **5:** 2892
government school relationship
school administration **2:** 1156
Institut Africain pour le Développement Economique et Social (INADES) **1:** 218, 220
language **2:** 1152
postsecondary education **2:** 1154
preschool education **2:** 1155
primary education **2:** 1154
private education **2:** 1153
secondary education **2:** 1154
student evaluation **2:** 1158
system of education **2:** ***1152–1161***
educational objectives **2:** 1153
enrollment **2:** 1154, 1155
major problems **2:** 1160
structure **2:** 1153
teacher recruitment **2:** 1157
teaching methodology **2:** 1158
textbook publication **11:** 6363
vocational education **9:** 5074
women's education **11:** 6736, 6738, 6739, 6740
Council for the Accreditation of Counseling and Related Education Programs (CACREP) (US) **9:** 5283
Council for the Accreditation of Teacher Education (England and Wales) **1:** 24 **10:** 5964
Council for Adult and Experiential Learning (US) **4:** 2185
Council for the Advancement of Citizenship (US)
CIVITAS curriculum **2:** 769
Council on Anthropology and Education **1:** 282, 283
Council for British Archaeology **1:** 279
Council of Chief State School Officers (US) **7:** 4053
Council for Cultural Cooperation (CDCC)
adult education counseling **2:** 1161, 1163
adult education project **6:** 3420
community development programs **2:** 905
training of adult educators **11:** 6433
Council of Europe (CE)
adult education and social change project **6:** 3420
Committee on Educational Research
training recommendations **11:** 6440
comparative education **2:** 921
definition of permanent education **6:** 3417, 3418
education
and information technology **4:** 1897
éducation permanente **5:** 2933
foreign language instruction **4:** 2348, 2352
policy **4:** 2340
information sources
comparative education **3:** 1586
international education **2:** 941
lifelong learning **1:** 179; **6:** 3420
second language instruction **6:** 3210
See also
Council for Cultural Cooperation
Council for Exceptional Children (CEC) (US) **2:** 631
Council for the International Evaluation of Educational Achievement
See International Association for the Evaluation of Educational Achievement (IEA)
Council for National Academic Awards (CNAA) (UK)
CATS program **2:** 663, 664
CONTACT program **2:** 663
flexible certification **2:** 664
and university adult education **11:** 6550
Council on Postsecondary Accreditation (US) **1:** 25
Counseling
distance education **3:** 1562
distinguished from guidance **2:** 1161
ethical issues **2:** 1164
evaluation and research **2:** 1164
Hindu theory **5:** 2601
Counselor evaluation **4:** 2130
Counselor qualifications
adult education **2:** 1163
Counselor role
adult education **2:** 1162
Counselor training
adult education **2:** 1163
standards **9:** 5283
Counting
See Computation
Course content
and decision-making theory **3:** 1424
and syllabi **10:** 5885
and teacher knowledge **10:** 6118
and teaching guides **10:** 6113
Course descriptions **10:** 5883
revision of
and curriculum theory **3:** 1353
See also
Syllabi
Course evaluation
and learning strategies
teaching of **6:** 3337
See also
Curriculum evaluation
Course selection (students)
and decision-making theory **3:** 1422, 1423
sex differences **10:** 5824
Courses
differential costs
and student fees **10:** 5753
Courseware
and computer literacy courses **2:** 975
copyrights **10:** 5620
criticisms of **7:** 4091
in curriculum **2:** 1172, 1174
design **2:** ***1165–1170***; **3:** 1775
attention–relevance–confidence–satisf (ARCS) model **2:** 1169
authoring aids for **10:** ***5622–5625***
compatibility **10:** 5624
content models **2:** 1166
content structure **2:** 1166
finance for **10:** 5622
interaction **2:** 1168
process models **2:** 1166
requirements for **2:** 1168
screen design **2:** 1168
student motivation **2:** 1169
team for **2:** 1169
development **10:** 5618
government initiatives **10:** 5618
teams for **10:** 5618
evaluation **2:** ***1170–1175***
Computer Courseware Evaluation Model (CCEM) **2:** 1173
criticism of practices **2:** 1174
and curriculum **2:** 1172, 1174
dimensions and indicators **2:** 1173
evaluation methods **2:** 1173
factors influencing **2:** 1171
objectives **2:** 1170
research **10:** 5671
special needs students **7:** 3807
and videotape recordings **11:** 6605
future trends **10:** 5621
illegal copying of **10:** 5620
integrated learning systems
and vocational education **4:** 1921
and language translation **10:** 5621
licensing **10:** 5619
multimedia systems **7:** 3994
networks **10:** 5620
production of **3:** ***1775–1779***; **10:** 5619
and Computers in the Curriculum Project (UK) **3:** 1778
future trends **3:** 1778
packaging and distribution **10:** 5619
system choice **10:** 5619
programming languages for **10:** 5621
protection systems **10:** 5620
publishers
types of **10:** 5619
publishing **10:** 5618
standards **10:** 5618
telesoftware **10:** 5621
types of **2:** 1171; **10:** 5623
versions **10:** 5620
vs. business software **3:** 1775

See also
Computer software, educational
Court litigation
and education **9:** 5255
and policy formation **5:** 2510
and syllabi **10:** 5883
Covariance analysis
See Analysis of covariance (ANCOVA)
Craft workers
and apprenticeships **1:** 310
guilds **11:** 6680, 6681
Creationism **5:** 2651
and anthropology teaching in high schools **1:** 299
and individual development
Christian theory **2:** 762
Creative development **2:** 1176
Soviet Union (former) **9:** 5096
Creative expression
special needs students
microcomputers **7:** 3804
Creative Research Group (Canada)
literacy legislation **7:** 4185
Creative thinking **2:** 1177
cognitive style
and teaching methods **2:** 871
and critical thinking **2:** 1206
problem-solving **8:** 4723
Purdue Creative Thinking Program **2:** 1181
teaching of
in industry **8:** 4729
See also
Divergent thinking
Productive thinking
Creativity **2:** ***1178–1183***
and art criticism **1:** 197
and art history **1:** 197
context **2:** 1178
and copyright **2:** 1101
and courseware design **2:** 1166
definitions of **2:** 1178
education for **2:** 1177
environmental influences
evaluation of **2:** 1180
evaluation of **2:** 1178
and expertise **2:** 1176, 1177
fundamental concepts of **2:** 1178
and giftedness **5:** 2727
individual characteristics **2:** 1176
and intelligence **2:** 1176; **5:** 2760
psychological approach **2:** ***1175–1178***
scientific **2:** 1176
Sternberg's Investment theory **5:** 2726
and teachers as artists **10:** 6084
teaching of **2:** 1180
evaluation **2:** 1181
problem-solving **2:** 1181
Creativity research **2:** ***1175–1178***
limitations **2:** 1178
Creativity tests **2:** 1176
assessment batteries
evaluation of **2:** 1180
and creative achievement
relationship between **2:** 1180
evaluation of **2:** 1179
and multiple regression analysis **9:** 4972
self-report measures
evaluation of **2:** 1180
Creativity training
CoRT program **2:** 1181
model for **2:** 1181
Purdue Creative Thinking Program **2:** 1181
Credentialism
developing nations **1:** 471
in public sector **8:** 4837
developing nations **8:** 4839
and screening hypothesis **3:** 1700, 1705, 1748; **9:** 5350, 5352
and social stratification **10:** 5734
and Weber's sociology of education **2:** 780
See also
Overeducation
Qualifications
Credentials
adult education **1:** 131; **2:** ***662–665***
Nordic countries **7:** 4176, 4177
and adult education curriculum **3:** 1309
and adult secondary education **1:** 181
and cultural capital
conflict theory **2:** 1069
and incentives **7:** 4254
inflation of
and academic repetition **6:** 3548
differential effects **6:** 3548
Japan **6:** 3078
and student evaluation **8:** ***4617–4623***
See also
Certification
Teacher certification
Credibility
and case studies **2:** 644
Credits
adult education
accumulation and transfer **2:** 664
transfer policy
Europe **4:** 2056, 2057
in vocational education
United States **11:** 6534
See also
College credits
Continuing education units
Crime
and educational background **4:** 2211
Criminals
and educational change **1:** 159
Crises (life events) **8:** 4717
assessment of developmental consequences **8:** 4717
developmental gains **8:** 4717
emotional response **8:** 4718
individual development **8:** ***4715–4719***
and mental health **8:** 4717
use of concept **8:** 4715
widespread in population
and social attitudes **8:** 4717, 4718
Criterion referenced tests **2:** ***1183–1189***; **4:** 2076; **10:** 6171
and academic records **8:** 4620
and achievement tests **1:** 33, 34
applications **2:** 1188
basic concepts of **2:** 1183
and behaviorism **4:** 1844
and competence **6:** 3469
and competency-based education **10:** 6114
content specifications **2:** 1184
content specificity **2:** 1184
definitions of **2:** 1183
development of **2:** 1185; **7:** 3703
domain specifications **2:** 1185
and educational assessment **1:** 367
grading **10:** 5819
and instructional alignment **5:** 2852
and item selection **2:** 1184
loss function **10:** 5723
measurement models **2:** 1188
and monitoring national standards **7:** 3908
and objective referenced tests **2:** 1183
objectives in **2:** 1183
and personality inventories **8:** 4396, 4397
preparation of **2:** 1188
purposes of **2:** 1184; **10:** 5721
reliability **2:** 1188
score generalizability **2:** 1184
setting standards in **2:** 1188; **10:** ***5721–5726***
Angoff's method **10:** 5723
arbitrary **10:** 5721
borderline-group method **10:** 5723
combination methods **10:** 5723
contrasting groups method **10:** 5724
Ebel's method **10:** 5722
empirical methods **10:** 5723
guidelines for **10:** 5724
judgmental methods **10:** 5722
methods **10:** 5722
Nedelsky method **10:** 5722
research **10:** 5725
trends **10:** 5725
in Standard Assessment Task and Teacher Assessment **7:** 3910
and test reliability **9:** 4993
trends **2:** 1189
use of term **2:** 1183
uses of **2:** 1183
vs. norm referenced tests **2:** 1184
See also
Achievement tests
Domain referenced tests
Mastery tests
Criterion validity (concurrent)
See Concurrent validity
Criterion validity (predictive)
See Predictive validity
Criterion variables **8:** 4652
categorization of **4:** 2182
definition and measurement of **8:** 4653
measurement units **4:** 2182

Critical path method
  and program management **8:** 4757
Critical pedagogy
  See Pedagogy, critical approach
Critical reading **2:** ***1194–1198***
  discourse analysis **2:** 1196, 1197
    classroom techniques **2:** 1197
  evaluation of **2:** 1198
  fundamental concepts **2:** 1194
  place in curriculum **2:** 1197
  psychological model
    cognitive processes **2:** 1195
  reader response model
    psychological criticism of **2:** 1195
    sociological criticism of **2:** 1194
  secondary school curriculum
    reader response model **2:** 1194
  as social analysis **2:** 1194
  sociological perspective **2:** 1195, 1197
Critical theory **1:** 276; **2:** ***1199–1204***
  and administrator education
    preservice **1:** 76
  and adult education **1:** 277;
      2: ***1189–1194***; **10:** 6055
  applications in education **2:** 1199
  and art education
    Germany **1:** 341
  communicative rationality **1:** 63
  and comparative education **2:** 926,
      929
  and context of learning **5:** 2883
  and critical thinking **2:** 1199
  criticism of **1:** 55
  and curriculum development **3:** 1264
  and curriculum research **3:** 1347
  in educational administration **1:** 55,
      63; **3:** 1772
  and educational research **9:** 5024
  feminism
    and the curriculum **4:** 2289
  grounding of **2:** 1201
  Habermas' version **2:** 1200, 1202;
      3: 1772
  and hermeneutics **5:** 2579
  and the hidden curriculum **3:** 1333;
      5: 2588
  and individual power **4:** 1982
  instruction **10:** 6196
  instrumental rationality **1:** 63
  interests and **2:** 1201
  and interpretivism **2:** 1199
  language **10:** 6197
  learning **10:** 6196
  and participatory research **7:** 4331
  and philosophy of education **8:** 4453,
      4454
  political orientation **2:** 1199
  and positivism **2:** 1199
  and social change **1:** 58; **2:** 1199
  and sociology of education **2:** 780;
      10: 5600
  and teacher education **10:** 5984
  and teacher supervision **10:** 6002
  validity **2:** 1200, 1203
Critical thinking
  and adult education **10:** 6055
  adults **1:** 164
  conceptions of **2:** 1204
  Cornell tests **2:** 1207
  courses **2:** 1206
  and creative thinking **2:** 1206
  and critical theory **2:** 1199
  and cultural analysis **2:** 1199
  curriculum and pedagogy **2:** 1206
  and educational reform **2:** 1204
  evaluation of skills **2:** 1207
  generalizability **2:** 1206
  humanities instruction **5:** 2695
  judgment **2:** 1205
  justification in education **2:** 1206
  normative aspects **2:** 1205
  origins **2:** 1204
  philosophical issues **2:** ***1204–1208***
  problem-solving **8:** 4723, 4724
  psychological aspects **2:** 1205
  rationality **2:** 1205
  reflective **2:** 1204
  relationship with formal logic **2:** 1206
  skepticism **2:** 1205
  Watson–Glaser Appraisal **2:** 1207
  weak/strong **2:** 1205
  See also
    Evaluative thinking
Cross age teaching
  Bell–Lancaster system **11:** 6482
  historical background **11:** 6482
  peer teaching
    special education **8:** 4372, 4373
  tutoring **11:** 6482
Cross-cultural studies
  of cognition **4:** 1849
  curriculum **4:** 1850
  educational anthropology
      2: ***1208–1213***
    future research **2:** 1212
  ethnocentrism **3:** 1244
  methodology **2:** 1208
  multilingualism **7:** 3973
  and test bias **11:** 6315
  and test translation **11:** 6328
    interpretation of results **11:** 6332
Cross-national comparisons
  See Comparative education
Cross-national studies
  See Comparative area studies
Cross-sectional studies **7:** 4051
  age–earnings profiles **3:** 1657
  classes of **2:** 1216
  conduct of **2:** 1217
  data analysis **2:** 1219
  and educational history **5:** 2604
  errors
    sources of **2:** 1218
  examples **2:** 1215
  and longitudinal studies **2:** 1214
    compared **6:** 3512
  pilot studies **2:** 1218
  pretests **2:** 1218
  purpose of **2:** 1215
  rate of return **8:** 4915
  research designs **2:** 1217
  research methods **2:** ***1213–1220***
    strategic choices **2:** 1214
  settings for **2:** 1214
  simultaneous **2:** 1216; **6:** 3515
  single **2:** 1216
  and surveys **10:** 5855
  time factors **2:** 1215
  treatment control **2:** 1215
  trend studies **2:** 1217
  types of **2:** 1215
  use of **2:** 1213
Cuba
  adult education **2:** 636
  educational change **3:** 1221, 1226;
      8: 4493
  educational planning
    and politics **3:** 1808
  farms into educational units **4:** 2366
  government school relationship
    school administration **3:** 1224
  illiteracy **2:** 637
  literacy campaigns **1:** 170
  literacy programs **2:** 637
  nonformal education **7:** 4144
    for social change **1:** 132
  popular education **6:** 3256
  preschool education **3:** 1223
  rural to urban migration
    determinants of **5:** 2943
  school enterprise
    externalities **9:** 5230
  schools into production units **4:** 2366
  secondary education
    vocational education **3:** 1222
  system of education **3:** ***1221–1227***
    educational objectives **3:** 1221
    major problems **3:** 1226
    structure **3:** 1222
  vocational education
    education with production **3:** 1686
    training with production **11:** 6447
Cultural awareness
  and core curriculum
    cultural literacy approach **2:** 1105
  cultural literacy list
    United States **2:** 1105
  and curriculum policies **3:** 1336
  and development education **3:** 1500
  program development **3:** ***1233–1236***
  and reading comprehension **8:** 4937
Cultural capital **9:** 5057
  and academic achievement **9:** 5019
  concept of **4:** 2267, 2269
  and family
    social differences **4:** 2269
  habitus of **4:** 2267, 2270
  intragroup differences **4:** 2270
  and occupational aspiration **1:** 356
  and peer influence **9:** 5219
  reproduction theory **9:** 5017
  and social values **4:** ***2267–2272***
  use of **4:** 2271
  variations in value **4:** 2268
  working class youth **9:** 5570

Cultural context
  cross-cultural studies **2:** 1210
  and decentralization
    developing nations **3:** 1414
  and dissemination of knowledge
      3: 1550
  and literacy **6:** 3453, 3454
  for literacy curriculum **6:** 3452
  situated learning **5:** 2882; **6:** 3342;
      7: 3885
    and transfer of training **11:** 6454,
      6455
Cultural continuities **1:** 290
  and academic achievement **3:** 1227
Cultural deficit theory
  and bilingual education **1:** 532
  criticism of **2:** 800; **3:** 1227; **4:** 2048
    and ethnography **4:** 2049
Cultural deprivation thesis
  and educational anthropology **1:** 281
  and poverty indicators **1:** 283
Cultural differences
  cognitive ability **3:** ***1246–1253***
  cross-cultural studies
    educational implications **3:** 1231
  educational anthropology **1:** 281
  and intelligence tests **4:** 1849
  and misunderstanding **1:** 292
  and power relations **1:** 292
  and reading comprehension **8:** 4937
  in schools
    and socialization **10:** 5590
  and second language learning
      6: 3210, 3212
  and test translation **11:** 6329
  urban schools **11:** 6562
Cultural discontinuities
  and academic achievement **5:** 2681
  educational anthropological studies
      1: 281, 290
  and ethnography **4:** 2049
  role of school **2:** 1209
  secondary
    and academic achievement **3:** 1228
  and underachievement **3:** 1233
  urban schools **2:** 916
Cultural ecology **1:** 286
Cultural education **1:** 96
Cultural influences
  beliefs
    individual development
      5: ***2651–2656***
  on cognitive development **3:** 1242
  on curriculum **9:** ***5518–5523***
  and formal adult education **10:** 5592
  and reproduction theory **9:** 5016
  and socialization **10:** 5586
  and textbook preparation **11:** 6365
Cultural pluralism **3:** 1726
  and the arts **7:** 3972
  and citizen participation **4:** 1981
  and communicative competence
      (language) **9:** 5218
  and comparative education **2:** 925
  and curriculum **6:** 3358, 3360
  and curriculum development
      7: ***3974–3978***
  and dominant cultural values **4:** 2268
  moral values **10:** 5987
  multicultural education **7:** 3962, 3964,
      3971
  and school-based curriculum planning
      3: 1270
  and sociology of education **10:** 5603
Cultural production
  concept of **9:** 5309
Cultural rationalization theory
  comparative education **2:** 929
Cultural reproduction **9:** 5057
  and academic achievement **3:** 1229
  culture and learning **3:** 1241
  and curriculum policies **3:** 1334
  and labor market forces **3:** 1229
  minority group students
    low achievement **9:** 5570
  resistance **3:** 1229; **9:** 5509
    concept of **9:** 5570
    and racial factors **9:** 5570
    rural schools **2:** 914
    and student attitudes **9:** 5571
    theory of **9:** 5570
    urban schools **2:** 915
  school role in **3:** 1229
  social capital **3:** 1229
  and social stratification **9:** 5570
Cultural traits
  and interviews **5:** 3005
Cultural transmission **3:** ***1724–1729***,
      1726
  and adult education **1:** 128
  communities
    and acculturation **2:** 914
  cross-cultural studies **2:** 1208
    cultural discontinuity model
      2: 1209
    instrumental model **2:** 1209
    interactionist model **2:** 1209
    systems model **2:** 1209
  educational anthropology
      9: ***5508–5510***
  and educational research **3:** 1727
  and family environment **5:** 2625
  indigenous populations **3:** 1751
  and nonformal education **4:** 2365,
      2367
  and slavery **3:** 1752
  See also
    Socialization
Culture
  and academic achievement
    trends in research **3:** 1230
    and use of computers **3:** 1231
  acquisition of **3:** 1725
    and language acquisition **3:** 1728
    research **3:** 1727
  anthropological concept of **7:** 3971
  anthropological studies **1:** 297
  circles of **1:** 133; **2:** 904, 1046
    Freire's pedagogy **3:** 1333
  concepts of **9:** 5309; **11:** 6798
    in educational research **3:** 1241
  definitions of **3:** 1242, 1751
  ethnography
    and program development
      3: ***1233–1236***
  evolutionary theory and education
      4: 2167
  formation
    research **11:** 6802
  high **3:** 1725
  high and popular **2:** 903
  impact of literacy on **3:** 1242
  as language
    and peer groups **9:** 5218
  and learning **3:** ***1241–1246***
  locus of **3:** 1725
  in other species **4:** 2168
  and personality
    diversity organization **3:** 1727
    uniformity replication **3:** 1727
  private
    propriospect **3:** 1726, 1727, 1728
  relationship with the individual
      3: 1725, 1726
  research
    and youth culture **11:** 6800
  in school organization **7:** 4243
  and social class
    conflict **9:** 5311
  use of term **5:** 2651
  youth **11:** ***6798–6803***
Culture and cognition approach
  and academic achievement **3:** 1230
  educational research **3:** 1243
Culture conflict
  domination
    and adult education **1:** 132
  and educational planning **3:** 1822
  and syllabi **10:** 5884
Culture fair tests
  and nonverbal tests **11:** 6344
  and test bias **11:** 6315
  and test translation **11:** 6328
  See also
    Test bias
Culture free tests
  See Culture fair tests
Culture and personality
  cross-cultural studies **1:** 282
Curiosity
  in child development
    Montessori method **7:** 3914
  and self-motivation **7:** 3939, 3940
Curriculum
  and academic freedom **6:** 3358
  adult education **3:** ***1308–1315***
    and credentials **3:** 1309
    and ideology **2:** 1191
    and social class bias **5:** 2733
    and values **3:** 1310
  adult literacy **3:** ***1257–1262***
    trends **3:** 1258
  as an instrument of social control
      3: 1303
  and aptitude tests **6:** 3314, 3315
  attained **3:** 1272

and beliefs about knowledge
6: ***3148–3151***
and censorship **6:** 3358
challenges to **9:** 5521
and children's rights **6:** 3359
and Christianity
Saint Augustine on **9:** 5116
and civil rights **6:** 3359
classroom coverage **3:** 1254
closed
and educational administration
6: 3274
cognitive development
and expertise **2:** 841
components
and teaching guides **10:** 6113
compromises
and information technology **7:** 4083
and computers
integration of **11:** 6283
concepts of **3:** 1262, 1263, 1272, 1309; **4:** 1842; **9:** 5518
and curriculum evaluation **3:** 1284
and educational change **4:** 1850
and multicultural education **7:** 3977
contribution of philosophers to content and policy **3:** 1327
and court litigation **6:** 3357
and critical thinking **2:** 1206
criticisms of **3:** 1317; **9:** 5519
and cultural awareness **7:** 3971
cultural influences **3:** 1289
and cultural pluralism **6:** 3358, 3360
and cultural reproduction **3:** 1304
and curriculum development **3:** 1323
definitions of **3:** 1263, 1320; **4:** 2287
departments of **3:** 1265
descriptions and definitions **3:** 1309
differences
cross-cultural studies **11:** 6332
economic factors **3:** 1288
and educational finance **9:** 5235
and educational reform **11:** 6561
effects on
political **10:** 5592
epistemological legitimation **4:** 1997
and equal education **6:** 3360
expanding environments **9:** 5573
expanding horizons **9:** 5579
factors affecting **9:** ***5518–5523***
population trends **9:** 5520
feminist approaches **4:** ***2287–2292***
liberal **4:** 2287
radical **4:** 2288
socialist **4:** 2289
in final grades of school
and recurrent education **8:** 4958
formal vs. informal **9:** 5580
for immigrant children **7:** ***3840–3848***
philosophical rationale **7:** 3842
indirect **6:** 3359
influence of postmodernism on
8: 4642
and information technology
7: ***4081–4088***
future impact **7:** 4087
impact **7:** 4085
innovations
implementation **3:** 1491
and instruction **3:** 1310
and instructional alignment **5:** 2853
and instructional materials **3:** 1323
integration **10:** 5813
intellectual influences **3:** 1289
issues **10:** 6089
and item banks **5:** 2783
learning strategies
teaching of **6:** 3336
legal control **6:** 3357
legal factors affecting **6:** ***3356–3360***
international **6:** 3359
national and regional interests
6: 3360
legislation **6:** 3357, 3358
federal **6:** 3357
and unitary administration **6:** 3357
levels
achieved **11:** 6322, 6326
implemented **11:** 6322, 6325
intended **11:** 6322, 6323
lifelong learning **6:** 3419
limitations
and school size **9:** 5292
for literacy **6:** 3455
Locke's theories **6:** 3498
mandatory **3:** 1272, 1273
and Marxian analysis of ideology
6: 3618
measurement-driven **7:** ***3722–3726***
and decentralization **7:** 3723
general curricula **7:** 3722
impact **7:** 3723
and public test results **7:** 3723
special purpose **7:** 3722
and metacognition
instruction **7:** 3790
for minority groups **7:** ***3840–3848***
philosophical rationale **7:** 3842
modular **7:** ***3886–3889***
multicultural education **6:** 3451;
7: ***3974–3978***
native language instruction
studies **11:** 6776
nongraded instructional grouping
7: ***4155–4157***
nonschool
and student experience **10:** 5815
for numeracy **6:** 3458
objectives
writing (composition) **11:** 6776
open
and educational administration
6: 3274
organization
and educational theories **10:** 5813
and outcomes of education **9:** 5260
philosophical perspectives
3: ***1325–1328***
political education **8:** 4569
political influences **3:** 1288
and politics of education **8:** 4582
preactive
definition of **9:** 5295
problem-based
and deep approach to learning
1: 193
and quality of life
Spencer's view **10:** 5706
racial bias **10:** 5824
ratings
and tests **11:** 6323
recommended **3:** 1272, 1273
religious education **9:** 5005
and reproduction theory **9:** 5021
resource room programs **9:** 5069
role of **9:** 5518
role of theory **3:** 1310
school business relationship **9:** 5188
school involvement **6:** 3358
and school organization **7:** 4231
coupling patterns **6:** 3525
and school size **9:** 5064
science education
primary school programs **9:** 5330
vs. classical-literary **9:** 5324
as self-actualization **3:** 1263
sex bias in **4:** 2409, 2448; **9:** 5441;
10: 5823
Islamic culture **11:** 6757
as social construction
research **9:** 5295
social influences **3:** 1289
social studies
in primary schools **9:** 5574
and socialism **3:** 1327
sociocultural critique of **9:** 5521
specification
science education **9:** 5330
student experience of **10:** ***5813–5818***
study of
historical background **9:** 5297
supported **3:** 1272, 1273
taught **3:** 1272
and teacher evaluation **10:** 6041
and teacher-led instruction **9:** 5170
and teaching methods **3:** 1323
technology education **11:** ***6287–6292***
tested **3:** 1272, 1273
and testing **11:** ***6321–6328***
and textbooks
readership size **11:** 6362
trends
economic factors **9:** 5519
and sociological values **9:** 5520
typology **3:** 1272
uniform
and government role in **5:** 2509
and utilitarianism **6:** 3149
and visual literacy **11:** 6623
vocational education **11:** 6250
with and without power **3:** 1272
women's education
North America **11:** 6764
written
historical background **9:** 5298
importance of **9:** 5296

See also
Core curriculum
Hidden curriculum
Modular curricula
Science curriculum
Secondary school curriculum
Student centered curriculum
Curriculum adaptation **3:** ***1253–1257***
definition of **3:** 1253
disadvantaged students **3:** 1254
ecological **3:** 1254
at policy level **3:** 1253
sociocultural patterns **3:** 1254
strategies **10:** 6089
teacher attitudes **3:** 1256
teacher influence **3:** 1254, 1255
time management **3:** 1254
types of **3:** 1254
within classrooms **3:** 1254
See also
Curriculum development
Curriculum advisory councils **2:** 890
Curriculum alignment **7:** 3723
minimum competency testing **7:** 3723
problems **7:** 3723
Curriculum analysis **10:** 6089
curriculum potential of **3:** 1365
Curriculum-based assessment
3: ***1355–1359***
developments in **3:** 1358
and noncategorical education **7:** 3832
and norm-referenced tests **3:** 1356
origins in special education **3:** 1356
problem-solving **3:** 1357
purposes of **3:** 1355
in special education **3:** 1356, 1357
special needs students **2:** 714
use of computers in **7:** 3805
use of term **3:** 1355
uses of **3:** 1357
Curriculum centers
See Curriculum development centers
Curriculum change
See Curriculum development
Curriculum control
feminist approaches **4:** 2287, 2288
Curriculum decision-making
community involvement **2:** ***888–893***
parent participation **2:** ***888–893***
Curriculum design **3:** 1323
and adult educators **3:** 1309
adult literacy
factors influencing **3:** 1258
and cognitive development **5:** 2666
components **10:** 5814
content-centered models
critical events model **5:** 2686
criteria for **3:** 1323
and educational history **3:** 1795
educational quality
and the law **6:** 3358, 3360
in effective schools **4:** 1931
and effective schools research **9:** 5377
and labor force development **5:** 2686
and learning factors **10:** 5747
levels **3:** 1313
models in context **3:** 1313
modular curricula **3:** 1313; **7:** 3887
and neo-Piagetian theory **8:** 4482
and printed materials **8:** 4697
racial discrimination
South Africa **7:** 3852
school organization **7:** 4233
science education **8:** 4645
selection of models **3:** 1313
student role in
and small group instruction
10: 6184
and syllabi **10:** 5883, 5884
teacher role in
and small group instruction
10: 6184
Twente model **3:** 1313
usefulness of models **3:** 1312
Curriculum development **3:** 1322
and accountability **7:** 3724, 3725
action research **10:** 6096
adult education
human traits based **3:** 1312
individual needs based **3:** 1312
social and cultural factors **3:** 1312
subject matter approach **3:** 1312
technology-based **3:** 1312
Africa **8:** 4681
behavioral objectives **3:** 1801
centralized **5:** 2497
teacher participation **10:** 6090
chemistry **8:** 4477
classroom techniques
discipline **10:** 6028
and community control **3:** 1235
for computer literacy **2:** 974
and concept maps **2:** 1029
and courseware **3:** 1776
and critical theory **2:** 1199; **3:** 1264
and cultural differences
core curriculum approach **3:** 1231
and ethnography **3:** 1235
multicultural education **3:** 1231
and cultural pluralism **7:** ***3974–3978***
curriculum research **3:** ***1262–1267***,
1319
and deskilling of teachers **10:** 6136
and developmental stages **5:** 2666
discovery learning **3:** 1538
economic factors **9:** 5519
and educational objectives **3:** 1264,
1322, 1325, 1327, 1801
and educational planning **3:** 1809
and educational principles **3:** 1803
and educational reform **9:** 5278
educational research **4:** 1869
and educational technology **3:** 1263
and equal opportunities **4:** 2289
United Kingdom **4:** 2290
expressive objectives **3:** 1801
feedback for
and vocational education **11:** 6668
and forms of knowledge **3:** 1326
and futures (of society) **4:** ***2327–2331***
Hirst's rational **3:** 1325
criticisms of **3:** 1326
impact of educational psychology on
4: ***1841–1848***
and individual development
Islamic theory **5:** 3022
and information technology **7:** 4081,
4086
integration
and vocational education **4:** 1919
and intellectual disciplines **9:** 5294
and intuition in cognition and **3:** 1263
and laboratory packages **6:** 3202
legal framework **6:** 3357
and literacy programs **8:** 4637
mathematical applications
6: ***3631–3634***
and monitoring national standards
7: 3907
multicultural education
United Kingdom **7:** 3845
national programs
and federal legislation **6:** 3357
naturalistic model **3:** 1330, 1802
organic **10:** 6090
policies for **9:** 5522
and political power **3:** 1306
preparation for **3:** 1321
primary school agriculture **8:** 4685
and principals
role of **9:** 5271
problem-solving objectives **3:** 1802
process model **3:** 1274; **10:** 6096
and professional autonomy **3:** 1346;
10: 6135
and public policy
multicultural education **7:** 3977
and reconstructionism **9:** 5522
renewal **3:** ***1338–1343***
and educational objectives **3:** 1339
end educational opportunities
3: 1340
future challenges **3:** 1342
government control **3:** 1341
holistic approach **3:** 1340
instructional materials **3:** 1339
national issues **3:** 1338
and professional autonomy of
teachers **3:** 1341
research and development projects
3: 1340
and social change **3:** 1339
targets for **3:** 1341
school-based **2:** 1106; **3:** ***1267–1272***
advantages and disadvantages
3: 1269
characteristics of **3:** 1268
evaluation of **3:** 1279
future prospects and research
3: 1270
history of **3:** 1267
procedures **10:** 6090
requirements **10:** 6090
and teachers **10:** 6090
variables in **3:** 1269
and school business relationship
8: 4337
science education **8:** 4461; **9:** 5326

secondary education
Sweden **11:** 6692
and social change **3:** 1263
United States **3:** 1299
strategies **3:** 1493
student characteristics and **3:** 1322
as symbolic action **3:** 1306
systems approach in **10:** 5899
and teacher attitudes **10:** 6209
and teacher effectiveness
prediction **4:** 2329
and teacher expectation of students
10: 6111
and teacher knowledge **10:** 6118
and teacher militancy **8:** 4582
and teacher participation **10:** 6080
teacher role **3:** 1267; **10:** 6079, 6097
first-order research **10:** 6097
multicultural education **7:** 3977
second-order research **10:** 6097
and teachers **10:** ***6089–6092***
technical education **11:** 6271
testing and **3:** 1322
and textbooks **3:** 1339; **11:** 6367
and training with production **11:** 6451
trends **9:** 5523
Tyler rationale **3:** 1801
United Kingdom **7:** 3907
use of educational objectives in
3: ***1800***, ***1800–1804***
and utilitarianism **3:** 1326
vocational education
Latin America **6:** 3260
Sweden **11:** 6692
trends **11:** 6667
vs. textbook publication **11:** 6365
See also
Curriculum adaptation
Curriculum planning
Curriculum development centers
3: 1267, ***1272–1278***
Canada **3:** 1274
Central and Eastern Europe **3:** 1276
context **3:** 1277
Denmark **3:** 1276
and educational practice **3:** 1278
features **3:** 1274
France **3:** 1275
future trends **3:** 1278
Germany **3:** 1275
India **3:** 1276
Indonesia **3:** 1276
international co-operation **3:** 1277
Japan **3:** 1276
Korea, Republic of **3:** 1276
Malaysia **3:** 1276
Netherlands **3:** 1275
Norway **3:** 1276
Pacific territories **3:** 1276
and professional development **3:** 1277
responsibilities **3:** 1273
role of **3:** 1273
South America **3:** 1275
Spain **3:** 1276
Sweden **3:** 1275
United Kingdom **3:** 1275
United States **3:** 1274
Curriculum differentiation **3:** 1318
Curriculum documents **3:** 1272, 1324
Curriculum evaluation **2:** 1058;
3: ***1279–1283***
and achievement tests **10:** 5769
based on field tests data **3:** 1280
case studies **3:** 1285
connoisseurship model **3:** 1281, 1286
and cost effectiveness studies **2:** 1134
criteria
economic **3:** 1359
external **3:** 1279
curriculum research **3:** 1319
curriculum-specific criteria
3: ***1359–1367***
balance **3:** 1360, 1361, 1366
potential **3:** 1365
relevance **3:** 1361
and educational quality
teacher role **3:** 1268
educational research **4:** 1869
and the law **6:** 3358
national standards
England and Wales **7:** 3908
parent participation **2:** 890
of products **3:** 1279
program evaluation **3:** 1280
qualitative **3:** ***1284–1288***
activities and aims **3:** 1285
characteristics of **3:** 1284
definition of **3:** 1284
origins **3:** 1284
phases of **3:** 1286
Tylerian model **3:** 1279, 1280;
7: 3722
See also
Program evaluation
Curriculum guides **3:** 1263
course descriptions
Tyler's **3:** 1263
modular curricula **7:** 3889
Curriculum history **3:** ***1301–1308***
administration and guidelines **3:** 1305
approaches **3:** 1302
areas of study **3:** 1302
China, People's Republic of **3:** 1291
and curriculum codes **3:** 1303
and curriculum studies **3:** 1302
as a discipline **3:** 1301, 1305
and educational history **3:** 1301, 1302
England and Wales **3:** 1293, 1294
Germany **3:** 1305
Germany, Federal Republic of
(former) **3:** 1289
ideas
theories and movements **3:** 1303
intellectual disciplines **3:** 1304
and intellectual history **3:** 1307
legitimization of **3:** 1305
national profiles **3:** ***1288–1301***
Nordic countries **3:** 1303
reform and practice **3:** 1305
research methodology **3:** 1307
scope and objectives **3:** 1302
and sociology of education **3:** 1302,
1303
United States **3:** 1296, 1303
Curriculum implementation **3:** 1324
research **3:** 1318, 1319
success factors **3:** 1324
theories of **3:** 1351
comparative research **2:** 954
Curriculum improvement
See Curriculum development
Curriculum kits
See Instructional materials,
curriculum packages
Curriculum management **3:** ***1320–1325***
curriculum research **3:** 1324
Curriculum materials
See Instructional materials
Curriculum models **3:** 1349
conference model **3:** 1349
FAL primary education **3:** 1352
Generatives Leitsystem **3:** 1349
Curriculum planning **3:** ***1328–1334***
and consciousness raising **3:** 1332
critical theory perspective **3:** 1332
deliberation approach **3:** 1330
implementation
evaluation (PIE) model **3:** 1331
levels of **3:** 1331
objectivity approach **3:** 1329
school focused **3:** ***1267–1272***
technical production perspective
3: 1329
Tyler rationale **3:** 1329, 1331
See also
Curriculum development
Curriculum policies
and curriculum politics **3:** ***1334–1338***
United States **3:** 1336
Curriculum politics
curriculum control
centralized or local **3:** 1335
Curriculum potential **3:** 1365
and teacher education **3:** 1366
Curriculum problems
technical education
teacher education **10:** 6065
Curriculum reform
See Curriculum development
Curriculum relevance
See Relevance (education)
Curriculum research **3:** ***1262–1267***
applied and developmental **3:** 1319
business administration education
3: 1354
cooperation **3:** 1320
coverage **4:** 1935
and critical theory **3:** 1347
curriculum development **3:** 1319
curriculum evaluation **3:** 1319
curriculum implementation **3:** 1318,
1319
curriculum management **3:** 1324
curriculum policy development
3: 1319
directions **3:** 1316
and educational history **3:** 1795

and educational practices **3:** 1264
forms of inquiry **3:** ***1316–1320***
analytic **3:** 1317
intentional **3:** 1318
narrative **3:** 1318
portrait **3:** 1317
Schwab's forms **3:** 1316
societal **3:** 1318
structure–functional **3:** 1318
generative curriculum **2:** 836
humanistic tradition **3:** 1316
IMPACT project **3:** 1350, 1354
interdisciplinary approach **3:** 1265, 1319
Marxist sociology **3:** 1346
Apple's influence **3:** 1346
resistance **3:** 1346
organicism **3:** 1344
phenomenology **3:** 1344
scientific tradition **3:** 1316
social reproduction theory **3:** 1345
sociology **3:** ***1343–1348***
and sociology of knowledge **3:** 1344
specializations **3:** 1319
themes **3:** 1262, 1263
Curriculum studies **3:** 1300
United Kingdom **3:** 1295
Curriculum theory **3:** 1264, ***1348–1355***
commonplaces in **3:** 1263
core issues **3:** 1352
critical
criticisms of **3:** 1335
defined **3:** 1348
Dewey on **3:** 1348
epistemological **3:** 1351
feminist **3:** 1335
Germany
educational theory **3:** 1291
information theory **3:** 1290
learning theory **3:** 1291
Herbart **3:** 1290, 1298
Humboldt **3:** 1290
and instructional process research **3:** 1348
issues **9:** 5518
legitimization **3:** 1349
mental discipline **3:** 1296
process–product approach **3:** 1348
process theories **3:** 1350
Schleiermacher **3:** 1290
structural theories **3:** 1350
and teacher education **3:** 1327
Tyler on **3:** 1348
Cutting scores
and decision theory **3:** 1419
Cybernetics
and systems approach **10:** 5895
Cyprus
adult education
nonformal education **3:** 1371
curriculum development **3:** 1373
educational change **3:** 1374
educational research **3:** 1373
ethnic groups **3:** 1367
government school relationship
financial support **3:** 1372
school administration **3:** 1371
language **3:** 1367
postsecondary education **3:** 1370
preschool education **3:** 1370
primary education **3:** 1369
secondary education **3:** 1369
structure of government **3:** 1368
system of education **3:** ***1367–1375***
degrees and qualifications **3:** 1373
educational objectives **3:** 1368
major problems **3:** 1374
structure **3:** 1369
teacher education **3:** 1372
teacher recruitment **3:** 1372
teaching methodology **3:** 1373
Czech Republic
adult education
history **2:** 656, 658, 659
osvsSta **1:** 112
apprenticeships **1:** 315
illiteracy **2:** 657
public education
management of contraction in **6:** 3605
special education
teams **10:** 6243
use of leisure time **6:** 3375
vocational education
administration of **11:** 6644
historical background **11:** 6642
policy formation **11:** 6646
Czechoslovakia
See Czech Republic
Slovak Republic

Dahomeans
ethnography of **3:** 1752
Daily living skills **1:** 96; **2:** 632, 633
mathematical applications **6:** 3634
stress variables **10:** 5736
training
for disabilities **11:** 6459
Dance
as an arts discipline **8:** 4385
intercultural communication **8:** 4384
Dance education **8:** ***4384–4388***
in physical education **8:** 4385
Data
classes of **7:** 4158
transformation of
and robustness (statistics) **9:** 5077
Data analysis
causal **3:** 1381
components of **3:** 1465
computers **4:** 2387
conclusion drawing **3:** 1470
sources of errors **3:** 1471
confirmation of findings **3:** 1471
strategies for **3:** 1472
in cross-national comparisons **4:** 2136
cross-sectional studies **2:** 1219
and data collection **3:** 1467
data reduction **3:** 1468
and databases
in education **3:** 1396
descriptive **3:** ***1464–1475***
background **3:** 1464
strategies **3:** 1465
design of investigations **3:** 1465
documentary records **3:** 1474
exploratory **4:** ***2199–2208***
integration of findings **3:** 1473
interactive model **3:** 1465
and management information systems **6:** 3595
matrix display **3:** 1469
and meaning
strategies for deriving **3:** 1470
methods
leadership studies **6:** 3281
multilevel analysis **4:** 2385
negative evidence **3:** 1473
outlier cases **3:** 1472
prescriptive **3:** 1382
public sector **3:** ***1381–1387***
rating scales **8:** 4930
replication of findings **3:** 1473
and researcher effects **3:** 1472
respondent feedback **3:** 1473
rival explanations **3:** 1473
surveys **10:** 5860
and weighting **3:** 1472
See also
Exploratory data analysis
Qualitative data analysis
Secondary data analysis
Data archives **3:** ***1377–1381***
access to **3:** 1379
data collection **3:** 1380
future trends **3:** 1380
item comparability **3:** 1380
social sciences **3:** 1379
Data banks **3:** ***1377–1381***
social sciences **3:** 1377
uses in education **3:** 1377
See also
Databases
Data collection
achievement studies **2:** 1217
case studies
methods **2:** 643
census figures **2:** 649
and cluster analysis **2:** 826
cross-sectional studies **2:** 1214
and data analysis **3:** 1467
and data archives **3:** 1380
and data banks **3:** 1377
data loggers
uses in education **3:** 1397
and databases
in education **3:** 1395
and descriptive data **3:** 1464
documentary records **3:** 1467
educational history
research methodology **5:** 2604
and event history analysis **4:** 2150
for generalizability theory **5:** 2458, 2460
and job analysis **6:** 3094
leadership studies **6:** 3281
for log-linear models **6:** 3501

and management information systems **6:** 3595
methods
and nonresponse **7:** 3854
and multivariate analysis **7:** 4012
nonresponse and missing data in surveys **7:** ***3853–3858***
and outcomes of education **9:** 5263
in participant observation **7:** 4317
phenomenography **8:** 4427
and program implementation evaluation **4:** 2072
questionnaires **8:** 4883
real time
and microcomputer-based laboratories **7:** 3808
and reliability **9:** 4989, 4991
in school evaluation **4:** 2382
choice of methods **4:** 2383
faulty procedures **4:** 2386
information overload **4:** 2386
multilevel issues **4:** 2384
respondent burden **4:** 2386
sensitivity of information **4:** 2387
timing of **4:** 2387
use of information technology **4:** 2387
school surveys **2:** 650
and single case research **9:** 5487
survey designs
and nonresponse **7:** 3853
surveys **10:** 5856, 5857
and Thurstone scales **11:** 6385
two wave **2:** 671
See also
Sampling
Data documentation
and data archives **3:** 1380
and data banks **3:** 1378
Data envelopment analysis **3:** ***1381–1387***
and changes over time **3:** 1386
model **3:** 1384
and school performance **3:** 1384
Data handling
See Data processing
Data interpretation
and observation **9:** 5046
and single case research **9:** 5487
Data needs
See Information needs
Data organization
codebook preparation **3:** 1379
coding **3:** 1378
and data banks **3:** 1378
Data processing
and case studies **2:** 644
and databases
in education **3:** 1396
educational surveys
and microcomputers **7:** 3814
and management information systems **6:** 3595
for multimedia systems **7:** 3988
and surveys **10:** 5859
Data protection **4:** 2387
Database design **3:** 1387
hierarchical data model **3:** 1390
network data model **3:** 1390
relational data model **3:** 1390
tasks **3:** 1392
and technological advancement **3:** 1398
Database management systems
advantages of **3:** 1388
characteristics of **3:** 1387
concepts of **3:** 1387
design and implementation **3:** 1392
in education **3:** ***1387–1394***
and educational planning **11:** 6296
example **3:** 1394
historical background **3:** 1388
and microcomputers **7:** 3815
Databases
adult education **1:** 141
and authoring aids
for courseware design **10:** 5624
availability in schools **3:** 1395
and computer-assisted instruction **2:** 989
computer software for **3:** 1392
educational applications **3:** 1392
and educational management information systems **5:** 2828, 2829
and educational planning models **3:** 1828
in educational research **3:** ***1387–1394***, 1554
and information networks **5:** 2993
international **5:** 2997
and information retrieval **5:** 2819
effectiveness factors **5:** 2822
instructional aspects of **3:** 1395
international collaboration **3:** 1398
and item banks **5:** 3042
learning strategies **3:** 1397
and management information systems **6:** 3594
and multimedia systems **7:** 3991
normalization of **3:** 1389
publications **5:** 2819
and query languages **3:** 1392
relational **3:** 1390
development of **3:** 1388
in science education **7:** 4101
and secondary data analysis
problems **9:** 5370
structure of **3:** 1390
and traditional archiving methods compared **3:** 1388
types of **3:** 1390
uses
by children **3:** 1395
instructional **3:** ***1394–1398***
and videotex **11:** 6302
See also
Data banks
Database design
Database management systems
Day care
child caregivers
skill level rating **3:** 1629
costs **2:** 690
demand for **2:** 690
economics of **2:** ***688–693***
effect on child development **3:** 1640
evaluation research
France **11:** 6396
Italy **11:** 6396
United States **11:** 6395
externalities **2:** 692
family day care **2:** 699
infants **5:** ***2803–2806***
policies
international overview **2:** ***693–701***
issues **2:** 691
and preschool education **8:** 4662
and preschool evaluation **4:** 2141, 2144
programs
Europe **11:** 6396
public policy
human resources argument **8:** 4671
public vs. private provision **8:** 4676
quality of **2:** 691
research **11:** 6395
and schools **5:** 2497
services
Europe **2:** 694, 696
international overview **2:** ***693–701***
Scandinavian model **2:** 695, 696
United Kingdom dual system **2:** 695
toddlers **11:** ***6395–6398***
type of **2:** 688
See also
Employer supported day care
Family day care
Day care centers **2:** 689, 690, 699
compared with parental caregiving **2:** 686
developing nations **3:** 1627
financial support **2:** 699
nursery schools **8:** 4670
quality
effect on child development **3:** 1640
United Kingdom **2:** 695
Day care programs
See Day care
Day release
See Released time
Day schools
full-time
and religious education **9:** 4997
supplementary
and religious education **9:** 4998
Deaf blind
etiology **3:** 1403
Deaf blind adults
education of **3:** 1405
Deaf blind children
characteristics of **3:** 1403
communication problems
language acquisition **3:** 1403

ecological approach to instruction **3:** 1405
educational needs **3:** 1403
educational programs **3:** 1403
functional curriculum **3:** 1405
individualized curriculum sequencing model **3:** 1405
integrated instruction programs **3:** 1405
mainstreaming **3:** 1405
movement-based instruction **3:** 1405
schools for **3:** 1402
sensory deprivation **3:** 1405
special education **3:** ***1402–1407***
historical background **3:** 1402
trends and issues **3:** 1405
teaching methods
augmentative communication **3:** 1404
finger spelling **3:** 1404
prelinguistic **3:** 1404
tactile cues **3:** 1404
tactual use of sign language **3:** 1404
Tadoma vibrotactile method **3:** 1404
total communication **3:** 1404
Deafness **3:** ***1398–1402***
adaptive behavior
emotional adjustment **3:** 1401
social adjustment **3:** 1401
cognitive ability
dynamic assessment **3:** 1401
cognitive processes **3:** 1401
communication **3:** 1399
and communicative competence
teaching methods **10:** 5659
curriculum
and attitudes **3:** 1400
individual development **3:** 1401
language acquisition **3:** 1399
sociolinguistic approach **3:** 1399
learning environments **3:** 1400
literacy
skill development **3:** 1399
mainstreaming **3:** 1400
and oral communication method **3:** 1399
and participative decision-making **3:** 1401
and reading skills **3:** 1399
social development **3:** 1401
special education **3:** 1400
history of **10:** 5658
preschool children **10:** 5661
and speech and language handicaps **10:** 5687
total communication **3:** 1400
Deakin University (Australia)
action research **1:** 44
Deans of students **10:** 5796
credentials **10:** 5802
females
North America **11:** 6763
Death
Christian theory of **2:** 763, 764
Debt crisis
See Economic crisis
Decentralization
advantages **3:** 1412
decision-making
costs and benefits **5:** 2793
and public schools **5:** 2796
requirements **5:** 2793
studies **5:** 2795
definitions of **3:** 1407, 1412
disadvantages **3:** 1412, 1413
educational administration **3:** ***1407–1412***; **7:** 4243
rationale for **6:** 3272
and educational change **5:** 2506
and educational contraction **6:** 3606
educational environment **3:** 1717
and educational planning **3:** 1817, 1827; **8:** 4496, 4503; **11:** 6295
Latin America **8:** 4494
politics of **8:** 4599
sub-Saharan Africa **8:** 4513
and educational policy **1:** 592
teacher role in **10:** 6080
and educational quality **8:** 4866
and educational reform **4:** 1855
failure
determinants of **3:** 1413
and federalism **6:** 3273
future trends **3:** 1411
geographical contexts **3:** 1407
and governance **6:** 3491; **8:** 4591
historical background **3:** 1407
and localism **6:** 3273
in manufacturing industry
policy implications **5:** 2795
matrices for **3:** 1408
and participative decision-making
costs **5:** 2797
politics of
research **1:** 592
and productivity **5:** 2795
reasons for **3:** 1407
and school administration **6:** 3493; **9:** 5165
educational reform **11:** 6555
studies **9:** 5183
and school-based management **9:** 5305
administrative effects of **3:** 1409
adoption of **3:** 1410
effects on learning **3:** 1410
structure of **3:** 1409
and school organization **7:** 4230, 4235
and school reform **9:** 5276
and school role **5:** 2602
and school as workplace **9:** 5177
of schools
developing nations **3:** ***1412–1416***
Mexico **2:** 1040
practice implications **3:** 1415
research implications **3:** 1415
and selection
secondary education **9:** 5389
stages of **3:** 1410
and state departments of education **7:** 3835, 3838
success
determinants of **3:** 1413
types of **3:** 1408
vs. centralization
and educational administration **8:** 4565
and educational equity (finance) **3:** 1791
and educational planning **8:** 4498
See also
Centralization
Decision-making
biophysics and sociocultural patterns
global approach **4:** 1994
classification of **3:** 1417
community
and smallest space analysis **9:** 5501
constraints and extensions **3:** 1419
devolution of
and vocational education **8:** 4529
and documentation systems **3:** 1592
and educational administration **6:** 3272
educational change **7:** 4235
and educational policy
comparative analysis **3:** ***1830–1835***
state departments of education **7:** 3838
by employees
categories of **5:** 2794
and management information systems **6:** 3596
occupations
factors affecting **6:** 3099, 3100
and organizational theories **4:** 2163; **9:** 5161
and participation
in educational reform **4:** 1855
policy-oriented research **8:** 4556
and principals
role of **9:** 5271
processes
and outcomes of education **9:** 5263
and school organization **7:** 4230
shared
in school policy **1:** 592
teacher participation
and school as workplace **9:** 5179
teachers **2:** 794
and educational technology **11:** 6283
techniques **5:** 2724
and idea generation **5:** ***2721–2725***
weighted decision matrix **5:** 2724
and vocational education
Central and Eastern Europe **11:** 6644
See also
Participative decision-making
Decision-making skills
and immigrants **5:** 2737
Decision-making theory **3:** ***1421–1425***
definitions of **3:** 1421
dichotomous outcomes **3:** 1424

educational applications **3:** 1424
expected values **3:** 1422
indifference curves **3:** 1422
individual
descriptive **3:** 1423, 1424
prescriptive **3:** 1422, 1424
interpretation of results **3:** 1424
procedures **3:** 1423
uncertainty **3:** 1422, 1424
utility function **3:** 1422, 1423, 1424
See also
Decision theory
Decision oriented evaluation **3:** 1282, ***1425–1431***; **4:** 2102
betting model **3:** 1428
Center for the Study of Evaluation model **4:** 2102
context, input, process, product (CIPP) model **3:** 1282; **4:** 2102
cost-effectiveness model **4:** 2102
and national education policies **3:** 1429
national models **4:** 2103
evaluability assessment **4:** 2103
rapid feedback evaluation **4:** 2103
stakeholder-based **3:** 1428
utilization-focused **3:** 1428; **4:** 2102
Decision support systems
See Management information systems
Decision theory
Bayesian **3:** 1419
and classification **3:** 1418, 1419
combination of elementary decisions **3:** 1418
in educational testing **3:** ***1416–1421***
and mastery tests **3:** 1417, 1420
optimization **3:** 1419
and placement **3:** 1418, 1420
and selection **3:** 1417, 1420
utility function **3:** 1419
See also
decision-making theory
Declarative knowledge **3:** ***1432–1434***; **4:** 1996; **6:** 3153; **8:** 4821; **10:** 5740
and artificial intelligence **5:** 2919
and cognitive development **2:** 855
concept formation
and long term memory **2:** 1018
definition of **3:** 1432
and educational research **4:** 1996
and epistemic structure **3:** 1433
examples and characteristics of **3:** 1432
experts' use of **4:** 2196
learning **6:** 3321
learning strategies
and second language learning **6:** 3332
measurement of **1:** 371
Declining enrollment
developed nations **6:** 3604
management of **6:** ***3603–3608***
strategies **6:** 3605
Decoding (reading) **8:** 4942, 4944
Deduction **8:** 4723, 4950
in children **8:** 4953
age differences **8:** 4953
inferences **8:** 4953, 4954
cognitive processes **8:** 4954
and data analysis **3:** 1465
learning processes
computer simulation **8:** 4721
Defining Issues Test (DIT) **7:** 3917; **10:** 5936
Definitions
operational
and logical positivism in educational research **8:** 4633
Degrees (academic)
educational researchers **11:** 6442
Japan **6:** 3087
Deinstitutionalization (of disabled) **3:** ***1434–1438***
administration **3:** 1434
and community services **3:** 1434
and daily living skills instruction **3:** 1435
definitional and conceptual factors **3:** 1434
implementation
United States **3:** 1435
and mainstreaming **6:** 3558
Norway **3:** 1435, 1437
and permanency planning **3:** 1437
Sweden **3:** 1435
Delinquency **1:** 86; **3:** ***1438–1441***
definitions of **3:** 1438
and disabilities **3:** 1438
causal explanations **3:** 1439
differential treatment hypothesis **3:** 1439
ineffective problem-solving hypothesis **3:** 1440
school failure hypothesis **3:** 1439
susceptibility hypothesis **3:** 1439
juvenile justice **3:** ***1438–1441***
runaways **1:** 86
treatment and rehabilitation methods **3:** 1440
and youth subcultures **11:** 6799
as social adaption **11:** 6799
Delinquency causes
and conflict in schools **11:** 6800
disabilities and **3:** 1439
research **11:** 6799
Delinquency prevention **1:** 87
Delivery systems
educational technology **9:** 5542
public services
and school-based management **9:** 5305
Delphi technique **3:** ***1441–1443***
advantages **3:** 1442
computer networks **3:** 1442
disadvantages **3:** 1443
exploratory vs. normative procedures **3:** 1442
multiple groups **3:** 1442
questionnaires **3:** 1441
research on independent study **9:** 5396, 5398
Demagogy **1:** 275
Demand for education
See Educational demand
Demand elasticity
See Elasticity of demand
Demand occupations
employment projections **11:** 6258
and technological advancement **11:** ***6256–6261***
Dementia **8:** 4820
Democracy
and adult education **1:** 134, 136
as a barrier to productivity **9:** 5203
and citizenship **8:** 4575
and educational benefits **1:** 511
effect on vocational education
Latin America **7:** 4153
and equal education **8:** 4587
and evaluation studies **4:** 2035
and governance **8:** 4592
and literacy **1:** 175
models of
and governance theory **5:** 2510
and moral education **7:** 3924
and political socialization **8:** 4575
individual power **4:** 1982
and sociology of education **10:** 5604
vs. meritocracy **7:** 3771
Democratic values
and adult education
Central and Eastern Europe **2:** 660
attitude measures
cross-cultural comparison **1:** 394
and control of curriculum **3:** 1327
and educational principles
Dewey **3:** 1523
and educational responsibility **10:** 5988
and history instruction **5:** 2619
and humanities **5:** 2695
just communities approach **1:** 379
and nationalism **3:** 1651
and teacher education **10:** 5982, 5984, 5985
trends in education **1:** 113
Demography
and census data **2:** 649, 651
and curriculum
factors affecting **9:** 5520
educational planning **3:** ***1449–1453***, 1827
and access to education **3:** 1449
Japan **6:** 3086
and population education **8:** 4608
and recurrent education **8:** 4963
Demonstration programs
mathematics education
studies **3:** 1551
Demonstrations (educational) **10:** ***6140–6143***
cooperation
computer-assisted instruction **10:** 6143
evaluation **10:** 6143

teaching skills **10:** 6142
communication **10:** 6140
evaluation **10:** 6143
learning processes **10:** 6140, 6141
mathematics instruction **10:** 6141
physical education **10:** 6141
program development **10:** 6140
roles **10:** 6140
science instruction **10:** 6142
teacher education **6:** 3197
teacher student relationship **10:** 6140
technological advancement **10:** 6140
Denmark
adult basic education **7:** 4178
adult education
folkeoplysning **1:** 112; **7:** 4176
legislation **6:** 3361, 3363; **7:** 4177
nonformal education **3:** 1457
provision **6:** 3419
research **7:** 4179
apprenticeships **1:** 314
boards of education
and parent participation **5:** 2507
curriculum development **3:** 1458
education of music teachers **7:** 4028
educational change **3:** 1459, 1460
English language instruction
primary schools **4:** 2349
folk high schools **2:** 895, 897, 1190; **4:** 2388
courses **4:** 2325
historical background **5:** 2733, 2734
for the unemployed **6:** 3419
general education and vocational education **7:** 4177
government school relationship
and educational change **6:** 3600
financial support **3:** 1458
school administration **3:** 1457
inservice teacher education
LEARN network **10:** 6007
language **3:** 1453
mental retardation **3:** 1505, 1507
open education **11:** 6550
postsecondary education **3:** 1455
preschool education **2:** 695, 696; **3:** 1455
primary education **3:** 1454
school-based management **5:** 2507
school reform **9:** 5279
science education **8:** 4461
secondary education **3:** 1454
degrees and qualifications **3:** 1455
vocational education **3:** 1454
sign language **3:** 1400
special education **2:** 723; **3:** 1455
state church relationship
accommodation **9:** 5011
structure of government **3:** 1453
system of education **3:** ***1453–1461***
degrees and qualifications **3:** 1459
educational objectives **3:** 1453
major problems **3:** 1460
structure **3:** 1454
teacher education **3:** 1458
education courses **3:** 1723, 1724
teacher salaries **10:** 5843
teaching methodology **3:** 1459
technical education **3:** 1456
university adult education **11:** 6549
vocational education **3:** 1456
Denver Developmental Screening Test (DDST) **3:** 1622
Department of Education (US)
adult literacy assessment (1992) **8:** 4635
Department of Education and Science (DES) (UK)
curriculum history **3:** 1295
and educational planning **8:** 4598
and school inspectors **9:** 5250
Department of Labor (US)
literacy assessments (1989) **8:** 4635
Departmentalization
See Departments
Departments
in secondary schools
and effective schools research **9:** 5376
Departments of education
See Schools of education
Depression (psychology)
in children
and pessimistic explanatory style **9:** 5405
and drug use **3:** 1611; **8:** 4422
psychological patterns **9:** 5404
Depth perception
infants **8:** 4380
stereogram research **8:** 4381
Deschooling **6:** 3419; **8:** 4574
and recurrent education **8:** 4960
Descriptive knowledge
See Declarative knowledge
Descriptive scales
advantages and disadvantages of **3:** 1475
classroom environment measures **3:** 1481
cross area comparisons **3:** 1480
and educational climate
measurement of **3:** ***1475–1483***
in educational research
uses for **3:** 1482
explanatory power of **3:** 1480
reliability **3:** 1475
estimates **3:** 1478
student **3:** 1479
studies
college characteristics index **3:** 1476
Learning Environment Inventory **3:** 1477
Organizational Climate Description Questionnaire **3:** 1477
teaching emphasis **3:** 1479, 1481
validity **3:** 1476, 1480
vs. attitude measures **3:** 1482
vs. classroom observation techniques **3:** 1475
Desegregated schools
See School desegregation
Desegregation (disabled students)
See Mainstreaming
Desegregation effects
academic achievement **3:** 1483
Desegregation methods
implementation **3:** 1484
Desegregation plans
recommendations for **3:** 1485
in schools **3:** ***1483–1486***
Design
activities
and prototyping **8:** ***4799–4803***
art education **1:** 340, 341
objectives
and material development **8:** 4800
and program management **8:** 4756
requirements
and project evaluation **8:** 4781
systems approach to **10:** ***5895–5901***
and technology education **11:** 6289
Design effect
index of sample complexity **7:** 3737
and sampling errors **9:** 5125
Deskilling
See Skill obsolescence
Desktop publishing (DTP) **4:** ***1954–1958***
copyright implications **4:** 1955
educational effects of **4:** 1956
and educational research
dissemination of **3:** 1555
educational uses for **7:** 3814
and electronic publishing
compared **4:** 1955
and information networks
international **5:** 2997
markets for **4:** 1956
origin of term **4:** 1955
uses for **4:** 1955
See also
Electronic publishing
Deutscher Lehrerverein (*DLV*)
objectives **10:** 6074
Deutsches Institut für Internationale Pädagogische Forschung **2:** 939
Developed nations
adult education
nongovernmental organizations **7:** 4146
adult literacy **1:** ***100–103***
instructional materials **3:** 1260
apprenticeships **1:** 312
birth rate and literacy **1:** 181
compulsory education
and population trends **3:** 1452
concept of leisure **6:** 3374
continuing education
costs **2:** ***1146–1152***
dropout rate **9:** 5225
early childhood education **8:** 4674
economic change
effects on education **9:** 5186
educational administration
legal procedures **6:** 3274
educational change
and inservice education **1:** 69
educational planning

Asia **8:** 4487
educational policy
global approach **5:** 2495
educational research
dissemination of **3:** 1554, 1555
educational technology **4:** 1915; **9:** 5542
educational television **4:** 1904
employment policy and on-the-job training **6:** 3616
evaluation of public job training programs **4:** ***2145–2150***
family education
and economic status **4:** 2275
growth rate **3:** 1692
higher education
rate of return **3:** 1662
illiteracy **6:** 3454, 3455
impact of education on birth rate **3:** 1673
job training **7:** 4197
life expectancy **3:** 1450
and participatory research **7:** 4331
population
school age **3:** 1451
private education
excess demand model **8:** 4832
public education
management of contraction in **6:** 3604
reading difficulties
programs for **8:** 4931
secondary education for adults **1:** ***181–184***
social change
anthropological research **9:** 5509
teacher certification **10:** 5925
teachers
work environment **10:** 5843
technological advancement
and division of labor **3:** 1708
trade regimes
choice of **11:** 6634
transitional programs in **5:** 2939
vs. developing nations
educational finance **5:** 2979
public expenditures **2:** 1123
taxes **4:** 2312
youth unemployment **3:** 1706
Developing nations
academic achievement
and instructional materials **8:** 4847
access to education **9:** 5535
adult basic education **6:** 3362
adult education **1:** 118, 123
colonial model **5:** 2934
consciousness raising and mobilization **2:** ***1045–1049***
ideologies **5:** 2733, 2734
legislation **6:** 3363
nongovernmental organizations **7:** 4146
participatory research **5:** 2734, 2735
adult literacy
instructional materials **3:** 1260
adult literacy programs **1:** ***169–176***
apprenticeships **1:** 315; **11:** 6657
art education **1:** 342
and brain drain **1:** 554, 557
class size
input output analysis **3:** 1760
colonialism
effect of **8:** 4680
community education **2:** 908
community schools **2:** 891
computer uses in education **4:** 1900
cost effectiveness studies **2:** 1131
cultural context
and decentralization **3:** 1414
curriculum development **9:** 5522
day care
policies for **2:** 688
definition of **4:** 1899
distance education **4:** 1900
organizations **3:** 1581
telecommunications **1:** 562, 563
dropout rate
and sex differences **9:** 5227
dual labor market theory **3:** 1681
early childhood education **8:** 4672
education
tuition fees **10:** 5752
education work relationship
time factors (learning) **6:** 3549
educational administration
and decentralization **7:** 4245
legal procedures **6:** 3274
trends **3:** 1823
educational development **11:** 6524
and labor markets **3:** 1682
and publishing industry **8:** 4845
and social equality **9:** ***5532–5539***
educational facilities
input output analysis **3:** 1760
educational facilities planning **4:** 2224, 2226
educational finance **8:** 4520
and economic adjustment **3:** ***1784–1789***
vocational education **8:** 4359
educational history **2:** 1060
educational planning
adaptive strategies **8:** 4518
Asia **8:** 4487
and decentralization **3:** 1414
and economic adjustment **3:** 1788
history of **8:** 4490, 4501
implementation problems **3:** 1821
for teacher effectiveness **8:** ***4519–4526***
educational policy
and public policy **4:** 1838
studies **4:** 1838
educational quality
improvement policies **8:** ***4865–4873***
and instructional materials **8:** 4859
schools **8:** 4865
educational radio **5:** 2890
educational reform
policy statements **8:** 4514
educational research
problems **3:** 1553
teacher effectiveness **8:** 4869
educational resources **8:** 4520
and equal education **9:** 5537
educational technology **4:** ***1899–1903***, 1915; **9:** 5542
and disabilities **10:** 5668
examples **4:** 1900
future research **4:** 1902
trends and issues **4:** 1902
educational television **4:** 1904
and cost effectiveness studies **2:** 1134
elasticity of supply
empirical research **3:** 1448
employed women
and education **3:** ***1666–1672***
employment
and informal sector **5:** 2814
enrollment rate **3:** 1826; **4:** 2412
family education
and economic status **4:** 2275
family life education **4:** 2262
financial support
international **5:** 2989
grade repetition rate **9:** 5225
homeless children **3:** 1733
human capital
investments **11:** 6652
illiteracy **1:** 169
impact of education on birth rate **3:** 1672
income distribution **5:** 2743
individual attitudes **1:** 129
information networks
problems **5:** 2995, 2997
information technology industry **4:** 1900
input output analysis
research **3:** 1759
internal labor market **5:** 2940
international agencies
assistance experts **5:** 2973
international aid
factors affecting **5:** 2963
nature of **5:** 2962
international education
problems with **5:** 2975
job security
effects on training **11:** 6636
job training **7:** 4197
labor force participation
females **3:** 1682
labor force planning **6:** 3609
labor market
and education **3:** ***1681–1685***
and productivity **3:** 1693
leadership training **1:** 69
learning disabilities
educational strategies for **10:** 5685
research recommendations **10:** 5685
life expectancy **3:** 1450
mathematics education
computer uses in **7:** 4098
national training tax system **1:** 110
nonformal education **4:** 2366; **6:** 3421
comparative analysis **7:** ***4132–4136***

policy **7:** ***4141–4145***
resource allocation **7:** 4140
resources **2:** 1150
and second chance education **9:** 5366
occupational mobility
and equal education **9:** 5537
occupational segregation **4:** 2430
and official development assistance **5:** 2961
onservice teacher education **10:** ***5977–5982***
open universities **7:** 4216
paraprofessional personnel
training of **11:** 6269
and participatory research **7:** 4330
and performance contracts **8:** 4714
policy formation
integrated **10:** 6035
population
school age **3:** 1451
post school training **11:** 6246
postsecondary education
and educational equity (finance) **3:** 1792, 1793
preschool education **2:** 681
benefits **8:** 4665
primary education
and economic crisis **9:** 5538
empirical studies **8:** 4702
financial support **7:** 4138, 4140
primary education finance **7:** 4138, 4140
principals
recruitment **1:** 68
private education
excess demand model **8:** 4832
private schools
costs **8:** ***4702–4708***
production
technology transfer models **11:** 6278
productivity
and equal education **9:** 5536
public education
management of contraction in **6:** 3603
public schools
costs **8:** ***4702–4708***
vs. private schools **8:** 4843
public sector employment **3:** 1706; **8:** 4838
policies **11:** 6634
recurrent education policies **8:** 4963
resource allocation
studies **2:** 1124
rural to urban migration **3:** 1682
determinants of **5:** 2943, 2945
and educational policy **5:** 2510
school administration
problems **9:** 5163
school enterprise
and cost recovery **9:** 5229
school statistics
trends **11:** 6297
schools
decentralization **3:** ***1412–1416***
science education **9:** 5326
and scientific literacy **9:** 5347
secondary education
access to **9:** 5388
empirical studies **8:** 4702
segmentation theory **6:** 3188
severance pay
studies **11:** 6636
skill development **11:** 6648
classification **10:** 5916
small business training **4:** 1988
social change
anthropological perspective **9:** 5508
social welfare education **1:** 116
student loan programs **10:** 5763, 5765
student textbook ratio **8:** 4696
syllabi **10:** 5883
tax deduction systems
geographic distribution **8:** 4361
teacher certification **10:** 5925
teacher education
input output analysis **3:** 1760
and special education **10:** 5940
trends **10:** 6042
teacher experience
input output analysis **3:** 1760
teacher salaries **8:** 4520
input output analysis **3:** 1760
teachers
work environment **10:** 5843
technical assistance **5:** 2999
technical education
coordination of **10:** 6064
technological advancement
and division of labor **3:** 1708
technology education **11:** 6288, 6291
textbook preparation
planning for **11:** ***6360–6366***
textbooks
availability **8:** 4694, 4696, 4846
input output analysis **3:** 1761
provision **11:** 6360
trade regimes
choice of **11:** 6634
training
government role in **11:** 6425
transnational publishing
influences on education **8:** 4846
underemployment **3:** 1682
vocational education
disadvantaged youth **11:** 6249
education with production **3:** 1687, 1688
and informal sector **5:** 2814
international aid **11:** 6660
planning for **8:** 4528
and private sector **11:** 6247
rate of return **9:** ***5071–5076***
and teacher shortage **10:** 6063
training with production **11:** 6447
vocational education and training
cost effectiveness improvement **11:** ***6648–6653***
vocational schools **11:** 6657
criticisms of **11:** 6267
vs. developed nations
educational finance **5:** 2979
public expenditures **2:** 1123
taxes **4:** 2312
women and leisure time **6:** 3375
and workplace literacy **5:** 2688
Development
and adult education
francophone Africa **1:** 215, 217
India **5:** 2756, 2758
adult education for **1:** ***127–135***; **5:** 2934, 2935, 2946
aid
and literacy programs **1:** 132
aid agencies
in adult education **1:** 132
concept of **3:** 1495
consciousness raising and popular education approaches **2:** ***1045–1049***
definitions of **3:** 1648
dominant approaches and social costs **2:** 1048
and education **3:** ***1648–1655***; **5:** 2663
and evolutionary processes **4:** 2168
as the goal of education **5:** 2664
institution building **4:** 2367
and literacy education **1:** 169; **6:** 3454
Asia **6:** 3464
and nonformal education **1:** 128
finance **2:** 1150
financial support **7:** 4140
as the prerequisite of education **5:** 2664
relationship of agents with client communities **4:** 2365, 2367
as a result of education **5:** 2664
and social justice **2:** 905
sustainable
and environmental influences **4:** 1994
systems approach to **10:** ***5895–5901***
See also
Educational development
Development education **3:** ***1494–1501***
Canada **3:** 1496
common characteristics of **3:** 1498
differences in practice **3:** 1499
financial support **3:** 1499
future directions **3:** 1500
historical background **3:** 1495
Netherlands **3:** 1496
Norway **3:** 1496
and population education **8:** 4609
problems in teaching **3:** 1499
tensions in **3:** 1499
United Kingdom **3:** 1498
United States **3:** 1497
working definition **3:** 1495
Developmental continuity
individual development **6:** ***3425–3428***
lifelong learning **6:** 3427
developmental reserve capacity **6:** 3427
longitudinal studies **6:** 3426

Developmental disabilities
behavior disorders **3:** 1516
handicap identification **3:** 1621
interdisciplinary approach **3:** 1519
longitudinal studies **3:** 1519
pervasive developmental disorders **3:** 1515
psychopathology **3:** ***1514–1520***
remedial programs
young children **5:** 2809
severe disabilities **3:** ***1504–1508***
definition of **3:** 1505
educational discrimination **3:** 1506
handicap discrimination **3:** 1506
mainstreaming **3:** 1506
normalization (handicapped) **3:** 1505
public policy **3:** ***1504–1508***
remedial programs **3:** 1505
residential care **3:** 1505
social attitudes **3:** 1504
social integration **3:** 1506
special education **3:** 1505
supported inclusion **3:** 1507
specific developmental disorders **3:** 1515
young children
screening tests **3:** ***1621–1624***
Developmental psychology **2:** 842; **8:** 4817
adult development **8:** 4817
biological differences **8:** 4817
lifespan development **8:** 4817
stage and process models **8:** 4817
adult education **8:** 4822
behaviorism **1:** ***495–497***
and child psychology **5:** 2656
constructivism in **5:** 2666
cross-sectional studies **5:** 2657
developmental continuity **6:** 3426
basic concepts **6:** 3426
ecological models **3:** ***1643–1647***
and educational practices **5:** ***2666–2670***
empiricism in **5:** 2667
and evolutionary theory **5:** 2656
historical background **5:** 2656
history of educational research **4:** 1865
individual development **5:** 2647
individual differences **5:** 2657; **8:** 4482
infant cognitive development **5:** 2799
interactional models **8:** 4716
maturation–degeneration hypothesis **5:** 2657
mechanistic model **5:** 2658
organismic model **5:** 2658
contextualism **5:** 2659
person-centered approach **5:** 2659
personality development **11:** 6310
pluralistic models **5:** 2660
and psychodynamics **8:** 4812
and resilience **8:** 4775
responses to crises
individual differences **8:** 4716
structuralist approaches **8:** 4482
task analysis **8:** 4482
theories of **5:** 2658
unidirectional models **5:** 2659
variable-centered approach **5:** 2659
Developmental psychopathology
See Psychopathology, developmental disabilities
Developmental research
individual development **5:** ***2673–2677***
cohort analysis **5:** 2675
cross-sectional studies **5:** 2673
designs **5:** 2673
intervention studies **5:** 2676
longitudinal studies **5:** 2674
microdevelopmental studies **5:** 2676
multivariate developmental paradigm **5:** 2673
single case studies **5:** 2676
time lag studies **5:** 2675
training studies **5:** 2676
univariate developmental paradigm **5:** 2673
Developmental screening
See Screening tests, developmental disabilities
Developmental stages
adulthood **8:** 4817
classic theories **5:** 2677
and curriculum development **5:** 2666
environmental theories **5:** 2677
and evolutionary theory **5:** 2656
individual development **5:** ***2677–2681***
interactional theories **5:** 2677
maturation theories **5:** 2677
measurement of **3:** ***1508–1514***
analysis method **3:** 1511
future trends **3:** 1513
methods **3:** 1509
models **3:** 1510
multiple tasks method **3:** 1509
partial credit method **3:** 1509
Saltus model **3:** 1512
Montessori method **5:** 2608
and primary school admission **5:** 2654
research methodology **5:** ***2673–2677***
and socialization **10:** 5587
statistical analysis **5:** 2679
theories involving **3:** 1508
and time factors (learning) **2:** 850
transition crises **8:** 4716
usefulness of concept **5:** 2680
See also
Child development
Cognitive development
Piagetian theory
Developmental tasks
adult development
teachers **10:** 5935
adult learning **6:** 3431
in adulthood **8:** 4819
and age **6:** 3427
Havighurst's sequence **8:** 4716
and individual development **8:** 4716
Piagetian theory
criticism of **2:** 851
sources of **8:** 4716
Developmental toxicology **1:** 13
and neurological impairment **1:** 14
Developmental verbal dyspraxia
See Verbal dyspraxia
Développement communautaire **6:** 3420
Diagnostic and Statistical Manual of Mental Disorders (DSM III-R) **1:** 487; **3:** 1515; **7:** 3826
Diagnostic teaching **5:** 2809; **10:** ***6086–6088***, ***6169–6173***
aptitude treatment interaction **10:** 6170
beliefs about
criticism of **10:** 6170
decision-making **10:** 6169
individualized instruction **10:** 6169
special education **10:** 6170
and student needs **10:** ***5768–5772***
relevance **10:** 5768
summative evaluation **10:** 6171
Diagnostic tests **10:** 6171
and cognitive development **1:** 5
development of **5:** 2875
and educational assessment **1:** 364, 366
giftedness
problems with **5:** 2728
reading **7:** 3931
special needs students **2:** 713, 715
and student needs **10:** 5770
Diagrams
and concept maps **2:** 1026
mathematical models **6:** 3659
Dialectical learning
adult capacity **8:** 4819, 4820, 4823
adult education **5:** 2734, 2735
Dialects **6:** 3225
characteristic features
socioeconomic influences **6:** 3225
and cultural differences **6:** 3225
and language styles **6:** 3225
Dialogs (language)
and questioning techniques **8:** 4877
Dialogs (literary)
Socratic **8:** 4532, 4535
Dictation
scholasticism **9:** 5123
Didacticism
and adult education
Central and Eastern Europe **2:** 657
conventional instruction
Israel **5:** 2533
United States **5:** 2533
Didactics
Germany **3:** 1289
Diethylstilbesterol (DES) **1:** 14
Difference scores
and change
measurement of **2:** 671
criticisms of **2:** 672
Differential aptitude tests (DAT) **1:** 1
and vocational evaluation **11:** 6671
Differential item performance
See Item bias

Differential psychology
  See Individual psychology
Differential test battery
  and vocational evaluation **11:** 6671
Difficulty level
  academic learning time **1:** 22
  test items
    and item bias **5:** 3044, 3049
    and sampling **9:** 5139
Diffusion (communication)
  innovations **3:** ***1549–1553***
  knowledge **3:** ***1549–1553***
  linkage **3:** 1550
  problem-solving **3:** 1550
  research–development–diffusion (RDD) model **3:** 1550
  theories of **3:** 1550
Diphenylhydantoin (DPH) **1:** 14
Direct instruction **3:** ***1524–1530***
  cognitive development **3:** 1528
  cognitive processes **3:** 1526
    academic achievement **3:** 1526
    reading comprehension **3:** 1526
  criticism of **3:** 1527
  fundamental concepts of **3:** 1527, 1528
  teacher effectiveness **3:** 1525
  See also
    Programmed tutoring
Disabilities
  and career education **2:** ***631–635***
  categories of **2:** 719
  census figures **3:** 1530
  in children
    effect on families **4:** ***1976–1980***
    social integration **2:** 723
  and civil rights **3:** 1435, 1437, 1506
  cohort analysis **3:** 1530
  communication disorders
    and educational opportunities **1:** 408
  conceptualization
    and mainstreaming **6:** 3557
  cultural attitudes
    and intervention models **5:** 2807
  deficit model **2:** 861; **3:** 1506
  definitions of **2:** 719
    international comparison **5:** 2908
  and deinstitutionalization (of disabled) **3:** ***1434–1438***
  and delinquency **3:** 1438
  education work relationship
    transition **11:** ***6457–6461***
  educational attainment
    and school attendance **3:** 1533
  and educational environment **3:** 1533
  and educational finance **9:** 5238
  and educational opportunities **3:** 1533
  and educational technology **10:** 5668
  gifted children with **5:** 2489
  and handicap identification **10:** 5665
  incidence **3:** 1532
    in children, United States **2:** 720
    by type **3:** 1533
  and interpersonal competence
    children **9:** 5564
  legislation
    on rights **2:** 712; **5:** 2574
  mainstreaming **5:** ***2903–2907***, ***2907–2910***; **6:** ***3556–3560***
  national surveys **3:** 1530
    comparative analysis **3:** 1530
  and need for career education **2:** 632
    functional curriculum **2:** 632
  peer teaching **8:** ***4372–4376***
  and preschool education **8:** 4663
  and preschool evaluation **4:** 2141
  registration programs **3:** 1530
  and resilience **8:** ***4775–4780***
  resource centers **5:** 2906
  special education **2:** ***719–730***; **5:** 2566
  statistical surveys **3:** ***1530–1534***
    data collection **3:** 1530
  and theories of evolution **10:** 5659
  types of **10:** 5692
  and unemployment rate **11:** 6457
  and vocational adjustment **2:** 633
  and vocational education
    United States **11:** 6532
  vs. disadvantaged
    semantics **8:** 4931
  See also
    Communication disorders
    Developmental disabilities
    Language handicaps
    Learning disabilities
    Mental disorders
    Mental retardation
    Perceptual handicaps
    Physical disabilities
Disabled
  See Disabilities
Disadvantaged
  adult education **1:** 112
  definition of **6:** 3213
  education of **8:** 4931
  and educational change **1:** 159
  and educational philosophy of justice **8:** 4574
  and educational voucher systems **9:** 5205
  equal opportunities (jobs) **11:** 6669
  and ethnicity **8:** 4892
  and functional illiteracy **8:** 4636
  and general education **5:** 2733
  gifted **5:** 2486
  language acquisition
    and learning **6:** ***3213–3216***
  and literacy skills **8:** 4635
  and nonverbal communication **7:** 4174
  outcomes of education **9:** 5508
  and participatory research **7:** 4332
  preschool education
    mediated effects **11:** 6382
  and related services personnel **9:** 5281
  in schools
    and Marxian analysis **6:** 3620
  and second chance education **9:** 5365
  and test bias **11:** 6317
  and universal basic education **6:** 3421
  and vocational education
    Latin America **7:** ***4148–4155***
    United States **11:** 6532
  vs. disabilities
    semantics **8:** 4931
  See also
    Economically disadvantaged
    Educationally disadvantaged
    Gifted disadvantaged
Disadvantaged environment
  and access to education
    nonformal education **7:** 4134
  high risk students **2:** 707
    early intervention **2:** 707
Disadvantaged youth
  curriculum adaptation **3:** 1254
  and motivation
    educational policies for **5:** 2499
  preschool education **8:** 4670
    cost effectiveness studies **2:** 1130
  and resilience **8:** ***4775–4780***
  and resource allocation **9:** 5062, 5238
  and social change **2:** 707
  vocational education **11:** 6249
Discipline **2:** ***816–820***; **3:** ***1534–1538***, 1537; **10:** ***6026–6031***
  behavior modification **1:** ***483–486***; **3:** 1536
  and beliefs **3:** 1537
  classroom techniques **3:** 1537
  and cultural context **3:** 1534
  and desegregation effects **3:** 1535
  Durkheim's views **2:** 778
  and educational environment **3:** 1537
  Herbart's views **5:** 2577
  and high school equivalency programs **3:** 1535
  individual approaches **3:** 1536
  interpretations of term **3:** 1535
  Locke's theories **6:** 3497
  positive reinforcement **9:** 4976
  research
    United States **3:** 1535
  and social values **3:** 1534
  teacher role **10:** 6027
Discipline policy **3:** 1536
  college students **10:** 5801
  corporal punishment **3:** 1536
  school policy **3:** 1535
Discipline problems
  and personality traits **11:** 6308
Disciplines (intellectual)
  See Intellectual disciplines
Discourse analysis
  classroom communication **2:** 798; **6:** 3237
  and critical thinking **2:** 1207
  and curriculum development
    sociology **3:** 1347
  feminist view **4:** 2300
    poststructuralism **5:** 2453, 2454, 2456
  function of **2:** 1196
  interpsychological studies **3:** 1249
  mathematics instruction **6:** 3635
  research **2:** 1207

stereotypes
teacher expectations of students **6:** 3237
and truth claims **2:** 1202
Discourse modes
in schools
initiation response evaluation (IRE) model **6:** 3215
Discourse participation
and learning experience **6:** 3298
Discovery learning **2:** 1177; **3:** ***1538–1544***; **7:** 3885
academic achievement **3:** 1542
and aptitude treatment interaction **10:** 6158
and computer-assisted instruction **2:** 990
criticisms of **3:** 1539
and curriculum development
AKTIF curriculum **3:** 1354
deduction **3:** 1540
discussion (teaching technique) **3:** 1541
induction **3:** 1540
instructional effectiveness **3:** 1542
science curriculum **3:** 1543
intellectual development **3:** 1538
learner controlled instruction **3:** 1540
learning motivation **3:** 1538
Piagetian theory **5:** 2881
retention (psychology) **3:** 1538
Discrete mathematics **6:** 3682
definition of **6:** 3682
mathematics curriculum **6:** 3683
secondary school curriculum **6:** 3683
Discriminant analysis **3:** ***1544–1549***
and career development **3:** 1544, 1548
and classification **3:** 1544, 1545
examples **3:** 1545, 1548
functions **3:** 1545, 1546
choice of scale **3:** 1546
interpretation of **3:** 1548
history of **3:** 1544
mathematics of **3:** 1546
multiple groups **3:** 1545
and multivariate analysis **7:** 4010
and prediction **8:** 4656
primary function of **3:** 1545
See also
Multivariate analysis
Discriminant function analysis
See Discriminant analysis, functions
Discrimination learning **5:** 2880
classificatory behavior **2:** 1017, 1018
computer simulation **8:** 4720
Discussion
cognitive outcomes **5:** 2531
group dynamics **2:** 803
history of **2:** 804
prerequisites **2:** 804
questioning techniques
scholasticism **9:** 5122
school environment **2:** 806
social environment **2:** 806
use of language
and philosophy of education **8:** 4460
See also
Interpersonal communication
Discussion (teaching technique) **2:** ***803–807***
and adult learning **10:** 6200
in classrooms **10:** 5791
cognitive processes **2:** 804
and computer-assisted instruction **2:** 990
educational effectiveness
criticism of **2:** 805
history of **2:** 804
and questioning techniques **8:** 4877
statistical analysis **2:** 803
student characteristics **2:** 805
student development **2:** 806
teacher attitudes **2:** 806
teacher characteristics **2:** 805
teacher role **2:** 805
vs. recitation
social studies **9:** 5582
Discussion groups
adult education **5:** ***2529–2532***; **10:** 6200
attributes of **5:** 2531
cohesion **5:** 2531
composition **5:** 2531
size **5:** 2531
and learning **6:** 3298
small group instruction **5:** 2528
workshops
learning strategies **1:** 192
Disease control
preventive medicine **5:** 2566
Disengagement theory **9:** ***5224–5228***
characteristics of **9:** 5224
and ethnicity **9:** 5227
and grade repetition rate **9:** 5226
measurement **9:** 5224
variables **9:** 5226
rural and urban areas **9:** 5227
and sex differences **9:** 5227
and socioeconomic status **9:** 5226
Disequilibrium theory
and productivity **3:** 1691
Disk drives
microcomputers **7:** 3812
Display aids
and profile analysis **8:** 4752
Display systems
and profile analysis **8:** 4752
screen design
and courseware design **2:** 1168
Dissemination
and project evaluation **8:** 4782
Dissertation Abstracts Online (DAO) **1:** 141
Distance education **6:** 3419
access to educational media **7:** 3758
access vs. advanced technology **3:** 1577
adult basic education **3:** 1571
Europe **7:** 4247
adult education **3:** ***1557–1563***; **10:** 5594
Nordic countries **7:** 4177
adult educators
teacher education **11:** 6434
and adult learning **1:** 166; **10:** 6201
Asia **1:** 350, 352
characteristics of **10:** 5594
classroom interaction vs. instructional design **3:** 1578
communications satellites
evaluation **5:** 2628
compared with conventional instruction **3:** 1557, 1562, 1568
and computer-assisted instruction **3:** 1561; **4:** 2185; **11:** 6301
and computer networks **2:** 978
continuing education **3:** 1559, 1571
cost effectiveness evaluation **3:** ***1567–1573***
costs **2:** 1149; **3:** 1576; **7:** 4139
counseling **2:** 1164; **3:** 1562
course development **3:** 1560
criticism of **4:** 1908
definitions of **3:** 1557, 1563, 1568
developing nations **4:** 1900
examples **4:** 1900
development of **3:** 1558
dropout research **3:** 1600
dual mode institutions **3:** 1575
economic impact
evaluation **3:** ***1567–1573***
and economic theory **3:** 1569
economics of **4:** 1907
educational broadcasting **3:** 1575
production standards **3:** 1575
and educational policy **3:** 1566
and educational technology **3:** ***1573–1580***; **9:** 5541
Ethiopia **4:** 2039
evaluation **3:** 1562
and file transfer **11:** 6299
functions of **3:** 1559
future research **3:** 1579
Guadeloupe and Martinique **5:** 2541
guidance **3:** 1562
historical background **3:** 1558, 1563
Hong Kong **5:** 2639
Iceland **5:** 2718
India **5:** 2749
Indonesia **5:** 2786, 2791
industrial model **3:** 1575
instructional materials **3:** 1560
international **5:** 2934
international organizations **3:** ***1580–1584***
Iran **5:** 3008
Ireland, Republic of **5:** 3016
large scale **7:** 4217
live interaction vs. flexibility **3:** 1577
mass media role in **2:** 884
media choice **3:** 1564
and media programs **7:** 3755
and media research **3:** 1571
mentors **3:** 1562
and modernity **10:** 5595

multimedia **3:** 1575
networks **7:** 4217
Norway **7:** 4190
open education **3:** 1557; **4:** 2330
outreach programs **7:** 4247
Pakistan **7:** 4267
Papua New Guinea **7:** 4277
periodicals **3:** ***1580–1584***
Portugal **8:** 4626
postsecondary education **3:** 1559, 1570
practice of **3:** 1559
in primary education **3:** 1558, 1571
programs **3:** 1559
provision **3:** 1558
rationales for **4:** 1899
rural education **1:** 240
Russia **9:** 5102
in schools **3:** ***1563–1567***
examples **3:** 1566
international review **3:** 1564
in secondary education **3:** 1559, 1571
single media **3:** 1574
small scale **7:** 4217
Soviet Union (former) **9:** 5093
Spain **10:** 5652
special education **5:** 2970
student support systems **10:** 5806
target population **3:** 1570
and teacher shortage **3:** 1570
teachers in **3:** 1570
and technological advancement stages **3:** 1574
and telecommunications **3:** 1561
teacher education **10:** 6007
two-way interactive **3:** 1576
typology of systems **3:** 1569
unit costs **3:** 1572
and universities **3:** 1570
university adult education **11:** 6549, 6550
vs. face-to-face instruction **3:** 1577
within school and out of school **3:** 1569, 1571
See also
Broadcast education
Correspondence study
Open universities
Distance learning
See Distance education
DISTAR
academic achievement
at risk persons **3:** 1527
Distinctive features (language)
and speech handicaps **10:** 5695
Distractors (tests)
and item bias **5:** 3047
Distribution-free statistics
See Nonparametric statistics
Distributions (statistical)
See Statistical distributions
Divergent thinking **8:** 4723
and cognitive style
gifted **5:** 2493
Division of labor
and economic change
government role in **3:** 1710
economic groups
categories **3:** 1709
female access to education **4:** 2407
international
and education **3:** ***1707–1713***
and information economy **3:** 1708
sexual **4:** 2281, 2282; **11:** 6741
Divorce
effects of education on **2:** 1054
and family life education **4:** 2264
Doctoral degrees
and educational researchers **11:** 6439
sex discrimination **11:** 6709
Doctoral dissertations
adult education **1:** 140
and educational researchers **11:** 6439, 6442
Doctoral programs
and educational researchers **11:** 6439, 6441, 6442
Document analysis
See Content analysis
Documentation
comparative education **3:** ***1584–1589***
international education **3:** ***1584–1589***
and management information systems **5:** 2830
production
and laser printers **8:** 4690
systems
regional education **3:** ***1589–1593***
Dogmatism
and values education **7:** 3922
Domain mastery tests
See Mastery tests
Domain referenced tests
and educational assessment **1:** 368
use of term **2:** 1183
See also
Achievement tests
Criterion referenced tests
Dominica
adult education **3:** 1596
curriculum development **3:** 1597
educational change **3:** 1598
educational research **3:** 1598
government school relationship
financial support **3:** 1597
school administration **3:** 1597
language **3:** 1593
postsecondary education **3:** 1595
preschool education **3:** 1596
primary education **3:** 1595
secondary education **3:** 1595
vocational education **3:** 1595
special education **3:** 1596
system of education **3:** ***1593–1599***
degrees and qualifications **3:** 1598
educational objectives **3:** 1594
structure **3:** 1595
teacher education **3:** 1595, 1597
teacher recruitment **3:** 1597
technical education **3:** 1596
Dominican Republic
educational radio **4:** 1906
interactive **5:** 2887
popular education **1:** 133
public schools vs. private schools **8:** 4843
Donors
and educational planning
Asia **8:** 4486
and educational policy **5:** 2511
and educational research **5:** 2964
role of **5:** 2962
textbooks
provision **11:** 6361
See also
Aid agencies
Dormitories
college students **10:** 5801
Downs syndrome
early reading **6:** 3461
effect on learning **5:** 2564
intelligence quotient **5:** 2463
and mainstreaming **6:** 3558
Drama
intercultural communication **8:** 4384
objectives and methods of educational programs **8:** 4386
in religious education **9:** 5002
Dramatic play **8:** 4541
Draw-a-person Test **8:** 4791
Dreams
achievement imagery
cultural differences **3:** 1238
Drills (practice)
computerized **2:** 988
science education **7:** 4103
variable interval performance **2:** 1168
feedback in **4:** 2280, 2282
and learning **6:** 3300
Dropout characteristics **1:** 183
Dropout prevention
adult education **3:** 1601
cost effectiveness studies **2:** 1130
remedies **3:** 1606
Dropout programs
Career Intern Program (US)
ethnographic evaluation **4:** 2044
Dropout rate
adult literacy **1:** 173
Argentina **1:** 334
Brunei Darussalam **1:** 572
calculation of **3:** 1603
comparative analysis
effect on Latin America **3:** 1831
Côte d'Ivoire **2:** 1153
Dominica **3:** 1595
El Salvador **4:** 1949
female blacks
South Africa **7:** 3851
females
India **11:** 6750
Guinea-Bissau **5:** 2561
Mali **6:** 3581
measurement problems **9:** 5225
problems **3:** 1604

and program evaluation **8:** 4759
types of **3:** 1603
United States **11:** 6540
urban schools **11:** 6554
United States **5:** 2688
Dropout research
adult basic education **3:** 1600, 1601
adult education **3:** ***1599–1602***
commitment and integration model **3:** 1601
congruence model **3:** 1601
expectancy-valence model **3:** 1601
program variables **3:** 1600
psychological variables **3:** 1600
situational variables **3:** 1600
teaching-learning variables **3:** 1600
theoretical issues **3:** 1601
distance education **3:** 1600
higher education **3:** 1600, 1601
Dropouts **9:** ***5224–5228***
adult education **3:** ***1599–1602***
and adult education provision **1:** ***181–184***
apprenticeships
Africa **1:** 223
categories of **9:** 5224
causal factors **3:** 1604
consequential factors **3:** 1605
definition of **3:** 1602
delinquency
and mild disabilities **3:** 1439
and grade repetition **5:** 2513
homeless children **3:** 1734
and literacy retention **6:** 3476
national ethnographic evaluation **4:** 2044
open universities **7:** 4218
screening hypothesis **9:** 5352
and sociology of education **10:** 5604
and student experience
of curriculum **10:** 5816
and truancy **3:** ***1602–1607***
See also
Expulsion
Truancy
Drug abuse
adolescents
and academic failure **5:** 2568
characteristics and effects **3:** 1618
drug education **3:** ***1607–1610***
effect on learning **3:** 1612
effects of drug education on
program evaluation **3:** 1610
identification by teachers **3:** 1618
Drug education **4:** 2330
curriculum **3:** 1618
drug abuse **3:** ***1607–1610***
background **3:** 1608
course content **3:** 1609
curriculum **3:** 1608
effectiveness factors **3:** 1610
evaluation studies **3:** 1609
ex-users **3:** 1609
health personnel **3:** 1609
objectives **3:** 1608
police **3:** 1609
prevention programs **3:** 1608
student volunteers **3:** 1609
target groups **3:** 1608
teachers **3:** 1609
teaching methods **3:** 1609
teaching methods
alternative activities approach **3:** 1609
authoritative source approach **3:** 1609
coping skills **3:** 1609
logical argument **3:** 1609
negative reinforcement **3:** 1609
peer teaching **3:** 1609
values clarification **3:** 1609
Drug prevention education
See Drug education, drug abuse
Drug therapy
behavioral and cognitive effects in **8:** 4420
in children **8:** ***4419–4424***
historical background **8:** 4419
management of
school personnel **8:** 4420
side effects **8:** 4423
Drug use
children
and parent attitudes **8:** 4420
effect on learning efficiency **3:** 1611
negative **3:** 1612
positive **3:** 1611
in pregnancy
and congenital impairment **1:** 13
stimulants **3:** 1611
teacher attitudes **3:** 1618
Drugs
and education **3:** ***1611–1619***
Dual labor market theory **6:** 3184; **8:** 4837
criticism of **6:** 3186
developing nations **3:** 1681
and efficiency wage model **6:** 3187
and feedback **6:** 3185, 3187
internal labor market **6:** 3184
on-the-job training **6:** 3184
and unemployment **6:** 3185
See also
Segmentation theory
Dual system
See Apprenticeships
Dualism
and constructivism **2:** 1049, 1050, 1051
Descartes' **3:** 1462
Duncan Socio-Economic Index (SEI) **7:** 3717
Dyslexia **7:** ***4077–4081***
and brain hemisphere functions **7:** 4078
as congenital impairment **7:** 4078
diagnostic problems **7:** 4078
as perceptual handicap **7:** 4078
prevalence of **10:** 5678
remedial reading **7:** 4080
use of term **8:** 4932
Early childhood
See Young children
Early childhood education
assessment **1:** ***358–362***
child development **3:** 1625
international studies **8:** 4670
definition of **3:** 1629
developed nations **8:** 4674
developing nations **8:** 4672
developmental programs **5:** 2808
early intervention **5:** 2808
female participation **3:** 1627
international studies **3:** ***1624–1629***
preschool children **3:** 1627
effect on primary school performance
developing nations **2:** 681
functions **3:** 1629
issues in 1990s **8:** 4675
long-range planning **4:** 2329
long-term effectiveness **2:** 679
parent education **7:** ***4294–4296***
parent participation **7:** ***4296–4302***
philosophy of education
Comenius **8:** 4667
Plato **8:** 4667
Quintilian **8:** 4888
Rousseau **8:** 4667
preschool education **8:** ***4666–4670***
preschool evaluation **4:** ***2141–2145***
as a profession **3:** 1629
professional personnel **3:** 1630, 1632
social influences **8:** 4667
teacher education **3:** ***1629–1636***
child development studies **3:** 1632, 1633
teaching methods **3:** 1632
variation in levels **3:** 1629
teacher qualifications **3:** 1629, 1634
teacher salaries **3:** 1634
teachers
working conditions **3:** 1634
See also
Preschool education
Primary education
Early childhood programs **5:** ***2806–2814***
caregiving **5:** 2808
child-centered approaches **5:** 2808, 2809
cultural differences **5:** 2806, 2807
family-centered approaches **5:** 2810
features **5:** 2808
parent participation **5:** 2806, 2810
program effectiveness **5:** 2812
UNESCO **11:** 6526, 6528
United States **5:** 2807
Early experience
and cognitive development **5:** 2661
effect on infant behavior **5:** 2799
individual development **3:** ***1636–1643***
and parent education **7:** 4294
and personality development **5:** 2661, 2662
Early intervention
and community development **3:** 1625
developmental disabilities
and screening tests **3:** 1621
disabled children

effect on child development
3: 1640
disadvantaged children
effect on child development
3: 1640
early childhood care
and developmental programs
3: 1625, 1626
early childhood education
international studies 3: ***1624–1629***
effect on primary school performance
3: 1625
and equal education 3: 1625
financial support 3: 1626
longitudinal studies
United States 3: 1625
parent education 7: 4298
young children 5: ***2806–2814***
Early reading
parent role 6: 3459
Early school leavers
See Dropouts
Early School Personality Questionnaire (ESPQ) 8: 4398
Early Screening Inventory (ESI)
3: 1623
Early Teaching of Modern Languages (ETML) 4: 2346
Earnings
and ability 3: 1659; 5: 2645
and education 3: ***1655–1660***
bias in estimates on 6: 3142
educational benefits 1: 513
empirical research 3: 1656
factors affecting 3: 1746
and education work relationship
3: ***1746–1750***
and educational background 3: 1702, 1703
factors affecting
internal labor market 5: 2938
noneducational 3: 1655
forgone
and time factors (learning) 6: 3547
internal labor market
used for analyses of 5: 2940
and job skill requirements
measurement 11: 6257
potential
and enrollment rate 6: 3099, 3100
productivity
and screening hypothesis 9: 5351
rural–urban differences 5: 2943
See also
Age–earnings profiles
Income
Earnings differentials
and academic achievement 3: 1657
cost per unit comparison 8: 4567
age–earnings profiles 3: 1658
causes of 4: 2444
sex bias 4: 2441
child care occupations
determinants 2: 689
and education 1: 517; 3: ***1655–1660***
cost effectiveness 2: 1128
vintage effects 11: ***6614–6615***
education work relationship 3: 1746
educational administration 8: 4406
and educational levels 3: 1703
effects on
on-the-job training model 7: 4207, 4209
and employment level 4: 2275
compensating differential method
4: 2275
empirical research 4: 2277
equalization of 3: 1747
ethnic groups 8: ***4896–4902***
experience–earnings profiles 3: 1658
factors affecting 3: 1659
human capital model 8: 4899
immigrant males vs. indigenous males
5: 2738
immigrants
and ability 5: 2737, 2738
and length of residence 5: 2739
in input output analysis measurement
3: 1757
and job skill requirements 11: 6260
and job training 8: 4711
research study 7: 4199
and labor market
labor market stratification model
6: 3181
labor market analysis
informal sector 3: 1677
as a measure of productivity 3: 1690; 11: 6629
measurement
vs. productivity 8: 4913
and monopsony discrimination
4: 2444
and multiple regression analysis
9: 4973
occupational segregation
and sex bias 4: 2427
public vs. private sector 8: 4837
and racial discrimination 1: 517;
8: ***4896–4902***
screening hypothesis 3: 1700; 9: 5353
sex bias 4: ***2440–2446***
cross-national comparisons 4: 2440
and education 4: 2416
sex discrimination 8: 4898
and supply and demand
market-clearing wage equation
6: 3179
and taste discrimination 4: 2443
teachers vs. other occupations
10: 5843
See also
Income distribution
Salary wage differentials
Earnings functions
and academic achievement 5: 2944
age–earnings profiles 3: 1703
alpha coefficient 5: 2645
inequality function
cross-sectional studies 5: 2741
and income distribution 5: 2741
and parental inequality aversion
in kinship studies 6: 3142
and race differences 8: 4897
recursive simultaneous equations
3: 1749
variables used 3: 1749
and vocational education 9: 5072
East Africa
educational finance studies
private vs. public resources 8: 4703
labor market analysis
informal sector 3: 1680
technical and vocational education and training 11: ***6251–6256***
vocational education
historical background 11: 6252
training with production 11: 6446
East Germany (former)
See German Democratic Republic (GDR) (former)
Eastern Europe
adult education 2: ***656–662***
goals under communism 2: 657
history 2: 656
houses of culture 2: 658, 660
independent under communism
2: 660
out of school 2: 659
research 1: 123; 2: 661
state systems 2: 658
in transition 2: 660
civic education 2: 768
educational planning
approaches 8: 4496
and educational change 8: 4498
educational research
problems 3: 1554
financial support
international 5: 2992
labor force planning
evaluations 6: 3613
social stratification
research 10: 5734
technology education
programs 11: 6291
vocational education
future trends 11: 6647
historical background 11: 6641
and international co-operation
11: 6645
International Labour Organization
programs 5: 3002
policies 11: 6665
post school programs 11: 6247
problems 11: 6645
training with production 11: 6447
vocational education and training
11: ***6641–6648***
See also
Central and Eastern Europe
Eating habits
disorders 3: 1516
Echolalia
autism
and interpersonal relationships
6: 3233
and word recognition skills 6: 3232

Ecodisc
  multimedia optical data disks **2:** 647
Ecole Polytechnique **8:** 4604; **11:** 6680, 6682
Ecological education **4:** ***1991–1996***
Ecological factors
  and urban education **11:** ***6551–6558***
Ecological psychology **1:** 286
Ecology
  and adult education **1:** 134; **2:** 1193
  and physical education **10:** 5710
  of schools **9:** 5207
  and urban schools
    definition **11:** 6552
Econometrics
  least squares method of analysis
    education work relationship **3:** 1749
Economic adjustment
  developing nations
    and educational finance **3:** ***1784–1789***
  educational finance
    policy formation **3:** 1788
    studies **3:** 1786
  effect on family income **3:** 1785
  effect on public education finance **3:** 1786
  effect on revenue expenditure
    and education **3:** 1786
  effects on education **3:** 1785
  policies for
    and International Monetary Fund **3:** 1785
    and World Bank **3:** 1785
  structural adjustment programs **3:** 1785
Economic change
  and access to education **5:** 2505
  and educational planning
    Latin America **8:** 4492
  effect on training with production **11:** 6448
  effects on education
    developed nations **9:** 5186
  effects on school role **5:** 2499
  global
    main features of **3:** 1707
  and governance **5:** 2506
  and international division of labor **3:** 1707
  national economy
    as a part of global economy **3:** 1708
  and vocational education
    Soviet Union (former) **10:** 5649
  and youth unemployment **11:** 6806
Economic crisis
  developing nations **6:** 3603
    and educational finance **3:** 1784, 1785
    and primary education **9:** 5538
  and educational change **6:** 3491
  and educational finance **5:** 2980; **8:** 4520; **9:** 5239
  and educational planning **8:** 4491
  effect on apprenticeships
    German Democratic Republic (former) **11:** 6656
  effects
    on administrator education **1:** 74
  and international aid **5:** 2961
  and national training agencies
    Latin America **6:** 3263
  and state departments of education **7:** 3834
  and teacher strikes **6:** 3193
Economic development
  accounting **3:** ***1660–1666***
  and adult education **1:** 129
  and adult literacy **1:** 103
  and continuing education **2:** 1088
  definition of **3:** 1648
  education and **3:** 1648, ***1660–1666***; **4:** 2211; **5:** 2646
    institutionalist approach **3:** 1649
    neoclassical view **3:** 1648
    radical perspective **3:** 1649
  and educational policy **3:** 1684
  and educational responsibility
    private sector **8:** 4831
  and human capital **5:** 2646
    theory of **3:** 1662
  postwar
    United Kingdom **11:** 6685
  and scientific literacy **9:** 5347
  strategies
    inward-looking **11:** 6633
    outward-looking **11:** 6633
  See also
    Modernization
    Social change
Economic education
  See Economics education
Economic factors
  and adult education **4:** ***2388–2394***
  and curriculum **9:** ***5518–5523***
  and social change **4:** 2328
    criticism of **11:** 6700
  and technological advancement **11:** 6275
  urban environment **11:** 6553
Economic growth
  See Economic development
Economic performance
  and entrepreneurial behavior **3:** 1678
  immigrants
    and education **5:** ***2737–2740***
Economic status
  and family status **4:** ***2274–2279***
Economically disadvantaged
  and formal education **9:** 5533
  grants vs. student fees **4:** 2314
  and nonformal education **7:** 4144
  and school desegregation **3:** 1484
  and school enterprise
    historical background **9:** 5229
  and special education placement **6:** 3293
Economics
  of apprenticeship **1:** ***306–310***
  of the brain drain **1:** ***554–561***
  of educational planning **3:** ***1810–1821***
  of educational technology **4:** ***1903–1911***
  of information
    and occupational information **6:** 3096
  institutional links with education
    anthropological studies **1:** 289
  of job training **7:** ***4197–4201***
  Marxism
    and employment contracts **3:** 1696
  planning
    quantitative methods **3:** 1811
  postwar development **3:** 1810
  of preschool education **8:** ***4662–4666***
  public choice theory **3:** 1813
  of teacher supply and demand **10:** ***5843–5846***
  See also
    Macroeconomics
    Microeconomics
Economics education
  computer-assisted instruction **9:** 5562
  concept teaching **9:** 5562
  research on learning in **9:** 5561
  simulation **9:** 5562
  and social studies **9:** 5577
  Soviet Union (former) **10:** 5646
  student understanding of concepts **9:** 5561
Economies of scale
  and cost effectiveness **2:** 1134
Ecuador
  adult education **6:** 3253
  educational finance
    and tax allocation **8:** 4360
  literacy campaigns **1:** 170, 175; **6:** 3256
ECUNET **3:** 1354
Editing
  of electronic periodicals **4:** 1957
  and printing **8:** 4690
Educable mentally handicapped
  See Mild mental retardation
Educação para Todos 1985 (Brazil) **11:** 6560
Educated labor
  demand for
    empirical research **11:** 6258
    factors affecting **11:** 6256
    and technological advancement **11:** ***6256–6261***
  vs. uneducated labor **6:** 3179
  elasticity of supply and demand **3:** ***1443–1449***
  strategies of **6:** 3182
Education
  anthropological concept of **7:** 3971
  concept of field
    and vocational education **6:** 3256
  and copyright **2:** ***1099–1102***
  crisis
    issues **11:** 6293
    worldwide **4:** 2364
  definitions of **9:** 4996
    and computers **2:** 1007

and development **3:** ***1648–1655***
and earnings **3:** ***1655–1660***, 1703
empirical research **3:** 1656
vintage effects **11:** ***6614–6615***
effect of economic adjustment on **3:** 1785
expansion of
and government policy **11:** 6634
as a field of study **3:** ***1720–1724***
international cooperation in **5:** ***2961–2965***
and international division of labor **3:** ***1707–1713***
joint production model **6:** ***3101–3106***
and labor market
developing nations **3:** ***1681–1685***
informal **3:** ***1676–1681***
labor relations in **6:** ***3189–3197***
legitimacy of
and conflict **2:** 1037
and measurement of judgement **6:** 3120
models
and educational administration **1:** 62
and organizational development **7:** 4237
power structure **9:** 5296, 5297
and productivity **3:** ***1690–1695***
rate of return to **8:** ***4913–4918***
religious factors in **9:** ***5008–5013***
role of
in socialist societies **11:** 6642
and social mobility **9:** ***5548–5554***
social nature of **10:** 6219
social psychology of **10:** 6223
and social stratification **9:** ***5548–5554***
and technological advancement **11:** ***6277–6283***
and technology
transformations **4:** 1884
and training
convergence between **11:** ***6412–6416***
differences between **11:** 6413
policy implications **11:** 6415
relationships between **11:** 6412
semantics **11:** 6412
technological advancement effects **11:** 6413
Education Act 1944 (England and Wales)
and school inspectors
role of **9:** 5250
Education for All Handicapped Children Act 1978 (US) **5:** 2574, 2904
Education continue (France) **6:** 3417, 3418
Education courses
experimental education **3:** 1722
historical development **3:** ***1720–1724***
social education **3:** 1722
teacher education **3:** ***1720–1724***
Education of the Handicapped Act (EHA) 1975 (US)
1983 amendment **11:** 6460
statistical surveys **3:** 1530
See also
Individuals with Disabilities Education Act (IDEA) (US)
Education indicators **3:** 1429, ***1740–1746***
categories of **3:** 1742
comparative analysis **2:** 960; **3:** 1834
international studies **3:** 1766
comparative education **2:** 957
context–input–process–output model **3:** 1742
definition of **3:** 1742
evaluation of cross-national **4:** 2139
generic **5:** 2986
international **5:** ***2984–2989***
problems and aims **5:** 2985
uses of **5:** 2986
levels of application **3:** 1742
policy relevance of **3:** 1742
trends **3:** 1742
utilization issues **3:** 1745
Education permanente (France) **6:** 3417, 3418; **8:** 4958
Council of Europe **5:** 2933
implementation **6:** 3417, 3419
Education populaire
in Africa **1:** 216, 218, 220
Education with production **3:** ***1685–1690***
evaluation **3:** 1688
historical background **3:** 1685, 1686
and Marxism **3:** 1686
policy issues **3:** 1689
and training with production compared **11:** 6445
See also
Training with production
Vocational education
Work experience programs
Education productivity relationship **3:** ***1690–1695***
agriculture **1:** ***244–254***
Education récurrente (France) **6:** 3417, 3418
Education Reform Act 1988 (UK)
and budgeting **9:** 5184
and decentralization **9:** 5211
and governance
schools **6:** 3493
and history instruction **9:** 5575
and information technology **2:** 976
measures **9:** 5278
provisions **9:** 5221
and religious education **9:** 5011
school-based management **9:** 5303; **11:** 6560
and school choice **1:** 591
and school inspectors **9:** 5249
Education Software Publishers Association (ESPA) (UK) **10:** 5619
Education work relationship **3:** ***1703–1707***, ***1736–1740***; **8:** ***4337–4339***
academic vs. vocational training **3:** 1700
apprenticeships **1:** ***306–310***
career education
disabilities **2:** 633
and community education
Brazil **2:** 909
consumers vs. products **11:** 6701
cooperatives
Soviet Union (former) **10:** 5646
correspondence theory **6:** 3185
curriculum issues **3:** 1737
criterion referenced tests **3:** 1738
differentiation **3:** 1737
relevance and motivation **3:** 1737
transition **3:** 1737
curriculum objectives **3:** 1736
developing nations
tendencies **3:** 1670
and earnings **3:** ***1746–1750***
and educational benefits **1:** 517
employment contracts **3:** ***1695–1703***
human capital theory **6:** 3186
and income distribution **5:** 2740
and labor market analysis **3:** 1679
and income distribution **5:** ***2740–2744***
and internal labor market theory of **5:** ***2937–2942***
job training
and earnings **3:** 1791; **7:** 4197
Kerschensteiner's view **6:** 3135
labor force participation
females **3:** 1669
labor force requirements
effect of technological advancement on **11:** ***6256–6261***
learning organizations **4:** 1923
and national surveys **2:** 651
occupational information **6:** ***3096–3101***
occupational segregation
and sex bias **4:** ***2427–2432***
organizational issues **3:** 1738
and overeducation **7:** ***4249–4255***
and school enterprise **9:** 5229
screening hypothesis **9:** ***5350–5355***
and time factors (learning) **6:** 3549
segmentation theory **6:** ***3184–3189***
and teaching **10:** 6138
technological advancement
and rate of return **3:** 1709
transition
definitions of **11:** 6457
and disabilities **11:** ***6457–6461***
trends **3:** 1739
vocational education
European Community **4:** 2066
Latin America **6:** 3258
planning methodologies **8:** 4526
and youth unemployment **11:** ***6803–6808***
See also
Relevance (education)

Educational administration
administrative organization
systems approaches **3:** 1770
applied science model of **9:** 5162
approaches **9:** 5160
behavioral science tradition **3:** 1769
careers **1:** ***78–83***, 81
contingencies **1:** 82
mobility **1:** 81
paths and patterns **1:** 81
centralization
rationale for **6:** 3272
vs. decentralization **8:** 4515
changing perceptions of **9:** 5166
coherence theory of justification **3:** 1773
and communicative competence **3:** 1773
community education **2:** 910
and constructivism **1:** 62
critical approaches **1:** ***60–67***
foundations **1:** 62
implications **1:** 65
and critical theory **1:** 55, 63; **2:** 1199; **3:** 1772
and cultural theory **3:** 1771
and curriculum development
sociology **3:** 1347
decentralization in **3:** ***1407–1412***
rationale for **6:** 3272
and decision-making **6:** 3272
values in **3:** 1771
and education indicators **3:** ***1740–1746***
and educational planning
contingency approach **8:** 4516
and educational policy **4:** 1837
teacher participation **10:** ***6079–6083***
effective schools **4:** ***1929–1934***
empirical research **1:** 61
employee motivation
and incentives **4:** 1967
ethical issues **3:** ***1769–1775***
evaluation-centered **3:** 1740
and expert systems
implications **5:** 2830
factors influencing **1:** 73
females
access and qualifications **4:** 2420
certification **11:** 6730
institutional constraints **4:** 2421
labor market **4:** 2420
occupational aspiration **11:** 6730
United States **11:** ***6727–6731***
and feminist approaches **1:** 64
field of study **1:** ***53–60***
historical background **1:** 60
improvement **11:** 6525
influences **1:** 56
inservice education **1:** ***67–73***
content **1:** 69
evaluation **1:** 71
functions **1:** 68
methods **1:** 70
policy issues **1:** 71
professional values **1:** 72
provision **1:** 69
research issues **1:** 71
types of **1:** 68
international **5:** ***2951–2955***
objectives **5:** 2951
trends **5:** 2954
international approach
periodicals **9:** 5162
international developments **5:** ***2504–2509***
International Institute for Educational Planning programs **11:** 6528
and law **6:** ***3272–3276***
and leadership **1:** 65
leadership
conceptual approaches **6:** 3277
findings **6:** 3282
future research **6:** 3283
research **6:** ***3276–3284***
theory of **6:** ***3276–3284***
trends **6:** 3283
leadership training **6:** 3278
and learning factors **10:** 5749
legal procedures in **6:** 3273
and logical empiricism **3:** 1769
critique **3:** 1771
management information systems **5:** 2828; **6:** ***3593–3597***
and micropolitics **7:** 3824
objectives **6:** 3274
and organizational development **7:** 4237
organizational theories
and evaluation **3:** 1740
personnel **8:** ***4404–4409***
philosophical issues **3:** ***1769–1775***
and postadministration **1:** 67
and postmodernism **1:** 56, 65
practice **1:** 66
preservice teacher education **1:** ***73–77***
professors of **1:** 74
public schools vs. private schools
implications **8:** 4844
recruitment **1:** 78
and religious education **9:** 5004
research **1:** 53
and resource allocation **9:** 5062
and school effectiveness
criticisms of **6:** 3492
school effectiveness research **3:** 1741
and school law **9:** 5254
school organization
theory of **7:** ***4240–4246***
and science history **1:** 56
scientific approach
criticism of **1:** 54
and sex differences **1:** 436; **10:** 5610
sex discrimination **11:** 6729
affirmative action **4:** 2422
developing nations **4:** ***2419–2423***
research trends **4:** 2422
and theories **4:** 2422
sex role socialization **4:** 2420
and social sciences **1:** 53
development **1:** 54, 57
theories of **9:** 5162
status of **9:** 5162
strategies
and educational planning **8:** 4518
studies **1:** 53, 55
classification of **9:** 5160
Latin America **8:** 4494
subjectivism **1:** 54; **3:** 1770
and teacher role
changes in **10:** 6082
theories of **1:** 54, 61; **9:** 5160
and inservice education **1:** 68
and intellectual fashions **1:** 57
transfers of authority **3:** 1412
trends **1:** 57, 59
developing nations **3:** 1823
use of term **9:** 5159
value neutral beliefs
vs. value-laden beliefs **1:** 65
and values **1:** 59
vs. classroom autonomy
and productivity **8:** 4563
See also
Administration
School administration
Educational Advisory Services Project (EASP) (UK)
public libraries **6:** 3394
Educational agencies
and scientific literacy **9:** 5348
Educational anthropology
academic orientation **1:** 282
analytical frameworks **1:** 284
areas of study **1:** 288
classroom environment **2:** ***796–803***
cross-cultural studies **2:** ***1208–1213***
cultural ecological model **1:** 287
cultural transmission model **1:** 284
development of discipline **1:** 281
ecological model **1:** 286
ethnography **4:** ***2046–2053***
future research **1:** 294
history and overview **1:** ***280–297***
indigenous populations **3:** ***1750–1756***
instrumental model **1:** 285
Instrumental Activities Inventory (IAI) **1:** 285
methodology **1:** 284
objectives **1:** 284
school community relationship **2:** ***914–918***
service orientation **1:** 280
and social change **9:** ***5508–5510***
social stratification **9:** ***5567–5572***
structural–functional model **1:** 286
technological functionalism **1:** 286
transactional model **1:** 285
United States **7:** 3972
Educational assessment **2:** 1058
and concept maps **2:** 1028
definition of **1:** 363
focus of **1:** 364
functions of **1:** 362
methods **1:** ***362–370***
criterion referenced **1:** 367
diagnostic **1:** 366
domain-referenced **1:** 368

mastery **1:** 366
minimum competency **1:** 367
norm referenced **1:** 368
performance-based **1:** 369
placement **1:** 365
standardized tests **1:** 369
national programs **3:** 1429
and prior learning **8:** 4702
purposes of **1:** 364
results
audiences for **1:** 365; **6:** 3470
reporting of **1:** 365
and scaling **1:** 370
Educational attainment
and adult education
measurement of **7:** ***3707–3711***
participation **1:** 107; **7:** 4320
and birth rate **3:** ***1672–1676***
and income levels
comparison by country **3:** 1660
and job skill requirements
measurement **11:** 6257
and race–earnings differentials
8: 4898, 4900
race and ethnicity **8:** ***4891–4896***
and vocational adjustment **9:** 5073
Educational attitudes
resistance **9:** ***5056–5061***
Educational benefits **1:** ***510–521***
classification of **1:** 511
dimensions of **1:** 510
elementary education **1:** 511, 514
empirical research **1:** 514
criticism of **1:** 515
and equal education **1:** 514
factors affecting **1:** 514
higher education **1:** 511, 512, 514, 516, 518
and institutional personnel **1:** 511
measurement **1:** 512
and achievement tests **1:** 513
monetary **1:** 511
nonfinancial
See Consumption benefits
nonmonetary **1:** 511
private **1:** 511
private education
excess demand model **8:** 4832
of school enterprise **9:** 5229
and skill development **10:** 5918
social **1:** 511
socio-economic status **1:** 515
use of knowledge concerning **1:** 514
value added approach **1:** 512
Educational broadcasting
objectives of **5:** 2885
See also
Educational radio
Educational television
Educational certificates
characteristics of **8:** 4617
Educational change
and administrator education
preservice **1:** 76
alternatives
and cost-effectiveness studies
2: 1135
building a system for **6:** 3599
and centralization **5:** 2506
characteristics of **5:** 2840
and conflict
Peru **2:** 1041
and curriculum development **3:** 1265
and decentralization **5:** 2506
decision-making **7:** 4235
definitions of **4:** 1848; **6:** 3597
determinants of **6:** 3492
criticism of **11:** 6701
educational administration
trends **6:** 3496
educational history **5:** 2614
and educational planning **8:** 4498
experiences of **8:** 4506
and educational research **4:** 1869
educational researchers
teachers as **10:** 6098
environmental philosophies **4:** 1851
failure of
symbolic perspective **9:** 5180
frame factors **4:** 2376
Germany **6:** 3417, 3419
early twentieth century
6: ***3133–3138***
global approach **5:** ***2495–2500***
components of **5:** 2496, 2498
global philosophies **4:** 1851
and governance
schools **6:** 3491
implementation of **6:** 3599, 3601; **9:** 5243
and industrial restructuring
5: ***2792–2799***
and inservice education **1:** 69, 71
and institutional self-evaluation
5: 2847
international comparisons **10:** 6126
international education **5:** ***2957–2961***
Japan **6:** 3075
and knowledge
emerging forms **4:** 1850, 1851
indigenous forms **4:** ***1848–1852***
language role **4:** 1850
management of commitment **6:** 3601
management of learning **6:** 3601
management of **6:** ***3597–3603***; **9:** 5243
measurement of
problems **5:** 2796
and middle-class standards
United States **9:** 5509
and minority groups **4:** 1850
objectives **6:** 3598
practicalities of **10:** 6208
processes **6:** 3599; **9:** 5243
and research findings **9:** 5042
resistance to
local elites **3:** 1414
passive **3:** 1414
and rural to urban migration **4:** 1850
and school effectiveness **6:** 3491
and school self-evaluation **5:** 2848
and skills shortages
China, People's Republic of **2:** 756
and state departments of education
7: 3838
role of **7:** 3834
studies
historical background **5:** 2839
and teacher attitudes **6:** 3597
and teacher socialization
developed nations **10:** 6126
developing nations **10:** 6126
teachers' beliefs **10:** 6099, 6102
United States **7:** 4053
America 2000 program **3:** 1358; **7:** 4053
American Achievement Tests
proposed **7:** 4053
World Class Standards proposed
7: 4053
and value conflicts **4:** 1850
vocational education
United States **11:** 6532
vs. system maintenance
and educational planning **8:** 4505
See also
Educational reform
Educational choice
See School choice
Educational computing
See Computer uses in education
Educational counseling
adult students **2:** ***1161–1165***
concepts and definitions of **2:** 1161
functions **2:** 1161
institutionally based **2:** 1162
international provision **2:** 1162
models and theory base **2:** 1163
settings and structures **2:** 1162
and outreach programs **7:** 4248
professionalization of **2:** 1163
Educational decisions
and labor market conditions **6:** 3099
and prospects for women **6:** 3100
Educational demand
adult education **8:** 4615
elasticity for **4:** 2390
and educational planning **3:** 1807
forecasting
fixed coefficient **3:** 1444
for graduates
public sector **8:** 4530
growth in **8:** 4792
and national surveys **2:** 651
and private resources **8:** 4704
and vocational education
4: ***2388–2394***
Educational development
developing nations **11:** 6524
and development **5:** 2957
and equal education
model of inequality **9:** 5534
factors influencing **2:** 951
and financial support
factors affecting **5:** 2990
and labor market
alternative models **6:** ***3179–3184***

bumping model **6:** 3181
labor market stratification model **6:** 3181
market-clearing labor market model **6:** 3179
patterns of
Asia **8:** 4487
and publishing industry
developing nations **8:** 4845
and recurrent education **8:** 4962
school-based **5:** 2849
and social equality
developing nations **9:** ***5532–5539***
historical background **9:** 5532
Educational diagnosis
learning disabilities **10:** 5683
special needs students **2:** ***711–719***
process **2:** 713
Educational discrimination
and race–earnings differentials
United States **8:** 4900
severe disabilities **3:** 1506
Educational economics
decentralization of **3:** 1408
and distance education **3:** ***1567–1573***
teacher education **10:** ***5948–5954***
See also
Educational finance
Educational effectiveness
concept of **3:** ***1779–1784***
definition of **3:** 1779
external **3:** 1781
of inputs **3:** 1783
internal **3:** 1780
Educational efficiency
concept of **3:** ***1779–1784***
and cost minimization **3:** 1782
definition of **3:** 1779
external **3:** 1781
internal **3:** 1780
constraints on improving **3:** 1782
cost of inputs **3:** 1783
Educational environment
and attendance **3:** 1605
as a barrier to women's education **4:** 2417
and computers **11:** 6284
decentralization trends **3:** 1717
and democratic values
Dewey on **3:** 1523
and descriptive scales **3:** 1475
development of **5:** 2496
and educational quality
vocational education **8:** 4860
and facilities planning **4:** 2219, 2226
and hypertext **5:** 2706
and interactive video **11:** 6601
and LOGO **6:** 3510
and mass media **2:** 885
measurement of
descriptive scales **3:** ***1475–1483***
and principals
role of **9:** 5270
and school size **9:** 5292
and science education **7:** 4101
and social development **9:** 5504
and social status
of teachers **10:** 6227
special needs students **2:** 713
and teacher expertise **10:** 6023
technologies for altering **4:** 1914
and urban education **11:** 6551
variables **4:** 2226
at work and everyday life **11:** 6394
workplace as **5:** 2687; **8:** 4964
See also
Classroom environment
Learning environment
School climate
Educational equity (finance) **3:** 1791
concepts of **9:** 5236
and educational contraction **6:** 3607
and efficiency **3:** 1781
fiscal neutrality
concept of **9:** 5239
and resource allocation **9:** 5238
and student loan programs **10:** 5765, 5767
Educational expansion
See Educational development
Educational experience
influences
classroom research **2:** 822
Educational facilities
developing nations
input output analysis **3:** 1760
evaluation of **4:** 2228
life cycle costing **4:** 2224
and physical plant **4:** ***2219–2225***
requirements **4:** 2227
and school administration **9:** 5163
and school organization **7:** 4229
as support to teaching and learning **4:** 2219
urban areas
deterioration of **11:** 6559
See also
School buildings
Educational facilities design
factors in **4:** 2223
and outcomes of education **9:** 5262
strategic planning **4:** 2227
systems approach in **10:** 5900
Educational facilities improvement
and educational research **8:** 4603
teachers
professional development **10:** 5934
Educational facilities planning **4:** 2227
Asia **8:** 4485
association charts **4:** 2220
common policy issues **4:** 2226
and educational environment **4:** 2226
factors **4:** 2221
future trends **4:** 2224, 2229
inventories for **4:** 2227
macrolevel vs. microlevel **4:** 2225
maintenance **4:** 2228
master plans **4:** 2227
and policy
macrolevel **4:** ***2225–2230***
process for **4:** 2219
scope **4:** 2226
specifications **4:** 2228
variations **4:** 2225
Educational finance **3:** ***1789–1793***; **9:** ***5233–5241***
adequacy of
measurement **3:** 1790
adult education **1:** 156; **6:** 3365
and judgments of educational worth **1:** 114
Afghanistan **1:** 207
Albania **1:** 258
Antigua and Barbuda **1:** 303
Argentina **1:** 336
Australia **1:** 419
bias in
and private resources **8:** 4705
Botswana **1:** 548
and brain drain **1:** 558
Brunei Darussalam **1:** 575
Bulgaria **1:** 585
Burkina Faso **1:** 597
Cameroon **2:** 614
Canada **2:** 613
and centralization
developing nations **3:** 1412
Chad **2:** 668
Colombia **2:** 877
cost constraints **9:** 5240
Côte d'Ivoire **2:** 1157
and debt
international **5:** 2990
decisions in **9:** 5234
developing nations **8:** 4520
and economic adjustment **3:** ***1784–1789***
public vs. private resources **8:** ***4702–4708***
and economic adjustment
studies **3:** 1786
and economic change **5:** 2506
and economic crisis **5:** 2980; **9:** 5239
and educational facilities planning **4:** 2221
educational history **2:** 1059
and educational planning
sub-Saharan Africa **8:** 4513
and educational resources **9:** 5236
educational vouchers **9:** 5204, 5239
and vocational education **11:** 6653
efficiency of
criteria **3:** 1790
and resource allocation **9:** 5238
and enrollment projections **9:** 5234
evaluation of research data **5:** 2978
factors affecting
type of education **9:** 5235
and federal government **5:** 2510
France **4:** 2382
future trends **9:** 5240
governance
structures **9:** 5236
and gross national product (GNP) **9:** 5234
India **5:** 2750
Indonesia **5:** 2787
inequalities

and resource allocation **9:** 5062
and input output analysis **3:** 1757
international **5:** ***2978–2984***, ***2989–2993***
comparative area studies **5:** 2979
evaluation of research data **5:** 2978
private vs. public resources **5:** 2978
strategies for **5:** 2992
International Institute for Educational Planning programs **11:** 6528
Iran **5:** 3009
Israel **5:** 3026
Kenya **6:** 3130
Kiribati **6:** 3147
Korea, Democratic People's Republic of **6:** 3158
Korea, Republic of **6:** 3166
Laos **6:** 3244
Latvia **6:** 3270
Lebanon **6:** 3353
lifelong learning **6:** ***3422–3425***
Maldives **6:** 3575
and management information systems **5:** 2828
market system vs. welfare system **6:** 3275
Mauritius **7:** 3695
Mongolia **7:** 3903
Morocco **7:** 3928
Mozambique **7:** 3957
Myanmar **7:** 4036
Namibia **7:** 4043
and national surveys **2:** 650
Nepal **7:** 4065
Netherlands **7:** 4073
New Zealand **7:** 4108
Nicaragua **7:** 4114
Niger **7:** 4122
Nigeria **7:** 4129
noneducational agencies
and adult education **1:** 154
Norway **7:** 4190
Oman **7:** 4204
Pakistan **7:** 4267
Panama **7:** 4273
Papua New Guinea **7:** 4191
Paraguay **7:** 4286
Peru **8:** 4412
Philippines **8:** 4437
Poland **8:** 4547
policy formation
and economic adjustment **3:** 1788
and policy-oriented research **8:** 4557
and politics of education **8:** 4593
Portugal **8:** 4627
and primary school agriculture **8:** 4687
and principals
role of **9:** 5271
projections **8:** 4786
public education
practices and trends **4:** ***2310–2316***
and school choice **9:** 5199
and religious education **9:** 5005
and resource allocation **9:** 5061
rural education
vs. urban education **3:** 1791
Russia **9:** 5103
Rwanda **9:** 5111
Saudi Arabia **9:** 5147
and school administration **9:** 5182
and school business relationship **9:** 5188
school choice
market approach **9:** 5202
school community relationship **2:** ***910–914***
and school size **9:** 5291
Senegal **9:** 5421
Seychelles **9:** 5447
Sierra Leone **9:** 5457
Singapore **9:** 5481
skill development **10:** 5918
and tax allocation **11:** 6651
Slovenia **9:** 5495
sources of **4:** 2311; **9:** 5235
deficit financing **4:** 2311
earmarked taxes **4:** 2314
private financial support **4:** 2313
taxes **4:** 2311
South Africa **10:** 5630
Spain **10:** 5655
Sri Lanka **10:** 5718
structural features of **9:** 5233
substitute teachers **10:** 5833
Sudan **10:** 5840
Suriname **10:** 5851
Swaziland **10:** 5864
Sweden **10:** 5870
Switzerland **10:** 5878
Syria **10:** 5892
Tanzania **10:** 5907
tax allocation **9:** 5236
and vocational education **8:** ***4359–4364***
tax deductions **8:** 4360
criticism of **8:** 4363
effect on businesses **8:** 4362
policy guidance **8:** 4363
rates **8:** 4362
technical education **10:** 6064
trends **8:** 4364
and teacher education **8:** 4524, 4525
and technical education **11:** 6271
and textbooks **11:** 6365
Thailand **11:** 6375
Togo **11:** 6401
Tonga **11:** 6408
for training **11:** 6425, 6426
training
and wage reductions **11:** 6427
Tunisia **11:** 6472
Turkey **11:** 6480
types of
and school organization **7:** 4231
Uganda **11:** 6499
United Arab Emirates **11:** 6514
United States **11:** 6543
Uruguay **11:** 6565
use of term **9:** 5233
Vanuatu **11:** 6583
Venezuela **11:** 6596
Vietnam **11:** 6612
vocational education
Japan **6:** 3091
Latin America **7:** 4154
levy–grant system **8:** 4360
sources **5:** 2817
and training with production **11:** 6449
United States **11:** 6531
vocational education and training
international aid **11:** ***6660–6664***
Yemen **11:** 6791
Zaire **11:** 6812
Zimbabwe **11:** 6818
See also
Expenditures
Resource allocation
School expenditures
School revenues
Educational games
behavioral objectives **9:** 5473, 5474
skill analysis **9:** 5473
Educational gerontology
trends **10:** 5596
Educational history **2:** ***1056–1064***; **3:** ***1720–1724***; **8:** 4452
adult education **1:** ***135–139***
Africa **2:** 1060
approaches to **5:** 2607
Arab nations **2:** 1061
Asia **2:** 1061
Australia **2:** 1062
background **3:** 1793
behavior
nature of **5:** 2606
in biographies **3:** ***1793–1797***; **5:** 2614
sources **3:** 1796
China, People's Republic of **2:** 1061
comparative education **5:** 2608, 2609
contextual factors **2:** 1056
control **2:** 1059
and curriculum history **3:** 1301, 1302
definition of **5:** 2615
developing nations **2:** 1060
Durkheim's views **2:** 778
educational finance **2:** 1059
educational planning **2:** 1060; **8:** ***4489–4491***
educational psychologists **3:** 1794
and educational researchers **3:** 1796
equal education **2:** 1062
sex discrimination **2:** 1063
females in **11:** 6741
India **2:** 1062
institutions **2:** 1057
interpretations **5:** 2614
Japan **2:** 1061
Latin America **2:** 1060
Luther's girls schools **11:** 6744
meritocracy issues **7:** 3769
oral **3:** 1796
and oral history **7:** 4223
philosophy of education **5:** 2608
political issues **2:** 1056
presentation **5:** 2606
quantitative methods **5:** 2603

research methodology **5:** ***2601–2607***
complementary **5:** 2605
problems **5:** 2605
as science **5:** 2601
science education **9:** ***5324–5328***
and social change **5:** 2607
socioeconomic influences **2:** 1056
South Africa **2:** 1061
strands of revisionism **5:** 2603
teaching characteristics **10:** 5608
topics of **5:** 2613
trends **5:** 2606
vocabulary used
problems **5:** 2605
vocational education
United States **11:** 6530
See also
Historiography of education
Educational improvement **9:** ***5241–5247***
centralization vs. decentralization **9:** 5245
change processes **9:** 5243
class size
cost effectiveness **2:** 772
and curriculum development **9:** 5519
and decentralization **9:** 5221
and declining resources **9:** 5245
and educational quality **9:** 5241
factors affecting **9:** 5242
management strategies
for school personnel **9:** 5244
model for **5:** 2844
objectives **9:** 5241
policies for **9:** 5241
development **9:** 5241
programs
characteristics of **9:** 5242
research
unit of analysis **9:** 5221
and school districts **9:** ***5221–5224***
influences **9:** 5222
school policy
vs. public policy **9:** 5244
teacher role
structural critique **10:** 6097
women faculty **10:** 6098
Educational inequality
See Equal education
Educational innovation
definitions of **6:** 3597
diffusion of **3:** ***1549–1553***
models and theories **3:** 1550
and educational planning **8:** 4516, 4517
history
adoption era **5:** 2839
implementation **3:** ***1491–1494***
factors affecting **3:** 1491
and information dissemination **3:** 1550
objectives **3:** 1552
and teacher role **3:** 1492
and industrial restructuring **5:** ***2792–2799***
issues in generalizing **3:** 1236
management of **6:** ***3597–3603***
and organizational theories **4:** 2164
process evaluation **3:** 1551
and school self-evaluation **5:** 2850
science education **8:** 4474
scope of
and educational improvement **9:** 5242
and small group instruction **10:** 6187
and student attitudes
research **10:** 5773
studies **9:** 5166
and teacher attitudes
age differences **10:** 6210
and vocational education
Chile **7:** 4152
See also
Educational reform
Educational legislation
and federal regulation **6:** 3361
history of **5:** 2609
Educational level
See Academic achievement
Educational management
See Educational administration
Educational materials
See Instructional materials
Educational media
attributes **7:** 3745
audiovisual **7:** ***3744–3753***
classification **7:** 3757, 3758
contextual theories **2:** 886
control of **7:** 3758
cost effectiveness
studies **2:** 1125
courses
and visual literacy **11:** 6624
definitions of **7:** 3756
in distance education **3:** 1573
issues and trends **2:** 887
and learning motivation **7:** 3741
low technology **4:** 1912
mental tool approach **7:** 3742
and novelty (stimulus dimension) **7:** 3740, 3742
organizations **3:** ***1797–1800***
continuing education of members **3:** 1798
decentralized groups **3:** 1797
electronic publishing **3:** 1799
functions of **3:** 1797
and government agencies **3:** 1798
growth in number of **3:** 1799
international **3:** 1799
periodicals **3:** 1800
and professionalism **3:** 1798
services to members **3:** 1797
trends **3:** 1799
types of **3:** 1797
periodicals **3:** ***1797–1800***
independent sources **3:** 1800
role of **2:** ***884–888***; **7:** 3745
and technology
relationship between **3:** 1573
theory
cone of experience **7:** 3744
tutoring function **7:** 3739
types of **7:** 3746
See also
Audiovisual aids
Autoinstructional aids
Educational broadcasting
Instructional materials
Educational Native American Network (US) **10:** 6008
Educational needs
adult education **8:** 4612
and educational finance **9:** 5234
and innovation **5:** 2840
and leadership training **6:** 3278
and school libraries **6:** 3395
and special education **10:** 5659
vs. commercial objectives **9:** 5543
Educational objectives
and administration **8:** 4564
and behavioral objectives **10:** 6161
change in
and science education **8:** 4475
and Christianity
Saint Augustine on **9:** 5115, 5116
and cognitive processes **10:** 5741, 5742
common
and educational vouchers **9:** 5203
and computer literacy **2:** 974
and computer uses in education
effectiveness of **11:** 6285
and cost effectiveness **2:** 1137
and criterion referenced tests **2:** 1185, 1188
and critical theory **1:** 64
curriculum development **3:** ***1800***, ***1800–1804***
cognitive psychological view **3:** 1803
means end model **3:** 1801
philosophical perspective **3:** 1325, 1326, 1327
taxonomy **3:** 1801
definition of **11:** 6576
determination of
and educational technology **4:** 1896
and educational planning **8:** 4595
consensus **3:** 1821
and educational research **5:** 2508
evaluation reports **4:** ***2074–2079***
and governance **5:** 2504
influences
frame factor theory **4:** 2375
tradition **4:** 2376
and innovation **5:** 2841
and instructional design theory **5:** 2863
justification
conceptual/logical/formal **11:** 6578
discourse **11:** 6579
empirical **11:** 6579
ethical **11:** 6579
legal **11:** 6579
and learning strategies **6:** 3336
and liberal–democratic values **3:** 1327
long range planning

curriculum development **4:** 2329
Marxism and **3:** 1326, 1327
and media selection **7:** 3757
and modular curricula **7:** 3886
and moral development **10:** 6167
and needs assessment **7:** 4058
and outcomes of education **3:** 1802
schools **9:** 5259
philosophy of education
Erasmus **4:** 2005
Locke **6:** 3498
Plato **8:** 4532
and politics of education **8:** 4587
preconceptions and misconceptions about **8:** 4650
scholasticism **9:** 5121
school organization **7:** 4233
science education
primary school programs **9:** 5331
specification
and systems approach **10:** 5897
and status of knowledge **6:** 3148
and student needs **10:** 5768
and study habits **10:** 5830
and syllabi **10:** 5885
and teacher education **10:** 5982, 5984, 6125
teaching
and cognitive development approach **10:** 6164
testing in evaluation **4:** 2102
accountability models **4:** 2102
discrepancy model **4:** 2102
EPIC model **4:** 2102
instructional objectives exchange **4:** 2102
Tylerian evaluation model **4:** 2102; **8:** 4763
values in **11:** 6578
See also
Outcomes of education
Relevance (education)
Educational opportunities
access to education
nonformal education **7:** 4133
and testing **1:** 371
and adult education **8:** 4611
adult rights to **6:** 3362, 3365
and cultural influences **9:** 5016
disabilities and **3:** 1533
and environmental research **4:** 2248
and family school relationship **4:** 2248
and internal migration **5:** ***2942–2945***
international studies
comparative analysis **10:** 6154
for labor force
and tax deductions **8:** 4363
and mental retardation **10:** 5664
and paid educational leave **7:** 4262
power structure
and sex discrimination **5:** 2454
and public examinations **4:** 2173
and school choice **9:** 5198, 5199
and sociology of education **10:** 5597
See also
Access to education
Educational organizations
See Organizations (groups), educational
Educational philosophy
See Philosophy of education
Educational planning
alternative approaches **8:** 4497
approaches **3:** 1812, 1818; **8:** 4497, 4502
choice of **8:** 4507
Arab nations **8:** ***4483–4485***
Asia **8:** ***4485–4489***
categories **8:** 4496
centralization vs. decentralization **8:** 4498, 4503
sub-Saharan Africa **8:** 4512
centralized
failure of **8:** 4513
challenges **11:** 6294
sub-Saharan Africa **8:** 4512
change
determinants of **3:** 1825
vs. system maintenance **8:** 4505
classification **3:** 1804
and communications **11:** 6297
comparative studies
Latin America **8:** 4493
computer software for **11:** 6296
conflict in **8:** 4598
contingency approach **8:** ***4514–4519***
analytical elements **8:** 4517
analytical procedure **8:** 4516
central features **8:** 4516
environmental assessment **8:** 4517
reform analysis **8:** 4517
and contraction **6:** 3605
and cost effectiveness **3:** 1813
and credibility **8:** 4597
and decentralization **3:** 1414, 1817, 1827; **11:** 6295
definitions of **8:** 4499
problems **3:** 1804
demands on
and educational reform **8:** 4515
demography **3:** ***1449–1453***
developing nations
and economic adjustment **3:** 1788
rate of return **8:** 4838
developments **8:** 4498
and documentation systems **3:** 1592
and economics
interaction between **3:** 1810
economics of **3:** ***1810–1821***
development **3:** 1810
and educational change **4:** 1849
experiences of **8:** 4506
educational history **2:** 1060
and educational research **8:** 4599
Europe **8:** ***4495–4499***
evolutionary
and implementation **6:** 3601
expanding existing services **3:** 1823
facilities
process for **4:** 2219
failure of **8:** 4501, 4596
and federal regulation **8:** 4508
future trends **3:** 1819; **8:** 4508
and games
application of **3:** 1828
gaps in **11:** 6525
and government **8:** 4598
government role **3:** 1816
history **8:** ***4489–4491***, 4500
capitalist nations **8:** 4490, 4500
developing nations **8:** 4490, 4501
socialist nations **8:** 4489, 4500
implementation problems **3:** ***1821–1825***
causes of failures **3:** 1823
developing nations **3:** 1821
full scale projects **3:** 1823
and inefficiency **3:** 1826
and information
role of **8:** 4598
and information manipulation **8:** 4597
information processing
and data collection **11:** 6293
interactive **8:** 4595
politics in **8:** 4599
international assistance experts
developing nations **5:** 2973
and labor force planning **6:** ***3608–3613***
Latin America **8:** ***4491–4495***
lead time **11:** 6294, 6295
legal constraints **3:** 1823
limitations
factors **11:** 6293
management skills **3:** 1822
management strategies **8:** 4518
adaptive **8:** 4518
mechanistic **8:** 4518
mixed **8:** 4518
manpower approach
effect of comparative analysis on **3:** 1833
methods **3:** ***1825–1830***
microcomputer uses in **11:** 6295
trends **11:** 6298
models **3:** ***1804–1810***, ***1825–1830***
algorithmic **3:** 1825
consensual **3:** 1808
cost effectiveness **8:** 4504
development of **3:** 1827
economic **8:** 4503
examples **3:** 1808
heuristic **3:** 1825, 1828
interactive **3:** 1805
labor needs **3:** 1827; **8:** 4503
linked systems **3:** 1827
management information systems **3:** 1828
multiple **3:** 1809
and neoclassical economics **8:** 4505
political **3:** 1807
political economy **8:** 4505, 4506
rational **3:** 1805
slow political consensus building **8:** 4508
social demand **3:** 1827; **8:** 4504
steady diffusion **8:** 4507
strategic **8:** 4600

technical **8:** 4508, 4595
technicist **3:** 1805
window of opportunity **8:** 4507
national plans **8:** 4490
and national surveys **2:** 650
needs assessment **7:** ***4056–4060***
and neoclassical economics
alternative views **3:** 1814
North America **8:** ***4495–4499***
objectives **3:** 1826; **8:** 4496, 4596
changes in **8:** 4490
overview **8:** ***4499–4510***
participation **3:** 1822
school personnel **9:** 5244
and participative decision-making **3:** 1817
perspectives **8:** 4499
policy constraints **3:** 1824
and policy dialogue **8:** 4599
and political attitudes **3:** 1816
political dimensions **3:** 1807
and political economy **3:** 1817
politics of **3:** 1821; **8:** ***4595–4602***
concepts **8:** 4595
and decentralization **8:** 4599
future trends **8:** 4600
implementation **8:** 4597
and power structure **8:** 4597
and private sector **3:** 1813
and privatization **3:** 1813
processes **11:** 6294
projections
uses of **8:** 4783
purpose of **3:** 1825
and rate of return
to education **8:** 4529
rational **8:** 4595, 4600
politics in **8:** 4596
role of **8:** 4499
and school administration **9:** 5167
and school law **9:** ***5252–5255***
and school mapping **9:** 5255
social process **10:** 5605
sub-Saharan Africa **8:** 4512
and social theories **10:** 5605
and socialism **8:** 4489
and sociology of education **10:** 5605
studies **8:** 4600
sub-Saharan Africa **8:** ***4510–4514***
supporting information for **3:** 1829
tasks of **3:** 1825
for teacher effectiveness
developing nations **8:** ***4519–4526***
and teacher salaries **8:** 4520
technical design **3:** 1822
technical vs. political **8:** 4502
and technology **11:** ***6292–6298***
time horizon **3:** 1824
traditional approach **8:** 4515
types of **8:** 4595
uncertainty in **3:** 1829
unexpected results **3:** 1824
vision building **6:** 3601
and vocational education
Africa **11:** 6255
and wastage **3:** 1826
Western Europe
approaches **8:** 4496
See also
Educational facilities planning
Educational policy
and administrator education
inservice **1:** 72
analytical criteria
and informal sector **3:** 1679
centralized
and educational quality **8:** 4872
comparative analysis **3:** ***1830–1835***
and comparative area studies **2:** 652
and comparative education **2:** 934
comparative research
and data envelopment analysis **3:** 1386
and education indicators **5:** 2985, 2987
and conceptions of teaching **10:** ***6035–6044***
coordination of
and state departments of education **7:** 3836
coordination with public and labor market policy **8:** 4958
cost effectiveness **2:** ***1121–1127***
and cost minimization **3:** 1782
curriculum development **9:** 5522
decentralization **1:** 592
and decision-making
state departments of education **7:** 3838
and development education **3:** 1500
and disabilities **10:** 6243
and distance education **3:** 1566
and economic development **3:** 1684
and education indicators **3:** ***1740–1746***
and educational research **4:** 1837
effect of unions on **10:** 6070
and ethnographic evaluation **4:** 2044
and facilities planning
macrolevel **4:** ***2225–2230***
formation
teacher role in **10:** 6080
global approach **5:** ***2495–2500***
professional implications **5:** 2499
and governance **5:** 2511
growth
and international division of labor **3:** 1707
influences on
division of labor **3:** 1711
and intergovernmental relations **5:** 2510
and the internal labor market **5:** 2941
interventions
and educational quality **8:** 4868
and learning factors **10:** 5749
legitimacy in **6:** ***3367–3368***
legitimatory research **6:** 3368
literacy programs **6:** 3451
minority females
South Africa **7:** 3850
and national surveys **2:** 650
nonformal education
developing nations **7:** ***4141–4145***
participation
and information networks **5:** 2996
and philosophy of education **10:** 5984
and politics of education **5:** ***2957–2961***; **8:** 4587
and popular preferences **8:** 4590
public schools vs. private schools **8:** 4843
implications **8:** 4843
quality improvement
developing nations **8:** ***4865–4873***
models for **8:** 4865, 4867
research **8:** ***4556–4562***
and resistance to change **9:** 5508
role of the state **3:** ***1713–1720***
and school choice **9:** 5192
and school desegregation **3:** 1485
school personnel
and outcomes of education **9:** 5263
and skill development
future trends **11:** 6702
and social rate of return **7:** 4254
and social scientific research
models **8:** 4559
and sociology of education **10:** 5605
studies **4:** ***1835–1841***
definitions of **4:** 1835
developing nations **4:** 1838
developing nations vs. developed nations **4:** 1838
influences of **4:** 1837
scope **4:** 1836
undervaluation **4:** 1839
teacher education **8:** 4523
and philosophy of education **10:** 5984
preservice vs. inservice **8:** 4524
teacher employment benefits **8:** 4521
and teacher evaluation **10:** 6041
and teacher participation **10:** 6080
teacher role
and teacher education **10:** 5983, 5985
and teachers **8:** 4519
management implications **10:** ***6079–6083***
and technological advancement **11:** 6279
and textbook preparation **11:** 6363
training
and market distortions **11:** 6637
and unions **10:** 6075
vocational education
Central and Eastern Europe **11:** 6646
China, People's Republic of **2:** 757, 759
comparative area studies **11:** 6697
effect of market forces on **11:** 6687, 6702
recommendations **5:** 2815
Sweden **11:** 6693
women's education
Islamic culture **11:** 6756

Educational practices
descriptive concept of **11:** 6576
impact of educational research on **4:** 1871
philosophy of education
Erasmus **4:** 2006
and psychology **4:** 1842
and research
translation of **9:** ***5038–5043***
Educational principles
and curriculum development **3:** 1326
and educational objectives
curriculum development **3:** 1803
prescriptive concept of **11:** 6576
values **11:** ***6576–6580***
Educational production functions
See Productivity
Educational programming
See Educational planning
Educational psychology
curriculum development
influence on **4:** ***1841–1848***
influence on, research **4:** 1846
and educational history **3:** 1793, 1794
emergence as a discipline **4:** 1841
factors in learning **8:** ***4400–4404***, ***4401***
and prior learning **8:** 4698
and psychoanalytic theory
ego development **8:** 4813
relationship with instructional psychology **5:** 2874
and theory practice relationship **9:** 5038
See also
Instructional psychology
Educational quality
and ability grouping **9:** 5170
and academic achievement **8:** 4866, 4868
and accreditation of teacher education **1:** 27
and balance between public and private schools **8:** 4824
basic education
International Institute for Educational Planning programs **11:** 6528
and centralized policy **8:** 4872
and characteristics of preservice teachers **10:** ***6103–6106***
and community support **2:** 912
comparative analysis **1:** 466, 469
components of **9:** 5241
curriculum design
and the law **6:** 3358, 3360
determinants of **8:** 4867
developing nations
improvement policies **8:** ***4865–4873***
and educational finance **9:** 5235
and educational research **8:** 4866
emerging models **8:** 4871
factors affecting **8:** 4866
research findings **8:** 4862
and governance of teacher education **10:** ***5961–5965***
and grade repetition **5:** 2514
improvement **9:** 5241
models for **8:** 4865
international education
crisis **5:** 2958
and learning factors **10:** 5749
measurement of
use of comparative analysis **3:** 1834
and outcomes of education **8:** 4858
policy models
production-function **8:** 4867
school organization **8:** 4870
teacher characteristics **8:** 4869
and private resources **8:** 4704
and private schools **8:** 4833
and racial discrimination **8:** 4900
reinforcement
and vocational education **8:** 4863
and resource allocation **9:** 5235
resource room programs **9:** 5069
and school business partnerships **9:** 5187
and school choice **9:** 5197
and school effectiveness **8:** 4865
and school mapping **9:** 5257
and school size **9:** 5291
schools and crisis **4:** 2269
and science education **8:** 4475
and teacher certification **10:** ***5925–5930***
and teacher recruitment **10:** 6044
and test results **7:** 3723
and testing programs
United States **7:** 3724
and training courses **2:** 1138
trends
developing nations **8:** 4865
vocational education **8:** ***4858–4865***
and classroom techniques **8:** 4863
and educational environment **8:** 4860
and institutional characteristics **8:** 4859
and instructional materials **8:** 4859
and leadership **8:** 4860
and teacher education **8:** 4859
and teacher selection **8:** 4859
Educational radio **5:** ***2884–2891***
Africa **5:** 2885
Asia **5:** 2886
characteristics of **5:** 2885
criticism of **4:** 1906
definition of **5:** 2884
distance education
adult education **1:** 562
developing nations **3:** 1559, 1561
future trends **5:** 2889
interactive **5:** 2884
characteristics of **5:** 2888
costs **5:** 2888
effectiveness of **5:** 2887
future trends **5:** 2889
historical background **5:** 2887
Latin America **5:** 2886
overview **5:** 2885
role of **4:** 1905
support for
factors **5:** 2890
sustainability problems **4:** 1906
technical problems **5:** 2885
See also
Radio
Educational reform
and academic achievement **10:** 6079
and adult education
definitions **1:** 159
analysis of **8:** 4517
commitment level **4:** 1852
contextual stability **4:** 1853
contextual suitability **4:** 1853
and environment
assessment of **8:** 4517
implementation of **4:** ***1852–1857***
cost effectiveness **4:** 1856
decision-making participation **4:** 1855
expertise for **4:** 1855
leadership role **4:** 1854
political strategies **4:** 1856
and school self-evaluation **5:** 2851
variables affecting **4:** 1852, 1857
internationalization **9:** 5280
and mainstreaming **11:** 6458
objectives **4:** 1854
and personnel management
United States **8:** 4407
and physical sciences **8:** 4475
planning
contingency approach **8:** ***4514–4519***
priorities **8:** 4515
rationale for **8:** 4514
scale of **4:** 1852
scope of **4:** 1852
and sex differences
trends **9:** 5431
and social mobility **9:** 5552
and teacher education **10:** 6042
and teacher responsibility **10:** 6209
and teaching
realities of **10:** 6208
and urban education **11:** ***6551–6558***
urban schools **11:** 6555, 6559
See also
Educational change
Educational innovation
School reform
Educational relevance
See Relevance (education)
Educational research
1900–1930 **4:** 1864, 1867
1930s to late 1950s **4:** 1864, 1869
1960s to 1970s **4:** 1864, 1870
1980s to 1990s **4:** 1871
and action research **1:** 42
agendas
choice of **8:** 4603
criticism of **8:** 4602
and politics **8:** 4602
applications **9:** 5042
approaches **9:** 5038
assignments **9:** 5359
audiotape recordings in **11:** ***6604–6608***

autonomous
criticism of **8:** 4557
autonomous institutions outside universities **2:** 938
and behavioral science research **10:** 6160
and case studies **2:** 642
methods **2:** 641
centers
documentation systems **3:** 1589
characteristics of **11:** 6439
collective nature of **9:** 5407
commercial television **5:** 2895
commissioned vs. academic **3:** 1556
comparative analysis **2:** ***948–958***, ***958–964***
adult education **1:** 179
future developments **2:** 956
computer uses in **4:** 1870; **9:** 5034
conduct of
and politics **8:** 4603
cooperative
teacher education **10:** 6039
and courseware design **2:** 1166
critical issues
response to **9:** 5035
critical paradigms **9:** 5022
and critical theory **2:** ***1199–1204***
criticisms of **9:** 5039
cross-disciplinary **9:** 5034, 5036
cross-sectional studies **2:** ***1213–1220***
curriculum coverage **4:** 1935
curriculum development **4:** 1869
curriculum evaluation **4:** 1869
databases in **3:** ***1387–1394***, 1554
descriptive
data analysis **3:** 1464
descriptive scales
and educational climate **3:** ***1475–1483***
design **8:** ***4873–4875***
historical background **4:** 1867
developmental stages **3:** ***1508–1514***
developments **9:** 5034
dissemination of **3:** ***1553–1557***
global context **3:** 1553
mechanisms **3:** 1555
policy impact **3:** 1556
and educational change **4:** 1869
educational history **5:** 2615
and educational planning **8:** 4599
Latin America **8:** 4493
lead time **11:** 6294
and educational policy **4:** 1837; **5:** 2499
developing nations **4:** 1838
and educational quality **8:** 4866
production-function model **8:** 4868
Educational Resources Information Center (US)
and information networks **5:** 2995
educational television **5:** 2894
empirical analytic paradigms **9:** 5022
epistemology **4:** 1871, 1996; **8:** 4631; **9:** ***5021–5031***
ethical issues **4:** 2032
ethnography **4:** ***2046–2053***
evaluation **9:** 5033
evaluations as objects of **11:** 6576
event history analysis **4:** 2150
experimental psychology **4:** 1864, 1865; **9:** 5053
experimental studies **4:** ***2186–2194***
experimental vs. quasiexperimental **4:** 2187
and exploratory data analysis **4:** 2200
and facet theory **4:** 2218
and factor analysis **4:** 2240
feminist **11:** ***6723–6727***
research methodology **4:** ***2297–2302***
finance for **8:** 4598
findings
and models of schooling **9:** 5042
functions of **9:** 5032
and Galois lattice method **4:** 2397, 2399
gaps in **11:** 6525
governance **5:** 2507; **8:** 4591
hermeneutics **9:** 5052
and hierarchical linear models **5:** 2590
historical methods **5:** ***2601–2607***
theory of **5:** 2605
traditional framework **5:** 2602
history of **4:** ***1864–1873***
key events **4:** 1866
holistic or systemic **2:** 948
humanistic tradition **4:** 1864, 1871
and hypothesis testing **5:** 2710
impact on educational practices **4:** 1871
and information networks **5:** 2994
institutions
establishment of **8:** 4602
instructional psychology **5:** ***2880–2884***; **8:** 4400
interaction effects **5:** ***2922–2931***
interactive video **11:** 6602
interdisciplinary approach **8:** 4400
interdisciplinary character of **11:** 6439
and international co-operation **5:** 2964
international indicators **5:** ***2984–2989***
international studies
comparative analysis **3:** ***1762–1769***
into microcomputer-based laboratories **7:** 3809
and knowledge **9:** 5054
knowledge utilization **8:** 4604
learning
approaches to **1:** ***318–322***
learning ability
studies **8:** 4424
learning processes **10:** 5783
and student characteristics **10:** 5745
legitimatory research **6:** ***3368–3373***
and logical positivism **4:** 1858
longitudinal studies **6:** ***3512–3524***
measurement **7:** ***3698–3707***
of change **2:** ***671–678***
of variation **7:** ***3726–3739***
media selection **7:** 3758
media vs. conventional treatments **7:** 3744
meta analysis **8:** 4402
future trends **7:** 3783
methodology
and politics **8:** 4603
and values **11:** 6576
microcomputers in **7:** ***3810–3816***
missing scores **7:** ***3858–3862***
and model building **7:** 3865
moderating and mediating effects in **4:** ***1873–1877***
multilevel analysis **7:** ***3978–3987***
multilevel nature of **9:** 5035
multiple regression analysis
applications **9:** 4972
multitrait multimethod techniques **7:** ***4000–4007***
multivariate analysis **7:** 3704, ***4007–4016***
narrative inquiry **7:** ***4046–4051***
nature of **9:** 5032
needs **9:** ***5031–5038***
criteria for priorities **9:** 5037
factors influencing **9:** 5035
vs. knowledge accumulation **9:** 5034
and neopositivism **4:** 1858
nongovernmental organizations **2:** 940
nonparametric statistics **7:** ***4157–4163***
nonverbal communication **7:** 4171
objectives
and politics **8:** 4602
oral history **7:** ***4220–4225***
organization of
concerns **9:** 5031
outcomes of education
productivity **8:** 4401
regression (statistics) **8:** 4401
outcomes of **9:** 5033
paradigms **9:** ***5051–5056***
characteristics of **9:** 5051
Continental **9:** 5051
historical background **9:** 5051, 5052
pluralistic approaches to **9:** 5054
types of **9:** 5051, 5053
utilization **9:** 5054
and partial credit model **7:** 4302
and path analysis **8:** 4339, 4352
pedagogical content knowledge **10:** 6181
personality inventories in **8:** 4398
phenomenography **8:** ***4424–4429***
phenomenology **9:** 5052
philosophical issues
positivism **8:** ***4630–4634***
and philosophy of education **8:** 4455
and policy analysis **8:** ***4550–4556***
and policy formation **4:** ***1857–1864***; **8:** 4602
historical background **4:** 1858
policy formation
international organizations **2:** 934
policy-oriented **3:** 1386; **5:** 2985, 2987; **8:** ***4556–4562***

functions of **8:** 4557, 4560, 4561
trends in **8:** 4557
utilization **8:** 4558
politics of **8:** ***4602–4604***
positivism **4:** 1864; **9:** 5051
postpositivism **9:** 5022, 5024
and practice
gap between **9:** 5038
historical background **9:** 5038
translation into **9:** ***5038–5043***
pre-1900 **4:** 1865
prediction in **8:** ***4652–4657***
priorities **9:** ***5031–5038***
criteria for setting **9:** 5036
dangers **9:** 5032
determination of **9:** 5036
problems **9:** 5035
statements of **9:** 5037
problems in **9:** 5031
productivity **11:** 6441
and progressive education **4:** 1864, 1866, 1869
prospective inquiry **9:** 5033
public schools vs. private schools **8:** ***4839–4845***
pure vs. applied **8:** 4556
qualitative research **9:** 4977, 5407
quasiexperimental design **4:** 1870; **8:** 4400
and questioning techniques **8:** 4875
and racial attitudes **3:** 1484
and rating scales **8:** 4924
realism (philosophy) and relativism **9:** ***4977–4981***
attitudes to **9:** 4977
religious education **9:** 5006
reporting of **3:** 1473
resource allocation **8:** 4602
response of anthropology to **1:** 283
responsive
criticism of **8:** 4557
sampling **9:** 5131
school-based management **9:** 5306
and school desegregation **3:** 1483
school organization **5:** 2848
schools
and sampling **9:** 5134
science education
primary school programs **9:** 5334
and scientific methodology **9:** 5052
and secondary data analysis **9:** 5369
selection bias in **9:** ***5379–5385***
self-report in **9:** ***5407–5411***
semiotics in **9:** ***5411–5417***
single case research **9:** ***5486–5490***
and social action **9:** 5033
and social background data
problems **7:** 3718
and social scientific research **9:** 5053
social studies **9:** 5580
and sociometric techniques **10:** 5614, 5616
Soviet Union (former) **4:** 1869, 1870
sport pedagogy **10:** ***5708–5713***
statistical analysis
historical development **4:** 1867
statistics
historical development **4:** 1865, 1867
and indicators **5:** 2986
international comparability **3:** 1429
strategies **9:** 5034
and politics **8:** 4603
studies
undervaluation **4:** 1839
surveys **10:** ***5854–5862***
administrative and normative **4:** 1868
symbolic paradigms **9:** 5022
and teacher education **9:** 5053
trends **10:** 6042
and teacher effectiveness **8:** 4521
teacher expectation of students **10:** 6106
and teacher expertise **9:** 5041
and teacher knowledge **10:** 6117
effects on **10:** 6120
teaching
imagery **10:** 6181
metaphors **10:** 6181
paradigms for **10:** ***6202–6208***
synthesizing **10:** ***6235–6240***
teaching methods
instructional effectiveness **5:** 2778
teaching skills
subject matter knowledge **10:** 6039
testing and assessment
historical development **4:** 1867
Thorndike's contribution **4:** 1867
traditions **9:** 5021
trend analysis **10:** 6197
types of
and sampling **9:** 5131
and secondary data analysis **9:** 5367
unintended effects in **11:** ***6507–6511***
unity thesis **9:** 5022, 5025, 5026, 5028
universities **2:** 935
utilization
models **4:** 1862
of results **8:** 4603
reviews **4:** 1861
value judgments in **11:** 6576
justifying **11:** 6578
variables **9:** 5034
classroom environment **2:** 809
leadership studies **6:** 3281
videotape recordings in **11:** ***6604–6608***
and visual literacy **11:** 6622
vocational education
Central and Eastern Europe **11:** 6641
writing instruction
and word processing **7:** 4090
Educational researchers
attitudes
and multivariate analysis **7:** 4007
beliefs of
educational change **10:** 6103
students **10:** 6102
characteristics of **4:** 1859; **8:** 4551; **9:** 5034
and educational history **3:** 1796
motivation of **9:** 5031
and participant observation **7:** 4317
and policy analysts
compared **8:** 4550, 4551
and policymakers compared **4:** 1859
role of **9:** 5035
and videotape recordings **11:** 6606
teachers as
Boston Women Teachers' Group **10:** 6098
curriculum development **10:** 6096
educational change **10:** 6098
feminism **10:** 6098
professional development **10:** 6097
social change **10:** 6098
theory practice relationship **10:** ***6096–6099***
and technological advancement
impact of **9:** 5035
training **11:** ***6438–6445***
degree programs **11:** 6442
examinations **11:** 6443
historical background **11:** 6438
incentives **11:** 6441
institutional arrangements **11:** 6443
recommendations **11:** 6440, 6443
recruitment **11:** 6441
specialized courses **11:** 6444
Educational resources
and academic achievement **3:** 1779
adult education **10:** 6200
allocation
and decentralization **3:** 1413
control of
and productivity **7:** 3817
decline in
and educational improvement **9:** 5245
and educational finance **9:** 5235, 5236
and educational planning **8:** 4520
and educational quality **8:** 4859
and educational technology **4:** 1889
and effects on academic achievement **7:** 3817
and equal education
developing nations **9:** 5537
and family environment **7:** 3721
and governance **5:** 2510
inequality in
and private resources **8:** 4705
and information technology **7:** 4083
libraries as **6:** ***3394–3399***
and national surveys **2:** 652
obtaining
and educational finance **9:** 5236
redistribution
Nordic countries **7:** 4176, 4177, 4178
and technical inefficiency **3:** 1784
vocational education
increasing efficiency in the use of **5:** 2817

Educational Resources Information Center (ERIC) (US) **1:** 141
activities **5:** 2823
comparative education data **3:** 1586
contact details **5:** 2827
document reproduction service **5:** 2824
and documentation systems **3:** 1590
educational research
and information networks **5:** 2995
and educational researchers **11:** 6438
educational technology
studies **4:** 1928
guides to **5:** 2824
international **5:** 2826
online systems **5:** 2824
optical data disks **5:** 2824, 2826
publications **5:** 2823
questioning techniques
research reports **8:** 4875
thesaurus of descriptors **5:** 2824
Educational responsibility
moral development **10:** 5987
public sector vs. private sector **8:** ***4831–4836***
Educational sociology
See Sociology of education
Educational software
See Courseware
Educational statistics
and projections **8:** ***4783–4788***
methods **8:** 4784
Educational strategies
and educational technology **9:** 5539
frame factors
piloting **4:** 2376
steering group **4:** 2375, 2376
and learning disabilities
comparative area studies **10:** 5684
learning processes **5:** 2500
mastery learning
formative evaluation **6:** 3626
and planning **3:** 1828
sex fairness **5:** 2455; **9:** ***5441–5445***
small classes **2:** 774
for social participation **3:** 1711
Educational supply
and national surveys **2:** 651
Educational surveys
See School surveys
Educational system
See System of education
Educational technology
and academically gifted
research **10:** 5672
and access to education **9:** 5542
adoption of
barriers to **11:** 6286
and adult education **1:** 148
applications **4:** 1887
audiovisual instruction
Hong Kong **5:** 2641
Sri Lanka **10:** 5719
autotelic activity **4:** 1895
broadcasting vs. audiocassette recordings **3:** 1577
classroom-level factors **4:** 1916
comparative area studies **4:** 1915
competencies required **4:** 1927
computer-assisted instruction **4:** 1922
computer networks **2:** ***977–982***
concepts of **4:** 1884
conceptual frameworks **4:** ***1882–1899***
consolidation period **4:** 1888
cost effectiveness
feasibility studies **2:** 1122
Costa Rica **2:** 1145
cultural factors **4:** 1916
current knowledge **9:** 5540
curriculum factors **4:** 1916
definitions of **4:** 1889, 1899, 1912, 1925
delivery systems **9:** 5542
developing nations **4:** ***1899–1903***
examples **4:** 1900
future research **4:** 1902
trends and issues **4:** 1902
development of **9:** 5040
sectors for **4:** 1885
development organizations **4:** 1881
in distance education **3:** ***1573–1580***
instructional issues **3:** 1577
economics of **4:** ***1903–1911***, 1916; **9:** 5540
criticism of **4:** 1904
and educational media
organizations **3:** 1797
and educational planning **11:** ***6292–6298***
Asia **8:** 4488
and educational technologists **4:** 1883
effects of **9:** 5540
in elementary education **4:** ***1911–1918***
realities of **4:** 1915
roles of **4:** 1912
ethics
code of **4:** 1927
field of study **4:** 1889, ***1924–1929***
challenges **4:** 1928
characteristics of **4:** 1925
definition of **9:** 5539
functions **4:** 1925
future research **9:** 5543
future trends **4:** 1928
hardware and software
availability **4:** 1915, 1916
historical background **7:** 3756
historical development **4:** ***1882–1899***
hypertext **5:** ***2706–2709***
and information technology **4:** 1897
and instructional design
special needs students **10:** 5670
theory of **5:** 2865
and instructional materials
trends **8:** 4847
and instructional psychology **5:** 2879
integrated learning systems
and vocational education **4:** 1921
interactionist concepts of **4:** 1895
interactive video **4:** 1921
international organizations
activities **4:** ***1878–1882***
interpretative paradigm **4:** 1892
issues **9:** 5539
in labor force development **4:** 1918, 1923
applications **4:** 1921
and learning **7:** ***3739–3744***
measurement of efficiency **7:** 3743
theories of **9:** 5040
and mass media **4:** 1893
mechanical aspects **7:** 3739
multimedia systems **7:** 3991
and neoclassical economics **4:** 1910
occupational information **4:** 1926
occupations in **4:** 1926
patterns of use **4:** 1915
in physical sciences
secondary school programs **8:** 4475, 4477
policy factors **4:** 1916
positivist paradigm **4:** 1892
potentialities of **4:** 1911, 1912
factors affecting **4:** 1915
professional certification **7:** 3755
professional organizations **4:** 1927
professional personnel **4:** 1925
categories of **4:** 1926
professional training **4:** 1926
project evaluation **8:** 4780
rationales for **4:** 1899
recognition of **4:** 1883
and religious education **9:** 5002
research **7:** 3759
role of **9:** 5540
school level factors **4:** 1916
in secondary education **4:** ***1911–1918***
realities of **4:** 1915
roles of **4:** 1912
semantics **4:** 1885
settings **4:** 1925
social implications of **9:** ***5539–5545***
in social studies **9:** 5582
special education **5:** 2970
student participation
increasing **9:** 5542
support personnel **4:** 1916
systems approach **4:** 1886
teacher education **10:** ***6004–6009***
and teacher role **11:** ***6283–6287***
teacher use of
patterns **11:** 6283
in technical education **4:** 1920
youth and adults **4:** ***1918–1924***, ***1922***
trends **7:** 3757; **9:** 5543
and issues **4:** 1917
types of **4:** 1891
and special needs students **10:** 5668
uses
special needs students **10:** ***5668–5674***
See also
Instructional systems
Educational television **4:** 1913; **5:** ***2891–2897***
barriers to use of **11:** 6286
constructivist perspective **7:** 3745

corporate television **5:** 2894
and cost effectiveness studies **2:** 1134
criticism of **4:** 1905
developments **5:** 2896
distance education
adult education **1:** 562
effects on children and youth **1:** 566
historical background **5:** 2892
impact of **5:** 2894
large-scale projects **5:** 2892
political issues **9:** 5541
preschool children **8:** ***4677–4680***
Australia **8:** 4678
Canada **8:** 4678
Japan **8:** 4679
programs **8:** 4678
research trends **8:** 4679
United Kingdom **8:** 4679
United States **8:** 4678
research studies **5:** 2894
role of **4:** 1904
school television **5:** 2893
teacher attitudes to **4:** 1905
United States **3:** 1566
Educational testing
computerized **2:** ***992–998***
decision theory in **3:** ***1416–1421***
evaluation procedures **2:** 992
item bias **5:** ***3043–3051***, ***3046***
multiple matrix sampling **5:** 3058
objectives **1:** 371
Educational Testing Service (ETS) (US) **3:** 1765
National Teachers Examination **10:** 5927
PRAXIS series **4:** 2128
Study I (1988) **4:** 2132, 2139
Study II (1991) **4:** 2132, 2139
Educational theories
and antipedagogy **8:** 4458
aptitude and instruction **8:** 4401
Dewey's **10:** 5813
and epistemology **4:** ***1996–2001***
Froebel's **4:** ***2385–2388***
Herbart's practical pedagogical enquiries **5:** 2577
Herbart's theoretical pedagogical enquiries **5:** 2578
history c. 1800 **5:** 2575
individual development debate **8:** 4457
influences **10:** 6179
international impact **5:** 2608
Kerschensteiner's **6:** 3136
and Marxism **6:** ***3617–3622***
operant model **1:** 483
productivity **8:** 4401
social theories **2:** ***1064–1074***
teacher attitudes toward **10:** 6094
teachers **10:** ***6178–6183***
participatory research **10:** 6180
relevance (education) **10:** 6179
research **10:** 6180
and value neutrality **11:** 6577
See also
Educational anthropology
Frame factor theory
Philosophy of education
Educational transfer
and international publishing
research relevance **8:** 4846
Educational trends
futures (of society)
teacher burnout **10:** 6061
teacher development **10:** 5934
Educational vouchers
and educational finance **9:** 5239
vocational education **11:** 6653
and educational information **9:** 5205
private schools **9:** 5198
regulations
requirements for **9:** 5204
and school choice **1:** 591; **4:** 2330; **8:** 4825; **9:** 5195
educational equity (finance) **3:** 1792
historical background **9:** 5202
social vs. family perspectives **9:** 5203
systems compared **9:** 5204
and tuition fees **8:** 4825
United States **3:** 1336
Educationally disadvantaged
at risk persons
compensatory education **4:** 1847
cultural differences **2:** 707
female blacks
South Africa **7:** ***3848–3853***
incidence
United States **2:** 709
outreach programs **7:** 4247
Edwards Personal Preference Schedule (EPPS) **8:** 4397
Effect size
analysis of
and meta analysis **7:** 3782
averaging of
and meta analysis **7:** 3781
estimating variation in
and meta analysis **7:** 3781
and hypothesis testing **5:** 2713
and meta analysis **7:** 3777, 3780
and research synthesis **7:** 3776
research synthesis
methods **10:** 6236
and sex differences
in academic achievement **9:** 5427
and statistical power **4:** 2192
in teacher expectation of students **10:** 6109
Effective schools
characteristics of **4:** 1930, 1932
creation of
practices and principles **4:** 1932
curriculum design in **4:** 1931
and educational change **6:** 3599
influences of **4:** 1932
management of **4:** ***1929–1934***
organizational objectives **4:** 1930
parent participation **4:** 1931
recognition (achievement) **4:** 1931
secondary **9:** ***5373–5379***
definition of **9:** 5374
See also
School effectiveness
Effective schools research
decision-making
and outcomes of education **9:** 5263
design approaches **4:** 1936
early beliefs **4:** 1931
experiments **4:** 1936
five factor theory **4:** 1930
future requirements **4:** 1933
historical background **4:** 1934
and inservice education **1:** 68
international studies **4:** 1929, 1931
interpretation of results **4:** 1938
issues **4:** 1938
and learning theories **10:** 5746
longitudinal designs
repeated measures on schools **4:** 1936
repeated measures on students **4:** 1936
methodological issues **4:** ***1934–1939***
methods **4:** 1929; **9:** 5373
and multilevel analysis **4:** 1937
objectives of **4:** 1934
and outcomes of education **4:** 1935; **9:** 5261
policy issues **4:** 1938
principals
role of **10:** 6082
and school-based management **6:** 3493
and school climate **9:** 5207
criticisms of **9:** 5208
schooling constructs
definition and measurement of **4:** 1935
secondary
historical background **9:** 5373
longitudinal studies **9:** 5377
studies **9:** 5373
and teacher administrator relationship **4:** 1930
United States **9:** 5276
See also
School effectiveness
Effective teaching
See Teacher effectiveness
Efficiency
definition of **3:** 1412
of education
and economic theory of markets **6:** 3614
and equal education **3:** 1654
external **3:** 1679
internal **3:** 1679
measurement
and educational planning **3:** 1814
public sector **3:** 1383
schools **3:** 1383, 1385
See also
Educational efficiency

Efficiency wage model
and employment contracts **3:** 1698
in stratification model **6:** 3187
Effort
See Energy expenditure
EFL
See English (foreign language)
Egalitarianism **8:** 4572, 4574
liberal
and justice **4:** 2002
Ego development
psychoanalytic theory **8:** 4813
Sentence Completion Test **10:** 5937
teachers **10:** 5937
Egocentrism
in childhood
Jewish theory of individual development **6:** 3114
and social cognition **9:** 5510
Egypt
academic achievement
effect of parents on **4:** 2417
adult education
nonformal education **4:** 1943
computer uses in education **4:** 1902
curriculum development **4:** 1945
educational change **4:** 1946
educational research **4:** 1946
ethnography of indigenous populations **3:** 1753
government school relationship
financial support **4:** 1944
school administration **4:** 1943
macroeconomics
and education level **11:** 6635
population growth **1:** 322
secondary school curriculum
citizenship education **9:** 5579
structure of government **4:** 1940
system of education **4:** ***1939–1947***
degrees and qualifications **4:** 1946
educational objectives **4:** 1940
major problems **4:** 1947
structure **4:** 1941
teacher education **4:** 1945
teacher recruitment **4:** 1945
technical education **4:** 1942
vocational education **4:** 1942; **10:** 5915
women's education **11:** 6754, 6755, 6758
Eigenstructures
and discriminant analysis **3:** 1545, 1546
Eigenvalues
and attitude measures **1:** 384
and discriminant analysis **3:** 1546
factor analysis **4:** 2234
Eigenvectors
and discriminant analysis **3:** 1546
factor analysis **4:** 2234
Eight-Year Study (US) **4:** 2080, 2093
and educational research **4:** 1868
and student participation **10:** 5814
Eire
See Ireland, Republic of
El Salvador
adult education
nonformal education **4:** 1951
curriculum development **4:** 1953
educational change **4:** 1953; **8:** 4493
educational research **4:** 1953
educational television **4:** 1904
large-scale projects **5:** 2892
ethnic groups **4:** 1948
government school relationship
financial support **4:** 1952
school administration **4:** 1951
postsecondary education **4:** 1950
preschool education **4:** 1950
primary education **4:** 1949
secondary education **4:** 1949
vocational education **4:** 1950
special education **4:** 1950
structure of government **4:** 1948
system of education **4:** ***1947–1954***
degrees and qualifications **4:** 1953
educational objectives **4:** 1948
enrollment **4:** 1949
major problems **4:** 1954
structure **4:** 1949
teacher education **4:** 1952
teacher recruitment **4:** 1952
teaching methodology **4:** 1953
technical education **4:** 1951
vocational education **4:** 1951
Elasticity of demand
day care **2:** 690
for educated labor **3:** ***1443–1449***
human capital theory **3:** 1446
measurement
and labor force planning **6:** 3612
Elasticity of substitution
empirical research **3:** 1445
function **3:** 1444
measurement
and labor force planning **6:** 3610
Elasticity of supply
and child care occupations **2:** 690
cobweb model **3:** 1447
for educated labor **3:** ***1443–1449***
and educational finance **4:** 2314
long-term **3:** 1447
and monopsony discrimination **4:** 2444
price **3:** 1448
short-term **3:** 1447
Elder hostels movement (US) **8:** 4806
Elderly
See Older adults
Elections
and unions
partisanship **10:** 6076
Electricity
education
laboratory packages for **6:** 3203
theory
and technical education **11:** 6414
Electronic blackboards
characteristics of **11:** 6300
Electronic control
laboratory packages for **6:** 3204
Electronic equipment
special needs students **7:** 3805
Electronic mail
applications **11:** 6303
characteristics of **11:** 6300
and computer networks **2:** 978
and educational research
dissemination of **3:** 1554
and electronic publishing **4:** 1955
foreign language instruction **4:** 2354
and information networks
international **5:** 2997
and language education **7:** 4089
and writing instruction **7:** 4089
Electronic publishing **4:** ***1954–1958***
copyright implications **4:** 1955
and desktop publishing
compared **4:** 1955
educational effects of **4:** 1956
in educational media organizations **3:** 1799
origin of term **4:** 1954
See also
Desktop publishing (DTP)
Electronic University (US) **11:** 6550
Elementary education
and educational equity (finance) **3:** 1791
educational technology in **4:** ***1911–1918***
enrollment
projections **8:** 4784
equal education
Germany **11:** 6742
moral development
Pestalozzi's views **3:** 1721; **8:** 4417
printed materials for
characteristics of **8:** 4695
See also
Adult basic education
Basic education
Primary education
Elementary school curriculum
problem-solving programs **8:** 4729
Elementary School Foreign Languages (ESFL) **4:** 2346
Elementary school teachers
and sex discrimination **9:** 5170
use of explanation **10:** 6146
Elementary schools
and bureaucracy **6:** 3525
curriculum
science education history **9:** 5325
and desegregation **3:** 1484
and educational television **5:** 2893
enrollment rate
francophone Africa **11:** 6738
expenditure
projections **8:** 4786
school counselors in **9:** 5283
and social studies **9:** 5572
See also
Primary schools

Elementary and Secondary Education Act (ESEA) 1965 (US) **4:** 2080, 2111; **8:** 4763
and educational research **4:** 1870
Title I and III Evaluation Programs (US) **4:** 2080; **8:** 4763
Title VII
on bilingualism **7:** 3972
Eleven-plus examination (UK)
selection **9:** 5386
and test coaching **11:** 6337
Elitism
education and leadership **3:** 1652
ELT (English language teaching)
See English (foreign language) English(second language)
Elton Report (UK) (1989)
discipline in schools **8:** 4368
Email
See Electronic mail
Embedded Figures Test **4:** 2335
Emotion
cognitive theories **4:** 1963
conceptualizations **4:** 1963
definitions and classification **4:** 1963
and learning **6:** 3641
psychoanalytic theories **4:** 1963
psychobiological approaches **4:** 1963
social learning conceptualizations **4:** 1963
theories and research traditions **4:** 1963
Emotional abuse
of children **1:** 15
Emotional development **4:** ***1963–1967***
of academically gifted **9:** ***5528–5532***
and cognitive development **4:** 1963, 1964
educational implications of research **4:** 1966
future research trends **4:** 1966
general principles **4:** 1964
integrative approaches **4:** 1964
and moral development **4:** 1965
primary emotions **4:** 1964
self-evaluative emotions **4:** 1965
Emotional disturbances
behavior disorders **1:** ***486–490***
behavior modification **1:** 489
and resilience **8:** 4776
severe **1:** 487
and social adjustment **1:** 488, 492
and social skills training **1:** 489
Emotional experience
effect on learning **1:** 199
and motivation
influence on cognitive processes **1:** 330
Emotional problems
effect on learning **1:** 200
sexual abuse and **1:** 17
and test anxiety **11:** 6355
Empathy
cross-cultural studies **5:** 2649
sex differences **9:** 5434
social cognition **9:** 5510
and social development **9:** 5524
young children **8:** 4797
Empiricism **8:** 4630
Berkeley's views **4:** 1997
challenges to **8:** 4631
characterization **8:** 4630
developmental psychology **5:** 2667
feminist **4:** 2299
and generalizations
educational research **4:** 1996
Hume's views **4:** 1997
and justification **8:** 4631
and learning processes **6:** 3316
Locke's views **4:** 1997; **8:** 4631
and positivism **8:** ***4630–4634***
and rationalism **4:** 1997
Kantian synthesis **4:** 1997
and scientific attitudes **5:** 2654
and sensory experience **8:** 4630
See also
Logical empiricism
Employed parents
leaves of absence **2:** 697
mothers
and child care services **2:** 693, 696
Employed women
increase in
and social change **9:** 5423
labor force participation
developing nations **3:** 1682
and education **3:** ***1666–1672***
factors affecting **3:** 1666
and preschool education **8:** 4662
and lifelong learning **11:** 6391
sex discrimination **4:** 2281, 2282
Employee absenteeism
teachers **10:** ***5832–5834***
causes **10:** 5832
developing nations **10:** 5832
resource allocation **10:** 5832
Employee attitudes
and job analysis **6:** 3095
motivation
and organizational economics **4:** 1969
in schools **4:** ***1967–1972***
Employee employer relationship
See Employer employee relationship
Employee evaluation
See Personnel evaluation
Employee involvement
See Participative decision-making
Employer attitudes
to females **4:** 2285
and job analysis **6:** 3095
Employer employee relationship
conflict **5:** 2794
decision-making **5:** 2793
employment contracts **3:** ***1695–1703***
implicit contracts **3:** 1697
and labor relations
in education **6:** 3189
and unions **5:** 2794
Employer supported day care **2:** 689
developing nations **3:** 1627
Employers
and alternation education **8:** 4962
expenditure on continuing education **2:** 1148
and financing lifelong learning **6:** 3424
and illiteracy **8:** 4636, 4638
incentives for firm-based training **4:** 1975
and labor force planning
survey **6:** 3610
and paid educational leave **7:** 4263
payment for general training **6:** 3615
rate of return
on-the-job training **6:** 3615, 3616
training costs **11:** 6417
training obligations **6:** 3616
training requirements **1:** 109, 110; **4:** 1974
Employment
and adult education
research **1:** 161
barriers to
and disabilities **11:** 6460
choice model
and earnings differentials **7:** 4198
contracts
and education **3:** ***1695–1703***
incomplete **3:** 1695, 1698
and education
earning **3:** ***1746–1750***
immigrants **5:** 2739
evaluation of effects of training policies on **4:** 1974
and informal sector **5:** 2814
and job training **8:** 4711
lifetime
Finland **5:** 2688
Japan **5:** 2687; **11:** 6696
and numeracy **6:** 3456, 3458
productive
and vocational education **3:** ***1685–1690***
public sector
developing nations **8:** 4838
and education **8:** ***4836–4839***
supply and demand
See Supply and demand, employment factors
at will system
vs. internal labor market **5:** 2941
See also
Work
Employment level
and academic achievement **7:** 3720
and earnings differentials **4:** 2275
empirical research **4:** 2277
and economic status
measurement **4:** 2275
and education
variables **4:** 2276
Wisconsin Longitudinal Study **4:** 2277
and family characteristics **4:** 2276
and intelligence quotient **7:** 3769
measurement **7:** 3716

and family environment **4:** 2278
and genetic endowments **4:** 2278
robustness **7:** 3719
sensitive measures **7:** 3720
and on-the-job training **6:** 3616
over life cycle **4:** 2275
of parents
and social mobility **9:** 5553
scales
females **7:** 3719
sibling correlation **4:** 2277
and social status **7:** 3716
and social stratification **9:** 5549
vocational education and **9:** 5072, 5074
and vocational qualifications
correlation **11:** 6535
mismatch **11:** 6640
Employment opportunities
female blacks
South Africa **7:** 3851
and intelligence **7:** 3769
and low achievement **9:** 5363
and nonformal education **7:** 4143
sex discrimination **4:** 2281
and career choice **4:** 2283
consequences **4:** 2282
and training **4:** 2282
and social stratification **10:** 5732
student expectations
factors affecting **11:** 6700
in teaching
females **10:** 5844
minority groups **10:** 5844
unskilled labor **6:** 3182
and vocational education
mismatch **11:** 6666, 6695
occupational mobility **11:** 6652
vs. academic achievement
in demand occupations **11:** 6258
women faculty **11:** 6709
Employment patterns
and social stratification **10:** 5731
and technological advancement **11:** 6258
urban areas **11:** 6553
and vocational education **4:** 2393
Employment policy
and adult education **4:** ***1972–1976***
and on-the-job training **6:** 3616
and vocational education **4:** ***1972–1976***
Employment projections
demand occupations **11:** 6258
Employment Training Panel (US)
and performance contracts **8:** 4710, 4712, 4713
Employment Training Scheme (ETS) (UK)
vocational education **11:** 6688
Empowerment **4:** ***1980–1985***
families of special needs children **4:** ***1976–1980***
and parent education **7:** 4295
See also
Individual power
Encoding (psychology)
and memorization strategies **7:** 3765
Encopresis
See Fecal incontinence
Enculturation **3:** 1724
Energy expenditure
and ability
and achievement need **1:** 29
compared with academic achievement **10:** 5820
in learning processes **1:** 202
Engineering
definitions of **4:** 1890
and educational technology **4:** 1891
Engineering technicians
functions of **11:** 6267
Engineering technology
and human factors engineering **4:** 2007
Engineers
and paraprofessional personnel
comparisons **11:** 6267
England and Wales
agricultural education
vocational education **1:** 242
art education **1:** 341
curriculum history **3:** 1293, 1294
gifted
special education for **5:** 2493
mathematics curriculum
secondary schools **6:** 3663
mathematics programs **6:** 3665
monitoring of standards **7:** 3907
Revised Code (1862) **3:** 1294
school health education **5:** 2571
special education legislation **2:** 722
teacher education
accreditation **1:** 24, 26; **10:** 5964
testing at age 14 **7:** 3909
See also
National Curriculum
United Kingdom (UK)
English (foreign language)
programs **4:** 2348
use of term **4:** 2346
English (second language)
basic interpersonal communication (BIC) skills **6:** 3228
for Chinese
computer simulation **7:** 4094
and educational innovation
Switzerland **3:** 1552
Hong Kong **2:** 1039
literacy provision **1:** 132
migrant adult education **6:** 3461
programs **4:** 2348
teaching
as art **10:** 6083
use of term **4:** 2347
See also
Limited English speaking
English for academic purposes
bilingual education **3:** 1231
English language teaching
See English (foreign language)
English (secondlanguage)
English native speakers
compared with non English speakers
academic achievement **6:** 3236
English as a second or other language (ESOL)
See English (second language)
English for special purposes
international communication **6:** 3210
factors affecting **5:** 2995
scientific research **5:** 2994
Enlightenment **1:** 112
and curriculum theory **3:** 1290
and moral values **10:** 5986
and people's education **1:** 135
and philosophy of education **8:** 4456, 4639, 4640, 4641
Rousseau and the **9:** ***5087–5091***
and vocational education **11:** 6680
Enrichment
teaching methods
mastery learning **6:** 3627
Enrichment activities
for the gifted **5:** 2493, 2730
Enrollment
adult education
studies **10:** 5593
college students
management model **10:** 5803
and resource allocation **9:** 5063
and school organization **7:** 4232
sex discrimination
francophone Africa **11:** 6739
Enrollment projections
and educational finance **9:** 5234
methods **8:** 4784
Enrollment rate
apprenticeships
Germany, Federal Republic of (former) **11:** 6654
college graduates
and earnings differentials **6:** 3183
comparative analysis
developing nations **1:** 467
developing nations **3:** 1826
and earnings potential **6:** 3099, 3100
educational finance
measurement of **3:** 1790
effect of excess demand on **8:** 4832
female
and birth rate **4:** 2415
India **11:** 6750
and infant mortality **4:** 2415
female blacks
South Africa **7:** 3851
formal education **9:** 5159
input output analysis
and economic adjustment **3:** 1787
job training
United States **11:** 6531
Latin America **8:** 4492
and Lorenz curves **7:** 3733
primary education **3:** 1692, 1826
private education **1:** 589; **8:** 4831

and racial discrimination **6:** 3099
sex differences
and academic persistence **9:** 5536
sub-Saharan Africa **8:** 4510
tuition fees
elasticity of supply **3:** 1447
vocational education
China, People's Republic of **2:** 757
Mexico **6:** 3259
United States **11:** 6534
vocational high schools
Japan **6:** 3088
and women's education **4:** 2412
Enrollment trends **1:** 471; **2:** 1057
academic achievement
comparative analysis **2:** 961
comparative analysis **2:** 961
effect on Latin America **3:** 1832
and formal education **9:** 5533
sex differences
comparative analysis **2:** 961; **3:** 1832
vocational education **11:** 6666
Enterprise
See Business
Entrepreneurship
and apprenticeships
Africa **1:** ***221–227***
attributes **4:** 1985
human capital theory
informal sector **3:** 1678
labor market analysis
informal sector **3:** 1677
and principals
role of **9:** 5270
training **4:** 1985
and universities **4:** 1987
women's education for
developing nations **11:** 6715
Enuresis
See Urinary incontinence
Environment
assessment of
and educational planning **8:** 4517
computer simulation of
and computer-assisted instruction **2:** 988
global problems **4:** 1994
and intelligence quotient **7:** 3770
Environmental education **4:** ***1991–1996***
attitudes and values **4:** 1992
and behavior modification **4:** 1991
conservation education **4:** 1992, 1993
curriculum
hierarchical approaches **4:** 1992
curriculum development **4:** 1994
definitions of **4:** 1991
interdisciplinary approach **4:** 1994
problems with **4:** 1995
learning for action **2:** 904
objectives **4:** 1991, 1992
and peace education **3:** 1730
and population education **8:** 4609
and primary school agriculture **8:** 4683
and responsible behavior **4:** 1992
and science education **9:** 5326
science and society **5:** 2902
and social studies **4:** 1994
teacher education **4:** 1994
UNESCO programs **11:** 6526
Environmental influences
and behavioral theories **10:** 6161
and human factors engineering **4:** 2011
and individual development **6:** 3513
Buddhist theory **1:** 580
Christian theory **2:** 764
Confucian theory **2:** 1043, 1045
Hindu theory **5:** 2598
Islamic theory **5:** 3021
and interpersonal competence
training for **9:** 5565
and learning performance **7:** 3943
and outcomes of education **4:** 2247
and panel studies **6:** 3518
and resilience **8:** 4775
and self-efficacy
of teachers **8:** 4564
and social change **4:** 2328
and testing **11:** 6313
and twin studies **11:** 6490
urban schools **11:** 6551
vs. genetic factors
twin studies **6:** 3140
Environmental measures
classroom **4:** ***2245–2250***
family **4:** ***2245–2250***
future research **4:** 2248
genetic influence on **11:** 6490
interpretative analyses **4:** 2247
press approach **3:** 1476; **4:** 2245
Environmental research
and educational opportunities **4:** 2248
Epidemiology
school health services **5:** 2573
and twin studies **11:** 6489
Epilepsy
characteristics of **8:** 4421
drug therapy for **8:** 4422
See also
Seizures
Epistemology
and action research tradition **9:** 5024
and behavioral science research **9:** 5045
central problems **4:** 1996
cognitive flexibility theory
and interactive video **11:** 6603
coherence **9:** 5027, 5028
culture and learning **3:** 1241
and curriculum legitimation **4:** 1997
and educational research **4:** 1996; **8:** 4631; **9:** ***5021–5031***
and educational theories **4:** ***1996–2001***
and empiricism **8:** 4630
feminist theories **4:** 2299; **11:** 6721
foundationalism **4:** 1997, 2000; **9:** 5027
criticism of **4:** 1998, 2030
genetics
Piagetian theory **8:** 4479
and hypermedia **4:** 1922
information processing in **10:** 5740
and interpersonal competence **9:** 5564
knowledge how and knowledge that **4:** 1996
linguistic aspects **4:** 1999
logic of justification **9:** 5023
and mass media **2:** 886
and metaphysics **4:** 1999
nature of **4:** 1996
nonfoundationalism **4:** 1999, 2000; **8:** 4632
dangers of **4:** 2000
and paradigms **9:** 5022, 5025
and pedagogy **4:** 1996
pluralism in **9:** 5024
praxis tradition (Freire) **9:** 5024
and prototyping **8:** 4801
and psychology
influence on educational theories **4:** 1997
relativism **9:** 4978
and scholasticism **9:** 5123
and science teachers **8:** 4463
social theories **10:** 6098
theoretical framework **10:** 5739
and theory of powers of the mind **9:** 5027
Equal education **1:** 169; **4:** ***2407–2412***; **5:** 2735, 2736; **8:** 4960
for adults **2:** 1193; **7:** 4166
Africa **11:** 6736, 6739
and aptitude treatment interaction **10:** 6156
Asia **8:** 4487, 4488
barriers to
in informal sector **3:** 1679
Coleman Report 1966 (US) **3:** 1756
and computer uses in education **4:** ***2423–2427***
concept of **9:** 5534
and conflict **2:** 1038
and curriculum **6:** 3360
trends **9:** 5522
and decentralization **3:** 1412
and democracy **8:** 4587
and educational benefits **1:** 514
educational history **2:** 1062
and educational planning **3:** 1826; **8:** 4496
and efficiency **3:** 1654
and empowerment **4:** ***1980–1985***
and equal respect
Rawls' views **4:** 2003, 2004
equality of access **9:** 5535
equality of outcome **9:** 5537
equality of output **9:** 5536
equality of survival **9:** 5535
and equity
definitions of **9:** 5534
ethnicity and **8:** 4892
and excellence in education **4:** 2031
feminist theories **5:** ***2453–2458***
and governance **5:** 2504; **8:** 4590
and heuristics **10:** 6173

and intervention **4:** 2001
and liberal theories of justice **4:** 2002
and lifelong education **6:** 3420
meritocracy **7:** 3769
dilemmas **7:** 3770
model of inequality **9:** 5534
negative interpretation **4:** 2001
philosophical issues **4:** ***2001–2004***
positive interpretation **4:** 2001
primary education
and school mapping **9:** 5256
private schools
and choice **8:** 4830
and racial differences **4:** 2001, 2003
and reading difficulties **8:** 4932
recurrent education **8:** 4957, 4960
resource allocation **9:** 5063, 5064
and school-based management **9:** 5305
and school choice **9:** 5192, 5198
science education **9:** 5326, 5334
and second chance education **9:** 5365
and sex differences **4:** 2003, 2031
sex discrimination
developing nations **3:** 1653
and social class **4:** 2003
and sociology of education **10:** 5602
South Africa **7:** 3850
and state departments of education **7:** 3834
and student experience
of curriculum **10:** 5816
Sweden **11:** 6691
and university adult education **11:** 6547
uses of term **10:** 5603
vocational education **4:** ***2281–2287***
and government intervention **11:** 6428
vs. school choice **1:** 591
women's education programs **4:** 2426
Equal opportunities (jobs)
academic rank (professional) **11:** ***6709–6712***
and curriculum development **4:** 2289
European Community **4:** 2068
and sex discrimination **4:** 2282
legislation
and vocational education **4:** 2284
minority groups **11:** 6669
race–earnings differentials **8:** ***4896–4902***
research **11:** 6677
vocational education
advocacy **4:** 2285
Equality of Educational Opportunity Survey (US)
and cross-sectional studies **2:** 1216
Equated scores **11:** ***6349–6355***
choice of design **11:** 6350
common-item nonequivalent groups design **11:** 6351
conditions for **11:** 6354
errors in **11:** 6353
essays **4:** ***2012–2017***
historical background **11:** 6349
inappropriate situations for using **11:** 6353
and item response theory **5:** 3054
and mastery tests **9:** 4993
methods **6:** 3520
and essays **4:** 2012
examples **11:** 6354
item response theory **11:** 6352
traditional **11:** 6351
properties **11:** 6350
and public examinations **4:** 2175
purpose of **11:** 6349
random groups design **11:** 6350
conditions for **11:** 6354
and scaling **11:** 6349
single group with counterbalancing design **11:** 6351
Equipment
international aid
for vocational education **11:** 6661
and skill development **10:** 5917
Equipment standards
optical data disks **2:** 646
Equity (educational finance)
See Educational equity (finance)
Equity (impartiality)
See Justice
ERASMUS **2:** 950; **4:** 2055; **5:** 2976; **7:** 3968; **8:** 4607
and international exchanges **5:** 2933
objectives **4:** 2063
Ergonomics
See Human factors engineering
Error analysis (language)
and contrastive linguistics **6:** 3438
foreign language instruction **6:** 3438
foreign language learning **4:** 2332
interlanguage **6:** 3439
Error correction
teaching methods
mastery learning **6:** 3627
Error of measurement
in bootstrap procedure **9:** 5469
and cross-sectional studies **2:** 1218
in experimental studies **4:** 2191
in generalizability theory **5:** 2458, 2461
item sampling **5:** 3055
and latent trait measurement models **6:** 3248
and mastery tests **9:** 4994
and partial least squares analysis **8:** 4356
problems in defining **9:** 4984
in profile analysis **8:** 4621, 4752
projections **8:** 4787
and rating scales **8:** 4927
regression (statistics)
and prediction **8:** 4654
and reliability **9:** 4982
sampling **9:** ***5124–5131***, 5135
formulas **9:** 5125
and selection bias **9:** 5380
two-stage **9:** 5140
Error patterns
cognitive psychology research
and curriculum development **4:** 1845
Error variance
See Error of measurement
Escuela Nueva (Colombia) **8:** 4507
ESL
See English (second language)
ESOL (English as a second or other language)
See English (second language)
Essay tests
alternatives to **4:** 2018
characteristics of **11:** 6343
constraints **4:** 2020
equated scores
example **4:** 2014
formats **4:** 2019
functions of **4:** 2018
objectives **4:** 2018
scoring of **4:** 2020
analytical schemes **4:** 2020
criteria **4:** 2021
external reference sets **4:** 2021
multiple independent ratings **4:** 2021
quantitative measures **4:** 2020
reliability and generalizability **4:** 2022
validity **4:** 2023
structure of **4:** 2019
vs. objective tests **7:** 4193
Essays
audiences for **4:** 2020
equated scores **4:** ***2012–2017***
model for **4:** 2012
and item response theory **4:** 2012
and multiple choice tests compared **4:** 2016
scoring of **4:** ***2018–2025***
Essentialism
sex education **9:** 5436, 5438
Esteem
See Prestige
Estimation (mathematics)
and achievement tests **1:** 38
and analysis of variance **11:** 6587, 6588
and hierarchical linear models **5:** 2591
individual effects **5:** 2592
and microeconomics **7:** 3816
Monte Carlo methods **9:** 5469
in multilevel analysis **7:** 3984
and reliability **9:** 4984
and robustness (statistics) **9:** 5077
sampling **9:** 5135
variance–covariance **5:** 2591
Estonia
adult education
nonformal education **4:** 2027
curriculum development **4:** 2028
educational change **4:** 2029
educational research **4:** 2029
government school relationship

financial support **4:** 2028
school administration **4:** 2027
postsecondary education **4:** 2026
preschool education **4:** 2027
primary education **4:** 2026
secondary education **4:** 2026
special education **4:** 2027
structure of government **4:** 2025
system of education **4:** ***2025–2029***
degrees and qualifications **4:** 2029
educational objectives **4:** 2025
historical background **4:** 2025
major problems **4:** 2029
structure **4:** 2025
teacher education **4:** 2028
teacher recruitment **4:** 2028
Ethical instruction
Locke's theories **6:** 3497
minimal negative consensus **7:** 3921
moral development
discussion courses **7:** 3919
just communities approach **7:** 3919
and moral values **4:** 2030
See also
Moral education
Values education
Ethics
and administration **4:** 2032
applied **4:** 2032
autonomy of **3:** 1771
of care
and teaching **10:** 6209
and case studies **2:** 645
communitarianism **4:** 2029
and curriculum development **3:** 1327
and educational administration **3:** 1771
in educational research **4:** 2032
evaluation methods **4:** ***2033–2037***
beneficence **4:** 2035
contractual **4:** 2034
definition of **4:** 2033
democratic values **4:** 2035
justice **4:** 2035
noncoercion **4:** 2035
nonmanipulation **4:** 2035
principles **4:** 2035
problems **4:** 2034
respect **4:** 2035
and feminism **4:** ***2292–2297***
fundamental concepts of **10:** 6048
Kantian **4:** 2029
and moral philosophy **4:** ***2029–2033***
and research methodology **4:** 2032
sex differences in approaches **4:** 2294
and surveys **10:** 5858
teacher education **10:** ***5985–5991***
ecologically based **10:** 5987, 5989
management-based **10:** 5988
pedagogy **10:** 5989
of teaching **4:** 2031, 2032
test coaching **11:** 6338
utilitarianism **4:** 2029
See also
Codes of ethics
Moral values
Ethiopia
adult education **1:** 213
nonformal education **4:** 2039
curriculum development **4:** 2041
distance education **1:** 218
educational change **4:** 2042
educational research **4:** 2042
ethnic groups **4:** 2037
government school relationship
financial support **4:** 2040
school administration **4:** 2039
literacy campaigns **1:** 171, 173
postsecondary education **4:** 2039
preschool education **4:** 2039
primary education **4:** 2038
enrollment rate **3:** 1790
private education **4:** 2040
secondary education **4:** 2038
structure of government **4:** 2037
system of education **4:** ***2037–2043***
degrees and qualifications **4:** 2041
educational objectives **4:** 2037
enrollment **4:** 2038
major problems **4:** 2042
structure **4:** 2038
teacher education **4:** 2040
teacher recruitment **4:** 2040
textbooks
provision **11:** 6361
vocational education
training with production **11:** 6447
Ethnic bias
job training
and earnings differentials **7:** 4197
and public examinations **4:** 2179
Ethnic groups
attitudes to social integration **7:** 3967
earnings differentials **8:** ***4896–4902***
educational strategies
small classes **2:** 775
and school desegregation **3:** 1483
See also
Minority groups
Ethnicity
and academic achievement **8:** 4892
Australia **8:** 4893
Israel **8:** 4893
parent influence **8:** 4895
United States **8:** 4892
and adult education **2:** 1193
and adult learning **1:** 166
and colonialism
United States **7:** 3840
and cultural pluralism **7:** 3971
and disadvantage **8:** 4892
and disengagement theory **9:** 5227
and educational attainment **8:** ***4891–4896***
meritocratic model **8:** 4894
problems in research **8:** 4891
revisionist model **8:** 4894
theoretical perspectives **8:** 4894
and employment level **7:** 3719
and equal education **8:** 4892
and high risk students **2:** 708
and mass media
effects on children and youth **1:** 567
measurement of **8:** 4891
and national unity **7:** 3966
and sex differences
educational anthropology **7:** 3973
special needs students **6:** 3292
and status attainment **8:** 4892, 4894, 4895
and test anxiety **11:** 6357
See also
Race
Ethnocentrism **6:** 3419
adult education **5:** 2936
and teaching of anthropology in high schools **1:** 298
United States **7:** 3842
Ethnoecology of schooling **1:** 287
Ethnography
as action research **4:** 2049
application to study of education **4:** 2047
and autobiographies **1:** 539
behaviorist approach **4:** 2049
and case studies **2:** 642, 644
classifications of **4:** 2049
of communication **4:** 2049
critical **4:** 2050, 2051
definition of **4:** 2048
design methodologies **4:** 2087
educational anthropology **3:** ***1233–1236***; **4:** ***2046–2053***
and educational innovation **3:** 1234
ethnomethodology **4:** 1871
ethnoscience **4:** 2049, 2050, 2051
evaluation in education **4:** ***2043–2046***
evaluation model **4:** 2103
factors in educational research **4:** 2048
feminism **4:** 2298, 2301
field studies
principles of research **4:** 2047
future trends **4:** 2052
generalizability **4:** 2051
goals of **7:** 3972
historical background **4:** 2047
holistic approach **4:** 2049, 2050, 2051
indigenous populations **3:** 1752
macroethnography **2:** 1210
microethnography **2:** 1210; **4:** 2049
and physical education **10:** 5710
reliability and validity issues **4:** 2050, 2051
research
cyclical **4:** 2048
development of **1:** 283, 284
early **2:** 1209
and literacy **6:** 3455
methodology **3:** 1248
paradigm **10:** 6205
and videotape recordings **11:** 6604
semiotic approach **4:** 2049
strengths and weaknesses **4:** 2050, 2051
and student experience
studies **10:** 5815, 5816

techniques **2:** 1208
topics of study **4:** 2048
types of educational **4:** 2049
Ethnology
historical
United States **4:** 2047
Ethnomethodology
and comparative education **2:** 926
Ethology **4:** 2169; **5:** 2648
and animal ethology **4:** 2169
educational research **4:** 2169
instinct and learning **4:** 2169
naturalistic observation **4:** 2169
EUDISED
See European Documentation and Information System for Education (EUDISED)
EUROFORM **4:** 2063
Europe
adult education **2:** ***656–662***; **10:** ***5635–5644***
ideology **5:** 2732
research **1:** 123
career education and disabilities **2:** 633
child care services **2:** 694, 696
community development **2:** 905
compulsory education
ages for **9:** 5386
continuing vocational education **4:** ***2059–2063***
day care for infants **5:** 2804; **11:** 6396
distance education
in schools **3:** 1565
education and fertility **3:** 1673
educational administration
characteristics of **9:** 5159
educational planning **8:** ***4495–4499***
historical background **8:** 4496
educational policy
and disabilities **10:** 6243
German-speaking
history of women's education **11:** ***6741–6748***
labor education **1:** 129
learning disabilities
prevalence **10:** 5683
organizational development
trends **7:** 4238
population
school age **3:** 1450
school reform
influences on **9:** 5279
secondary education
selection tests **9:** 5386
special education **10:** 5658, 5659
study circles **10:** 5829
vocational education
training with production **11:** 6448
See also
Central Europe
Eastern Europe
Western Europe
European Association of Distance Teaching Universities (EADTU) **7:** 4216
development of **3:** 1582
objectives **3:** 1582
European Association of Users in Satellites in Training and Education Programs (EUROSTEP) **4:** 1881
European Bureau of Adult Education **1:** 123; **5:** 2932; **8:** 4732, 4733, 4734
legislation and vocabulary **1:** 178
European Bureau of Library, Information, and Documentation Associations (EBLIDA) **6:** 3401
European Centre for the Development of Vocational Training (CEDEFOP) **4:** 2058, 2059
adult education
comparative analysis **1:** 177, 178
occupations
training levels for **4:** 2067
qualifications
recognition **4:** 2065
European Centre for Leisure and Education **6:** 3377
adult education research **1:** 123
European Community (EC)
continuing vocational education **4:** ***2059–2063***; **5:** 2933
credits
transfer policy **4:** 2056, 2057
degrees (academic)
recognition (achievement) **4:** 2056
DELTA program **4:** 1881
directives
general **4:** 2067
implementation of **4:** 2064
occupation-specific **4:** 2066
educational co-operation **4:** 2054
Educational Committee **4:** 2054
educational objectives **4:** ***2053–2059***
educational planning **4:** ***2053–2059***
educational quality
planning **4:** 2058
and equal opportunities
sex discrimination **4:** 2282
framework program **4:** 2055
harmonization
problems **4:** 2064
immigrant education
legislation **7:** 3845
information services **4:** 2057
intentions of
vocational education **4:** 2064
international aid
to Central and Eastern Europe **11:** 6646
involvement in education **4:** 2059
major educational programs **4:** 2055
migration patterns
of skilled workers **4:** 2065
occupational information **4:** 2068, 2069
principles of
vocational education **4:** 2064
qualifications
comparability system **4:** 2067
recognition (achievement) **4:** 2056
recognition studies
funding problems **4:** 2064
structure of **5:** 2509
teacher exchange programs **4:** 2057
training programs for unemployed **6:** 3420
vocational education **4:** 2054, 2056
common policy for **4:** 2064, 2065
curriculum **11:** 6250
future trends **4:** 2069
harmonization **11:** 6665
information dissemination **4:** 2068
learning modules **7:** 3894
training with production **11:** 6449
vocational evaluation
recognition (achievement) **4:** 2057
vocational qualifications
recognition **4:** ***2063–2070***
youth programs **4:** 2056, 2057
See also
EUROSTAT
European Conference on Educational Research (ECER)
ECUNET **3:** 1354
European Council for Cultural Cooperation **6:** 3209
European Curriculum Network
See ECUNET
European Documentation and Information System for Education (EUDISED) **3:** 1586
contact details **5:** 2827
scope **5:** 2825
European Forum on Educational Administration (EFEA)
activities **5:** 2953
European Information Network in the European Community (EURYDICE)
See EURYDICE
European Institute of Education and Social Policy **2:** 941
European Intervisitation Program (EIP) **5:** 2953
European Network for Women's Studies (ENWS) **11:** 6767
European Pool for Educational Software (EPES) **10:** 5621
European schools **4:** 2057
European Secondary Heads Association (ESHA) **5:** 2954
European University Institute **4:** 2057
EUROSTAT **2:** 951
labor force surveys and training **7:** 3712
training
definitions **11:** 6418
and vocational education **4:** 2062
EUROTECNET **4:** 2060
EURYDICE **3:** 1586; **4:** 2057

Evaluands
  See Evaluation, objects of
Evaluation **4:** ***2109–2119***
  accountability **4:** 2100, 2123, 2374, 2381
  adult education **4:** ***2119–2123***
    definition and purpose **4:** 2119
    developing nations **4:** 2122
    difficulties of measurement **4:** 2120
    future developments **4:** 2122
    and participant satisfaction **4:** 2120
    scope **4:** 2122
  and assessment
    semantic distinction **1:** 363
  communicational aspects **3:** 1428, 1430
  of cross-national comparisons **4:** ***2132–2140***
  curriculum-based **3:** ***1355–1359***
  definitions of **1:** 363; **4:** 2071, 2097, 2111; **8:** 4758
  as a discipline **4:** 2097, 2118
  distance education **3:** 1562
  of educational facilities **4:** 2228
  effects on attitudes **4:** 2094
  empirical framework **4:** ***2089–2097***; **11:** 6380
  of evaluations **4:** 2097, 2117
  evolving conceptions of **4:** 2111
  fields of **4:** 2097
  formal vs. informal **4:** 2109
  goal-based definitions **4:** 2109, 2111
  goal-free **3:** 1282; **4:** ***2097–2101***, 2103, 2370
  history of **4:** 2080, 2369
  impact on learning **6:** 3308
  of implementation **4:** ***2070–2074***
  industrial training **4:** 2122
  information-based **4:** ***2381–2389***
  internal and external **4:** 2109
  international educational indicators **5:** ***2984–2989***
  item banks in **5:** ***3036–3043***
  limitations of **4:** 2118
  of literacy programs **1:** 174
  managerialism in **4:** 2371
  mathematics education
    approaches **8:** 4643
  and measurement **4:** 2112, 2369; **8:** 4761
  medical education **4:** 2122
  metatheories of **4:** 2106, 2107
  nature of **4:** ***2109–2119***
  needs-based **7:** ***4056–4060***
  and nonformal transmission model **4:** 2365
  objects of **4:** 2097, 2110
  outcome-oriented **4:** 2090, 2098, 2123
  as a political activity **4:** 2112
  political context **3:** ***1425–1431***
  prescriptive **4:** 2101, 2106
  as a profession **4:** 2118
  prospective **3:** 1429
  public sector **3:** ***1381–1387***
  purposes of **3:** 1381; **4:** 2079, 2090
  quality of **8:** ***4736–4751***
  quantitative vs. qualitative **4:** 2115
  and research **4:** 2113; **8:** 4762
  research-oriented **4:** 2102; **11:** 6379
  role in educational process **8:** 4763, 4765
  school-based **4:** ***2381–2389***
  in schools
    methods **1:** ***362–370***
  as a scientific activity **4:** 2112
  standards **7:** ***4054–4056***; **8:** ***4736–4751***
    development of global **4:** 2117
    monitoring national **7:** ***3906–3912***
    national US **7:** ***4051–4054***
  student teaching **4:** 2125, 2128
  subject specialism in **4:** 2090
  technology of **4:** 2117
  theory-based **11:** ***6378–6385***
  theory and design **4:** 2088
  theory practice relationship **4:** 2106
  as a transdiscipline **4:** 2097, 2107
  types of **4:** 2097
  urban schools **11:** 6561
  user oriented **3:** 1283
  values-oriented **4:** 2370
  See also
    Decision-oriented evaluation
    Educational assessment
    Formative evaluation
    Fourth generation evaluation
    Measurement
    Meta evaluation
    Needs assessment
    Program evaluation
    Recognition (achievement)
    Self-evaluation (groups)
    Summative evaluation
    Testing
Evaluation criteria **4:** 2114
  adult education **4:** 2121
  curriculum evaluation **3:** ***1359–1367***
  outcomes of education **4:** ***2074–2079***
  utilization
    feasibility **4:** 2121
Evaluation methods
  adult education **4:** 2121
    qualitative research **4:** 2121, 2123
    research design **4:** 2122
    statistical analysis **4:** 2121
  analytical **4:** 2098
    component evaluation **4:** 2098
    dimensional evaluation **4:** 2098
  and case studies **2:** 642
  constant comparison analysis **4:** 2373
  criterion referenced tests **2:** 1183
  critical inquiry **4:** ***2381–2389***
  educational administration **3:** 1740
  ethics of **4:** ***2033–2037***
  ethnography **4:** ***2043–2046***
    nonjudgmental orientation **4:** 2043
  evolution of **4:** ***2079–2089***
  imbalance in emphasis **4:** 2090
  instructional materials **8:** 4800
  interviews **4:** 2130
  multilevel analysis **4:** 2384
  naturalistic **3:** 1279
  objectives-oriented **4:** 2114
  responsive **4:** 2371, 2373
  structural analysis **3:** 1382
  use of multiple models **4:** 2105
  See also
    Analysis
    Case studies
Evaluation models
  adversary-oriented **4:** 2103, 2114
    committee hearings model **4:** 2103
    judicial evaluation model **4:** 2103
  analyses **4:** 2104
  categories of **4:** 2114
  category systems **3:** 1280
  causal models **11:** 6379
  CIPP **4:** 2370
  classification of **4:** 2103
  consumer-oriented **4:** 2114
  countenance model **4:** 2370
  descriptive **3:** 1280; **4:** 2106, 2370
  differences in **4:** 2089
  ethnographic **4:** 2103
  expertise-oriented **4:** 2114
  integrations **4:** 2105
  management-oriented **4:** 2114
  naturalistic and participant-oriented **4:** 2114
  and needs assessment **7:** 4058
  prescriptive **3:** 1280
  theory-driven models **4:** 2103
  use of **4:** ***2101–2109***, 2115
  See also
    Delphi technique
    Tyler evaluation model
Evaluation reports **4:** ***2074–2079***
  for parents **4:** 2076
  for principals **4:** 2076
  for school districts **4:** 2077
    independent appraisal **4:** 2077
  for state agencies **4:** 2078
  for teachers **4:** 2076
Evaluation research
  comparative education **2:** 934
  experimental/quasi-experimental model **4:** 2103
  instructional model **4:** 2102
  and policy **5:** 2671
  use of causal models **11:** 6379
Evaluation Research Society (US)
  program evaluation standards **8:** 4737, 4745
Evaluation studies
  diversity of approaches **4:** 2114
  ideology **4:** 2036
  institutionalization of **4:** 2116
  of public training policies **4:** 1974
  reporting of results **8:** 4762
Evaluation utilization **3:** 1428; **4:** ***2074–2079***, ***2097–2101***, 2102, 2109
  approaches **4:** 2088
Evaluative thinking
  and emotional response
    effect on learning process **1:** 199, 201
  philosophy

relativism **9:** 4978
relativist realist positions **9:** 4979
self-efficacy
metacognition **9:** 5516
Evaluators
active rational reconstruction by **3:** 1429
adult education
collaboration **4:** 2121
external **4:** 2121
internal **4:** 2121
career opportunities **4:** 2116
and educational theorists **11:** 6380
ethics **4:** ***2033–2037***
clientism **4:** 2035
fallacies **4:** 2035
and methodologies **4:** 2036
pluralism/elitism **4:** 2036
relativism **4:** 2036
expertise **3:** 1281
and goal-free evaluation **4:** 2100
and political context **3:** 1426, 1427; **4:** 2112
role of **4:** 2096; **8:** 4760, 4765
in fourth generation evaluation **4:** 2371
training of **4:** 2090, 2117
training program
Kenya **4:** 2121
written contract **4:** 2034, 2036
Evening programs
adult education **1:** 138
Soviet Union (former) **9:** 5094
Asia **1:** 350
Germany **1:** 182
Event history analysis **4:** ***2150–2156***
censoring **4:** 2150
detection of predictors **4:** 2152
methods **4:** 2150
See also
Life events
Survival analysis
Evolution
concept teaching
problems **6:** 3415
and creationism **6:** 3414
Darwin's theory **4:** 2167; **5:** 2655
definition of **5:** 2681
ecological models **3:** 1647
education and culture **4:** 2167
and genetics **5:** 2655
human foundations of learning **5:** 2683
mammalian foundations of learning **5:** 2681
and physical anthropology **1:** 297, 299
primate foundations of learning **5:** 2681, 2682
scientific concepts **6:** 3413
Spencer's view **10:** 5705
theories of
and developmental psychology **5:** 2656
and individual development **4:** ***2167–2172***
and sex differences **9:** 5424
Examinations
associations responsible for development **3:** 1273
and certification **8:** 4617
and educational planning
Asia **8:** 4488
evaluation methods
criterion referenced tests **2:** 1183
and item banks
advantages of **5:** 3038
security issues **5:** 3038
and profiles **8:** 4618
public **4:** ***2172–2180***
comparability **4:** 2174
equity considerations **4:** 2178
historical background **4:** 2172
internal assessment **4:** 2174
item banks **4:** 2177
maintenance of standards **4:** 2173
moderation procedures **4:** 2174
placement of **4:** 2173
purposes of **4:** 2172
and school assessment **4:** 2174
publication of results by school
United Kingdom **7:** 3910
See also
Tests
Examiner characteristics
See Examiners, experimenter characteristics
Examiner examinee relationship **11:** 6313, 6314
and test translation **11:** 6329
Examiners
experimenter characteristics **11:** 6312
and test translation **11:** 6329
and testing
preparation **11:** 6312
Excellence in education
and equal education **4:** 2031
and mainstreaming **6:** 3559
national commission on (US) **9:** 5276
Exceptional child research
gifted **5:** ***2725–2732***
Exceptional persons
creativity **2:** 1176
Excess demand model
private education **8:** 4831
empirical research **8:** 4834
predictions **8:** 4832
Exchange programs
faculty development **5:** 2973, 2976
See also
Student exchange programs
Teacher exchange programs
Exemplary programs
See Demonstration programs
Existentialism **8:** ***4429–4433***
combined with phenomenology **8:** 4431
concept of dialog **8:** 4432
and humanistic psychology **5:** 2689, 2690
key themes **8:** 4430
Kierkegaard's views **8:** 4430
and philosophy of education **8:** 4453
and the self-concept **9:** 5390, 5391
Expectancy
See Expectation
Expectancy tables
construction of **4:** 2180
concrete methods **4:** 2182
technical issues **4:** 2182
theoretical methods **4:** 2182
definition of **4:** 2180
double entry **4:** 2181
in educational prediction **4:** ***2180–2183***
and prediction **8:** 4655
single entry **4:** 2181
smoothing techniques **4:** 2182
Expectation
causal variations **1:** 357
and cognitive theory of emotion **4:** 1963
compared with aspiration **1:** 355
of education
curriculum issues **9:** 5518
and educational attainment **1:** 356
future research **1:** 357
interpersonal
theory of **10:** 6220
and motivation **7:** 3945
of performance
and test anxiety **11:** ***6355–6360***
research **10:** 6107
and student development **6:** 3294
student interpretation of **1:** 356
by students **1:** ***354–358***
of students
factors affecting employment opportunities **11:** 6700
of success
sex differences in **9:** 5430
theory
and school dynamics **9:** 5171
Expenditure per student
Latin America **6:** 3603
and opportunity costs **3:** 1673
patterns **2:** 1123
and school size **9:** 5291
Expenditures
academic achievement
class size **2:** 772
comparative analysis **2:** 962
distribution of educational
comparative area studies **5:** 2981
educational statistics
and input output analysis **3:** 1757
international on education **5:** ***2978–2984***
private on education
sources **5:** 2982
public on education
developing nations **1:** 466
evaluation of research data **5:** 2978, 2979
and lifelong learning **6:** 3422
sources
family involvement **5:** 2983
industry **5:** 2983

private donors **5:** 2982
training **11:** 6417
and unit costs
studies **2:** 1123
See also
Educational finance
Experience
effect on learning **6:** 3286
life
and biographical research **1:** 539
and narrative inquiry **7:** 4046
and phenomenography **8:** 4426
and pragmatism **3:** 1521
and sociocultural systems **9:** 5309
Experience–earnings profiles
earnings differentials **3:** 1658
vintage effects **11:** 6614, 6615
Experiential learning **6:** 3348
and administrator education
inservice **1:** 70
adult education **4:** ***2183–2186***;
10: 5594
and certification **2:** 663
adults **1:** 164
and self-fulfilling prophecies **1:** 165
apprenticeship model **4:** 2184
and cognitive style **1:** 318
and computer networks **2:** 980
concept of **4:** 2184
cultural context of **1:** 165
and curriculum theory **3:** 1353
Dewey's contribution **3:** 1522;
4: 2184
games **9:** 5472
historical background **3:** 1722
indigenous populations **3:** 1751
and instructional materials **3:** 1494
international programs **4:** 2185
and interpretation **4:** 1884
Kolb's learning cycle **4:** 2184
limitations of **11:** 6414
and participation
in educational improvement
9: 5245
potential of **11:** 6414
programs
studies **10:** 6168
in science education **7:** 4101; **8:** 4645
simulation **9:** 5472
Experimental design
See Research design
Experimental pedagogy
See Educational research
Experimental psychology **5:** 2657
and educational history **3:** 1794
educational research **4:** 1864, 1865;
9: 5053
Wundt's laboratory **4:** 1865
Experimental schools
Adler's influence on **8:** 4816
Experimental studies **4:** ***2186–2194***
analysis of change **4:** 2193
classroom research designs **4:** 2193
error of measurement **4:** 2191
and heterogeneous grouping **4:** 2189
notation system **4:** 2187
research preparation **4:** 2187
sensitivity of **4:** 2189
statistical power **4:** 2191
validity **4:** 2188
variability **4:** 2190
Experimental Teaching Unit (ETU) (US)
and physical education **10:** 5711
Experimental World Literacy Program
(1966–74) (EWLP) **1:** 171;
5: 2935; **6:** 3453 **11:** 6505,
6506
evaluation of effect **1:** 175
Experiments
feminist criticism of **4:** 2298
limitations **3:** 1382
purpose of **4:** 2187
and research methodology **9:** 5047
Expert novice research
and automaticity of learning **2:** 850
and child development **2:** 839
cognitive development research
2: 845
cooperative learning **5:** 2668
and curriculum development **4:** 1845
and developmental psychology
5: 2667
and domain-specific knowledge
3: 1502
effect on memory **7:** 3762
and individual differences
in content-specific knowledge
2: 845
intellectual development
age differences **5:** 2913
metacognition **5:** 2667
modeling (psychology) of experts
5: 2668
problem-solving
computer simulation **8:** 4720
science education **9:** 5340
transfer of training
and task analysis **10:** 5913
Expert systems **8:** 4721
analysis-based **8:** 4721
and cognitive development **7:** 3742
and instructional design **5:** 2860
and management information systems
5: 2830
and models **2:** 986
task analysis
cognitive processes **10:** 5913
and technical education **4:** 1922
Expertise
acquisition of
and cognitive development
2: ***838–842***; **3:** 1503
in children
domain-specific **2:** 854
usefulness of training **2:** 854
cognitive development **2:** 836
cognitive psychological research
4: ***2194–2199***
educational implications **4:** 2197
and cognitive strategies **2:** 835
and cognitive structures **2:** 835
and creativity **2:** 1176, 1177
development of
stages **10:** 6021
domain specific **2:** 839; **4:** 2194, 2196
evaluation of component skills
4: 2198
identification of **2:** 839
individual differences **2:** 843
learning strategies **4:** 2197
measurement of **2:** 839
and test construction **1:** 371
and psychological studies **10:** 6021
research on **2:** 838
task analysis **10:** 5911
and transfer of training **11:** 6454
Explanation
concept teaching **10:** ***6143–6149***
evaluation criteria **10:** 6144, 6146
functions of **10:** 6143
given by students
evaluation criteria **10:** 6145
research methods **10:** 6147
Columbia University Instrument
10: 6148
Hermann's Pupil Awareness Rating
Form **10:** 6148
Illinois Instrument **10:** 6147
Rating Teacher Explanation
Instrument **10:** 6148
types of **10:** 6144
Explanatory learning
See Discovery learning
Explanatory style
heredity **9:** 5406
and individual development
9: ***5403–5407***
individual differences **9:** 5404
optimism **9:** 5404
pessimism **9:** 5404
Exploratory data analysis (EDA)
4: ***2199–2208***
applications **4:** 2200
box plots **4:** 2203, 2205
computer software for **4:** 2208
and cross-sectional studies **2:** 1219
data organization **4:** 2200
development of **4:** 2199
letter-value displays **4:** 2201
median
use of **4:** 2202, 2206
median polish
procedure **4:** 2207
methods **4:** 2199
models
data **4:** 2205
multiple batches **4:** 2205
for two-way classifications **4:** 2206
number summaries **4:** 2201
procedural objectives **4:** 2200
schematic plots **4:** 2203
stem-and-leaf display **4:** 2200, 2203
transformations **4:** 2203
Expository writing
organization of
and study skills **10:** 5830
Expulsion **9:** ***5224–5228***
factors affecting **9:** 5224

See also
Dropouts
Extended school day
and educational facilities planning **4:** 2222
Extended school year
comparative analysis
effect on Latin America **3:** 1831
Extended teacher education programs **10:** 5998
Extension agents
agricultural **1:** 252
Extension education **1:** 96; **6:** 3418, 3420
adult enrollment
Japan **6:** 3076
for adults **8:** 4807
polytechnics **8:** 4604
universities **1:** 89, 92
External benefits
See Externalities
External labor market **3:** 1696; **4:** 1973; **5:** 2937
Externalities **4:** ***2208–2212***
and educational choice
sex bias **4:** 2414
general education **11:** 6426
school enterprise **9:** 5230
of training **11:** 6426, 6429
vocational education **11:** 6426
Extracurricular activities
college students **10:** 5801
and disengagement theory **9:** 5225
and political education **8:** 4569
Extrinsic motivation
See Incentives
Extroversion introversion
and foreign language learning **4:** 2335
social development **9:** 5525
Eye contact
in classrooms **7:** 4173
cultural differences **7:** 4173
Eye movements
for computer control **10:** 5669
visual perception
psychological process **8:** 4377
Eyegaze system
and assistive technology **10:** 5669
Eysenck Personality Inventory (EPI) **8:** 4398
Eysenck Personality Questionnaire (EPQ) **8:** 4398

F-test
and analysis of variance **11:** 6588, 6589
and clustering **7:** 3734
and regression analysis **9:** 4966, 4967
Facet theory **4:** ***2213–2219***
cartesian designs
completion **4:** 2215
twists, nests, and loops **4:** 2215
content profile **4:** 2215
domain facets **4:** 2214
content facet **4:** 2213, 2214, 2218
focus facet **4:** 2213, 2214
examples **4:** 2216
and item writing techniques **5:** 3064
laws of monotonicity **4:** 2214
mapping sentences **4:** 2214
definitions of **4:** 2214
intension of **4:** 2215
recursive **4:** 2216
principles of **4:** 2213
purpose of **4:** 2213
range facets **4:** 2214
uses of **4:** 2215
formation of laws and theories **4:** 2217
variables
common meaning range **4:** 2213
Fachhochschulen **2:** 895
and technical education **11:** 6269
Fachoberschulen
vocational education
Germany, Federal Republic of (former) **11:** 6655
Fachschulen
vocational education
Germany, Federal Republic of (former) **11:** 6655
Facial expressions
research **7:** 4171
See also
Body language
Smiling
Facility requirements
and educational facilities planning **4:** 2221
specifications **4:** 2228
Facsimile transmission (FAX)
applications **11:** 6303
characteristics of **11:** 6300
Factor analysis **4:** ***2230–2241***; **7:** 3699
applications **4:** 2233, 2240
and attitude measures **1:** 384
basic factor model **4:** 2231
and canonical analysis **2:** 627
centroid method **4:** 2231
common factor model **4:** 2232
comparison of factors **4:** 2239
computer software for **4:** 2238, 2239
confirmatory
advances in **4:** 2238
applications **4:** 2238
and attitude measures **1:** 384
and cross-sectional studies **2:** 1219
development of **4:** 2233
and multitrait multimethod techniques **7:** 4002
vs. exploratory **4:** 2233
and construct validity **11:** 6572
and correspondence analysis **2:** 1121
and descriptive scales **3:** 1478
early development of **4:** 2230
educational research **7:** 3704
factor extraction **4:** 2231, 2234
factor rotation **4:** 2231, 2236
orthogonal vs. oblique **4:** 2231, 2236
and factorial modeling compared **4:** 2241
fundamental factor theorem **4:** 2231
generative methodology **4:** 2301
group factors **4:** 2230
hierarchical factor solutions **4:** 2239
and interests
measures of **11:** 6674
interpretation **4:** 2237
and latent trait measurement models **6:** 3247
linearity in
assumptions of **4:** 2239
in listening comprehension tests **7:** 3933
maximum likelihood statistics **4:** 2235
methodological aspects **4:** 2239
multiple
and models of intelligence **7:** 3874
and multivariate analysis **7:** 4010
nonmetric
and partial order scalogram analysis **7:** 4308
objectives **4:** 2230
and personality inventories **8:** 4396, 4397
principal **4:** 2234
and Q-methodology **8:** 4855
scaling **4:** 2239
methods **9:** 5156
segmentation theory
empirical research findings **6:** 3187
and smallest space analysis **9:** 5500
in speech tests **7:** 3934
and student evaluations of educational quality **10:** 6229
and transformations (mathematics) **4:** 2236
varimax criterion **4:** 2237
See also
Factor structure
Smallest space analysis (SSA)
Factor structure
matrices **4:** 2233, 2237
See also
Factor analysis
Factorial modeling **4:** ***2241–2245***
background to **4:** 2241
computer software **4:** 2242
example **4:** 2244
and factor analysis compared **4:** 2241
factor extraction **4:** 2241
mathematics **4:** 2241
and multivariate analysis **7:** 4011
rationale **4:** 2241
Faculty development
and learning role **10:** 6056
learning strategies
problem-solving **6:** 3347
Faculty mobility
in effective schools **4:** 1931
Failure
attribution theory
sex differences **9:** 5434
children's perceptions of
and motivation **1:** 30
fear of
and test anxiety **11:** 6358

student characteristics **1:** 191, 192
and theory of trainability **3:** 1692
Fair use (copyrights)
criteria for **2:** 1100
Family
attitudes of women to the **11:** 6768
definitions of **4:** 2258
employed women **5:** 2624
expenditures
international comparisons **5:** 2979
research studies **4:** 2251
as social capital **4:** ***2272–2274***
social differences
and cultural capital **4:** 2269
and socialization **10:** 5588
socioeconomic factors
and academic achievement **4:** 2252
ethnography **4:** 2251
of special needs children
empowerment **4:** ***1976–1980***
as unit of production **3:** 1667, 1669
See also
Foster family
Nuclear family
One parent family
Family attitudes
and academic achievement **9:** 5017
Family characteristics
and academic achievement
4: ***2250–2258***, ***2267–2272***
developing nations **4:** 2254, 2255
future research **4:** 2256
process variables **4:** 2254
and social class **4:** 2252
and attendance **3:** 1604
and child development **3:** 1637
education
and economic status **4:** 2275
and educational choice **4:** 2414
and educational opportunities **4:** 2251
and employment level **4:** 2276
and intellectual development
confluence model **4:** 2253
job training studies **7:** 4198
kinship studies
and academic achievement **6:** 3138
and language handicaps **10:** 5680
and learning factors **10:** 5748, 5749
Family choice (education)
See School choice
Family counseling **4:** 2260, 2261;
8: 4816
and incest **1:** 18
Family day care **2:** 688, 699; **11:** 6397
and parent child caregiver
relationship **7:** 4297
United Kingdom **11:** 6397
United States **11:** 6397
Family environment
and academic achievement
5: ***2624–2628***; **6:** 3293
cultural differences **5:** 2624
causal models of **7:** 3870
as center of leisure activities **6:** 3377
changes in **5:** 2624
and child rearing **5:** 2625
cultural background
and academic achievement **4:** 2254
disabled children
stress management **4:** 1978
education and cost-effectiveness
4: 2209
and employment level
measurement **4:** 2278
and environmental measures
4: ***2245–2250***
factors in learning **8:** 4400, 4401,
4402
and genetic studies
individual development **5:** 2463,
2464
and individual development
Judaic theory **6:** 3115
influence on learning in school
5: ***2624–2628***
age variables **5:** 2624
developmental psychology
perspective **5:** 2624
intelligence quotient
individual differences **5:** 2464
and learning factors **10:** 5749
measures
and interaction effects **5:** 2926
parent attitudes
and academic achievement **4:** 2254
physical environment **5:** 2625
developing nations **5:** 2625
and respect for the child
existentialist view **8:** 4432
and social background research
7: 3720
studies **4:** 2245
variables **4:** 2245, 2246
Family financial resources
and social mobility **9:** 5551
Family history
and oral history **7:** 4223
research **6:** 3426
Family income
and basic education
developing nations **1:** 468
and child development **3:** 1639
effect of economic adjustment on
and education **3:** 1785
and national surveys **2:** 651
Family influence
individual development **4:** ***2258–2261***
preschool education **7:** 4296
and socialization **10:** 5590
stress variables **10:** 5736
and student attitudes **9:** 5017
Family intervention
and individual development **4:** 2260
Family involvement
early childhood education
early intervention **5:** 2810
in education
and private resources **8:** 4704
educational expenditures **5:** 2983
Family life
behavior genetics **4:** 2258
enrichment **4:** 2264
and health **4:** 2258
heredity **4:** 2258
and social change **4:** 2328
and television viewing **1:** 565
Family life education **4:** ***2262–2267***
course content **4:** 2265
definitional questions **4:** 2262
developing nations **4:** 2262
evaluation studies **4:** 2266
and family relationship **4:** 2262
forms of **4:** 2263
historical background **4:** 2262
and mass media **4:** 2265
and modernization **4:** 2262
objectives **4:** 2263
organization formal/informal **4:** 2263
paradigms **4:** 2264
emancipating **4:** 2265
interpretative **4:** 2265
technical **4:** 2265
and population education **8:** 4609
and postmodernism **4:** 2262
religiously motivated **4:** 2264
and social work **4:** 2264
target groups **4:** 2265
teaching methods **4:** 2265
Family planning
and education **3:** 1675
and literacy **1:** 467
and population education **8:** 4608
Family problems
effect on children's play **8:** 4540
and family life education **4:** 2264
prevention **4:** 2261
Family programs **4:** 2261
public policy **5:** 2807
Family relationship **4:** 2259
couple relations **4:** 2259
and education
Pestalozzi's views **8:** 4417
and family life education **4:** 2262
cultural factors **4:** 2263
interactive factors **4:** 2263
risk factors **4:** 2263
social factors **4:** 2263
intergenerational relations **4:** 2260
parent child relationship **4:** 2259
sibling relationship **4:** 2260
Family role
behavior disorders
antisocial behavior **1:** 492, 493
human capital
investment **6:** 3139
and the production of education
6: 3101
analysis variables **6:** 3101
and school role
academic achievement **4:** 2250
and variance in educational mobility
6: 3141
Family school relationship **9:** 5265
and cultural capital **4:** 2269
and educational opportunities **4:** 2248
improvement **4:** 2255
and literacy **6:** 3449
and outcomes of education **9:** 5260

and resilience **8:** 4777
and school choice **9:** 5202
school community relationship
and special needs students **6:** 3294
and social capital **4:** ***2272–2274***
Family size
and academic achievement **4:** 2253
developing nations **4:** 2253
and birth order
relationships **7:** 3868
factors affecting **3:** 1451
influence of education on **3:** 1672, 1673, 1674
Family status
and economic status **4:** ***2274–2279***
and occupational success
measurement **4:** 2276
Family structure
and homeless people **3:** 1734
and parent participation in schools **2:** 892
and social mobility **9:** 5551
and social structure **4:** 2250
social support groups **4:** 2250
Family therapy
See Family counseling
Family violence **4:** 2259
child abuse **1:** 15
and intergenerational relations **4:** 2260
Family welfare
effect of women's education on **4:** 2414
Farmers
education of
and agricultural productivity **1:** 245; **3:** 1649, 1665, 1691; **4:** 2414
literacy
and productivity **1:** 467
Fathers
role in child care **8:** 4675
Fatigue (biology)
and human factors engineering **4:** 2010
and video display terminals **4:** 2010
Fear
in infants **4:** 1964
of technology
teachers **11:** 6286
Feasibility studies
cost effectiveness
and policy formation **2:** 1122
and material development **8:** 4799
and program management **8:** 4755
Fecal incontinence **3:** 1516
Federación Interamericana de Educación de Adultos (FIDEA) **5:** 2932
Federal aid
and vocational education
United States **11:** 6532
Federal government
framework of **5:** 2509
policy
and vocational education **11:** ***6530–6538***
state departments of education **7:** 3836
Federal legislation
equity
and personnel management **8:** 4405
Federal regulation
and educational planning **8:** 4508
and governance of teacher education **10:** 5962
Federal state relationship
vocational education
United States **11:** 6531
Federalism
educational administration **6:** 3273
Fédération de l'Education Nationale (FEN) (France) **10:** 6075, 6078
Feedback **4:** ***2279–2281***
and artificial intelligence **1:** 345
in behavioral modification **4:** 2279
between students
and microcomputer-based laboratories **7:** 3809
in classrooms
and teacher student relationship **10:** 6012
and computer-assisted instruction **2:** 988
and computer-assisted testing **5:** 2781
definition of **4:** 2279
in dual labor market theory **6:** 3185, 3187
educational uses **4:** 2279
in instruction
behaviorist views **4:** 2280
cognitive psychology views **4:** 2280
in instructional program divisions **6:** 3098
and interpersonal competence
training for **9:** 5566
in interviews **5:** 3004
in learning **4:** 2279
behaviorist views **4:** 2279
cognitive psychology views **4:** 2280
and learning performance **7:** 3944
and motivation **7:** 3945
and organizational development **7:** 4237
and partial credit model **7:** 4304
physical education
research **10:** 5709, 5711
and programmed instruction **8:** 4768, 4771
reinforcement
and educational quality **8:** 4863
respondent
and data analysis **3:** 1473
and school self-evaluation **5:** 2848
in skill development **4:** 2279
and student reaction **10:** 6013
in systems approach **10:** 5895
teaching methods
mastery learning **6:** 3627
Fees
and resource allocation **9:** 5064
student
See Student fees
Fellowships
international aid
for vocational education **11:** 6661
Female education
See Women's education
Female employment
and birth rate **3:** 1673
child care occupations
and academic achievement **2:** 689
and child rearing **3:** 1673
earnings
determinants **4:** 2276
status scales **7:** 3719
Female labor force
See Employed women
Female labor force participation
See Labor force participation, females
Female psychology
feminist theories **11:** 6721
Females
ability with computers
male attitudes **4:** 2425
academic achievement
single sex schools **2:** 832
academic rank (professional) **11:** ***6709–6712***
access to education **4:** 2407
developed nations **4:** 2408
developing nations **4:** 2407
distance from school **4:** 2408
factors affecting **4:** 2407
vocational education **4:** ***2281–2287***
admission to higher education
United Kingdom **3:** 1722
adult education **4:** 2411; **11:** ***6712–6719***
advanced schools
Germany **11:** 6745
and amount of leisure time **6:** 3375
attitudes to computers **4:** 2425
career choice **4:** 2410
changing roles
and child care services **2:** 693
and child rearing
family structure **3:** 1627
computer literacy
factors influencing **4:** 2423
education of **4:** ***2407–2412***
and fertility **3:** ***1672–1676***
Luther's view **6:** 3530
in educational administration
certification **11:** 6730
United States **11:** ***6727–6731***
educational attainment **4:** 2408
and fertility **3:** 1672
educational research on
South Africa **7:** 3850
enrollment rate **4:** 2407
China, People's Republic of **4:** 2408
Japan **4:** 2408
and evolution
theories of **9:** 5424
family role
and career development **11:** 6729
and career ladders **4:** 2421

gifted **5:** 2488
identity
variables **11:** 6725
illiteracy **4:** 2411
intellectual development **10:** 5938
and literacy **1:** 173, 174
moral development **10:** 5936
outcomes of education **9:** 5508
participation in adult education **1:** 107
participation in vocational education **4:** 2283
professional occupations
and family life **4:** 2410
role of
and adult education **1:** 160
safety within schools **2:** 834
self-esteem
and career development **11:** 6730
career planning **5:** 2489
teacher role models
and computer uses in education **4:** 2424
as teachers
developing nations **4:** 2419
teaching
professionalization of **11:** ***6719–6723***
Feminism
academic networking **11:** 6767
action research **4:** 2298
and adult education **1:** 134; **2:** 1192
analysis of teaching as work **11:** 6721
and anthropology **7:** 3972
and biographical research **1:** 542
coherence justification **4:** 2300, 2301
and comparative education **2:** 926
consciousness raising **4:** 2298
critique of communicative competence (Habermas) **4:** 2030
critique of professionalization **11:** 6720, 6721
and cultural pluralism **11:** 6768
and the curriculum **4:** ***2287–2292***
definitions of theories **5:** 2453
discourse analysis **4:** 2300
and educational administration **1:** 64
educational research **10:** 6098; **11:** ***6723–6727***
liberal **11:** 6725
materialist **11:** 6725
theoretical perspectives **11:** 6724
emancipatory approach **4:** 2298
and ethics **4:** ***2292–2297***
ethics of caring **4:** 2292, 2294; **11:** 6721
criticism of **4:** 2295
experiential analysis **4:** 2297
gender relations research **4:** 2297
gender theories **5:** ***2453–2458***
generative methodology **4:** 2300
heuristics **4:** 2301
and hidden curriculum **8:** 4582
history of women's education **11:** 6742
Australia **11:** 6732
biographies **11:** 6734
and importance of mothers **4:** 2294
and individual power **4:** 1983
and Kantian ethics **4:** 2293
liberal ethics **4:** 2292, 2295
liberal theories **5:** 2453
and moral education **4:** 2031, ***2292–2297***
and moral issues **4:** 2293
and moral philosophy **4:** 2030
and moral values in education **10:** 5990
new scholarship on women in education **11:** ***6723–6727***
criticisms of **11:** 6724
participatory research **4:** 2298; **7:** 4332
and patriarchy **2:** 831; **9:** 5437, 5438, 5439
pedagogy **11:** 6767
philosophy of education **11:** 6721
poststructuralism **5:** 2453, 2456
radical theories **5:** 2453, 2455
and Rawls' theory of justice **4:** 2293, 2295
rejection of positivism **4:** 2297
research methodology **4:** ***2297–2302***; **11:** 6725, 6726
research problems **4:** 2300
research on women in education **11:** ***6723–6727***
and sex differences research **9:** 5433
and sex education **9:** ***5435–5441***
and sexuality **9:** 5437
socialist theories **5:** 2453, 2456
teacher education **10:** 6097
and teaching **10:** 6134
theories on epistemology of females **11:** 6721
theories on female psychology **11:** 6721
values in research **4:** 2297
and women's studies **11:** 6766
Fertility rate
See Birth rate
Fetal alcohol syndrome **1:** 14
effect on learning **5:** 2564
fetal alcohol effects **5:** 2564
and learning disabilities **7:** 4079
and mental retardation **5:** 2564
Fiction
and student experience
of curriculum **10:** 5817
Field dependence independence **2:** 868, 870
cognitive processes
and social factors **3:** 1239
and cognitive style **1:** 318
Field experience programs
effects on student teachers **10:** 5809
student teaching **10:** ***5808–5812***
and teacher evaluation **4:** 2128
Field instruction
nonformal education **4:** 2365
Field interviews
and narrative inquiry **7:** 4048
Field notes
and data collection **3:** 1467
Field studies
ethics of **4:** 2032
and narrative inquiry **7:** 4048, 4049
randomization
in evaluation studies **4:** 2088
and videotape recordings **11:** 6606
Field tests
courseware **10:** 5618
Fiji
adult education
nonformal education **4:** 2306
curriculum development **4:** 2308
educational change **4:** 2310
educational research **4:** 2309
ethnic groups **4:** 2303
government school relationship
financial support **4:** 2307
school administration **4:** 2307
language **4:** 2303
postsecondary education **4:** 2304
preschool education **4:** 2305
primary education **4:** 2304
private education **4:** 2304
reading materials
and reading improvement **8:** 4696
school libraries
printed materials **8:** 4698
secondary education **4:** 2304
special education **4:** 2306
structure of government **4:** 2304
system of education **4:** ***2302–2310***
degrees and qualifications **4:** 2309
educational objectives **4:** 2304
enrollment **4:** 2305
major problems **4:** 2310
structure **4:** 2304
teacher education **4:** 2308
teacher recruitment **4:** 2307
Film study
United States **8:** 4387
Films
applications **7:** 3752
characteristics of **7:** 3751
as educational media **7:** 3751
and learning **6:** 3299
vs. videotape recordings **7:** 3752
Filmstrips
applications **7:** 3748
characteristics of **7:** 3748
Finance
See Educational finance
Finance reform
and urban education **11:** 6557
Financial aid
See Financial support
Financial audits
and school administration **9:** 5182
Financial policy
economic adjustment
and International Monetary Fund **3:** 1785

Financial problems
  municipalities **11:** 6553
Financial support
  adult education **10:** 5593
  higher education
    cost effectiveness studies **2:** 1130
  international
    conditions for **5:** 2991
    and education **5:** ***2989–2993***
    factors affecting **5:** 2990
    fungibility of **5:** 2990
    types of **5:** 2989
  public education
    international aspects of **4:** 2310
  vocational education
    and economic need **11:** 6533
    international aid **11:** 6660
  and world political environment
    changes in **5:** 2991
Fine arts **1:** 196
Finger spelling
  sign language
    for the deaf blind **3:** 1404
Finland
  adult education **1:** 123; **4:** 2319
    research **7:** 4179
  adult educators
    teacher education **11:** 6435
  curriculum development **4:** 2321
  education of music teachers **7:** 4028
  educational change **4:** 2323
  educational research **4:** 2322
  ethnic groups **4:** 2316
  folk high schools **4:** 2325
  folkeoplysning organizations **7:** 4176
  foreign language instruction policy
      4: 2340
  general education and vocational
      education **7:** 4177
  government school relationship
    financial support **4:** 2320
    school administration **4:** 2320
  labor force
    educational needs **10:** 5807
    surveys **11:** 6416
  language **4:** 2316
  lifetime employment **5:** 2688
  monitoring of standards **7:** 3907
  postsecondary education **4:** 2318
  preschool education **2:** 695, 696, 699
  primary education **4:** 2317
  reading campaigns **1:** 169
  second language learning needs in
      industry **6:** 3211
  secondary education **4:** 2318
    vocational education **4:** 2318
  special education **4:** 2319
  system of education **4:** ***2316–2324***
    degrees and qualifications **4:** 2322
    educational objectives **4:** 2317
    major problems **4:** 2323
    structure **4:** 2317
  teacher education **4:** 2321
    universities **3:** 1724
  teacher recruitment **4:** 2320
  technology education
    programs **11:** 6290
  university adult education **11:** 6549,
      6550
Finnish Adult Education Association
      7: 4148
Firm-based training
  See on-the-job training
First language
  See Native language
Fiscal crisis
  See Economic crisis
Fisher's exact test
  nonparametric statistics **7:** 4160
  and statistical significance **9:** 5461
Fisher's method of randomization
  nonparametric statistics **7:** 4158
Fisher's Z transformation **2:** 1111
  and meta analysis **7:** 3779
  uses of **2:** 1112
Flexible progression
  and tests of prior learning **8:** 4702
Flexible scheduling **3:** 1736; **5:** 2868;
      11: 6392
Flipcharts
  See Charts
Floppy disks
  characteristics of **10:** 5619
  and survey data **2:** 650
Flow charts
  and media selection **7:** 3758
Folk culture
  and achievement need **3:** 1236, 1238
  influences of
    Japan **11:** 6695
  and narrative inquiry **7:** 4047
Folk high schools **2:** 904; **4:** ***2324–2327***;
      11: 6393
  characteristics of **4:** 2326
  Denmark **2:** 895, 897, 1190; **4:** 2325,
      2388; **5:** 2733, 2734
  financial support **4:** 2325
  Finland **4:** 2325
  governance **4:** 2326
  history **4:** 2324
  and history of adult education **1:** 137
  Nordic countries **5:** 2733, 2734, 2735;
      7: 4176
  North America **5:** 2733, 2734
  Norway **4:** 2325
  Poland **2:** 660; **4:** 2325
  Sweden **4:** 2325; **10:** 5638
  teacher education for **4:** 2326
  trends and development **4:** 2327
  use of term **4:** 2324
Folkeoplysning **7:** 4175
  organizations for **7:** 4176, 4177
  research on **7:** 4178
Folklore
  See Folk culture
Followup studies
  and nonresponse adjustment **7:** 3856
  problems **7:** 3855
  technical education
    France **11:** 6269
Food and Agriculture Organization
      (FAO)
  educational technology
    activities **4:** 1880
Force field analysis
  and adult education participation
      7: 4327
FORCE
  See Formation Continue en Europe
      (FORCE)
Forced choice technique
  and rating scales **8:** 4924
Forecast
  See Prediction
Foreign aid
  educational finance **5:** 2979
    comparative area studies **5:** 2983
  vocational education
    Soviet Union (former) **10:** 5649
Foreign language instruction
      4: ***2339–2346***
  for adults **4:** 2340
  audiolingual method **4:** 2341, 2353
  audiovisual aids **4:** 2353
  communicative competence **4:** 2341,
      2353
  community language learning **4:** 2342
  content-based **4:** 2343
  definition of **4:** 2346
  eclectic methods **4:** 2341
  electronic mail **4:** 2354
  elementary schools
    United States **4:** 2340
    (US) (FLES) programs **4:** 2346, 2349
  error analysis (language) **6:** 3438
  examinations **4:** 2355
  graded objectives
    United Kingdom **4:** 2354
  grammar translation method **4:** 2341,
      2352
  history **4:** 2340, 2347
  immersion programs **4:** 2352, 2354
  individualized education programs
      4: 2353
  inductive vs. deductive methods
      4: 2341
  language laboratories **4:** 2353
  lifelong learning **4:** 2356
  methods **4:** 2341
  microcomputers **4:** 2354
  monitor theory **4:** 2342
  natural approach **4:** 2343
  notional functional syllabi **4:** 2342,
      2348, 2354
  objectives **4:** 2340
  pattern drills (language) **4:** 2341
  policy **4:** 2340
  primary schools **4:** ***2346–2351***
    characteristics of successful
        programs **4:** 2350
    Europe **4:** 2348
    foreign language experience (FLEX)
        4: 2349
    future prospects **4:** 2350
    global approach **4:** 2348
    immersion programs **4:** 2350

programs (US) **4:** 2347
research **4:** 2356
secondary schools **4:** ***2351–2357***
course descriptions **4:** 2354
instructional materials **4:** 2355
methods **4:** 2352
organization **4:** 2354
policy **4:** 2352
testing and examinations **4:** 2355
the silent way **4:** 2342
success **4:** 2356
suggestopedia **4:** 2342
tape recorders **4:** 2353
testing **4:** 2355
textbooks **4:** 2355
videotape recorders **4:** 2354
views of **4:** 2341
See also
Second language instruction
Foreign language learning
affective and social–psychological variables **4:** 2335
age effects **4:** 2334
attitudes and motivation **4:** 2335
Attitude Motivation Index **4:** 2336
cognitive style **4:** 2343
contextual factors **4:** 2336
developmental sequences **4:** 2332
individual differences **4:** 2333
aptitude **4:** 2334
cognitive style **4:** 2334
input and conversation **4:** 2336
and intelligence **4:** 2331
language aptitude **4:** 2343
learning motivation **4:** 2344
learning processes **4:** ***2331–2339***
learning strategies **6:** 3329
motivation **4:** 2336
process of **4:** 2344, 2345
role of native language **4:** 2333
standards
United Kingdom **4:** 2356
United States **4:** 2356
theories of **4:** 2343
psychological approaches **4:** 2343
sociolinguistic approach **4:** 2344, 2345
See also
Second language learning
Foreign language programs
See Second language programs
Foreign language testing **4:** ***2357–2364***
communicative ability
characteristics of **4:** 2359
developments in **4:** 2362
problems **4:** 2360, 2361
and specialization **4:** 2361
test items
direct **4:** 2362
discrete **4:** 2362
indirect **4:** 2362
integrative **4:** 2362
test requirements **4:** 2358
validity **4:** 2361
and washback effect **4:** 2363
See also
Second language testing
Foreign languages
and second languages
semantic differentials **4:** 2358
See also
Second languages
Foreign student advisers **10:** 5802
Foreign students
adult education **8:** 4607
tuition fees
United Kingdom **10:** 5753
Forethought
See Cognitive objectives, anticipatory outcomes
Form classes (languages)
and foreign language learning **4:** 2338
Formal education
and adult education **1:** 153; **10:** 5592
and agricultural productivity **1:** 247
definitions of **1:** 144; **7:** 4141
enrollment rate **9:** 5159
informal and nonformal
and development **3:** 1648
and occupational mobility **9:** 5538
role of
in meritocracy **7:** 3770
social influences of **10:** 5598
and social mobility **9:** 5533
vs. nonformal education **7:** 4143, 4197
See also
Conventional instruction
Formal operations
Piagetian theory **8:** 4480
Formation Continue en Europe (*FORCE*) **4:** 2061
Formative evaluation **4:** 2080, 2092, ***2097–2101***, 2109
activities **8:** 4780
and analytical evaluation **4:** 2099
appraisals **8:** 4764
clients of **8:** 4780
curriculum-based **3:** 1356
and curriculum design **4:** 1844
and educational assessment **1:** 364
feedback
remedial instruction **6:** 3626
individualized instruction **6:** 3626
instructional materials **8:** 4801
iterative
and courseware design **2:** 1169
mastery learning **6:** 3626
preferred periods for **8:** 4801
and preformative evaluation **4:** 2098
and program implementation **3:** 1493
purpose of
projects **8:** 4780
for school improvement
United States **4:** ***2381–2389***
student motivation **6:** 3627
and summative evaluation **4:** 2099
in teacher education **4:** 2125
teaching methods **6:** 3627
use of term **8:** 4761
Foster care
by children **2:** 732
Foster family
placement
and deinstitutionalization (of disabled) **3:** 1437
Foundations of education
See Philosophy of education
Fourth generation evaluation **3:** 1282; **4:** 2087, ***2369–2375***
action-oriented **4:** 2374
case report **4:** 2374
constructiveness inquiry **4:** 2088
contract in **4:** 2373
methodology
hermeneutic circle **4:** 2372, 2373
nature of **4:** 2371
negotiation **4:** 2087, 2374
procedural steps **4:** 2373
responsive focusing **4:** 2087, 2371
stakeholders in **4:** 2371, 2373, 2374
Fractions
and computer-assisted instruction
special needs students **10:** 5671
Frame factor theory **4:** ***2375–2377***
curriculum theory **4:** 2376
France
adult basic education **1:** 101, 102
adult education **4:** 2391; **10:** 5636
and age-related participation **1:** 105
continuation students **1:** 182
éducation populaire **1:** 112
formation continue **1:** 118
history **4:** 1972
nonformal education **4:** 2381
policies **4:** 1973, 1974, 1975
sociocultural **10:** 5636
agricultural education
vocational education **1:** 242
apprenticeship tax **1:** 182
apprenticeships **1:** 313
enrollment rate **11:** 6666
art education **1:** 341
compulsory education
teacher role in **9:** 5020
computer uses in education
organizations for **2:** 1015
consumption benefits
homemakers and **2:** 1054
curriculum development **4:** 2383
day care evaluation research **11:** 6396
développement communautaire **6:** 3420
école maternelle **2:** 695
education of music teachers **7:** 4029
éducation permanente **6:** 3417, 3418, 3419
educational change **4:** 2384
educational policy
government role in **5:** 2509
educational research **4:** 2384
employment
paraprofessional personnel **11:** 6268
employment policy and on-the-job training **6:** 3616

foreign language instruction
  primary schools **4:** 2348
government school relationship
  school administration **4:** 2381
grade repetition **5:** 2513, 2514
higher education
  communication efficiency in **9:** 5017
  social inequality in **9:** 5106
individualized training credits **8:** 4638
international aid
  for vocational education **11:** 6661
labor relations
  in education **6:** 3190
language **4:** 2377
literacy assessment **8:** 4636
literacy programs
  crédit-formation individualisé **8:** 4638
monitoring of standards **7:** 3907
paid educational leave **7:** 4258
parent participation
  legislation **9:** 5213
polytechnical education **8:** 4605
postsecondary education **2:** 895; **4:** 2381
preschool education **4:** 2381; **8:** 4667, 4668, 4669
primary education **4:** 2379
school administration
  centralization **9:** 5165
school choice
  conflicts **9:** 5195
  research **9:** 5194
school inspectors **9:** 5248
school mapping **9:** 5256
school organization **4:** 2159
science education history **9:** 5324
second language instruction for immigrants **6:** 3210
secondary education
  vocational education **4:** 2380
secondary school teachers
  recruitment **9:** 5016, 5018
state church relationship
  accommodation **9:** 5011
structure of government **4:** 2378
system of education **4:** ***2377–2385***
  degrees and qualifications **4:** 2384
  educational objectives **4:** 2378
  major problems **4:** 2385
  structure **4:** 2379
teacher militancy **6:** 3192
teacher recruitment
  women **4:** 2383
teacher role
  change in **9:** 5018
teaching
  professional recognition **9:** 5178
teaching methodology **4:** 2383
technical education
  and paraprofessional personnel **11:** 6269
track system (education) **9:** 5019
training **11:** 6416, 6417, 6418
  construction industry **11:** 6636
  legislation **7:** 3711
  and societal analysis **11:** 6419
transition programs
  and disabilities **11:** 6460
unions **10:** 6068
  state incorporation **10:** 6075
university adult education **11:** 6549
university institutes of technology **2:** 895
videotex
  historical background **11:** 6302
vocational education **11:** 6682
  curriculum change **11:** 6667
  legislation **6:** 3365
  three-tier structure **11:** 6664
France InterActive
  and language education **7:** 4092
Francophone Africa
  adult education **1:** ***215–221***
    institutions **1:** 220
    policies **1:** 217
  adult educators training **1:** 219
  history of women's education **11:** ***6735–6741***
  illiteracy **1:** 216
Frankfurt School
  See Critical theory
Fraternities
  Germany **10:** 5777
  United States **10:** 5777
Free education
  Hong Kong **2:** 1040
Free enterprise system
  and curriculum
    trends **9:** 5519
  and educational policy
    vocational education **11:** 6687, 6702
  market schools **8:** 4827
  and school-based management **9:** 5305
  and school choice **9:** 5202
Free market
  See Free enterprise system
Free schools **1:** 263
Freehand drawing **1:** 339; **11:** 6616
  reading writing relationship
    early experience **4:** 1959
French language
  dissemination of **6:** 3210
  and educational television **5:** 2892
  factors in learning
    international studies **3:** 1763
  as a second language
    and multimedia systems **7:** 3995
    and multimedia technology **7:** 4092
French-speaking Africa
  See Francophone Africa
Frequency distributions
  See Statistical distributions
Friedman test
  nonparametric statistics **7:** 4161
Friendship
  and academically gifted **9:** 5530
  and child development **10:** 5757
  choice
    conditions for **9:** 5173
    and reciprocity **9:** 5174
  conflict within **10:** 5758
  formation
    factors affecting **9:** 5174
  influence on student behavior **10:** 5756
  and moral development **10:** 5757
  patterns
    and sociometric techniques **10:** 5616
  and school dynamics **9:** 5173
  and school segregation **10:** 5755
  in schools **10:** ***5754–5759***
    and conformity **10:** 5755
    and cooperative learning **10:** 5756
    and ethnicity **10:** 5755
    and grouping (instructional purposes) **10:** 5756
    institutional characteristics **10:** 5755
    and racial relations **10:** 5756
    sex differences **10:** 5754
    and social class **10:** 5754
    and student participation **10:** 5756
    and tracking systems **10:** 5756
  and self-concept **10:** 5757
  and social development **8:** 4367
  and student characteristics **10:** 5754
Froebelian kindergarten **4:** ***2385–2388***
  art education **1:** 339
  Dewey's criticism of **4:** 2386
  educational principles **4:** ***2385–2388***; **8:** 4668
  financial support **8:** 4668
  "gifts" **4:** 2387; **8:** 4668
  influence of **8:** 4667, 4668
  instructional materials **4:** 2387
  "occupations" **4:** 2387; **8:** 4668
  spread of **8:** 4668
Frontier College (Canada) **1:** 102; **7:** 4182
Functional literacy **1:** 96, 172; **6:** 3443, 3445
  and completion of secondary education **6:** 3445
  and cultural differences **6:** 3475
  definition of **1:** 100
  females **11:** 6717
  France **1:** 182
  international education **5:** 2958
  legislation **6:** 3366
  measurement **8:** 4635
    Adult Performance Level (US) **8:** 4635
  national assessments **8:** 4635
  and secondary school completion **1:** 181
  and UNESCO **11:** 6501
  use of term **6:** 3474
Functionalism
  and adult education **10:** 5593
  definition of **2:** 776
  Durkheim's sociology **2:** 776
  and educational anthropology **1:** 281
  educational theories **2:** 1065
  and history of instructional psychology **5:** 2876, 2877

loosely coupled systems **6:** 3526
and occupational prestige **10:** 6225
and teacher roles
socialization **10:** 6133
and teacher socialization **10:** 6122
Functions (mathematics)
calculus **6:** 3681
Fund raising
community support
educational finance **2:** 911
effect of education on **4:** 2210
Fundamental education (adults)
See Adult basic education
Funding
See Financial support
Furniture design
educational facilities **4:** 2221
Further education
See Adult education
Vocational education
Futures (of society)
and curriculum development
4: ***2327–2331***
and prediction
research **4:** 2328
Futures planning
See Long range planning

Gabon
adult education **1:** 219, 220
Galois lattice method (G-Lattice)
4: ***2395–2400***
applications
in educational research **4:** 2397, 2399
binary variables **4:** 2395
and cognitive structures **4:** 2395, 2398
complexity **4:** 2399
Galois connection (G-connection)
4: 2395, 2398
procedures **4:** 2395
qualitative and quantitative methods
4: 2398, 2399
and Rasch measurement models
4: 2395, 2397, 2399
Gambia
adult education
nonformal education **4:** 2404
curriculum development **4:** 2405
educational change **4:** 2406
educational research **4:** 2406
ethnic groups **4:** 2401
government school relationship
financial support **4:** 2404
school administration **4:** 2404
language **4:** 2401
preschool education **4:** 2403
primary education **4:** 2403
printed materials
provision **8:** 4697
private education **4:** 2403, 2404
secondary education **4:** 2403
structure of government **4:** 2401
system of education **4:** ***2401–2407***
degrees and qualifications **4:** 2406
educational objectives **4:** 2402
enrollment **4:** 2403
major problems **4:** 2407
structure **4:** 2402
teacher education **4:** 2405
teacher recruitment **4:** 2405
technical education **4:** 2403
Game theory
and educational technology **4:** 1914
and teacher student relationship
7: 3818
Games **9:** ***5472–5476***
evaluation **9:** 5474
fundamental concepts of **9:** 5473
and individual instruction **5:** 2771
intercultural communication **9:** 5474
objectives of **9:** 5473
puzzles
transfer of training **11:** 6453
rewards **9:** 5473
rules of **9:** 5473
student attitudes toward **9:** 5474
student development **9:** 5474
student role
decision-making **9:** 5473
time factors (learning) **9:** 5475
See also
Computer games
Educational games
Real time games
Gaze
See Eye contact
Gemeinschaft
and sex differences **1:** 436
Gender (sex)
See Sex
Gender differences (sex)
See Sex differences
General Aptitude Test Battery (GATB)
and vocational evaluation **11:** 6671, 6677
General Certificate of Education (GCE) (UK)
Advanced level (A-level) **1:** 182
General Certificate of Secondary Education (GCSE) (UK)
1: 181
General education
and adult education **5:** 2732, 2733
universities **1:** 91
and apprenticeships
Germany, Federal Republic of (former) **11:** 6654
and businesses
financial factors **11:** 6635
criticisms of **5:** 2733
curriculum development
philosophical perspective **3:** 1326
externalities **11:** 6426
and humanism **6:** 3150
and international education **5:** 2975
and leisure for adult learning **6:** 3374
and on-the-job training **7:** 4208
relevance of
student attitudes **11:** 6703
to vocational education **6:** 3260; **11:** 6664, 6698
role in social change **5:** 2733, 2734
as social control **5:** 2733
and technology education **11:** 6288, 6291
and vocational education
China, People's Republic of **2:** 756
Soviet Union (former) **10:** 5645
vocationalization of **3:** 1736
vs. vocational education
and economic change **3:** 1711
and productivity **11:** ***6628–6633***
and productivity hypothesis
11: 6630
women's education **11:** 6713
General Educational Development Programs
See High school equivalency programs
General science **5:** ***2897–2903***
historical background **5:** 2898
and student centered curriculum
5: 2898
General Social Survey (GSS) (US)
and secondary data analysis **9:** 5368
General systems theory (GST)
See Systems approach
General Teaching Council for Scotland
1: 25
Generalizability theory **5:** ***2458–2462***
applications **5:** 2460, 2461
basic concepts of **5:** 2458
coefficient **5:** 2459
developments of **5:** 2459
essay tests **4:** 2022
illustration of **5:** 2460
and item sampling **5:** 3057
and judgments
measurement of **6:** 3121
measurement designs **5:** 2461
and multiple choice tests **4:** 2012
observed scores vs. universe scores
5: 2458
and reliability **9:** 4981
stages in the application of **5:** 2459
and student evaluations of teacher effectiveness **10:** 6230
true scores vs. universe scores
5: 2458
variance parameters **5:** 2458
Generalization
and case studies
methods **2:** 641
classificatory behavior **2:** 1017, 1018
cognitive development
and literacy **3:** 1244
computer simulation **8:** 4720
and research methodology **9:** 5046
Genetics
and behavior development **5:** 2465; **11:** 6488
disorders
behavioral consequences **5:** 2463
and employment level
measurement **4:** 2278
Galton's quantitative paradigm
5: 2462, 2463

heritability
twin studies **6:** 3140
individual development **5:** ***2462–2465***
Mendel's paradigm **5:** 2462
and sex differences **9:** 5428
vs. environmental influences
twin studies **6:** 3140
Genotypes
biological influences **7:** 3948
Geographic concepts
International Charter **5:** 2466
National Curriculum
England and Wales **5:** 2466
national educational goals
United States **5:** 2466, 2468
Geographic regions
effects on teacher supply and demand **10:** 5845
Geographical information systems (GIS)
and educational planning **3:** 1829
uses
in education **3:** 1397
Geography
curriculum **5:** 2466
development **5:** 2466
politicization **5:** 2467
educational programs **5:** ***2465–2470***
issues-based approaches **5:** 2466
liberalization **5:** 2468
locational knowledge base **5:** 2467
National Curriculum
England and Wales **5:** 2467, 2468
sense of place orientation **5:** 2467
social education issues **5:** 2466
and social studies
in primary schools **9:** 5573
status of **5:** 2468
Geography instruction
Australia **5:** 2468
history of **5:** 2466
International Charter **5:** 2466, 2469
methods **9:** 5573
objectives **5:** 2466
research **5:** 2468
resources **5:** 2468
values clarification **5:** 2466
Geometry
computer-assisted instruction **7:** 4097
concepts of **6:** 3679
curriculum development **6:** 3680
deductive course **6:** 3679
history of instruction **6:** 3643, 3645
mathematical applications **6:** 3680
mathematics instruction
cultural differences **6:** 3667
research on developmental thinking **6:** 3680
school curriculum **6:** 3679
German
international use of
scientific research **5:** 2994
German Association for Technical Cooperation (GTZ)
vocational education
Africa **11:** 6658
Asia **11:** 6657
Latin America **11:** 6659
German Democratic Republic (GDR) (former)
educational reform
implementation **4:** 1853
vocational education
and reunification **11:** 6656
German Reich
apprenticeships
historical background **1:** 311
Germany
adult basic education **1:** 101, 102
adult education **5:** 2475; **10:** 5636
age-related participation **1:** 105
Erwachsenenbildung **1:** 112, 118
financial support **10:** 5637
Hohenrodter Bund **6:** 3417, 3419
legislation **6:** 3362, 3363
participation **10:** 5636
policies **4:** 1973, 1975
provision **10:** 5636
research **1:** 124
Volksbildung **1:** 112
Weiterbildung **1:** 118
adult literacy **3:** 1261
alternation education **8:** 4962
andragogy **1:** 274
apprenticeships **1:** 108, 306; **6:** 3616; **11:** 6251, 6419
historical background **1:** 311
main features of **1:** 307
Arbeitschulen **6:** 3133, 3135
art education **1:** 341
citizenship education
and vocational schools **6:** 3134
community education **2:** 908
computer uses in education
organizations for **2:** 1015
curriculum development **5:** 2477
day care for infants **5:** 2805
debate on humanistic reform of education **6:** 3417, 3419
early twentieth century
educational change **6:** ***3133–3138***
education of music teachers **7:** 4029
educational administration
administrator selection **1:** 79
recruitment **1:** 79
educational change **5:** 2478
educational research **5:** 2478
questioning techniques **8:** 4878
ethnic groups **5:** 2470
evangelical Protestant schools
Melanchton's influence **6:** 3530
Fachhochschulen **2:** 895
folk high schools **1:** 123
fraternities **10:** 5777
government school relationship
financial support **5:** 2476
school administration **5:** 2476
history of adult education **1:** 136
history of vocational education **11:** 6681
history of women's education **11:** ***6741–6748***
industrial training costs **2:** 1149
internal labor market **5:** 2939
job training
program evaluation **4:** 2148
labor education **11:** 6770
labor relations
in education **6:** 3194
learning disabilities
intervention **10:** 5684
minority group and immigrant education **7:** 3845
multicultural education **7:** 3967
music education **7:** 4017
Nazism
and religion **9:** 5009
nontraditional education
Waldorf schools **1:** 262
on-the-job training **4:** 1975
organizational development
trends **7:** 4239
paid educational leave **7:** 4258, 4262
postsecondary education **5:** 2473
preschool education **2:** 696; **5:** 2474; **8:** 4667, 4669
primary education **5:** 2472
religious education **9:** 5011
research **9:** 5006
school inspectors **9:** 5249
school reform **9:** 5280
science education history **9:** 5324
second language instruction for immigrants **6:** 3210
secondary education **5:** 2472
parallel institutions **9:** 5386
special education **2:** 723; **5:** 2474; **10:** 5660, 6243
state church relationship
accommodation **9:** 5011
structure of government **5:** 2470
system of education **5:** ***2470–2480***
degrees and qualifications **5:** 2478
educational objectives **5:** 2471
historical background **5:** 2471
major problems **5:** 2478, 2479
structure **5:** 2472
teacher education **5:** 2477
teacher recruitment **5:** 2477
teaching methodology **5:** 2477
technical education
and paraprofessional personnel **11:** 6269
vocational education **1:** 112; **7:** 4206
after reunification **11:** 6656
Volkshochschulen **2:** 895, 898; **8:** 4806; **10:** 5637
See also
German Democratic Republic (GDR) (former)
Germany, Federal Republic of (FRG) (former)
Germany, Federal Republic of (FRG) (former)
adult education **1:** 124
developments **1:** 122
educators **1:** 122
research **1:** 121

science of **1:** 125
apprenticeships **11:** 6653, 6664, 6693
enrollment rate **11:** 6666
career choice **11:** 6654
civic education **2:** 767
curriculum development
vocational education **11:** 6668
curriculum history **3:** 1289
educational policy
and legitimacy **6:** 3368
educational research
questioning techniques **8:** 4880
Federal Employment Office **6:** 3424
postsecondary education **11:** 6666
public education
management of contraction in **6:** 3604
skilled occupations
and career ladders **11:** 6694
vocational education **11:** ***6690–6699***
curriculum change **11:** 6667
finance **11:** 6656
learning modules **7:** 3890
vocational education and training
Anglo–German comparisons **11:** ***6638–6640***
national and international dimensions **11:** ***6653–6660***
vocational schools **11:** 6694
Gerontology **6:** 3426
and adult education **1:** 128
Gesellschaft
and sex differences **1:** 436
Gestalt psychology
and art education
United States **1:** 340
and cloze procedure **11:** 6342
and human factors engineering **4:** 2009
learning theories **5:** 2876, 2880; **6:** 3316, 3340
problem-solving **8:** 4726
visual perception theory **8:** 4377
Gestalt therapy
and humanistic education **5:** 2691
Gestures (nonverbal communication)
See Body language
Getty Center for Education in the Arts (US) **11:** 6619
Gewerkschaft Erziehung und Wissenschaft (*GEW*) (Germany, Federal Republic of (former)) **10:** 6075
Ghana
adult education
nonformal education. **5:** 2483
curriculum development **5:** 2484
educational change **5:** 2485
educational planning **8:** 4511
Educational Reform Program (1987) **8:** 4511
educational research **5:** 2485
ethnic groups **5:** 2480
ethnography
of Sisala **3:** 1753
of Tallensi **3:** 1752
government school relationship
financial support **5:** 2483
school administration **5:** 2483
joint production model
empirical research **6:** 3105
postsecondary education **5:** 2482
preschool education **5:** 2482
primary education **5:** 2481
public sector employment **8:** 4838
rural to urban migration
determinants of **5:** 2943
secondary education **5:** 2482
selection **9:** 5388
special education **5:** 2482
system of education **5:** ***2480–2486***
degrees and qualifications **5:** 2484
educational objectives **5:** 2480
enrollment **5:** 2485
major problems **5:** 2485
structure **5:** 2481
teacher education **5:** 2484
teacher recruitment **5:** 2484
technical education **5:** 2482
Gifted
academic achievement **5:** 2492
acceleration (education) **5:** 2729
Study of Mathematically Precocious Youth (SMPY) **5:** 2729
child development **5:** ***2492–2495***
cognitive ability **5:** 2492
cooperative learning **5:** 2730
creative development **2:** 1177
cultural differences **5:** 2487
educational programs **5:** 2729
enrichment activities **5:** 2730
ethnographic evaluation studies **4:** 2045
females **5:** 2488
heterogeneous grouping **5:** 2730
homogeneous grouping **5:** 2730
as human capital **5:** 2492
identification **5:** 2492, ***2725–2732***
cultural differences **5:** 2493
individual development
longitudinal studies **5:** 2493
learning disabilities **5:** 2489
assessment and intervention **5:** 2489
social emotional adjustment **5:** 2490
mainstreaming **5:** 2490
minority group children
identification of **5:** 2492
minority groups **5:** 2487
assessment **5:** 2487
identification **5:** 2487
intervention strategies **5:** 2487
United States **5:** 2487
personality traits **5:** 2492
physical disabilities **5:** 2490
identification and intervention **5:** 2490
regular and special education relationship **5:** 2490
research **9:** 5528
sex differences **5:** 2489
social–emotional development of **9:** 5528
special classes **5:** 2491
special education **5:** ***2486–2491***; **10:** 5661
art therapy **5:** 2491
educational technology **5:** 2490
instructional materials **5:** 2491
trends and issues **5:** 2490
special education programs **5:** 2493
England and Wales **5:** 2493
and teacher behavior **5:** 2493
and teacher expertise **10:** 6025
teaching methods
research on **5:** 2493
underachievement **5:** 2488
intervention and prognosis **5:** 2488
See also
Academically gifted
Gifted disabled **5:** 2489
identification of **5:** 2492
Gifted disadvantaged **5:** 2486
Australia **5:** 2487
identification of **5:** 2492
intervention strategies **5:** 2487
Israel **5:** 2487
socio-economic status **5:** 2486
Gifted students
See Academically gifted
Gifted
Giftedness
behavior problems
prevention **5:** 2727
cognitive component approach **5:** 2726
cognitive development
predictive measures **2:** 844
and creativity **5:** 2727
definitions of **5:** 2492, 2726
descriptive approach **5:** 2726
explanatory approach **5:** 2726
Gagné's differential giftedness talent model **5:** 2726
Gardner's theory of multiple intelligences **5:** 2726
individual differences **5:** 2726
and intelligence quotient **5:** 2492
multidimensional concepts of
studies **5:** 2726
Munich giftedness model **5:** 2726
and parenting skills **5:** 2729
Renzulli's theory **5:** 2727
research on **5:** 2492
cognitive psychology information processing approach **5:** 2493
sociocultural model **5:** 2492
special programs
advocacy **5:** 2728
Gini coefficient
of inequality **7:** 3733
Girls
See Females
Global approach
educational policy and reform **5:** ***2495–2500***

future trends **5:** 2498
educational research **3:** 1553
Global education
and environmental education **4:** 1993
and social studies
research **9:** 5581
Global Tomorrow Coalition
environmental education
instructional materials **4:** 1994
Goal orientation
problems and crises
individual development
8: ***4715–4719***
Goal structures
See Learning strategies, behavioral objectives
Goals
See Objectives
Gompert curve
equation **6:** 3521
Goodman's index of association
nonparametric statistics **7:** 4162
Goodness of fit
and event history analysis **4:** 2154
and factor analysis **4:** 2238
and log-linear models **6:** 3502
and logit models **6:** 3504
in multitrait multimethod techniques
7: 4002
and Rasch measurement models
8: 4905
and regression analysis **9:** 4965
and structural equation models
8: 4349
and Thurstone scales **11:** 6386
Gordon Personal Profile and Inventory (GPPI) **8:** 4398
Governance
centers of power **5:** 2511
centralization **6:** 3491
vs. decentralization **8:** 4588
change of rules in
and principal role **9:** 5271
choice of
and organizational economics
4: 1969
control
locus of **5:** 2510
decentralization **6:** 3491
democratic
alternatives to **8:** 4590
problems **8:** 4588, 4593
wants vs. needs **8:** 4590
in democratizing societies **8:** 4592
educational
decentralization in **3:** ***1407–1412***
and educational policy **5:** 2511
educational research **5:** 2507; **8:** 4591
expert control **8:** 4591
frameworks
concept and theory of **5:** 2509
and information technology **7:** 4087
institutions of
effectiveness **8:** 4588
intergovernmental relations
5: ***2509–2512***
and learning factors **10:** 5748
local influence **5:** 2511
municipalities **11:** 6553
and politics of education
8: ***4587–4595***
schools
archaic structures **6:** 3492
and educational change **6:** 3491
international developments
5: ***2504–2509***
issues **5:** 2504
middle management roles in
6: 3495
and state departments of education
7: 3839
trends **5:** 2508
structures
and educational finance **9:** 5236
system of education
American Samoa **1:** 266
France **4:** 2382
Gambia **4:** 2404
India **5:** 2749
Kenya **6:** 3129
Korea, Democratic People's Republic of **6:** 3158
Latvia **6:** 3270
Lebanon **6:** 3353
Myanmar **7:** 4036
Namibia **7:** 4043
Nepal **7:** 4064
Netherlands **7:** 4073
New Zealand **7:** 4108
Nicaragua **7:** 4112, 4114
Niger **7:** 4121
Nigeria **7:** 4129
Norway **7:** 4190
Rwanda **9:** 5110
Swaziland **10:** 5864
Sweden **10:** 5870
Tanzania **10:** 5906
Thailand **11:** 6375
Togo **11:** 6401
Tonga **11:** 6407
Tunisia **11:** 6471
Turkey **11:** 6479
Uganda **11:** 6498
United Kingdom **11:** 6518
United States **11:** 6539, 6543
Yemen **11:** 6791
Zaire **11:** 6811
Zimbabwe **11:** 6818
and teacher education **10:** 6036
urban schools **11:** 6554
See also
Administration
Educational administration
Federal regulation
Governing boards
and school business relationship
8: 4337
Government (administrative body)
and educational planning **8:** 4598
expenditure
and state departments of education
7: 3834
interlevel relations
and governance **5:** ***2509–2512***
levels of
and educational finance **9:** 5236
and management of contraction
6: 3603
systems of
authoritarian **5:** 2511
confederation **5:** 2509
conservative authoritarian **5:** 2511
democratic **5:** 2510
federal **5:** 2509
radical authoritarian **5:** 2511
unitary **5:** 2509, 2510
union relationship with **10:** 6075
See also
Federal government
Local government
State government
Government employees
and documentation systems **3:** 1592
state departments of education
7: 3837
Government policy
See Public policy
Government role
courseware
design **10:** 5622
development **10:** 5618
publication **10:** 5619
day care
subsidization of **2:** 692
division of labor
and economic change **3:** 1710
policies affecting **3:** 1710
and educational finance **4:** 2311
and educational innovation
implementation of **5:** 2843
educational planning **3:** 1816; **8:** 4596
and educational quality **8:** 4872
and educational reform **8:** 4515
and educational technology **9:** 5540
in information economy **3:** 1711
in preschool education **8:** 4662
skill development
funds **11:** 6651
textbooks
provision **11:** 6363
in training **11:** ***6425–6431***
finance **11:** 6430
policy formation **11:** 6429
rationales **11:** 6426
Government school relationship
and educational change **6:** 3599
and educational reform **9:** 5276, 5277
and educational technology **9:** 5540
and legitimacy **6:** 3367
and principals
role of **9:** 5271
and religious education **9:** 5003
and school-based management
9: 5304
vocational education
Latin America **7:** 4153
Grade equivalent scores **4:** 2074

Grade levels
  See Instructional program divisions
Grade point average (GPA)
  and decision-making theory **3:** 1422
  and learning strategies
    teaching of **6:** 3337
Grade repetition **5:** ***2512–2515***
  and cost effectiveness **3:** 1791
  and credential inflation **6:** 3548
  and dropouts **5:** 2513
  effect on academic achievement **5:** 2513
  effect on adjustment **5:** 2513
  effect on dropout rates **5:** 2513
  evaluation research **7:** 4157
  France **5:** 2513, 2514
  and low achievement **5:** 2513
  policies and practices **5:** 2514
  and socioeconomic status **5:** 2513
  United States **5:** 2514
Grade repetition rate
  and age factors **9:** 5226
  comparative studies **5:** 2513
  developing nations **9:** 5225
  and disengagement theory **9:** 5226
  and enrollment
    projections **8:** 4784
  females and males compared **9:** 5225
Grades (program divisions)
  See Instructional program divisions
Grading
  with aptitudes **10:** 5819
  comparison of achievement with effort **10:** 5820
  criterion referenced tests **10:** 5819
    disadvantages **10:** 5819
  on the curve
  See Grading, norm referenced tests
  equating achievement with improvement **10:** 5820
  established standards
    comparison with **10:** 5819
  norm referenced tests **10:** 5818
  with other students **10:** 5818
  performance assessment **10:** 5821
  symbols used **10:** 5820
    checklists **10:** 5821
    letters **10:** 5820
    numerical **10:** 5821
    pass–fail **10:** 5821
  trends **10:** 5821
  United States **10:** ***5818–5822***
Graduate education
  See Graduate study
Graduate school faculty
  characteristics of
    and public policy **8:** 4551
Graduate study
  in education
    criticism of **11:** 6442
  educational researchers **11:** 6438
    training for **11:** 6438, 6439
  for public policy **8:** 4550
  study abroad **5:** 2976
Graduates
  demand for
    public sector **8:** 4530
  elasticity of substitution
    empirical research **3:** 1445
  and employment opportunities **3:** 1702
  in labor market
    trends **7:** 4252
  supply and demand
    in different intellectual disciplines **7:** 4251
  vintage effects **11:** 6614
Grammar **1:** 481
  definitions of **10:** 5698
  history of study **10:** 5697
  instruction **10:** ***5697–5705***
    effect on error reduction **10:** 5700
    influence on writing (composition) **10:** ***5697–5705***
    research **10:** 5699
  learning processes **10:** 5697
  pedagogic and scientific **6:** 3437
  and reading comprehension **8:** 4938
  stylistic **10:** 5698
    influence on writing (composition) **10:** 5699, 5701, 5702
  syntax **10:** 5697
    effectiveness of instruction **10:** 5700
Grammar schools
  teacher education for
    historical background **3:** 1721
Grammar translation method
  foreign language instruction **4:** 2341, 2352
Gramophone records
  See Audiodisks
Grandes écoles
  teacher role **9:** 5016, 5018
Grandparents
  influence on individual development **4:** 2260
  parent role
    and child development **3:** 1637, 1639
Grant maintained schools (UK) **9:** 5278, 5303
  and school choice **1:** 591
Grants
  and adult education **1:** 156
  and educational equity (finance) **3:** 1792, 1793
  impact on access to education
    comparative analysis **3:** 1834
  on-the-job training **6:** 3616
  to private sector
    comparative area studies **8:** 4835
    and private enrollment **8:** 4834
  providers **6:** 3364
  and resource allocation **9:** 5063
  for training
    and equity arguments **11:** 6428
    and government policy **11:** 6429
  vocational education
    United States **11:** 6538
  vs. student fees **4:** 2314; **10:** 5752
  vs. student loan programs **10:** ***5762–5768***
Graphemes
  and literacy **1:** ***480–483***
  nature of **1:** 480
Graphic arts
  and desktop publishing **4:** 1956
Graphical user interface (GUI)
  microcomputers **7:** 3813
  for printing **8:** 4689
  See also
    Windows (computer environment)
Graphs
  and concept maps **2:** 1026
  interpretation of
    and microcomputer-based laboratories **7:** 3809
  and profile analysis **8:** 4752
  and profiles **8:** 4752
  and single case research **9:** 5487
  and social networks **9:** 5555
  statistical information
    computer software for **7:** 3814
Great Britain
  See United Kingdom (UK)
Greece
  adult education **10:** 5641
    nonformal education **5:** 2519
    provision **10:** 5641
  curriculum development **5:** 2521
  educational change **5:** 2522
  educational research **5:** 2522
  government school relationship
    financial support **5:** 2519
    school administration **5:** 2519
  law
    and education **5:** 2516
  postsecondary education **5:** 2517
  preschool education **5:** 2518
  primary education **5:** 2517
  private education **5:** 2520
  public vs. private sector earnings comparison **8:** 4837
  school reform **9:** 5279
  secondary education **5:** 2517
    vocational education **5:** 2517
  social studies
    research **9:** 5581
  special education **5:** 2518
  system of education **5:** ***2515–2523***
    degrees and qualifications **5:** 2521
    educational objectives **5:** 2516
    major problems **5:** 2522
    structure **5:** 2516
  teacher education **5:** 2520
  teacher militancy **6:** 3191
  teacher recruitment **5:** 2520
  teaching methodology **5:** 2521
  technical education **5:** 2518
Greek civilization
  Stoics
    and semiotics **9:** 5411
  and teaching style **10:** 6173
Green University (Italy) **2:** 1193

Group activities
and cooperative learning **2:** 1097; **9:** 5547
and network learning **2:** 980
problem-solving
and cognitive development **9:** 5546
Group behavior
behavior standards **5:** 2525
and behavioral instruction **10:** 6162
theories of **5:** 2529
Group discussion **5:** 2534
adult education **5:** ***2529–2532***
conditions for productivity **5:** 2532
leadership **5:** 2530
objectives **5:** 2530
problems and issues **5:** 2531
classes (groups of students) **2:** ***803–807***
student characteristics **2:** 805
student participation **5:** 2524
Group dynamics **5:** ***2523–2529***
adult education **5:** 2529
definition of **5:** 2523
discussion **2:** 803
and individual behavior **11:** 6629
in informal education **10:** 5594
interaction process analysis **5:** 2534
helping relationship **5:** 2534
and network learning **2:** 979
and productivity **11:** 6629
more cooperative vs. less cooperative hypothesis **11:** 6630
and role theory **10:** 6220
in schools **9:** ***5169–5176***
small group instruction **5:** 2528
and systems approach **10:** 5899
teacher role **5:** 2536
training in **5:** 2535
Group instruction
compared with individual instruction **5:** 2770
mastery learning **6:** 3628
See also
Small group instruction
Group Investigation (GI) method
and small group instruction **5:** 2533; **10:** 6183, 6186
stages **10:** 6183
Group processes
See Group dynamics
Group structure
analysis of
and sociometric techniques **10:** 5614, 5615
Group testing
and student reaction **9:** 5486
vs. single case research **9:** 5486
Group therapy
and voice disorders **11:** 6705
Group unity **5:** 2525
and educational change **6:** 3602
Groupements d'établissements de l'éducation Nationale (France) **8:** 4806
Grouping (instructional purposes) **2:** ***821–825***; **6:** 3626
and academic achievement
research **9:** 5041
cognitive psychology approach **5:** 2532
comparative analysis **2:** 821
streaming **2:** 821
cooperative learning **5:** ***2532–2536***
and academic achievement **5:** 2534
cross-cultural studies **5:** 2533
and social development **5:** 2534
types of **5:** 2533
and ethnicity **1:** 8
and friendship **9:** 5173
interaction
sex differences **5:** 2535
intergroup relations **2:** 1097
mainstreaming **2:** 1098
mixed-age grouping **1:** 228
multigraded classes **1:** 227
nontraditional education **2:** 824
organization **2:** 822
pacing
teacher role **5:** 2868
and social class **1:** 8
social psychology approach **5:** 2532
student placement
teacher expectations of students **2:** 822
teacher student relationship
learner controlled instruction **2:** 823
teacher expectations of students **2:** 823
teachers
managerial behavior of **10:** 6027
United States
track system **2:** 822
See also
Ability grouping
Age grade placement
Heterogeneous grouping
Nongraded instructional grouping
Grouping effects
and multilevel analysis **7:** 3979
Groups
adult learning in **5:** ***2529–2532***
characteristics of **5:** 2523
and differential demand model **8:** 4832
communication **5:** 2524
conflict in **5:** 2525
classrooms **5:** 2528
development of **5:** 2523
interpersonal composition model **5:** 2524
and labor force development
in Japan **5:** 2687
leadership **5:** 2524
objectives **5:** 2524
performance standard setting **7:** 4055
problem-solving in **5:** 2535
size effects
and microeconomics **7:** 3818
Growth curves
and change
measurement of **2:** 674
equations **6:** 3521
Guadeloupe and Martinique
adult education
nonformal education **5:** 2541
cultural influences **5:** 2542
curriculum development **5:** 2542
educational change **5:** 2543
educational research **5:** 2542
ethnic groups **5:** 2537
government school relationship
financial support **5:** 2541
school administration **5:** 2541
language **5:** 2537
postsecondary education **5:** 2539
preschool education **5:** 2540
primary education **5:** 2538
secondary education **5:** 2539
special education **5:** 2540
structure of government **5:** 2537
system of education **5:** ***2536–2544***
degrees and qualifications **5:** 2542
educational objectives **5:** 2537
enrollment **5:** 2539, 2540
historical background **5:** 2538
major problems **5:** 2543
structure **5:** 2538
teacher education **5:** 2541
technical education **5:** 2540
Guatemala
adult education **5:** 2548
cultural influences **5:** 2544
curriculum development **5:** 2549
educational change **5:** 2551
educational research **5:** 2550
ethnic groups **5:** 2545
ethnography of indigenous populations **3:** 1755
government school relationship
financial support **5:** 2548
school administration **5:** 2548
postsecondary education **5:** 2547
preschool education **5:** 2547
primary education **5:** 2546
private education **5:** 2548
secondary education **5:** 2546
vocational education **5:** 2547
special education **5:** 2547
system of education **5:** ***2544–2551***
degrees and qualifications **5:** 2550
educational objectives **5:** 2545
major problems **5:** 2551
structure **5:** 2545
teacher education **5:** 2549
teacher recruitment **5:** 2549
teaching methodology **5:** 2549
Guessing (tests)
corrections for
confidence testing **7:** 3999
criticisms of **7:** 3996
elimination testing **7:** 3999
formula scoring **7:** 3996
item response theory approaches **7:** 3998

in multiple choice tests **2:** 788; **7:** ***3996–4000***
detection of **7:** 3999
and objective tests **7:** 4196
types of **7:** 3996
Guidance
distance education **3:** 1562
distinguished from counseling **2:** 1161
See also
Career guidance
Counseling
Guidance programs
for children **8:** 4816
Guilford–Zimmerman Temperament Survey (GZTS) **8:** 4397
Guilford's structure of intellect (SI) model **7:** 3874
Guinea, Republic of
adult education
nonformal education **5:** 2554
curriculum development **5:** 2554
educational change **5:** 2552, 2555
educational research **5:** 2555
ethnic groups **5:** 2552
government school relationship
financial support **5:** 2554
school administration **5:** 2554
postsecondary education **5:** 2553
primary education **5:** 2553
secondary education **5:** 2553
vocational education **5:** 2553
system of education **5:** ***2552–2556***
degrees and qualifications **5:** 2555
educational objectives **5:** 2552
major problems **5:** 2556
structure **5:** 2553
teacher education **5:** 2554
vocational education
training with production **11:** 6447
women's education **11:** 6738
Guinea-Bissau
adult education
nonformal education **5:** 2559
curriculum development **5:** 2560
educational change **5:** 2558, 2561
government school relationship
financial support **5:** 2560
school administration **5:** 2560
language **5:** 2556
popular education **1:** 133
preschool education **5:** 2559
primary education **5:** 2558
secondary education **5:** 2558
structure of government **5:** 2557
system of education **5:** ***2556–2562***
degrees and qualifications **5:** 2561
educational objectives **5:** 2557
major problems **5:** 2561
structure **5:** 2558
teacher education **5:** 2560
teacher recruitment **5:** 2560
Guttman scales
and attitude measures **1:** 382, 384, 387, 392
development of **7:** 3703, 3704
coefficient of reproducibility **1:** 384
coefficient of scalability **1:** 384
and descriptive scales **3:** 1477
and developmental stages **3:** 1510
and partial order scalogram analysis **7:** 4308, 4310, 4313
Guyana
distance teacher education **3:** 1559
Gymnasium **1:** 182; **9:** 5386
vocational education
Germany, Federal Republic of (former) **11:** 6655

Hadith
and Islamic individual development theory **5:** 3020, 3021
Haiti
dropout rate **9:** 5225
occupational segregation **4:** 2430
Han language education
China, People's Republic of **7:** 3847
Handicap discrimination
severe disabilities **3:** 1506
Handicap identification **3:** 1531
at risk persons
special programs **2:** 707
classification **2:** ***711–719***
developmental disabilities **3:** 1621
and disabilities **10:** 5665
disability screening approach **3:** 1532
impairment screening approach **3:** 1531
and intelligence tests **10:** 5660
international classification **3:** 1531
learning disabilities
preschool children **10:** 5685
Handicapped
See Disabilities
Handicaps
See Disabilities
Haptics
See Touching behavior
Harbison rules of thumb
labor force planning **6:** 3610
and school expansion **3:** 1811
Hard of hearing
See Partial hearing
Hardware (computers)
educational technology
maintenance of **4:** 1916
management information systems **5:** 2830
microcomputers **11:** 6295
central processing unit (CPU) **7:** 3811
input devices **7:** 3811
interfaces **7:** 3812
output devices **7:** 3812
printers **7:** 3812
multimedia systems
standards for **7:** 3993
science education **7:** 4102
technological
educational economics of **4:** 1903
Harvard Business School
case methods **10:** 5944
Harvard Institute for International Development
comparative education information **3:** 1585
Hauptschulen **9:** 5386
vocational education
Germany, Federal Republic of (former) **11:** 6655
Hawaii
reading instruction
methods **3:** 1234; **10:** 5792
resilience
research **8:** 4776
Hawthorne effect
definition of **11:** 6508
and educational research **11:** 6508
Head Start Program (US) **6:** 3451
early childhood education
disadvantaged **5:** 2807, 2808
effect on cognitive ability **2:** 680, 683
evaluation **4:** 2093
health aspect **5:** 2572
parent participation **7:** 4299
planned variation **2:** 682
and unintended effects **11:** 6510
Heads of households
mothers
and poverty **4:** 2282
and national surveys **2:** 650
Headteachers
See Principals
Health
academic achievement
adolescents **5:** 2568
assessment of status **5:** 2573
early intervention
developing nations **5:** 2572
and education **5:** ***2563–2567***
educational background and **4:** 2209
educational influences on **5:** 2566
effects
of physical education **10:** 5710
effects of education on **2:** 1053; **6:** 3100
and family life **4:** 2258
influences on education **5:** 2563
and learning **5:** 2572
and learning conditions **5:** 2563
and marital status **4:** 2258
and outcomes of education **5:** 2563
aptitude **5:** 2563
instructional effectiveness **5:** 2564
persistence **5:** 2564
time on task **5:** 2563
Health conditions
effect on learning **5:** 2564
screening
school health services **5:** 2573
Health education
curriculum **5:** 2566
definition of **5:** 2567
developing nations **1:** 116
factors in behavior modification **5:** 2567
objectives **5:** 2566
physical education **8:** 4466

and political issues **5:** 2566
role of school in **5:** 2568
school community programs **5:** 2570
in schools **5:** ***2567–2572***
Australia **5:** 2571
barriers to implementation **5:** 2570
Canada **5:** 2571
categorical programs **5:** 2569
and children as caregivers **2:** 731
comprehensive model **5:** 2568, 2569
England and Wales **5:** 2571
evaluation studies **5:** 2569
historical background **5:** 2567
models of **5:** 2568
program effectiveness **5:** 2569
trends **5:** 2571
worldwide status **5:** 2570
women's education
developing nations **11:** 6714
Health needs
special programs **5:** ***2572–2575***
Health promotion **5:** 2568
and adult education
research **1:** 161
behavior modification **5:** 2569
and chronic illness **5:** 2567
parenting skills disabled children **4:** 1976
Health services
clinics for adolescents
high schools **5:** 2574
college students **10:** 5801
first aid **5:** 2566
special education
design for **5:** 2575
See also
School health services
Hearing impairments **3:** ***1398–1402***
and achievement tests **3:** 1401
assessment
school health services **5:** 2573
and cleft palates **11:** 6706
demographic data **10:** 5687
detection problems **10:** 5689
and intelligence **3:** 1401
and speech communication **3:** 1399
and speech and language handicaps **10:** ***5686–5691***
factors **10:** 5690
future trends **10:** 5690
relationships **10:** 5687
See also
Deafness
Partial hearing
Hearing loss
See Hearing impairments
Hegemony
and adult education ideology **5:** 2733, 2734
concept of **3:** 1715
definition of **2:** 903
and educational objectives **6:** 3619
and popular culture **2:** 903
and popular education **2:** 1047
and social reproduction **9:** 5058
Helping relationship
and learning **8:** 4371
young children **8:** 4797
Helplessness
and achievement need **1:** 28
explanatory style **9:** 5404
females
classroom environment **9:** 5443
in learning **6:** 3295
Her Majesty's Inspectors (HMI) (UK)
recruitment **9:** 5250
reform of **9:** 5250
problems **9:** 5251
role of **9:** 5249
Heredity
congenital impairments **5:** 2463
and family life **4:** 2258
and individual development
Buddhist theory **1:** 580
Christian theory **2:** 764
Confucian theory **2:** 1043
Hindu theory **5:** 2598
Islamic theory **5:** 3021
and intelligence quotient **7:** 3770
and twin studies **11:** 6489
Heritability analysis
outcomes of education
function **6:** 3140
See also
Kinship studies
Heritage education
and native language instruction **11:** 6776
Hermeneutics **5:** ***2579–2586***
as the art of understanding **5:** 2581
as Biblical exegesis **5:** 2581
and critical theory **5:** 2579
and deconstruction **8:** 4641
in educational research **5:** 2580, 2585; **9:** 5052
and effect of literacy on cognitive development **3:** 1242
existential **5:** 2582, 2585
Geisteswissenschaften school **8:** 4448, 4449
hermeneutic circle **3:** 1772; **5:** 2580, 2585
in fourth generation evaluation **4:** 2372
hidden curriculum **5:** 2588, 2589
historical background **5:** 2580
humanities **5:** 2693
and language games (Wittgenstein) **5:** 2579
and Marxism **5:** 2579
meaning of term **5:** 2579
and phenomenology **5:** 2579
and philosophy of education **8:** 4453
and positivism **5:** 2583
and psychological impact of life events **8:** 4718
purpose of **5:** 2580
and social science **5:** 2583
text
model of **5:** 2583
as the theoretical foundation of human sciences (Dilthey) **5:** 2581
and triangulation **11:** 6462
and validity **5:** 2584
Heroin
drug abuse
effect on learning **3:** 1618
use in pregnancy
effect on newborn infant **1:** 14
Heterogeneous grouping **2:** 824
educational improvement **1:** 229
educational objectives **1:** 229
and experimental studies **4:** 2189
gifted **5:** 2494, 2730
and outcomes of education **9:** 5261
Heuristics **6:** 3457; **8:** 4821
and creativity **2:** 1177
feminism **4:** 2301
historical development **10:** 6173
instruction
and domain specific knowledge **8:** 4950
and instructional design **1:** 344
models
of teaching **10:** ***6173–6178***
and procedural knowledge **3:** 1432
in science education **8:** 4645
and training program design **3:** 1487
Hidden curriculum **3:** 1327, 1334; **5:** ***2586–2589***
adult education **3:** 1310
and classroom environment **2:** 798, 800
critical theory **3:** 1333; **5:** 2588
criticism of concept of **5:** 2587
definitions of **3:** 1334; **5:** 2586
and educational environment **5:** 2587
feminist approaches **4:** 2288; **8:** 4582
hedonic relevance **5:** 2588
hermeneutics **5:** 2588, 2589
and null curriculum **5:** 2589
and outcomes of education **5:** 2587
and political power **8:** 4582
as process of nonverbal communication **5:** 2587
and racial relations **8:** 4582
research on **5:** 2586, 2587
and rural schools **2:** 915
and social studies **9:** 5580
sociology of **3:** 1347
teacher education **10:** 5994
and transactional model
educational anthropology **1:** 286, 289
values **5:** 2587
in civic education **2:** 769
Hierarchical linear models (HLM) **5:** ***2590–2596***
aggregation bias **5:** 2593
algorithms
Fisher scoring **7:** 3983
general EM **7:** 3982
generalized least squares **7:** 3984
and aptitude treatment interaction **5:** 2930
basic two-level model **5:** 2590

- between-school model **5:** 2591
- cross-level effects **5:** 2593
- crossed random effects **5:** 2595
- educational applications **5:** 2590, 2592
- and educational improvement **9:** 5221
- EM algorithm **5:** 2591
- heterogeneity of regression **5:** 2593
- historical background **5:** 2590
- and multilevel analysis **7:** 3981, 3982
- non-normal errors **5:** 2594
- properties of estimators **5:** 2592
- standard errors
  - misestimated **5:** 2593
- statistical estimation **5:** 2591
- structural relations **5:** 2595
- three-level applications **5:** 2594
- within-school model **5:** 2590
- *See also*
  - Multilevel analysis

Hierarchical regression models
- interaction effects **5:** 2927

Hierarchy
- *See* Vertical organization

High achievement
- curriculum adaptation **3:** 1255
- learning strategies
  - group instruction **6:** 3626
- and teacher behavior **10:** 6109
- and teacher expectation of students **10:** 6108

High income groups
- vs. low income groups
  - and cost effectiveness **2:** 1128

High risk students
- acceleration (education) **2:** 710
- classroom change **2:** 710
- community-based learning **2:** 710
- cultural deprivation approach **2:** 707
- and educational environment **2:** 710
- educational programs **2:** 709
- identification **4:** 2329
- indicators **2:** 708
- individualized instruction **2:** 710
- learning strategies for **6:** 3325
- and poverty **2:** 708
- preschool education
  - benefits **8:** 4664
- prevention programs **2:** 710
- and race/ethnicity **2:** 708
- remedial instruction **2:** 707, 710
- and resilience **8:** 4775
- teacher role **2:** 710

High School and Beyond (HSB)
- database **8:** 4840
  - first follow-up study **8:** 4841
  - research findings **8:** 4840
- surveys **1:** 589

High school equivalency programs **1:** 181, 183; **8:** 4806, 4962
- testing **7:** 3722

High school graduates
- and decision-making theory **3:** 1424
- projections **8:** 4785

High school students
- and tutoring **11:** 6483

High schools
- loosely coupled systems **6:** 3525
- school counselors in **9:** 5283
- science education **9:** 5325
- and second chance education **9:** 5364
- *See also*
  - Folk high schools
  - Vocational high schools

Higher education
- accountability **3:** 1718
- adults in **1:** ***89–94***; **8:** 4958
  - Japan **6:** 3076
- costs **8:** 4960
- dropout research **3:** 1600, 1601
- Europe **4:** 2056
- expansion
  - effect of comparative analysis on **3:** 1833
- females in
  - United States **4:** 2408
- financial support
  - cost effectiveness studies **2:** 1130
- independent study **1:** ***184–194***
- nontraditional students in **7:** ***4163–4171***
- political socialization **8:** 4579
- private financial support **8:** 4338
- qualifications
  - recognition of **4:** 2064
- rate of return
  - developed nations **3:** 1662
- second chance education
  - trends **9:** 5365
- and social change **1:** 90, 93
- and the state **3:** 1718
- student loan programs **10:** ***5762–5768***
- studies
  - and selection bias **9:** 5382
- systems approach **4:** 1888
- vocational courses
  - Japan **11:** 6696
- and vocational education
  - global approach **2:** 1058
- *See also*
  - Universities

Hinduism
- beliefs about origin of man **5:** 2652
- counseling **5:** 2601
- gurus **5:** 2601
- individual development **5:** ***2597–2601***
  - and caste system **5:** 2597
  - childrearing implication of theory **5:** 2600
  - developmental stages **5:** 2600
  - educational implications of theory **5:** 2600
  - influences on **5:** 2598
  - length of **5:** 2598
  - motivation **5:** 2599
  - objectives **5:** 2598
- individual differences **5:** 2600
- intention **5:** 2599
- karma **5:** 2597, 2598
- learning process **5:** 2599
- levels of consciousness **5:** 2599
- meditation **5:** 2599
- reincarnation **5:** 2597
- and religious education **9:** 4999

Hispanic Americans
- achievement need **3:** 1239

Historical materialism
- and participatory research **7:** 4334

Historiography
- and curriculum history **3:** ***1301–1308***
- research methodology problems **5:** 2604

Historiography of education **5:** ***2607–2618***
- changes in emphasis **5:** 2611
- gaps in educational history **5:** 2616
- influence of social sciences on **5:** 2610
- interdisciplinary approach **5:** 2611
- international perspectives **5:** 2613
- methodology **5:** 2611, 2616
- sociocultural patterns **5:** 2610
- United States revisionism **5:** 2611

History
- changes in concept of **5:** 2618
- cognitive processes
  - critical thinking **5:** 2620
- in core curriculum **2:** 1104
- and cultural pluralism **5:** 2619
- discipline of **5:** 2618
- and educational objectives **5:** 2619
- educational programs **5:** ***2618–2623***
- elementary schools
  - textbook research **9:** 5560
- as a political instrument **5:** 2619
- psychological explanation of events **10:** 6145
- research on learning of **9:** 5560
- and social studies **9:** 5578
  - in primary schools **9:** 5573, 5574
- student conceptions and misconceptions **9:** 5560
- United Kingdom attainment target **7:** 3908

History curriculum **5:** 2620
- actualization **5:** 2622
- chronological approach **5:** 2621
- and concept of time **5:** 2621
- females in **5:** 2456
- geographical approach **5:** 2621
- holistic approach **5:** 2622
- interdisciplinary approach **5:** 2623
- local and global history **5:** 2622
- organization **5:** 2620
- postholing approach **5:** 2621
- selection of content **5:** 2621
- thematic approach **5:** 2621
- typological approach **5:** 2621
- and Western civilization **5:** 2622
- *See also*
  - History instruction

History of education
- *See* Educational history
  - Historiography of education

History instruction
- concept teaching **9:** 5562
- effect of changing concept of history on **5:** 2619
- historical awareness **5:** 2620

internationalization **5:** 2619
objectives **5:** 2619
story telling **5:** 2623
teacher explanations **9:** 5561
teaching methods **5:** 2623
values in **5:** 2620
for young children
research **9:** 5576
See also
History curriculum
Hodges–Lehmann test
nonparametric statistics **7:** 4161
Hogan Personality Inventory **8:** 4398
Holidays
and leisure time **6:** 3375
packaged **6:** 3377
and school organization **7:** 4233
Holistic approach
case studies
methods **2:** 640
and cognitive style **1:** 318
metaphysical **9:** 4979
and school self-evaluation **5:** 2850
semantic **9:** 4979, 4980
to teaching **10:** 6208
Holistic evaluation **4:** 2098
and teacher expertise **10:** 6022
Holland
See Netherlands, The
Holmes Group **9:** 5315
professional development schools **10:** 5811
teacher education curriculum **10:** 5994
Holtzman Inkblot Technique (HIT) **8:** 4789
Home computers
See Microcomputers
Home environment
See Family environment
Home management
effects of education on **2:** 1054
Home schooling **2:** 889; **5:** 2628
Home study
parent participation **2:** 890
Home visits
parent education **7:** 4294, 4295
Homeless children **3:** 1733
and child abuse **3:** 1733, 1734
children's rights **3:** 1734
citizenship education **3:** ***1733–1736***
developing nations **3:** 1733
dropouts **3:** 1734
educational programs **3:** ***1733–1736***
in employment **3:** 1733, 1735
family problems **3:** 1733
incidence **3:** 1734
Latin America **3:** 1734
and industrialization **3:** 1733
outreach programs **3:** 1735
and poverty **3:** 1734
social action **3:** 1734
Homework **5:** ***2628–2631***
academic achievement **5:** 2630; **11:** 6389
educational policy **5:** 2630
and effective schools **4:** 1931
evaluation **5:** 2628
High School Homework Helpers Program (US) **11:** 6482
learning processes **5:** 2629
feedback **5:** 2630
parent role
academic achievement **5:** 2630
and parent student relationship **5:** 2626
and skill development **6:** 3300
student motivation **5:** 2630
teacher role
teacher aides **5:** 2630
time factors (learning)
student motivation **5:** 2630
time on task **11:** 6392
comparative analysis **5:** 2628
Homogeneous grouping
academic achievement **2:** 821
gifted **5:** 2494, 2730
and outcomes of education **9:** 5261
See also
Ability grouping
Homosexuality
and religious education **9:** 5006
Honduras
adult education
nonformal education **5:** 2634
curriculum development **5:** 2635
educational planning
and enrollment rate **3:** 1823
government school relationship
financial support **5:** 2634
school administration **5:** 2634
preschool education **5:** 2634
primary education **5:** 2632
secondary education **5:** 2632, 2633
vocational education **5:** 2633
system of education **5:** ***2631–2636***
degrees and qualifications **5:** 2635
educational objectives **5:** 2632
enrollment **5:** 2633
major problems **5:** 2635
structure **5:** 2632
teacher education **5:** 2633, 2634
Hong Kong
adult education **1:** 349, 350
nonformal education **5:** 2639
curriculum development **5:** 2641
education
rate of return **8:** 4916
educational change **5:** 2641
educational finance
and school organization **7:** 4231
and tax allocation **8:** 4360
educational research **5:** 2641
ethnic groups **5:** 2636
government school relationship
financial support **5:** 2640
school administration **5:** 2639
polytechnical education **8:** 4607
postsecondary education **5:** 2638
preschool education **5:** 2638
primary education **5:** 2637
printed materials
provision **8:** 4697
school-based management **9:** 5303, 5304
schools
conflict in **2:** 1039
secondary education **5:** 2637
vocational education **5:** 2637
special education **5:** 2639
system of education **5:** ***2636–2643***
degrees and qualifications **5:** 2641
educational objectives **5:** 2636
enrollment **5:** 2638
major problems **5:** 2642
structure **5:** 2637
teacher education **5:** 2640
technical education **5:** 2639
vocational education **9:** 5073, 5074, 5075
Hopi
ethnography of **3:** 1754
HORIZON **4:** 2063
Hormones
sex differences **9:** 5434
Hostility
and peace education **3:** 1731
Household production theory
consumption benefits
and education **2:** 1052, 1053, 1054
Households
See Family
Human capital **1:** 471; **3:** ***1660–1666***; **4:** 2389; **11:** 6420
adult education **1:** 129; **4:** 1973
measurement of flow of **7:** 3707, 3709
measurement of stock of **7:** 3707, 3709
and brain drain **1:** 554, 556
continuing education **2:** 1087, 1151
depreciation of **3:** 1658
developed nations **3:** 1662
developing nations **3:** 1662; **11:** 6652
earnings
and labor market analysis **3:** 1677
and economic impact of education **3:** 1648, 1704; **7:** 4250
and educational benefits **1:** 512, 517
and educational change
global approach **5:** 2496
firm-specific **7:** 4208, 4209
and labor market structures **7:** 4209
general **7:** 4207, 4208
portability of **7:** 4208
types I and II **7:** 4208
investment **3:** 1658; **5:** ***2643–2647***
cost effectiveness **2:** 1127
and educational choice **4:** 2414
factors affecting **5:** 2937
family role in **6:** 3101, 3102, 3139
and immigration **5:** 2739
and income distribution **5:** 2740
and the labor market **3:** 1666
and occupational information **6:** 3097, 3100
in preschool education **8:** 4662

and rural to urban migration
5: 2943
and social objectives **3:** 1781
time factors affecting **6:** 3097
vs. inequality aversion **6:** 3141
on-the-job training **6:** 3614, 3615, 3616; **7:** 4207, 4210
and overeducation **7:** 4251
and physical capital **5:** 2644
and productivity **3:** 1691; **5:** 2644
effects on **3:** 1678; **11:** 6629
informal sector **3:** 1678
race–earnings differentials **8:** 4897, 4898
rate of return **3:** 1662; **5:** 2643; **9:** 5234
cross-national comparisons **3:** 1663
individual **3:** 1649
private **3:** 1662; **5:** 2644
social **3:** 1649, 1662; **5:** 2644
specific **7:** 4207
training
age effects on **1:** 104
general **6:** 3614
specific **6:** 3614
wage competition model **3:** 1704
Human capital theory
age–earnings profiles
cross-sectional studies **3:** 1657
and cost effectiveness **2:** 1125
criticisms of **1:** 130
and curriculum development **9:** 5519
and dual labor market theory **3:** 1681
earnings inequality function **5:** 2741
education work relationship **3:** 1697, 1746; **6:** 3186
and income distribution **5:** 2740
elasticity of demand **3:** 1446
historical background **3:** 1810
job training
and earnings differentials **7:** 4198, 4199
and screening hypothesis **6:** 3614, 3615
compared **9:** 5351, 5353, 5354
and continuing education **2:** 1087
vintage effects **11:** ***6614–6615***
and vocational education **10:** 5915
vs. occupation matching theory
3: 1748
Human development
behaviorist approaches **1:** ***495–497***
cross-cultural approaches
5: ***2647–2651***
cultural concepts of **5:** ***2651–2656***
ecological models **3:** ***1643–1647***
Bronfenbrenner's **3:** 1643
humanistic models **5:** ***2689–2692***
religious concepts of **5:** ***2651–2656***
research
and educational practice
5: ***2666–2670***
and social policy **5:** ***2670–2673***
See also
Evolution
Individual development
Human factors engineering
4: ***2007–2012***
arousal–performance hypothesis
4: 2008
and books **8:** 4693
controls **4:** 2010
educational facilities **4:** 2220, 2221
environmental influences **4:** 2011
fatigue **4:** 2010
historical background **4:** 2007
individual needs **4:** 2008
nature of **4:** 2007
operator machine system **4:** 2008
spare mental capacity hypothesis
4: 2008
and user environments **4:** 2008
video display terminals
health problems **4:** 2010
Human posture
teachers **7:** 4173
Human relations
and school as workplace **9:** 5176, 5178
Human relations movement
and organizational theories **9:** 5161
Human relations organizations
See Human relations programs
Human relations programs
and organizational theories **4:** 2158
Human resources development (labor)
See Labor force development
Human rights
See Civil liberties
Humanism **6:** 3417, 3420
administration and **3:** 1771
and curriculum development **5:** 2608
and education
historical background **4:** 2004
and humanistic education
ritualistic knowledge **6:** 3150
Luther's pedagogy **6:** 3528, 3530
Humanistic education
and adult education **5:** 2691
and business education **5:** 2691
consciousness raising **5:** 2691
and Gestalt therapy **5:** 2691
group instruction **5:** 2690
and self-actualization **5:** 2690
and the human potentials movement
5: 2690
and instructional design theory
5: 2866
Jesuit education **9:** 5119
and learner controlled instruction
5: 2691
learning theories **6:** 3210
and open education **5:** 2691
and special education **10:** 5659
Humanistic psychology
and anti-education **5:** 2691
assumptions and models **5:** 2689
and existentialism **5:** 2689, 2690
and individual development
5: ***2689–2692***
and individualism **5:** 2691
and phenomenology **5:** 2689, 2690
view of behaviorism **5:** 2689
view of psychiatry **5:** 2689
Humanities
classic ideal **5:** 2692
cultural criticism **5:** 2693
curriculum development
and teachers **5:** 2695
and democratic values **5:** 2695
didacticism **5:** 2693
and educational administration **1:** 63
educational programs **5:** ***2692–2697***
intellectual experience
participation **5:** 2693
interdisciplinary approach **5:** 2694
pedagogy **5:** 2693
and rhetoric **5:** 2693
and social structure **5:** 2695
Humanities curriculum
Belgium **5:** 2696
developing nations **5:** 2696
Hungary **5:** 2696
India **5:** 2696
Italy **5:** 2696
Spain **5:** 2696
Tanzania **5:** 2696
United Kingdom **5:** 2695
United States **5:** 2694, 2696
Humanities instruction
secondary schools
United States **5:** 2694
teaching methods **5:** 2694
See also
History instruction
Second language instruction
Hungarian Center for Evaluation (OKI-EK) **2:** 939
Hungary
adult education **2:** 658
nonformal education **5:** 2702
research **1:** 124
apprenticeships **1:** 315
comparative achievement data
4: 2136
core curriculum **3:** 1335
curriculum development **5:** 2703
day care for infants **5:** 2804
educational change **5:** 2700, 2705
educational research **5:** 2705
ethnic groups **5:** 2698
government school relationship
financial support **5:** 2703
school administration **5:** 2703
illiteracy **2:** 657
labor relations
in education **6:** 3193
postsecondary education **5:** 2701
preschool education **5:** 2702
primary education **5:** 2700
secondary education **5:** 2701
vocational education **5:** 2701
special education **5:** 2702
system of education **5:** ***2697–2706***, 2705
degrees and qualifications **5:** 2704
educational objectives **5:** 2699
enrollment **5:** 2701

historical background **5:** 2699
structure **5:** 2699
teacher education **5:** 2703
teacher recruitment **5:** 2703
teaching methodology **5:** 2704
technology education
programs **11:** 6291
vocational education
administration of **11:** 6644
decentralization **11:** 6645
historical background **11:** 6642
policy formation **11:** 6646
Huntington's chorea **5:** 2463
Hygiene
health education **5:** 2567
Hyperactivity
drug therapy **8:** 4420
and drug use **3:** 1611
and minimal brain dysfunction **1:** 491
sex differences **11:** 6309
See also
Attention deficit disorders
Hypermedia
and authoring aids
for courseware design **10:** 5624
and authorship **8:** 4690
in education **2:** 885
trends **4:** 1917
environments
characteristics of **2:** 885
and epistemology **4:** 1922
and hypertext
comparisons **5:** 2706
and independent study **5:** 2770
and instructional design **5:** 2861
and language education **7:** 4091
hardware (computers) **7:** 4092
software **7:** 4092
mathematics education **7:** 4095
and multimedia systems **7:** 3992
and systems approach **10:** 5899
See also
Hypertext
Multimedia instruction
Hypertext
concept maps **5:** 2707
definition of **5:** 2706
educational applications of
5: ***2706–2709***
historical background **5:** 2706
and instructional evaluation **5:** 2708
items
annotation of **5:** 2708
editing of **5:** 2708
learning environments **5:** 2706
navigation **5:** 2707
research findings **5:** 2708
simple **5:** 2706
structural rules for **5:** 2707
See also
Hypermedia
Hypotheses
definitions of **5:** 2709
derivation of **5:** 2709
restatement of **5:** 2710
Hypothesis testing **5:** ***2709–2714***
alpha level **4:** 2191
and analysis of covariance **11:** 6589
and analysis of variance **11:** 6587
and Bayesian statistics **1:** 476, 477
and bootstrap procedure **9:** 5470
composite alternative **9:** 5464
and configural frequency analysis
2: 1032, 1035
and contingency tables **2:** 1083;
6: 3499
and correlation **2:** 1111
data summarizing **5:** 2712
and decision-making theory **3:** 1423
effect size **5:** 2713
and experimental studies **4:** 2191
and factor analysis **4:** 2233
and hierarchical linear models
5: 2590
incorrect decisions **5:** 2712
measurement methods **5:** 2711
and models **7:** 3865
and moral development **7:** 3916
multiple tests **5:** 2713
and path analysis **8:** 4340
populations for **5:** 2711
power analysis **5:** 2713
procedures **5:** 2711
and Rasch measurement models
8: 4906, 4911
and research methodology **9:** 5048;
10: 6235
scientific methodology **3:** 1521, 1522
and statistical significance **9:** 5460
test statistic **5:** 2711, 2712
critical value **5:** 2712
twin studies **11:** 6490
Type I error **5:** 2713
Type II error **5:** 2713
See also
Null hypothesis

Iceland
adult education **7:** 4177
nonformal education **5:** 2718
curriculum development **5:** 2719
educational change **5:** 2720
educational research **5:** 2720
government school relationship
financial support **5:** 2719
school administration **5:** 2718
language **5:** 2715
postsecondary education **5:** 2717
preschool education **5:** 2717
primary education **5:** 2716
secondary education **5:** 2717
vocational education **5:** 2718
special education **5:** 2718
system of education **5:** ***2715–2721***
degrees and qualifications **5:** 2720
educational objectives **5:** 2716
enrollment **5:** 2718
major problems **5:** 2721
structure **5:** 2716
teacher education **5:** 2719
teacher recruitment **5:** 2719
technical education **5:** 2718
ICONS project (US)
communication programs
computer-assisted **6:** 3212
Idea generation
techniques **5:** 2722
and decision-making **5:** ***2721–2725***
group **5:** 2723
individual **5:** 2723
types of **5:** 2722
Identification (psychology)
and moral development **7:** 3916
and socialization **10:** 5586
Ideography
syllabographic languages **8:** 4938
Ideology
in adult education **1:** 114;
2: ***1189–1194***; **5:** ***2732–2737***
content **5:** 2732
pedagogy/andragogy **5:** 2733, 2735
and adult students **5:** 2734, 2735
definition of **3:** 1715
and epistemology **4:** 2000
evaluation studies **4:** 2036
feminism **5:** 2456
and patriarchy **2:** 831
history of women's education
11: 6744, 6746
Australia **11:** 6732
international education **5:** 2958
and knowledge **6:** 3148
and literacy education **5:** 2734
and Mannheim's sociology of
education **2:** 782
and Marxism **6:** 3618
new right **3:** 1716, 1717, 1719
and philosophical analysis **8:** 4444
private schools **8:** 4825
professionalism and power **11:** 6719,
6722
and structuralism **9:** 5056
and student activism **10:** 5780
use of term **5:** 2732
and women's education
North America **11:** 6761, 6762
Ijaw
ethnography of **3:** 1753
Illegitimate births
by teenagers **4:** 2210
Illiteracy **2:** 1058; **6:** 3420; **8:** 4634,
4635
adults
eradication programs **5:** 2950
Anglophone Africa **1:** 210
Arab nations **1:** 323
Asia **6:** 3464
Caribbean **2:** 635
Central America **2:** 635
China, People's Republic of **2:** 747,
748
comparative analysis **2:** 961
effect on Latin America **3:** 1833
international studies **1:** 178
developed nations **6:** 3455
developing nations **1:** 169

females **4:** 2411
developed nations **11:** 6716
developing nations **11:** 6715
francophone Africa **11:** 6739
Pakistan **11:** 6756
Turkey **11:** 6756
francophone Africa **1:** 216
and literacy **6:** 3445
new concepts **1:** 90
problem of definition **6:** 3476
recognition as a problem **1:** 100, 101
United Nations eradication programs **11:** 6524, 6526
See also
Adult literacy
Educationally disadvantaged
Literacy
Illustrations
types of **2:** 1026
Imagery
and memorization **7:** 3765
Imitation
and cultural transmission **4:** 2168
infant behavior **5:** 2800
Immersion programs
foreign language instruction **4:** 2352, 2354
multicultural education
Canada **7:** 3969
Immigrant children
bilingualism
sociolinguistic studies (US) **1:** 535
curriculum for **7:** ***3840–3848***
Immigrant education
Israel **7:** 3846
Immigrants
acculturation
United States **7:** 3844
and adult education
reform strategies **1:** 160
allocative skills **5:** 2737
assimilation
United States **9:** 5509
Canada **5:** 2738
characteristics of
self-selection model **5:** 2737
China, People's Republic of **5:** 2738
Cuba **5:** 2738
and curriculum
factors affecting **9:** 5520
earnings differentials
United States **8:** ***4896–4902***
economic performance
and education **5:** ***2737–2740***
education for
Germany **7:** 3845
North America **7:** 4182
Sweden **1:** 101
educational attainment
Australia **8:** 4893
employment vs. unemployment **5:** 2739
foreign language instruction policy for **4:** 2347
impact of education on
anthropological studies **1:** 293
and industrialization
United States **7:** 3842
and multicultural education **7:** 3975
and occupational status **5:** 2737
outcomes of education **9:** 5508, 5509
second language instruction **6:** 3210
Thailand **5:** 2738
Immunization programs
in schools **5:** 2567
Imperialism
and apprenticeships
Germany, Federal Republic of (former) **11:** 6654
teachers
and curriculum development **8:** 4583
Imports
restriction
and protectionist policies **11:** 6634
Impulsiveness
See Conceptual tempo
In school suspension **3:** 1536
Incentive grants
postsecondary education **3:** 1791
Incentives
financial
for training **11:** 6430
learning motivation **7:** 3938, 3939
and delay of gratification **7:** 3941
and organizational economics **4:** 1970
example **4:** 1970
in schools **4:** 1971
and productivity **4:** 1971
teacher student relationship **7:** 3819
and school administration **4:** ***1967–1972***
for training
factors affecting **11:** 6635
See also
Rewards
Incest **1:** 17
and family therapy **1:** 18
Income
age and on-the-job training **6:** 3614, 3615
correlation with qualifications **4:** 2393
and education **6:** 3185
and educational level **1:** 129, 130
impact of training on **11:** 6418
and literacy level **1:** 129, 130
and minimum wages
on-the-job training **6:** 3615, 3616
See also
Earnings
Income contingent loans
and student loan programs **10:** 5764
See also
Student loan programs
Income distribution
age and education related **3:** 1703
and developing nations **5:** 2743
earnings inequality function **5:** 2741
and education **5:** ***2740–2744***
and political economy **5:** 2742
empirical research **5:** 2741
equality in **3:** 1712
human capital theory
education work relationship **5:** 2740
job competition model
productivity and **5:** 2742
and public policy **5:** 2743
research **5:** 2740
and supply and demand **5:** 2740
wage-efficiency vs. labor discipline models
and labor control **5:** 2742
See also
Earnings differentials
High income groups
Low income groups
Income generation
women's education for
developing nations **11:** 6715
Income tax
See Tax deductions
Independent academic centers
and vocational education
Latin America **7:** 4152
Independent learning
See Independent study
Independent reading
parent influence **6:** 3461
Independent study **6:** 3376; **9:** ***5394–5399***
adult education **1:** 114; **10:** 5595, 6200
adults **1:** 163, 167
andragogy **9:** 5395
and assignments **9:** 5362
computer-assisted instruction **9:** 5395, 5396
definition of **9:** 5394
and educational reform
Indonesia **4:** 1854
and heuristics **10:** 6175
history **9:** 5395
and individual development **9:** 5395
and individual instruction **5:** 2770
institutional support **9:** 5395
and labor force
Japan **6:** 3090
learning readiness **9:** 5395
learning strategies **1:** ***184–194***; **6:** 3325; **10:** 5744
lifelong learning **6:** 3325
and measurement of literacy **7:** 3710
personal responsibility orientation (PRO) model **9:** 5397
and programmed instruction **8:** 4768
promotion of
and cognitive processes **10:** 5744
related concepts **9:** 5396
research **9:** 5395, 5396, 5398
role of facilitator **6:** 3346, 3347
in schools
problems **8:** 4772
second language learning **6:** 3212
skills
motivation **9:** 5042
self-instructive **6:** 3295
theoretical approaches **9:** 5396

trends and issues **9:** 5398
usefulness **9:** 5397
vocational education
Sweden **11:** 6691
See also
Individual instruction
Independent Television Authority (ITA) (UK)
and educational television **5:** 2895
Index of segregation **4:** 2428
aggregation sensitivity **4:** 2429
changes over time **4:** 2429
decline
due to integration within occupations **4:** 2430
Index terms
See Subject index terms
Indexing
processes **5:** 2819
India
adult education **5:** ***2753–2759***
financial support **5:** 2758
goals and scope **5:** 2754
legislation **6:** 3363
and literacy **5:** 2754, 2755, 2758
and nongovernmental organizations **5:** 2756
policies and programs **5:** 2754
problems **5:** 2757
research gaps **5:** 2757
target population **5:** 2754
Bangalore
industrial productivity **3:** 1693
community development programs **2:** 905
community education
and adult literacy **2:** 909
computer uses in education **4:** 1902
organizations for **2:** 1015
curriculum development **5:** 2750
distance education **4:** 1902
mass media role in **2:** 884
in schools **3:** 1565
educational finance studies
private vs. public resources **8:** 4703
educational history **2:** 1062
educational radio **5:** 2886
educational research **5:** 2752
educational television
large-scale projects **5:** 2893
ethnography of indigenous populations **3:** 1754
females
access to education **4:** 2288
Gram Shikshan Mohim **5:** 2755
history of women's education **11:** ***6748–6753***
Integrated Child Development Services (ICDS) **3:** 1625, 1626
job training **7:** 4197
labor force planning **6:** 3609
language **5:** 2744
literacy campaigns **1:** 171, 175
literacy rates **5:** 2753
National Open School (NOS) **3:** 1565
nonformal education **7:** 4133, 4135
primary education **7:** 4133
on service teacher education **10:** 5979
open university **1:** 563
popular education **1:** 133
Popular Science Movement **1:** 132
postsecondary education **5:** 2747
primary education **5:** 2747, 2753
finance **2:** 1150
financial support **7:** 4140
private schools
and minority groups **8:** 4832
production
technology transfer models **11:** 6278
screening hypothesis tests **9:** 5354
secondary education **5:** 2747
segmentation theory
studies **3:** 1683
social education **5:** 2754
social organizations **2:** 905
sociology of education
development of **10:** 5601
student evaluation **5:** 2751
system of education **5:** ***2744–2753***
educational objectives **5:** 2745
historical background **5:** 2745
major problems **5:** 2752
structure **5:** 2746
teacher education **5:** 2750
Andhra Pradesh Primary Education Project **10:** 5979
teacher recruitment **5:** 2750
teacher student ratio **8:** 4865
teaching methodology **5:** 2750
technical education **5:** 2748
unemployment
labor market stratification model **6:** 3181
vocational education **9:** 5072, 5073
education with production **3:** 1687
women's education **5:** 2756
World Education **7:** 4146, 4147
Indigenous populations
bilingual education
and academic achievement **3:** 1832
cultural transmission **3:** 1751
culture and education **3:** 1751
education and nonformal education **4:** 2365
educational anthropology **3:** ***1750–1756***
experiential learning **3:** 1751
history of education
United States **7:** 3841
impact of education on
anthropological studies **1:** 292
reproduction (biology) **3:** 1751
social reproduction **3:** 1751
Individual autonomy
See Personal autonomy
Individual characteristics
and existentialism **8:** 4430, 4432
workers
as measurement of job satisfaction **11:** 6630
and productivity **11:** 6629, 6630
Individual development **1:** 116; **8:** 4817, 4823
behavior development
sex differences **9:** ***5433–5435***
behaviorist approaches **1:** ***495–497***
beliefs
about causal forces **5:** 2653
about development **3:** 1636
cultural influences **5:** ***2651–2656***
religious factors **5:** ***2651–2656***
biological influences **5:** 2648; **6:** 3513
biopsychosocial aspects
sex differences **9:** 5435
Buddhist theory **1:** ***577–581***
and change
choice of model **2:** 675
measurement of **2:** 671
Christian theory **2:** ***760–767***
cognitive ability **3:** 1503
cognitive approaches **5:** 2658
Comenius' *pansophia* model **2:** 883; **8:** 4572
Confucian theory **2:** ***1042–1045***
and contextual influences **3:** 1645
cross-cultural studies **5:** ***2647–2651***
holistic approach **5:** 2650
cultural psychology **5:** 2648
cultural relativism **5:** 2648
culture and personality school **5:** 2647
developmental continuity **6:** ***3425–3428***
early experience **3:** ***1636–1643***
and educational practices **5:** ***2666–2670***
educational research **5:** ***2666–2670***
objectives **5:** 2666
and embryology
Spencer's view **10:** 5706
emotional development **4:** ***1963–1967***
environmental influences **6:** 3513; **8:** 4817
evolutionary theory **4:** ***2167–2172***
and experiential learning
Dewey **3:** 1522
factors affecting **6:** 3513
family influence **4:** ***2258–2261***
and friendship **10:** 5757
genetics **5:** ***2462–2465***
and heredity
ecological models **3:** 1646
Hindu theory **5:** ***2597–2601***
holistic approach **8:** 4392
and lifelong learning **8:** 4392
humanistic models **5:** ***2689–2692***
and independent study **9:** 5395
infants **5:** ***2799–2802***
and interpersonal competence **9:** 5564
and interpersonal relationships **3:** 1644
intervention influences **6:** 3513
Islamic theory **5:** ***3020–3023***
Judaic theory **6:** ***3113–3120***
language acquisition **6:** ***3219–3224***
learning processes **1:** 192
lifelong learning **6:** ***3285–3288***

and continuing education
6: ***3416–3422***
measurement of **3:** ***1508–1514***
memory **7:** ***3760–3763***
moral development **7:** ***3914–3920***
and narcissism **8:** 4815
nature nurture controversy **5:** 2647, 2648
overview of psychological studies
5: ***2656–2665***
and peer relationship **8:** ***4364–4368***
personal growth theories **8:** 4822
personality development
8: ***4388–4395***
phonology **10:** 5694
physical development **8:** ***4468–4474***
problems and crises **8:** ***4715–4719***
process–person–context model
3: 1644
psychoanalytic theory **5:** 2658; **8:** 4814
psychodynamic theories **8:** ***4812–4816***
psychological patterns **9:** ***5403–5407***
relevance (education)
epistemological view **3:** 1363
moral view **3:** 1363
psychological view **3:** 1363
social studies **3:** 1363
research
ethnocentrism in **5:** 2647, 2649
research methodology **5:** ***2673–2677***
Rousseau's view of **9:** 5089
self-concept **9:** ***5390–5394***
sex differences **9:** 5428
sex role **4:** ***2446–2449***
and social change **11:** 6391
social cognition **9:** ***5510–5512***
characteristics of **9:** 5517
theory **9:** ***5513–5518***
social development **9:** ***5523–5528***
social policy
and research **5:** ***2670–2673***
and sociocultural patterns **9:** 5513
sociological approaches **5:** 2658
stability and change in **8:** 4392
theories of maturation
and school readiness **9:** 5273, 5274
time budget for learning **11:** 6392
vs. maturation **10:** 5586
Vygotsky's zone of proximal development
and school readiness **9:** 5274
See also
Adolescent development
Behavior development
Career development;
Child development; Cognitive development; Creative development; Emotional
development; Moral development; Personality development; Physical
development; Skill development; Social development; Talent development

Individual differences
ability **1:** ***1–6***
and ability grouping **5:** 2766
and adult development **8:** 4817
aptitude **1:** ***1–6***
Buddhist theory **1:** 581
and change
measurement of **2:** 671, 674
model for **2:** 676
cognitive ability **5:** 2761
cognitive development **2:** ***842–847***
Confucian theory **2:** 1043, 1044
and developmental psychology
5: 2657
and developmental stages **3:** 1509
and educational practices **5:** 2666
Galton's genetic paradigm **5:** 2462, 2463
giftedness **5:** 2726
Hindu theory **5:** 2600
and individual instruction **5:** 2770
and instructional improvement
5: ***2759–2769***
intelligence
evolutionary approach **4:** 2168
learning strategies **1:** 186, 190
personality development
11: ***6307–6311***
and teacher student relationship
10: 5759
teaching methods
mastery learning **6:** 3627
See also
Sex differences
Individual Differences model (INDSCAL)
9: 5158
Individual instruction **5:** ***2770–2773***
adaptation factors **5:** 2772
advantages of **5:** 2770
approaches to **5:** 2770
classification of **5:** 2771
compared with group instruction
5: 2770
decision makers for **5:** 2771
future trends **5:** 2772
and independent study **5:** 2770
theoretical studies **5:** 2770
See also
Independent study
Individualized instruction
Tutoring
Individual needs
hierarchy theory **4:** 1967
human factors engineering **4:** 2008
Individual power
beliefs about **5:** 2653
and citizen participation **4:** 1981
and competence **4:** 1980
and consciousness raising **4:** 1982
educational programs **4:** ***1980–1985***
individual differences **4:** 1983
Individual psychology
individual differences **5:** 2760
Individual rights
See Civil liberties

Individual testing
in the classroom **5:** ***2779–2784***
Individualism **10:** 5989
achievement need **3:** 1237
and adult education ideology
5: 2733
and cognitive style **3:** 1238
and new right ideology **3:** 1719
political philosophy **8:** 4571, 4572, 4573, 4574
and teacher cultures **10:** 6213
and teaching **10:** 6134
Individualized Classroom Environment Questionnaire (ICEQ) **2:** 809; **3:** 1481; **4:** 2247
Individualized education programs
5: 2774, 2904
early examples **5:** 2770
parent participation **5:** 2904
special education **10:** 5662
Individualized instruction **5:** 2765, ***2773–2779***
Adaptive Learning Environments Model **5:** 2777
adult learning **6:** 3433
approaches **5:** 2772
and aptitude treatment interaction
10: 6156, 6157
and behavioral instruction **10:** 6162
Buddhism **1:** 581
computer-assisted instruction **4:** 1844
and computers **11:** 6285
cooperative learning **2:** 1096
decision-making **10:** 6171
diagnostic teaching **10:** ***6169–6173***
and educational technology **4:** 1890, 1894, 1914
educational trends
futures (of society) **5:** 2778
failure
factors affecting **5:** 2772
future trends **5:** 2772
history of **5:** 2774
Individually Guided Education
5: 2776
mastery learning **5:** 2777; **6:** 3626
and multimedia systems **7:** 3992
native language instruction **11:** 6776
outcomes of education **2:** 822
pacing **4:** 1844
instructional effectiveness **5:** 2776
Personalized System of Instruction (PSI) **5:** 2772, 2776
effectiveness of **5:** 2772
tutoring **11:** 6483
and tutoring **11:** 6481
See also
Diagnostic teaching
Flexible progression
Individual instruction
Individuals with Disabilities Education Act (IDEA) (US) **3:** 1506; **5:** 2574, 2808
1986 amendment **5:** 2807
1990 amendments **2:** 712

See also
Education of the Handicapped Act (EHA) 1975 (US)
Indoctrination
See Propaganda
Indonesia
academic achievement
effect of parents on **4:** 2414
adult education **1:** 351
adult literacy **1:** 173; **3:** 1260
attendance patterns **3:** 1604
community support
fund raising **2:** 912
computer uses in education **4:** 1901
cultural influences **5:** 2784
curriculum development **5:** 2789
distance education **4:** 1903
by radio **3:** 1561
educational change **5:** 2791
educational finance **5:** 2787
educational reform
implementation **4:** 1854
educational research **5:** 2790
educational television **9:** 5542
government school relationship
school administration **5:** 2787
item banks
establishment of **5:** 3039
Kejar program **1:** 351; **6:** 3465
language **5:** 2784
literacy education **6:** 3464, 3465
macroeconomics
salary wage differentials **11:** 6635
nonformal education **7:** 4133
onservice teacher education **10:** 5978
open university **1:** 563
postsecondary education **2:** 895; **5:** 2786
preschool education **5:** 2786
primary education **5:** 2786
religious education
day schools **9:** 4997
school fees
and resource allocation **9:** 5064
secondary education **5:** 2786
vocational education **5:** 2786, 2787
special education **5:** 2787
system of education **5:** ***2784–2792***
degrees and qualifications **5:** 2789
educational objectives **5:** 2785
enrollment **5:** 2791
structure **5:** 2785
teacher education **5:** 2788
Active Learning through Professional Support **10:** 5978
teacher recruitment **5:** 2788
vocational education **8:** 4794
census data **8:** 4528
women's education
barriers to **4:** 2417
Induction **8:** 4723, 4950
and data analysis **3:** 1465
learning processes
computer simulation **8:** 4721
thinking skills **6:** 3320
analysis of **1:** 4
Industrial arts
chambers of crafts **1:** 311
and craft guilds **1:** 310
and technology education **11:** 6287
Industrial development
vocational education
Germany **1:** 311
and learning modules **7:** 3891
Industrial education
and curriculum development **3:** 1262
Kenya **11:** 6255
Tanzania **11:** 6254
Industrial psychology
development of **5:** 2877
job analysis **5:** 2877
task analysis **5:** 2877
Industrial restructuring
See Industrial structure
Industrial sectors
and skill requirements **10:** 5916
Industrial structure
characteristics of
and learning **6:** 3302
and educational change **5:** ***2792–2799***
Industrial training **1:** 96
access
and age **2:** 1150
and educational level **2:** 1150
racial differences **2:** 1150
sex differences **2:** 1150
and work experience **2:** 1150
Central and Eastern Europe **2:** ***656–662***
and cognitive ability **6:** 3304
cognitive oriented conceptions **6:** 3303, 3305
cost effectiveness of courses **2:** 1136
costs **2:** 1148
comparative **2:** 1148
determinants **2:** 1149
per employee **2:** 1149
unit costs **2:** 1150
creative thinking **8:** 4729
employer support **10:** 5807
expenditures
comparative area studies **5:** 2983
international comparisons of **5:** 2979
history of **11:** 6681
internationalization **6:** 3304
Japan **6:** 3089; **11:** 6695
learning **6:** ***3302–3306***
learning strategies
problem-solving **6:** 3347
measurement **7:** ***3711–3715***
statistical development **7:** 3711
methods **6:** 3305
paid educational leave
United Kingdom **7:** 4262
population trends **6:** 3304
public support for **4:** 2146
and reform strategies **1:** 158
study circles **10:** 5827
and universities
Europe **4:** 2061
See also
Apprenticeships
Job training
on-the-job training
Industrial Training Act 1964 (UK)
levy–grant system **11:** 6685
criticism of **8:** 4361
Industrial training boards
United Kingdom **6:** 3424; **11:** 6685
criticism of **11:** 6685
decline of **11:** 6687
Industrialization
and homeless children **3:** 1733
and information technology **7:** 4082
and organizational theories **4:** 2159
and school organization **7:** 4241
and vocational education **11:** 6657, 6680, 6683
Industrializing countries
See Developing nations
Industry
and vocational education
Soviet Union (former) **10:** 5644
Inequality (mathematics)
index of **7:** 3733
Infant behavior
approach-avoidance **5:** 2800, 2801
behavior patterns **5:** 2800
change processes **5:** 2800
developmental stages **5:** ***2799–2802***
hedonic mediation **5:** 2800, 2801
implications of research for parenting **5:** 2802
prosocial **8:** 4797
reflexes **5:** 2800
Infant mortality
child health **5:** 2802
decline in **3:** 1450
and female enrollment rate **4:** 2415
global trends **8:** 4672
and literacy **1:** 467
United States **2:** 708
Infant schools
See Nursery schools
Infants
auditory perception **5:** 2801
characteristics of
environmentally sensitive **1:** 359
cognitive development **5:** 2799
day care **5:** ***2803–2806***
Berlin model (Germany) **5:** 2805
caregivers **5:** 2805
costs **2:** 691
and delinquency **5:** 2804
early intervention **5:** 2803
Europe **5:** 2804
Hungary **5:** 2804
Lally's infant program **5:** 2803
longitudinal studies **5:** 2804
program evaluation **5:** 2803, 2805
Reggio Emilia model (Italy) **5:** 2805
and social behavior **5:** 2804, 2805
Syracuse project **5:** 2803
development

Bayley Scales of Infant Development **5:** 2812
psychoanalytic theory **8:** 4814
early childhood programs **5:** ***2806–2814***
early experience **5:** 2799
early intervention **5:** 2809
emotional adjustment **4:** 1964
fear in **4:** 1964
individual development **5:** ***2799–2802***
learning processes **5:** 2800
nature nurture controversy **5:** 2799
perception **8:** 4380
depth perception **4:** 2446
physical development **8:** 4470
body composition **8:** 4469
and breastfeeding **8:** 4469
determinants **8:** 4470
maturity indicators **8:** 4469
size **8:** 4469
Piagetian theory **5:** 2800, 2801
play **8:** 4538
research issues **5:** 2799, 2801
resilience
research **8:** 4776
responses
genetic factors **5:** 2799
self-recognition **9:** 5391
sensory experience **5:** 2801
social and cultural influences
parent mediation **1:** 359
visual acuity **5:** 2801
visual perception **5:** 2801
Infectious diseases
See Communicable diseases
Inferences
and cognitive development
in children **8:** 4952
logical thinking **8:** 4951
and semiotics **9:** 5414
See also
Statistical inference
Inflation (economics)
control of **3:** 1785
deficit financing
and educational finance **4:** 2311
Infology
definition of **7:** 3772
field of **7:** 3772
Informal assessment
decision-making **10:** 6172
instructional effectiveness **10:** 6172
teacher effectiveness **10:** 6172
Informal education **4:** ***2364–2369***; **6:** 3418, 3420
for adults **10:** 5594
compared with nonformal and formal education **4:** 2368
definitions of **1:** 144; **4:** 2364; **7:** 4141
and do-it-yourself activities **6:** 3376
use of term **1:** 119
Informal labor market
See Labor market, informal
Informal sector
characteristics of **5:** 2814
and employment **5:** 2814
vocational education **5:** ***2814–2819***
future trends **5:** 2818
recommendations **5:** 2815
Informatics
See Information science
Information
provision
and management information systems **6:** 3595
role of
in policy formation **8:** 4560
types of **3:** 1549
Information brokers
See Information scientists
Information centers
and information retrieval **5:** 2821
international
comparative education **3:** 1584
policy formation
international organizations **2:** 934
regional
comparative education **3:** 1586
Information collection
See Data collection
Information design
definition of **7:** 3772
Information dissemination
in education **3:** 1549
evaluation of **3:** 1549
innovations **3:** ***1549–1553***
International Institute for Educational Planning programs **11:** 6529
knowledge **3:** ***1549–1553***
problems **3:** 1552
studies **3:** 1551
Information economy
government role in **3:** 1711
as a product of organizational change **3:** 1708
Information needs
and information retrieval **5:** 2819
and management information systems **6:** 3594
and messages
in information retrieval **5:** 2821
Information networks
in developed economies
occupational information **6:** 3097
and educational research
Latin America **8:** 4494
expansion of **5:** 2994
international **5:** ***2993–2998***, 2994
access to **5:** 2995
journal systems **5:** 2996
and technological advancement **5:** 2996
and international education indicators **5:** 2985
for teachers **10:** 6008
Information processing
and audiovisual aids **4:** 1884
and economic change **3:** 1707
educational planning
and data collection **11:** 6293
in epistemology **10:** 5740
and management information systems **5:** 2830
Information retrieval **5:** ***2819–2823***
definition of **5:** 2819
and educational planning **3:** 1829
and interactive video **11:** 6602
libraries **6:** 3396
problems **5:** 2821
special needs students
microcomputers **7:** 3803
systems **5:** 2819
components of **5:** 2822
effectiveness factors **5:** 2822
and libraries **5:** 2823
outputs of **5:** 2821
Information science
curriculum **2:** 969
Information science education
curricular approaches **2:** ***969–973***
and databases **3:** 1395
Information scientists
and information retrieval **5:** 2823
media program administration **7:** 3753
Information services
documentation systems **3:** 1589
functions of **5:** 2819
privatization of
and educational technology **9:** 5543
question–answer systems **5:** 2821
representations
of requests **5:** 2821
of texts **5:** 2821
types of
and management information systems **5:** 2829
See also
Libraries
Information sources
adult education **1:** ***139–142***
educational opportunities **1:** 139
fragmentation **1:** 139
networks **1:** 142
organizations **1:** 141
publications **1:** 140
resource centers **1:** 141
selection from **1:** 140
education **3:** 1551
and educational vouchers **9:** 5205
expanded **6:** 3398
and media programs **7:** 3755
and social background
measurement **7:** 3718
Information specialists
See Information scientists
Information storage **5:** ***2819–2823***
Information systems
confidentiality **11:** 6297
for education **5:** ***2823–2827***
contact details **5:** 2826
and educational planning **3:** 1829
Information technology
applications
incorporation into curriculum **7:** 4086
attitudes to **7:** 4082

characteristics of **7:** 4081
and the curriculum **7:** ***4081–4088***
challenges to **7:** 4082
definitions of **5:** 2828
and distance education **3:** 1576
in education
and databases **3:** 1397
finance for **7:** 4086
future role **7:** 4087
potential **7:** 4082, 4085
educational applications
research findings **7:** 4085
educational objectives **2:** 976
educational research **7:** 4083, 4086
dissemination of **3:** 1554
and educational technology
field of study **4:** 1925
and evaluation studies **4:** 2387
and industrial training **6:** 3303
industry
developing nations **4:** 1900
and information society **4:** 1897
in language education **7:** ***4088–4095***
and library instruction **6:** 3397
in mathematics education
7: ***4095–4100***
office automation **5:** 2828
and organizational change **3:** 1708
in science education **7:** ***4100–4104***
potentials of **7:** 4101
skills
and literacy **6:** 3395
teacher education curriculum
10: 6006
and technology transfer **11:** 6277
uses
in educational management information systems
5: ***2828–2831***
vs. conventional instruction **7:** 4083
Information transfer
and educational planning **11:** 6295
and educational research
dissemination of **3:** 1554
and information technology **7:** 4081
innovations
and vintage effects **11:** 6614
Information utilization **6:** 3596
and educational planning **8:** 4598
future research **3:** 1552
Inhibition
shyness
student behavior **11:** 6309
Initiation rites **3:** 1725
Injuries
effect on learning **5:** 2565
Inner city education
See Urban education
Innovation
definitions of **4:** 2071
and educational planning **3:** 1822
and educational policy **3:** 1712
and implementation **5:** 2839
implementation of **5:** ***2839–2847***
management of **6:** ***3597–3603***
in organizations (groups)
and decision-making **5:** 2794
and program evaluation **4:** 2070
technological advancement
importance to success in **3:** 1709
See also
Educational innovation
Input output analysis **3:** ***1756–1762***
adult education **7:** 3707
basic model **3:** 1756
and cost effectiveness **2:** 1121, 1125
developing nations
research **3:** 1759
and educational finance **3:** 1757
and efficiency **3:** 1779
enrollment rate
and economic adjustment **3:** 1787
and equal education
developing nations **9:** 5536
input variables **3:** 1757, 1759
time **6:** 3546
inputs
diminishing returns of **7:** 3817
technological **4:** 1903
measurement variables **8:** 4562
output variables **3:** 1757
and private resources
for education **8:** 4702
private sector vs. education **5:** 2796
problems **3:** 1783
and small business training **4:** 1989
substitutable inputs
interdependence of **7:** 3817
and systems approach **10:** 5896
and teacher effectiveness **10:** 6036
traditional model
criticism of **8:** 4562
and unions **10:** 6068
See also
Productivity
Inquiry
discussion (teaching technique)
3: 1541
and teaching
conceptions of **10:** 6040
teaching method **6:** 3298
Inquiry-based learning
and microcomputer-based laboratories **7:** 3809
Inservice education
educational administration **1:** ***67–73***
and educational change **1:** 71
and management development **1:** 71
methods **1:** 70
Soviet Union (former) **9:** 5095
Inservice teacher education
10: ***5966–5973***
for adult educators **10:** 6057;
11: 6434
anthropology programs
United States **1:** 298
apprenticeship model **10:** 5983
compared with on service teacher education **10:** 5978
computer literacy
and career ladders **10:** 6006
course provision **10:** 6006
costs **10:** 5966
developed nations **10:** 5949
costs **10:** 5950
distance education
telecommunications **10:** 6007
and educational policy **8:** 4525
effectiveness **10:** 5971
external support agencies **10:** 5971
financial support **10:** 5951
human resource development
10: 5966
laboratory training **6:** 3198
LEARN network
Denmark **10:** 6007
management of planned change
10: 5966
needs assessment **10:** 5967
individual teachers **10:** 5968
schools **10:** 5968
Organisation for Economic Co-operation and Development
definition **10:** 5966
and philosophy of education
10: 5985
policy trends **10:** 6037
professional development **10:** 5968, 5970
project-based models **10:** 5970
skill development **10:** 5968
reflective model **10:** 5969, 5984, 5985
relationship with preservice teacher education **10:** 5999
relationship with teacher orientation
10: 5999
self-development by schools and teachers **10:** 5966
and special education **10:** 5941, 5942
technical education **10:** 6066
types of **8:** 4525
for unqualified teachers **10:** 5966
INSET
See Inservice teacher education
Inspecteurs départmentals de l'Education nationale (IDEN) (France)
role of **9:** 5248
Inspecteurs généreaux de l'administration de l'Education nationale (IGAEN) (France)
role of **9:** 5248
Inspecteurs généreaux de l'Education nationale (IGEN) (France)
role of **9:** 5248
structure **9:** 5248
Inspection
schools
definition **9:** 5247
Inspectors of schools
See School inspectors
Institut Africain pour le Développement Economique et Social (INADES)
1: 218, 220
Institut canadien d'éducation des adultes (ICEA) **7:** 4181

Institut Européen pour la Formation Professionelle (*IEFP*)
educational technology
activities **4:** 1881
Institut National d'Education Populaire (France) **1:** 123
Institut für Schulenwicklungsforschung (*IFS*) (Germany)
and organizational development **7:** 4239
Institute of International Education (IIE) **2:** 941
Institute for Social Research (ISR) (US)
and organizational development **7:** 4236
Institutes of education
United Kingdom **3:** 1723
Institutional autonomy
and academic achievement
studies **1:** 590
Argentina **1:** 333
Bulgaria **1:** 583
and educational administration **6:** 3273
Italy **5:** 3030
Jordan **6:** 3110
Madagascar **6:** 3553
Mexico **7:** 3797
See also
Academic freedom
School-based management
Institutional characteristics
and attendance **3:** 1605
and educational quality
vocational education **8:** 4859
effect on educational finance **3:** 1786
and learning factors **10:** 5748
and outcomes of education **9:** 5261
and school choice **9:** 5193
and sociology of education **10:** 5600
Institutional development
See Organizational development
Institutional personnel
and educational benefits **1:** 511
Institutional role
downward expansion **5:** 2497
Institutional self-evaluation (groups)
critical inquiry
United States **4:** ***2381–2389***
and renewal **5:** ***2847–2852***
phases **5:** 2848
Institutional values
and academic achievement **8:** 4563
function **8:** 4564
Institutionalized persons
research on effects on behavior **3:** 1437
Institutions
concept of
and school organization **4:** 2157
costs
input output analysis **8:** 4702
demand
for academic achievement **8:** 4565
external
and governance **5:** 2511
and socialization **10:** 5586
Instituto Ajijc sobre Educación Internacional (*IASEI*) (Mexico) **2:** 940
Instituto Colombiano de Crédito Educativo y Estudios Técnicos en el Exterior (CETEX)
student loan programs **10:** 5764
Instruction
of adults **1:** 148
classroom
dimensions of **10:** 6184
cognitive participation in
variables **10:** 5739
cognitive processes **10:** ***6187–6193***
and computers
integration of **11:** 6283
concept formation **10:** ***6215–6219***
costs
effect of unions on **10:** 6071
criteria for successful **10:** 5983
critical theory **10:** 6196
and curriculum **3:** 1310
databases in **3:** ***1394–1398***
delivery of
mass media **2:** 884
domain-based theories of **5:** 2879
and educational reform **11:** 6561
evaluation
and hypertext **5:** 2708
explicit teaching model **10:** 6188
sequencing **10:** 6189
factors in learning **8:** 4400, 4402
feedback in **4:** ***2279–2281***
formative evaluation of
criticism of **2:** 794
frame factors
structuralist view **4:** 2375
Herbart's doctrine of stages **5:** 2577; **6:** 3135
inquiry-oriented instruction model **10:** 6190
and intelligence **5:** 2920
and learning
interaction **6:** 3290
intervention **6:** 3344
and learning strategies **6:** 3346
as a linguistic process **6:** 3236
linguistic theory **10:** ***6193–6197***
for literacy **1:** 172; **6:** 3455
for numeracy **6:** 3458
organization of **9:** 5169
peer groups **9:** 5171
planning of
educational resources **2:** 793
student characteristics **2:** 793
Plato on the nature of **8:** 4534
sequential approach
the Learning Cycle **3:** 1540
and questioning techniques **8:** 4879
science laboratories **3:** 1540
sociolinguistics **10:** ***6193–6197***
summative evaluation of **2:** 794
educational planning **2:** 795
influences **2:** 795
and teacher knowledge **10:** 6118
teacher led **3:** 1525; **9:** 5170
criticism of **3:** 1528
text comprehension **10:** 6190
and textbooks
role of **11:** 6368
theoretical framework **10:** 5739
theories of **4:** 1843; **7:** 3881, 3884
See also
Pedagogy
Instructional alignment
and transfer of training **5:** 2854, 2855
Instructional design
adaptive strategies **5:** 2865
affective learning **5:** 2866
and artificial intelligence **1:** ***343–348***
uses **1:** 346
and attention–relevance–confidence–satisfaction (ARCS) model **7:** 3945
authoring aids for **10:** 5623
automated systems **5:** 2860
constructivist strategies **5:** 2865
content analysis **2:** 1022
contextual analysis **2:** 1022
curriculum design
and vertical organization **4:** 1844
definitions of **1:** 344; **5:** 2856, 2862
and educational objectives **4:** 1844
and educational technology
special needs students **10:** 5670
field of study **5:** 2870
and Gagné's learning taxonomies **5:** 2920
implementation **3:** ***1491–1494***
and instructional psychology **5:** ***2870–2874***
contributions **5:** 2872
relationship **5:** 2870
and job analysis **6:** 3093
strategies **6:** 3093
and learning factors **10:** 5747, 5748
and learning problems
from misconceptions and preconceptions **8:** 4651
and media selection
intervention strategies **7:** 3758
minimalist instruction **5:** 2866
models **5:** ***2856–2862***
classification schema **5:** 2858
classroom-focused **5:** 2859
components of **5:** 2872
historical background **5:** 2857, 2858
product-focused **5:** 2859
purpose of **5:** 2857
system-focused **5:** 2860
trends **5:** 2860
motivation in **7:** ***3943–3947***
parameters **5:** 2872
and performance support systems (PSS) **5:** 2860
procedures **5:** 2873
processes **5:** 2873
and student needs **10:** 5768
systems analysis **10:** 5895, 5897

task analysis **10:** ***5910–5914***
selection of technique **10:** 5912
and teaching guides **10:** 6115
theories **5:** ***2862–2867***
attitudes **5:** 2866
characteristics of **5:** 2863
descriptive vs. prescriptive **5:** 2871
effects of information technology **5:** 2864
future trends **5:** 2866
historical background **5:** 2864
and learning theories **5:** 2863
level of detail **5:** 2864
pragmatic vs. ideological **5:** 2863
prescriptive vs. descriptive **5:** 2863
product vs. process **5:** 2864
trends **5:** 2865
validity vs. superiority **5:** 2863
training **3:** ***1486–1491***
Instructional development **2:** 836
and educational technology **4:** 1890
and instructional design models **5:** 2858
and media programs **7:** 3755
for mild disabilities **8:** 4933
models
and instructional design theory **5:** 2864
and project evaluation **8:** 4781
and testing **7:** 3724
Instructional effectiveness
and assignments **9:** 5360
and cognitive development **3:** 1503; **10:** 6188
and cognitive processes **10:** 5742
evaluation methods
paper and pencil tests **2:** 795
factors affecting **9:** 5039
instructional alignment **5:** ***2852–2856***
curriculum alignment **5:** 2853
philosophical approaches **5:** 2855
research **5:** 2854
stimulus control **5:** 2852
studies **5:** 2854
testing implications **5:** 2855
and misconceptions **8:** 4649
training **3:** ***1486–1491***
and vocational education **8:** 4861
See also
Teacher effectiveness
Instructional improvement
individual differences **5:** ***2759–2769***
and learning motivation **7:** 3943
Instructional innovation
and apprenticeships
Germany, Federal Republic of (former) **11:** 6656
Instructional leadership
vocational schools
and educational quality **8:** 4861
Instructional material development
See Material development
Instructional material evaluation
and dissemination **8:** 4782
during implementation stage **8:** 4782
processes **8:** 4800
and product development **8:** 4781
Instructional materials
adult literacy **3:** ***1257–1262***
analysis of
and artificial intelligence **1:** 346
attention arousing **1:** 376
censorship **6:** 3359
concept maps **2:** 1027
and content analysis **2:** 1076
and curriculum
adaptability **10:** 6089
and curriculum development **3:** 1492
curriculum packages **6:** 3202, 3203
design
and human factors engineering **4:** 2009
systems approach in **10:** 5899
distance education
quality control **3:** 1560
DISTAR **3:** 1527
and educational innovation **3:** 1492
and educational quality **8:** 4868
vocational education **8:** 4859
electronic
development **8:** 4800
evaluation **8:** 4800
and prototyping **8:** ***4799–4803***
English language in
dominance of **8:** 4847
evaluation
teacher role **2:** 794
international aid
for vocational education **11:** 6661
and international publishing
research **8:** 4845
international studies
comparative analysis **10:** 6150
for interpersonal competence training **9:** 5566
laboratory packages **6:** ***3202–3205***
learning resources centers **6:** 3396
and media programs **7:** 3753
and nonformal education **7:** 4143
and outcomes of education **9:** 5260
printing
image production **8:** 4690
and procedural specifications **3:** 1493
product development **4:** 1884
provision of
publishing industry **8:** 4846
publishing of
trends **8:** 4689
and resource allocation **9:** 5540
role of **10:** 5594
sex bias in **4:** 2448; **9:** 5442
sex fairness in **9:** 5444
and social studies **9:** 5576
and student participation **8:** 4871
and syllabi **10:** 5885
and test coaching **11:** 6337, 6339
transfer of
problems **8:** 4847
types of **11:** 6370
See also
Audiovisual aids
Printed materials
Programmed instructional materials; Textbooks
Instructional media
See Educational media
Instructional message design
See Message design
Instructional methods
See Teaching methods
Instructional processes
See Teaching methods
Instructional program divisions
aid to career development **6:** 3098
as feedback mechanism **6:** 3098
grouped subjects vs. learning modules **7:** 3891
and individualization **5:** 2771
and public examinations
placement of **4:** 2173
and questioning techniques **8:** 4879
and school organization **7:** 4230
secondary education **9:** 5385
small classes
academic achievement **2:** 774
and textbooks
readership size **11:** 6362
See also
Age grade placement
Instructional psychology
and behaviorism **5:** 2871
cognitive shift in **5:** 2871
and constructivism **5:** 2871
development of cognitive psychology **5:** 2878
and developmental psychology **5:** 2876, 2883
ecological validity **5:** 2883
and educational technology **5:** 2879
Europe **5:** 2875, 2876
experimental school **5:** 2875
history of **5:** ***2874–2880***
individual differences school **5:** 2875, 2883
influence of Gestalt **5:** 2876, 2880
influence of Münsterberg **5:** 2877
influence of Vygotsky **5:** 2876, 2881
influence of William James **5:** 2877
influence of Wundt **5:** 2877
influence of Würzburg **5:** 2876, 2881
and instructional design **5:** ***2870–2874***
relationship **5:** 2870
international influences **5:** 2878
learning theories **6:** 3317
and models of learning **7:** 3881
national developments in **5:** 2875
objectives **5:** 2874
paradigms in **5:** 2879, ***2880–2884***
quasiexperimental design **5:** 2883
and research design **5:** 2883
and Social Darwinism **5:** 2875
theories of
descriptive vs. prescriptive **5:** 2871
trends and developments **5:** 2883

See also
Educational psychology
Instructional radio
See Educational radio
Instructional software
See Courseware
Instructional systems
adaptation to individual differences **5:** 2765
and aptitude treatment interaction examples **10:** 6157
design models **2:** 1166
and instructional design **5:** 2862
and interactive video **11:** 6601
international studies
comparative analysis **10:** 6151
and programmed instruction **8:** 4772
Instructional technology
See Educational technology
Instructional television
See Educational television
Instructional time
See Time on task
Instrumental Enrichment Program **8:** 4729
Instrumentation
and mass media **2:** ***884–888***
Integrated activities
Computer Supported Intentional Learning Environment (CSILE) **6:** 3298; **11:** 6780
learning systems
computer-assisted instruction **7:** 3805
and computer-managed learning **2:** ***998–1002***
courseware **2:** 1171
Integrated curriculum **6:** 3207
and computers **2:** 975, 976
literature in **10:** 5958
Integrated learning
See Integrated activities, learning systems
Integrated rural development
See Rural development, integrated
Integrated science education **5:** ***2897–2903***
conceptual approaches **5:** 2897
curriculum evaluation **5:** 2903
developing nations **5:** 2900
dimensions **5:** 2901
environmental involvement **5:** 2902
intensity **5:** 2901
matrix **5:** 2902
scope **5:** 2901
and environmental problems **5:** 2900, 2902
historical background **5:** 2898
information sources for curriculum **5:** 2903
place of mathematics in **5:** 2901
principles **5:** 2900
rationale for **5:** 2898
common basic concepts **5:** 2899
epistemic argument **5:** 2898
psychological and pedagogical arguments **5:** 2899
societal and practical arguments **5:** 2899
scientific projects **5:** 2900
Integration (disabled students)
See Mainstreaming
Integrative analysis
See Meta analysis
Intellectual development
adult development
Piagetian theory **5:** 2912
teachers **10:** 5938
age differences **5:** 2910
children **5:** 2911, 2912, 2913
and cognitive ability **3:** 1503
contextual in adults **8:** 4819
contextual approach **5:** 2914, 2915
developmental stages **5:** 2912
and family size
effects of **7:** 3869
females **10:** 5938
individual development **5:** ***2910–2916***
individual differences **5:** 2911
influence of learning activities on **5:** 2654
information processing approach **5:** 2913, 2915
intelligence tests **5:** 2911
predictive validity **2:** 844
and interpersonal relationships **9:** 5546
issues in **5:** 2910
learning processes **5:** 2913, 2915
and literacy **6:** 3446
measurement
individual differences **5:** 2920
Piagetian theory **5:** 2912, 2915
and cognitive restructuring **2:** 857
psychometric approach **5:** 2911, 2915
age differences **5:** 2911
Spencer's view of **10:** 5707
Intellectual disciplines
analysis of
and artificial intelligence **1:** 346
change
international studies **9:** 5295
choice
sex differences **4:** 2287
classification schemes **3:** 1361
core curriculum **2:** 1104
interdisciplinary approach **2:** 1105
curriculum history **3:** 1304
and curriculum theory **3:** 1352
definition of **1:** 120
development of new **1:** 122
Dewey's organization of **3:** 1522
feminist view of **5:** 2456
future research **9:** 5298
grouping
based on models or theories **3:** 1360
in departments **3:** 1360
by function **3:** 1360
high status **9:** 5297
historical background **9:** 5296
humanities curriculum **5:** 2693
interests **1:** 201
knowledge of
and teacher expectation of students **10:** 6111
levels
and questioning techniques **8:** 4879
participation
and sex differences **9:** 5425
role of **1:** 120
studying **9:** ***5294–5299***
programs for **9:** 5296
rationale for **9:** 5295
research **9:** 5297
Intellectual freedom
Montessori method **7:** 3913
and moral development **5:** 2577
personal autonomy
Buddhism **1:** 581
and rights to pedagogical neutrality **4:** 2031
Saint Augustine on **9:** 5117
Intellectual history
and curriculum history **3:** 1307
and social history **5:** 2615
Intellectual property
copyrights **2:** 1100
electronic media **10:** 5620
See also
Copyrights
Intelligence **5:** ***2916–2922***
and acculturation **8:** 4818
and adjustment (to environment)
Piagetian theory **5:** 2912
and aptitude **6:** ***3312–3315***
attitudes to
and learning motivation **7:** 3938
and auditory perception **5:** 2760
beliefs about
and motivation **1:** 29, 31
bio-ecological approach (Ceci) **5:** 2914
and biological determinism **2:** 717
characterization of **5:** 2910
classifications of **7:** 3877
and cognitive processes **5:** 2918
correlation with prosocial behavior in children **8:** 4798
and creativity **2:** 1176; **5:** 2760
crystallized **5:** 2760, 2911; **6:** 3430; **8:** 4819
characteristics of **1:** 147
concept of **5:** 2921
theories of **5:** 2917
educational implications of research **5:** 2921
effects of learning on **5:** 2916
and employment opportunities **7:** 3769
entity theory **7:** 3784
ethological studies **4:** 2169
and facet theory **4:** 2214
fluid **5:** 2760, 2911; **6:** 3430; **8:** 4818
and aging (individuals) **1:** 235
characteristics of **1:** 147
concept of **5:** 2921

theories of **5:** 2917
general **5:** 2760
general theories of thinking **5:** 2919
giftedness
Sternberg's triarchic theory **5:** 2726
and hearing impairments **3:** 1401
hierarchical model **5:** 2911
incremental theory **7:** 3784
individual development **5:** ***2910–2916***
information processing theory **5:** 2918
and instruction **5:** 2920
and learning **5:** 2919
correlational studies **5:** 2920
taxonomies (Gagné) **5:** 2920
measurement of abilities **7:** 3878
measurement of **5:** 2916
and memory **5:** 2760
metacognitive beliefs about **7:** 3784
models of multiple (Thurstone) **2:** 845
models of **7:** ***3873–3880***
Carroll's three-stratum model **7:** 3875
Cattell–Horn model (Gf-Gc theory) **7:** 3875
choice **7:** 3873
Guilford's structure of intellect (SI) model **7:** 3874
Guttman's radex model **7:** 3876, 3878
hierarchical **7:** 3874, 3877
relationships between **7:** 3878
Thurstone's model **7:** 3874
Vernon's model **7:** 3875
multidimensionality of adult **8:** 4821
and nature nurture controversy **5:** 2916
nature nurture controversy
and cognitive restructuring **2:** 857
and neurophysiology **8:** 4818
and outcomes of education **7:** 3769
personal **8:** 4823
Piaget's definition **8:** 4480
and prior learning **8:** 4699
psychometric model **8:** 4818
and reaction time **5:** 2760
and resilience **8:** 4776
sex differences **9:** 5443
and social environment **7:** 3769
Spearman's two factor theory **5:** 2917
theories of **5:** 2911, 2914; **6:** 3430
and adult learning **1:** 147
Gardner's theory of multiple intelligences **7:** 3877, 3878
Sternberg's triarchic theory **5:** 2726, 2914, 2918; **6:** 3313; **7:** 3876, 3878
two-factor theory **7:** 3873
Thorndike's multifactor view **5:** 2917
training
enrichment activities **3:** 1503
variability
and sex differences **9:** 5428
and visual perception **5:** 2760
See also
Cognitive ability
Mental age
Intelligence differences **5:** 2918, 2919
correlation with learning **5:** 2920
evolutionary approach **4:** 2168
and sociometric techniques **10:** 5616
verbal ability **5:** 2918
Intelligence quotient (IQ) **2:** 844
adult
productivity relationship **3:** 1693
calculation of **11:** 6343
and classical test theory **2:** 788
cross-sectional studies **2:** 1215
effect of education on **5:** 2464
effects of preschool education on **2:** 679
and employment level **7:** 3769
and environment **7:** 3770
and heredity **7:** 3770
individual differences
family environment **5:** 2464
genetic factors **5:** 2464, 2465
influence on social development **9:** 5526
and intraindividual differences **2:** 845
and preschool evaluation **4:** 2142, 2143
sex differences **9:** 5433
and success **7:** 3770
Intelligence tests **1:** 1
abuse of **11:** 6344
adult performance
age differences **1:** 235
and aging (individuals) **8:** 4819
and specialization **8:** 4819
Binet's contribution **4:** 1866
characteristics of **11:** 6343
for children
predictive validity **2:** 844
crystallized and fluid intelligence **5:** 2917
and cultural differences **4:** 1849
culture fair tests **5:** 2918
and developmental psychology **5:** 2657
early **7:** 3873
and educational history **3:** 1793
Embedded Figures Test **4:** 2335
and factor analysis **4:** 2230
giftedness
problems with **5:** 2729
historical development **4:** 1867; **5:** 2917
influence on special education **10:** 5660
and learning disabilities
diagnosis of **10:** 5683
and Marxian analysis **7:** 3770
mental age **2:** 844; **11:** 6343
and mental retardation **10:** 5663
and meritocracy **7:** 3769
and objective tests **7:** 4193
predictive measurement **6:** 3312
pretests–posttests **6:** 3313
and reading achievement
discrepancies **8:** 4931
secondary education
selection **9:** 5387
and sex differences **9:** 5427
and smallest space analysis **9:** 5502
and social stratification **7:** 3770
special needs students **2:** 715
See also
Cognitive measurement
Intelligent tutoring systems
See computer-assisted instruction (CAI), programmed tutoring
Intention
and adult education participation **7:** 4322
and behavior **1:** 354, 356
and educational objectives **3:** 1803
and moral development
Buddhist theory **1:** 580
Christian theory **2:** 764
Hindu theory **5:** 2599
Islamic theory **5:** 3021
Intentional learning **6:** ***3325–3329***
learner controlled instruction **2:** 837
and motivation **7:** 3936
Inter-American Society for Educational Administration (ISEA) **5:** 2953
Interaction
and analysis of variance **11:** 6587
and artificial intelligence **1:** 345
as communicative action (Habermas) **2:** 1201
and computer-assisted instruction **2:** 990
configural frequency analysis **2:** 1034
and courseware design **2:** 1168
data analysis
vs. substantive claims **5:** 2922
disordinal **5:** 2922
and distance education **3:** 1578
effects
analysis **5:** 2925
analysis of polynomials **5:** 2926
case study **5:** 2926
detection of **5:** ***2922–2931***
future research **5:** 2930
regression surfaces **5:** 2927
significance **5:** 2926
testing **5:** 2925
hybrid **5:** 2922
learning
and simulation **2:** 986
ordinal **5:** 2922
treatment costs **5:** 2924
research designs
historical background **5:** 2922
residuals
examination of **5:** 2925
and school dynamics **9:** 5169
search procedures **5:** 2924
uses of **10:** 6155
See also
Aptitude treatment interaction
Group dynamics

Interaction process analysis
group dynamics **5:** 2534
time sampling
criticisms of **2:** 814
naturalistic units **2:** 815
uses of **2:** 815
Interactionism **2:** 1070
dramaturgical approach **2:** 1071
and learning **6:** 3307
and phenomenology **2:** 1071
and structuralism **2:** 1071
and teacher socialization **10:** 6124, 6125
internalized adjustment **10:** 6125
strategic compliance **10:** 6125
strategic redefinition **10:** 6125
teaching
educational research **10:** 6132, 6133
Interactive communication
electronic media
distance education **1:** 563
Interactive video **11:** ***6600–6604***
advantages of **5:** 2895
characteristics of **11:** 6600
design strategies
theory-based **11:** 6602
development of **11:** 6600
and distance education **3:** 1564
educational technology **4:** 1921
formats **11:** 6600
future trends **11:** 6603
hardware capabilities **11:** 6600
and learning **6:** 3299
as learning system **11:** 6601
and message design **7:** 3773
research **11:** 6602
and science education **7:** 4101
in social studies **9:** 5582
software for **11:** 6600
and technical education **4:** 1922
uses of **11:** 6601
and videodiscs **5:** 2896
Intercultural communication **6:** 3211
discontinuities in **1:** 291
multicultural education **7:** 3961, 3962, 3965
Intercultural education
See Multicultural education
Intercultural programs
Europe **4:** 2055
multicultural education **7:** 3965
United States **7:** 3975, 3976
Interdisciplinary approach
and educational research **11:** 6439
vocational education **4:** 1919
Interest inventories
equity issues **11:** 6676
innovations **11:** 6672
pictorial **11:** 6672
uses of **11:** 6670
Interests
cognitive structures **2:** 1200
in critical theory **2:** 1200
epistemological status **2:** 1201
definitions of **11:** 6669
emancipatory **2:** 1201, 1203; **3:** 1773
hierarchical model of **11:** 6674
individual differences
and motivation **5:** 2764
practical **2:** 1200; **3:** 1773
specific groups
educational media organizations **3:** 1798
structure of
research **11:** 6673
technical **2:** 1199, 1200; **3:** 1773
Intergenerational mobility
See Social mobility, intergenerational
Intergovernmental organizations
See International organizations
Intergroup relations
and facet theory **4:** 2216
peer relationship **8:** 4365
and school climate **9:** 5207
and school culture **9:** 5209
and school dynamics **9:** 5171
Interlanguage
error analysis (language) **6:** 3439
skill development **4:** 2332
Interlibrary loans **6:** 3396
Internal capital market
on-the-job training **7:** 4210
Internal labor market **3:** 1696, 1701; **4:** 1973; **8:** 4837
apprenticeship **5:** 2938
as control mechanism **5:** 2940
developing nations **5:** 2940
dual labor market theory **6:** 3184
criticism of **6:** 3186
earnings
factors affecting **5:** 2938
and education **5:** ***2937–2942***
Germany **5:** 2939
implications for educational policy **5:** 2941
Japan **5:** 2939
job clusters **8:** 4837
on-the-job training **5:** 2937; **7:** 4210
seniority promotion systems **8:** 4837
United States **5:** 2938
vertical organization **5:** 2938
vs. employment-at-will system **5:** 2941
Internal migration
See Migration, internal
Internalization
concept of **9:** 5319
International Academy of Education **2:** 941
International adult education **1:** 150; **5:** ***2931–2937***, ***2945–2951***; **7:** ***4146–4148***
as aid for development **7:** 4133
cooperation **5:** 2936
comparative analysis **5:** 2946, 2949
conferences **5:** 2936
donor agencies **5:** 2933
growth of **5:** 2931, 2936
national level interest **5:** 2934
normative action **5:** 2934
objectives **5:** 2946
political context **5:** 2946
and social change **5:** 2946
and vocational education **5:** 2947
See also
International Council for Adult Education
International aid
bilateral **5:** 2962
changing role of **5:** 2963
distribution of **5:** 2962
and economic crisis **5:** 2961
for education **5:** ***2961–2965***
and educational planning **3:** 1821
educational policy
influences on **4:** 1838
educational research
Latin America **8:** 4493
historical background **5:** 2962
multilateral **5:** 2962
nonformal education **7:** 4142
policy impact **5:** 2964
and private organizations
Latin America **7:** 4150
for vocational education
Africa **11:** 6255
bilateral aid **11:** 6660
development banks **11:** 6661
Germany, Federal Republic of (former) **11:** 6657
implications **5:** 2817
multilateral aid **11:** 6660
sources of **11:** 6660
and training with production programs **11:** 6449
for vocational education and training **11:** ***6660–6664***
International Assessment of Educational Progress (IAEP) **3:** 1765
mathematics and science studies **3:** 1765
mathematics studies
and sex differences **9:** 5426
Michigan Studies **3:** 1765, 1768
surveys
science education **9:** 5333
See also
Educational Testing Service (ETS) (US)
International Association for the Advancement of Educational Research
See World Association for Educational Research
International Association of Community Education **5:** 2948
International Association for Continuing Education and Training **8:** 4732
International Association for the Education of the Deaf–Blind **3:** 1402, 1406
International Association for Educational Assessment (IAEA) **2:** 940

International Association for the Evaluation of Educational Achievement (IEA) **2:** 942
attitude measures **1:** 390
and class size **6:** 3371
Classroom Environment Study **3:** 1764; **4:** 2132
research on teaching **10:** 6151
comparative analysis **2:** 921, 952; **3:** 1585, 1763, 1767; **11:** 6524
comparative area studies **9:** 5537
comparative education **2:** 925
Computers in Education Study **2:** 1002; **3:** 1764; **7:** 3808, 4084, 4096, 4102
computers in teacher education **10:** 6005
cross-sectional studies **2:** 1216; **6:** 3515
curriculum research **3:** 1317
educational policy studies **4:** 1837
and essay tests **4:** 2019
evaluation of cross-national comparisons **4:** ***2132–2140***
First Mathematics Study **3:** 1763; **5:** 2853
attitude measures **1:** 392
and curriculum validity **11:** 6326
and descriptive scales **3:** 1477
and multilevel analysis **7:** 3979
First Science Study **3:** 1764
and descriptive scales **3:** 1478
standard deviation **7:** 3730
foreign language instruction **4:** 2352, 2356
impact of studies on educational research and policy **4:** 2139
literature education study **2:** 734; **6:** 3481
mathematics studies
achievement **4:** 2132; **9:** 5126
achievement, sex differences **4:** 2433
and public examinations
social bias in **4:** 2178
reading comprehension tests **7:** 3931
Reading Literacy Study **1:** 482; **3:** 1765, 1766; **6:** 3471; **7:** 3721, 4056
and Rasch measurement models **8:** 4905
and rotated sampling **5:** 3059
science achievement studies
and analysis of variance **11:** 6588
and attitude measures **9:** 5321
female participation **9:** 5424
in United States **7:** 4053
second languages **5:** 2974
Second Mathematics Study (SIMS) **3:** 1764; **4:** 1937; **6:** 3663
research on teaching **10:** 6150
Second Science Study (SISS) **3:** 1764; **4:** 2134, 2135; **8:** 4646
attitude measures **1:** 394
and curricular validity **11:** 6325
and descriptive scales **3:** 1479
and sex differences **4:** 2179; **6:** 3410; **9:** 5430
and surveys **10:** 5854
and secondary data analysis **9:** 5369
Six Subject Study **3:** 1764; **4:** 2132, 2135, 2137; **7:** 3720
attitude measures **1:** 393
and multilevel analysis **7:** 3979, 3980
and sex differences **9:** 5426
standardized tests **1:** 470
studies
and selection bias **9:** 5380
surveys **11:** 6586
competence **6:** 3469
criticisms of **9:** 5333
third generation studies **3:** 1765
writing ability tests **7:** 3933
Written Composition Study **3:** 1764; **4:** 2019, 2022, 2134
International Association of Extension Workers **5:** 2933
International Baccalaureate (IB) **5:** ***2955–2957***, 2973, 2977
administration and affiliations **5:** 2956
content **5:** 2955
and curriculum development **5:** 2956
objectives **5:** 2955
origins and history **5:** 2956
statistical surveys **5:** 2955
and UNESCO **5:** 2956
use in public education **5:** 2955, 2957
International Bank for Reconstruction and Development (IBRD)
See World Bank
International Bureau of Education (IBE) **5:** 2947
comparative education surveys **2:** 950
conferences **11:** 6527
documentation **11:** 6527
functions **11:** 6527
information sources
comparative education **3:** 1585
Institute for Educational Planning **3:** 1585
Network for Educational Information **3:** 1585
International Center for Educational Evaluation (ICEE) (Nigeria) **2:** 938
International Classification of Diseases (ICD9-CM) **1:** 487; **3:** 1515, 1531; **7:** 3826
International Classification of Epileptic Seizures (ICES) **8:** 4422
International co-operation
changing role of **5:** 2965
copyright agreements **2:** 1100
in education **5:** ***2961–2965***
and educational research **5:** 2964
global approach **5:** 2974
historical background **5:** 2962
individual capacity-building **5:** 2964
international organizations
comparative education **2:** 935
and official development assistance (ODA) **5:** 2961
role of
in vocational education **11:** 6645
trends and actions **5:** 2963
International Commission on the Development of Education (1971–72) (Faure Report) **5:** 2957
International Commission on Mathematical Instruction (ICMI) **6:** 3646
International communication
and adult education **5:** 2946
use of English **6:** 3210
International Community Education Association (ICEA) **2:** 903; **5:** 2932
International Conference on Nonformal Education for Development (1979) **5:** 2959
International Conference on the World Crisis in Education (1967) **5:** 2958, 2959
International Congress for University Adult Education (ICUAE) **1:** 142; **5:** 2932, 2948; **8:** 4732, 4733
International Council for Adult Education (ICAE) **1:** 123; **5:** 2932, 2946, 2948, 2949
adult education publications **1:** 142
comparative analysis **3:** 1585
directory **8:** 4733
establishment of **5:** 2932
functional literacy **5:** 2958, 2959
learning for environmental action **2:** 904
peace education **2:** 1193
role of **7:** 4148
women's education **11:** 6712
International Council for Correspondence Education (ICCE)
development of **3:** 1580
International Council for Distance Education (ICDE) **4:** 2185; **5:** 2932; **7:** 4216
development of **3:** 1580
objectives **3:** 1580
International Council for Educational Development (ICED)
comparative analysis **3:** 1585
International Council on Educational Media (ICEM) **3:** 1800
International Development Association (IDA)
See World Bank
International Development Program (IDP) (Norway) **5:** 2849
International education **5:** ***2972–2978***
area studies **1:** ***331–332***
comparative analysis **2:** ***958–964***; **7:** 4227

and comparative education
2: ***918–923***, 925; 5: 2972, 2973
conferences **5:** ***2957–2961***
curriculum **5:** 2975
for development **5:** 2973
doctoral programs **5:** 2976
documentation **3:** ***1584–1589***
status and prospects **3:** 1587
educational change **5:** ***2957–2961***
educational information systems
5: 2826
heuristic approach **2:** ***923–933***
historical development **2:** 918;
5: 2973
ideology **5:** 2958
implementation **5:** 2975
information sources **3:** ***1584–1589***
publications **5:** 2977
institutionalization **5:** 2976
international co-operation **5:** 2973
and multicultural education **5:** 2972
objectives **5:** 2974
organizations and institutions
2: ***933–942***
survey **2:** 935
origins of **2:** 918
overview **2:** ***918–923***
paradigms and theories of **2:** ***923–933***
and peace education **3:** 1730; **5:** 2972
philosophy of education **5:** 2609
research **5:** 2977
textbooks **5:** 2975
See also
International adult education
International educational
administration
See Educational administration,
international
International educational exchange
5: 2973, 2976
contextual suitability **4:** 1853
International educational expenditures
See Expenditures, international on
education
International Extension College **5:** 2934
International Federation of Free
Teachers Unions (IFFTU)
6: 3190
International Federation for
Information Processing (IFIP)
World Conference (1990) **2:** 970
International Federation of Library
Associations and Institutions
(IFLA) **6:** 3401
International Federation of
Workers Educational
Associations (IFWEA) **5:** 2932;
11: 6772
International finance
of education
See Educational finance, international
International Foundation for Computer-
based Education in Banking
and Finance
(IFCEB)
educational technology
activities **4:** 1881
International Geographical Union
Commission on Geographical
Education
research **5:** 2468
International Institute for Educational
Planning (IIEP) **5:** 2947, 2974;
11: 6528
resource allocation
research **9:** 5062
and school mapping **9:** 5256
student loan programs **10:** 5763
International Institute for Rural
Reconstruction **7:** 4146, 4148
International Intervisitation Program in
Educational Administration
(IIP) **5:** 2952
development **5:** 2952
International Labour Office
research studies
skill acquisition **5:** 2815
International Labour Organization (ILO)
basic needs initiative **1:** 465
and dual labor market theory **3:** 1681
educational technology
activities **4:** 1879
future role **5:** 3001
historical background **5:** 2998
information sources
comparative education **3:** 1585
International Centre for Advanced
Technical and Vocational
Training **5:** 3000
national training agencies **6:** 3257
objectives **5:** 2998, 3002
paid educational leave **6:** 3362;
7: 4257
public sector wages **8:** 4838
regional strategies **5:** 3002
technical assistance **5:** 2999
trends **5:** 3000
vocational education **5:** ***2998–3003***
future policies **5:** 3001
policy recommendations **5:** 3000,
3001
women's education **11:** 6712
International League for Social
Commitment in Adult
Education **5:** 2932;
8: 4732
International Literacy Year (1990)
1: 169; **5:** 2947, 2950, 2951;
11: 6526
International Monetary Fund (IMF)
economic adjustment
policies for **3:** 1785
International Movement Toward
Educational Change (IMTEC)
and organizational development
7: 4237
International Networks in Education
and Development (INET)
2: 941; **5:** 2932
International organizations
affinity-based
and educational technology **4:** 1879
categories of
and educational technology **4:** 1878
for computer uses in education
listing **2:** 1013
development
and educational technology **4:** 1879
for distance education **3:** ***1580–1584***
and educational administration
5: 2951
and educational planning **3:** 1806
educational policy
and comparative education **2:** 934
educational technology **4:** 1881
activities **4:** ***1878–1882***
funding
and educational technology **4:** 1878
regional
and educational technology **4:** 1878
roles and activities
adult education **5:** 2947
and school law
influences on **9:** 5254
vocational training
and educational technology **4:** 1881
women's education **11:** 6712
Islamic culture **11:** 6759
International programs
disabilities
and education work relationship
11: 6460
International Reading Association (IRA)
2: 940; **7:** 4148
International relations
and adult education **5:** 2950
changes
and financial support **5:** 2991
International Social Survey Program
(ISSP)
and secondary data analysis **9:** 5369
International Society for Augmentative
and Alternative
Communication (ISAAC)
1: 408
International Society for Education
through Art (INSEA) **1:** 197,
340
International Sociological Association
(ISA) **10:** 5601
Biography and Society Group **1:** 537
International Standard Book Number
(ISBN)
and courseware **10:** 5619
International Standard Classification of
Education (ISCED) **1:** 95;
2: 959
and adult education provision **8:** 4805
International Standard Classification of
Occupations (ISCO)
coding systems **10:** 5734
International Standardization of
Educational Statistics
Revised Recommendation **2:** 959, 960

International Standing Committee for the History of Education **5:** 2613
International studies
area studies **5:** 2976
comparative analysis
design and implementation **3:** 1766
questionnaires **3:** 1767
target population **3:** 1766
test items **3:** 1767
topics **3:** 1766
comparative education
professional associations **2:** ***942–948***
cross-cultural studies **3:** 1767
cross-sectional studies **3:** 1767
longitudinal studies **3:** 1767
mathematics achievement **9:** 5361
multivariate analysis **3:** 1767
national systems of education **3:** 1767
public schools vs. private schools **8:** 4842
research design **3:** 1767
and test translation **11:** 6328
See also
Comparative area studies
International Telecommunications Union (ITU)
educational technology activities **4:** 1881
International Visual Literacy Association (IVLA) **11:** 6623, 6624
Internship programs
industry **5:** 2688
Interpersonal communication
discussion **2:** 803
and peer influence **9:** 5173
Interpersonal competence **9:** ***5504–5508***, ***5563–5567***
characteristics of **9:** 5563
and cognitive development
Piagetian theory **9:** 5507
Vygotskyian theory **9:** 5507
components of **9:** 5563
definitions of **9:** 5504, 5563
and disabilities
children **9:** 5564
future research **9:** 5566
importance of **9:** 5564
learning in school **9:** 5506
modeling (psychology) approach to learning **9:** 5506
and participant observation **7:** 4317
research **9:** 5565
skill development **9:** 5504
to reduce aggression **1:** 233
and social development **9:** 5525
individual differences **9:** 5526
influence of intelligence quotient on **9:** 5526
social reinforcement approach **9:** 5506
and social values **9:** 5504
training for **9:** 5565
and antisocial behavior **1:** 493
and behavioral instruction **10:** 6162
curriculum packages **9:** 5566
descriptive technology **9:** 5565
and emotional disturbances **1:** 489
interventions **9:** 5565
Interpersonal interaction
See Interpersonal relationship
Interpersonal relationship
and child development **9:** 5546
and cognitive development **9:** 5507, 5545, 5546
egocentrism and altruism
sociobiological approach **4:** 2170
and friendship
individual development **10:** 5757
and individual development **9:** 5545
Confucian theory **2:** 1043, 1045
and intellectual development **9:** 5546
and learning **9:** ***5545–5548***
and preconceptions **8:** 4649
research
and videotape recordings **11:** 6604
and school dynamics **9:** 5172
secondary schools
and effective schools research **9:** 5377
social development **9:** 5524
and social networks **9:** 5554
and socialization **10:** 5588
and sociometric techniques **10:** 5614
teaching and learning
and existential phenomenology **8:** 4432
Interpersonal skills
See Interpersonal competence
Interpreters
for test translation
selection of training **11:** 6330
Interpretive skills
hermeneutics **5:** ***2579–2586***
humanities **5:** 2693
and teacher expertise **10:** 6024
Interpretive sociology
and science education **8:** 4464
Weber's theory of education **2:** 781
Interrater reliability
and rating scales **8:** 4927
Interstate New Teacher Assessment and Support Consortium **10:** 5928
Interuniversity Consortium for Political and Social Research (ICPSR) (US)
data archives **3:** 1379
Interval scales **7:** 3700
definition of **9:** 5047
Intervention
and apprenticeships
Africa **1:** 225
and biographical research **1:** 542
cost
definition of **2:** 1132
influences
on individual development **6:** 3513
and instructional design **5:** 2871
and instructional psychology **5:** 2873
and interpersonal competence
training for **9:** 5565
and learning disabilities **10:** 5684
and learning strategies
teaching of **6:** 3336
programs
and reading difficulties **8:** 4930
and resilience **8:** 4778
and teacher expectation of students **10:** 6110
reading difficulties
mild disabilities **8:** 4934
and single case research **9:** 5486
studies
and longitudinal studies **6:** 3517
teacher-mediated
and interpersonal competence **9:** 5566
and teaching styles **9:** 5486
and team teaching **10:** 6240
and test anxiety **11:** 6357
See also
Prereferral intervention
Intervention assistance teams
See Prereferral intervention
Intervention
See Behavior modification
Interviewing
See Interviews
Interviews
bias in **5:** 3006
and conceptual understanding
charting of **10:** 5786
data
treatment of in research **5:** 3006
in educational research
phenomenography **8:** 4427
environmental factors **5:** 3005
feedback in **5:** 3004
intergroup relations
and facet theory **4:** 2216
and learning processes
research **10:** 5784
and learning strategies
evaluation **6:** 3338
and micropolitics research **7:** 3825
nature of **5:** 3003
and oral history **7:** 4221
problems **7:** 4222
procedures for
research **8:** 4405
questioning techniques
and speech communication **6:** 3440
types of **5:** 3004
and repertory grid technique **9:** 5014
role playing
and speech communication **6:** 3440
secondary education
selection **9:** 5387
for selection and clinical research **5:** ***3003–3007***
skills required **5:** 3004, 3005
structure of **5:** 3004
tape recorded
and data analysis **3:** 1468
techniques **5:** 3005
training of interviewers **5:** 3006
and videotape recordings **11:** 6604

  vs. questionnaires
    and nonresponse **7:** 3854
  See also
    Questioning techniques
Intragenerational mobility
  See Social mobility, intragenerational
Intrinsic motivation
  See Self-motivation
Intuition
  and mathematical applications
    6: 3634
Invalidity
  See Validity
Invented spelling **10:** 5703
Inventions
  and creativity **2:** 1176, 1177
Inventories (measurement)
  See Measures (individuals)
Investigations
  design of **3:** 1465
Investment
  and consumption
    brain drain **1:** 558
  and consumption benefits **2:** 1053
  primary education
    effect of comparative analysis
      3: 1830
  for training
    and cost effectiveness **2:** 1137
  in training
    government role in **11:** 6429
Investment in education
  See Human capital
IQ
  See Intelligence quotient
Iran
  curriculum development **5:** 3010
  educational change **5:** 3010
  educational research **5:** 3010
  ethnic groups **5:** 3007
  government school relationship
    school administration **5:** 3009
  postsecondary education **5:** 3008
  preschool education **5:** 3008
  primary education **5:** 3008
  private education **5:** 3008
  secondary education **5:** 3008
    vocational education **5:** 3009
  special education **5:** 3008
  state church relationship
    theocratic domination **9:** 5010
  system of education **5:** ***3007–3011***
    degrees and qualifications **5:** 3010
    educational objectives **5:** 3008
    enrollment **5:** 3008, 3009
    major problems **5:** 3011
    structure **5:** 3008
  teacher education **5:** 3009
  teacher recruitment **5:** 3009
Iraq
  adult education **1:** 324; **6:** 3362
  literacy programs **1:** 325
  vocational education **1:** 325
Ireland, Republic of
  adult education
    nonformal education **5:** 3016
  cultural influences **5:** 3012
  curriculum development **5:** 3017
  educational change **5:** 3019
  educational research **5:** 3018
  government school relationship
    financial support **5:** 3016
    school administration **5:** 3016
  language **5:** 3012
  postsecondary education **5:** 3014
  preschool education **5:** 3015
  primary education **5:** 3014
  private education **5:** 3014
  school inspectors in teacher
      evaluation **4:** 2126
  secondary education **5:** 3014
    vocational education **5:** 3014
  special education **5:** 3015
  structure of government **5:** 3012
  system of education **5:** ***3011–3020***
    degrees and qualifications **5:** 3018
    educational objectives **5:** 3012
    historical background **5:** 3013
    major problems **5:** 3019
    structure **5:** 3013
  teacher education **5:** 3017
  teacher recruitment **5:** 3017
  technical colleges **2:** 895
IRIS **4:** 2063
Irish Association of Speech and
      Language Therapists
  role of **10:** 5693
Islam
  individual development **5:** ***3020–3023***
    childrearing implications of theory
      5: 3022
    curriculum planning and theory
      5: 3022
    educational implications of theory
      5: 3022
    influences on **5:** 3021
    and intention **5:** 3021
    learning processes **5:** 3021
    length of **5:** 3020
    objectives **5:** 3021
Islamic culture
  Afghanistan **1:** 204, 206
  Bahrain **1:** 445
  Bangladesh **1:** 452
  Brunei Darussalam **1:** 573, 575
  Central African Republic **2:** 655
  Egypt **4:** 1940, 1941
  Indonesia **5:** 2784
  Iran **5:** 3007
  Jordan **6:** 3106
  Kuwait **6:** 3171, 3172
  Maldives **6:** 3572
  Mali **6:** 3580
  Morocco **7:** 3926
  Niger **7:** 4117
  Oman **7:** 4201
  Pakistan **7:** 4264, 4266
  Qatar **8:** 4849
  and religious education **9:** 4997, 4998
  Saudi Arabia **9:** 5142
  and school organization **7:** 4230
  sex stereotypes
    and female access to education
      4: 2408
  state church relationship **9:** 5010
  Sudan **10:** 5835
  United Arab Emirates **11:** 6512
  and women's education
    Africa **11:** 6736
    history of **11:** ***6753–6761***
  Yemen **11:** 6788
Islamic student movement **10:** 5778,
    5780
Isolation (perceptual)
  See Sensory deprivation
Israel
  academically gifted
    research **9:** 5530
  admission criteria
    university adult education **11:** 6548
  adult education **1:** 136
    nonformal education **5:** 3026
  career education and disabilities
    2: 634
  community support for families with
      disabled children **4:** 1978
  computer-managed learning **2:** 999
  computer uses in education
    organizations for **2:** 1015
  curriculum development **3:** 1492;
    5: 3027
  day care programs for toddlers
    11: 6396
  educational change **5:** 3027
  educational research **5:** 3027
  ethnic groups
    educational attainment **8:** 4893
  ethnography of Oriental Jews **2:** 1211
  evaluation standards **8:** 4745
  gifted disadvantaged **5:** 2487
  government school relationship
    school administration **5:** 3026
  immigrant education **7:** 3846
  kibbutzim
    teacher education curriculum
      10: 5992
  labor relations
    affiliations **6:** 3196
    in education **6:** 3190
  law
    and education **5:** 3024
  leadership
    research **6:** 3283
    theories of **6:** 3280
  multicultural education
    and discipline concerns **3:** 1535
  music education **7:** 4018
  physics curriculum **9:** 5341
  preschool education **5:** 3025
  primary education **5:** 3024
  principals
    role of **9:** 5214, 5270
  problem-solving
    teaching of **8:** 4729
  public education
    government aid **9:** 5010
  race earnings differentials **8:** 4901
  regional colleges **2:** 895, 896

religious education **9:** 5010
school-based management **9:** 5212
school desegregation **3:** 1484
second chance education **9:** 5365
secondary education **5:** 3024
special education **5:** 3025
state church relationship
theocratic domination **9:** 5010
structure of government **5:** 3023
system of education **5:** ***3023–3028***
educational objectives **5:** 3024
major problems **5:** 3027
structure **5:** 3024
teacher recruitment **5:** 3026
technical education **5:** 3024
test anxiety
studies **11:** 6357
test translation **11:** 6328
vocational education **9:** 5073, 5074, 5075
Italy
adult education **10:** 5642
ideology **5:** 2733, 2734
and labor education **10:** 5642
legislation **6:** 3363
nonformal education **5:** 3033
regional organization **10:** 5642
apprenticeships **1:** 314
enrollment rate **11:** 6666
computer uses in education
organizations for **2:** 1015
copyrights
historical background **2:** 1099
curriculum development **5:** 3034
day care evaluation research **11:** 6396
day care for infants **5:** 2805
educational administration
administrator selection **1:** 79
educational change **5:** 3035
educational research **5:** 3035
flexible job assignments **8:** 4637
government school relationship
financial support **5:** 3034
school administration **5:** 3033
Green University **2:** 1193
labor relations
in education **6:** 3190
need for vocational programs **2:** 899
nonverbal communication
touching behavior **7:** 4172
paid educational leave **7:** 4261
participatory research **7:** 4333
popular education **1:** 133
postsecondary education **5:** 3032
preschool education **2:** 695; **5:** 3032
primary education **5:** 3031
private education **5:** 3033
school organization
track system (education) **7:** 4231
secondary education **5:** 3031
special education **2:** 723; **5:** 3032
teams **10:** 6242
structure of government **5:** 3029
system of education **5:** ***3028–3036***
degrees and qualifications **5:** 3034
educational objectives **5:** 3029
historical background **5:** 3029
major problems **5:** 3035
structure **5:** 3030
teacher education **5:** 3034
technical education **5:** 3033
vocational education
three-tier structure **11:** 6664
Item analysis
and attitude measures **1:** 383
in cross-national comparisons **4:** 2136
and descriptive scales **3:** 1478
discrimination
procedures **5:** 3044
and item banks **5:** 3036
Item banks
administration of **5:** 3041
calibrated **5:** 3037
advantages of **5:** 3037
establishment of **5:** 3039
calibration of **5:** 2782
common items **5:** 3041
computer-assisted testing **2:** 994, 995; **5:** 2780
and computers **2:** 995
concept of **5:** 3037
and curriculum **5:** 2783
definitions of **5:** 3036
in item response theory **5:** 3053
new items
linking of **5:** 3041
organization of **5:** 3037
and partial credit model **7:** 4306
and personality inventories **8:** 4395
prestructured
and adaptive testing **1:** 49
problems **5:** 3042
and public examinations **4:** 2177
and science tests **8:** 4646
systems
procedures **2:** 995
in testing and assessment **5:** ***3036–3043***
unstructured
and adaptive testing **1:** 49
Item bias **5:** ***3043–3051***, ***3046***
and achievement tests **11:** 6319
categories of **5:** 3044
classical approaches **5:** 3044
delta plot method **5:** 3044
item response theory **5:** 3054
approaches **5:** 3048
procedures
examples **5:** 3046
future trends **5:** 3049
uses **5:** 3043
and standardization procedure **5:** 3046
Item characteristic curve theory
See Item response theory (IRT)
Item difficulty
See Difficulty level, test items
Item forms
and item writing techniques **5:** 3063
specific **5:** 3064
Item response theory (IRT) **3:** 1765; **5:** ***3051–3055***; **7:** 4055
and achieved curriculum **11:** 6327
and achievement tests **1:** 33
and adaptive testing **1:** 48, 49; **5:** 3054
computerized **2:** 993
advantages of **6:** 3250
applications **5:** 3053
assumptions **5:** 3051; **6:** 3249
basic concepts of **5:** 3051
and classical test theory **2:** 787
and competence **6:** 3470
and computer-assisted testing **2:** 992; **5:** 2780
computer software for **5:** 3053
conversions **1:** 41
development of **7:** 3700
and developmental stages **3:** 1510
dichotomous models **6:** 3248
disadvantages **5:** 3051
discrimination parameters **8:** 4907
and equated scores **11:** 6352
estimation methods
choice of **5:** 3053
and guessing (tests) **2:** 788; **7:** 3998, 3999
information functions **2:** 994; **5:** 3052
noise in **5:** 3052
invariance property **6:** 3250
and item banks **4:** 2177; **5:** 3037, 3039, 3042
and item bias **5:** 3048, 3054
item characteristic curves (ICC)
and item banks **5:** 3039
and Rasch measurement models **8:** 4907
item parameters **5:** 3051, 3054
item response functions **5:** 3051
and item sampling **5:** 3057
and latent trait theory **5:** 3051
in literacy measurement **7:** 3710
logistic models **6:** 3250
and longitudinal studies **6:** 3521
and mastery tests **5:** 3054
models **6:** ***3247–3253***
choice of **5:** 3052
multidimensional **6:** 3252
multicomponent latent trait model (MLTM)
and developmental stages **3:** 1511
and multiple choice tests **4:** 2012
nominal response model **6:** 3251
and nonresponse **7:** 3857
ordinal response model **6:** 3251
parameters
estimates of **4:** 2014
and programmed instruction **8:** 4773
and Rasch measurement models **8:** 4906
and rating scales **8:** 4926
redesigning an existing test **5:** 3053
relative efficiency functions **5:** 3052
response curve **2:** 994
scales
and achievement tests **1:** 36

test construction **5:** 3053
and test theory **1:** 373
and test translation **11:** 6333
and vocational aptitude **11:** 6673
See also
Latent trait measurement models
Item sampling
duplex design **5:** 3060
error of measurement **5:** 3055
incidence **5:** 3060
matrix sampling **5:** 3056
balanced incomplete block (BIB) **5:** 3058
multiple **5:** 3058
random **5:** 3056
rotated **5:** 3059
in testing **5:** ***3055–3061***
theory of
and achievement tests **1:** 33
and variance **5:** 3056
Item selection
and criterion referenced tests **2:** 1184
and norm referenced tests **2:** 1184
Item writing techniques **5:** ***3061–3066***
algorithms **5:** 3064
authoring aids (programming) **2:** 997
computer uses for **5:** 3064
concept learning approaches **5:** 3065
content–process matrices **5:** 3062
criterion referenced approaches **5:** 3062
development of **5:** 3061
facet design **5:** 3064
guidelines for **5:** 3061
and item banks **5:** 3039
linguistic-based approaches **5:** 3065
and objective tests **7:** 4195, 4196
paraphrasing **5:** 3065
student evaluations of teacher effectiveness **10:** 6228
transformational approaches **5:** 3065
Itinerant teachers
special education **2:** 722
visual impairments
special education **11:** 6626
Ivory Coast
See Côte d'Ivoire

Jackknife procedure
sampling errors **9:** 5127
and Stone–Geisser test **8:** 4356
Jackson Vocational Interest Survey (JVIS) **11:** 6674
Jamaica
adult education **6:** 3070
curriculum development **6:** 3072
educational change **6:** 3067, 3073
educational planning
and enrollment rate **8:** 4596
educational research **6:** 3073
ethnic groups **6:** 3067
government school relationship **6:** 3071
school administration **6:** 3070
language **6:** 3067
postsecondary education **6:** 3069
preschool education **6:** 3069
primary education **6:** 3068
private education **6:** 3070
school administration
control of **9:** 5166
secondary education **6:** 3068
vocational education **6:** 3069
special education **6:** 3069
structure of government **6:** 3067
system of education **6:** ***3067–3074***
degrees and qualifications **6:** 3072
educational objectives **6:** 3068
major problems **6:** 3073
structure **6:** 3068
teacher education **6:** 3071
teacher recruitment **6:** 3071
Japan
adult education **1:** 349, 350; **6:** ***3074–3078***
evaluation practices **6:** 3077
financial support **6:** 3077
institutions **6:** 3075
legislation **6:** 3074
nonformal education **6:** 3082
participation levels **6:** 3077
personnel **6:** 3077
policies **4:** 1973
private provision **6:** 3076
purposes and policies **6:** 3074
in schools **6:** 3076
structures **6:** 3075
telecommunications **1:** 561
art education **1:** 342
comparative achievement data **4:** 2136, 2137
compulsory education
and vocational education **6:** 3086
computer-managed learning **2:** 1000
computer uses in education
organizations for **2:** 1015
Confucianism
and achievement need **3:** 1238
continuing education expenditure **2:** 1148
correspondence study **1:** 109
cross-training **11:** 6418, 6419
cultural centers **6:** 3076
curriculum
urban schools **11:** 6561
curriculum development **6:** 3084
customs
as a barrier to mobility **7:** 4210
degrees (academic) **6:** 3087
demography **6:** 3086
education and productivity **3:** 1665
educational broadcasting **5:** 2886
educational change **6:** 3085
and information dissemination **3:** 1550
educational expenditures
family involvement **5:** 2983
educational history **2:** 1061
educational philosophy **11:** 6695
educational reform **6:** 3075
burakumin **11:** 6560, 6562
internationalization **9:** 5280
educational research **6:** 3084
educational television
elementary schools **5:** 2893
employment policy and on-the-job training **6:** 3616
employment practices
and decision-making **5:** 2796
lifetime employment **11:** 6696
equal education
barriers to **11:** 6562
female enrollment rate **4:** 2408
Fujinkai **8:** 4810
government school relationship
financial support **6:** 3083
school administration **6:** 3082
industrial training **6:** 3089; **11:** 6695
influence of Dewey's democratic ideas **3:** 1524
internal labor market **5:** 2939
on-the-job training **7:** 4210
job rotation **5:** 2687; **11:** 6418, 6419
junior colleges and special training schools **2:** 895, 897, 898
Kominkan **8:** 4810
labor force
and independent study **6:** 3090
labor force development **5:** 2687; **6:** 3090
lifelong learning
and community development **8:** 4339
and vocational education **6:** 3088
lifetime employment **5:** 2687; **6:** 3078, 3089; **11:** 6419
male retirement age **5:** 2688
mathematics education
and student role **10:** 5792
mathematics programs **6:** 3661, 3665
minority groups and social change
ethnography **2:** 1212
moral education
and civic education **2:** 768
nonverbal communication
touching behavior **7:** 4172
occupational tests **11:** 6697
off-the-job training **6:** 3090
on-the-job training **6:** 3090; **10:** 5915
parent participation **9:** 5213
postsecondary education **6:** 3081
preschool education **6:** 3081
primary education **6:** 3079
primary schools
social studies in **9:** 5575
private education **6:** 3083
private schools
and vocational education **11:** 6696
private tuition **11:** 6696
quality circles **5:** 2687
residential institutions for the disabled **3:** 1434, 1435
role of high school
macroethnography **2:** 1210
science education history **9:** 5325
secondary education **6:** 3080
decentralization **9:** 5177
vocational education **6:** 3082

Seinendan **8:** 4810
Shinto
theory of individual development **9:** ***5449–5453***
social education **1:** 348, 349; **6:** ***3074–3078***; **8:** 4810
social stratification
research **10:** 5733
special education **6:** 3081; **10:** 5660
special education programs
disabled children **3:** 1436
special training schools **1:** 349; **8:** 4795
structure of government **6:** 3079
student loan programs **10:** 5763
student teaching
field experience programs **10:** 5809
syllabi
and conflict **10:** 5884
system of education **6:** ***3078–3086***
degrees and qualifications **6:** 3084
educational objectives **6:** 3079
major problems **6:** 3085
structure **6:** 3079
teacher attitudes
and school as workplace **9:** 5178
teacher education **6:** 3083
teacher recruitment **6:** 3083
teaching
professional recognition **9:** 5178
teaching methods **6:** 3084; **8:** 4870
technical education **6:** 3082; **11:** 6697
and paraprofessional personnel **11:** 6269
training provision **1:** 109
training survey **11:** 6416, 6417, 6418, 6419
unions
and educational policy **10:** 6075
universities
and vocational education **6:** 3087
vocational education **6:** ***3074–3078***, ***3086–3092***; **11:** ***6690–6699***
course classification **6:** 3086
finance **6:** 3091
future policy **6:** 3091
and job rotation **6:** 3090
private sector provision **6:** 3089
public sector provision **6:** 3088
and quality circles **6:** 3090
work-based **11:** 6247
vocational high schools **6:** 3086
colleges of technology **6:** 3086
junior colleges **6:** 3087
vocational qualifications
and skills tests **6:** 3088
workplace learning **11:** 6393
Yobiko schools **9:** 5365
Japan Audio-Visual Education Association (JAVEA) **3:** 1799
Japanese
in Taiwanese education **2:** 1039
Japanese National Institute for Educational Research (NIER) **2:** 939
Java
See Indonesia
Jesness Inventory **8:** 4397
Jesuit education
educational principles **9:** 5119
pedagogy **9:** 5119
Saint Ignatius Loyola **9:** ***5118–5121***
study guides **9:** 5118
Jesuit schools
selective admission **9:** 5119
Jews
and religious education **9:** 4998
See also
Judaism
Job analysis
in corporate education **6:** ***3092–3096***
expertise for **6:** 3095
indeterminacy **10:** 6085
and instructional design
information provision **6:** 3093
integrative approach **6:** 3096
interpretative approach **6:** 3095
methods **6:** 3094
and needs assessment **6:** 3092
nomenclature **6:** 3092
perceptions of **6:** 3093
purposes **6:** 3093
surveys **6:** 3092
teaching **10:** 6085
type of **6:** 3095
underlying assumptions **6:** 3095
uses of **6:** 3092
See also
Task analysis
Job applicants
educational background **4:** 2210
Job characteristics
education
and productivity **11:** 6629
as a measurement of job satisfaction **11:** 6630
Job competition model
labor market **3:** 1705; **8:** 4836, 4837
productivity and **5:** 2742
Job development
task analysis **10:** 5910
Job information
See Occupational information
Job matching theory
continuing education **2:** 1087, 1091
vs. human capital theory **3:** 1748
Job performance
and aptitude
research **11:** 6671
Job rotation **6:** 3616
Japan **5:** 2687; **11:** 6418, 6419
and vocational education **6:** 3090
Job satisfaction
and adult education participation **7:** 4321
and continuing education **2:** 1093
measurement of **11:** 6630
and motivation **4:** 1968
paraprofessional personnel **11:** 6268
teachers
and school as workplace **9:** 5178
Job security
effects on training **11:** 6636
and motivation **5:** 2794
and paid educational leave **7:** 4258
Job segregation
See Occupational segregation
Job sharing
vs. redundancy **3:** 1697
Job simplification
limitations of **5:** 2938
Job skills
and adult education **1:** 104
essential **4:** 1919
and immigrants **5:** 2737
impact of technological advancement on **11:** 6257
and education **11:** 6259
labor force composition
United States vs. Japan **11:** 6259
and labor market
bumping model **6:** 3182
vocational education **11:** 6700
measurement of **11:** 6257, 6274
pay based on **6:** 3616
upgrading
and national training agencies **6:** 3264
and vocational education and training
Anglo–German comparisons **11:** 6639
Job training
and certification **2:** 662, 664
and communicative competence (languages) **6:** ***3209–3213***
cost effectiveness **3:** 1791; **7:** 4197
regression analysis **11:** 6424
costs
current vs. constant prices **11:** 6423
determinants **11:** 6424
direct **11:** 6421
establishment **11:** 6422
fixed **11:** 6421
marginal **11:** 6422
market vs. shadow prices **11:** 6423
measurement of **11:** ***6420–6425***
opportunity **11:** 6422
unit cost **11:** 6423
variable **11:** 6421
in developed nations **7:** 4197
in developing nations **7:** 4197
for disabilities **11:** 6459
and earnings
labor market analysis **3:** 1677
economics of **7:** ***4197–4201***
effects of minimum wage on **11:** 6635
employer-sponsored **1:** 108, 109
and race differences **1:** 107
and sex differences **1:** 107
and employment **8:** 4711
enrollment rate
United States **11:** 6531
evaluation research **2:** ***1084–1094***
and increased productivity **8:** 4712
labor market effects
developed nations **4:** ***2145–2150***
and literacy programs **8:** 4637

market failure of workplace
6: ***3614–3617***
motivation for
and performance contracts **8:** 4713
and performance contracts **8:** 4708, 4710
experiments **8:** 4710
impact on **8:** 4711
Peru
research study **7:** 4198
and productivity **2:** 1089; **3:** 1678
program evaluation
Germany **4:** 2148
and later employment rates **4:** 2146
Netherlands **4:** 2149
policy implications **4:** 2149
research implications **4:** 2149
Sweden **4:** 2148
United States **4:** 2147
psychomotor skill development
7: ***3950–3953***
public policy **7:** 4257
public programs
developed nations **4:** ***2145–2150***
evaluation **4:** ***2145–2150***
evaluation criteria **4:** 2146
evaluation methods **4:** 2146
objectives **4:** 2146
public support **4:** 2146
public sector vs. private sector
7: 4198
and segmentation theory **7:** 4197
sex discrimination **4:** ***2281–2287***
surveys **11:** 6417
for unemployed **4:** 2146
See also
Off the job training
On-the-job training
Vocational education
Job and Training Partnership Act 1983 (JTPA) (US) **4:** 2147; **8:** 4637
John Henry effect
definition of **11:** 6509
and educational research **11:** 6509
Joint Committee on Standards for Educational Evaluation (US)
evaluation criteria **4:** 2121
personnel evaluation standards
4: 2034, 2124, 2131; **8:** 4737, 4746
applicability of **8:** 4747
contents **8:** 4747
evaluations of **8:** 4747
program evaluation standards
4: 2034, 2079, 2088; **8:** 4737
applicability of **8:** 4741
citation form **8:** 4743
contents **8:** 4742
summary **8:** 4739
validity of **8:** 4743
Joint production model **6:** ***3101–3106***; **8:** 4563
achievement gains **6:** 3103
child achievement
effect of adult time on **6:** 3105
investment differentials
sources of **6:** 3104
measurement
empirical research **6:** 3105
parent attitudes
demand for education of children **6:** 3101
demand for educational quality **6:** 3103
school effort vs. academic achievement
functions **6:** 3105
and time management **6:** 3103
utility function **6:** 3103
voice function **6:** 3103
Jordan
adult education **6:** 3110
computer uses in education **4:** 1902
cultural influences **6:** 3107
curriculum development **6:** 3112
educational change **6:** 3113
educational research **6:** 3112
government school relationship
financial support **6:** 3111
school administration **6:** 3110
inservice teacher education **10:** 6066
postsecondary education **6:** 3109
preschool education **6:** 3109
primary education **6:** 3107
private education **6:** 3109, 3110
secondary education **6:** 3107
vocational education **6:** 3108
special education **6:** 3109
structure of government **6:** 3106
system of education **6:** ***3106–3113***
degrees and qualifications **6:** 3112
educational objectives **6:** 3107
major problems **6:** 3113
structure **6:** 3107
teacher education **6:** 3111
teacher recruitment **6:** 3111
teaching methodology **6:** 3112
Journal writing
and action research **1:** 44
effect on understanding of mathematical concepts **6:** 3208
Journals
See Periodicals
Scholarly journals
Judaism
child development
egocentrism **6:** 3114
individual development **6:** ***3113–3120***
and interpersonal relationships **6:** 3115
moral development **6:** 3116
rabbinic teaching **6:** 3114
state church relationship **9:** 5010
Judges
behavior of
and rating scales **6:** 3121
characteristics of
and testing **6:** 3124
Judgments
measurement of **6:** ***3120–3124***
dichotomously judged items **6:** 3122
equating **6:** 3124
generalizability theory **6:** 3121
inter-judge reliability **6:** 3121
rank ordering **6:** 3123
Rasch judging plans **6:** 3122
Rasch models **6:** 3121
true scores **6:** 3120
unidimensionality **6:** 3124
and objectivity **6:** 3120
Judicial action
See Court litigation
Junior Eysenck Personality Inventory (JEPI) **8:** 4398
Junior–Senior High School Personality Questionnaire (Jr–Sr HSPQ) **8:** 4397
Justice
and care **4:** 2030
and liberal egalitarianism **4:** 2002
and libertarianism **4:** 2002
moral development **10:** 5936
and moral philosophy **4:** 2030
and personnel management
United States **8:** 4405
in philosophy of education (Rawls) **8:** 4574
Rawls' theory **4:** 2030
and feminism **4:** 2293, 2295
and school choice **9:** 5198, 5199
Nozick's entitlement model **9:** 5199
Rawls' common good model **9:** 5198
social
and national surveys **2:** 652
theories of
educational implications **9:** 5199
universality of concept **4:** 2030
and utilitarianism **4:** 2002
Juvenile delinquency
See Delinquency
Juvenile justice
delinquency **3:** ***1438–1441***

Kafir
ethnography of **3:** 1752
Kamehameha Early Education Program (KEEP) (Hawaii) **3:** 1234; **10:** 5792
guiding principles **3:** 1234
reading program **3:** 1234; **6:** 3451
transfer attempts **3:** 1236
Kappa statistic (K)
and rating scales **8:** 4929
Karachi Plan for Primary Education 1959 (Pakistan) **8:** 4486
Kauai Longitudinal Study **8:** 4776
KEEP
See Kamehameha Early Education Program (KEEP) (Hawaii)
Keller Plan
See Individualized instruction, Personalized System of Instruction (PSI)
Kendall's coefficient of concordance
nonparametric statistics **7:** 4159

Kendall's correlation index
See Correlation, rank
Kent Mathematics Project 1978 (UK)
and programmed instruction **8:** 4773
Kent–Rosanoff Free Association Test **8:** 4790
Kenya
adult education
legislation **6:** 3363
nonformal education **6:** 3128
for socialism **1:** 132
business education **11:** 6250
citizenship education **9:** 5579
community support
educational finance **2:** 911, 913
self-help programs **2:** 911
computer uses in education **4:** 1901
curriculum development **6:** 3131
distance education **4:** 1901
in schools **3:** 1565
earnings differentials
and education **3:** 1659
educational change **6:** 3132
educational development
and labor market **6:** 3183
educational finance
and tax allocation **8:** 4360
educational radio **4:** 1906
interactive **5:** 2887
interactive programs **4:** 1913
educational research **6:** 3132
evaluation of national literacy program **4:** 2121
evaluator training program **4:** 2121
industrial education **11:** 6255
language **6:** 3125
nonformal education **7:** 4133
on-the-job training **7:** 4211; **10:** 5915
postsecondary education **6:** 3127
preschool education **6:** 3127
primary education **6:** 3127
primary school agriculture
tests **8:** 4686
public schools vs. private schools **8:** 4843
rate of return
to education **3:** 1710; **8:** 4916
secondary education **6:** 3127
diversified **11:** 6255
vocational education **6:** 3128
structure of government **6:** 3126
student evaluation **6:** 3131
system of education **6:** ***3125–3133***
educational objectives **6:** 3126
major problems **6:** 3132
structure **6:** 3126
teacher education **6:** 3130
by distance learning **4:** 1907
teacher recruitment **6:** 3130
teacher student relationship
research **10:** 5761
teaching methodology **6:** 3131
technical education **6:** 3128
coordination of **10:** 6064
vocational education
historical background **11:** 6252
Key words
in descriptive data analysis **3:** 1468
Keynesian economics
and unemployment **3:** 1697
Khit-Pen Movement
Thailand **1:** 118; **2:** 904
Kibbutzim
support for families with disabled children **4:** 1978
teacher education curriculum **10:** 5992
Kindergarten **4:** 2385; **5:** 2808
authoritarianism **4:** 2385
curriculum
and school readiness tests **9:** 5274
effect on literacy **6:** 3451
enrollment
projections **8:** 4784
Germany **4:** 2386
history of **8:** 4667
Monatsgegenstand approach **4:** 2385
in public schools **8:** 4668
United Kingdom **4:** 2386
United States **4:** 2385; **8:** 4670
use of name **4:** 2386
variations in definition **3:** 1629
See also
Early childhood education
Froebelian kindergarten
Preschool education
Kindergarten teachers
See Preschool teachers
Kinesics
See Body language
Kinesthetic perception
and speech handicaps **10:** 5696
Kinship studies
bias in **6:** 3143
and employment level
measurement **4:** 2278
latent variable–variance decomposition model
extended **6:** 3141
outcomes of education **6:** ***3138–3144***
sources of data **6:** 3138
social mobility
correlation tests **6:** 3139
variance decomposition estimates **6:** 3140
Kiribati
curriculum development **6:** 3147
language **6:** 3145
postsecondary education **6:** 3146
primary education **6:** 3145
secondary education **6:** 3145
vocational education **6:** 3146
structure of government **6:** 3145
student evaluation **6:** 3147
system of education **6:** ***3144–3148***
educational objectives **6:** 3145
major problems **6:** 3148
structure **6:** 3145
teacher education **6:** 3147
teacher recruitment **6:** 3147
teaching methodology **6:** 3147
technical education **6:** 3146
Knowledge
ancient
and participatory research **7:** 4333
as basis for social transformation **2:** 903
beliefs about
impact on curriculum **6:** ***3148–3151***
and cognitive development **6:** 3150, 3151
commercialization of
postmodernism **8:** 4640, 4642
comparative and international education
changing representations **2:** 923
mapping **2:** 932
taxonomy of perspectives **2:** 928
conceptual **10:** 5741
conditional **10:** 5740
content **10:** 5741
content-specific
individual differences **2:** 845
conversion from declarative to procedural **3:** 1433
conversion from procedural to declarative **3:** 1433
Descartes' theory
body–mind relationship **3:** 1462
development of expertise **8:** 4821
development stages **8:** 4821
discourse **10:** 5741
dissemination of **3:** ***1549–1553***
domain specific
and expertise **2:** 835, 839, 840, 841
and generalization **5:** 2669
influence on cognitive development **3:** 1502, 1503
and intellectual development **5:** 2914
and prior learning **8:** 4699
and reasoning **8:** 4951, 4952
and teacher expertise **10:** 6023
and educational research **9:** 5054
emerging forms of
and educational change **4:** 1850, 1851
evolution of **4:** 1849
experts proceduralization of **4:** 2196, 2197
explicit **10:** 5741
fragmentation of
and science education **8:** 4477
and ideology **6:** 3148
implicit and explicit **2:** 855
increasing **11:** 6614
indigenous forms of
and educational change **4:** ***1848–1852***
international networks **5:** ***2993–2998***
See also
Information networks
and learning strategies **6:** 3335
legitimation of
and postmodernism **8:** 4640, 4642
and legitimatory research **6:** 3370

measurement
and surveys **10:** 5856
metacognitive **7:** 3785; **10:** 5741
age differences **7:** 3785
nature of
and educational relevance **11:** 6703
organization of **6:** ***3151–3155***
in participatory research **7:** 4333
Plato on the nature of **8:** 4533
relationship with power
Foucault **8:** 4640, 4641, 4642
and rituals **6:** 3149
scientific
and scientific literacy **9:** 5349
social construction of **3:** 1725
and socialization **6:** 3149
sociocultural **10:** 5742
strategy **10:** 5742
tacit **10:** 5740
task **10:** 5741
teachers
and intellectual disciplines **9:** 5296
requirements **10:** 6227
tests
and partial order scalogram analysis **7:** 4314
theories of
and cognitive processes **10:** 5740
transfer of
and social psychology **10:** 6219
transmission of
and worthwhileness **1:** 114
transmission theory
and teacher education **10:** 5982, 5984
types of **3:** ***1432–1434***
See also
Declarative knowledge
Procedural knowledge
Knowledge acquisition
computer simulation **8:** ***4719–4722***
Cascade model **8:** 4721
KAGE model **8:** 4721
in context **2:** 841
expertise **2:** 839
increasing specialization **6:** 3098
Piagetian theory of internalization **3:** 1433
and problem-solving **2:** 839
and teacher behavior **10:** 6013
Knowledge characteristics
and learning **6:** 3295
Knowledge–communication–production system **4:** 2366
Knowledge level
prior learning **8:** ***4698–4702***
Knowledge representation **6:** ***3151–3155***
rule-based systems
computer simulation **8:** 4719
symbolic and distributed **6:** 3154
Knowledge structures
See Cognitive structures
Knowledge utilization
educational research
and politics **8:** 4604
enlightenment model **3:** 1428
instrumental model **3:** 1428
Kohlberg's Moral Judgment Scales **10:** 6165
Kolleg **1:** 182
Kominkan (Japan) **6:** 3076
Koran
and Islamic individual development theory **5:** 3020, 3021
and religious education **9:** 4999
Koranic schools **6:** 3455; **7:** 4134
Africa **11:** 6736, 6738
females **11:** 6754
and modernization **3:** 1651
sex discrimination **4:** 2421
Koranic study circles **1:** 322
Korea Air and Correspondence University **1:** 563
Korea, Democratic People's Republic of
adult education **1:** 349, 350
community development **2:** 905
Confucianism
and achievement need **3:** 1238, 1239
curriculum development **6:** 3159
educational change **6:** 3160
educational research **6:** 3159
mathematics achievement
cross-cultural studies **11:** 6332
postsecondary education **6:** 3157
social class
ethnography **2:** 1211
structure of government **6:** 3155
student evaluation **6:** 3159
system of education **6:** ***3155–3160***
educational objectives **6:** 3156
major problems **6:** 3160
structure **6:** 3156
teacher education **6:** 3158
teacher recruitment **6:** 3158
teaching methodology **6:** 3159
Korea, Republic of
adult education **1:** 349, 350
nonformal education **6:** 3165
community development **2:** 905
Confucianism
and achievement need **3:** 1238, 1239
cooperative education **11:** 6657
cultural influences **6:** 3161
curriculum development **6:** 3167
education
rate of return **8:** 4916
educational change **6:** 3169
government school relationship
school administration **6:** 3165
law
and education **6:** 3165
mathematics achievement
cross-cultural studies **11:** 6332
moral education
and civic education **2:** 768
postsecondary education **6:** 3162
preschool education **6:** 3164
primary education **6:** 3162
production
technology transfer models **11:** 6278
program management **8:** 4754
secondary education **6:** 3162
vocational education **6:** 3164
social class
ethnography **2:** 1211
special education **6:** 3164
teams **10:** 6242
student evaluation **6:** 3168
system of education **6:** ***3161–3170***
educational objectives **6:** 3161
enrollment **6:** 3161
historical background **6:** 3161
major problems **6:** 3169
structure **6:** 3162
teacher education **6:** 3167
teacher recruitment **6:** 3167
teacher salaries **10:** 5843
teaching methodology **6:** 3167
technical education **6:** 3164
vocational education **1:** 108
Korean Educational Development Institute (KEDI)
educational radio **5:** 2886
educational television **5:** 2894
Kpelle
ethnography of **3:** 1753
Kruskal–Wallis test
nonparametric statistics **7:** 4160
Kuder–Richardson formula
and classical test theory **2:** 786
and descriptive scales **3:** 1476
and reliability **9:** 4991, 4992
estimates **7:** 3730
Kurtosis
measures of **7:** 3733
Kuwait
adult education
nonformal education **6:** 3173
curriculum development **6:** 3174
educational change **6:** 3176
government school relationship
financial support **6:** 3174
school administration **6:** 3174
law
and education **6:** 3171
postsecondary education **6:** 3172
preschool education **6:** 3172
primary education **6:** 3172
private education **6:** 3172
secondary education **6:** 3172
special education **6:** 3172
student evaluation **6:** 3175
system of education **6:** ***3170–3177***
educational objectives **6:** 3171
enrollment **6:** 3172
major problems **6:** 3176
structure **6:** 3171
teacher recruitment **6:** 3174

teaching methodology **6:** 3174
vocational education **6:** 3173
Kwakiutl
ethnography of **3:** 1755
Kwoma
ethnography of **3:** 1754

Labeling (of persons)
learning disabilities **6:** 3558
and noncategorical education **7:** 3831
special education **2:** 725; **10:** 5664
special needs students **2:** 715
Labor
academic achievement
supply and demand **7:** 4251
output ratios
labor force planning **6:** 3611
substitution of capital for **11:** 6634
See also
Division of labor
Labor education **1:** 129, 132;
11: ***6769–6775***
access to **11:** 6773
Argentina **1:** 129
Brazil **1:** 129
Canada **1:** 129; **11:** 6772
Central and Eastern Europe **2:** 657
content **11:** 6772
definition of **11:** 6769
developed nations **7:** 4261
Europe **1:** 129
financial support **11:** 6773
formal sector **3:** 1684
Germany **7:** 4259; **11:** 6770
goals **11:** 6769
informal sector **3:** 1684
labor management partnership model
11: 6770
leadership training **11:** 6773
methods **11:** 6773
Mexico **1:** 129
organizing class model **11:** 6769
role of universities **11:** 6770
service-instrumental model **11:** 6770
Soviet Union (former) **10:** 5646
Sweden **11:** 6771
trends **11:** 6773
and unions **11:** 6770, 6771
United Kingdom **11:** 6688, 6771
United States **1:** 129; **11:** 6769, 6770
for women **11:** 6770, 6771
Labor force
academic achievement
and technological advancement
11: 6279
adult education
and mobility **1:** 128
aging (individuals)
Japan **5:** 2688
United States **5:** 2688
assessment
and educational planning **3:** 1806
changing nature and labor force
development **5:** 2688
cooperation
strategies **5:** 2742
competence
and technical education **4:** 1919
control of
radical theories **3:** 1696
educational needs **7:** 4249; **10:** 5807
effect of tax deductions on **8:** 4362
females
See Employed women
forecasting
and educational planning **8:** 4497
income distribution
wage-efficiency vs. labor discipline
models **5:** 2742
and independent study **6:** 3090
literacy **5:** 2688
United States **5:** 2688
peripheral
and adult education **2:** 1193
qualifications requirements **4:** 2393
retraining **4:** 1973
sex bias
and technological advancement
11: 6279
skill requirements
and literacy **8:** 4636
surveys
United States **7:** 4249
training and supply **1:** 131
Labor force development **1:** 119;
4: 2389; **5:** ***2685–2689***;
11: 6393, 6524
and administrator education
inservice **1:** 71
adult education **4:** 1973
and changing nature of workforce
5: 2688
comparative education **2:** 934
competency-based research **5:** 2686
concept of **5:** 2685
and continuing professional education
5: 2686
and cultural continuity **4:** 2367
definition of **5:** 2685
and educational planning **8:** 4512
educational technology **4:** 1918
educational problems **4:** 1920
role of **4:** 1923
Finland **5:** 2687
goals **5:** 2686
government role in **11:** 6425
graduate programs **5:** 2687
human augmentation theory **4:** 1923
and interactive television **4:** 1922
International Institute for Educational
Planning programs **11:** 6529
and international joint ventures
5: 2688, 2689
International Labour Organization
policies **5:** 3001
international perspective **5:** 2688,
2689
Japan **5:** 2687; **6:** 3074, 3090
and job satisfaction **2:** 1093
and nonformal education **4:** 2365,
2367
needs assessment **4:** 2365
and organization development
5: 2685, 2687
and performance improvement
2: 1136
as a profession **5:** 2686
research needs **5:** 2688
strategic **5:** 2687
and technology in workplace **5:** 2688
and training **11:** 6637
courses **2:** 1136
of practitioners **5:** 2686
programs **3:** ***1486–1491***
and university adult education
11: 6548
use of term **1:** 119
and vocational education **5:** 2686
and workforce literacy **5:** 2688
Labor force participation
females
added worker hypothesis **3:** 1668
agriculture **3:** 1667
and birth rate **3:** 1673
day care problems **2:** 690
developing nations **3:** 1682
discouraged worker hypothesis
3: 1668
and economic change **3:** 1709
and education **3:** ***1666–1672***
education work relationship
3: 1669
factors affecting **3:** 1667, 1668
historical stages of development
3: 1668
and lifelong learning **11:** 6391
and preschool education **8:** 4662,
4664
and race earnings differentials
8: 4899
rural to urban migration **3:** 1667
service occupations **3:** 1668
and sex discrimination **3:** 1667
and social change **9:** 5423
theories of **3:** 1666
urbanization **3:** 1667
labor market analysis
informal sector **3:** 1677
Labor force planning
approaches **6:** 3610
common characteristics of **6:** 3611
comparative area studies **6:** 3610
employer survey **6:** 3610
labor output ratios **6:** 3611
and educational planning
6: ***3608–3613***
evaluations
comparative area studies **6:** 3612
historical background **6:** 3609
input–output analysis
for predicting educational needs
11: 6279
measurement
elasticity of substitution **6:** 3610
reforms **6:** 3613
theories of **6:** 3609

See also
Mediterranean Regional Project (MRP)
Labor market
and adult education **1:** ***103–111***; **4:** ***1972–1976***
Nordic countries **7:** 4176, 4177, 4179
and age-related participation in adult education **1:** 105
and alternation education **8:** 4961
capital
deficient accumulation of **3:** 1682
changes
characteristics of **3:** 1709
and criticism of education system **6:** 3419
and literacy requirements **8:** 4636, 4637
and need for new skills **11:** 6391
and subcontracting **3:** 1709
conditions
and educational decisions **6:** 3099
and education **3:** ***1703–1707***
developing nations **3:** ***1681–1685***
and educational development
alternative models **6:** ***3179–3184***
market-clearing labor market model **6:** 3179
effect of adult education on **2:** ***1084–1094***
effect on qualifications **2:** 1057
effects of recurrent education **8:** 4960, 4961
evaluation of effects of job training on
developed nations **4:** ***2145–2150***
and firm-specific human capital **7:** 4209
forecasting
and national surveys **2:** 651
formal sector
developing nations **3:** 1681
labor education **3:** 1684
human capital theory
general training **6:** 3614
informal sector
and adult education **1:** 130
developing nations **3:** 1681
and education **3:** ***1676–1681***
labor education **3:** 1684
international
impact on educational programs **5:** 2973
job competition model **3:** 1705; **8:** 4837
links with vocational education **8:** 4337
neoclassical theory **3:** 1697
vs. segmentation theory **6:** 3186, 3187
occupational segregation
and sex bias **4:** 2427
primary segments **6:** 3184, 3188
proprietary schools
vocational education **8:** ***4792–4796***
public policy
and training **11:** 6427
public sector **8:** 4836
racial and sex discrimination **8:** ***4896–4902***
screening hypothesis **8:** 4837; **9:** ***5350–5355***
secondary segments **6:** 3184, 3188
sex bias
and earnings differentials **4:** 2441
sex differences
and earnings differentials **4:** 2413
sex discrimination **3:** 1666; **8:** ***4896–4902***
single
European Community **4:** 2065
stratification model
efficiency wage model **6:** 3187
nonmarket-clearing wages **6:** 3181
and teachers **10:** ***5843–5846***
theories of
and education **3:** 1704
and public sector employment **8:** ***4836–4839***
and vocational education **4:** ***2388–2394***; **9:** 5074
Europe **4:** 2059
Latin America **6:** 3258
Soviet Union (former) **10:** 5648
See also
Dual labor market theory
External labor market
Internal labor market
Segmentation theory
Teacher supply and demand
Labor market analysis
impact of education on
research methodologies **3:** 1677
informal sector **3:** 1676
characteristics of **3:** 1677
educational factors **3:** 1677
external efficiency **3:** 1679
internal efficiency **3:** 1679
Labor market information
See Occupational information
Labor market training
See Job training
Labor migration
See Occupational mobility
Labor needs
and curriculum **9:** 5519
and educational planning **3:** 1827; **6:** 3608; **8:** 4503
effect of technological advancement on **11:** ***6256–6261***
elasticity of demand **3:** 1443
forecasting
approaches **3:** 1811
criticisms of **3:** 1812
and social demand **3:** 1811
and national surveys **2:** 651
and personnel policy **9:** 5234
and school business partnerships **9:** 5187
skilled workers **7:** 4249
and vocational education
planning methodologies **8:** 4526
Labor relations
centralized **6:** 3194
characteristics of **6:** 3190
and collective bargaining **6:** 3192
decentralized **6:** 3194
in education **6:** ***3189–3197***
affiliations **6:** 3195
historical background **6:** 3190
and legislation **6:** 3193
and participative decision-making **5:** 2794, 2796
and policy **6:** 3193
structure of **6:** 3193
teacher
definitions of **6:** 3190
Labor segmentation
See Segmentation theory
Labor supply
employment policy
and vocational education **4:** 1974
and labor force planning **6:** 3609
skilled workers
factors influencing **7:** 4250
Labor turnover
control of **5:** 2938
and investment in training **11:** 6418
Laboratoire de Pédagogie Expérimentale (Belgium) **2:** 937
Laboratories
computers in **11:** 6284
microcomputer-based **7:** ***3808–3810***
See also
Language laboratories
Laboratory experiments
experimental psychology **5:** 2876
and microcomputer-based laboratories **7:** 3808
in science education **8:** 4645
Laboratory packages
characteristics of **6:** 3202
contents of **6:** 3202
future trends **6:** 3204
historical background **6:** 3202
and learning
views on **6:** 3203
for science learning **6:** ***3202–3205***
uses of **6:** 3203
Laboratory procedures
and science education history **9:** 5325
Laboratory schools
Dewey's **3:** 1298
teacher education **9:** ***5313–5318***
compared with professional development schools **9:** 5316
criticism of **9:** 5314
Dewey's influence **9:** 5313
history **9:** 5313
Laboratory training
student teacher attitudes **6:** 3198
teacher education **6:** ***3197–3202***
case studies **6:** 3200
computer simulation **6:** 3200
concept formation **6:** 3199
evaluation research **6:** 3198

factors influencing effectiveness **6:** 3199
feedback **6:** 3199
implications for practice **6:** 3200
participant observation **6:** 3199
research trends **6:** 3200
student teaching **6:** 3199
and transfer of training **6:** 3198, 3200
types of **6:** 3197
Language
and biographical research **1:** 538
characteristics of
and message design **7:** 3773
and cognitive structures **6:** 3214
communicative use of **4:** 2358
components of
texts **4:** 2358
in core curriculum **2:** 1104
critical theory **10:** 6197
and discovery learning **6:** 3205
form **6:** 3225
heuristic function **6:** 3205
and meaning
and relativism **9:** 4980
and preconceptions **8:** 4649
prestige
and social values **6:** 3436
role in learning **6:** 3308
processes **6:** 3205
and sociocultural factors **3:** 1250
visual
characteristics of **7:** 3773
Language acquisition
bilingual children **1:** 535
bilingualism
and connectionist theory **1:** 536
caregiver speech
and foreign language learning **4:** 2337
in children
and implicit and explicit knowledge **2:** 855
cultural discontinuities
family school relationship **6:** 3226
and culture acquisition **3:** 1728
disadvantaged children
language deficit theory **6:** 3213
language difference theory **6:** 3214
environmentalist perspectives **6:** 3213
family influence
and social class **9:** 5017
socialization **6:** 3225
and hearing impairments **10:** 5687
individual development **6:** ***3219–3224***
developmental stages **6:** 3219
prerequisites **6:** 3221
language handicaps **6:** 3222
early identification **6:** 3220, 3223
specifically language impaired (SLI) children **6:** 3222
language variation
and social attitudes **6:** 3225
and learning **6:** ***3213–3216***
educational implications **6:** 3215
nativist perspectives **6:** 3213
and nature nurture controversy **6:** 3213
and phonology **10:** 5694
role of mothers **6:** 3222
second languages
basic concepts **6:** 3228
social influences
dialects **6:** 3225
and speech handicaps
children **10:** 5696
vs. learning **4:** 2358
writing (composition) **11:** 6781
Language across the curriculum **6:** ***3205–3209***; **10:** 5958
constructive process **6:** 3206
context and use **6:** 3206
cooperative learning **6:** 3206
principles **6:** 3205
research **6:** 3207
speech communication **6:** 3440
and teacher role **6:** 3206
writing process approach **6:** 3456
Language aptitude
foreign language learning **4:** 2334
learning strategies **4:** 2334
Modern Language Aptitude Test **4:** 2334
Language arts
computer programs
writing instruction **11:** 6780
listening and speech instruction **6:** ***3439–3443***
place of literature in **6:** 3482
student-centered models **10:** 5958
teacher education **10:** ***5958–5961***
future trends **10:** 5961
models and programs **10:** 5959
pedagogical content knowledge **10:** 5959
subject area knowledge **10:** 5959
theory practice relationship **10:** 5959
text-based approach **10:** 5958
use of term **10:** 5958
Language attitudes
and language usage **6:** 3236
language variation **6:** 3225
racial differences
dialects **10:** 5822
sexism in language **10:** 5822
Language attrition (skills)
See Language skill attrition
Language comprehension
and hearing impairments **10:** 5687
Language development
See Language acquisition
Language disabilities
See Language handicaps
Language disorders
See Language handicaps
Language dominance
bilingual students **6:** 3228
Language education
hypermedia-supported **7:** 4091
information technology in **7:** ***4088–4095***
approaches **7:** 4088
pedagogy **6:** 3437
policy
beliefs influencing **6:** 3436
options **6:** 3436
rationales for **6:** 3436
and speech communication
simulations **7:** 4093
technology **6:** 3437
Language experience approach
beginning reading **8:** 4944
Language games
and cognitive development **3:** 1243
Language handicaps **10:** ***5691–5694***
assessment of **6:** 3226
autism **6:** ***3232–3235***
bilingual students **6:** ***3228–3232***
in children
classification **6:** 3226
definitions of **10:** 5691
dysphasia
and implicit knowledge of artificial grammars **2:** 855
factors affecting **10:** 5674
and genetics **10:** 5680
and hearing impairments **10:** ***5686–5691***
incidence **10:** 5674, 5692
language acquisition **6:** 3222
language processing **6:** 3223
and language variation **6:** ***3225–3228***
learning disabilities
disadvantaged children **6:** 3213
neurobiological advances **10:** 5679
and neurological impairments **1:** 553
organizations for **10:** 5692
and reading difficulties **10:** 5677, 5679
remediation **10:** 5680
research trends **10:** 5693
special needs students
microcomputers **7:** 3802
specific
of childhood **10:** ***5674–5681***
definition of **10:** 5674
subtypes of **10:** 5675
types of **10:** 5675
and temporal processing deficits **10:** 5679
types of **10:** 5691
Language of instruction
adult literacy programs **1:** 173
bilingual education programs **1:** 531, 532
and colonialism **4:** 2347
English
and teacher student relationship **10:** 5761
and history of women's education
francophone Africa **11:** 6737
and literacy measurement **6:** 3477, 3479
multicultural education **7:** 3963
official languages **4:** 2352
and textbooks
readership size **11:** 6362

Language laboratories **6:** ***3238–3241***
audiotape recorders
vs. computers **6:** 3240
computer uses in **6:** 3240
decline of **6:** 3239
definition of **6:** 3238
development of **6:** 3239
foreign language instruction **4:** 2353
functions of **6:** 3238
historical background **6:** 3238
and library services **6:** 3239
revival of **6:** 3240
teacher's console **6:** 3239
types of **6:** 3239
Language maintenance
and school choice **9:** 5193
Language policy
and adult literacy curriculum design **3:** 1258
francophone Africa **1:** 216
Language processing
effect of grammar instruction on **10:** 5700
language handicaps **6:** 3223
Language proficiency
bilingualism **6:** 3228
communicative competence
testing **6:** 3440
foreign language learning **4:** 2345
creative construction hypothesis **4:** 2345
and language tests **4:** 2360
and reading comprehension **8:** 4937
and reproduction theory **9:** 5017
second languages
cognitive/academic language proficiency (CALP) **6:** 3228
Language records (phonograph)
See Audiodisks
Language research
linguistic competence
comparative studies **6:** 3235
Language role
indigenous knowledge
and educational change **4:** 1850
Language skill attrition
in bilingualism **1:** 537
foreign language **1:** 537
native language **1:** 537
Language skills **1:** 96
assessment
bilingual students **6:** 3228
handicap identification **6:** 3228
and immigrants **5:** 2739
Language styles
and content analysis **2:** 1075
and dialects **6:** 3225
and social class **9:** 5017
Language teachers
teacher education **6:** 3437
Language teaching
communicative approach **6:** 3439
characteristics of **6:** 3439
classroom environment **6:** 3441
implementation **6:** 3441
methods of assessment **6:** 3440
programs **6:** 3440
research trends **6:** 3442
functional approach **6:** 3441
Language tests
bilingual students
cloze procedure **6:** 3229
handicap identification **6:** 3228
and language proficiency **4:** 2360
listening **7:** 3933
mother tongue **7:** ***3930–3936***
problems in cross-national comparisons **4:** 2133
reading **7:** 3930
requirements of **4:** 2358
social differences **9:** 5018
speech **7:** 3934
validity **4:** 2361
writing **7:** 3932
Language usage
Bernstein paradigm **6:** 3214
differences in **6:** 3214
in mathematics **6:** ***3634–3639***
science curriculum **6:** ***3216–3219***
Language variation
cultural linguistic **6:** 3225
and language handicaps **6:** ***3225–3228***
Laos
adult education **1:** 351
nonformal education **6:** 3244
curriculum development **6:** 3245
educational change **6:** 3246
educational research **6:** 3246
ethnic groups **6:** 3241
government school relationship
school administration **6:** 3244
secondary education
vocational education **6:** 3244
student evaluation **6:** 3246
system of education **6:** ***3241–3247***
educational objectives **6:** 3242
enrollment **6:** 3243
major problems **6:** 3246
structure **6:** 3243
teacher education **6:** 3245
teacher recruitment **6:** 3244
teaching methodology **6:** 3245
technical education **6:** 3244
Laser disks
See Optical disks
Latent class analysis
cluster analysis **2:** 830
and multivariate analysis **7:** 4012
Latent trait measurement models **6:** ***3247–3253***
linear **6:** 3247
local independence
assumption of **6:** 3248
nonlinear **6:** 3248
polytomous models **6:** 3251
See also
Item response theory (IRT)
Latent trait theory
See Item response theory (IRT)
Latent variable–variance decomposition model
extended
in kinship studies **4:** 2278; **6:** 3141
related models compared **6:** 3141
Latent variables
and canonical analysis **2:** 628
and correlation **2:** 1107
formation
and rating scales **8:** 4926
and path analysis **8:** 4346, ***4352–4359***
predictor specification **8:** 4353
Latin
curriculum history
United States **3:** 1296
and educational opportunities **9:** 5017
studies of
and transfer of training **11:** 6453
use in medieval university education **9:** 5121
Latin America
adult education **6:** ***3253–3256***
history **6:** 3253
and missionaries **1:** 128
popular **6:** 3255
providers **6:** 3256
and UNESCO **6:** 3254
basic education **1:** 465, 466
civic education **2:** 768
collective training corporations **6:** 3424
consciousness raising **2:** 1045
decentralization
and educational planning **8:** 4494
documentation systems
regional **3:** 1589
earnings differentials
and education **3:** 1712
economic change
and debt **3:** 1708
education and fertility **3:** 1672
education work relationship
tendencies **3:** 1670
educational administration
theories of **1:** 62
educational finance
private vs. public resources **8:** 4703
and tax allocation **8:** 4360, 4362
by tax deductions **8:** 4360
educational history **2:** 1060
educational planning **8:** ***4491–4495***
and analysis **8:** 4494
current issues **8:** 4494
and educational finance **8:** 4598
exchange of ideas **8:** 4493
problems **8:** 4495
research impact **8:** 4492
and revolution **8:** 4493
social contexts **8:** 4492
stages in **8:** 4491
educational policy
effect of comparative analysis on **3:** ***1830–1835***
educational radio **5:** 2886
interactive programs **4:** 1913
educational research

dissemination of **3:** 1555
homeless children **3:** 1734
job training **8:** 4714
labor force participation
females **3:** 1666, 1667
labor market
segmentation theory **6:** 3260
national training agencies
6: ***3262–3267***
evolution of **6:** 3263
functions of **6:** 3262
historical background **6:** 3262
nontraining services **6:** 3266
trends **6:** 3264
nonformal education
and consciousness raising **7:** 4144
and second chance education
9: 5366
participatory research **7:** 4330
popular education programs **2:** 903
population distribution
and educational planning **8:** 4492
private organizations
roles of **7:** 4154
public education
management of contraction in
6: 3603
public education finance
effect of economic adjustment on
3: 1787
radio schools **3:** 1559
rural to urban migration **7:** 4149
segmentation theory
studies **3:** 1683
skill development programs **10:** 5915
small business training **4:** 1989
student activism **10:** 5779
student loan programs **10:** 5764
study circles **10:** 5829
teacher rights
denial of **6:** 3191
teacher strikes **6:** 3193
teaching styles **3:** 1822
technical assistance **11:** 6659
technical education **7:** 4153
paraprofessional personnel **6:** 3260; **11:** 6270
training with production **7:** 4150
training programs
vocational education teachers
7: 4150, 4153
vocational education **8:** 4492
articulation (education)
6: ***3256–3262***
characteristics of **7:** 4150
comparative area studies **6:** 3258
curriculum change **6:** 3260
for the disadvantaged **7:** ***4148–4155***
finance **7:** 4154
historical background **6:** 3257
and independent academic centers
7: 4152
International Labour Organization
programs **5:** 3002
issues **6:** 3260
private vs. public sector roles
7: 4153
and research and development
centers **7:** 4152
and social groups **6:** 3258
vocational schools **11:** 6249
organization of **6:** 3262
quality of **6:** 3259
Latin American Educational Research Documentation Network (REDUC)
See Red Latinoamericano de Documentación en Educación (REDUC)
Latin schools movement
and problem-solving **8:** 4728
Lattice space analysis (LSA) **7:** 4311
Latvia
adult education
nonformal education **6:** 3269
curriculum development **6:** 3271
educational change **6:** 3271
ethnic groups **6:** 3267
language **6:** 3267
postsecondary education **6:** 3269
primary education **6:** 3268
secondary education **6:** 3269
vocational education **6:** 3269
special education **6:** 3269
student evaluation **6:** 3271
system of education **6:** ***3267–3272***
educational objectives **6:** 3268
major problems **6:** 3272
structure **6:** 3268
teacher education **6:** 3270
teacher recruitment **6:** 3270
teaching methodology **6:** 3271
Laubach Literacy International **1:** 214; **3:** 1259; **7:** 4146, 4147
Law
and education
Albania **1:** 258
Belgium **1:** 498
Bulgaria **1:** 583
Denmark **3:** 1453
Portugal **8:** 4624
South Africa **10:** 5626
See also
Legislation
Laws
and educational administration
6: ***3272–3276***
formation of
and facet theory **4:** 2217
Lead poisoning
effect on learning **5:** 2565
and learning disabilities **7:** 4078
and neurological impairment **1:** 14
Leaders
role of
and implementation **9:** 5243
Leadership
adult education **5:** 2735
characteristics of **6:** 3277
and outcomes of education **9:** 5262
and culture **7:** 4244
development **2:** 902
in education
role of **7:** 4241
educational
sex differences in **1:** 436
educational administration **1:** 65
conceptual approaches **6:** 3277
findings **6:** 3282
future research **6:** 3283
issues **6:** 3277
research **6:** ***3276–3284***
research limitations **6:** 3281
studies **6:** 3276
theory of **6:** ***3276–3284***
trends **6:** 3283
and educational improvement **9:** 5242
and educational quality
vocational education **8:** 4860
in effective schools **4:** 1931
group discussion **5:** 2530
groups **5:** 2524
importance of **6:** 3277
knowledge base construction **6:** 3277
and management
definitions **6:** 3597
and micropolitics **7:** 3824
organic intellectuals (Gramsci)
6: 3619
and organizational theories **4:** 2164
research **6:** 3280
international perspectives **6:** 3282
published studies **6:** 3281
quantitative vs. qualitative **6:** 3281
theory movement approach
6: 3278, 3279, 3280
and school effectiveness
research **5:** 2508
and school self-evaluation **5:** 2848
in secondary schools
and effective schools research
9: 5376
theories of **6:** 3279
grounded **6:** 3279
interactional perspectives **6:** 3280
open-systems **6:** 3279
published studies **6:** 3280
transformational
and organizational culture **1:** 435
See also
Instructional leadership
Student leadership
Leadership Behavior Description Questionnaire (LBDQ) **6:** 3279
Leadership responsibility
education and political socialization
3: 1652
in educational reform **4:** 1854
Leadership styles
and group dynamics **5:** 2524
and leadership theories **6:** 3280
sex differences **4:** 2423
Leadership training
adult education
North America **7:** 4180
educational administration **6:** 3278
female participation

developing nations **4:** 2420
and inservice education **1:** 69
and political education **8:** 4569
League of Arab States
objectives **8:** 4483
Learner characteristics
See Student characteristics
Learner controlled instruction **6:** 3325, 3328, 3342
and aptitude treatment interaction **10:** 6158
and attribution theory **2:** 837
cognitive strategy instruction
special education **2:** ***861–868***
community-based **8:** 4637
discovery learning **3:** 1540
inquiry **3:** 1540
intentional learning **2:** 837
outreach programs **7:** 4246
and self-concept **2:** 837
and socialization **2:** 837
Learning
and ability **5:** 2760
acquisition
and knowledge **10:** 5744
activity theory **6:** ***3289–3292***
as an active process **10:** 5783
approaches to
achieving **1:** 320
deep **1:** 320
information processing model **1:** 319
nature and measurement of **1:** ***318–322***
and outcomes of education **1:** 321
personal styles model **1:** 318
phenomenographic model **1:** 319
surface **1:** 320
systems model **1:** 320
attention dependent **1:** 328, 330
behaviorism and educational psychology **4:** 1843
child study movement **4:** 1843
classroom
studies of **9:** 5041
cognitive developmental **10:** 6165
and cognitive processes **2:** ***835–838***; **10:** ***5738–5745***
cognitive style in **2:** ***868–872***
collaborative roles in **10:** 5792
communities of practice in **3:** 1230
complementarity between school and other **8:** 4958
and constructivism **2:** ***1049–1052***; **6:** ***3297–3302***
critical theory **10:** 6196
cultural differences **6:** 3310
sources of **6:** 3311
and culture **3:** ***1241–1246***
definitions of **1:** 157
and development **5:** 2658
developmental stages
age differences **6:** 3285
domain specific **6:** 3344
effect of affective behavior on **1:** ***199–204***
evolution of
anthropological perspective on **5:** ***2681–2685***
by expanding **5:** 2688
factors affecting **9:** 5040; **10:** 5747
genetic perspective **3:** 1242
and health **5:** 2572
impact of evaluation on **6:** 3308
individual development **6:** ***3285–3288***
individual differences
special needs students **6:** ***3292–3297***
industrial training **6:** ***3302–3306***
and instructional psychology **5:** 2871, 2872
and intelligence **5:** 2919
by interaction **2:** 837; **6:** 3289
interactionist perspectives **6:** 3307
and knowledge characteristics **6:** 3295
and language acquisition **6:** ***3213–3216***
as a leisure pursuit **6:** 3374
leisure and work **6:** 3376
meaningful
characteristics of **6:** 3341
cognitive conceptions **6:** 3341
and memory **1:** 328
message design in **7:** ***3771–3775***
metacognitive beliefs about **7:** 3784
modalities **6:** 3291
models of **7:** ***3880–3886***
Bloom's school learning **7:** 3883
Brumer's theory of instruction **7:** 3884
Carroll's school learning **7:** 3882
Dahllöf's steering group **7:** 3883
and grouping (instructional purposes) **7:** 3880
and prediction **7:** 3881
relevance (education) **7:** 3880
and teaching methods **7:** 3881
validity **7:** 3880
models of school learning **4:** 1843
causal model, comparative research **2:** 955
nature nurture controversy **6:** 3307
nature of **6:** 3306
orientations
and learning strategies **2:** 870
and peer relationship **8:** ***4368–4372***
performance
and motivation **7:** 3943
personal autonomy in **6:** 3347
Plato on the nature of **8:** 4533
psychological factors **3:** 1387
psychological patterns **6:** 3344; **8:** ***4400–4404***
quality
and academic audits **1:** 193
receptive language
explanation **10:** 6146
redistribution across lifespan **11:** 6394
role of interpersonal relationship **2:** 1051
role of language in **6:** 3308
role of
in business **4:** 1923
semantic model of **7:** 3867
significance for cognitive development **3:** 1502
social context of **5:** 2684
social and cultural context **6:** 3342
and social differences **6:** 3310
social influences **6:** ***3306–3312***
social interaction model **6:** ***3306–3312***
social theories **6:** 3307
sociology of **6:** ***3306–3312***
stimulus–response theory **3:** 1725
and symbolic interactionism **6:** 3308, 3309
and teacher effectiveness **6:** 3308
and teaching
Heidegger's existential view **8:** 4433
theory practice relationship **6:** 3291; **7:** 3881
time factors in
See Time factors (learning)
traditional approaches **10:** 6165
and visual perception **8:** ***4376–4379***
See also
Cognitive processes
Individual development
Prior learning
Learning ability
and educational research studies **8:** 4424
Learning activities **6:** 3289
and computer-managed learning **2:** ***998–1002***
historical cultural development **3:** 1241
and learning motivation **7:** 3938
mediated through literacy **3:** 1242, 1243
participation in **6:** 3299
science education
primary school programs **9:** 5332
Learning characteristics
alterable vs. static variables **6:** 3292
special needs students **6:** ***3292–3297***
community influence **6:** 3293
ethnocultural and socioeconomic status **6:** 3292
family environment and influence **6:** 3293
peer influence **6:** 3293
Learning community
concept of **8:** 4339
Learning contracts
See Performance contracts
Learning difficulties
See Learning problems
Learning disabilities **2:** 720
comparative area studies **10:** 5683
context of **10:** 5665
definitions of **7:** 4077; **10:** 5682
and delinquency
United States **3:** 1438, 1439
diagnosis **10:** 5683
educational strategies
comparative area studies **10:** 5684
gifted **5:** 2489

historical background **10:** 5681
intervention **10:** 5683
knowledge
and production deficiency **6:** 3295
mainstreaming
socioemotional factors **5:** 2908
neurological impairments **1:** 553
prenatal influences **7:** 4079
prevalence **10:** 5683
research
recommendations **10:** 5685
and resource room programs **9:** 5066
special education
medical model **10:** 5665
specific **10:** ***5681–5686***
status of **10:** 5692
treatment **10:** 5684
Learning by doing
See Experiential learning
Learning environment **2:** 835, 837; **6:** ***3297–3302***, 3308
communication **6:** 3298
Computer Supported Intentional Learning Environment (CSILE) **6:** 3298; **11:** 6780
and distributed cognition **2:** 837
industry **6:** ***3302–3306***
performance **6:** 3301
problem-solving **6:** 3299
and teaching methods **6:** ***3297–3302***
training **6:** 3300
See also
Educational environment
Learning Environment Inventory (LEI) **2:** 808; **4:** 2247; **10:** 5772
and descriptive scales **3:** 1477
Learning experience
curriculum potential of **3:** 1365
evaluation of **8:** 4761
and library services **6:** 3394
use of term
Tylerian evaluation model **8:** 4763
See also
Mediated learning experience
Learning to learn
See Learning strategies
Learning materials
See Instructional materials
Learning modules
characteristics of **7:** 3890
coherence **7:** 3892
vs. choice **7:** 3893
and competence **7:** 3890
cost effectiveness **7:** 3892
criticism of
and evaluation **7:** 3892
and fragmentation of learning **7:** 3892
and retention (psychology) **7:** 3893
design
complementary approaches **7:** 3888
concentric model **7:** 3888
concurrent planning **7:** 3888
modular stratification **7:** 3888
sequential modules **7:** 3888
systems approach in **10:** 5899
in distance education **3:** 1559
and nonformal education **4:** 2365
objectives **7:** 3894
and open education **9:** 5541
prepackaged
and instructional design models **5:** 2859
teacher role
change in **7:** 3893
university adult education **11:** 6550
use of term **7:** 3890
in vocational education **7:** ***3890–3895***
Sweden **11:** 6692
See also
Modular curricula
Learning motivation **6:** 3344; **7:** ***3936–3942***
and academic achievement **7:** 3936
approaches to **7:** 3943
attention control **7:** 3938
and attribution theory **6:** 3328
and curriculum development **4:** 1846
effort avoidance **7:** 3937
goal orientation **7:** 3938
incentives **7:** 3938, 3939
individual development **6:** 3287
individual power **7:** 3937
and interest **6:** 3344
and learning strategies **6:** 3326, 3327, 3328
media research **7:** 3741
cognitive theories **7:** 3742
and self-efficacy **6:** 3328, 3344
self-motivation **7:** 3938, 3939
social sciences **9:** 5562
and test anxiety **7:** 3938
See also
Self-motivation
Student motivation
Learning networks
See Network learning
Learning objectives
See Behavioral objectives
Learning organization **6:** 3303
concept of the **5:** 2687; **6:** 3348
workers' needs in **5:** 2688
Learning outcomes
See Outcomes of education
Learning potential
See Aptitude
Learning problems
adult students
interventions **1:** 192
age differences
individual development **6:** 3286
and audio media **7:** 3749
disadvantaged children
sociolinguistic research **6:** 3214
and misconceptions **8:** 4650
neurological impairments **7:** ***4077–4081***
application of theory and research **7:** 4080
and environmental influences **7:** 4079
and physical sciences
secondary school programs **8:** 4476
and prereferral intervention **8:** 4657
and self-report **9:** 5409
Learning Process Questionnaire (LPQ) (Australia) **1:** 321
Learning processes **6:** 3346
and academic achievement **10:** 5783
research **10:** 5747
adult **8:** 4818
adult education **6:** 3428
analysis and formation **6:** 3290
apprenticeships
Africa **1:** 224
and aptitude treatment interaction **10:** 6155
and arousal **6:** 3319, 3432
as cognitive change **2:** 835, 836
cognitive development **10:** 6189
cognitive system model **2:** 1017
concept learning model **2:** 1017
executive control **2:** 1018
long term memory **2:** 1018
sensory receptors **2:** 1017
short term memory **2:** 1018
computer simulation **8:** ***4719–4722***
learning by chunking **8:** 4721
concept formation **2:** ***1016–1020***
and courseware **3:** 1775
deep **1:** 187, 188, 189, 190, 192
definition of **6:** 3319
discovery processes **3:** 1538, 1541
dynamics of
variables **10:** 5743
and educational media **7:** 3745
effect of prior learning on **8:** ***4698–4702***
and empiricism **6:** 3316
evaluative thinking
and emotional response **1:** 201
feedback in **4:** ***2279–2281***; **6:** 3432
functions **6:** 3342
guidance **3:** 1539
historical background **6:** 3316
and individual development **1:** 192
and individual instruction **5:** 2770
induction **3:** 1538
infants **5:** 2800
inquiry **3:** 1541
and interactive video **11:** 6602
Kolb's learning cycle model **4:** 2184; **6:** 3430
and LOGO **6:** 3510
macrostructure **6:** 3289
measurement of **7:** 3767
measurement techniques
academic learning time **1:** 21
and memory
research **7:** 3765
metacognition **10:** 6188
misconceptions **10:** 5744
models of **7:** 3880
and outcomes of education **6:** ***3315–3325***
instructional psychology model **6:** 3319, 3323

personal learning system **6:** 3431
and physical development **6:** 3286
preconceptions and misconceptions
resistance to change **8:** 4650
and prototypic learning tasks **6:** 3315
and qualitative research **9:** 5408
and rationalism **6:** 3316
research
historical background **10:** 5738
and videotape recordings **11:** 6604
schemata (cognition) **10:** 6189
science education **7:** 4102; **9:** 5329
sex differences **10:** 5824
strategic **1:** 188, 189
and student characteristics
research **10:** 5745
and study habits **10:** 5829
surface **1:** 188, 189, 190
and teacher behavior **10:** 6014
thinking skills
classroom ethnography **2:** 799
See also
Concept formation
Learning rate
See Time factors (learning), conceptual tempo
Learning readiness **9:** 5273
independent study **9:** 5395
Learning resources
See Educational resources
Learning resources centers
and educational technology **4:** 1889
libraries as **6:** 3395
and media program administration **7:** 3754
services **6:** 3396
Learning society
and adult education participation **8:** 4615
concepts of **5:** 2957; **6:** 3418, 3420; **11:** 6391, 6392
Learning strategies **6:** 3290, 3291, ***3325–3329***
and adult educators **10:** 6054
adults **1:** 165, ***184–194***; **6:** ***3345–3349***
and emotional maturity **1:** 166, 167
epistemic cognition **1:** 165
and lifelong learning **1:** 165
metacognition **1:** 165
reflective judgment **1:** 165
and affective factors **6:** 3328
age effects **6:** 3287
and aptitude treatment interaction **10:** 6158
associative learning **6:** 3287
behavioral objectives **5:** ***2500–2504***
intergroup relations **5:** 2500
characteristics of expertise **6:** 3325
and cognitive development **3:** 1502; **6:** 3327
cognitive mapping **2:** 966
cognitive processes **10:** 5742
cognitive style **6:** 3327
competition **5:** 2501
conclusion-oriented **2:** 870
and context effect **6:** 3327
cooperative learning **5:** 2501
critical reflection **6:** 3345, 3348
deep approach **9:** 5360
definitions of **6:** 3329, 3345
description-oriented **2:** 871
developmental stages
and teaching methods **5:** 2669
discussion workshops **1:** 192
educational objectives **5:** 2502
and educational research **8:** 4424
effort management study **1:** 188
evaluation **1:** 187; **6:** 3335
methods **6:** 3338
expert
and student role **10:** 5792
facilitation **6:** 3346
group instruction
high achievers **6:** 3626
holistic approach
comprehension learning **2:** 870
independent study **6:** 3325
individual development **6:** 3287
individual differences **1:** 186, 190; **5:** 2762; **6:** 3295
intervention **6:** 3295
research agenda **6:** 3296
training in development **5:** 2763
individualized instruction **5:** 2502
and information processing **1:** 187
informed strategies for learning program **4:** 1845
and interactive video **11:** 6602
inventories **1:** 187
knowledge required **6:** 3326
knowledge scaffolding **4:** 2197
learner controlled instruction **6:** 3325, 3328
mastery learning **6:** ***3625–3631***
and memory
research **7:** 3765
and metacognition **6:** 3295, 3326, 3327; **7:** 3785, 3789
methods and applications **6:** 3347
mnemonics **6:** 3287
models of **6:** 3336
and motivation **6:** 3326, 3327, 3328
and multimedia systems **7:** 3992
phenomenographic approach **5:** 2882
primary **1:** 186
problem-solving **8:** ***4722–4728***
proceduralization of knowledge **4:** 2196, 2197
promotion of **2:** 966
reciprocal teaching
and student role **10:** 5792
research **2:** 1095
and self-concept **6:** 3326
and self-efficacy **6:** 3332
and self-evaluation (individuals) **6:** 3328
serialist approach
operation learning **2:** 870
SMART operations **10:** 5743
and students **6:** 3335
characteristics **6:** 3335
teacher understanding of **10:** 6166
studies
and self-report **9:** 5410
study skills **6:** 3326
support **1:** 186
surface approach **9:** 5360
task analysis **6:** 3326; **10:** 5911
teaching of **6:** ***3335–3340***
adjunct instruction **6:** 3336
case study **6:** 3338
course evaluation **6:** 3337
courses in **6:** 3336
measurement **6:** 3337
metacurriculum **6:** 3337
types of **6:** 3335
testing of **6:** ***3335–3340***
and theories about intelligence **7:** 3784
thinking skills **8:** ***4722–4728***
training **1:** 186, 191; **2:** 835
training programs **2:** 966
educational effectiveness **2:** 966
transfer of training **11:** ***6452–6457***
types of **6:** 3335
use of metaphors in
and transfer of training **11:** 6455
visualization **6:** 3287
in the work environment **6:** 3348
See also
Study skills
Learning and Study Strategies Inventory (LASSI) **6:** 3337, 3339
Learning style
See Cognitive style
Learning theories
ability grouping **2:** 821
accessibility theory **8:** 4701
adult learning
transformative learning **1:** 164
behaviorism **1:** ***495–497***; **5:** 2880; **6:** 3316
United States **6:** 3340
cognitive development
Piagetian theory **6:** 3340
and cognitive psychology **6:** 3341
and cognitive restructuring **8:** 4701
and concept maps **2:** 1027
constructivism **6:** 3210
and task analysis **10:** 5913
and curriculum development **4:** 1842
and educational technology **9:** 5040
elaboration theory **8:** 4701
experimental psychology **7:** 3880
and Gagné's types of learning **6:** 3341; **10:** 5911
Gal'perin's stage by stage approach **6:** 3344; **7:** 3885
Gestalt psychology **5:** 2880; **6:** 3340
historical overview **6:** ***3340–3345***
Hull's motivational **1:** 495
humanistic education **6:** 3210
and individualism **6:** 3340
and industrial training **6:** 3303
information processing model **6:** 3340; **8:** 4701
and instructional design theory **5:** 2863

instructional psychology **6:** 3317
and instructional theories
5: ***2874–2880***
linguistic theory **10:** ***6193–6197***
interaction **10:** 6195
sociocultural patterns **10:** 6194
structuralist **10:** 6194
mental models **2:** 886
models
of school learning **9:** 5041;
10: 5746
and models of learning **7:** 3880, 3881
and nonformal education **4:** 2365
primary
associate and concomitant learning
5: 2588
and problem-solving **6:** 3340
psycholinguistics **10:** 6194
reflective learning **6:** 3316
relationship **10:** 6193
retrieval aid theory **8:** 4701
schemata (cognition)
and empowerment **6:** 3656, 3657
and mathematics instruction
6: 3656, 3657
selective attention theory **8:** 4701
social learning theory **1:** 495
sociolinguistics **10:** ***6193–6197***
and student attitudes **10:** 5772
and student characteristics **10:** 5738
and teaching guides **10:** 6113
and teaching methods
adult education **10:** 6198
transfer of training **11:** 6452
See also
Piagetian theory
Learning time
See Time on task
Learning by using
See on-the-job training
Least squares statistics
and correlation **2:** 1108, 1116
and decision-making theory **3:** 1424
and exploratory data analysis **4:** 2205
and factor analysis **4:** 2235
and hierarchical linear models
7: 3983, 3984
and individual development **2:** 676
and individual differences **2:** 677
and model testing **8:** 4341
in multilevel analysis **7:** 3984
and multivariate analysis **7:** 4009
parameter estimation
and path analysis **8:** 4345
and path analysis **8:** 4352, 4355
and prediction **8:** 4654
and regression analysis **9:** 4965
and robustness **9:** 5077
Leaves of absence
categories of educational **7:** 4257
and lifelong learning **11:** 6392, 6393
maternity leave **8:** 4958
See also
Paid educational leave
Released time
Lebanon
curriculum development **6:** 3354
educational change **6:** 3355
educational research **6:** 3355
language **6:** 3350
postsecondary education **6:** 3351
special education **6:** 3352
structure of government **6:** 3350
student evaluation **6:** 3355
system of education **6:** ***3349–3356***
educational objectives **6:** 3350
enrollment **6:** 3351
major problems **6:** 3355
structure **6:** 3351
teacher education **6:** 3354
teacher recruitment **6:** 3354
teaching methodology **6:** 3354
technical education **6:** 3352
Lecture method **6:** 3299
adult education **10:** 6199
and multimedia systems **7:** 3991
scholasticism **9:** 5123
Legal education (professions)
case methods **10:** 5944
Legal problems
and educational planning **3:** 1823
Legislation
adult education **6:** ***3360–3367***
curriculum **6:** ***3356–3360***
definition and scope of **6:** 3361
and educational administration
6: 3273
and governance of teacher education
10: 5962
and labor relations **6:** 3193
minority females
South Africa **7:** 3850
Legitimacy
in educational policy **6:** ***3367–3368***
compensatory strategies **6:** 3368
role of **6:** 3368
state
factors affecting **6:** 3367
problems **6:** 3367
Legitimatory research **6:** ***3368–3373***
characteristics of **6:** 3368, 3370
dissemination of findings **6:** 3369
examples of **6:** 3369, 3371
implications for conduct of **6:** 3372
models **6:** 3369
policy-oriented research **6:** 3368
power and knowledge **6:** 3370
problems with **6:** 3372
Leisure
concepts of **6:** 3373; **11:** 6794
as consummatory activity **11:** 6794
definitions of **6:** 3374
problems **11:** 6795
developed nations **11:** 6795
literature and art
Spencer's view **10:** 5707
and recreational activities **11:** 6795
residual **11:** 6794
youth and **11:** ***6794–6798***
commercialization of **11:** 6797
research methodology **11:** 6796
Leisure education **1:** 96
options and access **6:** 3375
Leisure industry **6:** 3377; **11:** 6795
and youth **11:** 6797
Leisure time **6:** 3374
and adult education **1:** 128;
6: ***3373–3378***
competing claims **6:** 3377
motivation **6:** 3375
amounts **6:** 3375
women **6:** 3375
and consumption benefits **2:** 1053
and learning **6:** 3374
passive activities **6:** 3377
work and learning **6:** 3376
Lesotho
curriculum development **6:** 3383
Distance Training Center **7:** 4148
educational change **6:** 3384
evaluation of national literacy
program **4:** 2121
government school relationship
financial support **6:** 3383
school administration **6:** 3382
postsecondary education **6:** 3381
primary education **6:** 3380
primary school agriculture
curriculum **8:** 4685
secondary education **6:** 3381
vocational education **6:** 3381
special education **6:** 3381
student evaluation **6:** 3384
system of education **6:** ***3378–3385***
degrees and qualifications **6:** 3384
educational objectives **6:** 3379
historical background **6:** 3379
major problems **6:** 3385
structure **6:** 3379
teacher education **6:** 3383
teacher recruitment **6:** 3383
technical education **6:** 3381
Lesson
concept of **6:** 3385
Lesson plans **6:** 3386
and program implementation **3:** 1493
and teacher knowledge **10:** 6119
Lesson structure **6:** ***3385–3389***
context **6:** 3388
factors influencing **6:** 3385
future research **6:** 3388
interaction process analysis **6:** 3388
learning activities **6:** 3387
and nongraded instructional grouping
6: 3386, 3387
pacing **6:** 3387
and small group instruction **6:** 3386
student attitudes research **6:** 3388
student role **6:** 3387
teacher role **6:** 3387
teaching methods **6:** 3386
Letters (alphabet)
recognition
prereading experience **4:** 1958
Letters (correspondence)
and narrative inquiry **7:** 4049

Levy–grant system
  skill development **11:** 6650
  vocational education **8:** 4360
Lexical-syntactic deficit syndrome
  characteristics of **10:** 5675
Liberal arts
  classical cycle **9:** 5116
  colleges
    teacher education programs **10:** 5996
  and curriculum legitimization **3:** 1349
  humanities **5:** 2693
  and mathematics education **6:** 3645
  teacher education **10:** 5989
  use in medieval university education **9:** 5121
Liberal education
  See General education
Liberalism
  and adult education **1:** 128
  feminist theories **5:** 2453
Liberia
  adult education **1:** 214
    nonformal education **6:** 3391
  curriculum development **6:** 3392
  educational change **6:** 3393
    resistance to **3:** 1414
  ethnic groups **6:** 3389
  ethnography of indigenous populations **3:** 1753
  ethnography of Kpelle **3:** 1245
  government school relationship
    financial support **6:** 3392
    nonformal education **6:** 3392
  intelligence tests **4:** 1849
  literacy project **6:** 3454
  mathematical skill of Kpelle **6:** 3457
  public sector employment **8:** 4838
  student evaluation **6:** 3393
  system of education **6:** ***3389–3394***
    educational objectives **6:** 3390
    enrollment **6:** 3391
    major problems **6:** 3393
    structure **6:** 3390
  teacher education **6:** 3392
  teacher recruitment **6:** 3392
  technical education **6:** 3391
  Vai script **1:** 482; **6:** 3454, 3460
    studies of **3:** 1242; **11:** 6453
Libertarianism
  and justice **4:** 2002
Librarians
  role of
    and educational technology **4:** 1889
    and electronic publishing **4:** 1956
Libraries
  and adult education **1:** 141; **8:** 4807
  expanded information sources **6:** 3398
  financial support **6:** 3395
  and history of adult education **1:** 137, 138
  as information retrieval systems **5:** 2823
  as learning resources **6:** ***3394–3399***
  as learning resources centers **6:** 3395
  and literacy education **6:** 3395
  search strategies **5:** 2823
  types of
    and educational resources **6:** 3397
  users **6:** 3397
  See also
    Academic libraries
Library administration
  and technological advancement **6:** 3396
Library associations **6:** ***3399–3401***
  characteristics of **6:** 3401
  objectives **6:** 3401
  periodicals **6:** ***3399–3401***
Library automation **6:** 3396
Library collection development **6:** 3399
Library development **6:** 3399
Library education
  and library development **6:** 3399
  types of **6:** 3396
Library instruction
  for users **6:** 3397
    and library development **6:** 3401
Library materials **6:** 3394, 3396, 3399
  formats **6:** 3396
Library organizations
  See Library associations
Library personnel
  and technological advancement **6:** 3396
Library research
  periodicals **6:** 3401
  studies **6:** 3401
Library role
  educational function **6:** 3394
  and library associations **6:** 3399
  research function **6:** 3394
  studies **6:** 3394
Library services
  and language laboratories **6:** 3239
Library technicians **6:** 3396
Libya
  adult education
    nonformal education **6:** 3404
  curriculum development **6:** 3405
  educational change **6:** 3406
  ethnic groups **6:** 3402
  government school relationship
    financial support **6:** 3405
    school administration **6:** 3404
  language **6:** 3402
  postsecondary education **6:** 3404
  primary education **6:** 3403
  secondary education **6:** 3403
  special education **6:** 3404
  structure of government **6:** 3402
  student evaluation **6:** 3406
  system of education **6:** ***3402–3407***
    educational objectives **6:** 3402
    enrollment **6:** 3403
    major problems **6:** 3407
    structure **6:** 3403
  teacher education **6:** 3405
  teacher recruitment **6:** 3405
  teaching methodology **6:** 3405
Licensing
  See Certification
Life cycle costing
  educational facilities **4:** 2224
Life events
  attitudes to
    and stress variables **10:** 3735
  and biographical research **1:** 539
  coping **8:** 4718
  individual development **9:** 5513
    problems and crises in **8:** ***4715–4719***
  and lifelong learning **11:** 6391
  and personality development **8:** 4390
  psychological impact of
    hedonistic value **8:** 4717
    and subjective interpretations **8:** 4717
  and social change **1:** 159
  teachers
    influences on **10:** 6210
  and university adult education **11:** 6549
  See also
    Crises (life events)
    Event history analysis
Life expectancy
  developed nations **1:** 235
  factors in **8:** 4818
  and literacy **3:** 1663
  and retirement **6:** 3375
  and time spent on learning **11:** 6392
Life sciences
  See Biological sciences
Life style
  individual psychology **8:** 4815
Lifelong development
  See Individual development
Lifelong education
  See Lifelong learning
Lifelong learning **1:** 89, 117; **4:** 2388; **6:** ***3416–3422***; **11:** 6391
  acceptance of concept **1:** 112
  adult education **1:** 144, 145; **8:** 4615
  Asia **1:** 351
  and certification **2:** 662
  China, People's Republic of **2:** 746
  cognitive ability **6:** 3429
  comparative analysis **1:** ***176–180***
  comparative aspects of timing **11:** 6391
  compared with continuing education **6:** 3420
  concept of **6:** 3416
    development **6:** 3417, 3419
  core of common elements **6:** 3418, 3420
  and cost effectiveness **2:** 1128
  criteria for evaluating **6:** 3422
  and criticism of conventional education **6:** 3417, 3419, 3420
  and cultural learning **3:** 1728
  curriculum **3:** 1311; **6:** 3419
  as deliberate learning **6:** 3418, 3420
  and developmental continuity **6:** 3427
  developmental stages **6:** 3431
  and education work relationship **3:** 1736

effectiveness **6:** ***3345–3349***
financial support **6:** ***3422–3425***; **8:** 4960
drawing rights model **6:** 3423
individual entitlements **6:** 3423
parafiscal funds **6:** 3424
self-financing model **6:** 3423
single employer **6:** 3424
state financing model **6:** 3424
future research **6:** 3421
goals **6:** 3422
growth of **1:** 119
horizontal articulation **6:** 3419
implications for educators **6:** ***3428–3435***
independent study **9:** 5396
individual development **6:** ***3285–3288***
developmental stages theory **6:** 3285
institutional patterns facilitating **11:** 6393
Japan **6:** 3074, 3075
legislation **6:** 3366
United States **6:** 3363
and libraries **6:** 3395
and nonformal education **4:** 2365
OECD concept **6:** 3418
and on-the-job training **7:** 4206
and open education **4:** ***2183–2186***
permanent education
comparison with French *éducation permanente* **6:** 3417, 3418
Council of Europe definition **6:** 3417, 3418
function of **6:** 3417
use of term **6:** 3417, 3419
principles **6:** 3420
public choice theory and financing of **6:** 3425
and public private provision **8:** 4338
radical nature **6:** 3419, 3420
and recurrent education **8:** 4958
second language learning **6:** 3211
social construction **11:** 6391
Soviet Union (former) **9:** 5096
time policies **11:** ***6390–6395***
and twin studies **11:** 6490
and UNESCO **11:** 6503
and university adult education **11:** 6548
use of term **1:** 119; **4:** 1973; **6:** 3417, 3418, 3420
Asia **6:** 3463
historical background **6:** 3417, 3419
and lifelong education **6:** 3417, 3418
vertical articulation **6:** 3419
and vocational education **11:** 6684
Japan **6:** 3088
See also
Recurrent education
Lifespan
beliefs about
religious traditions **5:** 2653
Lifespan development
See Individual development
Lifespan education
See Lifelong learning
Lighting design
educational facilities **4:** 2220
Likelihood function
See Maximum likelihood statistics
Likert scales **4:** 2384; **9:** 5153
and attitude measures **1:** 382, 387, 392; **7:** 3703, 3704
in science education **9:** 5319
and construct validity **11:** 6573
and descriptive scales **3:** 1477, 1478
and rating scales **8:** 4920, 4927
reliability of **8:** 4927
and vocational evaluation **11:** 6672
Limited English speaking
high risk students
United States **2:** 709
language handicaps **6:** 3231
language proficiency **6:** 3228
and vocational education
United States **11:** 6533
Linear Logistic Test Model (LLTM)
and developmental stages **3:** 1511
Linear programming **4:** 1844
and automated test design **2:** 996
Linear regression
See Regression (statistics)
Linear score conversions
and achievement tests **1:** 39
Linear structural relations analysis (LISREL)
See Structural equation models
Linearity
definition of **11:** 6385
LINGUA **4:** 2056, 2063
Lingua franca
language of instruction **4:** 2347
Linguistic anthropology
See Anthropological linguistics
Linguistic competence
individual differences **2:** 843
Linguistic philosophy
and analytic philosophy **8:** 4443, 4444
and foundationalist epistemology
Wittgenstein **4:** 1999
Habermas **8:** 4459
and hermeneutics **5:** 2579, 2582
language games (Wittgenstein)
and hermeneutics **5:** 2579
and postmodernism **8:** 4640
metalinguistics
and analytical philosophy **8:** 4450
and philosophy of education **8:** 4459
Wittgenstein **8:** 4450, 4459, 4633
Linguistics
and item writing techniques **5:** 3065
and phonology
research **10:** 5695
scope **6:** 3435
second language learning **6:** ***3435–3439***
Liquid crystal displays (LCDs)
and overhead projectors **10:** 5727
LISP (programming language)
programmed tutoring **2:** 972
LISREL type models
See Structural equation models
Listening comprehension
effect of sentence combining instruction on **10:** 5702
methods of improving **6:** 3442
Listening comprehension tests **6:** 3442; **7:** 3933
development of **7:** 3933
and language tests **4:** 2359
procedures **4:** 2363
Listening skills
instruction in **6:** ***3439–3443***
research **6:** 3441
integration with speech instruction **6:** 3439
and oracy skills tests **11:** 6345
and speech therapy **10:** 5696
tests **7:** 3934
Listening tests
See Listening comprehension tests
Literacy **6:** ***3443–3446***, ***3453–3459***
acquisition of **6:** 3475
and adult education **5:** 2735, 2736
nonformal education **6:** 3488
research **1:** 161
Afghanistan **1:** 206
anthropological study of **6:** ***3446–3453***
Asia **8:** 4487
scope of problem **6:** 3464
autonomous model **6:** 3453, 3454
Bangladesh **1:** 454
Botswana **1:** 548
Burkina Faso **1:** 595
campaigns
developing nations **1:** ***169–176***
and economic development **2:** 3454
and child-to-child programs
developing nations **2:** ***730–733***
China, People's Republic of **2:** 748, 752
cognitive effects **6:** 3447, 3454
comparative analysis
international studies **1:** ***465–475***
concepts of **6:** ***3453–3459***
cultural differences **3:** 1243
differences in national **1:** 100
constituent skills **6:** 3478
Costa Rica **2:** 1139
Côte d'Ivoire **2:** 1152
cross-cultural studies
ethnography **2:** 800
Cuba **3:** 1221, 1226
and cultural context **6:** 3453, 3454
cultural differences
and prior experience **6:** 3451
cultural influences
written language **1:** 482
cultural model **6:** 3453, 3454
curriculum **6:** 3455
in cultural context **6:** 3452
definitions of **1:** 100; **6:** 3443, ***3453–3459***, 3468, 3474
comparative **6:** 3454
political **6:** 3453
social practice **6:** 3454

UNESCO **6:** 3453
and democracy **1:** 175
developed nations **6:** 3454
developing nations
sex differences **1:** 467
and development **1:** 169; **3:** 1653
development of specific skills **6:** 3455
economic development and **3:** 1663
and educational history **5:** 2613
effect of written language on **6:** 3444
Egypt **4:** 1940, 1943
emergent **6:** 3456; **10:** 5958
preschool children **4:** ***1958–1963***
research **4:** 1962
use of term **4:** 1958, 1960
environmental **6:** 3445
Ethiopia **4:** 2039
and ethnographic research **6:** 3455
events **6:** 3454
and family environment **6:** 3447, 3448
and family school relationship **6:** 3449
francophone Africa **1:** 215
functions of **6:** 3444
Gambia **4:** 2401, 2404
Ghana **5:** 2482
and grapheme systems **1:** ***480–483***
Greece **5:** 2515
Guatemala **5:** 2548
Guinea, Republic of **5:** 2554
historical background **6:** 3443
and the Reformation **6:** 3531
household surveys **6:** 3477
and human rights **1:** 169, 175
and illiteracy **6:** 3445
impact on cognitive development **3:** 1242, 1243
impact on culture **3:** 1242; **6:** 3447
India **5:** 2744
individual differences **5:** 2654
information skills
and libraries **6:** 3395
intercultural **7:** 3972, 3973
international programs **5:** 2932, 2935
in interviews **5:** 3005
Iran **5:** 3007, 3009
Italy **5:** 3028
Jamaica **6:** 3070
Jordan **6:** 3110
Lebanon **6:** 3350
levels of **6:** 3475
levels in relation to length of school attendance **6:** 3445
and life expectancy **3:** 1663
Madagascar **6:** 3553
Malawi **6:** 3562
Mali **6:** 3582
Mauritania **6:** 3686, 3688
meaning of **8:** 4634
measurement **6:** ***3474–3480***; **7:** 3709
areas of debate **6:** 3476
direct **6:** 3477
and independent study **7:** 3710
of levels **6:** 3478
problems of comparability **6:** 3477
self-evaluation (individuals) techniques **6:** 3477
Mexico **7:** 3796
and middle class culture **6:** 3447
and mild disabilities **8:** 4932
Morocco **7:** 3927
Mozambique **7:** 3956
multiple **3:** 1230
national assessments **8:** 4635
national standard setting **7:** 4056
Nepal **7:** 4064
Niger **7:** 4121
and oral cultures **6:** 3447, 3451
Pakistan **7:** 4264
Panama **7:** 4270, 4273
Paraguay **7:** 4284, 4286
policy **8:** 4637
and economic goals **8:** 4635
United States **8:** 4637
postliteracy programs
females **11:** 6718
and power relations **6:** 3455
program financial support
United States **8:** 4637
program reforms **8:** 4636
rate
and economic development **3:** 1692
and grade attainment **8:** 4635
and women's education **4:** 2412
and reading comprehension
in second languages **8:** 4936
research **6:** ***3474–3480***
and design of instructional materials **6:** 3479
multisectoral **6:** 3479
and native language instruction **6:** 3477, 3479
and second language instruction **6:** 3479
and technology **6:** 3479
retention **1:** 174; **6:** 3476
India **5:** 2758
instructional materials for **3:** 1260
measurement **7:** 3710
Saudi Arabia **9:** 5147
Senegal **9:** 5420
Seychelles **9:** 5447
Sierra Leone **9:** 5456
and social change **6:** 3444, 3445
social and cultural differences **6:** 3476
social and family influences on learning **1:** 482
South Africa **10:** 5629
specialization
development of vocabulary skills **6:** 3446
expertise **6:** 3443, 3444, 3446
studies
and self-report **9:** 5410
Sudan **10:** 5834, 5840
Suriname **10:** 5850
Syria **10:** 5891
teachers **1:** 174
testing **6:** ***3468–3474***
domains **6:** 3472
studies **6:** 3471
text domains **6:** 3478
transfer of training **11:** 6453, 6454
Tunisia **11:** 6471
Turkey **11:** 6477
and UNESCO **11:** 6501
United Arab Emirates **11:** 6513
Uruguay **11:** 6563, 6565
and values education **11:** 6776
and work **8:** 4636
workforce **5:** 2688
United States **5:** 2688
written language
cultural differences **6:** 3443
historical development **6:** 3443
Yemen **11:** 6791
Zimbabwe **11:** 6815
See also
Functional literacy
Illiteracy
Scientific literacy
Literacy development
parent participation
children with special needs **6:** ***3459–3463***
Literacy education **6:** 3454, 3455
for adults **5:** 2733; **6:** 3420
Anglophone Africa **1:** 210
developing nations **2:** 1046
international **5:** 2935
social functions of **10:** 5593
approaches **1:** 172
consciousness raising **1:** 172
formal **1:** 172
functional **1:** 172
Arab nations **1:** 323
Asia **6:** ***3463–3467***; **8:** 4488
implementation **6:** 3465
policy **6:** 3466
program management and provision **6:** 3465
regional organization and co-operation **6:** 3464
research and evaluation **6:** 3467
China, People's Republic of **2:** 747
and economic development **1:** 129
and empowerment **1:** 134
Freirian critique **2:** 1195
critical pedagogy **2:** 1195
and ideology **5:** 2734
and libraries **6:** 3395
neglected populations **1:** 131
programs
conditions affecting **1:** 169
and development **6:** 3454
evaluation of **1:** 174
francophone Africa **1:** 216
nongovernmental organizations **7:** 4146, 4147
reciprocal teaching **10:** 5794
relevance of **2:** 903
and student reaction **10:** 5791
teacher education **8:** ***4945–4948***
terminology
Asia **6:** 3463
UNESCO programs
equal education **11:** 6716
use by revolutionary societies **1:** 132

women's education **11:** 6717
work-related **8:** 4635, 4636
Literacy Network (US) **7:** 4148
Literacy skills
See Literacy
Literacy Volunteers of America
7: 4146, 4147
Literary criticism **6:** 3481, 3482
humanities **5:** 2693
and narrative inquiry **7:** 4046
Literary styles
and narrative inquiry **7:** 4050
Literature
aesthetic values **6:** 3482
attitudes to **6:** 3481
circles
student role in **10:** 5793
in core curriculum **2:** 1104
and critical theory **6:** 3483
educational programs **6:** ***3480–3484***
content **6:** 3481
sequence **6:** 3483
student-centered models **10:** 5958
in integrated curriculum **10:** 5958
reader response
cultural differences **6:** 3481
literary criticism **6:** 3482
writing about **6:** 3482
and reading instruction **6:** 3483
role in secondary school curriculum
6: 3482
as a school subject **6:** 3482
teacher education **10:** ***5958–5961***
theory practice relationship
10: 5959
text-based approach **10:** 5958
whole language approach **10:** 5958
Literature appreciation **6:** 3481, 3482,
3483
scholasticism **9:** 5122
Lithuania
curriculum development **6:** 3489
development **6:** 3489
educational change **6:** 3490
government school relationship
financial support **6:** 3488
school administration **6:** 3488
language **6:** 3484
postsecondary education **6:** 3486
preschool education **6:** 3486
primary education **6:** 3485
secondary education **6:** 3485
vocational education **6:** 3487
special education **6:** 3487
structure of government **6:** 3485
student evaluation **6:** 3490
system of education **6:** ***3484–3491***
degrees and qualifications **6:** 3490
educational objectives **6:** 3485
structure **6:** 3485
teacher education **6:** 3489
teaching methodology **6:** 3489
technical education **6:** 3487
Living standards
urban areas **11:** 6557
Loan default
and student loan programs **10:** 5766
Lobbying
and politics of adult education
6: 3361, 3365
Local area networks (LANs)
and courseware **10:** 5620
and educational planning **11:** 6297
in schools **5:** 2830
special education **7:** 3805
Local education authorities (LEAs) (UK)
6: ***3491–3496***
budgeting **9:** 5184
and educational improvement **9:** 5221
organizational complexity **6:** 3493
and school-based management
9: 5303, 5304
and school inspectors **9:** 5251
use of term **6:** 3491
See also
School districts
Local government
and educational change **5:** 2506
schools
decentralization **3:** 1415
Localism
educational administration **6:** 3273
Locus of control
and aging (individuals) **1:** 237
attribution theory
and helplessness **9:** 5405
individual power **4:** 1981
teacher burnout **10:** 6061
Log-linear models **6:** ***3499–3508***
applications **2:** 1084; **6:** 3506
choice of **6:** 3500
computer software for **6:** 3500, 3502
conditions for **6:** 3500
and configural frequency analysis
6: 3507
for contingency tables **2:** 1083
and contingency tables
item bias procedures **5:** 3045
and correspondence analysis **6:** 3507
developments **6:** 3506
example **6:** 3501
follow-up methods **6:** 3502
historical background **6:** 3499
interpretation of results **6:** 3502
and mobility tables **7:** 3863
modes of inquiry **6:** 3500
and multivariate analysis **7:** 4012
ordered nominal data **6:** 3506
parameters
assessment of **6:** 3502
procedures for **6:** 3501
specifications **6:** 3501
variables
choice of **6:** 3501
See also
Logit models
Logic
formal **4:** 1998
and logical thinking **8:** 4950
See also
Mathematical logic
Logical empiricism
and analytical philosophy **8:** 4450
educational administration
and behavioral science tradition
3: 1769
and subjectivity in theory choice
3: 1770
Logical positivism **4:** 1998, 1999;
8: 4632; **9:** 5023
and antipositivism **8:** 4634
difficulties of **8:** 4633
and educational research **4:** 1858;
9: 5054
verifiability criterion of meaning
8: 4633
Logical thinking **8:** ***4948–4951***
analogical transfer theory **8:** 4724
and cognitive structures **8:** 4954
and critical thinking **2:** 1206
disadvantages of **8:** 4820
and heuristics **10:** 6176
inferences **8:** 4948
thinking skills **8:** 4950
LOGIST
and achievement tests **1:** 37
and item bias procedures **5:** 3049
Logistic models
See Rasch measurement models
Logit function
and event history analysis **4:** 2153
Logit models
Akaike's information criterion (AIC)
6: 3504
choice of **6:** 3504
computer software for **6:** 3503
and decision-making theory **3:** 1424
development of **7:** 3700
disadvantages **7:** 3701
follow-up methods **6:** 3505
interpretation of results **6:** 3505
method of focused comparisons
6: 3505
specification of **6:** 3503
See also
Log-linear models
LOGO **2:** 970
characteristics of **6:** 3509
cognitive development
and transfer of training **2:** 971
and computer-assisted instruction
2: 989
and computer uses in education
2: 1008
and culture of learning **2:** 971
definition of **6:** 3508
development of **6:** 3509
educational applications of
6: ***3508–3512***
effect on children's problem-solving
skills **2:** 1005
and mathematics education
research studies **7:** 4098
mathematics instruction
geometry **7:** 4097
microworlds concept of **6:** 3510
and models **2:** 986

philosophy of **6:** 3510
research **6:** 3511
studies **7:** 4084
turtle **6:** 3510
use in education **2:** 885
Long range planning
prediction
impact on curriculum **4:** ***2327–2331***
Long term memory (LTM) **1:** 328
and cognitive processes **10:** 5829
cognitive restructuring in **8:** 4701
concept formation
contextual knowledge **2:** 1018
and declarative knowledge **2:** 1018
procedural knowledge **2:** 1018
and prior learning **7:** 3764
Longitudinal studies **4:** 2383; **7:** 4051
adult education participation
Sweden **7:** 4322, 4323, 4328
and cross-sectional studies **2:** 1214, 1220; **6:** 3515
data analysis **6:** 3520
and educational history **5:** 2604
effective schools research **4:** 1936; **9:** 5377
intervention studies **6:** 3517
job training
and minimum wage **11:** 6635
measurement of adult education **7:** 3709, 3710
panel studies **6:** 3518
rate of return **8:** 4915
research methods **6:** ***3512–3524***
resilience **8:** 4776
sampling in **4:** 2387
in social stratification **10:** 5732
status of time in **6:** 3514
and surveys **10:** 5855, 5858
teacher expectation of students **10:** 6110
time series studies **6:** 3516
treatment control **2:** 1215
trend analysis **6:** 3515
twins **11:** 6490
types of **6:** 3514
validity **6:** 3519
external **6:** 3520
internal **6:** 3520
Loosely coupled systems
concept of **6:** 3524
definition of **6:** 3526
educational systems **6:** ***3524–3528***
epistemology **6:** 3526
future research **6:** 3526
school organization **6:** 3525
technical issues **6:** 3526
Lorenz curves **7:** 3733
Low achievement
cultural differences model **4:** 2048
cultural discontinuities approach **3:** 1227
ethnography **2:** 801
and cultural reproduction theory **3:** 1229
curriculum adaptation **3:** 1255
ethnocultural and socioeconomic status **6:** 3292
and grade repetition **5:** 2513
high risk students **2:** 708
and low expectation of school administrators **8:** 4566
minority group children
and peer influence **9:** 5219
minority group students
and cultural deprivation theory **3:** 1227
cultural theories **3:** ***1227–1233***
peer influence **9:** 5219
and secondary cultural discontinuity approach **3:** 1228
and teacher behavior **10:** 6109
and teacher expectation of students **10:** 6108
Good's passivity model **10:** 6109
See also
Academic failure
Low achievers
See Low achievement
Low income groups
educational strategies
small classes **2:** 775
vs. high income groups
and cost effectiveness **2:** 1128
Low vision training
deaf blind children **3:** 1404
Lower class
developed nations
educational anthropological studies **1:** 293
Lower class students
and motivation
educational policies for **5:** 2499
Luxembourg
adult education
nonformal education **6:** 3535
educational change **6:** 3537
government school relationship
financial support **6:** 3536
language **6:** 3531, 3533
postsecondary education **6:** 3534
preschool education **6:** 3535
primary education **6:** 3533
private education **6:** 3534
secondary education **6:** 3533
vocational education **6:** 3534
special education **6:** 3535
structure of government **6:** 3531
student evaluation **6:** 3537
system of education **6:** ***3531–3538***
educational objectives **6:** 3533
major problems **6:** 3537
structure **6:** 3533
teacher education **6:** 3536
teacher recruitment **6:** 3536
Lycées
teacher role **9:** 5016, 5018

M-estimation
robustness (statistics) **9:** 5077
Maastricht Treaty 1991 (EC)
Danish response to **4:** 2064
Macau
adult education **6:** 3542
cultural influences **6:** 3539
curriculum development **6:** 3543
educational change **6:** 3544
educational research **6:** 3544
ethnic groups **6:** 3539
government school relationship
financial support **6:** 3543
school administration **6:** 3542
postsecondary education **6:** 3541
preschool education **6:** 3542
private education **6:** 3541, 3542
second language instruction **4:** 2346
special education **6:** 3542
system of education **6:** ***3539–3545***
degrees and qualifications **6:** 3544
educational objectives **6:** 3539
major problems **6:** 3544
structure **6:** 3540
teacher education **6:** 3543
teacher recruitment **6:** 3543
Macroeconomics
and educational development **11:** 6634
environment
and vocational education and training **11:** ***6633–6638***
policies
development strategies **11:** 6633
skills development
incentives for **11:** 6634
and time factors (learning) **6:** ***3545–3550***
and vocational education **11:** 6251, 6700
See also
Economics
Madagascar
adult education **1:** 220
nonformal education **6:** 3553
curriculum development **6:** 3555
educational change **6:** 3556
ethnic groups **6:** 3550
government school relationship
financial support **6:** 3554
school administration **6:** 3553
postsecondary education **6:** 3552
preschool education **6:** 3552
primary education **6:** 3551
school business relationship **6:** 3553
secondary education **6:** 3552
special education **6:** 3552
structure of government **6:** 3551
system of education **6:** ***3550–3556***
degrees and qualifications **6:** 3555
educational objectives **6:** 3551
major problems **6:** 3556
structure **6:** 3551
teacher education **6:** 3554
teacher recruitment **6:** 3554
technical education **6:** 3553
Magazines
See Periodicals

Magnet schools **1:** 264
open enrollment **9:** 5198
and school choice **1:** 591; **9:** 5193, 5194
theater arts
United States **8:** 4384
United States **9:** 5197
Mail surveys
and nonresponse **7:** 3854
Mainframe computers
uses of
in educational research **7:** 3811
vs. microcomputers **7:** 3811
Mainstreaming **6:** ***3556–3560***
academic achievement **5:** 2908
administrator attitudes **5:** 2909
autism **6:** 3232
background **5:** 2907
behavior disorders **1:** 493
for blind students **11:** 6626
and career education **2:** 634
comparative analysis **6:** 3559
consequences for teaching methods **5:** 2905
cost effectiveness **5:** 2909
deaf blind children **3:** 1405
definition of **5:** 2907
and democratic values **6:** 3557
disabilities **6:** 3556
skill development **5:** 2906
educational innovation **5:** 2905
ideological aspect **6:** 3557
international trends **11:** 6458
and interpersonal competence **9:** 5565
misconceptions about **3:** 1506
primary education compared with secondary **5:** 2908
process
United Kingdom **5:** 2907
school policy **6:** 3559
severe disabilities **3:** 1506
socioemotional factors **5:** 2908
special education **2:** 722, 723; **5:** 2966; **10:** 5661
developed nations **2:** 723
developing nations **2:** 723, 728
and peer teaching **8:** 4372
special needs students **5:** ***2903–2907***, ***2907–2910***
student attitudes **5:** 2909
success
school and classroom factors **5:** 2909
teacher attitudes **5:** 2909
and teacher education **6:** 3559
and teacher education programs **10:** 5940
use of term **6:** 3556
Maintenance
educational facilities **4:** 2228
deferment of **4:** 2228
Majority attitudes
and minority interests
in democratic governance **8:** 4589
Malawi
adult education
nonformal education **6:** 3562
community support
and educational quality **2:** 912
curriculum development **6:** 3563
educational change **6:** 3564
educational research **6:** 3564
evaluation of national literacy program **4:** 2121
expulsion
females **9:** 5227
government school relationship
financial support **6:** 3563
school administration **6:** 3562
political education **8:** 4570
postsecondary education **6:** 3561
preschool education **6:** 3561
primary education **6:** 3561
public education finance
effect of economic adjustment on **3:** 1787
secondary education **6:** 3561
special education **6:** 3561
system of education **6:** ***3560–3564***
degrees and qualifications **6:** 3563
educational objectives **6:** 3560
major problems **6:** 3564
structure **6:** 3560
teacher recruitment **6:** 3563
teacher student ratio **8:** 4865
Malaysia
academic achievement
effect of parents on **4:** 2417
adult education **1:** 351; **6:** 3568
computer uses in education **4:** 1902
cultural influences **6:** 3565
curriculum development **6:** 3568, 3570
and disengagement theory **9:** 5227
distance education **4:** 1901
educational change **6:** 3571
educational demand
studies **8:** 4704
educational radio **5:** 2886
educational research **6:** 3571
ethnic groups **6:** 3565
government school relationship
financial support **6:** 3569
school administration **6:** 3568
language **6:** 3565
literacy education **6:** 3464
postsecondary education **6:** 3567
preschool education **6:** 3567
primary education **6:** 3566
private education **6:** 3567
public vs. private sector earnings comparison **8:** 4837
school inspectors **9:** 5249
secondary education **6:** 3566
vocational education **6:** 3570
special education **6:** 3567
system of education **6:** ***3564–3572***
degrees and qualifications **6:** 3571
educational objectives **6:** 3565
major problems **6:** 3572
structure **6:** 3566
teacher centers **7:** 3756
teacher education **6:** 3569
administration of **10:** 6064
teacher recruitment **6:** 3569
vocational education **8:** 4794; **9:** 5073
women's education
barriers to **4:** 2417
Malaysian Educational Technology Association (META) **3:** 1798
Maldives **7:** 4134
adult education
nonformal education **6:** 3574
curriculum development **6:** 3577
educational research **6:** 3577
government school relationship
school administration **6:** 3575
primary education **6:** 3573
secondary education **6:** 3574
vocational education **6:** 3574
special education **6:** 3574
system of education **6:** ***3572–3578***
educational objectives **6:** 3573
enrollment **6:** 3574
major problems **6:** 3577
structure **6:** 3573
teacher education **6:** 3576
teacher recruitment **6:** 3576
technical education **6:** 3574
Mali
adult education **1:** 220
curriculum development **6:** 3583
dropout rate **9:** 5225
educational change **6:** 3585
educational research **6:** 3584
ethnic groups **6:** 3578
government school relationship
financial support **6:** 3582
school administration **6:** 3582
Islamic culture **6:** 3580
language **6:** 3578
postsecondary education **6:** 3580
preschool education **6:** 3581
primary education **6:** 3580
public sector employment **8:** 4838
rural schools **7:** 4134
secondary education **6:** 3580
vocational education **6:** 3581
special education **6:** 3581
structure of government **6:** 3578
system of education **6:** ***3578–3586***
degrees and qualifications **6:** 3584
educational objectives **6:** 3579
historical background **6:** 3579
major problems **6:** 3585
structure **6:** 3580
teacher education **6:** 3583
teacher recruitment **6:** 3583
women's education **11:** 6738, 6739
colonial policy **11:** 6736
enrollment **11:** 6738
primary schools **11:** 6737
reforms **11:** 6738
youth training schemes **1:** 218

Malta
adult education
nonformal education **6:** 3589
educational change **6:** 3587
government school relationship
financial support **6:** 3590
school administration **6:** 3589
language **6:** 3586
postsecondary education **6:** 3588
preschool education **6:** 3589
primary education **6:** 3587
private education **6:** 3590
secondary education **6:** 3587
vocational education **6:** 3588
special education **6:** 3589
structure of government **6:** 3586
system of education **6:** ***3586–3593***
degrees and qualifications **6:** 3591
educational objectives **6:** 3587
historical background **6:** 3587
major problems **6:** 3591
structure **6:** 3587
teacher education **6:** 3591
teacher recruitment **6:** 3590
technical education **6:** 3589
Mammals
brain development **1:** 552
Man machine interface
See Man machine systems
Man machine systems
and educational technology **4:** 1886
and human factors engineering **4:** 2008, 2010
Management
See Administration
Management of contraction
See Declining enrollment
Management development
administrator education
inservice **1:** 68
definitions of **1:** 71
and educational management information systems **5:** 2830
humanistic model **6:** 3302
leadership training
self-actualization **6:** 3305
learning strategies **6:** 3348
and national training agencies
Latin America **6:** 3266
Management games
and educational planning **3:** 1828
Management information systems **6:** ***3593–3597***
characteristics of **6:** 3593
and comparative analysis **3:** 1833
conceptual framework **6:** 3594
and decision-making **6:** 3596
definitions of **5:** 2828
educational
definitions of **5:** 2828
and educational planning **3:** 1828
functions of **5:** 2828
human factors **5:** 2830
main services of **5:** 2829
model formation **5:** 2830
potential services **5:** 2830
structural framework **5:** 2829
uses of information technology in **5:** ***2828–2831***
and educational planning **11:** 6292
and educational research
Latin America **8:** 4494
and expert systems **5:** 2830
hardware (computers) **5:** 2830
operational procedures **6:** 3594
trends **6:** 3593
users of **6:** 3595
Management science
and educational planning **3:** 1807
Management skills
educational planning **3:** 1822
Management systems
and educational administration **1:** 65
and educational technology **4:** 1887
Management theory
contingency theory **4:** 2164
human relations tradition **4:** 2158
models **7:** 4240
and organizational theories **4:** 2164
in education **7:** 4240
and school administration **4:** 1929
and school organization **4:** 2158
and social theories
in organizational theories **4:** 2158
See also
Organizational theories
Management training
See Management development
Managerial occupations
and occupational segregation **4:** 2431
Managers
See Administrators
Mann–Whitney (Wilcoxon) test
nonparametric statistics **7:** 4159
Manpower
See Labor force
Manpower needs
See Labor needs
Manpower Services Commission (MSC) (UK)
employment programs **11:** 6686
Open Tech program **4:** 2185
training survey **7:** 3713
and vocational education **11:** 6686
Mantel–Haenszel statistic
and contingency tables
item bias procedures **5:** 3046
Manufacturing
production line model
training **6:** 3302
and vocational education **11:** 6681
Manufacturing industry
decentralization
policy implications **5:** 2795
and vocational education and training
Anglo–German comparisons **11:** 6639
Maori education **1:** 414
Maps
and concept maps **2:** 1026
Marijuana
drug abuse
effect on learning **3:** 1612
Marital instability
and child development **4:** 2259
Marital satisfaction
and child development **4:** 2259
Marital status
and health **4:** 2258
Market economy
See Free enterprise system
Market forces
See Free enterprise system
Market prices
See Cost indexes
Markov processes
and social networks **9:** 5558
Marriage
and disengagement theory **9:** 5227
effect on female employment **4:** 2418
effect on labor force participation
females **3:** 1669
effects of education on **2:** 1054
gender equality in **3:** 1674, 1675
Martinique
See Guadeloupe and Martinique
Marxian analysis
educational history **5:** 2612
and intelligence testing **7:** 3770
Marxism
and adult education **2:** 1191
Central and Eastern Europe **2:** 657
Althusser's structural **2:** 779
and education with production **3:** 1686
and educational history
research methodology **5:** 2605
and educational planning
history **8:** 4489
and educational theories **6:** ***3617–3622***
and employment contracts **3:** 1696
and formal education **9:** 5533
and governance **5:** 2511
Gramsci's humanistic **2:** 780
and hermeneutics **5:** 2579; **9:** 5052
and ideology **6:** 3618
and labor force participation
employed women **3:** 1667
and organizational theories **4:** 2161
and philosophy of education **8:** 4453, 4573
and polytechnical education **8:** 4605
and popular education **2:** 1047
and religious education **9:** 5009
and social change **1:** 58
and social class **6:** 3617
and social control **10:** 5597
and social labor concept **2:** 1201
and social stratification **7:** 3716
and socialization **10:** 5588
and sociology of education **2:** 779
and the state **6:** 3618
and student activism **10:** 5780
See also
Neo-Marxism

Marxist sociology
  curriculum research **3:** 1346
Mass communication
  See Mass media
Mass instruction
  mass media **2:** 884
Mass media
  access and control **4:** 1893
  audience response
    studies **1:** 564
  in education **4:** 1913
  impact of **6:** 3622
  influence in international education
    5: 2974
  information networks **5:** 2993
  and instrumentation **2:** ***884–888***
  issues and trends **2:** 887
  literacy **6:** ***3622–3625***
    rationale for **6:** 3622
  literacy programs **6:** 3623
    definition of **6:** 3622
    evaluation research **6:** 3624
    objectives **6:** 3624
  and preconceptions **8:** 4649
  and socialization **7:** 3741
  study courses on **8:** 4387
  and theater arts **8:** 4387
  theories of **2:** 885
  violence in
    and development of aggression in
      children **1:** 233
Mass media role
  and cognitive development **2:** 885
  in education **2:** 884
  instruction
    delivery of **2:** 884
  mediated educational environments
    2: 885
Mass media use
  and education **4:** 1891
  and media selection **7:** 3759
  reciprocal teaching **6:** 3625
  television viewing **6:** 3622
Massachusetts Institute of Technology
    (MIT) (US)
  Artificial Intelligence Laboratory
    development of LOGO **6:** 3509
Master plans
  educational facilities planning **4:** 2227
Master teachers **11:** 6720
  as artists **10:** 6083
Mastery learning **6:** ***3625–3631***; **7:** 3884
  and academic achievement **6:** 3625
    research **9:** 5042
  and achievement need **1:** 28, 30
  evaluative thinking
    and emotional response **1:** 202
  group instruction **6:** 3628
  and hypothesis testing **5:** 2710, 2712
  and individual achievement
    differences **3:** 1504
  individual differences **5:** 2777
  and individualized instruction **5:** 2772
  instructional effectiveness **5:** 2777
  model of **6:** 3545
Mastery tests **7:** 3703
  and achievement tests **1:** 33, 34
  and analysis of variance **11:** 6587
  and competence **6:** 3469
  and computer-assisted testing **5:** 2782
  consistency **9:** 4993
  and criterion referenced tests
    10: 5721, 5724
  and decision theory **3:** 1417, 1420
  and educational assessment **1:** 366
  and equated scores **9:** 4993
  and error of measurement **9:** 4994
  and individualized instruction **4:** 1914
  and item response theory **5:** 3054
  setting standards **7:** 4054
  specific subskill **3:** 1356
  and test reliability **9:** 4993
  United Kingdom **3:** 1336
Material development
  educational technology
    occupations **4:** 1926
  and human factors engineering
    4: 2009
  methods **8:** 4800
  problems **8:** 4800
  procedures **8:** 4799
  and prototyping **8:** 4801
Maternity leave
  See Leaves of absence, maternity
    leave
Mathematical applications
  computation **6:** 3653
  and creativity **6:** 3633
  cultural differences
    ethnography **6:** 3650
  curriculum development **6:** ***3631–3634***
  definition of **6:** 3632
  elementary schools
    Plato's view **6:** 3645
  fields of study **6:** 3632
  mathematical models **6:** 3632
    curriculum development **6:** 3647
    elementary schools **6:** 3656
  mathematics curriculum
    elementary schools **6:** 3655
  problem-solving **6:** 3632, 3653
    elementary schools **6:** 3656, 3658
  in school curriculum **6:** 3633
  secondary schools
    history of **6:** 3645
Mathematical concepts **6:** 3653
  Concepts in Secondary Mathematics
    and Science **6:** 3677
  misconceptions and mathematics
    instruction **6:** 3648
  teaching methods
    elementary schools **6:** 3644
Mathematical enrichment **6:** 3652, 3654
Mathematical formulas
  problem-solving
    elementary schools **6:** 3659
Mathematical logic **4:** 1998, 1999
  and cultural differences **4:** 1849
Mathematical models **7:** 3868
  and algorithms **6:** 3658
  confluence model **7:** 3868
  heuristics **6:** 3670
  and mathematical applications
    6: 3632
  phases of modeling process **6:** 3632
  response
    and rating scales **8:** 4919
  in school administration **9:** 5184
  and science education **7:** 4100
Mathematical vocabulary
  and bilingualism **6:** 3636
  history of English **6:** 3636
  language styles
    register **6:** 3636
Mathematicians
  development of mathematics
    education **6:** 3645
Mathematics
  attitude measures **1:** 392
    sex differences **1:** 392
  attitudes to **6:** 3639
    sex differences in **9:** 5430
  beliefs about **6:** 3639
  in core curriculum **2:** 1104
  and cost effectiveness studies **2:** 1134
  cultural model **6:** 3457
  culture differences in competence
    3: 1245
  Descartes' view of **3:** 1462
  emotional response to **6:** 3639
  and family environment **6:** 3449
  folk **6:** 3458
  in integrated science education
    5: 2901
  language of **6:** ***3634–3639***
  learning motivation **6:** 3642
    attribution theory **6:** 3640, 3642
    expectancy value theory **6:** 3642
  and psychology **6:** 3652
  pure **6:** 3457
  and reasoning skills **6:** 3457
  role of affective behavior
    sex differences **4:** 2434
  social context
    beliefs about **6:** 3639
  special needs students
    microcomputers **7:** 3803
  use of principles in public **6:** 3450
  as a way of thinking **6:** 3457
  whole maths position **6:** 3458
  See also
    Discrete mathematics
Mathematics achievement
  affective behavior and **6:** 3640
  and computer-assisted instruction
    7: 4096
  cross-cultural studies **11:** 6332
  and descriptive scales **3:** 1477
  and effective schools research **4:** 1936
  individual differences **4:** 2432
    and prior learning **5:** 2762
  and interaction effects **5:** 2927
  international studies **9:** 5361
  portfolio assessment **6:** 3670
  research
    sex differences **6:** 3650
    underachievement **6:** 3650

and self-efficacy **6:** 3639
and self-esteem **6:** 3639, 3640
sex differences **4:** ***2432–2436***; **6:** 3640; **9:** 5429, 5443
affective factors **6:** 3640
career choice **4:** 2434
and educational opportunities **4:** 2434
and sex stereotypes **4:** 2434
Mathematics anxiety **6:** 3450, 3639
females **4:** 2434
and tests **11:** 6359
Mathematics curriculum
abstract reasoning and problem-solving **6:** 3647
and affective behavior **6:** 3640
approaches to **6:** 3648
course selection
sex differences **4:** 2433
elementary schools **6:** 3656
influence of technological advancement on **6:** 3646
mathematical applications **6:** ***3631–3634***
National Curriculum (UK) **6:** 3458
new mathematics **6:** 3646, 3647
politicizing
Norway **3:** 1235
recommendations **6:** 3456
research **6:** 3647
secondary schools
England and Wales **6:** 3663
national reform initiatives **6:** 3663
United States **6:** 3664
Mathematics education
affective behavior and **6:** ***3639–3643***
ancient times **6:** 3643
attitude measures
sex differences in **9:** 5430
and cognitive psychology **6:** 3652
and computer-assisted instruction
special needs students **10:** 5671
and computer networks **7:** 4099
computer software
types of **7:** 4095
curriculum development
centralized **5:** 2497
demonstration programs
studies **3:** 1551
and educational technology **6:** 3667
ethnomathematics **6:** 3666
evaluation
approaches **8:** 4643
trends **8:** 4647
and heuristics **10:** 6174
history of **6:** ***3643–3647***
elementary schools **6:** 3644
as a scholarly field **6:** 3645
secondary schools **6:** 3645
universities **6:** 3645, 3646
and hypermedia **7:** 4095
information technology in **7:** ***4095–4100***
future trends **7:** 4098
learning theories
young children **6:** 3656, 3657
and LOGO
research studies **7:** 4098
mathematical modeling **6:** 3662
objectives **6:** 3661
preconceptions and misconceptions **8:** ***4648–4652***
problem-solving
design principals **8:** 4644
Realistic Mathematics Education (RME) **2:** 1050; **6:** 3654
reform movement **6:** 3646, 3647
research **6:** 3646, 3666
analytical approach **6:** 3651
anthropological approach **6:** 3651
behaviorist approach **6:** 3650
critical sociological approach **6:** 3651
systemic approach **6:** 3651
research methodology **6:** 3650
and sex discrimination **9:** 5170
social context **6:** 3650
student attitudes to **6:** ***3639–3643***
and student role **10:** 5792
studies
and selection bias **9:** 5381
and teacher expectation of students **10:** 6110
UNESCO program **6:** 3662
Mathematics instruction **6:** ***3652–3655***
assessment practice **6:** 3649
beliefs about **6:** 3639
changes in **6:** 3671, 3684
classroom communication **6:** 3635
computers **6:** 3647, 3649
constructivist approach **6:** 3672, 3673, 3684
cooperative learning **6:** 3654
courseware **6:** 3649
curriculum development **6:** ***3671–3686***
curriculum and evaluation standards
United States **6:** 3664, 3672
demonstrations (educational) **10:** 6141
didactical contract approach **6:** 3648
discourse analysis **6:** 3635
and educational technology **6:** 3671
elementary schools **6:** 3658
experimental teaching **6:** 3659
learning strategies **6:** 3659
word problems **6:** 3658
explanation in **10:** 6147
geometry
research studies **7:** 4097
learning processes **6:** 3648
listening and discussion **6:** 3635
and problem-solving **8:** 4643
problem-solving orientation **6:** 3672
proposals for change **6:** 3684
reading writing relationship **6:** 3635
research **6:** ***3647–3652***
trends **6:** 3648
and resource room programs **9:** 5067, 5069
secondary schools
history of **6:** 3645
small group learning **6:** 3654
social construction of knowledge **6:** 3650
and student role **10:** 5793
teacher knowledge and beliefs **6:** 3648
Mathematics materials
for algebra **7:** 4096
computer software **7:** 4095
for geometry **7:** 4097
Mathematics programs
Brazil **6:** 3666
components of successful **6:** 3662
developing nations **6:** 3662
elementary schools **6:** ***3655–3661***
Cognitively Guided Instruction Project **6:** 3660
Constructivist Teaching Project **6:** 3659
Problem Centered Primary Maths Program **6:** 3660
research projects **6:** 3659
England and Wales **6:** 3665
Japan **6:** 3661, 3665
Philippines **6:** 3666
secondary schools **6:** ***3661–3668***
comparative studies **6:** 3663
Sweden **6:** 3662
types available **6:** 3661
Mathematics skills
affective factors **6:** 3653
belief in usefulness **6:** 3639
heuristics **6:** 3653
and intellectual development **6:** 3645
learning **6:** ***3652–3655***
cultural constructivism **6:** 3654
dispositional view **6:** 3653
social constructivism **6:** 3653
learning processes
children **6:** 3668
metacognition **6:** 3653
research
and problem-solving **8:** 4643
testing of **8:** 4644
thinking skills **6:** 3669
views on nature of **6:** 3669
Mathematics teachers
beliefs **6:** 3648, 3650
expectations of females **4:** 2433
expert novice research **6:** 3650
inservice education **6:** 3668
knowledge **6:** 3648, 3649
and mathematical applications of mathematical models **6:** 3634
preservice education **6:** 3668
professional development **6:** 3649
teacher education **6:** ***3668–3671***
and children's mathematical thinking **6:** 3670
effectiveness **6:** 3669
history of **6:** 3646
mathematics skills **6:** 3670
provision **6:** 3668
skill development **6:** 3670
teacher effectiveness research **6:** 3650

Mathematics tests
and accountability **6:** 3649
anxiety **11:** 6359
evaluation research **6:** 3649
and expectancy tables **4:** 2181
items
types of **8:** 4643
and partial credit model **7:** 4302
performance tests **8:** ***4643–4648***
scholastic aptitude tests
sex differences **4:** 2433, 2434
SOLO superitems **8:** 4644
standardized tests
sex differences in performance **4:** 2433
and teaching experiments **8:** 4643
Mathematics textbooks
language usage **6:** 3637
Mathophobia
See Mathematics anxiety
Matrices
adjacency **9:** 5555
and basic factor model **4:** 2231
content–process
and item writing techniques **5:** 3062
and correlation **2:** 1114
factor analysis **4:** 2230
and data analysis
features of **3:** 1469
for decentralization **3:** 1408
displays
construction of **3:** 1470
distance **9:** 5556
factor **4:** 2231, 2233
and factorial modeling **4:** 2242
and item sampling **5:** 3056
in longitudinal studies **6:** 3515
in multitrait multimethod techniques **7:** 4005
and multivariate analysis **2:** 1115
in Q-methodology **8:** 4855
and Rasch measurement models **8:** 4903
reachability **9:** 5556
in regression analysis **9:** 4967
and reliability **9:** 4984
in scaling methods **9:** 5153, 5154, 5155
in smallest space analysis **9:** 5498
in social networks **9:** 5555
and sociometric techniques **10:** 5615
and structural equation models **8:** 4349
and test items **5:** 3065
transition
and mobility tables **7:** 3862
Maturity (individuals)
psychological characteristics **5:** 2690, 2691
Maudsley Personality Inventory (MPI) **8:** 4398
Mauritania **7:** 4134
curriculum development **6:** 3689
educational change **6:** 3690
educational research **6:** 3690
ethnic groups **6:** 3686
government school relationship
financial support **6:** 3689
school administration **6:** 3689
language **6:** 3686
postsecondary education **6:** 3688
preschool education **6:** 3688
primary education **6:** 3687
secondary education **6:** 3687
special education **6:** 3688
structure of government **6:** 3686
system of education **6:** ***3686–3691***
degrees and qualifications **6:** 3690
educational objectives **6:** 3687
historical background **6:** 3686
major problems **6:** 3690
structure **6:** 3687
teacher education **6:** 3689
teacher recruitment **6:** 3689
technical education **6:** 3688
Mauritius
adult education
nonformal education **7:** 3695
computer uses in education **4:** 1902
curriculum development **7:** 3696
educational change **7:** 3697
educational research **7:** 3697
ethnic groups **7:** 3691
government school relationship
school administration **7:** 3695
language **7:** 3691
postsecondary education **7:** 3694
preschool education **7:** 3694
primary education **7:** 3693
private education **7:** 3695
secondary education **7:** 3693
vocational education **7:** 3694
special education **7:** 3694
structure of government **7:** 3692
system of education **7:** ***3691–3698***
degrees and qualifications **7:** 3697
educational objectives **7:** 3692
major problems **7:** 3698
structure **7:** 3693
teacher education **7:** 3696
teacher recruitment **7:** 3696
Maximum likelihood factor analysis
See Factor analysis, maximum likelihood
statistics
Maximum likelihood statistics
and ability estimates **4:** 2014
and adaptive testing **1:** 50; **2:** 994
and hierarchical linear models **5:** 2591; **7:** 3983
and log-linear models **6:** 3502
and model testing **8:** 4341
in multilevel analysis **7:** 3985
and multivariate analysis **7:** 4009
and path analysis **8:** 4352
and Rasch measurement models **8:** 4911
and rating scales **8:** 4921
and statistical significance **9:** 5461, 5463
and tests **11:** 6326
and twin studies **11:** 6490
McKim diagram
and visual literacy **11:** 6622
Mean (statistics)
deviation
calculation **7:** 3728
use of **7:** 3727
Mean square error (MSE)
and sampling **9:** 5124, 5136
Meaning
conceptual role theory **9:** 5028
Measurement
and assessment
semantic distinction **1:** 363
of change **2:** ***671–678***
and longitudinal studies **6:** 3520
and classical test theory **2:** 785
conjoint **7:** 3700
curriculum-based model **3:** 1356
definitions of **1:** 363
adequate **11:** 6570
inadequate **11:** 6569
of developmental stages **3:** ***1508–1514***
educational
general sampling theory **5:** 3055
and physical measurement **7:** 3699
educational research **7:** ***3698–3707***
historical background **7:** 3698
effects
reactive **11:** 6508
estimation (mathematics) **6:** 3675
and evaluation **4:** 2112, 2369; **8:** 4761
general outcome model **3:** 1357
of judgments **6:** ***3120–3124***
mathematics curriculum **6:** 3674
mathematics programs **6:** 3674
multivariate approaches to **4:** 2384
in objective tests **7:** ***4193–4197***
physical
and educational measurement **7:** 3699
and research methodology **9:** 5047
research on readiness **6:** 3675
of social background **7:** ***3715–3722***
social variables
and Thurstone scales **11:** 6385
specific subskill mastery model **3:** 1356
as a transdiscipline **4:** 2098
and validity **11:** 6569
of variation **7:** ***3726–3739***
See also
Assessment
Evaluation
Testing
Measurement objectives
curriculum development **7:** ***3722–3726***
and instruction **1:** 371
Measurement techniques
historical background **7:** 3698
and hypothesis testing **5:** 2711
vocational education
and hypothesis testing **11:** 6631
See also
Sociometric techniques

Measures (individuals) **4:** 2113
  types of **7:** 3702
  vocational interests **11:** 6670
  See also
    Personality inventories
    Personality measures
Mechanical Institution (UK) **8:** 4731, 4733
Mechanical skills
  laboratory packages for **6:** 3204
Media (communication)
  See Mass media
Media literacy
  and media selection **7:** 3759
Media programs
  administration **7:** ***3753–3756***
    future trends **7:** 3756
    issues **7:** 3754
    role of **7:** 3753
  policies and procedures **7:** 3754
Media research
  comparative analysis **7:** 3740
  and educational technology **4:** 1893
  and learning **7:** ***3739–3744***
Media selection **7:** ***3756–3760***
  approaches **7:** 3757
    classroom-based **7:** 3757
  contextual issues **7:** 3759
  cost factors **7:** 3758
  criteria for **7:** 3758
  intervention strategies **7:** 3758
  and media literacy **7:** 3759
  models **7:** 3757
  research trends **7:** 3758
  teacher attitudes **7:** 3759
Media specialists
  and media program administration **7:** 3753
Median (statistics)
  measures of variation associated with **7:** 3732
Mediated learning experience
  characteristics of **2:** 858
  Feuerstein's view **2:** 858
Mediating effects
  See Mediation theory
Mediation theory
  in educational research **4:** 1874
  paradigm of **10:** 6205
  and path analysis **4:** 1875
  and prediction **4:** 1873
  See also
    Moderating effects
Medical education
  laboratory packages **6:** 3203
Medicine
  role of
    and learning disabilities **10:** 5682
Medieval history
  and teaching style **10:** 6173
Meditation **5:** 2691
  Buddhism **1:** 580
  Hinduism **5:** 2599
Mediterranean Regional Project (MRP)
  and educational planning **8:** 4490, 4492
  labor force planning **6:** 3611
    criticism of **6:** 3612
  labor needs
    and educational planning **3:** 1811
Memorization
  and associative learning **1:** 329
  encoding strategies
    elaboration **7:** 3765
    imagery **7:** 3765
    learning memory **7:** 3766
    prior knowledge activities **7:** 3765
    rehearsal **7:** 3765
    reorganization **7:** 3765
    retrieval **7:** 3766
    summarization **7:** 3765
    transformational mnemonics **7:** 3765
  hierarchical schemata **1:** 329
  and prior learning
    factors **7:** 3763
  and religious education **9:** 5001
Memory
  in bilingualism
    nature of **1:** 536
  concept of capacity **7:** 3760
    older adults **7:** 3762
  concept formation in **2:** 1017
  development
    in adults **7:** 3762
    in children **7:** 3760
    ethnography **3:** 1247
  and domain knowledge **7:** 3761
  effect of aging **8:** 4820
  evaluation of **7:** 3767
  expert performance **4:** 2194, 2195
    domain specific **4:** 2194
  implicit
    and priming **2:** 855
  incidental vs. intentional **7:** 3764
  individual development **7:** ***3760–3763***
  and information processing **8:** 4820
  and intelligence **5:** 2760
  and learning **1:** 328
  learning strategies **1:** 188; **7:** 3760
  measurement of **7:** 3767
  and metacognition **7:** 3761, 3762
  in observational learning **9:** 5514
  in older adults **7:** 3762
  and oral history **7:** 4221
  and prior learning
    role of **7:** 3764
  retrieval and acquisition **8:** 4820
  scientific study of
    historical background **7:** 3764
  sensory (SM)
    and cognitive processes **10:** 5829
  strategic processing
    coordination **7:** 3766
    role of **7:** 3764
  teaching and testing for **7:** ***3763–3769***
  tests
    types of **7:** 3764, 3767
  See also
    Long term memory (LTM)
    Recall (psychology)
    Recognition (psychology)
    Semantic memory
    Short term memory (STM)
Mende
  ethnography of **3:** 1753
Menstruation **1:** 84
Mental age
  of gifted **9:** 5528
  infant cognitive development **5:** 2799
  intelligence tests **2:** 844; **11:** 6343
  measurement
    and classical test theory **2:** 788
Mental disorders
  in children
    studies **8:** 4419
  classification systems **3:** 1515
    Diagnostic and Statistical Manual of (DSM III-R) **1:** 487; **3:** 1515
    International Classification of Diseases (ICD) **3:** 1515
  clinical diagnosis **3:** 1515
  and deinstitutionalization (of disabled) **3:** 1436
Mental health
  effect of education on **4:** 2210
  impact of life events on **8:** 4717
Mental health programs
  community health services **3:** 1436
  interdisciplinary approach **1:** 493
Mental retardation
  American Association on Mental Retardation
    classification **7:** 3826
  children **3:** 1515
  classification and diagnostic criteria **7:** 3826, 3829
  cognitive development
    predictive measures **2:** 844
  deinstitutionalization (of disabled)
    children **3:** 1436
    United States **3:** 1436
  Diagnostic and Statistical Manual of Mental Disorders (DSM III-R) **7:** 3826
  and educational opportunities **10:** 5664
  and ethnocentrism **10:** 5664
  genetic disorders **5:** 2463
  identification of groups **10:** 5660
  and intelligence tests **10:** 5663
  International Classification of Diseases **7:** 3826
  and learning disabilities **10:** 5681
  and psychiatric hospitals
    United States **3:** 1436
  special education **10:** 5659
    Montessori method **7:** 3913; **10:** 5659
  and speech handicaps **1:** 405
  use of Sigsymbols **1:** 407
  See also
    Mild mental retardation
    Moderate mental retardation
    Severe
  mental retardation
Mental tests
  See Psychological testing

Mentors **5:** 2685, 2688
  and adult education **10:** 5594
  distance education **3:** 1562
  and educational change **6:** 3598
  online **2:** 980
  teacher education **10:** 5947, 5983
Merit pay
  and teacher effectiveness **8:** 4523
  teachers **8:** 4407
Meritocracy **2:** 900; **7:** ***3769–3771***
  and education
    effect on occupational success **4:** 2276
  historical background **7:** 3769
  and Marxism **6:** 3618
  and school choice **9:** 5198
  scientific bases for **7:** 3770
  and social mobility **9:** 5550
  vs. democracy **7:** 3771
Message design
  in learning **7:** ***3771–3775***
  presentation **7:** 3772
  principles **7:** 3771
  relationships **7:** 3774
  verbal and visual combinations **7:** 3772
Meta analysis **3:** 1356; **7:** ***3775–3784***
  in attitude measures **9:** 5321
  coding precision **7:** 3780
  coding study characteristics **7:** 3780
  of computer-assisted instruction
    academically gifted **10:** 5673
  correlations **7:** 3779
  criticisms of **10:** 6237
  definition of **7:** 3776
  effect size **7:** 3776
    analysis of **7:** 3782
    averaging of **7:** 3781
    estimating variation in **7:** 3781
    strategies for **7:** 3781
  feminism **4:** 2298
  future trends **7:** 3783
  methodological characteristics
    coding of **7:** 3780
  and questioning techniques **8:** 4880
  research reports
    bias **7:** 3777
    identification of **7:** 3776
    quality of **7:** 3777
    quantification of findings **7:** 3777
    and sample selectivity **7:** 3778
    selection of **7:** 3777
  and resource room programs **9:** 5068
  and Scholastic Aptitude Test **11:** 6336
  and student evaluations of teacher effectiveness **10:** 6231
  substantive characteristics
    coding of **7:** 3780
  See also
    Research synthesis
Meta evaluation **4:** 2097, 2108, 2117
Metabolic diseases
  children
    and drug therapy **8:** 4423
Metacognition **1:** 191, 203; **5:** 2882; **7:** ***3784–3788***; **8:** 4820
  in children **8:** 4955
  and cognitive development **6:** 3321
  and cognitive processes **10:** 5741
  and cognitive strategies
    second language learning **6:** 3330
  cognitive strategy instruction **2:** 861
  comprehension monitoring **6:** 3327
  and curriculum development **4:** 1845
  definition of **7:** 3788
  development of **8:** 4652
  and energy expenditure **5:** 2764
  experts' use of **4:** 2196
  and industrial training **6:** 3303
  instruction
    choice of students for **7:** 3789
    content **7:** 3789
    curriculum issues **7:** 3790
    evaluation of **7:** 3790
    future research **7:** 3791
    guidelines **7:** 3791
    principles **7:** 3789
    tasks for **7:** 3790
    time factors **7:** 3790
  and learning factors **10:** 5749
  learning strategies **3:** 1503; **6:** 3295, 3327, 3345; **7:** 3785
    activities **6:** 3326
    and outcomes **6:** 3332
  and memory **7:** 3761, 3762, 3785
  and moral development **5:** 2669
  preconceptions and misconceptions **8:** 4650
  processes underlying **6:** 3321
  and reciprocal teaching **10:** 5792
  research **9:** 5042
    design **7:** 3790
    implementation problems **7:** 3790
    methodological issues **7:** 3790
    studies **7:** 3788
    trends **7:** 3787
  self-control **7:** 3784, 3785; **9:** 5401
    problem-solving **7:** 3785
    reading **7:** 3786
  and self-efficacy **7:** 3784; **9:** 5516
  and social affective strategies
    second language learning **6:** 3330
  strategies **7:** 3764
    and self-regulation **7:** 3766
    teaching and assessing **7:** ***3788–3792***
  thinking skills
    and transfer of training **11:** 6454
  training in **2:** 835
  and types of knowledge **3:** 1433
  use of concept **7:** 3784
Metamemory
  See Metacognition
Metaphysics
  and analytical philosophy **8:** 4450
  and epistemology **4:** 1999
  and philosophy of education **8:** 4448
Methadone
  use in pregnancy
    effect on newborn infant **1:** 14
Methods courses
  and teacher education **10:** 5960, 6038
Methylmercury
  fetal Minamata disease **1:** 14
Mexican Americans
  literacy **6:** 3448, 3451
Mexico
  adult education **2:** 639; **6:** 3253; **7:** 3796, 4181
    legislation **6:** 3363
    nonformal education **7:** 3797
  bilingual education **2:** 639
  curriculum development **7:** 3799
  education and economic growth **3:** 1663
  educational change **7:** 3800
  educational planning
    and decentralization **8:** 4599
  educational research **7:** 3800
  educational television **4:** 1905
  ethnography of indigenous populations **3:** 1755
  government school relationship
    financial support **7:** 3798
    school administration **7:** 3797
  illiteracy **2:** 639
  income distribution **5:** 2743
  inservice teacher education
    technical education **10:** 6067
  labor education **1:** 129
  labor force participation
    and industrial development **3:** 1668
  labor relations
    in education **6:** 3191
  language **7:** 3792
  occupational segregation **4:** 2431
  on-the-job training
    and educational objectives **11:** 6281
  postsecondary education **7:** 3794, 3795
  preschool education **7:** 3796
  primary education **1:** 130; **7:** 3793, 3794, 3795
  private education **7:** 3794
  production
    technology transfer models **11:** 6278
  rural to urban migration
    determinants of **5:** 2943
  school administration
    control of **9:** 5166
  schools
    conflict in **2:** 1040
  secondary education **7:** 3794, 3795
    vocational education **7:** 3795
  segmentation theory
    studies **3:** 1683
  socialist education **2:** 1047
  special education **7:** 3796
  state church relationship
    and dominant secular control **9:** 5009
  system of education **7:** ***3792–3802***
    degrees and qualifications **7:** 3800
    educational objectives **7:** 3793
    enrollment **7:** 3794

major problems **7:** 3801
structure **7:** 3793
teacher education **7:** 3798
administration of **10:** 6064
teacher recruitment **7:** 3799
technical education **7:** 3796
technology transfer **11:** 6278
textbooks
provision **11:** 6361
universities
and research training **11:** 6280
vocational education **2:** 639
technical **6:** 3258
Microcomputer-based laboratories (MBL)
components of **7:** 3808
development of **7:** 3808
educational research into **7:** 3809
and interactive video **7:** 4101
and learning processes **7:** 4102
in physical sciences
secondary school programs **8:** 4478
and science education **7:** ***3808–3810***, 4100
and science skills **7:** 4101
uses of **7:** 3808
Microcomputers
in adaptive testing **1:** 52
architecture of **7:** 3811
characteristics of **11:** 6295
and adaptive testing **2:** 993
and computer literacy **2:** 974
definition of **7:** 3810
development of
and computer software publishing **10:** 5618
in educational planning **11:** 6292, 6295
in educational research **7:** ***3810–3816***
dissemination of **3:** 1554
uses of **7:** 3810, 3814
for families with disabled children **4:** 1979
foreign language instruction **4:** 2354
hardware components **7:** 3811
historical background **7:** 3810
networks **7:** 3813
and printing **8:** 4689
in school administration **9:** 5184
software components **7:** 3812
special needs students **7:** ***3802–3808***
types of
and courseware **10:** 5621
and videotex **11:** 6302
in vocational education
applications **4:** 1922
Microeconomics
of cooperation **7:** 3818
of groups **7:** 3818
of productivity **7:** ***3816–3821***
research techniques **7:** 3816
Microelectronics
and technology transfer **11:** 6277
Microphones
characteristics of **1:** 398
types of **1:** 398
Micropolitics
characteristics of **7:** 3822
concept of **7:** 3821
control
forms of **7:** 3823
definitions of **7:** 3821
dimensions of
lateral **7:** 3823
vertical **7:** 3823
and leadership **7:** 3824
opposition
forms of **7:** 3823
research **7:** 3825
and school organization **7:** 4244
and school as workplace **9:** 5179
of schools **7:** ***3821–3826***
skills in
for teachers **7:** 3824
theory of
and conflict **7:** 3823
Microprocessors
See Microcomputers
Microteaching
and academic achievement **8:** 4869
discrimination training **10:** 5974
evaluation studies **6:** 3198
feedback **10:** 5975
modeling (psychology) **10:** 5974
models
behavior modification **10:** 5975
cognitive **10:** 5976
pragmatism **10:** 5975
social skills **10:** 5975
practice **10:** 5974
program evaluation
attitudes **10:** 5976
behavior change **10:** 5976
research on **10:** 5974
teacher education **6:** 3197; **10:** ***5973–5977***
Middle adulthood
adult education participation **8:** 4613
Middle-aged adults
adult education participation **8:** 4613
Middle class
history of women's education
Australia **11:** 6732
Middle-class standards
and adult education **5:** 2733
cultural bias
and literacy **6:** 3447
educational change and
United States **9:** 5509
resistance **2:** 916
Middle-class students
track system **3:** 1737
Middle East
See Arab nations
Middle schools
cores
United States **5:** 2526
Migraine headache
drug use
effect on learning **3:** 1611
Migrant adult education **5:** 2936
Migrant education programs
high risk students **2:** 707
Migrants
ideological
determinants of migration **5:** 2737
See also
Immigrants
Migration
behavior analysis in **5:** 2944
and brain drain **1:** ***554–561***
and cost effectiveness of public education **4:** 2211
and curriculum
factors affecting **9:** 5520
determinants of **5:** 2737
and direct measurement of literacy **7:** 3710
internal
and education **5:** ***2942–2945***
Todaro model **5:** 2945
of labor
and education **3:** 1413
motivation
self-selection model **5:** 2737
skilled workers **1:** 555
and multicultural education **2:** 1057
See also
Rural to urban migration
Migration patterns
and educational planning **3:** 1452
of skilled workers
within European Community **4:** 2065
Mild disabilities
classification problems **7:** 3831
and delinquency **3:** ***1438–1441***
early intervention **7:** 3832
instructional development for **8:** 4933
interpersonal competence
and delinquency **3:** 1439
learning
individual differences **6:** 3293
and noncategorical education **7:** ***3830–3833***
peer teaching **8:** 4373
programs for
costs **8:** 4934
and reading difficulties
incidence of **8:** 4932
intervention **8:** 4934
and reading instruction
principles of **8:** 4934
scope of term **7:** 3831
Mild mental retardation **7:** ***3826–3830***
anthropological perspective **7:** 3828
cognitive processes **7:** 3828
defining criteria **7:** 3827
diagnostic criteria
United States **7:** 3829
incidence **7:** 3827
longitudinal studies **7:** 3829
and mainstreaming **3:** 1506
minority groups **7:** 3828
and poverty **7:** 3827
remedial programs **7:** 3828
research and prospects **7:** 3829

and social context **7:** 3827
special classes **7:** 3829
special education
placement **7:** 3829
and test bias **11:** 6318
Mildly handicapped
See Mild disabilities
Militancy
See Activism
Military training
mass media role in **2:** 884
Mind
theories of
and children's cognitive development **2:** 854, 856
Mini-state theory
schools and school districts
key elements of **8:** 4564
and political considerations **8:** 4564
Minicomputers
and educational research **11:** 6297
vs. microcomputers **7:** 3811
Minicourses
social studies **9:** 5580
vocational schools
and educational planning **8:** 4529
Minimum competencies
basic skills **5:** 2695
and instructional design theory **5:** 2866
Minimum competency testing (MCT) **7:** 4055
and basic skills **11:** 6342
and curriculum alignment **7:** 3723
and educational assessment **1:** 367
and needs assessment **7:** 4058
and racial discrimination
United States **7:** 3724
and test bias **11:** 6318
Minimum wage
and job training
effects on **11:** 6635
Minimum wage legislation
and training
investment **11:** 6429
Ministries of education
See State departments of education
Minnesota Mother–Child Interaction Project (US) **8:** 4776
Minnesota Multiphasic Personality Inventory (MMPI) **8:** 4396, 4397
age differences **1:** 237
Minority group children
compensatory education **8:** 4892
urban schools **11:** 6562
Minority group students
academic achievement **3:** 1483
ethnography **2:** 800
and peer influence **9:** 5219
variability in **4:** 2050
cultural deprivation theory **3:** 1227
cultural discontinuities
school responses **3:** 1233
culture conflict
educational experience **2:** 801
low achievement
cultural reproduction **9:** 5570
and equal education **9:** 5569
family characteristics **9:** 5570
and stratification **9:** 5569
structural factors **2:** 916
and program development
ethnography **3:** ***1233–1236***
and social mobility **9:** 5219
socialization
ethnography **2:** 801
underachievement
and cultural discontinuities **3:** 1233
Minority group teachers
increased recruitment
Western societies **3:** 1232
Minority groups
academic achievement
effect of unions on **10:** 6071
academic failure
linguistic deficit view **6:** 3235
autonomous **2:** 1211; **3:** 1228
career counseling
and test bias **11:** 6318
cross-cultural studies **2:** 1211
curriculum for **7:** ***3840–3848***
domination by
in democratic governance **8:** 4589
earnings differentials **8:** ***4896–4902***
education in Germany **7:** 3845
and educational change **4:** 1850
employment opportunities
teaching **10:** 5844
equal opportunities (jobs) **11:** 6669
females
South Africa **7:** ***3848–3853***
gifted **5:** 2487
impact of education on
anthropological studies **1:** 293
indigenous populations
multicultural education **7:** 3963
involuntary **2:** 802, 1211; **3:** 1228
peer influence **9:** 5219
language handicaps **6:** 3226
language usage **6:** 3226
and multicultural education **7:** 3975
outcomes of education **9:** 5508
private schools **8:** 4824, 4827
and school desegregation **3:** 1483
small classes
academic achievement **2:** 774
and social class
cross-cultural studies **2:** 1211
and sociology of education **10:** 5603
and test bias **11:** 6317
test score decline
administrative change **2:** 771
social change **2:** 771
typology **3:** 1228
voluntary **2:** 802; **3:** 1228; **9:** 5219
See also
Ethnic groups
Misconceptions **8:** ***4648–4652***
cognitive psychology research
and curriculum development **4:** 1845
definition of **8:** 4649
patterns of
and learning problems **8:** 4650
scientific concepts
biological sciences **6:** 3409
sources of **8:** 4649
use of term **8:** 4649
Missing scores
common methods
listwise deletion **7:** 3859
pairwise deletion **7:** 3859
effects of **7:** 3858
imputation methods **7:** 3859
filling in estimated values **7:** 3860
filling in estimated values plus error **7:** 3860
filling in means **7:** 3860
hot decking **7:** 3860
multiple **7:** 3860
plausible values **7:** 3861
nonrandom **7:** 3861
reasons for **7:** 3858
in survey research **7:** ***3858–3862***
Mnemonics
effect on generalized measures of intelligence **8:** 4821
and memorization **7:** 3765
scholasticism **9:** 5123
Mobility
fluid
within European Community **4:** 2065
index **7:** 3862
Mobility aids
and assistive technology **10:** 5670
Mobility tables **7:** ***3862–3864***
analysis of **7:** 3862
association models **7:** 3863
definition of **7:** 3862
dimensions of **7:** 3863
future trends **7:** 3864
historical background **7:** 3862
loglinear methods **7:** 3863
mobility index **7:** 3862
multidimensional **7:** 3864
topological models **7:** 3863
Model
use of term **7:** 3881
Modeling (psychology)
and cultural transmission **4:** 2168
effects of **9:** 5515
explanatory style **9:** 5405
mass media **9:** 5514
and moral development **7:** 3915
observational learning **9:** 5514
role in social cognition **9:** 5514
Models
and computer-assisted instruction **2:** 989
computer simulation **2:** ***985–988***
tools for **2:** 985
computer software for **2:** 986
curriculum examples **2:** 987
definition of **2:** 985
educational planning **3:** ***1804–1810, 1825–1830***

hierarchical linear **5:** ***2590–2596***
instructional design **5:** ***2856–2862***
and model building **7:** ***3865–3873***
requirements of **7:** 3865
research implications **7:** 3872
and research methodology **9:** 5048
role of
and theory **8:** 4340
shortcomings of **7:** 3865
and simulation **9:** 5467
and teacher knowledge **10:** 6120
and teaching methods **10:** 6014
testing of **7:** 3866
approaches **8:** 4341
and theories
definitions **7:** 3865
types of **7:** 3866
See also
Paradigms
Moderate mental retardation
peer teaching **8:** 4373
Moderating effects
in educational research **4:** 1874
and profile analysis **8:** 4753
See also
Mediation theory
Moderation procedures
characteristics of candidatures **4:** 2176
group moderation **4:** 2177
moderator test **4:** 2175
prediction methods **4:** 2177
and public examinations **4:** 2174
requirements of **4:** 2175
sex differences **4:** 2179
Modern Language Association (US)
foreign language instruction **4:** 2347
Modern languages
educational programs **4:** ***2339–2346***
Modernization
and adult education **1:** 129
and education
empirical research **1:** 252
education and **3:** 1650
critique **3:** 1650
mass media **3:** 1650
and educational history **5:** 2610
and functional theories of education **2:** 1065
and vocational education
Central and Eastern Europe **11:** 6641
Modernization theory
comparative education **2:** 928
Modular curricula **7:** ***3886–3889***
building blocks **7:** 3886
course design **7:** 3887
course development **7:** 3887
definition of **7:** 3886
problems **7:** 3887
record keeping **7:** 3888
specifications **7:** 3887
tutorial guidance **7:** 3889
types of **7:** 3887
See also
Learning modules
Modular learning
See Learning modules
Modularization
See Learning modules
Money management
and school administration **9:** 5182
Mongolia
adult education **1:** 349, 350; **7:** 3903
audiovisual instruction **7:** 3904
curriculum development **7:** 3904
educational change **7:** 3904
government school relationship
school administration **7:** 3903
postsecondary education **7:** 3899
preschool education **7:** 3901
primary education **7:** 3897
secondary education **7:** 3897
special education **7:** 3901
structure of government **7:** 3896
system of education **7:** ***3895–3906***
degrees and qualifications **7:** 3904
educational objectives **7:** 3897
major problems **7:** 3905
structure **7:** 3897
teacher education **7:** 3904
teacher recruitment **7:** 3904
technical education **7:** 3902
Monolingualism
and test translation **11:** 6331
Monte Carlo methods
simulation **9:** 5467
studies **9:** 5468
and time series analysis **9:** 5488
Montessori method **7:** ***3912–3914***
classroom environment **7:** 3913
for the gifted **5:** 2494
implementation **7:** 3913
instructional materials **7:** 3913
and mental retardation
special education **10:** 5659
origin **7:** 3912
and preschool curriculum **8:** 4669
primary and secondary education **7:** 3914
schools **1:** 263
spread of **7:** 3914
Moods
effect on learning **1:** 199, 200
Mooney Problem Check List (MPCL) **8:** 4397
Moral development
and adult education **1:** 134
analysis of programs
role of philosophy of science **7:** 3921
Buddhist theory **1:** 579
Christian theory **2:** 760, 762
and cognitive development **5:** 2662; **7:** 3916
Piagetian theory **7:** 3916
Confucian theory **2:** 1043
and cooperative learning
Piagetian theory **9:** 5545
cross-cultural studies **5:** 2650
Defining Issues Test (DIT) **7:** 3917; **10:** 5936
educational objectives **5:** 2576; **8:** 4456; **10:** 6167
and educational practices **5:** 2668
educational responsibility **10:** 5987
and emotional development **4:** 1965
and equal education **4:** 2292
and ethical instruction **4:** 2031, 2293
and experience **8:** 4457
factors influencing
educational implications **7:** 3919
females **10:** 5936
and friendship **10:** 5757
individual development **7:** ***3914–3920***
Judaic theory **6:** 3116
Kantian duties toward self **7:** 3922
Kohlberg's theory **4:** 2031; **5:** 2668; **7:** 3916
and citizenship education **5:** 2668
developmental stages **7:** 3917
and ethnocentrism **7:** 3918
evaluation **7:** 3917
and feminism **7:** 3918
methods of research **7:** 3917
learning processes **1:** 379
Locke's theories **6:** 3497
and metacognition **5:** 2669
and motivation **7:** 3916, 3919
personal autonomy
Herbart's views **5:** 2576, 2577
psychoanalytic theories **7:** 3916
Saint Augustine on **9:** 5115
in schools **10:** 6167
self-motivation **9:** 5516
and disengagement practices **9:** 5516
sex differences **4:** 2292
and cultural differences **4:** 2295
social learning theories **7:** 3915
theories of **7:** 3915
value judgment
consistency with action **7:** 3919
values education **1:** ***377–380***
developmental stages **1:** 377
Moral education
approaches to **7:** 3923
content **7:** 3921
curriculum
Kohlberg's theory **4:** 2292
defining objectives **1:** 379
and democracy **7:** 3924
and discourse **7:** 3922, 3923, 3924
and Durkheim's sociology of education **2:** 777
and epistemology **4:** 1996
feminism **4:** 2031, ***2292–2297***
curriculum **4:** 2295
textbooks **4:** 2295
formal and procedural concepts **7:** 3921, 3922
liberalism and communitarianism **4:** 2031
moral development
and personal autonomy **7:** 3923
objectives **7:** 3920
and pedagogy **7:** 3923
Pestalozzi's views **8:** 4416

philosophical issues **7:** ***3920–3925***
provision **7:** 3921
role of philosophy in **7:** 3921
and socialization **4:** 2293
See also
Ethical instruction
Moral issues
and feminism **4:** 2293
Moral judgment
See Moral values, value judgment
Moral philosophy
and communitarianism **4:** 2030
and ethics **4:** ***2029–2033***
and feminism **4:** 2030
justice and rights **4:** 2030
Kantian duties toward self
and moral development **7:** 3922
and postmodernism **4:** 2030
Moral values **1:** 378
and behavior standards **7:** 3915
conventional **1:** 378
and curriculum development **3:** 1326
definitions of **7:** 3915
ecological approach **10:** 5986, 5987
and ethical instruction **4:** 2030
and evaluation methods **4:** ***2033–2037***
and individual power **7:** 3915
and intention **7:** 3915
moral development
Pestalozzi's views **8:** 4417
moral rules **7:** 3915
and personal autonomy **1:** 379
and social values **7:** 3915
teacher education **10:** ***5985–5991***
and teachers **11:** 6579
and teaching **10:** 6208
universalism debate **7:** 3918
utilitarianism **7:** 3915
value judgment
and moral development **7:** 3916
and social cognition **9:** 5512
teachers **10:** 5936
Morocco
adult education **7:** 3927
curriculum development **7:** 3928
educational change **7:** 3929
educational finance
and tax allocation **8:** 4362
educational research **7:** 3929
ethnography of indigenous populations **3:** 1753
French language
as determinant of success **9:** 5227
government school relationship
school administration **7:** 3927
postsecondary education **7:** 3927
preschool education **7:** 3927
primary education **7:** 3926
enrollment rate **3:** 1790
secondary education **7:** 3926
special education **7:** 3927
structure of government **7:** 3925
system of education **7:** ***3925–3930***
degrees and qualifications **7:** 3928
educational objectives **7:** 3926
major problems **7:** 3929
structure **7:** 3926
teacher education **7:** 3928
Mortality rate
children **2:** 706
decline in **3:** 1450
infant
education and **3:** 1674
Moslems
See Islamic culture
Mother attitudes
and child development **3:** 1627
Mother tongue
See Native language
Mothers
academic achievement
and child development **3:** 1638
employed
effect on child development **3:** 1639
and social mobility **9:** 5550
and ethical issues in feminism **4:** 2294
Froebel's views **11:** 6743, 6746
knowledge level
high risk students **2:** 709
parent education
and empowerment **7:** 4295
Motivation
and academic persistence **7:** 3937
academically gifted **9:** 5529
achievement need
anthropological approach **3:** ***1236–1241***
development of **1:** ***28–32***
individual differences **5:** 2763
action orientation **1:** 29
adult education **7:** 4322; **8:** 4821
Boshier's congruence model **7:** 4327
chain-of-response model **7:** 4328
and cognitive development **7:** 4326
expectancy-valence model **6:** 3433; **7:** 4324, 4326, 4327
and leisure **6:** 3375
measurement **7:** 3708
personal social interaction factors **7:** 4327
psychological factors **7:** 4326
psychological interaction model **7:** 4328
research **7:** 4328
adult learning **1:** 188; **6:** 3432; **7:** 4326; **10:** 6199
and artificial intelligence **1:** 345
and attention **1:** 374, 375
and attitudes **1:** 354
attribution theory
sex differences **9:** 5405
and behavior modification **9:** 5515
behavior theories **7:** 3937
and cognitive development **5:** 2662
content theories **7:** 3936
cultural discontinuities **1:** 292
developmental issues **1:** 29
and educational history **5:** 2602
and educational media **2:** 887
and educational quality **8:** 4866
and emotional experience
influence on cognitive processes **1:** 330
and grouping (instructional purposes)
cooperative learning **5:** 2533
hierarchy of needs (Maslow) **5:** 2690
and instructional design **7:** ***3943–3947***, 3943; **8:** 4822
attention–relevance–confidence–satisfac (ARCS) model **7:** 3944; **8:** 4822
macro-model **7:** 3943
and job security **5:** 2794
and learning strategies **6:** 3335
teaching of **6:** 3338
for literacy **1:** 173
and moral development **7:** 3916
in observational learning **9:** 5514
and organizational economics **4:** 1970
process theories **7:** 3937
psychological patterns in **7:** 3936
research
trends **7:** 3946
and school administration **4:** ***1967–1972***
state orientation **1:** 29
and testing **11:** 6313
theories of **4:** 1967; **8:** 4822
expectancy-value **7:** 3943
vocational education
curriculum development **11:** 6667
in vocational schools **11:** 6412, 6415
See also
Learning motivation
Self motivation
Student motivation
Teacher
motivation
Motivation techniques
and instructional improvement **7:** 3943
Motor development
and developmental psychology **7:** 3947
history of research **7:** 3947
origins of **7:** 3948
reaching behavior in infants **7:** 3948
reflex hypothesis **7:** 3948
walking in children **7:** 3948
perceptual motor learning **7:** ***3947–3950***
skill development **7:** ***3947–3950***
systems approach **7:** 3947
Motor skills
See Psychomotor skills
Mount Druitt Study (US) **6:** 3517
Movement disorders
See Psychomotor skills, disorders
Movement education
behaviorist approach **7:** 3951
cognitive approach **7:** 3951, 3952
ecological approach **7:** 3952
physical education **8:** 4465
psychomotor skills **7:** ***3950–3953***

Mozambique
adult literacy **1:** 173
curriculum development **7:** 3958
educational change **7:** 3959
educational finance **7:** 3957
educational research **7:** 3959
government school relationship
school administration **7:** 3957
language **7:** 3953
motivation techniques **7:** 3945
nonformal education for social change **1:** 132
postsecondary education **7:** 3956
preschool education **7:** 3956
primary education **7:** 3955
rehabilitation programs
boy soldiers **8:** 4778
secondary education **7:** 3955
vocational education **7:** 3955, 3956
special education **7:** 3956
structure of government **7:** 3954
system of education **7:** ***3953–3960***
degrees and qualifications **7:** 3959
educational objectives **7:** 3954
historical background **7:** 3954
major problems **7:** 3959
structure **7:** 3954
teacher education **7:** 3958
teacher recruitment **7:** 3958
MTMM methodology
See Multitrait multimethod techniques (MTMM)
Multicollinearity **1:** 516
and measurement of vintage effects **11:** 6615
and path analysis **8:** 4346
and regression analysis **9:** 4972
Multicomponent latent trait model (MLTM)
See Item response theory (IRT), multicomponent latent trait model (MLTM)
Multicultural education **3:** 1231; **7:** ***3960–3970***
anthropological perspectives **7:** ***3971–3974***
Canada **7:** 3969
categories **7:** 3963
cross-cultural studies **7:** 3973
and cultural differences **7:** 3975
cultural pluralism **7:** 3962, 3964, 3976
and culture **7:** 3964
and curricular unity **7:** 3976
curriculum **6:** 3230; **7:** ***3974–3978***
Afrocentrism (US) **7:** 3976
antiracism **7:** 3976
approaches and definitions **7:** 3975
global approach **7:** 3976
implementation **7:** 3976
for literacy **6:** 3451
social context **7:** 3974
United Kingdom **7:** 3844
definitions of **7:** 3960, 3961, 3963, 3971
differing views of **1:** 293
direct and indirect **7:** 3962
formal
informal and nonformal **7:** 3962
general and specific **7:** 3962
Germany **7:** 3967
and immigrants **7:** 3961
influence of Spencerian evolutionism on **1:** 281
intercultural communication **7:** 3961, 3962, 3965
and intercultural competence **7:** 3971
teacher education **7:** 3973
and intergroup relations **7:** 3975
international organizations **7:** 3965
methods **7:** 3964
minority groups
case study approach **7:** 3975
and nationalism **7:** 3974
negative attitudes to
United States **1:** 280
objectives **7:** 3964
and peer groups in schools **9:** 5219
and political power **7:** 3975
professional associations **7:** 3972
school types **7:** 3964
single group studies **3:** 1232
social reconstructionist approach **7:** 3976
and social studies **9:** 5576
and sociology of education **10:** 5603
teacher education **7:** 3964
and teaching of anthropology **1:** 278
terminology **7:** 3960, 3961
and testing **7:** 3967
United States **7:** 3969
use of term **7:** 3971
Multiculturalism
See Cultural pluralism
Multidimensional scaling
and facet theory **4:** 2217
multidimensional preference analysis (MDPREF) **9:** 5156
Shepard and Kruskal's nonmetric monotonic **9:** 5157
and smallest space analysis **9:** 5497, 5500
See also
Smallest space analysis (SSA)
Multidisciplinary approach
See Interdisciplinary approach
Multilevel analysis **7:** ***3978–3987***
aggregation bias **5:** 2590; **7:** 3980
analytical issues **7:** 3984
compositional and contextual effects **7:** 3985
different procedures **7:** 3985
estimation procedures **7:** 3984
random or fixed variables **7:** 3984
in assessment of classroom environment **7:** 3978
between groups **7:** 3979
between students over groups **7:** 3979, 3981
between students within groups **7:** 3979, 3981
and effective schools research **4:** 1937
framework of **7:** 3980
grouping analysis **7:** 3979
grouping effects **7:** 3979
hierarchical linear model **7:** 3981, 3982
methods **4:** 1937
and multivariate analysis **7:** 4012
pooling of data
conditions for **7:** 3981
and social stratification **10:** 5733
and structural equation models **8:** 4351
See also
Hierarchical linear models (HLM)
Multilevel linear models
See Hierarchical linear models (HLM)
Multilingualism **4:** 2340; **6:** 3210; **7:** 3961
bilingual education **4:** 2347
cross-cultural studies **7:** 3973
and literacy measurement **6:** 3477
Multimedia instruction
distance education
Asia **1:** 563
Pacific territories **1:** 563
in schools **3:** 1566
and individualized instruction **5:** 2773
and optical data disks **2:** 647
See also
Hypermedia
Multimedia systems
applications **7:** 3994
benefits of **7:** 3992
and copyright **7:** 3990
costs **7:** 3990
constraints **7:** 3994
and databases **3:** 1398
definitions of **7:** 3987, 3991
design **7:** 3988
distribution **7:** 3990
educational uses of **7:** 3990, ***3991–3996***
roles **7:** 3991
future developments **7:** 3995
hardware standards **7:** 3993
historical background **7:** 3991
implementation barriers **7:** 3993
integration of components **7:** 3989
and language education **7:** 4091
optical data disks for **11:** 6602
packages
production of **7:** ***3987–3991***
production stages **7:** 3987
production team **7:** 3989
and printing **8:** 4694
for professional market **7:** 3987
time constraints **7:** 3994
Multimedia technology
and audiovisual instruction **1:** 403
computer-assisted testing **2:** 997
and computer networks **2:** 981
educational impact of **2:** 648
in language laboratories **6:** 3240
and religious education **9:** 5003
Multiple choice tests **7:** 4051
and criterion referenced tests **10:** 5722

criticisms of **7:** 3723, 4195
and cross-cultural studies **11:** 6329
diagnostic **1:** 366
domain specifications **2:** 1185
and equated scores **11:** 6352
and essays compared **4:** 2016
and generalizability theory **5:** 2460
guessing in **2:** 788; **7:** ***3996–4000***
detection of **7:** 3999
and item response theory **5:** 3052
and item writing techniques **5:** 3061
for mathematics **8:** 4643
and objective tests **7:** 4195
and problem-solving **8:** 4729
and programmed instruction **8:** 4768, 4773
and reading tests **7:** 3930
and Rorschach tests **8:** 4789
theoretical methods **4:** 2012
and vocabulary skills **7:** 3932
and writing tests **7:** 3932
Multiple classification analysis (MCA)
and multivariate analysis **7:** 4011
Multiple correlation
See Correlation, multiple
Multiple disabilities **3:** 1505
and visual impairments **11:** 6626
Multiple regression analysis **9:** 4966
advantages of **9:** 4971
and analysis of variance **9:** 4969
applications **9:** 4972
and canonical analysis **2:** 627
and factorial modeling **4:** 2242
and interaction effects **5:** 2925
and prediction **8:** 4655
and school examination scores **7:** 3910
Multiple Wilcoxon test
nonparametric statistics **7:** 4162
Multishift schooling **7:** 4133
Multisite case studies
in educational research **2:** 643
Multitrait multimethod techniques (MTMM) **7:** ***4000–4007***
Campbell–Friske approach **7:** 4001
limitations of **7:** 4002
composite direct product model **7:** 4005
confirmatory factor analysis (CFA) **7:** 4002
classification of models **7:** 4003
recommendations **7:** 4005
convergent validity **7:** 4001
discriminant validity **7:** 4001
guidelines **7:** 4001
heterotrait-heteromethods (HTHM) **7:** 4001
heterotrait-monomethods (HTMM) **7:** 4001
latent variable approach **7:** 4002
method effects **7:** 4002
Multivariate analysis **7:** ***4007–4016***
and academic achievement **8:** 4840
and canonical analysis **2:** 626
of categorized data **7:** 4011
cluster analysis **2:** ***825–831***
comparisons of methods **7:** 4015
computer software **7:** 4014
configural frequency analysis **2:** 1031
and correlation **2:** 1115
and discriminant analysis **3:** 1544
educational research **7:** 3704
estimation in **7:** 4009
and generalizability theory **5:** 2459
and hypothesis testing **5:** 2711
and longitudinal studies **6:** 3522
and matrices **2:** 1115
and multilevel analysis **7:** 4012
multiple comparisons **11:** 6590
and nonparametric statistics **7:** 4161
normal model
assumptions **7:** 4008
pictorial representation **7:** 4013
and prediction **8:** 4656
problems **7:** 4012
of quantified data **7:** 4008
redundancy index **2:** 1116
sampling
complex survey data **9:** 5137
and secondary data analysis **9:** 5371
significance tests **7:** 4009
statistical significance **2:** 1115
and student evaluations of teacher effectiveness **10:** 6232
suppressor variables **7:** 4013
and surveys **10:** 5860
variables in **7:** 4007
variate values **7:** 4008, 4009
variates **7:** 4008
See also
Canonical analysis
Cluster analysis
Discriminant analysis
Partial order scalogram analysis
Smallest space analysis (SSA)
Multivariate analysis of covariance (MANCOVA) **7:** 4010
Multivariate analysis of variance (MANOVA) **7:** 4010; **11:** 6586
Municipal schools
history of women's education
Germany **11:** 6744
Municipalities
changing economic base of **11:** 6553
financial problems **11:** 6553
governance **11:** 6553
urban problems **11:** 6559
Musculoskeletal system
and human factors engineering **4:** 2010
Museums
and adult education **8:** 4807
Music
and core curriculum **7:** 4030
reproduction systems for **1:** 400
optical disks **2:** 646
See also
Applied music
Music education **11:** 6616
aesthetic argument for **7:** 4017
aesthetic preferences in **11:** 6617
anthropological argument for **7:** 4016
compensatory effect argument **7:** 4016
cultural–theoretical argument for **7:** 4016
curriculum **7:** ***4016–4027***
Dalcroze method **7:** 4019
definition of **7:** 4030
and Discipline-Based Arts Education **7:** 4017
educational-therapeutic argument for **7:** 4016
general approach
Germany **7:** 4017
Kodaly method **7:** 4019
Martenot method **7:** 4021
multicultural approach **7:** 4030
Israel **7:** 4018
Nigeria **7:** 4018
Orff method **7:** 4020
performance-oriented
United States **7:** 4017
programs **7:** 4017
research **7:** 4022
Suzuki method **7:** 4021
teaching methods **7:** 4019
Willems method **7:** 4020
Yamaha system **7:** 4022
Music teachers
elementary school teachers **7:** 4028
musicians **7:** 4028
specialists **7:** 4028
status of **7:** 4027
teacher education **7:** ***4027–4030***
cross-national trends **7:** 4028
curriculum **7:** 4027
Denmark **7:** 4028
Finland **7:** 4028
France **7:** 4029
future problems **7:** 4030
Germany **7:** 4029
models of **7:** 4028
Netherlands **7:** 4029
organization **7:** 4028
Sweden **7:** 4029
United States **7:** 4029
Music therapy **7:** 4016
Muslim
See Islamic culture
Mutism
elective **3:** 1516
My Class Inventory (MCI) **2:** 809; **4:** 2247
Myanmar
adult education **1:** 351
curriculum development **7:** 4037
educational change **7:** 4038
educational research **7:** 4037
ethnic groups **7:** 4031
ethnography of indigenous populations **3:** 1754
language **7:** 4031
postsecondary education **7:** 4033
preschool education **7:** 4035
primary education **7:** 4033
schools
decentralization **3:** 1414

secondary education **7:** 4033
special education **7:** 4035
structure of government **7:** 4032
student evaluation **7:** 4037
system of education **7:** ***4030–4038***
enrollment **7:** 4033
major problems **7:** 4038
structure **7:** 4033
teacher education **7:** 4036
teacher recruitment **7:** 4036
teaching methodology **7:** 4037
technical education **7:** 4035
vocational education **7:** 4035
Myers–Briggs Type Indicator (MBTI) **8:** 4397
Mythology
and knowledge evolution **4:** 1849
and narrative inquiry **7:** 4047

Namibia
adult literacy **1:** 175; **3:** 1259, 1260
cultural influences **7:** 4039
curriculum development **7:** 4045
ethnic groups **7:** 4039
language **7:** 4039
postsecondary education **7:** 4041
preschool education **7:** 4042
primary education **7:** 4041
program management **8:** 4754
secondary education **7:** 4041
vocational education **7:** 4041
special education **7:** 4042
system of education **7:** ***4039–4046***
educational objectives **7:** 4040
enrollment **7:** 4041
structure **7:** 4041
teacher education **7:** 4044
teacher recruitment **7:** 4044
teaching methodology **7:** 4045
Narcissism
and individual development **8:** 4815
Narcotics
cannabis
effect on learning **3:** 1612
Narration
writing (composition) **11:** 6779
Narrative inquiry **7:** ***4046–4051***
criteria for judging **7:** 4050
field tests **7:** 4048
personal **7:** 4047
process of **7:** 4047
related studies **7:** 4047
research reports
signature **7:** 4050
voice **7:** 4049
social **7:** 4047
theoretical context **7:** 4046
National Academy of Education (US)
educational research **4:** 1861; **9:** 5031
educational researchers
training recommendations **11:** 6440
National Assessment of Educational Progress (NAEP) (US) **7:** ***4051–4054***
curriculum-based assessment **3:** 1358
educational reform **7:** 4053
evaluation program **4:** 2078
Governing Board **7:** 4052
and item sampling **5:** 3058
literacy survey **8:** 4635
monitoring national standards **7:** 3906, ***4051–4054***
Reading Scale **1:** 37
reading tests **6:** 3471; **7:** 3931
reporting scheme **7:** 4056
and scaling **6:** 3521
secondary analysis **7:** 4052
sex differences
research **9:** 5425
standard setting **7:** 4056
state-by-state comparisons **7:** 3911, 4052
use of item response theory **7:** 3710
National Assessment of Vocational Education 1989 (NAVE) (US) **11:** 6534, 6536
recommendations **11:** 6537
National Association for the Education of Young Children (US) **3:** 1630, 1634; **11:** 6395
National Association of Educational Guidance Services (US)
advising adult learners **2:** 1162
National Association for Foreign Student Affairs (US) **2:** 919
National Association of Partners in Education (NAPE) (US) **9:** 5188
National Association of School Nurses (NASN) (US) **9:** 5284
National Association of School Psychologists (NASP) (US) **9:** 5286
National Association of Social Workers (NASW) (US) studies **9:** 5288
National Board for Professional Teaching Standards (NBPTS) (US) **10:** 5926, 5927
specialty competence **4:** 2128
National Centers for Community Education (US) **2:** 902
National Child Development Study (UK) **6:** 3512
National Commission on Excellence in Education (US)
and educational reform **9:** 5276
National Commission on Excellence in Educational Administration (NCEEA) (US) **1:** 76
National Commission for the Protection of Human Subjects of Biomedical and Behavioral Research (US) **4:** 2035
National Commission on Social Studies in the Schools (US)
curriculum recommendations **9:** 5574
National Continuing Education Association (NUCEA) (US) **8:** 4731, 4732
National Council for the Accreditation of Teacher Education (NCATE) (US) **1:** 25, 26; **10:** 5963, 5998
computers **10:** 6007
preschool teachers **3:** 1630
National Council for Educational Technology (NCET) (UK) **4:** 1912
National Council on Measurements Used in Education (NCME) (US)
Test Standards **8:** 4737
National Council for Vocational Qualifications (NCVQ) (UK) **11:** 6689
National Curriculum (UK) **3:** 1295, 1336; **7:** 3908
and academic achievement **11:** 6561
assessment **7:** 3908
publishing results **7:** 3910
reporting results **7:** 3910
attainment targets **7:** 3908
concept of **3:** 1288
core subjects **7:** 3908
and curriculum alignment **7:** 3725
curriculum development
evaluation of **3:** 1279
demands of **10:** 6209
equal education **4:** 2290
foundation subjects **7:** 3908
information technology **2:** 976
and intellectual disciplines **9:** 5295
mathematics **6:** 3458
place of geography in **5:** 2468
profile components **7:** 3908, 3909
science **8:** 4461
Standard Assessment Tasks **7:** 3909
Teacher Assessment **7:** 3909
and technology education **11:** 6288
National Education Association of the United States (NEA)
1893 Report of the Committee of Ten
curriculum development **3:** 1297
codes of ethics **10:** 5987
Department of Adult Education **8:** 4732, 4734
National Education Goals Panel (US) **7:** 4053
National Extension College (UK) **1:** 182
flexible scheduling **4:** 2185
National Governors' Association (US) **7:** 4053
National Home Study Council (US) **7:** 4216
National Institute of Adult Continuing Education (UK) **8:** 4732, 4733, 4735
Further Education Unit **2:** 1163
National Institute of Economic and Social Research (UK)
training survey **11:** 6419
National Institute of Education (NIE) (US)
and educational research **4:** 1860
National libraries
educational resources **6:** 3398

National Mental Health and Special Education Coalition (US) **1:** 488
National Policy Board for Educational Administration (NPBEA) (US) **1:** 76
National Science Foundation (NSF) (US) **7:** 4052, 4053
  science instruction **9:** 5343
National Science Teachers Association (US)
  Search for Excellence in Science Education **9:** 5344
National security
  and scientific literacy **9:** 5347
National Socialism
  See Nazism
National Society for the Study of Education (NSSE) (US)
  curriculum development **3:** 1262
  general education and core curriculum **3:** 1349
National Special Media Institutes (NSMI) (US)
  instructional design model **5:** 2856
National standards **7:** ***4054–4056***
  behavioral anchoring **7:** 4055, 4056
    item response theory **7:** 4055
  compromise methods **7:** 4055
  evaluation of cross-national comparisons **4:** ***2132–2140***
  misclassification adjustment methods **7:** 4055
    decision-theoretic **7:** 4055
  monitoring **7:** ***3906–3912***
    and accountability **7:** 3906, 3911
    assessment programs UK **7:** 3908
    technical issues **7:** 3911
    United States **7:** 3906, ***4051–4054***
    use of educational indicators **5:** 2987, 2988
  procedure examples **7:** 4056
  reference group methods **7:** 4055
  reporting **7:** 4056
  test content methods **7:** 4054
    Angoff **7:** 4054, 4056
    Ebel **7:** 4054
    Nedelsky **7:** 4054
  test-taker methods **7:** 4054
    borderline group **7:** 4055
    contrasting group **7:** 4055
  See also
    Achievement tests
National surveys
  and census data **2:** ***649–653***
  comparative education **4:** 1868
  on hearing impairments **10:** 5687
  intellectual development
    confluence model **7:** 3869
  publication of **2:** 650
  for research
    in social stratification **10:** 5733
  uses and limitations **2:** 650
  See also
    Census figures
National Teacher Assessment Project (US)
  and pedagogical content knowledge **8:** 4463
National Teacher Examinations (NTE) (US) **4:** 2128
  content validity
    academic knowledge **10:** 6017
  predictive validity
    functional knowledge **10:** 6017
National Technological University (NTU) (US) **11:** 6550
  and distance education **3:** 1576
National training agencies (NTAs)
  changing role of **6:** 3264
  Latin America **6:** ***3262–3267***
  nontraining services **6:** 3266
  organization of
    sectoral approach **6:** 3265
  trends **6:** 3264
  vocational education
    Brazil **6:** 3257
National Training Institute of Social Education (Japan) **6:** 3075
National Union of Elementary Teachers (UK) **3:** 1295
National Union of Teachers (NUT) (UK) **3:** 1295
  establishment of **10:** 6073
  objectives **10:** 6074
National University Extension Association (US) **8:** 4732, 4734
National Vocational Qualifications (UK) **3:** 1737; **11:** 6638
Nationalism
  and adult education **2:** 1193
  in civic education **2:** 769
  education and **3:** 1652
  and educational theories **5:** 2609
  and ethnicity
    and adult education **5:** 2946
  and history instruction **5:** 2619, 2622
  and humanities curriculum **5:** 2696
  and multicultural education **7:** 3974
  and political socialization **8:** 4580
  and social studies **9:** 5580
  and student activism **10:** 5779, 5780
Native language
  and foreign language testing **4:** 2360
  reading processes **8:** 4936
  tests **7:** ***3930–3936***
Native language instruction
  and academic achievement
    effect of comparative analysis on **3:** 1832
  heritage curriculum **11:** 6776
  and language education policy **6:** 3437
  and multicultural education **7:** 3967
Natural education
  Rousseau's concept of **9:** 5088, 5089
Naturalism
  holistic scientific **9:** 5029
Naturalistic inquiry
  design **4:** 2079, 2081, 2086
  differences from positivist paradigm **4:** 2087
  in fourth generation evaluation **4:** 2372
  trustworthiness/validity **4:** 2087
Nature nurture controversy
  cognitive development
    individual differences **2:** 845
  developmental psychology **5:** 2660
  genetics **5:** 2660
  individual development **5:** 2647, 2648
    cross-cultural studies **5:** 2648
    Mead's views **5:** 2648
  and language acquisition **6:** 3213
  and perception in infants **8:** 4380
  personality development **8:** 4389
Nature study **4:** 1993
Nazism
  children's literature
    didacticism in **2:** 736
  and curriculum development **3:** 1290
  and religion **9:** 5009
  and women's education **11:** 6747
Need gratification
  education and **3:** 1651
Needs
  adult students
    and counseling **2:** 1161
  concept of **7:** 4057
  definitions of **7:** 4057
    as deficit **7:** 4057
    as discrepancy **7:** 4057
    as want or preference **7:** 4057
  hierarchy theory
    and adult education participation **7:** 4326, 4327
  priorities **7:** 4059
  and transmission in nonformal education **4:** 2365
Needs assessment **7:** ***4056–4060***
  and accountability **7:** 4057, 4058
  and curriculum development **3:** 1321
    task analysis **3:** 1321
  design of **7:** 4059
  and job analysis **6:** 3092
  and labor force development **5:** 2686
  minimum satisfactory level **7:** 4058
  nonformal education
    labor force development model **4:** 2365
  purposes of **7:** 4058
  reporting and utility of results **7:** 4059
  special education
    national level **5:** 2968
  standards for educational **7:** 4058
  strategies and procedures **7:** 4058
  and task analysis **10:** 5913
Negative attitudes
  and individual development **9:** 5404
Negative reinforcement **9:** 4974
  drug prevention programs **3:** 1609
Negotiation
  and program implementation **4:** 2072

Neighborhood associations
  and adult education **1:** 134
Neighborhood centers
  See Community centers
Neighborhood improvement
  and education **4:** 2211
Neighborhood integration
  resistance **2:** 917
Nelson–Denny Reading Comprehension Test **6:** 3337
Neo-Marxism
  critical theory
    criticism of **1:** 55
    and educational administration **1:** 55
  and social sciences **1:** 54, 57
  See also
    Marxism
Neo-PI (personality inventory) **8:** 4398
Neoclassical economics
  and educational planning **8:** 4505
    alternative views **3:** 1814
    efficiency measurement **3:** 1814
    government role **3:** 1816
  and educational technology **4:** 1910
  and labor force planning **6:** 3609
  labor market **3:** 1697, 1704; **8:** 4836
    female participation in **3:** 1666
    informal sector **3:** 1677
    prevailing wage model **8:** 4836, 4838
  and motivation **4:** 1970
  stratification model **6:** 3187
  vs. labor needs forecasting **3:** 1812
  vs. political economy **3:** 1818
  vs. segmentation theory **3:** 1681, 1682; **6:** 3186, 3187
  vs. structuralist interpretation
    and labor force planning **6:** 3609
Neonates
  disabilities
    detection of **10:** 5692
Nepal
  adult education **5:** 2755, 2756
  agricultural extension agents **1:** 252
  agricultural productivity
    and education **1:** 252
  curriculum development **7:** 4066
  educational change **7:** 4067
  educational radio **9:** 5542
  educational research **7:** 4067
  language **7:** 4060
  literacy rates **5:** 2753
  postsecondary education **7:** 4063
  preschool education **7:** 4063
  primary education **7:** 4062
  secondary education **7:** 4062
    vocational education **7:** 4063
  special education **7:** 4063
  structure of government **7:** 4060
  student evaluation **7:** 4066
  system of education **7:** ***4060–4067***
    educational objectives **7:** 4061
    major problems **7:** 4067
    structure **7:** 4061
  teacher recruitment **7:** 4065
  teaching methodology **7:** 4066
  technical education **7:** 4063
  women's education
    barriers to **4:** 2417
Nervous system
  development of the brain **1:** 552
  Kennard principle of development **1:** 552
  myelination process **1:** 552
  neural development
    and motor development **7:** 3947
Netherlands, The
  adult basic education **1:** 101; **8:** 4806
  adult education **1:** 121; **10:** 5639
    expenditure and participation **10:** 5640
    general education **10:** 5640
    private provision **10:** 5640
    promotion **6:** 3365
  adult literacy **3:** 1261
  alternation education **8:** 4962
  andragogy **1:** 121, 125, 275
  apprenticeships **1:** 313
    enrollment rate **11:** 6666
    learning modules **7:** 3890, 3892, 3893
  classroom environment
    attitudes to **10:** 5773
  computer literacy for females **4:** 2426
  computer uses in education
    organizations for **2:** 1015
  curriculum design **4:** 1931
  curriculum development **7:** 4074
  development education **3:** 1496
  education of music teachers **7:** 4029
  educational change **7:** 4075
  educational research **7:** 4075
    priorities **9:** 5037
  evaluation standards **8:** 4745
  foreign language instruction policy **4:** 2340
  industrial training **10:** 5640
  information and computer literacy (ICL)
    objectives of **2:** 976
  information dissemination
    studies **3:** 1551
  information service for teachers **10:** 6008
  job analysis
    surveys **6:** 3092
  job training **10:** 5640
  language **7:** 4068
  literacy policy **8:** 4638
  monitoring of standards **7:** 3907
  nongraded instructional grouping
    Jenaplan Movement **7:** 4156, 4157
  organizational development
    trends **7:** 4239
  postsecondary education **7:** 4071
  preschool education **7:** 4071
  primary education **7:** 4069
  principals
    role of **4:** 1930
  private schools
    and religious minority groups **8:** 4832
  school choice **1:** 591
    research **9:** 5194
  school self-evaluation **5:** 2849
  science education **8:** 4461
  science and society
    integrated curriculum **8:** 4475
  secondary education **7:** 4070
    vocational education **7:** 4070
  special education
    assistive technology **10:** 5670
  state church relationship
    accommodation **9:** 5011
  structure of government **7:** 4068
  student evaluation **7:** 4075
  system of education **7:** ***4067–4077***
    educational objectives **7:** 4068
    enrollment **7:** 4070
    major problems **7:** 4076
    structure **7:** 4069
  teacher recruitment **7:** 4074
  teacher salaries **10:** 5843
  teaching methodology **7:** 4074
  technology education
    programs **11:** 6289
  vocational training centers
    evaluation **4:** 2149
Network analysis
  computer software for **9:** 5558
  limitations **9:** 5559
  and social networks **9:** 5554
Network learning
  characteristics of **2:** 979
  design and implementation **2:** 980
Networks
  characteristics of **9:** 5558
  and educational research
    dissemination of **3:** 1555
  See also
    Computer networks
    Information networks
    Social networks
Neurological impairments
  behavior disorders **1:** 491
  and developmental neurotoxicants **1:** 14
  diagnostic and clinical problems **7:** 4080
  influence of environment **1:** 552
  and learning disabilities **10:** 5681
  learning problems **7:** ***4077–4081***
    evidence **7:** 4078
  neurobiological
    and language handicaps **10:** 5679
Neurological organization
  brain hemisphere functions **7:** 4077
  models and learning **7:** 4079
  stimulation **1:** ***552–554***
Neurophysiology
  and intelligence **8:** 4818
Neurosis **8:** 4815
New Education Fellowship (UK) **3:** 1295
New information technology (NIT)
  See Information technology

New technology
  See Technological advancement
New Zealand
  adult education **1:** ***409–415***
    financial support **1:** 412
    general education **1:** 413
    nonformal education **7:** 4108
    polytechnics **1:** 413
    promotion **6:** 3365
    provision **1:** 414
    rural education **1:** 414
    school community relationship **1:** 413
    and universities **1:** 413
  adult vocational education **1:** 413
  community colleges **2:** 895, 898
  community education **2:** 910
  core curriculum
    sex bias **4:** 2290
  curriculum development **7:** 4109
  educational change
    and governance **5:** 2504
  educational policy
    and economic change **5:** 2506
  educational reform
    and decentralization **4:** 1855
  educational research **7:** 4110
  ethnic groups **7:** 4104
  governance
    schools **6:** 3493
  labor relations
    in education **6:** 3193
  language **7:** 4105
  literacy education
    Reading Recovery **10:** 5791
  Maori education **1:** 414
  polytechnical education **8:** 4607
  postsecondary education **7:** 4107
  preschool education **7:** 4107
  primary education **7:** 4106
  principals
    role of **9:** 5271
  school administration
    and centralization **6:** 3494
    changes in **5:** 2506
  school-based management **5:** 2507; **9:** 5211, 5303, 5304
  school reform
    influences on **9:** 5279
  secondary education **7:** 4106
    vocational education **7:** 4107
  sociology of education
    development of **10:** 5599
  state departments of education
    and educational change **7:** 3839
  structure of government **7:** 4105
  student evaluation **7:** 4110
  system of education **7:** ***4104–4111***
    degrees and qualifications **7:** 4110
    educational objectives **7:** 4105
    enrollment **7:** 4106
    major problems **7:** 4111
    structure **7:** 4106
  teacher education **7:** 4109
  teacher recruitment **7:** 4109
  technical education **7:** 4107
New Zealand Association for Community and Continuing Education **1:** 414
Newborn infants
  See Neonates
News media
  adult education
    francophone Africa **1:** 218
  television
    effects on children and youth **1:** 567
Neyman–Pearson tests
  statistical significance **9:** 5463
Ngoni
  ethnography of **3:** 1753
Nicaragua
  adult basic education **2:** 637, 638
  adult education **2:** 637; **7:** 4113
  curriculum development **7:** 4115
  educational change **7:** 4116
  educational quality
    and class size **8:** 4868
  educational radio **4:** 1905
    interactive **5:** 2887
    interactive programs **4:** 1913
  educational research **7:** 4116
  literacy campaign **2:** 637, 638; **5:** 2696; **10:** 6139
  literacy programs **1:** 170, 172; **2:** 1046; **3:** 1259; **7:** 4247
  nonformal education for social change **1:** 132
  popular education **1:** 133
  postsecondary education **7:** 4113
  preschool education **7:** 4113
  primary education **7:** 4113
  secondary education **7:** 4113
  special education **7:** 4113
  student evaluation **7:** 4115
  system of education **7:** ***4111–4117***
    degrees and qualifications **7:** 4115
    educational objectives **7:** 4112
    major problems **7:** 4116
    structure **7:** 4113
  teacher recruitment **7:** 4114
  teaching methodology **7:** 4115
  technical education **7:** 4113
Niger
  adult education
    nonformal education **7:** 4121
  Center for Training of Literacy and Adult Education Trainers **1:** 220
  curriculum development **7:** 4123
  educational change **7:** 4124
  educational television **4:** 1904
    large-scale projects **5:** 2892
  ethnic groups **7:** 4117
  language **7:** 4117
  nonformal education **7:** 4143
  postsecondary education **7:** 4119
  preschool education **7:** 4120
  primary education **7:** 4118
  secondary education **7:** 4119
  structure of government **7:** 4118
  student evaluation **7:** 4123
  system of education **7:** ***4117–4124***
    educational objectives **7:** 4118
    enrollment **7:** 4119
    major problems **7:** 4124
    structure **7:** 4118
  teacher education **7:** 4122
  teacher recruitment **7:** 4122
  teaching methodology **7:** 4123
  technical education **7:** 4120
  vocational education **7:** 4120
Nigeria
  adult education **1:** 213
    legislation **6:** 3363
  agricultural education
    vocational education **1:** 241
  apprenticeships
    studies **1:** 222
  community support
    fund raising **2:** 912
  curriculum development **7:** 4130
  distance education
    in schools **3:** 1565
  dreams
    achievement imagery **3:** 1238
  educational change **7:** 4131
  educational finance
    and tax allocation **8:** 4362
    vocational training centers **8:** 4362
  educational radio **5:** 2885
  educational research **7:** 4131
  educational television
    large-scale projects **5:** 2892
  ethnography of indigenous populations **3:** 1752, 1753
  job training vs. formal education **7:** 4197
  labor force planning **6:** 3611
  language **7:** 4125
  media selection **7:** 3759
  music education **7:** 4018
  postsecondary education **7:** 4127
  preschool education **7:** 4127
  primary education **7:** 4127
  public education finance
    effect of economic adjustment on **3:** 1787
  public sector employment **8:** 4838
  religious education **9:** 4999
  schools
    decentralization **3:** 1414
  secondary education **7:** 4127
    selection **9:** 5388
  special education **7:** 4127
  special needs students **2:** 717
  structure of government **7:** 4126
  student evaluation **7:** 4130
  system of education **7:** ***4124–4132***
    educational objectives **7:** 4126
    major problems **7:** 4132
    structure **7:** 4126
  teacher education **7:** 4129
  teacher recruitment **7:** 4129
  technical education **7:** 4128
    coordination of **10:** 6064
  technology education
    programs **11:** 6291

vocational education
apprenticeships **11:** 6658
and public sector support **11:** 6648
Nikkyoso (Japan)
and educational policy **10:** 6075, 6078
Noise (sound)
and hearing impairments **10:** 5690
and outcomes of education **9:** 5262
Nomadic schools **7:** 4134
Nomads
access to education **7:** 4134
Nominal data
and correspondence analysis **2:** 1117
and multivariate analysis **7:** 4009
and nonparametric statistics **7:** 4159
Nominal scales **7:** 3700
definition of **9:** 5047
Non-English speaking
compared with English native speakers
academic achievement **6:** 3236
Noncategorical education
and curriculum-based assessment **7:** 3832
and mild disabilities **7:** ***3830–3833***
organization of programs **7:** 3832
and special education **7:** 3831
teacher education **7:** 3832
Nonformal education **1:** 129; **2:** 1046; **4:** ***2364–2369***; **6:** 3418, 3420
access to education
comparative analysis **7:** 4133
for adults **10:** 5593
international conferences **5:** 2959
Nordic countries **4:** 2326
andragogical strategy **4:** 2365
Antigua and Barbuda **1:** 302
Australia **1:** 418
class organization
double class system **7:** 4134
community control **7:** 4133
comparative analysis **7:** ***4132–4136***
compared with formal and informal education **4:** 2368
concept of **7:** 4132
and consciousness raising **7:** 4144
cost effectiveness **2:** 1149; **4:** 2366
cost reduction **2:** 1147
costs
marginality of **2:** 1148
Côte d'Ivoire **2:** 1156
curriculum development **7:** 4134
data collection **1:** 97
data sources **1:** 97
database **1:** 98
decline of interest in **7:** 4145
definitions of **1:** 127, 144; **4:** 2364; **7:** 4141
developing nations **6:** 3421
comparative analysis **7:** ***4132–4136***
policy in **7:** ***4141–4145***
resource allocation **2:** 1150
for development
conferences **5:** 2946
economic and political dimensions **4:** 2366
economics of **2:** ***1146–1152***; **7:** ***4136–4141***
educational policy issues **7:** 4142
efficiency
improvement **7:** 4134
enculturation model **4:** 2365
females in
India **11:** 6751
financial support **4:** 2366
historical background **7:** 4141
and human ecology **4:** 2365
India **5:** 2748
innovative programs
international studies **7:** 4133
level equivalence **1:** 96
Namibia **7:** 4043
and national development **1:** 128
Netherlands **7:** 4072
Nigeria **7:** 4128
and on-the-job training **7:** 4206
out of school youth **1:** 96
Papua New Guinea **7:** 4278
paraformal education **1:** 96
pedagogical strategy **4:** 2365
performance of **7:** 4143
planning **4:** 2367
relevance (education)
improvement **7:** 4134
research agenda **4:** 2368
role of **7:** 4143
Russia **9:** 5102
school schedules
flexible scheduling **7:** 4133
second chance education **9:** 5366
self-financing **2:** 1148
significance of **2:** 1146; **7:** 4136
for social change **1:** 132
sociocultural dimensions **4:** 2367
statistics **1:** ***94–100***
aim of **1:** 95, 97
basic measurement units **1:** 98
identification and monitoring in census **1:** 98
indicators **1:** 99
need for **1:** 94
organization and collection **1:** 97
scope and coverage **1:** 95
trends and issues **1:** 99
strategies **7:** 4144
Sweden **10:** 5869
Tanzania **10:** 5905
teaching methods **7:** 4135
theory of **4:** 2364
transmission theory **4:** 2365
Turkey **11:** 6479
types of **1:** 96
Uganda **11:** 6498
United Kingdom **11:** 6518
United States **11:** 6543
use by revolutionary societies **1:** 132
use of term **1:** 94, 119; **4:** 2364; **7:** 4141
problem with **7:** 4142
vs. formal education **7:** 4197
Yemen **11:** 6791
Nongovernmental organizations (NGOs)
adult education **7:** ***4146–4148***
China, People's Republic of **2:** 748
design and development **7:** 4147
for development **1:** 132
financial support **7:** 4147
implementation **7:** 4147
improving programs **7:** 4147
policy formulation **7:** 4148
advocacy groups **7:** 4148
comparative education **2:** 940
and development education **3:** 1496, 1498, 1499
ideology **3:** 1499
financial support
developed nations **7:** 4146
local **7:** 4146
French
adult literacy programs **1:** 102
international **7:** 4146
and adult education **5:** 2948
international adult education **5:** 2932
literacy programs **1:** 170, 175; **7:** 4146, 4147
use of term **7:** 4146
See also
Private organizations
Nongraded instructional grouping **1:** 228; **2:** ***821–825***; **5:** 2514
ability grouping **1:** 228
and academic achievement **1:** 229; **7:** 4157
compared with age grade placement **7:** 4157
curriculum **7:** ***4155–4157***
individualized instruction
Individually Guided Education **1:** 228
influences on **7:** 4156
open education **1:** 228
research **7:** 4157
student development **1:** 229
theoretical bases for **7:** 4156
Nonmonetary benefits
of education
See Consumption benefits, of education
Nonparametric statistics **7:** ***4157–4163***
in blocking designs **7:** 4161
computer software for **7:** 4162
correlation coefficients
concordance **7:** 4159
nominal data **7:** 4159
ordinal data **7:** 4158
data
classes of **7:** 4158
for interaction **7:** 4162
k-sample tests **7:** 4162
matched-pairs tests **7:** 4160
methods **7:** 4158
procedures
classes of **7:** 4158
relative efficiency of **7:** 4162
repeated measures **7:** 4161
tests for behavior change **7:** 4161

tests for independent samples 7: 4159, 4160
Nonprofit organizations
private schools **8:** 4833
See also
Nongovernmental organizations (NGOs)
Nonprofit supply model
private education **8:** 4833
Nonresponse (data analysis)
and attitude measures **1:** 388
and cross-sectional studies **2:** 1218
effects on survey results **7:** 3854
item **7:** 3857
Politz–Simmonds method **7:** 3857
postratified estimator **7:** 3856
raking ratio estimation **7:** 3856
reduction of
data collection methods **7:** 3854
research on **7:** 3857
reweighting methods **7:** 3855
and sampling **9:** 5141
in school surveys **7:** 3853
statistical adjustment for **7:** 3855
surveys **7:** ***3853–3858***
unit **7:** 3853
Nonschool educational programs
curriculum
and student experience **10:** 5815
and preschool education **8:** 4663
Nontraditional education **1:** ***260–266***; **8:** 4827
characteristics of **1:** 261
comparative analysis **7:** ***4132–4136***
definitions of **1:** 260
fundamentalist schools **1:** 264
future trends **1:** 264
grouping (instructional purposes) **2:** 824
homeless children **3:** 1735
international examples **1:** 262
national indicators **1:** 260
open education
and group unity **5:** 2526
progressive schools **1:** 262
public schools **1:** 264
schools
categories **1:** 260
university adult education **11:** 6549
See also
Home schooling
Nontraditional students
adult students **7:** ***4163–4171***
Nonverbal behavior
See Nonverbal communication
Nonverbal communication
in classrooms **7:** ***4171–4175***
future research **7:** 4174
types of **7:** 4172
and development of language **6:** 3221
educational research **7:** 4171
ethological studies **4:** 2169
influences **7:** 4174
in interviews **5:** 3005
and projective measures **8:** 4791
studies
historical background **7:** 4171
Nonverbal tests
characteristics of **11:** 6344
Nordic Association for the Study of Education in Developing Countries **2:** 941
Nordic countries
adult education **1:** 122, 124; **6:** 3417, 3419; **7:** ***4175–4180***
financial support **7:** 4177
goals and scope **7:** 4175
legislation **7:** 4177
organization **7:** 4176
participation **7:** 4177
provision **7:** 4177
research **7:** 4178, 4179
adult learning tradition **6:** 3376
community colleges **2:** 896, 897
folk high schools **4:** ***2324–2327***; **5:** 2733, 2734, 2735
study circles **2:** 904; **7:** 4176, 4178, 4179
vocational education **6:** 3366
See also
Denmark
Finland
Iceland
Norway
Sweden
Nordic Folk High School Council **8:** 4732
Nordic Research Conference on Adult Education (1992) **1:** 124
Norm referenced tests **4:** 2077; **10:** 6171
and academic records **8:** 4620
and competence **6:** 3469
content specificity **2:** 1184
and curriculum-based assessment **3:** 1356
and educational assessment **1:** 368
grading **10:** 5818
and instructional alignment **5:** 2855
and item sampling **5:** 3056
and item selection **2:** 1184
purpose of **2:** 1184
score generalizability **2:** 1184
vs. criterion referenced tests **2:** 1184
See also
Achievement tests
Normal distribution (statistics)
See Statistical distributions, normal
Normal ogive model **7:** 3701
and item banks **5:** 3040
and latent trait measurement models **6:** 3248, 3249
Normalization (handicapped) **5:** ***2903–2907***; **10:** 5662
cultural values **3:** 1505
daily living skills **3:** 1505
and deinstitutionalization (of disabled) **3:** 1435
mainstreaming **5:** 2907; **6:** 3557
severe disabilities **3:** 1505
Normative philosophy
and philosophy of education **8:** 4449
Norms
school
and role theory **10:** 6220
and school mapping **9:** 5258
North America
aboriginal peoples
and attendance **4:** 1850
adult education **1:** 121, 124; **7:** ***4180–4185***
delivery systems **7:** 4181
financial support **7:** 4183
goals and scope **7:** 4180
ideology **5:** 2732
legislation **7:** 4183
participation **7:** 4182
policy and practice **7:** 4184
provision **7:** 4183
regional organization and co-operation **7:** 4181
research **7:** 4183
teacher education **7:** 4181
community-based organizations (CBOs) **7:** 4146
community development **2:** 906
educational planning **8:** ***4495–4499***
historical background **8:** 4496
ethnography of indigenous populations **3:** 1754
folk high schools **5:** 2733, 2734
history of women's education **11:** ***6761–6765***
information service for teachers
Physics Forum **10:** 6008
learning strategies projects **6:** 3347
literacy surveys **6:** 3478
organizational development
trends **7:** 4238
policy formation
and conceptions of teaching **10:** 6035
speech and language handicaps
incidence of **9:** 5286; **10:** 5692
study circles **2:** 904
teacher certification
alternatives to **10:** 6037
See also
Canada
United States (US)
Norway
adult education **7:** 4177
legislation **6:** 3363; **7:** 4177
research **1:** 124; **7:** 4179
sex differences in participation **1:** 107
voksenopplaering **1:** 112
adult educators
teacher education **11:** 6431
bully/victim research **8:** 4368
computer conferencing
applications **11:** 6302
curriculum development **7:** 4191
deinstitutionalization (of disabled) **3:** 1435, 1437
development education **3:** 1496

distance education
in schools **3:** 1565
educational change **7:** 4192
educational research **7:** 4191
folk high schools **4:** 2325
postsecondary education **7:** 4188
preschool education **7:** 4189
primary education **7:** 4187
principals
role of **1:** 68
regional colleges **2:** 895, 899
school-based management **1:** 592
school reform **9:** 5280
school self-evaluation **5:** 2849
secondary education **7:** 4187
vocational education **7:** 4189
special education **2:** 723; **7:** 4189
teams **10:** 6242
student evaluation **7:** 4191
survey of working life **7:** 3714
system of education **7:** ***4185–4192***
educational objectives **7:** 4186
major problems **7:** 4192
structure **7:** 4187
teacher education **7:** 4190
universities **3:** 1724
teacher recruitment **7:** 4190
teaching methodology **7:** 4191
technical education **7:** 4189
test anxiety
studies **11:** 6358
training statistics **7:** 3714
training survey **11:** 6416
university adult education **11:** 6549
vocational education and employment **4:** 1974
Notional functional syllabi
foreign language instruction **4:** 2342, 2348, 2354
NOW **4:** 2063
Nuclear family **2:** 1056
Nuclear technology **4:** 2328
Nuffield Foundation (UK)
curriculum design
science **8:** 4645
Null hypothesis
alpha level **4:** 2191
and analysis of covariance **11:** 6589
and analysis of variance **11:** 6587, 6588
composite **9:** 5465
and hypothesis testing **5:** 2711
testing
Bayesian statistics **1:** 475, 478
configural frequency analysis **2:** 1033
and correlation **2:** 1111
and statistical significance **9:** 5463
Number concepts
and phenomenography **8:** 4425, 4426
thinking skills **6:** 3673
Number systems
cultural differences **6:** 3450
Numbers
attribution of mystical properties **6:** 3457
Numeracy **6:** ***3453–3459***
in adults **6:** ***3453–3459***
anthropological study of **6:** ***3446–3453***
autonomous model **6:** 3453, 3457
change in meaning of word **6:** 3456
concepts
and computers **6:** 3458
and definitions **6:** ***3453–3459***
cultural model **6:** 3453, 3457
curriculum for **6:** 3458
definitions of **6:** 3456
and employment **6:** 3456, 3458
ideological model **6:** 3458
restricted **6:** 3450
teaching for **6:** 3458
testing **6:** ***3468–3474***
use of term **6:** 3456
whole maths position **6:** 3458
Nuns
contribution to history of women's education **11:** 6743
Nupe people
ethnography of **3:** 1752
Nurse practitioners
See School nurses
Nursery schools **8:** 4666, 4667, 4669
Bell–Lancaster monitorial system **8:** 4667
child caregivers
skill level rating **3:** 1629
and community education
Trinidad and Tobago **2:** 908
day care centers **8:** 4670
developmental programs **5:** 2808
and parent education
United States **7:** 4298
United Kingdom **2:** 695
Nursing education
teacher education for **11:** 6434
Nutrition
and academic achievement
early intervention **3:** 1626
in children
developing nations **5:** 2573
and preschool education
developing nations **2:** 681, 682
Nutritional deficiencies
iodine deficiency **5:** 2565
protein deficiency disorder **5:** 2564
vitamin deficiency disorders **5:** 2565

Object relations
psychoanalytic theory **8:** 4813
Objective referenced tests
See Criterion referenced tests
Objective tests
academically gifted
detection of **9:** 5531
advantages of **7:** 4196
applications **7:** 4193
characteristics of **11:** 6344
definition of **7:** 4193
disadvantages of **7:** 4195
error variance of **7:** 3702
item formats
matching items **7:** 4195
multiple choice **7:** 4195
supply items **7:** 4193
true/false **7:** 4195
and judgments **6:** 3120
in measurement **7:** ***4193–4197***
and Rasch measurement models **7:** 3700
See also
Multiple choice tests
Objectives
in criterion referenced tests **2:** 1183
and motivation **4:** 1968, 1970
See also
Educational objectives
Observation
and facet theory **4:** 2213
objective methods **7:** 4193
and research methodology **9:** 5046
social networks **9:** 5556
in sport pedagogy
research **10:** 5708
theory laden
and empiricism **8:** 4632
and triangulation **11:** 6464
See also
Participant observation
Observational learning
cognitive processes in **9:** 5514
mammalian foundations **5:** 2681
modeling (psychology) **9:** 5514
cognitive processes in **9:** 5514
mass media **9:** 5514
Occupation matching theory
See Job matching theory
Occupational aspiration
in environmental measures **4:** 2246
and expectation **1:** 355
females
in educational administration **11:** 6730
and risk of failure **6:** 3099
sex differences **1:** 355
and sex role **4:** 2411
social psychological approaches **1:** ***354–358***
Occupational information
and education **6:** ***3096–3101***
educational technology **4:** 1926
European Community **4:** 2068, 2069
imperfections in
as a function of increased specialization **6:** 3098
job analysts **6:** 3095
and resource allocation **6:** 3097, 3098
value to work experience **6:** 3098
Occupational mobility
administrators
state departments of education **7:** 3837
barriers to
and training **11:** 6427
and equal education
developing nations **9:** 5537
and facet theory **4:** 2216
and immigrants **5:** 2739
segmentation theory **6:** 3188

and social mobility **9:** 5552
and vocational education
in socialist societies **11:** 6642
Occupational segregation
horizontal
measurement **4:** 2429
measurement
index of segregation **4:** 2428
problems **4:** 2429
by race
over time **4:** 2429
relative attractiveness theory **4:** 2428
attributes **4:** 2428
resegregation by sex **4:** 2431
by sex
over time **4:** 2429
sex bias **4:** 2442
and earnings differentials **4:** 2445
and education **4:** ***2427–2432***
vertical
measurement **4:** 2429
and sex bias **4:** 2431
Occupational status
See Employment level
Occupational tests
Japan **11:** 6697
Tanzania **11:** 6252
Occupational training
See Job training
Occupations
classification of **7:** 3716
Australia **7:** 3717
Canada **7:** 3717
United Kingdom **7:** 3717
United States **7:** 3717
and vocational education planning
8: 4528
decision-making
factors **6:** 3099, 3100
definitions of **11:** 6669
measurement **7:** 3716
power scales **7:** 3718
prestige scale **7:** 3717
ranking of
and prestige scales **9:** 5549
regulation of
European Community **4:** 2067
role of **11:** 6669
and specialization **11:** 6667
teaching in hierarchy of professions
11: 6720
training levels for
European Community **4:** 2067
Odyssey (Venezuela)
problem-solving program **8:** 4729
Oedipal complex **8:** 4813
cross-cultural studies **5:** 2647
Off-the-job training **11:** 6417, 6420
characteristics of **10:** 5915
definition of **7:** 3713
evaluation studies **6:** 3305
Japan **6:** 3090
Office automation
types of **5:** 2828
Office of Economic Opportunity (OEO)
(US)
performance contracts
experiments **8:** 4709
Office of Education (US) **7:** 4051
Office of Educational Research and
Improvement (OERI) (US)
Leadership in Educational
Administration Development
Program (LEAD) **1:** 69
Official languages
and colonialism **4:** 2347
English in the United States **3:** 1231
and language of instruction **4:** 2352;
11: 6362
legislation **6:** 3358
and literacy measurement **6:** 3477
Older adults
adult education **1:** 238
participation **6:** 3376; **7:** 4321;
8: 4613
reform strategies **1:** 160
cognitive ability **5:** 2912, 2913, 2914
maintenance **1:** 236, 238; **5:** 2915
deafness **8:** 4818
educational needs **1:** 234, 235, 238
hearing impairments **8:** 4818
higher education for **7:** 4169
and the housebound
outreach programs **7:** 4247
learning processes **1:** 238; **6:** 3288
memory **7:** 3762
supplementary education
China, People's Republic of **2:** 747
and university adult education
11: 6548
Oman
adult education
nonformal education **7:** 4204
curriculum development **7:** 4204
educational change **7:** 4205
ethnic groups **7:** 4201
government school relationship
school administration **7:** 4204
literacy education
research studies **1:** 326
postsecondary education **7:** 4202
primary education **7:** 4202
secondary education **7:** 4202
vocational education **7:** 4202
special education **7:** 4203
system of education **7:** ***4201–4206***
degrees and qualifications **7:** 4204
educational objectives **7:** 4201
major problems **7:** 4205
structure **7:** 4202
teacher recruitment **7:** 4204
Onservice teacher education
10: ***5977–5982***
case studies **10:** 5978
compared with in service teacher
education **10:** 5978
India **10:** 5979
Indonesia **10:** 5978
Pakistan **10:** 5981
See also
Inservice teacher education
On-the-job training **4:** 1975; **6:** 3304;
7: ***4206–4211***; **9:** 5072
adult education **8:** 4338; **11:** 6417
age and earnings **6:** 3614, 3615
characteristics of **10:** 5915
compared with training with
production **11:** 6446
as a component of school education
9: 5230
and the Comprehensive Employment
and Training Act (US) **7:** 4197
and corporate classrooms **11:** 6393
costs **2:** 1148, 1149; **11:** 6420
definition of **7:** 3713
dual labor market theory **6:** 3184
earnings differentials
effects on **7:** 4207, 4209
Eastern Europe **2:** 659
economic theory of markets
failure in **6:** ***3614–3617***
and economics **7:** 4211
employer support **10:** 5807
evaluation studies **6:** 3305
evolution in **6:** 3304
financial support **6:** 3616
and financing lifelong learning
6: 3424
formal **6:** 3615; **11:** 6417
and general education **7:** 4208
history of **11:** 6682
human capital theory **7:** 4207, 4210
incentives for employers **4:** 1975
informal **6:** 3615; **11:** 6417, 6420
costs **11:** 6423
internal capital market **7:** 4210
internal labor market **5:** 2937;
7: 4210
and institutional adaptation to
change **7:** 4210
Japan **6:** 3090
lifelong learning **11:** 6394
limitations of **11:** 6414
and literacy **8:** 4636, 4637
market failure in **6:** ***3614–3617***
and national training agencies
Latin America **6:** 3265
nonschool-based providers **1:** 108
nontechnical usage **7:** 4206
policies **4:** 1975
productivity differentials
effects on **7:** 4207
rate of return **6:** 3614, 3615
surveys **1:** 109
teacher education **10:** ***5977–5982***
and technological advancement
11: 6281
and technology transfer **11:** 6278
United Kingdom **1:** 109
and vocational education **11:** 6665
and work experience **7:** 4207
See also
Apprenticeships
Work experience programs

One parent family **2:** 1056; **5:** 2624
and academic achievement **4:** 2251
and child development **3:** 1636, 1639
high risk students **2:** 708
and social background research **7:** 3719
One teacher schools **7:** 4134
Online catalogs
libraries **6:** 3396, 3399
Online public access catalogs
See Online catalogs
Online systems
and bibliographic databases **5:** 2823
for courses **2:** 978
libraries **6:** 3399
and multimedia systems **7:** 3991
user characteristics **2:** 981
Ontario Institute for Studies in Education (OISE) **2:** 937
Ontogeny
and phylogenesis **5:** 2656
Open classroom teaching (OCT)
See Open plan schools
Open College (OC) (UK)
and vocational education **11:** 6690
Open education **6:** 3419; **7:** ***4211–4215***
academic achievement **7:** 4214
for adults **4:** ***2183–2186***; **6:** 3434
Asia **1:** 350
characteristics of **4:** 2183
comparative analysis **7:** 4212
and computer networks **2:** 978
concepts of **4:** 2183; **7:** 4212
decline of **7:** 4214
and distance education **4:** 2330
and educational technology **9:** 5541
evaluation of **7:** 4214
history of **7:** 4211
international **4:** 2185
Israel
program development **7:** 4213
teacher characteristics **7:** 4213
issues and trends **4:** 2185
and nonformal education **4:** 2365
outcomes of education
student development **7:** 4214
program attitudes **7:** 4212
program design **7:** 4212
research **4:** 2186
student attitudes **7:** 4214
student behavior **7:** 4213, 4214
teacher attitudes toward **7:** 4213
student development **7:** 4213
teacher characteristics **7:** 4213
teacher education programs **10:** 6064
teacher motivation **7:** 4213
teacher role **7:** 4212, 4213
teaching methods
teacher student relationship **7:** 4213
United Kingdom **4:** 2185
United States **4:** 2185
Open enrollment
adult students **7:** 4166
apprenticeships
Germany, Federal Republic of (former) **11:** 6655
Open learning
See Open education
Open plan schools
and academic achievement
research synthesis **10:** 6238
and educational planning **3:** 1808
See also
Classroom design
Open schools
See Open education
Open universities **1:** 96; **7:** 4138, ***4215–4220***
adult education **11:** 6549, 6550
Asia **3:** 1581
characteristics of **7:** 4217
completion and dropout **7:** 4218
concept of **7:** 4215
cooperative education facilities **2:** 1148
developing nations **7:** 4216
development **7:** 4216
distance education **3:** 1558; **7:** 4215
Netherlands **3:** 1577
economics of **4:** 1907; **7:** 4219
and educational television **5:** 2894
evaluation **7:** 4218
institutions listed **7:** 4216
organization of teaching **7:** 4217
research **7:** 4219
South Africa **6:** 3419; **7:** 4216
students **7:** 4217
United States **11:** 6550
use of term **7:** 4215
See also
Distance education
Open University (OU) (UK) **4:** 2185, 2388; **10:** 5639; **11:** 6550
and audiovisual instruction **1:** 403
and computer networks **3:** 1576
counseling for adult students **2:** 1162
design of
systems approach in **10:** 5900
and distance education **1:** 561; **3:** 1575; **5:** 2628
economics of **4:** 1907
and educational technology **4:** 1894
research **3:** 1577
and educational television **5:** 2894
evaluation of **7:** 4218
historical background **7:** 4216
and independent study **9:** 5395, 5396
influences
developing nations **4:** 1903
mass media role in **2:** 884
media selection **7:** 3758
outreach programs **7:** 4247
and publishing industry **8:** 4692
telecommunications
applications **11:** 6303
Operant conditioning **1:** 495
and language **1:** 496
special education **2:** 861
Operating expenses
and education **8:** 4702
effect of economic adjustment on **3:** 1786
Operations research **3:** 1382
definition of **4:** 1887
Opinions
and narrative inquiry **7:** 4049
Opportunities
learning
and instructional alignment **5:** 2853
Opportunity cost
basic education
developing nations **1:** 468
continuing education **2:** 1146
and cost effectiveness **2:** 1121, 1129
and on-the-job training **7:** 4207, 4209
Optical data disks
CD-ROM XA
multimedia applications **2:** 647
CD-ROMs
advantages **2:** 646
bibliographic databases **5:** 2823
for consumer market **2:** 648
and courseware **10:** 5619
and databases **3:** 1397
development of **2:** 646
disadvantages **2:** 646
and educational research **3:** 1554
and electronic publishing **4:** 1957
hypermedia **7:** 4092
in libraries **6:** 3399
multimedia applications **2:** 647
and multimedia systems **7:** 3993
and special needs students **10:** 5671
standards for **2:** 646
and survey data **2:** 650
uses for **2:** 646
compact disc interactive (CD-I)
characteristics of **2:** 648
and educational television **5:** 2896
and message design **7:** 3773
digital video interactive (DVI)
and educational television **5:** 2896
multimedia applications **2:** 647
educational impact of **2:** 648
and multimedia systems **7:** 3987
premastering
and multimedia systems **7:** 3988
technology of **2:** ***646–649***
Optical discs
acoustic characteristics of **1:** 397
characteristics of **2:** 646; **7:** 3750
compact disc (CD)
characteristics of **1:** 397
compact disc digital audio (CD-DA) **2:** 646
and moving images **7:** 3751
technology of **2:** ***646–649***
Optics
Descartes' contribution to **3:** 1462
Oracy
skills test
characteristics of **11:** 6345
testing **6:** ***3468–3474***
United Kingdom **6:** 3470
use of term **6:** 3439
See also
Oral language

Oral communication
use of term **6:** 3439
See also
Speech communication
Oral history
and audio media **7:** 3749
and biographical research **1:** 541
development of **7:** 4220
in education **3:** 1796
in educational research **7:** ***4220–4225***
implications **7:** 4223
grass roots focus **7:** 4223
and narrative inquiry **7:** 4047, 4048
outside education **7:** 4222
periodicals **7:** 4222
as research methodology **7:** 4221
subjectivity in **7:** 4221
as teaching device **7:** 4224
techniques **7:** 4221
Oral language
parents as teachers
developing nations **6:** 3461
speech communication
skill development **6:** ***3439–3443***
and written language **6:** 3444
skill development **4:** 1958, 1960
See also
Oracy
Oral reading **7:** 3930
parents hearing children **6:** 3461
Oral tests
characteristics of **11:** 6345
Ordinal data
and multivariate analysis **7:** 4009
Ordinal scales **7:** 3700
definition of **9:** 5047
Organicism
curriculum research **3:** 1344
Organisation for Economic Co-operation and Development (OECD)
adult education **5:** 2948
concept of recurrent education **8:** 4957, 4958
development aid in adult education **1:** 132
economics of teacher education **10:** ***5948–5954***
education
and household expenditures **5:** 2979
education indicators **5:** ***2984–2989***
Education and Training Division **7:** 4226
educational activities **7:** ***4225–4227***
educational co-operation **7:** 4227
educational development **7:** 4226
educational finance and governance **7:** 4227
educational opportunities
for adults **1:** 178
educational policy
international education **7:** ***4225–4227***
educational programs
economic and social development **7:** 4226
educational achievement and economic development **7:** 4226
human capital **7:** 4226
objectives, policy and planning **7:** 4226
physical plant **7:** 4226
and structural change **7:** 4227
and educational quality **7:** 4226, 4227
and educational research **8:** 4558
finance for international adult education **5:** 2933
and financial support
international **5:** 2989
interdisciplinary approach **7:** 4226, 4227
International School Improvement Project (ISIP) **6:** 3599
and labor force
job training **7:** 4227
labor force planning **6:** 3609
and lifelong learning **7:** 4227
concept of **6:** 3418
member nations **5:** 2986
levy–grant system **8:** 4361
National Experts Group on Training Statistics **7:** 3712
and official development assistance **5:** 2961
paid educational leave
and recurrent education **7:** 4257
paraprofessional personnel
training of **11:** 6268
publications **7:** 4227
recurrent education **6:** 3420; **8:** 4958
research studies
skill acquisition **5:** 2815
school administration
levels of **9:** 5159
and social demand model **7:** 4226
survey of national assessment systems **7:** 3906
teacher characteristics **10:** 5609
training
definitions of **11:** 6418
international patterns **11:** 6416, 6418
training statistics **1:** 104, 107
transition programs **11:** 6460
See also
Centre for Educational Research and Innovation (CERI)
Organization
of schools **7:** ***4227–4236***
See also
School organization
Organization of American States (OAS)
special education **5:** 2969
Organizational change
and economic change
labor market demands on **3:** 1708
and labor force development **5:** ***2685–2689***
Organizational climate
and descriptive scales **3:** 1477
Organizational Climate Description Questionnaire (OCDQ) **3:** 1477; **4:** 2160
Organizational culture
and technological advancement **11:** 6275
Organizational development
characteristics of **7:** 4236
concept of **5:** 2685
and consultancy
in education **7:** ***4236–4240***
educational
characteristics of **7:** 4237
empirical research studies **7:** 4238
future trends **7:** 4239
historical background **7:** 4236
and industrial training **6:** 3302
objectives **7:** 4236
research
dissemination **7:** 4237
school restructuring **5:** 2526
and school self-evaluation **5:** 2848, 2851
in schools
guidelines **7:** 4238
trends **7:** 4238
Organizational economics (OE)
analytic framework **4:** 1969
axioms **4:** 1969
characteristics of **4:** 1969
incentives
in schools **4:** 1971
transaction costs **4:** 1969
Organizational effectiveness
external influences on **9:** 5374
internal influences on **9:** 5375
Organizational objectives
effective schools **4:** 1930
and organizational theories **4:** 2160
Organizational productivity
theory of **3:** 1691
Organizational research
schools **10:** 6132
Organizational theories
conflict model **6:** 3524
contingency theory **3:** 1741; **4:** 1930
control theory **3:** 1740
and decision-making **4:** 2163
developments
and schools **4:** 2162
in education
comparative management **7:** ***4240–4246***
contemporary developments **4:** ***2156–2167***
evolution **4:** ***2156–2167***
educational administration
cultural context **3:** 1771
and evaluation
educational administration **3:** 1740
fundamental approaches **4:** 2160
historical background **4:** 2157
and industrialization **4:** 2159
interpretative paradigm **4:** 2161
loosely coupled systems **6:** ***3524–3528***
open and closed models **6:** 3524

organizational objectives **4:** 1930
power and authority relationship **1:** 432
public choice theory **3:** 1741; **4:** 1930
radical structuralist paradigm **4:** 2161
rational and natural systems models **6:** 3524
and sociocultural systems **9:** 5308, 5310
and systems approach **4:** 2160; **10:** 5898
perspectives **4:** 2162
variables **4:** 2158
See also
Management theory
Organizations (groups)
as bureaucracies **9:** 5161
components of **4:** 2160
for computer uses in education **2:** ***1012–1016***
listing **2:** 1013
concept of **4:** 2156
and constructivism **1:** 62
and control **6:** 3525
culture of **9:** 5209
decentralization of **3:** 1408
domesticated **4:** 2164
educational
characteristics of effective **8:** 4858
conflict in **2:** ***1037–1042***
power structure **1:** ***432–437***
educational media **3:** ***1797–1800***
effects on outcomes of education **9:** ***5259–5264***
ideological
and private schools **8:** 4833
innovation
and decision-making **5:** 2794
library associations **6:** ***3399–3401***
management of
attributes **9:** 5160
and micropolitics **7:** 3821
professional
educational technology **4:** 1927
rationality in
criticisms of **4:** 2163
and symbolic interaction **1:** 62
and systems
use of term **4:** 2157
training courses
cost effectiveness of **2:** 1136
types of **4:** 2156
use of term **4:** 2156
wild **4:** 2164
Originality
See Creativity
Orthographic symbols
alphabetic **1:** 481
ideographic/logographic **1:** 481
and literacy **1:** ***480–483***
native language instruction **1:** 481
mixed **1:** 481
role of
in reading comprehension **8:** 4938
syllabic **1:** 481
types of **8:** 4938
Orthography
See Spelling
Orthopedically handicapped
See Physical disabilities
Otitis media
incidence of **10:** 5687, 5689
Out-of-school education
See Nonformal education
Out-of-school youth
leisure activities **11:** 6797
unemployment **11:** 6804
Outcomes of education
adult education and labor market performance **4:** 2389
anthropological research **9:** ***5508–5510***
and aptitude treatment interaction **10:** 6156
changes in
factors affecting **3:** 1711
cognitive
information processing model **10:** 5830
and international indicators **5:** 2987
and computer networks **2:** 980
continuing education **2:** ***1084–1094***
and course selection **3:** 1422
and curriculum development **3:** 1492
and data collection **9:** 5263
and decision-making theory **3:** 1423
democratic values **4:** 2210
and disabilities **11:** 6458
disadvantaged **9:** 5508
disengagement theory **9:** 5224
and educational objectives **3:** 1802
and educational quality **8:** 4858
and educational reform **4:** 1854
and educational research **8:** 4424
effect of unions on **10:** 6068, 6070
and effective schools research **4:** 1935, 1937
and environmental influences **4:** 2247
equality **9:** 5534, 5537
evaluation of **4:** 2092, 2094
females **4:** 2411
and general education **5:** 2733, 2734
and governance **5:** 2504
and hidden curriculum **5:** 2587
immigrants **9:** 5508, 5509
impact on working life
and international indicators **5:** 2987
input output analysis
measurement variables **3:** 1757; **8:** 4562
and instructional alignment **5:** ***2852–2856***
and instructional design theory **5:** 2863
and intelligence **7:** 3769
and internal assessment **4:** 2174
kinship studies **6:** ***3138–3144***
and learning
approaches to **1:** 321
learning processes and **6:** ***3315–3325***
measurement
comparative analysis **3:** 1762
quantitative **3:** 1782
standardized tests **3:** 1782
minority groups **9:** 5508
and needs assessments **7:** 4058
organizational effects on **9:** ***5259–5264***
outcomes-based education
United States **3:** 1358
personnel characteristics
effects of **9:** 5262
and predictive measurement **9:** 5040
preschool evaluation **4:** ***2141–2145***
private benefits **4:** 2209
public benefits **4:** ***2208–2212***
qualitative assessment of **1:** 321
and racial discrimination **8:** 4898
and resistance **9:** 5056
and school business partnerships **9:** 5189
school characteristics
effects of **9:** 5261
and school culture **9:** 5260
and school effectiveness **9:** 5221
and science
attitudes toward **9:** 5323
and secondary vocational education
United States **11:** 6535
sex differences in **9:** ***5423–5433***, 5443
and social change **9:** 5056
social change
indigenous populations **3:** 1752
and social stratification **10:** 5731
social structure
social change **9:** 5509
and student attitudes
studies **10:** 5773
and student characteristics **7:** 3881, 3883
women **9:** 5508
See also
Educational benefits
Outcomes of treatment
and experimental studies **4:** 2188
Outdoor education **4:** 1993
Outlining (discourse)
and study skills **10:** 5830
Outreach programs
adult education **7:** ***4246–4249***
target populations and methods **7:** 4246
adult literacy **7:** 4247
Belgium **7:** 4248
chronically ill children
and resilience **8:** 4778
distance education **7:** 4247
and educational counseling **7:** 4248
educationally disadvantaged **7:** 4247
feedback **7:** 4248
homeless children **3:** 1735
older adults and the housebound **7:** 4247
role of teachers **7:** 4248
Sweden **7:** 4247
and unemployment **7:** 4247
United Kingdom **7:** 4247, 4248

use of term **7:** 4246
working class **7:** 4247
Overeducation **7:** ***4249–4255***
effects on attitudes **7:** 4250
effects on earnings **7:** 4250
and employment **1:** 518
and human capital theory **7:** 4250
and job satisfaction **7:** 4250
and labor market **7:** 4249
measurement **7:** 4249
and productivity **7:** 4250
See also
Credentialism
Overhead projectors
applications **7:** 3747
characteristics of **7:** 3746; **10:** 5729
developments **10:** 5727
materials
production of **10:** 5727
uses of **7:** 3758; **10:** 5726
Overhead transparencies
See Transparencies
Overseas Development Agency (ODA)
women's education programs **5:** 2935
Ownership
role of
and program implementation **5:** 2846
Oxfam **2:** 905; **3:** 1497
Oxford University (UK)
moderation procedures **4:** 2174

p-values
and achievement tests **1:** 34
and item bias **5:** 3044
Pacific territories
distance education **1:** 562
Pacing
academic achievement **5:** 2869
educational effectiveness **5:** 2869
and educational quality
vocational education **8:** 4863
instruction **5:** ***2867–2870***
comparative analysis **5:** 2868
learner-controlled instruction **5:** 2868
learning theories **5:** 2868
and programmed instruction **8:** 4771
rate of **5:** 2868
teacher role **5:** 2868
grouping (instructional purposes) **5:** 2868
vocational education
learning modules **7:** 3891
Paid educational leave **11:** 6774
and access to education **7:** 4262
adult education **1:** 156; **6:** 3362
Canada **7:** 4257
and collective bargaining **7:** ***4257–4263***
Germany **7:** 4262
Italy **7:** 4261
United Kingdom **7:** 4262
comparative analysis **1:** 178
definition and scope **7:** 4257
employed parents
child rearing **2:** 697
Europe **10:** 5643
impact in developed nations **7:** 4262
and International Labor Organization **7:** 4257
and job security **7:** 4258
legislation **7:** 4258
France **7:** 4258
Germany **7:** 4258
Sweden **7:** 4260
lifelong learning
and OECD **7:** 4257
and recurrent education **1:** 179; **8:** 4611, 4959, 4960
special groups
developed nations **7:** 4261
and training programs **4:** 1974
Pakistan
academic achievement
effect of parents on **4:** 2414
adult education **5:** 2754, 2755, 2758; **7:** 4267
computer uses in education **4:** 1901
curriculum development **7:** 4268
distance education **4:** 1901
educational finance **7:** 4267
educational finance studies
private vs. public resources **8:** 4703
educational reform
political strategies **4:** 1856
educational research **7:** 4269
enrollment rate **3:** 1826
government school relationship
school administration **7:** 4267
language **7:** 4264
literacy rates **5:** 2753
Mosque School Program
female access to education **11:** 6757
nonformal education **7:** 4133, 4134
occupational segregation **4:** 2430
onservice teacher education **10:** 5981
open university **1:** 563
postsecondary education **7:** 4265
preschool education **7:** 4266
primary education **5:** 2753; **7:** 4265
private education **7:** 4269
secondary education **7:** 4265
special education **7:** 4266
system of education **7:** ***4263–4270***
degrees and qualifications **7:** 4269
educational objectives **7:** 4264
major problems **7:** 4270
structure **7:** 4264
teacher education
administration of **10:** 6064
Field Based Teacher development Program **10:** 5981
teacher recruitment **7:** 4267
teacher supply and demand **10:** 5845
teacher training **7:** 4268
technical education **7:** 4266
women's education **11:** 6755, 6759
barriers to **4:** 2417
Panama
curriculum development **7:** 4274
educational change **7:** 4275
educational finance **7:** 4273
educational research **7:** 4274
government school relationship
school administration **7:** 4273
language **7:** 4270
postsecondary education **7:** 4271
preschool education **7:** 4272
primary education **7:** 4271
secondary education **7:** 4271
vocational education **7:** 4273
special education **7:** 4272
system of education **7:** ***4270–4275***
degrees and qualifications **7:** 4274
educational objectives **7:** 4271
major problems **7:** 4275
structure **7:** 4271
teacher education **7:** 4274
teacher recruitment **7:** 4274
Panel studies
and longitudinal studies **6:** 3518
Pansophia
Comenius **2:** 882
Papago
ethnography of **3:** 1754
Papua New Guinea
adult education
nonformal education **7:** 4278
agricultural education
vocational education **1:** 241
community support
educational finance **2:** 913
cultural influences **7:** 4276
curriculum development **7:** 4192
educational change **7:** 4281
educational finance **7:** 4191
educational radio
interactive **5:** 2887
educational research **7:** 4281
effective schools
and teacher morale **4:** 1931
ethnography of indigenous populations **3:** 1754
government school relationship
school administration **7:** 4278
postsecondary education **7:** 4277
preschool education **7:** 4277
primary education **7:** 4277
schools
decentralization **3:** 1415
secondary education **7:** 4277
special education **7:** 4278
structure of government **7:** 4276
system of education **7:** ***4275–4282***
degrees and qualifications **7:** 4192
educational objectives **7:** 4276
historical background **7:** 4276
major problems **7:** 4282
structure **7:** 4277
teacher education **7:** 4191
teacher recruitment **7:** 4191
technical education **7:** 4278
Paradigms
concept of **10:** 6202
research **10:** 6203
schematic representation **10:** 6203
uses **10:** 6207
definitions of **10:** 6204, 6205, 6206

for educational research **9:** ***5051–5056***
and epistemology **9:** 5022, 5025
incommensurability **9:** 4979, 5025, 5028
interpretative (*Verstehen*) **9:** 5022
Kuhn's thesis **4:** 1998; **9:** 4977; **10:** 6202
criticisms of **9:** 4979, 5025
of planning **3:** 1805
for research
on teaching **10:** ***6202–6208***
scientific (*Erklären*) **9:** 5022
shifts and scientific revolutions **4:** 1999
of teaching
classification **10:** 6206
classroom ecology **10:** 6205
criterion of effectiveness **10:** 6203
extended process–product **10:** 6205
intact teaching styles **10:** 6206
machine **10:** 6204
mediating process **10:** 6205
process–product **10:** 6204
teacher cognition and decision-making **10:** 6206
teaching process **10:** 6204
uses of term **9:** 5025
criticisms of **1:** 56
See also
Models
Paraguay
adult education **6:** 3253
cultural influences **7:** 4282
curriculum development **7:** 4288
educational change **7:** 4289
educational finance **7:** 4286
educational research **7:** 4288
government school relationship
school administration **7:** 4286
postsecondary education **7:** 4285
preschool education **7:** 4285
primary education **7:** 4283
secondary education **7:** 4284
special education **7:** 4285
system of education **7:** ***4282–4290***
degrees and qualifications **7:** 4288
educational objectives **7:** 4283
enrollment **7:** 4284, 4285
major problems **7:** 4289
structure **7:** 4283
teacher education **7:** 4287
teacher recruitment **7:** 4287
technical education **7:** 4285
Paralinguistics
in classrooms **7:** 4173
Paraplegia
See Neurological impairments
Paraprofessional personnel
credentials **9:** 5282
definitions of **11:** 6267
and engineers
comparisons **11:** 6267
functions of **11:** 6267
role of
effect of technological advancement on **11:** 6268
Soviet Union (former) **10:** 5648
technical education
Latin America **6:** 3260
training of **11:** ***6266–6272***
comparative area studies **11:** 6270
in developing nations **11:** 6269
future trends **11:** 6270
historical background **11:** 6266
in OECD nations **11:** 6268
quality improvement **11:** 6271
Paraprofessional school personnel **7:** ***4290–4293***; **9:** ***5281–5291***
educational attainment **7:** 4290
educational effectiveness **7:** 4290
job training **7:** 4291
educational effectiveness **7:** 4291
noninstructional responsibility **7:** 4292
occupational information
comparative analysis **7:** 4291
evaluation **7:** 4292
parent role **7:** 4292
remedial programs **7:** 4293
research proposals **7:** 4292
special education **7:** 4293
statistical analysis **7:** 4290
teacher aides **7:** 4290
Parent aspiration **5:** 2627
in environmental measures **4:** 2245
Parent associations
curriculum advisory councils **2:** 890
Parent attitudes
and academic achievement **4:** 2254
and achievement need **3:** 1237
and aggression
in children **1:** 232
demand for education of children
joint production model **6:** 3101
demand for educational quality
joint production model **6:** 3103
developing nations **5:** 2625
and drug use
in children **8:** 4420
and educational quality **8:** 4866
in environmental measures **4:** 2245
influence on learning **5:** 2626
parent education **7:** 4294, 4295
to primary school agriculture **8:** 4684
and sex roles **4:** 2448
social psychology
status achievement model **4:** 2254
Parent background
and reading difficulties **8:** 4932
and social mobility
models **9:** 5550
Parent child relationship
and academic achievement **5:** 2625
achievement
and time management **6:** 3105
benefits of
and joint production model **6:** 3102
causal models **4:** 1877
and child abuse **1:** 16
and child development **3:** 1639; **4:** 2259
mothers and **3:** 1639
and mediation theory **4:** 1873
and resilience **8:** 4776
and social capital **4:** 2272
Parent education
and children's cognitive development **7:** 4294
and cognitive restructuring **2:** 860
compensatory education **7:** 4294
early childhood education **7:** ***4294–4296***
early intervention
more intelligent and sensitive child (MISC) program **2:** 860
educational programs **7:** 4294
Home Instruction Program for Preschool Youngsters **7:** 4294
effect on academic achievement of children **7:** 4294
and empowerment **7:** 4295
group discussion **7:** 4294
historical background
North America **7:** 4294
and lower class **7:** 4294
methods **7:** 4294
middle class **7:** 4294
parent effectiveness training **4:** 2265
and preschool education **7:** 4298
program effectiveness **7:** 4295
program evaluation **7:** 4295
psychotherapy **7:** 4294
and social support **7:** 4296
Parent financial contribution
basic education
francophone Africa **1:** 469
Parent influence
on academic achievement **5:** ***2624–2628***
education
and sex differences **4:** 2414, 2416
and educational objectives **8:** 4567
and social stratification **10:** 5732
Parent participation
and boards of education **5:** 2507
cultural differences **5:** 2626
in curriculum **2:** 888
in decision-making **9:** 5266
with disabled children **4:** 1977
school policy **9:** 5265
in educational reform **4:** 1855
effective schools **4:** 1931
and learning factors **10:** 5749
literacy development
children with special needs **6:** ***3459–3463***
parent school relationship **2:** 888
parents as teachers **4:** 2255
preschool education **7:** 4294, ***4296–4302***
programs **7:** 4299
school activities
and disabilities **11:** 6459
and school-based management **1:** 592; **3:** 1410
school choice
policies for **9:** 5192
research **9:** 5194
school councils

and governance **6:** 3494
and school effectiveness **9:** 5375
in school organization **9:** 5213
Parent rights
and curriculum decision-making **2:** 889
and history of parent school relationship **9:** 5265
and parent participation in preschool education **7:** 4296
and school choice **2:** 891
Parent role
as paraprofessional school personnel **7:** 4292
parent education **7:** 4294
school community relationship **9:** 5214
teacher student relationship
cooperation in **7:** 3819
Parent school relationship **9:** ***5264–5268***
academic achievement **9:** 5267
administrative problems **9:** 5267
communication problems **9:** 5266
cultural differences **9:** 5266
curriculum decision-making
values **2:** 889
educational experience of parents **9:** 5266
educational policy **9:** 5267
funding **9:** 5267
evaluation of **9:** 5266, 5267
history of
parent rights **9:** 5265
improvement **4:** 2255
interpersonal communication
participative decision-making **9:** 5267
objectives **9:** 5265
problems in **9:** 5267
public relations **9:** 5266
student attitudes **9:** 5267
teacher attitudes **9:** 5266
teacher influence **10:** 6129
teacher orientation **9:** 5267
See also
School community relationship
Parent student relationship
helping relationship
and cognitive development **5:** 2626
Parent teacher associations (PTAs)
community support
fund raising **2:** 912
Parent teacher co-operation **5:** 2626
preschool education **7:** 4297
and social capital **4:** 2274
sociobiological approach **4:** 2170
special education **10:** 5942
Parent teacher conferences
parent participation
and academic achievement **5:** 2626
preschool education **7:** 4297
Parenthood
and health **4:** 2259
Parenting skills
and academic achievement **7:** 4299
and child literacy **7:** 4299
disabled children
health promoting paradigm **4:** 1976
stress–resources–coping model **4:** 1976
and school readiness **7:** 4299
and socialization
via modeling (psychology) **5:** 2625
training programs
in cases of child abuse **1:** 18
Parents
child abuse
ecological model **1:** 16
psychopathology **1:** 16
sociocultural model **1:** 16
and child centered theory **8:** 4457
cognitive ability
and child development **3:** 1640
of disabled children
coping **4:** 1977
stress management **4:** 1976
and educational assessment
reports **1:** 365
results **6:** 3470
employment level of
and social mobility **9:** 5553
psychological characteristics
effect on child development **3:** 1640
Parents as teachers **2:** 889, 890; **7:** 4292; **9:** 5266
and academic achievement **5:** 2625
children with special needs **6:** 3461
parent participation **4:** 2255
problems **9:** 5267
school activities **9:** 5265
Pareto optimality **3:** 1384
Parochial schools
and school effectiveness **1:** 590
Part time employment
and education work relationship **3:** 1738
Part time students
adult students **7:** ***4163–4171***
universities **11:** 6549
Partial credit model **7:** ***4302–4307***
and achievement tests **10:** 5789
algebra of **7:** 4303
applications **7:** 4306
and computer-assisted testing **7:** 4306
constraints **7:** 4305
and developmental stages **3:** 1511
interactive items **7:** 4304
and item banks **7:** 4306
and item response theory **6:** 3251
mathematical example **7:** 4302
multistep problems **7:** 4304
ordered outcome categories **7:** 4304
and ordered partition model **7:** 4305
purpose of **7:** 4303
question clusters **7:** 4304
rating scales **7:** 4304, 4305
related models **7:** 4305
understanding
partial levels of **7:** 4304
variable definition **7:** 4306
Partial hearing
in adults **10:** 5690
and speech and language handicaps **10:** ***5686–5691***
Partial least squares analysis
historical development of **8:** 4353
limitations **8:** 4358
model estimation **8:** 4354
model evaluation **8:** 4356
indicators **8:** 4357
model trimming **8:** 4356
models
inner **8:** 4353
outer **8:** 4354
specification of **8:** 4353
parameter estimation
procedure **8:** 4355
reliability coefficients **8:** 4357
weights **8:** 4355
Partial least squares path analysis **4:** 2137
and attitude measures
science education **9:** 5322
and multivariate analysis **7:** 4011
Partial order scalogram analysis
computer software for **7:** 4308, 4310, 4313
concept of **7:** 4308
definition of **7:** 4313
dense scalogram **7:** 4311
diamond scalogram **7:** 4311, 4313
example **7:** 4308
four-test scalogram **7:** 4314
geometrical depiction **7:** 4308
lattice space analysis **7:** 4311
mathematical formulation **7:** 4310
of nonmetric data **7:** ***4308–4316***
standard scalogram **7:** 4311
two-dimensional configurations **7:** 4309
uses of **7:** 4308, 4313
See also
Multivariate analysis
Participant characteristics **7:** 4316
Participant observation
characteristics of **7:** 4316
classrooms **2:** 798
data analysis **7:** 4318
in educational anthropology **1:** 284
in environmental measures **4:** 2248
ethnography **4:** 2048
and physical education **10:** 5710
research biography **7:** 4319
researcher characteristics **7:** 4316
respondent validation **7:** 4318
role data relationship **7:** 4317
sampling
naturalistic **7:** 4318
theoretical **7:** 4318
and social networks **9:** 5556
social trajectory **7:** 4317
sociolinguistics **4:** 1846
and teacher socialization **10:** 6124
triangulation
data categories **7:** 4317
and verification **7:** ***4316–4319***

Participation
in classrooms
and questioning techniques **8:** 4878
and decentralization **3:** 1407
and decision-making
in educational reform **4:** 1855
education for **2:** 1048
education participation scale (EPS) **7:** 4322, 4327
educational planning **3:** 1822
and narrative inquiry **7:** 4047
and school culture **9:** 5209
and social studies
research **9:** 5581
and speech therapy **10:** 5696
See also
Student participation
Teacher participation
Participative decision-making **2:** 1059
and decentralization **5:** 2792
costs **5:** 2797
in education
and budgets **5:** 2797
and educational planning **3:** 1817
Japan **5:** 2687
Participatory research **7:** ***4330–4337***
and action research **1:** 42, 44, 45
adult education
international studies **5:** 2949
barriers to **7:** 4334
characteristics of **6:** 3369; **7:** 4330
and co-operation **7:** 4333
as counterhegemonic practice **7:** 4333
developing nations
adult education **5:** 2734, 2735
developments **7:** 4331
and evaluation **4:** 2123
feminist
guidelines **7:** 4332
and historical materialism **7:** 4334
issues **7:** 4332
local autonomy **7:** 4335
methods **7:** 4331
objectives of **7:** 4330
origins of **7:** 4330
participants in **7:** 4332
and popular education **2:** 903, 1048
power aspects **7:** 4335
and universities **7:** 4333
Participatory Research in Asia **5:** 2932
PASCAL **2:** 970, 972
goal-plan code editor (GPC) **2:** 972
Patents
historical background **2:** 1099
Path analysis
adult education participation studies **7:** 4323
approaches **8:** 4352
causal explanation **8:** 4340
and causal models **7:** 3870
computer software for **8:** 4349, 4351
decomposition of correlations **8:** 4343
in educational research
and mediation theory **4:** 1874, 1875
effects
direct and indirect **8:** 4343
example **8:** 4357
historical background **8:** 4339
identification **8:** 4344
indirect regression **8:** 4345
with latent variables **8:** ***4352–4359***
computer software for **8:** 4353
and least squares statistics
parameter estimation **8:** 4345
and linear structural relations analysis **8:** ***4339–4352***
models
causal **8:** 4342
choice of **4:** 1876
nonrecursive **8:** 4345
simple vs. latent variable **8:** 4346
specifications **8:** 4344
testing of **8:** 4344
and multivariate analysis **7:** 4011
and partial least squares analysis **8:** 4353
path diagrams
conventions for **8:** 4348
and rating scales **8:** 4926
and social mobility **9:** 5550
and social stratification **10:** 5734
theorem of **8:** 4342
two-stage least squares regression **8:** 4346
See also
Partial least squares path analysis
Patriarchy
and feminism **9:** 5437, 5438, 5439
feminist view of women faculty and **11:** 6724
and history of women's education **11:** 6742
Patriotism
and social studies **9:** 5580
Pattern drills (language)
foreign language instruction **4:** 2341
and language laboratories **6:** 3239
Pattern recognition **1:** 330
expertise in **4:** 2195, 2198
and teacher expertise **10:** 6024, 6025
Payment by results
See Performance contracts
Payroll levies
See Tax deductions
Peace
and development education **3:** 1500
Peace education **1:** 116; **3:** ***1729–1733***
for adults **2:** 1193; **5:** 2733
context of **3:** 1730
learning processes **3:** 1731
objectives **3:** 1730
and peace studies **3:** 1730
and politicization of curriculum **5:** 2467
as socialization **3:** 1731
target groups **3:** 1732
Peace studies
and education for peace **3:** 1730
Pearson product–moment correlation coefficient
See Correlation, coefficients of
Pedagogy
and adult education **1:** 121
ideology **5:** 2733, 2735
for liberation **2:** ***1045–1049***
ancient Greek and Roman
Quintilian on **8:** 4888
authoritarianism **9:** 5547
cooperation **9:** 5547
compared with andragogy **1:** 276, 277
critical approach
criticisms of **2:** 1196
and sociology of education **10:** 5602
and critical thinking **2:** 1206
and cultural awareness **7:** 3971
derivation of word **1:** 274
Dewey's beliefs **3:** 1523
and educational history **5:** 2613
and epistemology **4:** 1996
liberation **1:** 133
and nontraditional education **1:** 262
scholasticism **9:** 5121
social **1:** 275
theories
Herbart's **5:** 2577
Pestalozzi's **8:** ***4415–4419***
Rousseau's **9:** 5088
and values
philosophical issues **11:** ***6576–6580***
See also
Instruction
Pediatrics
voice disorders **11:** ***6704–6707***
Peer acceptance
and academically gifted **9:** 5530, 5531
peer groups **8:** 4365
Peer cooperation
cooperative learning **5:** 2528
Peer evaluation **4:** 2103
peer acceptance
and development **8:** 4366
sociometric techniques **8:** 4366
teachers **4:** 2126, 2129
Peer groups **8:** 4364
and academically gifted
research **9:** 5528
cooperative
and academic achievement **9:** 5171
and cultural continuity **9:** 5217
and culture theory **9:** 5218
instructional **9:** 5171
types of **9:** 5171
and multicultural education **9:** 5219
participation
and adult education **10:** 5594
in schools
ethnography **9:** ***5217–5220***
participant structures **9:** 5219
and social stratification **9:** 5217
and socialization **10:** 5589, 5590
structure
anthropology **9:** 5217
use of term **9:** 5217
vs. schools **9:** 5218

Peer influence
and academic achievement **6:** 3293
and disengagement theory **9:** 5225
effect on children's play **8:** 4541
factors in learning **8:** 4400, 4401, 4402
and learning in school **5:** 2624
personality development
and genetic factors **5:** 2464
proximate
research **9:** 5172
and school dynamics **9:** 5172
in schools **10:** 5756
secondary schools
and effective schools research **9:** 5377
special needs students **6:** 3293
stress variables **10:** 5736
Peer relationship
and academically gifted **9:** 5529, 5530
constructive aspects **8:** 4371
and cooperative learning **8:** 4369, 4370
and discovery learning **8:** 4370
helping relationship
and learning **8:** 4371
and individual development **8:** ***4364–4368***
interpersonal communication **8:** 4369
and learning **8:** ***4368–4372***
and personality development **8:** 4367
problems **8:** 4365
intervention programs **8:** 4367
in schools
friendship and conflict **10:** ***5754–5759***
and social capital **4:** 2274
and social development **9:** 5524, 5527
sociobiological approach **4:** 2170
and sociocognitive conflict **8:** 4371
Peer teaching **2:** 730; **8:** 4369; **9:** 5546
behavioral instruction **10:** 6162
and cognitive development **9:** 5507
critical thinking in **8:** 4370
definition of **8:** 4372
and educational change **6:** 3598
effect on tutors with behavior disorders **8:** 4373
evaluation research **8:** 4370
evaluation studies **8:** 4372
han **5:** 2631
learning experience **5:** 2534
peer influence **8:** 4365
regular and special education relationship **5:** 2906
and school dynamics **9:** 5171
special education **8:** ***4372–4376***
effectiveness **8:** 4373, 4374
ethics of **8:** 4374, 4375
evaluation studies **8:** 4373
issues and implications **8:** 4374
and teacher supervision **8:** 4375
and teacher training time **8:** 4374
tutoring **11:** 6482
and cost effectiveness studies **2:** 1135
and individual instruction **5:** 2771
and Vygotsky's zone of proximal development **8:** 4370
People's education
See Popular education
People's universities
Central and Eastern Europe **2:** 657, 660
Latin America **10:** 5806
Soviet Union (former) **9:** 5096
Spain **10:** 5806
Perception
concept formation
cognitive system model **2:** 1018
discrimination learning
and transfer of training **11:** 6454
and human factors engineering **4:** 2009
infants **8:** 4380
influence of research on **8:** 4559
integrative function **1:** 330
and phenomenography **8:** 4427
sensory experience
and memory **1:** 330
and spatial ability **1:** 330
visual perception
and learning **8:** ***4376–4379***
Perceptual development **8:** ***4379–4384***
children **8:** 4382
separability hypothesis **8:** 4382
and cognitive development **8:** 4380, 4382
depth perception
infants **4:** 2446
enrichment programs **8:** 4383
AGAM project (Israel) **8:** 4383
and motor development **7:** 3950
Perceptual handicaps **8:** 4382
compensation theory **8:** 4382
and attention control **8:** 4383
deaf blind children **3:** ***1402–1407***
effect on cognitive development **8:** 4383
learning disabilities **7:** 4078; **10:** 5681
Perceptual motor coordination **7:** 3949
feedback in **7:** 3949
Perceptual motor learning
development **7:** ***3947–3950***
psychomotor skills
and visual impairments **11:** 6626
skill development **7:** 3949
Performance
automaticity
in expert **2:** 984; **4:** 2196, 2198; **6:** 3323
and prior learning **1:** 376
distinguished from competence **3:** 1728
effects on
and test anxiety **11:** 6357
evaluation criteria **4:** 2113
expectation of
and test anxiety **11:** ***6355–6360***
human augmentation theory **4:** 1923
learning
and motivation **7:** 3943
as learning experience **6:** 3301
and learning motivation **6:** 3301
monitoring national standards **7:** ***3906–3912***
support systems
roles of **4:** 1923
See also
Expertise
Performance appraisal (personnel)
See Personnel evaluation
Performance contracts **7:** 4215
disadvantages **8:** 4713
in education and training **8:** ***4708–4715***
historical background **8:** 4708
and experiential learning **4:** 2185
experiments **8:** 4709
and individual instruction **5:** 2771
and institutions
types of **8:** 4711
issues **8:** 4710
and job training **8:** 4708, 4710
characteristics of **8:** 4714
impact on **8:** 4711
research findings **8:** 4711, 4712
skill development
cost effectiveness improvement **11:** 6653
and trainee selection **8:** 4713
Performance objectives
See Behavioral objectives
Performance support systems (PSS)
and instructional design **5:** 2860
Performance tests **4:** 1847
characteristics of **11:** 6345
effect on instruction **7:** 3724
and employment contracts **3:** 1696
in mathematics **8:** ***4643–4648***
and problem-solving **8:** 4730
reliability **1:** 373
in science **8:** ***4643–4648***
setting standards **7:** ***4054–4056***
See also
Intelligence tests
National standards
Nonverbal tests;
Standardized tests
Performing arts
See Theater arts
Perinatal influences
child development **3:** 1641
individual characteristics **3:** 1638
and resilience **8:** 4775
Periodicals
adult education **1:** 140
for computer uses in education **2:** ***1012–1016***
listing **2:** 1013
content analysis
and teachers as artists **10:** 6084
for distance education **3:** ***1580–1584***
educational administration
international approach **9:** 5162
educational media **3:** ***1797–1800***
and electronic publishing **4:** 1957
editing **4:** 1957

evaluation in education **8:** 4762
library associations **6:** ***3399–3401***
and narrative inquiry **7:** 4048
oral history **7:** 4222
personnel evaluation in education **4:** 2124
in postsecondary education **8:** 4695
research
information networks **5:** 2993
sociology of education **10:** 5598, 5599
See also
Scholarly journals
Perkins Act 1984 (US)
See Carl D Perkins Vocational Education Act 1984 (US)
Permanent education
See Lifelong learning
Permanent hearing loss
See Deafness
Perseverance
See Persistence
Persistence
in children
Japan **5:** 2625
in learning **6:** 3318
student behavior **11:** 6309
See also
Academic persistence
Person–environment interaction **10:** 6155
Person perception
See Social cognition
Personal autonomy
in children
United States **5:** 2625
and disabilities **11:** 6458
in evaluation studies **4:** 2036
and moral development **5:** 2576, 2577
and moral education **7:** 3923
and moral values **1:** 379
Personal computers
See Microcomputers
Personal construct theory
and repertory grid technique **9:** 5013
Personal development
See Individual development
Personal narratives
and biographical research **1:** 541, 542
and curriculum development **10:** 6091
and narrative inquiry **7:** 4048
and student experience **10:** 5815
and teacher expertise **10:** 6025
and teacher knowledge **10:** 6120
and teaching
conceptions of **10:** 6040
Personal space
classrooms
cultural differences **7:** 4172
and nonverbal communication **7:** 4172
Personality
in adult education **8:** 4822
and arousal patterns **11:** 6308
attitudes and adaptation in adults **8:** 4822
beliefs about structure of **5:** 2652
in children
research studies **11:** 6307
concept of **8:** 4388
and educational practices **11:** 6308
factors in learning **8:** ***4400–4404***, ***4401***
and heredity **11:** 6307
infant behavior **11:** 6308
in infants and children
longitudinal studies **11:** 6307
sex differences **11:** 6309
context effect **11:** 6310
and teaching methods **11:** 6308
Personality assessment
and adaptive testing **1:** 51
problems with **11:** 6309
and Q-methodology **8:** 4855
and teacher effectiveness **10:** 6036
by teachers **11:** 6309
Personality development **8:** ***4388–4395***
in adults **1:** 236
resistance to change **1:** 236
biological factors **8:** 4389
Buddhist theory **1:** 578
and Christianity **2:** 761
and cognitive development **5:** 2662
concept of **8:** 4388
dynamic interaction theory **8:** 4391, 4393
ecological model **5:** 2663
environmental factors **8:** 4390, 4393
Erikson's theory **8:** 4716
holistic approach **8:** 4389, 4392
and learning processes **6:** 3289
life events **8:** 4390
mental system **8:** 4389
peer influence
and genetic factors **5:** 2464
and peer relationship **8:** 4367
psychological patterns **11:** ***6307–6311***
in social context **5:** 2662
and trust (psychology) **9:** 5405
Personality inventories **8:** ***4395–4399***
characteristics of **8:** 4395
computer-assisted testing **8:** 4399
conditions for use of **8:** 4399
and content validity **8:** 4396, 4397
criterion-keyed **8:** 4396, 4397
definition of **8:** 4395
in educational research **8:** 4398
studies **8:** 4399
and factor analysis **8:** 4396, 4397
five-factor classification **8:** 4396
and personality theories **8:** 4397
response sets **8:** 4396
types of **8:** 4396, 4397
uses
in education **8:** 4398
Personality measures
development of **8:** 4395
factor analysis **7:** 3705
and projective measures **8:** 4788
and sentence completion tests **11:** 6346
and sex differences
development **9:** 5424
and vocational interests **11:** 6671
See also
Personality inventories
Personality problems
narcissism **8:** 4815
neurosis **8:** 4815
Personality rating
See Personality assessment
Personality Research Form **8:** 4397
Personality studies
attribution theory **5:** 2662
five factor model **5:** 2663; **11:** 6310
history
and conceptual approaches **11:** 6307
Personality theories
and environmental measures **4:** 2245
and personality inventories **8:** 4397
Personality traits
and adult education participation **7:** 4322
age differences
generation gap **1:** 237
cognitive style **2:** 868
and discipline problems **11:** 6308
genetic factors **5:** 2464
and guessing (tests) **7:** 3997
interpersonal competence
and delinquency **3:** 1439
interrelationships **11:** 6675
levels of analysis **8:** 4393
prosocial behavior **8:** 4798
protective factors in life crises **8:** 4718
sex differences **9:** 5434
and social development **9:** 5525
and vocational interests **11:** 6669
Personalized instruction
See Individualized instruction
Personnel
characteristics of
in state departments of education **7:** 3837
Personnel administration
See Personnel management
Personnel directors
and media program administration **7:** 3754
Personnel evaluation **6:** 3616
educational **4:** ***2123–2132***
and employment contracts **3:** 1696, 1698
and personnel management **8:** 4406
Personnel management **4:** 2389
andragogy **1:** 275
case study **8:** 4405
and collective bargaining **8:** 4407
in education **8:** ***4404–4409***
functions **8:** 4404
historical background **8:** 4404
objectives **8:** 4404
and educational reform
United States **8:** 4407
theoretical roots **8:** 4404
Personnel needs
and vocational education
policy formation **8:** 4528

Personnel policy
  educational administration **8:** 4404
  and labor needs **9:** 5234
  and school-based management
    8: 4408
  and vocational education
    new methodologies **8:** 4529, 4530
Personnel selection
  and personnel management **8:** 4405
  and program management **8:** 4754
  and school organization **7:** 4233
  state departments of education
    7: 3837
  task analysis **10:** 5910
    recruitment **10:** 5910
    training **10:** 5910
  See also
    Recruitment
Perspective taking
  explanation **10:** 6145
  programs
    studies **10:** 6168
  and social cognition **9:** 5510, 5511
    false belief paradigm **9:** 5511
Persuasive discourse
  and ability **8:** 4949
  development of field **2:** 1207
  and graduate study **8:** 4950
  and instruction **8:** 4949
  and learning **6:** 3298
    conversational teaching **6:** 3298
    Itakura method **6:** 3298
  logical thinking **8:** 4948
    in children **8:** 4948
    evaluation studies **8:** 4949
  normative study **2:** 1206
  role of attitude in **8:** 4949
  syllogisms **9:** 5123
Peru
  academic achievement
    effect of parents on **4:** 2414
  adult education **6:** 3253; **8:** 4412
  curriculum development **8:** 4413
  education
    and modernization **1:** 252
  education work relationship
    females **3:** 1671
  educational change **8:** 4414
  educational finance **8:** 4412
  educational planning
    implementation problems **3:** 1821
  educational research **8:** 4414
  government school relationship
    school administration **8:** 4412
  income distribution **5:** 2743
  job training
    research study **7:** 4198
  labor force participation
    females **3:** 1668
    and industrial development **3:** 1668
  labor market
    and productivity **3:** 1693
  language **8:** 4409
  occupational segregation **4:** 2430
  popular education **6:** 3256
  postsecondary education **8:** 4410
  preschool education **8:** 4411
  primary education **8:** 4410
  private education **8:** 4414
  schools
    conflict in **2:** 1040
  secondary education **8:** 4410
  special education **8:** 4411
  system of education **8:** ***4409–4415***
    degrees and qualifications **8:** 4414
    educational objectives **8:** 4409
    major problems **8:** 4415
    structure **8:** 4410
  teacher education **8:** 4413
  teacher recruitment **8:** 4413
  teaching methodology **8:** 4413
  technical education **8:** 4411
PETRA **4:** 2056, 2063
Pharmacotherapy
  See Drug therapy
Phenomenography **8:** ***4424–4429***
  analysis **8:** 4428
  applications **8:** 4429
  and developmental stages **3:** 1509
  models **1:** 319
  origins of **8:** 4424
  and phenomenology compared
    8: 4427
  research studies **8:** 4425
    methods **8:** 4427
Phenomenology **8:** ***4429–4433***
  concept of intentionality **8:** 4430
  curriculum research **3:** 1344
  educational research **9:** 5052
  existential **8:** 4431
    Heigegger **8:** 4431
    Sartre **8:** 4431
  and hermeneutics **5:** 2579
  and humanistic psychology **5:** 2689,
    2690
  Husserl's philosophical methodology
    8: 4430
  and interactionism **2:** 1071
  and phenomenography compared
    8: 4427
  and philosophy of education **8:** 4453
  and student experience
    of curriculum **10:** 5816
  and teacher supervision **10:** 6002
Phenylketonuria **5:** 2463
Philippines
  academic achievement
    effect of parents on **4:** 2414
  adult education **1:** 352
    nonformal education **8:** 4437
  adult literacy programs **2:** 1046
  community education **2:** 908
  comparative achievement data
    4: 2136
  computer uses in education **4:** 1901
  curriculum development **8:** 4439
  educational change **8:** 4441
  educational finance **8:** 4437
  educational planning
    textbook program **8:** 4508
  educational research **8:** 4440
  government school relationship
    school administration **8:** 4437
  language **8:** 4433
  literacy education **6:** 3463, 3464,
    3465; **7:** 4146, 4147, 4148
  malnutrition
    determinants of **4:** 2414
  mathematics programs **6:** 3666
  nonformal education **7:** 4133, 4134
  occupational segregation **4:** 2430
  postsecondary education **8:** 4436
  preschool education **8:** 4436
  primary education **8:** 4435
  school law
    and educational planning **9:** 5252
  secondary education **8:** 4435
    vocational education **8:** 4436
  special education **8:** 4436
  structure of government **8:** 4434
  student textbook ratio **8:** 4696
  system of education **8:** ***4433–4442***
    degrees and qualifications **8:** 4439
    educational objectives **8:** 4434
    major problems **8:** 4441
    structure **8:** 4435
  teacher education **8:** 4438
  teacher recruitment **8:** 4438
  technical education **8:** 4436
  textbooks
    provision **11:** 6361
  vocational education **8:** 4436, 4794,
    4796
  women's education
    barriers to **4:** 2417
Philosophy
  and aesthetics **1:** 194
  and Christianity
    Saint Augustine on **9:** 5115
  classification of branches of **8:** 4449
  and educational administration **1:** 62
  educational implications **8:** 4452
  and educational theories **10:** 5813
  nature and limits of **8:** 4448
  program for children **2:** 1207
    United States **5:** 2695
  and rhetoric
    Quintilian on **8:** 4889
  role in moral education **7:** 3921
  and use of language **8:** 4459
  See also
    Analytic philosophy
    Linguistic philosophy
    Political philosophy
Philosophy for children program **2:** 862
Philosophy of education **9:** 5051
  analytic philosophy **8:** ***4442–4447***,
    4449, 4454, 4574
    Peters' influence **8:** 4445
    in United Kingdom **8:** 4445
  and approaches to curriculum **3:** 1310
  Aristotle **3:** 1463
  Comenius **2:** ***880–884***; **3:** 1289
  common sense approach **8:** 4458
  contributions from other fields
    8: 4453
  critical emancipatory **8:** 4459
  critical theory **8:** 4453, 4454

and cultured reflection on education **8:** 4451
and curriculum **3:** ***1325–1328***
and curriculum history **3:** 1303
Descartes **3:** ***1461–1464***; **10:** 5986
Dewey **3:** ***1520–1524***; **10:** 5986
educational history **5:** 2608
and educational policy **10:** 5984
epistemology **4:** ***1996–2001***
and equal education **4:** ***2001–2004***
Erasmus **4:** ***2004–2007***
ethics and moral philosophy **4:** ***2029–2033***
feminist **11:** 6721
Hegelian **8:** 4453
Herbart **3:** 1721; **5:** ***2575–2579***
Herbart's critique of early 19th century **5:** 2576
historical overview **8:** ***4447–4456***
Japan **11:** 6695
Kant's influence on **5:** 2575; **8:** 4453
Kerschensteiner **6:** ***3133–3138***
liberalism and communitarianism **4:** 2031
Locke **6:** ***3496–3499***
and LOGO **6:** ***3508–3512***
Luther's views **6:** ***3528–3531***
as meta-activity **8:** 4449
metaphysical **8:** 4448, 4450
and moral education **7:** ***3920–3925***
moral issues **9:** 5115
and nontraditional education **1:** 261
normative **8:** 4449, 4454
Pestalozzi **3:** 1290, 1721; **8:** ***4415–4419***
and phenomenology **8:** 4453
phenomenology and existentialism **8:** ***4429–4433***
philosophical and religious positions **8:** 4451
Plato **8:** 4448, 4449, ***4532–4536***
views on women's education **11:** 6742
and political philosophy **8:** ***4571–4575***
and postmodernism **8:** ***4639–4642***
Rousseau **3:** 1290, 1720, 1721; **5:** 2576; **9:** ***5087–5091***
Saint Augustine **9:** ***5115–5117***
and self-determination **8:** 4458
and socialization **2:** 776
Spencer **10:** ***5705–5708***
system theory **8:** 4458
and teacher education **10:** ***5982–5985***
and theory practice relationship **8:** 4458
values **11:** ***6576–6580***
Western Europe **8:** ***4456–4461***
crisis in **8:** 4456
writings on **8:** 4452
See also
Educational anthropology
Philosophy of science
biological sciences **6:** 3412
feminist view **4:** 2300
and metaphysics **8:** 4450
and science education **8:** ***4461–4464***
Phoneme grapheme correspondence
spelling **10:** 5697, 5703
Phonemes
and speech evaluation **10:** 5694
target
and speech therapy **10:** 5695
Phonics
beginning reading **8:** 4944
Phonograph records
See Audiodisks
Phonologic programming deficit syndrome
characteristics of **10:** 5675
Phonological remediation
See Speech therapy
Phonological–syntactic deficit syndrome
characteristics of **10:** 5676
Phonology
acquisition
concepts of **10:** 5696
developmental lag hypothesis **10:** 5678
difficulties **10:** 5678
highly unintelligible
clinical research **10:** 5695
evaluation of **10:** 5695
therapy **10:** 5695
individual development **10:** 5694
and linguistics
research **10:** 5695
and reading difficulties **10:** 5678
speech handicaps **10:** ***5694–5697***
Photographs
characteristics of **7:** 3746
and narrative inquiry **7:** 4048
Phylogenesis
and ontogeny **5:** 2656
Physical abuse
of children **1:** 15
assessment and treatment **1:** 18
causes **1:** 16
effects **1:** 17
Physical attractiveness
and nonverbal communication **7:** 4174
Physical capital
and human capital **5:** 2644
Physical characteristics
and nonverbal communication **7:** 4174
Physical development **8:** ***4468–4474***
methods of assessment **8:** 4468
body composition **8:** 4468
Body Mass Index (BMI) **8:** 4468, 4470
maturity indicators **8:** 4468
Physical disabilities
and educational technology
special needs students **10:** 5671
gifted **5:** 2490
mainstreaming
socioemotional factors **5:** 2908
special classes **10:** 5660
Physical education
and athletics **8:** 4466
changing mission of departments **8:** 4465
curriculum **8:** 4465
dance education in **8:** 4385
demonstrations (educational)
educational technology **10:** 6141
health education **8:** 4466
movement education **8:** 4465
school programs **8:** 4465
teaching process
correlational approach **10:** 5710
descriptive approach **10:** 5708
See also
Sport pedagogy
Physical education teachers
behavior **10:** 5709
graduate study **8:** 4465, 4466
preparation
descriptive studies **10:** 5711
skill acquisition
studies **10:** 5712
and sport pedagogy **10:** 5708
teacher education **8:** ***4464–4468***
changes in programs **8:** 4465
curriculum **8:** 4466
exercise science courses **8:** 4465
research trends **8:** 4466
Physical environment
and outcomes of education **9:** 5262
and school organization **7:** 4228
Physical plant
See Educational facilities
Physical sciences
domains of
issues **8:** 4476
secondary school programs **8:** ***4474–4479***
and concepts **8:** 4477
constructivist approach **8:** 4476
and educational change **8:** 4475
and educational technology **8:** 4477
and learning problems **8:** 4476
reforms **8:** 4475
teacher role in **8:** 4477
Physicians
and occupational segregation **4:** 2431
Physics
educational programs
and achievement tests **10:** 5785, 5788
and learning processes **10:** 5785
Harvard Project Physics (HPP) (US) **3:** 1254
and descriptive scales **3:** 1477
Physical Science Curriculum Study (US) **9:** 5340
research method
Descartes' contribution to **3:** 1461, 1463
science curriculum
Israel **9:** 5341
and science history
United States **8:** 4462

Piagetian theory **5:** 2661, 2666, 2881; **8:** ***4479–4483***
and adult intellectual development **5:** 2912
cognitive development **3:** 1244, 1502; **5:** 2649; **10:** 6194
causes of **8:** 4480
cognitive conflict **8:** 4481, 4482
conservation experiments **2:** 853, 855
and learning **10:** 6165, 6166
and cognitive psychology **8:** 4480
cognitive restructuring **2:** 857; **6:** 3154
and controversy theory **10:** 6221
criticisms of **2:** 852; **8:** 4481
definition of intelligence **8:** 4480
developmental stages **3:** 1508; **5:** 2661, 2678; **8:** 4480
criticism of **2:** 851; **6:** 3285
horizontal *décalages* **2:** 843
infants **5:** 2800, 2801
moral development **7:** 3916
and educational history **3:** 1795
educational principles **8:** 4481
egocentrism
and social cognition **9:** 5506
and epistemology **8:** 4479
and heuristics **10:** 6174
and history instruction **9:** 5576
impact on curriculum design **5:** 2667; **8:** 4482
influence on educational practices **8:** 4481
intellectual development **5:** 2912
intelligence
and adjustment (to environment) **5:** 2912
and logical thinking **5:** 2655
and LOGO **6:** 3511
moral development
and cooperative learning **9:** 5545
and physical sciences
secondary school programs **8:** 4476
of play **8:** 4537
and social cognition **9:** 5510
and socialization **10:** 5587
and testing **5:** 2667
theoretical developments **8:** 4482
Pica (eating disorder)
and eating habits **3:** 1516
PICKUP program (UK)
adult vocational education **4:** 2391; **10:** 5807
Pictorial stimuli
concept maps **2:** 1026
and test bias **11:** 6329
Pilot projects
cross-sectional studies **2:** 1218
school mapping **9:** 5258
Placement
assessment **1:** 365
and decision theory **3:** 1418, 1420
decisions
and student evaluation **1:** 364
mainstreaming **6:** ***3556–3560***
special education
options **2:** 723
Plagiarism
and copyrights **2:** 1099
Planned activity check (PLA-check) **10:** 6161
Planning
definitions of **3:** 1804
educational effectiveness **10:** 6032, 6033
interaction
comparative analysis **10:** 6034
holistic approach **10:** 6034
and management information systems **6:** 3595
models of **10:** 6032
teacher attitudes
educational objectives **10:** 6032
objectives **10:** 6033
teacher role **10:** ***6031–6035***
context effect **10:** 6032
psychological evaluation **10:** 6032
research methodology **10:** 6031
teacher student relationship **10:** 6033
teachers
cognitive processes **10:** 6087
participatory research **10:** 6032
for vocational education **8:** ***4526–4532***
See also
Budgeting
Educational planning
Planning Programming Budget System (PPBS) (US) **3:** 1807
Platonism
and teaching style **10:** 6173
Play
and academically gifted **9:** 5530
and cognitive development **8:** 4539
curriculum influences **8:** 4541
definition of **6:** 3220
developmental stages **8:** 4538
dominance hierarchy **2:** 702
ecological influences **8:** 4541
Froebelian theory **4:** 2387
individual development **8:** ***4536–4542***
individual differences **8:** 4540
family influence **8:** 4540
and parent child relationship **8:** 4540
personality traits **8:** 4540
infants **8:** 4538
and interpersonal competence **9:** 5563
and interpersonal relationships **2:** 702
and language development **8:** 4539
media influence **8:** 4541
outdoor activities **8:** 4541
Piagetian theory **8:** 4537
preschool children **8:** 4539
psychoanalytic theory **8:** 4537
sex differences **2:** 702
and sex roles **4:** 2448
and sex stereotypes **4:** 2450, 2451
single sex groups
theories about **4:** 2450
and social development **8:** 4539
theories of **8:** 4536, 4537
toddlers **8:** 4538
Vygotsky's theory **8:** 4537
See also
Pretend play
Playground programs
conflict resolution **5:** 2525
Plowden Report 1967 (UK)
and cross-sectional studies **2:** 1216
family environment study **4:** 2254
Follow-up Study **6:** 3519
and multilevel analysis **7:** 3979
PLUTO International Network Project
teacher education **10:** 6007
Poisons
effect on learning **5:** 2565
See also
Lead poisoning
Poland
adult education **1:** 121, 124; **8:** 4547
history **2:** 656, 658, 659, 660
apprenticeships **1:** 315; **11:** 6643
curriculum development **8:** 4548
educational change **8:** 4549
educational finance **8:** 4547
educational research **8:** 4549
folk high schools **2:** 660; **4:** 2325
government school relationship
school administration **8:** 4547
illiteracy **2:** 657
postsecondary education **8:** 4545
preschool education **8:** 4546
primary education **8:** 4544
public education
management of contraction in **6:** 3605
secondary education **8:** 4545
vocational education **8:** 4546
social science research
and triangulation **11:** 6463
special education **8:** 4546
system of education **8:** ***4542***
degrees and qualifications **8:** 4549
educational objectives **8:** 4544
historical background **8:** 4542
major problems **8:** 4549
structure **8:** 4544
teacher education **8:** 4548
teacher recruitment **8:** 4548
teachers
social mobility of **10:** 5610
vocational education **8:** 4544
administration of **11:** 6644
crisis in **11:** 6644
decentralization **11:** 6645
historical background **11:** 6642
policy formation **11:** 6646
Policy
domestic
and educational policy **4:** 1835
economic
development strategies **11:** 6633
and evaluation research **5:** 2671
and labor relations **6:** 3193
studies
costs **4:** 1836

definitions of **4:** 1835
scope **4:** 1836
See also
Educational policy
Policy analysis **8:** ***4550–4556***
costs **4:** 1836
example **8:** 4552
historical background **8:** 4550
macro-macho approach **4:** 1836
models
percolation **8:** 4550, 4554
of research utilization **8:** 4550
types of activity **4:** 1836
Policy analysts
characteristics of **8:** 4550
and educational researchers
compared **8:** 4550, 4551
and policy intellectuals **8:** 4551, 4554
role of **8:** 4554
and political pressure **8:** 4555
problems facing **8:** 4553
time factors **8:** 4552
training of **8:** 4550
vs. interest groups **8:** 4554
Policy formation
abstracts
production of **3:** 1590
and adult education measurement
7: 3710
behavioral studies **2:** 1124
and case studies **2:** 643
determinants of
cost effectiveness **3:** 1791
discussion groups
and evaluation criteria **4:** 2078
in education
and cost effectiveness **2:** ***1121–1127***
motives **2:** 1123
education finance
and economic adjustment **3:** 1788
and educational contraction **6:** 3606
strategies for **6:** 3607
and educational facilities planning
4: 2225
and educational planning **8:** 4499
and educational reform **8:** 4515
and educational research
4: ***1857–1864***; **8:** 4602
historical background **4:** 1858
effect of program evaluation on
4: 2122, 2123
and evaluation of public job training
programs **4:** 2149
factors affecting
financial support **5:** 2991
private resources **8:** 4707
and federal government **5:** 2510
influences on
effect of educational research
3: 1556
integrated
developing nations **10:** 6035
and intergovernmental relations
5: 2510
legitimatory research **6:** 3368
and management information systems
6: 3596
policymakers
characteristics of **4:** 1858
and educational research **9:** 5054
and educational researchers
compared **4:** 1859
and program implementation **4:** 2072
projections
uses of **8:** 4783
and research
findings **8:** 4599
on individual development
5: ***2670–2673***
relationships **8:** 4559
and school law **9:** 5252
social factors
and school size **9:** 5293
for technical assistance **5:** 3000
and test results **4:** 2078
training
government role in **11:** 6429
and unions **10:** 6075
and vocational education
prediction **8:** 4528
Policy-making
See Policy formation
Policy-oriented research **6:** ***3368–3373***
types of **6:** 3369
Political affiliation
labor relations
in education **6:** 3195
Political attitudes
cross-cultural comparison **1:** 393
development and education **3:** 1651
and educational planning **3:** 1816,
1819
effects of education on **1:** 513
Spencer's view **10:** 5706
students
activism **10:** ***5775–5783***
Political economy
and educational planning **3:** 1817
and educational technology **4:** 1910
and income distribution **5:** 2742
of productivity **8:** ***4562–4568***
vs. neoclassical economics **3:** 1818
Political education **8:** ***4568–4571***
in Catholic schools **8:** 4570
China, People's Republic of **3:** 1292,
1293, 1294
curriculum and practices **8:** 4569
definitions of **8:** 4568, 4569
developmental trends **8:** 4569
future trends **8:** 4571
political literacy
United Kingdom **4:** 1981
Programme for Political Education
(UK) **10:** 5583, 5584
and sociology of education **10:** 5604
universal access to **5:** 2735, 2736
use of term **8:** 4568
See also
Citizenship education
Political influences
and syllabi **10:** 5884
Political literacy
definition of **8:** 4569
Political philosophy
anarchism **8:** 4573
collectivist model **8:** 4571, 4572
Comenius **8:** 4572
Dewey **8:** 4573
education in **2:** 775
individualism **8:** 4571, 4572, 4573,
4574
Locke **8:** 4572
Marx **8:** 4573
modern **8:** 4573
and philosophy of education
8: ***4571–4575***
Plato **8:** 4572
Rawls **8:** 4574
Rousseau **8:** 4573
scope of **8:** 4571
Political power
and education **3:** 1648, 1653
decentralization **3:** 1414
legitimacy of **8:** 4571, 4572, 4573
and multicultural education **7:** 3975
and nonformal education **7:** 4143
and racial segregation
South Africa **7:** 3849
of teachers **8:** ***4581–4587***
Political science
computer-assisted instruction
computer game format **9:** 5562
research on learning **9:** 5562
Political socialization **8:** ***4575–4581***
in adult education **8:** 4580
behaviorist perspective **8:** 4576
and cognitive development **8:** 4576
and curriculum **8:** 4577
and democratic values **8:** 4575, 4576,
4577
education and **3:** 1651
educational anthropological studies
1: 290
educational history **5:** 2612
educational implications **8:** 4580
effectiveness in education **8:** 4579
and family environment **8:** 4579
functionalist perspective **8:** 4576
and geography curriculum **5:** 2467
in Germany **8:** 4578
in higher education **8:** 4579
historical role of education **8:** 4575
historical and social context **8:** 4577
and individual power **4:** 1981
innovative approaches **8:** 4577
in Japan **8:** 4578
in military training **8:** 4580
and peace education **3:** 1730
and political education **8:** 4568
student organizations **10:** ***5775–5783***
in United Kingdom **8:** 4578
in United States **8:** 4578
Politicalization
See Political socialization

Politics **8:** 4582
change
effect on training with production **11:** 6448
and curriculum
effects on **10:** 5592
and educational planning **3:** 1808
of educational planning **8:** ***4595–4602***
and educational planning
support for **3:** 1821
and educational policy **6:** 3367
and educational quality **8:** 4866
of educational research **8:** ***4602–4604***
and identity **4:** 1983
and urban education **11:** ***6551–6558***
Politics of education
adult education
and interest groups **6:** 3361, 3365
changes in **6:** 3492
conflict in **8:** 4587
decentralization of **3:** 1408
democratic nations **8:** 4593
and educational finance **8:** 4593
equal education
vs. decentralization **8:** 4588
and governance **5:** 2509; **8:** ***4587–4595***
in schools **8:** 4582, 4583
and teachers **8:** ***4581–4587***; **10:** 6136, 6137
Polychlorinated biphenyls (PCBs)
and neurological impairment **1:** 14
Polynesia
ethnography of indigenous populations **3:** 1754
Polynomials
analysis of
and interaction effects **5:** 2926
Polytechnical education **8:** ***4604–4608***
China, People's Republic of **8:** 4605
comparative analysis **11:** 6263
concepts and definitions of **8:** 4604
France **8:** 4605
history **8:** 4605
international students **8:** 4607
New Zealand **8:** 4607
Soviet Union (former) **8:** 4605
United Kingdom **8:** 4606, 4607
use of term **8:** 4604
Polytechnics
and adult education
New Zealand **1:** 413
university status **8:** 4607
Poor
See Economically disadvantaged
Popular culture **2:** 903
and relevance (education) **3:** 1363
and resistance to sex stereotyping **11:** 6726
Popular education **1:** 145; **2:** 903, 1046, 1047
and adult education **2:** 635, 1190, 1192
Freire's concept of **2:** 1191, 1192
common features of projects **1:** 133
and consciousness raising **1:** 133
consciousness raising
mothers **7:** 4295
definition of **2:** 903
goals of **2:** 903
Latin America **2:** 903; **6:** 3254, 3255
and Marxism **2:** 1047
Nordic countries **10:** 5643
outcome evaluation **2:** 1048
and participatory research **2:** 903, 1048
Pestalozzi's views **8:** 4415
public popular schooling **1:** 133
for social change **2:** 904, 1047
Soviet Union (former) **9:** 5095
and study circles **10:** 5827
use of term **1:** 112
Popular enlightenment (Nordic countries)
See Folkeoplysning
Popular universities
See People's universities
Popularity
and friendship formation **9:** 5174
peer acceptance
sociometric techniques **8:** 4366
Population changes
See Population trends
Population distribution
and educational planning
Latin America **8:** 4492
Population education **1:** 116; **8:** ***4608–4610***
and Acquired Immune Deficiency Syndrome **8:** 4608
and demography **8:** 4608
and development education **8:** 4609
and environmental education **8:** 4609
and family planning **8:** 4608
historical development of **8:** 4608
information
education and communication (ICE) programs **8:** 4609
objectives **8:** 4608
and population studies **8:** 4609
and population trends **8:** 4608
relation to family life education **8:** 4609
school programs **8:** 4608
and sex education **8:** 4609
Population growth
literacy
and economic development **11:** 6524
Population trends **4:** 2328
and adult students **7:** 4169
baby boomers **1:** 235
and census data **2:** 649
characteristics of
and educational planning **3:** 1450
comparative area studies **3:** 1451
and curriculum development **9:** 5520
influence of education on **3:** ***1672–1676***
school age **3:** 1450, 1451
urban areas **11:** 6552
Portal schools
teacher education **9:** 5314, 5317
Portfolio assessment
and cognitive strategy instruction **2:** 866
effect on instruction **7:** 3724
Portfolios (background materials) **8:** ***4617–4623***
and student evaluation **8:** 4621
Portugal
adult education **8:** 4626; **10:** 5640
provision **10:** 5640
for socialism **1:** 132
curriculum development **8:** 4628
educational change **8:** 4629
educational finance **8:** 4627
educational research **8:** 4629
government school relationship
school administration **8:** 4626
popular education **2:** 904
postsecondary education **8:** 4625
preschool education **8:** 4625
primary education **8:** 4624
public vs. private sector earnings comparison **8:** 4837
secondary education **8:** 4625
special education **8:** 4625
structure of government **8:** 4624
system of education **8:** ***4623–4630***
degrees and qualifications **8:** 4628
educational objectives **8:** 4624
major problems **8:** 4629
structure **8:** 4624
teacher education **8:** 4628
teacher recruitment **8:** 4627
training survey **7:** 3712
vocational education **8:** 4625
Positive reinforcement **9:** 4974
discipline **9:** 4976
teacher response **9:** 4976
Positivism **4:** 1999; **8:** ***4630–4634***
and antipositivism **8:** ***4630–4634***
Comte **8:** 4632
and critical theory **2:** 1199
and educational administration **3:** 1769
criticisms of **1:** 56, 60
and educational history **3:** 1794
in educational research **9:** 5051
educational responsibility
and management paradigm **10:** 5988
and educational technology **4:** 1892
and empiricism **8:** ***4630–4634***
as a foundational epistemology **9:** 5022
and hermeneutics **5:** 2583
paradigms **9:** 5022
scientific research **4:** 1864
and social science research **9:** 5407
and teacher supervision **10:** 6002
and triangulation **11:** 6464
types of **9:** 5054
use of term **8:** 4632
See also
Logical positivism

Postliteracy
  See Adult literacy, second stage
Postmodernism **10:** 5986, 5989
  citizenship and **2:** 767
  and comparative education **2:** 930
  Derrida's deconstructionism **8:** 4641
  and educational administration **1:** 56, 65
  educational implications **8:** 4642
  and the end of epistemology **4:** 2000
  and family life education **4:** 2262
  feminist **4:** 2299
  Foucault **8:** 4640
  and legitimation of knowledge **8:** 4640, 4642
  Lyotard **8:** 4639
  metanarratives **8:** 4639, 4640
  and moral philosophy **4:** 2030
  and philosophy of education **8:** 4453, 4457, 4459, ***4639–4642***
  and sociology of education **10:** 5602
  and the state **3:** 1716
  use of term **8:** 4639
  See also
    Poststructuralism
Postpositivism
  educational research **9:** 5022, 5024
  and evaluation **3:** 1281
  and philosophy of science **9:** 5026
Postprimary education
  vocational education
    Latin America **6:** 3258
Postsecondary education
  access to **8:** 4958
  college entrance examinations
    and test bias **11:** 6317
  distance education **3:** 1559
  females
    Australia **11:** 6731
  financial support for
    United States **11:** 6534
  incentive grants **3:** 1791
  printed materials for
    type of **8:** 4695
  provision for adults **8:** 4806
  second chance education **9:** 5365
  single sex colleges
    developed nations **2:** 832
  vocational education **11:** 6246
    transition from secondary education **11:** 6683
  Western Europe **11:** 6665
  See also
    Community colleges
    Folk high schools
    Higher education
    Teacher education
    Universities
    Vocational education
Poststructuralism
  feminist theories **5:** 2453, 2456
  and individual power **4:** 1983
  See also
    Postmodernism
Posttest scores
  See Pretests–posttests
Posture
  See Human posture
Poverty
  and adult education **2:** ***1045–1049***
  as a barrier to migration **5:** 2944
  and child development **3:** 1641
  and children's well-being **3:** 1639
  and community development **2:** 905
  and high risk students **2:** 708
  and homeless children **3:** 1734
  and leisure **6:** 3377
  and literacy programs **1:** 132
  and preschool education **2:** 680
  and preschool evaluation **4:** 2141
  urban areas **11:** 6552
    causes of **11:** 6553
  See also
    Economically disadvantaged
Poverty programs
  urban schools **11:** 6556
Power
  Foucault's view
    and feminism **9:** 5439
  in legitimatory research **6:** 3370
  relationship with knowledge
    and adult education **2:** 1191, 1193
    Foucault **8:** 4640, 4641, 4642
  sexuality
    and sex education **9:** 5438
Power structure
  and collegiality **4:** 2163
  and community education **2:** 900
  consciousness raising and mobilization **2:** ***1045–1049***
  contemporary issues **1:** 434
  in education **9:** 5296, 5297
    and conflict **2:** 1041
  and educational administration **9:** 5160
  and educational planning **8:** 4503, 4597
  feminism
    and gender studies **11:** 6768
  and literacy **6:** 3455
  nature of **1:** 432
    persuasion and exchange **1:** 433
  in organizations
    educational **1:** ***432–437***
  and participatory research **7:** 4335
  and school organization **7:** 4229
  and sex discrimination **5:** 2453, 2455
  and sociocultural systems **9:** 5309
  teachers and **8:** ***4581–4587***
  and teaching **10:** 6135
Power tests
  characteristics of **11:** 6346
Practicum supervision
  student teaching **10:** ***6000–6004***
Practicums
  and teacher education **10:** 6038
Pragmatics **6:** 3225
Pragmatism
  Dewey's **3:** 1521
    and history of instructional psychology **5:** 2876
  feminist **4:** 2300
  James on **3:** 1521
  and neopragmatism **3:** 1524
  origins of
    United States **3:** 1521
  Pierce on **3:** 1521
Precision teaching **3:** 1356
  and behavioral instruction **10:** 6163
Precollege level
  See High schools
Preconceptions **8:** ***4648–4652***
  definition of **8:** 4649
  sources of **8:** 4649
Prediction
  of academic achievement **7:** 3874
  bias in
    and vocational evaluation **11:** 6675
  and case studies
    methods **2:** 641
  cross-validation **8:** 4653
  and the curriculum **4:** 2329
  and discriminant analysis **8:** 4656
  educational
    expectancy tables **4:** ***2180–2183***
  in educational research **4:** 1873; **8:** ***4652–4657***
  errors in
    and reliability **9:** 4995
  and explanation
    semantics **4:** 1873
  long range planning
    impact on curriculum **4:** ***2327–2331***
  mediating effects in **4:** 1873
  moderating effects in **4:** 1873
  and moderation procedures **4:** 2177
  and multiple regression statistics **8:** 4655
  outcomes of education
    and educational planning **8:** 4517
  and regression (statistics) **8:** 4654
  studies
    characteristics of **8:** 4653
  validity
    and reliability **9:** 4994
  and vocational education
    planning **8:** 4527
    policy formation **8:** 4528
  and vocational evaluation **11:** 6675
  See also
    Predictor variables
    Projections
Predictive measurement
  expectancy tables **4:** 2181; **8:** 4655
  and outcomes of education **9:** 5040
Predictive validity **11:** 6571
  and classical test theory **2:** 787
  and essay tests **4:** 2023
  and factorial modeling **4:** 2241
  predictive **1:** 387
  purpose of **11:** 6571
  and selection tests **9:** 5387
Predictor variables **8:** 4652
  categorization of **4:** 2182
  and criterion variables
    error of measurement **8:** 4654
  definition and measurement of **8:** 4653

and expectancy tables **4:** 2180, 2182; **8:** 4655
and interaction effects **5:** 2927
measurement units **4:** 2182
and regression (statistics) **8:** 4654
and regression analysis **9:** 4965
and validity **11:** 6572
See also
Prediction
Prefabrication
educational facilities **4:** 2223
Pregnancy
beliefs about **5:** 2653
and disengagement theory **9:** 5227
drug abuse
and learning disabilities **7:** 4079
drug use in **1:** 14
multiple
and twin studies **11:** 6488
substance abuse
and learning disabilities **7:** 4079
Premature infants
auditory sensitivity in **1:** 13
cognitive and social development
longitudinal studies **3:** 1519
responses to visual stimuli **1:** 13
Prenatal development
fetus
congenital impairments **1:** ***12–15***
Prenatal influences
resilience
research **8:** 4776
Prereading experience
and reading readiness **4:** 1958
Prereferral intervention **8:** ***4657–4662***
assistance teams **8:** 4660
assumptions **8:** 4658
definitions of **8:** 4657, 4658
future trends **8:** 4661
issues **8:** 4657
participants **8:** 4659
prevalence of **8:** 4658
procedures **8:** 4659
programs
evaluation **8:** 4661
implementation strategies **8:** 4660
rationale for **8:** 4657
related approaches **8:** 4658
use of term **8:** 4658
See also
Referral
Preretirement education **8:** 4613
Presbycusis
See Deafness
Hearing impairments
Preschool children
activities
sex differences in preference **4:** 2451
aggression in **1:** 230
sex differences **4:** 2450
cognitive curriculum for
Bright Start program **2:** 859
deafness
special education **10:** 5661
developmental disabilities
and screening tests **3:** 1621
early childhood programs **5:** ***2806–2814***
educational television **8:** ***4677–4680***
emergent literacy **4:** ***1958–1963***
environmental influences **1:** 359
handicap identification
learning disabilities **10:** 5685
play **8:** 4539
sex differences **4:** 2450
and prior learning **7:** 3764
prosocial behavior **8:** 4797
rating scales **1:** 361
Preschool curriculum
impact of progressive education on **8:** 4668
longitudinal studies **2:** 682
Bereiter–Engelman model **2:** 683
Darcee program **2:** 683
Head Start **2:** 683
Montessori model **2:** 683
and Montessori method **8:** 4669
sex fairness **4:** 2451
Ypsilanti demonstration project **2:** 682
Preschool education
and academic achievement **11:** 6560
Adler's influence on **8:** 4816
attitudes and ideologies **2:** 678
Austria **8:** 4669
Belgium **2:** 695; **8:** 4669
benefits of **8:** 4664
studies **8:** 4664
child rearing **2:** ***678–688***
and cognitive ability **2:** 680
comparative studies **2:** 681, 682
cost effectiveness of **8:** 4663
Denmark **2:** 695, 696
developing nations **2:** 681
disadvantaged children **8:** 4670
early intervention
advocacy **3:** 1628
integrated programs **3:** 1626
models **3:** 1626
and early school start **11:** 6393
ecological/mediating process paradigm **2:** 685
for economically disadvantaged children
and evaluation **11:** 6382
economics of **8:** ***4662–4666***
effects on intelligence quotient **2:** 679
effects of **2:** ***678–688***
enrollment trends
Europe **2:** 695
Europe **2:** 696
extension of
effect of comparative analysis on **3:** 1832, 1834
females
Islamic culture **11:** 6756
Finland **2:** 695, 696, 699
France **2:** 695; **8:** 4667, 4668, 4669
Germany **2:** 696; **8:** 4667, 4669
global approach **8:** ***4670–4677***
history of **8:** ***4666–4670***
investment in
cost effectiveness studies **2:** 1130
Italy **2:** 695
links with elementary schools **8:** 4676
mediated effects **11:** 6382
Montessori method **7:** 3914
organization **8:** 4669
parent cooperative programs
and parent education **7:** 4298
parent participation **7:** ***4296–4302***
policies and programs
international overview **2:** ***693–701***
and poverty **2:** 680
and primary schools
developing nations **3:** 1625
process–product paradigm **2:** 685
provision
developed nations **2:** 694
public education
United States **2:** 695
quality of life **2:** 683, 686
and referrals to special education **7:** 3832
role of **5:** 2497
Russia **8:** 4669
and sex role **4:** ***2449–2452***
sex stereotypes **4:** 2451
single sex groups **4:** 2450
Sweden **2:** 695, 696, 698
teacher response
sex differences **4:** 2451
term and concept **8:** 4666
terminology **2:** 678
concepts and focus **2:** 693
United Kingdom **8:** 4667, 4669
United States **8:** 4668, 4670
Child–Parent Centers **11:** 6382
universal policy choice **2:** 694, 696
See also
Kindergarten
Nursery schools
Preschool evaluation **4:** ***2141–2145***
disabilities studies **4:** 2141
ecological theory of human development **4:** 2141
economic evaluation **4:** 2144
effects on children generally **4:** 2143
effects on intelligence quotient
achievement and school success **4:** 2142, 2143
importance of program quality **4:** 2142, 2144
methods **4:** 2141
poverty studies **4:** 2141
public programs **4:** 2143
studies **2:** 678
longitudinal **2:** 679
Preschool teachers
teacher education **3:** ***1629–1636***
general education **3:** 1631
instructional knowledge **3:** 1632
practice **3:** 1632
professional foundations **3:** 1631
recruitment and selection **3:** 1630
and teacher student ratio **8:** 4663

Prescriptive knowledge
See Procedural knowledge
Prescriptive teaching
See Diagnostic teaching
Presentation boards
See Chalkboards
Preservice teacher education
adult educators **11:** 6434
curriculum **10:** ***5991–5995***
educational administration **1:** ***73–77***
and expectations of professional autonomy **10:** 5920
incentives **10:** 5964
laboratory training **6:** 3198
and philosophy of education **10:** 5985
policy
trends **8:** 4524; **10:** 6037
program content **1:** 73, 75
effect of administrative science movement on **1:** 75
trends **1:** 75
program structure **1:** 73, 74
rationalist model **10:** 5983
reflective model **10:** 5984
and relationship between schools and universities **10:** 5960
relationship with inservice teacher education **10:** 5999
relationship with teacher orientation **10:** 5999
and special education **10:** 5941
teacher attitudes to **10:** 6038
types of **8:** 4524
Preservice teachers
attitude change **10:** 6105
multicultural education **10:** 6105
attitudes **10:** 6105
characteristics of **10:** ***6103–6106***
cognitive ability **10:** 6104
emotional development **10:** 6105
values **10:** 6105
Prestige
concept of **10:** 6224
occupational
concept of **10:** 6224
teachers **10:** 5610
of teaching **10:** 6224
scales
and social stratification **9:** 5549; **10:** 5731
Pretend play
infants **8:** 4538
and parent child relationship **8:** 4540
preschool children
behavior development **8:** 4539
Pretesting
cross-sectional studies **2:** 1218
and test construction **11:** 6336
Pretests–posttests
change
measurement of **2:** 671, 672
and experimental studies **4:** 2188
and instructional alignment **5:** 2854
and meta analysis **7:** 3778
and programmed instruction **8:** 4769
and quasiexperimental design **8:** 4874
and standardized tests **2:** 995
survey instruments **10:** 5856
Prevention
and individual development **8:** 4815
Prevocational education
accreditation of curriculum **3:** 1737
features **3:** 1736
Prewriting **6:** 3207; **11:** 6778
Primary education
academic persistence
developing nations **9:** 5535
and agriculture
Africa **8:** ***4680–4688***
benefits of
and educational finance **9:** 5236
community schools **2:** 907
developing nations
costs **2:** 1148, 1150
empirical studies **8:** 4702
distance education **3:** 1558
educational radio
interactive **5:** 2888
enrollment rate **3:** 1692, 1826
developing nations **1:** 466
equal education
and school mapping **9:** 5256
equality of access **9:** 5535
finance
developing nations **7:** 4138, 4140
instructional materials
role of **8:** 4696
international aid **5:** 2962
World Bank **11:** 6662
investment in
effect of comparative analysis on **3:** 1830
rate of return **1:** 169; **3:** 1662; **5:** 2644
developing nations **3:** 1662
and science education **9:** ***5328–5335***
and vocational cost-effectiveness **9:** 5073
See also
Adult basic education
Universal primary education
Primary health care
adult education **8:** 4808
child-to-child programs **2:** 731
Primary mental abilities (PMAs) **7:** 3874
Primary school agriculture
Africa **8:** ***4680–4688***
characteristics of **8:** 4687
and child labor
Africa **8:** 4686
curriculum development **8:** 4685
and educational finance **8:** 4687
and environmental education **8:** 4683
historical background **8:** 4680
manual activity approach **8:** 4683
objectives **8:** 4681
parent attitudes to **8:** 4684
rural urban differences
Africa **8:** 4684
as separate subject **8:** 4683
survey studies **8:** 4682
and tests **8:** 4686
and theory practice relationship **8:** 4685
Primary schools
and educational television **5:** 2893
social studies in **9:** ***5572–5578***
textbook preparation for **11:** 6363
See also
Elementary schools
Principal components analysis
See Factor analysis
Principals
accountability
scope **9:** 5272
characteristics of
and inservice education **1:** 68
and outcomes of education **9:** 5262
and educational assessment
reports **1:** 365
results **6:** 3470
and educational innovation
implementation of **5:** 2842
ego development **10:** 5937
evaluation of **4:** 2130
assessment centers, United States **4:** 2130
biographical data method **4:** 2130
interviews **4:** 2130
females
North America **11:** 6762
United States **11:** 6727
influence on educational environment
and discipline **3:** 1537
and leadership research **6:** 3282
management style
and teacher burnout **10:** 5922, 5923
and micropolitics **7:** 3824
professional recognition
and organizational theories **1:** 434
role of
cultural **9:** 5269
and educational improvement **9:** 5223
and educational quality **8:** 4870
in effective schools **4:** 1931
environmental **9:** 5270
future trends **9:** 5272
and governance rules **9:** 5271
managerial **9:** 5270
new **9:** 5269
and new relationships **9:** 5271
political **9:** 5269
in restructured schools **9:** ***5268–5273***
school administration **4:** 1930
and school administration **9:** 5167
in school-based curriculum planning **3:** 1268
and school-based management **3:** 1410
and school community relationship **9:** 5214
in teacher evaluation **4:** 2127
and school districts
cooperation **9:** 5223
and school as workplace **9:** 5179

and teacher role
changes **10:** 6081
Print
See Printing
Printed materials
advantages and disadvantages **8:** 4697
bindings **8:** 4695
durability **8:** 4694
functions of **8:** 4696
life of **8:** 4695
minimum standards **8:** 4697
provision
coordination of **8:** 4698
role of
in education **8:** ***4694–4698***
targeting of **8:** 4697
types of **8:** 4694
See also
Books
Instructional materials
Periodicals
Textbooks
Printers
See Computer printers
Printing **8:** ***4688–4694***
binding and packaging **8:** 4692
computer software for **8:** 4689
and computers **8:** 4688, 4689
definition of **8:** 4688
educational materials
image production **8:** 4690
formats **8:** 4692
historical background **8:** 4689
in-house
benefits of **8:** 4694
methods
modern vs. traditional **8:** 4689
monopolies
and copyrights **2:** 1099
and multimedia systems **8:** 4694
and personal computers **8:** 4689
production stages **8:** 4690
and staff development **8:** 4693
textbooks
protection for **11:** 6364
typographic design **8:** 4691
Prior knowledge
See Prior learning
Prior learning **6:** 3342; **8:** ***4698–4702***
and academic achievement
causal models **8:** 4699
and aptitude treatment interaction
10: 6158
assessment
and adult education **1:** 154
cognitive ability **6:** 3314
cognitive development
and expertise **2:** 841
and cognitive structures **8:** 4699, 4701
concept of **8:** 4699
credentials
adult education **4:** 2183, 2185
effect on learning processes **8:** 4700
and evaluation **4:** 2091
and heuristics **10:** 6176
influence on learning processes
individual development **6:** 3286
and instruction **8:** 4648
and learning strategies
teaching of **6:** 3338
and memorization **7:** 3763, 3765
strategies **7:** 3766
and outcomes of education **8:** 4699
preconceptions and misconceptions
8: ***4648–4652***
and reading achievement **8:** 4937
role of
and memory **7:** 3764
and variance in pretest–posttest
scores **8:** 4699
Prisons
See Correctional institutions
Private agencies
voluntary
and educational support **5:** 2979
Private benefits
of education **1:** 511; **4:** 2209
Private costs
continuing education **2:** 1146
of education **8:** 4913
comparative area studies **2:** 1123
Private education
characteristics of
comparative area studies **8:** 4833
determinants of **8:** 4831
differential demand model **8:** 4832
empirical research **8:** 4833
excess demand model **8:** 4831
nonprofit supply model **8:** 4833
and public policy **8:** 4833
enrollment rate **1:** 589
history of women's education
Germany **11:** 6744, 6745
legislation
and curriculum choice **6:** 3358
role of
and educational administration
7: 3835
student fees **10:** 5751
vs. public education
and economic change **5:** 2505
student fees **10:** 5752
Private expenditures
See Expenditures, private
Private financial support
student fees **4:** 2313; **10:** 5752
See also
Private resources
Private organizations
and community development
Latin America **7:** 4153
and educational finance
Latin America **7:** 4154
roles of
Latin America **7:** 4154
and small business training **4:** 1988
and training programs
Latin America **7:** 4149
and vocational education
approaches to **7:** 4152
for the disadvantaged **7:** ***4148–4155***
historical background **7:** 4149
post school programs **11:** 6246
See also
Nongovernmental organizations
(NGOs)
Private resources
for education
classification **8:** 4703
input output analysis **8:** 4702
and educational resources
inequality in **8:** 4705
policy formation
factors affecting **8:** 4707
vs. public educational expenditure
8: 4703
See also
Private financial support
Private school aid
and school choice **9:** 5200
Private schools
characteristics of **8:** 4840
costs
in developing nations **8:** ***4702–4708***
definitions of **8:** 4826, 4831
and educational finance **6:** 3275;
9: 5235
enrollment
developed nations **8:** 4824
developing nations **8:** 4824, 4825
female blacks
South Africa **7:** 3852
females
Egypt **11:** 6754
Turkey **11:** 6754
financial support **8:** 4826, 4829
ideology **8:** 4825
impact on educational attainment
8: 4824
impact on society **8:** 4824
minority groups **8:** 4824, 4827
and nontraditional education
national indicators **1:** 260
power structure **7:** 4229
religious
and legislation **9:** 5012
school effectiveness **8:** 4827
and second chance education **9:** 5365
sociological perspective **8:** ***4824–4831***
teacher certification **10:** 5928
vocational education
Japan **6:** 3089; **11:** 6696
vs. public schools
research controversies
8: ***4839–4845***
vs. state schools
and private resources **8:** 4706
and student fees **10:** 5750
See also
Proprietary schools
Private sector
and educational planning **3:** 1813
effect on public schools **8:** 4828
links with public education
8: ***4337–4339***
and performance contracts **8:** 4712
and resource allocation **9:** 5063

textbook preparation **11:** 6363
training
markets for **11:** 6425
and vocational education **5:** 2816; **8:** ***4792–4796***; **11:** 6247
developing nations **11:** 6648
vs. public sector
and educational responsibility **8:** ***4831–4836***
job training **7:** 4198
and sociology of education **10:** 5604
Privatization
of education
and educational technology **9:** 5543
and educational finance **5:** 2506
and educational planning **3:** 1813
public education
and resource allocation **9:** 5063
and school choice **5:** 2498; **9:** ***5192–5197***; **11:** 6556
and school support **3:** 1826
of schools
pressures toward **8:** 4824
of vocational education **11:** 6649
Central and Eastern Europe **11:** 6641
constraints **11:** 6652
Probability
and Bayesian statistics **1:** 475
bootstrap procedure **9:** 5470
and cognitive development **6:** 3682
and configural frequency analysis **2:** 1032
and density distributions **1:** 478
elementary school programs **6:** 3672, 3682
and expectancy tables **4:** 2181
high school curriculum **6:** 3682
and item response theory **5:** 3051
and latent trait measurement models **6:** 3249
and logit models **6:** 3504
mathematics curriculum **6:** 3681
Monte Carlo methods **9:** 5468
and nonparametric statistics **7:** 4158
and partial credit model **7:** 4303
posterior distributions **1:** 478
prior distributions **1:** 478
and Rasch measurement models **8:** 4903
and rating scales **8:** 4919
and research methodology **9:** 5048
and research synthesis **7:** 3775
sampling **9:** 5132
simulation **9:** 5468
and statistical significance **9:** 5461
theory
alternative approaches **1:** 476
background to **1:** 476
and Thurstone scales **11:** 6385, 6386, 6387
Problem-solving **6:** 3457; **8:** 4820
and affective behavior **6:** 3640
classroom ethnography **2:** 799
and cognitive development **2:** 1019
cognitive processes **8:** 4724
creative development **2:** 1181
cognitive strategy instruction **2:** 861
cognitive style **8:** 4724
and comprehension program **2:** 862
and computer literacy **2:** 974
computer simulation **8:** ***4719–4722***
schemata **8:** 4720
search process **8:** 4720
constraint inclusion theory **4:** 2300
cooperative
and prereferral intervention **8:** 4659
coping in crises **8:** 4718
and creativity **2:** 1177
daily living skills **8:** 4726
deduction
in children **8:** 4953
definition of **8:** 4723
Dewey's pragmatic approach **3:** 1522
educational research
historical overview **8:** 4726
and educational research utilization **4:** 1862
and educational technology **4:** 1891
expert novice research **8:** 4727
heuristic models in **5:** 2881
information processing approach **8:** 4725
instruction
feedback **4:** 2280, 2281
intellectual disciplines **8:** 4727
and interactive video **11:** 6601
learning environments **6:** 3299
learning strategies **8:** ***4722–4728***
and learning theories **6:** 3340
mathematics
history of instruction **6:** 3643
mathematics education
design principals **8:** 4644
and mathematics instruction **8:** 4643
metacognition
executive control **7:** 3785
and motivation techniques **7:** 3945
nature of **5:** 2721
objectives of **5:** 2722
personal
and prereferral intervention **8:** 4659
and policy analysis **4:** 1836
problem representation
evaluation of **4:** 2198
expert approach **4:** 2195, 2197
and programming **2:** 982
research
and videotape recordings **11:** 6604
research projects **8:** 4726
role of facilitator **6:** 3346
science education
design principles **8:** 4646
skills
effect of LOGO on children's **2:** 1005
resilient children **8:** 4778
and social studies **9:** 5576
solution choice **10:** 5897
special needs students
microcomputers **7:** 3804
strategies
and cost effectiveness studies **2:** 1138
systematic **10:** 5896
systems approach to **10:** 5895
task analysis **8:** 4725
and teacher expertise **10:** 6024, 6025
teaching of
and assessment **8:** 4643
definitions of **8:** 4728
history **8:** 4728
programs **8:** 4729
theoretical framework **8:** 4728
teaching and testing for **8:** ***4728–4731***
and team teaching **10:** 6240
testable aspects of **8:** 4729
tests
future trends **8:** 4730
reliability **8:** 4730
validity **8:** 4730
use of educational media in **7:** 3742
See also
Creative thinking
Problems
Problems
categories **8:** 4715
coping with
and educational change **6:** 3601
definitions of **8:** 4722; **10:** 5896
individual development **8:** ***4715–4719***
nature of **5:** 2721
resolution strategies **5:** 2721
types of **5:** 2721; **8:** 4723
See also
Problem-solving
Word problems (mathematics)
Procedural knowledge **3:** ***1432–1434***; **6:** 3153; **8:** 4821; **10:** 5740
and artificial intelligence **5:** 2919
and cognitive development **2:** 855
and cognitive psychology **3:** 1432
concept formation
and long term memory **2:** 1018
definition of **3:** 1432
examples and characteristics of **3:** 1432
experts' use of **4:** 2196, 2197
females
intellectual development **10:** 5938
and heuristic structure **3:** 1433
learning **6:** 3319
learning strategies
and second language learning **6:** 3332
skill development **6:** 3323
See also
Expertise
Process education
and science education **9:** 5329
Process product research
paradigm of **10:** 6204
and teacher behavior **10:** 6013
Product development
and project evaluation **8:** 4781

Product–moment correlation
See Correlation, product–moment
Production
informal
educational factors **3:** 1678
technological advancement
and economic change **3:** 1707
Production functions
See Productivity
Production techniques
educational television **5:** 2895
and media programs **7:** 3754
multimedia systems **7:** 3988, 3989
videotape recordings **11:** 6606
Productive thinking **8:** 4723, 4724
explanation and **10:** 6146
model of **2:** 1178
Productive Thinking Program **8:** 4729
Productivity **3:** 1660, ***1756–1762***
in agriculture
and academic achievement **5:** 2944
barriers to
democracy **9:** 5203
and brain drain **1:** 557
classroom autonomy
vs. educational administration
8: 4563
and comparative international
indicators **5:** 2985
and continuing education **2:** 1087,
1088
and control of educational resources
7: 3817
and cost effectiveness **2:** 1121
and decentralization **5:** 2795
disequilibrium theory of **3:** 1691
earnings **9:** 5351
and on-the-job training **6:** 3615
and training **11:** 6418
earnings differentials
as a measure of **11:** 6629
and racial discrimination **1:** 517
and education **3:** ***1660–1666***
of farmers **3:** 1665
joint production model
6: ***3101–3106***
research studies **11:** 6628
in education
vintage effects **11:** 6614
education and industrial **3:** 1693
and educational quality
policy models **8:** 4867
and educational research **5:** 2507
effect on education
screening hypothesis **9:** ***5350–5355***
effects of education on **3:** ***1660–1666***,
1690–1695, 1704; **11:** 6420,
6421
screening hypothesis **1:** 517;
9: 5350
and social class **3:** 1704
women's education **4:** 2414
effects of group size on **7:** 3818
empirical research **3:** 1692
correlational studies **3:** 1692
and equal education
developing nations **9:** 5536
and group dynamics **11:** 6629
human capital **5:** 2644
human capital theory of **3:** 1678, 1691
informal sector **3:** 1678
international studies
comparative analysis **3:** 1762
and job competition model **5:** 2742
and job training **2:** 1089
measurement
vs. earnings differentials **8:** 4913
measurement of educational **3:** 1383
resource-based models **3:** 1383
and microeconomics **7:** ***3816–3821***
and need for industry training **7:** 3711
and nonformal education **2:** 1146;
4: 2366; **7:** 4137
and occupational segregation **4:** 2427
organizational
theory of **3:** 1691
and overeducation **7:** 4250
and political economy **8:** ***4562–4568***
research
and secondary data analysis **9:** 5371
research studies
and educational benefits **1:** 515
and resource allocation **7:** 3817
and school enterprise
historical background **9:** 5229
skills theory of **3:** 1691
standard economics models
vs. educational models **7:** 3816
and statistical discrimination **4:** 2444
of teacher educators
and log-linear models **6:** 3501
and technological advancement
11: 6280
and technology
educational inputs **4:** 1903
theory of educational
and evaluation **11:** 6382
traditional analysis
criticism of **8:** 4562
trainability theory of **3:** 1691
and training courses **2:** 1138
and unions **10:** 6068
and vocational education **9:** 5072;
11: ***6628–6633***
Anglo–German comparisons
11: 6639
China, People's Republic of **2:** 759
more cooperative vs. less
cooperative hypothesis
11: 6630
and work effort **11:** 6629
See also
Input output analysis
Productivity differentials
effects on
on-the-job training model **7:** 4207
vintage effects **11:** 6614
Productivity profiles
characteristics of **7:** 3819
teaching skills in **7:** 3819
Professional associations
adult education **8:** ***4731–4736***
benefits **8:** 4734
description **8:** 4732, 4734
directory **8:** 4733
harmful effects **8:** 4735
international **8:** 4732
issues in **8:** 4735
national **8:** 4733
networks **8:** 4734
purposes **8:** 4733
regional **8:** 4732
research **8:** 4735
typology **8:** 4735
United Kingdom **8:** 4731, 4732
United States **8:** 4731
Professional autonomy
and curriculum **10:** 6089, 6090
and curriculum development **3:** 1346
and governance of teacher education
10: 5962
international studies
comparative analysis **10:** 6153
and power structure **8:** 4584
and reproduction theory **9:** 5019
and teacher qualifications **6:** 3275
vs. bureaucratic control **4:** 2162
Professional continuing education **1:** 91;
6: 3416, 3417; **8:** 4338
financial support **1:** 91
and labor force development **5:** 2686
mandatory **8:** 4806
provision **8:** 4806
teacher education **10:** 5964
telecommunications **10:** 6007
Professional development
and adult educators **10:** 6057
and computer networks **2:** 978
inservice teacher education **4:** 2127
case studies **4:** 2127
and professional associations
adult education **8:** 4734
special education teachers **10:** 5941
teacher role **10:** 6179
use of evaluation for **4:** 2127
Professional development schools
definition of **9:** 5315
future of **9:** 5317
history of **9:** 5315
Holmes Group **10:** 5811
United States **4:** 2125
organization and activities **9:** 5315
teacher education **9:** ***5313–5318***
United States **10:** 6004
themes **9:** 5316
Professional education
Soviet Union (former) **9:** 5094
Professional occupations
codes of ethics
feminist ethic of care **4:** 2295
criteria
functionalist theory **10:** 6092
teaching **10:** 6093
in educational technology **4:** 1925
fundamental concepts **10:** 6093
social science research

sociology **10:** 6092
social theories
criticism of **10:** 6093
Professional personnel
categories of
educational technology **4:** 1926
in education
evaluation of **4:** ***2123–2132***;
8: 4737, 4745, 4746
use of evaluation in training of
4: 2124
international assistance experts
5: 2973
in schools
related services **9:** ***5281–5291***
support personnel
evaluation methods **4:** 2124, 2130
See also
Faculty
Professional recognition
and adult education **10:** 5595
and criterion referenced tests **2:** 1188
and educational technology **7:** 3755
ideology
and power structure **8:** 4584
teachers **5:** 2498; **6:** 3275; **10:** 6082
and organizational theories **1:** 434
teaching **9:** 5178; **10:** 5611
Professional standards
evaluation **4:** 2034, ***2123–2132***;
8: ***4736–4751***
accuracy **4:** 2034, 2079, 2124;
8: 4739
feasibility **4:** 2034, 2079, 2124;
8: 4739
propriety **4:** 2034, 2079, 2124;
8: 4739
utility **4:** 2034, 2079, 2124; **8:** 4739
See also
Standards
Professional standards and practices boards
and teacher unions **10:** 5928
Professional training
educational technology **4:** 1926
Professionalization
feminist critique of **11:** 6720, 6721
and sex discrimination **11:** 6719
of teaching
and females **11:** ***6719–6723***
and vocational education **11:** 6683
Professors
of educational administration **1:** 74
females **11:** 6710
teacher educators
historical background **3:** 1721, 1722, 1723
Profile analysis **8:** ***4752–4754***
definitions of **8:** 4752
Pearson product–moment correlation coefficient **8:** 4753
reliability **8:** 4753
of student evaluations of teacher effectiveness **10:** 6230
use of **8:** 4753
See also
Profiles
Profiles
advantages of **8:** 4618
characteristics of **8:** 4752
comparison of **8:** 4752
definitions of **8:** 4752
development of **8:** 4618
disadvantages of **8:** 4620
and examinations **8:** 4618
formats **8:** 4619
historical background **8:** 4618
and moderator effects **8:** 4753
and partial order scalogram analysis
7: 4308
prior learning in **8:** 4701
recording problems **8:** 4620
score **8:** 4752
student evaluation **8:** ***4617–4623***
technical issues **8:** 4621
use of term **8:** 4618
visual display of **8:** 4752
See also
Profile analysis
Profoundly hearing impaired
See Deafness
Program administration
See Program management
Program budgeting
and school administration **9:** 5183
Program content
characteristics of
and audiovisual aids **1:** 401
and educational planning
failure **8:** 4596
Program design
and implementation **3:** ***1491–1494***
for small business training
factors affecting **4:** 1989
Program development
and cultural differences **3:** ***1233–1236***, 1234
issues in generalizing **3:** 1236
ethnography and **3:** ***1233–1236***
functions **8:** 4754
instructional
occupations **4:** 1926
Program effectiveness
and cost effectiveness **2:** 1131
Program evaluation **4:** 2090, 2369;
5: 2766; **8:** ***4758–4766***
adult education **4:** ***2119–2123***;
10: 6201
older adults **4:** 2122
adversarial approaches **3:** 1282;
4: 2103
applied ethics **4:** 2034, 2035
connoisseurship model
curriculum evaluation **3:** 1281, 1286
costs **4:** 2093
decision-oriented approaches **8:** 4759, 4760; **11:** 6380
design **4:** ***2079–2089***
ethnographic techniques **4:** 2044
evaluability assessment **4:** 2103
evaluation methods **11:** 6380
experimental approaches **11:** 6378
expertise oriented valuing **3:** 1281
explanatory approach **11:** 6378
failure of **4:** 2093
feedback **4:** 2093
and goal-free evaluation **4:** 2100
history of **4:** 2080
information gathering **4:** 2091
judgment-oriented approaches
4: 2103; **8:** 4760
judicial **3:** 1282
and labor force development **5:** 2686
local relevance **8:** 4762
measurement outcome oriented
3: 1280
metatheory **4:** 2107
methodological models **3:** 1280
and national education policies
3: 1429
naturalistic **4:** 2079, 2081, 2086
and personnel evaluation **8:** 4746
pluralist–intuitionist approaches
4: 2103
policy analysis **4:** 2103
and policy formation **5:** 2671
process oriented valuing **3:** 1282
program theory **11:** 6378
project evaluation
use of terms **8:** 4780
public job training
developed nations **4:** ***2145–2150***
qualitative
curriculum evaluation **3:** ***1284–1288***
research **3:** 1281
quantitative
research **3:** 1281
research quality **3:** 1428, 1430
side effects **4:** 2095
and social change **4:** 2120, 2122, 2123
social justice based **3:** 1282
stakeholder approach **11:** 6378
standard setting procedures
7: ***4054–4056***
standards **8:** ***4736–4751***
criticisms of **8:** 4743
teacher education **10:** ***5954–5958***
theory-based **11:** ***6378–6385***
Tylerian approach **4:** 2080, 2102;
8: 4763
and unintended effects **11:** 6510
and videotape recordings **11:** 6605
See also
Project evaluation
Program evaluation and review technique (PERT)
advantages of **8:** 4757
and program management **8:** 4757
Program implementation
adaptation perspective **4:** 2072
alternative orientations **4:** 2072
characteristics of **5:** 2840
and cooperation **5:** 2844
complexity problems **5:** 2841
definitions of **4:** 2071
and design **3:** ***1491–1494***
and educational planning **8:** 4516

failure **8:** 4597
politics of **8:** 4597
evaluation of **4:** ***2070–2074***; **5:** 2845
concepts **4:** 2071
historical background **4:** 2070
procedures **4:** 2073
purposes of **4:** 2070
tasks **4:** 2071
evolutionary development **5:** 2844
factors affecting **5:** 2839
fidelity perspective **4:** 2072
illustrative study **3:** 1493
and innovation **5:** ***2839–2847***
issues **5:** 2846
and local characteristics of **5:** 2842
monitoring **5:** 2845
process
critical factors **5:** 2840
and projects **8:** 4757
quality and practicality factors **5:** 2841
restructuring **5:** 2845
and staff development **5:** 2844
themes in **5:** 2843
vision building **5:** 2844
Program management **8:** ***4754–4758***
analysis **8:** 4754
control **8:** 4755
definition of **8:** 4754
financial factors **8:** 4755
functions **8:** 4754
phases **8:** 4754
planning **8:** 4754
scope **8:** 4755
staffing **8:** 4754
supervision **8:** 4755
time factors **8:** 4755
See also
Project management
Program planning
See Program development
Programmed instruction **5:** 2880; **8:** ***4766–4775***
and behavioral instruction **10:** 6162
design
and feedback **8:** 4771
initial stages **8:** 4768
developmental testing **8:** 4771
early developments **8:** 4767
and educational history **3:** 1795
and educational technology **4:** 1883, 1913
and feedback **8:** 4768, 4771, 4773
feedback in **4:** 2280
frames **8:** 4767
design of **8:** 4770
large **8:** 4770
hierarchy approach **8:** 4769
and hypertext **5:** 2706
and instructional systems **8:** 4772
knowledge classification approach **8:** 4770
lean programs **8:** 4770
and learning **6:** 3300
linear programs **8:** 4770
master performer approach **8:** 4769, 4770
matrix approach **8:** 4769
and multiple choice tests **8:** 4768, 4773
and pacing **8:** 4771
prerequisites for **8:** 4769
and psychologists **4:** 1884
Skinner's work on **8:** 4767
structural communication **8:** 4773
for task analysis **8:** 4769
and teacher attitudes **8:** 4772
See also
computer-assisted instruction
Programmed tutoring
Programmed instructional materials
textbooks **8:** 4767
and teaching machines **8:** 4767
Programmed learning
See Programmed instruction
Programmed texts
See Programmed instructional materials, textbooks
Programmed tutoring **8:** 4774
and educational technology **4:** 1914
feedback in **4:** 2281
and skill development **6:** 3300
Programmers
attitudes
and programmed instruction design **8:** 4771
Programming **2:** 969
and cognitive development **2:** 970, 983
cognitive effects hypothesis **2:** 1005
computer-assisted instruction
programmed tutoring **2:** 972
computer literacy **2:** 974, ***982–985***
computer science education **2:** 969
curriculum development **2:** ***969–973***
discovery learning **2:** 983
educational psychology **2:** ***982–985***
expert novice research **2:** 984
expertise in **2:** 984
instruction in **2:** 983
mental model method **2:** 983
kinds of knowledge required **2:** 984
learning **2:** 983
and problem-solving
research studies **7:** 4084
and procedural knowledge **3:** 1432
sex differences **4:** 2425
in teacher education **10:** 6005, 6006
and thinking skills **2:** 969
skill development **2:** 1005
and transfer of training **2:** 983; **11:** 6453, 6454
Programming (broadcast)
content indifference **1:** 566
educational radio **5:** 2886
Programming languages **2:** 970, 983
BASIC **2:** 970
for courseware **10:** 5621
and courseware
authoring aids **10:** 5623
educational **10:** 5624
and item writing techniques **5:** 3064
LISP **2:** 972; **6:** 3509
LOGO **2:** 885, 970; **6:** 3508
microcomputers **7:** 3813, 3815
and models **2:** 986
PASCAL **2:** 970, 972
sex fairness **4:** 2425
Programs
definitions of **8:** 4754
and educational technology **4:** 1885
use of term **8:** 4766
See also
Projects
Progressive education
and art education **1:** 340
and Dewey's philosophy of education **3:** 1523
and educational research **4:** 1864, 1866, 1869
and preschool education **8:** 4668
schools **1:** 262
United States **4:** 2080; **5:** 2694; **6:** 3454
writings on **8:** 4451
Progressive Education Association (US)
and the Eight-Year Study **4:** 2093; **10:** 5814
Project evaluation **8:** ***4780–4783***
definition of **8:** 4780
and dissemination **8:** 4782
during implementation stage **8:** 4782
formative **8:** 4780
functions of **8:** 4780
procedures **8:** 4781
summative **8:** 4780
See also
Program evaluation
Project Literacy US (PLUS) **7:** 4148
Project management **8:** ***4754–4758***
analysis **8:** 4755
for computer software **8:** 4758
control **8:** 4757
design **8:** 4756
development **8:** 4757
estimations **8:** 4757
functions **8:** 4755
implementation **8:** 4757
phases **8:** 4754
time factors **8:** 4757
See also
Program management
Project monitoring **8:** ***4780–4783***
definition of **8:** 4780
Project PLAN (US)
and individualized instruction **5:** 2772
Project STAR
instructional materials **8:** 4476
Projection equipment
slides
characteristics of **7:** 3747
Projections
accuracy of **8:** 4786
assumptions **8:** 4785, 4786, 4787
and educational statistics **8:** ***4783–4788***
methods **8:** 4784

future developments **8:** 4787
limitations **8:** 4787
mean absolute percent error **8:** 4787
methods
exponential smoothing **8:** 4784, 4785, 4787
regression **8:** 4787
models
educational receipts **8:** 4786
elementary classroom teacher **8:** 4785
expenditure per pupil **8:** 4786
median voter **8:** 4786
public elementary enrollment **8:** 4784
public secondary enrollment **8:** 4784
secondary classroom teacher **8:** 4785
teacher salary **8:** 4786
uses of **8:** 4783
See also
Prediction
Projective measures **8:** ***4788–4791***
and attitude measures **1:** 386
classification of **8:** 4788
concepts of **8:** 4788
issues **8:** 4791
and nonverbal communication **8:** 4791
Thematic Apperception Test **3:** 1236, 1238, 1239
thematic methods **8:** 4789
uses of **8:** 4788
and verbal stimuli **8:** 4790
Projective tests
See Projective measures
Projects
definition of **8:** 4754
objectives
and design **8:** 4781
See also
Programs
Promotion (occupational)
evaluation of performance **11:** 6629
and vocational education and training
Anglo–German comparisons **11:** 6639
Pronunciation instruction
and simulation **7:** 4093
Propaganda
in education
and authoritarian governments **5:** 2511
Property taxes
and educational finance **9:** 5238
Propositional knowledge
See Declarative knowledge
Propositions
knowledge representations **6:** 3153
Proprietary schools
vocational education **8:** ***4792–4796***
accreditation **8:** 4794
attitudes toward **8:** 4793
Canada **8:** 4793
characteristics of **8:** 4792
China, People's Republic of **8:** 4794, 4795
definition of **8:** 4792
enrollment **8:** 4795
Indonesia **8:** 4794
Japan **8:** 4795
Malaysia **8:** 4794
Philippines **8:** 4794, 4796
regulation **8:** 4795
Thailand **8:** 4794
United States **8:** 4794
Prosocial behavior
child development **8:** ***4796–4799***
children
sex differences **8:** 4798
correlation with intelligence
in children **8:** 4798
cross-cultural studies **5:** 2649; **8:** 4797
developmental continuity **8:** 4797
parent influence **8:** 4798
peer relationship **8:** 4365
personality traits **8:** 4798
and socialization **8:** 4798
in subcultures **8:** 4797
teacher influence **8:** 4798
Protestantism
catechisms **6:** 3530
and development of literacy **6:** 3531
Luther's role in development **6:** 3529
Pestalozzi and pietism **8:** 4416
and religious education **9:** 5002, 5012
Protocol analysis
cognitive processes **10:** 5912
expert performance **2:** 839
verbal **7:** 3767
Prototyping
and authoring aids **10:** 5623
and computer software development **8:** 4801
courseware
for computer-assisted instruction **10:** 5624
as a design activity **8:** ***4799–4803***
and epistemology **8:** 4801
instructional materials
electronic **8:** 4801
and material development **8:** 4801
and teacher participation **8:** 4802
Proxemics
See Personal space
Proximity
and friendship **9:** 5173
Prussia
apprenticeships
historical background **1:** 311
Psychiatric hospitals
United States **3:** 1436
Psychiatric services
community health services **3:** 1436
Psychiatry
humanistic psychology view of **5:** 2689
See also
Psychoanalytic theory
Psychoanalytic theory
Freud's
of individual development **5:** 2658; **8:** 4812
Mahler's of child development
personal autonomy **8:** 4814
and moral development **7:** 3916
of play **8:** 4537
Psychodrama **5:** 2691
Psychodynamics
and developmental psychology **8:** 4812
theories of individual development **8:** ***4812–4816***
Adler's **8:** 4815
Psycholinguistics
language skills **10:** 5697
Psychological characteristics
academically gifted **9:** 5529
Psychological evaluation
and learning processes **1:** ***370–374***
Psychological patterns
affective behavior
and learning **1:** ***199–204***
cross-cultural studies **5:** 2648
individual development **9:** ***5403–5407***
and social cognition **9:** 5511
Psychological processes
microgenesis **3:** 1248
Psychological research
See Psychological studies
Psychological studies
and expertise **10:** 6021
historical background **9:** 5407
and learning **9:** 5041
moderating and mediating effects in **4:** 1873
and science and technology perspectives **4:** 1885
and secondary data analysis **9:** 5369
Psychological testing
and factor analysis **4:** 2230
historical development **4:** 1867
individual differences **5:** 2759
multivariate analysis
factor analysis **1:** 1
and security **11:** 6342
and Thurstone scales **11:** 6386
and true score theory **7:** 3702
Psychologists
and programmed instruction **4:** 1884
Psychology
of adult education **8:** ***4816–4824***
applied **8:** 4817
disciplinary perspective **8:** 4816
cross-cultural theories of cognition **3:** 1246
ecological
paradigm **10:** 6205
and educational practices **4:** 1842
and epistemology
influence on educational theories **4:** 1997
and human factors engineering **4:** 2007
of oppression **2:** 1046

theories
and artificial intelligence **1:** 344
Psychometrics **6:** 3307
and academic achievement measures **10:** 5787
and achievement tests **1:** 32
and adult learning **8:** 4818
alternative indexes of group level constructs **4:** 2385
aptitude tests **6:** ***3312–3315***
and attitude measures **1:** 386
child development
young children **1:** ***358–362***
cognitive development **5:** 2657
and cognitive psychology **1:** ***370–374***
construct indicator match **4:** 2385
and educational testing **3:** 1416
intellectual development
individual differences **2:** 844
and learning disabilities **10:** 5683
scale construction **4:** 2385
Psychomotor skills
analysis and categorization **7:** 3951
and curriculum objectives **3:** 1699
discovery learning
and direct instruction **7:** 3952
disorders
and drug therapy **8:** 4423
handicaps
and learning disabilities **10:** 5681
imitation **7:** 3950
instruction and training **7:** 3952
and interactive video **11:** 6601
learning and control **7:** 3951
movement education **7:** ***3950–3953***
patterned responses **7:** 3951
perceptual motor coordination **7:** ***3947–3950***, ***3950–3953***
retention and transfer **7:** 3951
scope and history of research **7:** 3950
skill development
ability requirements approach **7:** 3951
automatization **7:** 3953
behavior description approach **7:** 3951
behavior requirements approach **7:** 3951
degrees of freedom problem **7:** 3952
developmental stages **7:** 3951
feedback **7:** 3952
learner controlled instruction **7:** 3953
schema theory **7:** 3952
task characteristics approach **7:** 3951
Psychopathology **4:** 1963
developmental disabilities **3:** ***1514–1520***
etiological models **3:** 1516
mother infant relations **3:** 1517
prenatal and perinatal influences **3:** 1516
protective factors **3:** 1517
social deprivation **3:** 1516
levels of explanation **3:** 1517
biochemistry **3:** 1518
neuroanatomy **3:** 1518
neurophysiology **3:** 1518
psychology **3:** 1518
social adjustment **3:** 1519
Psychosexual development
in adolescents **8:** 4815
developmental stages **8:** 4813
behavior patterns **8:** 4813
Freud's views **8:** 4813, 4815
theories of
and socialization **10:** 5587
Psychosis
drug therapy for **8:** 4422
Psychotherapy
in child abuse cases **1:** 18
and self-actualization **5:** 2690
Psychotropic drugs
classification of **8:** 4420
Puberty **1:** 84
Public agencies
and governance of teacher education **10:** 5963
Public education
contraction in
determinants of **6:** 3603
issues **6:** 3607
management of **6:** ***3603–3608***
management strategies **6:** 3605
cost-effectiveness **4:** 2208
and migration **4:** 2211
and decentralization **3:** 1412
evaluation for improvement
United States **4:** ***2381–2389***
expenditure
vs. private resources **8:** 4703
finance
effect of economic adjustment on **3:** 1786, 1787
practices and trends **4:** ***2310–2316***
and private enrollment **8:** 4834
financial support
international aspects of **4:** 2310
labor relations in **6:** 3190
links with private sector **8:** ***4337–4339***
and moral values
Quintilian on **8:** 4889
and philosophical aspects of equal education **4:** ***2001–2004***
privatization of
and resource allocation **9:** 5063
rhetoric in Greek and Roman **8:** ***4887–4890***
role in capitalist democracies **4:** 2268
role of
and educational administration **7:** 3835
and school choice **9:** 5202
student fees **10:** 5751
United States
quality of **7:** 4052
vs. private education
and economic change **5:** 2505
student fees **10:** 5752
Public examinations
See Examinations, public
Public expenditures
See Expenditures, public
Public health
education and **4:** 2209
and school health education **5:** 2567
Public libraries
and adult students **6:** 3394
educational resources **6:** 3398
role of **6:** 3394
Public opinion
and vocational education **11:** 6702
Public policy
adult programs **1:** 155
and day care **2:** 691
employment and on-the-job training **6:** 3616
and income distribution **5:** 2743
labor markets
and training **11:** 6427
links with research **5:** ***2670–2673***
periodicals **8:** 4554
planning
for adult education **1:** ***152–158***
preschool education
effects on costs of **8:** 4663
and private education **8:** 4833
privatization
and vocational education **11:** 6688
schools for **8:** 4550
technical education
and educational technology **4:** 1918
for vocational education
comparative area studies **4:** 1920
vs. school policy
and educational improvement **9:** 5244
Public policy formation
bounded rationality model **3:** 1426
incremental model
and evaluation **3:** 1426
pure rationality model **3:** 1425
rational model
and evaluation **3:** 1425
and needs assessment **7:** 4057
Public school teachers
burnout rate **10:** 5921
faculty mobility
United States **10:** 5923
Public schools
bureaucracy in **1:** 589
and community education **8:** 4808
costs
in developing nations **8:** ***4702–4708***
and decentralization
decision-making **5:** 2796
and educational finance **9:** 5235
impact on educational attainment **8:** 4824
impact on society **8:** 4824
and Montessori method **1:** 263
nontraditional education **1:** 264
power structure **7:** 4229
religious education
and legislation **9:** 5013

sociological perspective **8:** ***4824–4831***
vs. Catholic schools
school organization **9:** 5375
vs. private schools
and decentralization **3:** 1407
research controversies
8: ***4839–4845***
Public sector
administrative organization
and state departments of education
7: 3834
and educational finance **6:** 3275
employment
and the Comprehensive
Employment and Training Act
(US) **7:** 4197
developing nations **3:** 1706; **8:** 4838
and education **8:** ***4836–4839***
evaluation models **3:** ***1381–1387***
decision systems model **3:** 1382
goal model **3:** 1382
operations research model **3:** 1382
system model **3:** 1382
and labor market segmentation
8: 4836
organizational theories **3:** 1741
textbook preparation **11:** 6363
and vocational education **5:** 2816
characteristics of **11:** 6648
developing nations **11:** 6648
vs. private sector
and educational responsibility
8: ***4831–4836***
job training **7:** 4198
and sociology of education
10: 5604
Public service
changing concept of **5:** 2505
Public support
for preschool education **8:** 4662
Publications
research
information networks **5:** 2993
Publishing industry
computer software **10:** ***5618–5622***
educational
state intervention **8:** 4848
trends **8:** 4848
and educational organizations
cooperation **8:** 4692
and educational research
dissemination of **3:** 1554
and electronic publishing
implications **4:** 1957
indigenous
and instructional materials **8:** 4847
instructional materials
provision of **8:** 4846
role of
and educational transfer **8:** 4846
and technological advancement
8: 4688
transnational influences **8:** ***4845–4848***
Puerto Rico
occupational segregation **4:** 2430
Punctuation **1:** 481
Punishment **9:** 4974
Pupil personnel services
historical background **9:** 5282
Pupil personnel workers
training of **9:** 5282
Pupil teacher ratio
See Teacher student ratio
Pushouts
See Expulsion
Pygmalion effect
See Self-fulfilling prophecies
Pyramid organization **3:** 1697, 1699

Q-methodology **8:** ***4855–4857***
criticisms of **8:** 4857
evaluation of **8:** 4856
and oral history **7:** 4221
Q-sort **8:** 4855
structured and unstructured **8:** 4855
Q-sort
See Q-methodology, Q-sort
Q-technique
See Q-methodology
Qatar
cultural influences **8:** 4849
index of segregation **4:** 2430
occupational segregation **4:** 2430
postsecondary education **8:** 4850
primary education **8:** 4850
secondary education **8:** 4850
system of education **8:** ***4849–4855***
educational objectives **8:** 4849
structure **8:** 4850
Quade test
nonparametric statistics **7:** 4161
Qualifications
correlation with earnings **4:** 2393
recognition
European Community
4: ***2063–2070***
and social stratification **10:** 5731
vocational schools **11:** 6667
Qualitative data analysis **3:** 1464
correspondence analysis **2:** ***1117–1121***
Qualitative research
of adult learning strategies **1:** 185,
188
complementary diversity thesis
9: 5022, 5024
in education **9:** 5407
educational administration **1:** 53
and educational administration
vs. quantitative research **1:** 59
epistemological integrity of **9:** 5025
ethnography **4:** 2046
role in educational policy formation
4: 2044
and narrative inquiry **7:** 4047
oppositional diversity thesis **9:** 5022,
5023
relationship with statistical analysis
2: 641; **9:** 5023
and research synthesis **10:** 6237
and teacher student relationship
10: 5761
terminology **9:** 5026
traditional vs. formalized
and case studies **2:** 643
and triangulation **11:** 6462
and validity **11:** 6574
Quality assurance
See Quality control
Quality circles **6:** 3616
Japan **5:** 2687
and vocational education
Japan **6:** 3090
Quality control
in vocational education **8:** ***4858–4865***
Quality of life
and continuing education **2:** 1092
disabilities
and transitional programs **11:** 6458
education and **3:** 1651; **4:** ***2208–2212***
environmental standards **4:** 1991
and family life education **4:** 2262
preschool education **2:** 683, 686
National Day Care study **2:** 865
Oxford research project **2:** 683
and research on individual
development **5:** ***2670–2673***
values
Spencer's view **10:** 5707
See also
Well-being
Quantitative ability
sex differences in **9:** 5427
Quantitative research (statistics)
See Statistical analysis
Quartiles
interquartile range **7:** 3732
semiquartile range **7:** 3732
skewness
indication of **7:** 3732
Quasiexperimental design **4:** 2081,
2082; **8:** ***4873–4875***
educational research **4:** 1870
ex post facto/static group comparison
4: 2083
and experimental studies **4:** 2187
interrupted time series **4:** 2082;
8: 4874
nonequivalent control group designs
4: 2082
procedure **8:** 4874
regression-discontinuity **8:** 4874
and replication studies **4:** 2084
selection of comparison group in
absence of randomization
4: 2083
validity **4:** 2084
Questioning techniques **8:** ***4875–4882***
and academic achievement
problems **8:** 4876
research synthesis **10:** 6238
contextual factors **8:** 4877
implications **8:** 4880
and interviews **5:** 3003
types of **5:** 3004
in questionnaires **8:** 4882
and research methodology **10:** 6235
and small group instruction **10:** 6185
social studies **9:** 5582

and student participation **8:** 4871
and student reaction
assistance **8:** 4879
and study skills **10:** 5831
and teacher behavior **10:** 6013
training students in **8:** 4880
training teachers in **8:** 4880
types of questions
clear **8:** 4879
discussion **8:** 4876
higher cognitive **8:** 4876
lower cognitive **8:** 4876
recitation **8:** 4876
test-relevant **8:** 4877
wait time **8:** 4879
See also
Interviews
Questionnaires **8:** ***4882–4887***
additional information **8:** 4884
assumptions in the use of **8:** 4882
and census data **2:** 649
coding schemes **8:** 4886
and content analysis **2:** 1076
development of **8:** 4883
in environmental measures **4:** 2246
field testing **8:** 4885
layout **8:** 4885
and learning
cognitive processes **1:** 319
systems approach **1:** 320
and partial credit model **7:** 4303, 4304
and personality measures **8:** 4395
pilot **8:** 4883
problems with in evaluation **4:** 2086
and Q-methodology **8:** 4856
and rating scales **8:** 4918
refinement of **8:** 4884
responses
data coding **3:** 1378
structure of items **8:** 4884
survey data
and secondary data analysis **9:** 5370
time constraints **8:** 4882, 4885
translation
in comparative analysis **3:** 1767
variables
identification of **8:** 4883
translation into questions **8:** 4883
vs. interviews
and nonresponse **7:** 3854
wording of **8:** 4885

Race
and disengagement theory **9:** 5227
and earnings differentials **8:** ***4896–4902***
and educational attainment **8:** ***4891–4896***
and employment level **7:** 3719
and high risk students **2:** 708
and school desegregation **3:** 1483
sex and social class **7:** 3849
and social stratification **9:** 5568
See also
Ethnicity
Racial attitudes
and evolutionary theory of social development
United States **7:** 3841
to immigrant children
United Kingdom **7:** 3844
and school desegregation **3:** 1484
Racial bias
educational improvement **10:** 5826
occupational segregation
relative attractiveness theory **4:** 2428
and public examinations **4:** 2179
and sex bias **7:** 3849
and social studies **9:** 5580
and teaching of anthropology in high schools **1:** 298
Racial differences **10:** ***5822–5827***
educational theories **10:** 5822
and equal education **4:** 2001, 2003
and school organization **9:** 5169
students
self-concept **10:** 5823
and teacher student relationship **9:** 5171
and test bias **11:** 6317
Racial discrimination
in administrative strategies **3:** 1696
curriculum for minorities
United States **7:** 3844
earnings differentials **8:** ***4896–4902***
and productivity **1:** 517
and enrollment rate **6:** 3099
equal education
South Africa **7:** ***3848–3853***
and gender differences in earnings **8:** 4896, 4899
and group unity **8:** 4894, 4895
and language proficiency **8:** 4894
occupational mobility
segmentation theory **6:** 3188
and productivity measures **3:** 1694
in schools **8:** 4894
in segmentation theory **6:** 3185
Racial identification
and resistance **9:** 5571
Racial integration
and democratic governance **8:** 4590
Racial relations
and friendship **9:** 5174
and hidden curriculum **8:** 4582
and school desegregation **3:** 1484
and teacher associations **8:** 4584
Racial segregation **7:** 3966
child care occupations **2:** 689
in schools
Africa **8:** 4681
South Africa **7:** 3849
United States **7:** 3844
Radiation effects
and video display terminals **4:** 2010
Radio
and distance education **3:** 1575
instruction
interactive **4:** 1905
and learning **6:** 3299
in religious education **9:** 5003
uses in education **1:** 401
See also
Educational radio
Radio drama
aesthetic education **1:** 197
Rampton Committee Report 1980–81 (UK)
multicultural education **7:** 3845
Random coefficient models
See Hierarchical linear models (HLM)
Random numbers
congruential generators **9:** 5468
generation of **9:** 5468
and simplex patterns **7:** 3705
Randomization
and experimental studies **4:** 2187
and sampling **5:** 2711
Range (statistics)
analysis of **7:** 3727
definition of **7:** 3731
uses of **7:** 3728
in analysis **7:** 3731
Rank correlation
See Correlation
rank
Rasch measurement models
acceptance **8:** 4903
and achieved curriculum **11:** 6327
and achievement tests **1:** 37
and attitude measures **7:** 3704; **9:** 5320
and computer-assisted testing **5:** 2780, 2781
and developmental stages **3:** 1510
dichotomous **8:** 4902
consequences of uniqueness **8:** 4904
and partial credit model **7:** 4305
uniqueness of **8:** 4903
and educational assessment **1:** 370
and equated scores **4:** 2012
and Galois lattice method **4:** 2395, 2397, 2399
general M-category **8:** 4902
goodness of fit **8:** 4905
historical background **8:** 4902
and item banks **4:** 2177; **5:** 3040
item characteristic curves **8:** 4907
and item discrimination
analysis of **8:** 4906
and item response theory **1:** 50; **5:** 3051; **8:** 4906
item bias procedures **5:** 3049
and judgments **6:** 3120
and latent trait measurement models **6:** 3250
and literacy testing **6:** 3472
many-facet
and judgments **6:** 3121
and objective tests **7:** 3700
objectivity in **8:** 4904
one-parameter logistic **8:** 4902
and partial credit model **7:** 4302
rank ordering **6:** 3123
and rating scales **8:** 4920

rejection **8:** 4903, 4905
scales
uses **1:** 38
scaling procedures
and attitude measures **1:** 385
and sex differences
determination of **8:** 4905
specific object comparisons **8:** 4904
specificity
proof of **8:** 4903
theory of **8:** ***4902–4913***
and Thurstone scales
distinctions **8:** 4923
two tests
comparison of results **8:** 4908
methods **8:** 4909
uses of **8:** 4902
Rate of return
and cost effectiveness **2:** 1129
to education **8:** ***4913–4918***
census studies **3:** 1814
cost effectiveness studies **2:** 1125
and educational finance **9:** 5234
and educational planning **8:** 4529
empirical research **8:** 4915
function **8:** 4913
implications **8:** 4917
and international labor market **3:** 1709
and labor market **11:** 6280
over time **8:** 4915
and time factors (learning) **6:** 3548
and educational planning **8:** 4497, 4504
estimates
by specialization **8:** 4530
estimation procedures
Mincerian **8:** 4914
traditional **8:** 4914
to investment
and occupational information **6:** 3097
social **8:** 4913
and cost effectiveness **2:** 1125
and labor market **11:** 6280
to vocational education
China, People's Republic of **2:** 759
See also
Cost effectiveness
Raters
characteristics of
and test bias **11:** 6319
employment of multiple **8:** 4928
leniency of **8:** 4922
training programs for **8:** 4928
Rating scales **8:** ***4923–4930***
analysis **8:** ***4918–4923***
anchoring of
methods **8:** 4924
categories **8:** 4922
characteristics of **8:** 4923
connecting to measurements **8:** 4922
content validity **10:** 6018
teacher effectiveness **10:** 6018
and contingency tables **8:** 4918
criterion scaling **8:** 4926
data analysis **8:** 4930
discrete categories
and judgments **6:** 3122
error of measurement **8:** 4927
minimizing **8:** 4928
and essay tests **4:** 2020, 2021
"halo" effect **8:** 4922
improvement **10:** 6018
individual classifications **8:** 4918
and judgments **6:** 3120
mathematical response models **8:** 4919
Rasch rating model **8:** 4920
traditional threshold **8:** 4919
monitoring procedures **8:** 4929
neutral category **8:** 4922
and partial credit model **7:** 4304
percentage
and test items **11:** 6325
predictive validity **10:** 6018
halo effect **10:** 6018
quality control **8:** 4922
reliability of **8:** 4929
reproducibility
assessment of **8:** 4929
response categories
scoring **8:** 4918
response pattern **8:** 4922
response sets **8:** 4922
scale categories
number of **8:** 4927
scale values
assignment of **8:** 4926
sufficient statistics for **8:** 4921
and test bias **11:** 6320
and test items **11:** 6325
and test translation **11:** 6329
Thurstone scales **11:** ***6385–6388***
types of **8:** 4924
unobserved categories
and judgments **6:** 3123
uses of **8:** 4918, 4923
year level
and test items **11:** 6325
See also
Behavior rating scales
Likert scales
Semantic differential
Ratio scales **7:** 3700
definition of **9:** 5047
Rational choice theory
comparative education **2:** 929
Rationalism
Descartes' views **4:** 1997, 1999; **8:** 4630
and empiricism **4:** 1997
and learning processes **6:** 3316
Raven Progressive Matrices Test **5:** 2927; **7:** 3879
Raw scores
in classical test theory **2:** 786
scales
and achievement tests **1:** 34
Reaction time
and intelligence **5:** 2760
Readability
and text analysis **2:** 1077
Readability formulas **2:** 1077
and comprehension **7:** 3930
Reader response **10:** 5959
school textbooks
and sex bias **9:** 5301
Reader text relationship
school textbooks
and sex bias **9:** 5301
and spatial conventions of written language **1:** 481
Readiness **9:** 5273
measurement research **6:** 3675
See also
Learning readiness
Reading readiness
School readiness
Writing readiness
Reading
basic vocabulary **6:** 3446
historical development of tradition **6:** 3530
learning by **6:** 3299
learning theories **8:** 4943
metacognition
executive control **7:** 3786
metacognitive knowledge
age differences **7:** 3785, 3786
and mild disabilities **8:** ***4930–4936***
models of
interactive **8:** 4936
national standard setting **7:** 4056
parent child interaction **6:** 3448
phenomenological approach **8:** 4947
prereading experience
and transition to school **6:** 3449
and speech **8:** 4942
and visual literacy **11:** 6623
See also
Basal reading
Beginning reading
Content area reading
Critical reading
Early reading
Independent reading
Oral reading
Reading aloud to others
Remedial reading
Silent reading
Speed reading
Story reading
Reading ability
and cluster analysis **2:** 826
and item sampling **5:** 3055
Reading achievement
and effective schools research **4:** 1936
and growth curves **2:** 674
and individual differences
growth model **2:** 676
and intelligence tests
discrepancies **8:** 4931
and prior learning **8:** 4937
and speech handicaps **10:** 5694
and visual literacy **11:** 6623
Reading aloud to others
parent audience **5:** 2626; **6:** 3461

Reading comprehension **8:** ***4940–4942***
affective factors **8:** 4942
and attention control **1:** 376
attitudes and achievement
cross-cultural studies **1:** 393
characteristics of **8:** 4936
cognitive linguistics **8:** 4942
cognitive processes **8:** 4940
cognitive strategies **8:** 4941
conceptual resources in **8:** 4937
error detection **7:** 3786
linguistic resources in **8:** 4937
measurement of **4:** 2075
metacognition **8:** 4941
motivation **8:** 4942
and orthography
role of **8:** 4938
and reading rate **7:** 3786
and reciprocal teaching **8:** 4941
reciprocal teaching **2:** 861
role of prior learning **8:** 4940
schemata in **8:** 4940
in second languages **8:** ***4936–4940***
automaticity **8:** 4938
instruction implications **8:** 4939
role of grammar **8:** 4938
utilization **8:** 4936
and summarization **7:** 3786
and teacher explanation **10:** 6147
tests **7:** 3930
content-referenced **7:** 3931
context-referenced **7:** 3931
latent trait scales in **7:** 3932
Nelson–Denny test **6:** 3337
proficiency measures **7:** 3932
See also
Reading tests
text reinspection **7:** 3786
and text structure **8:** 4940
use of literature in **6:** 3482
Reading consultants
alternatives to decoding methods **7:** 4080
Reading difficulties
causes of **10:** 5679
decoding (reading)
and cognitive processes **7:** 4080
diagnosis
and curriculum-based assessment **3:** 1358
disadvantaged children **6:** 3215
explanations of **8:** 4934
incidence of **10:** 5678
and mild disabilities **8:** 4932
intervention programs
research **8:** 4930
and language handicaps **10:** 5677
learning disabilities **7:** 4077
and mild disabilities
definitions **8:** 4931
neurobiological advances **10:** 5679
and parent background **8:** 4932
prevention of **8:** 4935
programs for
costs **8:** 4934
and Rasch measurement models **8:** 4909
and resource room programs **9:** 5067
special needs students
microcomputers **7:** 3802
and speech handicaps **10:** 5678
See also
Dyslexia
Remedial reading
Reading failure
cultural factors **6:** 3445
Reading improvement
and reading materials **8:** 4696
Reading instruction **8:** 4944
decoding (reading) **8:** 4942, 4944
effective
principles of **8:** 4934
literature-centered **2:** 735
parents as teachers **6:** 3451
paired reading **6:** 3461
parent listening **6:** 3462
pause, prompt, praise (PPP) approach **6:** 3461
SMART programs **6:** 3461
techniques **6:** 3461
reciprocal teaching method **3:** 1251
and resource room programs **9:** 5069
teaching guides for **10:** 6115
whole language approach **8:** 4944
Reading interests
adolescent literature **2:** 734
children's literature **2:** 733
Australia **2:** 734
cross-cultural studies **2:** 733, 737
India **2:** 734
literary devices **2:** 734
Scandinavia **2:** 734
sex differences **2:** 734
United States **2:** 733
Reading material selection
sex differences **10:** 5822
Reading materials
basal reading
sex bias **9:** 5299, 5441
and reading improvement **8:** 4696
Reading processes
interactive view **8:** 4945
and phenomenography **1:** 319
theories of **8:** 4936
Reading rate
and reading comprehension **7:** 3786
Reading readiness **4:** ***1958–1963***
and prereading experience **4:** 1958
spatial organization of print **4:** 1958
Reading Recovery program (US)
dyslexia **5:** 2514
research
New Zealand **10:** 5791
Reading skills
acquisition of
research **6:** 3475
cues **4:** 1961
and deafness **3:** 1399
early reading
context effect **6:** 3460
learning **8:** ***4942–4945***
native language
and literacy provision **6:** 3476
orthographic factors **1:** 481
protocol analysis **2:** 861
second languages
and literacy provision **6:** 3476
and reading comprehension **8:** 4937
selective attention strategies **1:** 376
and short term memory **1:** 375
SQ3R method **1:** 186
See also
Reading comprehension
Reading strategies
cognitive strategy instruction **2:** 863
special education **2:** 862
Reading teachers
teacher education **8:** ***4945–4948***
apprenticeship model **8:** 4945, 4946
competency-based model **8:** 4946
and empowerment **8:** 4947
inquiry-oriented model **8:** 4946, 4947
issues **8:** 4946
trends **8:** 4946
teacher educators
research **8:** 4947
Reading tests **7:** 3930
diagnostic **7:** 3931
and item response theory **1:** 37
and language tests **4:** 2359
and nonresponse
effects of **7:** 3854
procedures **4:** 2363
and quasiexperimental design **8:** 4874
and Rasch measurement models **8:** 4905
special **7:** 3931
and test bias **11:** 6316
United States **6:** 3471
See also
Cloze procedure
Reading comprehension, tests
Reading writing relationship **8:** 4942
early experience **4:** ***1958–1963***
learning processes **11:** 6781
literacy **6:** ***3443–3446***
Real time games **9:** 5474
FLEXIGAME **9:** 5475
Project Proteus **9:** 5475
Realism
causal **9:** 4980
construction of **9:** 4977
feminist pragmatic **4:** 2300, 2301
and relativism **9:** ***4977–4981***
varieties of **9:** 4978
Reality
representations of
and message design **7:** 3772
Realschulen **9:** 5386
vocational education
Germany, Federal Republic of (former) **11:** 6655
Reasoning
analogy
age differences **8:** 4955
child development

age differences **8:** 4952
in children
analogy **8:** 4953
cognitive development
8: ***4951–4957***
developmental stages **8:** 4955
factors influencing **8:** 4951, 4954
and cognitive style **8:** 4956
deduction **8:** 4953
definitions of **8:** 4951
inference
in children **8:** 4953
influence of experience on **8:** 4956
See also
Abstract reasoning
Thinking skills
Reasoning skills
See Thinking skills
Recall (psychology)
and children's cognitive development
2: 856
inferential **1:** 330
retrieval aid theory
and prior learning **8:** 4701
and state dependent memory **1:** 328
tests
and memory **7:** 3767
Receptive language
and sentence combining instruction
10: 5701
Recidivism
delinquency
and mild disabilities **3:** 1440
Reciprocal effects
and path analysis models **4:** 1877
Reciprocal teaching **5:** 2533; **7:** 3885;
10: 6189
and cognitive development **9:** 5507
cognitive strategy instruction **2:** 864
cultural differences **2:** 865
and practice **6:** 3300
reading comprehension **2:** 861;
8: 4941
reading instruction **3:** 1251
second language instruction **6:** 3331
and transfer of training **11:** 6454
Recitation
and learning **6:** 3301
Recognition (achievement)
definition of **4:** 2063
and effective schools **4:** 1931
vocational education
future trends **4:** 2069
vocational qualifications
European Community
4: ***2063–2070***
studies **4:** 2066
Recognition (psychology) **8:** 4820
tests
and memory **7:** 3767
and visual perception **8:** 4377, 4379
Recordkeeping
and action research **1:** 44
Records (forms)
and student evaluation **8:** ***4617–4623***
Records of achievement
See Academic records
Recreational activities
and academically gifted **9:** 5530
Recruitment
educational administration **1:** 78
educational researchers
training **11:** 6441
school personnel
and outcomes of education **9:** 5263
See also
Personnel selection
Recurrent costs
See Operating expenses
Recurrent education **4:** 1973; **6:** 3417,
3418; **8:** ***4957–4965***
admission criteria **8:** 4958
and adult vocational education **1:** 179
comparative analysis **1:** ***176–180***
compared with vocational education
4: 2389
concept of **6:** 3418, 3420
development **8:** 4957
criticisms of **8:** 4960
definition of **8:** 4957
economic value **8:** 4963
and educational leave of absence
11: 6393
goal **8:** 4958
guide to policy development **8:** 4962
impact **8:** 4962
and legislation **6:** 3366
and lifelong learning **6:** 3420; **8:** 4958
obstacles to implementation **8:** 4960
and paid educational leave **1:** 179;
8: 4611
as a planning strategy **8:** 4959
drawing rights system **8:** 4959
paid educational leave **8:** 4959
policy-making and **8:** 4958, 4963
principles **8:** 4958
alternation principle **8:** 4961
postponement principle **8:** 4961
uses of term **1:** 119; **6:** 3417, 3419
See also
Lifelong learning
Red Latinoamericano de Documentación en Educación (*REDUC*) **1:** 141;
3: 1555, ***1589–1593***
activities of **3:** 1589
common methodology **3:** 1591
contact details **5:** 2827
cooperative aspects **3:** 1590
finance **3:** 1589
funding **5:** 2826
future trends **3:** 1593
historical background **3:** 1590
limits to extension
factors affecting **3:** 1592
marketing of system **3:** 1591
scope **5:** 2826
training workshops **3:** 1591
users of **3:** 1591
Redundancy
in databases **3:** 1389
vs. job sharing **3:** 1697
Reference groups
and school dynamics **9:** 5172
Referral
special education
bilingual students **6:** ***3228–3232***
special needs students **2:** 713; **8:** 4657
See also
Prereferral intervention
Reflective teaching **10:** ***6215–6219***
cognitive development
educational strategies **10:** 6215
cognitive processes **10:** 6215, 6216
problem-solving **10:** 6215
cognitive structures **10:** 6217
creative thinking **10:** 6215
critical thinking **10:** 6216
evaluation of **10:** 6216
teaching skills **10:** 6216
inservice teacher education **10:** 5969,
5984, 5985
interaction
educational outcomes **10:** 6216
limited extent of **10:** 6218
model **8:** 4451; **10:** 5984, 5985
field experience programs
10: 6217
research methodology **10:** 6216
teacher attitudes
wholeheartedness **10:** 6215
teacher characteristics **10:** 6216
open-mindedness **10:** 6215
teacher education
evaluation **6:** 3198
language arts and literature
10: 5960
teacher responsibility
ethics **10:** 6215
teachers as researchers **10:** 5960
teaching skills **10:** 6218
Reformpädagogik **3:** 1290
Refugees
and adult education
reform strategies **1:** 160
determinants of migration **5:** 2737
Regional Center for Educational Innovation and Technology (INNOTECH) (Philippines)
activities **4:** 1878
Regional cooperation
educational finance
international **5:** 2992
Regional colleges
See Community colleges
Regional Council for Adult Education and Literacy in Africa (CREAA) **1:** 220
Regional organizations
for computer uses in education
listing **2:** 1014
Regional programs
International Labour Organization
5: 3002
Registrars (school) **10:** 5800
Regression (statistics) **3:** 1382, 1383
and aptitude treatment interaction
10: 6157

coefficients
determination of **9:** 4965
and hierarchical linear models **7:** 3982
and multilevel analysis **7:** 3979
in cross-national comparisons **4:** 2136, 2137
and earnings functions **3:** 1815
in educational research **1:** 516
in environmental measures **4:** 2246
and equated scores **11:** 6352
and hierarchical linear models **7:** 3983
logistic
and item bias **5:** 3047
models
choice of **9:** 4965
exponential **9:** 4965
linear quadratic **9:** 4965
multiple linear **9:** 4966, 4969
polynomial **9:** 4968
simple linear **9:** 4966
and multilevel analysis **7:** 3979
and multivariate analysis **7:** 4010
and partial least squares analysis **8:** 4353
and prediction **8:** 4654
and projections **8:** 4787
and quasiexperimental design **8:** 4874
in rate of return analysis **8:** 4914
ridge **9:** 4972
and robustness **9:** 5078
and selection bias **9:** 5379
sum-of-squares-and-cross-products (SSCP) matrix **9:** 4967, 4968
surfaces
and interaction effects **5:** 2927
and text analysis **2:** 1077
use in measurement of educational productivity **3:** 1383
See also
Multiple regression analysis
Regression analysis
Regression analysis
and coding techniques **9:** 4970
computer software for **9:** 4973
correction for shrinkage **9:** 4971
definition of **9:** 4965
loss function **9:** 4965
method **9:** 4965
predictor-weighting schemes **9:** 4972
of quantified data **9:** ***4965–4974***
uses of **9:** 4965
See also
Regression (statistics)
Regular and special education
relationship **2:** 723; **10:** 5661, 5666
cooperative learning **5:** 2906
individualized instruction **5:** 2905
mainstreaming **5:** ***2903–2907, 2907–2910***; **6:** 3557
and teacher education **6:** 3559
mild disabilities **8:** 4933
and noncategorical education **7:** 3832
peer teaching **5:** 2906; **8:** 4374, 4375
and prereferral intervention **8:** 4657
systems approach **8:** 4658
resource room programs **9:** 5067
problems **9:** 5069
studies **9:** 5069
second chance education **9:** 5364
service delivery
Adaptive Learning Environments Model **10:** 6241
teams **10:** 6241
special education teachers **5:** 2906; **10:** 5667
and special needs students **10:** 6241
teacher effectiveness **5:** 2905
team teaching **5:** 2906; **9:** 5070
United States **2:** 724
Regulations
requirements for
and educational vouchers **9:** 5204
Rehabilitation
special education
community-based programs **2:** 727; **5:** 2966
Rehabilitation programs
boy soldiers **8:** 4778
Rehearsal
and learning **6:** 3300
Reinforcement **4:** 2279; **9:** ***4974–4977***
autism **9:** 4976
behavior problems
parent participation **9:** 4975
and behavioral theories
of teaching **10:** 6159, 6160
contracting **1:** 485
differential
and stimulus control **10:** 6160
and educational quality
vocational education **8:** 4863
generalized reinforcers **9:** 4975
infant behavior **5:** 2800
learning **5:** 2852
primary (unlearned) reinforcers **9:** 4974
and programmed instruction **8:** 4767
schedules of **9:** 4975
in schools
and socialization **10:** 5590
secondary (learned) reinforcers **9:** 4974
self-management **1:** 485
student problems **9:** 4975
and student reaction **10:** 6013
tangible reinforcers **9:** 4974
and teaching methods
interaction effects **5:** 2922
token systems **4:** 1844
Rejection (psychology)
by peer group
and aggression **1:** 233
Relational databases
See Databases, relational
Relativism
criticisms of **9:** 4979
epistemological **9:** 4978
frameworks and judgments of truth **9:** 4978
modern
and standards **9:** 4978
origins **9:** 4978
and paradigms (Kuhn) **9:** 4978
problems with **9:** 4980
and realism (philosophy) **9:** ***4977–4981***
Relaxation training
stress management **10:** 5737
Released time **1:** 183; **8:** 4958, 4960
and apprenticeships
Germany, Federal Republic of (former) **11:** 6693
Relevance (education)
core curriculum **2:** 1105
in cross-national comparisons **4:** 2134
and curriculum evaluation **3:** 1361
definitions of **3:** 1361
individual development **3:** 1363
and motivation **7:** 3945
and popular culture **3:** 1363
and science or humanities debate **3:** 1363
and transfer to developing nations **1:** 466
vocational education **3:** 1363
Japan **11:** 6696
Reliability **9:** ***4981–4995***
attenuation of correlations **9:** 4994
and attitude measures **1:** 386
classical model **9:** 4981
assumptions **9:** 4981
effect of change in test length **9:** 4982
and classical test theory **2:** 786
clinical **9:** 4995
error variance **9:** 4995
coefficient **9:** 4982, 4991
coefficient alpha **9:** 4991, 4992
coefficient of generalizability **9:** 4988
coefficient of reducibility **9:** 4988
coefficients
and partial least squares analysis **8:** 4357
correction for attenuation **9:** 4984, 4994
and criterion referenced tests **2:** 1188
data collection strategies **9:** 4991
and descriptive scales **3:** 1475
of difference scores **2:** 672
of differences and discrepancies **9:** 4994
educational research
phenomenography **8:** 4428
equivalent forms **9:** 4991
error variance **9:** 4984, 4988
estimates **9:** 4984
internal consistency **9:** 4992
issues **9:** 4994
Kuder–Richardson formula **9:** 4991, 4992
and measurement validity **11:** 6569
and meta analysis **7:** 3778
multifacet model **9:** 4986
variance components **9:** 4988

nonrandom questions and readers **9:** 4988
problem-solving tests **8:** 4730
profile analysis **8:** 4753
and questionnaires **8:** 4885
retesting **9:** 4992
scoring
essay tests **4:** 2022
of student evaluations of teacher effectiveness **10:** 6229
variance components **9:** 4984
confounding of **9:** 4989
model **9:** 4986
See also
Test reliability
Religion
and beliefs **5:** 2651
and biological sciences **6:** 3414
concepts of **9:** 4996
and knowledge evolution **4:** 1849
major types of
statistics **9:** 4996
and national curriculum **3:** 1289
Religion studies
and religious education **9:** 5000
Religious conflict
and educational planning **3:** 1822
and science education
syllabi **10:** 5884
Religious cultural groups
Bhutan **1:** 526, 528
Bulgaria **1:** 582
Fiji **4:** 2302
Ghana **5:** 2480
India **5:** 2744
Mongolia **7:** 3895
Myanmar **7:** 4031
private education
and differential demand model **8:** 4832
schools
nontraditional education **1:** 261, 263
Swaziland **10:** 5862
Vanuatu **11:** 6580
Religious education **1:** 96; **9:** ***4995–5008***
administration **9:** 5004
Christianity **2:** 766
curriculum **9:** 5005
definitions of **9:** 4995
drama in **9:** 5002
evaluation **9:** 5005
exploitation **9:** 5000
finance **9:** 5005
forms of **9:** 4997
history of women's education **11:** 6744
and Marxism **9:** 5009
methods and media **9:** 5001
and multimedia technology **9:** 5003
and Nazism **9:** 5009
objectives **9:** 4998
cognitive vs. affective **9:** 5000
indoctrination vs. comparison **9:** 5000
overt vs. implied **9:** 4998
occasional classes **9:** 4998
and ordination
conflict **9:** 5006
participatory sermons **9:** 5002
personnel **9:** 5003, 5006
research **9:** 5006
ritualistic knowledge **6:** 3150
Shinto **9:** ***5449–5453***
and social change **9:** 5005
student centered projects **9:** 5002
teaching methods
Biblical model **2:** 766
terminology **9:** 5006
Religious factors
beliefs
individual development **5:** ***2651–2656***
in education **9:** ***5008–5013***
Religious instruction
and religious education
use of term **9:** 4996
Religious organizations
adult education **8:** 4808
and development education **3:** 1496
and literacy programs **7:** 4146, 4147
and private schools **8:** 4833
students
and political issues **10:** 5777
Remedial education
See Remedial instruction
Remedial instruction
and labor force basic skills **1:** 110
regular and special education relationship **3:** 1506
special classes **2:** 721
teaching methods
mastery learning **6:** 3627
Remedial programs
paraprofessional school personnel **7:** 4293
Remedial reading
dyslexia **7:** 4080
Reading Recovery program (US) **5:** 2514
Remediation
See Remedial instruction
Repeated measures analysis **11:** 6586
Repertory grid technique **9:** ***5013–5016***
applications
dynamic **9:** 5016
static **9:** 5016
constructs **9:** 5014
elements **9:** 5014
choice of **9:** 5015
laddering **9:** 5014
mathematical analyses **9:** 5015
origins **9:** 5013
procedures for **9:** 5015
pyramid construction **9:** 5015
Repetition rate
See Grade repetition rate
Repgrid technique
See Repertory grid technique
Report cards
daily
and behavioral theories **10:** 6161
and student evaluation **8:** ***4617–4623***
Reproduction (biology)
demographic trends
global consequences of education **4:** 2171
and social adjustment
sociobiological approach **4:** 2170
Reproduction theory **9:** ***5016–5021***, 5056
and academic autonomy **9:** 5019
cultural demands of schooling **9:** 5019
historical background **9:** 5016
and ideology **9:** 5056
importance of **9:** 5020
language differences **9:** 5017
origins of change **9:** 5020
resistance **9:** 5056
and hidden curriculum **5:** 2588
social class and culture **9:** 5016
and sociology of education **2:** 780
teacher role **9:** 5018
See also
Cultural reproduction
Social reproduction
Reprography
and copyright infringement **5:** 2997
and copyrights **2:** 1101
and information networks
international **5:** 2997
Research
case studies
methods **2:** ***640–646***
databases
and management information systems **6:** 3594
educational administration **1:** 53
empirical
precedence of **9:** 5039
and evaluation **4:** 2113; **8:** 4762
humanistic **3:** 1464
influence on perception **8:** 4559
international aspects **5:** 2975
nonexperimental
causation in **8:** 4340
paradigms
in education **9:** ***5051–5056***
and policy
relationship **8:** 4550
and policy formation
relationships **8:** 4559
presentation of **3:** 1473
priorities **8:** 4560
semantics **11:** 6439
See also
Action research
Educational research
Legitimatory research
Research administration
educational researchers vs. policymakers **8:** 4560
Research design **4:** 2079, 2080, 2081
blocking variables **4:** 2190
classroom **4:** 2193

data collection **4:** 2386
and effect size **4:** 2192
influences **8:** 4874
internal validity
threat to **8:** 4874
leadership studies **6:** 3281
metacognition **7:** 3790
notation system **4:** 2187
sensitivity of **4:** 2189
small studies **4:** 2082, 2086
treatment
random assignment to **4:** 2081
true
posttest-only control group **4:** 2081
pretest–posttest control group **4:** 2081
Solomon four-group **4:** 2081
validity **4:** 2081, 2084
See also
Quasiexperimental design
Research and development (R & D)
and educational reform **11:** 6556
model
in education **4:** 1858, 1862, 1863
and program evaluation **4:** 2070
of tests
and expectancy tables **4:** 2181
Research and development centers
business university links **8:** 4338
and vocational education
Latin America **7:** 4152
Research–development–diffusion (RDD) model
and information dissemination **3:** 1550
Research institutes
policy formation
international organizations **2:** 934
Research libraries
educational resources **6:** 3397
role of **6:** 3394
Research methodology
bias **9:** 5050
case studies **2:** 640
classes **9:** 5045
ethical issues **4:** 2032
experimental studies **4:** ***2186–2194***
experiments **9:** 5047
generalizations **9:** 5046
and hermeneutics **5:** 2585
historical methods **5:** ***2601–2607***
interviews
treatment of data **5:** 3006
measurement **9:** 5047
models **9:** 5048
naturalistic vs. positivist paradigms **4:** 2087
observations and data **9:** 5046
philosophy of science **9:** 5043
probability **9:** 5048
propositions **9:** 5045
scientific methods **9:** ***5043–5050***
scientific terms
semantics **9:** 5044
sequential **9:** 5039
simulation **9:** ***5467–5471***
statistical analysis
and educational evaluation **11:** 6380
statistics **9:** 5048
surveys **10:** ***5854–5862***
technics **9:** 5043
theories of **9:** 5049
validation of **9:** 5049
triangulation **11:** ***6461–6466***
values **9:** 5050
See also
Scientific methodology
Research practice relationship
See Theory practice relationship
Research projects
and learning **6:** 3300
Research reports
characteristics of
coding of **7:** 3780
language styles **6:** 3217
for meta analysis **7:** 3776
and narrative inquiry **7:** 4047, 4049
Research and Study Center for the Dissemination of the French Language **6:** 3210
Research synthesis
methods **10:** 6235
combined significance test models **10:** 6236
effect size **10:** 6236
narrative **10:** 6236
qualitative **10:** 6237
vote counting **10:** 6236
narrative methods **7:** 3775
objectives **10:** 6235
quantitative methods **7:** 3775
quantitative studies **7:** 3775
and secondary data analysis **9:** 5368, 5371
strategies for **7:** 3775
studies
literature for **7:** 3776
on teaching **10:** ***6235–6240***
comparative studies **10:** 6237
syntheses of **10:** 6238
See also
Meta analysis
Research utilization
legitimatory research **6:** 3369
models **4:** 1862
social science research
and policy formation **5:** ***2670–2673***
Researchers
communication skills **11:** 6621
and data analysis **3:** 1465
training for
graduate study **11:** 6438
See also
Educational researchers
Residential colleges
and student personnel services **10:** 5796, 5801
wardens of **10:** 5801
Residential institutions
disabilities
Japan **3:** 1434, 1435
Residential schools
for blind students **11:** 6626
folk high schools **4:** 2327
for labor education
United States **11:** 6770
Nordic countries **7:** 4179
special education **2:** 722
visual impairments **11:** 6626
Resilience
child
characteristics of **8:** 4778
concentration camp survivors
research **8:** 4778
definitions of **8:** 4775
programs **8:** ***4775–4780***
future research **8:** 4779
protective factors **8:** 4775
within child **8:** 4776
within community **8:** 4777
within family **8:** 4777
related research **8:** 4775
school-based programs **8:** 4777
studies **8:** 4775
Resistance (psychology)
critical **9:** 5058
and curriculum research **3:** 1346
educational attitudes **9:** ***5056–5061***
and educational practices **9:** 5059
educational research **9:** 5058
and family influence **4:** 2270
females **9:** 5057
ironic **9:** 5057
and reproduction theory **9:** 5056
schools as sites of **6:** 3619
use of term **9:** 5056
Resistance to change
and educational research
oral history approach **7:** 4223
Resistance theory
beginnings of **9:** 5057
and curriculum policies **3:** 1335
problems **9:** 5058
Resonance disorders
See Voice disorders
Resource allocation
adult education **4:** 2393
and basic education
developing nations **1:** 470
in education
studies **2:** 1124
and education cost function (ECF) **2:** 1124
and educational contraction **6:** 3607
and educational efficiency **3:** 1780, 1782
and educational finance **9:** 5238
and educational quality **9:** 5235
educational research **8:** 4602
grants
implications of **9:** 5063
and instructional materials **9:** 5540
and management information systems **5:** 2828
nonformal education
developing nations **2:** 1150; **7:** 4140

and occupational information
6: 3097, 3098
and outcomes of education
effect of unions on **10:** 6069
and private sector **9:** 5063
and productivity **7:** 3817
research
obstacles **9:** 5065
and school-based management
3: 1409; **9:** 5305
school districts
origins of interest in **9:** 5061
in schools **9:** ***5061–5066***
inequalities **9:** 5062
research **9:** 5061
substitute teachers **10:** 5832
and tax efficiency **9:** 5237
Resource centers
adult education **1:** 141
disabilities **5:** 2906
Resource room programs **5:** 2904
alternatives to **9:** 5070
for children with disabilities **2:** 722
efficacy research
analysis of **9:** 5068
weaknesses **9:** 5068
empirical studies **9:** 5068
historical background **9:** 5066
pull-out model
research **9:** 5068
shortcomings **9:** 5069
as special education model
9: ***5066–5071***
subject-specific **9:** 5067
teacher responsibility **9:** 5067
teams for **10:** 6241
types of **9:** 5066
visual impairments
special education **11:** 6626
Respite care
and deinstitutionalization (of
disabled) **3:** 1437
Respondent validation
participant observation **7:** 4316, 4318
Response contingent testing
See Adaptive testing
Response rates (questionnaires)
8: 4882, 4885
maximizing **7:** 3854
and surveys **10:** 5859
Response style (tests)
and measurement effects **11:** 6508
and personality inventories **8:** 4396
and projective measures **8:** 4788
in questionnaires **8:** 4882
Responses
active
and programmed instruction
8: 4771
in attitude measures **9:** 5319
errors
and social background research
7: 3719
and rating scales **8:** 4924
Responsibility
and ethics **4:** 2030
and ideology **3:** 1535
moral issues **10:** 6049
Resúmenes Analíticos en Educación
(*RAE*)
annual index **3:** 1591
development of **3:** 1590
Retention (in grade)
See Grade repetition
Retention (in school)
See School holding power
Retention (psychology)
and study skills **10:** 5830
vocational education
learning modules **7:** 3893
Retirement
higher education in **7:** 4169
and life expectancy **6:** 3375
and recurrent education **8:** 4963
Retraining **6:** 3418
Europe **4:** 2059
for high quality production
Anglo–German comparisons
11: 6639
institutions
Soviet Union (former) **9:** 5095
technological advancement and
6: 3304
Return to basics
See Back to basics
Revenue costs
See Operating expenses
Revenue expenditure
See Operating expenses
Review (reexamination)
and secondary data analysis **9:** 5368
Revision (written composition)
writing processes **11:** 6778
Revolution
and educational planning
Latin America **8:** 4493
Iran
state church relationship **9:** 5010
and Marxist educational thought
6: 3617, 3619
teacher participation **8:** 4585
Rewards
as incentives **4:** 2280
and interpersonal competence
training for **9:** 5566
student
and sex discrimination **9:** 5170
See also
Incentives
Rhetoric
Greek textbooks **8:** 4888
and humanities **5:** 2693
and logical thinking **8:** 4948
moral issues **8:** 4888
persuasive discourse **8:** 4888
Quintilian **8:** ***4887–4890***
Rhetorical invention
Quintilian **8:** 4888
Rhetorical theory
criticism of
Saint Augustine **9:** 5115
Risk
individual attitudes toward
and employment **3:** 1747
Rituals
and knowledge **6:** 3149
Robbins Report 1963 (UK)
and polytechnical education **8:** 4606
Robotics
laboratory packages for **6:** 3204
Robustness (statistics) **9:** ***5077–5082***
and adaptive testing **1:** 51
and analysis of variance **9:** 5080
example **9:** 5080
computer software for **9:** 5079
employment level
measurement **7:** 3719
and exploratory data analysis **4:** 2199
M-estimation **9:** 5077
alternative functions **9:** 5078, 5081
example **9:** 5078
outlying observations **9:** 5077
detection of **9:** 5077
and regression **9:** 5078
example **9:** 5079
and secondary data analysis **9:** 5371
Rock music
and youth culture **11:** 6802
Role conflict
in schools **10:** 6220
teachers **10:** 6131
Role of education
and segmentation theory
developing nations **3:** 1682
Role perception
teachers
role conflict **10:** 6131
Role playing
and computer-assisted instruction
2: 989
and computer simulation **2:** 987
and individual instruction **5:** 2771
and religious education **9:** 5003
Role taking
See Perspective taking
Role theory
and social organizations
educational **10:** 6219
Roman Catholic Church
See Catholicism
Romania
adult education
history **2:** 656, 658
adult education legislation **6:** 3364
cultural influences **9:** 5082
curriculum development **9:** 5086
educational finance **9:** 5085
educational research **9:** 5086
English language instruction **4:** 2350
government school relationship
school administration **9:** 5085
illiteracy **2:** 657
nonformal education **9:** 5085
postsecondary education **9:** 5084

preschool education **9:** 5084
primary education **9:** 5084
secondary education **9:** 5084
special education **9:** 5085
system of education **9:** ***5082–5087***
degrees and qualifications **9:** 5086
educational objectives **9:** 5083
enrollment **9:** 5083
major problems **9:** 5086
structure **9:** 5083
teacher education **9:** 5085
technical education **9:** 5085
Romanticism
and adult education **1:** 138
and Froebelian theory **4:** 2387; **8:** 4667
Root mean square deviation
See Standard deviation (statistics)
Rorschach tests
criticisms of **8:** 4789
interpretation **8:** 4788
method **8:** 4788
Rote learning
and comprehension **8:** 4724
criticisms of **10:** 6165
historical background **10:** 6165
mathematics instruction
history of **6:** 3644
and religious education **9:** 5001
Spencer's criticism of **10:** 5707
Rotter Incomplete Sentences Blank **8:** 4791
Routines **2:** ***816–820***
and classroom environment **2:** 819
formal **2:** 818
fundamental concepts of **2:** 817
informal **2:** 818
instructional effectiveness **2:** 817
research into **2:** 818
objectives of **2:** 817
research methodology **2:** 818
Rubella
and deaf–blind children **3:** 1402
Rudolf Steiner Schools
See Waldorf schools
Rules **2:** ***816–820***
categories of **2:** 818
and classroom environment **2:** 819
formal **2:** 818
fundamental concepts of **2:** 817
informal **2:** 818
instructional effectiveness
research into **2:** 818
research methodology **2:** 818
Runaways **3:** 1733
child abuse **3:** 1734
Rural areas
dropout rate **9:** 5227
education–earnings relationship **3:** 1704
and educational technology **9:** 5542
United States **1:** 240
Rural development **1:** 96
integrated
adult education **8:** 4809
India **2:** 905
use of term **1:** 119
and small business training **4:** 1988
Rural education **1:** 131, ***240–244***
and agricultural education **1:** 240
developed nations **1:** 240
distance education **1:** 240
new ideologies **1:** 240
and quality of life **1:** 240
vs. urban education
and educational finance **3:** 1791
Rural extension **1:** 96
for adults **8:** 4807
Canada **7:** 4182
costs **2:** 1149
Latin America **6:** 3254
programs **7:** 4139
United States **7:** 4182
women's education
developing nations **11:** 6715
Rural extension agents
exposure to
farmers **1:** 252
farming community **1:** 252
and formal education **1:** 252
Rural schools
culture conflicts in **2:** 914
and hidden curriculum **2:** 915
local cultures **2:** 915
France **2:** 915
Germany **2:** 915
United States **1:** 240
Rural sociology
rural schools **1:** 240
Rural urban differences
educational administration **8:** 4565
and literacy testing **6:** 3472
primary school agriculture
Africa **8:** 4684
and school size **9:** 5293
and skill development **10:** 5918
Rural to urban migration
determinants of
and education **5:** ***2942–2945***
developing nations **3:** 1682
and educational change **4:** 1850
and educational policy **5:** 2510
and homeless children **3:** 1734
labor force participation
females **3:** 1667
Latin America **6:** 3262; **7:** 4149
Ruskin College
Oxford (UK) **2:** 1190
Russia
adult education **9:** 5101
curriculum development **9:** 5104
educational change **9:** 5106
educational finance **9:** 5103
educational research **9:** 5105
foreign language instruction **4:** 2354
language **9:** 5098
nonformal education **9:** 5102
postsecondary education **9:** 5100
preschool education **8:** 4669; **9:** 5100
primary education **9:** 5099
secondary education **9:** 5100
vocational education **9:** 5101
special education **9:** 5101
system of education **9:** ***5098–5107***
degrees and qualifications **9:** 5105
educational objectives **9:** 5099
major problems **9:** 5106
structure **9:** 5099
teacher education **9:** 5103
teacher recruitment **9:** 5104
teaching methodology **9:** 5105
See also
Soviet Union (USSR) (former)
Rwanda
adult education **1:** 219
nonformal education **9:** 5110
curriculum development **9:** 5112
distance education **1:** 218
educational change **9:** 5113
educational research **9:** 5113
ethnic groups **9:** 5107
language **9:** 5107
postsecondary education **9:** 5109
preschool education **9:** 5110
primary education **9:** 5108
secondary education **9:** 5109
special education **9:** 5110
student evaluation **9:** 5112
system of education **9:** ***5107–5114***
degrees and qualifications **9:** 5113
educational objectives **9:** 5107
enrollment **9:** 5108
major problems **9:** 5113
structure **9:** 5108
teacher recruitment **9:** 5112

Saemaul Education
Korea **2:** 905
Safety
and educational facilities planning **4:** 2227
within schools
females **2:** 834
Salaries
and career choice
teaching **10:** 5844
See also
Teacher salaries
Salary expectations
labor market
bumping model **6:** 3182
Salary wage differentials
and public policy **11:** 6635
See also
Earnings differentials
Saltus model
and developmental stages **3:** 1512
example **3:** 1512
Samoan Islands
See American Samoa
Samoans
ethnography of **3:** 1754
Sample size
choice of **9:** 5140
effective **9:** 5138
and factor analysis **4:** 2236
in generalizability theory **5:** 2459
and nonresponse effects **7:** 3854

in Q-methodology **8:** 4857
and statistical power **4:** 2192
and time series analysis **9:** 5488
Sampling
accuracy **9:** 5135
advantages **4:** 2387
balanced incomplete block (BIB) **5:** 3058
example **5:** 3059
and Bayesian statistics **1:** 477
bias **9:** 5135, 5141
and case studies **3:** 1467
comparability in national **4:** 2135
and correlation **2:** 1110, 1112
and descriptive data **3:** 1464
design
efficiency **9:** 5137
survey samples **9:** 5137
design effect (Deff) **9:** 5137
dimensions
and participant observation **7:** 4318
distribution
and correlation **2:** 1111
and nonparametric statistics **7:** 4158
effective size **9:** 5138
equal probability of selection method (EPSEM) **9:** 5133
estimation **9:** 5135
and factorial modeling **4:** 2241
frames **9:** 5132
general theory of **5:** 3055
and hypothesis testing **5:** 2711
incidence **5:** 3060
intraclass correlation coefficient
estimation of **9:** 5139
mean square error (MSE) **9:** 5136
and microcomputers **7:** 3814
multiple matrix
in evaluation **4:** 2092
multistage **9:** 5133
and multivariate analysis **7:** 4012
complex survey data **9:** 5137
and national surveys **2:** 649
nonprobability **9:** 5132
and nonrepresentative data **3:** 1472
nonresponse **9:** 5141
planning equation **9:** 5140
population inference **9:** 5135
populations **9:** 5131
precision **9:** 5135
estimates of **9:** 5136
probability **9:** 5132
methods **9:** 5133
probability proportional to size (PPS) **9:** 5134
lottery method **9:** 5135
random
in bootstrap procedure **9:** 5469
cross-sectional studies **2:** 1214
and generalizability theory **5:** 2458, 2460
and research design **8:** 4874
and test construction **11:** 6321
and videotape recordings **11:** 6606
randomization **5:** 2711
replication **5:** 2711
rotated **5:** 3059
and selection bias **9:** 5380
simple two-stage **9:** 5138
design tables for **9:** 5139
and social networks **9:** 5557
standard error
in cross-national comparisons **4:** 2135
and statistical significance **9:** 5460
and stratification **9:** 5133
and survey designs **7:** 3853
in survey research **9:** ***5131–5142***
and surveys **10:** 5854, 5857
systematic selection **9:** 5134
target populations
in cross-national comparisons **4:** 2134
and time series studies **6:** 3517
weighting **9:** 5135
See also
Item sampling
Sampling errors
Sampling errors
complex samples **9:** 5125
modeling **9:** 5129
and cross-sectional studies **2:** 1219
definition of **9:** 5124
and design effect **9:** 5125
estimation of **9:** 5124
balanced repeated replication **9:** 5127
bootstrap procedure **9:** 5128
empirical techniques **9:** 5126
jackknife procedure **9:** 5127
random subsample replication **9:** 5126
Taylor's series approximations **9:** 5128
and item sampling **5:** 3057
mean square error **9:** 5124
random samples **9:** 5124
in survey research **9:** ***5124–5131***
use of range in determining **7:** 3731
See also
Error of measurement
Sarvodaya Shramadana Movement
Sri Lanka **1:** 118, 132; **5:** 2756; **8:** 4809
Satellite Instructional Television Experiment (India) **2:** 884
Satellites (aerospace)
applications **11:** 6303
See also
Communications satellites
Satisfaction
and motivation **7:** 3945
Saturn (Europe)
open learning network
objectives **3:** 1582
Saudi Arabia
adult education
nonformal education **9:** 5147
curriculum development **9:** 5148
educational finance **9:** 5147
and school organization **7:** 4231
educational planning **8:** 4484
educational research **9:** 5150
government school relationship
school administration **9:** 5147
preschool education **9:** 5146
private education **9:** 5145
social studies **10:** 5583
special education **9:** 5146
system of education **9:** ***5142–5151***
degrees and qualifications **9:** 5149
educational objectives **9:** 5143
enrollment **9:** 5144, 5147
major problems **9:** 5150
structure **9:** 5144
teacher education **9:** 5148
teacher recruitment **9:** 5148
teaching methodology **9:** 5149
technical education **9:** 5146
vocational education **9:** 5146
women's education **11:** 6755, 6758
Scaffolding **2:** 836; **4:** 2197
and computer-assisted learning **2:** 1004
science instruction **9:** 5340, 5341
writing instruction **11:** 6779
Scales
type of **7:** 3700
See also
Measures (individuals)
Rating scales
Scaling
achievement tests **1:** ***32–42***
and attitude measures **1:** 382, 383
categorized ratings
analysis of **9:** 5156
and computers **9:** 5156
criterion
and rating scales **8:** 4926
distances between objects **9:** 5157
and educational assessment **1:** 370
and equated scores **11:** 6349
equipercentile
in longitudinal studies **6:** 3520
and exploratory data analysis **4:** 2203
free clustering **9:** 5154
Individual Differences model (INDSCAL) **9:** 5158
item response theory
in longitudinal studies **6:** 3521
judgments **9:** 5151
of similarity **9:** 5155
linear
in longitudinal studies **6:** 3520
methods **9:** ***5151–5159***
balanced incomplete block (BIB) **9:** 5153
multidimensional preference analysis (MDPREF) **9:** 5156
multiple
and partial order scalogram analysis **7:** 4313
ordered category ratings **9:** 5153
ordered preferences
analysis of **9:** 5155
and partial order scalogram analysis **7:** 4308

preferences **9:** 5151
psychological objects **9:** 5151
responses to **9:** 5151
and public examinations **4:** 2175
rank methods **9:** 5152
variance stable rank sum **9:** 5155
Rasch model **7:** 4055
and attitude measures **1:** 385
and robustness (statistics) **9:** 5078
similarities
analysis of **9:** 5158
and smallest space analysis **9:** 5497
types of tasks **9:** 5152
See also
Multidimensional scaling
Scalogram analysis
and attitude measures **1:** 384
See also
Partial order scalogram analysis
Scandinavia
educational policy
and disabilities **10:** 6243
organizational development
trends **7:** 4239
special education **10:** 5660
student loan programs
studies **10:** 5766
transition programs
and disabilities **11:** 6460
work experience programs **3:** 1687
See also
Nordic countries
Scheduling
in projects **8:** 4757
Schemata (cognition) **6:** 3152, 3322
frames **6:** 3153
hierarchical **1:** 329
and language **8:** 4649
mental images **6:** 3153
mental models **6:** 3153
modification by new experience **6:** 3154
scripts **6:** 3153
Schematic models **7:** 3868
Scholarly journals
audiences for **5:** 2996
information networks
international **5:** 2996
ownership of **5:** 2996
See also
Periodicals
Scholarships
international aid
for vocational education **11:** 6661
Scholastic aptitude
See Academic aptitude
Scholastic Aptitude Test (SAT) **11:** 6341
and equated scores **11:** 6354
and item sampling **5:** 3058
moderation procedures for **4:** 2176
and scaling **6:** 3521
scores
and birth order **7:** 3870
studies
and selection bias **9:** 5381
and test bias **11:** 6317
and test coaching **11:** 6334, 6336, 6337
and trend analysis **6:** 3515
Scholasticism
compared with Cartesianism **3:** 1463
educational objectives **9:** 5121
literature appreciation **9:** 5122
pedagogy **9:** 5121
Saint Thomas Aquinas **9:** ***5121–5124***
teacher education **9:** 5123
School accounting
and cost effectiveness studies **2:** 1133
School activities
and disabilities
quality **11:** 6459
effective
and disabilities **11:** 6459
and resilience **8:** 4777
and school size **9:** 5293
School administration
and budgeting **9:** ***5181–5186***
definition **9:** 5182
and centralization **6:** 3494
centralization vs. decentralization **9:** 5165
factors **9:** 5165
research **6:** 3494
changing perceptions of **9:** 5166
computer software for **9:** 5184
constraints and limitations **9:** 5162
decentralization **6:** 3493
and educational reform **11:** 6555
and educational finance **9:** 5182
and educational planning **9:** 5167
effective schools **4:** ***1929–1934***
females
aspirations **11:** 6730
barriers to **11:** 6729
comparative analysis **11:** 6727
developing nations **11:** 6727
effectiveness **11:** 6728
United States **11:** ***6727–6731***
history of **9:** ***5159–5169***
international developments **5:** ***2504–2509***
and learning factors **10:** 5748
levels of **9:** 5159
microcomputer applications **9:** 5184
nature of **4:** 1929
and organizational theories **9:** 5161
and principals
role of **9:** 5270
research
factors **5:** 2507
scope of **9:** 5181
secondary schools
effective schools research **9:** 5376
and sex discrimination
developing nations **4:** 2422
and sex fairness **4:** 2422
urban schools **11:** 6554
vocational schools
and educational quality **8:** 4860
See also
School-based management
School administrators
See Administrators
School of the Air (Australia) **3:** 1564
School architecture
See Educational facilities design
School attendance
See Attendance
School attendance legislation **6:** 3358
and educational history **5:** 2606
immigrants
United States **7:** 3842
School attitudes
comparative analysis **1:** ***390–396***
sex bias **4:** 2409
School-based curriculum planning **3:** ***1267–1272***
School-based management **9:** ***5302–5308***
administrative effects of **3:** 1409
adoption of **3:** 1410
approaches **9:** 5303
and budgeting **9:** 5183
and bureaucracy **1:** 592
characteristics of **9:** 5183
concept of **9:** 5305
concerns **9:** 5305
decentralization
and role of the state in education **3:** 1718
and educational policy **10:** 6080
global approach **5:** 2498
and educational reform **9:** 5276
effects on learning **3:** 1410
historical background **9:** 5304
impact of **9:** 5306
issues **9:** 5307
national curriculum
and centralized testing **3:** 1719
and organizational development **7:** 4238
and personnel policy **8:** 4408
problems **9:** 5307; **11:** 6555
recruitment and orientation **10:** 6046
and school councils **6:** 3491
school district role in **9:** 5221
and school effectiveness **5:** 2507
and school self-evaluation **5:** 2849
structure of **3:** 1409
United Kingdom **9:** 5197
urban schools **11:** 6560
vs. centralization **9:** 5211
See also
School enterprise
School restructuring
School self-evaluation (SSE)
School boards
See Boards of education
School buildings
adaptation for wheelchairs **5:** 2909
long range planning **4:** 2330
School business management
See School administration
School business officials
competencies needed **9:** 5182
and computer system design **9:** 5185
guidelines for **9:** 5182

School business partnerships
9: ***5186–5192***
and apprenticeships **9:** 5186
criticisms of **9:** 5190
definition of **9:** 5187
effectiveness of **9:** 5189
evaluation of **9:** 5188
issues **9:** 5189
future development **9:** 5190
individual **9:** 5187
international development **9:** 5190
objectives **9:** 5190
origins of **9:** 5186
rationales **9:** 5187
reinforcement technique **9:** 5189
replication and influence **9:** 5188
scope **9:** 5187
significance of **9:** 5188
trends **9:** 5186
types of **9:** 5187
School business relationship **8:** 4337
Albania **1:** 257
and curriculum development **8:** 4337
and educational finance **9:** 5188
Egypt **4:** 1943
Ireland, Republic of **5:** 3013
Madagascar **6:** 3553
motivation **9:** 5187
and school culture **9:** 5207
technical education **11:** 6271
vocational education
participation **11:** 6649
Sweden **11:** 6693
training with production **11:** 6449
See also
School business partnerships
School characteristics
See Institutional characteristics
School choice **9:** ***5197–5201***
and access to education
regulations **9:** 5200
aim **9:** 5197
Australia **8:** 4825
and bureaucracy **1:** 589
and civil liberties **9:** 5199
and earnings differentials **6:** 3103
and educational opportunities
9: 5198, 5199
and educational quality **9:** 5197
and educational reform **9:** 5276
educational vouchers **4:** 2330; **8:** 4825
historical background **9:** 5202
effects of
research **9:** 5194
and equal education **9:** 5198
and freedom of conscience
policies for **9:** 5193
and governance **5:** 2505; **8:** 4592
and human capital theory
parental attitudes **6:** 3102
and institutional characteristics
policies for **9:** 5193
and justice
theoretical perspectives **9:** 5198
and language maintenance
policies for **9:** 5193
market mechanisms **9:** ***5201–5206***
and meritocracy **9:** 5198
objections to **9:** 5196
parental
policies for **9:** 5192
by parents **2:** 891
United Kingdom **3:** 1336
policies **9:** 5197
Australia **9:** 5197
Canada **9:** 5197
responses to **9:** 5198
United Kingdom **9:** 5197
United States **9:** 5197
policy issues **9:** 5195
popularity of
research **9:** 5194
private and public schools **9:** 5199
and private school aid **9:** 5200
private schools and tax rates **9:** 5199
and privatization **5:** 2498;
9: ***5192–5197***
public vs. private education **8:** 4831
and racial desegregation
policies for **9:** 5193
research **9:** 5194
and role of the state in education
3: 1717
and sex differences
economics of **4:** ***2412–2419***
and social values
conflict **9:** 5198
sociological perspective **8:** ***4824–4831***
strategies for
public vs. market **9:** 5202
support for **9:** 5195
tax credits
tuition **9:** 5202
theories of **4:** 2413
altruistic parents model **4:** 2413
household choice model **4:** 2413
parent-centered model **4:** 2413
trends **9:** 5196
United States **8:** 4825
and urban education **11:** 6556
and urban schools **11:** 6560
vs. equal education **1:** 591
School climate
change in
research **9:** 5208
components of **9:** 5207
concept of **9:** 5207
criticisms of **9:** 5208
and culture **9:** ***5206–5211***
measurement of
descriptive scales **3:** ***1475–1483***
surveys
uses of **9:** 5210
use of term **9:** 5206, 5207
See also
School culture
School community relationship
9: ***5211–5217***
adaptation **2:** 914, 915, 916
anthropological study **2:** ***914–918***
communications **9:** 5265
discontinuities in **1:** 291
educational finance **2:** ***910–914***
and micropolitics **7:** 3822
and outcomes of education **9:** 5260
parent attitudes **2:** 917
parent role
and professional role **9:** 5214
Plato on **8:** 4534
and principals
role of **9:** 5269
research **9:** 5214
resistance **2:** 914
rural schools **2:** 915
and school-based management
9: 5306
and sociocultural systems **9:** 5311,
5312
student attitudes **2:** 916
trends **9:** 5215
urban schools **2:** 915
vocational schools **8:** 4860
School councils **6:** ***3491–3496***
parent participation
and governance **6:** 3494
and school-based management
6: 3491
use of term **6:** 3491
School counseling
organizations (groups) **9:** 5283
periodicals for **9:** 5283
School counselors
historical background **9:** 5282
as related services personnel **9:** 5282
role of **9:** 5283
School culture
alternative perspectives **9:** 5209
and climate **9:** ***5206–5211***
common traits
and research **9:** 5208
concept of **9:** 5207, 5208
definitions of **9:** 5208
and educational improvement **9:** 5242
and outcomes of education **9:** 5260
and principals
role of **9:** 5269
research studies **9:** 5209
and school law **9:** 5253
and social psychology **10:** 6223
and student role **10:** 5794
studies
uses of **9:** 5210
subcultures of **9:** 5209
use of term **9:** 5206
See also
School climate
School demography
analog model of **7:** 3867
and learning factors **10:** 5748
School desegregation **3:** ***1483–1486***
and busing
United States **9:** 5199
and democracy **8:** 4587
and effective schools research **9:** 5375
effectiveness of **3:** 1483
equal status contact theory **3:** 1485
and friendship **9:** 5174
implementation **3:** 1484

issues **3:** 1483
policies for **3:** 1485
racial attitudes **3:** 1484
research studies **3:** 1483
and school choice **9:** 5193
School Development Plans (SDPs) (UK) **5:** 2850
School district autonomy
and school effectiveness **5:** 2507
School districts
administration
and educational expectation **8:** 4567
characteristics of
and political economy **8:** 4563
co-operation between
benefits **7:** 3819
corruption in **6:** 3493
and decentralization **9:** 5221
and educational improvement **9:** ***5221–5224***
influences **9:** 5222
and educational innovation
implementation of **5:** 2842
inequalities **9:** 5062
influences
on schools **9:** 5222
and information technology **5:** 2828
and micropolitics
research **7:** 3823
mini-state theory
key elements of **8:** 4564
and political considerations **8:** 4564
organizational complexity **6:** 3493
and principals
cooperation **9:** 5223
and resource allocation **9:** 5061
role of
and school-based management **3:** 1410
in school governance **6:** 3495
United States
civic values **2:** 770
use of term **6:** 3491
See also
Local education authorities (LEAs) (UK)
School dropouts
See Dropouts
School dynamics **9:** ***5169–5176***
cognitive processes **9:** 5169
instructional processes **9:** 5169
interactive processes **9:** 5169
social processes **9:** 5172
School effectiveness
and academic achievement **5:** 2508; **8:** 4870
and administrator education
inservice **1:** 71
and bureaucracy **1:** ***589–594***
creation of
practices and principles **4:** 1932
and decentralization **3:** 1407
determinants of **4:** 1932
and discipline **3:** 1537
and educational change **6:** 3491
and educational quality **8:** 4865
vocational education **8:** 4859
evaluation for improvement
United States **4:** ***2381–2389***
external influences on **9:** 5374
factors **4:** 1932
and family characteristics
developing nations **1:** 470
and free market approach **5:** 2505
and governance **8:** 4591
and hidden curriculum **5:** 2588
internal influences on **9:** 5375
measurement of **3:** 1383
movement
and teaching experience **10:** 6132
United Kingdom **7:** 3910
and organizational theories **4:** 2164
and parent school relationship **2:** 888
and politics of education **8:** 4587
private education
vs. public education **1:** 590
private schools **8:** 4827
public schools vs. private schools **8:** 4839
and publication of examination results
United Kingdom **7:** 3910
research **9:** 5221
and educational administration **3:** 1741
methodological issues **4:** ***1934–1939***
and resource room programs **9:** 5068
and role theory **10:** 6220
and school administration **9:** 5166
and school-based management
research **9:** 5306
and school business partnerships **9:** 5189
and school climate **9:** 5207
and school district autonomy **5:** 2507
and school self-evaluation **5:** 2847
selection bias **4:** 1936
and socio-economic status **4:** 1935
standardized tests
and input output analysis **3:** 1759
studies **1:** 593; **9:** 5373
urban schools **11:** 6554
See also
Effective schools
Effective schools research
School enterprise
benefits **9:** 5229
educational **9:** 5229
constraints **9:** 5232
economics of **9:** ***5228–5233***
externalities **9:** 5230
studies **9:** 5231
teacher control of **9:** 5230
School entrance age
comparative analysis **2:** 959
effect in Latin America **3:** 1831
school readiness **9:** 5274
and individualized education programs **9:** 5274
School environment
See Classroom environment
Educational environment
School expenditures
allocation of **9:** 5239
definition of **9:** 5233
increase
factors affecting **9:** 5234
School failure
See Academic failure
Low achievement
Underachievement
School finance
See Educational finance
School funds
United Kingdom **9:** 5197
School government relationship
See Government school relationship
School health education
See Health education, in schools
School health services **5:** 2566, 2573
definitions of **9:** 5284
organization **5:** 2574
special education students **5:** 2574
financial support **5:** 2575
surveys **9:** 5284
School holding power
comparative analysis
international studies **1:** 470
and public examinations **4:** 2173
School improvement
See Educational facilities
improvement
School inspectors
centralized model
France **9:** 5248
decentralized model
England and Wales **9:** 5249
federal models **9:** 5249
historical background **9:** 5247
power structure **9:** 5247
role of **9:** ***5247–5252***
in teacher evaluation **4:** 2126
Australia **4:** 2126
Ireland, Republic of **4:** 2126
United States **4:** 2126
types of **9:** 5247
See also
Her Majesty's Inspectors (HMI) (UK)
School law
characteristics of **9:** 5252
and cognate law **9:** 5253
concept of **9:** 5252
and educational planning **9:** ***5252–5255***
effectiveness of
and educational planning **9:** 5255
framework for approaching **9:** 5252
jurisdictional limits to **9:** 5252
mandatory **9:** 5253
permissive **9:** 5253
process of **9:** 5254
purpose of **9:** 5254
sources of **9:** 5253
substance of **9:** 5253
trends **9:** 5254
weight of **9:** 5253

School leavers
  educational strategies for unemployed **8:** 4961
  expectations of work **8:** 4962
  unemployment **3:** 1706
School libraries
  books
    and censorship **11:** 6367
  educational resources **6:** 3397
  and media programs **7:** 3755
  and printed materials **8:** 4696
    provision **8:** 4697
  role of **6:** 3394
School location
  access to education
    and school mapping **9:** 5257
School location planning
  See School mapping
School maintenance **4:** 2224
  and educational facilities planning **4:** 2228
School management
  See School administration
School managers
  See Administrators
School mapping **9:** ***5255–5259***
  administration of **9:** 5258
  characteristics of **9:** 5255
  definition of **9:** 5255
  generalization
    requirements **9:** 5258
  historical background **9:** 5256
  introduction of **9:** 5258
  methods **9:** 5257
    uses **9:** 5259
  objectives **9:** 5256
  scope of **9:** 5256
  training courses **9:** 5258
School nurses
  historical background **9:** 5284
  organizations (groups) **9:** 5284
  periodicals **9:** 5286
  as related services personnel **9:** 5284
  role of **9:** 5284
  specialized
    definitions of **9:** 5285
    functions of **9:** 5285
School organization **7:** ***4227–4236***
  and academic achievement **5:** 2505
  academic work
    and effective schools research **9:** 5377
  Catholic schools vs. public schools **9:** 5375
  characteristics of **4:** 1930; **7:** 4242
  and class organization
    anthropological studies **2:** 798
  co-operation **5:** 2503
  contingency model **9:** 5177
  curriculum design **7:** 4233
  and educational change **6:** 3492
  and educational improvement **9:** 5242
  educational objectives **7:** 4233
  and educational quality
    policy models **8:** 4870
  efficiency **8:** 4828
    and school size **8:** 4828
  ethnography **9:** ***5217–5220***
  and feminist approaches **1:** 64
  formal vs. small societies **9:** 5374
  governance rules
    change of **9:** 5271
  and hierarchical linear models **5:** 2593
  loosely coupled systems **6:** 3525
  models
    borrowing of **7:** 4241
    bureaucratic **4:** 2157
    bureaucratic–governmental **7:** 4242
    climate **4:** 2159
    culture **4:** 2159; **7:** 4243
    industrial–business **7:** 4241
    limitations **7:** 4242, 4244
    loose-coupling **4:** 2162
    multiple **7:** 4245
    political **7:** 4244
  and nontraditional education **1:** 261
  personnel
    supplying **7:** 4233
  and principals
    role of **9:** ***5268–5273***
  procedures
    definitions of **7:** 4228
  and professionalism **6:** 3525
  public schools vs. private schools **8:** 4841
  and reform **9:** ***5275–5281***
  and resource allocation **9:** 5062, 5064
  school as workplace
    concept of **9:** 5176
  standardization **7:** 4235
  and structuralism **4:** 2159
  structures
    attendance **7:** 4233
    authority **7:** 4229
    curriculum **7:** 4231
    definitions of **7:** 4228
    enrollment **7:** 4232
    funding **7:** 4231
    physical **7:** 4228
    stage **7:** 4230
    system **7:** 4230
    track **7:** 4230
  student evaluation **7:** 4234
  teachers
    personal autonomy **10:** 6094
  theories of **9:** 5160
    classical management **4:** 2158
    comparative management **7:** ***4240–4246***
    contemporary developments **4:** ***2156–2167***
    developments **4:** 2162
    historical background **4:** 2157
School–parent relationship
  See Parent school relationship
School personnel
  characteristics of
    and outcomes of education **9:** 5262
  drug therapy
    management of **8:** 4420
  management strategies for
    and educational improvement **9:** 5244
  related services **9:** ***5281–5291***
    concept of **9:** 5281
    deployment of **9:** 5289
    future trends **9:** 5289
    issues **9:** 5289
    professionalism in **9:** 5282
    and specialization **9:** 5282
School policy
  development processes **9:** 5241
  and educational improvement **9:** 5241
  and reading difficulties **8:** 4931
  shared decision-making **1:** 592
  vs. public policy
    and educational improvement **9:** 5244
School principals
  See Principals
School programs
  See School activities
School psychologists
  historical background **9:** 5286
  organizations (groups) **9:** 5286
  periodicals for **9:** 5287
  professional standards **9:** 5286
  as related services personnel **9:** 5286
  services **9:** 5287
  and student attitudes
    to classrooms **10:** 5774
  to student ratio **9:** 5287
School psychology
  use of curriculum-based assessment in **3:** 1358
School readiness **9:** ***5273–5275***
  broad-based assessment approaches **9:** 5275
  concepts of **9:** 5273
  criteria
    United States **9:** 5275
  individual development
    maturational view **9:** 5273, 5274
  school entrance age **9:** 5274
School readiness tests **9:** 5273
  attitudinal consequences **9:** 5274
  compared with developmental screening tests **3:** 1621
  curricular and equity issues **9:** 5274
  use of test results **9:** 5274
School reform
  and restructuring **9:** ***5275–5281***
School responsibility
  noninstructional **9:** 5265
  and socialization **10:** 5589
School restructuring
  and ability grouping **1:** 10
  aspects of **5:** 2849
  concept of **9:** 5269
  and deskilling of teachers **10:** 6133
  and information technology **7:** 4086
  and new relationships **9:** 5271
  organizational development **5:** 2526
  and parent participation **9:** 5214
  and principals
    role of **9:** ***5268–5273***
  and professional autonomy **10:** 6137

and school choice **9:** 5198
and school reform **9:** ***5275–5281***
teachers
and sex bias **10:** 6137
See also
School-based management
School revenues
definition of **9:** 5233
School role
effects of economic change on
5: 2499
and friendship formation **9:** 5174
history
research methodology **5:** 2601
Kerschensteiner's view **6:** 3135
noninstructional responsibility **9:** 5265
and outcomes of education **9:** 5260
perceptions of **3:** 1741
and production **3:** 1669
and the production of education
6: 3101
and related services personnel
9: 5281
and social change **7:** 4241
and sociocultural systems **9:** 5311
and teacher student relationship
10: 5759
vertical organization
formation **9:** 5174
School schedules
effect of comparative analysis on
3: 1831
and school organization **7:** 4233
and value conflicts **4:** 1850
School self-evaluation (SSE)
5: ***2847–2852***
holistic school improvement **5:** 2850
influences **5:** 2848
school-based development **5:** 2849
schools **3:** 1429
trends **5:** 2851
School site management
See School-based management
School size **9:** ***5291–5294***
economics of **9:** 5291
educational implications **9:** 5292
optimum **9:** 5294
and organizational effectiveness
9: 5374
and outcomes of education **9:** 5261
and policy formation
social factors **9:** 5293
research
summaries **9:** 5292
and resource allocation **9:** 5064
and school dynamics **9:** 5169
School social workers
historical background **9:** 5287
organizations (groups) **9:** 5288
periodicals **9:** 5288
as related services personnel **9:** 5287
services **9:** 5288
standards **9:** 5288
training of **9:** 5288
School space
planning of **4:** 2219, 2220, 2221
School statistics
and educational planning **11:** 6294
and microcomputers **11:** 6297
School subjects
See Intellectual disciplines
School support
external
and educational improvement
9: 5245
and privatization **3:** 1826
School surveys
data collection **2:** 650
and educational planning **11:** 6294
problems **7:** 3853
reading tests
and nonresponse **7:** 3854
and school mapping **9:** 5257
School to work transition
See Education work relationship
School as workplace
concept of **9:** 5176
human relations approaches **9:** 5178
and decision-making **9:** 5179
and professionalism **9:** 5178
perspectives **9:** 5176
political approach **9:** 5176, 5179
reform implications **9:** ***5176–5181***
structural approaches **9:** 5176
studies **9:** 5180
symbolic approach **9:** 5176, 5180
teacher attitudes **9:** 5178
teacher role **9:** 5177
trends **9:** 5180
urban areas **11:** 6554
Schools
as agents of social control **1:** 516
anthropological study of **1:** 281
behavior standards **5:** 2526
belief systems
and school effectiveness **9:** 5375
as a cause of unemployment **11:** 6700
concepts of **9:** 5308
conflict in **2:** 1037
avoidance of **2:** 1039
and crisis of education
expectations **8:** 4457
critical inquiry
United States **4:** ***2381–2389***
culture of the schools project **1:** 281
decentralization of
developing nations **3:** ***1412–1416***
and defining of cultural capital
4: 2268
definition of **7:** 4227
educational administration
and critical theory **1:** 63
educational policy
and crisis **4:** 2268
educational research
and sampling **9:** 5134
and educational television **5:** 2893
employees
motivation and incentives
4: ***1967–1972***
evaluation
measurement of social usefulness
3: 1383
production functions **3:** 1383
ranking **3:** 1384
external context of
and educational improvement
9: 5243
as "firms"
in input output analysis **8:** 4562
governance
and state departments of education
7: 3839
group dynamics **5:** 2525
history of **5:** 2609
independent study in
problems **8:** 4772
inequalities in
and resource allocation **9:** 5064
influences
resistance to **9:** 5222
information technology in **7:** 4082
innovations in
management of **6:** 3597
labor relations within **10:** 6137
and management theory **7:** 4240
as mass education systems **10:** 6211
micropolitics of **7:** ***3821–3826***
mini-state theory
key elements of **8:** 4564
and political considerations **8:** 4564
objectives
and outcomes of education **9:** 5259
organization of
racial bias **10:** 5824
and organizational development
7: 4237
integration strategies **7:** 4238
organizational viability **3:** 1409
as organizations **7:** 3822
and outcomes of education
effects on **9:** ***5259–5264***
as political and public institutions
8: 4563
politics of education **8:** 4582, 4583
power structure
professional autonomy **10:** 6129
resource allocation in **9:** ***5061–5066***
school district influences on **9:** 5222
self-renewing
concept of **5:** 2847
as sites of resistance **6:** 3619
small business training **4:** 1988
as social institutions
and existential phenomenology
8: 4432
and social stratification **10:** 5732
and socialization **10:** 5589
sociocultural milieu **1:** 283, 289
as sociocultural systems **9:** ***5308–5313***
future trends **9:** 5312
qualitative research **9:** 5310
sociological views of **9:** 5374
stability of
and hierarchical linear models
5: 2594
subsystems as groups **5:** 2526

types of
and academic achievement **8:** 4840
Schools Council for Curriculum and Examinations 1964 (UK) **3:** 1295
foreign language instruction
student attitudes to **4:** 2356
Guidelines for Internal Review and Development (GRIDS) project **5:** 2849
and public examinations **4:** 2179
Schools Council Integrated Science Project (SCISP) (UK) **5:** 2900
Schools of education
and educational research **9:** 5031
teacher education programs **10:** 5995
types of
and technical education **10:** 6063
in universities
United Kingdom **3:** 1723
Science
See Sciences
Science and society **5:** 2898, 2900
agriculture education and **1:** 243
and biological sciences **6:** 3410
educational programs **9:** 5344
environmental education **4:** 1993; **5:** 2902
Girls into Science and Technology (GIST) **4:** 2288
instructional materials **6:** 3219
and physical sciences
secondary school programs **8:** 4475
programs **8:** 4461; **9:** 5326
and scientific literacy **9:** 5347, 5349
and technology education **11:** 6290
Science careers
equal opportunities **4:** 2438
female participation **4:** 2438
Science curriculum
access to
equal education **4:** 2437
agriculture in **1:** 243
children's contribution to popularizing **2:** 732
effect of information technology on **7:** 4102
female participation **4:** 2438
general science **5:** ***2897–2903***
and laboratory packages **6:** 3203
language styles
research reports **6:** 3217
language usage
supplementation of peripheral meaning **6:** 3216
National Curriculum
United Kingdom **8:** 4461
new curriculum reform **5:** 2898
physics
Harvard Physics project **3:** 1254
reform
and attitudes to science **9:** 5318
role of language in **6:** ***3216–3219***
modern views **6:** 3217
and teaching methods **6:** 3218
Russian Biological Science curriculum study **3:** 1254
science history in **8:** 4462
United States **8:** 4462
science programs **9:** 5340
science teacher education **9:** 5343
Scottish Integrated Science curriculum **3:** 1254
sex fairness **4:** 2438
West Indian Science Improvement project **3:** 1253
Science education
affective measures in **9:** 5320
attitude measures in **9:** 5319
Canada **8:** 4461, 4462
and cognitive tests **11:** 6343
computer uses in **7:** 4100
effects **7:** 4103
problems **7:** 4103
concept learning perspective **9:** 5339
and constructivism **8:** 4464
cross-national comparison research
IEA **4:** 2134
curriculum design **8:** 4645
curriculum development
centralized **5:** 2497
Denmark **8:** 4461
developmental perspective **9:** 5339
developments **7:** 4101; **8:** 4647
differential perspective **9:** 5340
educational innovation **8:** 4474
equal education **9:** 5326
evaluation
approaches **8:** 4645
trends **8:** 4647
and heuristics **10:** 6176
history and philosophy of science
and teacher education **8:** 4463
influences on **9:** 5325
information technology in **7:** ***4100–4104***
future trends **7:** 4103
potentials of **7:** 4101
integration with other subjects **9:** 5331
laboratory packages for **6:** ***3202–3205***
and language usage **6:** 3218
learning processes **9:** 5329
research **10:** 5784
and microcomputer-based laboratories **7:** ***3808–3810***
microworlds **7:** 4100
Netherlands **8:** 4461
objectives **8:** 4645; **9:** 5340
out of school
and scientific literacy **9:** 5348
and paradigms
concept of **10:** 6203
perspectives on **9:** 5338
and philosophy of science **8:** ***4461–4464***
United States **8:** 4462
practical work in **8:** 4645
preconceptions and misconceptions **8:** ***4648–4652***
primary school programs **9:** ***5328–5335***
content approach **9:** 5329
evaluation **9:** 5334
historical background **9:** 5328
implementation problems **9:** 5333
learning activities **9:** 5332
objectives **9:** 5331
process approach **9:** 5329
resources for **9:** 5334
structure **9:** 5330
teacher background **9:** 5333
problem-solving
design principles **8:** 4646
problem-solving perspective **9:** 5340
program implementation **3:** 1493
and scientific literacy **9:** 5346, 5347
Spencer's view **10:** 5707
and student attitudes
descriptive scales **3:** 1479, 1480
studies
and selection bias **9:** 5380
and teaching emphasis **3:** 1479, 1481
teaching guides for **10:** 6113
and technology education **11:** 6290
See also
General science
Integrated science education
Science education history **9:** ***5324–5328***
curriculum development **9:** 5326
definition of **9:** 5324
elementary schools
curriculum **9:** 5325
teaching methods **9:** 5325
Science equipment
laboratory packages **6:** ***3202–3205***
sex differences in informal use **4:** 2438
Science experiments
planning of **6:** 3217
Science history
biological sciences **6:** 3412
and educational administration **1:** 56
and philosophy of education **8:** ***4461–4464***
in science education **8:** 4462
and scientific language **6:** 3218
and scientific literacy **9:** 5347
Science instruction **9:** ***5338–5342***
demonstrations (educational) **10:** 6142
teacher effectiveness **10:** 6142
laboratories **9:** ***5335–5338***
cognitive processes **9:** 5336
educational objectives **9:** 5335
inquiry **9:** 5336, 5337
learning processes **9:** 5336
student behavior **9:** 5337
teacher behavior **9:** 5337
teaching methods **9:** 5335
technical skills **9:** 5336
observational learning
preconceptions and misconceptions **8:** 4650
and prior learning **8:** 4651
sex fairness **4:** ***2436–2440***

teaching methods **9:** 5341
scaffolding **9:** 5340, 5341
through agriculture **1:** 243
Science Laboratory Environment Inventory (SLEI) **10:** 5774
Science laboratory instruction
See Science instruction, laboratories
Science parks **8:** 4338
Science Processes and Concepts Exploration (SPACE) **9:** 5332
Science teachers
and epistemology **8:** 4463
expectations of females **4:** 2438
role of language in teaching methods **6:** 3218
sex bias **9:** 5340
teacher education **9:** 5341, ***5342–5345***
basic principles **9:** 5344
future directions **9:** 5344
history of **9:** 5342
and history and philosophy of science **8:** 4463
science curriculum **9:** 5343
Science Teacher Education Project (UK) **9:** 5344
Search for Excellence in Science Education (US) **9:** 5344
trends **9:** 5343
use of explanation **10:** 6144
Science teaching centers
and laboratory packages **6:** 3204
Science Teaching through its Astronomical Roots
See Project STAR
Science technology and society (STS)
See Science and society
Science tests
approaches **8:** 4645
and item banks **8:** 4646
sex differences in performance **4:** 2437
Sciences
achievement
and Rasch measurement models **1:** 38
sex differences **4:** 2436; **9:** 5429, 5443
and surveys **10:** 5854
attitudes toward **9:** ***5318–5324***
and academic achievement **9:** 5321, 5322
comparative area studies **9:** 5321
cross-cultural studies **1:** 395
domain of **9:** 5320
future research **9:** 5323
measures **1:** 393, 394; **9:** 5319
nature of **9:** 5318
and outcomes of education **9:** 5323
research findings **9:** 5322
research studies **9:** 5320
sex differences in **1:** 395; **9:** 5430
variables **9:** 5322
in core curriculum **2:** 1105
definitions in
language usage **6:** 3216
disciplinary
development of **10:** 6203
and educational change **4:** 1851
epistemology **4:** 2370
integrated activities
teaching methods **5:** 2898, 2899
and interests
critical theory **2:** 1200
learning **9:** ***5338–5342***
methodology **4:** 2370
neutrality debate **2:** 1200
ontology **4:** 2370
performance tests in **8:** ***4643–4648***
popularization of **9:** 5347
professionalization of **9:** 5347
public understanding of **9:** 5348
as school subject
historical background **9:** 5324
sex bias **4:** 2288
specialization **8:** 4463
Spencer's view of **6:** 3149
use of metaphors **6:** 3218
vocabulary in **6:** 3216
Scientific attitudes
cultural influences **5:** 2651, 2654
and scientific literacy **9:** 5348
sex fairness **4:** 2439
See also
Sciences, attitudes toward
Scientific concepts **5:** 2900
biological sciences **6:** 3413
characteristics of student concepts **9:** 5339
concept teaching **9:** 5339
energy **6:** 3413
evolution **6:** 3413
learning **9:** 5339
misconceptions **9:** 5339
and sex bias **4:** 2439
molecular biology **6:** 3413
sex differences in understanding **4:** 2437
understanding
and microcomputer-based laboratories **7:** 3809
Scientific enterprise
and scientific literacy **9:** 5347
Scientific language **6:** ***3216–3219***
Scientific literacy **9:** ***5345–5350***
beliefs about
sex differences **4:** 2437
benefits of **9:** 5346, 5347
and biological sciences **6:** 3409
concept of **9:** 5345
deficit model of **9:** 5348
definitions of **9:** 5346
functional **9:** 5346
interpretations of **9:** 5347
issues **9:** 5349
measurement of **9:** 5346, 5348
sex differences **4:** 2436
programs
agencies **9:** 5348
science curriculum **4:** 2438
and science education **9:** 5327, 5347
types of **9:** 5346
Scientific management
influence on curriculum development **3:** 1299
Scientific methodology
cognitive processes **3:** 1540
discovery learning **3:** 1542
and educational research **9:** 5052
and evaluation **4:** 2370
fashions in **9:** 5044
functions **5:** 2654
theories in **3:** 1770
Scientific principles **9:** 5341
Scientific processes
Science—A Process Approach (US) **5:** 2900
Scottish Integrated Science **5:** 2900
Scientific reports
See Research reports
Scientific research
and humanistic research compared **3:** 1465
information networks **5:** 2993
international education **5:** 2974
Lakatos' views **4:** 1998
role of questions in **4:** 2213
Scientism
and research methodology **9:** 5044
Scores
and attitude measures **1:** 388
and classical test theory **1:** 33
corrections to
and guessing **7:** 3996
effect of test coaching on **11:** 6337
equated
See Equated scores
missing
in survey research **7:** ***3858–3862***
normalized
and classical test theory **2:** 787
rescaling of
and standard deviation **7:** 3729
residual
and measurement of change **2:** 673
standardized
use in teacher evaluation **4:** 2129
Scoring
concept maps **2:** 1030
of essays **4:** ***2018–2025***
criteria **4:** 2021
and objective tests **7:** 4193, 4196
partial credit analysis **1:** 373
and test construction **11:** 6312
Scotland
computer conferencing
applications **11:** 6303
computer literacy for females **4:** 2426
curriculum guides
sex bias **4:** 2290
General Teaching Council **10:** 5962
monitoring of standards **7:** 3907, 3911
school choice **1:** 591
research **9:** 5194
school size
studies **9:** 5291
science curriculum **3:** 1254
teacher education

accreditation **1:** 25, 26
historical background **3:** 1722
videotex
applications **11:** 6305
vocational education
learning modules **7:** 3890, 3892
modular programs **9:** 5364
See also
United Kingdom (UK)
Scottish Centre for Education Overseas
language skills program **6:** 3212
Scottish Council for Research in Education
sex differences
studies **9:** 5427
Scottish Institute of Adult and Continuing Education **8:** 4735
Scottish Mental Survey (1932)
and cross-sectional studies **2:** 1215
Scottish Report Profile **8:** 4618
Screening hypothesis **3:** 1660, 1705
credentialism **3:** 1700, 1748; **9:** 5350, 5352
earnings differentials **3:** 1700; **9:** 5353
and education **3:** 1699; **9:** ***5350–5355***
empirical research **3:** 1701, 1748; **9:** 5352
sheepskin hypothesis **9:** 5352
Wiles hypothesis **9:** 5352
and employment contracts **3:** 1699
human capital and **5:** 2645
implications of **3:** 1700
labor market **8:** 4837
productivity
effect of education on **1:** 517
and self-employment **3:** 1701; **9:** 5353
self-selection **9:** 5351
signalling theory **9:** 5350
vs. human capital theory **9:** 5351, 5353, 5354
weak version vs. strong version **3:** 1700; **9:** 5353
Screening tests
developmental disabilities
background **3:** 1621
characteristics and criteria **3:** 1622
Denver Developmental Screening Test **3:** 1622
Early Screening Inventory **3:** 1623
effect on parents **3:** 1623
referrals from **3:** 1622
sensitivity and specificity **3:** 1622
young children **3:** ***1621–1624***
and predictive validity **11:** 6571
Screens (display)
design
and authoring aids **10:** 5623
Search strategies
and information retrieval **5:** 2819
processes **5:** 2820
libraries **5:** 2823
Seating arrangement **9:** ***5355–5359***
academic achievement **9:** 5357
instructional effectiveness **9:** 5355
interpersonal relationship **9:** 5356
language enrichment **9:** 5356
student attitudes **9:** 5358
memorization **9:** 5356
student behavior **9:** 5357
behavior modification **9:** 5357, 5358
student motivation **9:** 5357
teacher attitudes **9:** 5358
teacher expectations of students **9:** 5358
teacher role
educational objectives **9:** 5358
teacher student relationship **9:** 5356
Seatwork
assignment and supervision of **9:** ***5359–5363***
and cognitive processes **10:** 5741
definitions of **9:** 5359
future trends **9:** 5362
perspectives **9:** 5359
Second chance education **1:** 116, 129; **6:** 3420; **11:** 6393
administration of **9:** 5364
and alternative routes **9:** ***5363–5367***
concept of **9:** 5363
distance education **3:** 1558
Europe **10:** 5642
frameworks of **9:** 5363
France **10:** 5636
higher education
trends **9:** 5365
nonformal education **9:** 5366
outside-school programs **9:** 5365
postsecondary education **9:** 5365
preventative approach **9:** 5364
rehabilitation approach **9:** 5364
remedial instruction **7:** 4135
research **9:** 5366
secondary education
within-school programs **9:** 5364
special programs for **9:** 5364
trends **9:** 5366
Second language instruction
age of beginning **6:** 3437
definition of **4:** 2346
employer sponsored provision **6:** 3212
immigrants **6:** 3210
literacy in
cultural differences **1:** 482
provision by adult educational institutions **6:** 3211
reciprocal teaching **6:** 3331
and underachievement **6:** 3236
See also
Foreign language instruction
Second language learning
adult education **6:** ***3209–3213***
needs assessment **6:** 3211
aptitude and opportunity approach **6:** 3330
audiolingual methods **6:** 3330
and biculturalism **6:** 3210
bilingualism
abstract language properties **1:** 535
age effects **1:** 535
principles of development **1:** 535
cognitive academic language learning approach (CALLA) **6:** 3333
cognitive academic language proficiency (CALP) **6:** 3228, 3333
compared with foreign language instruction **4:** 2331
and cultural differences **6:** 3210, 3212
developments and trends **6:** 3212
experiential learning **6:** 3212
immigrant education
Europe **7:** 3845
independent study **6:** 3212
industrial training
needs assessment **6:** 3211
intensive language courses **6:** 3437
international education **5:** 2976
job training **6:** ***3209–3213***
needs assessment **6:** 3211, 3212
language proficiency
evaluation **5:** 2974
learning strategies **6:** ***3329–3335***
associative vocabulary learning **6:** 3330
classification **6:** 3330
and cognitive psychology **6:** 3331
and content area instruction **6:** 3333
protocol analysis **6:** 3330
reading strategies **6:** 3330
typology **6:** 3331
linguistics **6:** ***3435–3439***
minority groups
learning strategies **6:** 3329
natural approach **6:** 3330
for partial credit model **7:** 4306
theories of **6:** 3210
written and verbal communication skills
rhetoric **1:** 482
See also
Foreign language learning
Second language programs
for adult students **6:** 3211
Europe **4:** 2056
objectives of **4:** 2360
and unintended effects **11:** 6510
vocational education
Europe **4:** 2063
Second language testing **4:** ***2357–2364***
See also
Foreign language testing
Second languages
cognitive/academic language proficiency (CALP) **6:** 3229
and foreign languages
semantic differentials **4:** 2358
learning strategies **6:** 3347
reading comprehension in **8:** ***4936–4940***
reading processes **8:** 4937
See also
Foreign languages
Secondary data analysis **9:** ***5367–5373***
advantages of **9:** 5367
and disadvantages **9:** 5372
and educational research **9:** 5367, 5369

ethical issues **4:** 2032
future trends **9:** 5372
issues **9:** 5370
methods **9:** 5370
research study **9:** 5371
research synthesis **9:** 5371
uses of **9:** 5368
Secondary education
access to
equal **9:** 5388
and school mapping **9:** 5256
benefits of
and educational finance **9:** 5236
community schools **2:** 907
curriculum change
Sweden **11:** 6692
developing nations
empirical studies **8:** 4702
distance education **3:** 1559
diversified
Africa **11:** 6254
educational technology in
4: ***1911–1918***
enrollment
projections **8:** 4784
equal education
global approach **2:** 1057
history of vocational education
11: 6682
industrial
Latin America **6:** 3257
instructional program divisions
9: 5385
nonvocational
school business relationship **8:** 4337
printed materials for
type of **8:** 4695
and public examinations **4:** 2173
second chance education
within-school programs **9:** 5364
selection mechanisms in **9:** ***5385–5389***
examination **9:** 5387
nonexamination **9:** 5387
single sex schools
developed nations **2:** 832
and streaming
China, People's Republic of **2:** 756
student options
Soviet Union (former) **10:** 5644
and technology education **11:** 6289
terminal stage of
and female participation **9:** 5424
and vocational education **11:** 6245, 6628
China, People's Republic of **2:** 756
vocationalization of **3:** 1736
Secondary education for adults
See Continuation students, adult education
Secondary school curriculum
job training
for disabilities **11:** 6459
mainstreaming **11:** 6459
physical sciences **8:** ***4474–4479***
social history of **9:** 5297
social studies **9:** ***5578–5583***
Secondary school students
in part time employment **5:** 2624
and sex discrimination **9:** 5170
Secondary school teachers
contexts **10:** 6213
recruitment
France **9:** 5016, 5018
Secondary schools
administration
and effective schools research
9: 5376
alienation in **9:** 5378
and educational television **5:** 2893
effective **9:** ***5373–5379***
expenditure
projections **8:** 4786
females
Islamic culture **11:** 6755
interpersonal relationship
and effective schools research
9: 5377
organization
formal **9:** 5376
specialization in
and effective schools research
9: 5376
See also
Adult secondary schools
Comprehensive schools
High schools
Segmentation theory
and dual labor market theory **3:** 1681
empirical research findings
developing nations **3:** 1683; **6:** 3188
factor analysis in **6:** 3187
occupational mobility **6:** 3188
and job training **7:** 4197
labor market **3:** 1705; **8:** 4836
and adult basic education **1:** 130
and adult education **4:** 1973
and education **6:** ***3184–3189***
empirical research findings **6:** 3187
and employed women **3:** 1666
informal sector **3:** 1677
Latin America **6:** 3260
and mobility **3:** 1683
and public sector employment
8: ***4836–4839***
radical
labor market **3:** 1696; **6:** 3185
and racial discrimination **6:** 3185
and role of education
developing nations **3:** 1682
vs. neoclassical economics **3:** 1681, 1682; **6:** 3186, 3187
See also
Dual labor market theory
Segmented labor markets (SLM)
See Segmentation theory
Seizures
characteristics of **8:** 4421
disorders
and drug therapy **8:** 4420, 4421
See also
Epilepsy
Selection
coaching for
effects of **9:** 5388
cultural
and reproduction theory **9:** 5019
and decision theory **3:** 1417, 1420
in education
and internal migration
5: ***2942–2945***
interviews for **5:** ***3003–3007***
bias in **5:** 3003
types of **5:** 3003
labor market
screening hypothesis **9:** ***5350–5355***
microdeterminants of **5:** 2943
and public examinations **4:** 2172
in sampling **9:** 5134
in secondary education **9:** ***5385–5389***
agencies for **9:** 5389
mechanisms of **9:** 5387
need for **9:** 5386
private schools vs. public schools
9: 5388
tests
characteristics of **11:** 6346
reliability and validity **9:** 5387
Selection bias
adjustment methods **9:** 5380
and attitude measures **9:** 5321
definitions of **9:** 5379
in educational research **9:** ***5379–5385***
examples **9:** 5380
methods
allocation designs **9:** 5383
common group designs **9:** 5384
experimental designs **9:** 5384
imputation adjustment **9:** 5384
mixture modeling **9:** 5384
modeling **9:** 5383
regression adjustment **9:** 5383
and sex differences
research **9:** 5431
and test bias **11:** 6317
Selective schools
intellectual basis **8:** 4826
social elite **8:** 4826
Self
as a subject and object **9:** 5390
Self-actualization
adult education **2:** 1047
characteristics of **5:** 2690
Froebelian theory **4:** 2387
and humanistic psychology **5:** 2689, 2690
and socialization **5:** 2691
Self-concept
academically gifted **9:** 5529
and aging (individuals) **1:** 237
sex differences **1:** 237
attribution theory **9:** ***5403–5407***
success and failure **1:** 201
child development
changes in structure **9:** 5391
and cognitive processes **10:** 5741
cross-cultural studies **5:** 2650
developmental stages **9:** 5391

- early development **9:** 5391
- effect on performance **1:** 200
- functional view **9:** 5390
- individual development **9:** ***5390–5394***
- and literacy testing **6:** 3472
- mainstreaming **5:** 2908
- parent influence on development **9:** 5393
- performance
  - and learning motivation **7:** 3938
- and Q-methodology **8:** 4855
- self-efficacy **9:** 5392
  - educational strategies **9:** 5393
  - realism in judgments **9:** 5392
  - role of classroom environment **9:** 5392
- and self-evaluation **9:** 5390, 5391
  - dimensionality **9:** 5391
  - stability issue **9:** 5392
- and sex role **4:** 2446
- social cognition
  - and social development **9:** 5524
- and socialization **10:** 5587
- students
  - research **10:** 5772
- teacher burnout **10:** 6061
- and teacher knowledge **10:** 6119
- teachers
  - adult development **10:** 5937
- theoretical view of nature of **9:** 5390

Self-confidence
- *See* Self-esteem

Self-control **9:** ***5400–5403***
- attention control **9:** 5402
  - individual differences **5:** 2764
- and conflict resolution **9:** 5400
- definition of **9:** 5400
- and delay of gratification **9:** 5400
- and emotional response **9:** 5402
- and individual power **9:** 5400
- information processing model **9:** 5400
- Judaic theory **6:** 3118
- and learning **1:** 203
- learning strategies **6:** 3335; **9:** 5401
- in maturity (individuals) **9:** 5402
- and metacognition **9:** 5401
- ontogenetic development theory **9:** 5400
- and personal autonomy **9:** 5400, 5403
- resistance to temptation **9:** 5400
  - and cognitive restructuring **9:** 5403
- and self-motivation **9:** 5402
- self-regulation test for children **9:** 5402
- skill development **9:** 5401
- theory of self-regulatory deficit **9:** 5400

Self-determination
- beliefs about **5:** 2653
- and community education
  - Thailand **2:** 908
- individual power **9:** 5515
- and self-motivation **7:** 3939, 3940
- *See also*
  - Personal autonomy

Self-directed groups
- adult learning **5:** 2530, 2531

Self-directed learning
- *See* Independent study

Self-efficacy
- and academic achievement **1:** 200; **6:** 3295; **9:** 5393
- attention control
  - and academic achievement **1:** 376
- and competence **4:** 1980
- and energy expenditure
  - individual differences **5:** 2764
- evaluative thinking **9:** 5516
- and metacognition **9:** 5516
- and self-concept **9:** 5392
- and self-motivation **7:** 3939, 3940, 3942
- social cognition
  - and social development **9:** 5524
- stress variables **10:** 5736, 5737
- of teachers
  - and academic achievement **8:** 4565
  - and environmental influences **8:** 4564
  - as a function of centralized administrative control **8:** 4565
- and test anxiety **11:** 6358

Self-employment
- and business education **11:** 6250
- and job training **7:** 4199
- screening hypothesis **3:** 1701; **9:** 5353
- *See also*
  - Small businesses

Self-esteem
- academically gifted **9:** 5529
- and artificial intelligence **1:** 345
- career planning
  - females **5:** 2489
- and construct validity **11:** 6572
- definition of **11:** 6570
- and mathematics achievement **6:** 3639, 3640
- and measurement validity **11:** 6570
- and motivation **7:** 3945
- and narcissism **8:** 4815
- personality trait **3:** 1611
- and self-evaluation **9:** 5390
- theory
  - in education **10:** 6222

Self-evaluation (groups)
- institutional
  - and renewal **5:** ***2847–2852***
- organizational development **5:** 2848, 2851
- school-based review **5:** 2848
- *See also*
  - School self-evaluation

Self-evaluation (individuals) **4:** 1846
- and aptitude treatment interaction **5:** 2929
- cognitive measurement **1:** 372
- learning strategies **6:** 3328
- and learning strategies **6:** 3335
- and metacognition **7:** 3766
- and self-esteem **9:** 5390
- and sociometric techniques **10:** 5614
- young people
  - and occupational choice **6:** 3099

Self-expression
- art expression **1:** 339, 340; **11:** 6616
- and sexuality **9:** 5440

Self-fulfilling prophecies
- definition of **11:** 6509
- and educational research **11:** 6509
- and teacher expectation of students **10:** 6107
  - Brophy–Good model **10:** 6107

Self-help programs
- adult education
  - employer support **10:** 5807
- educational finance **2:** ***910–914***

Self-instruction
- *See* Independent study

Self-knowledge
- *See* Self concept

Self-motivation
- and academic achievement **9:** 5400
- and computer-assisted instruction **7:** 3938, 3939
- and coping with failure **9:** 5402
- and feedback **9:** 5515
- and homogeneous grouping **7:** 3938, 3939
- and learning motivation **7:** 3938, 3939
- and self-control **9:** 5402
- types of
  - academically gifted **9:** 5529
- and underachievement **9:** 5400

Self-paced instruction
- *See* Individualized instruction, pacing

Self-perception
- *See* Self-concept

Self-regulated learning
- *See* Independent study

Self-regulation
- *See* Self-control

Self-report
- in educational research **9:** ***5407–5411***
- perspectives **9:** 5410
- research findings based on **9:** 5409
- vs. introspection **9:** 5408

Self-supporting students
- adult education **4:** 2394

Self-verbalization
- *See* Verbalization

Semantic differential
- and attitude measures **1:** 382
- and scaling **9:** 5154

Semantic memory
- and levels of consciousness **2:** 856
- semantic priming **1:** 328

Semantic models **7:** 3867
- example **7:** 3867

Semantic/pragmatic deficit syndrome
- characteristics of **10:** 5676

Semantics **6:** 3225
- contamination across fields **6:** 3636
- and semiotics **9:** 5412

Semiology
- *See* Semiotics

Semiotics
  codes **9:** 5413
    anchoring **9:** 5416
    in educational activities **9:** 5414
    issues **9:** 5415
  definitions of **9:** 5411
  didactic efficacy **9:** 5416
  in educational research **9:** ***5411–5417***
  historical background **9:** 5411
  icons **9:** 5412
  indexes **9:** 5412
  interpretant **9:** 5412
  and nonverbal communication **7:** 4171
  relations
    paradigmatic **9:** 5413
    syntagmatic **9:** 5413
  semiosis **9:** 5412
  signs **9:** 5411
    definition of **9:** 5412
  and sociocultural systems **9:** 5308
  symbols **9:** 5412
  theories of
    developments **9:** 5412
    and mass media **2:** 886
Senegal
  adult education **1:** 220; **9:** 5420
  curriculum development **9:** 5422
  educational change **9:** 5418
  educational finance **9:** 5421
  ethnic groups **9:** 5417
  government school relationship
    school administration **9:** 5421
  nonformal education **7:** 4143
  postsecondary education **9:** 5419
  primary education **9:** 5419
    academic persistence **9:** 5536
  public sector employment **8:** 4838
  secondary education **9:** 5419
    vocational education **9:** 5420
  special education **9:** 5420
  structure of government **9:** 5417
  system of education **9:** ***5417–5423***
    degrees and qualifications **9:** 5422
    educational objectives **9:** 5417
    historical background **9:** 5417
    major problems **9:** 5422
    structure **9:** 5419
  teacher education **9:** 5422
  teacher recruitment **9:** 5421
  textbook publication **11:** 6363
  vocational education **9:** 5420
  youth training schemes **1:** 218
Sensitivity training **5:** 2691
  and individual instruction **5:** 2771
Sensory aids
  hearing impairments **3:** 1399
Sensory deprivation
  deaf–blind children **3:** 1405
Sensory experience
  and preconceptions **8:** 4649
Sensory integration
  neonates
    prenatal influences **1:** 12
Sensory training
  deaf--blind children
    use of residual sensory channels **3:** 1404
Sentence combining
  and receptive language **10:** 5701
  in stylistic grammar **10:** 5701
Sentence completion tests
  See Cloze procedure
Separation anxiety **3:** 1516
Sequential approach
  and adaptive testing compared **1:** 48
Serbocroatian
  orthography of **8:** 4938
Serial learning
  and cognitive style **1:** 318
Service occupations
  labor force participation
    females **3:** 1668
Servicio Nacional de Aprendizaje (*SENA*) (Colombia)
  labor education **3:** 1684
Sesame Street (US) **5:** 2893
Severe disabilities
  and communication disorders
    behavior modification **1:** 407
  developmental disabilities **3:** ***1504–1508***
Severe mental retardation **3:** 1505
  peer teaching **8:** 4374
  and segregation **10:** 5660
Sex
  and educational change **4:** 1851
  and educational choice
    economics of **4:** ***2412–2419***
  race and social class **7:** 3849
  resegregation
    and occupational segregation **4:** 2431
Sex bias
  career counseling **11:** 6318
  changes in
    and occupational segregation **4:** 2431
  in children's literature **9:** 5442
  in classroom communication **9:** 5443
  in curriculum **4:** 2409; **9:** 5441
  curriculum **4:** 2448
  earnings differentials **4:** ***2440–2446***
    factors affecting **4:** 2441
  and education
    earnings differentials **4:** 2416
    theories of **4:** 2413
  educational administration **1:** 64
    and recruitment **1:** 78
  educational environment **4:** 2410
  educational improvement **10:** 5826
  instructional materials **4:** 2448; **9:** 5442
  job training
    and earnings differentials **7:** 4197, 4199
  occupational segregation **4:** 2442
    and education **4:** ***2427–2432***
  and public examinations **4:** 2178
  and racial bias **7:** 3849
  and Rasch measurement models **8:** 4906
  in research
    feminist view **4:** 2299
  school attitudes **4:** 2409
  teacher attitudes **4:** 2409, 2448
  in teacher student relationship **9:** 5442
  textbook research **9:** ***5299–5302***
  in textbooks **4:** 2409; **9:** 5441
Sex differences **10:** ***5822–5827***
  in abilities
    origins of **9:** 5428
  and academic achievement **10:** 5824
    changes over time **9:** 5427
    comparative area studies **9:** 5426
    research **9:** 5423, 5425
  and academic persistence **9:** 5536
  behavior development **9:** ***5433–5435***
  biological **9:** 5428
  brain laterality **9:** 5429
  course selection (students) **10:** 5824
  determination of
    and Rasch measurement models **8:** 4905
  and disengagement theory **9:** 5227
  in education
    fundamental concepts of **10:** 5822
  and educational administration **10:** 5610
  in educational leadership **1:** 436
  and educational resources **8:** 4705
  educational theories **10:** 5822
  and equal education **4:** 2003
  and ethnicity
    educational anthropology **7:** 3973
  expectancy of success **9:** 5430
  and feminist educational research **11:** 6725
  genetic **9:** 5428
  history of research on **9:** 5433
  hormonal **9:** 5429
  intellectual disciplines
    participation **9:** 5425
  learning processes **10:** 5824
  and literacy testing **6:** 3472
  and mass media
    effects on children and youth **1:** 567
  mastery tests
    and analysis of variance **11:** 6587
  and mathematics achievement **4:** 2181; **5:** 2927
  and mathematics anxiety **11:** 6359
  maturational **9:** 5428
  and mediation theory **4:** 1874
  moderation procedures **4:** 2179
  nature nurture controversy **9:** 5433, 5435
  and outcomes of education **9:** ***5423–5433***
    academic ability **9:** 5427
    attitude effects **9:** 5429
    historical background **9:** 5424
    participation **9:** 5424
    research reviews **9:** 5423

trends **9:** 5431
and public examinations **4:** 2178
reading material selection **10:** 5822
research
developmental continuity **9:** 5433
meta analysis **9:** 5433
problems **9:** 5431
and selection bias **9:** 5431
sex bias in **9:** 5433
and school organization **9:** 5169
and science
attitudes toward **9:** 5323
socialization **4:** 2416; **9:** 5429
and sociology of education **10:** 5603
stereotypes **9:** 5433
students
self-concept **10:** 5823
studies
and self-report **9:** 5410
teacher associations
and power structure **8:** 4584
and teacher behavior **10:** 5760
in questioning techniques **8:** 4878
teaching **10:** 5609
prestige of **10:** 6226
and test anxiety **11:** 6357
and test bias **11:** 6317
Scholastic Aptitude Test **11:** 6317
and twin studies **11:** 6491
vs. gender
semantics **9:** 5423
vs. women's education
benefits from **4:** 2416
writing (composition) **10:** 5822
and youth culture
research **11:** 6801
Sex discrimination
in administrative strategies **3:** 1696
earnings differentials
factors affecting **4:** 2442
policy issues **4:** 2444
theories of **4:** 2442
educational administration **11:** 6729
developing nations **4:** ***2419–2423***
job training
and earnings differentials **7:** 4199
in labor market **3:** 1666
and power structure **5:** 2453, 2455
and race earnings differentials **8:** 4896, 4899
in schools **10:** 5824
statistical discrimination
and productivity **4:** 2444
by teachers **9:** 5170
and vocational education **11:** 6533, 6535
Sex education **9:** ***5435–5441***
controversial aspects **9:** 5436
females and ideology **4:** 2409
and feminism **9:** ***5435–5441***
and population education **8:** 4609
sex bias in **9:** 5440
subjectivity and power **9:** 5438
Sex fairness
educational strategies **4:** 2449; **9:** ***5441–5445***
in research
feminist view **4:** 2299
school districts policy **9:** 5444
technological advancement **4:** ***2423–2427***
Sex role
attitudes
and female access to education **4:** 2407, 2408
definitions of **4:** 2446
family influence **4:** 2448
feminist theories **5:** ***2453–2458***
individual development **4:** ***2446–2449***
cognitive development theories **4:** 2446
developmental stages **4:** 2447
educational implications **4:** 2448
gender schematic processing theory **4:** 2447
psychoanalytic theory **4:** 2446
social influences **4:** 2447
social learning theories **4:** 2446
media influence **4:** 2447
and occupational aspiration **4:** 2411
peer influence **4:** 2448
perceptions
and intellectual disciplines **9:** 5429
and preschool education **4:** ***2449–2452***
role models **5:** 2455
school influence **4:** 2448
socialization **4:** ***2407–2412***
Sex stereotypes
Arab nations **4:** 2408
and career counseling **4:** 2285
and child development **4:** 2447
and the curriculum **4:** 2287
and gender schematic processing theory **4:** 2447
and play **4:** 2450, 2451
preschool education **4:** 2451
in school textbooks **9:** ***5299–5302***
and single sex schools
female attitudes **2:** 833
socialization **10:** 5823
and computer uses in education **4:** 2424
in textbooks **9:** 5442
Islamic culture **11:** 6759
Sexism
See Sex bias
Sexism in language
textbooks **9:** 5300
Sexual abuse
of children **1:** 15
assessment and treatment **1:** 18
effects **1:** 17; **5:** 2573
and emotional problems **1:** 17
preventive programs **1:** 19
Sexual harassment
discourse analysis
feminist poststructuralist **5:** 2456
in schools **10:** 5824
Sexual identity
developmental disorders **3:** 1516
and identification (psychology) **4:** 2446
and liberal feminist theory **5:** 2454
observational learning **4:** 2446
and peer influence **9:** 5218
and sex role **4:** 2446
Sexuality
feminism and **9:** 5437
role of
Judaic theory **6:** 3119
and self-expression **9:** 5440
social constructivism
Foucault's view **9:** 5436, 5439
women's studies **11:** 6768
Seychelles
adult education **9:** 5447
curriculum development **9:** 5448
educational change **9:** 5449
educational finance **9:** 5447
educational research **9:** 5449
government school relationship
school administration **9:** 5447
language **4:** 2037
postsecondary education **9:** 5446
preschool education **9:** 5447
primary education **9:** 5446
secondary education **9:** 5446
special education **9:** 5447
system of education **9:** ***5445–5449***
degrees and qualifications **9:** 5449
educational objectives **4:** 2037
major problems **9:** 5449
structure **4:** 2037
teacher education **9:** 5448
teacher recruitment **9:** 5448
vocational education **9:** 5447
Shadow school system
See Nonformal education
Sharing behavior
young children **8:** 4797
Sheepskin hypothesis
empirical research **9:** 5352
Shinto
beliefs about origin of man **5:** 2652
ethics of **9:** 5451
individual development **9:** ***5449–5453***
educational implications **9:** 5452
expectations in **9:** 5452
goal of **9:** 5451
implications for childrearing **9:** 5450, 5452
nature of *kami* **9:** 5450
and personality development **9:** 5450
Short courses
See Minicourses
Short cycle institutions
See Community colleges
Short term memory (STM) **1:** 328
and accessibility theory **8:** 4701
and cognitive processes **10:** 5829
concept formation **2:** 1018
and development of memory span **7:** 3760
and induction **6:** 3321
and learning **6:** 3317
processes **10:** 5740
role of attention in **1:** 375

Shyness
  student behavior **11:** 6309
Sibling relationship
  caring behavior **2:** 730
  and individual development **4:** 2260; **8:** 4816
Sibling studies
  bias in **6:** 3143
  outcomes of education **6:** 3138
  See also
    Kinship studies
    Twin studies
Siblings
  children's responsibility for **2:** 730
  and social mobility
    research **9:** 5551
Sierra
  analysis system
    and textbook evaluation **1:** 347
Sierra Leone
  adult education **9:** 5456
  community education **7:** 4134
  cultural influences **9:** 5453
  curriculum development **9:** 5458
  educational change **9:** 5459
  educational finance **9:** 5457
  educational research **9:** 5459
  ethnic groups **9:** 5453
  ethnography of indigenous populations **3:** 1753
  government school relationship
    school administration **9:** 5457
  postsecondary education **9:** 5455
  preschool education **9:** 5455
  primary education **9:** 5455
  secondary education **9:** 5455
    vocational education **9:** 5456
  special education **9:** 5455
  system of education **9:** ***5453–5460***
    degrees and qualifications **9:** 5455, 5459
    educational objectives **9:** 5454
    historical background **9:** 5453
    major problems **9:** 5460
    structure **9:** 5454
  teacher education **9:** 5458
  teacher recruitment **9:** 5458
  technical education **9:** 5456
Sign language **10:** 5658
  American sign language **3:** 1400
  and cultural deafness **3:** 1398
  tactual use in teaching deaf blind children **3:** 1404
  total communication
    simultaneous communication **3:** 1400
Signalling theory
  and screening hypothesis **3:** 1748; **9:** 5350
    employment contracts **3:** 1699
Significance
  See Statistical significance
Signs
  semiotics **9:** 5411
Silence
  in classrooms **7:** 4174
Silent reading **7:** 3930
Simulation **9:** ***5472–5476***
  advantages and disadvantages **9:** 5473
  bootstrap procedure **9:** 5469
  courseware
    authoring aids for **10:** 5624
  deterministic models **9:** 5467
  and educational planning **3:** 1828
  and educational technology **4:** 1914
  evaluation **9:** 5474
  formative evaluation **9:** 5472
  fundamental concepts of **9:** 5472
  as interaction **9:** 5472
  intercultural communication **9:** 5474
  and learning **6:** 3300
  learning interactions **2:** 986
  and multimedia systems **7:** 3992, 3993
  planning of
    teacher role **9:** 5472
  as research methodology **9:** ***5467–5471***
  stochastic models **9:** 5467
  student development **9:** 5474
  teacher role **9:** 5472
  teaching methods
    early childhood education **3:** 1632
  tests
    characteristics of **11:** 6347
  See also
    Computer simulation
    Monte Carlo methods
    Role playing
Singapore
  adult education **1:** 352
  adult education promotion **6:** 3365
  computer uses in education **4:** 1902
  curriculum development **9:** 5482
  educational change **9:** 5484
  educational finance **9:** 5481
    and tax allocation **8:** 4360, 4362; **11:** 6651
  educational research **9:** 5484
  ethnic groups **9:** 5476
  government school relationship
    school administration **9:** 5480
  language **9:** 5476
  polytechnical education **8:** 4607
  postsecondary education **9:** 5477
  preschool education **9:** 5479
  primary education **9:** 5477
  private education **9:** 5479
  school-based management **9:** 5212
  science education
    primary school programs **9:** 5330
  secondary education **9:** 5477
  segmentation theory
    studies **3:** 1683
  special education **9:** 5480
  system of education **9:** ***5476–5485***
    degrees and qualifications **9:** 5483
    educational objectives **9:** 5476
    enrollment **9:** 5478
    major problems **9:** 5485
    structure **9:** 5476, 5480
  teacher education **9:** 5481
  teacher recruitment **9:** 5481
  teaching methodology **9:** 5482
  technical education **9:** 5477, 5478
  vocational education **9:** 5480
    and media programs **7:** 3755
  vocational training centers **7:** 3755
Single case research
  detecting change in **9:** 5487
  interrupted time series (ITS) **9:** 5486, 5487
    procedures **9:** 5486
  measuring change in **9:** ***5486–5490***
  nomenclature **9:** 5486
  statistical analysis **9:** 5488
  visual analysis **9:** 5487
  vs. group testing **9:** 5486
Single European Market
  See European Community (EC)
Single parent family
  See One parent family
Single sex colleges
  developed nations **2:** 832
  effects of **2:** 832
  historical trends
    United States **2:** 831
  North America **11:** 6761
Single sex schools
  advantages **4:** 2290
  Australia
    ladies schools **11:** 6732
  and coeducation **2:** ***831–834***; **4:** 2410
  developed nations **2:** 832
  developing nations **2:** 833
  female enrollment
    developing nations **2:** 833
  and radical feminism **5:** 2455
  sex fairness **4:** 2421
  types of **2:** 831
  vs. coeducation **2:** ***831–834***; **4:** 2410; **9:** 5444
Single subject research
  See Single case research
Sisala people
  ethnography of **3:** 1753
Site development
  educational facilities **4:** 2223
Site selection
  educational facilities **4:** 2223
Situated learning **2:** 841; **5:** 2668
Situational tests
  characteristics of **11:** 6347
Sixteen Personality Factor Questionnaire (16PF) **8:** 4397
Skewness (statistics)
  indication of
    and quartiles **7:** 3732
  measures of **7:** 3732
Skill analysis
  skills rules and knowledge (SRK) **10:** 5913
  task analysis **10:** 5911
    learning hierarchy (Gagné) **10:** 5911
Skill development
  accountability
    funds **11:** 6651
  and automaticity of learning **2:** 850

classification **10:** ***5914–5919***
elements of **10:** 5916
courseware for
design **10:** 5622
developing nations **11:** 6648
educational finance
and tax allocation **11:** 6651
and expertise **10:** 6021
finance **10:** 5916
funds
external factors **11:** 6650
government role **11:** 6651
incentives for **11:** 6634
and learning **6:** 3300
levy–grant system
and educational finance **11:** 6650
motor development **7:** ***3947–3950***
in observational learning **9:** 5514
perceptual motor learning **7:** 3949
performance contracts
and cost effectiveness improvement **11:** 6653
for prereferral intervention **8:** 4661
procedural knowledge **6:** 3323
recommendations **10:** 5918
sources for **8:** 4527
specific subskill mastery tests **3:** 1356
training
and educational policy **11:** 6702
types of **10:** 5914
and vocational education
funds **11:** 6650
Skill obsolescence
of teachers
and teacher-proof curriculum **11:** 6720
and technological advancement **11:** 6257, ***6272–6277***
Skilled occupations
career ladders
Germany, Federal Republic of (former) **11:** 6694
Skilled workers
history of industrial training **11:** 6681
migration of
within European Community **4:** 2065
poaching of **11:** 6426
Skills
dimensions of
autonomy control **11:** 6274, 6279
substantive complexity **11:** 6274, 6279
effects of technological advancement **11:** 6279
evaluation of
and certification **2:** 662
individual-based approaches **2:** 663
program-based approaches **2:** 663
international transferability
model of **5:** 2737
and labor market
bumping model **6:** 3182
meaning of **11:** 6273
measurement of **11:** 6273
and migration **1:** 554
testing of **6:** 3469
theory of
of productivity **3:** 1691
utilization and training **11:** ***6416–6420***
Skills shortages
and educational change
China, People's Republic of **2:** 756
postwar
United Kingdom **11:** 6685
Slavery
and cultural transmission **3:** 1752
Slides
advantages of **10:** 5729
applications **7:** 3748
characteristics of **7:** 3747; **10:** 5727, 5730
production of **10:** 5727
Slovak Republic
apprenticeships **1:** 315
Slovenia
adult education **9:** 5494
curriculum development **9:** 5495
educational change **9:** 5496
educational finance **9:** 5495
educational research **9:** 5496
government school relationship
school administration **9:** 5494
language **9:** 5490
postsecondary education **9:** 5493
preschool education **9:** 5494
primary education **9:** 5491
secondary education **9:** 5492
vocational education **9:** 5492
special education **9:** 5494
structure of government **9:** 5490
system of education **9:** ***5490–5497***
degrees and qualifications **9:** 5496
educational objectives **9:** 5491
historical background **9:** 5491
major problems **9:** 5496
structure **9:** 5491
teacher education **9:** 5495
teacher recruitment **9:** 5495
See also
Yugoslavia (former)
Slow learners
special education for **10:** 5660
Small businesses
definitions of **4:** 1985
and labor market analysis **3:** 1677
role of **4:** 1985
training **4:** ***1985–1991***
business plans **4:** 1986
future trends **4:** 1990
government intervention **11:** 6428
institutions and agencies **4:** 1987
models of **4:** 1985
and national training agencies **6:** 3266
program characteristics **4:** 1990
program design factors **4:** 1989
See also
Self employment
Small classes **2:** ***770–775***
academic achievement **2:** 770, 771, 774
instructional program divisions **2:** 774
educational strategies **2:** 774
evaluation **2:** ***770–775***
and group unity **5:** 2526
minority groups
academic achievement **2:** 774
outcomes of education **2:** 773, 775
problems **2:** 774
cost effectiveness **2:** 774
teacher attitudes **2:** 773
teacher behavior **2:** 773
teacher morale **2:** 770
teacher student relationship **2:** 770
Small group instruction **2:** ***1094–1099***; **10:** ***6183–6187***
behavior standards **5:** 2528
and classroom communication **10:** 6185
classroom design for **10:** 6185
cooperative learning **5:** 2533
and curriculum design **10:** 6185
effective
requirements for **10:** 6186
group dynamics **5:** 2528
group unity **5:** 2528
reciprocal teaching **5:** 2533
student teams achievement divisions (STADS) **5:** 2533
and teacher administrator relationship **10:** 6186
teacher control function **10:** 6184
teacher role
observers **10:** 6186
teaching methods
teamwork **2:** 1095
and time on task **5:** 2535
United Kingdom **5:** 2533
vs. conventional instruction **10:** 6186
vs. large group instruction **10:** 6184
See also
Group Investigation (GI) method
Small schools **9:** ***5291–5294***
environmental problems **9:** 5292
and teacher effectiveness **9:** 5293
Smallest space analysis (SSA) **9:** ***5497–5504***
and attitude measures **1:** 385
computer software for **9:** 5497, 5499
definition of **9:** 5497
distance functions **9:** 5500
examples **9:** 5501
and facet theory **4:** 2217
faceted **9:** 5498
generalizations for research **9:** 5503
input matrix **9:** 5499
and multivariate analysis **7:** 4010
and other techniques **9:** 5500
and partial order scalogram analysis **7:** 4308, 4311
similarity data
example **9:** 5498
representation of **9:** 5498
space relationships **9:** 5501
and theory construction **9:** 5498, 5501
ties

treatment of **9:** 5500
uses of **9:** 5501
versions of **9:** 5499
Smiling
and student behavior **7:** 4173
and teacher behavior **7:** 4173
Smith–Hughes Act 1917 (US)
vocational education **11:** 6531
Smoking **3:** 1608
children
and contingency tables **2:** 1082
and education **4:** 2210
prevention
health promotion **5:** 2569
Social action **1:** 129, 132, 134
nature of
and educational research **9:** 5033
and philosophy of education
Comenius **2:** ***880–884***
programs
and religious education **9:** 5002
structure vs. agency **10:** 5602
teachers **10:** 6138
Social adjustment
and emotional disturbances **1:** 488, 492
peer relationship **8:** 4365
Social agencies
and sociology of education **10:** 5601
Social anthropology
United States **3:** 1725
Social background
measurement **7:** ***3715–3722***
and academic achievement **7:** 3720
and family environment **7:** 3720
issues **7:** 3716
problems **7:** 3718
Social behavior
age related changes **9:** 5523
individual differences **9:** 5525
stability and change **9:** 5526
sex differences **9:** 5434
Social benefits
of education **1:** 511; **3:** 1413; **8:** 4913
and vocational education **11:** 6700
Social bias
and public examinations **4:** 2178
Social capital **4:** 2267, ***2272–2274***
forms of **4:** 2272
types of **4:** 2272
use of term **4:** 2272
Social change **2:** 902
and adult education **1:** ***127–135***; **6:** 3420; **10:** 6055
ideology **5:** 2733, 2734
reform strategies **1:** 161
consensus model **2:** 902
and critical theory **2:** 1199
economic determinants of
criticism of **11:** 6700
education and **3:** 1648, 1650
educational anthropological studies **1:** 292
education for **2:** ***1045–1049***
and educational administration **1:** 57
and educational anthropology **9:** ***5508–5510***
and educational history **5:** 2607
educational researchers
teachers as **10:** 6098
effects of
and religious education **9:** 5005
and ethics of teacher education **10:** 5990
and higher education **1:** 90, 93
and lifespan development **11:** 6391
Mannheim's sociology of education **2:** 782
and nonformal education **7:** 4143
outcomes of education
indigenous populations **3:** 1752
pluralist model **2:** 902
and popular education **2:** 904, 1047
and program evaluation **4:** 2120, 2122, 2123
and school organization **7:** 4241
and sex differences
and outcomes of education **9:** 5423
and social studies **9:** 5579
structuralist model **2:** 902
teacher role **8:** 4585
and textbook content **11:** 6367
and youth culture
studies **11:** 6801
Social characteristics
academically gifted **9:** 5529
and measurement **7:** 3716
of teaching **10:** 6225
Social class
and academic achievement **6:** 3307
and adult education **10:** 5593
ideologies **5:** 2733
and culture
conflict **9:** 5311
effect on children's play **8:** 4540
effect on educational and employment opportunities **3:** 1704
and equal education **4:** 2003
family influence
and cultural discernment **9:** 5017
and Marxism **6:** 3617
minority groups
cross-cultural studies **2:** 1211
race and sex **7:** 3849
and racial stratification **9:** 5568
closure and affiliation **9:** 5568
cognitive orientation **9:** 5569
status summation **9:** 5569
and vertical social mobility **9:** 5569
and reproduction theory **9:** 5016
and social stratification **10:** 5730
teacher background **10:** 6226
See also
Lower class
Middle class
Working class
Social cognition **2:** 837; **9:** ***5510–5512***, ***5545–5548***
and aggression **1:** 231, 233
bilingualism **1:** 535
causal model **9:** 5513
cognitive structures **9:** 5505
communication skills **9:** ***5504–5508***
impairment
autism **6:** 3232
individual development **9:** ***5513–5518***
interpersonal competence **9:** ***5504–5508***
learning theories **1:** 495
moral values **9:** 5511
observational learning
cognitive processes in **9:** 5514
processes **9:** 5511
role of culture **9:** 5512
social development **9:** 5524
social psychology **9:** 5511
social values **9:** 5511
symbolic learning **9:** 5513
vicarious experiences **9:** 5514
Social competence
See Interpersonal competence
Social constructivism
See Constructivism
Social control
and intellectual disciplines **9:** 5297
legitimacy of **8:** 4571
and sociology of education **10:** 5597
Social costs
and apprenticeships
in Germany **1:** 309
continuing education **2:** 1146
Social Darwinism
Spencer's **2:** 782
Social demand
and educational planning
criticisms of **3:** 1812
and labor needs forecasting **3:** 1811
Social development
of academically gifted **9:** ***5528–5532***
in adolescents **5:** 2684
and adult education
Canada **7:** 4182
and cognitive development **9:** 5505
communication skills **9:** ***5504–5508***
and educational practices **5:** 2668; **9:** 5527
and friendship **8:** 4367
hierarchical model of **9:** 5564
individual development **9:** ***5523–5528***
and environmental change **9:** 5525, 5527
interpersonal competence **9:** ***5504–5508***
and peer relationship **9:** 5524, 5527
person-oriented view **9:** 5526
personality studies **9:** 5526
and personality traits **9:** 5525
and play **8:** 4539
self-motivation **9:** 5516
social cognition **9:** 5524
and social experience
developmental stages **9:** 5505
and social networks **9:** 5524, 5527
and socialization **9:** 5505
Turiel's view of social understanding **5:** 2668

Social differences
  criteria **9:** 5533
  and education **9:** 5533, 5535, 5536
  and family
    cultural capital **4:** 2269
  language tests **9:** 5018
Social discrimination
  as a barrier to school enterprise **9:** 5232
  and education
    informal sector **3:** 1679
Social education
  Japan **1:** 348, 349
    national training institute **6:** 3075
    and Shinto **9:** 5450, 5452
Social environment
  changes in
    and social development **9:** 5524
  cross-cultural studies **2:** 1210
  factors in learning **8:** ***4400–4404***
  and individual development **9:** 5525
  and intelligence **7:** 3769
  and personality development
    dynamic interaction **8:** 4393
Social equality
  and educational development
    developing nations **9:** ***5532–5539***
  See also
    Civil rights
Social experience
  and social development **9:** 5505
Social factors
  See Social influences
Social history
  and educational history
    research methodology **5:** 2603
  and historical sociology **5:** 2615
  of secondary school curriculum **9:** 5297
  of teaching **10:** 5608
Social indicators
  and curriculum development **3:** 1321
  and education indicators **3:** 1742
  research utilization **5:** 2671
Social influences
  on curriculum **9:** ***5518–5523***
  and educational planning **8:** 4504
  exchange
    and authority **1:** 434
  of formal education **10:** 5598
  persuasion
    and authority **1:** 434
  and sociometric techniques **10:** 5616
Social institutions (organizations)
  See Institutions
Social insurance
  effects on training **11:** 6636
Social integration **7:** 3966
Social isolation
  effect on development **8:** 4367
    aggression **8:** 4367
    behavior problems **8:** 4367
  peer relationship **8:** 4365, 4366
  protection from
    and social capital **4:** 2273
Social learning
  See Socialization
Social mobility
  circulation **9:** 5552
  and education **9:** ***5548–5554***; **10:** 5605
    factors affecting **6:** 3138
    labor market analysis **3:** 1677
  factors affecting **9:** 5548
  factors in developing socioeconomic status **8:** 4716
  and formal education **9:** 5533
  and functional theories of education **2:** 1065
  intergenerational **10:** 5730
    definition of **9:** 5548, 5550
    and education **9:** 5550
    models **9:** 5550
  intragenerational **10:** 5730
    definition of **9:** 5548, 5550
    and education **9:** 5552
  kinship studies
    and education **6:** 3138
  measurement
    mobility tables **7:** 3862
  and nonformal education **7:** 4143
  and occupational mobility **9:** 5552
  outcomes of education
    correlation tests **6:** 3139
  structural **9:** 5552
  of teachers **10:** 5610
  See also
    Mobility tables
Social movements
  See Activism
Social networks
  adult child relationships
    and social capital **4:** 2273
  analysis **9:** ***5554–5560***
  characteristics of **9:** 5558
  computer software for **9:** 5558
  concepts of **9:** 5554
  definition of **9:** 5554
  dissonance theory **9:** 5174
  and friendship choice **9:** 5175
  inference and analysis **9:** 5557
  Markov models **9:** 5558
  matrices in **9:** 5555
  name generators **9:** 5556
  nodes **9:** 5554
  observation **9:** 5556
    designs for **9:** 5556
  and school dynamics **9:** 5174
  and social development **9:** 5524, 5527
  studies **9:** 5554
Social organizations
  educational
    and role theory **10:** 6219
  and socialization **10:** 5586
Social philosophy
  and political philosophy **8:** ***4571–4575***
Social policy
  and deinstitutionalization (of disabled)
    comparative studies **3:** 1434
Social problems
  and behavior disorders **1:** 494
  controversial issues (course content)
    and core curriculum **2:** 1104
  global approach **4:** 2328
Social psychology
  aspiration
    and educational and occupational attainment **1:** ***354–358***
  and attitudes
    research **9:** 5319
  contact theory **9:** 5171
  of education **10:** 6223
  expectation states theory **9:** 5171
  prosocial behavior
    and values **1:** 378
  and school culture **10:** 6223
  and social mobility
    models **9:** 5551
  theories
    achievement motivation **10:** 6221
    attribution **10:** 6222
    conflict **10:** 6221
    distributive justice **10:** 6221
    interdependence **10:** 6220
    self-esteem **10:** 6222
    of teaching **10:** ***6219–6224***
  uses of **10:** 6223
Social reproduction
  Bernstein's theory **3:** 1345
  Bourdieu's theory **3:** 1345
  correspondence theory **9:** 5057
  and cultural capital **4:** 2267, 2269
  curriculum research **3:** 1345
  and hegemony **9:** 5058
  Marxism **6:** 3618
  and peer influence **9:** 5219
  resistance **6:** 3619
  and textbook research **3:** 1345
Social science research
  and action research **1:** 46
  and educational policy
    models **8:** 4559
  and educational research **9:** 5053
  empirical studies **1:** 58
  feminist research methodology **4:** ***2297–2302***
  historical background **9:** 5407
  individual development
    and policy formation **5:** ***2670–2673***
  and intellectual disciplines **9:** 5296
  learning
    issues **9:** 5562
  and policy formation **5:** 2670
    contextual factors **5:** 2671
    measurement of outcomes **5:** 2671
    values in **5:** 2670
  and scaling **9:** 5153
  and secondary data analysis **9:** 5369
  and socialization **10:** 5587
  and sociology of education **10:** 5600
  Statistical Package for the Social Sciences (SPSS) **7:** 4052
  textbook research **9:** 5560
  and triangulation **11:** 6462

utilization
models **4:** 1862
Social Science Research Council (SSRC) (UK)
survey archive **3:** 1379
Social sciences
attack on alleged objectivity **3:** 1770
data archives **3:** 1379
data banks **3:** 1377
development
and educational administration **1:** 54, 57
influences **1:** 56
and educational administration **1:** 53
theories **9:** 5162
generalizations in **3:** 1770
and hermeneutics **5:** 2583
learning and instruction **9:** ***5560–5563***
learning motivation **9:** 5562
and social studies **9:** 5578
and student activism **10:** 5781
syllabi
and political influences **10:** 5884
textbooks
explanation in **10:** 6145
theoretical trends
and educational administration **1:** 58
thinking skills **9:** 5562
variables
and Thurstone scales **11:** 6385
Social skills
See Interpersonal competence
Social status
measurement **7:** 3716
scales **7:** 3717
and social stratification **10:** 5730
of teachers **8:** 4522
of teaching **10:** ***6224–6227***
Social stratification
concept and types of **9:** 5568
definitions of **9:** 5548, 5549, 5568
and education **9:** ***5548–5554***, 5569
educational anthropology **1:** 290; **9:** ***5567–5572***
in educational systems **10:** ***5730–5735***
structures **10:** 5733
and intelligence testing **7:** 3770
issues **10:** 5730
and measurement **7:** 3716
methodological issues **10:** 5734
and outcomes of education **10:** 5731
status attainment model **10:** 5732
scales of **9:** 5549
and schools **10:** 5732
studies **10:** 5733
and Veblen's sociology of education **2:** 783
Social structure
social change
outcomes of education **9:** 5509
and sociology of education **10:** 5601
Social studies
African Social and Environmental Studies Program **10:** 5583, 5584
anthropology in **1:** 279
characteristics of **10:** 5583
and citizenship education **10:** 5583
and civic education
Africa **2:** 768
and core curriculum **2:** 769
curriculum **4:** 2330
expanding environments **9:** 5574
issues **9:** 5579
for United States immigrants and minority groups **7:** 3843
definitions of **9:** 5573, 5578
educational research **9:** 5580
and environmental education **4:** 1994
functions of **9:** 5572, 5573
inservice teacher education **10:** 5584
interdisciplinary approach **10:** 5583
issues **9:** 5578
and issues-based geography instruction **5:** 2467
new movement in **9:** 5578
objectives of **9:** 5572, 5573
issues **9:** 5578
in primary schools **9:** ***5572–5578***
historical background **9:** 5573
materials and strategies **9:** 5576
program context **9:** 5574
research trends **9:** 5577
reform **9:** 5578
Saudi Arabia **10:** 5583
secondary school curriculum **9:** ***5578–5583***
and social change **9:** 5579
socialization **10:** 5583
teacher education **10:** ***5583–5585***
issues **10:** 5583, 5585
models and programs **10:** 5584
reflective/critical inquiry approach **10:** 5584
trends **10:** 5584
and teaching guides **10:** 6114
teaching methods **9:** 5579
trends **9:** 5582
use of term **9:** 5578
Social systems
concept of
and organizations (groups) **4:** 2157
Social theories
conflict theory **2:** 1066; **10:** 5608
education in **2:** 775
and educational planning **10:** 5605
functional theories of education **2:** 1065
and interactionism **2:** 1070
interpretive **10:** 5608
and management theory
in organizational theories **4:** 2158
sociology of education **2:** ***1064–1074***
structural–functionalism **10:** 5608
utilitarian theories of education **2:** 1066
Social values
conventional **1:** 378
and cultural capital **4:** ***2267–2272***
and moral values **7:** 3915
school enterprise
benefits on **9:** 5231
Social welfare
politics of
and adult education **1:** 128
See also
Well-being
Social welfare education **1:** 116
Social work
andragogy **1:** 275
Socialism
and adult education **2:** 1189, 1193
Soviet Union (former) **9:** 5092
adult education for **1:** 132
adult education legislation **6:** 3364
and adult educators **10:** 6055
and curriculum **3:** 1327
and education **3:** 1653
Central and Eastern Europe **11:** 6642
and educational administration **6:** 3274
and educational planning **8:** 4489
feminism
and the curriculum **4:** 2289
feminist theories **5:** 2453, 2456
and general education **5:** 2733, 2734
and literacy programs **1:** 170
and Marxist educational thought **6:** 3617
and peace education **3:** 1730
Socialist nations
compulsory education **8:** 4497
educational planning
Asia **8:** 4487
history of **8:** 4489, 4500
Socialization **1:** 116; **6:** ***3306–3312***; **10:** ***5586–5591***
achievement need
in children **1:** 30
work ethic **3:** 1237
and adult education **1:** 110, 128
agents of **10:** 5586
and aggression **1:** 232
and antipedagogy **8:** 4458
black stereotypes **10:** 5823
and child development
cultural differences **4:** 2260
of children
and educational quality **8:** 4866
and comparative national achievement levels **4:** 2138
components of **10:** 5586
concept of **10:** 5586
conflict approach **10:** 5587
contexts of **10:** 5588, 5589
cooperative learning **2:** 1095
and course selection (students) **10:** 6125
definitions of **10:** 5586, 6122
and developmental psychology **6:** 3426
and emotional development **4:** 1963, 1964
employment objectives
Japan **11:** 6696

and enculturation **3:** 1724
and family **10:** 5588
influence of school
communication skills development **9:** 5506
interactive nature of **10:** 5586
and knowledge **6:** 3149
maturation vs. development **10:** 5586
Mead's views
and social cognition **9:** 5510
and mediation of learning **3:** 1243
minority group children
ethnography **2:** 801
minority groups
and bilingual education **1:** 534
and moral development **7:** 3915
and moral education **4:** 2293
and nonformal education **4:** 2365
occupational **10:** 5589
organic approach **10:** 5587
peer groups **10:** 5589, 5590
and individual variability **9:** 5218
and philosophy of education **2:** 776
processes
in schools **10:** 5590
professional development of teachers **10:** ***6122–6127***
and prosocial behavior **8:** 4798
research **10:** 5588
role of language in **6:** 3214
and school choice **8:** 4829
and school context **10:** 5589
by schools
and conflict **2:** 1038
in schools
and discipline **3:** 1535
sex differences **3:** 1737; **4:** 2416; **9:** 5429
francophone Africa **11:** 6736
sex role **4:** ***2407–2412***, 2446, 2449
and ideology **4:** 2407
sex stereotypes **10:** 5823
social class
and aspiration **1:** 355
and social development **9:** 5505
social learning theory
personality development **8:** 4390
social studies **10:** 5583
and state education relationship **3:** 1715
systems of **10:** 5587
and teacher education **10:** 5612
of teachers **10:** 6208
theory of
current trends **10:** 5588
historical background **10:** 5587
and values education **1:** 377
and Znaniecki's sociology of education **2:** 784
See also
Cultural transmission
Political socialization
Society for Anthropology in Community Colleges (US) **1:** 279
Society for the Study of Curriculum History (US) **3:** 1288, 1300, 1302
Sociobiology **4:** 2170
and individual development
adjustment (to environment) **4:** 2170
parents' and teachers' roles **4:** 2170
peer relationship **4:** 2170
Sociocultural animation
adult education **8:** 4810
Africa **1:** 216, 217
Sociocultural patterns
and curriculum development **9:** 5520
development **3:** 1648, 1650
educational anthropology **9:** 5508
Sociocultural systems
concepts of **9:** 5308
schools as **9:** ***5308–5313***
qualitative research **9:** 5310
Socioeconomic influences
and prestige scales **9:** 5549
Socioeconomic status (SES)
and disengagement theory **9:** 5226
educational benefits **1:** 515
and effective schools research **9:** 5375
measurement **7:** 3716
and peer influence **9:** 5172
scale of **7:** 3717
scales of
and social stratification **9:** 5549
and school desegregation **3:** 1484
and school effectiveness **4:** 1935
special needs students **6:** 3292
Socioeconomic techniques
and social networks **9:** 5554
graph theory **9:** 5555
Sociograms
See Sociometric techniques, sociograms
Sociolinguistics
classroom communication **2:** 798; **3:** 1229
disadvantaged children
and language usage **6:** 3214
foreign language learning **4:** 2344, 2345
and linguistic deprivation model **6:** 3235
United States **6:** 3214
urban schools
anthropological research **2:** 916
Sociology
age stratification model **6:** 3426
and biographical research **1:** 537
and educational research
educational opportunities **4:** 1869
Sociology of education **10:** ***5596–5607***
adult education **10:** ***5591–5596***
approaches
macro vs. micro **10:** 5601
classical theories **2:** ***775–785***
and critical pedagogy **10:** 5602
criticisms of **10:** 5598
and curriculum history **3:** 1302, 1303
curriculum research **3:** ***1343–1348***
definitions of the field **10:** 5597
changes **10:** 5599
developments **10:** 5601
Durkheim **2:** 776
and educational administration **1:** 55, 61, 62
future trends **10:** 5605
historical background **10:** 5596, 5598
as international discipline **10:** 5601
learning **6:** ***3306–3312***
Mannheim **2:** 782
Marx **2:** 779
methods
developments **10:** 5599
periodicals **10:** 5598, 5599
perspectives **10:** 5597
and postmodernism **10:** 5602
social theories **2:** ***1064–1074***
categories **2:** 1064
special **10:** ***5663–5668***
Spencer **2:** 782
teaching **10:** ***5607–5614***
and school organization **4:** 2159
themes **10:** 5601
theories **2:** 1064
developments **10:** 5599
Veblen **2:** 783
Weber **2:** 780
Znaniecki **2:** 783
Sociology of knowledge
and curriculum research **3:** 1344
Sociology of work
teaching **10:** ***6132–6139***
Sociometric techniques **10:** ***5614–5618***
classroom interaction **10:** 5617
and cognitive development **10:** 5617
computer software for **10:** 5617
and educational research **10:** 5616
future research **10:** 5617
graphic representation **10:** 5615
historical background **10:** 5614
limitations **10:** 5615
nomination method **10:** 5614
origins and development **10:** 5614
peer evaluation **8:** 4366
quantitative methods **10:** 5615
self-rating method **10:** 5614
social influences **10:** 5616
sociograms **10:** 5614, 5615
misuse of **10:** 5615
uses of **10:** 5615
Software publishing
See Computer software, publishing
Software
See Computer software
Software tools
See Authoring aids (programming)
Solvents
inhalant abuse
effect on learning **3:** 1612
Somalia
adult education
radio **1:** 326
literacy campaigns **1:** 170
schools
decentralization **3:** 1415

Sororities
United States **10:** 5777
Sound
See Acoustics
South Africa
adult education **10:** 5629
cultural influences **10:** 5626
curriculum
sex bias **4:** 2290
curriculum development **10:** 5633
educational change **10:** 5634
educational finance **10:** 5630
educational history **2:** 1061
educational research **10:** 5634
educational technology
interactive video **4:** 1902
ethnic groups **10:** 5625
ethnography of Kafir **3:** 1752
female blacks
educationally disadvantaged
7: ***3848–3853***
governance
and politics of education **8:** 4591
government school relationship
school administration **10:** 5630
language **10:** 5625
media selection **7:** 3759
multilingualism
bilingual education **4:** 2347
open universities **7:** 4216
postsecondary education **10:** 5628
preschool education **10:** 5629
primary education **10:** 5627
secondary education **10:** 5627
special education **10:** 5629
system of education **10:** ***5625–5635***
degrees and qualifications **10:** 5633
educational objectives **10:** 5626
enrollment **10:** 5632
structure **10:** 5627
teacher education **10:** 5632
by distance learning **4:** 1907
teacher recruitment **10:** 5632
technical and vocational education
and training **11:** ***6251–6256***
vocational education **10:** 5629
historical background **11:** 6252
South America
community colleges **2:** 895
educational research
action research **1:** 45
South-East Asia and Pacific Region
Educational Administrators
and Managers
Symposium (SEAPREAMS) **5:** 2954
South East Asian Ministers of
Education Organization
(SEAMEO) **5:** 2933; **6:** 3464
educational technology
activities **4:** 1878
Southport Institute for Policy Analysis
(US)
Jumpstart study **7:** 4148
literacy legislation **7:** 4185
Soviet Union (USSR) (former)
adult education **9:** ***5091–5098***
coverage **9:** 5093
finance **9:** 5093
future strategies **9:** 5096
governance and legislation **9:** 5093
history **2:** 1191; **9:** 5091
institutional organization **9:** 5094
participation **9:** 5093
research **1:** 124; **9:** 5097
structures **9:** 5093
art education and ideology **1:** 340
civic education **2:** 768
collective settlements
and education **10:** 5646
computer uses in education
and media programs **7:** 3755
cooperatives
education work relationship
10: 5646
dissolution of **10:** 5645
management of contraction in
public education **6:** 3604
economic change
and vocational education **10:** 5649
economics education **10:** 5646
educational planning **8:** 4496
history of **8:** 4489, 4500
educational reform
implementation **4:** 1854
educational research **4:** 1869, 1870
ethnicity
and national unity **7:** 3966
general education
and vocational education **10:** 5645
influence of Dewey's democratic ideas
3: 1524
labor education **10:** 5646
labor force development **5:** 2688
labor market
vocational education and **10:** 5648
literacy campaigns **1:** 171; **9:** 5092
paraprofessional personnel **10:** 5648
polytechnical education **8:** 4605
school administration
centralization **9:** 5165
secondary education
student options **10:** 5644
technical education **10:** 5647
vocational education **10:** ***5644–5650***
agriculture **10:** 5648
characteristics of **10:** 5644
finance **10:** 5649
historical background **10:** 5644
policies **10:** 5645, 5647
reforms **10:** 5644
vocational schools **10:** 5644; **11:** 6245
organizational change in **10:** 5647
rural **10:** 5648
See also
Russia
Spain
adult education **10:** 5652
adult education promotion **6:** 3365
computer uses in education
organizations for **2:** 1016
cooperative education **1:** 132
cultural influences **10:** 5650
curriculum development **10:** 5656
educational administration
administrator selection **1:** 80
educational change **10:** 5657
educational finance **10:** 5655
educational research **10:** 5657
female participation in adult
education **1:** 107
government school relationship
school administration **10:** 5654
monitoring of standards **7:** 3907
postsecondary education **10:** 5652
preschool education **10:** 5653
primary education **10:** 5653
principals
recruitment **1:** 68
private education **10:** 5652
school-based management **1:** 592
school reform **9:** 5279
secondary education **10:** 5653
vocational education **10:** 5654
sociology of education
development of **10:** 5601
special education **10:** 5652
system of education **10:** ***5650–5658***
degrees and qualifications **10:** 5656
educational objectives **10:** 5650
enrollment **10:** 5652
major problems **10:** 5658
structure **10:** 5651, 5653
teacher education **10:** 5656
Classified Practice Centers **10:** 5811
teacher recruitment **10:** 5656
vocational education **10:** 5652
Spatial ability **5:** 2761
process analyses **1:** 3
sex differences **4:** 2434; **9:** 5428, 5443
spatial relations **1:** 3
visualization **1:** 3
Speaking ability
See Speech evaluation
Spearman–Brown formula **9:** 4983
and classical test theory **2:** 786
and item sampling **5:** 3057
and rating scales **8:** 4927
Spearman's rank order correlation
coefficient
See Correlation, rank
Special classes
for children with disabilities **2:** 722
and diagnostic tests **2:** 712
school readiness
Scandinavia **10:** 5660
special education **10:** 5660
transitional programs
school readiness **9:** 5274
visual impairments **11:** 6626
Special education
administration **2:** 722; **5:** 2968
Albania **1:** 257
Argentina **1:** 335
behavior disorders **1:** 491
bilingual students
language handicaps **6:** ***3228–3232***

Bulgaria **1:** 584
Canada **2:** 621
and career education **2:** 631
Chile **2:** 741
classification **2:** 724
for educational purposes **2:** 724
cognitive strategy instruction
2: ***861–868***
and compulsory education **10:** 5659
computer software **7:** 3805, 3806
correctional education **3:** 1440
Côte d'Ivoire **2:** 1155
critical theory **10:** 5664
curriculum-based assessment in
3: 1356, 1357
Cyprus **3:** 1370
degrees of mainstreaming **6:** 3558
Denmark **2:** 723; **3:** 1455
diagnostic practices
mild disabilities **7:** 3831
diagnostic teaching **10:** 6170
diagnostic tests **10:** 5660
disabilities **5:** 2566
disabilities model
labeling (of persons) **10:** 5664
distance education **5:** 2970
educational needs
developing nations **5:** 2966
global approach **5:** 2966
educational objectives **10:** 5658
educational technology **5:** 2970
curriculum integration **7:** 3806
enrollments **2:** 720
developing nations **2:** 720; **5:** 2966
Europe **10:** 5658, 5659
evaluation studies **2:** 727
expansion of **10:** 5660
extension of **10:** 5941
France **4:** 2381
Germany **2:** 723; **10:** 5660
gifted **5:** ***2486–2491***
health needs of students **5:** 2574
historical development **2:** 720
history of **10:** ***5658–5663***
and humanistic education **10:** 5659
India **5:** 2747
international activities **2:** 727
international agencies **5:** 2966
international co-operation
5: ***2965–2972***
recommendations **5:** 2971
international conferences **5:** 2970
international educational exchanges
and sabbatical leaves **5:** 2969
international perspective **2:** ***719–730***
Italy **2:** 723
Japan **10:** 5660
Kenya **6:** 3128
labeling (of persons) **2:** 725
and learning disabilities concept of
10: 5664
least restrictive environment approach
6: 3558
legislation **2:** 721
England and Wales **2:** 722
United States **2:** 721; **5:** 2572
legitimation of programs **10:** 5663, 5667
local area networks **7:** 3805
and mainstreaming **10:** 5661
medical model **6:** 3294, 3557
mental retardation
Montessori method **7:** 3913
microcomputer uses **7:** ***3802–3808***
model
resource room programs
9: ***5066–5071***
modes of delivery **10:** 5942
needs
and teacher education
10: ***5939–5943***
Netherlands **7:** 4072
New Zealand **7:** 4107
and noncategorical education **7:** 3831
Norway **2:** 723
outcomes of education
and aptitude treatment interaction
10: 6157
paraprofessional school personnel
7: 4293
peer teaching **8:** ***4372–4376***
philanthropic foundations **10:** 5658
placement
and test bias **11:** 6318
policies **2:** 722
problems and issues **2:** 728
professional organizations **2:** 728
provision
and training **10:** 5940
United Kingdom **2:** 720
rationale of **8:** 4931
recent trends **2:** 721
reconceptualizing
and supported inclusion **3:** 1507
referrals **10:** 5667
research **2:** 726; **8:** 4933
financial support for **2:** 727
problems of **2:** 726
university sponsored **5:** 2969
respect for individual differences
2: 729
Scandinavia **10:** 5660
school-based **10:** 5942
scope of **10:** 5940
service delivery
teams for **10:** 6241
services
and learning disabilities **10:** 5684
severe disabilities **3:** 1505
and social control **10:** 5663, 5665
sociology of **10:** ***5663–5668***
Sweden **5:** 2906
talent **5:** ***2486–2491***
Tanzania **10:** 5904
teaching models
data-based program modification
3: 1356, 1358
exceptional teaching **3:** 1356
precision teaching **3:** 1356
resource/consulting teaching
3: 1356
teaming arrangements for
10: ***6240–6245***
Thailand **11:** 6373
trends **9:** 5070
Tunisia **11:** 6470
United States **2:** 724; **10:** 5659;
11: 6542
use of technology in **10:** ***5668–5674***
visual impairments **11:** ***6625–6628***
vocational education **2:** 632
Special education personnel **2:** 725
auxiliary professional staff **2:** 725
Special education teachers
administration
microcomputers **7:** 3804
burnout **2:** 726
computer-assisted instruction
implementation **7:** 3806
international supply **5:** 2966
professional development **5:** 2968;
10: 5941
qualifications of **10:** 5939
regular and special education
relationship **10:** 5667
resource room programs **9:** 5067
teacher education **2:** 725; **5:** 2968;
6: 3559; **10:** 5661, 5662
curriculum **2:** 726
initial **10:** 5940
noncategorical education **7:** 3832
teaching methods **5:** 2968
team teaching **6:** 3558
training for mainstreaming **5:** 2906
Special health problems **5:** ***2572–2575***
Special libraries
educational resources **6:** 3398
Special needs children
empowerment of families
4: ***1976–1980***
literacy development
parent participation **6:** ***3459–3463***
parents as teachers **6:** 3461
Special needs students
and adult programs **1:** 155
characteristics of **10:** 5668
classification **6:** 3294
medical model **6:** 3294
social system model **6:** 3294
and computer-assisted instruction
10: 5671
diagnosis and classification
and cultural differences **2:** 715
issues in **2:** 715
legal considerations **2:** 712
models of **2:** 713
purposes **2:** 712
educational diagnosis **2:** ***711–719***
Africa **2:** 717
practices **2:** 712
procedures **2:** 714
and educational finance **9:** 5235
educational technology
uses of **10:** ***5668–5674***
identification **6:** 3294
intelligence tests **2:** 715
learning characteristics **6:** ***3292–3297***

literacy development
parent participation **6:** ***3459–3463***
mainstreaming **5:** ***2907–2910***
microcomputers **7:** ***3802–3808***
parents as teachers **6:** 3461
and prereferral intervention **8:** 4657
provision and responsibilities for **6:** 3558
and resource allocation **9:** 5061
and resource room programs **9:** 5066
teams for **10:** ***6240–6245***
and testing **11:** 6314
Special programs
disabled children
Japan **3:** 1436
health needs **5:** ***2572–2575***
individualized programs **2:** 713, 714
visual impairments **11:** 6627
Special schools
for children with disabilities **2:** 722; **8:** 4827
Specialization
and cognitive ability **8:** 4819, 4821
in development of new disciplines **1:** 122
and educational researchers **11:** 6439, 6443
intellectual disciplines
and evaluation **4:** 2090
recognition of outstanding teacher competence **4:** 2127
and teacher certification **4:** 2126
and occupations **11:** 6667
and related services personnel **9:** 5282
and school mapping **9:** 5257
in secondary schools
and effective schools research **9:** 5376
and teaching guides **10:** 6116
and textbooks
readership size **11:** 6362
and vocational education **11:** 6250
Specific language disorders
See Language handicaps, specific
Specific learning disabilities
See Learning disabilities, specific
Specifications
and project evaluation **8:** 4781
and prototyping **8:** 4801
Speech
characteristics of **11:** 6704
reproduction systems for **1:** 400
Speech acts
ideal speech situation
communicative competence **2:** 1202
Speech communication
and hearing impairments **10:** 5688
and language education
simulations **7:** 4093
and language tests **4:** 2359
listening and speech instruction **6:** ***3439–3443***
and narrative inquiry **7:** 4049
and voice disorders **11:** 6704
See also
Oral communication
Speech disorders
See Speech handicaps
Speech evaluation **7:** 3934
measurement **7:** 3934
and phonemes **10:** 5694
requirements **10:** 5695
Speech handicaps **3:** 1516; **10:** ***5691–5697***
cluttering **3:** 1516
communication disorders
augmentative and alternative communication **1:** ***404–409***
congenital impairments **1:** 405
definitions of **10:** 5691
and hearing impairments **10:** ***5686–5691***
incidence and prevalence **10:** 5692
and mental retardation **1:** 405
neurological impairments **1:** 405
organizations for **10:** 5692
and reading achievement **10:** 5694
and reading difficulties **10:** 5678
research trends **10:** 5693
special needs students
microcomputers **7:** 3802
types of **10:** 5691
See also
Articulation impairments
Cleft palate
Stuttering
Voice disorders
Speech instruction **6:** ***3439–3443***
integration with listening skills **6:** 3439
teaching methods **6:** 3441
Speech pathology
and cleft palates **11:** 6706
language handicaps
changing role **10:** 5693
intervention **6:** 3227
and voice disorders **11:** 6705
Speech perception
and hearing impairments **10:** 5688
Speech recognition systems
and assistive technology **10:** 5669
Speech–sound disorders
See Speech handicaps
Speech–sound system
See Phonology
Speech tests **7:** 3934
situations for **7:** 3934
Speech therapy
active participation approach **10:** 5696
articulation **10:** 5694
for cleft palates **11:** 6706
concepts of **10:** 5696
cycles approach **10:** 5695
future research **10:** 5696
for highly unintelligible phonologies **10:** 5695
optimal match approach **10:** 5696
voice disorders **11:** 6705
Speed reading
and reading comprehension **1:** 186
selective attention strategies **1:** 376
tests of **7:** 3931
Speed tests
See Timed tests
Spelling **1:** 481
phoneme grapheme correspondence **10:** 5697, 5703
skill development
developmental stages **10:** 5702
testing **10:** 5704
tests
and analysis of variance methods **11:** 6586
See also
Finger spelling
Invented spelling
Spelling instruction **10:** ***5697–5705***
teaching methods
and developmental stages **10:** 5703
Sponsorship
and nonformal education **7:** 4142
Sport pedagogy
definitions of **10:** 5708
future research
problems **10:** 5713
research in **10:** ***5708–5713***
observation by deduction **10:** 5708
observation by induction **10:** 5710
teacher preparation
descriptive studies **10:** 5711
teaching process
correlational approach **10:** 5710
descriptive approach **10:** 5708
teaching skills
studies **10:** 5712
See also
Physical education
Spreadsheets
and educational planning **11:** 6296
models **3:** 1827, 1828
and microcomputers **7:** 3815
in physical sciences
secondary school programs **8:** 4478
in school administration **9:** 5184
Sri Lanka
adult education **1:** 118; **5:** 2755
nonformal education **10:** 5718
computer uses in education **4:** 1902
curriculum development **10:** 5719
educational change **10:** 5720
educational finance **10:** 5718
educational research **10:** 5720
ethnic groups **10:** 5714
government school relationship
school administration **10:** 5718
inservice teacher education **10:** 6066
nonformal education **7:** 4133
postsecondary education **10:** 5716
preschool education **10:** 5716
primary education **5:** 2753
private education **10:** 5715
public sector employment **8:** 4838, 4839
social movement **1:** 132

special education **10:** 5717
structure of government **10:** 5714
system of education **10:** ***5713–5721***
degrees and qualifications **10:** 5720
educational objectives **10:** 5715
major problems **10:** 5720
structure **10:** 5715
teacher education **10:** 5719
administration of **10:** 6064
and cost effectiveness studies **2:** 1135
teacher recruitment **10:** 5719
vocational education **10:** 5717
and public sector support **11:** 6648
See also
Sarvodaya Shramadana Movement
Staff development
action research **10:** 5938
collaborative problem-solving **10:** 5938
inservice teacher education **10:** 5967, 5971
and printing **8:** 4693
and program implementation **5:** 2844
teams
and specialization **10:** 6242
use of evaluation for **4:** 2127
Stage theory
See Developmental stages
Standard Assessment Tasks (SATs) (UK) **3:** 1295
Standard deviation (statistics)
calculation **7:** 3728
frequency distribution format
formula **7:** 3728
and meta analysis **7:** 3777
use of **7:** 3727
Standard error of estimate
See Error of measurement
Standard error of measurement
See Error of measurement
Standard International Occupational Prestige Scale (SIOPS) **7:** 3718; **10:** 5731, 6225
Standard scores (statistics)
calculation **7:** 3729
Standardized tests
achievement
input output analysis measurement **3:** 1757
administration of **11:** 6311
and educational assessment **1:** 369
history of **4:** 2080
input output analysis
measurement **8:** 4562
and language styles **6:** 3237
national policies **3:** 1336
norm-referenced tests
historical development **4:** 1868
and norms for needs assessments **7:** 4058
and outcomes of education **3:** 1782
and performance contracts **8:** 4709
procedures for **2:** 994, 995
and school effectiveness **1:** 590
special needs students
and cultural differences **2:** 716
and student needs **10:** 5769
and teacher effectiveness **8:** 4521
test bias
curriculum content **3:** 1356
test items
and outcomes of education **4:** 2075
unsuitability for young children **1:** 360
Standards
classroom techniques
effect of unions on **10:** 6071
courseware **10:** 5618
in criterion referenced tests **10:** ***5721–5726***
educational
and decentralization **9:** 5212
and educational objectives
curriculum development **3:** 1801
evaluation **8:** ***4736–4751***
compliance with **4:** 2034
global **4:** 2117
and management information systems **6:** 3595
minimum
printed materials **8:** 4697
setting **7:** ***4054–4056***
and teacher certification **10:** ***5925–5930***
test translation **11:** 6333
use of term **7:** 3911
world class proposed
United States **7:** 4053
See also
Academic standards
National standards
Professional standards
Stanford–Binet intelligence test
adaptive testing **2:** 993
and sex differences **9:** 5427
Stanford International Development Education Committee (SIDEC) (US) **2:** 937
Stanine scale
and achievement tests **1:** 35
State
adult education
direct commitment **6:** 3364
enablement **6:** 3364
finance of **6:** 3365
regulation **6:** 3364
and support services **6:** 3365
and adult education ideology **2:** 1191
adult education obligations **6:** 3362
concept of **3:** 1713
and education **3:** ***1713–1720***
financing of lifelong learning **6:** 3424
and higher education **3:** 1718
ideological apparatus **3:** 1715
ideological trends **3:** 1717
legitimacy of **6:** 3367
liberal–pluralist theories **3:** 1716
and literacy campaign objectives **1:** 170
Marxist theories **3:** 1715; **6:** 3618
and new right ideology **3:** 1716, 1717, 1719
and politics of adult education **6:** 3365
and postmodernism **3:** 1716
power **3:** 1714
regulatory powers over adult education **1:** 115
role in capitalist democratic education **4:** 2268
Rousseau's view of the **9:** 5088
and status of adult education **6:** 3361
theories of **3:** 1715
State boards of education
teacher certification
standards **10:** 5926
State church relationship
accommodation
pluralist politics of **9:** 5010
dominant secular control **9:** 5008
and governance **5:** 2511
and religious education **9:** 5004
and school choice **9:** 5193, 5195
theocratic domination **9:** 5010
State church separation
concept of **9:** 5012
and educational administration **6:** 3274
State departments of education **7:** ***3833–3840***
administrative organization **7:** 3836
changing context **7:** 3834
centralization vs. decentralization **7:** 3838
coordination problems **7:** 3836
decision-making processes **7:** 3838
and educational change **7:** 3838
functions **7:** 3835
future trends **7:** 3839
and governance of teacher education **10:** 5962
multiple agency model **7:** 3835
organizational patterns **7:** 3835
personnel **7:** 3837
administrator characteristics **7:** 3837
powers of **7:** 3838
responsibilities **7:** 3836
role of
and educational change **7:** 3834
single agency model **7:** 3835
teacher certification **10:** 5926
State government
teachers
professional autonomy **10:** 6095
State policy
See Public policy
State schools
educational history
research methodology **5:** 2602
females in
Germany **11:** 6746
sex discrimination
South Africa **7:** 3852
vs. private schools

and private resources **8:** 4706
and student fees **10:** 5750
Statistical analysis
change
measurement of **2:** 676
choice of method
and secondary data analysis **9:** 5370
comparative education **2:** ***958–964***
computer software for **3:** 1388
correlation
historical development **4:** 1867
and evaluation **4:** 2371
and expectancy tables **4:** 2182
and microcomputers **7:** 3815
multilevel **4:** 2384
in program evaluation **11:** 6380
relationship with qualitative research **2:** 641; **9:** 5023
and research synthesis **7:** 3775
robust **9:** ***5077–5082***
social science
Statistical Package for the Social Sciences (SPSS) **7:** 4052
terminology **9:** 5026
test selection
and experimental studies **4:** 2191
See also
Bayesian statistics
Robustness (statistics)
Statistical bias
in research reports
and meta analysis **7:** 3777
Statistical distributions
and achievement tests **1:** 32
in bootstrap procedure **9:** 5469
and classical test theory **2:** 787
and criterion referenced tests **10:** 5724
and educational measurements **7:** 3701
in equated scores **11:** 6350, 6351
marginal
and mobility tables **7:** 3862
multivariate analysis **7:** 4008
multivariate normal
and achievement tests **1:** 40
naturally occurring **1:** 36
normal
formula **1:** 477
and sampling **9:** 5137
test for **7:** 3732
normal score
and achievement tests **1:** 35
and psychological measurements **7:** 3701
rectangular
and achievement tests **1:** 35, 39
and research synthesis **7:** 3776
and robustness (statistics) **9:** 5077
and sampling **9:** 5137
shapes of **7:** 3732
standard deviation
formula **7:** 3728
and statistical significance **9:** 5464
and Thurstone scales **11:** 6385
Statistical inference
in educational research **7:** 4157
Statistical significance **9:** ***5460–5467***
and analysis of variance **11:** 6587, 6588
asymptotic tests **9:** 5462
in canonical analysis **2:** 630
and clustering **7:** 3735
omega squared **7:** 3735
composite alternative hypothesis **9:** 5464
composite null hypothesis **9:** 5465
and correlation coefficients
in meta analysis **7:** 3779
and educational history **5:** 2604
exact tests **9:** 5461
Fisherian tests **9:** 5461
and models **7:** 3866; **9:** 5460
and multilevel analysis **7:** 3981
multiple comparisons **11:** 6590
Bonferroni method **11:** 6591
and multivariate analysis **7:** 4009
Neyman–Pearson tests **9:** 5463
power of **9:** 5464
and experimental studies **4:** 2191
problems **9:** 5466
and regression analysis **9:** 4968
and research synthesis **7:** 3776
test models
and research synthesis **10:** 6236
tests **2:** 1110
and logit models **6:** 3505
multiple correlation **2:** 1114
multivariate analysis **2:** 1115
partial correlation **2:** 1113
Statistical surveys
in adult education measurement **7:** 3707
methodologies **7:** 3712, 3713, 3714, 3715
and microcomputers **7:** 3814
proxy responses **7:** 3708, 3709
questionnaires **7:** 3709
selection bias in **9:** 5380
and terminological diversity **7:** 3708
Statistics
and cognitive development **6:** 3682
concept of **7:** 3726
discrimination
by sex **4:** 2444
and educational indicators **5:** 2986
elementary school programs **6:** 3672, 3682
estimation (mathematics)
and microeconomics **7:** 3816
high school curriculum **6:** 3682
mathematics curriculum **6:** 3681
and research methodology **9:** 5048
See also
Bayesian statistics
Educational statistics
Status
attainment
and education **10:** 5605
and social stratification **10:** 5732
and sociology of education **10:** 5600
concept of **10:** 6224
effects
and student participation **9:** 5171
and friendship formation **9:** 5174
mobility system in anthropology **1:** 287
occupational
concept of **10:** 6224
Stealing **3:** 1536
Steiner Schools
See Waldorf schools
Steinmetz Archive (Netherlands)
data archives **3:** 1379
Stem-and-leaf display
exploratory data analysis **4:** 2200, 2203
Sten scale
and achievement tests **1:** 36
Stereopsis
See Depth perception
Stereotypes
teacher expectations of students
and discourse analysis **6:** 3237
See also
Sex stereotypes
Teacher stereotypes
Still media
See Visual aids
Stimulants
dosage of **8:** 4421
effects
on cognitive functions **8:** 4421
Stimuli
control
and reinforcement **10:** 6160
and Q-methodology **8:** 4855
related vs. unrelated
and idea generation **5:** 2722
unrelated
and idea generation **5:** 2723
Stockholm University
Institute for International Education **2:** 937
Stone–Geisser test (SG-test) **8:** 4356
Story reading
contribution to reading skill development **4:** 1961
by parents **6:** 3460
children with special needs **6:** 3460
picture books **4:** 1961
story telling
retellings **4:** 1961
Story telling
history instruction **5:** 2623
and narrative inquiry **7:** 4046, 4048
parents as teachers
developing nations **6:** 3461
Strategic learning
See Learning strategies
Strategy to Develop Arab Education **8:** 4483
Stratification
forms of **9:** 5568
and sampling **9:** 5133

See also
Social stratification
Stratification model
efficiency wage model **6:** 3187
in neoclassical economics **6:** 3187
Streaming
See Ability grouping
Street children
See Homeless children
Stress (psychological)
fundamental concepts of **10:** 6058
in young children
family influence **1:** 359
See also
Anxiety
Stress management
adolescents **10:** 5737
attitudes
transactional stress theory **10:** 5736
coping **10:** 5736
and learning **10:** ***5735–5738***
for parents of disabled children **4:** 1976
resistance resources **4:** 1977
in schools **10:** 5737
social support groups **10:** 6060
teachers **10:** 6061
Stress variables
in adolescents **10:** 5735
burnout **10:** 6061
in children **10:** 5735
in schools **10:** 5735
student responses **11:** 6309
teacher burnout **10:** 6061
teachers **10:** 6059
research and development **10:** 6061
role ambiguity **10:** 6060
role conflict **10:** 6060
school organization **10:** 6060
social influences **10:** 6059
student attitudes **10:** 6060
and teaching **10:** 6212
and test anxiety **11:** 6355
Structural communication
programmed instruction **8:** 4773
Structural equation models **4:** 2137; **11:** 6382, 6383
assumptions **8:** 4347
and attitude measures
science education **9:** 5322
and causal models **7:** 3870
computer programs for
LISREL **11:** 6381, 6383
and correlation **2:** 1110
in estimation of preschool benefits **8:** 4664
and factor analysis **4:** 2238
and factorial modeling **4:** 2242
fit functions **8:** 4349
goodness of fit **8:** 4349
input data **8:** 4349
measurement model **8:** 4347
model refinement **8:** 4350
model testing **8:** 4349
moment matrices **8:** 4349
and multilevel analysis **8:** 4351
and multivariate analysis **7:** 4011
partial least squares path analysis **4:** 2137
and path analysis **8:** ***4339–4352***
methods **8:** 4347
in program evaluation **11:** 6381
and social stratification **10:** 5734
specification **8:** 4347
structural model **8:** 4347
and test translation **11:** 6333
and theoretical validity **11:** 6327
and twin studies **11:** 6490
Structural–functional analysis
United Kingdom **4:** 2047
Structural–functionalism
and teacher role **10:** 5608
Structural linguistics
mathematics and language **6:** 3635
and semiotics **9:** 5413
Structuralism
and history of instructional psychology **5:** 2876
and ideology **9:** 5056
and interactionism **2:** 1071
and occupational prestige **10:** 6225
and school organization **4:** 2159
and social studies **9:** 5578
teaching
and social reproduction **10:** 6133
Structure of Observed Learning Outcomes (SOLO) taxonomy **1:** 321
and developmental stages **3:** 1508, 1511
and mathematics **8:** 4644
STS (Science technology and society)
See Science and society
Student achievement
See Academic achievement
Student aid
See Student financial aid
Student alienation
and sociology of education **10:** 5604
Student aptitude
See Academic aptitude
Student assignments
See Assignments
Student attitudes
approaches to learning **1:** ***318–322***
and assignments **9:** 5361
classroom environment **4:** 2247
to classrooms **10:** ***5772–5775***
factors **10:** 5773
future research **10:** 5774
measurement of **10:** 5772
personal **10:** 5774
trends **10:** 5774
computer uses in education
factors **11:** 6284
to courses and assessment procedures
effect on learning **1:** 190
individual differences **1:** 190
to educational media **2:** 887
futures (of society) **4:** 2330
intellectual disciplines
content of **10:** 5793
to learning
and student role **10:** 5794
managerial behavior **10:** 6030
and outcomes of education
studies **10:** 5773
to primary school agriculture **8:** 4682
to religious education **9:** 5001
research **10:** 5772
and school size **9:** 5293
science education
computer uses in **7:** 4103
and science education
descriptive scales **3:** 1479, 1480
and self-report **9:** 5410
sex differences
secondary school students **10:** 5825
and social studies
research **9:** 5580
to teacher behavior
differential **10:** 6109
vocational education **11:** 6703
Soviet Union (former) **10:** 5646
Student behavior
analysis of **1:** ***483–486***
body language **7:** 4173
and classroom environment **8:** 4871; **10:** 5791
classroom techniques
discipline **1:** 486
conflicts at school **10:** 5758
evaluation
and videotape recordings **11:** 6604
evaluation methods **2:** 795
influence of friendship on **10:** 5756
and measurement effects **11:** 6508
modification of **1:** ***483–486***
physical education
research **10:** 5709
and self-concept **10:** 5772
sex differences
elementary school students **10:** 5825
and single case research **9:** 5487
and sociometric techniques **10:** 5616
and teacher expectation of students **10:** 5761, 6108
teacher guidance **10:** 6029
teacher response **10:** 6027
and teacher student relationship
research **10:** 5760
Student centered curriculum **6:** 3150, 3151
adult education **3:** 1309
curriculum history
United States **3:** 1297
differentiated for gifted **5:** 2494
and religious education **9:** 5002
social action programs **9:** 5002
Student certification
and evaluation **8:** ***4617–4623***
vocational schools **11:** 6667
Student characteristics
adult students **7:** 4164
affective entry **10:** 5746
and aptitude treatment interaction **10:** 6155

and attendance **3:** 1604
and audiovisual instruction **1:** 400
change in
and science education **8:** 4475
cognitive entry **10:** 5746
and cognitive processes **10:** 5740
and communication patterns **9:** 5170
and descriptive scales **3:** 1475
emotions
teacher perceptions of **10:** 5771
failing students **1:** 191, 192
individual differences
individualized instruction **5:** 2774
and learning factors **10:** 5748, 5749
and learning theories **10:** 5738
and multilevel analysis **7:** 3978
naturalistic observation **2:** 793
noncognitive
data sources for **10:** 5771
for physical sciences
in secondary school programs **8:** 4475
in preservice teacher education **1:** 75
and questioning techniques **8:** 4878
racial differences **10:** ***5822–5827***
sex differences **10:** ***5822–5827***
and student needs **10:** 5768
and student personnel services **10:** 5799
successful students **1:** 187
and teacher effectiveness **8:** 4520
teacher evaluation of **2:** 792, 793
and student needs **10:** 5770
and teacher expectation of students **10:** 5760
and teacher student relationship **10:** 5759
and teaching **10:** ***5745–5750***
and teaching guides **10:** 6116
urban schools **11:** 6559
Student culture
and women's education
North America **11:** 6763
Student developed materials
and desktop publishing **4:** 1956
Student development
and computer-assisted testing **5:** 2783
and school psychologists **9:** 5286
and student personnel services **10:** 5797
Student differences
See Student characteristics
Student educational objectives
and learning **1:** 320
and technology education **11:** 6289
Student engaged time
See Time on task
Student evaluation **7:** 4054
borderline group method **7:** 4055
certification **8:** ***4617–4623***
and computer-assisted testing **5:** 2782
contrasting group method **7:** 4055
data interpretation
teacher role **2:** 795
diagnostic teaching **10:** 6172
discourse analysis
stereotypes **6:** 3237
ethics **2:** 796
formative **10:** 6170
and multimedia systems **7:** 3992
and portfolios (background materials) **8:** 4621
purposes of **1:** 364; **7:** 4234
research
and videotape recordings **11:** 6605
resource room programs **9:** 5067
and school organization **7:** 4234
standardized tests **2:** 795
standards
types of **10:** 5769
and student needs **10:** 5769
and teacher behavior **10:** ***6012–6015***
trends **10:** 6015
types of **10:** 6014
and teacher effectiveness **8:** 4521
studies **10:** 6013
and teacher participation **10:** 6080
and teacher role **10:** 5770
teacher role **2:** ***792–796***
decision-making **2:** 793
techniques **7:** 4234
and track system (education) **7:** 4234
vs. teaching styles
and mediation theory **4:** 1874, 1876
Student evaluation of teacher performance **4:** 2129; **10:** ***6227–6235***
international studies
comparative analysis **10:** 6154
See also
Student evaluations of teacher effectiveness (SETs)
Student evaluations of educational quality (SEEQ)
content validity **10:** 6228
factors of **10:** 6228
Student evaluations of teacher effectiveness (SETs) **10:** ***6227–6235***
bias in **10:** 6232
dimensions of **10:** 6228
generalizability of **10:** 6229
measurement of **10:** 6229
multiple evaluators **10:** 6231
profile analysis of **10:** 6230
purposes of **10:** 6228
reliability of **10:** 6229
research
implications **10:** 6234
primary and secondary schools **10:** 6233
research studies **10:** 6232
stability of **10:** 6229
utilization **10:** 6233
validity
construct **10:** 6230
multisection **10:** 6230
research implications **10:** 6232
See also
Student evaluation of teacher performance
Student exchange programs **5:** 2973, 2976
and comparative education societies **2:** 947
and development education **3:** 1500
multicultural education **7:** 3963, 3968
Student experience
of curriculum **10:** ***5813–5818***
autobiographical studies **10:** 5814
biographical studies **10:** 5814
critical interpretations **10:** 5816
empirical studies **10:** 5815
ethnographic studies **10:** 5815
historical background **10:** 5813
models **10:** 5813
phenomenological interpretations **10:** 5816
in research reports **10:** 5813
stories **10:** 5816
and memorization **7:** 3763
Student fees **10:** ***5750–5754***
differential **10:** 5751
determinants of **10:** 5753
private education **10:** 5751
vs. public education **10:** 5752
public education **10:** 5751
public vs. private financial support **10:** 5752
vs. grants **4:** 2314
See also
Tuition fees
Student financial aid **10:** 5800
objectives **10:** 5763
officers
United States **10:** 5800
and tuition fees **10:** 5753
type of **10:** 5762
See also
Student loan programs
Student government **10:** 5778
Student improvement
learning strategies **6:** 3347
Student leadership
females
North America **11:** 6764
Student loan programs **10:** ***5762–5768***
characteristics of **10:** 5764
developing nations **10:** 5763, 5765
and educational equity (finance) **3:** 1793; **10:** 5765, 5767
evaluation of **10:** 5766
and income contingent loans **10:** 5764
loan default **10:** 5766
objectives **10:** 5763
reforms **10:** 5767
vs. grants
factors **10:** 5765
vs. student fees **10:** 5752
See also
Income contingent loans
Student financial aid
Student mobility
Europe **4:** 2055
Student motivation
and correlation **2:** 1112
and course selection **3:** 1423

and courseware design **2:** 1169
and cross-cultural studies **11:** 6332
individualized instruction **5:** 2776
and information technology
in science education **7:** 4101
lower class
educational policies for **5:** 2499
and microcomputer-based laboratories **7:** 3809
and modular curricula **7:** 3886
teacher judgments of **10:** 5771
teachers' beliefs **10:** 6100
urban schools **11:** 6554
Student needs
diagnosis of **10:** ***5768–5772***
and achievement tests **10:** 5769
alternative approaches **10:** 5769
methods **10:** 5769
trends **10:** 5771
and educational facilities planning **4:** 2221
measurement
and educational equity (finance) **3:** 1792
and prereferral intervention **8:** 4657, 4658
and student characteristics
teacher evaluation of **10:** 5770
Student organizations
activism **10:** 5778
activities **10:** 5776
political power **10:** 5776
student participation **10:** 5776
Student outcomes
See Outcomes of education
Student participation
curriculum design **10:** 5814
and educational technology **9:** 5542
influences
on teaching **10:** ***5759–5762***
and instructional materials **8:** 4871
and questioning techniques **8:** 4871
and school dynamics **9:** 5171
vocational education
learning modules **7:** 3891
Student perceptions
See Student attitudes
Student personnel services
administrative organization
United States **10:** ***5796–5805***
and cultural pluralism **10:** 5803
history **10:** 5796
organizational structures **10:** 5798
orientation programs **10:** 5800
programs **10:** 5799
purposes and philosophy **10:** 5797
theory and practice **10:** 5798
Student personnel workers **10:** 5796
credentials **10:** 5802
Student placement
testing problems **10:** 6171
Student problems
and attendance **3:** 1605
teams for **10:** 6240
Student progress
See Academic achievement
Student promotion
policies of automatic **5:** 2513, 2514
Student publications **10:** 5776
Student reaction
to educational objectives
and behavioral theories **10:** 6161
and educational television **5:** 2895
and feedback **10:** 6013
and group testing **9:** 5486
to information technology
in science education **7:** 4101
and nonverbal communication **7:** 4174
and questioning techniques **8:** 4879
assistance **8:** 4879
and reinforcement **10:** 6013
and social background research **7:** 3719
and teacher behavior
risks **10:** 6109
and teacher diagnosis **10:** 5791
and teacher expertise **10:** 6024
Student records
and databases **3:** 1390, 1394
and management information systems **5:** 2829
See also
Academic records
Student recruitment
and school mapping **9:** 5257
Student responsibility
and assignments **9:** 5361
and learning strategies **6:** 3337
Student role
in classrooms **10:** ***5791–5796***
change in **10:** 5791
factors **10:** 5793
in small group instruction **10:** 6185
transformation of
factors **10:** 5794
Student selection
See Admission criteria
Student subcultures **6:** 3311; **10:** 5778
group unity **5:** 2527
Student support systems
adult education **10:** ***5805–5808***
background and philosophy **10:** 5805
co-operation **10:** 5807
government support **10:** 5806
regional centers **10:** 5806
rural areas **10:** 5806
Student support teams
See Prereferral intervention
Student t-test
See t-test
Student teacher attitudes
laboratory training **6:** 3198
Student teacher evaluation **10:** 6001
Student teacher ratio
See Teacher student ratio
Student teacher supervisors
cooperating teachers **10:** 6000
criticism of role **10:** 5810
university supervisors **10:** 6001, 6003
Student teachers
attrition rate **10:** 5845
educational theories
relevance (education) **10:** 6179
instructional innovations **10:** 6126
preconceptions **10:** 5812
self-efficacy **10:** 5810
and teachers
mismatch problems **10:** 6168
Student teaching **10:** 5612
early childhood education **3:** 1632
cooperating teachers **3:** 1633
evaluation **4:** 2125, 2128
field experience programs **10:** ***5808–5812***
Canada **10:** 5809
comparative analysis **10:** 5809
criticisms of **10:** 5809
international comparisons **10:** 5809
Japan **10:** 5809
time factors **10:** 5809, 5811
trends and recommendations **10:** 5811
United States **10:** 5809
practicum supervision **10:** ***6000–6004***
practicums **10:** 5993
and professional development **10:** 5810
supervision
apprenticeship model **10:** 6000, 6003
laboratory model **10:** 6000
theory practice relationship **10:** ***5808–5812***
Student unions **10:** 5778
and political action organizations **10:** 5799
and student personnel services **10:** 5799, 5802
Student welfare
administrative organization
United States **10:** ***5796–5805***
Students
aspirations **1:** ***354–358***
and documentation systems **3:** 1591
and educational assessment
reports **1:** 365
expectations **1:** ***354–358***
extracurricular activities
political aspects **10:** 5775
interpersonal relationship
racial bias **10:** 5825
peer influence
sexuality **10:** 5825
social groups **5:** 2526
clubs **5:** 2526, 2527
friendship **5:** 2526
socialization
teacher influence **10:** 6101
Study
intellectual disciplines **9:** ***5294–5299***
Study abroad
graduate study **5:** 2976
multicultural education **7:** 3963

Study circles **2:** 904; **10:** ***5827–5829***; **11:** 6393
- and adult education **10:** 5593
- cost effectiveness **10:** 5807
- definition of **10:** 5827
- Europe **10:** 5829
- evening programs
  - Scandinavia **1:** 138
- goals **2:** 904; **10:** 5827
- history **10:** 5827
- international aspects **10:** 5829
- and labor education **11:** 6773
- Latin America **10:** 5829
- Nordic countries **7:** 4176, 4178, 4179
- origins **8:** 4809
- pedagogy **10:** 5828
- and popular education **10:** 5827
- state financial support **10:** 5828
- Sweden **4:** 2388; **10:** 5638, 5807, ***5827–5829***
- trends **10:** 5828

Study facilities
- libraries **6:** 3396

Study habits
- and cognitive processes **10:** 5829
  - guiding of **10:** 5830
- definitions of **10:** 5829
- future research **10:** 5831
- and study skills **10:** ***5829–5831***

Study Process Questionnaire (SPQ) (Australia) **1:** 321

Study skills **6:** ***3325–3329***
- adult learning **1:** ***184–194***
- future research **10:** 5831
- manuals **1:** 185
- and metacognition **7:** 3789
- organizational habits **1:** 186
- and study habits **10:** ***5829–5831***
- summarization strategies **10:** 5830
- traditional training **1:** 185
- types of **10:** 5830

Study strategies
- *See* Study skills

Stuttering **3:** 1516

Sub-Saharan Africa
- civic education **2:** 768
- educational crisis **8:** 4510
- educational planning **8:** ***4510–4514***
  - centralization **8:** 4512
  - challenges **8:** 4512
  - decentralization **8:** 4513
  - fiscal issues **8:** 4513
  - and human resources development **8:** 4512
  - local participation **8:** 4513
  - objectives **8:** 4510, 4512
  - rational for investment **8:** 4510
  - structural adjustment **8:** 4514
- enrollment rate **8:** 4510
- ethnographies of indigenous populations **3:** 1752
- international aid **5:** 2962
- international cooperation **5:** 2963
- public education
  - management of contraction in **6:** 3604
- social process **8:** 4512

Subcultures
- concepts of **11:** 6798
- of poverty
  - urban schools **2:** 916
- youth **9:** 5217; **11:** ***6798–6803***
- *See also*
  - Student subcultures

Subject disciplines
- *See* Intellectual disciplines

Subject index terms
- selection of **5:** 2819

Subject specialism
- *See* Specialization, intellectual disciplines

Subjectivism
- educational administration **1:** 54
- and social sciences **1:** 54, 57

Subjectivity
- and case studies **2:** 644

Subsidies
- *See* Grants

Substance abuse
- and contingency tables **2:** 1080

Substitute teachers **10:** ***5832–5834***
- educational finance **10:** 5833
- educational trends
  - futures (of society) **10:** 5833
- incentives **10:** 5832
- instructional effectiveness **10:** 5833
- job satisfaction
  - problems **10:** 5833
- quality of working life **10:** 5832
  - problems **10:** 5833
- stress variables **10:** 5832
- teacher background **10:** 5832

Subtraction
- learning strategies **6:** 3657

Success
- attribution theory
  - sex differences **9:** 5434
- and intelligence quotient **7:** 3770
- in occupations
  - and education **4:** 2276
  - and family status **4:** 2276
- prediction of **8:** 4653
  - and vocational evaluation **11:** 6675
- and productivity **3:** 1691
- at school
  - and preschool evaluation **4:** 2142, 2143
- student characteristics **1:** 187

Successive categories
- *See* Likert scales

Sudan
- adult education **1:** 325; **10:** 5840
- curriculum development **10:** 5841
- educational finance **10:** 5840
- educational research **10:** 5842
- ethnic groups **10:** 5835
- government school relationship
  - school administration **10:** 5840
- literacy programs **1:** 325
- macroeconomics
  - salary wage differentials **11:** 6635
- postsecondary education **10:** 5837
- preschool education **10:** 5839
- private education **10:** 5837, 5838
- public sector earnings **8:** 4839
- rural education **7:** 4134
- secondary education
  - vocational education **10:** 5839
- special education **10:** 5839
- structure of government **10:** 5835
- system of education **10:** ***5834–5843***
  - degrees and qualifications **10:** 5842
  - educational objectives **10:** 5836
  - enrollment **10:** 5837
  - major problems **10:** 5842
  - structure **10:** 5836
- teacher education **10:** 5841, 5981
- teacher recruitment **10:** 5841
- teaching methodology **10:** 5842
- vocational education **10:** 5839

Sufficient statistics
- and rating scales **8:** 4921

Suggestopedia
- foreign language instruction **4:** 2342

Summated rating scales
- *See* Likert scales

Summative evaluation **3:** 1356; **4:** 2092, ***2097–2101***, 2109; **7:** 3906
- administration of **8:** 4781
- clients of **8:** 4781
- consumption benefits
  - and education **2:** 1054
- and curriculum design **4:** 1844
- and educational assessment **1:** 364
- and experimental design **4:** 2080
- and formative evaluation **4:** 2099
- instructional materials **8:** 4800
- purpose of
  - projects **8:** 4780
- science education
  - primary school programs **9:** 5334
- stage at which conducted **4:** 2098
- and student needs **10:** 5769
- in teacher education **4:** 2126
- use of term **8:** 4761

Summer Institute of Linguistics **7:** 4146, 4147

Superintendents
- and leadership research **6:** 3282

Supervision
- and program management **8:** 4755
- *See also*
  - Practicum supervision
  - Teacher supervision

Supplementary education
- for the elderly
  - China, People's Republic of **2:** 747

Supply and demand
- educated labor
  - functions **6:** 3179
- effect on occupational segregation **4:** 2428
- employment factors **3:** 1746
  - ability **3:** 1747
  - compensating earnings differentials **3:** 1747

education costs **3:** 1747
imperfect information **3:** 1747
licenses **3:** 1747
monopolies **3:** 1747
regional immobility **3:** 1747
risk **3:** 1747
human capital theory
and income distribution **5:** 2740
labor force planning **6:** 3608
labor needs
and vocational education **8:** 4526
market-clearing wage equation **6:** 3179
for primary education **9:** 5535
and private education **8:** 4833
sex bias
and earnings differentials **4:** 2441
teaching skills
allocation of **7:** 3820
and technological advancement **11:** 6275
See also
Teacher supply and demand
Supply elasticity
See Elasticity of supply
Supply of teachers
See Teacher supply and demand
Supported employment
role of **11:** 6459
Suppressor variables
and multivariate analysis **7:** 4013
Suriname
adult education **10:** 5850
curriculum development **10:** 5852
educational change **10:** 5853
educational finance **10:** 5851
educational research **10:** 5853
ethnic groups **10:** 5847
government school relationship
school administration **10:** 5851
language **10:** 5847
postsecondary education **10:** 5849
preschool education **10:** 5850
primary education **10:** 5848
private education **10:** 5851
secondary education **10:** 5848
vocational education **10:** 5849, 5850
special education **10:** 5850
structure of government **10:** 5847
system of education **10:** ***5846–5854***
degrees and qualifications **10:** 5852
educational objectives **10:** 5848
major problems **10:** 5853
structures **10:** 5848
teacher education **10:** 5851
teacher recruitment **10:** 5851
Surveys
analysis **10:** 5860
analytic **10:** 5854
cooperation in **10:** 5858
conceptual framework **10:** 5856
conduct of **10:** 5858
cross-sectional **7:** 3855
studies **2:** 1217
data collection **10:** 5856, 5857
quality of **10:** 5859
data preparation **10:** 5859
data verification **10:** 5859
descriptive **10:** 5854
design
program evaluation **4:** 2081, 2086
and sample selection **7:** 3853
and sampling **9:** 5137
documentation **10:** 5861
for educational facilities planning **4:** 2227
educational research **4:** 1868
enterprise **11:** 6416
ethical issues **4:** 2032; **10:** 5858
instruments **10:** 5856
development of **10:** 5856
types of **10:** 5856
item comparability **3:** 1380
labor force
training statistics **11:** 6416, 6417
literacy **6:** 3468
longitudinal **7:** 3855
methods
comparisons **7:** 3854
and microcomputers **7:** 3814
noncontacts
and nonresponse adjustment **7:** 3856
nonresponse and missing data **7:** ***3853–3858***
numeracy **6:** 3468
objectives **10:** 5855
oracy **6:** 3468
populations
and sampling **9:** 5131
types of **10:** 5857
purpose of **10:** 5854
research
missing scores in **7:** ***3858–3862***
sampling errors in **9:** ***5124–5131***
sampling in **9:** ***5131–5142***
strengths and weaknesses **8:** 4400
research cycle **10:** 5855
research methods **10:** ***5854–5862***
developments **10:** 5854
research questions **10:** 5856
research results **10:** 5861
response rate **4:** 2086
sample **10:** 5857
and secondary data analysis **9:** 5368
studies
problems **7:** 3853
types of **10:** 5854
See also
Statistical surveys
Survival analysis
discrete-time vs. continuous-time **4:** 2151, 2155
effects of predictor change over time **4:** 2155
hazard function **4:** 2151, 2153
interpretation **4:** 2154
proportional odds model **4:** 2155
and time-varying predictors **4:** 2154
survivor function **4:** 2152
See also
Event history analysis
Suspension **3:** 1536
and school desegregation **3:** 1536
and truancy **3:** 1536
Sustaining Effects Study (US) **6:** 3517
Swann Report 1985 (UK)
education for all **7:** 3845
Swaziland
curriculum development **10:** 5865
educational change **10:** 5865
educational research **10:** 5865
language **10:** 5862
postsecondary education **10:** 5863
preschool education **10:** 5863
primary education **10:** 5863
science curriculum **3:** 1254
secondary education **10:** 5863
special education **10:** 5864
structure of government **10:** 5862
student evaluation **10:** 5865
system of education **10:** ***5862–5866***
educational objectives **10:** 5863
historical background **10:** 5862
major problems **10:** 5866
structure **10:** 5863
teacher education **10:** 5864
teacher recruitment **10:** 5864
Sweden
adult basic education
financial support **1:** 101
legislation **1:** 101
adult education **7:** 4177; **8:** 4611; **10:** 5637
expenditure **10:** 5637
and labor market policy **10:** 5637
legislation **6:** 3363
participation **7:** 4322, 4323, 4328; **10:** 5637; **11:** 6392
provision **8:** 4805, 4806; **10:** 5637
research **1:** 123, 124, 126; **7:** 4179
studies **10:** 5593
vuxenuntervising **1:** 112
apprenticeships **11:** 6691
civic education **2:** 767
comprehensive schools
vocational education **11:** 6691
computer-managed learning **2:** 1000
continuing education expenditure **2:** 1147
curriculum development **10:** 5871
day care
costs **2:** 692
elasticity of demand **2:** 690
deinstitutionalization (of disabled) **3:** 1435
education of music teachers **7:** 4029
educational change **10:** 5872
and local government **5:** 2506
studies **6:** 3600
educational improvement
and decentralization **9:** 5245
educational policy
vocational education **11:** 6693
educational research **10:** 5872
educational researchers
training **11:** 6441
employment level

research **4:** 2277
employment policy and on-the-job training **6:** 3616
English language instruction **4:** 2352
folk high schools **4:** 2325; **10:** 5638
foreign language instruction
needs assessment **4:** 2340
GRUNDVUX program **8:** 4805; **10:** 5638
incentives for firm-based training **4:** 1975
job training
program evaluation **4:** 2148
KOMVUX program **8:** 4806; **10:** 5638
labor education **11:** 6771
labor force surveys **11:** 6416, 6417, 6419
labor relations
affiliations **6:** 3196
language **10:** 5866
life expectancy and lifelong learning **11:** 6392
lifelong learning **6:** 3417, 3419
and on-the-job training **7:** 4206
literacy policy **8:** 4638
longitudinal studies **6:** 3512
mathematics programs **6:** 3662
paid educational leave **7:** 4260
popular education **1:** 101
postsecondary education **10:** 5868
preschool education **2:** 695, 696, 698; **10:** 5868
primary education **10:** 5868
public education
and economic change **5:** 2506
reading campaigns **1:** 169
recurrent education **11:** 6390, 6392
religious education **9:** 5000
school administration
decentralization **8:** 4825
school-based management **1:** 592
schools
conflict in **2:** 1038
screening hypothesis tests **9:** 5354
second language instruction for immigrants **6:** 3210
secondary education **10:** 5868
vocational education **10:** 5868
sign language **3:** 1400
special education **5:** 2906; **10:** 5869
assistive technology **10:** 5670
teams **10:** 6242
structure of government **10:** 5866
student evaluation **10:** 5871
study circles **4:** 2388; **10:** 5638, 5807, ***5827–5829***
system of education **10:** ***5866–5873***
degrees and qualifications **10:** 5871
educational objectives **10:** 5867
major problems **10:** 5872
teacher education
universities **3:** 1724
teacher militancy **6:** 3192
teacher recruitment **10:** 5871
teacher salaries **10:** 5843
teacher training **10:** 5871
twin studies **11:** 6491
union participation in literacy programs **8:** 4637
university adult education **11:** 6549
admission criteria **11:** 6548, 6549
upper secondary schools **2:** 895
vocational education **4:** 2391; **11:** ***6690–6699***
historical background **11:** 6692
vocational schools **11:** 6691
workplace study organizers **11:** 6771
youth culture
research **11:** 6802
Swedish Commission on Internationalization of Higher Education **5:** 2974
language skills **5:** 2976
Swedish Education Commission
recurrent education **8:** 4957
Switzerland
adult education **10:** 5877
apprenticeships **1:** 313; **4:** 1919
curriculum development **10:** 5880
educational administration **1:** 68
educational change **10:** 5881
educational finance **10:** 5878
educational research **10:** 5880
English (second language)
and educational innovation **3:** 1552
government school relationship
school administration **10:** 5878
language **10:** 5873
popular education **1:** 133
postsecondary education **10:** 5876
preschool education **10:** 5876
primary education **10:** 5875
secondary education **10:** 5875
special education **10:** 5877
structure of government **10:** 5874
system of education **10:** ***5873–5883***
degrees and qualifications **10:** 5880
educational objectives **10:** 5874
historical background **10:** 5874
major problems **10:** 5882
structure **10:** 5874
teacher education **10:** 5879
teacher recruitment **10:** 5879
teaching methodology **10:** 5880
vocational education **10:** 5877
Syllabi **10:** ***5883–5887***
centralized **10:** 5884
content of **10:** 5884
definitions of **10:** 5883, 6089
and educational objectives **10:** 5885
evaluation **10:** 5886
formats of **10:** 5884
future trends **10:** 5886
importance of **9:** 5296
legal status of **10:** 5883
macro objectives **10:** 5885
micro objectives **10:** 5885
modes of transaction **10:** 5885
need for **10:** 5883
organization of **10:** 5883, 5885
and political influences **10:** 5884
types of **10:** 5883
utilization **10:** 5886
See also
Course descriptions
Symbolic interactionism
Habermas **2:** 1201
learning and **6:** 3308, 3309
Mead's views **9:** 5545
and role theory **2:** 1070
and the self-concept **9:** 5390, 5393
Symbolic learning
mammalian foundations **5:** 2681, 2682
and mass media **2:** 885
social cognition **9:** 5513
Symbolic logic
See Mathematical logic
Symbols (mathematics)
early history of **6:** 3644
mathematical formulas **6:** 3637
Syntax **1:** 481
and reading comprehension **8:** 4938
Syracuse University
Adult Education Network (AEDNET) **1:** 142
International Information Sharing Network (IISN) **1:** 142
Resources for Educators of Adults **1:** 141
Syria
adult education **6:** 3362
nonformal education **10:** 5891
curriculum development **10:** 5893
educational change **10:** 5894
educational finance **10:** 5892
educational research **10:** 5894
government school relationship
school administration **10:** 5891
language **10:** 5887
postsecondary education **10:** 5890
preschool education **10:** 5890
primary education **10:** 5889
secondary education **10:** 5889
vocational education **10:** 5890
structure of government **10:** 5887
system of education **10:** ***5887–5895***
degrees and qualifications **10:** 5893
educational objectives **10:** 5889
enrollment **10:** 5889
historical background **10:** 5888
major problems **10:** 5894
structure **10:** 5889
teacher education **10:** 5893
teacher recruitment **10:** 5892
teaching methodology **10:** 5893
System for Adult Basic Education Support (SABES) (US) **7:** 4147
System of education
Afghanistan **1:** ***204–210***
Albania **1:** ***254–260***
American Samoa **1:** ***266–274***
Antigua and Barbuda **1:** ***300–306***
Argentina **1:** ***332–338***
Australia **1:** ***415–423***
Austria **1:** ***423–432***
Bahamas **1:** ***439–444***
Bahrain **1:** ***444–450***

Bangladesh **1:** ***450–457***
Barbados **1:** ***458–465***
Belgium **1:** ***497–504***
Belize **1:** ***504–510***
Benin **1:** ***521–525***
Bhutan **1:** ***525–531***
Botswana **1:** ***543–552***
Brunei Darussalam **1:** ***570–577***
Bulgaria **1:** ***581–588***
Burkina Faso **1:** ***594–598***
Burundi **1:** ***598–607***
Cameroon **2:** ***609–618***
Canada **2:** ***618–626***
Central African Republic **2:** ***653–656***
Chad **2:** ***665–670***
Chile **2:** ***738–746***
China, People's Republic of **2:** ***750–755***
Colombia **2:** ***872–880***
Costa Rica **2:** ***1139–1146***
Côte d'Ivoire **2:** ***1152–1161***
Cuba **3:** ***1221–1227***
Cyprus **3:** ***1367–1375***
Denmark **3:** ***1453–1461***
Dominica **3:** ***1593–1599***
Egypt **4:** ***1939–1947***
El Salvador **4:** ***1947–1954***
Estonia **4:** ***2025–2029***
Ethiopia **4:** ***2037–2043***
Fiji **4:** ***2302–2310***
Finland **4:** ***2316–2324***
France **4:** ***2377–2385***
Gambia **4:** ***2401–2407***
Germany **5:** ***2470–2480***
Ghana **5:** ***2480–2486***
Greece **5:** ***2515–2523***
Guadeloupe and Martinique **5:** ***2536–2544***
Guatemala **5:** ***2544–2551***
Guinea, Republic of **5:** ***2552–2556***
Guinea-Bissau **5:** ***2556–2562***
Honduras **5:** ***2631–2636***
Hong Kong **5:** ***2636–2643***
Hungary **5:** ***2697–2706***
Iceland **5:** ***2715–2721***
India **5:** ***2744–2753***
Indonesia **5:** ***2784–2792***
Iran **5:** ***3007–3011***
Ireland, Republic of **5:** ***3011–3020***
Israel **5:** ***3023–3028***
Italy **5:** ***3028–3036***
Jamaica **6:** ***3067–3074***
Japan **6:** ***3078–3086***
Jordan **6:** ***3106–3113***
Kenya **6:** ***3125–3133***
Kiribati **6:** ***3144–3148***
Korea, Democratic People's Republic of **6:** ***3155–3160***
Korea, Republic of **6:** ***3161–3170***
Kuwait **6:** ***3170–3177***
Laos **6:** ***3241–3247***
Latvia **6:** ***3267–3272***
Lebanon **6:** ***3349–3356***
Lesotho **6:** ***3378–3385***
Liberia **6:** ***3389–3394***
Libya **6:** ***3402–3407***
Lithuania **6:** ***3484–3491***
Luxembourg **6:** ***3531–3538***
Macau **6:** ***3539–3545***
Madagascar **6:** ***3550–3556***
Malawi **6:** ***3560–3564***
Malaysia **6:** ***3564–3572***
Maldives **6:** ***3572–3578***
Mali **6:** ***3578–3586***
Malta **6:** ***3586–3593***
Mauritania **6:** ***3686–3691***
Mauritius **7:** ***3691–3698***
Mexico **7:** ***3792–3802***
Mongolia **7:** ***3895–3906***
Morocco **7:** ***3925–3930***
Mozambique **7:** ***3953–3960***
Myanmar **7:** ***4030–4038***
Namibia **7:** ***4039–4046***
Nepal **7:** ***4060–4067***
Netherlands **7:** ***4067–4077***
New Zealand **7:** ***4104–4111***
Nicaragua **7:** ***4111–4117***
Niger **7:** ***4117–4124***
Nigeria **7:** ***4124–4132***
Norway **7:** ***4185–4192***
Oman **7:** ***4201–4206***
Pakistan **7:** ***4263–4270***
Panama **7:** ***4270–4275***
Papua New Guinea **7:** ***4275–4282***
Paraguay **7:** ***4282–4290***
Peru **8:** ***4409–4415***
Philippines **8:** ***4433–4442***
Poland **8:** ***4542***
Portugal **8:** ***4623–4630***
Qatar **8:** ***4849–4855***
Romania **9:** ***5082–5087***
Russia **9:** ***5098–5107***
Rwanda **9:** ***5107–5114***
Saudi Arabia **9:** ***5142–5151***
Senegal **9:** ***5417–5423***
Seychelles **9:** ***5445–5449***
Sierra Leone **9:** ***5453–5460***
Singapore **9:** ***5476–5485***
Slovenia **9:** ***5490–5497***
South Africa **10:** ***5625–5635***
Spain **10:** ***5650–5658***
Sri Lanka **10:** ***5713–5721***
Sudan **10:** ***5834–5843***
Suriname **10:** ***5846–5854***
Swaziland **10:** ***5862–5866***
Sweden **10:** ***5866–5873***
Switzerland **10:** ***5873–5883***
Syria **10:** ***5887–5895***
Tanzania **10:** ***5903–5910***
Thailand **11:** ***6371–6378***
Togo **11:** ***6398–6403***
Tonga **11:** ***6403–6412***
Tunisia **11:** ***6466–6476***
Turkey **11:** ***6476–6481***
Tuvalu **11:** ***6484–6488***
Uganda **11:** ***6493–6501***
United Arab Emirates **11:** ***6511–6515***
United Kingdom **11:** ***6515–6523***
United States **11:** ***6538–6547***
Uruguay **11:** ***6563–6567***
Vanuatu **11:** ***6580–6586***
Venezuela **11:** ***6591–6600***
Vietnam **11:** ***6608–6614***
Yemen **11:** ***6787–6794***
Zaire **11:** ***6809–6814***
Zimbabwe **11:** ***6814–6821***
Systematic Analysis for School Improvement (SAS) (Netherlands) **5:** 2849
Systems analysis
of education
global approach **5:** 2497
instructional design **10:** 5895, 5897
and organizational theories **4:** 2160
structural components **10:** 5896
Systems approach
boundary definition **10:** 5896
definition of
and educational technology **4:** 1886
to design and development **10:** ***5895–5901***
in education
applications **10:** 5899
definitions **10:** 5895
flowchart **10:** 5897
higher education **4:** 1888
and instructional design **5:** 2858
instructional design **5:** 2860
to learning **1:** 320
origins of **10:** 5895
to prereferral intervention **8:** 4658
systematic problem-solving **10:** 5896
systematic thinking **10:** 5895
trends **10:** 5900
Systems of education
history of **5:** 2609
levels of **5:** 2862
loose coupling **6:** ***3524–3528***
social stratification in **10:** ***5730–5735***
Systems engineering
See Operations research

T groups
See Sensitivity training
t-test
compared with bootstrap procedure **9:** 5470
and effect size **4:** 2192
and experimental studies **4:** 2190
one-tailed **4:** 2191
and regression analysis **9:** 4966
and statistical significance **9:** 5465
two-tailed **4:** 2191
Tables (data)
mobility **7:** ***3862–3864***
Tachistoscopes
visual stimuli
and perception studies **8:** 4378
Tactile stimuli
responses by fetus to **1:** 12
Tactual behavior
See Touching behavior
Tailored testing
See Adaptive testing
Taiwan
adult education **1:** 349, 350
aesthetic education **1:** 342

career education and disabilities **2:** 634
educational choice
sex bias **4:** 2416
educational technology
support personnel **4:** 1916
parent participation
research **9:** 5215
schools
conflict in **2:** 1039, 1040
Talent
ethnographic evaluation studies **4:** 2045
special education **5:** ***2486–2491***
Talent development
art education **11:** 6617
and cultural differences **11:** 6617
Talent identification **5:** ***2725–2732***
child development **5:** 2729
functions of **5:** 2727
methodological problems **5:** 2728
and talent development **5:** 2727
Talking books
and assistive technology **10:** 5670
Tallensi
ethnography of **3:** 1752
Tanzania
adult education **1:** 212
legislation **6:** 3363
community education **7:** 4135
community support
educational finance **2:** 912
cooperative education **7:** 4138
cooperative education facilities **2:** 1147
curriculum development **10:** 5908
earnings differentials
and education **3:** 1659
educational change **10:** 5909
educational finance
and tax allocation **8:** 4362
educational reform
commitment to **4:** 1853
educational research **10:** 5908
educational resources
inequality in **8:** 4705
farms into educational units **4:** 2366
folk development colleges **2:** 904
industrial education **11:** 6254
literacy campaigns **1:** 171, 172, 173
literacy rate and adult education **5:** 2735, 2736
nonformal education for social change **1:** 132
on-the-job training **10:** 5915
participatory research **7:** 4331
postsecondary education **10:** 5904
preschool education **10:** 5904
primary education **10:** 5903
academic persistence **9:** 5536
primary school agriculture **8:** 4685, 4686
public schools vs. private schools **8:** 4843
schools into production units **4:** 2366
secondary education **10:** 5904
diversified **11:** 6254
vocational education **10:** 5905
student evaluation **10:** 5908
system of education **10:** ***5903–5910***
educational objectives **10:** 5903
major problems **10:** 5909
structure **10:** 5903
teacher education **10:** 5907
by distance learning **4:** 1907
teacher recruitment **10:** 5907
teaching methodology **10:** 5908
technical education **10:** 5905; **11:** 6252
Ujamaa integrated rural development scheme **8:** 4809
vocational education
education with production **3:** 1687
historical background **11:** 6252
training with production **11:** 6447
vocational training centers **11:** 6252
Taoism
beliefs about origin of man **5:** 2652
Tape recorders
characteristics of **11:** 6605
Tape recordings
for interviews
procedures **3:** 1468
and learning **6:** 3301
Task analysis
and cognitive processes **10:** 5741, 5743
computers in **10:** 5913
content analysis **10:** 5911
definition of **10:** 5910
functions of **10:** 5910
information sources **10:** 5912
instructional design **10:** ***5910–5914***
and instructional psychology **5:** 2873
and job analysis **6:** 3095
learning theories
constructivism **10:** 5913
procedural **10:** 5911
elaboration theory **10:** 5911, 5913
path analysis **10:** 5911
for programmed instruction **8:** 4769
research issues and directions **10:** 5912
techniques **10:** 5911
See also
Job analysis
Task Group on Assessment and Testing (TGAT) (UK) **3:** 1295
National Curriculum assessment **7:** 3908
Tasmania
school-based management **5:** 2849
Tax allocation
and educational finance **4:** 2314; **9:** 5236
vocational education **8:** ***4359–4364***
Tax credits
tuition
and school choice **9:** 5202
United States **9:** 5198
Tax deductions
and educational finance
effect on businesses **8:** 4362
rates **8:** 4362
and skill development **11:** 6651
vocational education **8:** ***4359–4364***
geographic distribution of systems
developing nations **8:** 4361
Tax effort
and educational finance **9:** 5239
Tax rates
and incidence of tax **9:** 5237
Taxes
and educational finance **4:** 2311
effects on efficiency and growth **4:** 2312
incentives
and adult education **1:** 156
and national training agencies **6:** 3265
reform of
and optimization of revenue **4:** 2313
types of **4:** 2312
and educational finance **9:** 5237
Taxonomy
See Classification
Taylor's series approximations
and sampling errors **9:** 5128
Teacher administrator relationship **8:** 4583
and effective schools research **4:** 1930
group dynamics **5:** 2526
micropolitical perspective **7:** 3825; **9:** 5179
and small group instruction **10:** 6186
and teacher evaluation **10:** 6041
types of **4:** 1929
Teacher aides
academic achievement **2:** 774
occupational information
comparative analysis **7:** 4292
Teacher alienation
and burnout **10:** 5919, 5920
and sociology of education **10:** 5604
Teacher assistance teams
See Prereferral intervention
Teacher associations
historical background **6:** 3191; **10:** 6073
and personnel evaluation **8:** 4745
political influences **8:** 4583
and power structure
sex differences **8:** 4584
and racial relations **8:** 4584
and teacher militancy **8:** 4584
world confederation **5:** 2973
Teacher attendance
employee absenteeism **10:** ***5832–5834***, 5923
Teacher attitudes **10:** ***6099–6103***
beginning teachers
evaluation **10:** 5956
behavior disorders **1:** 488
to classrooms **10:** 5773
computer-assisted instruction

and geometry **7:** 4097
and computer networks **2:** 981
computer uses in education
factors **11:** 6284
to computers
anxiety **11:** 6286
positive **11:** 6286
courseware **3:** 1777
and curriculum development **10:** 6209
and distance education **3:** 1564
drug use **3:** 1618
and educational change **6:** 3597; **10:** 6208
and educational innovation
age differences **10:** 6210
to educational radio **4:** 1907
to educational television **4:** 1905
effect of unions on **10:** 6070
external evaluation **5:** 2859
graduates **10:** 5956
and information technology **7:** 4085
intellectual disciplines
content of **10:** 5793
to learning
and student role **10:** 5794
to learning modules **7:** 3894
managerial behavior **10:** 6030
and mathematics education **6:** 3642
measurement
and partial order scalogram analysis **7:** 4315
media selection **7:** 3759
to micropolitics **7:** 3822
political influences **8:** 4583
professional autonomy **10:** 6135
and programmed instruction **8:** 4772
and school-based management **3:** 1409; **9:** 5306
and school as workplace **9:** 5178
and self-report **9:** 5410
sex bias **4:** 2409, 2448
sex discrimination **5:** 2454; **9:** 5170
sex fairness **5:** 2455
and student personality traits **11:** 6309
students
moral issues **10:** 6052
to teacher evaluation
traditional **10:** 6037
and teacher student relationship **10:** 5761
to teaching guides **10:** 6116
tutoring **11:** 6483
value judgement **10:** 6052
Teacher autonomy
See Professional autonomy
Teacher background
and science education **9:** 5333
social class **10:** 6226
teachers' beliefs **10:** 6178
Teacher behavior
and academic achievement
comparative analysis **10:** 6153, 6154
body language **7:** 4173
and class activities **10:** 6013
thinking tasks **10:** 6014
and classroom environment **10:** 5791
cultural differences
ethnography **2:** 801
decision-making **10:** 6050
differential
student attitudes to **10:** 6109
and discipline **3:** 1537
educational environment
and computers **11:** 6285
evaluation
and videotape recordings **11:** 6604
of expert teachers **10:** 6022
functional analysis **10:** 6128
and knowledge acquisition **10:** 6013
modification
and teacher expertise **10:** 6023
and organizational climate **3:** 1477
and participant observation **7:** 4317
physical education
research **10:** 5709, 5712
and power structure
United States **8:** 4583
process product research **4:** 1846
and questioning techniques **8:** 4876
reactive **10:** 6027
research methodology
classroom observation techniques **10:** 6128
questionnaires **10:** 6128
self-evaluation **10:** 6217
sex bias **4:** 2291
and sex differences **10:** 5823
in questioning techniques **8:** 4878
and single case research **9:** 5487
small classes
academic achievement **2:** 773
and small groups **10:** 6183
and student evaluation **10:** ***6012–6015***
trends **10:** 6015
and student evaluations of teacher effectiveness **10:** 6231
studies
and correspondence analysis **2:** 1119
teacher background **10:** 6178
and teacher expectation of students **10:** 6108
and teacher student relationship
research **10:** 5760
teachers' beliefs about **10:** 6178
and teaching experience **10:** 6021
Teacher burnout **10:** ***5919–5925***, ***6058–6062***
and collegiality **10:** 5923
and demographic and organizational factors **10:** 5922
and individual personality traits **10:** 5921
magnitude of problem **10:** 5921
and politics of education **10:** 6138
and principal's management style **10:** 5922, 5923
psychological patterns **10:** 6059
psychological view **10:** 5919
research **9:** 5178
research and development **10:** 6061
and social support (groups) **10:** 5923
sociological view **10:** 5604, 5920
stress variables **10:** 5920
and teacher persistence **10:** 5924
and type A behavior **10:** 5921
and work attitudes **10:** 5923
Teacher centers
Malaysia **7:** 3756
professional continuing education **10:** 5978
Teacher certification
adult educators **11:** 6432, 6436
alternative teacher certification **10:** 5961
control of **10:** 6037
developed nations **10:** 5925
developing nations **10:** 5925
future of **10:** 5929
and governance of teacher education **10:** 5964
job performance **10:** 6017
outstanding competence
United States **4:** 2128
policy context
United States **10:** 5926
processes **10:** 5926
testing **10:** 5927, 5928
transcript analysis/credit count **10:** 5927
validated programs **10:** 5927
specialization
intellectual disciplines **4:** 2126
and standards **10:** ***5925–5930***
by states
United States **4:** 2126
and teacher education
United States **3:** 1336
teacher education curriculum **10:** 5928
use of evaluation in **4:** 2126
use of terms **10:** 5926
Teacher characteristics **10:** 6208
and academic achievement **8:** 4869
and coping strategies **10:** 6211
and descriptive scales **3:** 1475
and discipline **3:** 1537
and educational innovation
implementation of **5:** 2843
and educational quality
policy models **8:** 4869
exemplary
computer users **11:** 6287
expectation **10:** 6130
generalized
research syntheses **10:** 6238
international studies
comparative analysis **10:** 6151
and questioning techniques **8:** 4878
Quintilian on **8:** 4889
social **10:** 5609
and social studies
research **9:** 5581
and teacher expectation of students **10:** 5760
and teacher expertise **10:** 6022, 6024

and teacher student relationship
10: 5759
Teacher competency tests
content knowledge **10:** 6016
improvement **10:** 6017
National Teacher Examinations (US)
content validity **10:** 6016
predictive validity **10:** 6016
professional knowledge **10:** 6016
teacher effectiveness **10:** 6017
technological advancement **10:** 6017
Teacher Corps Program (US)
and educational planning **3:** 1808
Teacher cultures
content of **10:** 6213
forms of **10:** 6213
balkanization **10:** 6213
collaborative **10:** 6213
contrived collegiality **10:** 6214
individualism **10:** 6213
Teacher developed materials
achievement tests **10:** 5770
and desktop publishing **4:** 1956
Teacher education
and academic achievement **10:** 6036
academic vs. professional schools
8: 4524
accreditation **1:** ***24–28***
administration of **10:** 6064
cooperative approach **10:** 6039
adult development **10:** ***5935–5939***
adult educators **11:** ***6431–6438***
and aesthetic education **1:** 195
portfolio method **1:** 198
Afghanistan **1:** 206
Albania **1:** 257, 258
alternative routes
costs **10:** 5950
and anthropology **7:** 3973
apprenticeship model **10:** 5983
balance between initial and inservice
10: 5952
behavior disorders **1:** 493
and black students **10:** 5845
Burundi **1:** 604
Cameroon **2:** 614
case methods **10:** ***5943–5948***
academic orientation **10:** 5945
context for research **10:** 5943
critical/social orientation **10:** 5947
definition of **10:** 5943
expert novice research **10:** 5946
heuristics **10:** 5945
personal orientation **10:** 5947
practical orientation **10:** 5945
research issues **10:** 5947
technological orientation **10:** 5946
Classified Practice Centers
Spain **10:** 5811
codes of ethics **10:** 5987
and cognitive development **10:** 6167
computer literacy **10:** 6005
qualifications **10:** 6006
computer uses in education
organization **10:** 6005
conceptions of
alternative **10:** 6038
expert–novice **10:** 6039
traditional **10:** 6038
and conceptions of teaching
policies **10:** ***6035–6044***
conceptual development research
10: 5937
and cost effectiveness studies **2:** 1135
costs **10:** 5844, 5949
institutional context **10:** 5950
participants and staff time **10:** 5949
scale and variation **10:** 5950
unit costs **10:** 5951
coursework
student teachers attitudes **10:** 5810
and critical theory **2:** 1199
critical thinking **10:** 6216
Cuba **3:** 1225
and cultural awareness **3:** 1232
cultural transformation model
10: 5959
and curriculum potential analysis
3: 1366
and curriculum theory **3:** 1327
definitions of **10:** 5977
developing nations
input output analysis **3:** 1760
and development education **3:** 1500
distance education
costs **10:** 5950
developing nations **3:** 1559
telecommunications **10:** 6007
by distance learning **4:** 1907
early childhood education **3:** 1630,
1633
program components **3:** 1630, 1634
economics of **10:** ***5948–5954***
and educational history **3:** ***1720–1724***;
5: 2608, 2609
and educational objectives **3:** 1802
and educational policy **8:** 4523
and educational quality
vocational education **8:** 4859
and educational reform **10:** 6042
and educational research **9:** 5053
educational statistics
and input output analysis **3:** 1758
effect on careers **10:** 5952
elementary schools
history of **6:** 3644
and epistemology **4:** 1996
ethics **10:** ***5985–5991***
evaluation models **10:** 5954
competency-based **10:** 5955
countenance **10:** 5954, 5955
documentation and assessment
10: 5955
objectives-based **10:** 5954
outcomes-based **10:** 5955
Stufflebeam's **10:** 5954
evaluation studies **10:** 5956
females
Islamic culture **11:** 6759
feminism **10:** 6097
financial support
sources and methods **10:** 5951
foundations of education courses
10: 5992
France **4:** 2383
governance **10:** ***5961–5965***
administrative organization
10: 5963
admission criteria **10:** 5963
curriculum **10:** 5964
functions **10:** 5963
issues in **10:** 5965
level of preparation **10:** 5963
policy formation **10:** 5962
processes **10:** 5964
and heuristics
problems **10:** 6177
history
United Kingdom **10:** 5996
influence of Pestalozzi on **8:** 4418
institutions **10:** 5991, 5995
internal efficiency **10:** 5951
international **5:** 2935
international studies
comparative analysis **10:** ***6149–6155***
knowledge **3:** 1632
content **3:** 1632
curriculum **3:** 1632
pedagogy **3:** 1632
laboratory schools **9:** ***5313–5318***
laboratory training **6:** ***3197–3202***
language arts **10:** ***5958–5961***
length of **10:** 5612
literature **10:** ***5958–5961***
and mainstreaming **5:** 2906; **6:** 3559
masters degrees **10:** 5998
mathematics
comparative analysis **10:** 6150
mathematics teachers **6:** ***3668–3671***
mentors **10:** 5947, 5983
and methods courses **10:** 6038
microteaching **10:** ***5973–5977***
and moral values **10:** ***5985–5991***
multicultural education
anthropological perspective **7:** 3972
and intercultural competence
7: 3973
music teachers **7:** ***4027–4030***
Netherlands **7:** 4074
noncategorical education **7:** 3832
on-the-job training **10:** ***5977–5982***
outcomes of education **10:** 5952
performance assessment **10:** 5955
performance-based evaluation **4:** 2125
philosophical issues **10:** ***5982–5985***
and philosophical and religious
positions **8:** 4452
philosophy of education
and educational policy **10:** 5984
physical education teachers
8: ***4464–4468***
PLUTO International Network Project
10: 6007
policy issues **10:** 6036
preschool teachers **3:** ***1629–1636***
preservice vs. inservice **8:** 4524
professional continuing education
4: 2330

professional development schools **9:** ***5313–5318***
United States **4:** 2125
programming in **10:** 6005, 6006
rationalist model **10:** 5983
reading teachers **8:** ***4945–4948***
and religious education **9:** 5004
Research About Teacher Education (US) **10:** 5809
role of cooperation in **10:** 5960
role of schools and universities **10:** 5960
scholasticism **9:** 5123
science teachers **9:** ***5342–5345***
self-evaluation **10:** 6216
sex fairness
Principal Effectiveness Pupil Achievement Program (PEPA) **9:** 5444
teacher student relationship **9:** 5444
simulated environment **6:** ***3197–3202***
social studies **10:** ***5583–5585***
and socialization **10:** 5612
and special education
accreditation criteria **10:** 5941
future trends **10:** 5942
specialized courses **10:** 5941
and special education needs **10:** ***5939–5943***
and sport pedagogy **10:** 5708
supervision **10:** ***6000–6004***
supply and demand **10:** 5949
teacher certification
and socioeconomic status **10:** 5953
Teacher Education Project (UK)
lesson structure and student ability **6:** 3386
teacher effectiveness
and teacher education **10:** 6064
and teacher expertise **9:** 5041
teacher qualification
historical background **3:** 1722
teacher role
and school-based curriculum planning **3:** 1271
and teacher supply and demand **10:** 5609
teaching skills
teacher attitudes **10:** 6216
technical education
problems with **10:** 6065
technology **10:** ***6004–6009***
theory practice relationship **10:** 5983, 5992, 5994
efficiency **10:** 5951
training vs. supervision **8:** 4523
university studies
vs. practical experience **10:** 6038
use of evaluation in **4:** 2125
use of term **10:** 5958
and validation of competence in schools **4:** 2125
visual arts **11:** ***6618–6621***
vocational and technical education **10:** ***6063–6068***
See also
Competency-based teacher education
Inservice teacher education
On service teacher education
Preservice teacher education
Reflective teaching
Student teaching
Teacher education curriculum **10:** ***5991–5995***, 5998
audiovisual aids **10:** 6005
Carnegie Forum on Education **10:** 5994
comparative education in **2:** 947
computer uses in education **10:** 6004, 6005
consecutive mode **10:** 5991
content knowledge **10:** 5998
and educational innovation **10:** 5994
general education **10:** 5998
hidden curriculum **10:** 5994
Holmes Group **10:** 5994
information technology **10:** 6006
integrated **10:** 6217
intellectual disciplines **10:** 5992
issues and directions **10:** 5994
kibbutzim **10:** 5992
methods courses **10:** 5992
null **10:** 5994
pedagogical content knowledge **10:** 5999
pedagogy **10:** 5999
practicums **10:** 5993
traditional **10:** 6038
word processing **10:** 6005
Teacher education programs **3:** ***1720–1724***
computer oriented **10:** 6007
content **10:** 5808
developing nations **10:** 5997
evaluation **10:** ***5954–5958***
and accountability **10:** 5954
criterion variables **10:** 5955
independent variables **10:** 5956
methods **10:** 5956
problems with **10:** 5955
field experience
cognitive development **10:** 6217
student teachers' attitudes **10:** 5810
four year **10:** 5997
general
and special education **10:** 5940
graduate study **10:** 5998
parent school relationship
interpersonal communication **9:** 5266
problems with **10:** 6065
provision **10:** 5964
special needs students **9:** 5266
structure of **10:** ***5995–6000***
time and organization **10:** 5997
United Kingdom **3:** 1722
and vocational education **10:** 6064
and work experience programs **10:** 6065
Teacher educators
characteristics of **10:** ***6009–6012***
computer literacy **10:** 6006
demography **10:** 6009
females **10:** 6009
minority groups **10:** 6010
productivity of
and log-linear models **6:** 3501
reflective teaching
educational objectives **10:** 6217
research and scholarship of **10:** 6010
and social class **10:** 6009
student teacher supervisors **10:** 6011
and teacher accreditation **1:** 27
work environment **10:** 6011
Teacher effectiveness **10:** 5960
and academic achievement **8:** 4872
classroom observation techniques **8:** 4521
and cognitive development approach **10:** 6166
components of **10:** 6229
and computer uses in education **11:** 6285
conceptions of **10:** 6035
data collection
and outcomes of education **9:** 5263
definitions of **8:** 4520
development of
by feedback **7:** 3820
direct instruction **3:** 1525
and educational quality **8:** 4870
and educational reform **10:** 6208
and educational technology **4:** 1916
evaluation **10:** 6017
academic achievement **10:** 6018
evaluation criteria **10:** 6019
student characteristics **10:** 6019
and eye contact **7:** 4173
factors affecting
and teacher education **10:** 6064
and hypothesis testing **5:** 2710, 2711
and learning **6:** 3308
measurement techniques **10:** 6019
pretests–posttests **10:** 6019
and merit pay **8:** 4523
paradigm of **10:** 6203
and personality traits **10:** 6036
and physical education **10:** 5710
planning
developing nations **8:** ***4519–4526***
performance factors **10:** 6033
pretests–posttests
test validity **10:** 6019
process–product model **3:** 1525; **10:** 6036
productivity
and student development **7:** 3817
recognition of outstanding **4:** 2127
research
teacher attitudes to **10:** 6037
and school size **9:** 5293
standardized tests
and input output analysis **3:** 1759
student evaluation of **10:** 6228
studies **10:** 6013

and subject matter knowledge
10: 5584
and teacher attitudes
preservice teachers **10:** 6105
and teacher knowledge **10:** 6118
research **10:** 6119
and teacher salaries **10:** 6081
scales **8:** 4522
and teacher supply and demand
10: 5844
use of explanation **10:** 6147
and videodiscs **10:** 5670
Teacher employment
uses of evaluation in **4:** 2126
Teacher employment benefits
differential levels **8:** 4522
educational policy **8:** 4521
overall level **8:** 4522
Teacher evaluation **4:** ***2123–2132***;
10: ***6015–6020***
and aptitude treatment interaction
10: 6155
competency-based teacher education
10: 6016
conceptions of
alternative **10:** 6040
curriculum **10:** 6041
policies **10:** ***6035–6044***
supervised reflective practice
10: 6041
criteria **10:** 6016
and educational change **6:** 3598
and employment **4:** 2126
faculty development
criteria **1:** 25
improvement **10:** 6017
job performance **10:** 6016
judgment accuracy approach **10:** 5770
research **10:** 5770
low-inference observation schedules
10: 6018
methods
career ladder-merit pay programs
4: 2126, 2129
classroom observations **4:** 2128
clinical supervision **4:** 2126, 2129
field experience evaluation **4:** 2128
peer evaluation **4:** 2126, 2129
rating scales **4:** 2128
student ratings **4:** 2129
student test scores **4:** 2129
teacher competency tests **4:** 2128
teacher performance portfolios
4: 2126, 2130
performance-based **4:** 2125
problems **10:** 6017
qualitative approaches **10:** 6041
rating scales **10:** 6018
Rating Teacher Explanation
Instrument **10:** 6148
research
and videotape recordings **11:** 6605
school-based models **4:** 2126
duties-based **4:** 2126
on-the-job performance **4:** 2126
total systems **4:** 2126
and school districts
influences **9:** 5222
standards **8:** 4737, 4745, 4746
student improvement
test validity **10:** 6019
systems for
research **8:** 4406
and teacher administrator relationship
10: 6041
teacher improvement **10:** 5933
traditional
teacher attitudes to **10:** 6037
United States **3:** 1336
See also
Student evaluation of teacher
performance
Teacher effectiveness
Teacher exchange programs
and comparative education societies
2: 947
and development education **3:** 1500
international **5:** 2973, 2976
Teacher expectations of students
10: ***6106–6112***
academic achievement **10:** 6220
and classroom interaction **10:** 5605
definitions of **10:** 6107
differential
and teacher behavior **10:** 6108
and discipline **3:** 1537
effects
types of **10:** 6107
explanatory style
sex differences **9:** 5404, 5405
future research **10:** 6112
importance of **10:** 6108
increasing
effects of **10:** 6110
induced **10:** 6107
influences **2:** 793
intervention programs **10:** 6110
findings **10:** 6111
and low achievement
Good's passivity model **10:** 6109
natural **10:** 6107
personality traits **11:** 6309
physical education **10:** 5709
preconceptions and misconceptions
about **8:** 4650
racial bias **10:** 5823
and reproduction theory **9:** 5019
research **10:** 5759, 5760, 6106
directions **10:** 6111
types of **10:** 6107
secondary school students
sex bias **10:** 5825
and self-fulfilling prophecies **10:** 6107
Brophy–Good model **10:** 6107
sex bias **10:** 5823
and student needs **10:** 5770
and test anxiety **11:** 6356
variations over time **10:** 6110
Teacher experience
See Teaching experience
Teacher expertise **10:** ***6020–6026***
and automaticity **10:** 6023
cognitive skills **10:** 6039
and computers **11:** 6285
context factors **10:** 6023
and curriculum **10:** 6089
and curriculum development **10:** 6091
descriptive propositions **10:** 6022
and educational environment
10: 6023
and educational research **9:** 5041
and flexibility **10:** 6024
management skills **10:** 6039
and pattern recognition **10:** 6024,
6025
and problem-solving **10:** 6024, 6025
stages
advanced beginner **10:** 6021
competent **10:** 6021
expert **10:** 6022
novice **10:** 6021
proficient **10:** 6022
studies **10:** 6022, 6025
and teacher expectation of students
10: 6111
and teaching guides **10:** 6116
vs. teaching experience **10:** 6020
See also
Teacher knowledge
Teacher guidance
Socratic Method **3:** 1541
testing **6:** 3626
Teacher guides
See Teaching guides
Teacher improvement **10:** ***5930–5935***
clinical supervision (of teachers)
10: 5933
collegiality **10:** 5933
cooperative planning **10:** 5933
self-actualization **10:** 5933
teacher evaluation **10:** 5933
Teacher indirectness
and academic achievement
research synthesis **10:** 6237
Teacher induction
See Teacher orientation
Teacher influence
curriculum adaptation **3:** 1254, 1255
on curriculum policies **3:** 1337
educational change **10:** ***6096–6099***
and resilience **8:** 4777
social change **10:** ***6096–6099***
students
socialization **10:** 6101
Teacher knowledge **10:** ***6117–6122***
of content **10:** 6118
domains **10:** 6117
integration of **10:** 6119
dynamic nature of **10:** 6119
future research **10:** 6121
and instruction **10:** 6118
and intellectual disciplines **9:** 5296
level
teacher student relationship
10: 6016
research **10:** 6117

  and self-concept **10:** 6119
  types of **10:** 6117
    and classroom techniques **10:** 6120
    narrative **10:** 6120
    paradigmatic **10:** 6120
  See also
    Teacher expertise
Teacher militancy
  and curriculum development **8:** 4582
  teacher attitudes to **6:** 3191
  United Kingdom **8:** 4583
Teacher morale
  and burnout **10:** 5922, 6059
  See also
    Teacher burnout
    Teachers, occupational stress
Teacher motivation
  and burnout **10:** 6059
  expectancy theory **4:** 1968
  goal theory **4:** 1968
  and incentives **4:** 1967
  influences
    professional development **10:** 5931
  needs hierarchy theory **4:** 1967
  two-factor theory **4:** 1968
  See also
    Teacher burnout
    Teachers, occupational stress
Teacher organizations
  See Teacher associations
Teacher orientation
  beginning teacher induction
      10: ***6044–6048***
  mentors **10:** 6046
  and national policies **10:** 6047
  preservice and inservice teacher
      education **10:** 5999
  program content **10:** 6045
  relevance (educational) **10:** 6046
  trends
    issues and research **10:** 6046
Teacher parent cooperation
  See Parent teacher cooperation
Teacher participation
  and action research **1:** 43, 45
  curriculum development **10:** 6080
    centralized **10:** 6090
    factors **10:** 6091
    science education **9:** 5331
  decision-making
    and school as workplace **9:** 5179
  and educational policy **10:** 6080
  in educational reform **4:** 1855
  job security
    and motivation **5:** 2797
  and prototyping **8:** 4802
  in revolution **8:** 4585
  and school-based management
      9: 5306
  and school culture **9:** 5260
  and school organization **4:** 2163
  and student evaluation **10:** 6080
  unions
    penalties **10:** 6073
Teacher performance
  See Teacher effectiveness
Teacher persistence **10:** 5924
  barriers to
    research **9:** 5178
  in effective schools **4:** 1931
  factors affecting **10:** 6210
  and teacher burnout **10:** 5924
Teacher preparation
  See Teacher education
Teacher promotion
  sex discrimination **11:** 6709
    developing nations **4:** 2421
    United Kingdom **4:** 2421
Teacher qualifications **10:** ***5925–5930***
  adult educators **11:** 6436
  early childhood education **3:** 1629,
      1634
  and educational reform **10:** 6082
  and professional recognition **6:** 3275
  professionalization of **5:** 2498
  resource room programs **9:** 5067
  and social class **10:** 6226
  and teacher supply and demand
      10: 5612
  and technical education **10:** 6065
Teacher quality
  See Teacher effectiveness
Teacher recruitment **10:** ***6044–6048***
  approaches to **10:** 6045
  and career structure **10:** 6044
  factors affecting **10:** 5612
  policy context **10:** 6044
  and population trends **3:** 1452
  problems in **10:** 6104
  and social class **10:** 6226
  and teacher effectiveness **10:** 6044
  and teacher employment benefits
      8: 4522
  and teacher shortage **10:** 6044
  trends
    issues and research **10:** 6046
Teacher remuneration
  See Teacher employment benefits
Teacher response
  and artificial intelligence **1:** 345
  individual differences **5:** 2766
  and instructional materials **3:** 1492
  positive reinforcement **10:** 6014
  preschool children
    sex differences **4:** 2451
  and questioning techniques **8:** 4880
  sex bias in **9:** 5442
  and teacher behavior **10:** 6013
  test coaching **7:** 3724
Teacher responsibility **10:** ***6048–6053***
  changes in **10:** 6081
  conflict resolution
    moral issues **10:** 6050
  and educational reform **10:** 6209
  Erasmus on **4:** 2006
  moral values **10:** 6048, 6052
  research
    theory practice relationship
      10: 6048
  teacher effectiveness **10:** 6052
  and teaching experience **10:** 6021
Teacher rights
  denial of **6:** 3191
  and labor relations **6:** 3190
Teacher role **10:** ***6048–6053***, ***6127–6132***
  and acting **10:** 6084
  in andragogy **1:** 276
  behavior **10:** 6128
  and centralization **9:** 5177
  changes in **10:** 6081
    and administrators **10:** 6082
    and computer uses in education
      11: 6286
    and learning modules **7:** 3893
    origins of **10:** 6079
  in classrooms **10:** 5791
  cognitive development **10:** 6194
  computers
    and educational environment
      11: 6284
  constructivist learning theory **6:** 3669
  and curriculum development **10:** 6089
  decision-making
    classroom environment **2:** 792
  development of **10:** 5934
  drug therapy
    in schools **8:** 4420
  and educational innovation
    implementation **3:** 1492
  educational technology **11:** ***6283–6287***
    adoption of **11:** 6283
  evaluation **10:** 6093
  expectation **10:** 6130
    research methodology **10:** 6130
    role conflict **10:** 6130, 6131
    teacher behavior **10:** 6131
  fundamental concepts of **10:** 6127
    behavior **10:** 6127
    expectation **10:** 6127
    social status **10:** 6127
  group instruction **9:** 5170
  and heuristics **10:** 6177
  and intensification **10:** 6212
  intervention procedures
    and interpersonal competence
      9: 5566
  language arts and literature **10:** 5959
  language styles **2:** 799
  and LOGO **7:** 4098
  and media program administration
      7: 3754
  in physical sciences
    secondary school programs **8:** 4475,
      4477
  planning **10:** ***6031–6035***
    research methodology **10:** 6031
  and professionalization **10:** 6212
  regulation of **10:** 6079
  reproduction theory **9:** 5018
  research **9:** 5177
  research problems **10:** 6128
  role models
    listening skills **6:** 3441
    speech skills **6:** 3441
  school community relationship
      9: 5214
  and school organization **9:** 5177

and science education **9:** 5333
in secondary schools
and effective schools research **9:** 5376
and small groups **10:** 6183
social structure
evaluation methods **10:** 6128
sociological perspectives **10:** 5607
and student evaluation **10:** 5770
Teacher salaries **10:** 5843, 6129
beginning teachers
and costs of teacher education **10:** 5949
comparative analysis
effect on Latin America **3:** 1832
continuing education **2:** 1150
developing nations **8:** 4520
input output analysis **3:** 1760
early childhood education **3:** 1634
and educational planning **8:** 4520
and educational reform **10:** 6081
effect of unions on **10:** 6069
and event history analysis **4:** 2154
females
North America **11:** 6763
and legitimatory research **6:** 3371
nonformal education **2:** 1148; **7:** 4138
and occupational prestige **10:** 5610
and personnel management **8:** 4406
projections **8:** 4786
scales
and teacher effectiveness **8:** 4522
and school size **9:** 5291
sex discrimination
developing nations **4:** 2421
and teacher effectiveness **10:** 6081
and unions **10:** 6074
variations
United States **9:** 5062
vs. other occupations **10:** 5843
Teacher selection
and anticipatory socialization **10:** 6124, 6125
and educational quality
vocational education **8:** 4859
and personnel policy **8:** 4404
Teacher shortage
and teacher recruitment **10:** 6044
vocational education
developing nations **10:** 6063
Teacher stereotypes **10:** 6104, 6130
Teacher strikes
legal rights **6:** 3193
types of **10:** 6076
Teacher student ratio
comparative analysis
effect on Latin America **3:** 1833
in day care **2:** 691
effect of unions on **10:** 6069
and preschool teachers **8:** 4663
and school size **9:** 5291
Teacher student relationship
and assignments **9:** 5361
and attendance **3:** 1605
classroom design
seating arrangement **9:** 5357
and cleft palates **11:** 6706
cooperation
and curriculum design **10:** 5814
commitment **10:** 6209
communication
for small group instruction **10:** 6185
and correspondence analysis **2:** 1119
disadvantaged children
sociolinguistic approach **6:** 3215
and disengagement theory **9:** 5225
expectation studies **10:** 5760, 5761
feedback
in classrooms **10:** 6012
and game theory **7:** 3818
incentives
and productivity **7:** 3819
and learning disabilities **10:** 5683
and learning factors **10:** 5748
and learning strategies **6:** 3337
and lesson structure **6:** 3388
mismatch problems **10:** 6168
mutual cynicism **9:** 5310
negotiation
and academic records **8:** 4620
parent role
cooperation in **7:** 3819
physical education **10:** 5709, 5712
process–product studies **10:** 5760, 5761
qualitative studies **10:** 5761
racial bias **10:** 5824
and school dynamics **9:** 5170
secondary schools
and effective schools research **9:** 5377
and semiotics **9:** 5414
sex bias **9:** 5442; **10:** 5824
in secondary schools **10:** 5825
sex differences **10:** 5824
elementary schools **10:** 5825
and social status **10:** 6227
and status
problems **10:** 6213
student characteristics **4:** 2376
systems approach **2:** 819
and teaching methods **10:** 5759
tutoring **11:** 6483
Teacher supervision **10:** ***6000–6004***
alternative approaches **10:** 6003
applied behavioral approach **10:** 6002
costs **10:** 5950
counseling **10:** 6002
directive and nondirective **10:** 6002
models **10:** 6002
problems of **10:** 6001
purposes **10:** 6000
theoretical paradigms **10:** 6002
trends and issues **10:** 6003
vs. training **8:** 4523
Teacher supply and demand **10:** ***5843–5846***
attrition rate **10:** 5845
demographic effects on **10:** 5846
determinants of **10:** 5843
developed nations **10:** 5949
factors affecting **10:** 5609
females **10:** 5844
as a function of geographic regions **10:** 5845
and inservice teacher education **10:** 5966
minority groups **10:** 5844
number of preservice teachers **10:** 6103
projections **8:** 4785
and teacher certification **10:** 5925
and teacher effectiveness **10:** 5844
and teacher qualifications **10:** 5612
Teacher trainers
See Teacher educators
Teacher training
See Teacher education
Teacher turnover
See Faculty mobility
Teacher unions
See Unions
Teacher workshops
early childhood education **3:** 1632
Teachers
academic achievement of **10:** 6226
and action research
reports **1:** 43
affective behavior
research **10:** 6030
as *animateurs* **8:** 4585
as artists **10:** ***6083–6086***
and creativity **10:** 6084
research **10:** 6084
types of **10:** 6084
use of metaphor **10:** 6083
aspirations
limiting factors **7:** 3818
beliefs of **10:** ***6099–6103***
academic ability **10:** 6101
academic achievement **10:** 6100
educational change **10:** 6102
educational research **10:** 6102, 6182
research **10:** 6100
student motivation **10:** 6100
and teacher attitudes **10:** 6210
values education **10:** 6101
See also
Teacher attitudes
career development **10:** 5930, 5931, 5935
factors affecting **10:** 6210
career prospects
and school inspectors **9:** 5247
and child centered theory **8:** 4457
code of ethics for **11:** 6579
cognitive ability
planning **10:** 6033
cognitive development **10:** 5930
developmental stages **10:** 5936
cognitive processes **10:** 6087
curriculum agenda **10:** 6087
curriculum script **10:** 6087
decision-making **10:** ***6086–6088***
interactive teaching **10:** 6087
reflection-in-action **10:** 6087
teacher education **10:** 6088
cognitive structures

evaluation **10:** 6094
research utilization **10:** 6088
commitment **10:** 6209
community involvement
political influences **8:** 4585
and computer-assisted instruction **2:** 990
as cultivators
use of metaphor **10:** 6084
and curriculum
implementation **10:** 6089
and curriculum development **10:** 6090
as curriculum makers **10:** ***6089–6092***
concepts of **10:** 6091
decentralization
decision-making **5:** 2797
decision-making
educational history **10:** 6086
ethics **10:** 6049
policy-capturing studies **10:** 6086
research methodology **10:** 6086, 6087
stimulated recall studies **10:** 6086
developmental stages **10:** 5930
and documentation systems **3:** 1591
and educational assessment
reports **1:** 365
results **6:** 3470
and educational innovation
implementation of **5:** 2842
and educational policy **8:** 4519
and educational research **9:** 5054
as educational researchers **11:** 6441
educational theories **10:** ***6178–6183***
empowerment of **10:** 6080
as ethnographers **6:** 3455
and event history analysis **4:** 2151, 2153
individual development
teacher education **10:** 5947
international studies
sex differences **10:** 6150
isolation of
and educational improvement **9:** 5222
and labor relations **6:** 3190
life events of
influences **10:** 6210
literacy **1:** 174
lives
research **10:** 6211
managerial behavior of **10:** ***6026–6031***
academic tasks **10:** 6028
influences **10:** 6027
preventive strategies **10:** 6028
procedures **10:** 6028
reactive strategies **10:** 6028
research **10:** 6030
routines **10:** 6028
moral development **10:** 5936
influence of school environment **10:** 5936
needs of
and educational facilities planning **4:** 2221
occupational stress **10:** ***6058–6062***
personal autonomy
in learning **6:** 3348
and role in state **10:** 6122
school organization **10:** 6094
and personnel policy **8:** 4404
and policy
management implications **10:** ***6079–6083***
political attitudes **8:** ***4581–4587***; **10:** 6137
political influences **8:** ***4581–4587***
and politics of education **8:** ***4581–4587***
prestige **10:** 6129
productivity of
and incentives **4:** 1971
professional autonomy **10:** 6129
bureaucratic constraints **10:** ***6092–6096***
existentialist view **8:** 4432
and lesson structure **6:** 3385
organizational climate **10:** 6094
state government **10:** 6095
professional continuing education **10:** ***5977–5982***
professional development **10:** ***5930–5935***, 5935, 6094
educational facilities improvement **10:** 5934
environment **10:** 5931
futures (of society) **10:** 5934
individual characteristics **10:** 5930
instructional leadership **10:** 5932
and market forces **10:** 6126
participant observation **10:** 6124
peer influence **10:** 5932
school attitudes **10:** 5932
school policy **10:** 5932
social influences **10:** 5931
socialization **10:** ***6122–6127***
teaching methods **10:** 5932
professional knowledge **10:** 6016
evaluation **10:** 6017
as professional personnel
and political power **8:** 4582, 4584
professional recognition **6:** 3275
and organizational theories **1:** 434
and power structure **8:** 4584
relationship between
and educational innovation **5:** 2843
of religious education **9:** 5003
as researchers
reflective teaching **10:** 5960
teacher education **10:** 5946
reserve pool of
source of supply **10:** 5845
retraining **10:** ***5977–5982***
schemata
educational research **10:** 6182
sex discrimination
action research **4:** 2422
sex stereotypes
and Christianity **4:** 2421
Islamic culture **4:** 2421
social characteristics of **10:** 5609
social mobility of **10:** 5610
social status **8:** 4522; **10:** 6128, 6129
socialization
and attitude changes **10:** 6123
and values **10:** 6123
staff development **10:** 5930
status of
and teacher education **8:** 4523
theory practice relationship
and curriculum adaptation **3:** 1256
unionization of **10:** ***6068–6073***
unqualified
and inservice teacher education **10:** 5966
work environment **10:** 5843
as workers
and teaching **10:** 6135
Teachers' colleges
See Schools of education
Teaching
adult education research **1:** 124
of adults
andragogical approach **1:** 276
as an activity
factors **10:** 6226
aptitude treatment interaction model of **10:** ***6155–6159***
art or science **10:** 6083
attitudes to
and social status **10:** 6227
behavioral theories of **10:** ***6159–6164***
characteristics **10:** 6159
field of study **10:** 6159
future research **10:** 6163
principles **10:** 6159
trends **10:** 6163
career choice
factors affecting **10:** 5844
characteristics of
historical background **10:** 5608
classroom
and student characteristics **10:** ***5745–5750***
cognitive apprenticeship model **3:** 1251
cognitive development approach
framework **10:** 6164
and students **10:** 6166
and teachers **10:** 6166
theories **10:** ***6164–6169***
conceptions of
alternative **10:** 6038
inquiry process **10:** 6040
organizational **10:** 6039
personal narratives **10:** 6040
and policies **10:** ***6035–6044***
reflective practice **10:** 6040
subject matter knowledge **10:** 6039
traditional **10:** 6035
contexts
contemporary **10:** 6212
continuing **10:** 6211
of diversity **10:** 6212
coping strategies **10:** 6211
educational research
ethnography **10:** 6133

ethics of **4:** 2031, 2032
ethnographic studies **10:** 6054
females
caring role **10:** 6125
feminization of **10:** 5609
heuristic models of **10:** ***6173–6178***
characteristics **10:** 6177
direct strategy **10:** 6175
generative **10:** 6175
historical development **10:** 6173
interactive **10:** 6175, 6176
logical argument **10:** 6176
modern **10:** 6174
reciprocal **10:** 6174
self-instructional strategy **10:** 6175
transactional strategy **10:** 6175
humanistic theories of **10:** ***6164–6169***
indeterminacy of **10:** 6085
interactive
and cognitive development approach **10:** 6164
international studies
comparative analysis **10:** ***6149–6155***
job analysis **10:** 6085
and labor market **10:** 6135
sex differences **10:** 6135
metaphors **10:** 6179
as moral enterprise **10:** 6208
occupational prestige of
and sex differences **10:** 6226
studies **10:** 6224
paradigms for research on **10:** ***6202–6208***
as performing art **10:** 6083
and power structure **10:** 6135
as profession **10:** 5611
professional recognition **9:** 5178; **10:** ***6092–6096***
professional values
client centeredness **10:** 6095
professionalization of
and females **11:** ***6719–6723***
realities of **10:** ***6208–6215***
reflective approach **10:** 5984, 5985
relational approach **10:** 6134
research
lessons for **10:** 6085
research synthesis **10:** ***6235–6240***
importance of **10:** 6235
and responsibility
policy formation **10:** 5988
in small groups **10:** ***6183–6187***
social characteristics of **10:** 6225
social functions of **10:** 6225
and social mobility **10:** 6124, 6125
social status **10:** ***6224–6227***
evaluation **10:** 6093
sociology of **10:** ***5607–5614***
teacher role **10:** 5607
sociology of work **10:** ***6132–6139***
status as profession
and educational policy **8:** 4523
student evaluation of **10:** ***6227–6235***
student influences on **10:** ***5759–5762***
assumptions **10:** 5759
research **10:** 5759
and teachers as workers **10:** 6135
technology of
and behavioral theories **10:** 6161
theories of
social psychological **10:** ***6219–6224***
traditional approaches **10:** 6165
trend to graduates **10:** 5949
as women's work **11:** 6720
Teaching (process)
See Instruction
Teaching experience
and audiotape recordings **11:** 6607
and curriculum development **10:** 6091
developing nations
input output analysis **3:** 1760
educational statistics
input output analysis **3:** 1758
and expertise **10:** 6021, 6023
field experience
early childhood education **3:** 1632
international studies
comparative analysis **10:** 6150, 6154
and outcomes of education **9:** 5262
and politics of education **10:** 6137
and school effectiveness movement **10:** 6132
and socialization **10:** 5612
and teacher knowledge **10:** 6120
vs. teacher expertise **10:** 6020
Teaching guides **10:** 6089, ***6113–6117***
content of **10:** 6113
for universities **10:** 6114
development of **10:** 6115
effectiveness **10:** 6116
examples **10:** 6113, 6114
historical background **10:** 6113, 6114
management system **10:** 6114
modular curricula **7:** 3889
need for **10:** 6113
and specialization **10:** 6116
and student characteristics **10:** 6116
subject differences **10:** 6115
teacher attitudes to **10:** 6116
and textbooks **8:** 4696
types of **10:** 6114
utilization **10:** 6116
studies **11:** 6369
Teaching load
and computer uses in education **11:** 6286
research **10:** 6212
Teaching machines **4:** 1844
and audiovisual instruction **4:** 1884
autotutors **8:** 4768
characteristics of **8:** 4767
and educational history **3:** 1795
and learning theories **9:** 5040
paradigm of **10:** 6204
and programmed instruction **8:** 4766; **10:** 6162
Teaching materials
See Instructional materials
Teaching methods
ability
and learning **5:** 2761
academic achievement
academic learning time **1:** 20
adult education **10:** ***6198–6202***
direction **10:** 6199
and discovery learning **10:** 6199
evaluation **10:** 6201
expository **10:** 6199
and learning theories **10:** 6198
adult literacy **3:** 1258
basic **6:** 3454
censorship **6:** 3359
characteristics of
for individualization **5:** 2771
and cognitive development **5:** 2666
cognitive processes **3:** 1526; **10:** 5742
collaborative dialog **8:** 4877
computer uses in education
sex fairness **4:** 2426
conversations **8:** 4877
debate **6:** 3454
Dewey's **3:** 1522
discussion **2:** ***803–807***
and educational quality **8:** 4861, 4868
and educational television **5:** 2895
explanation **10:** ***6143–6149***
and group testing **9:** 5486
higher education
and needs of labor market **8:** 4338
historical background **3:** 1721
improvement of
implications **10:** 5749
individual instruction **5:** ***2770–2773***
influence of adult education on **6:** 3419
and instructional design models **5:** 2859
and instructional design theory **5:** 2863
instructional sequencing **3:** 1540
international studies
comparative analysis **10:** 6151
as labor process
relational approach **10:** 6136
and learning environments **6:** ***3297–3302***
and learning factors **10:** 5747, 5748
learning strategies (strategy instruction) **6:** 3329
Locke's theories **6:** 3498
and media research **7:** 3740
and models **10:** 6014
oral history **7:** 4224
paradigm of **10:** 6204
Pestalozzi's views **8:** 4415, 4417
physical education **10:** 5712
program implementation **3:** 1493
and questioning techniques **8:** 4876
questioning techniques
and teacher behavior **10:** 6013
and reinforcement
interaction effects **5:** 2922
and reproduction theory **9:** 5020
research
developments **10:** 6206
resource room programs **9:** 5068
Saint Augustine on **9:** 5117
and school dynamics **9:** 5169

science education history **9:** 5325
social studies **9:** 5576, 5579
research **9:** 5581
student centered **6:** 3454, 3456
and student needs **10:** 5768
studies
and self-report **9:** 5410
and teacher knowledge **10:** 6118
research **10:** 6119
and teaching guides **10:** 6114
and test wiseness
ethics **11:** 6338
tutoring **11:** ***6481–6484***
and unintended effects **11:** 6510
and videotape recordings **11:** 6605
vocational education
Uruguay **7:** 4151
See also
Demonstrations (educational)
Direct instruction
Reflective teaching
Teaching models
and artificial intelligence **1:** 345
pedagogical content knowledge **10:** 6182
Teaching practices
See Teaching methods
Teaching skills
and academic achievement **8:** 4869
allocation of
supply and demand **7:** 3820
improvisation **10:** 6033
and productivity profiles
microeconomic analysis **7:** 3819
requirements **10:** 6227
and teacher effectiveness
measurement **10:** 5844
Teaching styles
adaptation to student characteristics **5:** 2766
and body language **7:** 4172
and correspondence analysis **2:** 1119
of expert teachers **10:** 6022
expert vs. novice **10:** 6023
frontal teaching **3:** 1822
intact
paradigm of **10:** 6206
and intervention **9:** 5486
and lesson structure **6:** 3387
and outcomes of education **9:** 5261
and teacher effectiveness **8:** 4521
vs. student evaluation
and mediation theory **4:** 1874, 1876
Team accelerated instruction (TAI)
and educational technology **4:** 1914
Team teaching
and incentives **4:** 1971
and interdisciplinary approach **5:** 2694
regular and special education
relationship **5:** 2906; **9:** 5070; **10:** 6241
special education **6:** 3558
types of **10:** 6240
Teams
child study **10:** 6240
collaborative consultation **10:** 6242
purposes of **10:** 6242
intervention assistance **10:** 6240
school-based resource **10:** 6240
for special education
factors affecting **10:** 6243
international perspectives **10:** 6242
service delivery **10:** 6241
student support **10:** 6240
teacher assistance **10:** 6240
types of
for special needs students **10:** ***6240–6245***
Teamwork
cooperative learning **2:** 1095
and productivity **11:** 6629
school personnel
related services **9:** 5289
Technical assistance
Africa **11:** 6658
Asia **11:** 6657
future policies **5:** 3001
International Labour Organization **5:** 2999
trends **5:** 3000
Latin America **11:** 6659
policy formation **5:** 3000
and private organizations
Latin America **7:** 4149, 4152
to training with production programs **11:** 6449
vocational education and training
international aid **11:** ***6660–6664***
Technical colleges
See Technical institutes
Technical cooperation
See Technical assistance
Technical education
Afghanistan **1:** 206
Albania **1:** 257
area studies **11:** 6261
Botswana **1:** 547
Brunei Darussalam **1:** 574
Bulgaria **1:** 584
Burundi **1:** 602
Cameroon **2:** 612
Canada **2:** 621
Central African Republic **2:** 654
Chad **2:** 668
Chile **2:** 741
comparative analysis
data requirements **11:** 6264
enrollment rates **11:** 6262
future trends **11:** 6264
methods **11:** 6264
taxonomy **11:** 6262
thematic approach **11:** 6264
coordination of
developing nations **10:** 6064
Côte d'Ivoire **2:** 1155
curriculum development **11:** 6271
task analysis **11:** 6261
Cyprus **3:** 1371
definitions of **11:** 6268
Dominica **3:** 1596
East Africa and South Africa **11:** 6252
and economic development **11:** 6261
educational finance **11:** 6271
tax deductions **10:** 6064
educational innovations **11:** 6261
and educational technology
role of **4:** 1920
and electrical theory **11:** 6414
Fiji **4:** 2306
inservice teacher education **10:** 6066
interdisciplinary approach
comparative analysis **11:** 6263
International Labour Organization **5:** 2999; **11:** 6261
international studies **11:** 6261
comparative analysis **11:** ***6261–6266***
Israel **5:** 3025
Japan **11:** 6697
Latin America **7:** 4153
macroeconomic context **11:** 6251
multiple locations of **11:** 6245
Namibia **7:** 4042
national case studies **11:** 6262
and national training agencies
Latin America **6:** 3264
nuclear personnel
computer-assisted instruction **4:** 1922
Oman **7:** 4203
participation
patterns **11:** 6248
post school programs **11:** 6246
provision **11:** 6261
regional studies
comparative analysis **11:** 6262, 6263
resources **10:** 6064
role of **11:** 6250
Rwanda **9:** 5110
school-based **11:** 6245
school business relationship **11:** 6271
and skill development **10:** 5917
and small business training **4:** 1986
Soviet Union (former) **10:** 5647
teacher education **10:** ***6063–6068***
problems with **10:** 6065
and teacher qualifications **10:** 6065
and technological advancement **11:** 6268
Thailand **11:** 6374
training with production **11:** ***6445–6452***
Uganda **11:** 6498
UNESCO and **11:** 6261, 6264
United Kingdom **11:** 6518
United States **11:** 6542
vocational education
Latin America **6:** ***3256–3262***
vocational evaluation
policy studies **11:** 6262
work-based **11:** 6247
youth and adults
educational technology **4:** ***1918–1924***, ***1922***

See also
Technical and vocational education and training (TVET)
Vocational education
Technical institutes
small business training **4:** 1987
types of
and teacher education **10:** 6063
Technical occupations
and school nurses **9:** 5285
and vocational education **11:** 6667
Technical schools
See Vocational schools
Technical skills
and promotion (occupational) **11:** 6629
training programs **4:** 1986
Technical and Vocational Education Initiative (TVEI) (UK) **8:** 4337; **11:** 6689
flexible learning **4:** 1896
sex roles **4:** 2290
Technical and vocational education and training (TVET) **11:** ***6245–6251***
Eastern and Southern Africa **11:** ***6251–6256***
See also
Technical education
Vocational education
Vocational education and training (VET)
Technical writing
science curriculum **6:** 3217
Technicians
See Paraprofessional personnel
Technikerschulen
and technical education **11:** 6269
Technological advancement
and adult education **1:** 128
aggregate studies **11:** 6273, 6274
conclusions **11:** 6274
and apprenticeships
Germany, Federal Republic of (former) **11:** 6656
case studies **11:** 6273
conclusions **11:** 6275
changes and criticism of education system **6:** 3419
conditional theory **11:** 6273
contingency theory **11:** 6273
and copyrights **2:** 1101
and cultural numeracy **6:** 3457
and curriculum change **7:** 4081
and curriculum development **9:** 5521
and database design **3:** 1398
and demand for adult education **11:** 6391
and demand for educated labor **11:** ***6256–6261***
demonstrations (educational) **10:** 6140
and desktop publishing **4:** 1955
developed nations
and division of labor **3:** 1708
developing nations
and division of labor **3:** 1708
and distance education
stages **3:** 1574
downgrading thesis **11:** 6272, 6279
and economic change **3:** 1708
and education **4:** 2211; **11:** ***6277–6283***
and educational facilities planning **4:** 2229
and educational media organizations **3:** 1799
and educational planning
Asia **8:** 4488
and educational policy **5:** 2499; **11:** 6279
educational programs
Europe **4:** 2055
and educational researchers
impact on **9:** 5035
and educational technology **4:** 1893
and educational television **5:** 2891, 2896
effects **11:** 6288
on education and training **11:** 6413
on job skills **11:** 6257
on labor force participation **3:** 1668
on skills **11:** 6279
and electronic publishing **4:** 1955
and employment patterns **11:** 6258
futures (of society) **4:** 2328
hardware (computers)
in education **4:** 1903
influence on adult education **5:** 2735, 2736
and information networks
international **5:** 2996
and instructional design theory **5:** 2865
labor force
and academic achievement **11:** 6279
sex bias **11:** 6279
and libraries **6:** 3399
and library materials **6:** 3396
and management information systems **6:** 3593
and managerial prerogatives **11:** 6275
and market forces **11:** 6275
and new skill requirements **1:** 181
and oral history **7:** 4224
and organizational change **3:** 1708
and organizational culture **11:** 6275
and paraprofessional personnel
effect on role of **11:** 6268
production
and economic change **3:** 1707
factors for the development of **11:** 6278
vocational education vs. on-the-job training **11:** 6281
and productivity **11:** 6272, 6280
and psychomotor skill development **7:** 3953
and publishing industry **8:** 4688
and recurrent education **8:** 4963
sex fairness **4:** ***2423–2427***
and skill obsolescence **11:** 6257, ***6272–6277***
future research **11:** 6276
and special education **10:** 5942
and supply and demand **11:** 6275
and technical education **11:** 6268
uncertainty–contingency hypothesis **11:** 6273, 6275
vs. skill–training life cycle model **11:** 6276
upgrading thesis **11:** 6279
industrialization thesis **11:** 6272
and visual aids **10:** 5726
and vocational education **4:** 1923; **9:** 5074
and vocational education programs
Europe **4:** 2060
Technological change
See Technological advancement
Technological diffusion
See Technology transfer
Technological literacy
concept of **11:** 6288
Technology
competencies
classification **11:** 6291
and continuing education **2:** 1089
and education
transformations **4:** 1884
and educational change **4:** 1851
educational economics of **4:** ***1903–1911***
and educational planning **11:** ***6292–6298***
effects on children and youth **1:** ***564–570***
soft
in education **4:** 1913
and teacher role **11:** ***6283–6287***
and training requirements **1:** 110
uses
in special education **10:** ***5668–5674***
in workplace
and labor force development **5:** 2688, 2689
Technology education
curriculum development
centralized **5:** 2497
problems **11:** 6288
and educational change
influences **11:** 6288
evaluation **11:** 6292
historical background **11:** 6287
objectives **11:** 6289
production-orientated **11:** 6290
programs **11:** ***6287–6292***
conceptual frameworks for **11:** 6291
content **11:** 6289
developments **11:** 6288
future trends **11:** 6291
progression **11:** 6291
subject components **11:** 6290
and science education **11:** 6290

Technology transfer **8:** 4338
consumer electronics **11:** 6277
factors affecting **11:** 6277
information technology **11:** 6277
microelectronics **11:** 6277
on-the-job training **11:** 6278
and production of advanced technological goods **11:** 6278
and the production of traditional goods and services **11:** 6277
telecommunications **11:** 6277
universities
role of **11:** 6280
Teleclassrooms
applications **11:** 6304
characteristics of **11:** 6301
Telecommunications
adult education **1:** ***561–564***
access **1:** 562
advantages **1:** 562
constraints **1:** 562
objectives and uses **1:** 561
between schools **2:** 978
and computers **11:** 6298
definition of **11:** 6298
developments
and educational television **5:** 2896
and distance education **3:** 1561
in education **4:** 1913; **11:** ***6298–6307***
applications **11:** 6302
future trends **11:** 6306
and educational media organizations **3:** 1799
and electronic publishing
advantages and disadvantages **4:** 1955
file transfer **11:** 6299
applications **11:** 6303
historical background **11:** 6298
and language education **7:** 4089
hardware (computers) **7:** 4090
software **7:** 4090
PLUTO International Network Project
teacher education **10:** 6007
special needs students
microcomputers **7:** 3803
technical systems **11:** 6299
and technology transfer **11:** 6277
Teleconferencing
applications **11:** 6304
characteristics of **11:** 6301
and computer networks **2:** 978
and distance education **3:** 1564, 1566, 1576, 1578
United States **3:** 1566
and educational research
dissemination of **3:** 1555
and language education **7:** 4089
and writing instruction **7:** 4089
See also
Computer conferencing
Telecourses
adult education
United States **1:** 561, 562
See also
Educational television
Telekolleg **1:** 183
Telematics
definition of **11:** 6299
Telephone instruction **7:** 4247
Telesoftware
courseware **10:** 5621
Television
and audiovisual instruction
characteristics of **1:** 402
digital
characteristics of **5:** 2896
and distance education **3:** 1575
bandwidth restrictions **3:** 1576
effects on children and youth **1:** 564
high definition (HDTV) **5:** 2896
influences
behavioral **1:** 569
on children and youth **1:** 566
interactive **4:** 1921
production styles
multicamera **1:** 402
single camera **1:** 402
program choice
children and youth **1:** 565
in religious education **9:** 5003
sex bias **4:** 2448
uses in education **1:** 401; **4:** 1904
vs. books
children and youth **1:** 565
See also
Broadcast television
Cable television
Commercial television
Educational television
Television commercials
critical viewing **6:** 3624
effects on children and youth **1:** 567
Television curriculum
critical viewing **7:** 3741
Television research
effects on academic achievement
findings **1:** 568
Television surveys
audience response **1:** 564
Television viewing
and academic achievement **1:** 568; **7:** 3741
causal factors **1:** 568
acculturation **9:** 5514
active vs. passive **8:** 4677
age patterns **1:** 564
and antisocial behavior **7:** 3741
attitudes to **6:** 3622
children and youth **1:** 564
children's behavior studies **6:** 3623
and comprehension **6:** 3623
content indifference **1:** 566
critical viewing **6:** 3623
daily patterns **1:** 564
effect on children's play **8:** 4541
effects on behavior of young children **8:** 4677
factors in learning **8:** 4400, 4401, 4402
and family life **1:** 565
individual experience
characteristics of **1:** 566
learning effects **8:** 4677
and literacy testing **6:** 3472
low involvement **1:** 566
monitoring
and comprehension **1:** 566
and partial order scalogram analysis **7:** 4314
patterns
and education **2:** 1053
preschool children
adult guidance **8:** 4678
comprehension **8:** 4678
programming (broadcast) **6:** 3622
prosocial behavior **8:** 4798
television research **4:** 2330
time **6:** 3622
and values **6:** 3622; **7:** 3741
violence
and development of aggression in children **1:** 233
effects on children **6:** 3624
Temperament
See Personality
Temperature
control
educational facilities **4:** 2220
Temporal processing deficits
and language handicaps **10:** 5679
TEMPUS (EC program) **4:** 2056
and international exchanges **5:** 2933
Tenured faculty
females **11:** 6709
Teratogens
and congenital impairments **1:** 13, 14
Teratology **1:** 13
Terminology
See Vocabulary
Terry–Hoeffding test
nonparametric statistics **7:** 4160
Tertiary education
See Postsecondary education
Tertiary libraries
See Academic libraries
Test administration
See Testing
Test administrators
See Examiners
Test anxiety **4:** 1963, 1965
and academic achievement **4:** 1965
and achievement need **5:** 2763; **7:** 3939, 3940
aspects of **11:** 6355
attention-deficit hypothesis **1:** 200
background variables
effects of **11:** 6357
and cognitive appraisal **11:** 6356
and computer-assisted testing **5:** 2782
conceptualization of **11:** 6356
conditions for **11:** 6357
control of **11:** 6357
controllable factors **11:** 6356
effect on cognitive processes **1:** 199
expectation of performance **11:** ***6355–6360***

experiences of success and failure **11:** 6358
and factorial modeling **4:** 2244
and mathematics **11:** 6359
significance of **11:** 6355
and testing **11:** 6313
therapy **4:** 1966
treatments for **11:** 6356
Test bias **5:** ***3043–3051***, ***3046***; **11:** ***6315–6321***
and achievement tests **10:** 5769
in attitude measures **9:** 5319
definition of **11:** 6315
and group differences **11:** 6315
methodology **11:** 6318
research
trends **11:** 6320
and test format **11:** 6319
and test theory **11:** 6316
and test translation **11:** 6328
and test use
settings for **11:** 6316
See also
Culture fair tests
Item bias
Test coaching **11:** ***6334–6340***
and curriculum development **7:** 3722
definitions of **11:** 6335
effects of **11:** 6336
equity in **11:** 6337
ethics **11:** 6338
historical background **11:** 6334
and instructional alignment **5:** 2853
main issues **11:** 6335
types of **11:** 6335
Test construction **11:** 6334
and automation **2:** 992, 996
items
and computer-assisted testing **5:** 2780
parameters for **11:** 6311
procedure **11:** 6321
racial bias **10:** 5824
and scoring **11:** 6312
sex bias **10:** 5824
and test translation **11:** 6330
two-way grid **11:** 6321
Test design
See Test construction
Test development
See Test construction
Test format **11:** 6311
and test bias **11:** 6319
and test validity
cross-cultural studies **11:** 6329
Test interpretation
factors
sociopolitical **11:** 6332
Test items
achievement tests **10:** 5783
bias **5:** ***3043–3051***, ***3046***
domain specifications **5:** 3064
and facet theory **4:** 2215
and foreign language testing **4:** 2362
higher level
construction of **5:** 3065
intentional vs. incidental **8:** 4877
mathematics
types of **8:** 4643
and objective tests **7:** 4193; **11:** 6345
formats **7:** 4193
and problem-solving **8:** 4730
replicable
construction techniques **5:** 3061
and test construction **11:** 6311
translation
in comparative analysis **3:** 1767
validity of
in computer-assisted testing **5:** 2781
See also
Item writing techniques
Test manuals
and test translation **11:** 6329
Test reliability **11:** 6340, 6348
and criterion-referenced tests **9:** 4993
examples **9:** 4984
and factor analysis **4:** 2232
and judgments
measurement of **6:** 3121
and language tests **4:** 2358
and mastery tests **9:** 4993
Test results
and curriculum development **7:** 3722
item analysis **4:** 2076
psychometric approach **4:** 2074
reporting **4:** ***2074–2079***
scores
misinterpretation **4:** 2074
teachers' use of **4:** 2074
Test score decline
and educational change **6:** 3492
Test scoring machines
and reliability **9:** 4995
Test selection
experimental studies **4:** 2191
Test taking anxiety
See Test anxiety
Test taking skills
See Test wiseness
Test theory
classical
See Classical test theory
implications of cognitive measurement for **1:** 373
standard **1:** 371
and test bias **11:** 6316
See also
Item response theory (IRT)
Test translation
and attitude measures **11:** ***6328–6334***
and cultural differences **11:** 6329
empirical designs **11:** 6331
interpretation of results **11:** 6332
interpreters
selection of training **11:** 6330
judgmental designs
backward **11:** 6331
forward **11:** 6331
problems **11:** 6331
methods **11:** 6328
process **11:** 6330
reasons for **11:** 6328
research trends **11:** 6333
standards **11:** 6333
technical factors **11:** 6330
test items
in cross-national comparisons **4:** 2133
Test use **4:** ***2074–2079***
effects of
undesirable **11:** 6340
grouping (instructional purposes) **6:** 3626
learning problems
remedial instruction **6:** 3626
settings for **11:** 6316
Test validity **11:** 6340, 6348
achievement tests **10:** 5769
in cross-national comparisons **4:** 2133
curriculum coverage index **4:** 2134
curriculum relevance index **4:** 2134
item validity **4:** 2133
motivational **4:** 2134
test relevance index **4:** 2134
differential item functioning **1:** 373
of essay scores **4:** 2023
and foreign language testing **4:** 2361
and item banks **5:** 3039
and language tests **4:** 2358
and test coaching **11:** 6336
and test format
cross-cultural studies **11:** 6329
and test translation **11:** 6329
technical factors **11:** 6330
See also
Construct validity
Content validity
Test wiseness
ethics **11:** 6338
and test anxiety **11:** 6356
Testing **2:** 1059; **11:** ***6311–6315***
changes in conditions for **11:** 6314
and cognitive psychology **1:** ***370–374***
constraints **11:** 6340
and curriculum **11:** ***6321–6328***
trends **11:** 6327
and curriculum development **3:** 1322; **7:** ***3722–3726***
emotional setting for **11:** 6313
environmental factors **11:** 6313
and examinee preparation **11:** 6312
and examiner preparation **11:** 6312
feedback
error correction **6:** 3626
implications of instructional alignment for **5:** 2855
individualized
problems with **11:** 6314
and instructional effectiveness
instructional alignment **5:** ***2852–2856***
item banks in **5:** ***3036–3043***
item sampling in **5:** ***3055–3061***
as a learning experience **6:** 3301
matrix sampling **4:** 2077
memory **7:** ***3763–3769***
of models **7:** 3866
national norms

legislation **6:** 3358
problem-solving **8:** ***4728–4731***
procedures
and foreign language testing **4:** 2363
purpose of **11:** 6311
standardization of procedures for **11:** 6312
and test translation **11:** 6329
young children **1:** ***358–362***
concurrent validity **1:** 361
negative effects **1:** 360
predictive validity **1:** 361
problems **1:** 360
test construction **1:** 361
test items **1:** 359
See also
Adaptive testing
Assessment
computer-assisted testing
Confidence testing
Educational testing
Evaluation
Group testing
Individual testing
Measurement
Minimum competency testing
Psychological testing
Tests

Testing programs
dynamic **3:** 1251

Tests
and achieved curriculum **11:** 6326
characteristics of **11:** 6340
cheating in **11:** 6314
conventional instruction
behavioral objectives **1:** 371
curriculum ratings **11:** 6323
equated scores **11:** ***6349–6355***
external **11:** 6341
and implemented curriculum **11:** 6325
indexes
coverage **11:** 6323, 6324
curriculum coverage **11:** 6323, 6324
and intended curriculum **11:** 6323
relevance **11:** 6323, 6324
uses of **11:** 6325
internal **11:** 6341
materials for **11:** 6312
presentation of **11:** 6314
and primary school agriculture **8:** 4686
prior learning in **8:** 4701
and security **11:** 6342
timing of **11:** 6313
types of **11:** 6311, ***6340–6349***
and test bias **11:** 6315
uses of **11:** 6340
young children
role of context **1:** 359
See also
Achievement tests
Examinations
Testing

Tests of significance
See Statistical significance

Text analysis
and comprehension **2:** 1077
and content analysis **2:** ***1074–1079***
use of computers in **2:** 1077
See also
Content analysis

Text processing
See Word processing

Text structure
and study skills **10:** 5830

Textbook bias
sex bias **4:** 2409; **9:** 5441
elementary education **9:** 5300
research **9:** ***5299–5302***
secondary education **9:** 5300

Textbook content
criticisms of **11:** 6367
factors affecting **11:** 6367
politics of **11:** 6365
and social change **11:** 6367

Textbook development
See Textbook preparation

Textbook evaluation
and artificial intelligence models **1:** 347
and feedback **11:** 6370
and Hawthorne effect **11:** 6508
methods **11:** 6368
for selection **11:** 6368
Sierra analysis system **1:** 347
United States **3:** 1279

Textbook preparation
criticisms of **11:** 6369
and curriculum development centers **3:** 1273
in developing nations
planning for **11:** ***6360–6366***
issues **11:** 6362
and paper supply **11:** 6365
problems **11:** 6369
public sector vs. private sector **11:** 6363

Textbook publication **11:** 6369
and adoption **11:** 6368
bindings **8:** 4692
and copyrights **11:** 6365
costs **11:** 6370
and courseware **10:** 5619
local
protection for **11:** 6364
vs. international **11:** 6362, 6363
market research **8:** 4692
public policy
multicultural education **7:** 3977
and school libraries **8:** 4698
and teaching guides **10:** 6115
vs. curriculum development **11:** 6365

Textbook research
history **9:** 5560
sex bias **9:** ***5299–5302***
guidelines for eliminating **9:** 5301
issues **9:** 5301
and social reproduction **3:** 1345
social sciences **9:** 5560

Textbook selection **11:** 6368
procedures **11:** 6368

Textbook writing
See Textbook preparation

Textbooks **2:** 793; **11:** ***6366–6371***
adoption **11:** 6368
authors
classical literature **9:** 5121
availability of
developing nations **8:** 4694, 4696, 4846
controversies **11:** 6367
criticisms of **11:** 6369
cultural differences in utilization **3:** 1243
and curriculum **10:** 6089
and curriculum development **3:** 1339
developing nations
input output analysis **3:** 1761
effective use of **11:** 6366
finance for **11:** 6365
functions of **8:** 4696
historical background **11:** 6366
impact
on academic achievement **3:** 1834
on learning **11:** 6368
on teaching **11:** 6368
learning from
and curriculum development **9:** 5520
marketing **11:** 6369
mathematics
language usage **6:** 3637
and programmed instruction **8:** 4766
provision
activities **11:** 6361
developing nations **11:** 6360
problems **11:** 6361, 6362
ratio per student
developing nations **8:** 4696
readership size **11:** 6362
sex stereotypes in **9:** 5442
and teaching guides **10:** 6113, 6115
utilization **11:** 6366
studies **11:** 6368
See also
Printed materials

THAID **5:** 2925
and multivariate analysis **7:** 4011

Thailand
adult education **1:** 118, 153, 352; **6:** 3362
nonformal education **11:** 6374
adult literacy programs **2:** 1046
community development **2:** 904
community education **2:** 908
computer uses in education **4:** 1901
curriculum development **11:** 6376
distance education **4:** 1901
educational change **11:** 6377
educational demand
studies **8:** 4704
educational finance studies
private vs. public resources **8:** 4703, 4704
educational quality
and instructional materials **8:** 4859
educational radio **4:** 1906; **5:** 2886

educational research **11:** 6377
educational resources
inequality in **8:** 4705
effective schools research **4:** 1937
ethnic groups **11:** 6371
index of segregation **4:** 2430
language **11:** 6371
literacy education **6:** 3463, 3464, 3465
open university **1:** 563
postsecondary education **11:** 6372
preschool education **11:** 6373
primary education **11:** 6372
public schools vs. private schools **8:** 4843
religious education **9:** 4999
second chance education **7:** 4135
secondary education **11:** 6372
state schools vs. private schools
and private resources **8:** 4706
student evaluation **11:** 6376
system of education **11:** ***6371–6378***
educational objectives **11:** 6372
enrollment **11:** 6373
major problems **11:** 6377
structure **11:** 6372
teacher education **11:** 6375
teacher recruitment **11:** 6375
teaching methodology **11:** 6376
videotex
applications **11:** 6306
vocational education **8:** 4794
apprenticeships **11:** 6658
women's education
barriers to **4:** 2418

Thalidomide **1:** 14

Theater arts
educational programs **8:** ***4384–4388***
future trends **8:** 4387
instructional psychology **11:** ***6616–6618***
and the mass media **8:** 4387
national policies **8:** 4384
popular theater **2:** 903
agitprop **2:** 903
consciousness raising **2:** 903
participatory **2:** 903
teaching as **10:** 6083
traditional and popular **8:** 4387
United Kingdom **8:** 4384, 4385
United States **8:** 4384

Thematic Apperception Test (TAT) **8:** 4789
achievement need **3:** 1236, 1238, 1239

Theological education
and scholasticism **9:** ***5121–5124***

Theories
construction of
and smallest space analysis **9:** 5498, 5501
conversion into problem-solving procedures **3:** 1433
definition of
Feigl's ideal **3:** 1769
development of
and case studies **2:** 641
formation of
and facet theory **4:** 2217
and models
definitions **7:** 3865
Popper's views **4:** 1998
precedence of **9:** 5039
as problem-solving devices **9:** 5029
and research methodology **9:** 5049
and scientific attitudes **5:** 2654
See also
Hypothesis testing

Theory practice relationship
and critical theory **2:** 1200, 1203
declarative and procedural knowledge **3:** ***1432–1434***
education **9:** ***5038–5043***
issues **9:** 5039
models **9:** 5040
and research findings **9:** 5042
and educational research **4:** 1857
Herbart's philosophy of education **5:** ***2575–2579***
and instructional design **5:** 2871
and primary school agriculture **8:** 4685
proposals **9:** 5039
and relevance (educational) **8:** 4458
and sport pedagogy **10:** 5708
and traditions in philosophy of education **8:** 4458

Thermodynamics
studies
and microcomputer-based laboratories **7:** 3809

Thesauri
and indexing **5:** 2819

Thinking
See Cognitive processes

Thinking aloud protocols
See Protocol analysis

Thinking skills **2:** 1205, 1206; **8:** ***4948–4951***
children
mathematics skills **6:** 3669, 3670
cognitive strategy instruction **2:** 861, 862, 865
development
mass media role in **2:** 885
effect of educational media on **7:** 3742
and heuristics **10:** 6176
instruction in
influence of Piagetian theory **8:** 4482
and intellectual disciplines **8:** 4950
and intelligence
general theories **5:** 2919
intracultural variation
ethnography **3:** 1247
and knowledge level **8:** 4950
lateral
and idea generation **5:** 2723
learning strategies **8:** ***4722–4728***
literacy
and cognitive development **3:** 1244
and long term memory **1:** 329
and mathematics **6:** 3457
philosophical approach to development **2:** 1205, 1206
and physical sciences
secondary school programs **8:** 4476
reproductive **8:** 4723, 4724
skill development
training in **3:** 1503
social sciences **9:** 5562
theoretical and practical development **3:** 1327

Third age
and lifelong learning **11:** 6391
University of the **7:** 4169, 4247

Third World
See Developing nations

Three-parameter models
and item response theory **7:** 3998
item bias procedures **5:** 3048

Threshold level (languages)
programs for immigrants **6:** 3210

Thurstone scales **7:** 3699; **11:** ***6385–6388***
and attitude measures **1:** 382, 387, 392; **7:** 3703, 3704
defining a continuum **11:** 6385
and Rasch measurement models
distinctions **8:** 4923
and rating scales **8:** 4918
statistical formulations **11:** 6385
attitude and mental testing **11:** 6386
equal appearing intervals **11:** 6386
law of comparative judgement **11:** 6385
pair comparison design **11:** 6386
successive intervals **11:** 6386
and unidimensionality **11:** 6385
validity checks **11:** 6386
person measurement **11:** 6387
principles of invariance **11:** 6387
statistical tests **11:** 6386

Thurstone Tests of Primary Mental Abilities
and vocational evaluation 6671 11.

Tics
Gilles de la Tourette disorder **3:** 1516
and drug therapy **8:** 4423

Tikopians
ethnography of **3:** 1754

Time
committed **6:** 3374, 3375
concept of
and history instruction **9:** 5576
contracted **6:** 3374, 3375
financial dimension of **6:** 3547
free and nonwork **6:** 3375
for learning **6:** 3377
necessary **6:** 3374
residual **6:** 3374
types of **6:** 3374
use in longitudinal studies **6:** 3514

Time factors (learning) **7:** 3880; **10:** 5747; **11:** ***6388–6390***
academic achievement **1:** 22; **11:** 6389

administrative schedules
characteristics of **6:** 3546
behavioral objectives **2:** 1021
Carroll's model **1:** 21
conceptual tempo
individualized instruction **5:** 2776
and cost effectiveness **2:** 1129
decision-making units **6:** 3546
as a dimension of macroeconomics **6:** ***3545–3550***
education work relationship
screening hypothesis **6:** 3549
effect of unions on **10:** 6070
and group size **7:** 3818
impact on academic achievement **6:** 3547
individual differences **3:** 1504
and investment in education
competition **6:** 3548
knowledge acquisition **2:** 1022
as measures of exposure **6:** 3545
memory systems
storage **2:** 1022
opportunity to learn **1:** 21
and outcomes of education **9:** 5260
and rate of return
to education **6:** 3548
research methodology **1:** 22
substitute teachers **10:** 5833
United States **1:** 20
Time management
classroom techniques
comparative analysis **10:** 6151, 6154
in classrooms **7:** 4174
curriculum adaptation **3:** 1254
and instructional effectiveness
vocational education **8:** 4862
and joint production model **6:** 3103
in lifelong learning **11:** ***6390–6395***
in projects **8:** 4757
schools **11:** ***6388–6390***
comparative analysis **11:** 6388
homework **11:** 6388
literacy **11:** 6388
mathematical concepts **11:** 6388
policy formation **11:** 6390
time on task **11:** 6389
and semiotics **9:** 5415
See also
Time on task
Time on task **1:** 21
and academic achievement **8:** 4870; **11:** 6389
comparative analysis **5:** 2628
effects of increasing **6:** 3547, 3548
elementary school students **1:** 22
factors affecting **6:** 3546
and learning motivation **7:** 3937
and mediation theory **4:** 1874
and outcomes of education **9:** 5260
physical education **10:** 5709, 5711
religious education **9:** 4997
resource room programs **9:** 5067, 5068
schools **11:** ***6388–6390***
comparative analysis **11:** 6389
See also
Academic learning time
Time management
Time series analysis
computer software
DMITSA2 **9:** 5489
ITSE **9:** 5488
TMS **9:** 5488
interrupted **8:** 4874
and single case research **9:** 5486
and longitudinal studies **6:** 3516
model identification **9:** 5488
number of observations **9:** 5488
projections
exponential smoothing **8:** 4784
and quasiexperimental design **8:** 4874
retrospective **6:** 3517
and social background research **7:** 3720
Timed tests
characteristics of **11:** 6346
cross-cultural studies **11:** 6330
Timetables
See School schedules
Title I and III Evaluation Programs (US)
See Elementary and Secondary Education Act (ESEA) 1965 (US)
Title VII
See Elementary and Secondary Education Act (ESEA) 1965 (US)
Tobago
See Trinidad and Tobago
Toddlers
accordion grouping **11:** 6397
classroom research **11:** 6396
day care **11:** ***6395–6398***
future provision **11:** 6397
research **11:** 6396
day care programs
Israel **11:** 6396
United States **11:** 6396
early childhood programs **5:** ***2806–2814***
early intervention **5:** 2809
play **8:** 4538
prosocial behavior **8:** 4797
Togo
educational change **11:** 6402
educational research **11:** 6402
language **11:** 6398, 6399
postsecondary education **11:** 6399
preschool education **11:** 6400
primary education **11:** 6399
secondary education **11:** 6399
vocational education **11:** 6400
student evaluation **11:** 6402
system of education **11:** ***6398–6403***
educational objectives **11:** 6399
historical background **11:** 6399
structure **11:** 6399
teacher recruitment **11:** 6401
technical education **11:** 6400
textbook publication **11:** 6363
women's education **11:** 6736, 6737, 6738, 6739
Token economy
behavior modification
delinquency **4:** 1844
behavioral instruction **10:** 6162
Tonga
curriculum development **11:** 6409
educational change **11:** 6411
educational research **11:** 6411
language **11:** 6404
postsecondary education **11:** 6406
preschool education **11:** 6407
primary education **11:** 6405
secondary education **11:** 6406
special education **11:** 6407
structure of government **11:** 6404
student evaluation **11:** 6410
system of education **11:** ***6403–6412***
educational objectives **11:** 6405
enrollment **11:** 6406
major problems **11:** 6411
structure **11:** 6405
teacher education **11:** 6409
teacher recruitment **11:** 6409
teaching methodology **11:** 6409
Total communication
deaf blind children **3:** 1404
deafness **3:** 1400
Total costs
continuing education **2:** 1146
impact of lifelong learning on **6:** 3422
Total learning systems
and nonformal education **4:** 2365
Totalitarianism
and adult education **2:** 657
and conformity via education **8:** 4576
Touching behavior
and nonverbal communication **7:** 4172
Tourette syndrome
See Tics, Gilles de la Tourette disorder
Trace line
See Item response theory (IRT)
Tracer studies
and longitudinal studies **6:** 3512
in vocational education **8:** 4530
Botswana **11:** 6253
Tanzania **11:** 6253
Track system (education) **1:** ***6–12***
and academic achievement **2:** 824
Catholic schools **8:** 4841
elementary schools
Japan **1:** 6
United States **1:** 6
flexible progression **2:** 823
France **9:** 5019
and school organization **7:** 4230
school restructuring
United States **1:** 10
secondary schools **1:** 6
and use of standardized tests
racial factors **1:** 9
Trade schools
See Vocational schools

Trade unions
  See Unions
Traditional grammar **10:** 5698, 5958
  content **10:** 5698
  influence of Latin on **10:** 5698
  influence on writing (composition) **10:** 5699
Traditional instruction
  See Conventional instruction
Traditional schools
  cost effectiveness **7:** 4134
  vs. nontraditional education **1:** 260
Trainees
  and skill development **10:** 5917
Trainers
  characteristics of
    and small business training **4:** 1989
  selection of
    and performance contracts **8:** 4713
  and skill development **10:** 5917
Training
  and adult education **8:** 4338
  application of psychology to **5:** 2878
  concepts and statistics **11:** ***6416–6420***
  courses
    cost effectiveness of **2:** ***1136–1139***
    cost factors **2:** 1137
    effectiveness factors **2:** 1137
  definitions of **3:** 1486, 1487; **11:** 6417, 6418
  for the disadvantaged
    Latin America **7:** ***4148–4155***
  earnings and productivity **11:** 6418
  and education
    convergence between **11:** ***6412–6416***
    differences between **11:** 6413
    relationships between **11:** 6412
    semantics **11:** 6412
    technological advancement effects **11:** 6413
  of educational researchers **11:** ***6438–6445***
  empirical studies **11:** 6418
    individual wage effects **11:** 6418
    institutional **11:** 6419
  by equipment vendors **1:** 109
  expenditure surveys **7:** 3712, 3713
  expenditures
    concept of **11:** 6417
  finance **11:** 6425, 6426
    and wage reductions **11:** 6427
  general **11:** 6421
    costs **11:** 6421
    and labor market **1:** 104
    rate of return **6:** 3614
  government role in **11:** ***6425–6431***
    equity arguments **11:** 6428
    external benefits **11:** 6426, 6429
    finance **11:** 6430
    and market imperfections **11:** 6426
    policy formation **11:** 6429
    small businesses **11:** 6428
  human resources
    development **11:** 6637
  incentives for **11:** 6430
    factors affecting **11:** 6635
  incidence of
    and occupational category **1:** 107
  informal
    costs **11:** 6423
  international agencies **5:** 2934
  international comparisons **11:** 6416, 6417
    and level of education **11:** 6419
  International Institute for Educational Planning programs **11:** 6529
  and learning strategies **6:** 3346
  levels in organization **3:** 1488
  market distortions
    effects of **11:** 6637
  markets
    and adult education **1:** ***103–111***
  measurement of **11:** 6416
  narrow concept of **5:** 2685
  national agencies for
    Latin America **6:** ***3262–3267***
  occupational
  See Job training
  off-the-shelf programs **1:** 109
  paraprofessional personnel **11:** ***6266–6272***
  and payment by results **11:** 6419
  performance contracts in **8:** ***4708–4715***
  private markets for **11:** 6425
  small businesses **4:** ***1985–1991***
  specific **11:** 6421
    rate of return **6:** 3614
  standards
    and apprenticeships **6:** 3616
  statistics **11:** 6416
    sources **11:** 6416
  tax system
    developing nations **1:** 110
  as a tool of management philosophy **3:** 1488
  types of **11:** 6420
  See also
    Industrial training
    Job training
    Vocational education
Training abroad
  investment in
    and brain drain **1:** 557
Training agencies
  private **1:** 109
  See also
    National training agencies (NTAs)
Training Agency (UK) **10:** 5639
  costs survey **11:** 6418
Training allowances **4:** 1974
Training councils
  vocational education **11:** 6649
Training methods
  national training agencies
    Latin America **6:** 3263
  and videotape recordings **11:** 6605
Training Opportunities Programme (TOPS) (UK)
  administration of **11:** 6686
Training with production **11:** ***6445–6452***
  and curriculum development **11:** 6451
  development of **11:** 6449
  for the disadvantaged
    Uruguay **7:** 4151
  and education with production compared **11:** 6445
  effect of economic change on **11:** 6448
  effect of political change on **11:** 6448
  historical background **11:** 6446
  implementation methods **11:** 6450
  Latin America **7:** 4150
  relationship between training and production **11:** 6450
  socialism and capitalism compared **11:** 6447
  types of **11:** 6445
  See also
    Education with production
    Vocational education
Training programs
  characteristics of
    Latin America **7:** 4150
  design **3:** ***1486–1491***
    Chile **7:** 4152
    human resource results model **3:** 1487
    systems models **3:** 1486, 1487
    and transfer of training **3:** 1490
  effectiveness **3:** ***1486–1491***
    learning results **3:** 1489
  evaluation **3:** 1488
    for policy formation **8:** 4528
  mismatched
    and job analysis **6:** 3093
  and paid educational leave **4:** 1974
  and private organizations
    Latin America **7:** 4149
  private vs. public organizations
    Latin America **7:** 4151, 4152
  vocational **9:** 5072
Training statistics
  concepts and definitions of **7:** 3712, 3713, 3714
  development **7:** 3711, 3712, 3713, 3714
Transfer of learning
  See Transfer of training
Transfer policy
  credits
    adult education **2:** 664
  university adult education **11:** 6549
Transfer of training **3:** 1490; **11:** ***6452–6457***
  and cognitive theories **5:** 2877
  conditions of **11:** 6454
  definition of **11:** 6452
  and industrial training **6:** 3303
  instruction for **11:** 6456
  and instructional alignment **5:** 2854, 2855
  international transferability of skills model
    immigration **5:** 2737
  learning strategies **2:** 837

mechanisms of **11:** 6455
near vs. far **11:** 6453, 6454
positive and negative **11:** 6452
and problem-solving **8:** 4728
and program design **3:** 1490
prospects for **11:** 6453
Transformational generative grammar
influence on writing (composition) **10:** 5699
Transformations (mathematics)
and exploratory data analysis **4:** 2203
and factor analysis **4:** 2236
mathematics instruction
computer software for **7:** 4097
and partial order scalogram analysis **7:** 4309
of raw scores
linear **1:** 34
Transient children
access to education **7:** 4134
Transitional programs
bridge jobs **5:** 2939
in developed nations **5:** 2939
and disabilities
adult service agencies **11:** 6459
common characteristics **11:** 6458
education work relationship **11:** ***6457–6461***
future trends **11:** 6460
issues **11:** 6457
planning **11:** 6460
quality **11:** 6458, 6459
responsibilities **11:** 6458
individualized **11:** 6459
Translation
and copyright **2:** 1101
See also
Test translation
Translators
See Interpreters
Transparencies
applications **7:** 3747
characteristics of **7:** 3746
developments **10:** 5727
Transportation costs
and educational vouchers **9:** 5204
Transsexualism **3:** 1516
Trauma (psychological)
See Emotional disturbances
Trend analysis
and cross-sectional studies **2:** 1217
and longitudinal studies **6:** 3515
Triangulation **4:** 2383; **11:** ***6461–6466***
criticisms of **11:** 6464
and data analysis **3:** 1472
definition of **11:** 6461
historical background **11:** 6462
interpretation
hermeneutic **11:** 6462
multiple
design problems **11:** 6463
example **11:** 6463
need for **11:** 6462
and participant observation
data categories **7:** 4317
problems **11:** 6465
strategies
variations **11:** 6463
types of
data **11:** 6462, 6464
investigator **11:** 6463, 6464
methodological **11:** 6463, 6465
multiple **11:** 6463, 6465
theory **11:** 6463, 6464
uses **11:** 6462
Tribal colleges
United States **2:** 905
Trinidad and Tobago
community education **2:** 908
public sector employment **8:** 4838
Truancy
and attendance patterns **3:** 1603
Australia **3:** 1536
causal factors **3:** 1604
definition of **3:** 1602
and dropouts **3:** ***1602–1607***
incidence of **3:** 1603
suspension for **3:** 1536
True scores
equating
and item response theory **5:** 3054
and item sampling **5:** 3057
and judgments **6:** 3120
ordinal theory **2:** 789
problems in defining **9:** 4984
and psychological testing **7:** 3702
and reliability **9:** 4981
strong theory **2:** 789
vs. observed scores **11:** 6352
vs. universe scores
in generalizability theory **5:** 2458
weak theory **2:** 786
Trust (psychology)
continuity of relationships
and social capital **4:** 2274
and personality development **9:** 5405
Trusts (financial)
and adult education **1:** 156
Tuition
private
Japan **11:** 6696
Tuition fees **10:** ***5750–5754***
Colombia **2:** 877
Mongolia **7:** 3903
Senegal **9:** 5421
See also
Student fees
Tuition tax credits
See Tax credits, tuition
Tunisia
computer uses in education **4:** 1902
curriculum development **11:** 6473
educational change **11:** 6474
educational research **11:** 6474
literacy education **1:** 326
postsecondary education **11:** 6469
preschool education **11:** 6470
primary education **11:** 6468
academic persistence **9:** 5536
secondary education **11:** 6469
social insurance
and training **11:** 6636
structure of government **11:** 6466
system of education **11:** ***6466–6476***
educational objectives **11:** 6467
enrollment **11:** 6469
historical background **11:** 6467
major problems **11:** 6475
structure **11:** 6468
teacher education **11:** 6472
teacher recruitment **11:** 6472
teaching methodology **11:** 6473
technical education **11:** 6471
Turkey
adult literacy programs **2:** 1046
apprenticeships **1:** 315
curriculum development **11:** 6480
educational change **11:** 6481
educational research **11:** 6481
ethnic groups **11:** 6477
language **11:** 6477
postsecondary education **11:** 6479
preschool education **11:** 6479
primary education **11:** 6478
enrollment rate **3:** 1790
rural to urban migration
determinants of **5:** 2943
secondary education **11:** 6478
special education **11:** 6479
student evaluation **11:** 6480
system of education **11:** ***6476–6481***
educational objectives **11:** 6477
major problems **11:** 6481
structure **11:** 6477
teacher education **11:** 6480
teacher recruitment **11:** 6480
teaching methodology **11:** 6480
vocational education **1:** 316; **6:** 3366
women's education **11:** 6754, 6758
Tutorial programs
and computer-assisted instruction **2:** 988
Tutoring **11:** ***6481–6484***
and administrator education
inservice **1:** 70
adolescents **11:** 6483
benefits of **11:** 6483
of children **11:** 6482
course **11:** 6483
definition of **11:** 6481
emergency **11:** 6483
evaluation
studies **11:** 6482
future trends **11:** 6484
guidelines **11:** 6483
high school
types of **11:** 6483
Personalized System of Instruction **11:** 6483
research **11:** 6484
resources **11:** 6483
structured **11:** 6483
uses of **11:** 6481
young adults **11:** 6483
See also
Programmed tutoring

Tutors
characteristics of **11:** 6482
types of **11:** 6482
Tuvalu
adult education
nonformal education **11:** 6487
curriculum development **11:** 6487
educational change **11:** 6488
government school relationship
financial support **11:** 6487
school administration **11:** 6487
language **11:** 6485
preschool education **11:** 6486
primary education **11:** 6485
secondary education **11:** 6485
vocational education **11:** 6486
student evaluation **11:** 6487
system of education **11:** ***6484–6488***
educational objectives **11:** 6485
major problems **11:** 6488
structure **11:** 6485
teacher education **11:** 6487
teaching methodology **11:** 6487
technical education **11:** 6486
Twin studies **11:** ***6488–6492***
and behavioral sciences **11:** 6489
bias in **6:** 3143
clinical **11:** 6489
and employment level
measurement **4:** 2278
environmental influences **11:** 6490
epidemiological **11:** 6489
family characteristics
outcomes of education **6:** 3138
fields of research **11:** 6488
genotype–environment correlation
11: 6489
genotype–environment interaction
11: 6489
and language handicaps **10:** 5680
lifelong development **11:** 6490
methodological problems **11:** 6489
model fitting **11:** 6490
partial variance decomposition
estimates **6:** 3140
phenotypes in **6:** 3140
trends **11:** 6491
types of **11:** 6488
Twins
biology of **11:** 6488
dizygotic (DZ) **6:** 3140; **11:** 6488
genetic factors in cognitive
development **5:** 2465
monozygotic (MZ) **6:** 3140; **11:** 6488,
6491
multiple pregnancy **11:** 6488
personality
and nature nurture controversy
11: 6308
quantitative genetic studies **5:** 2463,
2464
Two-factor theory
and factor analysis **4:** 2230, 2231
Tyler evaluation model **4:** 2080, 2102;
8: 4763
curriculum evaluation **3:** 1279, 1280
curriculum planning **3:** 1329, 1331
Typographic design
computer software for **8:** 4691
discourse issues **8:** 4691
and reading strategy **8:** 4691
research **8:** 4691
typefaces **8:** 4691
Typology
See Classification

Uganda
child-to-child programs **2:** 732
curriculum development **11:** 6500
educational change **11:** 6500
educational finance **11:** 6499
postsecondary education **11:** 6495
primary education **11:** 6495
secondary education **11:** 6495
special education **11:** 6497
student evaluation **11:** 6500
system of education **11:** ***6493–6501***
degrees and qualifications **11:** 6500
educational objectives **11:** 6494
major problems **11:** 6501
structure **11:** 6495
teacher education **11:** 6500
teaching methodology **11:** 6500
Ulpanim
Hebrew language
adult education **1:** 136
Hebrew as a second language **7:** 3846
Underachievement
gifted **5:** 2488
language acquisition
and cultural discontinuities **6:** 3226
and second language instruction
6: 3236
Undereducation **7:** 4254
Underemployment
developing nations **3:** 1682
and job skill requirements **11:** 6257
Understanding
and assignments **9:** 5360
categories of description **8:** 4424
and cognitive processes **6:** 3341
and concept maps **2:** 1029
and heuristics **10:** 6176
realist constructivism **2:** 1049
See also
Verstehen
Uneducated labor
labor market stratification model
6: 3181
supply and demand analysis **6:** 3179
Unemployment
and adult education **4:** 1973; **6:** 3420;
8: 4821
participation **6:** 3377
and employment contracts **3:** 1697
factors affecting
dual labor market theory **6:** 3185
schools **11:** 6700
and job training **7:** 4257
and Keynesian economics **3:** 1697
and nonformal education **4:** 2367
and on-the-job training **6:** 3616
orthodox vs. radical explanation
3: 1698
and outreach programs **7:** 4247
problem of educated **8:** 4838
training programs **6:** 3420
and selection bias **9:** 5382
and vocational education
programs **11:** 6687
See also
Youth unemployment
Unemployment rate
and disabilities **11:** 6457
in screening hypothesis **9:** 5354
UNESCO
adult basic education **5:** 2933
adult education **1:** 153, 158; **5:** 2947;
11: ***6501–6507***
Anglophone Africa **1:** 212
concepts of **1:** 178
conferences **5:** 2946, 2947
definition of **1:** 113
and distance education conferences
6: 3420
Latin America **6:** 3254
legislation **6:** 3362
normative role **11:** 6502
publications **1:** 141
recommendations **6:** 3362;
11: 6502, 6503
regional agencies **5:** 2932
terminology **1:** 119
Asia Pacific Program of Education for
All (APPEAL) **1:** 353; **6:** 3463,
3464
Asian Center of Educational
Innovation for Development
(ACEID)
educational technology, activities
4: 1879
Asian Cultural Center **6:** 3464
basic education **1:** 465
comparative education surveys **2:** 950
Conferences on Adult Education
6: 3254, 3417, 3419; **11:** 6503
and educational administration
international **5:** 2951
educational development
activities **11:** 6526
priority themes **11:** 6526
educational finance
statistics **5:** 2979
educational planning **8:** 4501
Arab nations **8:** 4483
Asia **8:** 4486, 4488
educational statistics **5:** 2988
educational technology **3:** 1800
evaluation of literacy programs **1:** 175
Exchange Network on Literacy and
Postliteracy in Developed and
Developing Countries
11: 6505
functional literacy campaign
Liberia **1:** 214

fundamental education program **5:** 2932
information sources
comparative education **3:** 1584, 1586
Innovation, Technology and Research Section (ITR) **4:** 1878
international adult education **5:** 2933
and International Baccalaureate **5:** 2956
International Committee for the Advancement of Adult Education **6:** 3418, 3420
international statistical data **2:** 958, 959
labor force planning
and educational planning **6:** 3609
lifelong learning **4:** 2184; **6:** 3420; **8:** 4958
programs **1:** 178
promotion **6:** 3417, 3420
literacy education **1:** 132
literacy programs **6:** 3453
Asia **6:** 3464
Medium-Term Plan (1990–95) **11:** 6503
adult basic education **11:** 6505
adult education **11:** 6506
and nonformal education **7:** 4142
promotion of intellectual co-operation **11:** 6505
promotion of international education **5:** 2973
Regional Center on Higher Education (CRESALC)
documentation systems **3:** 1591
right to learn declaration **11:** 6502, 6504
science education
surveys **9:** 5328
special education programs **5:** 2966
objectives **5:** 2967
special needs in the classroom project **2:** 728
statistical comparisons of literacy **6:** 3475
statistics on nonformal education **1:** ***94–100***
technical cooperation **11:** 6506
textbooks
provision **11:** 6361, 6362
Universal Copyright Convention **2:** 1100
world education indicators **5:** 2984, 2988
World Education Reports **5:** 2988
and literacy **6:** 3468
World Surveys of Education (1950s and 1960s) **5:** 2988
UNESCO Institute for Education (UIE) **3:** 1585; **11:** 6506
adult education instructional materials **1:** 141
basic education programs **11:** 6528
foreign language instruction
primary schools **4:** 2347
lifelong learning **1:** 179; **5:** 2947; **11:** 6528
literacy network **5:** 2935
literacy programs **11:** 6527
nonformal education **7:** 4133
UNFPA
See United Nations Fund for Population Activities (UNFPA)
UNICEF
early intervention
and child development **3:** 1626
educational technology
activities **4:** 1880
special education **5:** 2969
Unidimensionality
and achievement tests **1:** 33
and Thurstone scales **11:** 6385
Unintended effects
in educational research **11:** ***6507–6511***
sources of **11:** 6507
after effects **11:** 6510
Golem effect **11:** 6509
Hawthorne effect **11:** 6508
John Henry effect **11:** 6509
reactive measurement effects **11:** 6508
self-fulfilling prophesies **11:** 6509
side effects **11:** 6510
Unions **10:** ***6073–6079***
and academic achievement
empirical research **10:** 6070
and adult education **5:** 2932; **8:** 4810
and apprenticeships **1:** 108
Germany **1:** 311
as a barrier to school enterprise **9:** 5232
benefits of **10:** 6072
and collective bargaining
personnel management **8:** 4407
consolidation of **10:** 6075
cost effects
categories of **10:** 6072
developments **10:** 6077
economics of **10:** ***6068–6073***
education
effects on **10:** 6068
and educational finance
effects on **5:** 2507
effect on resource allocation **10:** 6069
effects on decentralization **5:** 2793
and employer employee relationship **5:** 2794
formation of
factors preventing **10:** 6073
factors required **10:** 6073
fragmentation of **10:** 6077
government relationship with **10:** 6075
growth of **10:** 6073
industrial agendas in **10:** 6074
international role of **10:** 6078
and investment in training **11:** 6418, 6419
and labor education **11:** 6770, 6771
and labor relations **6:** 3190
and legitimatory research **6:** 3371
membership **10:** 6077
militancy **10:** 6076
new
formation of **10:** 6075
and paid educational leave **7:** 4262
participation in literacy programs **8:** 4637
and primary segment employment **8:** 4837
and productivity
costs **10:** 6071
professional recognition
teachers **1:** 435
and professional standards and practices boards **10:** 5928
and school-based management **1:** 592; **9:** 5306
and sponsored apprenticeships **1:** 307
state incorporation **10:** 6074
and teacher associations **6:** 3191
teachers
and industrial democracy **10:** 6137
and power structure **8:** 4584
and vocational education
effect on policies **11:** 6697
See also
Collective bargaining
Unit costs
comparative analysis
effect on Latin America **3:** 1832
continuing education **2:** 1150
and expenditures
studies **2:** 1123
factors affecting
technology **2:** 1124
Unit for the Development of Continuing Adult Education (UK)
educational guidance **2:** 1163
United Arab Emirates
curriculum development **11:** 6514
educational change **11:** 6515
educational finance **11:** 6514
educational research **11:** 6515
government school relationship
school administration **11:** 6513
index of segregation **4:** 2430
postsecondary education **11:** 6513
preschool education **11:** 6513
primary education **11:** 6513
secondary education **11:** 6513
special education **11:** 6513
structure of government **11:** 6512
system of education **11:** ***6511–6515***
degrees and qualifications **11:** 6514
educational objectives **11:** 6512
major problems **11:** 6515
structure **11:** 6512
teacher education **11:** 6514
teacher recruitment **11:** 6514
technical education **11:** 6513
United Kingdom (UK)
academic records **8:** 4618
access courses **8:** 4606, 4608
adult basic education **1:** 101, 102
adult education **1:** 125; **10:** 5638

colleges **11:** 6689
financial support **10:** 5592
and local education authorities **10:** 5638
participation **10:** 5638
participation rates **1:** 104
provision **10:** 5638
telecommunications **1:** 561
use of term **1:** 111
adult educators
teacher education **11:** 6431
andragogy **1:** 275, 276
apprenticeships **1:** 314
modular programs **11:** 6685
attendance
and truancy **3:** 1603
Campus 2000 network **10:** 6008
Central Labour College **2:** 1190
child care services **2:** 695
civic education **2:** 767
colleges of further education **1:** 182; **2:** 895, 896; **10:** 5639
community education **2:** 902, 907
competency-based education **1:** 71
computer uses in education **11:** 6689
and media programs **7:** 3755
organizations for **2:** 1014
curriculum
historical background **9:** 5297
curriculum development **11:** 6520
vocational education **11:** 6668
department of education **3:** 1723
development education **3:** 1498
economic development
postwar **11:** 6685
educational administration
administrator selection **1:** 79, 80
inservice education **1:** 69
theories of **9:** 5162
educational change **11:** 6521
and governance **5:** 2510
educational history
immigrants **7:** 3844
minority groups **7:** 3844
educational planning
conflict **8:** 4598
educational reform
historical background **9:** 5277
educational research **8:** 4558; **11:** 6521
action research **1:** 45
curriculum coverage **4:** 1935
educational technology
professional training **4:** 1927
educational television
research studies **5:** 2895
effective schools
studies **4:** 1932
foreign language instruction **4:** 2354
foundation programs **8:** 4606
governance
schools **6:** 3493
government policies
and vocational education **11:** 6688
government school relationship
and educational reform **9:** 5277
grant maintained schools **1:** 591; **9:** 5278
higher education
profiles **8:** 4621
and student fees **10:** 5750
tuition fees **10:** 5752, 5753
immigrant education
legislation **7:** 3845
income contingent loans **10:** 5764
Industrial Language Training project **6:** 3210, 3211
industrial training boards **11:** 6685
criticism of **11:** 6685
decline of **11:** 6687
industrial training costs **2:** 1149
job analysis
surveys **6:** 3092
labor education **11:** 6771
labor force surveys **7:** 3713
labor relations
affiliations **6:** 3196
in education **6:** 3193
learning strategies project **6:** 3347
levy–grant system
criticisms of **8:** 4361; **11:** 6685
local education authorities
role of **6:** 3495
longitudinal studies **6:** 3512
mainstreaming
legislation **3:** 1506
process **5:** 2907
mathematics education
surveys **8:** 4644
meritocracy **7:** 3769
minority groups
and discipline concerns **3:** 1535
multicultural education **7:** 3845
multimedia systems
Doomsday Project **7:** 3994
nontraditional students
higher education **7:** ***4163–4171***
occupations
classification of **7:** 3717
on-the-job training **1:** 109
Open College project **10:** 5639
oracy testing **6:** 3470
organizational development
characteristics of **7:** 4238
trends **7:** 4239
paid educational leave **7:** 4262
performance contracts
historical background **8:** 4708
political education
curriculum **8:** 4569
historical background **8:** 4569
program **4:** 1981
polytechnical education **8:** 4606, 4607
polytechnics **10:** 5639
postsecondary education **11:** 6517, 6666
initiatives **11:** 6665
preschool education **8:** 4667, 4669; **11:** 6518
studies **8:** 4665
primary education **11:** 6517
primary schools
history instruction **9:** 5575
principals
recruitment **1:** 68
role of **4:** 1930; **9:** 5167, 5270
printing monopolies
and copyrights **2:** 1099
private education **11:** 6517
private schools
Assisted Places Scheme **8:** 4825
professional associations
adult education **8:** 4731, 4732
profiles **8:** 4618
public schools vs. private schools **8:** 4842
public vs. private sector earnings comparison **8:** 4837
publishing industry
instructional materials **8:** 4846
religious education **9:** 5011
research
priorities **9:** 5032
sandwich courses **8:** 4606
school administration
budgeting **9:** 5184
changes in **5:** 2506
control of **9:** 5166
decentralization **9:** 5166
school-based management **5:** 2507; **9:** 5211, 5303, 5304
urban schools **11:** 6560
school business partnerships
evaluation **9:** 5189
government role in **9:** 5187
school choice **5:** 2505; **9:** 5202; **11:** 6556
research **9:** 5194
school inspectors **9:** 5249
school organization
studies **4:** 2159
school reform
influences of **9:** 5278
school size
studies **9:** 5293
science education
history **9:** 5325
research **8:** 4645
second language instruction for immigrants **6:** 3210
secondary education **11:** 6517
parallel institutions **9:** 5386
social class
conflict **9:** 5311
social studies **10:** 5583, 5584
sociology of education
development of **10:** 5599
special education **11:** 6518
special education provision
historical development **2:** 720
state church relationship
accommodation **9:** 5011
state schools
opting out scheme **8:** 4825, 4826
student evaluation **11:** 6520
system of education **11:** ***6515–6523***
degrees and qualifications **11:** 6521
educational objectives **11:** 6516

enrollment **11:** 6516
major problems **11:** 6522
structure **11:** 6516
teacher administrator relationship **9:** 5179
teacher education **11:** 6520
education courses **3:** 1722
teacher recruitment **11:** 6519
teaching
professional recognition **9:** 5178
teaching methods debate **6:** 3454
technology education
programs **11:** 6288
test anxiety
studies **11:** 6358
theater arts **8:** 4384, 4385
training
construction industry **11:** 6636
training and enterprise councils (TECs) **10:** 5639
training statistics **7:** 3713
training survey **11:** 6419
unions
state incorporation **10:** 6074
use of time **6:** 3374
universities **10:** 5639
university extension **2:** 1190
videotex
applications **11:** 6305
historical background **11:** 6301
vocational education **7:** 4206; **8:** 4337
initiatives **11:** ***6685–6690***
learning modules **7:** 3890
postwar history of **11:** 6685
vocational education and training (VET)
Anglo–German comparisons **11:** ***6638–6640***
vocational schools **11:** 6689
working men's colleges **2:** 1190
youth subculture
research **11:** 6800
youth unemployment
and vocational education **11:** 6686
See also
England and Wales
National Curriculum (UK)
Scotland
United Nations (UN)
comparative education **2:** 921
educational co-operation **11:** 6529
and educational planning **8:** 4490
educational research **11:** ***6523–6530***
comparative education **11:** ***6523–6530***
future research **11:** 6529
international education **11:** ***6523–6530***
information sources
comparative education **3:** 1584
institutional response to educational needs **11:** 6525
National Household Survey Capability Program **6:** 3478
population studies
school age **3:** 1451
United Nations Development Programme (UNDP)
educational technology activities **4:** 1880
technical assistance **5:** 3001
United Nations Educational, Scientific, and Cultural Organization
See UNESCO
United Nations Fund for Population Activities (UNFPA)
literacy programs
Asia **6:** 3464
United Nations International Children's Emergency Fund
See UNICEF
United States (US)
academic achievement
national surveys **10:** 6165
administrator education
preservice **1:** 73
adult basic education **1:** 101
legislation **1:** 101
adult education **1:** 121, 122, 124; **7:** 4181
legislation **6:** 3363
and training markets **1:** ***103–111***
use of term **1:** 111
adult educators
teacher education **11:** 6431, 6434
adult literacy programs **2:** 1046
agricultural education
vocational education **1:** 242
andragogy **1:** 275, 277
apprenticeships **1:** 109, 306, 313
main features of **1:** 306
art education **1:** 340
assistive technology
access to **10:** 5669
attendance
and truancy **3:** 1603
black education **8:** 4900
and brain drain **1:** 555, 560
civil rights **8:** 4896, 4900
classroom environment
attitudes to **10:** 5773
communication disorders
prevalence of **11:** 6704
community-based education
compared with community education **2:** 900
community colleges **4:** 2388, 2391; **6:** 3418
community education **2:** 907
comparative achievement data **4:** 2137
computer literacy for females **4:** 2426
computer-managed learning **2:** 999
computer uses in education **11:** 6284
organizations for **2:** 1014
continuing education expenditure **2:** 1147
curriculum
historical background **3:** 1296; **9:** 5297
curriculum development **11:** 6544
curriculum development centers **3:** 1274
day care market **2:** ***688–693***
day care programs for toddlers **11:** 6396
decentralization
research **1:** 592
development education **3:** 1497
distance education
broadcasting **3:** 1575
research **3:** 1567
in schools **3:** 1566
teleconferencing **3:** 1576
dropout rate **3:** 1604
early childhood programs **5:** 2807
early intervention
infants and toddlers **5:** 2809
education
and economic growth **3:** 1660, 1663; **5:** 2646
rate of return **8:** 4916
educational administration
inservice education **1:** 69
theories of **1:** 62
educational change **11:** 6546
research studies **6:** 3599
educational development
and labor market **6:** 3183
educational evaluation **4:** 2111
educational finance
and school organization **7:** 4232
educational funding and accountability **7:** 4057
educational history
immigrants **7:** 3840
indigenous populations **7:** 3841
minority groups **7:** 3840
educational personnel evaluation **4:** ***2123–2132***
educational planning **3:** 1808
strategic **8:** 4600
educational policy
minority groups **8:** 4589
teacher role in **10:** 6080
educational radio
studies **5:** 2890
educational reform **7:** 4053
AMERICA 2000 program **3:** 1358; **7:** 4053
historical background **9:** 5276
participation in **4:** 1855
and urban schools **11:** 6559
educational research **11:** 6545
action research **1:** 45
descriptive scales **3:** 1477
politics of **8:** 4602
priorities **9:** 5037
questioning techniques **8:** 4876
educational technology
professional training **4:** 1927
educational television
large-scale projects **5:** 2892
effective schools research **9:** 5276
longitudinal studies **9:** 5377
studies **4:** 1936
employment patterns

and technological advancement
11: 6258
employment projections
demand occupations **11:** 6258
equal education **4:** 2426
and resource allocation **9:** 5063
equal opportunities (jobs)
research **11:** 6677
ethnic groups **11:** 6539
educational attainment **8:** 4892
ethnicity
and national unity **7:** 3966
evaluation for school improvement
4: ***2381–2389***
evaluation standards **4:** 2117;
8: ***4736–4751***
farmer education and productivity
3: 1665
females
and curriculum development
4: 2291
in educational administration
11: ***6727–6731***
film study **8:** 4387
foreign language instruction policy
4: 2340
gifted
minority groups **5:** 2487
governance
schools **6:** 3494
government school relationship
and educational reform **9:** 5276
grade repetition **5:** 2514
hearing impairments
in adults **10:** 5689
national surveys **10:** 5687
high schools
and educational change **6:** 3599
science education **9:** 5325
higher education
and student fees **10:** 5752
immigrants
earnings **5:** 2738
industrial training costs **2:** 1148
institutional support for independent
study **9:** 5395
investment in education **4:** 2208
job analysis
surveys **6:** 3092
job training **7:** 4197
program evaluation **4:** 2147
labor education **1:** 129; **11:** 6769,
6770
labor force development in **5:** 2686,
2688
labor force surveys **11:** 6416, 6417,
6419
labor relations
in education **6:** 3190, 3194
learning disabilities
educational strategies **10:** 5684
prevalence **10:** 5683
learning strategies
teaching of **6:** 3336
literacy
and culture programs **6:** 3455
low achievement **8:** 4933
programs **7:** 4146, 4147
studies **8:** 4635
mathematics curriculum
secondary schools **6:** 3664
mathematics instruction
curriculum and evaluation
standards **6:** 3664
minimum competency testing
and test bias **11:** 6318
monitoring national standards
7: ***4051–4054***
multicultural education **7:** 3969
multimedia systems **7:** 3995
multiple choice tests **11:** 6329
music education **7:** 4017
music teachers
education of **7:** 4029
occupations
classification of **7:** 3717
organizational development
historical background **7:** 4236
overeducation
and employment **1:** 518
parent participation **9:** 5213
studies **1:** 593
peer teaching **11:** 6482
programs **10:** 6162
performance contracts
historical background **8:** 4709
personnel management
case study **8:** 4405
and collective bargaining **8:** 4407
and educational reform **8:** 4407
national trends **8:** 4405
policy analysis **8:** 4553
postsecondary education **11:** 6541
financial support for **11:** 6534
preschool education **8:** 4668, 4670;
11: 6382, 6542
primary education **11:** 6540
primary schools
social studies in **9:** 5574
principals
recruitment **1:** 68
role of **4:** 1930; **9:** 5167, 5270
private education
vs. public education **1:** 589
productivity
effect of education on **3:** 1694
professional associations
adult education **8:** 4731, 4734
program evaluation requirement
8: 4763
progressive education movement
6: 3454
public education
school districts **4:** 2078
public policy
schools for **8:** 4554
public schools vs. private schools
research **8:** 4840
race earnings differentials
8: ***4896–4902***
reading tests **6:** 3471
returns to education **5:** 2644
school administration
centralization **6:** 3494
decentralization **9:** 5165
school-based management **1:** 592;
9: 5211, 5303, 5304
school business partnerships
evaluation **9:** 5190
school choice **8:** 4825; **11:** 6556
policy issues **9:** 5195
research **9:** 5194
school desegregation
effective schools research **9:** 5375
school districts
role of **6:** 3495
school effectiveness
studies **1:** 593
school enterprise
studies **9:** 5231
school organization
studies **4:** 2159
school personnel
related services **9:** 5281
school reform
influences of **9:** 5278
school restructuring **5:** 2849
nongraded instructional grouping
7: 4156
school role
and decentralization **5:** 2602
school size
studies **9:** 5291, 5293
schools
resource allocation in **9:** 5061
science education
American Project 2061 **8:** 4461
science education history **9:** 5325
secondary education **11:** 6540
selection **9:** 5386
sex differences
and outcomes of education **9:** 5423
research **9:** 5425
social class
conflict **9:** 5311
social studies
trends **9:** 5582
sociology of education
development of **10:** 5598
special education **2:** 724; **10:** 5659
legislation **2:** 721
use of curriculum-based assessment
3: 1357
state church separation **9:** 5012
student evaluation **11:** 6545
portfolios **8:** 4622
student loan programs **10:** 5763
student teaching
field experience programs **10:** 5809
study circles **10:** 5829
system of education **11:** ***6538–6547***
educational objectives **11:** 6539
enrollment **11:** 6541, 6542
major problems **11:** 6546
structure **11:** 6540
teacher administrator relationship
9: 5179
teacher certification

alternatives to **10:** 6037
and standards **10:** ***5925–5930***
teacher education **11:** 6544
accreditation **1:** 25, 26
teacher licensing by states **4:** 2126
teacher militancy **6:** 3192
teacher recruitment **11:** 6544
teacher salaries **10:** 5611
variations **9:** 5062
teachers
social mobility of **10:** 5610
teaching methodology **11:** 6544
teleclassrooms **11:** 6304
teleconferencing **11:** 6305
textbook publication **11:** 6369
textbook selection **11:** 6368
textbooks
historical background **11:** 6367
theater arts **8:** 4384
transition programs
and disabilities **11:** 6460
tribal colleges **2:** 905
union participation in literacy programs **8:** 4637
unions
membership levels **10:** 6068
university adult education **11:** 6549, 6550
admission criteria **11:** 6548, 6549
urban schools
dropout rate **5:** 2688
governance **11:** 6554
videotex
applications **11:** 6305
vocational education **1:** 112; **11:** 6683
disadvantaged youth **11:** 6249
federal policy **11:** ***6530–6538***
proprietary schools **8:** 4794
youth apprenticeships
proposals for **1:** 309
youth culture
research **11:** 6799
See also
North America
United States Agency for International Development (USAID)
and educational radio
interactive **5:** 2887
and educational research
Latin America **3:** 1590
educational technology
activities **4:** 1878
Units of study
lesson structure **6:** ***3385–3389***
Univariate analysis
and surveys **10:** 5860
Universal Copyright Convention (UCC) **2:** 1100, 1101
Universal Declaration of Human Rights 1948 (UN)
and education **11:** 6503
and school choice **9:** 5192
Universal education
See Equal education
Universal primary education (UPE) **1:** 169, 465
and democracy **1:** 467
and educational quality **1:** 472
francophone Africa **1:** 216
and population trends **3:** 1452
and promotion of literacy **6:** 3451
UNESCO campaign **1:** 465, 466
Universe scores
See True scores
Universities
adult education **1:** 89, 92; **11:** ***6547–6551***
alternative teaching and learning models **11:** 6549
characteristics of **11:** 6548
definitions and terms **11:** 6547
distance education **11:** 6549, 6550
extension programs **5:** 2732, 2733
financial support **11:** 6549
graduate programs (US) **1:** 122
national enrollment patterns **11:** 6548
national policy support structures **11:** 6549
New Zealand **1:** 413
policies **11:** 6550
trends and developments **11:** 6550
adult educators
teacher education **11:** 6432
Arab nations **1:** 322
changing definition of **11:** 6547
and comparative education **2:** 934
Costa Rica **2:** 1142
courseware
publication **10:** 5619
departments of education
United Kingdom **3:** 1723
and distance education **3:** 1570
dual mode
Australia **7:** 4216
educational history **5:** 2614
entrance tests
and predictive validity **11:** 6571
Ethiopia **4:** 2039
and extension education
history of adult education **1:** 136, 137
faculty
political attitudes **10:** 5776
female access to **5:** 2454
females in
Australia **11:** 6734
Germany **11:** 6746
India **11:** 6751
North America **11:** 6763
historical development of **9:** 5121
and history of vocational education
United States **11:** 6683
and industrial training
Europe **4:** 2061
influence of Descartes' theories on **3:** 1463
Jamaica **6:** 3071
laboratory packages **6:** 3203
links with business **8:** 4338
links with community colleges **2:** 899
Mongolia **7:** 3899
and open education **7:** 4216
Panama **7:** 4271
and participatory research **7:** 4333
private education
excess demand model **8:** 4834
and public schools
Carnegie Task Force **9:** 5315
Holmes Group **9:** 5315
teacher education **9:** 5314, 5316, 5317
recognition of women's studies **11:** 6767
role of
in technology transfer **11:** 6280
scholasticism in medieval **9:** 5121, 5123
small business training **4:** 1987
and student evaluations of teacher effectiveness **10:** 6232
teacher education
doctoral programs **10:** 5997
and field experience programs **10:** 5811
historical background **3:** 1721, 1723
programs **10:** 5996
and schools **10:** 5585
and teachers as researchers **10:** 5585
teaching guides for **10:** 6114
and vocational education
Japan **6:** 3087
See also
Open universities
People's universities
Universities without walls
See Open universities
University of the Air (Japan) **1:** 349, 561, 562; **4:** 2388
courses **1:** 109
historical background **6:** 3077
University of California (US)
and policy analysis **8:** 4552
University Council for Educational Administration (UCEA) (US) **1:** 53, 76
activities of **5:** 2952
University extension
See Extension education
University industry relationship
training with production **11:** 6450
University of London (UK)
Institute of Education
comparative education **2:** 935
University role
See College role
University of Sussex (UK)
Institute of Developmental Studies (IDS) **2:** 937
University of the Third Age **7:** 4169, 4247
Unskilled workers
employment opportunities **6:** 3182
Upper Volta
See Burkina Faso

Urania Houses
  Austria and Germany **1:** 137, 138
Urban areas
  living standards **11:** 6557
Urban education **11:** ***6551–6558***
  dropout rate **9:** 5227
  and finance reform **11:** 6557
  and urban environment
    changes **11:** 6552
  vs. rural education
    and educational finance **3:** 1791
Urban environment
  changes
    and urban education **11:** 6552
Urban language
  bilingualism
    communicative competence **6:** 3236
Urban Native Indian Education Society
    (Canada) **7:** 4183
Urban population
  reduction in
    and urban education **11:** 6552
Urban problems
  municipalities **11:** 6559
  poverty **11:** 6552
Urban rural differences
  See Rural urban differences
Urban to rural migration
  and quality of life **1:** 240
  and urban education **11:** 6552
Urban schools **11:** ***6558–6563***
  academic climate **11:** 6554
  accountability **11:** 6561
  and bureaucracy **11:** 6554
  characteristics of **11:** 6559
  culture conflicts in **2:** 915
  educational finance for **11:** 6555
  and educational reform **11:** 6552, 6555, 6559
    future trends **11:** 6562
    programatic investment **11:** 6556
    strategies **11:** 6557
  environmental influences **11:** 6551
    ecological **11:** 6553
  evaluation **11:** 6561
  governance **11:** 6554
  interventions **11:** 6562
  problems **11:** 6558
  and school choice **11:** 6560
Urban teaching
  and teacher burnout **10:** 5921
Urbanization
  and educational policy **5:** 2510
  and female enrollment rate **4:** 2408
  labor force participation
    females **3:** 1667
Urinary incontinence **3:** 1516
Uruguay
  adult education **6:** 3253; **11:** 6565
  cultural influences **11:** 6563
  curriculum development **11:** 6566
  educational change **11:** 6567
  educational finance **11:** 6565
  educational research **11:** 6567
  postsecondary education **11:** 6565
  preschool education **11:** 6565
  primary education **11:** 6564
  secondary education **11:** 6564
    vocational education **11:** 6565
  special education **11:** 6565
  structure of government **11:** 6564
  system of education **11:** ***6563–6567***
    degrees and qualifications **11:** 6566
    educational objectives **11:** 6564
    major problems **11:** 6567
    structure **11:** 6564
  teacher education **11:** 6566
  teacher recruitment **11:** 6566
  vocational education
    for the disadvantaged **7:** 4151
User needs (computer systems)
  multimedia systems **7:** 3988
User needs (information)
  and educational innovation **3:** 1552
  and management information systems **6:** 3595
  and search strategies **5:** 2821
Users (information)
  libraries **6:** 3394, 3397
    characteristics of **6:** 3397
  and multimedia systems design **7:** 3989
  and operational contexts **3:** 1551
USSR
  See Soviet Union (USSR) (former)
Utilitarianism
  and curriculum development **3:** 1326
    United Kingdom **3:** 1294
  educational theories **2:** 1066
  and human capital theory **2:** 1066
  and justice **4:** 2002
  and knowledge in curriculum **6:** 3149
  moral values **7:** 3915
  and public choice theory **2:** 1066
  and rights **4:** 2030
Uzbekistan
  employment
    and education **10:** 5648
  vocational education
    policies **10:** 5647
  vocational schools
    rural **10:** 5648

Validated programs
  adult education **2:** 662, 663
Validity **11:** ***6569–6576***
  and achievement tests **11:** 6321
  convergent **4:** 2383; **7:** 4001
  in cross-national comparisons **4:** 2133
  curricular
    and tests **11:** 6321
    use of indexes of **11:** 6325
  definitions of **11:** 6569
    new **11:** 6573
  and descriptive scales **3:** 1476, 1480
  discriminant **7:** 4001
  in educational research
    and videotape recordings **11:** 6607
  and expectancy tables **4:** 2181
  and experimental studies **4:** 2188
  external **4:** 2084
    and attitude measures **1:** 387
    and experimental studies **4:** 2189
  internal **4:** 2084
    and experimental studies **4:** 2188
  and longitudinal studies **6:** 3519
  nonquantitative methods **11:** 6573
  and political correctness **11:** 6574
  problem-solving tests **8:** 4730
  and questionnaires **8:** 4885
  and reliability **9:** 4981
  statistical conclusion **4:** 2084
    and experimental studies **4:** 2189
  strategies **11:** 6574
  and test bias **11:** 6316
  theoretical **11:** 6327
  types of **11:** 6570
  See also
    Concurrent validity
    Construct validity
    Content validity;
    Predictive validity
    Test validity
Value judgment
  and cultural pluralism **1:** 379
  in educational research **11:** 6576
Values
  in civic education
    nationalism **2:** 769
  concept of **11:** 6576
  conflicts **1:** 378
    and educational change **4:** 1850
  contextual factors **1:** 379
  cultural
    discontinuities in **1:** 291
  cultural pluralism
    public and private schools **8:** 4829
  and curriculum
    adult education **3:** 1310
  and educational administration **1:** 59, 65; **3:** 1771
  in educational objectives **11:** 6578
  in educational research **9:** 5024
  and moral development
    parental influence **8:** 4457
  philosophical issues **11:** ***6576–6580***
  pluralism
    and evaluation **4:** 2370, 2371
    and problems of child rearing **8:** 4457
  and postmodernism **8:** 4642
  respect for human life **11:** 6577, 6579
  and science
    attitudes toward **9:** 5322
  vertical organization (Hodgkinson) **3:** 1771
  See also
    Aesthetic values
    Democratic values
    Moral values
    Social values
Values clarification **1:** 378
  geography instruction **5:** 2466
Values education **1:** ***377–380***
  civic education **2:** 767
  and dogmatism **7:** 3922
  and humanities **5:** 2694
  indoctrination vs. value relativism **1:** 379

Kerschensteiner's pedagogy **6:** 3136
and literacy **11:** 6776
pluralism **7:** 3922
and relativism **7:** 3922
teachers' beliefs **10:** 6101
Van der Waerden test
nonparametric statistics **7:** 4159
Vanuatu
curriculum development **11:** 6584
educational change **11:** 6585
educational finance **11:** 6583
ethnic groups **11:** 6580
government school relationship
school administration **11:** 6583
language **11:** 6580
postsecondary education **11:** 6582
preschool education **11:** 6582
primary education **11:** 6581
private education **11:** 6582
secondary education **11:** 6581
system of education **11:** ***6580–6586***
degrees and qualifications **11:** 6584
educational objectives **11:** 6580
major problems **11:** 6585
structure **11:** 6581
teacher education **11:** 6583
teacher recruitment **11:** 6583
teaching methodology **11:** 6584
technical education **11:** 6582
vocational education **11:** 6582
Variables
continuous **2:** 1109
control **2:** 1112
correlation of **2:** 1107, 1109
dichotomous **2:** 1109
manifest
and partial least squares analysis **8:** 4353
and path analysis **8:** 4352
polychotomous **2:** 1109
relationship between
and multivariate analysis **7:** 4007
Variance
and canonical analysis **2:** 629
in classical test theory **2:** 786, 791
and correlation **2:** 1108, 1112
definition of **7:** 3727
and discriminant analysis **3:** 1546
estimates of
pooled **7:** 3729
in generalizability theory **5:** 2458
and item sampling **5:** 3056
and meta analysis **7:** 3782
in models of intelligence **7:** 3878
and reliability **9:** 4982, 4984
and sampling errors **9:** 5124
See also
Analysis of variance (ANOVA)
Variation
Variation
characteristics of **7:** 3726
coefficient of **7:** 3730
measures of **7:** ***3726–3739***
associated with the mean **7:** 3727
associated with the median **7:** 3732
clustering **7:** 3734
distribution shapes **7:** 3732
range **7:** 3727
variance **7:** 3727
See also
Variance
Venezuela
adult education **11:** 6596
concentrated wealth
and governance **5:** 2510
curriculum development **11:** 6597
educational change **11:** 6598
educational finance **11:** 6596
central control of **2:** 913
ethnic groups **11:** 6592
government school relationship
school administration **11:** 6596
individualized instruction **5:** 2772
postsecondary education **11:** 6594
preschool education **11:** 6595
primary education **11:** 6593
private education **11:** 6594, 6597
problem-solving
teaching of **8:** 4729
public education finance
effect of economic adjustment on **3:** 1787
secondary education **11:** 6592, 6594
special education **11:** 6595
structure of government **11:** 6592
system of education **11:** ***6591–6600***
dg **11:** 6598
educational objectives **11:** 6592
enrollment **11:** 6592, 6593
historical background **11:** 6592
major problems **11:** 6599
structure **11:** 6593
teacher education **11:** 6597
teacher recruitment **11:** 6597
university adult education **11:** 6550
Verbal ability
and aging (individuals) **1:** 235
process analyses **1:** 3
sex differences in **9:** 5427, 5444
sources of individual differences **1:** 3
and twin studies **11:** 6491
Verbal auditory agnosia
characteristics of **10:** 5676
Verbal communication
in interviews **5:** 3005
and learning strategies
evaluation **6:** 3338
and message design **7:** 3772
and voice disorders **1:** 404
Verbal development
vocabulary development **6:** 3220
production of sentences **6:** 3220
Verbal dyspraxia
characteristics of **10:** 5677
Verbal learning **6:** 3316
and audiovisual aids **7:** 3744
Verbal tests
reasoning
characteristics of **11:** 6347
See also
Language tests
Verbalization
cognitive processes
and heuristics **10:** 6175
Verstehen
and biographical research **1:** 538
in comparative education **2:** 919
Dilthey **5:** 2580; **8:** 4453
and educational administration **3:** 1772
interpretive paradigm **9:** 5022
Weber's sociology of education **2:** 781
Vertical mobility
See Social mobility
Vertical organization
in capitalism
and education **7:** 3770
formation
school role in **9:** 5174
Vestibular apparatus
in fetus **1:** 12
Veterans education **4:** 2184
Victorian Science Achievement Study **10:** 5789
Video cameras
See Video equipment
Video display terminals
and health problems **4:** 2010
Video equipment
and education
developing nations **4:** 1902
and educational research **11:** 6605
standards **1:** 403
uses in education **1:** 401
Video games
participation
children and youth **1:** 565
Videodisc recordings
See Videodiscs
Videodiscs
characteristics of **5:** 2896; **7:** 3751; **11:** 6600, 6606
and computer-assisted instruction
special needs students **10:** 5671
constant angular velocity (CAV) **11:** 6600
constant linear velocity (CLV) **11:** 6600
formats **11:** 6600
and hypermedia environments **2:** 885
in language laboratories **6:** 3240
production of **7:** 3990
and teacher effectiveness **10:** 5670
Videotape cassettes
and copyrights **2:** 1102
Videotape recorders
availability of **5:** 2896
barriers to use of **11:** 6286
characteristics of **11:** 6605
foreign language instruction **4:** 2354
Videotape recordings
applications **7:** 3752
educational **5:** ***2891–2897***
as educational media **7:** 3751
in educational research **11:** ***6604–6608***

analytic issues **11:** 6607
settings for **11:** 6606
techniques **11:** 6606
uses **11:** 6604
validity **11:** 6607
formats **11:** 6606
and learning **6:** 3299
technical considerations **11:** 6605
and television
children and youth **1:** 565
vs. films **7:** 3752
Videotex
applications **11:** 6305
characteristics of **11:** 6302
historical background **11:** 6301
Vietnam
adult education **1:** 352; **11:** 6611
curriculum development **11:** 6612
educational change **11:** 6613
educational finance **11:** 6612
educational research **11:** 6613
ethnic groups **11:** 6609
government school relationship
school administration **11:** 6611
literacy campaigns **1:** 170, 171
literacy education **6:** 3464, 3465
nonformal education **7:** 4134
nonverbal communication
in classrooms **7:** 4173
smiling **7:** 4173
preschool education **11:** 6610
primary education **11:** 6610
secondary education **11:** 6610
vocational education **11:** 6611
system of education **11:** ***6608–6614***
degrees and qualifications **11:** 6613
educational objectives **11:** 6609
enrollment **11:** 6610
major problems **11:** 6613
structure **11:** 6610
teacher education **11:** 6612
teacher recruitment **11:** 6612
Vintage effects
and cohort size **11:** 6615
and education **11:** ***6614–6615***
interpretations of **11:** 6614
measurement of **11:** 6614
Violence
and idolatry
Judaic theory **6:** 3118
and peace education **3:** 1730
and television research **1:** 569
Virgin Islands
occupational segregation **4:** 2430
Vision
and aging (individuals) **8:** 4818
representation in
concept maps **2:** 1026
system of
effect of deprivation of stimuli
1: 553
Visual acuity
assessment
school health services **5:** 2573
infants **8:** 4381
measurement **11:** 6625
Visual aids
and audiovisual instruction **1:** 402
classification problems **10:** 5726
computer uses for **10:** 5729
concept maps **2:** 1027
and formal education **7:** 3744
and message design **7:** 3772
production of **10:** ***5726–5730***
changes **10:** 5726
selection criteria **10:** 5729
still pictures
applications **7:** 3746
characteristics of **7:** 3746
Visual arts
aesthetic preferences **11:** 6617
industrial arts
Bauhaus **1:** 340
instructional psychology
11: ***6616–6618***
and moral education **11:** 6616
teacher education **11:** ***6618–6621***
admission criteria **11:** 6620
curriculum development **11:** 6619
educational quality **11:** 6620
future trends **11:** 6619
knowledge base **11:** 6619
models and programs **11:** 6618
pedagogy **11:** 6619
responsibilities **11:** 6620
theory practice relationship
11: 6621
teacher education programs
administration **11:** 6620
validated **11:** 6620
Visual display units
See Video display terminals
Visual equipment
See Visual aids
Visual impairments
and assistive technology **10:** 5670
congenital impairments
effects on development **11:** 6626
definitions and criteria **11:** 6625
demographic characteristics **11:** 6625
developmental characteristics
11: 6626
etiology **11:** 6625
issues in education **11:** 6627
and multiple disabilities **11:** 6626
and reading difficulties **10:** 5679
special classes **11:** 6626
special education **10:** 5659;
11: ***6625–6628***
computer-assisted instruction
11: 6627
history **11:** 6626
itinerant teachers **11:** 6626
provision and models of service
11: 6626
residential schools **11:** 6626
resource room programs **11:** 6626
teaching methods **11:** 6627
vocational education **11:** 6627
special programs **11:** 6627
Visual Interests Test (TTVIT)
and vocational evaluation **11:** 6672
Visual literacy **11:** ***6622–6625***
courses **11:** 6624
curriculum issues **11:** 6623
definitions of **11:** 6622
official **11:** 6623
domains of **11:** 6624
and educational television **5:** 2896
historical background **11:** 6622
and message design **7:** 3772
perspectives **11:** 6624
teaching issues **11:** 6623
theoretical framework **11:** 6622
Visual materials
See Visual aids
Visual media
See Visual aids
Visual perception
cognitive or indirect approach **8:** 4377
color
infants **8:** 4381
ecological or direct approach **8:** 4378
Gibsonian theory **8:** 4378
hypothesis testing theory **8:** 4378
illusion research **8:** 4378
impoverished stimuli research **8:** 4378
and intelligence **5:** 2760
and learning **8:** ***4376–4379***
and message design **7:** 3773
and movement
optic flow **8:** 4378
psychological process **8:** 4376
psychological theories
elementary attributes **8:** 4377
Gestalt theory **8:** 4377
scanning
infants **8:** 4381
size constancy **8:** 4377
See also
Depth perception
Visual acuity
Visual stimuli
responses by fetus to **1:** 13
and smallest space analysis **9:** 5501
and test bias **11:** 6319
Visualization **1:** 3; **6:** 3135, 3287
and visual literacy **11:** 6624
vs. verbal information **2:** 886
Vitamin A compounds
and congenital impairment **1:** 14
Vocabulary
controlled
and indexing **5:** 2819
second languages
and reading comprehension **8:** 4938
tests
characteristics of **11:** 6347
Vocabulary development
and hearing impairments **10:** 5688
preschool children **4:** 1962
Vocabulary skills
and reading comprehension tests
7: 3932
Vocational adjustment
career education
and disabilities **2:** 632

Vocational agriculture education (VAE)
See Agricultural education, vocational education
Vocational aptitude
definitions of **11:** 6669
measures **11:** ***6669–6678***
alternative methods **11:** 6676
equity issues **11:** 6676
innovations **11:** 6673
instruments for **11:** 6671
methods **11:** 6671
purposes of **11:** 6670
research foci **11:** 6673
prediction
effectiveness in **11:** 6675
See also
Vocational evaluation
Vocational education
and academic education
for development **3:** 1654
administration
Eastern and Central Europe **11:** 6643
and adult education
in socialist societies **11:** 6642
Afghanistan **1:** 206
apprenticeships
historical background **11:** 6654
history and development of **1:** ***310–318***
articulation (education)
Latin America **6:** ***3256–3262***
attendance patterns
Japan **6:** 3089
Austria **11:** 6682
Botswana **1:** 547
Brunei Darussalam **1:** 574
Bulgaria **1:** 584
Burundi **1:** 602
Cameroon **2:** 612
Canada **2:** 621
Central African Republic **2:** 654
Central and Eastern Europe
delivery **11:** 6644
Chad **2:** 668
change
Central and Eastern Europe **11:** 6645
characteristics of
Latin America **7:** 4150
Soviet Union (former) **10:** 5644
Chile **2:** 741
China, People's Republic of **2:** ***755–760***
comparative analysis **11:** 6262
problems of **11:** 6679
comparative area studies
Latin America **6:** 3258
competency-based education
and learning modules **7:** 3890
in compulsory education
Japan **6:** 3086
content
Central and Eastern Europe **11:** 6644
and context effect **11:** 6412
cooperative education
and productivity **11:** 6629
core curriculum **2:** 1103
cost effectiveness **9:** 5071, 5072
objectives **11:** 6649
Côte d'Ivoire **2:** 1155
course classification
Japan **6:** 3086
courses
Japan **6:** 3088
curriculum **3:** 1736; **11:** 6250
curriculum change
trends **11:** 6667
curriculum development **9:** 5521; **11:** 6684
feedback for **11:** 6668
integration **4:** 1919
Cyprus **3:** 1371
decision-making
devolution of **8:** 4529
developing nations **1:** 316
rate of return **9:** ***5071–5076***
differentiation in **11:** 6249
for the disadvantaged
Chile **7:** 4151
Latin America **7:** ***4148–4155***
United States **11:** 6532
Uruguay **7:** 4151
disadvantaged youth **11:** 6249
dual system **7:** 4257
Germany **6:** 3134
history of **11:** 6681
Eastern and Southern Africa **11:** ***6251–6256***
economic factors
Latin America **6:** 3259
education with production **3:** ***1685–1690***
educational change
United States **11:** 6532
educational field
concept of **6:** 3256
and educational planning
Asia **8:** 4488
effect of unions on policies **11:** 6697
effective
characteristics of **8:** 4858
empirical research **11:** 6631
limitations of findings **11:** 6632
and employment opportunities
occupational mobility **11:** 6652
enrollment rate
United States **11:** 6531, 6534
enrollment trends **11:** 6666
and enterprise **11:** 6250
equal education **4:** ***2281–2287***
and equal opportunities legislation **4:** 2284
equity effect **9:** 5075
Estonia **4:** 2027
Ethiopia **4:** 2039
Europe **4:** 2056
European Community
common policy **4:** 2064, 2065
comparability **4:** 2067
harmonization **11:** 6665
evaluation studies **9:** 5072
externalities **11:** 6426
and federal aid
United States **11:** 6532
federal policy
United States **11:** ***6530–6538***
federal state relationship
United States **11:** 6531
female access to **4:** ***2281–2287***
obstacles **4:** 2283
female participation **4:** 2283
factors influencing **4:** 2283
image problem **4:** 2285
participatory research **4:** 2284
females
Islamic culture **11:** 6758
Fiji **4:** 2306
finance
Central and Eastern Europe **11:** 6643
Germany, Federal Republic of (former) **11:** 6656
Japan **6:** 3091
Russia **10:** 5649
sources of **5:** 2817
Soviet Union (former) **10:** 5649
and tax allocation **8:** ***4359–4364***
financial support
and economic need **11:** 6533
Finland **4:** 2319
France **11:** 6682
future policy
Japan **6:** 3091
future trends **11:** 6637
general education
history of **11:** 6682, 6684
and German reunification **11:** 6656
Germany **1:** 182; **5:** 2474
Germany, Federal Republic of (former) **11:** ***6690–6699***
Ghana **5:** 2482
and government policies
privatization **11:** 6688
government role in **11:** ***6425–6431***
equity arguments **11:** 6428
finance **11:** 6425
provision **11:** 6425
support services **11:** 6425
grants
United States **11:** 6538
Greece **5:** 2518
Guadeloupe and Martinique **5:** 2540
Guinea-Bissau **5:** 2559
historical background **11:** ***6678–6684***
China, People's Republic of **2:** 756
cooperative system **11:** 6681
Germany **11:** 6681
Latin America **6:** 3257
United States **11:** 6530
Honduras **5:** 2634
Hong Kong **5:** 2639, 2640
Hungary **5:** 2702
Iceland **5:** 2718
India **5:** 2748
Indonesia **5:** 2787
and industrialization **11:** 6657

informal sector **5:** ***2814–2819***
  future trends **5:** 2818
  global context **5:** 2814
  recommendations **5:** 2815
initiatives
  United Kingdom **11:** ***6685–6690***
and instructional effectiveness **8:** 4861
international aid
  development banks **11:** 6661
  Germany, Federal Republic of (former) **11:** 6657
  implications **5:** 2817
  types of **11:** 6660
International Labour Organization **5:** ***2998–3003***
  policy recommendations **5:** 3000, 3001
international perspectives
  China, People's Republic of **2:** 758
Ireland, Republic of **5:** 3015
Israel **5:** 3025
issues
  West Africa **5:** 2815
Italy **5:** 3033
Jamaica **6:** 3069, 3070
Japan **6:** 3082, ***3086–3092***; **11:** ***6690–6699***
  private sector provision **6:** 3089
job training **2:** 1058
Jordan **6:** 3109, 3110
Korea, Democratic People's Republic of **6:** 3157
Kuwait **6:** 3173
and labor market
  developing nations **9:** 5074
and labor market analysis
  informal sector **3:** 1678
Latin America **8:** 4492
  private vs. public sector roles **7:** 4153
and learning disabilities **10:** 5685
learning modules **7:** ***3890–3895***
  cost effectiveness **7:** 3892
  pacing **7:** 3891
  and student participation **7:** 3891
  vs. grouped subjects **7:** 3891
Lebanon **6:** 3352
links with labor market **8:** 4337
Macau **6:** 3542
macroeconomic view **11:** 6251
  criticism of **11:** 6700
Malawi **6:** 3562
Malaysia **6:** 3567
Mauritania **6:** 3688
Mauritius **7:** 3694
and microcomputers
  applications **4:** 1922
models
  Western Europe **11:** 6664
modes **11:** ***6690–6699***
  comparisons **11:** 6697
and modular curricula **7:** 3888
Morocco **7:** 3927
Mozambique **7:** 3956
multiple locations of **11:** 6245
Namibia **7:** 4042
Nigeria **7:** 4128
Oman **7:** 4203
organization
  Central and Eastern Europe **11:** 6643
  and educational quality **8:** 4858
Papua New Guinea **7:** 4278
Paraguay **7:** 4285
participation
  patterns **11:** 6248
Philippines **8:** 4436
planning for **8:** ***4526–4532***
  and classification of occupations **8:** 4528
  criticism of labor needs approach **8:** 4527
  labor needs approach **8:** 4526
  new methodologies **8:** 4529, 4530
  prediction **8:** 4527
Poland **8:** 4544
policies
  Eastern Europe **11:** 6665
  Russia **10:** 5647
  Soviet Union (former) **10:** 5645
  Uzbekistan **10:** 5647
policy formation
  and personnel needs **8:** 4528
Portugal **8:** 4625
post school programs **11:** 6246
postwar history of
  United Kingdom **11:** 6685
preferred systems
  characteristics of **10:** 5914
prior to the Industrial Revolution **11:** 6680
and private organizations
  historical background **7:** 4149
and private sector **5:** 2816; **8:** ***4792–4796***
privatization of **11:** 6649
  constraints **11:** 6652
and productivity **3:** 1678; **11:** ***6628–6633***
  more cooperative vs. less cooperative hypothesis **11:** 6630
and professionalization **11:** 6683
programs
  flexibility **5:** 2817
  and unemployment **11:** 6687
and promotion (occupational) **11:** 6629
proprietary schools **8:** ***4792–4796***
  and the labor market **8:** ***4792–4796***
and public opinion **11:** 6702
public sector **5:** 2816
  characteristics of **11:** 6648
public sector provision
  Japan **6:** 3088
quality control in **8:** ***4858–4865***
rate of return to **3:** 1710
  China, People's Republic of **2:** 759
reforms
  China, People's Republic of **2:** 755
regional programs **5:** 3002
relevance of general education to **11:** 6664, 6698
research
  Central and Eastern Europe **11:** 6641
resources
  increasing efficiency in the use of **5:** 2817
restructuring **11:** 6250
role of **11:** 6250
Romania **9:** 5085
Rwanda **9:** 5110
Saudi Arabia **9:** 5146
school-based **11:** 6245
school business relationship
  participation **11:** 6649
and second chance education **9:** 5364
Senegal **9:** 5420, 5421
sex bias **507020:** 90. 4.2285
sex discrimination **4:** 2284; **11:** 6533, 6535
  promotion **4:** 2285
  recruitment **4:** 2285
sex fairness
  enrollment trends **4:** 2283
Seychelles **9:** 5447
since the Industrial Revolution **11:** 6680
Singapore **9:** 5480
skill development
  funds **11:** 6650
and small business training **4:** 1986
social factors **11:** 6700
and social groups
  Latin America **6:** 3258
social integration effect **9:** 5075
sources for **8:** 4527
South Africa **10:** 5629
Soviet Union (former) **10:** ***5644–5650***
special education **7:** 4266
and specialization **11:** 6250
  vs. general education **11:** 6703
Sri Lanka **10:** 5717
statistical data **11:** ***6416–6420***
strategies for
  China, People's Republic of **2:** 757, 759
structure
  Central and Eastern Europe **11:** 6643
Sudan **10:** 5839
Swaziland **10:** 5864
Sweden **11:** ***6690–6699***
Switzerland **10:** 5877
Syria **10:** 5891
and teacher education **10:** ***6063–6068***
and teacher education programs **10:** 6064
teaching methods
  Uruguay **7:** 4151
technical education
  comparative analysis **11:** ***6261–6266***
  International Labour Organization **5:** 2999
  international studies **11:** ***6261–6266***

and technological advancement **4:** 1923; **11:** 6281
case for **11:** 6281
and technology education **11:** 6288
Thailand **11:** 6374
theory of **11:** ***6699–6704***
time management
and instructional effectiveness **8:** 4862
Tonga **11:** 6407
and track system (education) **7:** 4231
training councils **11:** 6649
training methods
Germany, Federal Republic of (former) **11:** 6638
United Kingdom **11:** 6638
training with production **11:** ***6445–6452***
Tunisia **11:** 6471
Turkey **1:** 316
types of **1:** 312
Uganda **11:** 6498
United Kingdom **11:** 6518
United States **11:** 6542, 6683
universal
trend toward **11:** 6248
Vanuatu **11:** 6582
vs. academic education
and primary school agriculture **8:** 4684
United States **11:** 6531, 6534
vs. general education
and economic change **3:** 1711
and productivity hypothesis **11:** 6630
work-based **11:** 6247
work efficiency function
as a measure of productivity **11:** 6630
See also
Adult vocational education
Apprenticeships
Education with production
Technical education
Technical and vocational education and training (TVET)
Training with production
Vocational education and training (VET)
Vocational Education Act 1963 (US) **11:** 6532
Vocational education teachers
and training programs
Latin America **7:** 4150, 4153
Vocational education and training (VET)
Anglo–German comparisons **11:** ***6638–6640***
Central and Eastern Europe **11:** ***6641–6648***
developing nations
cost effectiveness improvement **11:** ***6648–6653***
international aid **11:** ***6660–6664***
and macroeconomic environment **11:** ***6633–6638***
national and international dimensions of
Germany, Federal Republic of (former) **11:** ***6653–6660***
Western Europe **11:** ***6664–6669***
See also
Technical and vocational education and training (TVET)
Vocational
education
Vocational evaluation
methods **11:** 6671
Vocational high schools
colleges of technology
Japan **6:** 3086
Japan **6:** 3086
junior colleges
Japan **6:** 3087
Vocational interests
definitions of **11:** 6669
hierarchical model of **11:** 6674
measures **11:** ***6669–6678***
alternative methods **11:** 6676
equity issues **11:** 6676
innovations **11:** 6672
instruments for **11:** 6670
inventories **11:** 6671
methods **11:** 6670
purposes of **11:** 6670
research findings **11:** 6672
research foci **11:** 6673
prediction
effectiveness in **11:** 6675
See also
Vocational evaluation
Vocational qualifications
and employment level
correlation **11:** 6535
mismatch **11:** 6640
Germany, Federal Republic of (former) **11:** 6638
recognition
European Community **4:** ***2063–2070***
and skills tests
Japan **6:** 3088
United Kingdom **3:** 1737; **11:** 6638
Vocational rehabilitation
and the International Labour Organization **5:** 3000
Vocational school fallacy **11:** 6248
China, People's Republic of **2:** 759
and educational development
developing nations **1:** 466
and primary school agriculture **8:** 4684
Vocational schools **1:** 108; **9:** 5072
administration of **11:** 6644
and apprenticeships
Germany **1:** 311
Central and Eastern Europe **11:** 6643
characteristics of **10:** 5916
China, People's Republic of **2:** 756
developing nations **11:** 6657
criticisms of **11:** 6267
development of
China, People's Republic of **2:** 756
effect of economic change on
Soviet Union (former) **10:** 5646
enrollment trends in **11:** 6666
finance
and training with production **11:** 6449
future of
Latin America **6:** 3261
Germany, Federal Republic of (former) **11:** 6694
historical development of **11:** 6680, 6682
Germany **6:** 3134
Latin America **6:** 3257
libraries
educational resources **6:** 3397
maintenance
and educational quality **8:** 4861
minicourses
and educational planning **8:** 4529
and motivation **11:** 6412, 6415
organization of
Latin America **6:** 3262
organizational change in
Soviet Union (former) **10:** 5647
provision of **11:** 6245
qualifications **11:** 6667
quality of
China, People's Republic of **2:** 758
Latin America **6:** 3259
rural
Soviet Union (former) **10:** 5648
school administration
and educational quality **8:** 4860
school community relationship **8:** 4860
social rate of return **9:** 5073
Soviet Union (former) **10:** 5644
student certification **11:** 6667
Sweden **11:** 6691
training for production **11:** 6650
transfer of control
Soviet Union (former) **10:** 5646
types of **10:** 5914
Germany, Federal Republic of (former) **11:** 6655
United Kingdom **11:** 6689
Western Europe **11:** 6664
Vocational training
See Vocational education
Vocational training centers
Botswana **11:** 6253
Japan **6:** 3088
Singapore **7:** 3755
Tanzania **11:** 6252
Vocationalism
theory of **11:** ***6699–6704***
See also
Vocational education
Vocations
See Occupations
Voice disorders
in children **11:** ***6704–6707***
diagnosis of **11:** 6705
future trends **11:** 6707

laryngeal **11:** 6704
causes of **11:** 6705
characteristics of **11:** 6705
management of **11:** 6705
prevalence of **11:** 6704
resonance problems
characteristics of **11:** 6706
prevalence of **11:** 6705
and speech handicaps **1:** 405; **10:** 5691
and verbal communication **1:** 404
Volition
See Individual power
Volkshochschulen
Germany **2:** 895, 898; **8:** 4806; **10:** 5637
Volksschulen
development by Kerschensteiner **6:** 3135
Voluntary agencies
adult education **5:** 2735
and development education **3:** 1497
on governance of teacher education
developing nations **10:** 5963
private
and educational support **5:** 2979
Volunteers
literacy programs **7:** 4146, 4147
adult **1:** 102
Vote counting methods
and research synthesis **10:** 6236
Vouchers
See Educational vouchers
Vulnerability
sex differences **9:** 5434

Wald test
statistical significance **9:** 5462
Waldorf schools **1:** 262
art education **1:** 341
War
and peace education **3:** 1730
Philippines
and community education **2:** 908
and social change **1:** 58
and teaching compared **10:** 6164
Warnock Report 1978 (UK)
education for disabled children **5:** 2907
mainstreaming **3:** 1506
Washington University Sentence Completion Test **8:** 4791
Wechsler Adult Intelligence Scale (WAIS)
age differences **1:** 235
Well-being
and aging (individuals) **1:** 237
and child development
risk and vulnerability model **3:** 1637
and evaluative thinking
learning processes **1:** 202
individual development **3:** 1637
West Africa
apprenticeships **11:** 6247
ethnography of indigenous populations **3:** 1752
research studies
skill acquisition **5:** 2815
vocational education
issues **5:** 2815
West African Examinations Council (WAEC)
and selection **9:** 5388
West Germany
See Germany, Federal Republic of (FRG) (former)
West Indies
science curriculum **3:** 1253
Western civilization
cultural bias **6:** 3419
and curriculum policies **3:** 1336
Western Europe
adult education **10:** ***5635–5644***
research **1:** 122, 124
apprenticeships **11:** 6664
civic education **2:** 767
educational planning
approaches **8:** 4496
philosophy of education **8:** ***4456–4461***
postsecondary education **11:** 6665
vocational education
age groups **11:** 6666
vocational education and training **11:** ***6664–6669***
vocational schools **11:** 6245
Wheelchairs
and assistive technology **10:** 5669, 5670
school environment **5:** 2909
White collar occupations
and blue collar occupations
demarcation **7:** 3770
and employment level **7:** 3716
and incidence of training **1:** 107
Whiteboards
See Chalkboards
Whole class instruction
teacher role **10:** 6027
Whole language approach **6:** ***3205–3209***
beginning reading **8:** 4944
literature **10:** 5958
Wilcoxon matched-pairs signed-ranks test **7:** 4160
Wiles hypothesis
empirical research **9:** 5352
Windows (computer environment)
and courseware development **3:** 1778
mathematics instruction
geometry **7:** 4097
microcomputers **7:** 3813
and models **2:** 986
and physical sciences
secondary school programs **8:** 4477
See also
Graphical user interface (GUI)
Wisconsin Longitudinal Study
employment level
and education **4:** 2277
Wisconsin model
and social mobility **9:** 5551
Withdrawal (psychology)
and social development **9:** 5525
Wogeo
ethnography of **3:** 1754
Wolof
and test translation **11:** 6329
WOMBAT (teaching model) **1:** 345
Women
See Females
Women faculty
academic rank (professional)
sex discrimination **11:** 6709
status **11:** 6709
and age
event history analysis **4:** 2153
educational improvement **10:** 6098
effect of ideology of professionalization on **11:** 6722
feminist research on **11:** 6723
history of women's education **11:** 6746
and male ideology
Australia **11:** 6733
North America **11:** 6762
participatory research **11:** 6724
and religious education
conflict **9:** 5006
social influences **10:** 5609
and social status **10:** 6226
Women In Development (WID) **11:** 6759
Women teachers
See Women faculty
Women's Action Alliance Sex Equity in Education Program (US) **4:** 2426
Women's clubs
North America **11:** 6764
Women's education **4:** ***2407–2412***; **5:** 2733
adult education **11:** ***6712–6719***
Bahrain **1:** 450
barriers to **4:** 2417
distance factors **4:** 2417
family financial resources **4:** 2417
school environment **4:** 2417
benefits from **4:** 2414
cross-national comparisons **4:** 2415
vs. sex differences **4:** 2416
and birth rate **3:** ***1672–1676***
compared with women's studies **11:** 6766
continuing education **11:** 6714
continuing vocational
Europe **4:** 2063
disequilibrium theory of and **3:** 1691
domestic education
Australia **11:** 6732
educational choice
economics of **4:** ***2412–2419***
and effect on health **2:** 1053
for entrepreneurship
developing nations **11:** 6715
and family size **3:** 1672, 1673, 1674

future directions
Australia **11:** 6734
Gambia **4:** 2401
general education **11:** 6713
Greece **5:** 2518
health education
developing nations **11:** 6714
history of
Australia **11:** ***6731–6735***
francophone Africa **11:** ***6735–6741***
German-speaking Europe **11:** ***6741–6748***
India **11:** ***6748–6753***
Islamic culture **11:** ***6753–6761***
North America **11:** ***6761–6765***
for income generation
developing nations **11:** 6715
India **5:** 2756
international **5:** 2935
Japan **6:** 3076
job training
and earnings differentials **7:** 4198
for literacy **1:** 131, 132
literacy education **11:** 6717
Luther's views **11:** 6744
Madagascar **6:** 3550
Mongolia **7:** 3903
Plato's views **11:** 6742
and productivity **4:** 2414
rural extension
developing nations **11:** 6715
Saudi Arabia **9:** 5145
Sierra Leone **9:** 5456
single sex colleges
developing nations **2:** 832, 833
Sudan **10:** 5838
UNESCO programs **11:** 6526
Women's International Studies Europe (WISE) **11:** 6767
Women's rights
See Feminism
Women's studies **2:** 1190, 1192; **4:** 2410; **11:** ***6765–6769***
and adult education **1:** 160
ambiguities of term **11:** 6723
biographies **4:** 1983
categories of programs **11:** 6767
criticisms of **11:** 6766
definition of **11:** 6766
ideological debate
Australia **11:** 6733
interdisciplinary approach
permeation model **11:** 6768
issues **11:** 6767
lesbian studies **11:** 6768
models of courses **11:** 6766
national groups or organizations **11:** 6767
North America **11:** 6765
radical feminist theory **5:** 2455
sexuality **11:** 6768
Women's World Banking Organization **11:** 6715
Word association tests **8:** 4790
Word associations (reading)
See Associative learning
Word blindness
See Word recognition, difficulties
Word deafness
See Verbal auditory agnosia
Word knowledge tests
See Vocabulary tests
Word problems (mathematics)
and computation **6:** 3658
language usage **6:** 3637
sex differences **4:** 2433, 2434
Word processing
educational uses for **7:** 3813
elementary schools **11:** 6780
and language skills
writing processes **2:** 1004
and management information systems **5:** 2830
and prototyping **8:** 4802
and revision (written composition) **2:** 1004
software tools **7:** 4091
teacher education curriculum **10:** 6005
and test item writing **2:** 997
and writing (composition) **7:** 4090
issues **7:** 4091
and writing skills **7:** 4084
Word processors
intelligent
and special needs students **10:** 5671
Word recognition
and computer-assisted instruction **10:** 5671
difficulties
and learning disabilities **10:** 5681
Work
alternating with education **8:** 4958, 4961
concept of **3:** 1738
evolving attitudes as a social phenomenon **11:** 6679
hours competing with leisure time **6:** 3377
leisure and learning **6:** 3376
and literacy **8:** 4636
organization and utilization of skills **11:** 6419
reduction in hours **6:** 3375; **11:** 6392
and technical interest (Habermas) **2:** 1200
See also
Employment
Work adjustment
See Vocational adjustment
Work attitudes
and socialization **10:** 5589
Work effort
and productivity **11:** 6629
effect of education on **11:** 6629, 6630, 6632
Work environment
as learning environment **5:** 2687; **8:** 4964
new technology
and labor force development **5:** 2688, 2689
reform
and education work relationship **8:** 4636
and socialization **10:** 5589
teachers **10:** 5843
Work ethic
and concept of leisure **11:** 6794
Work experience **3:** 1736, 1738; **8:** 4337; **11:** 6421
and admission to recurrent education **8:** 4958
and career choice **3:** 1738
as a component of school education **9:** 5230
evaluation of effect **3:** 1738
and on-the-job training **7:** 4207
as a source of occupational information **6:** 3098
Work experience programs **3:** 1686
and the Comprehensive Employment and Training Act (US) **7:** 4197
and teacher education programs **10:** 6065
and youth unemployment **3:** 1687
See also
Education with production
On-the-job training
Work schools (Germany)
See Arbeitsschulen
Work study programs **11:** 6393
Workbooks
and assignments
research **9:** 5359
Worker evaluation
See Personnel evaluation
Workers' education
See Labor education
Workers' Educational Association (WEA) (UK) **2:** 1190; **5:** 2732, 2733; **8:** 4731, 4732; **11:** 6772
adult education
financial support **10:** 5592
adult educators
teacher education **11:** 6432
historical background **8:** 4732, 4733
transfer of programs **5:** 2934
Workers' educational associations **1:** 136
international federation **5:** 2932; **11:** 6772
Working class
and adult education **5:** 2733, 2734
ideology **2:** 1190
Marx on education for the **2:** 779
outreach programs **7:** 4247
studies
and youth culture **11:** 6800
Working class students
track system **3:** 1737
Working class youth
cultural reproduction **9:** 5570
gender differences **9:** 5570
and race **9:** 5570

Working life
education for 3: ***1736–1740***
Working memory
See Short term memory (STM)
Workshops
and learning strategies 6: 3346
World Association for Adult Education
5: 2932
World Association for Educational
Research 2: 941
World Bank
comparative education 2: 921
curriculum development
Africa 8: 4681
decentralization
strategies for 6: 3606
documentation
comparative education 3: 1585
economic adjustment
policies for 3: 1785
Education and Employment Division
2: 942
and educational administration
international 5: 2951
educational finance 5: 2979
effect of economic adjustment on
3: 1786
for projects 3: 1783
educational planning
Asia 8: 4486
implementation problems 3: 1823
educational policy
studies 4: 1838
educational radio
studies 5: 2889
educational technology
activities 4: 1878
financial support
international 5: 2989, 2991
instructional materials
finance for 8: 4696
international aid
for vocational education 11: 6646,
6662
loans to primary education 1: 169
research studies
skill acquisition 5: 2815
and school administration 9: 5164
studies
educational diversification
11: 6254, 6255
textbooks
provision 11: 6361, 6362, 6363
vocational education 9: 5071;
11: 6245, 6247, 6660
planning methodology 8: 4528
policies 11: 6251, 6449, 6657,
6698
policy recommendations 5: 3001
World Confederation of Organizations
of the Teaching Profession
(WCOTP) 6: 3190; 10: 6078
World Conference on Education for All
1990 (WCEFA) 1: 468; 3: 1831;
5: 2936, 2959, 2988; 11: 6526
adult education 1: 130
and adult literacy 5: 2935, 2947
and basic education 1: 169
children with no access to education
2: 720
comparative educational indicators
2: 960
Declaration 11: 6503
developing nations 6: 3366
and dimensions of education 6: 3455
educational planning 8: 4486, 4502
and international co-operation
5: 2963
objectives 1: 144, 473; 5: 2960;
6: 3420
barriers to 7: 4140
special education 2: 727
World Council of Comparative
Education Societies 2: 921, 945
congresses 2: 946
legal status 2: 945
membership 2: 945
objectives 2: 946
relationship with UNESCO 2: 945, 947
World Development Report
primary education
enrollment rate 3: 1826
World Health Organization (WHO)
and adult education 1: 161
educational technology
activities 4: 1880
World history 5: 2622
World Intellectual Property
Organization (WIPO) 2: 1100
World studies
and politicization of curriculum
5: 2467
Writers
See Authors
Writers in Electronic Residence
Program (Canada) 7: 4089
Writing (composition) 11: ***6781–6785***
classical rhetorical model 10: 5958
cognitive processes 11: 6783
curriculum objectives
studies 11: 6776
discourse modes
and social context 11: 6779
domains of 4: 2019
effect of grammar instruction on
10: ***5697–5705***
feedback 11: 6783
teacher response 11: 6783
language acquisition 11: 6781
and language tests 4: 2359
learning strategies 11: 6781, 6782
student motivation 11: 6783
metacognition 11: 6779
narration 11: 6779
persuasive discourse 11: 6779
rating of 7: 3933
sex differences 10: 5822
and telecommunications 7: 4089
and thinking skills 11: 6780
and visual literacy 11: 6623
and word processing 7: 4090
writing across the curriculum 6: 3207
Writing ability
and telecommunications 7: 4089
tests 7: 3932
Writing across the curriculum 6: 3206,
3208
Writing development
See Writing improvement
Writing difficulties
special needs students
microcomputers 7: 3803
Writing evaluation
and configural frequency analysis
2: 1035
methods 11: 6784
and writing skills 11: 6779
Writing improvement
cognitive development 11: 6781
learning processes 11: 6782
Writing instruction 11: ***6778–6781***
composition 11: ***6775–6778***
functions of 11: 6775
methods 11: 6777
objectives 4: 2018; 11: 6775
scaffolding 11: 6779
in schools
objectives 11: 6775
special education
protocol analysis 2: 861
student motivation 11: 6782
and teleconferencing 7: 4089
and word processing 7: 4090
Writing processes 11: 6778
knowledge-telling model 11: 6778,
6780
knowledge-transforming model
11: 6778, 6780
National Writing Project (US)
10: 5958, 5960
problem-solving 11: 6782
revision (written composition)
11: 6778
See also
Prewriting
Writing readiness 4: ***1958–1963***
invented spelling 4: 1960
letters (alphabet) 4: 1958
pattern recognition 4: 1960
Writing skills
and composition 11: 6777
curriculum-based assessment 3: 1358
effects on learning 6: 3207
and essay tests 4: 2019
expertise 11: 6779, 6780
learning 11: ***6778–6781***
peer teaching 5: 2528
skill development 11: 6779
Writing strategies
learning disabilities 6: 3331
and student role 10: 5793
Writing systems
See Written language

Writing tests **4:** 2076; **7:** 3932
interactive group tests **4:** 2362
and partial credit model **7:** 4306
and test bias **11:** 6319
Written composition
See Writing (composition)
Written language **8:** 4942
alphabets
and literacy **6:** 3443, 3444
and reading **8:** 4942, 4943, 4944
conventions of **1:** 480
linguistic **1:** 481
spatial **1:** 480
structural **1:** 481
development of understanding
preschool children **4:** 1958
early experience
family influence **4:** 1960
grapheme recognition
preschool children **4:** 1958
historical development of functions
6: 3444
and historical development of literacy
6: 3443
logographic systems
and literacy **6:** 3443
and reading **8:** 4942, 4943
and mathematics
origins of **6:** 3643
and oral language development
4: 1958, 1960
orthographic symbols **1:** ***480–483***
phoneme grapheme correspondence
8: 4943, 4944
standardization of **1:** 481
syllabary systems
and literacy **6:** 3443
and reading **8:** 4942, 4943
of Vai
Liberia **1:** 482; **3:** 1242; **6:** 3454, 3460; **11:** 6453

X-irradiation **1:** 14

Yemen
curriculum development **11:** 6792
educational change **11:** 6793
educational research **11:** 6793
enrollment rates **9:** 5536
language **11:** 6787
law
and education **11:** 6788
postsecondary education **11:** 6789
preschool education **11:** 6790
primary education **11:** 6788
secondary education **11:** 6788
special education **11:** 6790
student evaluation **11:** 6792
system of education **11:** ***6787–6794***
educational objectives **11:** 6788
enrollment **11:** 6788
major problems **11:** 6793
structure **11:** 6788
teacher education **11:** 6792
teacher recruitment **11:** 6792
technical education **11:** 6790
textbooks
provision **11:** 6361
vocational education **11:** 6790
Young Adult Literacy Assessment (US)
6: 3478
Young adults
adult education participation **8:** 4613
physical development **8:** 4473
Young children
development **1:** 359
multiple factors in **1:** 359
early intervention **5:** ***2806–2814***
history instruction for
research **9:** 5576
measurement of development
1: ***358–362***
prosocial behavior **8:** 4797
resilience
research **8:** 4776
and school readiness tests **9:** 5274
screening tests
developmental disabilities
3: ***1621–1624***
testing **1:** ***358–362***
See also
Infants
Toddlers
Youth
changing conceptions of **11:** 6795
culture **11:** ***6798–6803***
age factors **11:** 6802
issues **11:** 6799
male **11:** 6801
research **11:** 6801
studies **11:** 6800
definition of **11:** 6804
effects of broadcasting and technology on **1:** ***564–570***
effects of leisure on **11:** 6795
extracurricular activities
participation **11:** 6796
and leisure **11:** ***6794–6798***
and antisocial behavior **11:** 6795
demographic factors **11:** 6796
effects of participation **11:** 6797
impact of school on **11:** 6796
research methodology **11:** 6796
role of
and youth organizations **10:** 5794
subcultures **9:** 5217; **11:** ***6798–6803***
and conflict in schools **11:** 6800
and delinquency **11:** 6799
formation **11:** 6801
issues **11:** 6799
technical education
and educational technology
4: ***1918–1924***
See also
Disadvantaged youth
Out of school youth
Youth Opportunities Programme (YOP) (UK)
and vocational education **11:** 6687
Youth organizations
and political education **8:** 4570
Youth problems
and delinquency prevention **1:** 87
Youth programs
Europe **4:** 2056, 2057
Youth Training Scheme (YTS) (UK)
7: 3713; **11:** 6246, 6806
vocational education **11:** 6687
Youth unemployment **3:** 1706;
11: ***6803–6808***
and apprenticeship **11:** 6806
consequences of **11:** 6804
and cultural identity **11:** 6807
developed nations **3:** 1706
developing nations **11:** 6803
educational strategies **8:** 4960, 4961
effects on social life **11:** 6805
effects on working life **11:** 6804
and gang membership **11:** 6806
identifying high risk groups **11:** 6804
and job development **11:** 6806
levels **11:** 6804
policy solutions
developed nations **11:** 6806
and professional education **11:** 6806
and qualifications **11:** 6804
and after school programs **11:** 6806
and skill obsolescence **11:** 6805
and social identity problems **11:** 6805
and technical education **11:** 6806
and vocational education
China, People's Republic of **2:** 759
United Kingdom **11:** 6686
and work experience programs
3: 1687
Ypsilanti Perry Pre-School Project (US)
6: 3517
Yugoslavia (former)
adult education **1:** 121, 124
andragogy **1:** 275
ethnicity
and national unity **7:** 3966
See also
Slovenia

Zaire
adult education **1:** 220; **11:** 6811
curriculum development **11:** 6812
educational change **11:** 6813
educational research **11:** 6813
language **11:** 6809
postsecondary education **11:** 6810
preschool education **11:** 6810
primary education **11:** 6810
secondary education **11:** 6810
vocational education **11:** 6811
special education **11:** 6810
student evaluation **11:** 6813
system of education **11:** ***6809–6814***
educational objectives **11:** 6809
historical background **11:** 6809
major problems **11:** 6814
structure **11:** 6810
teacher education **11:** 6812
teacher recruitment **11:** 6812
teaching methodology **11:** 6812
technical education **11:** 6811

women's education **11:** 6737, 6738, 6740
Zambia
adult education legislation **6:** 3363
agricultural education
vocational education **1:** 241
apprenticeships
studies **1:** 222
distance education
in schools **3:** 1565
elementary schools
disabilities in **9:** 5564
ethnography of indigenous populations **3:** 1753
macroeconomics
salary wage differentials **11:** 6635
public education finance
effect of economic adjustment on **3:** 1787
public sector employment **8:** 4838
schools
decentralization **3:** 1415
teacher education programs **10:** 6065
technical education
coordination of **10:** 6064
vocational education
education with production **3:** 1688
Zimbabwe
adult education **1:** 213; **11:** 6817
community support
educational finance **2:** 911
computer uses in education **4:** 1901
curriculum development **11:** 6819
distance education **4:** 1901
in schools **3:** 1565
distance teacher education **3:** 1559
educational change **11:** 6820
educational research **11:** 6819
language **11:** 6814
literacy campaigns **1:** 171
postsecondary education **11:** 6817
primary education **11:** 6815
reading achievement
and sampling **9:** 5131
secondary education **11:** 6815
diversified **11:** 6254
special education **11:** 6817
system of education **11:** ***6814–6821***
degrees and qualifications **11:** 6819
educational objectives **11:** 6815
major problems **11:** 6820
structure **11:** 6815
teacher education **11:** 6819
teacher recruitment **11:** 6818
teaching methodology **11:** 6819
technical education **11:** 6817
technology education **11:** 6288
training
and minimum wage **11:** 6636
vocational education **11:** 6817
education with production **3:** 1688
historical background **11:** 6252
Znanie
Central and Eastern Europe **2:** 659
Soviet Union (former) **8:** 4810

List of Foreign Terms

Abitur
Agence de Coopération Culturelle et Technique (ACCT) (France)
Animateurs
Animation socio-culturelle
Arbeit und Leben
Arbeitsschulen
Association Nationale pour la Formation Professionelle des Adultes (France)

Baccalauréat
Burakumin
Berechtigungswesen
Berufliches Gymnasium
Berufsaufbauschulen
Berufsfachschulen
Berufsschulen

Centre d'Enseignement par Correspondance (France)
Centre International d'Etudes Pédagogiques (CIEP)
Centre National D'Enseignement à Distance (France)
Centro de Cooperación Regional para la Educación de Adultos en América Latina y el Caribe
Centro de Investigación y Desarrollo de la Educación (CIDE) (Chile)
Centro Europeo Dell'Educazione (CEDE) (Italy)
Consejo de Educación de Adultos de América Latina (CEAAL)
Conservatoire National des Arts et Métiers (France)
Crédit-formation

Décalages
Deutscher Lehrerverein (DLV)
Deutsches Institut für Internationale Pädagogische Forschung
Développement communautaire

Ecole maternelle
Ecole Polytechnique
Educação para Todos 1985 (Brazil)
Education continue (France)
Education permanente (France)
Education populaire
Education récurrente (France)
Erklären
Erwachsenenbildung
Escuela Nueva (Colombia)

Fachhochschulen
Fachoberschulen
Fachschulen
Federación Interamericana de Educación de Adultos (FIDEA)
Fédération de l'Education Nationale (FEN) (France)
Folkeoplysning
Formation continue
Formation Continue en Europe (FORCE)
Fujinkai

Geisteswissenschaften
Gemeinschaft
Gesellschaft
Gewerkschaft Erziehung und Wissenschaft (GEW) (Germany, Federal Republic of [former])
Grandes écoles
Groupements d'établissements de l'éducation Nationale (France)
Gymnasium

Habitus
Han
Hauptschulen
Hohenrodter Bund

Individualisé
Inspecteurs départmentals de l'Education nationale (IDEN) (France)
Inspecteurs généreaux de l'administration de l'Education nationale (IGAEN) (France)
Inspecteurs généreaux de l'Education nationale (IGEN) (France)
Institut Africain pour le Développement Economique et Social (INADES)
Institut canadien d'éducation des adultes (ICEA)
Institut Européen pour la Formation Professionelle (IEFP)
Institut für Schulenwicklungsforschung (IFS) (Germany)
Institut National d'Education Populaire (France)
Instituto Ajijc sobre Educación Internacional (IASEI) (Mexico)
Instituto Colombiano de Crédito Educativo y Estudios Técnicos en el Exterior (CETEX)

Kami
Kibbutzim
Kolleg
Kominkan (Japan)

Laboratoire de Pédagogie Expérimentale (Belgium)
Lingua franca
Lycées

Monatsgegenstand

Nikkyoso (Japan)

Osveta

Pansophia

Realschulen
Red Latinoamericano de Documentación en Educación (REDUC)
Reformpädagogik
Resúmenes Analíticos en Educación (RAE)

Seinendan
Servicio Nacional de Aprendizaje (SENA) (Colombia)

Technikerschulen
Telekolleg

Ulpanim

Verstehen
Voksenopplaering
Volksbildung
Volkshochschulen
Volksschulen
Vuxenundervising

Weiterbildung

Yobiko

Znanie

List of Abbreviations and Acronyms

16PF	Sixteen Personality Factor Questionnaire
A-level	Advanced level (UK)
AACD	American Association for Counseling and Development
AACTE	American Association of Colleges for Teacher Education
AALAE	African Association for Literacy and Adult Education
AAMR	American Association on Mental Retardation
AAOU	Asian Association of Open Universities
AASCU	American Association of State Colleges and Universities
AASL	American Association of School Librarians
ABC	Australian Broadcasting Corporation
ACA	American Counseling Association
ACCT	*Agence de Coopération Culturelle et Technique* (France)
ACEID	Asian Center of Educational Innovation for Development
ACER	Australian Council for Educational Research
ACHE	Association for Continuing Higher Education (US)
ACO	African Curriculum Organization
ACSTT	Advisory Committee for the Supply and Training of Teachers
ACT	American College Testing
AECS	Association of European Correspondence Schools
AECT	Association for Educational Communications and Technology (US)
AEDNET	Adult Education Network
AEI	Australian Education Index
AERA	American Educational Research Association
AETT	Association for Educational Training and Technology (UK)
AIAET	All India Association for Educational Technology
AIC	Akaike's information criterion
AID	Automatic interaction detection
AIDS	Acquired Immune Deficiency Syndrome
AIT	Agency for Instructional Television
ALA	American Library Association
ALBSU	Adult Literacy and Basic Skills Unit (UK)
ALECSO	Arab League Educational, Cultural, and Scientific Organization
ALEM	Adaptive Learning Environments Model
ANCOVA	Analysis of covariance
ANOVA	Analysis of variance
AOECS	Arab Organization of Education, Culture, and Science
APA	American Psychological Association
APEID	Asia and Pacific Program of Educational Innovation for Development
APPEAL	Asia Pacific Program of Education for All
APU	Assessment of Performance Unit (UK)
ARCS	Attention–relevance–confidence–satisfaction model
ARLO	Arab Literacy Organization
ASBO	Association of School Business Officials (US)
ASCD	Association for Supervision and Curriculum Development (US)
ASEAN	Association of South East Asian Nations
ASEP	Australian Science Education Project
ASET	Australian Society for Educational Technology
ASI	Approaches to Study Inventory (UK)
ASPBAE	Asian South Pacific Bureau of Adult Education
ASVAB	Armed Services Vocational Aptitude Battery
ATI	Aptitude treatment interaction
BAAS	British Association for the Advancement of Science
BASIC	Beginner's All-purpose Symbolic Instruction Code
BBC	British Broadcasting Corporation
BBCP	Bristol Bay Curriculum Project (Alaska)
BEI	British Education Index
BEMAS	British Educational Management and Administration Society
BETA	Bibliography of Education Theses in Australia
BETI	British Education Theses Index
BIB	Balanced incomplete block
BIC	Basic interpersonal communication
BMI	Body Mass Index
BNB	British National Bibliography
CAAE	Canadian Association for Adult Education
CACREP	Council for the Accreditation of Counseling and Related Education Programs
CAEO	Coalition of Adult Education Organizations
CAETA	Commonwealth Association for the Education and Training of Adults
CAI	Computer-assisted instruction
CAL	Computer-assisted learning
CALLA	Cognitive academic language learning approach
CALP	Cognitive/academic language proficiency
CARCAE	Caribbean Regional Council for Adult Education
CARN	Classroom Action Research Network
CASAE	Canadian Association for the Study of Adult Education
CASEA	Center for the Advanced Study of Educational Administration (US)
CAT	Children's Apperception Test
CAV	Constant angular velocity
CBE	Community-based education
CBOs	Community-based organizations

CCCS	Centre for Contemporary Cultural Studies (UK)
CCEA	Commonwealth Council for Educational Administration
CCEM	Computer Courseware Evaluation Model
CD	Compact discs
CD-DA	Compact disc digital audio
CD-I	Compact disc interactive
CDA	Child Development Associate program (US)
CDCC	Council for Cultural Cooperation
CDI	Composite Development Index
CE	Council of Europe
CEAAL	*Consejo de Educación de Adultos de América Latina*
CEC	Council for Exceptional Children
CEDC	Community Education Development Centre (UK)
CEDCAR	Cooperative Education Data Collection and Reporting (US)
CEDE	*Centro Europeo Dell'Educazione* (Italy)
CEDEFOP	European Centre for the Development of Vocational Training
CEI	Canadian Education Index
CERI	Centre for Educational Research and Innovation
CES	Classroom Environment Scale
CESE	Comparative Education Society in Europe
CETA	Comprehensive Employment and Training Act (US)
CETEX	*Instituto Colombiano de Crédito Educativo y Estudios Técnicos en el Exterior*
CFA	Configural frequency analysis
CFA	Confirmatory factor analysis
CGI	Cognitively Guided Instruction
CIC	Computers in the Curriculum Project (UK)
CIDA	Canadian International Development Agency
CIDE	*Centro de Investigación y Desarrollo de la Educación*
CIEP	*Centre International d'Etudes Pédagogiques*
CIES	Comparative and International Education Society
CIPP	Context, input, process, product model
CIVITAS	CIVITAS curriculum (US)
CLES	Constructivist Learning Environment Survey
CLV	Constant linear velocity
CML	Computer-managed learning
CNAA	Council for National Academic Awards (UK)
CNIER	Chinese National Institute for Educational Research
COL	Commonwealth of Learning
CP	Community Programme (UK)
CPQ	Children's Personality Questionnaire
CPU	Central processing unit
CRAPEL	Center for Research and Pedagogical Applications (France)
CREAA	Regional Council for Adult Education and Literacy in Africa
CRESALC	Regional Center on Higher Education (UNESCO)
CSILE	Computer Supported Intentional Learning Environment
CTC	City Technology Colleges (UK)
CTP	California Test of Personality
CTW	Children's Television Workshop (US)
DAO	Dissertation Abstracts Online
DAT	Differential aptitude tests
DDST	Denver Developmental Screening Test
Deff	Design effect
DELTA	DELTA program (EC)
DES	Department of Education and Science (UK)
DES	Diethylstilbesterol
DIT	Defining Issues Test
DLV	*Deutscher Lehrerverein*
DPH	Diphenylhydantoin
DSM III-R	Diagnostic and Statistical Manual of Mental Disorders (revised version)
DTP	Desktop publishing
DVI	Digital video interactive
DZ	Dizygotic
EADTU	European Association of Distance Teaching Universities
EASP	Educational Advisory Services Project (UK)
EBLIDA	European Bureau of Library, Information, and Documentation Associations
EC	European Community
ECER	European Conference on Educational Research
ECF	Education cost function
ECUNET	European Curriculum Network
EDA	Exploratory data analysis
EFEA	European Forum on Educational Administration
EFL	English (foreign language)
EHA	Education of the Handicapped Act 1975 (US)
EIP	European Intervisitation Program
ELT	English language teaching
ENWS	European Network for Women's Studies
EPES	European Pool for Educational Software
EPI	Eysenck Personality Inventory
EPPS	Edwards Personal Preference Schedule
EPQ	Eysenck Personality Questionnaire
EPS	Education participation scale
EPSEM	Equal probability of selection method
ERIC	Educational Resources Information Center (US)
ESEA	Elementary and Secondary Education Act 1965 (US)
ESFL	Elementary School Foreign Languages
ESHA	European Secondary Heads Association
ESI	Early Screening Inventory
ESL	English as a second language
ESOL	English as a second or other language
ESPA	Education Software Publishers Association (UK)
ESPQ	Early School Personality Questionnaire
ETML	Early Teaching of Modern Languages
ETS	Educational Testing Service (US)
ETS	Employment Training Scheme (UK)
ETU	Experimental Teaching Unit (US)
EUDISED	European Documentation and Information System for Education
EUROSTEP	European Association of Users in Satellites in Training and Education Programs
EURYDICE	European Information Network in the European Community
EWLP	Experimental World Literacy Program (1966–74)

FAO	Food and Agriculture Organization
FAX	Facsimile transmission
FEN	*Fédération de l'Education Nationale* (France)
FIDEA	*Federación Interamericana de Educación de Adultos*
FLES	Foreign language elementary schools programs (US)
FLEX	Foreign language experience programs (US)
FORCE	*Formation Continue en Europe*
FRG	Federal Republic of Germany (former)
G-connection	Galois connection
G-Lattice	Galois lattice method
GATB	General Aptitude Test Battery
GCE	General Certificate of Education (UK)
GCSE	General Certificate of Secondary Education (UK)
GDR	German Democratic Republic (former)
GEW	*Gewerkschaft Erziehung und Wissenschaft* (Germany)
Gf-Gc theory	Cattell-Horn model of fluid and crystallized intelligence
GI	Group Investigation method
GIS	Geographical information systems
GIST	Girls into Science and Technology
GNP	Gross national product
GPA	Grade point average
GPC	Goal-plan code editor (PASCAL)
GPPI	Gordon Personal Profile and Inventory
GRIDS	Guidelines for Internal Review and Development project (UK)
GSS	General Social Survey (US)
GST	General systems theory
GTZ	German Association for Technical Cooperation
GUI	Graphical user interface
GZTS	Guilford–Zimmerman Temperament Survey
HDTV	High definition television
HIT	Holtzman Inkblot Technique
HLM	Hierarchical linear models
HMI	Her Majesty's Inspectors (UK)
HPP	Harvard Project Physics (US)
HSB	High School and Beyond
HTHM	Heterotrait-heteromethods
HTMM	Heterotrait-monomethods
IAEA	International Association for Educational Assessment
IAEP	International Assessment of Educational Progress
IAI	Instrumental Activities Inventory
IASEI	*Instituto Ajijc sobre Educación Internacional* (Mexico)
IB	International Baccalaureate
IBE	International Bureau of Education
IBRD	International Bank for Reconstruction and Development
ICAE	International Council for Adult Education
ICC	Item characteristic curves
ICCE	International Council for Correspondence Education
ICD	International Classification of Diseases
ICDE	International Council for Distance Education
ICDS	Integrated Child Development Services (India)
ICE	Information, education and communication programs
ICEA	*Institut canadien d'éducation des adultes*
ICEA	International Community Education Association
ICED	International Council for Educational Development
ICEE	International Center for Educational Evaluation (Nigeria)
ICEM	International Council on Educational Media
ICEQ	Individualized Classroom Environment Questionnaire
ICES	International Classification of Epileptic Seizures
ICL	Information and computer literacy
ICMI	International Commission on Mathematical Instruction
ICONS	ICONS project (US)
ICPSR	Interuniversity Consortium for Political and Social Research (US)
ICUAE	International Congress for University Adult Education
IDA	International Development Association
IDEA	Individuals with Disabilities Education Act (US)
IDEN	*Inspecteurs départmentals de l'Education nationale* (France)
IDP	International Development Program (Norway)
IDS	Institute of Developmental Studies (University of Sussex)
IEA	International Association for the Evaluation of Educational Achievement
IEFP	*Institut Européen pour la Formation Professionelle*
IFCEB	International Foundation for Computer-based Education in Banking and Finance
IFFTU	International Federation of Free Teachers Unions
IFIP	International Federation for Information Processing
IFLA	International Federation of Library Associations and Institutions
IFS	*Institut für Schulenwicklungsforschung* (Germany)
IFWEA	International Federation of Workers Educational Associations
IGAEN	*Inspecteurs généreaux de l'administration de l'Education nationale* (France)
IGEN	*Inspecteurs généreaux de l'Education nationale* (France)
IIE	Institute of International Education
IIEP	International Institute for Educational Planning
IIP	International Intervisitation Program in Educational Administration
IISN	International Information Sharing Network
ILO	International Labour Organization
IMF	International Monetary Fund
IMPACT	IMPACT project
IMTEC	International Movement Toward Educational Change

INADES *Institut Africain pour le Développement Economique et Social*
INET International Networks in Education and Development
INNOTECH Regional Center for Educational Innovation and Technology (Philippines)
INSEA International Society for Education through Art
IQ Intelligence quotient
IRA International Reading Association
IRE Initiation response evaluation model
IRF Initiation, response, feedback sequence
IRT Item response theory
ISA International Sociological Association
ISAAC International Society for Augmentative and Alternative Communication
ISBN International Standard Book Number
ISCED International Standard Classification of Education
ISCO International Standard Classification of Occupations
ISEA Inter-American Society for Educational Administration
ISR Institute for Social Research (US)
ISSP International Social Survey Program
ISSTAL ISSTAL model
ITA Independent Television Authority (UK)
ITR Innovation, Technology and Research Section (UNESCO)
ITS Interrupted time series
ITU International Telecommunications Union
IVLA International Visual Literacy Association

JAVEA Japan Audio-Visual Education Association
JEPI Junior Eysenck Personality Inventory
Jr–Sr HSPQ Junior–Senior High School Personality Questionnaire
JTPA Job and Training Partnership Act 1983 (US)
JVIS Jackson Vocational Interest Survey

K Kappa statistic
KEDI Korean Educational Development Institute
KEEP Kamehameha Early Education Program (Hawaii)

LANs Local area networks
LASSI Learning and Study Strategies Inventory
LBDQ Leadership Behavior Description Questionnaire
LCDs Liquid crystal displays
LEAD Leadership in Educational Administration Development Program
LEAs Local education authorities
LEI Learning Environment Inventory
LISP LISt Processing (programming language)
LISREL Linear structural relations analysis
LLTM Linear Logistic Test Model
LOGO LOGO (programming language)
LPQ Learning Process Questionnaire (Australia)
LSA Lattice space analysis
LTM Long-term memory

MANCOVA Multivariate analysis of covariance
MANOVA Multivariate analysis of variance
MBL Microcomputer-based laboratories
MBTI Myers–Briggs Type Indicator
MCA Multiple classification analysis
MCI My Class Inventory
MCT Minimum competency testing
MDPREF Multidimensional preference analysis
META Malaysian Educational Technology Association
MISC More intelligent and sensitive child program
MIT Massachusetts Institute of Technology (US)
MLTM Multicomponent latent trait model
MMPI Minnesota Multiphasic Personality Inventory
MPCL Mooney Problem Check List
MPI Maudsley Personality Inventory
MRP Mediterranean Regional Project
MSC Manpower Services Commission (UK)
MSE Mean square error
MTMM Multitrait multimethod techniques
MZ Monozygotic

NAEP National Assessment of Educational Progress (US)
NAPE National Association of Partners in Education (US)
NASN National Association of School Nurses (US)
NASP National Association of School Psychologists (US)
NASW National Association of Social Workers (US)
NAVE National Assessment of Vocational Education 1989 (US)
NBPTS National Board for Professional Teaching Standards (US)
NCATE National Council for the Accreditation of Teacher Education (US)
NCEEA National Commission on Excellence in Educational Administration (US)
NCET National Council for Educational Technology (UK)
NCME National Council on Measurements Used in Education (US)
NCVQ National Council for Vocational Qualifications (UK)
NEA National Education Association of the United States
NGOs Nongovernmental organizations
NIE National Institute of Education (US)
NIER Japanese National Institute for Educational Research
NIT New information technology
NOS National Open School (India)
NPBEA National Policy Board for Educational Administration (US)
NSF National Science Foundation (US)
NSMI National Special Media Institutes (US)
NSSE National Society for the Study of Education (US)
NTAs National training agencies
NTE National Teacher Examinations (US)
NTU National Technological University (US)
NUCEA National Continuing Education Association (US)
NUT National Union of Teachers (UK)

OAS	Organization of American States
OC	Open College (UK)
OCDQ	Organizational Climate Description Questionnaire
OCT	Open classroom teaching
ODA	Official development assistance
ODA	Overseas Development Agency
OE	Organizational economics
OECD	Organisation for Economic Cooperation and Development
OEO	Office of Economic Opportunity (US)
OERI	Office of Educational Research and Improvement (US)
OISE	Ontario Institute for Studies in Education
OKI-EK	Hungarian Center for Evaluation
OS	Operating systems
OU	Open University (UK)
PASCAL	PASCAL (programming language)
PCBs	Polychlorinated biphenyls
PEPA	Principal Effectiveness Pupil Achievement Program
PERT	Program evaluation and review technique
PICKUP	PICKUP program (UK)
PIE	Planning implementation evaluation model
PLA-check	Planned activity check
PLAN	Project PLAN (US)
PLUS	Project Literacy US
PLUTO	PLUTO International Network Project
PMAs	Primary mental abilities
PPBS	Planning Programming Budget System (US)
PPP	Pause, prompt, praise approach
PPS	Probability proportional to size
PRAXIS	PRAXIS series (Educational Testing Service)
PRC	People's Republic of China
PRO	Personal responsibility orientation model
PSI	Personalized System of Instruction
PSS	Performance support systems
PTAs	Parent teacher associations
R & D	Research and development
RAE	*Resúmenes Analíticos en Educación*
RDD	Research–development–diffusion model
REDUC	*Red Latinoamericano de Documentación en Educación*
RME	Realistic Mathematics Education
SABES	System for Adult Basic Education Support (US)
SAS	Statistical Analysis System
SAS	Systematic Analysis for School Improvement (Netherlands)
SAT	Scholastic Aptitude Test
SATs	Standard Assessment Tasks (UK)
SCISP	Schools Council Integrated Science Project (UK)
SCT	Sentence Completion Test
SDPs	School Development Plans (UK)
SEAMEO	South East Asian Ministers of Education Organization
SEAPREAMS	South-East Asia and Pacific Region Educational Administrators and Managers Symposium
SEEQ	Student evaluations of educational quality
SEI	Socio-Economic Index
SENA	*Servicio Nacional de Aprendizaje* (Colombia)
SES	Socio-economic status
SETs	Student evaluations of teacher effectiveness
S–G test	Stone–Geisser test
SI	Guilford's structure of intellect model
SIDEC	Stanford International Development Education Committee (US)
SIMS	Second Mathematics Study (IEA)
SIOPS	Standard International Occupational Prestige Scale
SISS	Second Science Study (1986-88) (IEA)
SLEI	Science Laboratory Environment Inventory
SLI	Specifically language impaired
SLM	Segmented labor markets
SM	Sensory memory
SMPY	Study of Mathematically Precocious Youth
SNOWMAN	System for Knowledge Management
SOLO	Structure of Observed Learning Outcomes taxonomy
SPACE	Science Processes and Concepts Exploration
SPQ	Study Process Questionnaire (Australia)
SPSS	Statistical Package for the Social Sciences
SRK	Skills rules and knowledge
SSA	Smallest space analysis
SSCP	Sum-of-squares-and-cross-products matrix
SSE	School self evaluation
SSRC	Social Science Research Council (UK)
STADS	Student teams achievement divisions
STM	Short-term memory
STS	Science technology and society
SWITCH	Scottish Women into the Computing Habit
TAI	Team accelerated instruction
TASH	The Association for Persons with Severe Handicaps
TAT	Thematic Apperception Test
TGAT	Task Group on Assessment and Testing (UK)
TOPS	Training Opportunities Programme (UK)
TTVIT	Visual Interests Test
TVEI	Technical and Vocational Education Initiative (UK)
TVET	Technical and vocational education and training
UCC	Universal Copyright Convention
UCEA	University Council for Educational Administration (US)
UIE	UNESCO Institute for Education
UK	United Kingdom
UN	United Nations
UNDP	United Nations Development Programme
UNESCO	United Nations Educational, Scientific, and Cultural Organization
UNFPA	United Nations Fund for Population Activities
UNICEF	United Nations International Children's Emergency Fund
UPE	Universal primary education
US	United States

USAID	United States Agency for International Development
USSR	Union of Soviet Socialist Republics
VAE	Vocational agriculture education
VET	Vocational education and training
WAEC	West African Examinations Council
WAIS	Wechsler Adult Intelligence Scale
WCEFA	World Conference on Education for All 1990
WCOTP	World Confederation of Organizations of the Teaching Profession
WEA	Workers' Educational Association (UK)
WHO	World Health Organization
WID	Women In Development
WIPO	World Intellectual Property Organization
WISE	Women's International Studies Europe
YOP	Youth Opportunities Programme (UK)
YTS	Youth Training Scheme (UK)

LIST OF MAJOR EDUCATION JOURNALS

The list of journals given below is a representative selection of periodical publications, particularly those published in English, devoted primarily to the dissemination of research on education and includes all those frequently referred to in this *Encyclopedia*. The field of education emanates from many diverse scholarly disciplines and this list reflects that situation, citing not only journals dealing with education, but also those with bearings upon the field of education. For the purposes of this list the word "journal" has been loosely defined to include not only journals but also periodicals, bulletins, and yearbooks.

Academe	Academe (formerly *AAUP Bull.*)
Acad. Ther.	Academic Therapy
Acta Psychol.	Acta Psychologica
Acta Sociol.	Acta Sociologica
Adolescence	Adolescence
Adm. Sci. Q	Administrative Science Quarterly
Adult Educ.	Adult Education
Adult Educ. Q.	Adult Education Quarterly (formerly *Adult Educ.*)
Adult Lead.	Adult Leadership
Adult Learn.	Adult Learning (formerly *Lifelong Learn.*)
Aging Hum. Dev.	Aging and Human Development
Altern. Higher Educ.	Alternative Higher Education (now Inner Higher Education)
AAHE Bull.	American Association for Higher Education Bulletin
AAUP Bull.	American Assocation of University Professors Bulletin
Am. Econ. Rev.	American Economic Review
Am. Educ.	American Education (ceased publication 1985)
Am. Educ. Res. J.	American Educational Research Journal
Am. J. Clin. Hypn.	American Journal of Clinical Hypnosis
Am. J. Dis. Child.	American Journal of Diseases of Children
Am. J. Distance Educ.	American Journal of Distance Education
Am. J. Educ.	American Journal of Education (formerly *Sch. Rev.*)
Am. J. Orthopsychiatry	American Journal of Orthopsychiatry
Am. J. Physiol.	American Journal of Physiology
Am. J. Sociol.	American Journal of Sociology
Am. Psychol.	American Psychologist
Am. Schol.	American Scholar
Am. Sch. Brd. J.	American School Board Journal
Am. Sci.	American Scientist
Am. Sociol. Rev.	American Sociological Review
Am. Sociol.	American Sociologist
Ann. Am. Acad. Polit. Soc. Sci.	Annals of the American Academy of Political and Social Science
Ann. Hum. Genet.	Annals of Human Genetics
Annu. Rev. Inf. Sci. Technol.	Annual Review of Information Science and Technology
Annu. Rev. Psychol.	Annual Review of Psychology
Anthropol. Educ. Q.	Anthropology and Education Quarterly
Appl. Econ.	Applied Economics
Appl. Psychol. Meas.	Applied Psychological Measurement
Appl. Psychol.	Applied Psychology: An International Review (formerly *Int. Rev. Appl. Psychol.*)
Appl. Psychol. Monogr.	Applied Psychology Monographs
Appl. Stat.	Applied Statistics

Arch. Genet.	Archiv für Genetik
Arch. Gen. Psychiatry	Archives of General Psychiatry
Arch. Neurol.	Archives of Neurology (Chicago)
ADE Bull.	Association of Departments of English Bulletin
Aud. Vis. Commun. Rev.	Audio–Visual Communication Review
Audio–Vis. G.	Audio–Visual Guide
Aust. Educ. Rev.	Australian Education Review
Aust. Educ. Res.	Australian Educational Research
Aust. Sci. Teach. J.	Australian Science Teachers Journal
Aust. Univ. Rev.	Australian Universities Review
Behav. Disord.	Behavioral Disorders
Behav. Neurosci.	Behavioral Neuroscience (formerly *J. Comp. Physiol. Psychol.*)
Behav. Sci.	Behavioral Science
Behav. Res. Ther.	Behaviour Research and Therapy
Beitr. Hoch.	Beiträge zur Hochschulforschung
Betr. Erz.	Betrifft Erziehung
Bild. Erz.	Bildung und Erziehung
Bild. Wiss.	Bildung und Wissenschaft
Br. Educ. Res. J.	British Educational Research Journal
Br. J. Disord. Commun.	British Journal of Disorders of Communication
Br. J. Educ. Psychol.	British Journal of Educational Psychology
Br. J. Educ. Stud.	British Journal of Educational Studies
Br. J. Educ. Technol.	British Journal of Educational Technology (formerly *J. Ednl. Technology*)
Br. J. Guid. Couns.	British Journal of Guidance and Counselling
Br. J. Math. S.	British Journal of Mathematical and Statistical Psychology
Br. J Med. Educ.	British Journal of Medical Education
Br. J. Psychiatry	British Journal of Psychiatry
Br. J. Psychol.	British Journal of Psychology
Br. J. Relig. Educ.	British Journal of Religious Education (formerly *Relig. in Educ.*)
Br. J. Sociol.	British Journal of Sociology
Br. J. Sociol. Educ.	British Journal of the Sociology of Education
Bull. Oxf. Univ. Stat.	Bulletin of the Oxford University Institute of Statistics
Calif. J. Ed. Res.	California Journal of Educational Research
Calif. J. Teach. Educ.	California Journal of Teacher Education
Camb. J. Educ.	Cambridge Journal of Education
Can. J. Higher Ed.	Canadian Journal of Higher Education
Career Dev. Q.	Career Development Quarterly (formerly *Vocat. Guid. Q.*)
Change	Change
Child Abuse Neglect	Child Abuse and Neglect
Child Dev.	Child Development
Child Develop. Absts. Biblio.	Child Development Abstracts and Bibliography
Child Wel.	Child Welfare
Child. Today	Children Today
Chron. Higher Educ.	Chronicle of Higher Education
Clin. Work	Clinical Social Work Journal
Cog.	Cognition
Cognit. Psychol.	Cognitive Psychology
Cognit. Sci.	Cognitive Science
Coll. Teach.	College Teaching
Coll. Univ.	College and University
Commun. Res.	Communication Research

Communicator	Communicator
Comm. Dev. J.	Community Development Journal
Community Tech. Jr. Coll. J.	Community, Technical, and Junior College Journal
Comp. Educ.	Comparative Education
Comp. Educ. Rev.	Comparative Education Review
Comput. Educ.	Computers and Education
Contemp. Educ.	Contemporary Education
Contemp. Educ. Psychol.	Contemporary Educational Psychology
Context	Context
Convergence	Convergence
Couns. Psych.	Counseling Psychologist
Counsel. Val.	Counseling and Values
Couns. Educ. Superv.	Counselor Education and Supervision
Crime Delinq.	Crime and Delinquency
Curr. Issues Higher Ed.	Current Issues in Higher Education
Curric. Inq.	Curriculum Inquiry (formerly *Curric. Theo.*)
Curric. Theo.	Curriculum Theory Network

Daedalus	Daedalus
Demography	Demography
Development	Development
Dev. Psychol.	Developmental Psychology
Dev. Rev.	Developmental Review
Distance Educ.	Distance Education

Econometrica	Econometrica
Econ. Development Q.	Economic Development Quarterly
Econ. Rec.	Economic Record
Economica	Economica
Econ. Educ. Rev.	Economics of Education Review
Econ.	The Economist
Education	Education
Educ. Chem.	Education in Chemistry
Educ. Comp.	Education Comparée
Educ. Cult.	Education and Culture
Educ. et Dévelop.	Education et Développement
Educ. Libr. Bull.	Education Libraries Bulletin
Educ. Perm.	Education Permanente
Educ. Psychol. Meas.	Education and Psychological Measurement
Educ. Sci.	Education in Science
Educ. Soc.	Education and Society
Educ. Spec. Training Sch.	Education in Special Training Schools
Educ. Tech. Training Int.	Education and Training Technology International (formerly *Program. Learn. and Educ. T.*)
Educ. Urb. Soc.	Education and Urban Society
Educ. Comm. Tech. J.	Educational Communications and Technology Journal
Educ. Eval. Policy Anal.	Educational Evaluation and Policy Analysis
Educ. Leadership	Educational Leadership
Educ. Phil. Theor.	Educational Philosophy and Theory
Educ. Policy	Educational Policy
Educ. Psychol. Meas.	Educational and Psychological Measurement
Educ. Psychol.	Educational Psychologist
Educ. Psychology	Educational Psychology
Educ. Psychol. Rev.	Educational Psychology Review

Educ. Rec.	Educational Record
Educ. Res.	Educational Research
Educ. Res. Q.	Educational Research Quarterly (formerly *Calif. J. Ed. Res.*)
Educ. Researcher	Educational Researcher, AERA
Educ. Stud.	Educational Studies
Educ. Stud. Math.	Educational Studies in Mathematics
Educ. Technol.	Educational Technology
Educ. Tech. Res. Dev.	Educational Technology Research and Development (formerly *Educ. Comm. Tech. J.*)
Educ. Theory	Educational Theory
El. Engl.	Elementary English
Elem. Sch. Guid. Couns.	Elementary School Guidance and Counseling
Elem. Sch. J.	Elementary School Journal
Eng. Educ.	Engineering Education
Engl. Lang. Teach.	English Language Teaching
Engl. Lang. Teach. J.	English Language Teaching Journal (formerly *Engl. Lang. Teach.*)
Enseignement Math.	Enseignement Mathématique
Envir. Behav.	Environment and Behavior
Erz. Wiss.	Erziehung und Wissenschaft
Eur. J. Educ.	European Journal of Education (formerly *Paedag. Eur.*)
Eur. J. Psychol. Educ.	European Journal of the Psychology of Education
Eur. J. Sci. Educ.	European Journal of Science Education
Educ. J. Spec. Need. Educ.	European Journal of Special Needs Education
Eval. Educ.	Evaluation in Education
Eval. Rev.	Evaluation Review
Ex. Ch. Ab.	Exceptional Child Education Abstracts
Ex. Ch. Res.	Exceptional Child Education Resources (formerly *Ex. Ch. Ab.*)
Excep. Child.	Exceptional Children
Fam. Community Health	Family and Community Health
Fam. Coord.	Family Coordinator
Fam. Proc.	Family Process
Fam. Relat.	Family Relations (formerly *Fam. Coord.*)
Genet. Psychol. Monogr.	Genetic Psychology Monographs
Genet. Soc. Gen. Psych.	Genetic, Social and General Psychology (formerly *Genet. Psychol. Monogr.*)
Gerontologist	Gerontologist
Harv. Bus. Rev.	Harvard Business Review
Harv. Educ. Rev.	Harvard Educational Review
Harv. Mo.	Harvard Monthly
Heilpädag. Forsch.	Heilpädagogische Forschung
High. Educ.	Higher Education
Higher Educ. Eur.	Higher Education in Europe
Higher Educ. Policy	Higher Education Policy
Higher Educ. Q.	Higher Education Quarterly
High. Educ. R & D	Higher Education Research and Development
High. Educ. Res. Neth.	Higher Education and Research in the Netherlands
Hist. Child. Q.	History of Childhood Quarterly
Hist. Educ. Q.	History of Education Quarterly
Hist. Ed. R.	History of Education Review
Hist. Higher Educ. Ann.	History of Higher Education Annual
Home Econ. Res. J.	Home Economics Research Journal

Human Commun. Res.	Human Communications Research
Hum. Dev.	Human Development (formerly *Vita Hum.*)
Hum. Relat.	Human Relations
Hum. Resource Dev. Q.	Human Resource Development Quarterly
Indiv. Psy.	Individual Psychology (formerly *J. Individa. Psychol.*)
Ind. Arts Voc. Ed.	Industrial Arts and Vocational Education
Ind. Educ.	Industrial Education (formerly *Ind. Arts Voc. Ed.*)
Ind. Higher Educ.	Industry and Higher Education
Innov. Higher Educ.	Innovative Higher Education (formerly *Altern. Higher Educ.*)
Instr. Sci.	Instructional Science
Intelligence	Intelligence
Interchange	Interchange
Int. Econ. Rev.	International Economic Review
Int. J. Aging Hum. Dev.	International Journal of Aging and Human Development
Int. J. Disabil. Dev. Educ.	International Journal of Disability Development and Education (formerly *Aging Hum. Dev.*)
Int. J. Early Child.	International Journal of Early Childhood
Int. J. Educ.	International Journal of Education
Int. J. Educ. Dev	International Journal of Educational Development
Int. J. Educ. Res.	International Journal of Educational Research (formerly *Eval. Educ.*)
Int. J. Inst. Mangt. Higher Educ.	International Journal of Institutional Management in Higher Education
Int. J. Instr. Media	International Journal of Instructional Media
Int. J. Lifelong Educ.	International Journal of Lifelong Education
Int. J. Phys. Educ.	International Journal of Physical Education
Int. J. Psychiat.	International Journal of Psychiatry
Int. J. Psychoanal. Psychother.	International Journal of Psychoanalytic Psychotherapy (formerly *Int. J. Psychiat.*)
Int. J. Sci. Educ.	International Journal of Science Education
Int. J. Spec. Educ.	International Journal of Special Education
Int. J. Univ. Adult Educ.	International Journal of University Adult Education
Int. Lab. Rev.	International Labor Review
Int. Rev. Appl. Psychol.	International Review of Applied Psychology
Int. Rev. Educ.	International Review of Education
Int. Soc. Sci. J.	International Social Science Journal
Issues Sci. Technol.	Issues in Science and Technology
J. Erz. Schulgesch.	Jahrbuch für Erziehungs- und Schulgeschichte
J. Abnorm. Child Psychol.	Journal of Abnormal Child Psychology
J. Abnorm. Psychol.	Journal of Abnormal Psychology (formerly *J. Abnorm. Soc. Psychol.*)
J. Abnorm. Soc. Psychol.	Journal of Abnormal Social Psychology
J. Appl. Behav. Anal.	Journal of Applied Behavior Analysis
J. Appl. Commun. Res.	Journal of Applied Communication Research
J. Appl. Psychol.	Journal of Applied Psychology
J. Autism Child. Schizo.	Journal of Autism and Childhood Schizophrenia
J. Autism Dev. Disord.	Journal of Autism and Developmental Disorders (formerly *J. Autism Child. Schizo.*)
J. Br. Soc. Ind. Tutors	Journal of the British Society of Industrial Tutors
J. Child Psychol. Psychiatry Allied Discip.	Journal of Child Psychology and Psychiatry and Allied Disciplines
J. Coll. Sci. Teach.	Journal of College Science Teaching

J. Coll. Stud. Dev.	Journal of College Student Development (formerly *J. Coll. Stud. Pers.*)
J. Coll. Stud. Pers.	Journal of College Student Personnel
J. Coll. Univ.	Journal of the College and University Personnel Association
J. Commun.	Journal of Communication
J. Community Psychol.	Journal of Community Psychology
J. Comp. Physiol. Psychol.	Journal of Comparative and Physiological Psychology
J. Comp. Psychol.	Journal of Comparative Psychology (formerly *J. Comp. Physiol. Psychol.*)
J. Comput. Sci. Math. Educ.	Journal of Computers in Science and Mathematics Education
J. Consult. Clin. Psychol.	Journal of Consulting and Clinical Psychology
J. Couns. Psychol.	Journal of Counseling Psychology
J. Cross-cult. Psychol.	Journal of Cross-cultural Psychology
J. Curric. St.	Journal of Curriculum Studies
J. Curr. Theor.	Journal of Curriculum Theorizing
J. Dev. Econ.	Journal of Developmental Economics
J. Dev. Planning	Journal of Developmental Planning
J. Dev. Rem. Educ.	Journal of Developmental and Remedial Education
J. Economet.	Journal of Econometrics
J. Econ. Lit.	Journal of Economic Literature
J. Econ. Theo.	Journal of Economic Theory
J. Educ.	Journal of Education
J. Educ. Adm.	Journal of Educational Administration
J. Educ. Finance	Journal of Educational Finance
J. Educ. Meas.	Journal of Educational Measurement
J. Educ. Psychol.	Journal of Educational Psychology
J. Educ. Res.	Journal of Educational Research
J. Ed. Stat.	Journal of Educational Statistics
J. Ednl. Technology	Journal of Educational Technology
J. Eng. Educ.	Journal of Engineering Education
J. Environ. Educ.	Journal of Environmental Education
J. Exp. Educ.	Journal of Experimental Education
J. Exp. Psychol.	Journal of Experimental Psychology (now split into four parts—see below)
J. Exp. Psychol. (Animal Behav. Proc.)	Journal of Experimental Psychology: Animal Behavior Processes
J. Exp. Psychol. Gen.	Journal of Experimental Psychology: General
J. Exp. Psychol. Hum. Percept. Perform.	Journal of Experimental Psychology: Human Perception and Performance
J. Exp. Psychol. Learn. Mem. Cognit.	Journal of Experimental Psychology: Learning, Memory, and Cognition
J. Gen. Educ.	Journal of General Education
J. Gen. Psychol.	Journal of General Psychology
J. Genet. Psychol.	Journal of Genetic Psychology
J. Geogr.	Journal of Geography
J. Geogr. Higher Educ.	Journal of Geography in Higher Education
J. Geront.	Journal of Gerontology
J. Higher Educ.	Journal of Higher Education
J. Hum. Resources	Journal of Human Resources
J. Hum. Psy.	Journal of Humanistic Psychology
J. Individ. Psychol.	Journal of Individual Psychology
J. Instr. Dev.	Journal of Instructional Development
J. Labor Econ.	Journal of Labor Economics
J. Learn. Disabil.	Journal of Learning Disabilities
J. Marriage Fam.	Journal of Marriage and the Family

J. Math. Psy.	Journal of Mathematical Psychology
J. Mem. Lang.	Journal of Memory and Language (formerly *J. Verbal Learn. Verbal Behav.*)
J. Multivar. Exp. Pers. Clin. Psychol.	Journal of Multivariate Experimental Personality and Clinical Psychology
J. NAWDAC	Journal of the National Association of Women Deans, Administrators and Counsellors
J. Pediat. Psychol.	Journal of Pediatric Psychology
J. Pediat.	Journal of Pediatrics
J. Pers.	Journal of Personality
J. Pers. Soc. Psychol.	Journal of Personality and Social Psychology
J. Phil. Educ.	Journal of Philosophy of Education
J. Phys. Educ. Rec.	Journal of Physical Education and Recreation
J. Phys. Educ. Recreat. Dance	Journal of Physical Education, Recreation and Dance (formerly *J. Phys. Educ. Rec.*)
J. Pol. Econ.	Journal of Political Economy
J. Psychohist.	Journal of Psychohistory (formerly *Hist. Child. Q.*)
J. Publ. Econ.	Journal of Public Economics
J. Public Policy	Journal of Public Policy
J. Read.	Journal of Reading
J. Read. Behav.	Journal of Reading Behaviour
J. Res. Dev. Educ.	Journal of Research and Development in Education
J. Res. Math. Educ.	Journal of Research in Mathematics Education
J. Res. Sci. Teach.	Journal of Research in Science Teaching
J. Rural Sml. Sch.	Journal of Rural and Small Schools
J. Soc. Issues	Journal of Social Issues
J. Soc. Psychol.	Journal of Social Psychology
J. Soc. Work Educ.	Journal of Social Work Education
J. Soc. Research Administrators	Journal of the Society of Research Administrators
J. Spec. Educ.	Journal of Special Education
J. Spec. Educ. Technol.	Journal of Special Education Technology
J. Stud. Financial Aid.	Journal of Student Financial Aid
J. Teach. Educ.	Journal of Teacher Education
J. Tertiary Educ. Adm.	Journal of Tertiary Educational Administration
J. Verbal Learn. Verbal Behav.	Journal of Verbal Learning and Verbal Behavior
Junior Coll. J.	Junior College Journal
Lbr. Studies J.	Labor Studies Journal
Labour Soc.	Labour and Society
Lang. Arts	Language Arts (formerly *El. Engl.*)
Lang. Soc.	Language in Society
Lang. Teach.	Language Teaching (formerly *Lang. Teach. Ling. Abstr.*)
Lang. Teach. Ling. Abstr.	Language Teaching and Linguistics: Abstracts
Lib. Educ.	Liberal Education
Lifelong Learn.	Lifelong Learning
Math. Teach.	Mathematics Teacher
Math. Teaching	Mathematics Teaching
Meas. Eval. Couns. Dev.	Measurement and Evaluation in Counseling and Development (formerly *Meas. Eval. Guid.*)
Meas. Eval. Guid.	Measurement and Evaluation in Guidance
Ment. Retard.	Mental Retardation
Merrill-Palmer Q.	Merrill-Palmer Quarterly
Minerva	Minerva

Monogr. Soc. Res. Child Dev.	Monographs of the Society for Research in Child Development
Month. Lab. Rev.	Monthly Labor Review
Mt. Sinai J. Med.	Mount Sinai Journal of Medicine
Multivar. Exp. Clin. R.	Multivariate Experimental Clinical Research (formerly *J. Multivar. Exp. Pers. Clin. Psychol.*)
NASPA J.	NASPA Journal
Nat. Forum	National Forum: Phi Kappa Phi Journal
N. Sammlung	Neue Sammlung
New Dir. Community Coll.	New Directions for Community Colleges
New Dir. Inst. Res.	New Directions for Institutional Research
New Educ.	New Education
NY Times	New York Times
NZ J. Educ. Stud.	New Zealand Journal of Educational Studies
Nouv. Rev. Pédag.	Nouvelle Revue Pédagogique
Open Learn.	Open Learning
Orientat. Sc.	Orientation Scolaire et Professionelle
Oxford B. Econ. Statis.	Oxford Bulletin of Economics and Statistics
Oxford Rev. Educ.	Oxford Review of Education
Päd.	Pädagogik
Pädagog. Forsch.	Pädagogische Forschungen
Pädagog. Rundsch.	Pädagogische Rundschau
Paedag. Eur.	Paedagogica Europae
Paedag. Hist.	Paedagogica Historica
Pedagog. Sem.	Pedagogical Seminary
Pedia.	Pediatrics
Percept. Mot. Skills	Perceptual and Motor Skills
Pers. Soc. Psychol. Bull.	Personality and Social Psychology Bulletin
Pers. Guid. J.	Personnel and Guidance Journal
Phi Del. Kap.	Phi Delta Kappan
Phys. Educ.	Physics Education
Phys. Teach.	Physics Teacher
Phys. Didakt.	Physik und Didaktik
Phys. Schule	Physik in der Schule
Plan. Higher Educ.	Planning for Higher Education
Proc. Nat. Acad. Sci. USA	Proceedings of the National Academy of Sciences of the United States of America
Program. Learn. Educ. T.	Programmed Learning and Educational Technology
Prospects	Prospects
Psychoanal. Rev.	Psychoanalytic Review
Psychol. Abstr.	Psychological Abstracts
Psych. Bull.	Psychological Bulletin
Psychol. Iss.	Psychological Issues
Psychol. Med.	Psychological Medicine
Psychol. Rec.	Psychological Record
Psychol. Rep.	Psychological Reports
Psychol. Rev.	Psychological Review
Psychologie	Psychologie (Paris)
Psychologie (Bern)	Psychologie (Bern)
Psychologies	Psychologies (formerly *Psychologie (Paris)*)
Psychol. Rundsch.	Psychologische Rundschau
Psychol. Sch.	Psychology in the Schools
Psychol. Today	Psychology Today

Psychol Women Q.	Psychology of Women Quarterly
Psychometri.	Psychometrika
Psychos. Med.	Psychosomatic Medicine
PsycInfo	PsycInfo (formerly *Psychol. Abstr.*)
Public Interest	Public Interest
Publ. Policy	Public Policy
Q. J. Econ.	Quarterly Journal of Economics
Read. Res. Q.	Reading Research Quarterly
Read. Teach.	Reading Teacher
Rehab. Lit.	Rehabilitation Literature
Relig. in Educ.	Religion in Education
Relig. Educ.	Religious Education
Rem. Educ.	Remedial Education
Rem. Spec. Educ.	Remedial and Special Education
Res. Dev. Educ.	Research in Developmental Education
Res. Educ.	Research in Education
Res. Higher Educ.	Research in Higher Education
Res. Higher Educ. Abstr.	Research into Higher Education Abstracts
Res. Lab. Econ.	Research in Labour Economics
Res. Rural Educ.	Research in Rural Education
Rev. Econ. Stud.	Review of Economic Studies
Rev. Econ. Stat.	Review of Economics and Statistics
Rev. Educ.	Review of Education
Rev. Educ. Res.	Review of Educational Research
Rev. Higher Educ.	Review of Higher Education
Rev. Res. Educ.	Review of Research in Education
Rev. Invest. Educ.	Revista de Investigación Educacional
R. Franç. Pédag.	Revue Française de Pédagogie
Rev. Psy. App.	Revue de Psychologie Appliquée
Rural Educ.	Rural Educator
Scand. J. Educ. Res.	Scandinavian Journal of Educational Research
Scand. J. Psychol.	Scandinavian Journal of Psychology
Sch. Couns.	School Counselor
Sch. Rev.	School Review
Sch. Sci. Math.	School Science and Mathematics
Sch. Sci. Rev.	School Science Review
Sch. Soc.	School and Society
Science	Science
Sci. & Educ.	Science and Education
Sci. Educ.	Science Education
Sci. Paedagog.	Scientia Paedagogica
Sci. Paedagog. Exp.	Scientia Paedagogica Experimentalis (formerly *Sci. Paedagog.*)
Sci. Am.	Scientific American
Semin. Psychiatry	Seminars in Psychiatry
Signs	Signs: Journal of Women in Culture and Society
Soc. Educ.	Social Education
Soc Forces	Social Forces
Soc. Prob.	Social Problems
Soc. Psychol. Q.	Social Psychology Quarterly
Soc. Serv. Rev.	Social Service Review
Sociol. Foc.	Sociological Focus
Sociol. Q.	Sociological Quarterly

Sociol. Rev.	Sociological Review
Sociology	Sociology
Sociol. Educ.	Sociology of Education
South Pac. J. Teach. Educ.	South Pacific Journal of Teacher Education
Sov. Ped.	Sovetskaya Pedagogika
Stud. Adult Educ.	Studies in Adult Education
Stud. Educ. Eval.	Studies in Educational Evaluation
Stud. Fam. Pl.	Studies in Family Planning
Stud. High. Educ.	Studies in Higher Education
Stud. Sci. Educ.	Studies in Science Education
Supplry. Educ. Monogr.	Supplementary Educational Monographs
Supp. for Learn.	Support for Learning (formerly *Rem. Educ.*)
Teach. Educ. Q.	Teacher Education Quarterly (formerly *Calif. J. Teach. Educ.*)
Teach. Educ. Spec. Educ.	Teacher Education and Special Education
Teach. Coll. Rec.	Teachers College Record
Teach. Distance	Teaching at a Distance
Teach. Excep. Child.	Teaching Exceptional Children
Teach. Sociol.	Teaching Sociology
Techniques	Techniques
Technol. Soc.	Technology and Society
Theol. Educ.	Theological Education
Theory Pract.	Theory into Practice
TES	Times Educational Supplement
THES	Times Higher Educational Supplement
Training	Training
Train Dev. J.	Training and Development Journal
Unicorn	Unicorn
UnterWiss.	Unterrichtswissenschaft
Urban Educ.	Urban Education
Vergl. Pädag.	Vergleichende Pädagogik
Vita Hum.	Vita Humana
Vocat. Guid. Q.	Vocational Guidance Quarterly
West Afr. J. Educ. Vocat. Meas.	West African Journal of Educational and Vocational Measurement
World Bank Econ. R.	World Bank Economic Review
World Bank Res. Obs.	World Bank Research Observer
World Dev.	World Development
World Yr. Bk. Ed.	World Yearbook of Education (formerly *Yb. Educ.*)
Yb. Educ.	Yearbook of Education
Yearb. Int. Assoc. Child Psychiat.	Yearbook of the International Association for Child Psychiatry and Allied Professions (formerly *Int. Yearb. Child Psychiat.*) (also known as *The Child in His Family*)
Yearbook (Natl. Soc. Stud. Educ.)	Yearbook of the National Society for the Study of Education
Youth Soc.	Youth and Society
Z. Entwick. P.	Zeitschrift für Entwicklungspsychologie und Pädagogische Psychologie
Z. Heilpädagog.	Zeitschrift für Heilpädagogik
Z. Kinderpsychiatr.	Zeitschrift für Kinderpsychiatrie
Z. Pädagogik	Zeitschrift für Pädagogik